T4-AHV-656

PROBLEMS IN PREHISTORY: NORTH AFRICA AND THE LEVANT

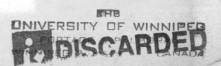
UNIVERSITY OF WINNIPEG
DISCARDED
CANADA

DISCARDED

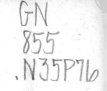
GN
855
.N35P76

PROBLEMS IN PREHISTORY: NORTH AFRICA AND THE LEVANT

Edited by

FRED WENDORF and ANTHONY E. MARKS

SMU PRESS · DALLAS

ⓒ   1975   ·   Southern Methodist University Press   ·   Dallas

Southern Methodist University Contributions in Anthropology, No. 13

Library of Congress Cataloging in Publication Data

Main entry under title:

Problems in prehistory: North Africa and the Levant.

(Southern Methodist University contributions in anthropology, no. 13)

Papers presented at "a conference on pleistocene paleoenvironments and prehistory of northeast Africa and the Levant" held Dec. 5-8, 1973.

Bibliography: p.
1. Man, Prehistoric—Near East—Congresses.
2. Man, Prehistoric—Africa, North—Congresses.
3. Near East—Antiquities—Congresses.
4. Africa, North—Antiquities—Congresses.
5. Paleoclimatology—Near East—Congresses.
I. Wendorf, Fred, ed.
II. Marks, Anthony E., ed.
III. Series: Dallas. Southern Methodist University contributions in anthropology, no. 13
GN855.N35P76   913.39'7   74-14722
ISBN 0-87074-146-2

CONTENTS

PROBLEMS IN PREHISTORY: NORTH AFRICA AND THE LEVANT

INTRODUCTION

Since World War II there has been an ever increasing tempo of research on prehistory throughout the world. One of the most active areas has been the region which borders on the southern and eastern shores of the Mediterranean. Part of the stimulus for this new work was the quest for the origins of food production in the Old World. Another factor was the awakening of concern for the preservation of the archaeological heritage which increasingly faced destruction as the region rapidly became urbanized and industrialized. Thus, the international campaign in Nubia and the proliferation of salvage excavations in the Levant, which now account for much of our recent knowledge concerning the area, can be attributed to these conservation efforts.

In spite of the acceleration of research, the unfortunate but longstanding regional political instability has hampered direct communication between the scholars involved. Many prehistorians working the region rarely, if ever, have the opportunity for face-to-face discussions of mutual problems. The faculty of the Department of Anthropology at Southern Methodist University were acutely aware of this problem since they were conducting simultaneous research in both Egypt and Israel.

In 1971, a friend of the Department, Mr. A. C. Greene of Dallas, Texas, also became aware of this problem while serving as a volunteer member of the staff on the excavation at Ubedeiya, Israel, under the direction of Dr. Ofer Bar-Yosef. Upon his return to Dallas, Mr. Greene brought his concern to our attention and suggested that a conference be organized with his assistance where scholars from the entire region could meet and discuss their mutual interests.

The conference was called for December 5 to 8, 1973, and was held at Southern Methodist University in the Institute for the Study of Earth and Man, the sponsoring organization. Twenty-five scholars participated, representing the archaeological interests of six countries. While additional scholars might well have been included, the value of informal interaction by a small group was of paramount consideration.

FRED WENDORF
ANTHONY E. MARKS

Southern Methodist University
Institute for the Study of Earth and Man
May 20, 1975

PART I

North Africa and the Nile

THE GEOLOGICAL EVOLUTION OF THE RIVER NILE

Rushdi Said

The Geological Survey of Egypt

INTRODUCTION

This paper deals with the geologic history of the river that followed a course closely associated with the present-day valley of the Nile, which seems to have been cut during the Upper Miocene. The earlier pre–Upper Miocene rivers that drained the elevated lands of Egypt do not seem to have been associated with the valley in its present form and, therefore, do not constitute the subject of this paper. Relics of these earlier rivers are preserved in fluviatile sand and gravel spreads and in deltaic sediments recorded in several places in northern Egypt. The earliest of the fluviatile Tertiary deposits dates back to Late Eocene and Early Oligocene times. They are in the form of a 310-470 m-thick section of deltaic and associated offshore and barrier beach deposits (Qasr el Sagha and Qatrani Formations) in the Fayum region to the north of Birket Qarun at an elevation of 350 m above sea level. The Fayum deltaic deposits have been extensively studied (Beadnell, 1905; Vondra, 1974, etc.). The most interesting feature of these deposits is their inclusion of important and unique vertebrate remains that have attracted the attention of numerous scholars (Beadnell, 1901, 1905; Von Stromer Reichenbach, 1902; Andrews, 1906; Simons, 1968; and others). No fluviatile sediments have been recorded so far that would give a clue to the course of the Upper Eocene–Oligocene river that made up this delta which must have formed along the edge of a marine gulf that protruded inside the elevated lands of Egypt up to the Fayum region. Recent drilling in the area extending from the Mediterranean to the Fayum has given the first indication of the presence of this embayment by the discovery of the only record so far known in Egypt of marine Oligocene. Blanckenhorn (1901) was the first to visualize the presence of this bay, and he and Beadnell (1905) attempted to reconstruct the course of the river that debouched into this estuary, claiming that it probably took its headwaters from Bahariya oasis at lakes in which the iron ores known in that region must have been deposited. Recent studies, however, have shown that the ores are not lagoonal in origin (Said and Issawi, 1964) and that their age is earlier than that of the delta of the Fayum.

River deposits in the form of extensive sand and gravel spreads that overlie the deposits of this early Upper Eocene–Oligocene river are known in the Western Desert of Egypt over the plateau which extends between Minia and Bahariya oasis. They form part of the "gravel spreads" marked on the new geological map of Egypt (as a patch on this plateau), trending in a northwestern direction. These deposits form part of the fluviatile facies of the lower Miocene deposits of the Western Desert of Egypt (Said, 1962*b*).

These fluviatile deposits represent rivers which probably opened into the delta at Moghra Oasis at the eastern tip of the Qattara depression. Here again the presence of land and semiaquatic fossil vertebrates in Moghra shows that the deltaic deposits of this area were formed by a prograding delta.

The present paper, which deals with the sediments associated with the Nile Valley in an attempt to understand its geologic evolution, is based on observations carried out in the field during the seasons extending from 1961 to 1973. The field work was first carried out in conjunction with the Prehistoric Expedition of Southern Methodist University (1961-1969) and later in association with the Geological Survey of Egypt (1970-1973). During the first period emphasis was given to the later sediments of the river, whereas during the second period emphasis shifted to the earlier sediments.

The cross sections of the valley (fig. 1) and the delta (fig. 2) and the longitudinal section of the delta (fig. 3) were constructed from the stratigraphic data gained from the field or provided by the numerous wells drilled in the delta and valley of the Nile after the search for oil and water. Figure 9 gives the logs of some of the measured sections (the locations of which are given in fig. 10).

This writer owes a great debt to a large number of persons. Foremost among these is Professor Fred Wendorf, who aroused the writer's interest in the Quaternary geology of Egypt, initiated and organized the work of the Prehistoric Expedition, and arranged for numerous scientists to visit the field over the seasons. The writer also owes a great debt to Professors Claude Albritton, Jean de Heinzelin, and Romuald Schild for their stimulating discussions. The Geological Survey camp was organized by geologists M. S. Abdel Ghany and Elsayed Zaghloul, who mapped large stretches of the Nile valley and who, together with geologists Samir Massoud and Hoda Shawky, helped in the preparation of the maps, profiles, and geological sections which accompany this paper. Mrs. S. Kharlamova Rustum drafted the accompanying geological maps. A special note of thanks is due to Dr. M. K. Ayouty and the staff of the Egyptian General Petroleum Organization for providing the basic data of the deep boreholes drilled in the delta and samples from four cores of the Sidi Salem well no. 1.

THE NILE

The field mapping of the fluviatile and associated sediments of the Nile valley and the examination of a large number of boreholes, both deep and shallow, have shown that it is possible to conceive of the Nile as having passed through five main episodes. Each of these episodes was

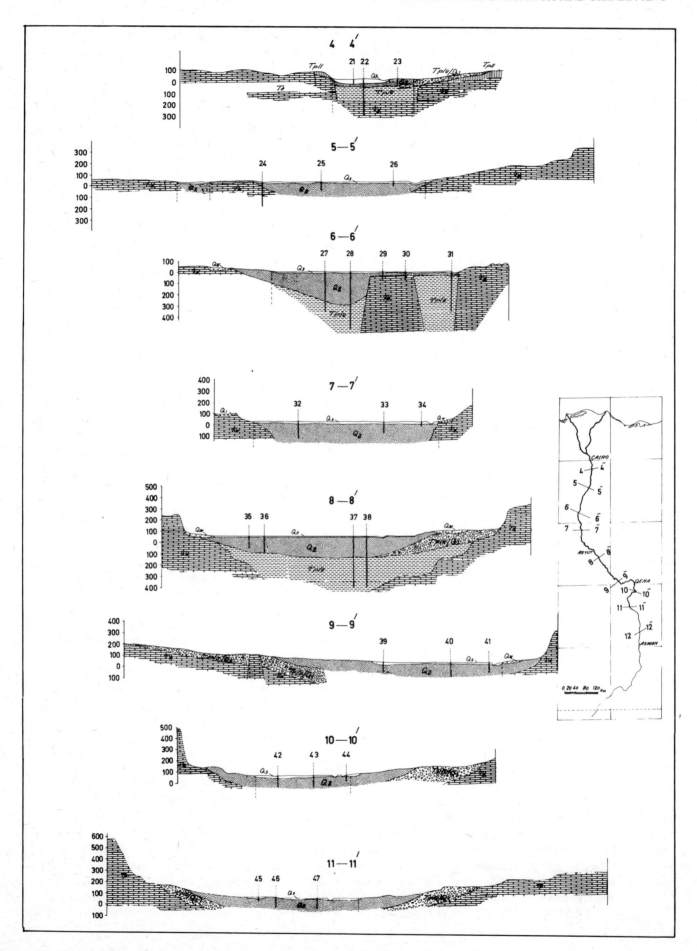

characterized by a river which drew the larger part of its waters from sources outside Egypt. Toward the end of the first four episodes (the last is still extant), the river seems to have declined or ceased entirely to flow into Egypt. These major recessional phases were relatively short in duration and were accompanied by major physical, climatic, and hydrologic changes. There is evidence that during two of the three episodes of recession there occurred ephemeral torrential rivers which drew their waters solely from Egypt. These five rivers are here termed the Eonile (Tmu), Paleonile (Tplu), Protonile (Q^1), Prenile (Q^2), and Neonile (Q^3).

THE EONILE (Tmu)

The cutting of the valley of the Nile seems to have taken place during the Messinian (Upper Miocene). This stage has long been recognized as an episode of regression and erosion in northern Africa. Barr and Walker (1973) have recently reviewed the earlier records of Messinian in northeastern Africa and have come to the conclusion that all lack definitive paleontologic evidence. In the case of Egypt in particular, these authors agree with the currently accepted view of the complete absence of marine Upper Miocene deposits in Egypt. The Deep Sea Drilling Project cruise leg 13 covering the Mediterranean Sea has revealed the widespread occurrence of an evaporitic suite beneath the bottom of this sea which has now been proven to be of Upper Miocene age. The evaporitic suite obtained from drilling during leg 13 comprises halite, anhydrite, gypsum, and dolomite. Hsü, Ryan and Cita (1973) have given evidence that these were deposited in a "desiccated deep-sea basin model" that allowed the formation of these evaporites in a series of shallow salt lakes or playas which represented the relics of a desiccated Mediterranean. All available evidence from mineralogical, petrographical, sedimentological, and geochemical investigations indicates that the Mediterranean sea bottom was a bare exposed surface during the Upper Miocene. The inferred lowering of the sea level by several thousand meters below the Atlantic sea level has supporting geomorphological evidence from adjacent land areas where channels cut by streams rejuvenated during the regression of the sea have been recorded from all areas draining into this emptied Mediterranean basin.

Channels cutting deep into the elevated north African plateau and graded to this new base level have been recorded from several places in Libya and Egypt. Squyers and Bradley (1964) have recorded an abandoned channel in the Qattara scarp. Bellini (1969) has recorded another channel in the area between Jaghbub and Giallo in Libya, while Barr and Walker (1973) have reported a deeply incised channel south of the Cyrenaican platform on the northeastern flank of the Sirte Basin in Libya, which has cut more than 430 m below sea level into middle Miocene rocks. These latter authors suggest a sudden drop in the Mediterranean sea level of considerably more than 430 m to explain this deep drainage erosion in Upper Miocene times. The same authors have also reported that geophysical crews prospecting for oil along the eastern margin of the Sirte basin, northern Libya, experienced severe velocity problems in the upper 1,000 to 2,000 feet of surface sediments, indicating rapid lithologic changes. These sharp velocity changes coincided in many cases with dry drainage systems that seem to be of considerable magnitude and depth.

The drilling in the delta and valley of the Nile has also fathomed the great depth to which the Nile channel was excavated during the Upper Miocene. South of Aswan and in the abandoned channel between Shallal and Aswan the granitic bedrock was hit at a depth of 220 m below sea level. To the west of Cairo at Tamuh water well the middle Eocene bedrock was reached at a depth of 568 meters. Recent drilling in the delta of the Nile has shown the presence of an evaporitic suite at exactly the same horizon recorded beneath the Mediterranean Sea by the Deep Sea Drilling Project cruise leg 13 at depths ranging from 3,963 m (Kafr el Sheikh well no. 1) to 2,034 m (Tabia well no. 1) below sea level.

Figure 4 is a structure contour map of the base of the Upper Miocene in the delta region. It shows that at the advent of this epoch the southern part of the delta (here termed the South Delta Block) was a positive area which represented in fact the northern margin of the African continent. To the north and beyond the cliffy edge of this block a deep embayment (here termed the North Delta Embayment) covered the northern reaches of the delta and formed part of the Eastern Mediterranean Basin. The

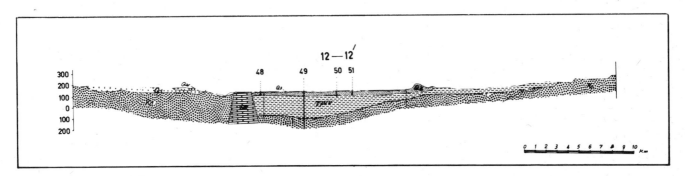

FIG. 1—Cross sections in Nile Valley. *Kn* = Cretaceous Nubian Sandstone; *Te* = Eocene; *Tpll* = Lower Pliocene; *Tplu* = Upper Pliocene Paleonile; *Tplu/Q_1* = Protonile; Q_2 = Prenile; Q_3 = Neonile.

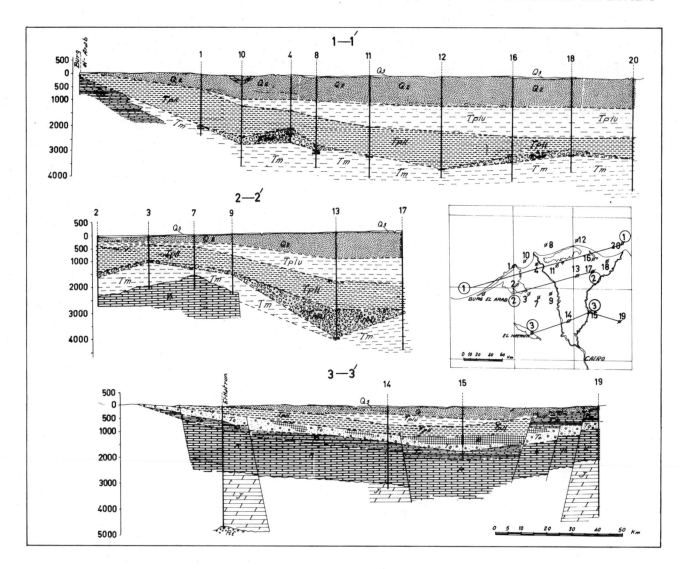

FIG. 2—Cross sections in Nile Delta. *PC* = Precambrian; *J* = Jurassic; *K* = Cretaceous; *Te* = Eocene; *To* = Oligocene; *B* = Basalt sheets; *Tm* = Miocene; *Tmu* = Eonile (Upper Miocene); *Tpll* = Lower Pliocene; *Tplu* = Paleonile (Upper Pliocene); Q_2 = Prenile; Q_3 = Neonile; *Dark lines* = Anhydrite bands.

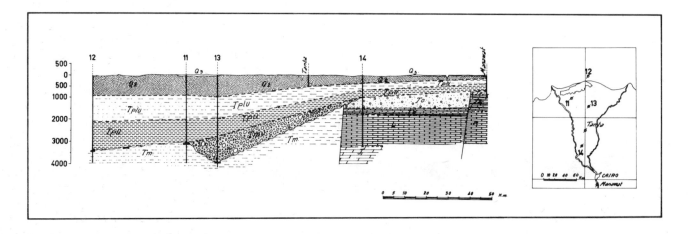

FIG. 3—Longitudinal Section in Nile Delta.

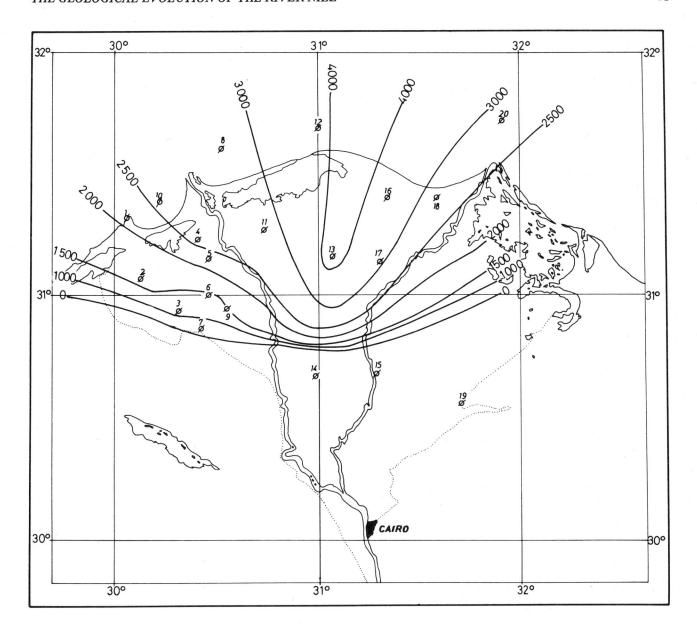

FIG. 4—Structure Contour Map of Base of Miocene.

southern limit of this basin seems to have been controlled by the east-west fault which marks the present coast of the Mediterranean to the west of the Gulf of Arabs; the continuation of this fault limited the northern edge of the South Delta Block. During the middle Miocene open marine deep water sediments were deposited in the northern embayment. To the east and west of this embayment were deposited shallow marine reefal limestones which seem to have accumulated in the shelf areas of the African continent that were overlapped by the middle Miocene sea.

The Eonile must have eroded its bed deep into the elevated Egyptian plateau along a path which defined the course of the Nile. The Eonile must have also received waters from the numerous wadis that debouch into the valley today; their courses must have also been molded during this epoch. Many of these wadis are filled with sedi-

ments of the succeeding rivers which abut against their slopes, indicating that they were already in existence when these rivers started to flow. The Eonile must have cascaded over the northern cliffs of the South Delta Block into the dried Northern Delta depression distributing its load over its surface. In some of the wells drilled in the North Delta Embayment such as Kafr el Dawar, Hosh Isa, Buseili, Mahmudiya, Damanhour, N. Dilingat, Rosetta offshore, Ityay el Baroud, Abu Qir offshore, Kafr el Sheikh, Abu Madi, El Wastani and Bilqas, Upper Miocene Eonile sediments have been recorded. In most of these wells these sediments rest over the evaporites and form thin sections of less than 100 m in thickness. In some, however, they attain thicknesses of more than 300 m (Buseili). In Kafr el Sheikh they overlie and interfinger the evaporites and attain a thickness of more than 1,300 meters. The sediments are coarse clastics, unstratified, and include chert granules and rolled fossils derived from the Cretaceous and Eocene rocks of mainland Egypt. The presence of these thick sediments in Kafr el Sheikh indicates that this area represented the overdeepened part of the basin which lay at the foot of the South Delta Block waterfall of the Eonile.

THE EONILE/PALEONILE INTERVAL (Tpl 1)

During the lower Pliocene the rise in sea level caused a marine ingression into the excavated valley of the Eonile. Marine lower Pliocene sediments follow on top of the Upper Miocene or older rocks in the wells drilled in the delta. In the wells drilled in the North Delta Embayment, the lower Pliocene sediments include a rich planktonic foraminiferal assemblage. Viotti and Mansour (1969) recognized four planktonic zones which they considered belonging to the Miocene. They are: the *Globigerina nilotica* Zone, the *G. nepenthes* Zone, the *Sphaeroidinellopsis seminula grimsdalei* Zone, and the *Globorotalia fohsi peripheroronda* Zone. An unconformity is present separating the lowermost zone from the upper three zones. The oldest zone, the *Globorotolia fohsi peripheroronda* Zone, is of middle Miocene age. However, in a reevaluation of this work, Mansour et al. (1969) now consider the upper three zones as lower Pliocene. The evidence, therefore, indicates that in the North Delta Embayment an open sea planktonic facies of lower Pliocene age overlies an open sea facies of the middle Miocene. As previously noted, the interval that separates these two epochs is represented by evaporites and fluviatile sediments of the Eonile phase. In the South Delta Block, the open marine lower Pliocene sediments are far thinner and rest directly over Oligocene sands and gravels. In Mit Ghamr well no. 1 and Shebin el Kom well no. 1, the lower Pliocene sediments attain a thickness of 350 and 307 m respectively. In contrast, the thickness of the lower Pliocene in the North Delta Embayment ranges from 700 (Ityay el Baroud well no. 1) to 1,400 m (Abu Qir offshore well no. 1) (see fig. 3).

Away from the delta the distribution of the lower Pliocene sediments is limited in extent. In the Burg el Arab well No. 1, 45 km west of Alexandria, the lower Pliocene is represented by a 50 m-thick shale section which rests unconformably on middle Miocene limestones (Omara and Ouda, 1969). In Wadi Natrun well no. 1, half way along the Cairo-Alexandria desert road, the marine lower Pliocene rests over sands that follow a basalt sheet of supposed Oligocene age. In the Abu Roash well no. 1, marine lower Pliocene sediments are recorded from depths of 94-161 m, resting unconformably over Cenomanian shales. In addition to these marine records Chumakov (1967), using materials from numerous boreholes, has documented a large channel in the Nile Valley in Aswan. This was cut into igneous bedrock by an ancestral Nile River 310 m below the Nile's present level. The basal sediments filling this ancient channel consist of gray, montmorillonitic clays with thin lenses of fine-grained, micaceous sands and sandy loams

that are rich in plant detritus. A uniform suite of authigenic minerals is present including glauconite, zeolite, pyrite, and siderite. The sands are partially cemented by secondary calcite. Rare ostracods belonging to the genera *Cypridea*, *Cyprinotus*, *Limnocythere*, *Eucypris*, and *Candoniella* were recovered, which suggests a brackish environment of deposition and a lower Pliocene age for the lowermost channel fill. Chumakov believes this channel to have been cut during the late Miocene, resulting in the formation of an enormous marine estuary in the Nile Valley during the early Pliocene. The presence of this marine estuary has long been inferred from the study of the distribution of sediments of the Pliocene in Egypt (Sandford and Arkell, 1939; Butzer and Hansen, 1968).

Although the origin of this elongate channel that was flooded by the lower Pliocene marine embayment could be the result of erosion by a river that graded its bed to a lowered base level, it is possible that tectonics played an important role in its formation. The Egyptian part of the Nile Valley which lies not very far from the seismoactive east African fault zone seems to represent the consolidated part of the early platform which was rejuvenated by recent faulting movements and block dislocations. Gorshkov (1963) lists the major historic earthquakes that are known to have taken place along the Nile Valley from the data published by the National Astronomical Centre, Cairo (Ismail, 1960; Sieberg, 1932). Most of the epicenters pass along the valley of the Nile which is shown to be seismoactive. The stratigraphic data compiled in this paper show that the distribution of several rock units that were formed in the valley cannot be explained rationally without assuming faulting movements along the entire valley. Furthermore, the presence of slipped masses and thick breccias at the footslopes of the cliffs of the valley show that these must have slid along the slopes by the trigger action of earthquakes. The centers of earthquake activity in Egypt coincide to a remarkable degree with the areas that were effected by the submergence of the Pliocene gulf.

Furthermore, as will be noted later, many of the major changes in the regimen, sources and courses of the rivers that filled the valley of the Nile since the termination of this gulf phase are connected in one way or another with major events that took place during the development of the Red Sea. Although there is no geodetic record of uplift or tilting of the land through which the Nile passes and there is no record of movement along the numerous faults that cross or run parallel to the Nile, there is no doubt that further research will prove the presence of these movements which are to be expected if the idea of Red Sea spreading is accepted.

Indication that the Nile Delta and the northern reaches of the valley form a structural depression representing a gap originating by an incipient crustal separation arrested at an early stage comes from the scanty geophysical data available. Gergawi and Khashab (1968) have shown, from a survey of the seismic wave velocities, that the thickness of the crust in the seismic belt across the delta to the north of Helwan which they have marked on their seismic map (1968) is 24 km, smaller than usual, so much so that they called this crust "semicontinental," or "intermediate transitional between continent and water." Several transverse faults with an almost east-west direction cut across the delta forming a series of horsts and grabens. The most conspicuous of the horsts is the South Delta Block, the northern boundary of which seems to have controlled the limit to which the middle Miocene sea advanced over the delta. Basalts issuing along these faults are known in many places in the block either in outcrop or in the subsurface. In Mit Ghamr well no. 1 a basalt sheet about 300 m thick is recorded in the subsurface at a depth of 1,117 meters. In Wadi el Natrun well no. 1, in Khatatba well no. 1, and in many of the shallow water wells drilled to the northwest of Cairo basalts of lesser thicknesses have been recorded recently in the subsurface and in association with Oligocene sands and gravels. In addition to the numerous northwest/southeast faults that cross the river in many places, particularly in the Minia–Beni Suef reach, a large number of east-west faults are known to cut across the valley in many places. One of the most spectacular of these is the Wadi Tarfa fault which is shown in the space photographs to cut across the entire Eastern Desert up to the Red Sea. Less spectacular of this set of faults are the Wadi Assiuti–Gebel Drunka east-west fault, the Kom Ombo graben fault, the Wadi Abu Sibeira fault (north of Aswan), and the Kalbsha–Khor Rahma fault, which seem to form the continuation of one of the great east-west faults known in the southern part of the Western Desert and which runs along the Sinn el Kaddab scarp for a distance close to 200 kilometers. All these faults show horizontal displacements along their path.

Even more significant are the numerous reentrants along the cliffs that bound the Nile Valley in its middle course and which cannot be explained by normal weathering processes. These reentrants assume the shape of a rhomb (Nag Hamadi, Akhmim, Tel el Amarna, Assiut), or of a sphene (Tahta, Sannur). Many have no drainage into them, but some form the mouths of some of the wadis that drain into the Nile. The fact that these reentrants become suddenly wider and the wadis debouch into them shows that they cannot owe their origin to normal erosion. The rhomboid-shaped reentrants may best be explained by wrench faulting along an original deflected or sinuous fracture, which brought about the separation of the adjoining blocks and the development of gradually lengthening gaps. A similar origin has been given to the Dead Sea "rhombochasm" by Quennell (1958). The Tahta and Sannur sphenes also could represent gaps separating two blocks bound by faults which converge toward a point. These gaps do not only involve rotation of one block relative to another but also a certain amount of trans-current movement.

Toward the end of the Lower Pliocene the marine gulf which occupied the long and narrow excavated valley of the Nile witnessed a phase in which the sea retreated to the north up to the latitude of Biba (Beni Suef province) to the north. Into this marine embayment were deposited shallow marine sediments, mainly marls, sandstones, and coquinal limestones which make up numerous outcrops that skirt the cultivation and abut the bounding Eocene rocks of the valley in its northern reaches. The classical locality of these deposits is that of Kom el Shelul to the south of the Gizeh Pyramids. The remarkable abundance of fossils in this locality makes it one of the most frequently visited areas. It has been described by Blanckenhorn (1901), Mayer-Eymar (1898), Sandford and Arkell (1939), and many others. The section begins by a basal 10 m oyster bed made up almost exclusively of *Ostrea cucullata* shells. This is followed by a 2 m sandstone bed crowded with *Pecten benedictus* and *Chlamys scabrella*. Upon this lies a sandstone bed only ½ m thick full of remains of *Clypeaster aegyptiacus* casts of large gastropods (*Strombus coronatus*, *Xenophora infundibulum*, etc.), the same Pectens in the underlying bed, and many other fossils. Then follows a 10 m bed of nonfossiliferous yellow quartzone sand and brownish sandstone with large flint pebbles.

Several other exposures are known along the cultivation edge on both banks of the Nile. Many of the exposures listed by Blanckenhorn (1901), Sandford and Arkell (1939), and Little (1935) have been tilled up or have become the sites of habitation of local villagers and are, therefore, difficult to reexamine. Perhaps the best preserved of these exposures is in Helwan (Tebin) and the Nile-Fayum divide. In Helwan the exposure is about 20 m thick and is made up of a series of marls, sandstones, shales, and thin limestone bands rich in typical Pliocene fossils. Farag and Ismail (1959) describe the section and Said (1955) gives a list of the foraminifera which he separated from a marl bed in this locality.

Blanckenhorn (1901) and Little (1935) give several sections in Wadis El Hai and Nuumiya on the east bank of the river opposite El Ayat and Iskar villages. Both sections are in the form of a thin (1 m) bed of sandstones or marls rich in *Ostrea cucullata* and/or *Pecten benedictus* which are topped by coarse conglomerates of local derivation. Both sections abut middle Eocene limestone. In Wadi Sannur a 6 m section is described from this locality by Blanckenhorn. It is made up of sandstone and oyster banks as well as hardened shaley bands topped by a ½ m bed of boulders of local derivation. In Gebel Um Raqaba, the most southerly extension of the marine Pliocene exposures along the east bank of the Nile, Abdel Ghany and Zaghloul (1973) describe a section of sandstone with oyster casts about 7 m thick which overlies unconformably the upper Eocene and which is overlain by an 8 m-thick section of conglomerates and sandy marls.

On the opposite (western) bank of the Nile in Fayum several sections of Pliocene have been described by Sandford and Arkell (1929) and Little (1935). The best exposure is that of Shakluf bridge in the Gebel Naalun area. Here the section is about 36 m thick of which the top layers—made up of false-bedded nonfossiliferous yellow to brown quartz sands (12 m) and a hard conglomerate bed of coarse gravel cemented by travertines (2 m)—may not belong to the Pliocene. The lower part of the section is made up of thin sandstone beds, somewhat cemented sand beds alternating with thick, blue to purple gypseous shales. The hard yellow sandstone beds include casts of *Pecten benedictus*, *Chlamys scabrella*, and *Ostrea cucullata* shells. From a bird's eye view, these late lower Pliocene exposures form undulating, gravelly-to-cobbly lands, often with shallow soils and local rock outcrops.

In all these exposures the Pliocene rests over older rocks with angular unconformity, and there is no stratigraphic evidence that would help in placing the deposits of this episode within the sequence of stratigraphic rock units that fill the valley of the Nile. No Pliocene occurrences with similar faunas or lithology have so far been noted in the boreholes drilled in the Nile or the delta region, and it is possible that the shallow marine Pliocene was never deposited in many parts of the delta region. The regressive Pliocene deposits were restricted to channels in the delta that have yet to be found; but it is also possible that the regressive marine lower Pliocene sediments were deposited in the Nile Valley and the delta and were then removed by later erosion. Said and Yousri (1964) describe a fauna from the clay beds in the Abu Sir well, one of the boreholes of the Cairo area between a depth of 474 to 572 m, which they ascribe to the Pliocene. On paleogeographic and paleotectonic evidence it is difficult to correlate this unit with the nearby shallow marine Pliocene exposures, and it may well be more fitting to correlate this unit with the overlying clays which top the marine Pliocene in many parts of the Cairo area.

In the boreholes of the delta, marine to fluvio-marine upper Pliocene faunas are recorded in the clay section above the lower Pliocene, but the section rests directly without unconformity or change of facies over the lower Pliocene. The only locality where the *Ostrea cucullata* shallow marine beds fall within a complete Pliocene-Pleistocene section is in the Wadi Natrun area where these beds overlie unconformably the lower Pliocene and underlie the deltaic marls and clays correlatable with the estuarine clays of the Paleonile (*vide infra*). In this particular locality the lower beds of the Garet el Meluk section carry the usual marine Pliocene faunas of the Kom el Shelul Formation, and these pass unconformably into the clays of the Paleonile. The elevation of this shallow marine Pliocene is in the range of 4 to 6 m above sea level.

The Pliocene beds in the floor of Wadi el Natrun are, therefore, different from any other in that they are very low in altitude as compared to those in the Cairo-Fayum reach on the western bank and to those on the eastern bank. These elevations show the intense movements to which the delta and the Nile must have been subjected prior to this regressive phase of the lower Pliocene. Indications that these movements must have taken place since the Pliocene will be discussed later in this paper.

THE PALEONILE (Tplu)

Sediments belonging to the Paleonile river system consist of a long series of interbedded, red brown, fluviatile to fluvio-marine clays and thin, fine-grained sands and silt laminae which crop out along the banks of the valley and many of the wadis that drain into it. They are also recorded from the subsurface in practically all the boreholes that were drilled in the valley or the delta. They occur consistently below the sand-gravel layer that underlies the agricultural silt layer characteristic of the fertile lands of Egypt.

In the north the fluviatile clays become fluvio-marine in character and seem to represent deposition under estuarine conditions. These fluvio-marine clays are noted on the well logs of the deep boreholes drilled in the delta region where they are given the name "Kafr el Sheikh Formation" by geologists of the oil companies. This formation, as defined by these geologists, includes the clay section which lies underneath the sand and gravel beds deposited by the succeeding river. The lower limit of the formation is fixed at the point where a lithological change takes place or where an unconformity surface is encountered. The formation as such includes in many cases, in addition to the Paleonile fluvio-marine clays, the purely marine clay beds of the lower Pliocene. In Kafr el Sheikh well no. 1, considered by the oil company geologists as the type section of this clay unit, the formation has a thickness of 1,960 m and extends from depths of 775 m to 2,735 m below sea level. The lower 885 m of this unit is of lower Pliocene age and includes a rich, open marine planktonic foraminiferal assemblage. The upper 905 m, however, includes, in addition to marine faunas, a brackish water foraminiferal assemblage which increases relative to the marine assemblage both in the number of species and individuals as one progresses toward the upper levels of the section. This indicates the relative increase with time of riverine versus marine forces in the construction of the Nile Delta.

These fluviatile to fluvio-marine clays and silts appear also on the surface in many parts of the valley. They have been noted by previous workers and referred to in the literature as the *Melanopsis* Stufe by Blanckenhorn (1901, 1921), the chocolate brown clays of the Gulf phase by Sandford and Arkell (1939), the plastic clay layer by Fourtau (1915) and Said (1973), or the Helwan Formation by the Geological Survey of Egypt (Said, 1971).

The Paleonile sediments are exceedingly uniform in lithological and mineral composition. An examination of four clay samples from these sediments in Sidi Salem well no. 1 (kindly supplied by the Petroleum Organization) shows that the clay is composed mainly of montmorillonite with little kaolinite and some accessory minerals including quartz, biotite, muscovite, pyrite, epidote, and zircon. Minor feldspars and pyroxenes are recorded from the topmost sample. Save for the presence of minor interbedded sand beds especially noted in the upper levels of the formation, the Paleonile sediments form an almost solid clay unit. Phillip and Yousri (1964) describe the mineralogy of the sand layers which intercalate this unit in the Abu Sir well near Cairo and state that about one-half of the heavy mineral fraction separated is made up of opaques. Epidote and other accessory minerals such as zircon, kyanite, andalusite, staurolite, and others make up the other half of the heavy mineral fraction. No pyroxenes such as characterize the modern Nile sediments (Shukri, 1950) are found in these sand layers. This points to a source which is different from that of the present-day Nile.

Structure contour maps constructed on the base of the Paleonile sediments (fig. 5) show that the delta region had at the inception of the Paleonile riverine sedimentation a northward sloping surface with a downward dip at the northern edge of the older South Delta Block. This block, as pointed out earlier, was overlapped by the lower Pliocene transgression, but its effects persisted during the upper Pliocene. This effect can be seen on examination of the isopach map of the Paleonile sediments (fig. 6) where they reach a thickness of 250-500 m in the South Delta Block, and in the northern embayment they attain a thickness which exceeds 1,000 meters. This figure shows also that the Paleonile had a delta whose outline coincided more or less with the modern delta along its eastern edge, but along its western borders the Paleonile delta seems to have extended farther west.

The fluvio-marine and deltaic beds of the Wadi el Natrun area (Gar el Muluk Formation) seem to represent the western peripheral swampy deposits of this old delta in its early phases. The Wadi Natrun fluvio-marine beds have attracted the attention of authors since the discovery within them of fossil mammals by Struder in 1889. The area has been visited since then by numerous scholars, and a good description of the classical Gar el Muluk section is given in Lyons (1906), Blanckenhorn (1901), Andrews (1902), and Von Stromer Reichenbach (1902). The latter author describes the vertebrate faunas as well as the stratigraphic relationships of the fossil vertebrate-bearing bed within the section. A review of the earlier work on the vertebrates found in this region and a description of additional materials is to be found in James and Slaughter (1974).

The exposure at Gar el Muluk forms a prominent topographic feature in the flat surrounding terrain of the Natrun depression. The hill is capped by about 14 m of alternating gypsiferous clay, sandstone, silt, and limestone beds of both marine and brackish water origin. These beds contain, in addition to crocodilian and fish remains, a late lower Pliocene invertebrate assemblage. Below this unit is a 1 m-thick resistant sandstone bed followed underneath by slope-forming carbonaceous sandstone, clay, and limestone beds 8 m thick. Underlying this are the main vertebrate-bearing beds which include 6 m of alternating sand and clay layers with cross-bedded channel-fill deposits of sand and gravel. These beds seem to be a fresh water habitat. *Hipparon*, *Hippopotamus*, and *Hippotragus* sp. are among the vertebrates that have been described from this unit.

The Wadi Natrun Pliocene exposures seem, therefore, to represent the oldest beds deposited by the Paleonile which began with the retreating seas of the lower Pliocene. The river then seems to have overstepped the area to build a large delta toward the north. Figure 6 shows that the Paleonile sediments increase in thickness progressively northward. It seems reasonable, therefore, to believe that these sediments were deposited by a prograding river which built up a progressively advancing delta, the northern limits of which within the Mediterranean cannot be delineated at present. The Nile cone is known to extend from the continental shelf and slope across the continental rise to the long, narrow Herodotus abyssal plain. The western part of this cone, the so-called Rosetta fan, is close to 60,000 km^2 in extent and is indented by the Alexandria submarine canyon which forms the extension of the modern Rosetta branch of the delta. The canyon bifurcates in this deltaic fan. The eastern part of the cone, the Damietta fan, is separated from the western Rosetta fan by a mass of abyssal hills. The Damietta fan seems to have received contribution from the Nile in relatively recent times. The area of the delta cone made up of both these fans and the continental delta is, therefore, in the range of 125,000 km^2, almost four times the size of the modern delta.

The drillholes of the Deep Sea Drilling Project cruise leg 13 in the delta cone (holes 129, 130, and 131) are shown to be made up of turbidites with rare pelogic oozes which obviously resulted from the Nile sediment discharge into the Mediterranean (Nesteroff, 1973). Although these drillholes did not penetrate into the Pliocene, it is feasible to believe that deeper drilling in the margins of the African continent off the Nile Delta would reveal the presence of other turbidites such as those found beneath the Quaternary sediments in the offshore deep wells of the delta.

The thickness of the deltaic sediments since the beginning of river sediment contribution to the Mediterranean is in the range of 2 km in the northern reaches of the delta, decreasing toward the apex of the delta to about 500 m; and the volume of the entire sediment is, therefore, about 200,000 km^3. This figure is larger than the 140,000 km^3 figure given by Harrison (1955) based upon an interpretation of gravity anomalies in the eastern Mediterranean. Of the estimated 200,000 km^3 of the Nile Delta cone, it can be safely stated that about 60% of this detritus was accumulated by the Paleonile system. It also can be assumed that the delta of the Nile is an old feature which started to build by the advent of the upper Pliocene and took form by the beginning of the Pleistocene.

The paleontology of the Paleonile sediments suggests a gradual filling of the valley and the delta by a river system that debouched into the marine Pliocene gulf with the fluviatile sediments progressively moving northward. Thus, in the south the formation carries no recognizable fossils and is of proper fluviatile origin, while in the north the formation carries a fauna of estuarine to brackish water habitat. Blanckenhorn (1901, 1921) had already described some of the more characteristic fossils found in this unit— *Melanopsis aegyptiacus*, *Melania tuberculata*, *Hydrobia*

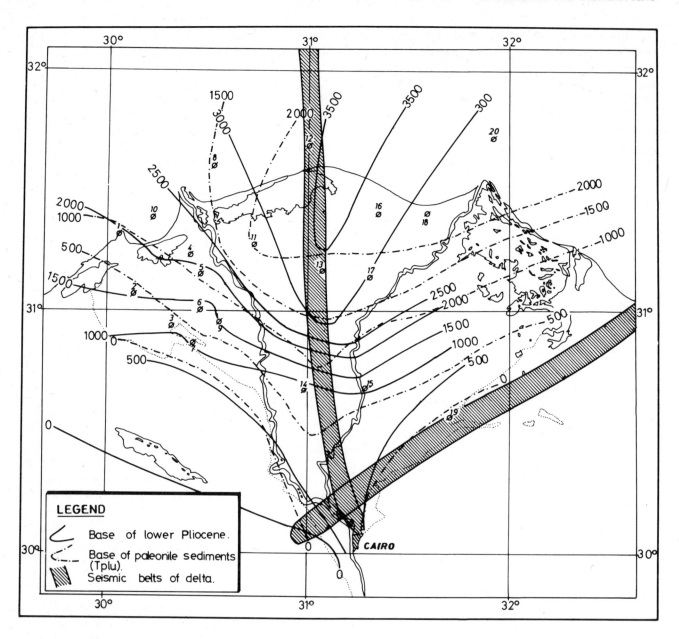

FIG. 5—Structure Contour Map of Base of Pliocene and Base of Paleonile (*Tplu*).

stagnalis, Vivipara martensi, Mactra subtruncata elongata, and others. Said and Yousri (1964) describe a rich brackish water foraminiferal assemblage of boreal habitat and Atlantic affinities from a well near Cairo in the upper levels of the clays of the Paleonile which was correlated with the Castellarquato faunas, now considered as of upper Pliocene age (see discussion by Berggren, 1969; Hays et al., 1969; Ciaranfi and Cita, 1973). The logs of many of the wells drilled in the northern reaches of the delta show the influx of brackish water foraminiferal assemblage following on top of the open marine assemblages of lower Pliocene age in the Kafr el Sheikh Formation.

The height to which the Paleonile sediments accumulated is difficult to determine. These old riverine deposits appear at a depth that ranges from -2,214 m in the Abu Madi well no. 1 to -308 m in the Kafr el Dawar well no. 1.

The elevations of the Paleonile sediments measured in outcrop and encountered in the subsurface of the wells of the valley, respectively, show heights which range from -183 to +180 meters. Whether the formation in any one area formed a column that extended from the lowest point within the valley to the highest point on its fringes is difficult to ascertain. It is possible that tectonics played a role in the lowering of the axial parts of the Nile trough in post-Paleonile times; but it is also certain that the upper part of the formation was trimmed by erosion in later times.

The Paleonile sediments crop out along the footslopes of the bounding cliffs of the present major wadis that drain into the southern reaches of the Egyptian Nile, indicating that these wadis were not only in existence when the Paleonile started flowing but that they also represented major

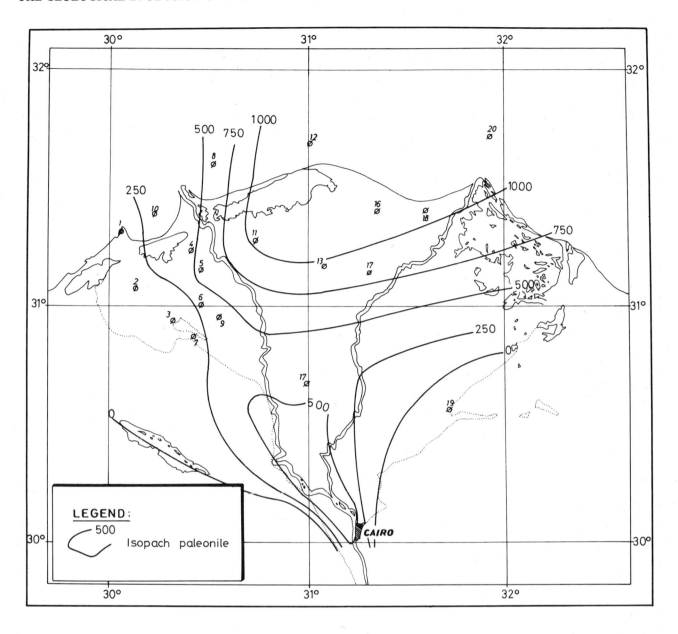

FIG. 6—Isopach Map of Paleonile (*Tplu*) Sediments. (Numbers refer to well locations.)

tributaries of this river. Perhaps the largest of these tributaries is the Kharit-Garara branch on the sides of which the present writer was able to identify Pliocene fluviatile sediments. The discovery of these Paleonile sediments fringing the present-day course of the Kharit-Garara wadis of the southern part of the Eastern Desert of Egypt represents one of the most significant contributions of this work. Further work is needed before a full description of this important tributary of the Paleonile can be given, and the following remarks must be regarded as preliminary.

Wadi Kharit, one of the present great trunk wadis of Egypt, has its principal head at Gebel Ras el Kharit on the main Nile—Red Sea watershed at altitude 24°09′N. and longitude 35°E. Pursuing a course the prevailing direction of which is a little north of west, and collecting the drainage from numerous great wadis on its way, it debouches in the Kom Ombo plain and reaches the Nile at the same point as another great wadi, Shait, at latitude 24°35′ N. The length of the main channel is over 260 km and of its tributaries probably more than twenty times as great. It drains an area of more than 25,000 km². Its average fall is about 2 m/km, but in its lower reaches its gradient is less than half this amount. The principal tributaries of Wadi Kharit are wadis Natash, Antar, Khashab, Abu Hamamid, and Karara. Wadis Karara, Timsah, and Ghadarib are great feeders and in direct continuation with the main trunk of Wadi Kharit. Together they run in a great tectonic graben that extends from the Kom Ombo plain down to Gebel Hodein. The sediments that fill this graben and overlie the Nubia Sandstone already have been separated by the Hunting geology report (1967) which carried out a photogeological survey of the southern part of the Eastern Desert of Egypt. They were noted as thinly bedded sediments of "quite distinct photo characteristics." They were related to post-Nubian Early Tertiary—Cretaceous sediments of the Kom Ombo and Wadi Abad areas. The distinguishing photo characteristics are "the generally light tone (although darker material is occasionally present), smooth surface, rather thin bedding, and pronounced dips and folds near major fault zones." The distribution of the Wadi Karara—Wadi Abad sediments is clearly fault controlled. They occupy downthrown blocks in the Nubia Sandstones.

The Paleonile sediments of the Wadi Kharit—Wadi Karara complex occur as enormous terrace embankments about 10-12 m high on either side of the present water channel. They are made up of well-stratified, alternating thinly bedded friable sands and sandy clays, ending abruptly against the granites and schists of the hill masses. They contain ferruginous scales and show suncracks in places. The material is fine and well stratified and must have been laid down under different climatic conditions than those prevailing at present. The deposits are indeed very similar to the Pliocene thinly bedded sediments that were described by Chumakov (1967) as occurring at depth in the boreholes of the Aswan region. The ferruginous scales are exclusively in the ferrous form indicating reducing conditions. This can be explained by deposition of a river that had its source in a moist region with effective vegetation cover and little or no torrential runoff, so that stream discharge includes little or no coarse detritus.

The Kharit-Karara Paleonile sediments run in a northwesterly direction and end in the Kom Ombo graben. Another similar deposit trending in the same direction fringes the tectonic graben of Wadi Um Sellim which opens up at present to the south of Idfu. The deposits here are more sandy than the Kharit-Karara sediments. Whether this wadi was, during the Pliocene, in continuation with the Kharit-Karara drainage remains to be seen; but it is almost certain that northwest-southeast grabens of Wadis Um Sellim and Kharit-Karara are older than the east-west Wadi Shait—Silsileh, Wadi Natash, and Abu Sibeira—Allawi—Khashab faults which control the Kom Ombo graben.

The uniformity of the Paleonile sediments, its mineralogy, and its fine-grained lithological composition suggest that the Paleonile had its sources in moist areas with effective vegetation cover. Indeed, southern Egypt must have enjoyed a wet climate during the Pliocene. It is interesting to note that the Paleonile coincided with the greatest first global cooling, which must have brought in a great pluvial episode in tropical and equatorial Africa. The distribution of these sediments suggests that the wadis draining the southeastern massif of Egypt formed a source of this river. Other sources which must have existed in order to account for the enormous volume of sediments of the Paleonile have to be sought outside Egypt. There is a good possibility that the equatorial and subequatorial highlands of Africa contributed sediment to this river.

The question of the history of the equatorial Nile and its breakthrough into Egypt is unknown. No data are available on the subsurface geology of the Bahr el Gebel and White Nile basins. These basins are covered by the Um Ruwaba

Formation which is a thick deposit of lacustrine origin. In the absence of more detailed study, the concensus is that the equatorial Nile did not reach Egypt except during the Late Pleistocene. Even if further research should corroborate this view, this would not preclude the possibility of another equatorial or subequatorial source. It is possible to assume the feeding of the Nubian-Egyptian Nile from equatorial Africa via the large and impressive Wadis el Milk and Hawar which drain the highlands of Western Sudan (Gebel Marra volcanic massif which receives today a mean monthly rainfall of 800 mm). These seasonally fed wadis emanate today from this massif, and their waters fail to reach the Nile and die out in the plains of the sand-covered country of Northern Sudan. It is feasible to assume that under more favorable climatic conditions, such as are assumed to have occurred during the Upper Pliocene, these wadis reached the Nubian Nile in the Debba-Dargola reach. Andrew (1948) and Whiteman (1971) claim that there is an uplift of the country between the massif and the Nile (Wadi el Milk—Sodiri axis). It may be that in later times this uplifting coupled with a period of lesser precipitation prevented the water of this subequatorial source from flowing into Egypt. There is no doubt that the detailed mapping of these regions will help in the reconstruction of the paleogeography of the Paleonile basin.

THE PALEONILE-PROTONILE INTERVAL $(Tplu/Q_1)$

The Paleonile-Protonile interval covers the period which elapsed from the time the Paleonile stopped flowing to the beginning of the breaking through of the succeeding Protonile into Egypt. This interval was essentially one of great seismicity, during which the climate was exceedingly arid. This period of hyperaridity was interrupted in its early part by a short pluvial, here termed the Armant "Pluvial," during which semiarid climatic conditions with winter season runoff prevailed. The result of this "pluvial" was the deposition, over the eroded surface of the Paleonile sediments, of locally derived detritus in the form of alternating beds of conglomerate and sands or marls. These choke today many of the mouths of the side wadis that drain into the Nile. Thicknesses of as much as 40 m of this material have been noted in the Armant area to the south of Luxor. During the end phases of this pluvial bedded horizontal or slope travertines were deposited and tufaceous materials cementing the Armant beds were formed.

During the latter part of this interval, here termed the Issawia, great seismic activity set over the Nile Valley. Great talus breccias accumulated along the slopes of the valley and the side wadis.

The Paleonile-Protonile interval was one in which wind activity was most active; and it was during this interval that some, if not all, of the famous depressions of Egypt were formed, or at least started to form. The Wadi Natrun depression which was filled by the Paleonile sediments, relics of which still stand in the form of isolated hills within the depression, was subjected during this interval of hyperaridity to enormous lowering. The amount of lowering during this particular episode cannot be determined, for the depression must have been the site of further lowering by wind erosion in succeeding periods of aridity.

Deposits of this interval will be dealt with in the following paragraphs under the headings of Armant and Issawia Formations.

The Armant Formation

The early part of the hyperarid Paleonile-Protonile interval seems to have been characterized by torrential winter season runoff. During this episode there accumulated in many of the wadis that drain into the Nile conglomeratic deposits which are very similar to those that have accumulated in the recent past.

The conglomeratic deposits of the Armant Formation crop out along the footslopes of the bounding cliffs of the valley and in the deltas of the wadis that open into it. They also occur at depth in many of the floors of these deltas. The formation has not been recognized in the boreholes drilled in the valley or delta of the Nile. The Armant Formation skirts the cliffs that border the valley or the wadis that drain into it as well as the open deltas of these wadis. Some of the finest exposures are found at the footslopes of the towering cliffs of the plateau in the Thebaid hills on both the east and west banks, and on the east bank of the Minia—Beni Suef stretch where later erosion has exposed sections of this formation, composed of layer upon layer of conglomerate made up of the coarse disintegration products of the surrounding plateaus, washed and rounded by tributary streams. Away from the cliffs, the fine-grained calcareous component of this formation becomes increasingly conspicuous. These fine-grained sediments are marls composed largely of small chips of Eocene rocks cemented in some places (such as in the Valley of the Kings, Luxor) by later action of springs into fine-grained hard rock.

The most complete section of this formation is in Wadi Bairiya, Luxor district, which opens into the Nile near Armant (sec. 64, fig. 9). The formation is made up of conglomerate beds of locally derived Eocene gravels of limestone and chert of different sizes, alternating with thick marl beds which have numerous pebble intercalations. Sandford and Arkell (1933) give a photograph of this section (Pl. III, A and B) and a good description of it under their "Pliocene Gulf Deposits." This section is also the subject of the study of Coque and Said (1972).

To this formation belong also the east-west gravel-filled inverted channels that seem to have drained the elevated Fayum region and opened in the Rus channel of the Nile. Sandford and Arkell (1929) were the first to delineate these channels, and a good description of them is given in their work and in Pfannenstiel (1953). These authors interpret these channels as interdigitating the marine Pliocene sediments in the Nile Valley. The reexamination of these deposits, however, leads the author to the belief that the

sediments follow unconformably on top of the marine Pliocene sediments.

Deposits that belong to the Armant Formation have been recognized by Sandford and Arkell (1933, 1939) where they are classified among the "Pliocene Gulf Deposits," by Blanckenhorn (1901, 1921) where they are separated as "Diluvium II deposits" and by Giegengack (1968) as the "Wadi Conglomerates."

The composition of the rock fragments that make up the deposits of the Armant Formation differs from place to place, being, on the whole, of calcareous nature due to the derivation of most of them from the Eocene limestone plateaus that tower the valley along most of its middle course; but in some areas the fine-grained rock is made up of the products derived from the disintegration of the Cretaceous to Paleocene Dakhla and Esna Shales. These can be easily recognized because they are extensively quarried for use as Sebakh or fertilizer used by local villagers for spreading on the fields. In other areas, such as Wadi Um Silimat, the Nubia sandstone and the phosphate formation give the rock a phosphatic or arenaceous composition. In many areas, such as in Beni Suef, the gravel ridge made up of loose siliceous to dolomitic gravels are quarried for local construction. In the Qena and Ballas regions the calcareous silts have become famous since ancient Egyptian times, for they were, and are still, used as raw material for the famed Qena potteries of Upper Egypt.

The Armant Formation lies unconformably over the Paleonile or older sediments. The thickness ranges from a few meters to more than 40 meters. Its absolute elevation ranges from +120 to 230 m above sea level. On the whole, the elevation increases as one moves from the mouth to the source of the side wadi, indicating a steep gradient (1:200, in the case of Wadi Qena) and formation after an intense period of erosion. Figure 9 depicts the logs of those sections of the Armant Formation measured in the field by Abdel Ghany and Zaghloul (1973).

One of the characteristics of the Armant Formation which distinguishes it from later modern wadi conglomerates is the yellow red color which it assumes as a result of the presence of iron oxide cement within its particles. Most of the Armant occurrences form rolling surfaces. The top gravel layers (up to 2 m deep from the surface) have, in between the pebbles, sandy loam which is reddish brown in color (5 YR 4/4 moist - 4/7 dry) and is rich in lime with numerous soft gypsum aggregates. Many of the gravel beds have calcium carbonate hard pans.

The lithological characteristics of the Armant Formation are not different from those of another more recent (Neolithic[?]) but much thinner deposit which is also attributed to torrential activity of winter rains and cloudbursts. The climate of the Armant time also must have been similar to that of the Neolithic (?), but it was of a much longer duration and perhaps had more frequent rains. It must be assumed that during Armant time the Paleonile had stopped flowing into Egypt and that its sediments were cut down by the locally derived ephemeral streams of Armant times. At present the depth of this erosion cannot be estimated, but it was probably in the range of 200 m judging from the difference in elevation of the Paleonile sediments in the thalweg and in the sides of the Nile Valley. The Armant master stream seems to have first cut into the Paleonile sediments and then built up its bed in a course that is yet to be defined. The extent of the volume of the deposits of the Armant times can be visualized from a study of these sediments in Wadi Sannur. Here the thickness of the Armant Formation exceeds 15 m of which 9 m have been recorded from the subsurface in a pit that was dug in the bottom of the wadi without reaching the bedrock. The volume of sediment deposit by the Armant torrents must have exceeded 3 km^3 in this locality alone.

The end phase of this pluvial was marked by the deposition of travertines and tufaceous rocks. The best known of these travertines are those which occur in Issawia along the east bank of the river in the vicinity of Akhmim. The famous 7 m-thick, horizontally bedded travertines of Issawia are quarried on a large scale for their peculiar property as water-resistant rocks. The Issawia travertines are separated from the underlying chocolate brown clays of the Paleonile by a one-half-meter-thick bed of conglomerate made up of cemented, rounded to subrounded, limestone pebbles. The travertine itself, although porous, is very hard, easily dressed, and has no tendency to split or break, but can be worked in any direction and cut into any shape. The specific gravity is 2.4 to 2.5, while crushing strengths reach up to 188 kgm/cm^2. It is almost made up of pure CaCO$_3$ (99.60%) deposited in thin imbricating laminae as evaporites around algae that thrived in the Issawia lake in post—Kafr el Sheikh times. Although the rock itself is creamy white in color, the cavities in the limestone are often lined with red or yellow ochre. Mineralogically, the rock is made up of fine-grained microcrystalline calcite which is cloudy gray to white in color. The mineral is in the form of very fine anhedral to euhedral crystals, and there are few and scattered quartz grains.

Travertines that belong to this episode are known in many places along the slopes of the Eocene limestone cliffs of middle Egypt. The largest occurrence is in Nag Hammadi west where the travertines form an unbedded mass of vesicular rock that follows on the slope of the cliff. They seem to owe their origin, as in the case of the Kharga Oasis slope travertines, to the evaporation of the oozing waters spilling from the cliff around reeds whose roots must have taken hold on it.

Other travertines that belong to the same episode are found west of Beni Adi and Deir el Muharraq and in the Valley of the Kings around Luxor where the conglomerate and marl beds of the Armant Formation are cemented by tufaceous materials that seem to be the result of the evaporation of the CaCO$_3$—bearing waters that percolated through them.

Since the formation of the travertines and other tufaceous materials is the result of evaporation at the end phases of a pluvial period, it is obvious that travertines could be of different ages. Our work, however, has shown that the end phase of the Armant "Pluvial" is the episode *par excellence* of travertine formation in the Nile Valley.

The Issawia Formation

The Issawia Formation follows on top of the Armant Formation in many places in the Nile Valley. It is made up of massive rubble breccias which are topped in many places by the characteristic hard red breccias which are quarried for ornamental use in many places along the Nile. The type locality of this formation is in the Issawia rhomboid reentrant along the east bank of the river in the vicinity of Akhmim. The section (fig. 9, sec. 51) is made up of a 15 m-thick massive bed of breccia, made up of angular limestone pebbles, which overlies unconformably the thick travertines of this locality. It is characterized by poorly sorted angular pebbles, boulders, and occasional large blocks of stone. Usually, however, most of the pebbles are in the size range of 4-6 cm, or less, which gives the land surface a rather smooth appearance. The beds occupy the piedmonts of the nearby cliff, and their slope is rather steep (between 10 and 20%). The breccia was obviously not laid down by running water, but largely by gravity.

The top smooth surface of the formation forms a hard and cemented red breccia, 6.5 m deep in Issawia, which has been quarried since ancient Egyptian times for use as an ornamental stone. The commercial name of this stone in Egypt today is "Brocatelli." The color of the breccia is due to iron oxides of red brown color which seem to have filled the pore spaces of the breccia during a period of soil formation in a later episode of humidity; the breccias were later cemented by the evaporating CaCO$_3$—bearing waters that percolated through the pebbles.

Red breccias which also seem to form during the end phases of pluvials are recorded in Luxor, Issawia, Tahta, and Wadi Assiuti.

As previously stated, the massive breccias of the Issawia Formation are accumulations due to gravity and mass movements which seem to have been triggered by earth movements that must have affected the valley during the Issawia episode. The fact that most of the pebbles are angular chips indicates that these movements occurred during and after a long period of great aridity. Red breccias have been recorded outside the valley by Sandford in five areas in minor depressions in the plateau to the west of Minia (1934, p. 34). One of these occurrences falls within the range of the map that accompanies this paper and is marked as "fanglomerate of older age." All these occurrences lie along northwest-southeast faults that cross the Nile in this region, producing the rugged topography of the east and causing several isolated outliers of Eocene to appear within the valley on the west bank. Basalt dikes occur on both sides of the Nile in the Samalut—Beni Mazar highly faulted region. The presence of red breccias in these depressions indicates that these transverse northwest faults must have been activated during Issawia times to produce these massive breccias.

It is interesting to note that the Issawia highly seismic time interval coincides with the Plio-Pleistocene interval which Ross and Schlee (1973) have recently demonstrated to be the interval of sea-floor spreading, resulting in the formation of the axial zone of the Red Sea. This spreading also seems to have tilted the African subequatorial highlands in a way that prevented the waters of these sources of the Paleonile from coming into Egypt.

It also may be of interest to point out that formations similar to the Armant and Issawia have been recorded from many parts of north Africa (Coque, 1962), and they have been assigned to the Villafranchian Aidian stage (Chavaillon, 1964).

THE PROTONILE (Q_1)

Fluviatile deposits that belong to the third river system that occupied the present Nile basin are in the form of complex gravel, coarse sand, and loamy materials. The best and most extensive exposure of the remains of this river is to be found in the Kom Ombo west bank stretching across Darb el Gallaba plain from Wadi Kubaniya to the north of Aswan as far as El Sibaiya. This Formation, named Idfu, has its type locality in Wadi el Qura where the Geological Survey of Egypt has recently completed a detailed study of the gravels of this region as a possible source of silica for use in the ferrosilicon and phosphorous complex industries.

The Darb el Gallaba area is almost completely covered by these Idfu gravels, only interrupted by some areas where the Nubia Sandstone bedrock crops out. Between these isolated outcrops of bedrock the Idfu river gravels are present everywhere, more or less eroded by gullies formed in later erosion stages which drain mostly to the present river. Certain outcrops of Nubia Sandstone have relics of the Idfu gravels on their tops. This indicates that these gravels must have been at least 30 m higher than their present level estimated to be about 50 to 60 m above the level of the Nile.

The Darb el Gallaba plain represents the floodplain deposits of a braided river where strong floods carried mainly gravel over an ever changing system of stream beds. Wadi el Qura is a small wadi which cuts through the Idfu gravels and opens up near the village of el Hassayia west, 11 km south of Idfu. Pit no. 1, in the Geological Survey work (Abdel Razik and Nour el Din, 1970), to the south of this wadi, is taken as the type of this formation. The pit was sunk in one of the ridges which form the surface of the relatively higher parts of the rolling plain for a total depth of 7 meters. It hit at the depth of 4.5 m a loose, yellow, coarse sand layer with occasional quartz pebbles, and continued for the remaining 2½ m of the pit without reaching its base. The upper 4½ m are made up of a top thin 10 cm layer of cemented conglomerate made up of large (+50 mm), well-sorted quartz pebbles, mainly milky white in color, cemented in a matrix of medium to fine-grained red

brown compact sandstone. This is underlain by a gravel bed made up of loose, well-sorted rounded to subrounded quartz pebbles, mainly milky white in color, but becoming pale brownish at depth. The whole section is topped unconformably by a surface gravel layer 10 to 30 cm thick which is made up of locally derived Eocene and chert pebbles from the plateau in the hinterland.

In the hundred wells that were drilled in this area the section was more or less the same. The loose gravel layer ranged in thickness from 2 to 4.5 m, and it always rested over a bed of coarse sand which exceeded, in some pits, 6 m in thickness. The mechanical analysis of the loose gravel layer in Pit no. 1 shows that 60% of the pebbles are in the size range of 10 to 50 mm, 6.7% are in the size range of 5 to 10 mm, 1½% are in the size range over 50 mm, while 31% are finer than 5 mm in size. Analyses of a hundred other representative samples of this bed show that more than one-half of the gravels are in the size range of 10 to 50 mm (reaching up to 83% in one composite sample), and the rest is distributed in the other ranges, mostly in the finer-than-5-mm range. The mineral analysis of the gravels shows that they are overwhelmingly siliceous (92-96%), while other igneous rock fragments make up the remainder of the ingredients. The chemical analysis shows that the percentage of silica may reach up to 96%.

The overlying conglomeratic layer is cemented by yellowish red, coarse sandy loam (5YR 4/8 moist - 4/6 dry). A thin hard pan of iron compounds is frequently present in the middle reaches of this bed. The underlying coarse sand bed is always reddish, predominantly of the 5YR hue.

Butzer and Hansen (1968) give a short description of the undulating Darb el Gallaba gravel plain and appear to be of the belief that the plain originated during the Late Pliocene as a lacustrine basin fed by a southern river that passed through Wadi Kubaniya and the modern valley. These authors correlated the Wadi Gallaba gravels with the 150-60 m high gravels in the Kom Ombo graben and consequently concluded that both were related, during the Lower Pleistocene, to one drainage system that derived its waters from the wadis of the Eastern Desert. It is now apparent that the gravels on the two sides of the Nile are different as to their mineralogy—the western Idfu gravels are almost exclusively made up of quartz, while the eastern Kom Ombo gravels are of polygenetic origin including a large variety of igneous and metamorphic pebbles.

The Idfu gravels have been noted in many parts of Nubia and Egypt. Giegengack (1968) describes similar beds in Nubia under the term "Early Nile gravel" where the typical representative of this unit includes cobbles 10 to 20 cm in diameter and a finer-grained sediment that fills the interstices in the gravel. The cobbles are mostly "pegmatite quartz, metamorphic quartzite, a very small percentage of other crystalline lithologies, and a variable proportion of chert." In addition, large cobbles and boulders of Nubia Sandstone are observed in the base of these gravels. The fine-grained fraction of Giegengacks's Early Nile Gravel consists of quartz grains coated and imperfectly cemented together by iron oxide in the form of hematite. The section, reinterpreted from Giegengack, repeats almost exactly the section of the Idfu pits described above. After passing through a 25 cm-thick superficial layer of surface gravels which is drab in color (5 YR 8/4), the section turns to a cemented conglomerate layer, 2.75 m thick, of deep brick red color (2½ YR 4/4) which is followed underneath by a loose gravel layer whose top is pallid in color (5 YR 8/4) and seems to mark the depth to which intense oxidizing conditions prevailed either during or after the concentration of Fe_2O_3 in the section.

Giegengack (1968) gives a map of the distribution of these Idfu gravels in Nubia which are seldom observed farther than one kilometer from the present Nile. Patches of these gravels appear parallel to the Nile at Adindan east, Abu Simbel east, Aniba west, Tomas west, Korosko east, Wadi el Sibu east, Seiyala east, Allaki east, Meriya east, and Aswan east where they then join with Wadi Kubaniya and the great expanse of Darb el Gallaba. In Nubia as in many areas in the north of Egypt, the Idfu gravels are restricted to an area whose constant width and general configuration is similar to the shape of the modern Nile. In Nubia the Idfu gravels are preserved as caprock strata which lie on mesas 40 to 60 m above the present height of the flood plain and attain a thickness of about 5 meters. They rest directly and unconformably over the Nubia Sandstone bedrock.

To the north of Darb el Gallaba plain, where the Idfu river seems to have branched into numerous braided channels, the path of the river is less defined. Patches of the Idfu Formation are seen along the western bank of the Nile as far north as Esna and reappear again at the latitude of Ninia, where they continue in a more or less defined channel about 10 to 15 km to the west of the modern Nile until Cairo. Here the river seems to have negotiated its way through the Abu Rowash outlier and continued to the north forming a more or less continuous channel, the relics of which are seen along a path that is 10 to 15 km to the west of the Rosetta branch of the modern delta of the Nile. The Idfu Formation in this northern reach coincides with the Plio-Pleistocene gravel terraces of Sandford and Arkell (1929, 1939). In the middle latitudes of Egypt relics of the old channel of the Idfu river may be sought in the gravel terraces to the west of Minia, which appear on the older geological map of Egypt (1928) under "gravel spreads of uncertain age." These occur again as spreads of gravel running parallel to the Nile which rest directly over Eocene bedrock. Drilling over the plateau in this reach, done by the Geological Survey of Egypt in search of suitable limestones for the iron and steel industry in Egypt, has shown that these fluviatile gravels (composed mainly of rounded flint pebbles and cobbles) have a thickness of 30 meters. Otherwise, the channel seems to have been exhumed and buried under a more recent cover of dune sand and local outwash. It remains for geophysical work to delimit this old channel if remains of it are still extant.

The Idfu gravels differ conspicuously from those of the Armant Formation since they contain pebbles which are not derived from a local source but are transported from a distant source. Also, they are conspicuously smaller than the boulders of the Armant Formation. The pebbles are mainly of flint with a small influx of igneous metamorphic material; this distinguishes the formation from earlier or later gravel formations. Good exposures exhibiting the whole section are few, but at Mena House to the north of the Pyramids of Gizeh Shukri and Azer (1952) describe a 26 m-thick section made up mainly of sands of different color shades with few intercalating beds of gravels made up of flint pebbles. The mineral analysis of 13 samples of this section shows that close to two-thirds of the heavy fraction is composed of iron-ores, while the other third is made up of the following minerals in decreasing order of abundance: amphiboles, epidote, garnet, staurolite, tourmaline, zircon, pyroxenes, and other minor accessories. This assemblage is shown to be different from that of the modern river and points to a derivation from a southern sedimentary terrain.

In Nubia and in the entire stretch of Upper and Middle Egypt, the Idfu gravels are mostly deposited on a bedrock surface forming the bottom of a through-flowing river that occupied a course which lay to the west of the modern Nile and the Paleonile. At the time of deposition such a surface must have constituted the lowest part of the valley. This valley must have cut its way in the bedrock that lay then at lower elevations than the surface of the older pre-Idfu sediments of the Nile. Whether such a cross section could have been obtained solely by erosion is open to doubt. Judging from the distribution of the sediments of the Paleonile, which occupied more or less the same course of the modern Nile and that of the Protonile, which occupied a more westerly channel, it would seem that some tilting must have occurred along the axial course of the modern valley, perhaps during Issawia times, which caused the lowering of its western part. This tilting seems to have affected the whole valley and the delta, and the Idfu Protonile seems to have had a single westerly channel in the delta region. This channel passed by the eastern tip of the Wadi Natrun depression.

The path of the Idfu Protonile in the Fayum region seems to indicate that the Protonile did not have access to the Fayum depression which started forming during the Issawia time.

The height of the present Idfu Protonile sediments indicates a gradient that might have been even smaller than that of the modern Nile. In Nubia and in the southern reaches of Upper Egypt the gravels are in the range of 60 m higher than the modern floodplain, while to the north the gravels are 30 to 100 m higher than the modern floodplain. Since these elevations do not represent the actual surfaces of deposition, which were since their elevation the sites of erosion and lowering, it is difficult to come to any conclusions regarding the gradient of the original river.

The Idfu Protonile sediments seem to be archaeologically sterile. Records of rolled "Chellean" artifacts are frequently mentioned. Said and Issawi (1964) and Giegengack (1968), however, report the presence of a heavy concentration of fresh artifacts at a locality in the Abu Simbel west directly overlooking the river. Kleindienst (in Giegengack, 1968) gives a preliminary assessment of these artifacts and shows that they do not seem to belong to the latest Acheulean of Nubia. Judging from the scanty description of the occurrence, as given by Giegengack, it is possible to assume that these artifacts are associated with the period of soil formation rather than with the period of formation of the gravels themselves. Hayes (1965, p. 26) gives a date of 660,000 years B.P. to the "320 terrace" of Sandford and Arkell, which is here considered as belonging to the Idfu Protonile sediments. If this date is accepted for the Protonile—and there is very good geological evidence to believe that it is reasonably correct—then the geological context of the artifacts discovered by Giegengack in Nubia has to be reexamined.

To recapitulate, it can be stated that the Idfu sand/gravel complex was deposited by a through-flowing river capable of transporting cobble-size gravel for long distances. This river seems to have had the same sources as the Paleonile, and the climate of Egypt seems to have been wet and similar to that which prevailed during the Pliocene. The Idfu Pluvial, therefore, is different from all other "pluvials" of the Pleistocene in Egypt inasmuch as the rains were evenly distributed throughout the year.

If the author's earlier contention of the equivalence of the Idfu gravels with the gravels described by Arkell (1949) from Khor Anga near Khartoum is correct, then the sources of the sediments of the river have to be sought, in addition to the areas already mentioned, in a provenience to the south of Khartoum. The river had a course parallel to the modern Nile but lying 10 to 15 km to the west, and at an elevation that ran as high as 100 m above the modern flood-plain. Its course followed that of lower Nubia and Egypt. Judging from the volume of sediment deposited by this river, which is estimated not to exceed 300 km³, the river seems to have been of short duration, probably centered around the 700,000 years B.P. episode of cooling and deterioration of climate in the northern hemisphere (Hays et al., 1969). Apparently the river did not fan out into a delta in the land of Egypt, but it seems to have flowed in a single, although braided, channel. It is difficult at present to know whether this river continued northward in the elevated Rosetta fan of the Mediterranean basin or not. Thus far, sediments from the deep boreholes off the shore of the Mediterranean have not been described as being similar to those of the Idfu Protonile.

The Idfu Protonile sediments are characterized by a mineral assemblage which is different from that of the modern Nile. The gravels are well-sorted, rounded, and composed mainly of flint and quartz with minor ingredients of igneous and metamorphic pebbles. In this respect the Idfu gravels differ from the earlier and later gravels in the Nile section. The gravels of the Idfu Protonile have a red soil which is probably the most distinctive characteristic of

the sediment. The formation of this soil occurred at a later time, after the elevation of the river bed and in a period of intense rain. In the mature terrace of the Idfu Protonile along the Darb el Gallaba plain the gravels of the river are now seen capping the high rock outcrops of Nubia Sandstone that interrupt the monotony of the plain, indicating that the gravels had a greater thickness and that they represent a lag surface that was developed during an intense period of aridity. Sand was removed and the gravels were lowered as much as 30 m below their original surface. It was only after this period of aridity that the brick red soils of the Idfu gravels developed, presumably in the late Acheulean Abbassia "Pluvial" (*vide infra*). It is of interest to point out here that this episode begins the long period of aridity which the author postulated to have affected the Sahara up to pre-Late Acheulean times and which resulted in the formation of the major surfaces of erosion in the Western desert of Egypt (Said MS). Presumably it was during this period that most, if not all, the depressions of Egypt, and in particular the Fayum depression, were thoroughly hollowed out and assumed, more or less, their present shape.

THE PRENILE (Q₂)

Fluviatile sediments belonging to this complex river system crop out in a most conspicuous way along the banks of the Egyptian Nile valley and the delta margins, forming an important element in the landscape of the valley. They seem also to fill the deeper parts of the channel and floodplain of the modern Nile valley and delta where they appear consistently on the logs of all wells drilled in these reaches. The graded sand/gravel unit belonging to this formation lies unconformably beneath the famed agricultural silt layer of the land of Egypt.

The Prenile sediments comprise a complex group of deposits including the fluviatile graded sands of the Qena Formation and the silts of the Dandara Formation. The Prenile extends for a period of more than 500,000 years, terminating somewhere around 120,000 years B.P. During this long period covering a good part of the pre-Würm glacial ages of Europe, great changes took place over the Nile and the lands from which it derived its waters. These changes are reflected in the sedimentary sequence of the Prenile system. The Prenile sediments have been divided previously into the Qena and Dandara Formations which are fluviatile sediments of through-flowing rivers which obtained a large proportion of their waters from sources outside Egypt. The Qena-Dandara sediments represent deposits of large and competent rivers. The deposits are very thick with numerous breaks and extensive facies changes. In the regional mapping of the sediments of the Qena-Dandara complex, it was difficult to separate the deposits of these rivers into time-rock units; and it was thought advisable to map these deposits according to their lithology, retaining the term "Qena Formation" for the sand facies of these deposits and the term "Dandara Formation" for the clay-silt facies, attaching no time connotation to them. In the following paragraphs, therefore, the description of these two rock units is given under the heading "The Qena-Dandara complex." In a previous publication, Said, Wendorf, and Schild (1970) proposed the erection of the two Formations, Dandara and Qena, to represent the deposits of two succeeding rivers that preceded the oldest of the Neonile sediments. The Dandara in its type section (ibid., p. 46, fig. 2) was shown to underlie a sand unit which was equated in that paper with the type Qena Formation which crops out on the opposite bank of the river. It was believed, therefore, that the Dandara was older than Qena. However, further more elaborate field mapping in the Qena region has convinced the author that the sand unit overlying unconformably the ,Dandara belongs to yet another unit which most probably represents the deposits of a younger river in the Prenile sequence. Thus, it would now seem that the Qena Formation (as described by Said, Wendorf, and Schild, 1970) could be the oldest formation in the group; it is followed by the Dandara Formation which, in turn, is followed by fluviatile sands carrying shells of *Unio* and *Aspatharia* which are best represented in the Rus channel along the eastern edge of the Nile-Fayum divide (Sandford and Arkell, 1929; Little, 1935). However, it was difficult to separate this younger sand unit from the Qena sands on the map; the two units look very much the same for a field mapper. Consequently, the accompanying geological map does not separate the deposits of Qena-Dandara which further work may prove to be the deposits of a number of rivers that succeeded one another. Fortunately the mineralogy of the type Qena sands, the Dandara silts, and the younger sand unit overlying the Dandara Formation are more or less the same, indicating most probably that these units belonged to a natural group of rivers that had the same sources and regimen.

The Qena-Dandara complex as defined above includes the Qena sand facies and the Dandara silt-clay facies of the Prenile system. The Qena sands are extensively distributed along the eastern banks of the river in the Qena region and also occur in isolated patches on the western bank of the river. The type section of these sands is in Wadi Abu Manaa, the quarry face of which exhibits a magnificent section of these cross-bedded floodplain deposits of an extremely competent river. The section is made up of a massive 20 m-thick bed of sand with very few bands of conglomerate whose pebbles are well rounded and made up of a variety of basement rocks. Mechanical analyses of 5 samples collected along the face of this quarry show these sands to be well sorted. More than 60% of the sediment by weight falls in the 200-630-m size range. Only in one sample did its bulk fall in the >1,000-m size range. The clay fraction of the samples never exceeded 8% by weight of the sample.

The mineral analysis shows that the heavy minerals constitute about 2% of the sand fraction of these samples. The opaque minerals make up about 50% of the heavy minerals present. The other 50% is made up of the following minerals in decreasing order of abundance (average of 5 samples)—epidotes (25%), pyroxenes (12%), garnet (6%),

tourmaline, zircon, staurolite, rutile, and other minor accessories (7%).

The mineral analysis of the 44 m terrace of Sandford and Arkell (1929) in Fayum was published by Shukri and Azer (1952). This terrace is considered in this work as correlatable with the sand unit which overlies the Dandara Formation in its type locality forming part of the Qena-Dandara complex. The average composition of the heavy minerals separated shows that the opaque minerals also form about 50%. Amphiboles come next in abundance—then epidotes, pyroxenes, garnet, and other accessories. The mineral analysis of both sand units (believed to overlie and underlie the Dandara type section as described by Said, Wendorf, and Schild [1970]) are, therefore, the same, except for the presence of amphiboles in the supposedly younger sands. This is certainly not due to provenience but to the size of the fraction from which the heavy minerals were separated. The fact that these two sand units have more or less the same mineral composition and similar lithological appearance gives support to the idea that both form a natural group that belongs to one complex hydrological system.

The mineral analysis of the Qena sands shows that they differ from the older Idfu sediments by the presence of pyroxenes in greater abundance. In spite of the fact that the varieties of the pyroxene minerals found in the Qena sands are similar to those of the modern tributaries of the Nile in Ethiopia, the Qena sands differ from the modern sediments of the Nile in having smaller amounts of the pyroxenes and larger amounts of epidote. It is feasible, therefore, to believe that the Ethiopian highlands contributed sediments to the Prenile. Ryan et al. (1973) studied the heavy mineral composition of the sand layers in the piston cores from the Western Nile cone (Damietta) collected during the deep Sea Drilling Project cruise leg 13 in the Mediterranean. They report that, while the surface samples have a mineral composition similar to that of the modern Nile, the drill core samples which are "of an appreciably older Pleistocene age than the surface piston cores" have a higher epidote content. The samples thus described from the core of the Damietta cone seem to belong to the Prenile sediments. This seems to indicate that the Prenile must have reached as far seaward as the Strabo trench of the Eastern Mediterranean basin. Since certain beds in the Qena-Dandara Formations have pebbles of local derivation it must also be assumed that there were, on the whole, more frequent rains during Prenile times in Egypt than at present, even though it is almost certain that these rains did not add but a very small fraction of the sediment of this river; most of the sediment came from sources to the south. It is also certain that periods of wetter climatic conditions were episodic, representing short and intermittent periods of wadi activity during Qena-Dandara times.

The Qena-Dandara complex includes several units that were previously described by Sandford and Arkell (1929, 1933, 1939) under different headings ranging from the "Pliocene" to the "Lower Paleolithic." The type Qena formation was described as part of the deposits of the "Plio-cene gulf" interfingering and interdigitating the marl-conglomerate materials of what is considered, in this paper, as the Armant Formation and the masses of limestone breccia of what is now called the Issawia Formation. This was advocated in spite of the fact that these authors (1933, p. 13) admitted that the sands of Qena had a different source from that of the other locally derived formations for they were "brought from the south by the main stream which fed the headwaters of the gulf above Kom Ombo." Our observations during these long field seasons seem to show beyond any doubt that the Qena sands form a unit which lies above the other units mentioned by Sandford and Arkell and are, in fact, separated from them by a marked unconformity and a long period of time.

The Dandara silts are exposed in many areas in Upper Egypt. The type locality, as described by Said, Wendorf, and Schild (1970), lies at a point 3 km south of the temple of Hathor, Dandara, where a cut shows a unit of gray poorly sorted, compact, and massive silty sand with occa-sional gravel bands of Eocene and Precambrian derivation and lenses of coarse sand. This unit is about 2 m-thick (base unexposed). It is unconformably overlain by a 70 cm-thick bed of rubble made up of gravels of different sizes and composition. The largest majority is of pebble size, but occasional cobbles are also present. Fresh Late Acheulean tools were found on the surface of this gravel cover, and several flakes and one core were obtained from a depth of 1 m within the silt and under this cover, indicating that the Dandara silts are of pre-Late Acheulean age.

To the north of Dandara this unit reaches its maximum development. It is 15 m thick and is made up of a lower gray, loose and fine sandy-silt bed, and an upper unit of brown silt with a number of thin carbonate interbeds in the upper part of the section. A sample of carbonaceous marl collected from these beds dated more than 39,900 years B.P. The whole is covered unconformably by a veneer of gravel of local derivation including slightly rolled imple-ments belonging to Sangoan-Lupemban tradition. A thick red soil is preserved on the eroded surface of this formation below the gravel veneer. It is possible that the two units described in this locality are those that were noted by Sandford (1934) as the gray and brown marls in this same stretch. Otherwise the Dandara silts could be equated, in part, with the 15 m terrace of Sandford and Arkell (1933).

Sands and gravels of very similar lithology and miner-alogy are found in all boreholes drilled in the valley and delta of the Nile beneath the agricultural clay-silt layer of the fertile lands of Egypt. They represent the water-bearing horizons in the valley and delta. These are correlated on lithological grounds with the Qena-Dandara complex. These riverine sands also appear in outcrop as isolated low mounds or "islands" in the agricultural fields of the Nile Delta representing the higher parts of the eroded surface of this complex. These are the turtlebacks described by Sand-ford and Arkell (1939). The most famous of these turtle-backs is that of Quesna to the north of Cairo. The Qena-

Dandara suite of sediments is a widely distributed unit which can be seen fringing the western part of the cultiva-tion edge all along the Nile on its western banks. The most continuous patch of Qena-Dandara sediments is that which extends all along the western bank of the Nile from Man-falut to Wasta—and from there to Cairo. Seen from the valley it forms a continuous bluff usually incised by small gullies. In this stretch sand dunes interfinger these deposits in a manner which is very similar to that occurring within the Neonile sediments (Wendorf and Said, 1967). This seems to indicate that climatic and physical conditions pre-vailing over Egypt during the deposition of the Prenile sedi-ments must have been similar to those prevailing over Egypt during most of the Holocene.

The Qena-Dandara deposits outcrop along the margins of the delta on both sides of Wadi Tumailat, which forms the southern fringe of the lands to the east of the modern delta, and these deposits seem to extend across the Suez Canal into eastern Sinai. On the western margins of the delta the Qena sands appear again as low terracelike extensions cover-ing the desert fringes of Beheira province.

The thickness of the Qena-Dandara suite of sediments exceeds 250 m in the valley and reaches thicknesses ex-ceeding 1,000 m in the north of the delta. Figure 7 gives the isopachs of the Prenile sediments which show that the thickness is at its maximum in the axial parts of the modern delta and becomes increasingly greater as one proceeds toward the Mediterranean Sea. Thus, in the middle latitudes of the delta thicknesses of 600 m are common, while near Cairo the thickness decreases to about 250 meters. Many boreholes dug outside the recent floodplain of the river in the fringes of the delta show that the deposits of the Prenile extend for long distances outside the reaches of the modern delta. The maximum thickness of the Prenile sediments lies to the west of the modern channel, and it is in this western channel that the main stream seems to have run. Occasion-ally, along many parts of the Nile the thickness becomes exceptionally thin, such as to the south of Helwan where a kind of fall must have existed during the Prenile and also during the Paleonile (fig. 1).

Judging from the distribution and thickness of the Qena-Dandara sediments, it is safe to say that the Prenile was the largest and most effective river in outlining the modern landscape of the valley, the delta and the coastline. The delta of this river was twice as large as the modern delta in surface area. The volume of sediments that this complex Prenile system of rivers carried exceeded 60,000 km^3; and if this volume was built up in the span of 500,000 years, then this river must have carried an annual load of suspended matter which is double that which the modern river carried prior to its control.

The younger sediments of the Prenile carry casts of African species of molluscs. Said, Wendorf, and Schild report from the Dandara area the presence of arenaceous casts of *Unio abyssinicus* and *Aspatharia cailliaudi* in a sand unit above the Dandara Formation. Sandford and Arkell (1929) report the presence of shells of *Corbicula artini*,

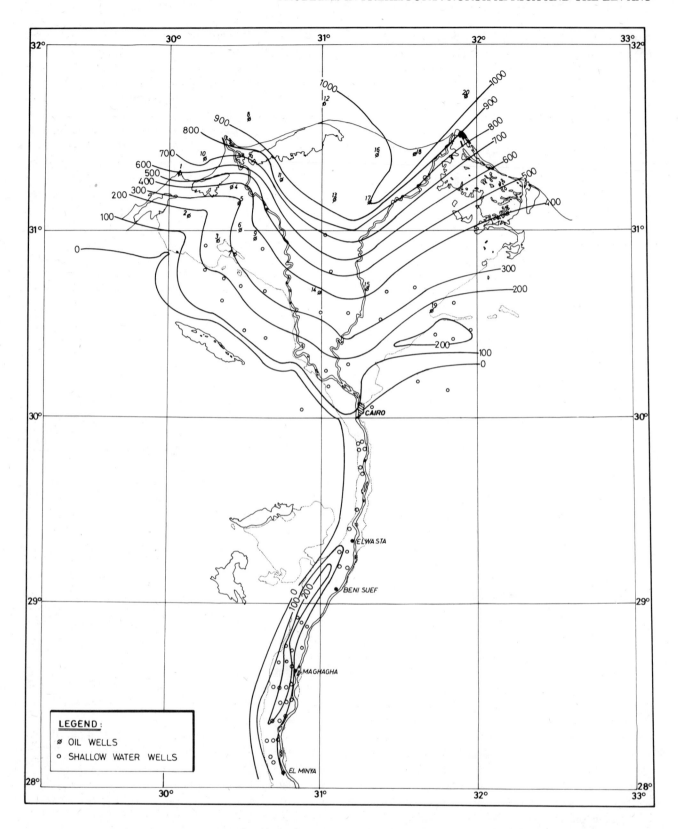

FIG. 7—Isopach Map of Prenile (Q_2) Sediments. (Numbers refer to well locations.)

Unio, and *Mutelina* spp. in their Lower Paleolithic terraces, which are here considered as the final stage of the Qena-Dandara complex. The fossils are obviously African in origin and show clearly that the river had access to the Abyssinian Highlands. The fossils are still extant. Thus far, no *in situ* archaeological materials have been separated from the Prenile sediments, save for the record already mentioned from the Qena area. The Prenile sediments, however,

lie below gravels that carry fresh Late Acheulean implements, indicating that these deposits are of pre-Late Acheulean age. Hayes (1965) gives dates for the 44 m terrace of
Fayum (late Qena-Dandara) and the 15 m terrace of middle
Egypt (Dandara) as 150,000 years B.P., a date which is
consistent with geological observations and the sequence of
events as described in this paper.

The Prenile occupied a course which lay to the west of
the modern Nile and to the east of that which was occupied
by its predecessor, the Protonile. This may be related to
some tilting of the land to the west of the Nile. The Prenile
sediments also appear quite conspicuously in the eastern
reaches of the delta; this may be explained as due to an
activation of the old east-west echelon fault extending from
Gebel Shabrawet, near Ismailia, to Gebel Um Qamar, to the
northwest of Cairo which brought these reaches within
access of the Prenile. This line of faults lies along one of the
modern seismic zones of Egypt (Gergawi and Khashab,
1968). It seems also that at some late time in its history,
the Prenile broke through the Fayum depression; terraces
of young Qena sands, indistinguishable from those of the
Nile-Fayum divide, encircle the depression in many places
at an elevation of 44 to 46 m above sea level (Little, 1935).
Previously, Said et al. (1972) had noted the deposits of this
beach but had expressed doubts as to its lacustrine character and association with the Fayum depression. Our field
work has now established the fact, already noted by Little,
that the Prenile in its late phases entered the Fayum depression, and relics of its deposits are now seen encircling it at a
constant elevation on all sides.

To recapitulate, it can be stated that the Prenile deposits
are varied. They include fluviatile sediments of a major
stream whose main channel occupied the western part of
the modern Nile Valley and whose floodplain covered larger
stretches than the modern Nile covers. The sediments of
this stream reach great thicknesses, about 250 m in Upper
Egypt, of which about 200 m are known from the subsurface of the modern valley beneath the fluviatile sediments of the Neonile. In the delta region the thickness of
the deposits of this river may exceed 1,000 meters. The
area of the delta of this river was twice as large as the
modern delta, and the volume of sediment that this river
deposited exceeded 60,000 km³. The river, which excavated its channel to the east of the channel of the Protonile,
started flowing into the land of Egypt shortly after the
Protonile had ceased to flow and continued with vigor and
competence until Late Acheulean times, a period which
extends for close to half a million years. The annual suspended matter that this river carried, therefore, must have
been in the range of 0.12 km³, an amount higher than that
which entered the land of Egypt by the modern Nile prior
to its control. Ball (1939) points out that of the 110 million tons of suspended matter passing Wadi Halfa in an
average year by the modern Nile, only 58 million tons
remain in suspension in the river at its passage past Cairo,
corresponding to 0.05 and 0.027 km³ of sediment com-
pacted to 10% moisture content by dry weight.

Most of the waters of this river came from sources
outside Egypt. The mineralogy of the sediment suggests
that for the first time in the history of the Nile a sizeable
part of the waters came from the Ethiopian highlands. The
climate in Egypt itself was arid, but cloudbursts were more
frequent than at present, and the wadis draining into the
Nile were more active. Occasional pebble beds derived from
local sources are frequent in the lower part of the section of
the river, decreasing in number and frequency in the upper
parts; this may point to increasing desiccation with the
passage of time. The mineralogy of the sediments also
suggests that the contribution of the Ethiopian highlands
was probably as great as that from other equatorial sources.
The modern Nile, in contradistinction, receives close to
80% of its waters from the Ethiopian highlands. Wind
erosion during this period of aridity helped in bringing
about a landscape of desert lands which is more or less
similar to that which exists today. During the later times of
the Prenile the river entered the Fayum depression which
seems to have been fully excavated for the first time.

THE PRENILE/NEONILE INTERVAL (Q₂/Q₃)

The Prenile/Neonile (Q₂/Q₃) interval covers the span of
time which elapsed between the ceasing of the flow of the
Prenile in Late Acheulean times and the breaking through
of the Neonile about 30,000 years B.P. During the early
part of this interval a great pluvial occurred over Egypt, and
rains falling on the uncovered basement rocks of the
mountainous areas of the Eastern Desert brought down to
the Mediterranean great quantities of gravel which were
deposited unconformably over the Prenile sands and silts.
The new ephemeral river seems to have followed the
channels of the older river. Red and yellow red soils were
formed, and man made a grand appearance in the Nile
Valley and in many parts of Egypt. The duration of this
Pluvial, which is here termed the "Abbassia Pluvial," is not
known; but an estimate of 30,000 years (perhaps contemporaneous with Riss I in the Alpine classification) is reasonably supported by dates that precede and succeed this
"Pluvial."

With the termination of this "Pluvial" arid conditions set
over Egypt again and continued to the Mousterian subpluvial. During this episode of aridity the valley and the lands
around it were eroded by wind and by frequent cyclonic
winter rains into a landscape which is quite similar to that
of the present. Gypseous soils developed in places. In the
late times of this period, more frequent rains were known
in Egypt (Mousterian subpluvial), producing slope and
sheetwash that covered many surfaces of the eroded valley.
These include implements of Mousterian tradition by men
who made their reappearance during this episode. The
entire interval which covers the arid period of erosion and
the Mousterian wet period with its slope and sheetwash is
here called the Makhadma Interval.

In the following paragraphs a description of the sediments of the Q₂/Q₃ intervals is given under the headings of
Abbassia Formation and Makhadma Formation.

The Abbassia Formation

The Prenile sediments are capped in many areas of the valley by a thick fluviatile gravel cover, mostly of pebble size and diversified mineral composition. The thickness of this cover varies from place to place. It averages 6 m in thickness, although in places the thickness may reach 15 meters. The most famous of these gravel beds is that of Abbassia, near Cairo, from which Bovier-Lapierre, more than 50 years ago, described *in situ* implements from what was then described as a stratified site about 10 m thick including eoliths(?) in its lower parts up to Acheulean materials in its upper parts. Bovier-Lapierre (1926) gives a photograph of the locality and a schematic description of the occurrence. Because of the fame of this locality these important gravel beds are given the name of Abbassia, even though Bovier-Lapierre's site may never again be seen, for it is now being tilled down to form the foundation of the buildings of Nasr City, a new suburban area which is being developed near Cairo. It is proposed, therefore, to take as a type the Rus section situated at the mid-desert station of Rus along the state railway line from Wasta to Medinet el-Fayum traversing the Prenile bed at its broadest part in the Nile-Fayum divide. The Rus station is the center of extensive quarrying of the gravels for railroad ballast. The ballast pits, about 8 m thick, expose a massive gravel bed made up of well-rounded and well-sorted (mostly 5 to 10 cm) pebbles of red, green, and purple rocks derived from the basement rocks of the Eastern Desert of Egypt. The whole rests, as in Abbassia, over sands of the Qena-Dandara complex. Sandford and Arkell (1929) had remarked that the archaeological materials which they had separated from the lower parts of this formation were waterworn, while those separated from the upper parts—rare examples of beautiful Acheulean work—were "almost as fresh and as sharp as on the day of their manufacture." These authors, therefore, described the Abbassia *terrace* as the Acheulean terrace, a contention with which the present author is in full agreement. Bovier-Lapierre's Abbassia site must be similar, and it can by no means be considered a stratified site ranging, as claimed, from the Eolithic to the Late Acheulean.

The Abbassia gravels are widely distributed in the valley and delta regions of the Nile. They make some of the best quarrying sites for gravel in Egypt. They follow on top of the Qena-Dandara complex with a clear-cut unconformity, although in places such as in the Cairo area, the lower part of the Abbassia section includes several thin bands of the Qena sands. This indicates that the Abbassia Pluvial was not separated by a long lapse of time from the Prenile riverine conditions, and, in fact, it probably started during the waning stages of the Prenile.

The Abbassia gravels differ from the Idfu gravels in composition, the latter being made up of quartz and quartzite pebbles derived from deeply leached terrain, while the former contain abundant crystalline rocks and feldspathic sands derived from a deeply disintegrated but little leached terrain. The Abbassia gravels are widely spread in the valley and form characteristic beds in many parts of Egypt; they seem to include rich archaeological material. Of these, one may mention the 100 ft terrace at Sebaiya and east of Esna (Sandford and Arkell, 1933); the 50 ft terrace of the Kom Ombo plain and El Kab near Idfu, the 30 ft terrace near Armant, and the 10 ft terrace of the Valley of Queen's Tombs at Thebes. All these *terraces* are characterized by similar lithology and archaeological materials, and they seem to belong to one formational unit which assumes these different elevations due to later erosion. The futility of using elevations in correlation is obvious in a valley with as complex a history as that of the Nile Valley which was formed by several streams following one another and separated by periods of intense tectonics and erosion. The mechanical analyses of the Sebaiya and Kom Ombo gravels show that about 30% of their pebbles are made up of quartz, 50% of basement materials (granodiorite, diorite, gaboro, syenite), and 20% of fine-grained materials, mainly sand and clay.

The Abbassia gravels owe their origin to deposition in a stream which had its headwater in the Egyptian deserts which at that time must have enjoyed a much wetter climate to justify calling this episode the Abbassia Pluvial. The age of this Pluvial is Late Acheulean. There is archaeological evidence that this was a period when man lived over most of the desert areas of Egypt, as well as in the valley, and there is also evidence that there was a savanna of vegetation in many of the now barren areas of these regions. The deposition of gravel beds derived from the Egyptian basement to the east of the Nile suggests an enormous wadi activity that seldom has been witnessed since then.

The effect of this Pluvial also can be seen in the number of soils that are preserved on older surfaces. The brick red to yellow red soils of the Idfu surface have already been described. The Abbassia gravels themselves have red brown soils of the 10-5YR hue. If the archaeological materials found by Giegengack (1968) in the Idfu gravels prove to be of the same period as those found in the Abbassia gravels, it would be fair then to assume that both were formed during the same period and that the difference in color could be the result of different stages of maturity of the soils. The amount of rain that would be required to develop soils of this nature was discussed by Flint (1959), Giegengack (1968), Butzer (1964), and many others. According to most authorities red soils form in climates having an annual precipitation in excess of 40 inches and a semitropical to tropical mean annual temperature. Giegengack cites Walker (1967) whose work in Baja California showed that red iron oxide pigment in Pleistocene soils could develop under conditions where the mean annual precipitation is believed not to have exceeded 6 inches as a result of diagenetic alteration of ferromagnesian minerals, chiefly hornblende. Giegengack compares the mineralogy of both soils to show that the Idfu soils display characteristics significantly different from those of Baja California. While in the California soil

CaCO$_3$ is present in abundance throughout the soil profile, clay is absent, and the little that may be found of it is in the form of montmorillonite; the Nubian soil, according to Giegengack, is conspicuously different. In Egypt proper, however, the soils which developed over Dandara Formation in its type locality show an abundance of CaCO$_3$ bands immediately underneath the soil. Iron minerals are abundant, and the significant clay fraction is montmorillonite.

A typical soil profile in the Darb el Gallaba plain which developed over the Idfu gravels in its type locality is as follows:

0- 50 cm	Coarse gravel, with slightly silty coarse sand between the gravel.
50-150 cm	Yellowish red cemented coarse sandy silt (5YR 4/8 moist - 4/6 dry). Thin hard pan of iron compounds at about 70 centimeters. Very rich in lime.
150-180 cm	Strong brown, medium-fine sand cemented with soft lime segregations (7.5YR 5/8 moist - 5.5/8 dry).
180-200 cm	Gray silt to clay with soft and hard lime segregations (10YR 6/1 moist - 6.5/1 dry).

It thus seems that the Abbassia Pluvial was a period in which extensive rains fell over Egypt to produce a through-flowing river which deposited thick polygenetic gravels in channels that followed the modern wadis and a master stream that closely followed that of Qena-Dandara times. Soils developed over old surfaces; they are mostly in the 5YR hue in the younger formations and in the 2½YR hue in the older formations.

The Makhadma Formation

Subsequent to the Abbassia Pluvial, there seems to have occurred over Egypt an extensive period of aridity which extended from Late Acheulean to "Mousterian" times, a period which continued for more than 60,000 years. During this interval the dried beds of the Qena-Abbassia Intervals were subjected to intensive erosion, mostly by wind, but also by frequent cyclonic winter rains which dissected the sands and gravels of the Qena-Dandara and Abbassia Formations. The result of this period of erosion was the formation of a landscape which is, in its important elements, very similar to the modern landscape. The final shape of this landscape was accomplished during the Mousterian-Aterian time when more frequent rains produced the shape of the slopes of the valley and excavated it to a relief which is represented by the numerous cross sections of the valley and delta given in figs. 1-3. The sheetwash deposits of the Mousterian episode cover unconformably the slopes and many of the lowered surfaces of the previous formations. In this sheetwash implements of Mousterian tradition are known. The best known of these occurrences is in Makhadma to the north of Qena where the slopewash overlying the Qena sands includes implements of Sangoan-Lupemban tradition (Wendorf, Said, and Schild, 1970c). Other occurrences include the Abbassia area where Bovier-Lapierre (1926) separated Mousterian implements from the sheetwash overlying unconformably the Abbassia gravels. A similar situation is reported by Sandford and Arkell (1933) in regard to the sheetwash that covers the 10 ft "Middle Paleolithic" terrace in the Luxor area. These latter authors note (p. 84) that these Mousterian implements which they had separated from the gravel are "found in the basal part of the later deposits, which consist mainly of micaceous silts almost indistinguishable from that brought down by the Nile today."

The Makhadma sheetwash deposits are thin gravelly deposits with pebbles of local derivation which could not have been transported for long distances. The pebbles are mostly in the 10 to 15 mm size range and are embedded in a matrix of yellow red soils in the 7.5 to 10YR hue. They overlie unconformably the slopes and eroded benches of older deposits and underlie the sediments of the Neonile.

During the arid episode of Makhadma gypseous soils developed over the Prenile sediments and the Abbassia gravels. To the north and all along the western bank of the Nile, from the north of Assiut to Cairo, the soil profile developing on top of the Abbassia gravels is characterized by the presence of gypsum and salt pans of later genesis and probably of local derivation from the nearby rocks. A typical profile in this reach is in Darb Gerza where a gypsum pan has developed at depth in thicknesses that warrant quarrying it on a small scale. These gypsum incrustations occur just below the surface frequently at a depth of 40 to 100 centimeters. Here the soil is mainly a gravel soil, though more often coarse sandy in part. The surface shows a gravelly desert pavement over a sandy-silt desert topsoil some 5 cm thick, (color 7.5YR 5/8 dry - 5/6 moist), very rich in lime and platy in appearance. The gravel subsoils are underlain by a 50 cm thick layer of gravel with very coarse sand in between, rich in salt crystals and rich in lime, having a color of 5YR (5/6 dry - 5/8 moist). Frequently a salt pan underlies this zone.

THE NEONILE (Q$_3$)

The deposits of the Neonile are made up of silts and clays indistinguishable in aspect and composition from those which have been deposited over the land of Egypt by the modern Nile up to the very recent past. They rest over the eroded surface of the Prenile/Neonile Interval with a marked unconformity. These deposits form the top layer of the floodplain of the modern Nile and are also found in many parts of Egypt outside this plain in the form of benches that fringe the valley at elevations ranging from 1 to 12 m above the modern floodplain. These sediments seem to have been deposited by a river which could not have been very much different in regimen and source from that of the modern river.

The sediments of the Neonile which were formed during a time span extending for close to 30,000 years recently have been subjected to detailed studies as a result of the international campaign to salvage the archaeological treasures of Nubia. The detailed studies of the stratigraphy of the Neonile sediments in Nubia are given in de Heinzelin, 1968*a*, and Butzer and Hansen, 1967, 1968; and in Egypt in Wendorf and Said, 1967, 1970, Said, Wendorf, and Schild, 1970, Albritton, 1968, and Said et al., 1972. A review of the work carried out in both Nubia and Egypt is given in Wendorf and Schild (in press). Since this latter work includes a detailed survey of our present knowledge of the Neonile sediments, the following paragraphs on this important episode will be brief. Recent work has shown that the Neonile sediments were laid down during five, if not six, aggradational episodes during which structured silts with interfingering dune sands were deposited (particularly obvious along the western banks of the river). These are separated from each other by recessional episodes during which pond or playa sediments and/or diatomites accumulated and during which wadis draining into the Nile were more active.

A study of the distribution of the sediments of the older aggradational episodes in Egypt (Korosko[?], Dibeira-Jer, Ballana, and Sahaba Formations) shows that these occupy sloping benches that fringe the present valley and follow one another in stratigraphic order. Information about the two older episodes is scanty, the deposits being deeply buried or badly eroded beyond recognition in most places, but the succeeding two episodes have outcrops that have been extensively studied (see Wendorf and Schild, in press). The deposits recur all along the Nile, and although there are indications that the slope of the river was slightly higher in the older aggradational episodes, it is evident that this was of minor magnitude. The layer of Nile mud which caps the column of sediment in the river valley and delta, and which forms the famed fertile agricultural land of Egypt, represents the composite deposits of all the aggradational episodes of the Neonile.

The cross and logitudinal sections of the Nile Valley in its different places (figs. 1-3) show the disposition and isopach distribution of the Nile agricultural clay layer, while fig. 8 gives the isopachous variations of the Nile mud cap in the Nile Delta. This cap seems to have been built up during the period after the modern regimen of the river had been established, a period stretching for close to 30,000 years from the Korosko(?) episode to the present. The composite thickness of this layer differs from place to place, but in the valley it averages about 10 meters.

About 30,000 years ago the river, with a regimen not very much different from that of today, cut its way to Egypt in a valley filled with a layer of sand and gravel deposited by the Prenile. The surface of this fill was uneven. During the earlier part of this period the river continued to build its bed to a level higher than the present level of its floodplain by at least 12 meters. This is the period which stretches from the Korosko(?) to the Sahaba episodes of aggradation (27,000 B.P. to 10,000 B.P.). During the aggradational episodes of this period the river had

floods which fluctuated in a manner not very much different from that which prevailed in the recent past. During the recessional episodes the river became low, or even waning. During the first episode of normal floods (i.e., similar to the present) silt and mud filled the valley gradually, up to a level slightly higher than the present level of the floodplain. In many places the upper parts of these early deposits are recognizable in outcrops outside the valley. During the succeeding three aggradational episodes the river continued to build up its bed over the eroded surface of the preceding phase until it reached, in Sahaba times, the highest elevation known to have been reached by the Neonile. It was certainly in Sahaba times that the river had its maximum floods, and the column of sediment in Upper Egypt by the end of Sahaba times must have reached about 22 m in thickness, of which 12 m are now exposed. The exposed section shows in many places the four aggradational phases of deposition as well as the intercalating recessional deposits. The older aggradational deposits of the Neonile were thus laid down during 17,000 years. Of these, less than 4,000 years represent recessional episodes.

The post-Sahaba sediments of the Neonile are the deposits of the Holocene. They begin with the deposits of the very short Dishna recessional episode and are followed by alluvial deposits of an almost continuous episode of aggradation extending to the present time. Recessions during the Holocene represent very minor events in an otherwise regular curve of accretion of Nile silts over the valley and delta of the river. Indeed, one can say that the regimen of the river (prior to its control) has been more or less constant for the past 9,000 years and that the Nile in Egypt must have assumed at the inception of this period its modern gradient. The distributaries of the delta were more numerous, fanning out as far eastward as the old Pelusiac branch. Seven major deltaic branches of the Nile Delta are mentioned in various historical documents and in ancient maps. Five of them have degenerated and have silted up in the course of history, whereas two, the present-day Damietta and Rosetta branches, remain active. During the Holocene sedimentation, at an average rate of about 1 cm/century, continued almost uninterruptedly. On the other hand, the delta coastline must have been on the retreat since the beginning of the Holocene, due partially to the general rising of sea level during this Interval (Fairbridge, 1963). This retreat of the coast has been noted during the recent past over most of the coast (Said, 1958). In a recent work Sneh and Weissbrod (1973) studied the defunct Pelusiac branch and showed that in the Sinai stretch of the Neonile Delta the coastline seems to have been built up as it is being built up today in the Damietta—Port Said stretch as a result of the accumulation of the sediments of the Nile which are moved toward the east by the Mediterranean longshore currents. Save for this eastern stretch of the coast of the delta, it can be safely assumed that the sea advanced continuously during the Holocene, an advance that was counteracted by aggradation over the land of Egypt. This indeed would make most unlikely the finding of outcropping *in situ* archaeological sites of the Holocene within the Nile Valley.

The places where the Holocene Neonile sediments can best be examined in outcrop are in Nubia and in the Fayum province. There is evidence that degradation was active during the Holocene over most of the stretch of Sudanese and Egyptian Nubia where numerous cataracts interrupt the river, and many more must have been present in the very recent past. The Arkin, which represents the first aggradational episode of the Holocene, built up its bed to a level which reached 10 m above the modern floodplain in Nubia (de Heinzelin, in Wendorf, 1968), while the post-Arkin sediments form a series of recessional beaches marking the decline from the maximum of the Arkin aggradation. The lowering of the valley by at least 10 m since Arkin times is noted in many places in Nubia, and evidence at hand shows that this degradation was due partly to the fact that the Nubian Nile ran in a shear zone, thus resulting in episodic uparching of this area.

The Fayum is a circular depression to the west of the Nile which formed an escape for the river waters, especially during flood periods throughout the Holocene and earlier times, ever since the Nile cut its access to it, the Hawara channel (for details, see Wendorf and Schild, in press). It was King Amenemhat (XII Dynasty) who widened and deepened this channel, clearing away the rocky barriers, and converted the lake into a veritable reservoir. The later history of this lake is obscured, but it seems that the silting up of the channel and its later reopening to allow enough waters to irrigate Fayum lands took place sometime prior to the Arab invasion. The Fayum depression, therefore, offers one of the few places in Egypt proper where Holocene outcrops can be examined. Indeed, Fayum also offers the only evidence which shows that the Arkin and post-Arkin sediments did not form a continuous series but, rather, were broken by intervals of low floods. The unconformities which separate the Premoeris, Protomoeris, and Moeris Lakes seem to represent short periods of low floods. The last episode (between 5200 and 400 B.C.) corresponds perhaps to the stage of lower levels of the Nile and wetter climates in the deserts of Egypt described by de Heinzelin (in Wendorf, 1968), and Butzer (1959*a*, 1959*b*, 1960*a*, 1960*b*). The fluctuations shown by the Fayum lakes, however, could represent a normal curve of a reservoir fed by a river with a regimen very similar to that of the present Nile.

The study of the records of the Nile levels which are preserved for a long period (641 A.D. to present, with short breaks) may help in understanding the nature of this regimen. In spite of the inaccuracies inherent in these records, they nevertheless form a valuable series which has been examined by numerous scholars. A valuable review of these records is given in Popper (1951). Hurst et al. (1966) analyzed the available data and showed that no periodicity seems to have governed the fluctuations of the floods of Egypt. Brooks (1949) showed that there is a fairly good

agreement between the flood level and low-water stage, although the fluctuations of the latter are the more violent. Both show a minimum about 755 A.D., a maximum about 870 A.D., a minimum about 960 A.D., a maximum at 1110 A.D., and a double minimum at 1220 A.D. and 1300 A.D. It can be generally stated that starting from the fifteenth century the flood levels become progressively higher than during the earlier eight centuries. A study of the means of the maximum flood and low-water levels per century, corrected for the progressive rise of the river bed due to deposition of silt, shows that the difference between the highest and lowest level becomes much larger starting from the fifteenth century (6.4 m) and continues to rise until it reaches 7.3 m in the nineteenth century. The difference prior to this, however, fluctuates between 6.5 and 6.1 m with an average of 6.25 meters. No conclusion can be made from these readings with regard to the volume of the floods, as these changes could be attributed more properly to the fact that during these latter centuries the bifurcation of the delta has been receding away from Cairo with the result that the water surface rose in response to this retreat.

Surviving historical records indicate that abnormally low floods were recorded between 2180 and 2130 B.C., while unusually higher floods were recorded between 1840 and 1775 B.C. (Bell, 1970, 1971). Toussoun (1922) and Brooks (1949) show that high floods were recorded around 500 B.C.

In conclusion, it can be stated that the Nile, with more or less its modern regimen, has been in existence for at least 10,000 years. The only observable physical break in this continuous record lies between 5200 and 4100 B.C., discernible through a break in sedimentation in the Fayum succession of Neonile sediments. These short breaks in the Fayum succession could be looked upon as episodes of low floods within the larger cycle of the regimen of the river. A survey of the fluctuations of the river during historical times shows that similar episodes of low floods, though on a smaller scale, occurred in the past. Indeed, none of the breaks in the Fayum succession deserves to be described as a recessional episode of the magnitude of the Deir el Fakhuri episode which separates the Ballana and Sahaba aggradational phases of the Neonile.

The Modern Nile

It may not be out of place to terminate these notes on the Neonile by giving a brief description of the most salient features of the topography and hydrology of the modern Nile. The literature on the modern Nile is extensive, and the following notes touch only upon those aspects of the river that may contribute to a better understanding of the past behavior of the river, its evolution, and its utilization by early man.

The course of the Nile from the mouth of the Atbara to the Mediterranean Sea may be divided roughly into two parts. The first, stretching as far as Aswan, is the part in which the river flows in a rocky channel with alternations of rapids and reaches of more gentle slope and where, on the whole, it is eroding its bed. The second is from Aswan to the sea, where it traverses its own floodplains. In neither portion does it receive any appreciable addition to its volume. However, due to percolation and cultivation it is continuously losing water, but little is known about the actual volume of this loss. In connection with this it should, though, be noted that seepage through the bed into the surrounding areas is by no means a dead loss, since great portions of the water which is thus drained from the river at its higher stages (when its level is above that of the surrounding water table) percolates back again during the period of lower level when conditions are reversed. Thus, the discharge reading at Aswan prior to the erection of the artificial means of flood control during the periods of lower level is larger than that at Wadi Halfa. This is an extremely important point with regard to the regimen of the river in past geological episodes.

It is to be noted that the Main Nile from Khartoum to Aswan falls 295 m in 1,810 kilometers. The so-called six cataracts occupy 565 km with a slope of 1:3,000 and a total drop of 192 m, and the ordinary channel occupies 1,245 km and has a slope of 1:12,000 and a total drop of 103 meters. From Aswan to Cairo, a length of 970 km, the Nile falls 76 m with a mean slope of 1:13,000.

The velocities of the river in flood and low supply are greatest in the cataract region (averaging 2.3m/sec. and 1.2m/sec., respectively); while they are lower in other reaches of the Main Nile (e.g., 1.7 m/sec. and .85 m/sec. between Aswan and the Mediterranean). The time for traversing the different reaches differs from place to place. From Khartoum to Aswan the Nile takes eleven days in flood and twenty-two days in low supply, while from Aswan to Cairo it takes six days in flood and twelve days in low supply.

From Aswan to the Barrages (north of Cairo) the length of the river is 973 km in summer and 923 km in flood. The slope in summer is 1:13,000 and in flood 1:12,000. The mean fall of the valley is 1:10,800. The slopes vary in the different mean reaches, the least being 1:14,800 in Qena province and the greatest being 1:11,400 in Beni Suef. In a high flood with a rise of 9 m in Aswan, the rise in Qena will be 9.5 m and only 8.2 m in Beni Suef. Omitting spill channels, it may be stated that in a high flood the mean area of the Nile is 7,500 m^2 and the mean width 900 meters. In the province of Qena the area is 7,000 m^2 and the width 800 m, while in Beni Suef the mean area is 8,000 m^2 and the mean width 1,000 meters. Speaking generally, it may be stated that where the Nile Valley is narrow, the slope of the river is small, its depth great, and width contracted; while where the valley is broad, the slope is great, the depth small, and the width enlarged. It may be said that the Nile in summer has a natural section whose width in flood is 100 times its depth, while its mean velocity is 1.50 m/second.

In spite of the great strides that were made in the past hundred years with regard to the study of the Nile, its

water balance (especially after the building of the great Aswan High Dam) is not yet fully understood. Even more difficult to unravel is the hydrology of the natural river unhampered by man's structures and interference. Since the dawn of civilization in Egypt about 5,000 years ago the problems of water storage and flood control have occupied the attention of every enlightened ruler of Egypt. During this long history the harnessing of the river ranged from the laying down of gigantic blocks on both banks of the river to the strengthening of the natural levees of the Nile, to the erection of the great structures of the water schemes of the nineteenth and twentieth centuries. These, as well as the continuous interference by man through wise and unwise measures, make it difficult to understand the natural regimen of the river. The following notes attempt to summarize the salient features of the nearest system to the natural regimen of the river (i.e., before the filling of the Aswan reservoir in 1902). For full details of the hydrology of the river and the effects of the building of the reservoirs on its regimen the reader is referred to the classical works of Lyons (1906), Garstin (1904), Willcocks (1889, 1904), Willcocks and Craig (1913), and the compendium on the Nile written by Hurst et al., volume 10 of which appeared in 1966.

The Egyptian Nile derives its waters almost exclusively from the rain which falls over two elevated areas—the Equatorial Plateau of Central Africa and the Ethiopian Plateau. The rainfall over the two main regions follows the sun, coming, broadly speaking, to a maximum after the sun is in the zenith, and falling away as it recedes. Consequently there are two wet seasons over the Equatorial Plateau corresponding closely with the equinoxes, although of the two the spring rains are the more pronounced, while there is only one in Ethiopia coinciding with the summer solstice when the sun is at the zenith in the Northern Hemisphere.

The runoff from the two plateaus plays very different roles in the regimen of the modern Nile. The Equatorial Plateau contributes a small but regular amount to the Nile in Egypt, and were this source of supply to be cut off there is little doubt that the River Nile would run dry in the spring months unless new sources were to come into operation. The rainfall on the Ethiopian Highlands, on the other hand, produces the regular flood effect upon which, until recent times, the whole agriculture of the country depended for its annual watering. Furthermore, owing to the rich deposit brought down every year from the disintegration of the hill surfaces on which the rains fall, it was, and continued to be until the building of the High Dam, both the architect and fertilizer of the floodplain which alone makes Egypt today a habitable country.

At Wadi Halfa the river begins to rise in June, and in the next two months it rises about 7 m, reaching a maximum at the beginning of September. It then falls more slowly than it rose, reaching a minimum flow in May. Three streams—the Blue Nile, the White Nile, and Atbara—are responsible for the water supply of the Main Nile here. The average discharge of the Main River at Aswan, unaffected by reservoirs, has the maximum discharge occurring about September 8, when it totals 712 million m³/day, of which the White Nile contributes about 70 million m³/day, or 10% of the total, while the Blue Nile and the Atbara contribute about 485 and 157 million m³/day, or 68% and 22% of the total respectively. The minimum discharge, however, is about 45 million m³/day from the Blue Nile (or about 17% of the total). The average discharge at Halfa is about 230 m³/day amounting to a total discharge of about 80 thousand million m³/year, of which close to 16% comes from the Equatorial Highlands. Discharges as low as 41 thousand million m³/year and as high as 140 thousand million m³/year are recorded, depending on the amount of flood.

It is clear that the biggest quantity is contributed by the Blue Nile and the least by Atbara; but that at the time of year when the level is lowest, February to June, the White Nile is the most important source of supply. The Atbara contributes nothing from January to June. On the average, 84% of the water of the Main Nile comes from Abyssinia and 16% from the Lake Plateau of Central Africa.

Except for small and isolated tracts of land that have been recently reclaimed, the agricultural land of Egypt is the area that used to be flooded annually by the rise of the Nile. All land out of reach of the flood was a virtual desert. The regular and stately precision of the rise and fall of the waters of the Nile, the composition and nature of the silt it carried, and the fact that the floods preceded the cool weather of Egypt all contributed in developing and perfecting the basin system of irrigation. This remained, until very recent times, the only system of irrigation of Egyptian lands. Basin irrigation, as it was practiced in Egypt for thousands of years, was one of the most effective methods of utilizing the river. It can be started by the sparsest of populations, and yet it can support in wealth a multitude of people, while the direct labor of cultivation is reduced to an absolute minimum.

The rate of sedimentation of the Nile mud over the lands of Egypt has attracted the attention of authors for a long time. Ball (1939) summarized the earlier attempts and gave a detailed account of his calculation of the rate of accumulation of the Nile mud over the basin lands of Upper Egypt based upon a study of the fate of the suspended matter which enters the Nile in Wadi Halfa. Of 110 million tons per year of suspended matter which enters the Nile at Wadi Halfa, only 58 million tons pass by Cairo. The difference settles over the floodplain of the Nile between these two points. Ball estimated the rate of increase of thickness of the Nile mud in basin lands of Upper Egypt prior to the establishment of the Aswan Dam at 10.3 cm/century. In the case of Cairo and the Delta, no studies similar to those carried out by Ball are available, and probably none ever will be made. The lands were converted to perennial irrigation at the beginning of the last century prior to the establishment of a scientific body to record the amounts of suspended matter carried past the canals. If, however, it is assumed that the layer of Nile mud which caps unconformably the underlying Prenile sand and gravel bed has been deposited during the same period in which the top agricultural layer in Upper Egypt has been deposited, then it must be assumed that rates of accumulation of the mud in the delta region are slightly larger than those in Upper Egypt. This seems a reasonable conclusion since the delta, up to historical times, was a swampy place where the water slowed down and its surface lowered as it branched off in the numerous distributaries of the delta. At present the fall of the water surface is considerable at every bifurcation, and the difference between the mean high and low supply at the Barrages today is 6 m as compared to 7.2 m in Cairo.

The Rosetta branch in its middle reaches is from 1.5 to 2 m above the level of the country in a high flood, and the Damietta branch is from 2.5 to 3 meters. The slope of the first part of the Damietta branch is considerably less than that in the first part of the Rosetta branch; this results in the gradual silting up of the former. This may help in explaining the greater thickness of the agricultural clay (Nile mud) layers along the Damietta branch (fig. 8) and the lower equivalent blackbody temperature (T_{bb}) along this branch of the delta as recorded by the Nimbus Meteorological satellite, for here water retention would be at a minimum.

The history of the numerous branches of the delta and their gradual silting up was summed up Toussoun (1922). It seems that most of the water of the silted-up channels went into the Rosetta branch with the greatest slope. The strong flow from this branch would account for the Alexandria canyon which indents the shelf break, off the delta in the Mediterranean (Emery et al., 1966). It is to be noted, however, that the thorough control of the water going into the delta distributaries since 1833 (date of the erection of the Barrages) doubtless has reduced the deposition of silt in the delta. Ball (1939) found out that the controlled perennial irrigation schemes in the delta had reduced to a minimum the accumulation of Nile muds there. He estimated the rate of deposition per century, if one projects the figures gathered from a fully controlled river in the twenties of this century, to be 0.6 cm/century.

The figures of the rates of accumulation obtained from a study of the amount of suspended matter settling in basins of Upper Egypt could compare with the rates of a natural river, the flow of which is unhampered by irrigation projects and the floodwater of which are entirely uncontrolled by man. There is no doubt, however, that the figures obtained from a study of the amount of deposit laid down in the perennially irrigated lands of lower Egypt are completely unacceptable. Figures given by Ball, for example, for the amount of Nile mud laid on the perennially irrigated lands in Upper Egypt are about 30% less than those given for the rate in basin lands of the same district. In a natural delta where the

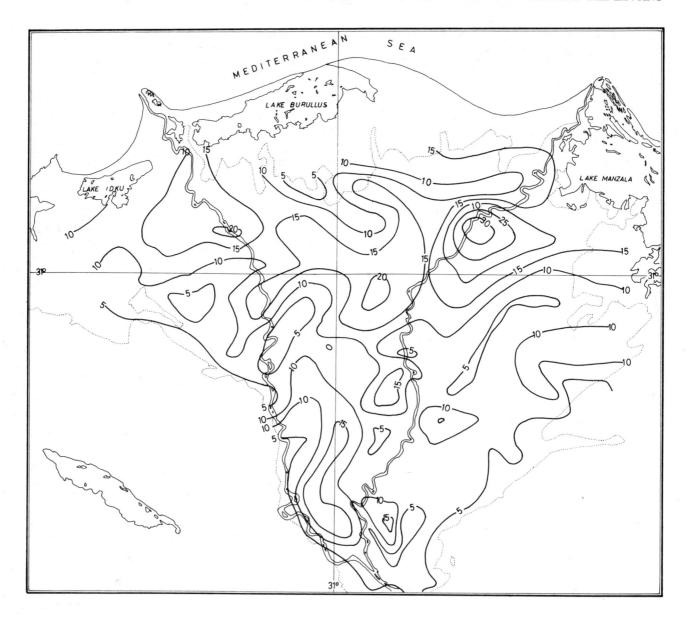

FIG. 8—Isopach Map of Neonile (Q_3) Sediments.

distributaries are free to overflow their banks, scour fresh channels, and form swamps, a greater rate of sedimentation is expected. The slightly thick silt and clay bed that forms the upper layers of the delta seems to have been deposited in the same period in which the same layer was deposited in Upper Egypt and at rates that could be only slightly higher than those prevailing in Upper Egypt. The amount of sediment that would build this bed in the delta would make up 22% of the total amount of suspended matter that passes Wadi Halfa, the rest would then go to the Mediterranean for the building up of the delta cone. If this figure is projected back in time to the beginning of the Neonile system, then the share of the Neonile sediments to the total volume of the sediments of the delta cone would be negligible indeed. They could hardly have formed anything more than a thin layer on the top of the delta cone.

To recapitulate, it can be stated that a river very similar to the modern Nile in its sources and regimen broke into Egypt about 30,000 years B.P. The breaking of this river, which is here termed the Neonile, followed a period of aridity and a short pluvial in which the preceding Prenile had almost dried up, or at least had been lowered down to levels which cannot be determined. It is almost certain that the breaking of the Neonile into Egypt occurred as a result of a bigger flow of the Blue Nile and Atbara which made possible the erosion of the elevated Nubian massif and the establishment of a connection across this massif into Egypt. During the Neonile the Nubian Nile was continuously lowering its course at a rate of 1 m/1,000 years; the older sediments of the Neonile appear as benches 27 m higher than the river, and the newer sediments appear at successively lower elevations. It may be of interest to point out here that the breaking of the Neonile coincides with the age

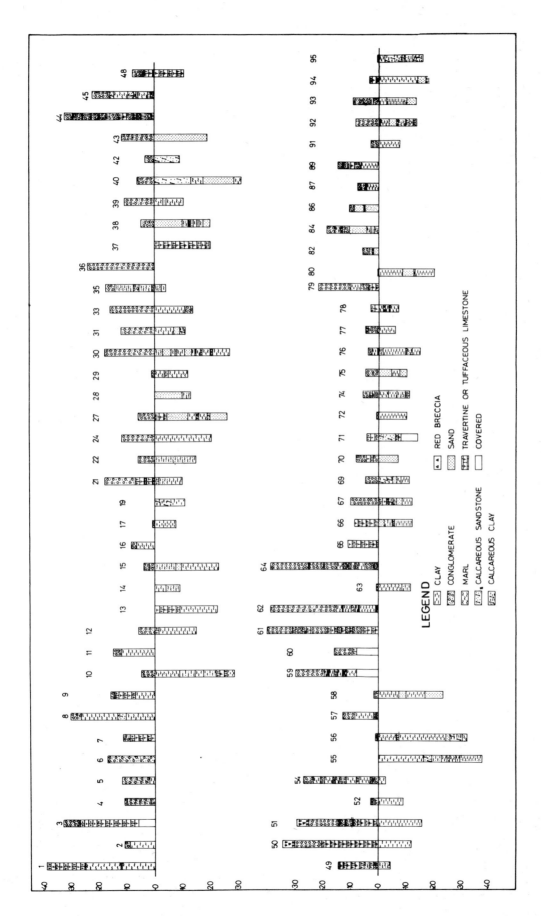

FIG. 9—Logs of Measured Sections of Paleonile (*Tplu*) Sediments and Armant and Issawia Formations. (Numbers refer to sections, the locations of which are shown in fig. 10.)

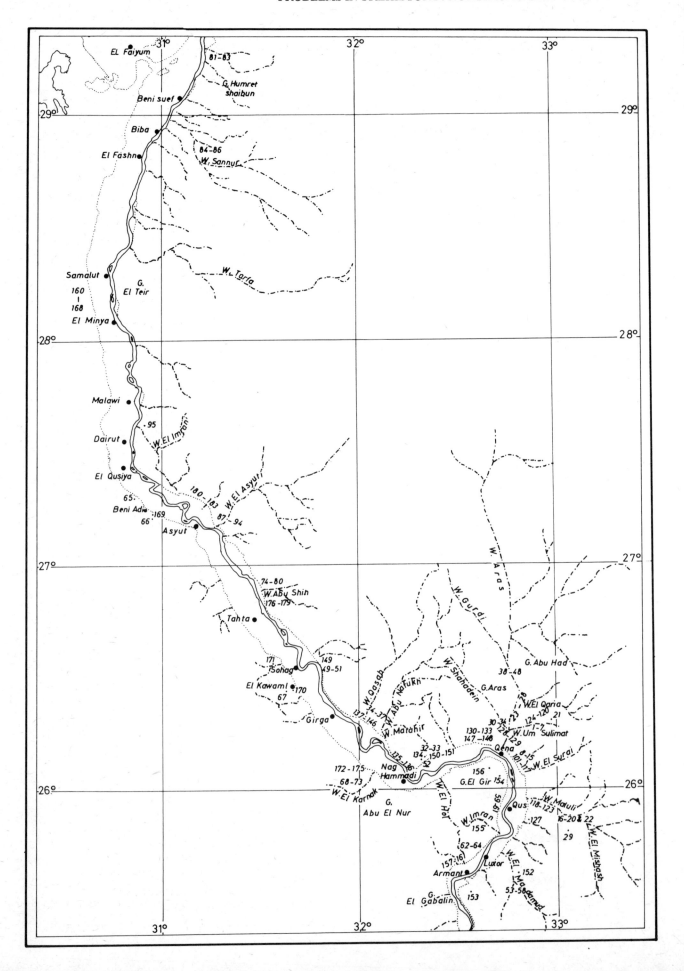

of the deeps in which hot brines have been discovered recently in the Red Sea Basin (Hackett and Bischoff, 1973). The fissuring of these deeps seems to have marked an episode of tectonic activity which affected the Ethiopian highlands and the direction and intensity of the flow of the water that fell on them.

In the Egyptian Valley itself, the Neonile was aggrading its bed and depositing its sediments over the eroded and uneven surface of the floodplains of the Prenile molded during the Makhadma interval. The composite thickness of the sediments deposited by the Neonile represents but a small fraction of the fluviatile sediments of the valley. The composite thickness (of both outcrop and subsurface) varies from place to place and is approximately 12 m in the valley and approximately 15 m in the delta, a thickness which represents less than 1% of the total sediments deposited by the earlier rivers that occupied the valley. The Neonile sediments have been subjected lately to extensive studies both in Nubia and Egypt. A good synthesis of the evolution of the Neonile is given in Wendorf and Schild (in press). The history of the Neonile is that of long episodes of aggradation, when the river had normal floods reaching to the edges of the valley, interrupted by periods of recession, when extended episodes of lower floods seem to have been the rule. The earlier aggradational episodes had higher floods than are known today, and this trend continued up to the Sahaba aggradation which seems to have had the highest floods known in the history of the Neonile. Judging from the elevation assumed by the Sahaba sediments, the floods probably averaged 140,000 million m^3/year, a volume that has seldom been reached by the modern Nile. Prior to this aggradation and after a short recession (Dishna recession) the Neonile at 10,000 B.P. assumed a regimen and gradient very similar to the modern Nile. The floods seem to have averaged over the years, as in modern times, about 80,000 million m^3/year. The episodes of recession which interrupted the periods of aggradation were episodes when the floods were low. The longest of these recessions, and perhaps also the best known, was that of Deir el Fakhuri (15,000 to 12,000 B.P.) which separated the Ballana and the Sahaba aggradational episodes. The floods during this period perhaps averaged about 40,000 million m^3/year, a volume which was recorded by the modern Nile during the years of pestilence known in the history of Egypt. The Holocene Nile seems to have aggraded its bed in response to an advancing sea; the delta must have had, at the beginning of the Holocene, a coast which lay probably 50 km to the north of the modern coast. The longshore currents, which also must have established a regimen like the present, transported the detritus of the river toward the east, causing the building up of numerous barrier beaches in the Gulf of Pelusium. These beaches were gradually incorporated with the land, causing the coast of Pelusium to advance at the rate of 5 m/year.

FIG. 10—Key Map Showing Locations of Measured Sections.

During the aggradational episodes the climate was very similar to the present-day climate prevailing over Egypt. Save for very occasional cloudbursts, the wadis were not active. Windblown sands interfingered the deposits of the Nile, and especially along the west bank of the river where an enormous supply of sand and great fetch produced dunes of sizeable dimensions. Dunes interfingering the Ballana aggradational deposits already have been noted (Wendorf and Said, 1967; Wendorf and Schild, in press). The most spectacular of the dunes are those which interfinger the Sahaba sediments along the western bank of the Minia-Mallawi stretch of the Nile. These form the famous Khefoug landscape which makes a distinct mappable rock unit. It is interesting to note that the Prenile sediments in this same stretch have thick interfingering dunes. The Khefoug deserves special attention, for this is the only stretch on the banks of the river where sand dunes form the major component of the exposed Nile terrace. Thin laminae of Nile silts interfinger the deposit which is otherwise made up of dune sand which is now stabilized. The mechanical analysis of twenty samples from these dunes shows that 30% of the sample, by weight, falls in the size range of 100 to 200 m, 17% between 50 and 100 m, and 50% greater than 200 meters.

The path of the Neonile lay to the east of that of the Prenile. However, there was a tendency for the river to shift its course toward the west during the Holocene. Thus, in many parts of the Nile the Sahaba channel, which silted up during the Dishna recession, was abandoned by the succeeding Arkin river to newer westward channels which, in most cases, lay in hard rock. The classical example of this tendency can be demonstrated by the Aswan-Shallal abandoned channel which seems to have formed the channel of the river during the Paleonile, the Prenile, and the Neonile up to Sahaba times (a drillhole in the channel repeats bed by bed the section of the Aswan High Dam made famous by descriptions of Chumakov, 1967). The Arkin river abandoned this well-established channel and followed the difficult path across the granitic mass of Aswan, interrupted today by the well-known Aswan cataract. Another example of this tendency of the river to shift its bed to the west is in the Silsila region to the north of Kom Ombo where again, in Arkin times, the river abandoned its established channel to follow the difficult path through siliceous sandstones of Gebel Silsila, cutting its way through a gorge. Less spectacular examples can be given in the Armenna region of Nubia, now under water but shown on the map of Butzer and Hansen (1968), where again the Holocene river abandoned its old channel and followed a westward course through the Nubia Sandstone. In Abnub, Assiut province, a similar phenomenon is also noted. In the Cairo area Said (1973) compared Napoleon's map of Cairo with that of the modern city and concluded that the eastward shift of the river in the city was due to the interference of the city planners during the nineteenth century.

Thus, the Neonile followed a course that lay to the east of its predecessor, washing, in many places, the Eocene eastern cliffs that border the valley in its middle latitudes and bypassing the ridge of Eocene limestone that lies underneath the surface at shallow depth within this reach (fig. 1). This trend shifted in Holocene times and, in several places all along the Nile, started to move toward the west. This trend seems to have been in response to movements at the inception of the Holocene which tilted the older silted beds of the Nile in certain localized areas.

These movements also seem to have affected the Rosetta branch of the delta which became, since Holocene times, the distributary with the greatest slope and discharge. The silting of the distributaries of the delta started only after this early Holocene movement, which also seems to have affected the position of the branching of the delta distributaries. These distributaries are known to have shifted northward during the Holocene.

Studies on the mineral composition of the Nile sediments have been carried out by Shukri (1950), El Gabaly and Khadr (1962), Hamdi (1967), and Butzer and Hansen (1968). Venkatarathnam and Ryan (1971) studied the clay mineralogy of surface sediments of the Nile cone in the Mediterranean and showed that a distinct clay assemblage with high amounts of well-crystallized smectite (>50%) and 15-25% kaolinite occurs in these surface sediments. These two minerals characterize the Neonile sediments. Their distribution in the Mediterranean, like that of modern sands of the river, appears to be related to easterly moving surface currents which form part of the counterclockwise gyre present in the modern eastern Mediterranean. These currents seem to have continued for the duration of the Holocene, contributing, as previously stated, to the building up of the advanced coastline of the Gulf of Pelusium.

The factors that influence and control the shape of a delta have been discussed recently by Wright and Coleman (1973). In general, it can be stated that the Nile Delta belonged, throughout the Holocene and perhaps also throughout the Würm, to the type of delta in which the wave regime is totally expended in redistributing the fluviatile sediments of the river. The Neonile Delta, therefore, must have had features similar to that of the modern delta, even though in earlier times it seems to have been more fluvially dominated, with a more arcuate coastline, higher and broader sand beaches with larger eolian dunes, and even larger linear beach ridges and swales. The eolianites (so-called Kurkar) today form parallel ridges along the coast and have been incorporated in the delta sediments with the advance of the sea. The presence of some of these indurated eolianites in the upper part of many boreholes indicates closeness to the coast. Several boreholes drilled in the offshore and the northern reaches of the delta have these eolianites at depths ranging from 15 to 100 m below the surface.

SUMMARY AND CONCLUSIONS

The study of the fluviatile and other associated sediments of the Nile Valley shows that the river has undergone great changes since its downcutting during the Upper Miocene Five rivers succeeded one another in the valley. These are from the oldest to the youngest: the Eonile (Upper Miocene), the Paleonile (Upper Pliocene), the Proto-, the Pre-, and Neoniles (Pleistocene). These rivers are separated from each other by episodes in which the river declined or ceased to flow into Egypt probably in response to tectonic activity and/or climatic changes.

During the Eonile/Paleonile episode the advancing waters of the Mediterranean invaded the excavated valley of the Nile, leaving behind fossiliferous marine to fluvio-marine beds which have been recorded as far south as Aswan and Wadis Kharit and Karara. During the Paleonile/Protonile interval, which coincided with the lower Pleistocene, great climatic change occurred over the Sahara in general and the land of Egypt in particular. Perhaps one of the most important results of the present work is the discovery that arid conditions did not set over Egypt except during the Pleistocene. Prior to this epoch and during most of the Cenozoic, there is evidence that the climate in Egypt was wet. There was a good mat of vegetation, little surface denudation, and, during several episodes, moderate to intense chemical weathering. The rains during these epochs seem to have been gentle but probably evenly distributed throughout the year. It was only during the Pleistocene that major climatic changes set over Egypt, leading to aridity with occasional winter cloudbursts. During short episodes of the Pleistocene these cloudbursts were intense and more frequent, leading to accumulation of thick coarse gravels derived from local sources along many wadi beds. Two of these episodes, the Armant and Abbassia, have been termed Pluvial. Their duration was not long, and they occurred around one and a half million years ago and 100,000 years B.P., respectively. Two other submaxima have also been noted around 50,000 and 7,000 years B.P. It is no wonder, therefore, that practically all archaeological sites hitherto found in Egypt are associated with the dependable supplies of the river or the springs of the desert.

The hyperaridity to which Egypt was subjected resulted in the lowering of the desert surface and the destruction of its earlier relief. It also resulted in the formation of the great depressions known in the deserts of Egypt, shown in this paper to be Pleistocene features which did not take their present shape except very late in time.

The source and hydrographic setups of the succeeding rivers which occupied the Nile Valley have changed with time. While the Paleonile seems to have had its sources in equatorial and subequatorial Africa as well as in Egypt itself, the Prenile and Neoniles seem to have had, in addition to the equatorial sources, Ethiopian highland sources, first by the capture of the Atbara system during Prenile times and finally by the capture of the Blue Nile system in Neonile times.

UNIVERSITY OF WINNIPEG
PORTAGE & BALMORAL
WINNIPEG 2. MAN.   CANADA

BIBLIOGRAPHY

ABDEL GHANY, M. S., and ZAGHLOUL, E., 1973. "Results of Three Mapping Seasons in the Nile Valley." Geological Survey of Egypt, internal report.

ABDEL, RAZIK, T. M., and NOUR EL DIN, M., 1970. "The Occurrence of Quartz Gravels in Esna-Aswan District (Nile Valley) and Its Preliminary Evaluation." Geological Survey of Egypt, internal report No. 12/70.

ALBRITTON, C. C., 1968. "Geology of the Tushka Site: 8905." *The Prehistory of Nubia*, edited by F. Wendorf, 2:856-64. Dallas: Fort Burgwin Research Center and Southern Methodist University Press.

ANDREW, G., 1948. "Geology of the Sudan." In *Agriculture in the Sudan*, edited by J. D. Tothill, pp. 84-128. Khartoum: Government Printing Press.

ANDREWS, C. W., 1902. "Note on a Pliocene Vertebrate Fauna from the Wadi Natrun, Egypt." *Geological Magazine* 9(460):433-39.

————, 1906. *The Extinct Animals of Egypt*. London: British Museum of Natural History.

ARKELL, A. J., 1949. *The Old Stone Age in the Anglo-Egyptian Sudan*. Sudan Antiquities Service, Occasional Paper No. 1.

BALL, J., 1939. *Contributions to the Geography of Egypt*. Cairo: Survey and Mines Department.

BARR, F. T., and WALKER, B. R., 1973. "Late Tertiary Channel System in Northern Libya and Its Implications on Mediterranean Sea Level Changes." In *Initial Reports of the Deep Sea Drilling Project*, edited by W. B. F. Ryan, K. J. Hsü, et al., 13:1244-51. Washington: U. S. Government Printing Office.

BEADNELL, H. J. L., 1901. *Some Recent Geological Discoveries in the Nile Valley and Libyan Desert*. London: Stephen Austin and Son. (An English translation of a paper communicated to the International Geological Congress, Paris, 1900).

————, 1905. *The Topography and Geology of the Faiyum Province of Egypt*. Cairo: Survey Department of Egypt.

BELL, B., 1970. "The Oldest Records of the Nile Floods." *Geographical Journal* 136:569-73.

————, 1971. "The Dark Ages in Ancient History." *American Journal Archaeology* 75:1-26.

BELLINI, E., 1969. "Biostratigraphy of the Al Jaghbub (Giarabub) Formation in Eastern Cyrenaica (Libya)." *Proceedings Third African Micropaleontology Colloquium, Cairo*, pp. 165-84.

BERGGREN, W. A., 1969. "Rates of Evolution in Some Cenozoic Planktonic Foraminifera." *Micropaleontology* 15:351-69.

BLANCKENHORN, M. L. P., 1901. "Neues zur Geologie und Palaentologie Aegyptens: IV, Das Pliocaen und Quartaerzeitalter in Aegypten ausschliesslich des Rothen-Meergebietes." *Zeitschrift D. Geol. Ges.* 53:307-502.

————, 1921. *Handbuch der Regionalen Geologie: Aegyptens*. Heidelberg.

BOVIER-LAPIERRE, P., 1926. "Les gisements paléolithiques de la plaine de l'Abbassieh." *Bull. de l'Institut d'Egypte* 8:257-75.

BROOKS, C. E. P., 1949. *Climate through the Ages*. New York: McGraw-Hill.

BUTZER, K. W., 1959a. "Contributions to the Pleistocene Geology of the Nile Valley." *Erdkunde* 11:46-67.

————, 1959b. *Die Naturlandschaft Aegyptens während der Vorgeschichte und dem dynastischen Zeitalter*. Abhandlungen Akademie der. Wissenschaften und die Literatur (Mainz), Mathematische-Naturwissenschaftliche Klasse 1959, 2.

_____, 1960*a*. "On the Pleistocene Shore Lines of Arabs' Gulf, Egypt." *Jour. Geol.* 68:626-37.

_____, 1960*b*. "Archeology and Geology in Ancient Egypt." *Science* 132:1617-24.

_____, 1964. *Environment and Archeology*. Chicago: Aldine-Atherton.

_____, and HANSEN, C. L., 1967. "Upper Pleistocene Stratigraphy in Southern Egypt." In *Background to Evolution in Africa*, edited by W. W. Bishop and J. D. Clark, pp. 329-56. Chicago: University of Chicago Press.

_____, and HANSEN, C. L., 1968. *Desert and River in Nubia*. Madison: University of Wisconsin Press.

CHAVAILLON, J., 1964. *Étude stratigraphique des formations quaternaires du Sahara nord-occidental*. Paris: CNRS.

CHUMAKOV, I. S., 1967. "Pliocene and Pleistocene Deposits of the Nile Valley in Nubia and Upper Egypt." *Trans. Geol. Inst. Acad. Sci. USSR* 170:1-110. (In Russian).

CHURCHER, C. S., 1972. *Late Pleistocene Vertebrates from Archaeological Sites in the Plain of Kom Ombo, Upper Egypt*. Toronto: Royal Ontario Museum Life Science Contribution No. 82.

CIARANFI, N., and CITA, M. B., 1973. "Paleontological Evidence of Changes in the Pliocene Climates." In *Initial Reports of the Deep Sea Drilling Project*, edited by W. B. F. Ryan, K. J. Hsü, et al., 13:1387-99. Washington: U. S. Government Printing Office.

CITA, M. B., 1973*a*. "Pliocene Biostratigraphy and Chronostratigraphy." In *Initial Reports of the Deep Sea Drilling Project*, edited by W. B. F. Ryan, K. J. Hsü, et al., 13:1343-79. Washington: U. S. Government Printing Office.

_____, 1973*b*. "Inventory of Biostratigraphical Findings and Problems." In *Initial Reports of the Deep Sea Drilling Project*, edited by W. B. F. Ryan, K. J. Hsü, et al., 13:1045-73. Washington: U. S. Government Printing Office.

_____, and RYAN, W. B. F., 1973. "Time Scale and General Synthesis." In *Initial Reports of Deep Sea Drilling Project*, edited by W. B. F. Ryan, K. J. Hsü, et al., 13:1405-15. Washington: U. S. Government Printing Office.

COQUE, R., 1962. *La Tunisie présaharienne: étude géomorphologique*. Paris: A. Colin.

_____, and SAID, R., 1972. "Observations préliminaires sur la géomorphologie et le Quaternaire de piemont Thebaine." *Grafitti de la montagne Thebaine 1, Centre de documentation et Études sur l'Ancienne Egypte, le Caire*, pp. 12-22.

EL GABALY, M. M., and KHADR, M., 1962. "Clay Mineral Studies of Some Egyptian Desert and Nile Alluvial Soils." *Jour. Soil Sci.* 13:333-42.

EMERY, K. O.; HEEZEN, B. C., and ALLAN, T. D., 1966. "Bathymetry of the Eastern Mediterranean Sea." *Deep-Sea Res.* 13:173-92.

FAIRBRIDGE, R. W., 1963. "Mean Sea Level Related to Solar Radiation during the Last 20,000 Years." In *Symposium on Changes of Climate, Proc. Unesco and the World Meteorological Organization*, pp. 229-40.

FARAG, I. A. M., and ISMAIL, M. M., 1959. "Contribution to the Stratigraphy of the Wadi Hof Area (Northeast of Helwan)." *Bull. Fac. Sci. Cairo Univ.* 34:147-68.

FLINT, R. F., 1959. "Pleistocene Climates in Eastern and Southern Africa." *Bull. Geol. Soc. Amer.* 70:343-74.

FOURTAU, R., 1915. "Contribution à l'étude des Dépôts nilotiques." *Mém. Inst. Egypte* 8:57-94.

GARSTIN, W., 1904. *Report on the Basin of the Upper Nile*. Blue Book Egypt (2).

GERGAWI, A., and KHASHAB, H. M. A., 1968*a*. *Seismicity of U. A. R.* Helwan Obs. Bull. No. 76.

————, and KHASHAB, H. M. A., 1968*b*. *Seismic Wave Velocities in U. A. R.* Helwan Obs. Bull. No. 77.

GIEGENGACK, R. F., 1968. "Late Pleistocene History of the Nile Valley in Egyptian Nubia." Ph.D. dissertation, Yale University.

GORSHKOV, G. P., 1963. "The Seismicity of Africa." In *A Review of the Natural Resources of the African Continent*, pp. 101-51. Paris: UNESCO.

HACKETT, J. P., and BISCHOFF, J. L., 1973. "New Data on the Stratigraphy, Extent and Geologic History of the Red Sea Geothermal Deposit." *Economic Geology* 68:553-64.

HAMDI, H., 1967. "The Mineralogy of the Fine Fraction of the Alluvial Soils of Egypt." *U. A. R. Jour. Soil Sci.* 7:15-21.

HARRISON, J. C., 1955. "An Interpretation of Gravity Anomalies in Eastern Mediterranean." *Phil. Trans. Roy. Soc.* (A)248:283-325.

HAYS, J. D.; SAITO, T.; ORDYKE, N. D., and BURCKLE, L. H., 1969. "Pliocene-Pleistocene Sediments of the Equatorial Pacific: Their Paleomagnetic, Biostratigraphic and Climatic Record." *Geol. Soc. Amer. Bull.* 80:1481-1513.

de HEINZELIN, J., 1968. "Geological History of the Nile Valley in Nubia." In *The Prehistory of Nubia*, edited by F. Wendorf, 1:19-55. Dallas: Fort Burgwin Research Center and Southern Methodist University Press.

————, and PAEPE, R., 1965. "The Geological History of the Nile Valley in Sudanese Nubia: Preliminary Results." In *Contribution to the Prehistory of Nubia*, edited by F. Wendorf, pp. 29-56. Dallas: Fort Burgwin Research Center and Southern Methodist University Press.

HSÜ, K. J., and CITA, M. B., 1973. "The Origin of the Mediterranean Evaporite." In *Initial Reports of the Deep Sea Drilling Project*, edited by W. B. F. Ryan, K. J. Hsü, et al., 13:1203-31. Washington: U. S. Government Printing Office.

————, and RYAN, W. B. F., 1973. "Summary of the Evidence for Extensional and Compressional Tectonics in the Mediterranean." In *Initial Reports of the Deep Sea Drilling Project*, edited by W. B. F. Ryan, K. J. Hsü, et al., 13:1011-19. Washington: U. S. Government Printing Office.

————; RYAN, W. B. F., and CITA, M. B., 1973. "Late Miocene Desiccation of the Mediterranean." *Nature* 242:240-44.

HUNTING GEOLOGY AND GEOPHYSICS, 1967. Assessment of the Mineral Potential of the Aswan Region U. A. R., Photogeological Survey. Unpublished report of Hunting Geology and Geophysics, Ltd., England. U. N. Development Program and U. A. R. Regional Planning of Aswan.

HURST, H. E., et al., 1931-1966. *The Nile Basin.* Cairo: Physical and Nile Control Department, Ministry of Irrigation.

————, 1944. *A Short Account of the Nile Basin.* Physical Department Ministry of Public Works Paper No. 45.

ISMAIL, A., 1960. *Near and Local Earthquakes at Helwan from 1903-1950.* Helwan Obs. Bull. No. 49.

JAMES, C. T., and SLAUGHTER, B. H., 1974. "A Primitive New Middle Pliocene Murid from Wadi el Natrun, Egypt." *Annals Geol. Survey Egypt* 4 (in press).

LAWSON, A. C., 1927. "The Valley of the Nile." *Univ. Calif. Chron. Berkeley* 29:235-59.

LITTLE, O. H., 1935. "Recent Geological Work in the Faiyum and in the Adjoining Portion of the Nile Valley." *Bull. Inst. Egypt* 18:201-40.

LONGINELLI, A., and CITA, M. B., 1973. "Isotopic Evidence of Changes in Oceanic Circulation." In *Initial Reports of the Deep Sea Drilling Project*, edited by W. B. F. Ryan, K. J. Hsü, et al., 13:1400-1404. Washington: U. S. Government Printing Office.

LYONS, H. G., 1906. *The Physiography of the River Nile and Its Basin*. Cairo: Egypt Survey Department.

MANSOUR, A. T.; BARAKAT, M. G., and ABDEL HADY, Y. S., 1969. "Marine Pliocene Planktonic Foraminiferal Zonation Southeast of Salum, Egypt." *Riv. Ital. Paleont.* 75(4):833 f.

MAYER-EYMAR, C. D. W., 1898. "Systematisches Verzeichniss der Fauna des unteren Saharianum (marines Quartaer) der Umgegend von Kairo, nebst Beaschreibung der neuen Arten." *Palaeontographica* 30:60-90.

NESTEROFF, W. D., 1973. "The Sedimentary History of the Mediterranean Area during the Neogene." In *Initial Reports of the Deep Sea Drilling Project*, edited by W. B. F. Ryan, K. J. Hsü, et al., 13:1257-61. Washington: U. S. Government Printing Office.

OMARA, S., and OUDA, K., 1969. "Pliocene Foraminifera from the Subsurface Rocks of Burg el Arab Well No. 1, Western Desert, Egypt." *Proc. Third African Micropal. Colloquium, Cairo*, pp. 581-665.

PFANNENSTIEL, M., 1953. "Das Quartaer der Levante. II—Die Entstehung der aegyptischen Oasendepressionen." *Akademische Wissenschaft und Literatur Mathematik Natur Klasse, Mainz*, 7:337-411.

PHILLIP, G., and YOUSRI, F., 1964. "Mineral Composition of Some Nile Delta Sediments near Cairo." *Fac. Sci. Cairo Univ. Bull.* 39:231-52.

POPPER, W., 1951. *The Cairo Nilometer*. Berkeley: Univiversity of California Press.

QUENNELL, A. M., 1958. "The Structural and Geomorphic Evolution of the Dead Sea Rift." *Geol. Soc. London Quarterly Jour.* 114:1-24.

ROSS, D. A., and SCHLEE, 1973. "Shallow Structure and Geologic Development of the Southern Red Sea." *Geol. Soc. Amer. Bull.* (in press).

RYAN, W. B. F., 1973. "Paleomagnetic Stratigraphy." In *Initial Reports of the Deep Sea Drilling Project*, edited by W. B. F. Ryan, K. F. Hsü et al., 13:1380-87. Washington: U. S. Government Printing Office.

_____, HSÜ, K. J., et al., 1973. *Initial Reports of the Deep Sea Drilling Project*, vol. 13, part 2:515-1441. Washington: U. S. Government Printing Office.

_____; VENKATARATHNAM, K.; and WEZEL, F. C., 1973. "Mineralogical Composition of the Nile Cone, Mediterranean Ridge and Strabo Trench Sandstones and Clays." In *Initial Reports of the Deep Sea Drilling Project*, edited by W. B. F. Ryan, K. J. Hsü et al., 13:731-46. Washington: U. S. Government Printing Office.

SABATINI, R. R.; RABCHEVSKY, G. A.; and SISSALA, J. E., 1971. *Nimbus Earth Resources Observations*. Techn. Rep. 2, Nat. Aeronautics and Space Administration, Goddard Space Flight Center, Greenbelt, Md.

SAID, R., 1955. "Foraminifera from Some 'Pliocene' Rocks of Egypt." *Jour. Washington Acad. Sci.* 45:8-13.

_____, 1958. "Remarks on the Geomorphology of the Deltaic Coast between Rosetta and Port Said." *Soc. Géogr. Egypte Bull.* 31:115-25.

_____, 1962a. *The Geology of Egypt*. New York: Elsevier Publishing Co.

_____, 1962b. "Das Miozaen in der westlichen Wueste Aegypten." *Geol. Jb.* 80:349-66.

_____, 1971. *Explanatory Notes to Accompany the Geological Map of Egypt*. Geol. Survey Egypt Paper No. 56.

_____, 1973. *Subsurface Geology of Cairo Area*. Inst. Egypte Mem. 60.

_____; ALBRITTON, C.; WENDORF, F.; SCHILD, R.; and KOBUSIEWICZ, M., 1972. "A Preliminary Report on the Holocene Geology and Archaeology of the Northern Fayum Desert." In *Playa Lake Symposium*, edited by C. C. Reeves, Jr., pp. 41-61. Lubbock: Icasals Publication No. 4.

————, and ISSAWI, B., 1965. "Preliminary Results of a Geological Expedition to Lower Nubia and to Kurkur and Dungul Oases." In *Contributions to the Prehistory of Nubia*, edited by F. Wendorf, pp. 1-28. Dallas: Fort Burgwin Research Center and Southern Methodist University Press.

————, and ISSAWI, B., 1965. *Geology of Northern Plateau, Bahariya Oasis, Egypt*. Geol. Survey Egypt Paper No. 29.

————; WENDORF, F.; and SCHILD, R., 1970. "The Geology and Prehistory of the Nile Valley in Upper Egypt." *Archeologia Polana* 12:43-60.

————, and YOUSRI, F., 1964. "Origin and Pleistocene History of River Nile near Cairo, Egypt." *Inst. Egypte Bull.* 45:1-30.

SANDFORD, K. S., 1934. *Paleolithic Man and the Nile Valley in Upper and Middle Egypt*. University of Chicago Oriental Institute Publication 18:1-131.

————, and ARKELL, W. J., 1929. *Paleolithic Man and the Nile-Fayum Divide*. University of Chicago Oriental Institute Publication 10:1-77.

————, and ARKELL, W. J., 1933. *Paleolithic Man and the Nile Valley in Nubia and Upper Egypt*. University of Chicago Oriental Institute Publication 17:1-92.

————, and ARKELL, W. J., 1939. *Paleolithic Man and the Nile Valley in Lower Egypt*. University of Chicago Oriental Institute Publication 46:1-105.

SHUKRI, N. M., 1950. "The Mineralogy of Some Nile Sediments." *Geol. Soc. London Quart. Jour.* 105:511-34.

————, and AZER, N., 1952. "The Mineralogy of Pliocene and More Recent Sediments in the Faiyum." *Inst. Desert Egypt Bull.* 2(1):10-39.

SIEBERG, A., 1932. "Erdebengeographie." *Handbuch der Geophysik* 4(6):687-1006.

SIMONS, E. L., and WOOD, ALBERT E., 1968. *Early Cenozoic Mammalian Faunas, Faiyum Province, Egypt*. Peabody Museum Natural History, Yale University, Bulletin No. 28.

SNEH, A., and WEISSBROD, T., 1973. "Nile Delta: The Defunct Pelusiac Branch Identified." *Science* 180:59-61.

SQUYERS, C. H., and BRADLEY, W., 1964. "Notes on the Western Desert of Egypt." In *Guidebook to the Geology and Archaeology of Egypt*, pp. 99-105. Sixth Annual Field Conference, Petroleum Exploration Society, Libya.

TOUSSOUN, O., 1922. *Anciennes branches du Nil*. Mém. Inst. Egypte No. 4.

VENKATARATHNAM, K., and RYAN, W. B. F., 1971. "Dispersal Patterns of Clay Minerals in the Sediments of the Eastern Mediterranean Sea." *Marine Geology* 11:261-82.

VIOTTI, C., and MANSOUR, A., 1969. "Tertiary Planktonic Foraminiferal Zonation from the Nile Delta, Egypt, U. A. R." In *Miocene Planktonic Foraminiferal Zonation*, pp. 425-60. Proc. Third African Micropal. Colloquium, Cairo.

VONDRA, C. F., 1974. *The Upper Eocene Transitional and Near-Shore Qasr el Sagha Formation, Faiyum Depression, Egypt, U. A. R.*. Annals Geol. Survey Egypt No. 4.

VON STROMER REICHENBACH, B. E., 1902*a*. "Wirbelthierreste aus dem mittleren Pliocaen des Natrontales und recente Saeugetierreste aus Aegypten." *Zeitschr. D. Geol. Ges., Berlin* 3:108-16.

————, 1902*b*. "Die alttertiaeren Saeugetiere des Fajum." *Naturw. Wochenschr. Berlin* 18:145-47.

————, 1905. "Fossile Wirbeltier-Reste aus dem Uadi Faregh und Uadi Natrun in Aegypten." *Abhandlungen Senckenberg Naturforschende Gesellschaft Frankfürt a. M.* 2:99-132.

WENDORF, F. (ed.), 1968. *The Prehistory of Nubia*, 2 vols. Dallas: Fort Burgwin Research Center and Southern Methodist University Press.

————, and SAID, R., 1967. "Palaeolithic Remains in Upper Egypt." *Nature* 215:244-47.

————; SAID, R.; and SCHILD, R., 1970*a*. "Egyptian Prehistory: Some New Concepts." *Science* 169:1161-71.

————; SCHILD, R.; and SAID, R., 1970*b*. "Problems of Dating the Late Paleolithic Age in Egypt." In *Radiocarbon Variations and Absolute Chronology*, edited by I. U. Olsson, pp. 57-79. Nobel Symposium 12, Upsala. Stockholm: Almqvist and Wiksell.

————; SAID, R.; and SCHILD, R., 1970*c*. "Late Paleolithic Sites in Upper Egypt." *Archaeologia Polona* 12:19-42.

————, and SCHILD, R., in press. *Paleolithic of the Nile Valley, Egypt*. New York: Academic Press.

WHITEMAN, A. J., 1971. *The Geology of the Sudan Republic*. Oxford: Clarendon Press.

WILLCOCKS, W., 1889. *Egyptian Irrigation*. London: William Clows and Sons, Ltd.

————, 1904. *The Nile in 1904*. London: Spon, Ltd.

————, and CRAIG, J. I., 1913. *Egyptian Irrigation* 3rd ed. London: Spon, Ltd.

WRIGHT, L. D., and COLEMAN, J. M., 1973. "Variations in Morphology of Major River Deltas as Functions of Ocean Wave and River Discharge Regimes." *Amer. Assoc. Petrol. Geol. Bull.* 57:370-98.

POLLEN ANALYSES IN THE SAHARA

Madeleine Van Campo

Laboratoire de Palynologie

Centre National de la Recherche Scientifique, U.S.T.L.

INTRODUCTION

Analyses have been made of sediments from the Saoura valley, the wadis of the Ougarta mountains, from lacustrine depressions, and from wadis of the Sahara mountains. Only analyses in which at least 200 pollen grains could be counted have been included for publication (table 1).

Sediments from the Upper Pliocene or Plio-Villafranchian and from an altitude above 1800 m in the Sahara mountains yielded pollen spectra which reveal a vegetation much more varied than that of today, and in particular a considerable percentage of pollen grains from trees of the Mediterranean basin.

All the other analyses presented difficulties of interpretation which we have tried to resolve by the use of two types of tests of present-day pollen deposit: (1) analysis of weekly pollen rain near Béni-Abbès, and (2) analysis of pollen from the ground dust raised while crossing the northern Sahara from north to south.

Research on present-day pollen rain, based on the simple model provided by the absence of vegetation in the Sahara, provides understandable data on the extent of present-day long distance pollen transport and clarifies its causes.

PRESENT-DAY POLLEN RAIN IN THE BÉNI-ABBÈS REGION (N. W. SAHARA)

Spores and pollen rain have been collected regularly since October 15, 1969, by a trapping station 7 km west of the palm grove of Béni-Abbès on the hamada of Guir.

Pollen grains and spores transported by air currents are trapped by means of vertical filters. The quantity of spores and pollen thus trapped is collected by horizontal filtration units with a surface of 400 cm^2, consisting of eight layers of hydrophilic gauze coated with silicon oil to make them adhesive; these units are exposed for a week on a horizontal support one meter from the ground (fig. 1).

In order to extract the spore and pollen content, the filters are treated as is usual for sandy sediments.

The data given in Figure 2 and in the table were obtained from a set of weekly filters (one per month) exposed over a year's cycle (from November, 1969 to October, 1970).

A summary presentation of the 12 spectra obtained is given, in which only the largest pollen masses are considered. To give a clear idea of the precision of the analyses, the complete analysis for one week in May is also presented. There are distinct differences among these spectra. (In general, evidence such as this is of interest to doctors specializing in allergies; the reference criterion used by palynologists is generally the mean annual spectrum.) The first and most striking feature is the quantity of pollen collected on the filters, considering the sparsity of the ground vegetation. A very large number of these pollen grains are allochthonous—for example, pollen grains from the mountains of the Mediterranean basin. The prevailing winds are ENE (fig. 10), and a portion of the pollen comes from Pontic regions. In June, for instance, 25% of the total pollen is from trees.

The *Artemisia* are wind-pollinated Compositae which produce a very large quantity of pollen and which grow very widely in cold steppes or in pseudosteppes with a Mediterranean climatic cycle. They are also found in the more diffuse steppes (with open vegetation distributed independently of the relief). They are very numerous in Würmian steppes. In the Sahara these allochthonous pollen grains are only identified as far as the genus.

The rest of the pollen grains from Compositae, except for *Artemisia*, will be classified as echinulate (pollen grains of *Tubiflorae*) and as fenestrate (pollen grains of *Liguliflorae*). *Carduaceae* (large echinulate pollen grains) are Mediterranean and Saharan, and it is of interest to consider them separately. The ratio of echinulate to fenestrate diminishes from the north to the south of the Sahara, this being due to the gradual disappearance of the *Carduaceae*. In the *dayas* the Compositae are quite numerous.

The *Cyperaceae* play a very small role in these spectra, but their pollen grains are transported over great distances by atmospheric currents. The *Ephedra* are likewise in small numbers, but for another reason; the pollen of *Ephedra* falls out rapidly except during exceptionally violent storms.

The periporates are represented by three families: the *Chenopodiaceae*, the *Amaranthaceae*, and the *Caryophyllaceae*. The *Chenopodiaceae*, numerous in arid zones and in places with high salinity, produce a large quantity of pollen.

The *Graminae* supply large quantities of pollen, but it is difficult to identify their genera. Ovoid pollen tends to come from northern Gramineae and spherical pollen from tropical Gramineae (1948). This test is an excellent one, as will be seen from our traverse.

In Europe the pollen of cultivated Gramineae is identified by its larger size. It is difficult to use this test in the Mediterranean region and in Africa. Analyses made with phase contrast and the scanning microscope would certainly enable a greater number to be identified. Only *Triticum*, *Pennisetum*, and *Aegliops* have been identified.

In the column "others" pollen grains have been included which appear in the spectra only irregularly, albeit some-

TABLE 1

DETAILS OF FIVE ANALYSES OF PRESENT-DAY FALLOUT

GROUND DUST FLOW SAMPLING ON A CROSSING OF THE SAHARA

HORIZONTAL FILTER

	High Algerian Plateau Point C$_{15}$ 33°00 lat. N 23 Sept. 1972			Point C$_{12}$ 30°00 lat. N (Béni-Abbès) 22 Sept. 1972			Point C$_1$ 28°45 lat. N 15 Sept. 1972			Point C$_9$ PK 600 21°40 lat. N 18 Sept. 1972			Béni-Abbès 11-18 May 1970		
	Number Counted	%	Total	Number Counted	%	Total	Number Counted	%	Total	Number Counted	%	Total	Number Counted	%	Total
TAXA NOT REPRESENTED IN THE SAHARA															
Temperate and Mediterranean															
Abietineae *Pinus*	11	0.39	616	13	0.36	133	6	0.22	56	2	0.07	20	12	0.41	3,955
Cedrus	1	0.03	56	6	0.16	61	1	0.03	9				1	0.03	315
Buxaceae *Buxus*															
Compositae *Artemisia*	339	11.87	19,004	370	10.46	3,770	181	6.71	1,698	12	0.42	123	57	1.96	18,830
Corylaceae *Corylus*				1	0.02	10							1	0.03	315
Cupressaceae	102	3.57	5,718	88	2.49	897	46	1.70	431	1	0.03	10	10	0.34	3,318
Ericaceae	1	0.03	56	2	0.05	20	3	0.11	28				1	0.03	315
Euphorbiaceae *Mercurialis*							2	0.07	19						
Fagaceae *Castanea*				1	0.02	10	2	0.07	19	1	0.03	10			
Quercus	54	1.89	3,027	113	3.19	1,151	78	2.89	732	7	0.24	72	239	8.24	78,911
Oleaceae *Fraxinus*				1	0.02	10	2	0.07	19						
Phillyrea							2	0.07	19						
Olea	27	0.94	1,513	119	3.37	1,213	90	3.34	844	4	0.14	41	372	12.84	122,850
Solanaceae *Lycium*				1	0.02	10									
Terebinthaceae *Pistacia*	3	0.10	168	3	0.08	31	10	0.37	94	1	0.03	10	5	0.17	1,631
Thymeleaceae	1	0.03	56				2	0.07	19						
TOTAL	539	18.85	30,214	718	20.24	7,316	425	15.72	3,987	28	0.96	286	698	24.05	230,440
Tropical															
a) Sahelian and Soudanese															
Combretaceae				8	0.22	82	5	0.18	47	21	0.73	215			
1) Sahelian															
Rubiaceae *Borreria*										1	0.03	10			
2) Soudanese															
Acanthaceae *Blepharis*							2	0.07	19	13	0.45	133			
Monechma				1	0.02	10	1	0.03	9	1	0.03	10			
Anacardiaceae *Lannea*										1	0.03	10			
Euphorbiaceae *Acalypha*										1	0.03	10			
Phyllantus reticulatus										1	0.03	10			
Rubiaceae *Mitracarpus scadera*				1	0.02	10									
b) Soudano-Guinean							2	0.07	19	4	0.14	41			

TABLE 1 (cont.)

Taxon	Point C_{15}			Point C_{12}			Point C_1			Point C_9 PK 600			Béni-Abbès		
Palmae *Elais guineensis*										1	0.03	10	5	0.17	1,631
TOTAL				10	0.26	102	10	0.35	94	44	1.50	449	1	0.03	315
TAXA PRESENT IN THE SAHARA															
Significative Saharian Taxa															
Boraginaceae *Moltkia*				8	0.22	82	9	0.33	84	2	0.07	20			
Capparidaceae *Cleome arabica*				3	0.08	31	1	0.03	9						
Caryophyllaceae *Polycarpea*	27	0.94	1,513	178	5.03	1,814	169	6.27	1,585	8	0.28	82	42	1.44	13,867
Gnetaceae *Ephedra* > 1%							1	0.03	9	19	0.66	195			
Mimosaceae *Acacia*				4	0.11	41				1	0.03	10	6	0.20	2,002
Palmae Phoenix (cult.)							3	0.11	28						
Polygonaceae *Calligonum*				12	0.33	122	13	0.48	122						
Solanaceae *Hyocyamus*				2	0.05	20									
Zygophyllaceae *Nitraria*							1	0.03	9						
Zygophyllum													21	0.72	6,909
TOTAL	27	0.94	1,513	207	5.82	2,110	197	7.28	1,846	30	1.04	307	75	2.56	24,724
TAXA NOT EXCLUSIVE TO THE SAHARA															
a) Holarctic															
Boraginaceae *Echium* sp.	17	0.59	953	5	0.14	51	23	0.85	216				12	0.41	3,955
Lappula sp.							2	0.07	19	160	5.60	1,638	211	7.28	69,678
Chenopodiaceae-Amaranthaceae	251	8.79	14,071	804	22.75	8,193	767	28.47	7,194						
Cistaceae *Helianthemum* sp.	12	0.42	673	6	0.16	61	5	0.18	47	3	0.10	31	18	0.62	5,901
Compositae Liguliflores	50	1.75	2,803	87	2.46	887	37	1.37	347	1	0.03	10			
Convolvulaceae *Cressa cretica*							1	0.03	9						
Geraniaceae				1	0.02	10							1	0.03	315
Holorageae *Myriophyllum*	1	0.03	56												
Liliaceae *Androcymbium punctatum*							1	0.03	9						
Asphodelus p.p.				3	0.08	31	1	0.03	9				1	0.03	315
Papaveraceae	89	3.11	4,989				117	4.34	1,097						
Plantaginaceae *Plantago* sp.	1	0.03	56	102	2.88	1,039				8	0.28	82	243	8.38	80,227
Plumbaginaceae				5	0.14	51							1	0.03	315
Polygonaceae *Emex* sp.	3	0.10	168	22	0.62	224							42	1.45	13,867
Rumex sp.	2	0.07	112	2	0.05	20	17	0.63	159				3	0.10	1,001
Renonculaceae				4	0.11	41	1	0.03	9				2	0.06	679
Resedaceae				7	0.19	71									
Reseda sp.	3	0.10	168	9	0.25	92	8	0.29	75	2	0.07	20	7	0.24	2,317
Tamaricaceae *Tamarix* sp.	3	0.10	168	46	1.30	469	2	0.07	19	1	0.03	10	2	0.06	679
Umbelliferae	12	0.42	672	1	0.02	10	44	1.59	413	3	0.10	31	73	2.51	24,101
Zygophyllaceae *Fagonia* sp.	4	0.14	224				9	0.33	84	1	0.03	10	15	0.51	4,956
b) Cosmopolitan															
Compositae Tubiflores	130	4.55	7,287	340	9.62	3,465	185	6.86	1,735	55	1.92	563	80	2.76	26,544
Cruciferae	161	5.64	9,025	243	6.87	2,476	109	4.04	1,022	111	3.88	1,137	83	2.86	27,426

TABLE 1 (cont.)

	Point C_{15}			Point C_{12}			Point C_1		Point C_9 PK 600			Béni-Abbès		
Cyperaceae	6	0.21	336	131	3.70	1,335	938	3.71	838	29.35	8,581	31	1.07	10,227
Euphorbiaceae *Euphorbia* sp.	1,452	50.87	81,399	5	0.14	51	38	0.14	18	0.63	184	4	0.13	1,316
Gramineae	1	0.03	56	692	19.58	7,051	5,206	20.60	1,446	50.64	14,807	1,120	38.68	369,831
Labiatae	4	0.14	224	3	0.08	31	9	0.03				2	0.06	679
Papilionaceae				10	0.28	102	47	0.18	13	0.45	133	30	1.03	9,912
Lotus sp.				3	0.08	31	19	0.07						
Rhamnaceae				1	0.02	10	28	0.11				16	0.55	5,271
Rubiaceae *Galium* sp.	2	0.07	112	1	0.02	10	9	0.03						
Scrophulariaceae							9	0.03						
Celsia sp.				2	0.05	20						1	0.03	315
Linaria sp.							9	0.03				6	0.20	2,002
Veronica sp.												2	0.06	679
Typhaceae *Typha* sp.				2	0.05	20	9	0.03	7	0.24	72			
Urticaceae				5	0.14	51	56	0.22	2	0.07	20	8	0.27	2,632
Zygophyllaceae *Tribulus* sp.							9	0.03	24	0.84	246			
TOTAL	2,204	77.16	123,552	2,542	71.80	25,903	18,849	74.42	2,693	94.26	27,575	2,014	69.41	665,140
c) Tropical Sahelian														
Capparidaceae *Boscia*							9	0.03	4	0.14	41			
Gynandropsis gynandra									2	0.07	20			
Maerua									3	0.10	31			
Euphorbiaceae *Crozophora*									3	0.10	31			
Nyctaginaceae									1	0.03	10			
Palmae *Hyphaene thebaica*									1	0.03	10			
Papilionaceae *Indigofera*									1	0.03	10			
Zygophyllaceae *Balanites aegyptiaca*									1	0.03	10			
TOTAL							**9**	**0.03**	**15**	**0.50**	**153**			
PLANTED														
Caesalpiniaceae *Ceratonia* sp.												1	0.03	315
Casuarinaceae *Casuarina* sp.	1	0.03	56											
Myrtaceae *Eucalyptus* sp.	2	0.07	112				28	0.11	1	0.03	10	2	0.06	679
Sapotaceae	2	0.07	112				47	0.18				23	0.79	7,595
Vitaceae *Vitis vinifera*												11	0.37	3,633
TOTAL	**5**	**0.17**	**280**				**75**	**0.29**	**1**	**0.03**	**10**	**37**	**1.25**	**12,222**
UNIDENTIFIED	1	0.03	56	5	0.14	51	75	0.29	1	0.03	10	36	1.24	11,865
UNIDENTIFIABLE	77	2.69	4,316	38	1.07	387	328	1.29	43	1.50	440	34	1.17	11,235
Number of pollen grains counted	2,853			3,533			2,694		2,855			2,894		
Number of taxa	33			53			57		45			44		
Total pollen collected on filters of 400 cm^2 per km	159,931			36,002			25,263		29,230					
Total pollen deposited on one sq m in 7 days												955,626		

FIG. 1–Trapping Station at Béni-Abbès. In the foregound is the support for the horizontal filter which collects the pollen fallout, behind a meteorological tower at the top of which are fixed–to the right, a horizontal filter and–to the left, a weather vane which holds into the wind two vertical filters intercepting pollen flow. *Photograph by Pierre Cour, 1972.*

times in large quantities: *Cruciferae, Resedaceae,* and *Zygophyllaceae.*

SPORES

Very few fern spores are found in the air, spores being transported by water. In a small enclosed basin a large number of spores always indicates the presence of populations of Pteridophytes.

This analysis of the atmosphere at Béni-Abbès indicates the important and sometimes preponderant role that allochthonous pollen grains play. This is a point which will have to be included in all discussions of pollen spectra. Later we

shall see that the mean annual pollen spectrum is repeated more or less exactly in sediments from the Quaternary.

PRESENT-DAY POLLEN RAIN IN THE SAHARA TRAVERSE FROM BOUGTOUB TO MALI

By far the most exciting experiment among those concerned with the sampling of pollen from the ground is the work of P. Cour, in which pollen was raised and caught during a traverse of the Sahara (from Bougtoub–high Algerian Plateau–latitude 34° N, to the frontier of Mali at 21°40') (fig. 3). He had the idea of exposing filter units in the cloud of dust raised by a vehicle traveling off the road (fig. 4); these filter units, composed of five layers of hydrophilic gauze coated with silicon oil, were exposed for ten kilometers, this sampling being repeated every 100 km, giving 13 collections in all (fig. 5).

This technique of dust sampling allows selective collection of the finest particles deposited on the surface. A large number of pollen grains and spores (particularly those of fungi) are generally found among the dust thus raised.

After exposure of the filters, the gauze with the mineral and organic particles, trapped at the same time as the pollen grains, was destroyed by a series of chemical treatments. In the analysis, very precise volumetric measures made on the initial centrifugation pellet and on fractions of the pellet actually counted under the microscope make it possible to estimate the number of pollen grains (per taxon) collected on the filters.

It was possible to collect on a 400 cm² filter exposed in 10 km of dust flow a minimum of 45,900 pollen grains at point C6 (latitude 24°10' N) situated at the center of Tanezrouft in a hyperarid region, and a maximum of 1,600,000 pollen grains in the heart of the alfa-grass and *Artemisia* steppes of the high Algerian Plateau (point C15 at a latitude of 33° N).

In figure 5a the graph of the distribution of pollen rain along the Sahara crossing is shown with a solid line. For a clearer graphic presentation, the quantities of pollen grain collected per kilometer of dust flow at each point have been expressed as a percentage of the total pollen mass obtained over all 13 points (which was 468,729 pollen grains for 13 dust flow samples).

We will assume that the large quantities of pollen collected by this method provide a sample which is perfectly representative of the pollen rain over a considerable area. Thus rain provided by Mediterranean flora will allow us to define the term of "pollen influence"–in fact, it was determined that for each taxon there exists a nonrandom latitudinal distribution shown by the graphs in figures 7, 8, and 9. These graphs, as well as the frequency tables, clearly demonstrate that:

1. The pollen fallout of Mediterranean origin has a very perceptible influence in the pollen spectra as far as the center of Tanezrouft: at a latitude of 26° N. Five hundred seventy-six "Mediterranean" pollen grains collected per kilometer of dust flow made up 9.25% of the spectrum.

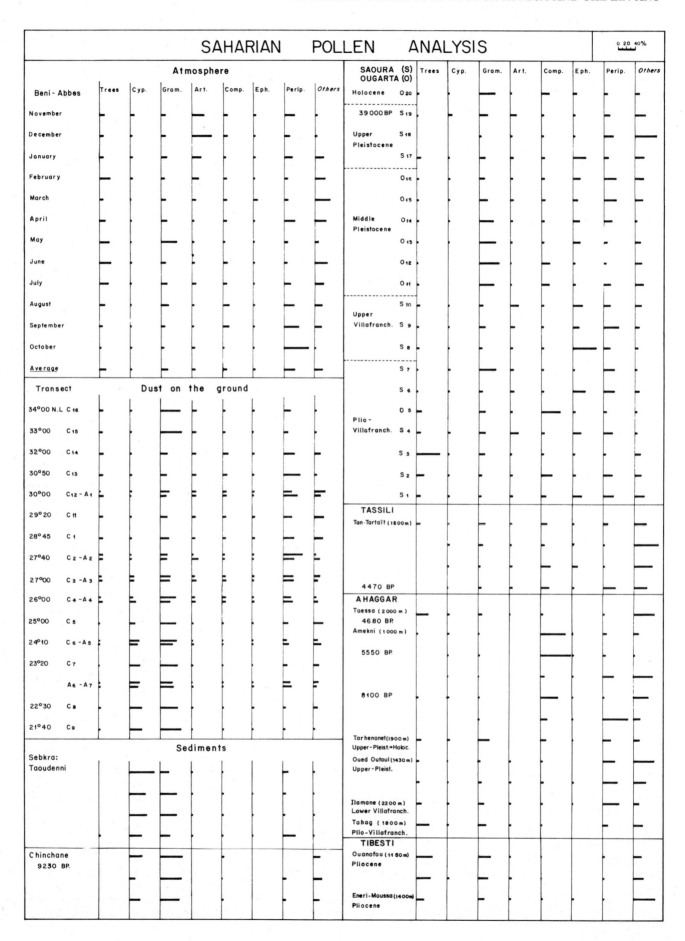

This rain reaches the southern limit of the Sahara; at latitude 21°30′ N, 256 pollen grains per kilometer of dust flow, or 0.96% of the spectrum, were still collected. The principal component of this deposit comes, for the trees, from *Olea, Quercus, Pinus, Cupressus,* and *Juniperus,* and from the genus *Artemisia.* The pollen of *Olea* and that of *Artemisia* have been included in the rain of Mediterranean origin, although these genera are present on the Ahaggar and in the northern pre-Saharan regions (these regions being subject to only a semidesert climate).

2. The pollen rain originating from tropical regions (emitted from taxa not represented in the Saharan flora) do not reach the northern limit of the Sahara (latitude 32° N) (fig. 6); pollen rain of this type first appeared at Béni-Abbès (latitude 30°) (fig. 6), where 102 pollen grains were collected per kilometer of dust flow, and these pollen grains only represent 0.26% of the local spectrum.

The rain originating from exclusively tropical taxa constitutes only a small part of the pollen rain collected in the southern part of the traverse (449 pollen grains, or only 1.50% of the spectrum). Both the total absence of vegetation ground cover and the increase toward the south in the number of pollen grains from a large number of taxa (see in particular the rising distribution curves for the pollen rain from the *Gramineae, Cyperaceae, Typha, Tribulus*. . ., figs. 8 and 9) point to the conclusion that this rain came largely from the semidesert (Sahel) southern regions situated more than 500 km away.

COMMENTS ON THE POLLEN SPECTRA OBTAINED FROM QUATERNARY SEDIMENTS IN THE VALLEY OF WADI SAOURA OR ITS TRIBUTARIES AND IN THE OUGARTA MOUNTAINS

Only wadi bed deposits give pollen in sufficient quantity to attempt paleoecological and paleoclimatic interpretations. Furthermore, only spectra based on counts of more than 200 pollen grains have been retained. If these samples correspond, as is probably the case, to more regular periods of wadi flow, and thus to periods of greater wetness toward the source, then they constitute mere short episodes in the complex history of the deposition of sediments in these wadis; the age of these sediments is not known precisely, and some, even thick ones, may have been deposited by a limited number of large floods.

The only divisions that geologists have thought distinguishable are the following: Plio-Villafranchian, Upper Villafranchian, Middle Pleistocene, Upper Pleistocene, and Holocene. The pollen analyses were performed by F. Beucher (1971) and are taken from her thesis.

If on the one hand one looks at the present-day pollen spectra for the region under consideration, and on the other at spectra coming from dusts from alfa-grass and *Aristida* steppe and from the desert, and if one compares with these the spectra obtained in the valley of the Saoura and in the Ougarta mountains, various vegetational landscapes of the Pleistocene can be reconstructed more confidently.

The first conclusion is that never, during the periods covered by the pollen spectra, was the Béni-Abbès region under the pollen influence of tropical steppe or of grass savanna. In other words, in none of these periods did the limit of the grass savanna experience a northerly displacement of more than 300-400 km from its present position, for had such been the case the influence of its pollen would have been widely felt in the region of Béni-Abbès. Indeed, the picture of the pollen grains from the grassy savanna as it is today, south of 25° N, is dominated by *Cyperaceae-Graminae.* In the Sebkra of Taoudeni at 22°40′ N, and Chinchane, at 21°10′ N, (Assemien, 1971), it is exclusively of *Cyperaceae-Graminae,* and likewise in the center of the Tchad depression the muds of stagnant pools give a spectrum comprising 65% Cyperaceae and 22% Graminae, making 87% in all (Maley, 1972). Further reinforcing this effect of the grass pollen grains is the weakness of the tree pollen component. Since the majority of these trees are zoogamous, they contribute practically nothing to the atmospheric pollen.

A reliable reference point for the interpretation of the pollen content of the deposits is obtained by comparing this to present-day pollen spectra. However, there is a point which must be borne in mind; a slight increase in humidity in the Béni-Abbès region would not lead to a modification of the flora itself, but only to an increase in the vegetation ground cover (fig. 11). Such a change is usually estimated from absolute values, that is from the total quantity of pollen found in equal amounts of sediment. These changes are completely undetectable in the "fossil spectra," which are difficult to compare with one another since we do not know the precise conditions under which the pollen grains

FIG. 2—Table Summarizing the Pollen Analyses. Sediments: Taoudenni—four levels, 6.30, 4.80, 4.80, and 2.60 m; Chinchane (Assemien, 1971)—three levels, 625, 500, and 400 cm, wells in the sebkra of Chinchane; Saoura (S) and Ougarta (O) (Beucher, 1971)—S[1], S[2], S[3], and S[4]—formations of Aidian age, near Hassi-Ali bel Hadj el Aid, in the "Gilfe de Mazzer"; O[5]—sandy Aidian formations at Mekitla south of the Ougarta mountains; S[6] and S[7]—Aidian formations at Foum Marouga; S[8] and S[9]—Mazzerian riverine formations at Mazzer (Saoura Valley); S[10]—cemented Mazzerian conglomerate of Foum Marouga; O[11], O[12], O[13], and O[14]—varicolored fluviatile formations of Ougartian age in Wadi Farès; O[15] and O[16]—formations of Ougartian age, right bank of Wadi Ali; S[17] and S[18]—fluvio-lacustrine Mazzerian sedimented formations in the "rukna" of Tamtert; S[19]—lignitic level identified at Bou-Hadid, lower part of the Saourian terrace; O[20]—guirian formations of the "Catherine Butte." Tassili (Alimen, Beucher, Lhote, Delibrias, 1968)—Neolithic deposits of Tan-Tartait and of d'I-n-Itinen, Tassili-N-Ajjer (central Sahara), four levels—limestone with large nodules, Bed III, manure, manure in the process of decomposition *b,* and manure in the process of decomposition *a.* Ahaggar—Tahag (Van Campo, Cohen, Guinet, Rognon, 1965); Ilamane (Van Campo, Aymonin, Guinet, Rognon, 1964); Oued Outoul (Van Campo, Guinet, Cohen, Dutil, 1967), two levels, 5 and 3 m; Tarhenanet (Van Campo, Aymonin, Guinet, Rognon, 1964); Amekni (Guinet, Planque, in G. Camps, 1969), five levels, 1.60, 1.40, 0.90, 0.75, and 0.60 m; and Taessa (Pons, Quezel, 1958). Tibesti (Maley, Cohen, Faure, Rognon, Vincent, 1970)—Eneri-Moussa and Ouanofou.

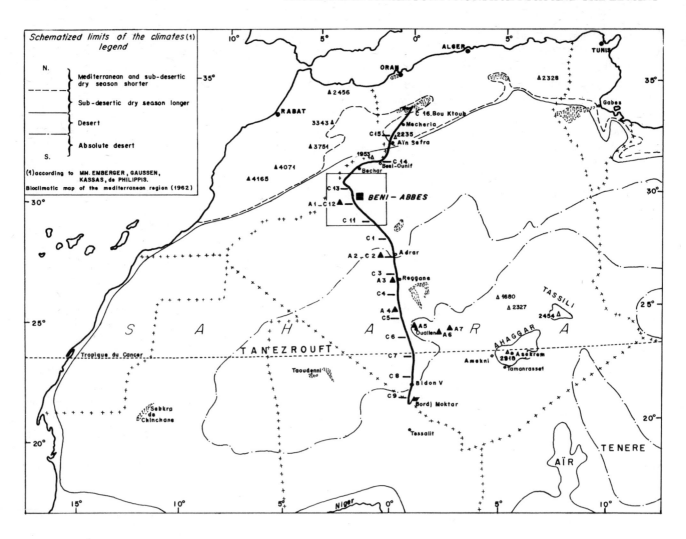

FIG. 3—Map of the principal climatic zones in the Sahara, indicating the places mentioned in the text and the course of the transect.

were deposited. Pollen content can be compared only from deposits laid under the same conditions.

On the other hand, an increase in the local ground cover induces a greater local pollen release and thus a lowering of the percentage of allochthonous forms. In the current state of our knowledge we cannot make precise calculations of the percentage of allochthonous forms, since we cannot identify pollen grains of the *Gramineae*, even as to genera. It is only the pollen from Mediterranean trees that gives us some idea—the mean percentage of tree pollen grains in the air today near Béni-Abbès is 15%, and from the dust of the Sahara traverse it is 10%. In mud from the Saoura (December flood, collected in June), the percentage of trees goes down to 3%. Thus at present, depending on the sediment chosen, the percentage of trees varies from a high of 15% to a low of 3%. Should the percentages vary from the range indicated for trees, it is to be considered that conditions were other than those obtaining today.

Considering cases outside this range, several interpretations may be possible:

1. A decline of pollen emission by allochthonous trees, corresponding to periods of deteriorating climate in the

Mediterranean regions; in other words, periods when these regions were invaded by steppes of *Artemisia-Chenopodiaceae*. In fact, during the Würm, a telescoping of the zones of vegetation is seen, the type of climate favorable to mixed oak forest having disappeared. The deciduous forests were either in refuges where the microclimate and nature of the soil could assure the maintenance of a number of species, or in the form of a belt of vegetation in the mountains of the Mediterranean basin, in any case in isolated pockets (Van Campo, 1969). The *Artemisia* and *Chenopodiaceae* steppes should not necessarily be considered characteristic of very cold climates, but rather, in the Mediterranean plains, of an arid and sunny climate, with a wide temperature differential between night and day. Thus, simultaneous with a diminution in numbers of tree pollen grains, the *Artemisia* increase in the Saoura valley (sample S19, trees 2%, *Artemisia* 15%). Hence it is difficult to get a precise idea of changes in local vegetation. All that can be said is that the *Compositae* are rare, that the flora is limited in species, fitting in well with a thinning of the vegetation ground cover, and thus with greater dryness. This being the case, simultaneous with reduction in the release of pollen grains

FIG. 4—The dust cloud raised by the vehicle moving at 40 kph (dust flow sampling). Behind the vehicle is a thin pole 1 m long, at the end of which are fixed two filters to which the dust adheres. *Photograph by Pierre Cour, 1972.*

in the surrounding regions, there would also have been a reduction in the local pollen emission, reflecting greater dryness.

2. The ground cover is less extensive, but this is not synchronous with a cold dry period in the Mediterranean basin—such appear to be the conditions in S4 and S10. The presence of pollen from *Olea* and *Acacia* suggests that it was no colder. Thus what these spectra represent are periods of enhanced local aridity, pollen of *Artemisia* reaching considerable proportions. Such an interpretation is confirmed by the presence of a substantial quantity of pollen of *Calligonum* and *Ephedra*. It is clear that in such an environment conditions slightly more arid than those of today would have an immediate effect on the extent of ground cover.

It is also possible that a less extensive ground cover could be due to instability of the surface, as for example in the case of constant sandstorms. Under such conditions, however, it is difficult to see how polliniferous sediments could be deposited at all.

3. Extensive vegetation ground cover. This is evidently a present-day characteristic of the wadi beds or of *dayas*. Such a possible origin of the sediment must be borne in mind when interpreting the analysis. Samples O^{20}, O^{12}, O^{11}, and S^{18} suggest a more extensive ground cover.

S^{18} may represent the flora of a *daya*. Spectra O^{11}, O^{12}, and O^{20}, from wadi Farès, are remarkable for the dominance of *Gramineae*, with very low percentages of *Artemisia* and *Chenopidiaceae*. *Acacia* pollen grains are present. Such a spectrum corresponds to the present-day vegetation in the bed of wadi Farès where precise surveys were made by Ph. Guinet (1958). It is evident from these that the association *Acacia-Panicum* + *Compositae* is such that it gives a very comparable spectrum.

Levels S^6, S^7, S^8, S^9, and O^{14} are easily placed with respect to the reference spectra of today. O^{14} in particular gives a spectrum of the same type as alfa-grass steppe, while the others would suggest an *Aristida* steppe. Thus it was wetter, especially in O^{14}.

Spectra S^1, S^6, O^{15}, and O^{16} are in precise accordance with the present-day spectra of Béni-Abbès. Spectrum S^{17},

near the Erq, with 34% *Ephedra*, is also "present-day." Spectrum O^{13}, from wadi Farès, is perhaps a little "drier" than that of today.

Two spectra quite different from those of today remain to be considered: S^2 and S^3.

In S^3 the percentage of tree pollen grains reaches 56%, and it is quite clear that such a percentage cannot be explained on the basis of an hypothesis of dominance by allochthonous pollen grains.

Details from the analysis S^3 of sediments from the Aïdian age (Plio-Villafranchian) from the Gulf of Mazzer, altitude 506 m, are as follows—percentages: *Cyperaceae* 1.30%, trees 55.65% (*Erica arborea* 1, *Fraxinus excelsior* 7, *Platanus orientalis* 4, *Myrtus communis* 1, *Alnus* 1, *Aesculus* 9, *Betuloides* 25, *Carpinus* 8, *Corylus* 2, *Fagus* 1, *Olea* cf. *europea* 4, *Quercus* 39, *Pinus* 3, *Salix* 1, *Ulmus* 1, *Taxus* 7, cf. *Zelkova* 2, *Celtis* 1, *Juglans* 2), *Gramineae* 12.60%, *Artemisia* 2.60%, *Compositae tubuliflorae* 4.78%, *Ephedra* 3.47%, *Chenopodiaceae* 3.04%, *Caryophyllaceae* 0.86%, *Cruciferae* + *Polygonaceae* 1.30%, *Umbelliferae* 0.43%, *Acacia* 0.43%, *Myrtaceae* 0.43%, indeterminate and miscellaneous 12.60%.

In the Pliocene the Saoura therefore siphoned off the northern forest toward the south, implying extensive rain in the Mediterranean basin where the dry season was either shorter or more subjected to storms than that of today, or had a more extensive cloud cover.

COMMENTS ON THE POLLEN SPECTRA OF THE MOUNTAINS OF THE SAHARA

Studies have been made of sediments coming from Tassili N'Agger, from the Ahaggar, and from the Tibesti.

The first striking fact is that the low altitude Pliocene sediments and the high altitude Quaternary sediments are rich in tree pollen grains.

In the Pliocene strata of the Tibesti numerous tree pollen grains are accompanied by a large quantity of pollen grains of *Gramineae*; this pollen analysis is typical of wind-pollinated flora. The pollen flora suggests an Oro-Mediterranean open forest, but it is quite clear that trees from tropical tree savanna or from riparian forest, mostly entomogamous, release little pollen into the air—they are insufficiently represented. Thus only under exceptional circumstances can the tropical nature of the flora be detected in pollen masses from the atmosphere. It can be brought out, however, by precise analyses which lead to the identification of species.

One of the samples from the Pliocene Formation at Wanofu is quite remarkable because of the presence of large quantities of pollen grains from both plane trees and a holly. Pollen of plane is very abundant in the three samples published, which refutes the hypothesis that its presence is due to chance. Holly is anemophilous—thus the *Ilex* were *in situ*. It is not *Ilex aquifolium*, but probably an *Ilex* of tropical origin. In one of the samples there are pollen grains of *Loranthoideae* and two of *Combretaceae*. A flora

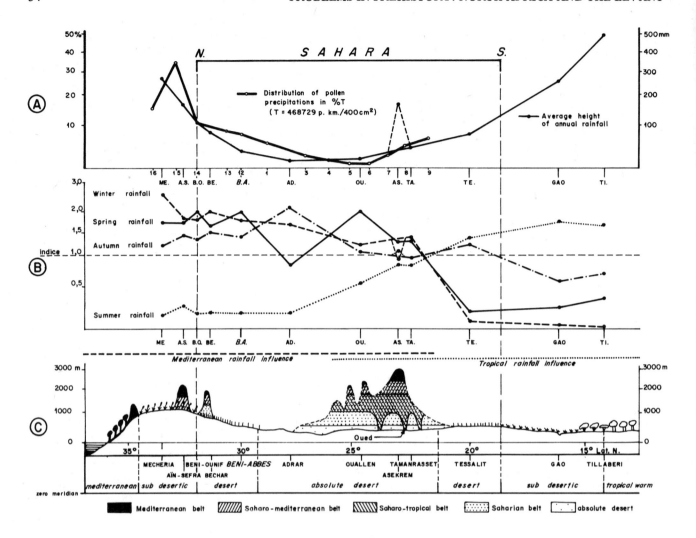

FIG. 5—A The thin line indicates mean annual rainfall measured between 1926 and 1950 at the principal meteorological stations situated in
the desert in the vicinity of zero meridian, between Mecheria in Algeria (a subdesert region, under Mediterranean influence) and
Tillaberi on the Niger (a subdesert region under tropical influence). *After J. Dubieff, 1963, pp. 138-45, and after G. Rippstein and B.
Peyre de Fabregues, 1972, p. 45, for the rainfall figures at Tillaberi. Broken lines* indicate the rainfall data for the plateau of
Assekrem (2,726 m) and for Tamanrasset (1,395 m), both in the Ahaggar Massif, near longitude 5° 30′. *The thick line* on the graph
of mean annual rainfall, in mm, indicates the latitudinal distribution of pollen fallout; these pollen data are derived from ground
surface deposits over a NS crossing of the Sahara, between the latitudes 34° and 21° N. Each point of this distribution is expressed as
a percentage of the sum of all the pollen collected during the crossing. *The dotted line* shows the mean rainfall at Ahaggar.
B Indices of latitudinal distribution of seasonal rainfall in the Sahara and in the adjacent northern and southern regions. The
distribution index for seasonal rainfall, collected at different meteorological stations, is calculated from the following proportion for
each station: the mean seasonal rainfall expressed as a percentage of the total fall of water during each season at all the stations (in
spring Sp = 279.0 mm; summer Su - 775.2 mm; in autumn A - 453.4 mm; in winter W - 203.1 mm) divided by the annual rainfall
expressed as a percentage of the total fall of water recorded annually by all the stations (T - 1,710.7 mm of rain).
Examples of calculations: for the station at Béni-Abbès the rainfall collected between 1926 and 1950 gives a mean annual rainfall of
32.1 mm, or 1.87% of this fall; the spring rainfall (March, April, and May) adds up to 10.9 mm, or 3.90% of the spring fall, and the
summer rains (June, July, and August) add up to 2.4 mm, or 0.30% of the summer fall. By giving the latitudinal distribution of
rainfall recorded annually at Béni-Abbès (1.87%) a reference index of 1.00, we obtain, for example, a springtime rainfall distribution
index of 1.08. (3.90% of $Sp \div 1.87\%$ of T = 2.08). And a summertime rainfall distribution index of 0.16 (0.30% of $Su \div 1.87\%$ of T =
0.16). Such a system of representation as this shows clearly the seasonal distribution of rain at any one station and the relationship of
this to the patterns found at all the other stations.
C Diagrammatic section of the climatic zones; in the background is given a summary of the vegetational belts on the Ahaggar.

tropical in character was thus present in association with a
Caducifolieae flora of an Oro-Mediterranean nature.

An analysis of sediments from the Natron Gap, on the
other hand, emphasizes the tropical nature of a scattered
fern flora. J. Maley gives the following information on the
flora of two diatomites: the two samples analyzed (other

analyses are currently being carried out) were collected in
the Natron Gap by P. Rognon in April, 1965, in an isolated
mound of diatomite in an eroded depression at about 1850
m altitude and about 425 m below the southwest edge of
the crater.

The mound is three m high. Sample number 688 was

FIG. 6–*Upper*: Point C^{16} (Bougtoub area at latitude 34° N). Steppe with *Tipa tenacissima*, *Lygeum spartum*, *Artemisia herba-alba* of the High Algerian Plateaus. *Middle*: Point C^{14} (Beni Oumf area, at latitude 32° N). Diffuse vegetation with *Anabasis aretioides*, *Gymnocarpos decander*, *Helianthemum aristida*, etc. *Lower*: Point C^{12} (Béni-Abbès area, at latitude 30° N). Desert type ground apart from the hollow and the wadi beds. *Photographs by Pierre Cour, 1972.*

taken toward the base of a layer of thin slabs, and number 689 was taken one m from the top of the section in a layer containing molluscs. These two and also others from a neighboring mound in a similar stratigraphic position gave two dates: 14,970 B.P. ± 400 years (sample no. 689) and 14,790 B.P. ± 400 years (sample no. 688) (H. Faure, 1969).

A third date, 12,400 B.P. ± 400 years, was obtained from limestone deposits probably of algal origin. H. Faure (1969) states "that the three dates quoted could be too old because of possible concentrations of carbon dioxide of

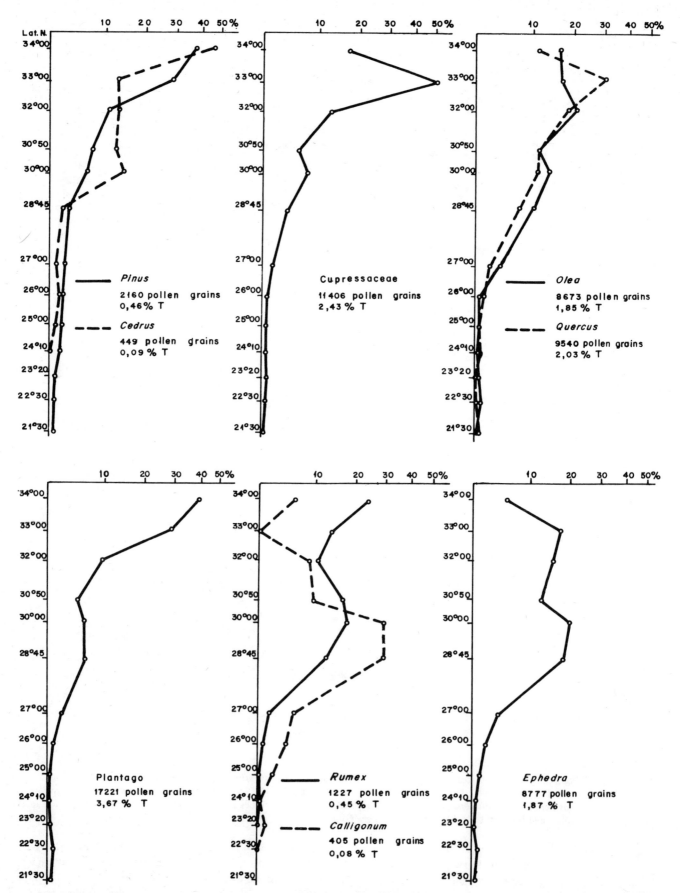

FIGS. 7, 8, and 9—The number shown after each taxon is the total number of pollen grains for this taxon collected over all thirteen points; the number in brackets is a percentage indicating the relative place of the taxon in the global pollen spectrum obtained over all the thirteen dust flow samples. (For example, in the top left of fig. 7, the 2,610 pollen grains of *Pinus* collected over the whole transect is

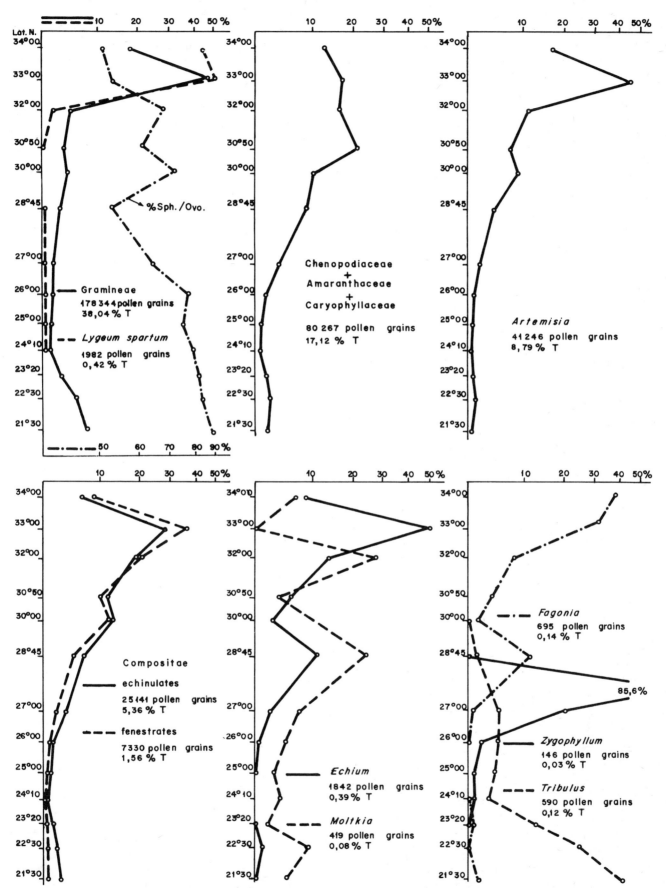

equal to 0.46% of the total pollen mass obtained from the thirteen samples—that is, 468,729 pollen grains.) The graph of latitudinal distribution of each taxon is calculated as a percentage of the sum of pollen grains collected over the whole transect for that taxon. (For example, at latitude 30° N, at Béni-Abbès point C^{12}, the 133 pollen grains of *Pinus* collected per km of dust flow sampling on a

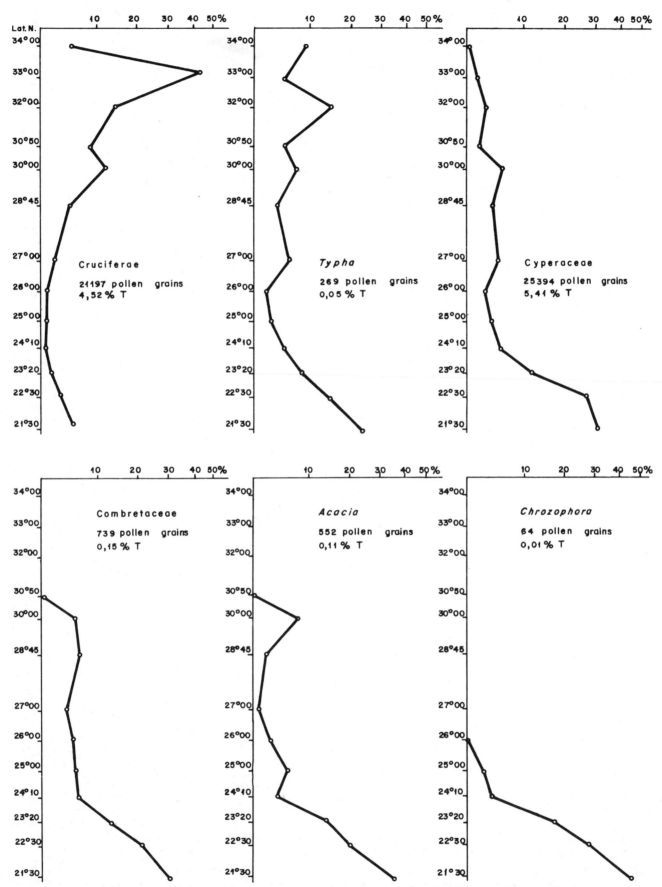

filter of 400 cm^2 represent 5.09% of the 2,610 pollen grains of *Pinus* which were collected over all thirteen dust flow samples; likewise, the 61 pollen grains of *Cedrus* give 13.58% of the 449 pollen grains collected over the whole transect of the Sahara.)

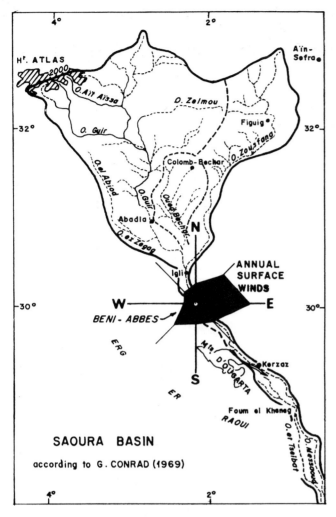

FIG. 10—Saoura Basin. For the region of Béni-Abbès wind direction indicator has been drawn at the borders of the Saoura basin, showing that the prevailing winds are ENE.

volcanic origin in the lake water; release of CO_2 in the natron springs occurs today in the bottom of the Gap."

Comparison with similar lacustrine formations in other craters of the Tibesti might enable the verification of these dates. No date exists for the base of the formations, whereas the summit of a lacustrine formation has been dated as from 8,055 B.P. ± 90 years in the Tarso Yega at an altitude of about 2,100 m (U. Bottcher et al., 1972). According to these authors the most recent dates for lacustrine formations 1,000 m high are between 7,000 and 8,000 years B.P., and the oldest between 13,000 and 14,000 years B.P.

POLLEN ANALYSIS OF SAMPLE NUMBER 688

Gramineae 12, *Cyperaceae* 1, *Pteris dentata* 182, *Pteris vittata* 1, *Cheilanthes* sp. 10, *Actiniopteris radiata* 5, *Ophioglossum* sp. 2, *Anogramma leptophylla* 1, monolete spores 50, *Riccia* sp. (liverworts) 1, indeterminate 3, nonidentifiable 1, total 271; total spores 254; total other taxa 13.

POLLEN ANALYSIS OF SAMPLE NUMBER 689

Gramineae 30, *Cyperaceae* 5, *Typha* 1, *Artemisia* sp. 3, *Erica arborea* 2, *Pteris dentata* 75, *Pteris vittata* 1, *Cheilanthes* sp. 21, *Actiniopteris radiata* 4, *Asplenium* cf. *aethiopicum* 1, *Ophioglossum* sp. 6, *Anogramma leptophylla* 6, monolete spores 45, *Riccia* sp. (liverworts) 1, indeterminate 15, nonidentifiable 13, total 238; total spores 169; total other taxa 41.

Almost all the spores belong to ferns of tropical origin. Only *Anogramma leptophylla* can be traced as far as the Atlantic coast.

Numerous tree pollen grains are found again on the Ahaggar in the Plio-Villafranchian at an altitude of 1,800 m, including *Aesculus*. This impoverished "forest" is found again 4,680 years ago at 200 m and perhaps would still be found but for the depredation by animal herds over thousands of years. These holarctic trees reach the southern limit of their range in the high Saharan mountain massifs. As stressed by P. Quezel in 1957, the Oro-Mediterranean taxa were present in the Burdigalian since numerous species are found on the summit of the Macronesian islands.

Each oscillation toward a drier climate destroyed a little of this high altitude flora, be it Mediterranean or tropical; it was at its extreme limits for survival and was unable to find a refuge from which to spread out again afterwards. Nevertheless, the picture it presents today is a consequence of the action of man. We might cite as a single proof of this the luxuriance of the pink laurel (*Nerium oleander*) and of the fig (*Ficus*), the first being toxic to animals and the second only browsed upon to a limited extent and protected by man.

It is certain that the wadis flowing down from the Ahaggar or from the Tassili N'Agger ran far more continuously during different epochs, but to find the chronological indicators the vegetation would have had to change each time. Its density increased or decreased, but the vegetation did not change (fig. 12), at least as far as the palynologists have been able to determine.

We can assume that a wetter climate at an altitude corresponding to a lowering of temperature of ± 4° must favor both Mediterranean and tropical flora.

The fact that the high Saharan summits had a far higher rainfall and thus that the wadis were in continuous flow does not necessarily imply that the low altitudes and plains were always wetter in the regions between the rivers. It is therefore not impossible that at certain periods the wadis flowed through a zone of desert even more arid than today.

COMMENTS ON THE POLLEN SPECTRA OF TROPICAL PSEUDOSTEPPE AND OF SAVANNA

The spectra obtained from the ground dust at 22°30′ and at 21°40′ (fig. 2) are under the pollen influence of grassy savanna. It is largely the *Gramineae* and the *Cyperaceae* which dominate the spectrum.

The pollen analysis of the Holocene sebkra of Taoudeni gives spectra where *Cyperaceae-Gramineae* predominate

FIG. 11—*Upper*: Contracted vegetation, confined in the depressions (*daya*) of hamada of Guir around latitude 30° N in the region of Béni-Abbès. These depressions are largely colonized by arborescent plants, notably—*Launaea arborescens, Anvillea radiata, Bubonium graveolens, Zilla macroptera, Randonia africana* as well as a certain number of plants, such as *Lotus jolyi, Convolvulus supinus, Polycarpea confusa*, some asphodels and Gramineae. *Lower*: Vegetation of nonsalty wadi beds, between latitude 31° and 29° N, with *Acacia raddiana, Panicum turgidum, Anvillea radiata, Pituranthos chloranthus*, etc. *Photographs by Pierre Cour, 1972.*

(fig. 2); likewise in the sebkra of Chinchane.

J. Maley (1972), studying the muds of stagnant ponds of Lake Tchad, also obtains spectra dominant in *Gramineae-Cyperaceae.*

Thus it is sufficiently clear that tropical pseudosteppe and tropical grassy savanna give a spectrum where *Gramineae-Cyperaceae* are dominant.

To the southwest of Abidjan there is a savanna which A.

Aubreville (1962) has classified as an aberrant savanna; this savanna is marked with a 1 on the map (fig. 13). In fact, it is situated in a forest zone, and edaphic conditions would not be against the existence of a forest here. The savannas at 2 and 3 (fig. 13) are also considered as aberrant. Furthermore, it is a known fact that natural savannas exist around and within the African or Amazonian tropical forest which the forest is in the process of reconquering. Two pollen

FIG. 12—*Upper*: Saharo-Tropical zone: Amekni wadi at approximately 1,100 m with *Panicum, Aristida*, various Compositae, *Zilla spinosa*, etc., and with *Acacia, Tamarix, Balanites*, and *Calotropis* not visible on the photograph. *Middle and Lower*: Saharo-Mediterranean zone—*middle*, Guelta Tarhenanet (1,814 m) with *Nerium oleander, Tamarix gallica, Typha, Phragmites, Juncus*, etc.; *Lower*: Ilamane wadi, at approximately 1,950 m, with *Olea laperrini, Pituranthos scoparius, Atriplex halimus, Artemisia campestris*, etc. *Photographs by Pierre Cour, 1972.*

analyses (P. Assemien, 1971) have been carried out in this savanna near Abidjan. A sample of peat near the level -65 m (regressive) dates from 23,000 B.P. ± 1,000 years, and the other sample from the level -63 m (transgressive) dates from 11,900 B.P. ± 250 years. The main component of the pollen flora from the sediment dated at 23,000 years is comprised of *Gramineae, Cyperaceae*, and some spores from *Pteridophytes*. The sample dated at 11,900 years B.P.

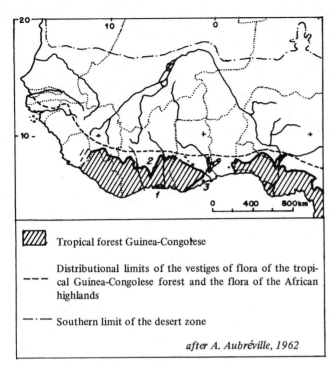

Tropical forest Guinea-Congolese

Distributional limits of the vestiges of flora of the tropical Guinea-Congolese forest and the flora of the African highlands

Southern limit of the desert zone

after A. Aubréville, 1962

FIG. 13–Distributional Limits; Major Floral Zones in West Africa. shows a fairly varied flora, but the pollen of large trees is rare (*Pentaclethra, Meliaceae*). This characteristic would suggest a much more open forest than that which can be seen today.

It is thus clear that 23,000 years ago the low latitudes had a drier climate than today, which confirms the results of geomorphology, and that the southern limit of the Sahara was below that of today.

The hypercold periods therefore correspond to hyperdry periods, but the "hot" periods do not necessarily correspond to wet periods. This phenomenon has been studied very precisely by J. Maley at Lake Tchad. Taking the levels of the lake during various historical periods as reference points, he shows that the "small ice age" (from the middle of the sixteenth century to the end of the eighteenth century) was a period of high water level in the lake.

A similar situation was found for the cool period at the end of the last century. Recently (1953-64) a slight drop in temperature was recorded which also corresponded to flooding of the lake. Periods of warmer climate, such as those of recent years (1964-73), correspond to a lowering of the water level in the lake and to a lessening of rainfall in the tropical zone. These correlations show that the intensification of the monsoon must be associated with increased winter cold in the southern hemisphere. The attraction of the low pressures of the Sahara plays but a secondary and incidental role. Viewed like this, the position of the meteorological equator of zones of intertropical convergence (I.T.C.) depends on the antagonistic action of the polar fronts of the two hemispheres.

Thus it can be seen that fluctuations in the monsoon follow the fluctuations in advance and retreat of the glaciers. Thus toward the end of the last glacial period the

rapid retreat of the Arctic ice cap involved a comparable retreat of the North Polar front which encouraged a very great extension of the monsoon to the north of the equator. Indeed, during the winter of the southern hemisphere the air of the Antarctic Pole was colder than it is today. The south polar front was therefore capable of vigorously pushing subtropical anti-cyclones toward the equator, particularly the St. Hélène which generates the African monsoon. Its maximum displacement was produced, it seems, several millennia in advance of the climatic optimum, which occurs broadly around 6,000 years B.P.

CONCLUSION

Pollen analysis in desert regions can lead to interesting conclusions, but pollen deposits can only be interpreted in conjunction with an understanding of the diverse pollen influences to which the desert is subject.

Large populations of anemophilous plants, even distant ones, are the principal pollen producers. Since in the desert zone north of the tropics the pollen influence originates largely in the Mediterranean basin, it will of necessity give a "cooler" and wetter picture. Trees of tropical and equatorial regions release little pollen into the air. One should, therefore, pay particular attention to the less numerous pollen grains and identify them carefully.

South of the tropic the spectra are made up of *Gramineae* and *Cyperaceae*, which are largely anemophilous.

A quite precise idea of the extent of the vegetation ground cover can be obtained from the spectra in all cases where one can differentiate between the pollen grains which are definitely allochthonous and those which are definitely autochthonous.

The pollen spectra of Middle and Upper Pleistocene and Holocene sediments have been of use only in the detection of periods which were drier or wetter than today.

It has been emphasized that a colder and drier period in the northern periphery of the Mediterranean basin coincided with a dry period in the lower valley of the Saoura. A very cold period in Europe was drier on the Ivory Coast.

Conditions are very different in the mountainous regions of the Sahara where a fall in temperature induces a weaker evapo-transpiration in the vegetation. On the other hand, by contrast with the low altitudes, all the raindrops reach the ground. The colder periods thus favored more regular and more extensive flow of the wadis rising in the mountains.

Certain cold periods in the Quaternary would thus have made the plains of the Sahara a far more varied landscape than that of today, with drier areas between rivers and wetter river valleys.

There is no simple correlation between glacial periods and wetter or drier periods within the tropics, except during the periods of maximal deterioration when extreme cold in boreal regions is synchronous with extreme dryness in low latitudes. We have observed this phenomenon at 23,000 years B.P. for the savanna and 19,000 years B.P. for the Würmian *Artemisia* steppe of the Mediterranean basin.

BIBLIOGRAPHY

ALIMEN, H.; BEUCHER, F.; LHOTE, H.; and DELIBRIAS, G., 1968. "Les gisements néolithiques de Tan-Tartait et d'I-n-Itinen Tassili-n-Ajjer (Sahara Central)." *Bulletin de la Société Préhistorique Française* 65(1):421-58.

ASSEMIEN, P., 1971. "Étude comparative des flores actuelles et quaternaires récentes de quelques paysages végétaux d'Afrique de l'Ouest." Thèse Doct. Sci. nat. Abidjan: Arch. orig. Centre Document no. 5868. Paris: CNRS.

_____; FILLERON, J. C.; MARTIN, L.; and TASTET, J. P., 1970. "Le Quaternaire de la zone littorale de Côte d'Ivoire." *Bull. Ass. sénég. ét. Quatern. Ouest afr.* 25:65-78.

AUBRÉVILLE, A., 1962. "Savanisation tropicale et glaciations quaternaires." *Adansonia* 2(1):16-91.

BEUCHER, F., 1971. "Étude palynologique de formations néogènes et quaternaires au Sahara nord-occidental." Thèse de Doct. Sci. Nat. Arch. orig. Centre Document no. 5408. Paris:CNRS.

BOTTCHER, V; ERGENZINGER, P. J.; JAECKEL, S. H.; and KAISER, K., 1972. "Quartäre Seebildungen und ihre Mollusken-Inhalte im Tibestigebirge und seinen Rahmenbereichen der zentralen Ostsahara." *Z. Geomorph.* 16(2):182-234.

BUTZER, K. W., 1966. "Climatic Changes in the Arid Zones of Africa during Early to Mid-Holocene Times." In *World Climate from 8000 to 0 B.C.*, edited by J. S. Sawyer, pp. 73-83. London: Royal Meteor. Society.

CONRAD, G., 1969. *L'Évolution continentale post-Hercynienne de Sahara Algerien.* Paris: CNRS.

COUR, P.; GUINET, P.; COHEN, J.; and DUZER, D., 1971. "Reconnaissance des flux polliniques et de la sédimentation actuelle au Sahara Nord-Occidental." III International Palynological Conference, sec. 9, Novosibirsk, U.S.S.R.: July, 1971 (sous presse).

DUBIEF, J., 1952. "Le vent et le déplacement du sable au Sahara." *Travaux de l'Institut de Recherches Sahariennes* 8:123-64.

_____, 1963. "Les précipitations. La Pluie." In *Le climat du Sahara*, tome 2, 3me partie: "L'eau atmosphérique au Sahara." Inst. Rech. Sahar., Alger.

FAURE, H., 1969. "Lacs quaternaires du Sahara." *Mitt. Internat. Verein. Limnol.* 17:131-46.

GILLET, H., 1968. "Tchad et Sahel tchadien." *Acta Phytogeogr. Suec.* 54:54-58.

GUINET, P., 1958. "Notice détaillée de la feuille Béni-Abbès (coupure spéciale) de la carte de la végétation de l'Algérie au 200000 e." *Bull. Serv. Carte Phytogéogr., sér. A*, 3(1):21-96.

_____, and PLANQUE, D., 1969. "Résultats de l'analyse pollinique." In *Amekni. Néolithique ancien du Hoggar*, by G. Camps. Mém. Centre Rech. anthropol. préhist. ethnograph. 10:186-88.

KOUPRIANOVA, L. A., 1948. "Morphologie des pollens et phylogénie des Monocotylédones (en russe)." *Comm. Komarow Inst. Acad. Sci.* 1(7):163-262.

LIVINGSTONE, D. A., 1971. "Speculations on the Climatic History of Mankind." *American Scientist* 59(3):332-37.

MALEY, J., 1972. "La sédimentation pollinique actuelle dans la zone du Lac Tchad (Afrique centrale)." *Pollen et Spores* 14(3):263-307.

_____ 1973. "Les variations climatiques dans le bassin du Tchad durant le dernier millénaire; essai d'interprétation climatique de l'Holocène africain." *C. R. Acad. Sci. Paris, sér. D* 276:1673-75.

_____1974. "Mécanisme des changements climatiques aux basses latitudes." *Palaeogeogr., Palaeoclimatol., Palaeoecol.* 14(4). (sous presse).

————; COHEN, J.; FAURE, H.; ROGNON, P.; and VINCENT, P. M., 1970. "Quelques formations lacustres et fluviatiles associées à différentes phases du volcanisme au Tibesti (Nord du Tchad)." *Cah. O.R.S.T.O.M., sér. Géol.* 2(1):127-52.

MARTIN, L., and TASTET, J. P., 1972. "Le Quaternaire du littoral et du plateau continental de Côte d'Ivoire. Rôle des mouvements tectoniques et eustatiques." *Bull. Ass. Sénég. ét. Quatern. Ouest Afr.* 33-34:17-32.

MONOD, T., 1971. "Remarques sur les symétries floristiques des zones sèches Nord et Sud en Afrique." *Mitt. Bot. Staatssamml. München* 10:375-423.

OZENDA, P., 1958. *Flore du Sahara septentrional et central.* Paris: CNRS.

PONS, A., and QUÉZEL, P., 1958. "Premières remarques sur l'étude playnologique d'un guano fossile du Hoggar." *Note Acad. Sci.* Paris.

QUÉZEL, P., 1957. "Peuplement végétal des hautes montagnes de l'Afrique du Nord." *Encyclop. Biogéogr. Ecol.* 10. Éd. Lechevalier.

————, 1965. "La végétation du Sahara, du Tchad à la Mauritanie." *Geobotanica selecta* 2.

RIPPSTEIN, G., and PEYRE DE FABREGUES, B., 1972. "Modernisation de la zone pastorale du Niger." Étude Agrostologique no. 33. Institut d'Elevage et de Médecine Vétérinaire des Pays Tropicaux Lab. Nat. Elev. Rech. Vét. Niamey.

VAN CAMPO, M., 1964. "Quelques pollen pleistocènes nouveaux pour le Hoggar." *C.R. Acad. Sci.* 258(4):1297-99.

————, 1964. "Représentation graphique de spectres polliniques des régions sahariennes." *C.R. Acad. Sci.* 258(6):1873-76.

————, 1969. "Végétation würmienne en France - Données bibliographiques - Hypothèses." In "Études françaises sur le Quaternaire," pp. 104-11. *Suppl. Bull. A.F.E.Q.*

————; AYMONIN, G.; COHEN, J; DUTIL, P.; GUINET, P.; and ROGNON, P., 1964. "Contribution à l'étude du peuplement végétal quaternaire des montagnes sahariennes: l'Atakor." *Pollen et Spores* 6(1):169-94.

————; COHEN, J.; GUINET, P.; and ROGNON, P., 1965. "Contribution à l'étude du peuplement végétal quaternaire des montagnes sahariennes II - Flore contemporaine d'un gisement de mammifères tropicaux dans l'Atakor." *Pollen et Spores* 7(2):361-71.

————; GUINET, P.; COHEN, J.; and DUTIL, P., 1967. "Contribution à l'étude du peuplement végétal quaternaire des montagnes saharaennes III - Flore de l'oued Outoul (Hoggar)." *Pollen et Spores* 9(1):107-20.

————; GUINET, P.; and COHEN, J., 1968. "Fossil Pollen from Late Tertiary and Middle Pleistocene Deposits of the Kurkur Oasis." In *Desert and River in Nubia,* by K. W. Butzer and C. L. Hansen, pp. 515-20. Madison: University of Wisconsin Press.

VAN DER HAMMEN, T., 1972. "Changes in Vegetation and Climate in the Amazon Basin and Surrounding Areas during the Pleistocene." *Geologie en Mijnbouw* 51(6):641-43.

WIJMSTRA, T. A., 1969. "Palynology of the First 30 Meters of a 120 M Deep Section in Northern Greece." *Acta Bot. Neerl.* 18(4):511-27.

NEW EXPLORATIONS IN THE EGYPTIAN SAHARA

Romuald Schild
Institute for the History of Material Culture
Polish Academy of Sciences

and

Fred Wendorf
Southern Methodist University

INTRODUCTION

In 1972 the Combined Prehistoric Expedition began a long-range study of the Quaternary geology and prehistoric remains in the Great Western Desert of Egypt, one of the most remote places of the world (fig. 1). This area was selected because it appeared to be extremely promising. The work of Caton-Thompson and Gardner at Kharga Oasis and the Fayum, along the fringe of this huge mass of stone and sand, the prehistoric discoveries in the Gebel Uweinat area, and the recent work of J. Hester in the Dungul section suggest the presence of numerous archaeological remains, although these are perhaps not as rich or as complex as those in the Nile Valley.

Two field seasons have thus far been completed, both conducted by the regular parties of the Combined Prehistoric Expedition and jointly sponsored by Southern Methodist University, the Institute of the History of Material Culture, Polish Academy of Sciences, and the Geological Survey of Egypt. Financial support was provided by all these institutions, and especially by two NSF Grants (GS-1886 and GS-36959) and two Smithsonian grants (2423, SF3-00101).

The first season, regarded initially as a feeler before making a major commitment to systematic exploration of the Great Barren Waste, was spent in the Dakhla-Abu Mingar area with a week long trip southward across the center of the depths. The work began with an extensive survey of the area around Dakhla Oasis, including the fringe of the Eocene Plateau just north of the village of Balat; the territory between the scarp at the eastern edge of the Great Sand Sea up to the abandoned oasis of Abu Mingar in the northwest; and finally, the Oasis of Kharga in the east. This did not disclose any important sites, except in the vicinity of Kharga. All of the sites which were found had been derived or completely deflated, and the prospects looked very bleak. Eventually, however, an area just west of Balat yielded our first significant sites, identified as E-72-1 and E-72-2. The excavations at these sites formed the backbone of the season.

Near the end of the work near Balat a reconnaissance flying camp moved to the Bir Sahara area to evaluate the discovery of archaeological materials made in 1971 by Dr. Bahay Issawi, during a short trip organized by the Geologi-cal Survey of Egypt. The survey in the area between Balat and Bir Sahara disclosed two prehistoric sites, which were numbered E-72-4 and E-72-5. No collections were made during this survey trip at Bir Sahara, but numerous sites were noted in the area, and a full season there was planned for 1973.

THE DAKHLA AREA

THE GEOMORPHOLOGY AND GEOLOGY

The Oasis of Dakhla is situated at the very edge of two geomorphologic units of the Eastern Sahara Desert, the Libyan Plateau, and the Libyan Sand Plain (Raisz, 1952). It is the middle oasis of the Kharga-Abu Mingar chain, all located in enclosed basins carved out in the plateau.

The basin of Dakhla extends for more than 80 km along the southern edge of the limestone plateau marked by an impressive scarp elevated from 300 m to 400 m above the bottom of the oasis. The edge of the plateau bends to the northwest at the extreme western part of the oasis and runs in this direction after passing the small abandoned oasis of Abu Mingar, located on the road to Farafra. To the east, toward Kharga, the scarp runs for some 130 km in a general easterly direction along the huge mass of Abu Tartur, and then turns north and again east to see the famous Oasis of Kharga incised as a long meridionally placed hollow in the eastern edge of the southern peninsula of the Libyan Plateau.

The clifflike face of the Eocene scarp at Dakhla is made up of Paleocene limestone, chalky limestone, and inter-calated bands of gray cherts. This upper section, 60 m thick, is underlain by the Dakhla Shale assuming a thickness of 250 meters. The footslope of the plateau, which has the form of a 30 m thick step, is made up, in descending order, of phosphates, shale, limestone, and marl beds, all lower Maestrichtian in age.

The floor of the basin is at an elevation close to 100 m above sea level and is covered in its eastern part by red clays forming the top part of the Qusseir Shale or Variegated Shale Member of the Nubia Formation. The basal strati-graphic unit in the area, however, is the Taref Sandstone Member of the Nubia Formation, the same unit which forms the floor of the Western Desert plateau to the south (Herminia et al., 1961; Said, 1962; Issawi, 1972, MS).

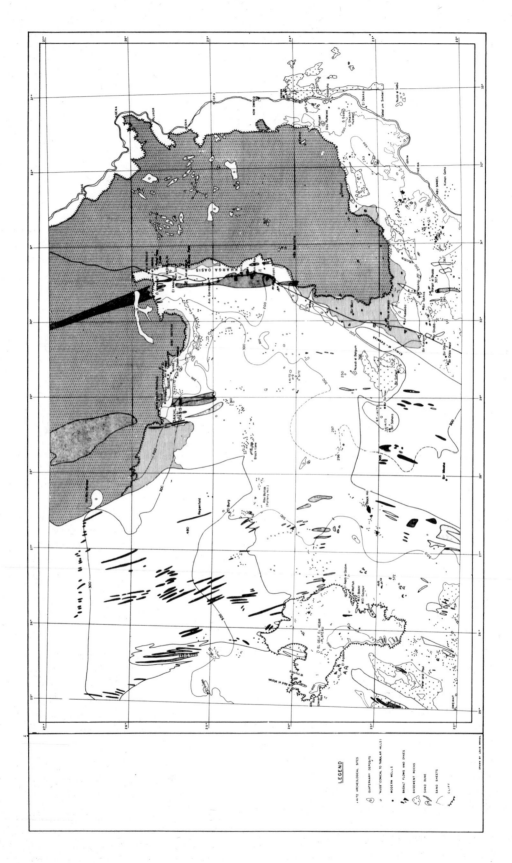

FIG. 1.—Map of southern part of the Egyptian Sahara. Composition, R. Said in March 1973.

Toward the south the floor of the depression rises slowly up to vanish within the Sandstone Plateau of the Western Desert. At a few places, however, a minuscule scarp, 10 m to 15 m in height, borders the oasis.

The modern floor of Dakhla Oasis consists of several villages with adjacent fields fed by natural and artificially drilled wells which receive their water from the depths of the Nubia Sandstone. Several fields are separated by dry, barren surfaces, some of which are made up of silts and clayey playalike deposits associated with spring mounds. An extensive survey of these large patches of silt and clays failed to disclose earlier evidence of occupation prior to the Neolithic, but even these were not *in situ* and were never sufficiently dense to justify further work. On the other hand, the silty deposits which could be considered of pre-Neolithic age were archaeologically sterile. In a few cases, presumably late playa silts yielded Pharaonic or later remains well *in situ*.

The adjacent rim of the gloomy *charafish* landscape of the Libyan Plateau contains numerous supposedly deflational and/or solution-formed pans filled with thin silts showing poorly developed closed drainage systems. Here, numerous possibly Neolithic sites were noted associated with the pans, yet only a few of them had any material *in situ*.

Finally, just west of the village of Balat an extensive area of erosional remnants made up of the Variegated Shale and containing fossil springs with associated tufas and spring caps was discovered. A few of these, later numbered as sites E-72-1 and E-72-2, yielded the Upper Acheulean materials which can be counted among the richest finds of this age in the whole of Africa.

The remnants are located in a large mouth of highly deflated wadi cut out in the Variegated Shale and descending from the foot of the Eocene Plateau. The limits of the mouth are very inconspicuous and masked by cultivation, flat eolian sand sheets, and playa silts (fig. 2). Numerous shale hillocks, from one to six m in height, capped by iron and/or sulfur cemented sands and clays, betray fossil spring vents whose cemented caps and conduits served to resist the erosion. Farther down, several larger remnants or flat-topped mounds are covered with typical spring tufas.

Upstream, big remnants of the preerosional surface show a thick bed of chert and limestone boulders in a reddish pebbly sand matrix unconformably covering the Qusseir Shale.

More than fifty of the spring vents and tufa hills were closely examined, but only a few yielded any traces of occupation, none associated with tufas. On the other hand, the floor of the wadi and wind-eroded deflational concavities contained numerous stone artifacts in a typical lag situation. Most of these appeared to be of Aterian and possibly Mousterian affiliations. Numerous Levallois pieces, Mousterian and Levallois points, and rare Aterian pedunculates were noted scattered on the surface. These entirely destroyed and mixed occupations did not seem to be suitable for further work.

A cluster of five spring conduits located on a lower, southern part of the Variegated Shale remnant was found clearly associated with two joined but thin concentrations of deflated Acheulean material. The northern concentration dispersed around only one conduit was labeled Site E-72-1, while the southern one, tied with four separate but clearly smaller conduits, was numbered Site E-72-2. The surface material was collected and plotted on the map. Its spatial distribution shows semirandom pattern generally following the shape of the remnant. There was no sterile surface separating the two concentrations; therefore, the question is whether the deflated material came from a single site associated with a spring fed by several conduits or had been originally contained within two or more separate occupation areas.

A small elongated conical mound with its top and slopes covered with well-rolled chert and limestone boulders and pebbles forms a part of this remnant. It stands just behind the sites, overlooking them from the north and witnessing for a lowering of the preerosional surface to at least seven m below its initial top (fig. 3).

Three of the spring conduits were excavated, one at Site E-72-1 and two others, numbered vents 1 and 3, at Site E-72-2. The first one gave a large quantity of archaeological material and yielded basic observations on its lithostratigraphic setup, permitting limited reconstructions.

The spring vent at Site E-72-1 was irregularly oval in shape and measured 5.5 m by 3.5 meters. Its base formed by the Nubia Sandstone was reached at the very top of the reverted cone of the conduit at 266 cm below the surface (compare fig. 4:1). The cone is cut in the Qusseir Variegated Shale (fig. 4:2), an obvious aquifuge whose cracks and fissures evidently permitted the ascending water to penetrate and subsequently to erode the conduit up to the floor of the depression. A reworked Variegated Shale, cemented and unstratified, coats the base of the conduit (fig. 4:3). A few artifacts (eight pieces) were recorded in its upper portion. The reworked shale is, in turn, conformably overlain by a sterile lense of an amorphous white clay (10YR 8/1) containing 10% to 12% of quartzite grains (fig. 4:4). The clay lense is covered by a loose to cemented, unstratified layer of gravels and pebbles in a coarse sand matrix. The sediment is highly stained and dusky red (5R 3/4) to yellow (10YR 7/8) from the admixture of sulfates and iron oxides resulting from the breakdown of the shale (Servello, 1973, MS). These base gravels contained 1,424 chipped artifacts, of which 8.9% were highly rolled, the highest proportion of rolled artifacts recovered from the cone (fig. 4:5).

The walls of the vent show very characteristic benches and pockets. These are usually filled with side wall gravel in a coarse sand matrix which also forms a sort of coating around the walls (compare fig. 4:6). The gravels are slightly sorted, with larger-sized specimens deposited over the benches and in the pockets together with more concentrated heavy artifacts. This sediment yielded 2,355 artifacts, of which 5.8% were heavily rolled. Concentrations of

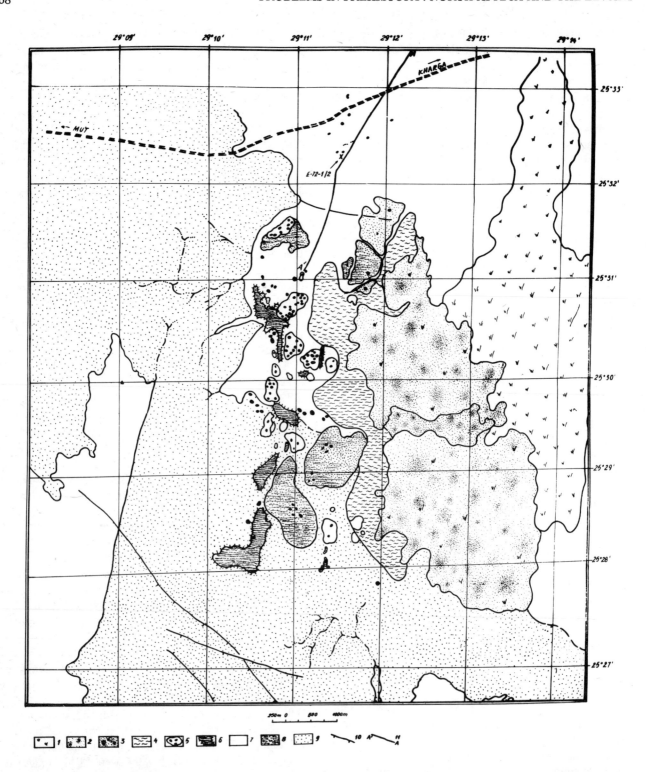

FIG. 2—Geological map of the Balat area. Key: 1) cultivated land; 2) eolian sands; 3) eolian sands with bushes; 4) playa sediments; 5) spring mounds; 6) tufa deposits; 7) Variegated Shale; 8) Nubia Sandstone with shaley bands; 9) Nubia Sandstone undifferentiated; 10) faults; 11) section line. Mapped by B. Issawi in March, 1972.

iron oxides and sulfates produce a characteristic dusky red (5R 3/4) and brownish yellow (2.5YR 5/4) staining. A narrow, horizontal fissure in the eastern wall filled with sand contains dispersed gypsum crystals (fig. 4:6a).

The central part of the cone was filled with medium to coarse-grained sands containing steeply sloping lenses of gravel, conformable to the general lamination of the sedi-

ment. The lamination was near vertical to very steep and also roughly conformable to the side walls (compare fig. 4:7). The very center of the vent was unstratified and loose, white to light gray (2.5Y 7/2). Sulfates and iron oxides stain the sands in the parts located closer to the side walls. A large lump of the Qusseir Shale (fig. 4:7a) was also recorded in this sediment. The recovered archaeological mate-

FIG. 3–Sites E-72-1 and E-72-2 as seen from the remnant. Group of people stands near the vent at Site E-72-1; Site E-72-2 is located behind and slightly left of the truck. Numerous spring mounds in background.

rial amounted to 788 pieces, a much smaller value than before, especially considering the volume of this sediment which makes the largest part of the fill.

Along the eastern wall an extensive area of jarosite (potassium iron hydroxy sulfate), positively identified through X-ray defraction (Servello, 1973, MS), was found deposited in a coarse sand matrix over a steep bench of the wall, near the base of the conduit cone (fig. 4:7b). The sediment contained numerous artifacts (1,158 pieces).

The dynamic interpretation of the fill suggests a greater discharge and velocity at the beginning of the activity with considerable sorting of the worked down archaeological materials through constant winnowing of the outpouring water in the conduit. The central portion of the fill may suggest a somewhat declining productivity of the spring. The presence of jarosite indicates that the outpouring water should have been warm as it is today in the Dakhla Oasis, where the temperature of modern springs fluctuates between 24° C. and 40° C. (Abu Al-Izz, 1971, p. 210). Heavy admixture of iron oxides and sulfates also suggests that the mineral content of the water was again very high, as it is today.

THE ARCHAEOLOGY

An impressive collection of worked stone contains 7,002

pieces from Site E-72-1 and 2,847 artifacts from E-72-2. A comparison of the two collections shows very high similarity in all sections with a few discrepancies, some of which should be attributed to quantitative inequality of the samples (compare fig. 5). Almost all of the dissimilarities are of the quantitative character and have no statistical significance.

Statistical comparisons within the collections show that the means of measured material, especially bifaces, may differ significantly according to their stratigraphic environment. Thus, the one-way analysis of variance (calculated by Nancy Singleton) shows that the amygdaloids and backed bifaces collected on the surface have all or most of their attributes significantly smaller than those from the conduit. It is most likely that the above discrepancies may be accounted for by differentiated depositional selection during which heavier pieces were more easily worked down, toward the bottom, while lighter specimens had been left at a somewhat higher elevation. The latter certainly constitute most of the surface material.

In spite of some minor dissimilarities, the material from both collections is highly homogeneous not only in its quantitative and qualitative content but also in the raw material preference. In both samples more than 99% of all artifacts are made from local Eocene chert redeposited as boulders over the pre-spring surface.

EGYPT 72/1

EAST   WEST

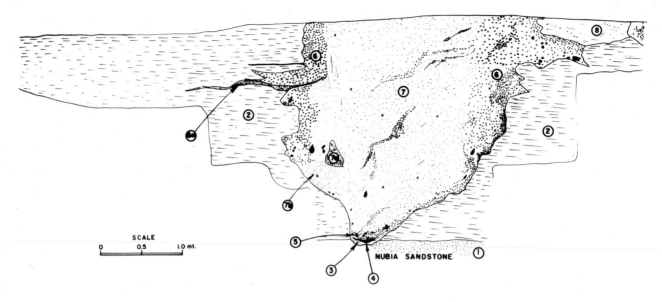

FIG. 4—Section of the spring conduit at Site E-72-1. Key: 1) Nubia Sandstone; 2) Qusseir Variegated Shale; 3) reworked Variegated Shale; 4) lense of amorphous clay; 5) base gravels; 6) side wall gravels; 6a) gypsum crystals; 7) central gravels and sands; 7a) lump of Qusseir Shale; 7b) potassium iron hydroxy sulfate in sand matrix; 8) lump of reworked Qusseir Shale. Profile, Servello and Schild.

The General Structure (restricted) of the assemblages indicates the following main features: relatively high values of primary flakes; weak Flake Group; high rate of flakes obtained from changed orientation cores; very low Blade Group, evidently composed of accidental blades removed from flake cores; strong Tool and Tool Production Waste Group (compare fig. 5). The latter shows clear discrepancy between high index of bifaces and relatively low index of biface trimming flakes. The divergence could have suggested a tool production economy in which a large portion of bifaces had been brought to the site from somewhere else. However, an apparent depositional selection indicates that lighter pieces were more concentrated at upper parts of the conduit and obviously in the surrounding area. Therefore, these lighter pieces were apparently the first to be destroyed or removed.

The non-Levallois cores are exploited by hard hammer and are of a flake group only. The most numerous are those with changed orientation of both the flat and globular categories. Simple, single platform flake cores are the next. The preparation is always limited to striking platforms. A restricted number of sub-discoidal and opposed platform flake cores complete this group (fig. 5).

A few Levallois flake cores (four specimens) are rather crude and can be classified within the proto-Levallois category. The only Levallois point core, collected on the surfaces of Site E-72-2, has semi-Nubian preparation with two radiating bladelet scars coming from its distal end.

The bifaces certainly make up the strongest tool group in both assemblages, totaling 910 pieces. Their index fluctuates between 64.3 and 80.5 at E-72-1. The most numerous group is formed by amygdaloids (fig. 9:2) of both the regular (fig. 6a:25-26) and short (fig. 6a:27-28) varieties.

The majority of these have thick unworked butts. Among those with thinned butts a small quantity characterized by oblique bases were found. Next comes a very characteristic group of backed bifaces, with both natural and worked backs, amounting to 20% of all defined specimens. These broke down into a few categories, of which the most important are symmetric (fig. 10:2), thick (m/e > 2.35) backed specimens. However, a considerable number of asymmetric, thick examples also occur. These are characterized by angled backs with thick lower parts and sharp, worked half-backs at the distal end. The half-backs are either straight (Klausennische) or convex varieties. Possibly, the most interesting of all are thin (m/e < 2.35) asymmetric backed bifaces with straight or convex half-backs which have to be classified as Prodnik (fig. 10:1) or thin Klausennische knives. Some of these have short longitudinal spalls removed from the distal end, a technique usually associated with these and similar forms (Krukowski, 1939; Kowalski, 1967a, 1967b, 1969; Bosinski, 1969, 1972; Bordes, 1972), although also reported as used on Mousterian, Mousterian-like points, and convergent scrapers (Wendorf and Schild, 1974). It is interesting to note that a few characteristic resharpening spalls also occurred at Site E-72-1.

Two groups of bifaces occurred in similar quantities. These are the peculiar double backed specimens with natural or worked butts and short tips accounting for 15.6% at E-72-1 and 16.7% at E-72-2. Similar values are shown by the triangular group, which is mainly composed of subtriangular specimens with thick worked (fig. 9:1) and unworked butts. A small number of pelecyform bifaces complete the group.

The group of cordiforms, which account for 9.4% at

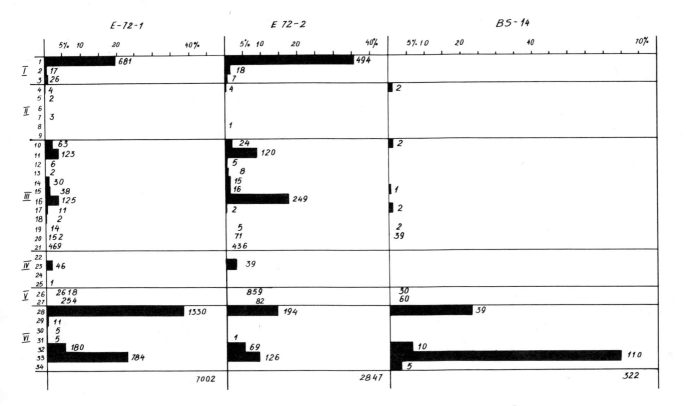

FIG. 5—Restricted General Structure of inventories from Sites E-72-1, E-72-2, and Bir Sahara 14. Figures indicate number of pieces in each category. Key: Group I (Initial) - 1) primary flakes; 2) primary blades; 3) initially struck cores; Group II (Levallois) - 4) Levallois flake cores; 5) Levallois flakes; 6) Levallois blade cores; 7) Levallois blades; 8) Levallois point cores; 9) Levallois points; Group III (Flake) - 10) single platform flake core; 11) flakes from single platform core; 12) opposed platform flake cores; 13) flakes from opposed platform cores; 14) changed orientation flake cores, flat; 15) changed orientation flake cores, globular; 16) flakes from changed orientation cores; 17) sub-discoidal cores; 18) flakes from sub-discoidal cores; 19) fragments of undetermined flake cores; 20) undetermined flakes; 21) rolled, undetermined flakes; Group IV (Blade) - 22) single platform blade cores; 23) blades from single platform cores; 24) opposed platform blade cores; 25) blades from opposed platform cores; Group V (Chip) - 26) simple chips; 27) crushed chips; 29) notch spalls; 30) resharpening spalls; 31) naturally backed knives; 32) retouched tools plus burins; 33) bifaces; 34) spheroidal hammerstones. Categories 19, 20, 21, 16, and 27 are excluded from the restricted percentages.

E-72-1 or 15% at E-72-2, is basically made up of sub-cordiforms among which the handaxes with thick butts form a clear majority (fig. 6b).

Minor quantities of other bifaces were recorded. Among these are rare discoidal and lanceolate, occasional oval, limande, proto-limande, rostro-carinate, amygdaloids with cleaverlike tips, and very atypical Micoquian.

The non-handaxe tools (figs. 7 and 8) show negligible Levallois indices (IGL, IL, and ILty), medium-high side-scraper index, low indices of the IIId Group, and relatively high index of denticulates (IV Group).

A pronounced inequality of the systems of publication and classification of Acheulean materials from Northern Africa makes it extremely difficult to compare recovered assemblages, especially since most of the worked sites are only briefly mentioned and/or described. However, it seems that the Acheulean material obtained by Caton-Thompson from a spring conduit, designated as K-10, at Kharga Oasis (Caton-Thompson, 1952, pp. 60-72) constitutes the closest analogy to our assemblages from E-72-1 and E-72-2. This impression is mainly given by the occurrence, at K-10, of numerous double backed handaxes, amygdaloids, and a large proportion of thick butts.

The surface assemblages described by the Guichards (1965, 1968) from Nubia, although also characterized by complete absence of cleavers, differ very significantly from the Dakhla assemblages mainly because of an expanded group of lanceolates and Micoquian handaxes in supposedly Middle and Upper Acheulean, or primitive forms in the collections believed to be of Lower Acheulean age.

The assemblage reported by Chmielewski (1968) from Arkin 8 in Nubia stands out considerably from the remaining mass of surface collections chiefly because of an extremely high percentage of ovates and discs accompanied by rare amygdaloids. The material from Arkin 8 does not appear to have any real points in common with the assemblages recovered at Dakhla.

Tempting comparisons with the Maghreb and Sahara meet a number of difficulties, impassable in the present state of publication. The well-publicized site in Tunisia at Sidi Zin, near Kef (Gobert, 1950; Balout, 1955; Vaufrey, 1955), however, offers very few common points in its lower and upper layers, and still fewer in the middle one. Aesthetically enjoining surface finds at Al-Ma el-Abiod, south of Tebessa, in Algeria (Vaufrey, 1955; Balout, 1955), certainly represent mixed assemblages with a remarkable final Acheu-

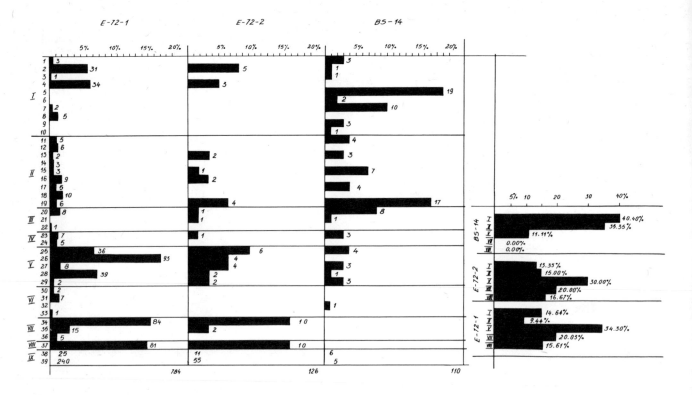

FIG. 6—Quantitative distribution of biface categories. Key: I, Group of sub-triangulars: 1) sub-triangular with thinned butt; 2) sub-triangular with thick butt; 3) sub-triangular elongated with thinned butt; 4) sub-triangular elongated with thick butt; 7) pelecyform with thinned butt; 8) pelecyform with thick butt; 9) shark-tooth with thinned butt; 10) shark-tooth with thick butt; II, Group of Cordiforms: 11) cordiform with thinned butt; 12) cordiform with thick butt; 13) cordiform elongated with thinned butt; 14) cordiform elongated with thick butt; 15) sub-cordiform with thinned butt; 16) sub-cordiform with thick butt; 17) sub-cordiform elongated with thinned butt; 18) sub-cordiform elongated with thick butt; 19) sub-cordiform with oblique thinned butt; III, Group of Ovals: 20) discoidal; 21) oval; 22) limande; IV, Group of Thick Elongates: 23) lanceolate; 24) atypical Micoquian; V, Group of Amygdaloids: 25) amygdaloid with thinned butt; 26) amgdaloid with thick butt; 27) amygdaloid short with thinned butt; 28) amygdaloid short with thick butt; 29) amygdaloid with oblique thinned butt; VI, Group of Diverse: 30) protolimande; 31) cleaver-biface; 32) ficron; 33) rostro-carinate; VII, Group of Backed Bifaces: 34) backed symmetric, thick; 35) backed asymmetric, thick; 36) backed asymmetric, thin (Prondnik etc.); VIII, Group of Double-Backed Bifaces: 37) short-tipped; IX, Others: 38) undetermined and fragments; 39) unfinished.

lean component expressed in nice, fine, elongated cordiforms, lanceolates (?), and regular cordiforms with thinned and unworked bases. On the other hand, the Acheulean sites from Central Sahara at Erg Tihoidaine and Tabelbalat-Tachenghit seem to be characterized by high proportions of cleavers (Arambourg and Balout, 1955; Balout, 1955). A seemingly later site from Bir Sahara 14 (see below) is also clearly different, as shown by comparison of the main indices and type frequencies (compare figs. 5 to 8).

Surprisingly enough, the high proportions of backed bifaces, together with thin backed specimens of the *Klausennische* or *Prondnik* type, are found within the assemblages which are classified as belonging to the so-called Micoquian of Central Europe known from Klause, near Essing, and Bocksteinschmiede in Bavaria (Wetzel and Bosinski, 1969), the latter believed to date with the Last Interglacial. Roughly similar typological components, although clearly quantitatively differentiated, are found on a slightly younger level in the Micoco-Prondnikian or post-Micoquian assemblages from Wylotne and Okiennik in southern Poland (Krukowski, 1939; Chmielewski, 1969), and in Buhlen in Hessia (Bosinski, 1969) dated with the Early Würm. According to Bordes (1968, p. 110; 1972, p.

159) some backed handaxes occur in Upper Acheulean at Combe Grenal and in La Micoque in Dordogne. Similarly, the resharpening technique using longitudinal spalls is also reported to be applied in the Upper Acheulean of France (Bordes, 1972, p. 159).

Obviously, there are serious differences separating the assemblages from Dakhla Oasis and those in Central Europe. First of all, the whole structure of the handaxe group is different, as well as the proportions of categories within the backed cluster. The transverse section of the backed handaxes from Dakhla is usually less asymmetric than that from Central Europe. Furthermore, the quantitative distribution of non-biface tools differs considerably, although, as at Dakhla, the assemblages from Europe may also contain flat, bifacial side-scrapers. At the present moment the degree of taxonomic similarity cannot be measured; however, it would oscillate highly because of a relative instability of the indices and the large time period covered by the Central European sites.

It seems that the resemblances discussed could be better explained by the nature of limited abilities of morphological evolution of the bifaces, some of which were undoubtedly streaming toward more functionally adapted

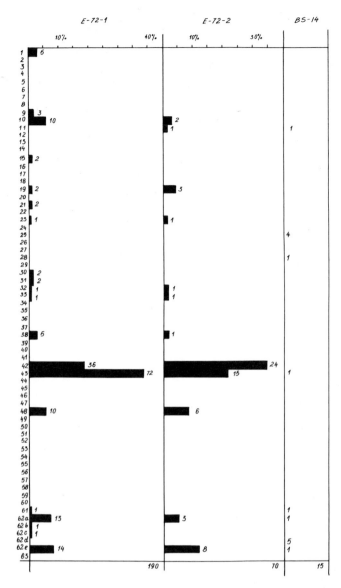

FIG. 7—Quantitative distribution of tools. Categories 1 to 61 and 63
according to type list of F. Bordes; n. 62a) bifacial edge pieces;
62b) atypical side-scrapers; 62c) bifacially worked pebble; 62d)
spheroidal hammerstones; 62e) undetermined and fragments.
Figures indicate number of pieces.

cutting tools or knives. It is natural to expect that the
experiments with backed thick handaxes could eventually
have led to thin backed bifacial tools with or without longitudinal resharpening technique. This explanation may also
suggest a serious functional variability within the group of
bifaces strongly associated with their forms. Unfortunately,
the material recovered from the vent is not suitable for
microscopic wear studies.

The secondary position of the artifacts on the surface,
the differential preservation of the material resulting from
the depositional pattern in the conduit and during erosion,
and the lack of any organic remains all prohibit further
analyses relating to spatial distribution of artifacts, raw
material economy and procurement system, subsistence
pattern, etc. The extreme richness of both localities, pre-

sumably initially deposited around a single spring pool,
seems to suggest that the pool was used repeatedly over a
long period of time, most possibly during its full cycle of
activity as suggested by sedimentary contents of the conduit. The high proportion of clearly unfinished and
broken-when-chipped handaxes made out of the picked-at-
the-place material shows that the occupation and formation
of the spring took place after the deposition of the
boulder/pebble mantle which covers the Variegated Shale.

THE DYKE AREA

During the reconnaissance trip southward to the area
around Bir Sahara and Bir Terfawi, several prehistoric sites
were recorded in a stretch of desert located some 150 km
due south from the village of Balat.

After crossing the badlands of the southern rim of
Dakhla Oasis, made up of very soft and powdered Variegated Shale, the surface of the desert slowly rises up,
becoming hard and relatively flat. Here, it is the Taref Sandstone Member which is exposed over enormous waste of
this part of the Nubia Sandstone Plateau. The area is generally flat or slightly undulated, with sand sheets here and
there. The monotony of the landscape is broken by
unnamed nunatak-like jebels rarely dotting the scene. The
most conspicuous of all is the White Knoll, standing lonely
25 km south of Balat. Incidentally, the straight, unmarked
course south followed old car tracks which had doubtless
been left by Prince Kemal el-Din Hussein during one of his
trips to Uweinat in the 1920s.

Nearly 140 km south of Balat traces of various dykes
appear on the surface. These seem to form an extension of
a huge dyke area stretching out toward the northwest from
the Nusab el-Belgum igneous mount and the Pre-Cambrian
mass of El Tawila (Issawi, 1971).

Scattered in the area, but not clearly associated with the
dykes, are numerous large oval or circular sand pans
spotting the landscape. These are large and shallow basins
excavated in the Nubia Sandstone and filled with sand.
Drainage lines are very inconspicuous, appearing only in the
nearest vicinity of the basins. Several prehistoric sites were
discovered in the area, of which the two best ones were
worked from a flying camp in the desert. Most of the sites
are highly deflated, often deposited over a rocky surface,
especially at the dykes where most of them seem to be
associated with the procurement of the raw material which
appears here in quantities. The most expanded of all is a
brown quartzitic sandstone.

SITE E-72-4

One of the pans, measuring ca. 300 m by 500 m and
encircled by the bare Nubia Sandstone, contained a Mousterian settlement which was designated as Site E-72-4 (Site
E-72-3, located at Dakhla, gave only a few worked artifacts). The artifacts appeared entirely on the surface (fig.
11), spatially arranged in three inconspicuous concentrations which were labeled one to three. The concentrations occupied ca. 70 square meters with the artifact

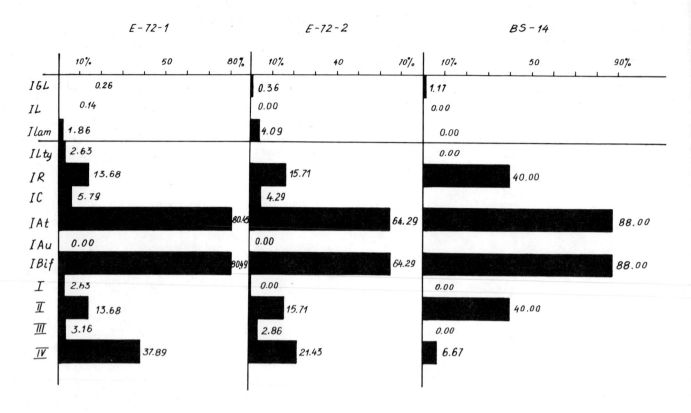

FIG. 8—Main indices (large). IGL—General Levallois Index totaling all categories of the Levallois Group (compare fig. 5). Figures indicate percentages.

density of 5 per square meter. The total collection contains 371 artifacts of which 41 were tools.

Because of the paucity of concentrations and resulting limited sizes of the measured samples it is impossible to test the significance of the difference separating the three concentrations. On the other hand, there are no apparent qualitative differences in the tool kit contained within the clusters, permitting a functional interpretation of the grouping. Furthermore, an obviously limited test of articulation showed that two parts of a large double sidescraper found in Concentrations 1 and 2 fit together, making less valid the initial impression that the three clusters represent three separate, internally contained units (compare fig. 12).

Three types of raw material were present: a red brown quartzitic sandstone, the so-called ferrocrete sandstone; a dark brown, almost black ferruginous grit sandstone occurring in blocks in the nearest vicinity; and rarely, a light-colored petrified wood.

The technological and typological indices indicate a low emphasis on Levallois technology (IL = 0.9), and heavy dominance of side-scrapers (IR = 64.1) among the tools (figs. 13 and 18). The group of denticulates is rather low (Group IV - 11.1).

A comparison with Middle Paleolithic from Kharga is of a very limited range, mainly because of the extreme smallness of the samples from Kharga (Caton-Thompson, 1952). However, judging from the high proportions of Levallois cores in the Kharga collections it is imaginable that the Levallois content at Kharga must have been much more significant.

The much more satisfactory comparative data for the Nubian section of the Nile Valley (Marks, 1968; Guichard and Guichard, 1965, 1968) indicate very little resemblance of the Type A and B Mousterian to the material from Site E-72-4. Similarly, the Nubian Middle Paleolithic described by the Guichards (Guichard and Guichard, 1965, pp. 98-100) differs highly by the presence of the distinctive Nubian cores, Nubian scrapers, and bifacial foliates. On the other hand, the low index of Group IV, not counting other differences, excludes a closer formal similarity with the Denticulate Mousterian in Nubia or Bir Sahara as shown on fig. 38 (see also below).

A small trench dug at the site and the extensive scraping of the surface did not reveal any material *in situ*. Judging from the fresh appearance of some of the tools or their toward-the-ground faces, the deflational drop should not have been too large. The trench demonstrated that the artifacts were lying on a coarse-grained sand with occasional small pebbles, both obviously derived from the Nubia Sandstone. The sand is reddish-yellow (5YR 6/6) in color, consolidated, unstratified. The base formed by the Nubia Sandstone slopes gently toward the center of the pan. The top is only slightly more reddish in color and shows a small net of desiccation cracks, truncated and filled with modern dune sand.

SITE E-72-5

Some 18 km farther south from Site E-72-4 is another large, oval sand pan measuring roughly 600 m by 400 meters. The floor of the pan is clearly deflated, showing

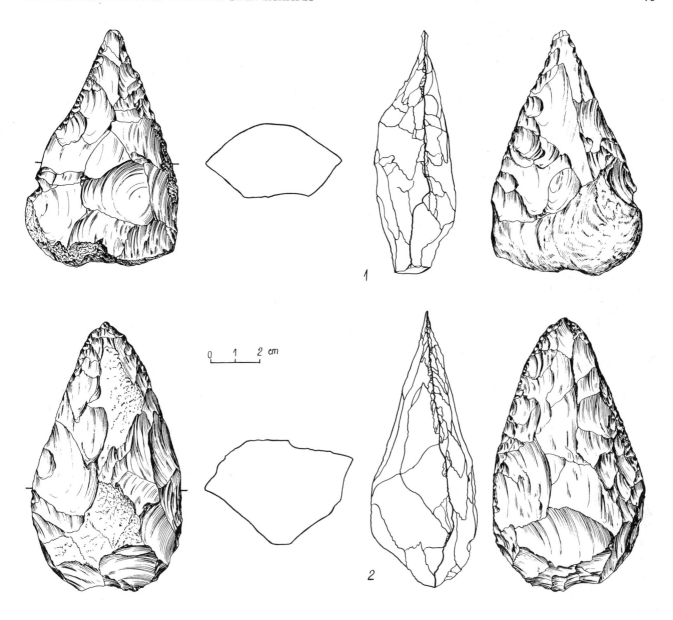

FIG. 9—Bifaces from Site E-72-1: 1) sub-triangular with unworked butt; 2) amygdaloid with worked thinned butt.

numerous low and usually flat elevations containing archae-ological material on top (fig. 14). These elevated concen-trations of archaeological material seem to represent two distinct taxonomic characteristics. The first, appearing in tight smaller clusters with relatively clear external limits, contains numerous chipped stone artifacts, among which long blades, bladelets, and geometrics are immediately noticed. The second appear as poorly delimited, usually larger, and highly deflated concentrations of artifacts and burnt stones. The density of chipped stones is very low, a few per square meter. The occasional presence of retouched bifacial pieces made on thin slabs may indicate a Neolithic of Predynastic age for these more deflated occupations.

The whole sand pan contained six concentrations of the first type, of which two were very dense and roughly equal in size and were found one beside the other. The eastern one of the two was subsequently worked and designated as Site E-72-5.

The worked concentration shows up as a very well demarcated, almost circular, very dense cluster of artifacts measuring ca. 7 m in diameter. Almost 50 heavy sandstone slabs and chunks, some of them measuring more than 30 cm in diameter, are scattered around the perimeter of the cluster, together with a few big and flat heavy grinding stones made of the Nubia Sandstone slabs (fig. 15). The patterning is statistically significant and suggests a large tent or enclosure with its floor covered by tools and debitage.

The spatial distribution of the tools and debitage does not seem to indicate any reliable clustering inside the struc-ture except for a more accentuated presence of retouched, notched and denticulated blades and bladelets in the central portion. On the other hand, the arrangement of the surface material is somewhat altered by the reduction of small, light pieces, especially triangles. These were most certainly blown away during heavy sandstorms. The explanation is suggested by the significantly larger proportions of triangles

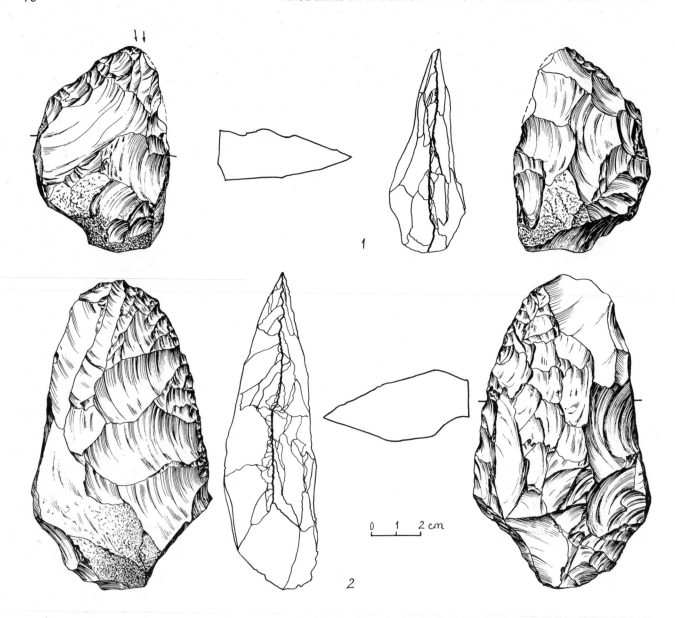

FIG. 10—Bifaces from Site E-72-1: 1) Prondnik with convex half-back and lamellar longitudinal thinning along slight convex front edge; 2) backed biface, thick, symmetric.

and their fragments in the *in situ* material (compare fig. 18) recovered from a trench on squares D-F(1-4).

The *in situ* material occurs down to 20 cm below the surface and is characterized by high density of artifacts as shown by the comparison of the two recovered samples containing 2,651 specimens from the whole surface and 1,245 specimens from the trench. Unfortunately, it was impossible for us to excavate the whole concentration, not to speak of the western cluster. These operations would have required a few weeks of work and manual help, neither of which was readily available at the time.

Four stratigraphic trenches directed toward the center of the pan showed an uneven surface of the Nubia Sandstone, sloping toward the center, conformably covered by a thin bed of laminated sand, pink (5YR 7/4) in color, fluctuating in thickness from 40 cm, near the site, to less than 15 cm in the central portion (fig. 16). The sand is coarse to fine-

grained and clearly derived from the Nubia Sandstone. The lamination, although conformable with the general dip of the sandstone floor, is not uniform. Numerous small swales and wavy sections are observed, together with alternations of coarser and finer material.

The raw material used at the site is characterized by a heavy predominance of a dark reddish brown quartzitic sandstone, followed by cherts, most certainly obtained in the vicinity of the dykes. Far behind these two materials are somewhat lighter and softer quartzitic sandstones, petrified wood, and other stones.

Blade cores are heavily dominant. Most numerous are the single platform elegant cores, elongated with flat or rounded flaking surfaces and full or almost full pre-core preparations of backs, and pre-flaking surfaces and sides. Yet since most of these cores were made from sandstone slabs, their preparation usually followed the shape of these

FIG. 11—Site E-72-4 before collection, looking north.

slabs. Several blade cores show changed orientations, and only a few can be classified within the category of conical ones. Opposite platform elongated blade cores are well represented. Some of these show traces of pre-core preparation on their backs and sides. All blade cores were exploited by punch flaking.

The flake cores, clearly less numerous, are mostly of the unorganized change of orientation variety followed by the single platform category. Opposed platform cores are rare. Several of the flake cores show traces of previous blade core stages.

Blades are obviously dominant. However, flakes are also well represented. Most of these are of the category of flakes removed from single platform cores, while those obtained during core preparation are very scarce. Cortex flakes made of quartzitic sandstone are totally absent. The above facts point to a specific raw material economy in which all of the pre-cores were most certainly prepared at the place of extraction. The presence of more numerous cortex flakes made of chert indicates a more local provenience of this material, a fact positively established during the survey of the neighboring dykes.

The tool kit is characterized by very heavy values for notched and denticulated blades and bladelets, including notched or denticulated and retouched pieces (fig. 17:10 to 12), fluctuating between 28.6% and 39.8% of all tools.

These are closely followed by the geometrics (up to 24.3%) of which the heaviest proportions are made up of elongated scalene triangles and elongated scalene triangles with small short sides (fig. 17:5-8), often concave (fig. 17:9). Backed blades are absent, and backed bladelets are not too numerous. Most of the latter are classified within the so-called shouldered bladelet category (fig. 17:3-4) which, in fact, should be considered as unfinished triangles abandoned before removal of microburins. The "real" backed bladelets (fig. 17:1-2) are very sparsely represented (between 1.9% and 4.4%). End-scrapers run very low (1.3% to 0.0%), while burins (fig. 17:13) form a considerable, though not too well represented, group (between 10.3% and 2.1%). Microburins are, as expected, rather high, accounting for up to 11.4%.

Organic material was almost wholly dissolved, except for a few little scraps of ostrich egg shells recovered from the trench.

The cumulative curves plotted on Tixier's type list (Tixier, 1963, 1967) show a very characteristic flat curve in the first three quarters, and a high jump in the section of notches (C) and geometrics (M.G.).

Several surface finds collected during the work of Caton-Thompson and Gardner in the vicinity of Kharga, at Ghuata, Gala Hill, in the mud pans of the Abu Sighawal and Bulaq Pass, contain typologic elements similar to those from Site E-72-5. The microlithic sites near Kharga, called

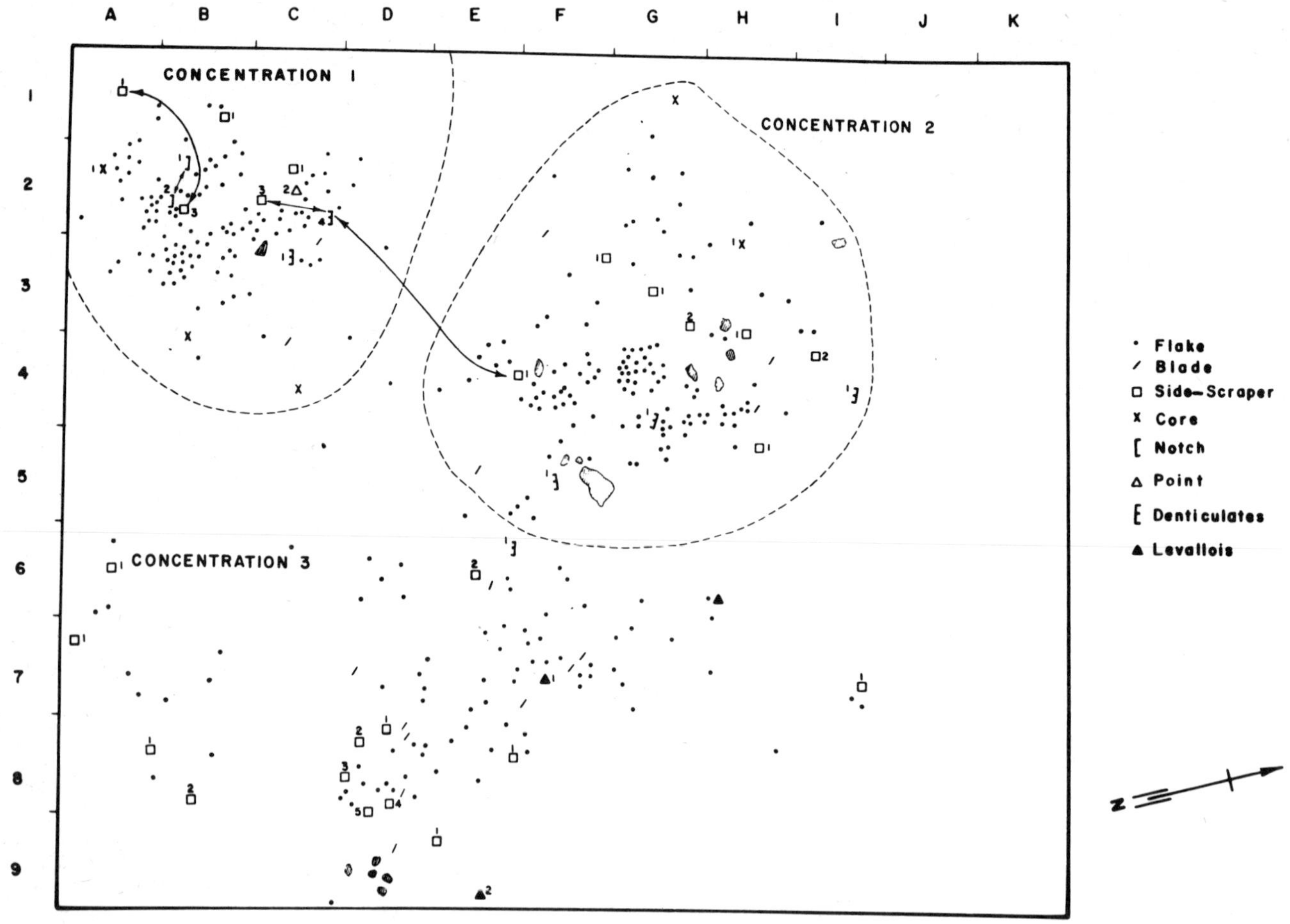

FIG. 12–Site E-72-4, horizontal distribution of artifacts. Shaded blocks indicate sandstones.

"Bedouin Microlithic," are certainly mechanically mixed and show pronounced Neolithic or later elements. However, a clear presence of notched blades and elongated scalene triangles in some of the assembled collections may suggest traces of occupations similar to Site E-72-5.

In March 1973 Dr. Bahay Issawi collected a small grab sample of artifacts from a desert site located some 40 km northeast of the Bir Sahara–Bir Terfawi area, ca. 100 km farther south from Site E-72-5. A casual study of this collection, deposited at the Geological Museum of Cairo, leaves a strong impression that this assemblage is closely similar to that from E-72-5. The impression is mainly supported by the presence of roughly the same proportions of used raw materials as well as metrical and technical characteristics of the debitage.

The typology of the assemblage from Site E-72-5 fits well into the general typological variability of the Terminal Paleolithic (Epipaleolithic) of Northern Africa. However, a close statistical comparison with well-known Nilotic taxonomic units of supposedly similar age shows pronounced, and statistically significant, dissimilarities. Thus, both the Shamarkian from Sudanese Nubia (Schild et al., 1968), and the Idfu area (Vermeersch, 1970) clearly display basic differences concerning several tool groups. First of all, the group of backed bladelets in the Shamarkian constitutes the main tool group while notched and denticulated bladelets run very low and triangles are almost absent, none being of the elongated scalene group. The debitage, methods of core preparation, their forms, and finally, raw material preferences are also significantly divergent. A short glance at the cumulative curve suffices to show the basic disagreements (figs. 19-20).

The Qarunian from sites located on the northern shores of the Fayum Lake shows large similarities to the Shamarkian, especially in the technology, and heavy emphasis on backed bladelets together with low interest in geometrics (compare figs. 18 and 20). Both the Shamarkian and Qarunian are closely associated with either riverine or lacustrine environment and demonstrate certain subsistence stress on fishing, as indicated by enormous quantities of fish bones at several sites, e.g., E29G3, Area E. Their age is also very similar, placed by several radiocarbon dates in the sixth millenium B.C. (Schild et al., 1968; Vermeersch, 1970; Said et al., 1972*a*, 1972*b*).

Another unnamed, supposedly Terminal Paleolithic from Sudanese Nubia (Locality 265 and Site 394 of SJE) reported by Marks (1970) shows very little in common with the material from Site E-72-5. Here the biggest dissimilarity is manifested in a much higher index of backed bladelets, considerable indices of burins and scaled pieces, almost

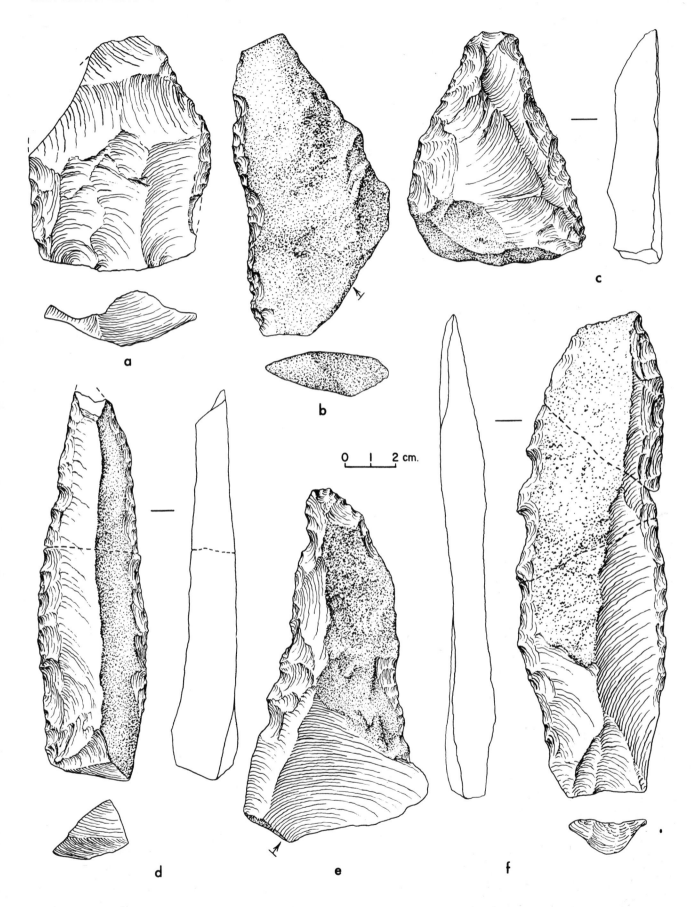

FIG. 13–Tools from Site E-72-4: *a*) bilateral side-scraper on flake; *b*) concave side-scraper on flake; *c*) converging side-scraper on flake; *d*) point on blade; *e*) bilateral denticulate on flake; *f*) bilateral convex side-scraper.

FIG. 14—Site E-72-5, before collection, looking west.

total absence of geometrics, and finally, greatly differing technology and material preference (Marks, 1970, pp. 74-75).

A quick glance up to the northwest, through the immense wastes of the Libyan Rocky Lowland, Serir of Tibesti, Fezzan Plateaus, and the Siritian Plateaus, takes us to the area of Tunisian *chott* where numerous and highly differentiated Capsian sites are located. There, north of the great *chott* of Djerid, in the southeastern dry steppe of the Algero-Tunisian Plateau, a few Upper Capsian sites show several similar quantitative and qualitative characteristics to those from Site E-72-5. These are the sites which are classified as the Chacal and Ain Aachena Variants of Upper Capsian (Tixier, 1963, 1967, personal communication). It is also mentioned that some other Upper Capsian sites, this time classified as belonging to the so-called Sétif Face, located on the Algerian Plateau north of Chott el Hodna, and/or Phase III of the Upper Capsian, are marked by numerous pieces encochées and elongated geometrics with concave base. The Terminal (IIId) Phase of the Upper Capsian is chronologically placed in the fifth and fourth millenia B.C. (Camps et al., 1968, pp. 20-21; Camps, 1968; Camps and Camps-Fabrer, 1972, pp. 31-35).

The main points of similarity between the Tunisian inland sites mentioned and the assemblage from the Dyke area lie in the following characteristics: high indices of notched, denticulated, and notched or denticulated retouched blades and bladelets (Chacal, Lalla, Ain Aachena, Dakhlat es-Saadane B); low proportions of backed bladelets, among which those with shouldered backing play an important role (Chacal, Lalla); high values of geometrics with a clear stress on elongated scalene triangles. The similarities are apparent when one compares the jumps of cumulative curves (fig. 19), although their runs are not entirely identical, reflecting some points of dissimilarity such as the higher proportion of endscrapers (Chacal, Lalla, Dakhlat es-Saadane B) more abundant trapezes (Dakhlat es-Saadane, Chacal) and usually more pronounced indices of notches and denticulates (Tixier, 1963, p. 119; 1967, p. 804). The differences are in most cases statistically significant.

In summary, the assemblage from the deep desert of the Dyke area diverges significantly from the known, chronologically comparable, archaeological entities recognized along the Nile and associated with either riverine or lacustrine environment. Instead, the best analogies are provided by some Upper Capsian sites located in an inland situation, a dry steppe of today, far from the *chotts*.

The clear taxonomic dichotomy shown by the Nilotic sites and those found deep in the desert probably reflects, at least partially, different adaptive technological systems of procurement reechoed in entirely contrasted tool kit structures and settlement patterns, assuming smaller and

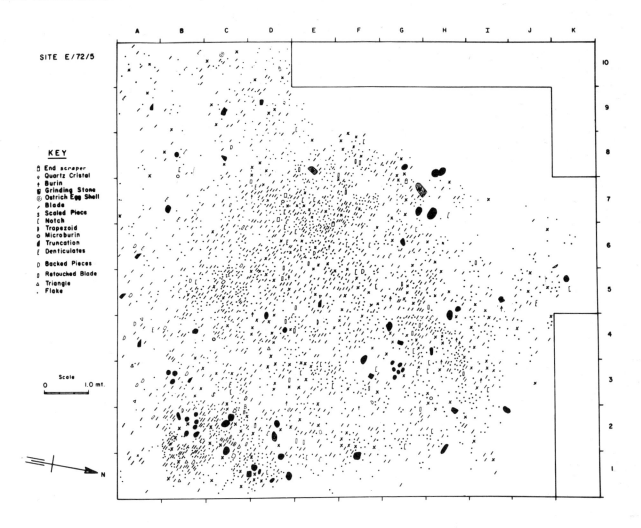

FIG. 15—Site E-72-5, horizontal distribution of artifacts. Sandstone slabs totally blackened; milling stones shaded.

more isolated clusters of artifacts, etc. On the other hand, this situation ostensibly contravened older ideas postulating the Sahara as a possible source for the Shamarkian (Schild et al., 1968, p. 705). One can hardly negate a great techno-morphological unity of the Terminal Paleolithic of Northern Africa, however, as demonstrated by repetition of types, techniques, and methods of stone work in the Upper Capsian Variants, Shamarkian, Qarunian, Site E-72-5, and other Saharan assemblages. The environmental patterning of the composition and quantitative structures of tool kits, raw material preferences, flint working methods, and consequently the interdependence of these elements seem to look more and more convincing when regarded from the Nile Valley and Western Desert perspective.

The tight and clearly limited distribution of the artifacts at Site E-72-5, suggesting confinement within a closed structure, possibly a tent, should indicate a homogeneous occupational unit in which most of the camp chores of the members were performed at the same place. This situation may suggest a family, either extended or nuclear. The presence of an apparently similar occupational unit just beside the worked one may imply a two occupational unit camp. However, since the other cluster was left untouched the hypothesis remains only a guess.

The sand pan sites in the deep desert of the Dyke area were obviously witnessing climatic conditions much different from those that obtain today in the Western Desert of Egypt. The lithostratigraphic situation at Site E-72-5 and the complete lack of any significant traces of drainage, even in the near vicinity of the basins, seems to suggest climatic conditions inhibiting heavy erosion and runoff. The observed alternations of coarse and fine-grained silty sand laminae in the section at Site E-72-5 could indicate a diffused surface wash somehow alternating with more violent transport, but still dispersed over large surfaces. Such effects could have been produced by unpatterned overlapping of rare low to moderately intense rains and heavier showers over a flat, grass covered, but basically rocky surface, with slightly reduced permeability and practically nonexistent drainage.

A heavy occurrence of artifacts within a single occupation unit often indicates a long, unbroken period of dwelling. If this is the case at Site E-72-5, then the water resources in the pan should have been large enough to cover more than one short season. Such a situation is possible when one assumes an alternation of winter and summer rains and/or a high ground water level.

The conjecture of the long-lived settlement at Site

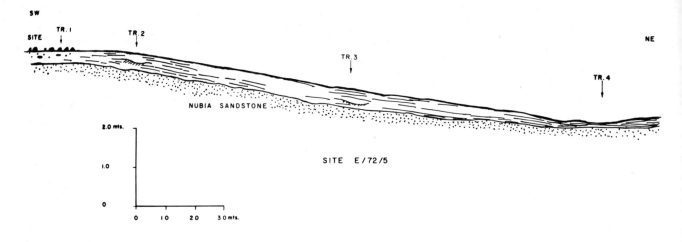

FIG. 16—Cross-section through Site E-72-5 toward pan center.

E-72-5 is reinforced by the occurrence of large, well used grinding stones some of which are hardly transportable because of their size and weight (fig. 21). It is imaginable that these stones were used for grinding grass seeds, a use which one could have expected in the reconstructed environment, as it exists today in the Tchad area (Monod, 1963, p. 194 after Créac'h). The biggest of the stones does not show any trace of paint grinding.

THE BIR SAHARA—BIR TERFAWI AREA

Forty kilometers south of Ain Dab, in the Kharga Depression, a right turn on the Darb El-Arbain road begins a much less known caravan track which runs almost straight southwest passing the mont of Nusab el-Belgum, and after some 230 km, hits the depressions of Bir Terfawi and Bir Sahara, one of the most desolate places in the world. The track runs farther down, passes the artificially drilled Bir Misaha, and at the border with the Republic of Sudan meets the ancient road from Selima Oasis to Kufra. This remote place has rarely been visited by scientists and travelers. J. Ball and Prince Kemal Del Din Hussein were there in 1923, 1925, and 1926; H. J. L. Beadnell in 1927-28, L. E. Almasy in 1933, and B. Issawi with a Geological Survey party in 1971. Extensive traces of a World War II British Army base were scattered in the area.

The brief visit to the *Birs* during the Desert Campaign of 1972 convinced us that the area offers a unique opportunity for a complex, multidisciplinary research project on the Egyptian Sahara. Subsequently, the entire season of 1973 was spent in this area. The enormous logistical problems caused by the work of a party which included thirteen scientific personnel and thirty-one workers, drivers, mechanics, and other support staff were overcome by Dr. B. Issawi, who organized the camp. A large car park composed of ten vehicles, including four jeeps, two pickups, three lorries, and a gasoline tanker made the group easily movable. Most fortunately, good water was available at both wells.

THE GEOMORPHOLOGY AND GEOLOGY

The central part of the southern portion of the Western Desert is undoubtedly one of the lesser known areas of the Sahara. The available maps are only of the 1:500,000 scale, and the air photos are not accessible. The geological mapping is practically nonexistent.

An extensive geological work conducted in the area by Drs. R. Said, B. Issawi, V. Haynes, P. Mehringer, and the present authors resulted in a preliminary reconstruction of the geological history which will most certainly be more fully expanded when the final accounts of several accompanying analyses are made available.

The landscape at the Bir Terfawi—Bir Sahara area is almost absolutely flat, except for the depressions in which the wells are located. Morphologically, the area forms a westward continuation of the Atmur El Kobeish peneplain (Issawi, 1971, 1973 MS), which extends much farther east to the Darb El-Arbain road and the Limestone Plateau. A large field of basement rocks, the so-called Terfawi or El Tawila mass, borders the area from the east, while unlimited sand sheets with occasional rock saddles, ridges, and dunes surround the territory from the south and southwest, extending down to the Sudan Republic. A smaller outcrop of basement rocks, known as the Black Hill, marks the horizon halfway to the Gilf El Kebir Plateau. Some 70 km toward the north, dark sandstone mesas and buttes break the monotony of the seemingly endless plain (Issawi, 1973, MS).

The exact size and shape of the whole area containing Quaternary deposits is still unknown because of the lack of airphotos and adequate maps. The initial mapping which started during the 1973 season was limited to the area of the depressions (mapping was done by Dr. B. Issawi). An estimation suggests an elongated patch of Quaternary deposits ca. 50 km long and 30 km wide (fig. 1), or perhaps even larger, assuming a size of 150 km by 100 km (fig. 22).

The general elevation of the area is 250 m above sea level, except for the shallow deflational depressions of Bir

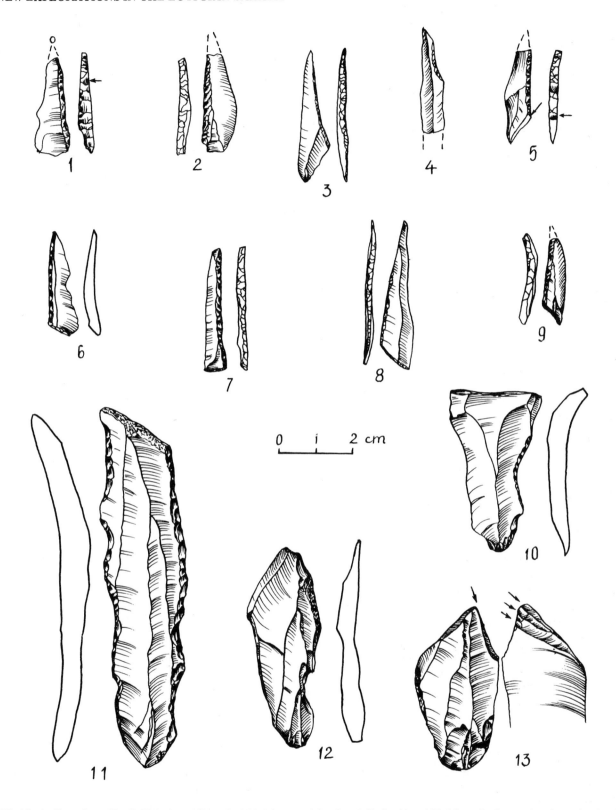

FIG. 17—Artifacts from Site E-72-5: 1 and 2) backed bladelets, straight; 3 and 4) shouldered bladelets; 5) elongated scalene triangle with small short side formed by still unretouched microburin scar; 6 - 8) elongated scalene triangles with small short side; 9) elongated scalene triangle with concave short side; 10 and 12) notched blades; 11) denticulated and retouched blade; 13) dihedral asymmetric burin.

Sahara, Bir Terfawi, and an unnamed basin to the north-west from Bir Sahara. The basins have their deepest points some 10 m below the surrounding flat plain. Both larger deflation basins are elongated in shape, extending for a distance of 15 km (Bir Terfawi) to 8 km (Bir Sahara). A discontinuous, narrow stretch of date palm, dom, acacia and tamarisk trees over the dunes and in the between-dune lows marks the axis of Bir Terfawi. At Bir Sahara the

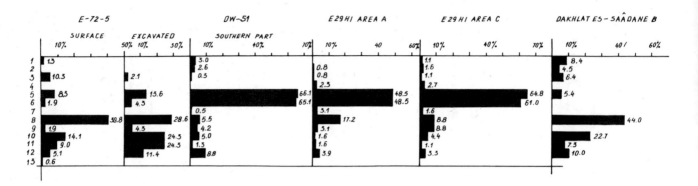

FIG. 18—Main tool indices from Site E-72-5: Dibeira West 51 (Sudanese Nubia); Site E19H1, Area A and Area C (Northern Fayum); and Dakhlat es-Saadane B (Algeria). Key: 1) Endscraper Index; 2) Perforator Index; 3) Burin Index; 4) Backed Blade Index; 5) Backed Bladelet Index; 6) Backed Bladelet Index with n. 64 excluded; 7) Ouchtata Index; 8) Index of Notches and Denticulates; 9) Index of Truncations; 10) Index of Geometrics; 11) Index of Triangles; 12) Index of Microburin Technique; 13) Index of Scaled Pieces.

central chain of recent dunes is covered by low tamarisk bushes, while the only trees, also tamarisks, are seen near the well.

Both depressions are irregularly elongated, with their long axes laid out in NNE-SSW direction. Their outlines are very capricious, with numerous "bays," "peninsulas," and

buttes, while the central part contains modern dunes, abundant spring circles (truncated conduits), and mounds rising from just above the surface to ca. 10 m above the floor. Considerable remnants of the pre-deflational surface appear here and there overlooking the floor of the basins (fig. 23). All sediments are usually discontinuous, thus making

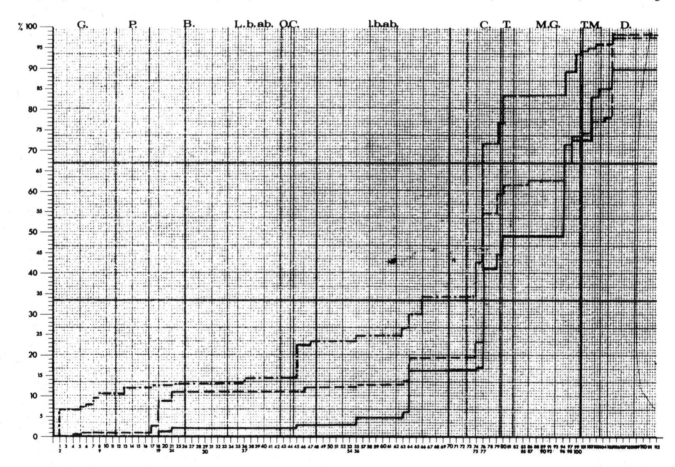

FIG. 19—Cumulative diagrams of assemblages from Site E-72-5, Surface (156 pieces), *broken line*; Site E-72-5, Excavated (140 pieces), *solid line*; and Lalla (Tunisia) collected by R. Vaufrey, count by J. Tixier, *broken and dotted line*.

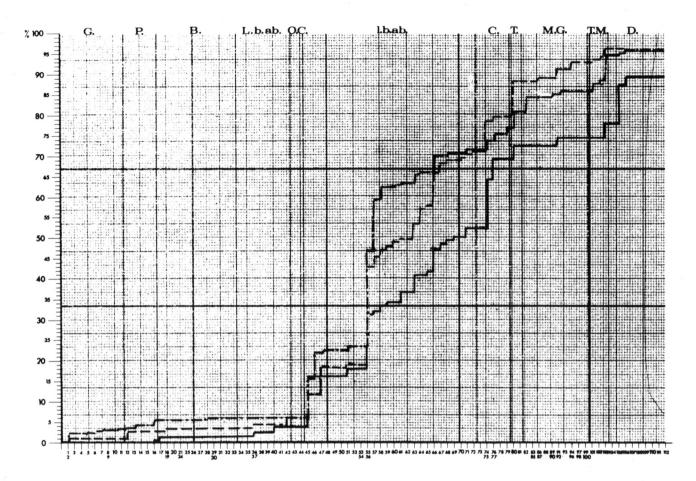

FIG. 20—Cumulative diagrams of assemblages from Site E29H1, Area A (128 pieces), *solid line*; E29H1, Area C (182 pieces), *broken line*; and Dibeira West 51, Southern Part (622 pieces), *broken and dotted line*.

impossible an expanded aerial reconstruction of the fill at every stage of its history. Very shallow, flat, inconspicuous wadis can be observed entering the depressions and disappearing on the plain after a few hundred meters. Patches of salt crust dot the floor near modern wells or at abandoned, sanded up water holes. The water occurs ca. two m below the floor of the depressions at 238 m above sea level; the discharge was extensive, estimated at 440 gallons per day at Bir Sahara (Issawi, 1973, MS).

The general stratigraphic situation of the Quaternary patch at the Bir Sahara—Bir Terfawi area indicates, according to Issawi (1973, MS), that the deposition of these sediments took place in a faulted syncline of the Nubia Sandstone underlain by late Paleozoic—Early Mesozoic sandstones emerging farther west at the Gilf El Kebir Plateau. To the east the upthrown igneous mass of the Precambrian Granite of El Tawila domes the synclinal basin in which the Quaternary sediments were blocked.

Basing his assumptions on the study of the Darb El-Arbain area, Issawi (1973, MS) believes that the last transgression of Thetys had occurred during early Eocene, and since then the area was generally a dry land over which the weathering processes helped the peneplanation. Some relief observed at a few places resulted from igneous activity and structural deformations.

Plateau Carbonate and Underlying Sands

Almost the whole flat plain surrounding the depressions at an elevation of ca. 250 m above sea level displays on its surface a nearly continuous sheet of carbonate crust in form of flakes, plates, and large rectangular to hexagonal structures. The carbonate is gray, cemented, rarely porous to cavernous. At some places a friable gray clay containing carbonate nodules and quartz grains was observed to underlie the carbonate covered surface (Issawi, 1973, MS). In most places, however, the carbonate crust rests immediately on a sand unit whose upper portion is sometimes made up of two different sands. The lower, which certainly constitutes the lowest recognized unit in the area, is a white, friable, medium-grained, well-sorted sand. It contains coarse quartz grains and very rare sub-angular to sub-rounded feldspar grains (Issawi, 1973, MS). The thickness of this sand most certainly exceeds 10 m as shown by its large remnants sticking out from the floor of the basins. The upper unit, rarely present, is made up of a very coarse gritty sand containing small quartz pebbles and is friable, poorly to moderately sorted with sub-rounded to sub-angular feldspars. Its thickness only slightly exceeds 20 cm (Issawi, 1973, MS).

Toward the west from Bir Sahara several very low, inconspicuous mounds dot the carbonate covered surface,

FIG. 21.—Some milling stones from Site E-72-5.

suggesting their association with fossil springs; however, none of these mounds appearing on the plateau were tested.

Numerous Acheulean sites were recorded on the surface of the carbonate plateau. Most of these are clearly in a lag situation dropped from a higher surface, although some offer slight suggestion of at least a small portion of the material remaining *in situ*. These are characterized by less abraded tools, some of which have their toward-the-ground faces almost completely fresh. Because of their secondary position only a few grab samples were collected. The stratigraphic relationship of the Acheulean sites and flaky carbonate crust is not clear, for both are certainly lowered. The taxonomic formal classification of the surface Acheulean is also to be established. An impression, however, based on heavy presence of the amygdaloid and cordiform groups, together with a lower frequency of lanceolates, lack of backed forms, and an extreme rarity of cleavers would rather point to an Upper Acheulean, yet different from that at Dakhla Oasis.

Final Acheulean Spring

At the southern rim of the depression of Bir Sahara several pronounced mounds of fossil springs have been recorded (fig. 23). One of these, a large hill, elevated slightly more than three m above the surrounding wind-scoured oldest sands, contained, on its carbonate cemented surface and sandy slopes, numerous Acheulean bifaces arranged in a typical radiating slide pattern. The locality was designated as Site BS-14.

The central part of the flat-topped hill was highly cemented by a solid mass of carbonates of unknown thickness, but a small five m long trench, dug at the rim of the carbonate cap, yielded the data which permit preliminary assumptions (fig. 24). Here, the lowest archaeologically sterile sediment is the described basal sand unit, which is loose to slightly consolidated, white (10YR 8/2), coarse to medium-grained. The upper part of this sand is clearly truncated. Over the truncation is deposited a very coarse, well-sorted sand with Acheulean artifacts, faunal remains, and rootlike carbonized sand rods. Its thickness fluctuates between 70 cm and 90 cm, but the base slopes gently toward the center of the hill. In turn, a 30 cm thick unit of medium blocky evaporates made up of carbonate cemented sand with more than 70% of carbonate covers the sand, thickening toward the center. Its upper part contains more rounded and smaller concretions of carbonates. The whole carbonate unit wedges out at the rim of the spring hill. A thin coarse-grained, reddish yellow (7.5YR 7/6) sand overlaps the external part of the evaporate rim.

All gathered data seem to suggest that the trench is located at the rim of a spring pool containing archaeological remains deposited mostly during the period of its major

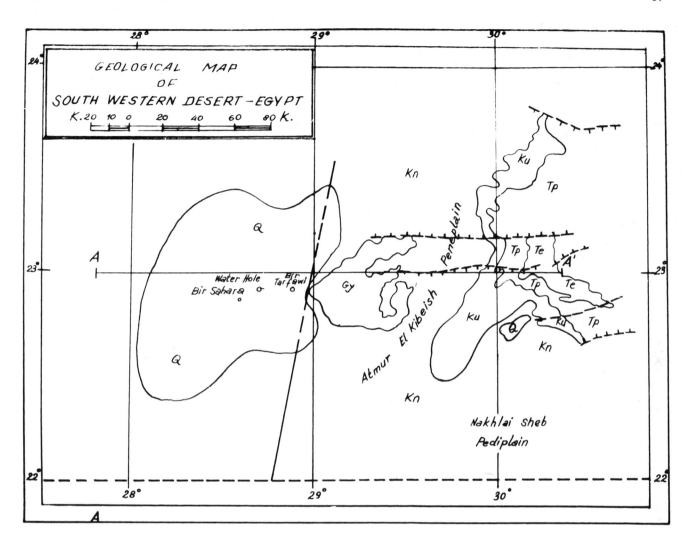

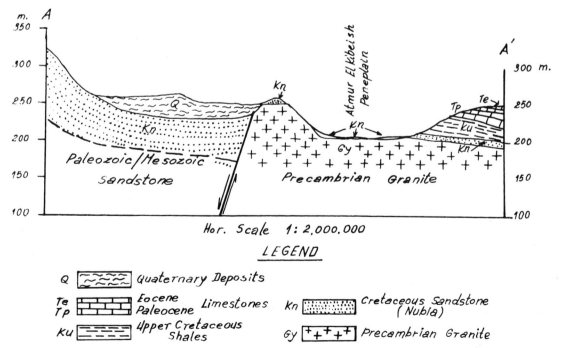

FIG. 22—Geological map and west/east cross section of southern part of the Egyptian Sahara. Mapped by B. Issawi.

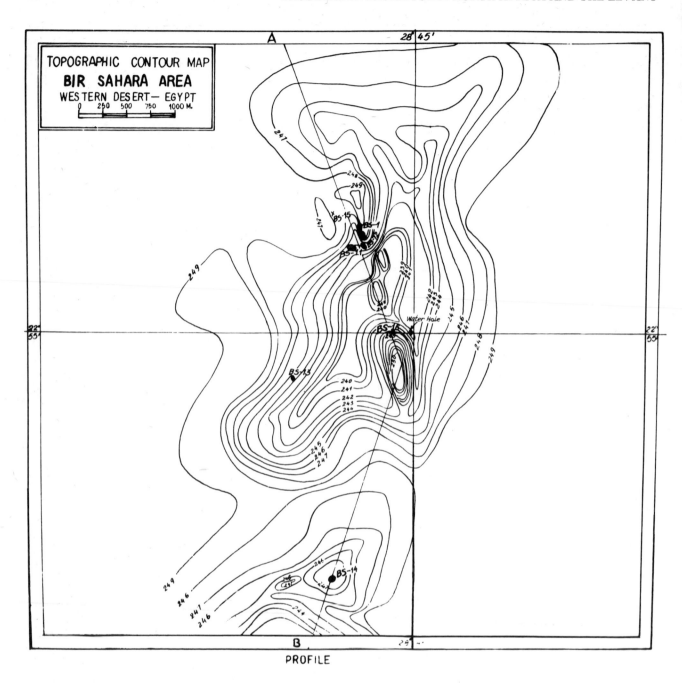

FIG. 23–Topographic contour map of the Bir Sahara basin showing
location of sites and general cross-section. Map by B. Issawi,
February 1973.

activity. The bed made up of evaporates indicates a somewhat lesser discharge, a dying source, marked by the
decayed vegetation which eventually covered the spring
eye.

The precious faunal remains which were recovered from
the spring sand bed contained tooth enamel fragments of a
medium-sized or large ruminant, and some pieces of ostrich
egg shell. A few other bones were collected when eroding
from the supposedly basal part of the carbonate seal. The
analysis indicated one upper r   ariform tooth of an equid,
probably *Equus asinus*; a jaw fragment, and one acetab-

ulum, both also belonging to an equid (Gautier, 1973, MS).

The morphological situation of the fossil spring at Site
BS-14 and very limited excavation do not suffice to establish a precise relationship of the site to the previously
mentioned units, especially the plateau carbonates. However, some suggestions may be offered. The top of the
mound located at ca. 247 m above sea level is slightly more
than two m below the surface of the plateau. This observation could indicate that a period of deflation took place
before the formation of the spring and after the plateau
carbonates had been deposited.

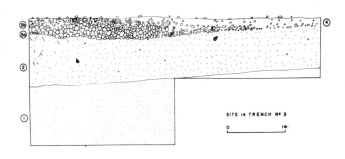

FIG. 24—Cross-section at Site BS-14. Key: 1) basal sand unit; 2) coarse, sorted sand with Acheulean artifacts and carbonized sand rods, spring sands; 3a) lower part of blocky evaporates with rare Acheulean artifacts at base; 3b) upper part of blocky evaporates; 4) eolian sand with weak red soil.

Older Mousterian Dune

After the death of the spring at Site BS-14, a considerable period of eolian erosion followed during which the depression was excavated for the first time down to at least 242 m above sea level, thus more than eight m below the surrounding plateau. Slightly later, this hole of an unknown size was filled with sand dunes, exposed today over a large portion of the floor. A long section pertaining to this event was exposed by a series of trenches in Bir Sahara at archaeological sites BS-1 and BS-12.

Here, the foreset and topset dune beds extend laterally for more than 200 m (fig. 25:1) assuming a thickness of at least five m with their topmost section at just below 245 m above sea level. At Site BS-12 the topset beds contained numerous, but heavily sand blasted, Mousterian artifacts with denticulates and notches as the only recovered tools. The dune is consolidated to cemented, medium to coarse-grained, white (2.5Y 8/0), with iron stains and destroyed lamination in its upper part.

Older Lacustrine Series

An intricate series of lacustrine, shore, and in-blown sediments follows after the deposition of the dune. It starts with the so-called black layer (fig. 25:2b), a black to grayish brown (10YR 5/2) sand, heavily stained with concentrated manganese. The unit is uniformly deposited at similar elevations in several places of the basin, indicating a primarily continuous bed. At the lowest point, at Site BS-16, its base is 243.8 m above sea level, while at Site BS-1 it reaches 245.1 m, gradually disappearing upward from this point on. Laterally, the black layer slopes very gently toward the center of the basin, becoming more intense and thick while descending. Upward, it passes gradually into a vegetation layer at Site BS-1 (fig. 25:2a), marked (figs. 26 and 27) by a thick mat of carbonized root casts (Lower Vegetation Layer at Site BS-1), and a slight rise in the $CaCO_3$ content (fig. 32), while its texture is not significantly different from that of the underlying and overlying sands.

The black sand seems to grade down very gently, but at some places it shows a clear erosional contact with the underlying dune (Site BS-13). Here it fills numerous small channels excavated in the dune. The deeper parts of these channels are usually a more intense black.

At Site BS-16, where the black layer assumes its lowest elevation above sea level, it grades up into a powdered, entirely mineralized, slight laminated peatlike sediment.

The thickness of the black layer usually fluctuates between 20 cm and 40 cm with maximal values of ca. 70 cm in the erosional channels at Site BS-13.

Several extensive Mousterian sites were recorded at Site BS-11, or in the layer at Sites BS-1, BS-12, and BS-13. At BS-12 fragments of tooth enamel from the black layer probably can be attributed to the white rhinoceros, *Ceratotherium sinium,* and to a large bovid—probably the extinct buffalo, *Homoioceros antiquus.*

The exact environmental conditions in which this manganese rich horizon was deposited are still mysterious. The channeling at Site BS-13 and the lateral differentiation suggest a near shore or shore environment which, on the other hand, is reinforced by the occurrence of the *in situ* Mousterian settlements imbedded in the layer. It was established that the black color is entirely due to the admixture of manganese (V. Haynes, personal communication).

The top of the black layer is slightly truncated at places and, in turn, covered by a bed of iron-stained gray sand (5Y 6/1) sloping gently toward the center of the basin. The thickness of this bed varies according to its lateral place. Thus it thickens considerably upward, toward the edges of the basin. At some places (BS-13) its lower portion is conformably laminated over minuscule swale excavated in the surface of the black layer. Numerous carbonate cemented beautiful root casts form a thick mat, especially at the downslope located sections of the bed, while the upward placed and thicker parts show a noticeably smaller number of root casts. Again farther up the slope this sand bed thickens to more than one and one-half meters (fig. 25:3-5). Here, numerous brown iron stains mark the whole bed. Its upper portion contains a clear vegetation layer (Upper Vegetation Layer at Site BS-1). It is again an extremely thick mat of carbon-cemented micro-rootlet casts which appear as spongy structures tightly knotted together. This horizon is also marked by a slightly higher $CaCO_3$ content and considerably finer texture (fig. 32). The vegetation horizon is, in turn, covered by inconspicuously laminated sands, identical to those in the level below (fig. 32).

At Site BS-13 at the very base of the sand an extensive, partially destroyed Mousterian settlement was deposited. The cultural horizon yielded a distal moiety of a tibia from a large camel (probably *C. thomasi*), metapodial fragments of the white rhinoceros (*Ceratotherium simum*), mandibular fragments of an equid probably wild ass (*Equus asinus*), and an upper molar ascribed to the extinct buffalo (*Homoioceras antiquus*).

At Site BS-1 the vegetation horizon, located near the top of the sand bed, contained another Mousterian settlement.

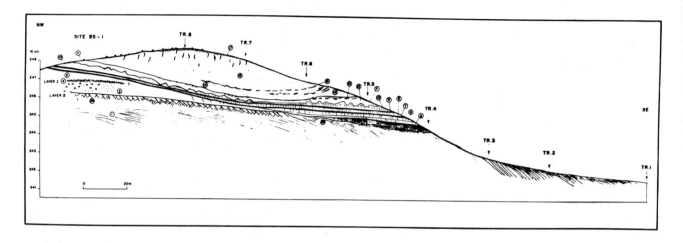

FIG. 25—Cross section at Sites BS-1 and BS-12. Key: 1) older Mousterian dune; 2a) lower vegetation horizon passing down into black layer; 2b; 3) iron-stained, patchy sand; 4) upper vegetation layer at Site BS-1; 5) iron-stained patchy sand with inconspicuous traces of lamination at places; 6, 8, 10) silt layers; 7 and 9) burnt layers; 11) white marl; 12) sag structures; 13) white marl with lenses of silt and platey evaporates or spongy evaporates at places; 14) base of upper dune interfingering with spongy evaporates; 15) platey to slightly spongy evaproates; 16) main body of upper dune with carbonate cemented root casts in top part; 17) reddish-yellow soil.

Unfortunately, the fragments of bones found in the cultural horizon of this site were unidentifiable.

The environmental interpretation of the gray, patchy sand bed is similar to the black layer. Most likely, it is a shore and near shore sandy sediment reflecting some minor pulsations of the lake recorded as slight erosion of the black layer and stabilization marked by the Upper Vegetation Horizon at Site BS-1. It is not unlikely that the sand beach was fed by in-blown eolian sands.

A series of alternating light gray (5Y 7/2), thin layers of sandy silts with medium blocky structure (fig. 25:6, 8, 10) conformably overlies the described sandy layers. At its basal part two to three reddish brown (2.5YR 5/4) or pink (5YR 8/3) burnt layers intercalate between the silts

FIG. 26—Site BS-11, black layer passing up into vegetation horizon at site's highest point; patchy sands and gray marl above.

FIG. 27–Site BS-1, two vegetation horizons separated and overlain by patchy, iron-stained sands. Person indicates upper vegetation horizon with main cultural layer.

(fig. 25:7, 9). The thickness of the bed does not exceed one meter.

A bed of light gray (2.5Y 7/2) to white or white gray highly calcareous limestonic silt (fig. 32) with medium to coarse blocky structure overlies alternating silt beds (fig. 28). The contact, however, is erosional at places (BS-13) and/or displaying very pronounced sag structures (fig. 25:12). Its upper part grades up into platey evaporates alternating with thin streaks of silt (fig. 25:13), and again, slightly higher, into a cemented bed of spongy evaporates. At some places this lacustrine silty series is reduced to one bed of whitish limestonic silt (BS-11, BS-16). The thickness of the whole bed rarely exceeds one meter.

At Site BS-11 the very base of the upper silt, displaying an erosional contact with the lower silt, contains numerous washed-down animal bones seemingly redeposited from the nearest shore now completely removed. Among the recovered bones the following are represented: tooth enamel of the extinct buffalo (*Homoioceras antiquus*), an upper molar probably from the wild ass (*Equus asinus*), and a mandible fragment of the warthog (*Phacochoerus aethiopicus*).

Slightly farther down the sloping bed of the upper silt unit, and nearer the axis of the depression, a collection of molluscs from the snail-laden upper portion of this bed gave the following identifications: *Melanoides tuberculata*,

Lymnaea natalensis, *Biomphalaria alexandrina*, and *Gyraulus costulatus* - all very frequent, and less abundant *Hydrobia sp. ?* and *Bulimus truncatus*. A sample of *Melanoides* shells collected from the surface of this calcareous silt yielded a radiocarbon date of 32,780 years B.P. ± 900 years (SMU-80). This undoubtedly too-recent date seems to be the result of surface contamination. At Site BS-16 another molluscan sample collected from the base of the same white limestonic silt unit gave very frequent *Melanoides tuberculata*, *Lymnaea natalensis*, *Gyraulus costulatus*, and less frequent *Biomphalaria alexandrina* (Gautier, 1973, MS).

A cleaned and selected sample of large *Melanoides* shells from this locality gave a radiocarbon date of > 41,500 years B.P. (SMU-81). A sample of small *Melanoides* shells from the same spot indicated a radiocarbon age of 40,710 years B.P. ± 3,270 years (SMU-82). The difference in age of the two dates is attributed to carbonate contamination which could not be removed from the small shells.

Both major beds of silts are clearly representing water-laid sediments of an expanding lake which certainly exceeded 248 m above sea level (the highest recorded elevation). Despite a persistent search for the beach face of this lake, nothing resembling a near-shore or shore environment was found; it obviously was destroyed by subsequent erosions. The alternating homogeneous layers of silts in the

FIG. 28—Older lacustrine series downslope from Site BS-1. Black sands at base covered by patchy sands with rootlet casts and, in turn, by silts overlain by white marls; burnt layer seen as horizontal erosional fissure within silts; platey and spongy evaporates just above white marl.

basal part of the unit, burnt plant growth layers, traces of erosion between the lower and upper unit as well as the sag structures, all point to the fact that the level of the lake had never been stable, but had undergone considerable and fast changes. Some of these may be associated with a seasonal rhythm. Near the top of the upper unit a recession of the lake is heralded by the appearance of rich evaporite layers obviously formed at the near-beach environment and often displaying beautiful plant casts.

Upper Dune

An invading dune is recorded at Site BS-1/BS-12 interfingering at the base with spongy evaporites (fig. 25:14). The dune is friable, medium-grained, pale yellow (2.5Y 8/4) in color. Several thin layers of platey to slightly spongy carbonate cemented sand structures occur in the lower part of the dune (fig. 25:15). Near the top numerous carbonate cemented root casts and patches of lime are observed. A thin reddish yellow (5YR 7/6) soil with fine crumbly structure tops the dune sand at Site BS-1. The formation of the soil clearly postdates the development of carbonate cemented root-drip structures, as shown by their broken sections displaying white, discolored sand grains. The whole thickness of the preserved dune slightly exceeds three m in its thickest portion.

The sections at Sites BS-11 and BS-15 reveal a large ca. 400 m long and almost two m thick, lense of the upper dune sand which overlies the truncated lower silt bed (fig. 29:7) and, in turn, is covered by a unit of later silts (fig. 29:8).

Upper Lacustrine Series

New units of silts unconformably overlie the dune (fig. 29:8). Only two medium extensive patches of these sediments are recorded at Bir Sahara, both at elevations close to 247.5 m above sea level. At Site BS-15 a thin (ca. 30 cm), gray (10YR 7/1) sandy silt displaying irregular blocky structure contains numerous snails and clams. It rests on the upper dune. The molluscan assemblage includes frequent specimens of *Melanoides tuberculata, Biomphalaria alexandrina, Gyraulus costulatus*, and lesser quantities of *Bulimus truncatus, B. forskalii, Corbicula consorbina*, and small land snails ascribed to *Pupoides coenopictus* (Gautier, 1973, MS and personal communication). Clam shells, some of which were collected from the surface, gave a radiocarbon date of 30,870 B.P. ± 1,000 years (SMU-75). Another sample of selected large *Melanoides* shells yielded a date of > 44,700 years B.P. (SMU-79). The younger date is possibly contaminated by younger carbonates from the surface.

The basal silt grades up into a darker, loose to slightly

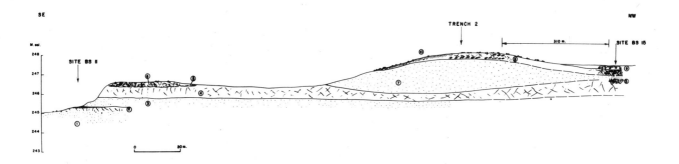

FIG. 29—Cross section between Sites BS-11 and BS-15 (geological locality). Key: 1) older Mousterian dune; 2) black layer passing upslope into vegetation layer; 3) patchy, iron-stained sands; 4) silts; 5) platey evaporates; 6) spongy evaporates; 7) upper dune; 8) upper lacustrine series, basal marl; 9) upper lacustrine series, brown upper marl; 10) reddish soil.

consolidated horizon of brown (10YR 5/3), thin (ca. 20 cm) sandy silt displaying fine crumbly structure possibly resulting from pedogenetical alterations (soil A horizon) subsequent to deposition. Again, it contains rich molluscan fauna. The assemblage here includes more land snails than before and contains frequent *Melanoides tuberculata, Biomphalaria alexandrina, Gyraulus costulatus, Zootecus insularis*, less numerous *B. truncatus, B. forskalii, Lymnaea natalensis*, and the same small land snail, *Pupoides coenopictus* (Gautier, 1973, MS and personal communication).

The top of the upper silt is slightly truncated.

The upper lacustrine unit is archaeologically sterile in the depression of Bir Sahara; however, an apparently analogous silt unit deposited in closely similar lithostratigraphic sequence in the Bir Terfawi basin contained, in its uppermost portion, a huge Aterian kill site with numerous bones scattered over an area measuring a few thousand square meters. Work at this site is planned for the next field season.

The upper lacustrine series certainly marks out a new

FIG. 30—Plateau remnant southeast of Sites BS-11, BS-12, and BS-1, in foreground with rod-like and crumbly carbonates on slightly deflated surface. Line of trenches in background located at Sites BS-12 and BS-1. Site BS-11 is at left corner, across sand sheet separating it from Sites BS-12 and BS-1. Camp is at picture's right corner.

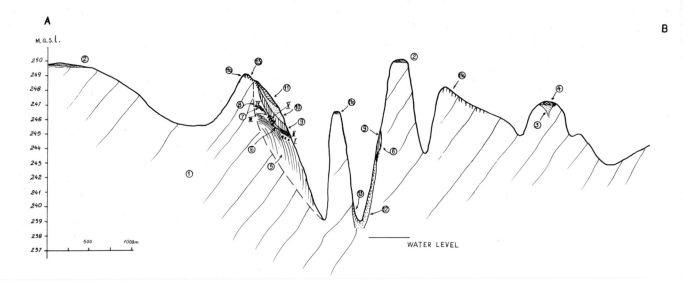

FIG. 31—Schematic cross section through Bir Sahara basin along line indicated on Fig. 22 (slightly overpassed). Key: 1) basal sand unit; 2) plateau carbonate crust; 3) Acheulean spring conduit; 4) Acheulean spring evaporates; 5) older Mousterian dune; 6) black layer passing upslope into lower vegetation horizon; 7) patchy, iron-stained sands; 8) upper vegetation horizon; 9) silts and marls of older lacustrine series; 10) upper dune; 11) upper lacustrine series; 11a) rod-like and crumbly carbonates; 12) recent eolian sands; 13) reddish-yellow recent soil. Cultural horizons indicated by Roman numerals I to V and crosses.

aggradation in the basins. The highest recorded elevation of the already truncated silts is at 247.5 m above sea level, but the beaches are not preserved. Because of the high stand of the lake it is quite possible that the carbonate cemented root casts which are observed in upper portions of the younger dune, at an elevation slightly overpassing 248 m above sea level, were formed during this phase of the lake. Similarly, the rodlike carbonates occurring on the plateau remnants (fig. 30) in the basin as well as in the northern part of the rim could have been formed during this time. These are marked on the map as Sand (Carbonate Unit - Issawi, 1973, MS) and are identical to those on the upper dune. Both seem to form a single mantle when followed on the surface.

Truncation and Recent Sediments

There is no record of younger Pleistocene sediments in either depression. The next recognized event is expressed in a pronounced deflation which cut through the accumulated lacustrine and preceding eolian sediments to a level which could have been very close to the modern water table. It is believed that the general morphology of the area was developed during this time. This assumption is indicated by the presence of several chipped stone sites of Early Kingdom age, located close to the modern wells, only a few meters above the present water level. These sites are only partially *in situ*, but they clearly display preserved occupational patterning. The tools are fresh to semi-fresh, which shows that these sites were only recently exposed. A radiocarbon date obtained on ostrich egg shells at one of these sites (BT-20) gave a date of 4,510 B.P. ± 70 years (SMU-74).

Still more recent sand dunes partially fill the depressions. They contain small traces of occupations of Later

Historic age with wheel-made pottery, a hand-made pottery with design motifs resembling that of Early Khartoum ware, occasional pieces of iron and bronze, scraps of faience, together with camel and human bones.

ARCHAEOLOGY

The Acheulean

For all practical purposes only one Acheulean site, BS-14, was worked. It yielded a considerable surface collection, and a much more restricted *in situ* material recovered from the edge of the spring pool.

The spatial distribution of artifacts demonstrates a typical slide pattern, with most of the handaxes concentrated on the eroded slopes of the cone, and a few resting on the edges of its carbonaceous seal.

The raw material is almost entirely composed of quartzitic sandstones with rare quartz pieces. Debitage is poorly represented, undoubtedly a repercussion of the surface environment as shown by clearly different quantitative proportions in the small assemblage recovered from the trench. The strongest debitage group is formed by biface trimming flakes, although their number is significantly smaller than the minimal required figure to shape the bifaces found at BS-14. A few recovered cores include two semi-discoidal ones, one single platform for flakes, one globular of the changed orientation group, and two Levallois specimens.

The bifaces certainly form the strongest tool group (IB = 88.0) totaling 110 specimens. Their quantitative and qualitative distributions show pronounced stress on two major groups (compare fig. 6), triangular (Group I), and cordiform (Group II), which account for 40.4% and 35.3% respectively. The two groups are mainly made up of fine, elongated ogivo-triangular and pelecyform bifaces with

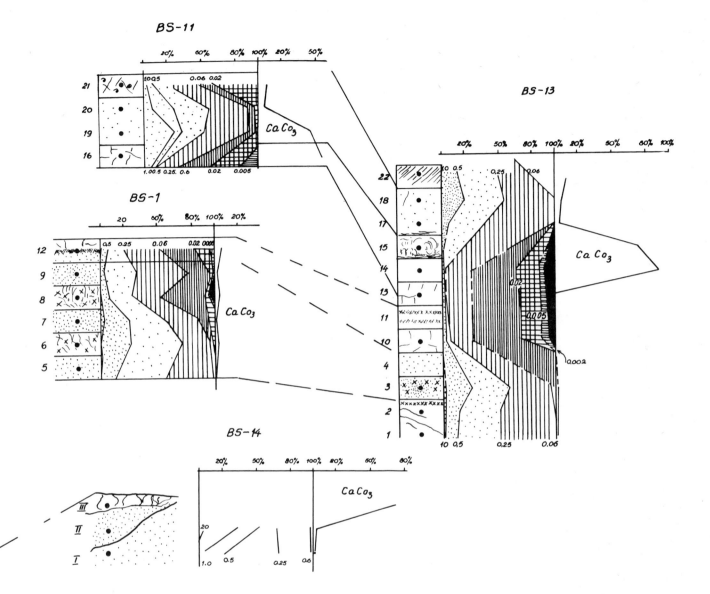

FIG. 32–Grain size and CaCO$_3$ curves of sediments from Bir Sahara basin. Analyses by J. Kossakowska-Such and T. Wesolowska. Key: I–Basal sands. II–Coarse sorted sand. III–Blocky evaporates: 1) Foreset beds of lower Mousterian dune; 2) Topset beds of lower Mousterian dune; 3) Black layer; 4) Iron-stained patchy sand; 5) Iron-stained patchy sand below lower vegetation layer; 6) Lower vegetation layer; 7) Patchy sand between two vegetation layers; 8) Upper vegetation layer; 9) Patchy sand above upper vegetation layer; 10) Basal silt; 11) Silt with burnt layers; 12) Sandy silt with burnt layer; 13) Silt above burnt layers; 14) White highly calcareous silt; 15) Spongy evaporates; 16) Sandy silt truncated at top; 17) Base of younger Mousterian dune; 18) Upper part of younger Mousterian dune; 19 and 20) Younger Mousterian dune; 21) Lower portion of younger lacustrine silt; 22) Reddish-yellow recent soil. Crosses indicate presence of human occupation. No scale.

thinned butts, both slightly tending to cordiforms; and cordiforms and sub-cordiforms with thinned butts, of which some have distinctly oblique bases. The amygdaloids, which make the third strongest group (Group V), account for 11.1%, and thus are far behind the first two groups. The group of discoidal oval and limandes is relatively strong, attaining slightly over 8% (compare fig. 6). It is dominated by discoidal bifaces (eight specimens). Among other forms, a few (three specimens) fine lanceolates attract attention.

The other tools (15 specimens) include five spheroids, four inverse sidescrapers, two other sidescrapers including one bifacial, and single specimens of bifacial edge piece, chopping tool, denticulate, and an undetermined fragment.

Certainly, the assemblage from BS-14 is quite different from those recovered at Dakhla (compare figs. 5 and 8), Nubia, or on the plateau in the Bir Sahara area. It seems that the closest analogy is offered by the collection from El-Ma el-Abiod in Algeria (Vaufrey, 1955; Balout, 1955). Yet, more detailed comparisons of these two sites are practically impossible. The general resemblance of both is mirrored in a great elegance of biface trimming, high frequency of cordiforms, especially elongated, and an entire lack of cleavers.

Generally speaking, the above characteristics, together with somewhat more pronounced occurrence of the Levallois Group, although manifested only in cores, would rather

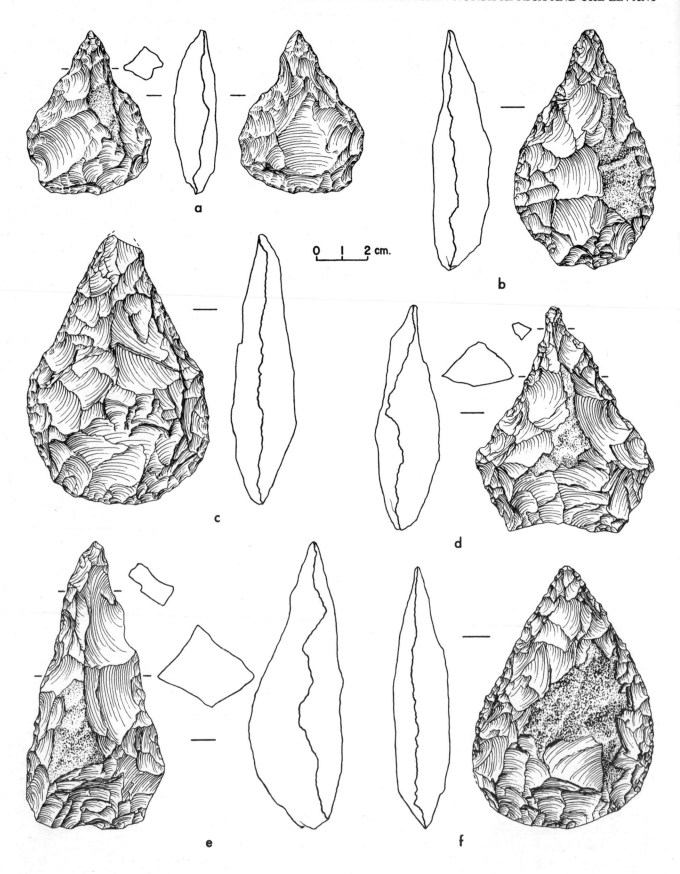

FIG. 33–Bifaces from Site BS-14, surface. *a-c*, Micoquian with rounded base; *d*, triangular with constricted tip; *e*, ficron; *f*, short cordiform.

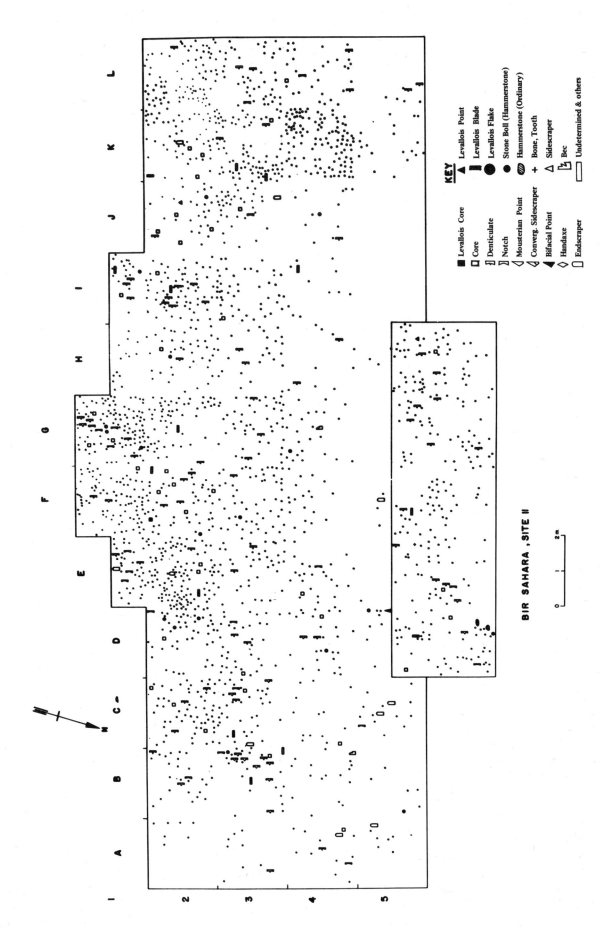

FIG. 34—Site BS-11, horizontal distribution of artifacts. Excavated area in the block at northern edge.

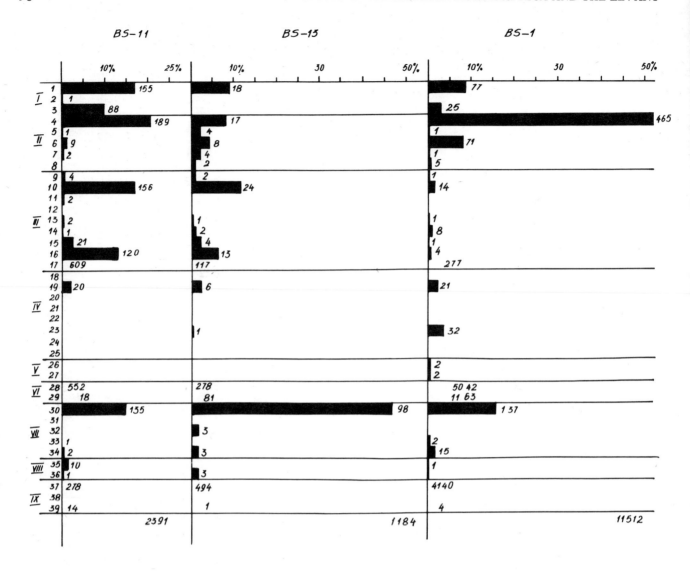

FIG. 35—Restricted General Structure of inventories from Sites BS-11, BS-13, and BS-1. Key: Initial Group (I): 1) Primary flakes; 2) primary blades; 3) early stage core preparation flakes; Levallois Group (II): 4) Levallois core preparation flakes; 5) Levallois cores; 6) Levallois flakes; 7) Levallois blades; 8) Levallois points; Flake Group (III): 9) single platform flake cores; 10) flakes from single platform cores; 11) opposed platform flake cores; 12) flakes from opposed platform flake cores; 13) discoidal cores; 14) flakes from discoidal cores; 15) changed orientation cores; 16) flakes from changed orientation cores; 17) undetermined flakes; Blade Group (IV): 18) single platform blade cores; 19) blades from single platform cores; 20) opposed platform blade cores; 21) flakes from opposed platform blade cores; 22) single platform bladelet cores; 23) bladelets from single platform cores; 24) opposed platform bladelet cores; 25) bladelets from opposed platform cores; Core Rejuvenation and Early Removal from Pre-cores (V): 26) core tablets; 27) core "trimming" blades; Chip Group (VI): 28) regular chips. 29) retouch chips; Tool and Tool Production Waste Group (VII): 30) retouched tools; 31) resharpening (longitudinal) spalls; 32) biface trimming flakes and chips; 33) burin spalls; 34) notch spalls; Hammerstone Group (VIII): 35) spheroidal hammerstones (?); 36) regular hammerstones; Undetermined Group (IX): 37) crushed chips; 38) chunks; 39) undetermined cores. Categories 28, 29, 37, 38, and 39 are excluded from the restricted percentages.

incline to the classification of the assemblage from BS-14 as an Evolved or Final Acheulean, even though the meaning of these terms in Northern Africa is practically insignificant.

The Mousterian

One of the most striking scenes awaiting an unwarned traveler coming to the depressions of the Bir Sahara–Bir Terfawi area are large dark portions of the deflated floor literally covered by carpets of Mousterian artifacts. The impression of the presence of hundreds of sites concentrated in these relatively minuscule basins is certainly exceptionally strong. It must have been the same impres-

sion shared by K. S. Sandford when he had reached the Laqiya Depression in the southern Libyan Desert and saw enormously rich concentrations of "late middle Paleolithic implements" (Sandford, 1933).

Unfortunately, almost all of the concentrations in the Bir Sahara–Bir Terfawi area are entirely destroyed by deflation which had removed once imbedded sites. Nevertheless, the reconstructed sequence of Mousterian sites in the area is most certainly one of the richest in the whole of north Africa. Five consecutive Mousterian horizons were recognized as follows, all associated with the lower lacustrine series:

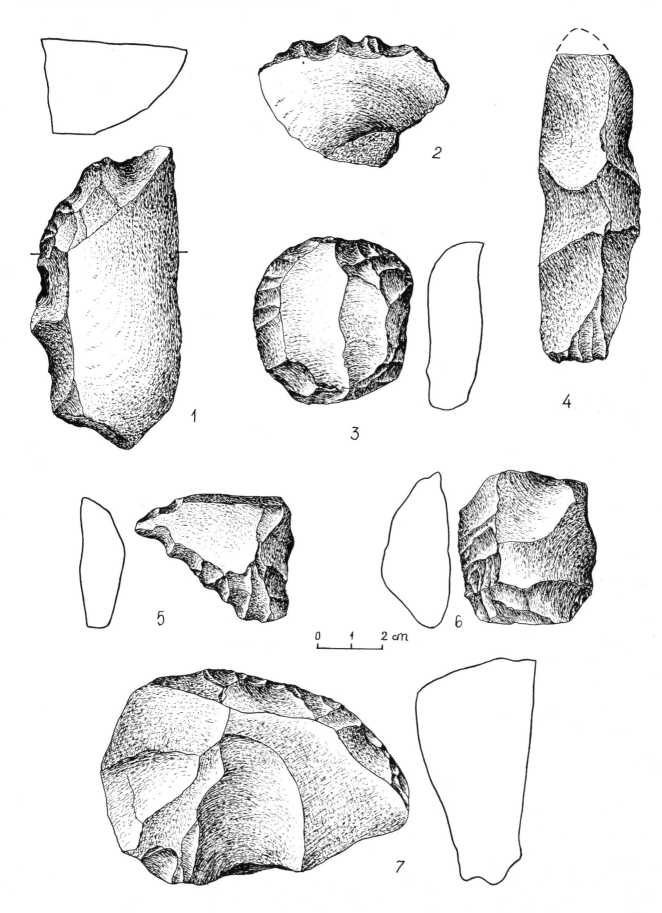

FIG. 36—Artifacts from Site BS-11: 1) thick, single blow notched, lateral denticulate; 2) inverse, transversal denticulate; 3) endscraper on retouched flake; 4) Levallois blade; 5) bilateral denticulate passing into triangular; 6) small Levallois flake core; 7) semi-Quina transversal scraper.

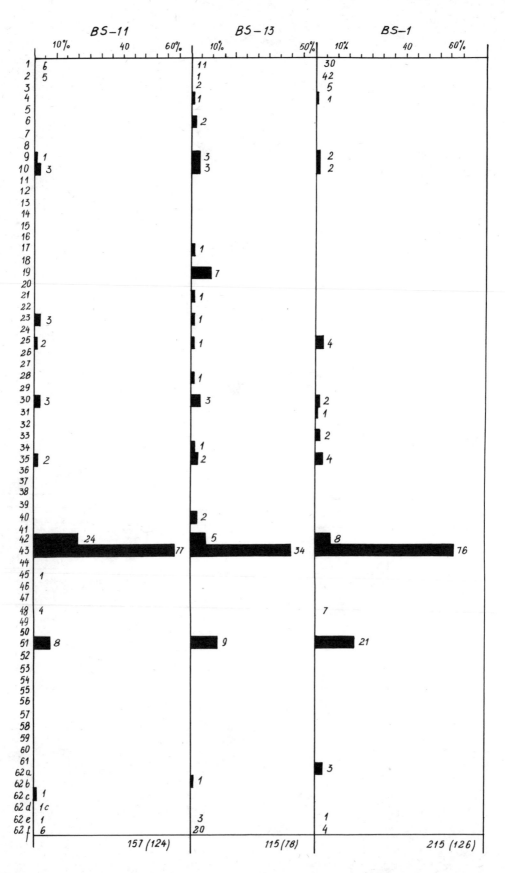

FIG. 37—Quantitative distribution of tools from Sites BS-11, BS-13, and BS-1 (restricted percentages). Categories 1 to 61 according to type list of F. Bordes; n. 62a) undetermined sidescrapers; 62b) bifacial triangular points; 62c) bifacial edge pieces; 62d) spheroids; 62e) regular hammerstones; 62f) undetermined and fragments. Figures indicate number of pieces in each category. Figures in parentheses at base give restricted totals.

I. Traces of Mousterian occupation contemporaneous with sedimentation of the lower dune (Site BS-12, Lower Level).

II. Extensive Mousterian settlements imbedded in the so-called black layer formed at the very beginning of the older lacustrine series. The settlements are included either in the thick black layer low and close to the center occurrence, approximately at an elevation between 244.5 m and 245.0 m above sea level (Site BS-12, Upper Level, Site BS-13, Lower Level); or just below the black layer and in its lower portion at places located slightly higher, at an elevation of 245.0 m to 245.5 m above sea level (BS-11). Still farther up the slope some traces of occupation were recorded at Site BS-1 in the Lower Vegetation Horizon, an upslope stratigraphic continuation of the black layer. It is highly possible that these slight differences in the absolute elevations and lateral place of settlements reflect minor fluctuations of the shore.

III. An extensive Mousterian settlement in gray patch sands just above slightly truncated black layer at Site BS-13 (Middle Level).

IV. Two huge adjoining concentrations in Upper Vegetation Horizon shortly before maximal aggradation of the lower lacustrine series (Site BS-1, Upper Level).

V. A redeposited bone horizon possibly associated with a Mousterian settlement located on the shore of maximal aggradation of the lower lacustrine series (Site BS-13, Upper Level).

The lowest horizon recorded at Site BS-12 yielded a very limited collection of artifacts totaling 86 pieces. Several of these cannot be classified due to the high level of abrasion. However, one Levallois core for flakes, one discoidal, and one globular were recognized. The tools include five denticulates and one Clactonian notched flake.

On the second horizon, the two excavated sites provided considerable collections. The assemblage from BS-12, Upper Level, is very limited and comes mainly from the surface. A few test trenches provided no more than two dozen artifacts. The technological and typological characteristics of this assemblage containing only 29 tools, including Levallois pieces, is undoubtedly affected by the size of the sample; however, considering its paucity, the assemblage is not significantly different from that collected at Site BS-11 (compare indices on fig. 38).

At Site BS-11, across a flat concavity from Sites BS-12 and BS-1 (fig. 30), a large deflational remnant contained on its almost leveled surface a freshly exposed settlement eroding from a low scarp. Subsequent work on this site proved that only the upper portion had been exposed by the deflation. It is, therefore, assumed that the spatial distribution of artifacts, as recorded by scatter diagram, largely reflects

original pattern of the settlement. On the other hand, it is well to remember that the settlement was primarily larger than its actual extension, a result of later erosion which left only a portion of the artifact-bearing sediments.

The scatter diagram shows very little differentiated spatial distribution without any statistically significant concentrations or tool clusters. The density is low, characterized by a mean of 19 artifacts per square meter, of which 1.3 are tools (fig. 34).

Gray and brown quartzitic sandstones were the most preferred raw materials; however, a few pieces of the Eocene chert also occurred. The sources of quartzitic sandstones are known to occur at the rim of the Quaternary filled basin, some 30 km to 40 km from the site.

The General Structure (restricted) of the assemblage indicates a raw material economy in which the unworked lumps of rock had been brought to the settlement and then shaped there. Large values of the Initial Group (fig. 35), accompanied by significant figures of Levallois preparation flakes, demonstrate that most of the cores were shaped at the place. A low index of Levallois pieces (fig. 36:4) suggests that some of the unexploited or partially exploited Levallois cores were removed from the settlement, a sign characteristic for workshop-related occupations.

The debitage is mainly based on changed orientation cores for flakes displaying an unpatterned change of orientation. Both the flat and globular variety are present. Single platform cores for flakes come next while discoidal, opposed platform, and Levallois cores are very scarce (fig. 36:6). This setup is partially reflected in the low IL values. Blade index is very low, suggesting fortuitousness of the recovered blades. Heavy hammerstones were used as strikers.

The tool kit (157 pieces, including Levallois) is characterized (compare fig. 37) by extremely heavy values of denticulates reaching almost 70% (restricted index of Group IV + n. 51). The group includes a large number of varieties among which the bilateral, transversal (fig. 36:2), simple, lateral (fig. 36:1), triangular (fig. 36:5), and converging are most common, all made on flakes and elongated bladelike flakes. Notches form the next important group, accounting for almost 20% (restricted count). Sidescrapers are low with with IR (compare fig. 38) slightly overpassing the value of 7.0 (restricted). ILty is at 7.0 while the Upper Paleolithic Group is scarcely represented (fig. 36:3). A collection of ten beautiful, large spheroids completes the assemblage.

On the third horizon, represented by the settlement at BS-13, the spatial distribution of artifacts essentially recalls that at BS-11. Here too the settlement is preserved on an erosional remnant and is partially wind exposed. The artifacts are distributed in an elongated thin concentration measuring ca. 18 m by 7 meters. Their mean density of 22 artifacts per square meter in which 1.9 are tools is also generally similar. An important but inconspicuous cluster of 14 tools was recorded on squares Y-Z/1-3 (fig. 39). This unusual aggregation of tools is important not because of its higher density, which is only slightly different, but chiefly

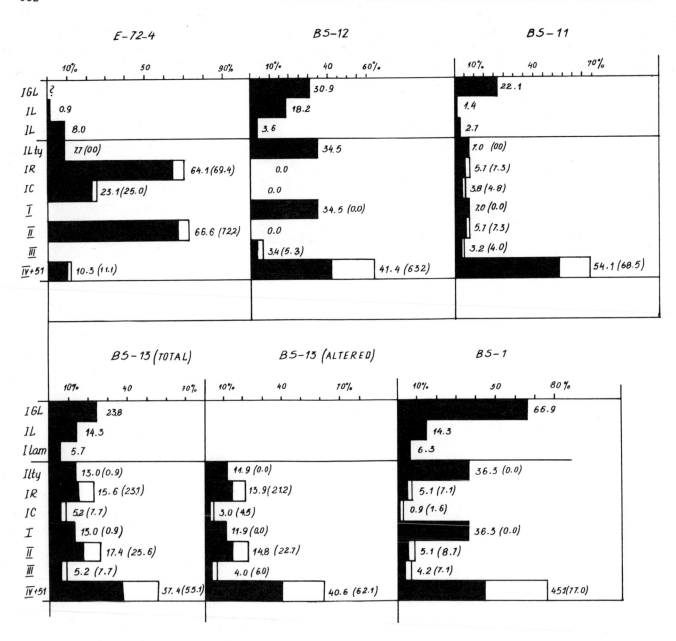

FIG. 38—Main indices of assemblages from Sites E-72-4, BS-12, BS-11, BS-13 (total altered by removal of tools from supposed activity cluster), and BS-1. Black bars indicate large percentages while white ones show restricted percentages if these are bigger than large ones. Figures without parentheses give large percentages; restricted ones are shown in parentheses.

by the reason of the assocation of types. Thus, over a surface measuring slightly more than two square meters the following types were deposited: three Levallois points, one of which is retouched; three converging sidescrapers; one Mousterian point; one bifacial triangular point of Stillbay appearance; one notched flake; and two denticulates. Bearing in mind the general type frequency at the site, which is heavily denticulate dominated, the above tool association is significant, suggesting a special activity area.

The preferred raw material is basically the same as at Site BS-11. The General Structure of the assemblage indicates a slightly lesser stress on primary flakes and the whole Initial Group including Levallois core preparation flakes. On the other hand, Levallois pieces are more numerous (fig.

35). These characteristics, together with the lesser number of cores, suggest that most of the Levallois flakes and points as well as some other blanks must have been brought there in a finished form. This observation agrees quite well with a high index of Group VII (Tools and Tool Production Waste). Levallois technical index (IL) is higher than before, 14.3; although the value of the whole Levallois Group (IGL) is not different from previous figures, mainly because of low presence of the Levallois preparation flakes. The variability of core types is almost identical with that at Site BS-11; however, the ILam figure is slightly higher than before.

On the tool level (115 pieces), the assemblage is strongly denticulate oriented (figs. 37 and 38), especially when

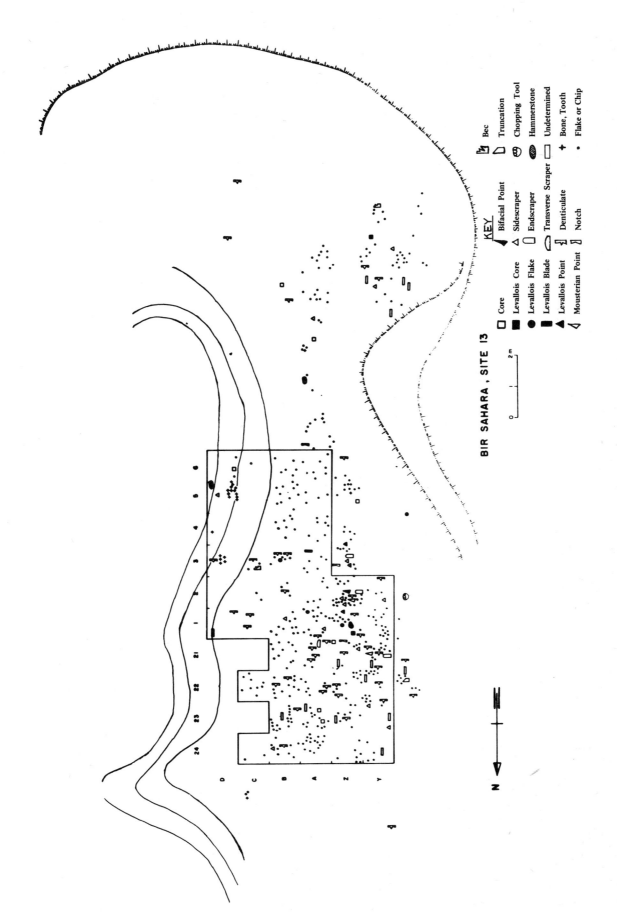

FIG. 39—Site BS-13, horizontal distribution of artifacts.

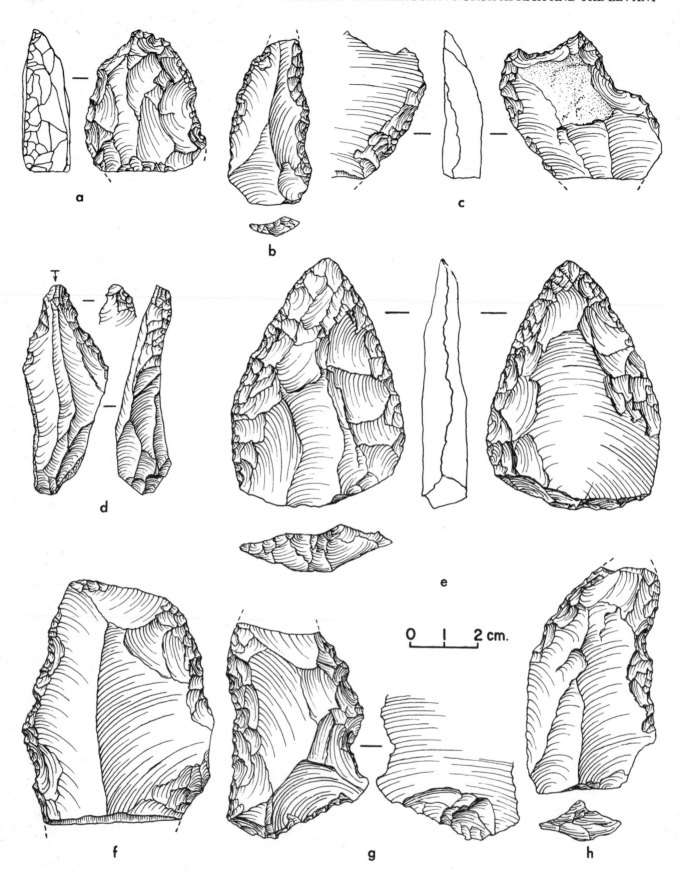

FIG. 40—Tools from Site BS-13. *a*, converging sidescraper; *b,g*, converging denticulate; *c*, bec; *d*, borer; *e*, Mousterian point; *f*, bilateral denticulate; *h*, bilateral sidescraper.

excluding from the count the mentioned activity cluster. The variability of tool types is almost the same as at Site BS-11. However, the side-scrapers are nearly twice as numerous as before, similar to the ILty figures. Upper Paleolithic elements are not abundant and mostly include end-scrapers and becs. Spheroids are not present, although some heavy hammerstones were recovered.

On the fourth horizon, at Site BS-1, two large, adjoining concentrations were recorded, almost entirely imbedded in the sediment. Both were oval in shape, approximately 30 m in diameter, and were likely overlapped in the unexcavated area. Limited excavations at one of these concentrations occupied only 50 square meters, but did furnish a good sample of spatial distribution pattern highly different from those at Sites BS-11 and BS-13. Here the density of artifacts is very prominent, reaching some 230 artifacts per square meter, of which 4.3 are tools. The distribution within the excavated area (fig. 41) does not show any significant clustering or activity areas.

The raw material preference and economy are eminently dissimilar to those observed at BS-11 and BS-13. First of all, the preferred material was a brownish quartzitic sandstone accompanied by an insignificant number of other rocks.

The observations suggested by the General Structure of the assemblage are of interest. Thus, the Initial Group (fig. 35), containing primary and early stage preparation flakes, is rather low, while the Levallois core preparation flakes run as high as over 50% of the total restricted count. These high values for the Levallois preparation flakes do not find their expected counterparts in the number of recovered Levallois cores, which is extremely low, or in the value of IL, placed at a relatively mediocre level. The implication of these anamalous proportions seems to be obvious. Most certainly, a large portion of the prepared Levallois cores had been taken away from the site, thus indicating some emphasis on the secondary workshop type of activities.

As already mentioned, cores are almost nonexistent, accounting for eight pieces, of which one was Levallois (fig. 41:1), one semi-discoidal, one globular, and one single platform for flakes.

The tool assemblage (215 pieces) is also highly denticulate dominated (fig. 41:4-7) which here seems to reach the climax, arriving at the 77.0 level (compare fig. 38). All previously identified type variations are present. Side-scrapers are very low (fig. 42:10), and the Upper Paleolithic component (fig. 42:11) runs at a level similar to that recorded before. The ILty value rises up to its highest point, slightly over the 36.0 mark (compare figs. 36 and 38).

Except for the above characteristics, some stylistic changes in the assemblage from BS-1 are observed. These refer mostly to the size of tools and blanks, which are significantly smaller than before. It is very unlikely that this change could have been explained by the observed switch in raw material preference.

On the fifth level, only the bone material suggested the existence of a settlement in the near vicinity, possibly at the shore which today is destroyed. There are no indications as to its taxonomic classification; however, a possibility that it had been a Mousterian settlement is indicated by an apparently short time gap separating the assemblage from BS-1 and the maximal aggradation of the lake.

Summarizing all taxonomic characteristics of the described Mousterian settlements, one has to stress that all of them are highly denticulate oriented and should be formally classified as the Denticulate Mousterian Variant. On the other hand, all of the noted differences separating particular assemblages demonstrate random distribution and do not show any evolutive trends when plotted on the time scale. Certainly, several of the quantitative dissimilarities, especially those touching the Levallois Group, may be explained by slightly divergent raw material economies and varying stress on workshop type activities. The tool cluster at Site BS-13, with strong characteristics of a Typical Mousterian of Levallois Facies, submerged in the strongly denticulate dominated environment, vividly suggests its functional interpretation and has far-reaching implications.

The distributional analysis of the recorded settlement samples indicates large occupied areas without any internal clustering, except for rare activity grouping observed at BS-13. Most important of all is the positive lack of any traces of clustering which could have suggested smaller homogeneous occupation units within areally extensive settlement mantles, a situation highly divergent from those found at several Upper and Late Paleolithic sites in Europe and North Africa, where scatter-patterning of artifacts was put into operation. This observation might suggest, in spite of the very limited experience with Mousterian spatial distribution of artifacts, a radically different social and/or functional patterning of the settlements from Bir Sahara from all other Middle Paleolithic settlements. Small, internally contained, homogeneous occupational units, which often make up the larger settlements of Upper or Late Paleolithic, are frequently interpreted as representing closely tied small social units partially isolated within larger structures and identified with families.

The Denticulate Mousterian from Bir Sahara is similar to those denticulate oriented assemblages reported from Nubia as well as from elsewhere. Indices of Group IV + n. 51, however, are noticeably higher than in Nubia (compare Marks, 1968, p. 282), Syria (Bordes, 1965), the Denticulate Mousterian assemblages from southwestern France (Bordes et al., 1954; Bordes, 1957, 1963; Bourgon, 1957, pp. 108-16), and all of the northwest Mediterranean Denticulate Mousterian sites, including those with Group IV slightly exceeding the 40.0 level, as at Abri Romani (compare de Lumley and Isetti, 1965; de Lumley and Ripoll-Perello, 1962; Ripoll-Perello and de Lumlev. 1965; de Lumley, 1969; etc.). It seems that only some of the Middle Paleolithic sites from the southern part of the European USSR, e.g., Kiyk-Koba, Old Drouytor, and Krouglik, often classified as Moustero-Tayacian (Gladilin, 1970, p. 270), may contain similarly high indices of denticulates and notches.

From the point of view of formal taxonomic classifica-

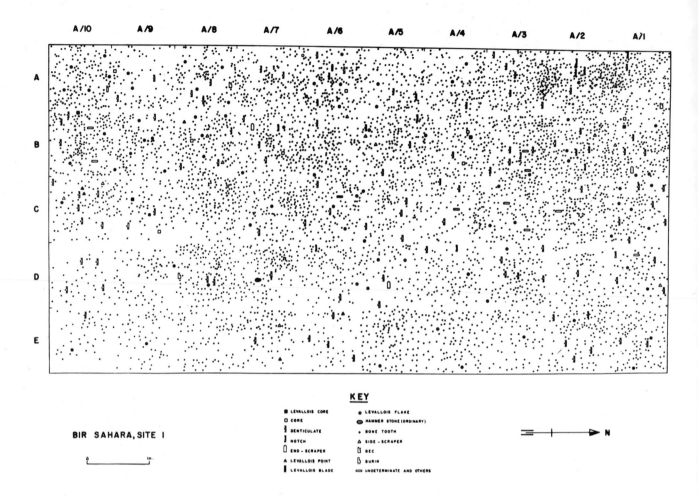

KEY

BIR SAHARA, SITE I

FIG. 41—Site BS-1, horizontal distribution of artifacts.

tion, the Denticulate Mousterian from Bir Sahara, because of its medium high Levallois technological indices, is to be placed close to the lower limit of the Levallois variant. The low blade values (ILam), small to medium sidescraper frequencies (IR), and the low Upper Paleolithic component all are well within the variability limits of the classical Denticulate Mousterian from Europe. Yet it is obvious from the technological studies that the level of Levallois indices at Bir Sahara is highly interrelated with actual employed raw material economy. Furthermore, the recovered activity cluster at Site BS-13 strongly advises a functional interpretation of the tool variability in the Mousterian of Bir Sahara, especially the significance of denticulates, converging sidescrapers, Mousterian and Levallois points.

Any comparisons with the supposedly numerous Middle Paleolithic sites in the southern Libyan Desert mentioned in the literature are practically impossible. ([Sandford, 1933]; the Gilf El Kebir and Djebel Uweinat areas [Bagnold et al., 1939; Peel and Bagnold, 1939]; and the Western Desert of Egypt [Murray, 1951; Caton-Thompson, 1952]).

CONCLUSIONS

Recent research in the Egyptian Sahara, although in its initial stage, permits limited reconstruction of climatic vari-

ations reflecting only a general tendency of climate pulsations in Eastern Sahara (fig. 43).

It seems that the sequence at hand starts with the boulder/pebbly mantle at Dakhla, near Balat. It is almost certain that the deposition of this mantle preceded the activity of the Upper Acheulean spring at E-72-1/2. Environmental circumstances of this sedimentation are unknown, although it is obvious that the dynamics of transportation must have required a high velocity for the stream. Torrential rains and relatively steep and hard depositional surfaces could have been responsible for this sedimentation.

The next noted event is the sedimentation of the oldest sands in the Bir Sahara—Bir Terfawi area, also preceding Upper Acheulean remains. Although the exact thickness of the bed is still unknown, it is presumed that it must be well over 10 meters. Preliminary studies of the grains indicate eolian transportation as the main depositional source, thus suggesting a long period of desert environment during which the Bir Sahara—Bir Terfawi basin was filled up to an elevation slightly above that of today. It is very likely that the lower sands do not form the lowest Quaternary sediment in the basin, but that some other earlier deposits may rest on the Nubia Sandstone base.

The formation of the plateau carbonate crust is most

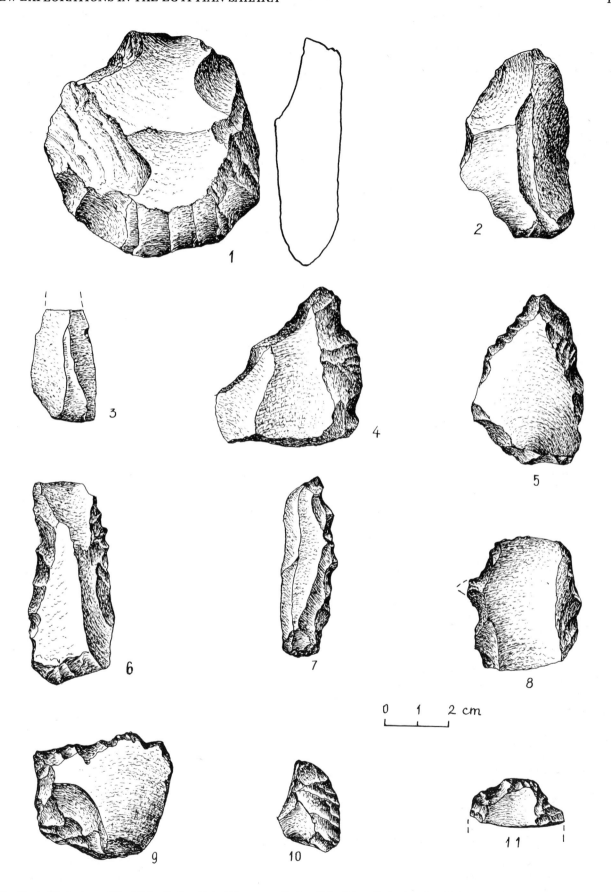

FIG. 42–Artifacts from Stie BS-1: 1) Levallois flake core; 2) Levallois flake; 3) broken Levallois point; 4) converging, asymmetric denticulate; 5) converging denticulate, inverse; 6) bilateral denticulate; 7) lateral denticulate; 8) side bec and lateral denticulate; 9) corner bec and transversal denticulate; 10) micro sidescraper, convex; 11) flat-nosed endscraper.

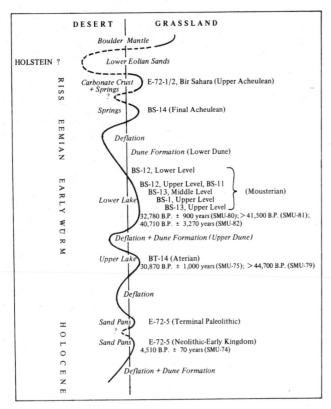

FIG. 43–Schematic climatic curve of the Egyptian Sahara and two tentative correlations with Europe.

likely connected with the beginning of spring discharge and an associated high ground water table. The origin of several springs in the *Birs* area is most certainly correlated with the birth of Acheulean springs at Kharga and Dakhla, and consequently was connected with a much greater hydrostatic pressure head. The rise of the pressure seems to be associated with increased water supply of the aquifer, not necessarily by a very local rainfall but, more likely, through the rain-catching highlands of the Gilf El Kebir Plateau and Djebel Uweinat, discharging their numerous wadis on the flats of the Libyan Sand Plain. The sloping sandstones, which certainly acted as the aquifer, dammed by the upthrown granite mass of El Tawila, formed an underground basin (compare fig. 23) with its maximal hydrostatic pressure just below the *Birs* area.

Numerous crust-filled desiccation hexagons observed on the plateau of Bir Sahara suggest a climate with considerable dryness and, most of all, marked dichotomy of the dry and wetter seasons.

The separation of the Upper Acheulean springs located on the plateau of Bir Sahara from the Final Acheulean pool at Site BS-14 by a relatively short period of deflation is not yet too well demonstrated, though quite conceivable (fig. 31). The recovered fauna suggest a dry steppe environment, yet a more expanded sample may easily change this initial impression.

A pronounced period of deflation obviously occurred after the Acheulean occupation, and several deep basins were excavated to a depth most certainly below that of the modern water table, thus indicating a huge drop of the water level in this part of the desert. Subsequently, the Bir Sahara basin was partially filled with dunes to an elevation close to 246 m above sea level at their highest crests. Most likely, the deposition of dune has been partially associated with a slightly rising water table, as suggested by the oldest Mousterian occupation, traces of which were left during the time when the dunes were still forming. Succeeding Mousterian sites in the Bir Sahara basin witness to a rising water table and, most possibly, progressing humidity of the area. However, the thick sandy beaches over which Site BS-1 is located may indicate that a certain amount of air-transported sand was still coming into the basin.

The maximal development of the Mousterian lake in Bir Sahara is possibly contemporary with a less dry grassland environment with Ethiopian fauna dominating. At that time, during its maximal stand, the lake reaches an elevation of at least 248 m above sea level. Most likely this is the very moment when the Mousterians spread more freely over the desert, as suggested by the sand pan site of E-72-4 and the lack or scarcity of settlements in the Bir Sahara area.

Quiet water with much plant growth is indicated in the depression by the recovered molluscan assemblages (Gautier, 1973, MS), while the lack of pronounced incoming wadis and numerous spring rings on the floor strongly suggest that the lake was essentially fed by spring discharge. The observed sharp fluctuations may denote "bad years" in spring activity, reflecting dry years in the rain catchment area.

It is most possible that the revival of spring activity at Bir Sahara is entirely contemporaneous with the development of new springs at Kharga, as suggested by the Levalloisian conduit of KO8A (Caton-Thompson, 1952, pp. 75-80). An increase in local rainfall is also indicated by wadi silts and tufas containing Levallois elements in Refuf Pass, near Kharga Oasis (Caton-Thompson, 1952, pp. 95, 103-5).

A progressing climatic deterioration is recorded in the receding lake and invading dunes, with better years marked by thin streaks of silts and layers of crust-cemented sand in the basal part of the younger dune at Bir Sahara. At some places, both the deflation and succeeding eolian sand deposition may mark this period of the returning desert. The depth to which the water table receded is unknown, but the entire lack of traces of human occupation could suggest a level close to modern.

Once again, a considerable rise of the water table and spring discharge caused formation of lakes with generally the same water characteristics as before (Gautier, 1973, MS). The maximal extension is certainly slightly above the 247.7 m above sea level mark. The assemblage of molluscs from the topmost lacustrine beds containing more land snails indicates fluctuations of the lake and/or progressing dryness. This interpretation is, furthermore, reinforced by the presence of a large Aterian kill area imbedded in the uppermost lake bed at Bir Terfawi, and the pedogenetically changed upper marl at BS-15.

The renewal of spring activity is also observed at Kharga, where rich Aterian assemblages were recovered from KO6E (Caton-Thompson, 1952, pp. 86-90). An increase in local rainfall is suggested by the association of Aterian sites with the so-called tufaceous pans and wadis of the Eocene Plateau in Bulaq Pass, near Kharga Oasis (Caton-Thompson, 1952, pp. 126-32).

A sizable deflation marking the obvious return of the desert and the drop of the water table is recorded at Bir Sahara as a pronounced deflation which cut through the accumulated lacustrine and preceding eolian sediment to a level two to four m higher than that of the modern water table. The recent morphology of the *Birs* area was mostly formed in that time. However, the Terminal Paleolithic sites associated with sand pans, which certainly collected rain water, denote an amelioration of the climate and possible return of the dry grassland during that period. Curiously enough, this event is not recorded in the spring-fed areas of Bir Sahara and Kharga, which may indicate an entirely different rain pattern, possibly more associated with the Nile Valley and avoiding the highlands of the Libyan Desert.

Another, possibly slight, increase in precipitation is recorded in the Dyke area by the presence of the Neolithic—Early Kingdom (?) sites, and a slightly higher water table at Bir Sahara—Bir Terfawi fluctuating around 240 m above sea level, as indicated by the location of supposedly Neolithic sites. Numerous Neolithic—Early Kingdom sites associated with huge mud and sand pans of the Nakhlal-Sheb peneplain, in the area west of Abu Simbel, certainly mark this event (Combined Prehistoric Expedition survey in March 1973).

In summary, the observed characteristics of climatic changes in the Eastern Sahara during the Upper Pleistocene seem to stress a few points of interest. First of all, it appears that this part of the desert was always relatively dry. Important changes in the environment could have been produced only by an increase in local rainfall, reinforced by the discharge of underground waters, which certainly were supplied through the rain-catching Libyan highlands. Climatic changes on the opposite side indicate the importance of deflational processes in the basin forming, a phenomenon so characteristic for the old depression of the Western Desert of Egypt (Ball, 1927; Said, 1962; Smith, 1972), and one which was again accentuated in the creation of much younger Quaternary basins.

The comparison with climatic changes recorded in other parts of Saharan Africa yields several points of similarity, although a serious lack of reliable absolute chronology prevents far-reaching conclusions. A more humid climate is apparently associated with some Upper Acheulean sites in Sahara, e.g., lacustrine beds of Tihoudaine (Arambourg and Balout, 1955). In Tunisia the increased spring activity at Sidi Zin (Gobert, 1950) may also mark this time. Similarly, the Mousterian sites of Tunisia at Ain el Guettar and Oued el Akarit, connected with spring or spring-fed organo-genic sediments (Oued el Akarit), furnished relatively rich pollen spectra (Van Campo, 1960; Van Campo and Coque, 1960; Coque, 1962) suggesting colder and moister conditions than those of today (see also discussion in Butzer, 1971, p. 320).

On a later level, some Aterian sites are also reported as associated with lacustrine sediments with pollen grains suggesting cooler and moister conditions, e.g., at Ardar Bous in Central Sahara (Quezel and Martinez, 1962). Numerous radiocarbon dates on lacustrine sediments in the Sahara, including Tchad, indicate two Early Holocene wetter fluctuations well comparable with the data from the Western Desert of Egypt (see Butzer, 1971, pp. 581-85 for summary).

It is obvious that the very essence of Late Pleistocene paleoclimates in various parts of North Africa may differ significantly according to the geographic location of the area; however, an apparent similarity of general trends is imaginable.

Comparison with Europe is certainly much more difficult and hardly possible without firm absolute dating. The extreme complexity of climates during the two last glaciations, and especially during the Würm glaciation, prohibits an exact correlation with numerous recognized and named oscillations. On the other hand, some rather wild guesses may be offered. There are several possibilities. Thus, one can correlate the Upper Acheulean spring activity with Riss and the pronounced deflations, responsible for the formation of the basins at Bir Sahara and Bir Terfawi, with the Eemian interglacial. On the other hand, one might assume that the Final Acheulean together with Mousterian should be placed in Early Würm (compare fig. 33). The present authors favor a longer chronology, allocating the Eemian Interglacial between our Acheulean and Mousterian occupations, and consequently placing the Aterian from Bir Terfawi in the Early or Lower Middle Würm (compare Camps et al., 1968, p. 15, and the dates from Dar es Soltan), thus making it at least partially contemporary with the Mousterian of Europe.

ACKNOWLEDGEMENTS

We would like to express our great appreciation to many persons who helped organize the project and carry it through. Dr. Rushdi Said, General Director of The Geological Survey of Egypt, whose assistance resolved most of the logistical problems, had also kindly offered his great scientific experience. Dr. Bahay Issawi was responsible for the excellent camp, mapping, and the endless geological discussions in which Drs. Vance Haynes and Peter Mehringer were always taking a very active role. The present authors feel that these long discussions inspired their actual understanding of the Quaternary Geology of the area. Drs. Michal Kobusiewicz, Thomas R. Hays, and Messrs. Frank A. Servello, Jacek Lech, Thomas M. Ryan, Owen Henderson, and Russ Morrison all contributed enormously to the success of the expedition.

BIBLIOGRAPHY

ABU AL-IZZ, M.S., 1971. *Landforms of Egypt*. Cairo: American University.

ARAMBOURG, C. and BALOUT, L., 1955. "L'ancien lac de Tihodaine et ses gisements préhistoriques," pp. 281-92. *Actes de la IIe session, Congrès Panafricain de Préhistoire, Alger 1952.*

BAGNOLD, R. A., MYERS, O. H.; PEEL, R. F.; and WINKLER, H. A., 1939. "An Expedition to the Gilf Kebir and Uweinat 1938." *Geographical Journal* 93:281-313.

BALL, J., 1927. "Problems of the Libyan Desert." *Geographical Journal* 70:21-38, 105-28, 209-24.

BALOUT, LIONEL, 1955. *Préhistoire de l'Afrique du Nord*. Paris: Arts et Métiers Graphiques.

BORDES, F., 1955. "Le Paléolithique inférieur et moyen de Jabrud (Syrie) et la question du Pré-Aurignacien." *L'Anthropologie* 59:486-507.

————, 1957. "Le Moustérien de Haute-Roche, comparaison statistique." *L'Anthropologie* 61:436-41.

————, 1963. "Le Moustérien à denticulés." *Archeolosski Vestnik* 13-14:43-49.

————, 1968. *The Old Stone Age*. London: Weidenfeld and Nicolson.

————, 1972. "Discussion" after Bosinski, 1972. *The Origin of Homo Sapiens*, edited by F. Bordes, p. 159. Proceedings of the Paris Symposium, 2-5 September 1969. Paris: UNESCO.

————; FITTE, P.; and BLANC, S., 1954. "L'Abri Armand Chadourne." *Bulletin de la Société Préhistorique Française* 51:229-54.

BOSINSKI, G., 1969. "Eine Variante der Micoque-Technik am Fundplatz Buhlen, Kreis Valdeck." *Jahreschrift für Mitteldeutsche Vorgeschichte* 53:59-74.

————, 1972. "Late Middle Paleolithic Groups in Northwestern Germany and Their Relations to Early Upper Paleolithic Industries." *The Origin of Homo Sapiens*, edited by F. Bordes, pp. 153-60. Proceedings of the Paris Symposium, 2-5 September 1969. Paris: UNESCO.

BOURGON, MAURICE, 1957. *Les industries moustériennes et pré-mousteriennes du Périgord*. Paris: Masson.

BUTZER, KARL W., 1971. *Environment and Archaeology*. Chicago: Aldine-Atherton Press.

CAMPS, G., 1968. "Tableau chronologique de la préhistoire récente du Nord de l'Afrique. Première synthèse des datations absolues obtenues par le Carbone 14." *Bulletin de la Société Préhistorique Française* 65:609-22.

————, and CAMPS-FABRER, H., 1972. "L'Épipaléolithique récent et le passage au Néolithique dans le Nord de l'Afrique." In *Die Anfänge des Neolithikums vom Orient bis Nordeuropa*, pp. 19-59. Cologne, Vienna: Böhlau.

————; DELIBRIAS, G.; and THOMMERET, J., 1968. "Chronologie absolue et succession des civilisations préhistoriques dans le Nord de l'Afrique." *Libyca* 16:9-28.

CATON-THOMPSON, GERTRUDE, 1952. *Kharga Oasis in Prehistory*. London: Athlone Press.

CHMIELEWSKI, W., 1968. "Early and Middle Paleolithic Sites near Arkin, Sudan." In *The Prehistory of Nubia*, edited by F. Wendorf, 1:110-47. Dallas: Fort Burgwin Research Center and Southern Methodist University Press.

————, 1969. "Ensembles Micoquo-Prondnikiens en Europe Centrale." *Geographia Polonica* 17:371-86.

COQUE, ROGER, 1962. *La Tunisie présaharienne*. Paris: A. Colin.

GAUTIER, A., 1973, MS. "Preliminary Report on Some Animal Remains from Bir Sahara—Bir Terfawi Area."

GLADILIN, V., 1970. "Les variantes techniques et les types d'industrie dans le Moustérien de la Plaine Russe et de la Crimée." *Actes 7ᵉ Congrès International des Sciences Préhistoriques et Protohistoriques, Prague 1969*, pp. 269-74.

GOBERT, E. G., 1950. "Le gisement paléolithique de Sidi Zin." *Khartago* 1:1-63.

GUICHARD, J., and GUICHARD, G., 1965. "The Early and Middle Paleolithic of Nubia: A Preliminary Report." In *Contributions to the Prehistory of Nubia*, edited by Fred Wendorf, pp. 57-116. Dallas: Fort Burgwin Research Center and Southern Methodist University Press.

————, and GUICHARD, G., 1968. "Contributions to the Study of the Early and Middle Paleolithic of Nubia." In *The Prehistory of Nubia*, edited by Fred Wendorf, 1:148-93. Dallas: Fort Burgwin Research Center and Southern Methodist University Press.

HALLET, JEAN-PIERRE, 1973. *Animal Kitabu* (Polish translation). Warsaw: Iskry.

HERMINA, M.; GHOBRIAL, M.; and ISSAWI, B., 1961. "The Geology of the Dakhla Area." *Geological Survey of Egypt* 33:1-33.

ISSAWI, B., 1971. "Geology of Dar El-Arbain, Western Desert, Egypt." *Annals of the Geological Survey of Egypt* 1:53-92.

————, 1972. "Review of Upper Cretaceous—Lower Tertiary Stratigraphy in Central and Southern Egypt." *American Association of Petroleum Geologists Bulletin* 56:1448-63.

————, 1972. MS, "Geology of the Dakhla Area."

————, 1973. MS, "Quaternary Geology of Bir Sahara, Western Desert."

KOWALSKI, S., 1967a. "Ciekawsze jabytki paleolityczne z najnowszych badan archeologicznych (1963-1965) w Jaskini Ciemnej w Ojcowie, pow. Olkusz." *Materialy Archeologiczne* 8:39-46.

————, 1967b. "Zagadnienie przejscia od paleolitu srodkowego do gornego na obszarze Polski w swietle elementow postępu technicznego." *III Sympozium Paleolityczne*, Krakow: PAU.

————, 1969. "Zagadnienie przejscia od paleolitu srodkowego do gornego w Polsce poludniowej w aspekcie postępu technicznego." *Swiatowit* 30-5-21.

KRUKOWSKI, S., 1939. "Paleolit." *Prehistoria ziem polskich*. Krakow: PAU.

de LUMLEY, HENRI, 1969. *Le Paléolithique inférieur et moyen du Midi méditerranéen dans son cadre géologique* 1. Paris: CNRS.

————, and RIPOLL-PERRELLO, E., 1962. "Le remplisage et l'industrie moustérienne de L'Abri Romani." *L'Anthropologie* 66:1-35.

————, and ISETTI, G., 1965. "Le Moustérien à denticulé tardif de la station de San Francesco (San Remo) et de la Grotte Tournal (Aude)." *Cahier ligures de la Préhistoire et d'Archeologie* 14:5-30.

MARKS, A. E., 1968. "The Mousterian Industries of Nubia." In *The Prehistory of Nubia*, edited by Fred Wendorf, 1:194-314. Dallas: Fort Burgwin Research Center and Southern Methodist University Press.

————, 1970. *Preceramic Sites*. The Scandinavian Joint Expedition to Sudanese Nubia Publications, vol. 2, edited by Torgny Save-Söderbergh. Helsinki: Scandinavian University Books.

MONOD, T., 1963. "The Late Tertiary and Pleistocene in the Sahara and Adjacent Southerly Regions." In *African Ecology and Human Evolution*, edited by F. Clark Howell and François Bourlière, pp. 117-229. Chicago: Aldine.

MURRAY, G. W., 1951. "The Egyptian Climate." *Geographical Journal* 117:422-34.

PEEL, R. F., and BAGNOLD, R. A., 1939. "Archaeology, Additional Notes." *Geographical Journal* 93:291-95.

QUEZEL, P., and MARTINEZ, C., 1962. "Premiers résultats de l'analyse palynologique de sédiments recueillis au Sahara méridional à l'occasion de la Mission Berliet." In *Mission Berliet Ténéré-Tchad*, pp. 313-21. Paris: Arts et Métiers Graphiques.

RAISZ, ERWIN, 1952. *Landform Map of North Africa*. Cambridge, Mass.

RIPOLL-PERELLO, E., and de LUMLEY, H., 1965. *El Paleolitico medio en Cataluna*. Barcelona: Diputacion Provincial de Barcelona.

SAID, RUSHDI, 1962. *The Geology of Egypt*. New York: Elsevier Publishing Co.

————; ALBRITTON, C.; WENDORF, F.; SCHILD, R.; and KOBUSIEWICZ, M., 1972*a*. "Remarks on the Holocene Geology and Archaeology of Northern Fayum Desert." *Archaeologia Polona* 13:7-22.

————; ALBRITTON, C.; WENDORF, F.; SCHILD, R.; and KOBUSIEWICZ, M., 1972*b*. "A Preliminary Report on the Holocene Geology and Archaeology of the Northern Fayum Desert." In *Playa Lake Symposium*, edited by C. C. Reeves, Jr., pp. 41-61. Lubbock: Icasals Publication No. 4.

SANDFORD, K. S., 1933. "Past Climate and Early Man in the Southern Libyan Desert." *Geographical Journal* 82:219-22.

SCHILD, R.; CHMIELEWSKA, M.; and WIECKOWSKA, H., 1968. "The Arkinian and Shamarkian Industries." In *The Prehistory of Nubia*, edited by Fred Wendorf, 1:651-767. Dallas: Fort Burgwin Research Center and Southern Methodist University Press.

SERVELLO, F. A., 1973. MS, "Site E-72-1 and Site E-72-2, Sediment Analysis and Interpretation."

SMITH, H. T. U., 1972. "Playas and Related Phenomena in the Saharan Region." In *Playa Lake Symposium*, edited by C. C. Reeves, Jr., pp. 63-87. Lubbock: Icasals Publication No. 4.

TIXIER, JACQUES, 1963. *Typologie de l'Epipaléolithique du Maghreb*. Paris: Arts et Métiers Graphiques.

————, 1967. "Procédés d'analyse et questions de terminologie concernant l'étude des ensembles industriels du Paléolithique récent et de l'Epipaléolithique dans l'Afrique du Nord-Ouest." In *Background to Evolution in Africa*, edited by W. W. Bishop and J. D. Clark, pp. 771-820. Chicago: University of Chicago Press.

VAN CAMPO, M., 1960. "Analyse pollinique des dépôts würmiens d'El Guettar (Tunisie)." *Verhandlungen der 4 International Tagung der Quartarbotaniker, Veroff. Geobotanische Institut Rubel* 134:133-35.

————, and COQUE, R., 1960. "Palynologie et géomorphologie dans le Sud tunisien." *Pollen et Spores* 2(2):275-84.

VAUFREY, RAYMOND, 1955. *Préhistoire de l'Afrique, Vol. I. Le Maghreb*. Paris: Masson.

VERMEERSCH, P., 1970. "L'Elkabien." *Chronique d'Egypte*. 45:45-67.

WENDORF, FRED, and SCHILD, ROMUALD, 1974. *A Middle Stone Age Sequence from the Central Rift Valley, Ethiopia*. Wroclaw: Ossolineum.

WETZEL, R., and BOSINSKI, G., 1969. *Die Bocksteinschmiede im Lonental*. Stuttgart.

THE ATERIAN IN NORTH AFRICAN PREHISTORY

C. Reid Ferring
Southern Methodist University

INTRODUCTION

The Aterian is a lithic complex widespread in North Africa and the Sahara. Its name is derived from the site of Bir el Ater in eastern Algeria, where Reygasse (1922) found pedunculated tools in association with a Levallois assemblage. Since that time, a large number of Aterian habitations have been located and excavated, and several interpretations of this industry and its relations to other North African industries have been presented (Caton-Thompson, 1946; Antoine, 1950; Ruhlmann, 1952; Balout, 1955). Research in the last two decades has revealed substantial data which provoke new considerations of this industry and its place in North African prehistory. This paper will examine the current status of that research.

DISTRIBUTION

The Aterian has an exceptionally wide distribution (fig. 1). It is most heavily concentrated on the Mediterranean littoral from eastern Morocco to Cap Blanc in Tunisia, on the Algero-Tunisian Plateau, and on the Moroccan Atlantic Coast north of the High Atlas (Balout, 1955; Tixier, 1967). Less numerous habitations are reported along the Wadi Saoura, south of the pre-Saharan Plateau (N. Chavaillon, 1957, 1969, 1971; J. and N. Chavaillon, 1957), and southeast into Mauritania and Mali (Hugot, 1963b, 1967; N. Chavaillon, 1956). In the Sahara proper it is located primarily near the Hoggar and Aïr massifs (Hugot, 1963a; Arambourg and Balout, 1952). Other Saharan localities include Ténéré, the northern periphery of the Tchad basin (Hugot, 1962), and the Wanyanga Kebir, east of Tibesti (Arkell, 1962). A few sites have been reported from Tripolitania (McBurney, 1967). In the Egyptian Sahara, Aterian assemblages are known from the oases of Siwa and Kharga (Caton-Thompson, 1946, 1952), Dungul (Hester and Hoebler, 1969), Jebel Uweinat (de Heinzelin, Haesaerts and Van Noten, 1969) and Bir Terfawi (Schild and Wendorf, this volume). The extensive surveys in the Nile Valley in the last decade have failed to substantiate the earlier claims for its presence there, making the Egyptian oases the eastern limit of its spread.

ORIGINS OF THE ATERIAN

There is general agreement that the Aterian had its origins in the Mousterian of northwestern Africa. This Mousterian was very sparse relative to Acheulean and Aterian habitation, with only about a dozen sites with clear Mousterian assemblages known, as well as a meager number of *possible* sites (Balout, 1965a). Most of the sites are in Tunisia, with a few in northern Algeria and Morocco. No firm claims for Mousterian in the Central Sahara have been made, yet one "Mousteroid" find near Adrar Bous in the Aïr has been indicated recently (Hall et al., 1971, p. 456).

These few Mousterian assemblages are quite homogeneous typologically, being characterized by very high proportions of sidescrapers, lower frequencies of Mousterian points and denticulates, and very low burin and endscraper frequencies. Several of these assemblages, particularly El Guettar, Ain Metherchem, and Taforalt, contain rare but typical Aterian pedunculates or bifacial foliates. All of the Mousterian assemblages exhibit a Levallois technology, with Levallois and discoidal core techniques and fairly low production of Levallois blades. The scarcity of this Mousterian, as well as the inclusion of Aterian elements within certain assemblages, obviously complicates the delineation of early Aterian manifestations from Mousterian ones, although the problems are largely theoretical.

It is not possible to approximate the absolute chronological relationships between the Mousterian and Aterian at this time. On stratigraphic evidence the age of the former may be Eemian, or within the first part of Würm, but the exact position is not firmly demonstrated (Balout, 1965a, p. 57). Also it has been argued that some contemporaneity may exist between the Mousterian and Aterian (Camps et al., 1968, p. 15). Only one radiocarbon determination has been obtained on the Mousterian, that of > 32,000 B.P. (ny-72) from Djebel Irhoud, Morocco (Ennouchi, 1962). With the exception of Taforalt (Roche, 1969), and possibly Mugharet el 'Aliya (Howe, 1967), the Mousterian cannot be clearly related stratigraphically to the Aterian. The Tunisian Mousterian habitations are largely restricted to spring deposits and are associated with mixed Ethiopian and Palearctic faunas. Palynological analysis from El Guettar indicates that the climate was deteriorating to more arid conditions from those which prevailed during the earlier and denser occupations at this site (Gruet, 1959). The faunal assemblages from the Mousterian layers at Djebel Irhoud and Mugharet el 'Aliya are exceedingly rich and suggest more favorable environmental conditions than existed in Tunisia, yet the settlement was nonetheless sparse.

The earliest Aterian is very much like the Mousterian, but with low frequencies of pedunculates. It occurs along the Mediterranean, as at Camp Franchet d'Esperey (to be discussed below), and occurs inland also, as at Ain Fritissa, located on the Wadi Moulouya in eastern Morocco. The assemblage from Ain Fritissa (table 1) is quite similar to the Mousterian from El Guettar, with the addition of low per-

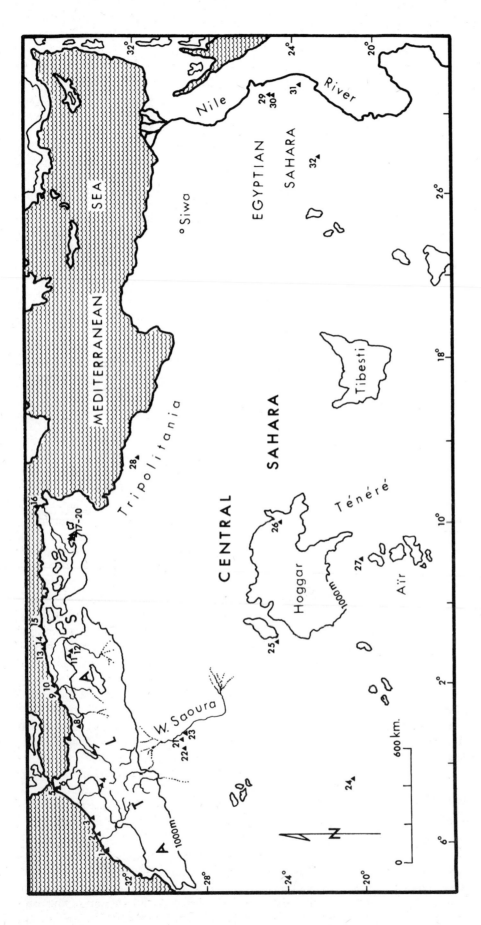

FIG. 1—Map of North Africa showing some major Aterian site localities. Contours shown are all 1,000 m above sea level.

1. Khenzira
2. Tit Mellil
3. Dar es Soltan
4. Ain Maarouf
5. Mugharet el 'Aliya
6. Station III, Merdja Seguira
7. Ain Fritissa
8. Taforalt
9. Camp Franchet d'Esperey
10. Karouba
11. Vignes Deloache
12. Pierre à Sacrifices
13. Kaouli
14. Berard
15. Ain Taya
16. Cap Blanc
17. Puits de Chaachas
18. Djouf el-Djemel
19. Oued Djebbana
20. Oued Serdiesse
21. Kheneg et Thaia
22. Anchal
23. Zaouia el Kebira
24. Mreyye
25. Meniet
26. Tiouririne
27. Adrar Bous
28. Wadi Gan
29. Kharga Oasis
30. Bulaq Pass
31. Dungul Oasis
32. Bir Sahara-Bir Terfawi

centages of pedunculates and bifacial foliates (Tixier, 1960). Like several of the Mousterian habitations in Tunisia, the occupation at Ain Fritissa is associated with a spring deposit, but it is probably representative of the beginning of the expanse of the Aterian beyond the range of Mousterian habitations. Very little is known of this earliest Aterian, however, as it is apparently as scarce as the preceding Mousterian.

The Aterian which follows this earliest phase is that which has the full distribution mentioned earlier. This "typical" or developed Aterian has been defined as a facies of the Mousterian characterized by Levallois debitage (often with numerous blades with faceted platforms), numerous sidescrapers, relatively abundant points, more endscrapers than other facies of the Mousterian, and a "non-negligible" portion of the pedunculated tools (Tixier, 1967, p. 795). Some typical Aterian artifacts are shown as Figure 2. This definition must be tempered by the presence of phases (diachronic) and facies (synchronic) within the Aterian itself. The delineation of phases within the Aterian on the basis of typological changes has been applied by several authors. Here the use of the term *phase* is used in only a general sense and is not intended to conform to any of the numbered or lettered schemes presented elsewhere. The lack of control over functional or regional variations make clear division of phases on the basis of typological seriation dangerous at this time.

TEMPORAL AND REGIONAL DEVELOPMENT OF THE ATERIAN

In the Northwest Sahara a series of Aterian habitations has been defined and located within the local Saouran sequence, which appears to span the greater part of Würm (J. Chavaillon, 1964; see Butzer, 1971, pp. 317-18 for discussion). The Aterian in the Saoura area occurs in Unit I and the lower part of Unit II of the five-unit Saouran sedimentation cycle (J. Chavaillon, 1964, pp. 190-244). Samples from a lignite within Unit II at Bou Hadid have provided two radiocarbon dates which allow a minimal determination of the age of the Aterian in this area of the Sahara. These are > 38,000 B.P. (I-1761) and > 39,900 B.P. (I-1787) (Alimen, Beucher, and Conrad, 1966, p. 5). The stratigraphic hiatus between Late Acheulean and Aterian in this area (N. and J. Chavaillon, 1957, 1962), in addition to the absence of any Mousterian sites, points toward an introduction into the northwestern Sahara, and probably into the Central Sahara as well, of an Aterian population, not simply its cultural traits.

Pollen analysis from Saoura indicates that this population occurred when a more Mediterranean-type climate prevailed there, but that aridification set in after the Aterian occupation (Alimen, Beucher, and Conrad, 1966, p. 7). Additional dates from this sequence, along with small pollen samples, indicate that deposition of Unit II may have continued until as late as about 33,000 B.P., and that at about that time another brief humid phase may have set in.

Aterian artifacts are apparently restricted to the lower part of that unit, however, suggesting that only the earlier part of the Unit II sequence is applicable to dating Aterian habitation of this area.

The assemblages from the northwestern Sahara exhibit a fair amount of typological variability. The assemblage from Zaouia el Kebira has been placed stratigraphically between Units I and II; it has quite rare Upper Paleolithic tool elements, but the increase in pedunculates and denticulates over the frequencies found at Ain Fritissa is striking (N. Chavaillon, 1971). This assemblage, along with many of the others (table 1), illustrates a trait common to the Aterian—that of a much lower frequency of scrapers than has been seen in all of the Mousterian assemblages from northwestern Africa. Endscrapers and pedunculates achieve even higher frequencies at several other sites from this area, especially at Kheneg et Tlaia (N. Chavaillon, 1957), but almost all of the scrapers are still made on flakes. Sites in the vicinity of Mreyye in the western Sahara (Chavaillon and Fabre, 1968), and also the site at Anchal (N. Chavaillon, 1956) have almost equal proportions of endscrapers and sidescrapers, while the latter site also has a quite high percentage of points. This variability found within the assemblages from the western and northwestern Sahara is difficult to assess at this time. Stricter chronological control is needed here, as elsewhere, to determine what synchronic variability may exist in any region of Aterian occupation. Functional factors could, and most probably did, require different tool inventories in synchronous habitation of areas as widespread and ecologically variable as those where Aterian sites occur. In any event, the presence of Aterian assemblages greater than 40,000 years ago is documented quite firmly for the northwestern Sahara. Evidence from other areas now offers other confirmation of this minimal age for Aterian industries.

Recent work in the Egyptian Sahara has recovered Aterian assemblages from the Bir Sahara—Bir Terfawi area, associated with the upper lacustrine unit (Schild and Wendorf, this volume). This occupation is stratigraphically above the Mousterian occupations in this area. Some initial radiocarbon samples from the upper lacustrine unit at Bir Sahara have provided two readings—30,870 B.P. ± 1,000 years (SMU-75) and > 44,700 years B.P. (SMU-79)—(Wendorf, personal communication). The younger date is from a sample found partially on the surface and possibly contaminated by more recent carbonates. The earlier date came from a sample fully *in situ* and is probably the more accurate of the two. Further excavation should clarify the dates, as well as provide data on the assemblages which have only been inspected in the field thus far. However, these dates tentatively confirm the Middle Würm or older age for the Aterian habitation there, an age which is complementary to that determined in the northwestern Sahara. Like the Aterian in the northwestern Sahara, that of the Egyptian Sahara also seems to be marked by considerable variability among the reported assemblages. Two of the Aterian

TABLE 1
Selected Essential Tool Frequencies and Available Technological Indices†
from Aterian Sites in North Africa

	Mousterian Points	Sidescrapers	Endscrapers	Burins	Denticulates	Bifacial foliates	Pedunculates	IL	IF	IFs	Ilam
Morocco											
Ain Fritissa (1720)	5.7	63.3	3.3	0.5	8.3	2.7	1.1		54.9	43.4	
Taforalt H (158)	3.1	61.0	7.5			1.3	0.0	36.3	65.5	53.7	29.7
Taforalt F(?)	2.1	41.3	8.0		9.5	0.8	1.3	32.0	64.9	49.7	28.4
Taforalt D(?)		27.2	15.9			12.5	4.5	42.2	69.3	50.0	28.3
Dar es Soltan											
I (96)	4.1	40.6	5.2	0.0	11.5	2.1	30.2	36.1	51.7	41.4	20.0
C_2(121)	4.1	36.4	0.0	1.7	9.9	3.3	24.8	29.1	49.0	30.0	13.7
Mugharet el Aliya											
6 (503)	14.9	17.1	0.4			14.3	1.2				
5 (270)	24.4	17.4	0.4			2.6	2.2				
Maghreb											
Pierre à Sacrifices (143)	9.1	79.0	5.6			0.0	5.6				
Vignes Deloache (220)	0.0	64.0	11.8			1.8	16.8				
West and Northwest Sahara											
Zaouia el Kebira (693)	4.0	28.3	4.0	3.6	24.8	0.1	11.8	20.2	39.1	21.8	12.9
Anchal (226)	13.7	12.4	11.5	2.7	14.2	6.6	19.5		54.0	53.5	
Point I, Mreyye (84)	1.2	10.7	8.3	0.0	25.0	1.2	14.3	11.0	31.0	13.0	24.0
Kheneg et Tlaïa (135)	6.7	4.4	20.7	2.2	8.1		28.1				
Central Sahara											
Meniet (223)*	1.3	17.0	28.3		5.4	few	3.1		81.3	75.4	
Egyptian Sahara											
Dungul 8735 (73)	0.0	6.9	6.9	5.5	19.2	0.0	1.4	26.1	75.0	55.9	16.3
Dungul 8708 (60)	3.3	16.7	11.7	0.0	10.0	1.7	11.7	25.0	76.1	41.3	19.6

†Blanks indicate index unavailable. See text for discussion of regional variability and of sites not shown here. Compiled with modifications from Tixier, 1960; Roche, 1956, 1969; Howe, 1967; de Bayle des Hermens, 1964, 1965; N. Chavaillon, 1956, 1957, 1971; Chavaillon and Fabre, 1968; Hugot, 1962; Marks, n.d.

*Varia removed from sample.

sites from Dungul Oasis (Hester and Hoebler, 1969; Marks, n. d.) illustrate, despite the small tool sample sizes, general Aterian characteristics, while the differences in frequencies of certain tools, particularly pedunculates and denticulates, may reflect functional variability. The Aterian industries from Site KO6e at Kharga Oasis and from Site A near Bulaq Pass (Caton-Thompson, 1952, pp. 86-90; 126-32) also show marked variability, particularly in the frequencies of scrapers and pedunculates. The former site has an abundance of pedunculates and few scrapers, while the reverse is found at Bulaq Pass. Both of these sites exhibit a dominance of endscrapers or end/sidescrapers over sidescrapers, a trait which also is present at Wadi Gan in Tripolitania (McBurney and Hey, 1955, pp. 225-29).

It is clear that considerably more information is needed for a fuller understanding of the appearance of Aterian industries in the Egyptian Sahara as well as in Tripolitania and Cyrenaica. The dates from Bir Sahara, though in need of clarification, indicate an age for these assemblages at least as great as those found in the northwestern Sahara, though the relative periods of occupation for these two areas cannot be determined. Without doubt they confirm the quite early presence of Aterian influences a tremendous distance from their origin. While a stratigraphic hiatus separates the Aterian material from the Mousterian at Bir Terfawi, the state of habitation at the Egyptian oases at the time Aterian influences appear is not established firmly. That populations were well established throughout this time period in Cyrenaica (McBurney, 1967), and most probably in the Nile Valley as well, makes the delineation of the mechanisms by which these Aterian influences entered the area exceedingly problematical. A few artifacts suggestive of Aterian influence have been found in levels XXXI/XXX at Haua Fteah, dated between 41,450 B.C. ± 1,300 years and 45,050 B.C. ± 3,200 years (GrN-2564, GrN-2023) (McBurney, 1967). This sample of artifacts is unfortunately small and allows no confirmation of its being "Aterian," but the age of that sample is now quite well within the range one would expect for Aterian influences in that area.

Aterian assemblages of at least two phases occur in the Algerian and Tunisian coastal deposits upon the Tyrrhenian beach deposits and within the red silts and sands above them. The stratigraphic position of the late Aterian in these deposits west of Algiers has been clarified recently by Roubet (1969). In that area two silt layers, separated by a regressional dune deposit, are superimposed above the *Strombus* beach. The upper silt which contains the Aterian in that locality is marked by crusting at its top, is surmounted by another dune, and is finally capped by various Late Upper Pleistocene and post-Pleistocene soils and sands containing Epipaleolithic and Neolithic industries (Roubet, 1969, p. 126). A date of 31,800 B.P. ± 1,900 years (I-3951) has been obtained from the Aterian at this locality (Hebrard, 1970, p. 41). This evidence greatly strengthens the argument that the Aterian found upon the beach and within the silt directly over it at Camp Franchet d'Esperey belongs to a phase which is early Würm in age, as has been contended for some time on the basis of stratigraphic evidence (Camps, 1955). The assemblage from Camp Franchet d'Esperey is characterized by Mousterian points, a dominance of sidescrapers over endscrapers, and moderately frequent pedunculates. Aterian artifacts in a similar stratigraphic position are recorded at Karouba (Vaufrey, 1955). The assemblages from Pierre à Sacrifices and Vignes Deloache (Bayle des Hermens, 1964, 1965), appear to have typological affinities to the early Aterian of the coastal region, but chronological relations cannot be established.

The late Aterian of the coast is poorly described (Marchand and Ayme, 1935; Vaufrey, 1955), yet several sites to the east in the Tebessa region appear to exhibit facies of the late Aterian. All of these sites have abundant pedunculates and a high incidence of Levallois blades (Balout, 1955; Tixier, 1967). Endscrapers are more common than sidescrapers at such sites as Oued Djebbana (Balout, 1955, p. 287) and Djouf el-Djemel (Le Du, 1934), yet other assemblages including Puits de Chaachas (Balout, 1955, p. 294) and Oued Serdiesse (Balout, 1955, pp. 300-301) have a dominance of sidescrapers over endscrapers. Chronological controls over these sites are inadequate to clarify the relationships between these assemblages, and either temporal or functional factors may again be involved. These sites most likely represent a facies of the late Aterian present at Taforalt cave in eastern Morocco (Roche, 1969). Levallois blades are abundant there as well, and while sidescrapers are more frequent than endscrapers, the latter are common nonetheless. This assemblage also has a dominance of bifacial foliates over pedunculates, a trait which is not evident in the sites to the east. This terminal layer from Taforalt has provided two radiocarbon dates—30,400 B.C. and 32,600 B.C. (Camps, this volume).

As proposed by Balout, western Morocco does not seem to have evidence of early Aterian habitation, and Mousterian sites are exceedingly rare as well (Balout, 1955, p. 312; 1965a, pp. 46-50). The Aterian of that area is known largely from cave deposits ascribed to the Soltanian continental cycle (Biberson, 1970, pp. 63-67). These have provided several stratified Aterian assemblages associated with abundant faunal samples, particularly from Mugharet el 'Aliya (Howe, 1967), Dar es Soltan (Ruhlmann, 1951; Roche, 1956), El Khenzira (Ruhlmann, 1936; Caton-Thompson, 1946; Vaufrey, 1955), and the spring deposit of Tit Mellil (Antoine, 1938; Arambourg, 1938). On the basis of several bifacial tanged and shouldered points (Moroccan and/or pseudo-Saharan points), the assemblages from the upper Aterian layers at Mugharet el 'Aliya and Dar es Soltan have been viewed as the most highly evolved, and—at the former site—just "pre-Neolithic" (Antoine, 1950). This argument no longer seems tenable. Similar point forms from the upper Aterian layer at Dar es Soltan have been dated to >27,000 B.P. (UCLA-678B), and the analogously high proportion of foliated artifacts is present at Taforalt at a similarly early date. The Aterian layers from Mugharet el 'Aliya are undated, but both are part of the same depositional sequence, with the upper layer being weathered, indicating a hiatus between it and the surmounting Neolithic layer (Howe, 1967, p. 146).

The assemblages from western Morocco display some internal variability and some general dissimilarity from the Algerian Aterian. They are characterized at Dar es Soltan in layers I and C_2 by a dominance of sidescrapers over endscrapers in the lower layer and a total absence of endscrapers in the upper. Both have very high frequencies of pedunculates and low foliate frequencies (Roche, 1956). The lower Layer (I) has been dated > 30,000 B.P. (UCLA-678A). Endscrapers are exceedingly rare in the Aterian

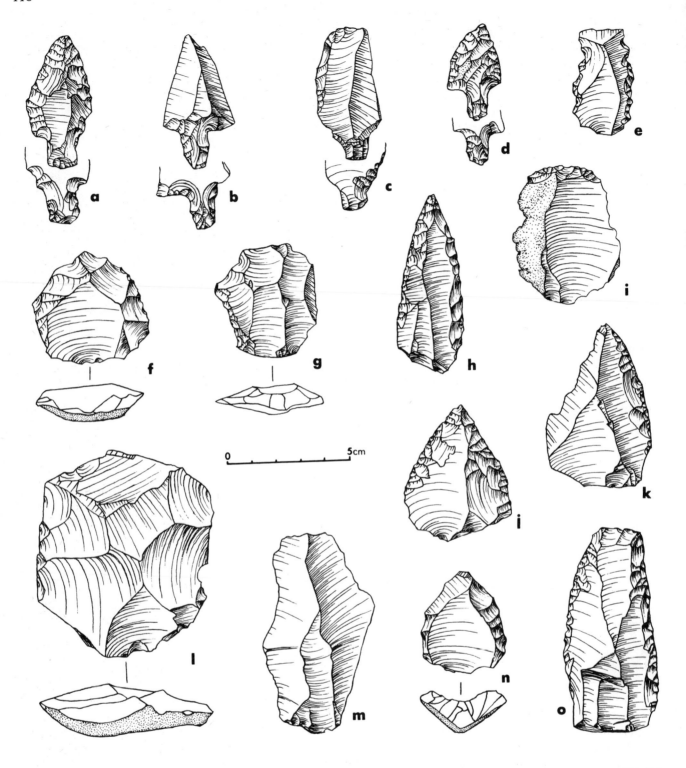

FIG. 2—Aterian artifacts from Zaouia el Kebira: *a, b, d*—pedunculated points; *c*—pedunculated scraper; *e*—denticulate; *f*—Levallois flake core; *g*—Levallois flake; *h*—elongated Mousterian point; *i*—endscraper; *j*—Mousterian point; *k*—simple sidescraper; *l*—Mousterian discoidal core; *m*—Levallois blade; *n*—Levallois point core; *o*—double sidescraper. (Redrawn from N. Chavaillon, 1971.)

from Mugharet el 'Aliya, while the low sidescraper index seems to be due to differences in classification (McBurney, 1960, p. 184). Open-air sites in western Morocco seem to bear strong affinities with the cave assemblages. Tit Mellil, a spring deposit southeast of Casablanca, contains two Aterian layers which exhibit distinct changes in the frequencies of scrapers. These are dominated in the lower layer (B) by sidescrapers, while in the upper layer (A) the total scraper index drops, and endscrapers become very rare. Both have low foliate and pedunculate frequencies. A small sample of artifacts from an *in situ* Aterian habitation, Station III, Merdja Seguira, associated with a lacustrine deposit south of Cap Ashakar, shows a similar dominance of sidescrapers (Howe, 1967, p. 147). An undescribed "typical" Aterian assemblage from Ain Maarouf has been dated to 32,000 B.P. ± 600 years (GrN-3165) (Choubert et al., 1967, p. 435).

The dates from Dar es Soltan, Ain Maarouf, and Taforalt are all indicative of a rather ubiquitous appearance of the last phase of the Aterian, one which is considerably earlier than had been proposed before. Termination of the Aterian habitation in this area as well as others will be discussed below.

Discussion of the Aterian on the Central and southern Sahara has been delayed to this point because it is the most poorly known region in terms of Aterian habitation, and also because it has been claimed to be among the latest of Aterian occupations (Balout, 1955, p. 312; Hugot, 1967). Sites are apparently always associated with swamp or lacustrine deposits, and in most cases artifacts are not found *in situ*, but heavily rolled or wind-abraded. Recent work in the Aïr has located several *in situ* Aterian sites in silts overlain by eolian sand. They are characterized by the Levallois and discoidal core technique, blades made by direct percussion, sometimes having faceted platforms, side- and endscrapers, some of which are denticulated, and some pedunculates and lanceolate bifaces. Rare burins and spheroids were also found (Hall et al., 1971, p. 456). These assemblages promise to offer new information concerning the occupation of this area, and to clarify the problematic nature of similar assemblages from other Central Saharan locations. The above assemblages appear to bear strong affinities to those reported from Meniet (Hugot, 1962, pp. 48-70), which has low frequencies of pedunculates and quite common endscrapers, many of which are denticulated. Spheroids, or bolas, occur with these Central Saharan assemblages, as well as at Anchal and Zaouia el Kebira in the northwestern Sahara and at one site, Puits de Chaachas, in eastern Algeria. (Their association with sites in desertic or semi-arid environments is an interesting contrast to the more western Aterian, and is suggestive of a hunting technique adapted to an open environment. They also occurred in a great heap at the Mousterian site of El Guettar in Tunisia [Gruet, 1955]).

The stratigraphic position of the Aterian in the Central Sahara is exceedingly problematical. No absolute dates have been obtained as yet on *in situ* assemblages, although the horizontal association of Aterian artifacts with lacustrine deposits has resulted in the tendency to apply dates from those deposits to the artifacts. This practice is unsound and can lead to seemingly erroneous conclusions. The number of dates on Saharan lacustrine deposits indicate that they were being formed much earlier than the often quoted dates from Fachi initially indicated. One of these dates was 21,350 B.P. ± 350 years (T340B) (van Zinderen Bakker, 1966, p. 126). That date correlates with the end of lacustrine depositions in the Tchad basin to the south of Fachi, which is followed by about ten millennia of aridity accom-

panied by eolian deposition (Servant, Servant, and Delibrias, 1969; Servant and Servant-Vildary, 1972). Carbondated lacustrine deposits from the Erg Chech and the Ahnet-Mouydir basin indicate that these lacustrine depositions began as early as about 35,000 B.P., making correlation of Aterian artifacts with simply "lacustrine" deposits entirely ambiguous (Conrad, 1969b). Only the dating of Aterian assemblages in firm contexts will clarify these ambiguities. Rognon in 1967 (summarized by Butzer, 1971, pp. 327-29) outlined a climatic sequence for the Hoggar and placed Aterian occupation there sometime after the arid interval following late Acheulean habitation. Aterian habitation in the lower elevations around Hoggar are associated with lacustrine deposits such as those found at Tiouririne, where Aterian artifacts occur in derived positions stratigraphically below a pre-Neolithic diatomite (Arambourg and Balout, 1952, p. 285).

Surface collections of Aterian artifacts which are often found in close proximity to Neolithic sites where mixture (particularly of the bifacial projectile points known to both industries) is a problem, can lead to equally ambiguous, if not wholly misleading, conclusions. The greater than 40,000 year age of the Aterian assemblages in the northwestern Sahara can be viewed as a minimum age for the introduction into the Central Sahara of this industry, although typological comparisons suggest that it could have been somewhat later. The latter, however, are unsatisfactory for solving the problem. The apparent hiatus, though not extensively defined as yet, between Late Acheulean and Aterian assemblages in both the northwestern and Central Sahara (J. Chavaillon, 1964; Arambourg and Balout, 1952; Rognon, 1967), points strongly toward a migration into the Sahara by Aterian populations.

The higher elevations of the Central Sahara have functioned as biotic refuges during the Pleistocene (Van Campo et al., 1964), and conditions during Main Würm there were apparently cold, with conditions elsewhere in the Sahara evidently arid (Butzer, 1971, pp. 328-33). Yet the possibility that these highlands served as a cultural refuge throughout this period, and until the appearance of the technologically distinct Neolithic or pre-Neolithic industries, seems remote and is at this time without convincing stratigraphic, or any radiometric, evidence for support. The age and duration of the Aterian of the Central Sahara is, in any event, up to further research to clarify; one certainly looks forward to the continuation and products of that research.

In the Egyptian Sahara, Aterian settlement is followed by a period of pronounced deflation with no reoccupation of the springs in the Bir Sahara—Bir Terfawi region until the Terminal Paleolithic (Schild and Wendorf, this volume). This hiatus is also evidenced at Dungul Oasis, which was abandoned following Aterian habitation and not reoccupied until the appearance of a "Libyan Culture," with a developed blade technology and ground stone (Hester and Hoebler, 1969). A date of 5,950 B.C. ± 150 years (WSU-

TABLE 2

SOME FAUNAS FROM MOUSTERIAN AND ATERIAN SITES
IN NORTHWEST AFRICA †

	*MUGHARET el ALIYA 9	*DJEBEL IRHOUD	Tit Mellil	Dar es Soltan I	Dar es Soltan C	Mugharet el Aliya 6	Mugharet el Aliya 5	El Khenzira	Ain Taya	Taforalt H, F, D	Ain Fritissa	*RETAIMIA	*SIDI ZIN	Ain Metherchem	El Guettar	Puits de Chaachas	Wadi Djebbana
Elephas antiquus			+														
Elephas sp.	+					+	+										
Rhinoceras sp.				+							+						
Rhinoceras simus			+							+					+		
Rhinoceras mercki	+	+				+		+		+					+	+	
Equus mauritanicus	+	+	+	+	+	+	+	+	+	+	+	+	+	+	+	+	+
Equus asinus (?)		+															
Hippopotamus amphibius	+		+	+		+											
Sus scrofa	+		+		+	+		+									
Sus sp.									+								
Phacochoerus africanus	+			+		+	+	+									
Bos primigenius	+	+	+	+	+	+	+	+		+	+	+	+	+	+		
Alcephalus buselaphus	+	+	+	+	+	+	+	+	+	+		+	+	+	+		+
Homioceras antiquus		+		?		+		+									
Ovis aries	+						+										
Ammotragus lervia	+			+						+	+	+		+			
Conn. (Gorgon) taurinus	+	+	+		+	+		+				+			+	+	
Redunca sp.							+										
Cervus algericus	+		+													+	
Taurotragus oryx	+		+														
Gazella dorcas	+	+			+	+	+	+				+					
Gazella cuvieri	+	+				+	+			+		+			+		
Gazella atlantica	+	+				+	+	+	+								
Gazella rufina	+	+					+										
Gazella tingitana	+	+				+	+										
Gazella sp.			+	+													
Capra sp.												+					
Felis leo	+					+	+										
Felis pardus	+			?	+	+			+				+				
Hyaena striata	+					+	+			+							
Hyaena crocuta	+	+	+			+	+	+									
Hyaena sp.																+	
Canis anthus	+	+	+	+		+	+	+	+								
Camelus thomasi										+					+	+	
Vulpes vulpes atlant.	+		+	+	+	+	+	+	+								
Hystrix cristata	+	+	+	+	+	+	+	+									
Struthio camelus		+															

† Compiled with modification from Dolloni, 1952; Ennouchi, 1962; Gruet, 1955; Howe, 1967; Roche, 1952; Ruhlmann, 1951; Tixier, 1960; Vaufrey, 1955.

* Mousterian Sites indicated by All Cap Type.

316) has been recorded for this culture (Hester, 1968, p. 498). A period of hyperaridity between ca. 27,000 and 17,000 B.P. is recorded for this area by Butzer (1971, p. 332) which appears to be coeval with the cultural hiatus at the oases.

In the far western Sahara an analogous period of aridity is recorded following the Inchirian transgression in Senegal. The last phase of that transgression, dated between 32,000 and 31,000 B.P., is followed by a period of heavy dune formation and the transition of the Senegal River to an internal drainage. This aridity lasted there until some time after 20,000 B.P. (see van Zinderen Bakker, 1969, pp. 103-4, and Butzer, 1971, pp. 329-30, for summaries; Faure and Elouard, 1967, for dates).

Van Campo and Coque (1960) have characterized "pluvial" conditions in Tunisia as semi-arid periods with cold winters. For the presumably Early Würm spring deposits at the Mousterian site of El Guettar, their pollen analysis indicates about 10% arboreal pollens, which are dominated by cedar and cyprus, indicative of conditions more humid than are now present in the area. At Ain Brimba the pollen spectrum contains even fewer arboreal pollens (ca. 4%). These are of a different character from those of the El Guettar sample, having a fair representation of pine. The inclusion of "Upper Paleolithic" implements with the Mousterian artifacts led the authors to apply the same climatic conditions to that period (Van Campo and Coque, 1960, p. 281). The deposits near Oued el Akarit containing Mousterian and Iberomaurusian assemblages (Gobert, 1962) revealed a pollen spectrum with 2% arboreal pollens, with pine also well represented. It seems probable that these latter two pollen samples contain elements present at the time of Iberomaurusian occupations (late Würm). The Würm climatic sequence for Cyrenaica proposed by Hey (1963) suggests correlations here with a moist early Würm, with contemporary Mousterian habitation, and a drier and colder Main Würm. Climatic conditions shortly after the latter phase would have been cooler than after the moister early Würm. Very cold conditions during Würm, resulting in glaciation of the Jurjura Mountains southeast of Algiers (Butzer, 1971, p. 295), are probably correlated with the very cold conditions described for the Main Würm in the Hoggar (Rognon, 1967).

The stratigraphic hiatus which is apparent between the Aterian and the Iberomaurusian assemblages in northwestern Africa, on the basis of available radiometric datings, coincides with the period of an apparently cold and dry Main Würm. Available data certainly imply these conditions during this period, as the arid conditions suggested elsewhere in the Sahara, although substantial evidence, particularly palynological, is obviously needed to substantiate them. These conditions are suggested here as a possible explanatory factor for the apparent abandonment of the Eastern Atlas and coastal regions prior to the arrival of the Iberomaurusian, as suggested on stratigraphic evidence by Balout (1955, p. 309). Radiometric evidence now supports

this as well. Subsequent to terminal Aterian occupations in the Berard area, and also at Taforalt, both dated to about 32,000 B.P., sterile depositions in the form of crusting and dune deposition at the former, and a thin layer of roof fall at the latter, separate Aterian from the later industries. Dates for the Iberomaurusian at Taforalt (Camps et al., 1968; Camps, this volume) indicate that this hiatus was of considerable duration. The final Aterian at Dar es Soltan is followed by a sterile accumulation, and then by an industry which has been dated to 5,860 B.P. ± 70 years (GrN-2805) (Maarleveled, 1964, p. 355). A thin layer of roof fall separates the Aterian from the Iberomaurusian at El Khenzira and at Mugharet el 'Aliya. Howe proposes that there was probably a hiatus with either little sedimentation or scouring of the upper surface of layer 5 corresponding to the low sea level of Main Würm (1967, p. 146). Typological comparisons with other western Moroccan assemblages are not demonstrative of any technological changes beyond those exhibited by the material from Dar es Soltan or Mugharet el 'Aliya.

Distinct faunal changes in this area with loss of certain palearctic species, documented by Arambourg (1962), occurred between the Aterian and Iberomaurusian periods. This may reflect either climatic changes during that interval or, possibly, increased pressure from an Aterian population inhabiting a more restricted western Moroccan environment. The disappearance of several species from the faunal assemblages between the lower and upper Aterian habitations at Dar es Soltan and Mugharet el 'Aliya (table 2) may indicate that process could have been happening just prior to the termination of Aterian habitation of those caves.

CONCLUSIONS

The Aterian is one of the most widely distributed Paleolithic industries of North Africa, extending from the Atlantic almost to the Nile Valley and throughout much of the Sahara. It had its origins in the Mousterian of North Africa, sometime in the Early Würm, with radiometric evidence for its spread from its place of origin in excess of 40,000 years ago. During this spread the Aterian lithic complex maintained the same Levallois-based technology and production of pedunculated and foliated artifacts. Regional differentiation may be observed, but present data do not permit assessment of the functional and temporal variables which undoubtedly will explain much of this variability.

Other radiometric and stratigraphic evidence indicates that the final facies of the Aterian occur prior to the Main Würm, a period which is evidenced in several areas of North Africa by markedly colder and drier conditions than had existed in Early Würm. In northwestern Africa a hiatus from about 30,000 B.P. to about 15,000 B.P. apparently existed between the final Aterian and the introduction of Epipaleolithic populations. At the least, a rather pronounced decrease in the size of Aterian populations is implied during this period. In the eastern Sahara the hiatus at the oases seems to extend into the Holocene, when these areas were reoccupied by radically different groups. Evidence from the Central Sahara does not offer any firm support for the persistence of Aterian habitation until the arrival of the quite distinct Holocene industries, yet no radi-

ometric or clear stratigraphic evidence is available to define the range of Aterian occupation there.

The evidence thus far indicates that further study of Aterian subsistence patterns and culture change is highly warranted and would contribute greatly to our understanding of the prehistory of North Africa.

BIBLIOGRAPHY

ALIMEN, H.; BEUCHER, F.; and CONRAD, G., 1966. "Chronologie du dernier cycle pluvial-aride au Sahara nord-occidental." *Comptes Rendus des Séances de l'Academie des Sciences* 263:5-8.

ANTOINE, M., 1938. "Notes de préhistoire marocaine. Un cone de resurgence du Paléolithique moyen à Tit Mellil, près de Casabalanca." *Bulletin de la Société de Préhistoire du Maroc* 4:1-4.

————, 1950. "L'Atérien du Maroc atlantique, sa place dans la chronologie Nord-Africaine." *Bulletin de la Société Préhistoire du Maroc* ns 1950:5-47.

ARAMBOURG, C., 1938. "La faune fossile de l'Ain Tit Mellil (Maroc)." *Bulletin de la Société Préhistorique Française* 12:97-101.

————, 1962. "Les faunes mammalogiques du Pléistocène Circumméditerranéan." *Quaternaria* 6:97-109.

————, 1965. "Le gisement Moustérien et l'Homme du Jebel Irhoud (Maroc)." *Quaternaria* 7:1-8.

————, and BALOUT, L., 1955. "L'ancien lac de Tihodaine et ses gisements préhistoriques," pp. 281-93. *Actes de la IIe session, Congrès Panafricain de Préhistoire, Alger, 1952*. Paris: Arts et Métiers Graphiques.

ARKELL, A. J., 1962. "The Aterian of Great Wanyanga (Ounianga Kebir)." In *Actes du IVe Congrès panafricain de préhistoire et de l'étude du Quaternaire, Léopoldville, Congo, 1959, section 3, pré- et protohistoire*, edited by G. Mortelmans and J. Nenquin, pp. 233-42. Tervuren, Belgium: Musée royal de l'afrique centrale.

BALOUT, LIONEL, 1955. *Préhistoire de l'Afrique du Nord*. Paris: Arts et Métiers Graphiques.

————, 1965a. "Le Moustérien du Maghreb." *Quaternaria* 7:43-58.

————, 1965b. "Données nouvelles sur le problème du Moustérien en Afrique du Nord." *Actas del V Congreso Panafricano de Prehistoria y de estudio del Cuaternario, Tenerife, 1963* 1:137-45.

de BAYLE des HERMENS, R., 1964. "Les industries préhistoriques de la station de 'La Pierre à sacrifices.' Tiaret (Algérie)." *Libyca* 12:72-94.

————, 1965. "L'Atérien des Vignes Deloache à Guertoufa, Tiaret (Algérie)." *Libyca* 13:59-81.

BIBERSON, P., 1970. "Index Cards on the Marine and Continental Cycles of the Moroccan Quaternary." *Quaternaria* 13:1-76.

BUTZER, KARL W., 1971. *Environment and Archaeology*. Chicago and New York: Aldine-Atherton Press.

CAMPS, G., 1955. "Le gisement Atérien du Camp Franchet d'Esperey." *Libyca* 3:17-56.

————; DELIBRIAS, G.; and THOMMERET, J., 1968. "Chronologie absolue et succession des civilisations préhistoriques dans le Nord de l'Afrique." *Libyca* 16:9-28.

CATON-THOMPSON, G., 1946. "The Aterian Industry: Its Place and Significance in the Paleolithic World." *Huxley Memorial Lecture, Journal of the Royal Anthropological Institute* 76(2):87-130.

————, 1952. *Kharga Oasis in Prehistory*. London: Athlone Press.

CHAVAILLON, JEAN, 1964. *Étude stratigraphique des formations quaternaries du Sahara Nord-Occidental (de Colomb Béchar à Reggane)*. Paris: CNRS, série géologie, 5.

————, and CHAVAILLON, NICOLE, 1957. "Présence d'industries Acheuléenne, Atérienne et Néolithique dans les alluvions du Kheneg et Tlaia (Sahara Nord-Occidental)." *Bulletin de la Société Préhistorique Française* 54:636-44.

————, and CHAVAILLON, NICOLE, 1962. "Rapports stratigraphiques de l'Acheuléen final et de l'Atérien (Sahara Nord-Occidental)." *Bulletin de la Société Préhistorique Française* 59:440-44.

CHAVAILLON, NICOLE, 1956. "L'Atérien d'Anchal, Monts d'Ougarta, Sahara Occidental." *Bulletin de la Société Préhistorique Française* 53:637-47.

————, 1957. "L'Atérien du Kheneg et Tlaia (Monts d'Ougarta, Sahara Occidental)." *Bulletin de la Société Préhistorique Française* 54:645-51.

————, 1969. "L'Atérien de la Région d'Adrar Reggane (Sahara)." *Palaeoecology of Africa* 4:130.

————, 1971. "L'Atérien de la Zaouia el Kebira au Sahara Nord-Occidental." *Libyca* 19:9-51.

————, and FABRE, J., 1968. "L'Atérien et le Néolithique au Nord-Est du Mreyye (Sahara Occidental)." *Bulletin de la Société Préhistorique Française* 65:399-420.

CHOUBERT, G.; FAURE-MURET, A.; and MAARLEVELD, G. C., 1967. "Nouvelles dates isotopiques du Quaternaire marocain et leur signification." *Comptes Rendus des Séances de l'Académie des Sciences* 264:434-37.

CONRAD, G., 1963. "Synchronisme du dernier pluvial dans le Sahara Septentrional et le Sahara Méridional." *Comptes Rendus des Séances de l'Académie des Sciences* 257:2506-9.

————, 1969*a*. "L'Évolution climatique du Sahara Occidental Algérien pendant le Quaternaire récent." *Palaeoecology of Africa* 4:42-49.

————, 1969*b*. *L'Évolution continentale post-Hercynienne du Sahara Algérien*. Paris: CNRS.

ENNOUCHI, ÉMILE, 1962. "Une crâne d'homme ancien au Jebel Irhoud (Maroc)." *Comptes Rendus des Séances de l'Académie des Sciences* 254:4330-32.

FAURE, H., 1969. "Recherches sur le Quaternaire littoral du Sénégal et de la Mauritanie." *Palaeoecology of Africa* 4:104-8.

————, and ÉLOUARD, P., 1967. "Schéma des variation du niveau de l'Océan Atlantique sur la côte de l'Ouest d'Afrique depuis 40,000 ans." *Comptes Rendus des Séances de l'Académie des Sciences* 265:784-87.

————; MANGUIN, E.; and NYDAL, R., 1963. "Formations lacustres du Quaternaire supérieur du Niger Oriental: diatomites et âges absolues." *Bulletin Bureau Recherches Géologiques Minéral* 3:41-63.

GOBERT, E. G., 1962. "La préhistoire dans la zone littorale de la Tunisie." *Quaternaria* 6:271-308.

GRUET, M., 1955. "Le gisement d'El Guettar." *Karthago* 5:3-79 (followed by a note on the fauna by Vaufrey, pp. 83-87).

————, 1959. "Le gisement d'El Guettar et sa flore." *Libyca* 6-7:101-26.

HALL, D. N.; WILLIAMS, M. A. J.; CLARK, J. DESMOND; WARREN, A.; BRADLEY, P.; and BEIGHTON, P., 1971. "The British Expedition to the Air Mountains." *Geographical Journal* 137(4):445-57.

HEBRARD, L., 1970. "Fichier des âges absolues du Quaternaire d'Afrique au nord de l'equateur." *Association Sénégalaise pur l'Étude du Quaternaire de l'Ouest Africain* 26:39-56.

de HEINZELIN, J.; HAESAERTS, P.; and VAN NOTEN, F., 1969. "Géologie récent et préhistoire au Jebel Uweinat." *Africa-Tervuren* 15:120-25.

HESTER, JAMES J., 1968. "Comments on Origins of African Agricultural Symposium." *Current Anthropology* 9(5):497-98.

_____, and HOEBLER, P., 1970. *Prehistoric Settlement Patterns in the Libyan Desert*. University of Utah Papers in Anthropology 92, Nubia Series 4. Salt Lake City: University of Utah Press.

HEY, R. W., 1963. "Pleistocene Screes in Cyrenaica (Libya). *Eiszeitalter und Gegenwart* 14:77-84.

HOWE, BRUCE, 1967. *The Paleolithic of Tangier, Morocco*. American School of Prehistoric Research, Peabody Museum, Harvard, Bulletin 22.

HUGOT, H., 1962. *Mission Berliet Ténéré Tchad*. Paris: Arts et Métiers Graphiques.

_____, 1963*a*. *Recherches préhistoriques dans l'Ahaggar Nord-Occidental, 1950-57*. Mémoires du Centre de Recherches Anthropologiques Préhistoriques et Ethnographiques I.

_____, 1963*b*. "Limites méridionales de L'Atérien." *Actas del V Congreso Panafricano de Prehistoria y de estudio del Cuaternario, Tenerife, 1963*, pp. 95-108.

_____, 1967. "Le Paléolithique terminal dans l'Ouest." In *Background to Evolution in Africa*, edited by W. W. Bishop and J. D. Clark, pp. 528-56. Chicago: University of Chicago Press.

LE DU, R., 1934. "Station Atérienne de l'Oued Djouf el-Djemel." *Recueil des Notices et Mémoires de la Société Archéologique de Constantine* 62:2.

MAARLEVELD, G. C., 1964. "Dar es-Soltane, Morocco." *Radiocarbon* 6:355.

McBURNEY, C. B. M., 1960. *The Stone Age of Northern Africa*. Hammondsworth, Middlesex: Penguin Books.

_____, 1967. *The Haua Fteah (Cyrenaica) and the Stone Age of the Southeast Mediterranean*. Cambridge: At the University Press.

_____, and HEY, R. W., 1955. *Prehistory and Pleistocene Geology in Cyrenaican Libya*. Cambridge: At the University Press.

MARCHAND, D., and AYME, A., 1935. "Recherches stratigraphiques sur l'Atérien." *Bulletin de la Société d'Histoire National de L'Afrique du Nord* 26:340-41.

MARKS, ANTHONY, n.d. *A Restudy of Collections from the Dungul Oasis, Egypt*. Unpublished manuscript.

PIROUTET, M., 1930. "La station préhistorique d'Ain Taya, près d'Alger." *Bulletin de la Société Préhistorique Française* 27(11):513-17.

QUEZEL, P., and MARTINEZ, C., 1961. "Le dernier interpluvial au Sahara Central. Essai de chronologie palynologique et paléoclimatique." *Libyca* 6-7:211-27.

REYGASSE, M., 1922. "Note au sujet de deux civilisations préhistoriques africaines pour lesquelles deux termes nouveaux me paraissent devoir être employés," pp. 467-72. *XLVIe Session de l'Association française pour l'Avancement des Sciences, Montpellier*.

ROCHE, J., 1956. "Étude sur l'industrie de la grotte de Dar-es-Soltan." *Bulletin d'Archéologie Marocaine* 1:93-118.

_____, 1969. "Les industries paléolithiques de la grotte de Taofralt (Maroc Oriental). Methodes d'étude. Évolution technique et typologique." *Quaternaria* 11:89-100.

ROGNON, P., 1967. *Le massif de L'Atakor et ses bordures (Sahara Central)*. Paris: CNRS.

ROUBET, F. E., 1969. "Le niveau atérien dans la stratigraphie côtiere à l'Ouest d'Alger." *Palaeoecology of Africa* 4:124-29.

RUHLMANN, A., 1936. "Les grottes préhistoriques d'El Khenzira." *Publication du Service des Antiquities du Maroc* 2.

————, 1951. *La grotte préhistorique de Dar es Soltan*. Hesperis 11.

————, 1952. "The Moroccan Aterian and its Subdivisions." *Proceedings of the First Pan-African Congress on Prehistory, Nairobi, 1947*. Oxford: Basil Blackwell.

SERVANT, M., and SERVANT-VILDARY, S., 1972. "Nouvelles données pour une interprétation paléoclimatique de séries continentales du Bassin Tchadien (Pleistocène, Récent, Holocène)." *Palaeoecology of Africa* 6:87-92.

————, and DELIBRIAS, G., 1969. "Chronologie du Quaternaire récent des basses régions du Tchad." *Comptes Rendus des Séances de l'Académie des Sciences* 269:1603-9.

TIXIER, J., 1959. "Les industries lithique d'Aïn Fritissa (Maroc oriental)." *Bulletin d'Archéologie Morocaine* 3:107-248.

————, 1967. "Procédés d'analyse et questions de terminologie concernant l'étude des ensembles industriel du Paléolithique récent et de l'Épipaléolithique dans l'Afrique de Nord-Ouest." In *Background to Evolution in Africa*, edited by W. W. Bishop and J. D. Clark, pp. 771-820. Chicago: University of Chicago Press.

VAN CAMPO, M., and COQUE, R., 1960. "Palynologie et géomorphologie dans le Sud Tunisien." *Pollen et Spores* 2(2):275-84.

————; AYMONIN, G.; COHEN, J.; DUTIL, P.; GUINET, P.; and ROGNON, P., 1964. "Contribution à l'étude du peuplement végétal quaternaire des montagnes sahariennes: l'Atakor." *Pollen et Spores* 6(1):169-94.

VAUFREY, R., 1955. *Préhistoire de l'Afrique. Vol. I: Le Maghreb*. Paris: Masson.

van ZINDEREN BAKKER, E. M. (ed.), 1966. *Palaeoecology of Africa*, vol. 1.

————, (ed.), 1969. *Palaeoecology of Africa*, vol. 4.

————, 1972. "Late Quaternary Lacustrine Phases in the Southern Sahara and East Africa." *Palaeoecology of Africa* 6:15-27.

THE PALEOLITHIC OF THE LOWER NILE VALLEY

Fred Wendorf
Southern Methodist University
and
Romuald Schild
Institute for the History of Material Culture
Polish Academy of Sciences

INTRODUCTION

The study of Paleolithic materials from the Nile Valley can perhaps best be characterized as sporadic. There was considerable interest in the area before World War I (Schweinfurth, 1903, 1904, 1905, 1909; Curelly, 1913; Sterns, 1917), but the most important period was the two decades of the 1920s and 1930s when the first systematic surveys and excavations were undertaken which resulted in the classic studies by Caton-Thompson and Gardner (1934); Caton-Thompson (1946, 1952); Sandford (1934); Sandford and Arkell (1929, 1933, 1939); and Vignard (1921a, 1921b, 1923, 1928, 1934a, 1934b, 1935, 1955a, 1955b, 1957). These research activities were disrupted by the onset of World War II and the subsequent political developments in Egypt. The erroneous impression obtained from the earlier work that Nilotic Paleolithic materials were both scarce and culturally retarded in comparison with adjacent areas of the Near East efficiently inhibited interest in the area even when work was again possible. As a consequence, no significant research on Paleolithic materials in the Nile Valley was undertaken for a period of over twenty years until 1961, when construction began on the New High Dam at Aswan and the international campaign was mounted to salvage the archaeological and historical treasures threatened by the new dam.

Several of the Nubian expeditions, although concerned primarily with Pharaonic and later materials, undertook limited excavations at Paleolithic sites (Chavaillon and Maley, 1966; Siirianen, 1965; and Vinogradov, 1964), but there were three major groups concerned primarily with prehistoric materials: the University of Colorado group working in a small area on the west bank near Wadi Halfa, Sudan (Irwin et al., 1968); the joint Yale University—Canadian National Museum party with a major effort at Kom Ombo, just north of Aswan, but also doing some work in Egyptian Nubia, mostly along the east bank of the river (Reed, 1966; Smith, 1966; Butzer and Hansen, 1968); and the Combined Expedition sponsored by several American, Belgium, British, Egyptian, French, and Polish organizations, and working in both Egyptian and Sudanese Nubia and the adjacent desert (Wendorf, 1965, 1968; Hester and Hoebler, 1970). As a result of this concentrated activity during a four year period, between 1961 and 1966, over 100 Paleolithic sites were intensively studied in the reservoir and Kom Ombo areas. Not surprisingly, the data from

these sites have completely altered our concepts of Nilotic prehistory.

When the Aswan Reservoir began to fill and field work in Nubia was discontinued in 1966, interest in the prehistory of the Nile Valley continued, but was shifted to adjacent areas. In Sudan, one group from the Combined Prehistoric Expedition moved upstream near Dongola, Sudan, then to Khashm el Girba on the upper Atbara, along the Ethiopian frontier (Marks et al., 1968, 1971). The outbreak of hostilities and the accompanying political disturbances in the summer of 1967 terminated this project. A second group in 1967 and 1968 worked downstream from Aswan to Sohag, in central Egypt (Wendorf et al., 1967, 1970a, 1970b, 1970c; Said et al., 1970), and then in 1969 moved to the Fayum, just south of Cairo (Said et al., 1972a, 1972b). No work was undertaken in the area between Sohag and the Fayum, a distance of approximately 400 kilometers. Although a hundred additional Paleolithic sites were studied during these most recent projects, the work must be regarded as essentially a preliminary reconnaissance to determine the potential of the Paleolithic materials in the area and the gross stratigraphic framework in which the sites occur. Detailed excavations at several selected localities were planned to begin after the survey had been carried northward to the Mediterranean, but in late 1969 political events again terminated field investigations in the Nile Valley. It seems highly likely that another long span of time will pass before active research will begin again in this area.

One of the most important results of the Paleolithic research which has been done in the Nile Valley since 1961 has been a complete revision of the geologic history of the river (de Heinzelin, 1968; Butzer and Hansen, 1968; Said et al., 1970). The previous investigations of the 1920s and 1930s had concentrated on broad correlations of riverine terrace levels, on relating these to the Pleistocene fluctuation of the Mediterranean, and on dating these terraces through occasional finds of artifacts. These efforts had resulted in a sequence presumably extending from Early Acheulean to the Neolithic; but the poor chronological controls, based mostly on derived artifacts, and the absence of detailed measured sections resulted in widespread skepticism concerning the details of the sequence and consequently reduced the usefulness of much of that work.

A different approach has characterized the investigations

undertaken since 1961. Major emphasis has been given to detailed studies of local areas and the development of local stratigraphic sequences based on numerous profiles and sections. Furthermore, the geologic studies were often accompanied by extensive excavations at living sites which can be directly related to the local sequences.

No attempt will be made here to summarize the concepts which were in vogue before 1961, or to repeat the already adequately published interpretations of the Nubian and Kom Ombo regional sequences. Instead, we propose to discuss the more recently obtained data and to consider how these have modified the interpretation of climatic and sedimentary events which had emerged at the conclusion of the Nubian Campaign. There are also significant modifications in the interpretations acquired since the close of the Nubian Campaign, as they were offered in the preliminary accounts of the work, and in the methodology utilized in the synthesis of the geological history of the lower Nile Valley. In the preliminary accounts we attempted to utilize the formal geologic terminology developed in Nubia and extend it downstream into Upper Egypt. This was probably an error, for it requires some redefinition of the terms used, and it may conceal regional differences of significance in the dynamic history of the river. In lieu of formal geologic names we propose to discuss the geologic history of the lower Nile in terms of an informal chronicle of events, using the same approach as that generally followed by students of the European Pleistocene. This paper is a much abbreviated summary of a synthesis now in the final stages of preparation by the present authors.

THE OLDER EVENTS

THE GEOLOGY

One of the major conclusions which emerged from the geological studies conducted during the Nubian Campaign was the belief that the Nile River, as a stream connecting the Ethiopian Highlands with the Mediterranean, was a fairly recent phenomenon, almost surely of Late Pleistocene age, and possibly post-Mousterian. This interpretation is now known to be incorrect, for downstream from Nubia there are extensive deposits containing heavy minerals of Ethiopian origin stratigraphically below Late Acheulean artifacts. Obviously, then, the Nile clearly precedes the Late Acheulean, and could well be considerably earlier.

These earlier Nile sediments have not been systematically examined, thus their complexity, extent, and chronological positions remain largely unknown; but as presently understood the sequence is as follows from early to late (Said et al., 1970):

a) The earliest unit in this series, named the Dandara silts, occurs on both the east and west banks between Luxor and Qena. There is a single radiocarbon date from the top of these silts "greater than 39,000 B.P.," a not unexpected age since they underlie a Late Acheulean occupation in the same unit. While handaxes also occur in the Dandara silts, no living floor is known.

b) A thick suite of gravels and sands, derived from the Eastern Desert of Egypt and named the Qena Sands, overlies the Dandera silts. These gravels seemingly record a period of heavy local rainfall and a *markedly* different Nilotic regime from that which prevailed previously. A thick red soil caps this unit, but no identifiable archaeological materials were recovered from it.

c) A thick mantle of locally derived pebbles and cobbles in a red soil matrix covers the Qena sands and the underlying Dandara silts. These gravels are wadi-like in character and suggest sizable stream velocity and thus, presumably, heavy seasonal rainfall. The deposition of the gravels was followed by a long period of erosion during which the modern rolling topography of the Nile Valley in central Egypt was formed and the morphology of the preceding wadi beds was inverted.

d) A thick unit of slopewash was then deposited over the rolling landscape, along both sides of the river. In the base of this slopewash are numerous derived artifacts of Middle Paleolithic aspect, at least one of which (Site E6103) contained a few bifacial foliated points. Higher in this unit, the slopewash gradually becomes a true colluvium, and at one locality (Site E6104) it contains a living site which is both typologically and technologically of early Late Paleolithic aspect.

In Nubia deposits which could record any of the above older Nilotic events were not recognized except in the Older Pediments which were seen as of non-Nilotic origin, and pre-Nilotic in age. These Older Pediments contained Acheulean materials in the lower portion and Middle Paleolithic in the upper part.

On the basis of detailed study of the geology of the Wadi Halfa area in Sudan and adjacent southernmost Egypt, de Heinzelin (1968) concluded that there were three major phases of Nile aggradation separated by intervals of downcutting and dune migration, and that these occurred during the Late Upper and Final Pleistocene. Each of the aggradations could be separated from the others primarily through their different elevations. Numerous trenches and profiles were recorded to document this sequence. Although there were a few areas of conflicting data, this concept of Nilotic sedimentary history was strongly supported by the sequence of associated archaeological industries, by a substantial series of radiocarbon dates obtained from the various units, and by the absence of any clear-cut evidence of earlier archaeological materials associated with deposits of Nilotic origin.

A slightly earlier episode of Nile siltation than those defined by de Heinzelin was recorded in the Korosko Formation at Kom Ombo and Egyptian Nubia (Butzer and Hansen, 1968, pp. 87-97). A sample of marl from this unit yielded a date of 25,250 ± 1,000/900 years (I-2061), but this did not alter the basic concept held by most of those working in Nubia that true Nile sediments were deposited no more than 30,000 years ago. The discovery of earlier Nile deposits downstream in Egypt has, of course, suggested the possibility that some of the Nile silts observed in Nubia were older than first believed. Unfortunately, with the Nubian localities now deeply buried beneath Lake Nasser, the question probably can never be resolved satisfactorily, but it seems highly likely that several of the "problem" localities for which the dating or interpretation of the stratigraphy was then controversial could well represent earlier episodes of Nilotic deposition.

A possible earlier Nile silt was reported by Chmielewski (1965, p. 154) at Site Arkin 14, associated with Late Acheulean handaxes. The stratigraphic situation was unclear, however, and there is a possibility that the Nile silts were later.

One of the most important of the "problem" localities is Site 440, near Wadi Halfa (Shiner, 1968b). The details of the stratigraphy at Site 440 are recorded by de Heinzelin (1968, figs. 14-16) who offered two interpretations: first, that the silts in which the site occurred were a part of the Sahaba Formation and thus late; or second, that they were much older and at the base of the Debeira-Jer Formation. The site undoubtedly would have been classified as Middle Paleolithic had we not been convinced from our observations elsewhere that the Middle Paleolithic occupation in Nubia predated the Nile. Unfortunately, the extensive trenches excavated at the site failed to establish conclusively the stratigraphic position of the overlying silts in the local sequence. In the field, the most favored interpretation placed the occupation at the base of the earliest phase of siltation then known (the Debeira-Jer), but the possibility that the silts were from the later Sahaba aggradation could not be eliminated. Thus, when the radiocarbon date of 12,390 B.C. ± 500 years (WSU-290) was obtained on charcoal from the upper living floor, the interpretation of a Sahaba age for the silts prevailed.

The occupation of Site 440 occurs in a dune sand separating two thick layers of silt. The upper silt is deeply altered by a thick vertisol. Fluvial sands and gravels overlie the upper silt.

In the absence of detailed studies of the older silts which occur downstream in Upper Egypt it is not possible to relate the events at Site 440 with any of those of Upper Egypt. At present there is no means of determining the stratigraphic relationship between these scattered occurrences of older Nile silt. As a group they probably represent small segments from a considerable time interval ranging from early Upper Pleistocene through the middle Upper Pleistocene, and it seems likely that there may have been several episodes of aggradation and recession during this period. A convincing sorting out of the sequence of these earlier events must await further work both in Sudan and Egypt.

THE ARCHAEOLOGY OF THE OLDER EVENTS

Except for scattered finds, the only information available on the Early and Middle Stone Age along the Nile comes from Nubia where thirteen sites near Wadi Halfa yielded lithic assemblages which are typologically and technologically within the range of the Acheulean complex, and twenty-one other studied localities in the same area were assigned to one of three or four distinct Middle Stone Age industries. This is not to suggest that Early and Middle Stone Age sites are not present elsewhere along the Nile, for they are known to occur in Upper Egypt; but neither the Acheulean locality found in Nile silts below Luxor nor the two Middle Stone Age sites near Qena and Dandara have yet been analyzed (fig. 1).

The Wadi Halfa Early Stone Age localities share many resemblances with the Middle and Late Acheulean from Khor Abu Anga near Khartoum, as well as other Acheulean assemblages from central and northern Sudan (Chmielewski, 1965, 1968; Guichard and Guichard, 1965, 1968). In some assemblages handaxes, ovates, choppers, and chopping tools occur in nearly equal proportions, with handaxes always becoming more frequent in the Late phase. Characteristic central African Acheulean forms, such as cleavers, trihedrals, and para-Levallois flakes, are rare to absent. Levallois technology appears in the Middle phase and gradually increases in importance, as do flake tools, although the latter are never numerous. All of the known sites are workshops near quarries (fig. 2).

The northern limit of the Khor Abu Anga Acheulean in the Nile Valley is not known, but it apparently does not extend westward into the Sahara, at least during the Late Acheulean. The presumably contemporary materials from Kharga Oasis (Caton-Thompson, 1952), Dakhla Oasis, Bir Sahara, and Bir Terfawi (Schild and Wendorf, this volume) are significantly different.

As originally described, the Nubian Middle Stone Age was comprised of three distinct industries: a Nubian Mousterian divided into two subgroups based on the presence or absence of handaxes, and closely similar to the typical Mousterian of Europe except for a higher frequency of Upper Paleolithic type tools; a Denticulate Mousterian, known only from two sites, but both well within the range of Denticulate Mousterian in Europe and the Near East (Marks, 1968a); and the Nubian Middle Paleolithic which is believed to have some resemblances with the Sangoan and Lupemban complexes of central and east Africa (Guichard and Guichard, 1968). All of the known Middle Paleolithic sites of these industries were situated either on the tops of inselbergs or buried in the upper part of the Older Pediments, and usually well back from the river. This was one of the factors which contributed to the conclusion, now known to be erroneous, that the modern Nile was a comparatively recent stream.

A possible fourth industry, or a variation of the Nubian Denticulate Mousterian, possibly also containing bifacial foliates, may be represented at Site 440 and at several sites along the Nile near Dongola, farther south in Sudan. (Fig. 3)

There were two living floors at Site 440, clearly differing in economic exploitative emphasis. The lower floor yielded numerous large mammal remains, mostly Bos, Equus, gazelle, and hippo; while the upper floor was predominately fish. The lower assemblage had a higher frequency of Levallois pieces, but this may be due to sampling (only 30 pieces

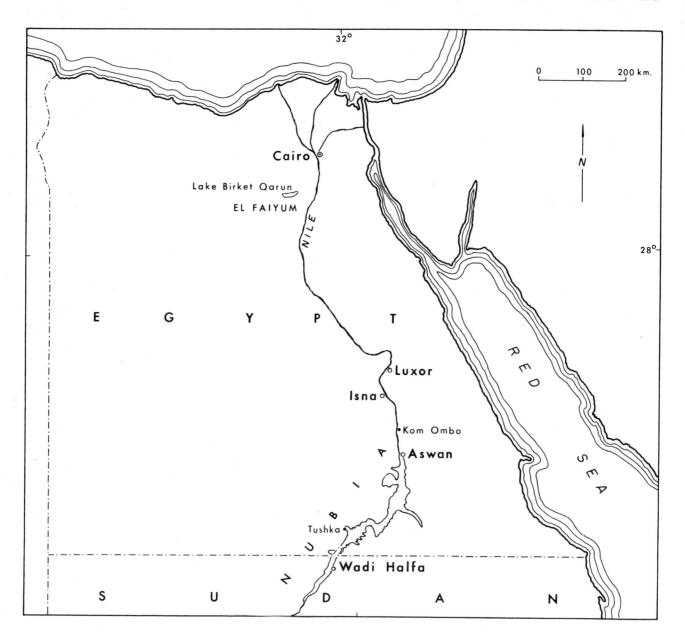

FIG. 1—Map of Lower Nile Valley.

were recovered from this unit); they are otherwise clearly similar, in spite of the obvious exploitative differences. Both assemblages utilize moderately large flakes, and the tool group is dominated by denticulates (around 40%), with sidescrapers (13%), retouched pieces (13%), and notches (12%) of secondary importance. Endscrapers, burins, and truncated flakes also occur, but at frequencies of around 3% or less. A single biface foliate occurred on the surface.

Farther south, in the vicinity of Dongola, three sites with closely similar lithic assemblages to those at Site 440 were also found associated with Nile silts of the Goshabi Formation (Marks et al., 1971; de Heinzelin, 1971). On the basis of similarity in geomorphic expression, de Heinzelin also correlated the Goshabi Formation with the Sahaba in the Wadi Halfa area, thus indicating a comparatively late age for the associated living sites. No radiocarbon dates are

available, but the assemblages have moderate Levallois indices. The tools are executed on medium sized flakes and consist mostly of denticulates (20% to 22%) with notches and sidescrapers each representing from 6% to 13%. Rare bifacial foliates also occur (figs. 4 and 5).

The Dongola sites and the two assemblages from Site 440 are clearly of Middle Paleolithic aspect, and are formally classifiable as Denticulate Mousterian. The extensive data now available from both Upper Egypt and the adjacent Sahara would strongly suggest that it is highly unlikely that a Middle Paleolithic industry survived in this area as late as 12,000 B.C., in spite of the radiocarbon date at Site 440. Consequently, it seems reasonable to reject this date and to suggest that the silts at Site 440 and those of the Goshabi Formation record an episode of Nile aggradation contemporary with the Middle Paleolithic in this area.

FIG. 2—Acheulean Site Arkin 5, near Wadi Halfa, Sudan.

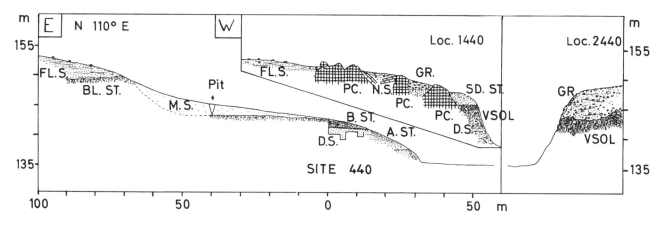

FIG. 3—Profile of Site 440 and adjoining localities (from de Heinzelin, 1968).

Downstream along the Nile in Egypt materials of Middle Paleolithic age are known to occur (Caton-Thompson, 1946), but only as occasional flakes or as reworked pieces in gravels. Living sites, either on the surface or *in situ*, have thus far not been reported. This is not to suggest that the sites are not present along the Nile in Egypt, but only that the deposits of the appropriate age have not been closely examined.

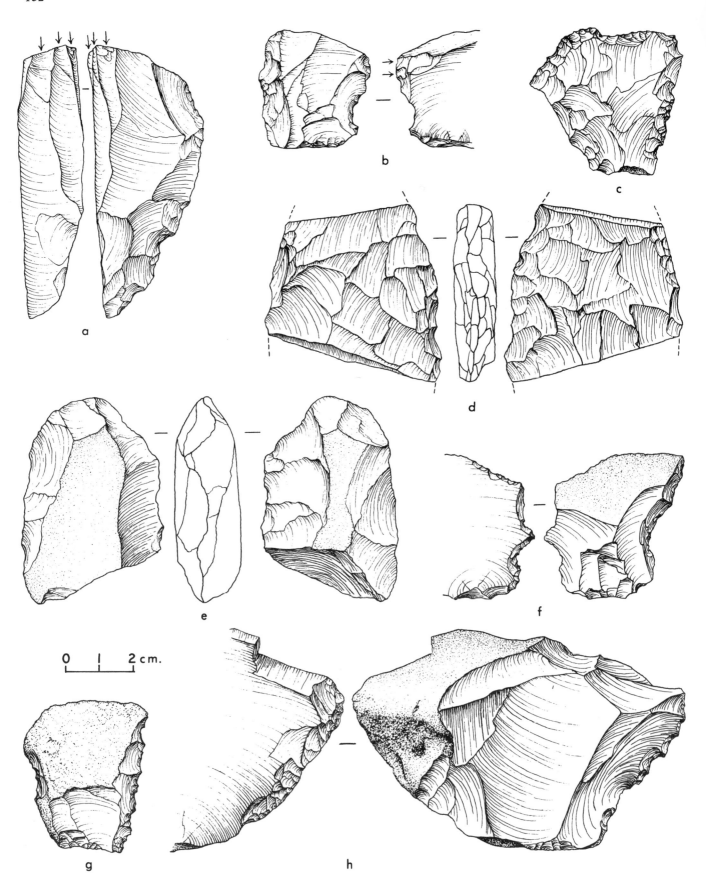

FIG. 4—Tools from Site N2, probable Denticulate Mousterian assemblage from near Dongola, Sudan. From Marks et al., 1971, fig. 2.

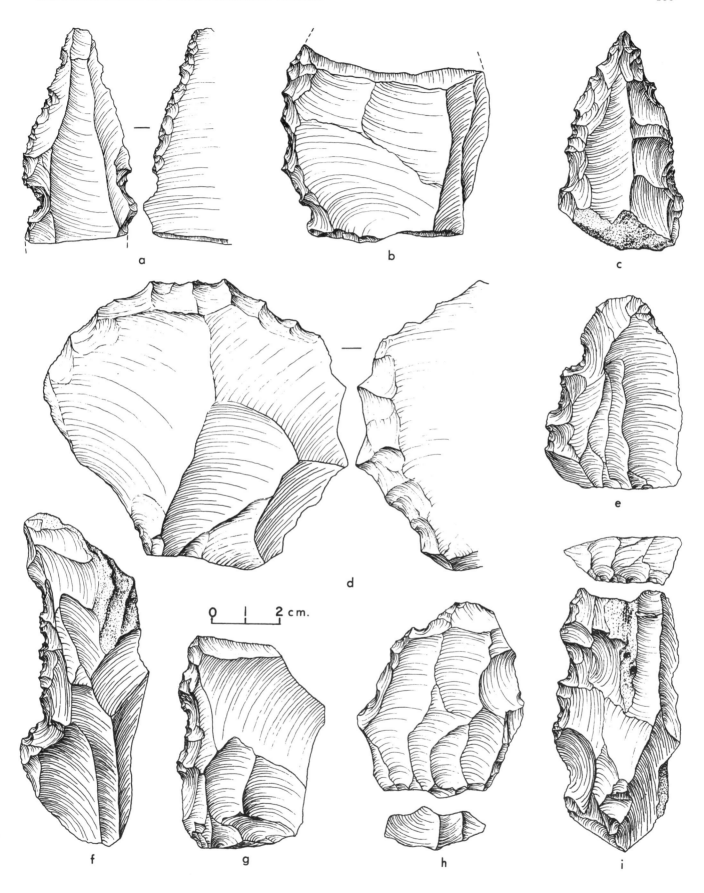

FIG. 5—Tools from Site N2, probable Denticulate Mousterian assemblages from near Dongola, Sudan. From Marks et al., 1971, fig. 3.

A transition from the Middle Paleolithic to the Late Paleolithic cannot be demonstrated along the Nile. The earliest assemblages which could be classified as Late Paleolithic have either a fully developed blade technology (in Upper Egypt) or a tool typology which is dominated by Upper Paleolithic types combined with a Levallois technology (in Nubia).

LATER PLEISTOCENE EVENTS

THE GEOLOGY

The situation in regard to the later Nile deposits is much more satisfactory than for those of earlier events. There are numerous measured sections and many localities with associated archaeological materials and radiocarbon dates. Here too, however, certain revisions seem appropriate. In the original scheme, the threefold Upper Pleistocene units of Nile aggradation in Nubia were named in order from early to late: the Debeira-Jer, reaching an elevation of 34 m above the modern floodplain; the Sahaba at 20 m above the floodplain (it had two phases); and the Arkin some 10 m–14 m above the floodplain (de Heinzelin, 1968). These were separated by episodes of regression, down-cutting, and dune aggradation, which were termed the Ballana and the Birbet.

Subsequent work in central Egypt and reexamination of the sites attributed to the Debeira-Jer Formation in Nubia suggest the possibility that two separate episodes of siltation may be represented in this unit. The earliest of these, to which the name Debeira-Jer is restricted, is recorded at Site 1017, where a Khormusan industry occurs and which yielded a revised radiocarbon date of 18,950 B.C. ± 280 years (WSU-203).

The second phase of this event, or in our present view a slightly later and separate episode of Nile aggradation, is recorded at several localities in both Nubia and Upper Egypt. Along the west bank the sediments of this event indicate that the aggradation of the silts during this period was accompanied by extensive migration of aeolean sand. These sands appear to be the same unit which in Nubia were named the Ballana Formation, and the silts in Upper Egypt are apparently the chronological equivalent of the Masmas Formation at Kom Ombo. We propose, therefore, to refer to this event as the Ballana-Masmas aggradation. The dune activity and the absence of any evidence for local runoff in the wadis suggest a climate during the Ballana-Masmas aggradation similar to that which prevails in Egypt today. There are sixteen consistent radiocarbon dates between 15,000 B.C. and 17,000 B.C. which refer to this event. The dates are listed below and include two groups, only one of which is acceptable.

All of the dates in the last group are rejected, or considered questionable, because if correct they would imply a longer time range for the associated archaeological materials than seems probable, or they overlap with older or younger geological events.

AREA	DATE	ASSOCIATED ARCHAEOLOGY
Nubia	14,550 B.C. ± 500 years (WSU-201)	(Minimal date) Halfan Industry
	15,850 B.C. ± 500 years (WSU-215)	Late Khormusan Industry
	16,155 B.C. ± 1,200 years (I-863)	Dabarosa Complex
	16,650 B.C. ± 550 years (WSU-318)	Halfan Industry
	17,200 B.C. ± 375 years (WSU-332)	Halfan Industry
Kom Ombo	15,150 B.C. ± 400 years (I-2178)	No associated archaeology
	16,350 B.C. ± 310 years (I-2060)	No associated archaeology
Upper Egypt, Idfu	15,000 B.C. ± 350 years (I-3248)	Idfuan, Halfan variant
	15,300 B.C. ± 300 years (I-3249)	Idfuan, Halfan variant
	15,500 B.C. ± 300 years (I-3418)	Idfuan, Halfan variant
	15,650 B.C. ± 300 years (I-3419)	Idfuan, Halfan variant
	15,850 B.C. ± 330 years (I-3417)	Idfuan, Halfan variant
Isna	14,880 B.C. ± 290 years (I-3420)	No associated archaeology
	15,640 B.C. ± 300 years (I-3415)	Fakhurian Industry
	16,070 B.C. ± 330 years (I-3416)	Fakhurian Industry

There are also several dates which must be regarded with skepticism:

4,200 B.C. ± 400 years (I-864)		Dabarosa Complex
7,325 B.C. ± 600 years (GXO-122a)		Dabarosa Complex
13,020 B.C. ± 1,420 - 1,730 years (GXO-576)		Halfa Complex
13,150 B.C. ± 750 years (GXO-122b)		Dabarosa Complex
19,638 B.C. ± 1,518 years (Thermoluminescence, Oxford Laboratory for Archaeology, 161-C-1)		Idfuan Industry
23,750 B.C. ± 2,500 - 3,700 years (GXO-410)		Halfa Complex

Following the maximum of the Ballana-Masmas aggradation, the level of the Nile fell significantly. This event is referred to as the Deir El-Fakhuri recession. Previously, the present authors and others (Wendorf et al., 1970a, b, c; and Said et. al., 1970) proposed the term "Deir El-Fakhuri Formation" in reference to a series of pond sediments believed to represent this recessional feature. Additional data, however, suggest that these ponds may, in fact, have developed in a closed dune field adjacent to the river during an early phase of the subsequent aggradation.

A recession did occur, however, although the maximum extent to which the level of the river was depressed during this recession is not known. Butzer and Hansen (1968, p. 149) indicate that it fell at least 20 m at Kom Ombo, while in Upper Egypt the only data are that a decline of more than 2 m occurred. Wadi deposits, a good exposure of which occurs in the Dishna area, just north of Qena, are the best record now available of sediments during this period of recession. There are few archaeological sites known for this period, and the time span represented is not well established. A consistent series of dates like that for the preceding aggradation is not available. There are, however, several conflicting radiocarbon determinations from Kom Ombo which may refer to this period:

DATE	ASSOCIATED ARCHAEOLOGY
14,050 B.C. ± 800 years (M-1551)	Sebekian
13,250 B.C. ± 700 years (M-1642)	Sebekian
12,290 B.C. ± 370 years (I-1291)	Sebekian
12,150 B.C. ± 400 years (I-1292)	Sebekian
11,661 B.C. ± 600 years (M-1641)	Sebekian

The problem with these dates is that they come from a living floor which overlies a "Silsillian" assemblage, and at a nearby site the Silsillian occurs in the early part of the subsequent Sahaba-Darau aggradation and has two dates of 13,360 B.C. ± 200 years (Y-1376), and 12,440 B.C. ± 200 years (I-5180). Because of the long time span represented by the first group of dates and the suggested cultural sequence in reference to the Silsillian dates, it seems appropriate to have some reservations about the entire group. The current view is that the latest dates, located around 12,000 B.C., in the Sebekian series are more likely to be correct (Phillips and Butzer, in press), and thus the sites in question probably were occupied during the Sahaba-Darau aggradation and not during the Deir-El-Fakhuri recession.

There is yet another possible date for this event at Kom Ombo of 15,450 B.C. ± 300 years (I-2179) on freshwater marl from the base of wadi alluvium attributed to the Malki member, which is considered to be younger than the Masmas aggradation and contemporaneous with the Gebel Silsila Formation of Butzer and Hansen (1968, p. 116). This date may be slightly too old, or possibly our correlation with the Deir El-Fakhur event may be in error, as well as its chronological association with the beginning of the Gebel Silsila siltation.

As described by de Heinzelin (1968), the Sahaba Formation of Nubia represented the second large Nile aggradation associated with the modern Nile regime. This large aggradation was originally subdivided into two segments separated by an episode of downcutting. It is now apparent, on the grounds of numerous radiocarbon dates, that the early segment of the Sahaba has to be considered as chronologically contemporaneous with the period of simultaneous siltation and dune sedimentation which we are here terming the Ballana–Masmas aggradation. On the other hand, the Late Sahaba is exactly correlative both with the Darau member of the Gebel Silsila Formation at Kom Ombo and with numerous "upper silts" exposed farther downstream in central Egypt (Wendorf et al., 1970b). For this reason, we propose to name this event the Sahaba-Darau aggradation.

The beginning date for the Sahaba-Darau aggradation is not well established. Butzer and Hansen (1968, p. 149) have suggested that it began around 15,000 B.C., based on a date of 15,050 B.C. ± 600 years (I-1297) for the Manshiya Channel, which they regard as broadly contemporaneous with the basal deposits of Channel A at Gebel Silsila 2, the oldest of all the channels within the Darau member. There is, however, only a general geomorphic association of the Manshiya Channel with the Fatira Channel, of which both Channel A and B at Gebel Silsila are the bifurcating parts (Butzer and Hansen, 1968, fig. 3-1). Furthermore, there is another radiocarbon date on shell "in a position of growth" at Channel A at Gebel Silsila 2A of 11,900 B.C. ± 200 years (I-1806). This last date closely agrees with others available from Sahaba silts elsewhere in Nubia.

As previously noted, the series of pond sediments, at first assigned to the Deir El-Fakhuri recession, are now believed to have developed as seepage ponds in topographic lows in dune fields adjacent to the Nile when it was rising during the Sahaba-Darau aggradation. There are several dates on these pond sediments. The earliest is at Tushka in Egyptian Nubia, where charcoal from the base of a pond dated 12,550 B.C. ± 490 years (WSU-315). There are several other dates from this same locality which are rejected as much too recent (see Wendorf, 1968, p. 940 for discussion):

400 B.C. ± 300 years (WSU-315a);
7,780 B.C. ± 120 years (WSU-444);
8,580 B.C. ± 126 years (WSU-415b);
9,540 B.C. ± 70 years (WSU-417 and 442 combined).

In Upper Egypt near Esna, carbonates at the base of another small pond, which was later covered by silts of the Sahaba-Darau event, yielded a date of 10,740 B.C. ± 240 years (I-3421).

In addition to these dates from the pond sediments, there is a large series of radiocarbon dates attributed to the Sahaba-Darau silts. These dates cluster between 12,000 B.C.

and slightly after 10,000 B.C. Those not previously mentioned are:

AREA	DATE
Nubia	12,850 B.C. ± 100 years (WSU-107)
	11,700 B.C. ± 300 years (GX-421)
	11,020 B.C. ± 300 years (GX-422)
	10,770 B.C. ± 350 years (I-929)
	10,690 B.C. ± 400 years (Y-1644)
	10,600 B.C. ± 460 years (WSU-202)
	10,440 B.C. ± 120 years (Y-1645)
	10,300 B.C. ± 100 years (WSU-109)
	10,150 B.C. ± 160 years (Y-1810)
	10,060 B.C. ± 200 years (Y-1809)
	10,060 B.C. ± 160 years (Y-1808)
	9,700 B.C. ± 300 years (I-532)
	9,460 B.C. ± 270 years (WSU-189)
	9,250 B.C. ± 150 years (WSU-106)
Kom Ombo	11,160 B.C. ± 120 years (Y-1447)
	11,120 B.C. ± 120 years (Y-1375)
	10,500 B.C. ± 120 years (Y-1446)
	10,070 B.C. ± 205 years (HV-1265)
	9,770 B.C. ± 195 years (HV-1264)
Upper Egypt	11,430 B.C. ± 770 years (I-3440)
	10,550 B.C. ± 230 years (I-3424)

In the above series the date of 12,850 B.C. from Nubia is regarded as too old for the stratigraphic position of the sample at the top of the Sahaba-Darau silts. Also, the Nubian samples which yielded dates of 10,770 B.C. and 9700 B.C. are from the same level in the same exposure at the base of a thick unit of silt believed to be the Sahaba. The more recent of the two would seem to be in error, if the overlying silt is correctly assigned to the Sahaba-Darau aggradation. The date of 10,550 B.C. from Upper Egypt is of particular interest since it refers to a burned layer near the top of silts attributed to the Sahaba-Darau aggradation. This burned layer is widespread in this portion of the Valley, and must record an extensive fire which swept the vegetation along the margin of the stream from at least Dishna in the north to Esna in the south.

Several of the more recent dates, as well as some of the earlier ones in the above series, come from fluvial deposits at considerably higher elevations than the bulk of the silt assigned to this event. It is not known if these higher fluvial deposits refer to the final and highest phase of aggradation, or if they record a series of exceptionally high floods at various times during the Sahaba-Darau.

There is some evidence suggesting a climatic sequence beginning with greater local rainfall during the early part of the Sahaba-Darau aggradation, then a decline in rainfall, followed by a final period of increased moisture. At Dishna, in Upper Egypt, wadi gravels clearly interfinger with the lower silts of this event. The gravels gradually reduce in size as the base of erosion rises with the aggrading Nile. During the main phase of aggradation, however, there was no interfingering of wadi deposits with the silt. The final phase is characterized by the development of playas in the blocked wadi mouths behind the natural levee, suggesting another small increase in local rainfall. This sequence is partially confirmed in Egyptian Nubia, where Giegengack (1968, pp. 115-24) reports interfingering wadi deposits and Nile silts along the east banks of the river during most of the period which can be attributed to the Sahaba-Darau aggradation, but the heaviest were at the beginning of the sequence. In the Kom Ombo area Butzer and Hansen consider the wadi alluviation at the Malki subunit to be contemporaneous with the Sahaba siltation (Butzer and Hansen, 1968, p. 116).

Cooler summer temperatures are also indicated for this period by the diatoms from the ponds which developed along the margin of the river. Not only do these ponds appear to have survived longer than is possible today—some of them may even have been perennial—but the diatom fauna contains very few forms with tropical affinities. This contrasts markedly with the Holocene assemblages from the Fayum, where tropical forms comprise a strong component (Aleem, 1958). At the same time, judging from the pollen analyses, these ponds do not appear to have supported an abundant aquatic flora; instead, the total spectra throughout point to a short grass prairie landscape.

There is no evidence that the Sahaba-Darau aggradation was accompanied by widespread dune migration in any way comparable with that which occurred with the maximum of the preceding Ballana-Masmas event. This suggests that local climatic conditions were significantly different during these two episodes, even though both were marked by a major rise in the level of the Nile. If so, then we must conclude that these climatic events in East Africa responsible for the increased flow and aggradation downstream in Sudan and Egypt do not have a simple one-to-one relationship with the climatic phenomena which determine the local climate in the northeastern Sahara. Periods of heavy rainfall in the Ethiopian highlands seemingly do not consistently correlate in Egypt and Sudan either with periods of greater local rainfall or with periods of increased aridity.

The Sahaba-Darau aggradation is followed by a major recession in the level of the Nile. In Nubia the Nile is believed to have fallen more than 20 m; elsewhere in Egypt the extent of decline is unknown, since the evidence is usually buried beneath the modern cultivated areas. There are two dates which refer to this event: 9610 B.C. ± 180 years (I-3760) on a recessional bar inset against Sahaba-Darau silts, and 9250 B.C. ± 285 years (I-531) on shell at the base of silts assigned to the succeeding Arkin aggradation. If these dates are correct, then the Sahaba-Darau aggradation and the final phase of high floods probably ended around 9700 B.C. (this would reject the two most recent Sahaba-Darau dates of 9250 B.C. and 9460 B.C. as too young).

THE ARCHAEOLOGY OF THE
LATER PLEISTOCENE EVENTS

Far more sites of Late Pleistocene age are known and have been excavated along the Nile than for the much longer time span represented by the older sediments. Furthermore, these sites appear to reflect a far greater diversity than previously existed in the lithic technologies and typologies. It is conjecture whether these various industries reflect different patterns of adaptation to the Nilotic microenvironment, a variety of specialized activities by the same or closely related groups, or the concentration into a limited area in a short period of time of various groups from other areas and with different cultural traditions. At present, the evidence favors the latter interpretation, but the question must be left open until more data are available.

The earliest dated Late Paleolithic site in Nubia is designated 6G30 and is assigned to the Khormusan industry (Irwin et al., 1968, pp. 111-12, use the term "Buhen Complex," but they note the close resemblance with other sites grouped into the Khormusan industry. The confusion of terms is the unfortunate result of near-simultaneous publication of the final reports; however, the use of the term Khormusan industry in reference to this lithic complex has priority, see Wendorf, 1965, p. 16). It has a radiocarbon date of "greater than 34,000 B.C." (GXO-409), which seems too old, for it would suggest that for a period of around 20,000 years there were only minor changes in lithic technology and typology along the Nile in Nubia. One of the more recent sites of the Khormusan industry (ANW-3) is dated 15,850 B.C. ± 500 years (WSU-215), while another assemblage, not the earliest of the same industry (Site 1017), is dated 18,950 B.C. ± 280 years (WSU- 203). There are clearly minor changes in the industry through time—a decrease in the frequency of Levallois, a shift in types of raw materials utilized, and some fluctuations in tool frequencies—but if the dates are correct, then the tempo of change during the Khormusan was much slower than in the period immediately following.

The Khormusan is a flake industry with a strong and well-developed Levallois technology (Marks, 1968b). It is typologically dominated by burins (well-made and in a variety of forms) and denticulates. Although there are some resemblances with contemporary materials in East Africa identified as Stillbay, the Khormusan is clearly distinct. It lacks, for example, the unifacial and bifacial points characteristic of the East African assemblages. There may be a closer resemblance between the Khormusan and the "Upper Levalloisian" of Kharga; however, the emphasis on sidescrapers and Mousterian points in the latter suggests that the similarities may be superficial at best and limited to the parallels in Levallois technology. The Khormusan sites are usually extensive, probably because of repeated reoccupation of the same locality, and contain numerous large mammal bones and a few remains of fish.

Apparently coeval with the latter part of the Khormusan and in the same general area was another and radically different lithic industry known as the Halfan. Whereas the Khormusan predominately utilized macrolithic flakes and had a strong preference (at least in the earlier sites) for ferrocrete sandstone in the manufacture of tools, the Halfan was a microlithic blade industry with a distinctive and highly specialized Levallois technology and with heavy emphasis on Nile chert and agate for raw materials (Marks, 1968c). The Halfan microlithic blade tools may record one of the earliest occurrences of composite tools in northeast Africa.

Ten sites of this industry have been reported, with five radiocarbon dates ranging from 23,750 B.C. ± 2,500 years (GXO-410) to 13,020 B.C. ± 1,730 years (WSI-201). The time span suggested by the two extreme dates may be too long, since the other three dates closely group between 15,000 B.C. and 17,000 B.C. The ten sites appear to cluster into four stages or groups. As originally presented, the four groups of sites were viewed as sequential stages; however, changes through time may account for only part of the variety seen in the Halfan sites. It seems equally possible that some of the evident shifts in typology and technology are the result of seasonal variation or specialized activity. Unfortunately, the available dates appear to overlap between stages and do not clearly cluster in a manner which would give confidence to any particular interpretation. The sites assigned to the earliest stage or cluster have low frequencies of backed microblades and have high values for the specialized Halfa flake. Other tools, all of which are frequently microlithic, include scrapers, burins, and denticulates. In the later stages or clusters the frequency of Halfa flakes progressively declines and backed microblades become increasingly important.

The Halfa settlements are small, densely concentrated camps supported by both hunting and fishing. The compactness and density of the Halfan sites suggest extended occupation of the same locality by a small group, perhaps confined to a limited area by a fence, house, corral, or other structure.

Downstream along the Nile in Upper Egypt during this period the known lithic assemblages are significantly different from those in Nubia. Possibly the earliest known site (E6104) is situated on the east bank of the Nile near Dishna, in the upper part of the slope sediment which lies between an old Nile silt, possibly of Late Acheulean age or similar to the Korosko silts of Butzer and Hansen, and silts of the Sahaba-Darau aggradation. The position of the cultural layer bearing colluvium in relation to the sequence of later Nile silts is not known, but numerous derived Middle Paleolithic artifacts occur in the base of the unit along with numerous pebbles and cobbles in a coarse sand matrix, while the fresh to only slightly eolized or abraded lithic materials of early Late Paleolithic aspect occur in the upper colluvial part. Extensive quarrying for salt by the local residents had destroyed most of the site; thus its true dimensions and character could not be determined, although its size suggested more than one concentration. The lithic assemblage included numerous opposed and single platform blade cores, many showing typical Upper Paleolithic lateral preparation and at the same time frequently displaying carefully prepared, sometimes convex, faceted platforms reminiscent of those on typical Levallois cores. They appear to represent a blend of Middle and Upper Paleolithic technology. Of debitage other than chips, blades represent slightly more than 9%, while primary flakes account for nearly 2% and the remainder are flakes. The blades are poorly made, wide and thick, and are usually incurvate. (Fig. 10)

About 15% of the tools are made on blades. The tool kit is dominated by three tool categories: retouched flakes and blades (about 37%), notches (34%), and denticulates (21%). Endscrapers and truncated pieces occur (each about 2%) as do rare burins, sidescrapers, and backed pieces (each less than 1%). The assemblage shares several characteristics with the slightly later Idfuan industry, especially the importance of retouched pieces, notches, and denticulates, but it lacks several features characteristic of the Idfuan, particularly the long pointed blades with blunted bases, the Ouchtata bladelets, and the emphasis on burins.

Possibly of about the same age as the locality near Dishna, but more likely of slightly later date, are sites of three other lithic groups, both known along the west bank of the Nile. One of these groups, named the Idfuan industry, is recorded at seven sites in two areas: one group near Idfu, and another at Esna. The Idfuan has two quite distinct facies; one with a moderate Levallois and Halfan component, the other without Levallois or Halfan. (Fig. 6)

There are two localities (E71P1 and E71K8) which have the Halfan facies, but both are extensive and each probably records multiple occupations. Both of them are associated with sediments correlated with the Ballana-Masmas aggradation. There are five dates from various parts of Site E71P1. These range from 15,850 B.C. ± 330 years (I-3417) to 15,000 B.C. ± 350 years (I-3248). The several areas of that site do not appear to differ insofar as core and debitage is concerned, but they do have significantly different tool kits. Nearly half the cores are Levallois, and most of these are of the Halfan variety. Other important forms are single and opposed platform flake and blade cores, some with opposite side utilization, and changed orientation cores. Most were exploited with a punch, but some of these also have well-prepared convex faceted striking platforms. Most are made on local wadi chert.

Variations in tool frequencies suggested that Site E71P1 could be divided into two distinct areas. At the north end of the site, both burins and Ouchtata bladelets are rare to absent, and the most common tools are retouched blades and flakes, including numerous elongated pointed blades with basal blunting. Notches and denticulates are also common. At the south end of the site there are high to moderate frequencies for Ouchtata backed bladelets, burins, and scaled pieces, while the value for retouched pieces is only half that in the northern section. End- and sidescrapers as well as borers and groovers are present, but rare.

The Halfan variety of the Idfuan industry has several parallels with the Halfan industry in Nubia. The most obvious similarity is the highly distinctive Halfan technology, but the Ouchtata backed bladelets and many of the burin categories are also equivalent. There are, however, several important differences. One of the most striking is size. The Halfan has a Microlithic Index of 90 or more, while very few of the Idfuan tools are below 30 m in length. Another important difference is the emphasis on retouched pieces in the Idfuan and particularly the long pointed blades with basal blunting. The Halfan facies might be regarded as a regional variant of the Halfan, but it also shares many close typological features with nearby and contemporary sites which lack any trace of Halfan and Levallois technology, and for this reason we have grouped the two facies into a single industry. (Figs. 11 and 12)

The non-Levallois/Halfan facies of the Idfuan industry is represented at five sites, all of which also occur in deposits correlated with the final phase of the Ballana-Masmas aggradation. They share a common technological base with emphasis on opposed platform blade and bladelet cores, usually with typical lateral preparation, closely similar to the technology at Site E6104 near Dishna, but better executed. The tool categories display considerable variation from site to site, but all share an emphasis on burins, retouched flakes and blades, including elongated blades with basal blunting, notches, and denticulates, while endscrapers, backed elements, and truncations are rare to absent. The variations between sites are reflected in the shifts in Ouchtata bladelets, which vary between 5% and 15%, in the frequencies of burins (ranging from less than 1% to more than 22%), and in the values of the elongated basal blunted points which vary from slightly less than 2% to more than 17%. (Figs. 7 and 8)

Only one site (E71K9) in this non-Levallois group has been dated. A piece of burned clay from a hearth yielded a thermoluminescent date of 21,588 B.P. ± 1,518 years (Oxford Laboratory for Archaeology); but confidence in the reliability of this date probably should be restrained at this time, since we have only very limited experience on which to base an evaluation of the technique. It should be noted, however, that this date is about 5,000 years older than is expected, if the geological interpretation of that site is correct, and if the several radiocarbon dates for the Ballana-Masmas event elsewhere are accurate. On the other hand, if the thermoluminescent date is correct, then consideration would have to be given to the possibility that the non-Levallois facies of the Idfuan had a greater antiquity than the Levallois/Halfan variant, in spite of the stratigraphic interpretation of near-contemporaneity of the two groups.

There is no evident difference in the fauna recovered from the two facies of the Idfuan industry. A diverse subsistence economy is indicated for both. Animal remains with both facies indicate hunting of large mammals, particularly *Bos* and hartebeest, and less commonly, hippopotamus and gazelle. In addition there is evidence for considerable fish-

FIG. 6–View of Site E71P7, Idfuan industry, non-Levallois facies, looking southeast. Site is located at foot of low hill. Note area in near foreground destroyed by local residents quarrying for salt.

ing, especially for the Nile catfish, and gathering of *Unio* shellfish. Many of the sites are large, suggesting that many camp localities were frequently reoccupied. (Fig. 9)

In the same general area (at Esna) as some of the Idfuan sites, and associated with the same episode of silt aggradation, are five other sites containing a significantly different lithic complex known as the Fakhurian industry. The two radiocarbon dates on these sites, 16,070 B.C. ± 330 years (I-4316) and 15,640 B.C. ± 300 years (I-3415), also support the placement of the Fakhurian as contemporary with the Idfuan. Whereas the Idfuan is macrolithic, however, the Fakhurian is microlithic, and based on a true bladelet technology. In tool frequencies there are virtually no points of similarity between the Idfuan and Fakhurian industries, and many of the tool groups in one do not even occur in the other. It would be extremely difficult to explain those differences as reflecting either seasonality or specialized activities. Instead, they suggest occupation of the same area by two groups with totally different lithic traditions, not necessarily simultaneously, but certainly within a short period of time. (Fig. 13)

The Fakhurian sites are all small and are known to occur in only one restricted area, but they represent two distinct site situations: the first is at the margin of a moving dune field at the border between the dune and the flood-plain; the other is within the dune field well back from the floodplain (Lubell, 1971). Different faunal assemblages were recovered from the sites in these two situations, but it is not clear if this reflects a different economic emphasis or merely differential preservation. Fish remains dominate in the sites at the floodplain margin, but occur with numerous large mammal bones, especially hartebeest, but also including rabbit, *Bos*, gazelle, and hippopotamus. At the interior dune site fewer bones were preserved, and these limited to hartebeest and *Bos*. (Figs. 14 and 15)

The Fakhurian is a non-Levallois bladelet and micro-blade industry utilizing opposed platform and single platform cores. Changed orientation cores are also common (ranging from 8% to 18%). The tool kit includes four major classes: backed bladelets (ranging from 20% to 51%), including both straight and arch-backed, and in some assemblages numerous Ouchtata backed bladelets; retouched pieces (from 16% to 32%); perforators, mostly double-backed with both ends pointed (9% to 15%); and notches and denticulates (7% to 15%). There are also endscrapers (which range from 3% to 10%), truncations (around 6%), and a few burins (from 1% to 3%). (Fig. 16)

Two fragmentary human skeletons were recovered at one of the Fakhurian sites, but unfortunately they were too poorly preserved for definitive description. They were not,

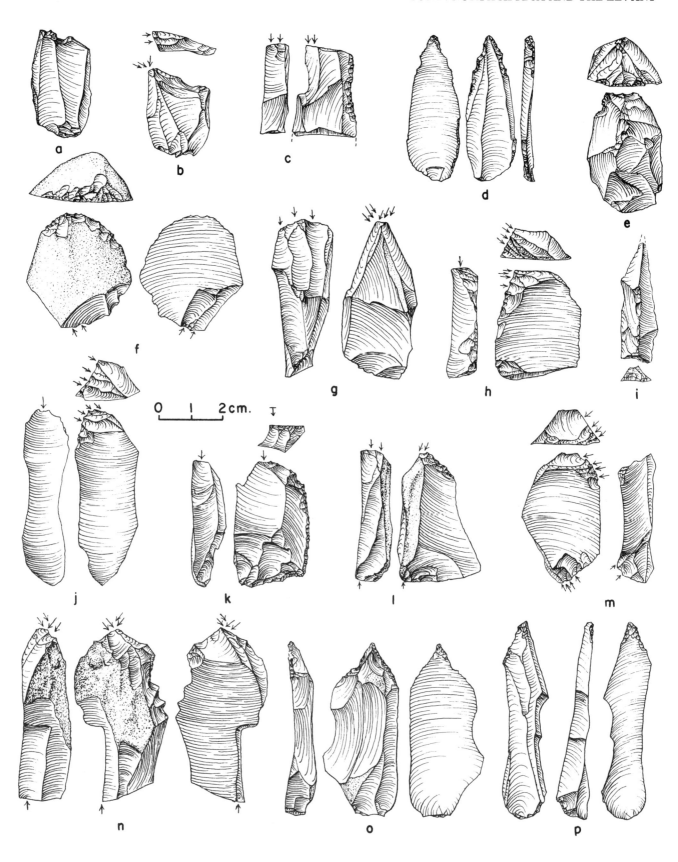

FIG. 7—Tools from Site E71K9C: *a*, notch; *b-c,g-h,j-n*, burins; *d*, borer; *e*, endscraper with notch; *f*, endscraper with multiple burin; *i*, basal truncated bladelet; *o-p*, borers.

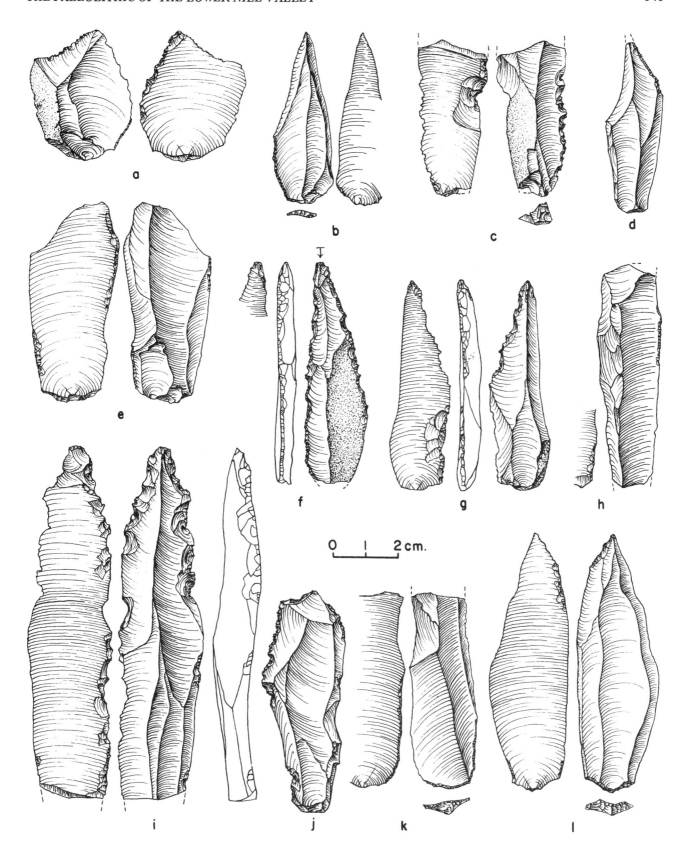

FIG. 8—Tools from Site E71K9C: *a,c,i-j*, denticulates; *b*, basal blunted bladelet; *d,e*, retouched bladelets; *f,g*, borers on denticulated blades; *h*, retouched blade; *k*, basal blunted blade; *l*, pointed arch tipped blade with basal blunting.

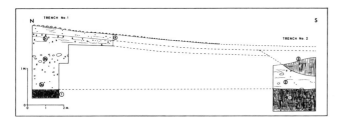

FIG. 9—Profile of Trenches 1 and 2 at early Late Paleolithic site of E6104, Area C, near Dishna, Egypt: 1) dark, grayish brown silt (possibly Dandara Formation); 2) brown, unsorted sand with numerous pebbles and cobbles, especially in middle part, rolled Middle Paleolithic artifacts throughout 2a and 2b, and early Late Paleolithic cultural layer at top of unit (colluvium); 3) sterile brown silt, Sahaba-Darau aggradation; 4) light, yellowish brown sand with local pebbles and gravels, upper slopewash.

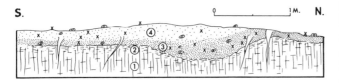

FIG. 10—Profile of Trench 2 at Idfuan Site E61K9 near Esna, Egypt: 1) brown, calcareous silt; 2) same as "1" but weathered; 3) yellowish dune sand with numerous artifacts throughout and dehydration cracks protruding into silt, thermoluminescent date of 19,638 B.C. ± 1,518 years from lower part of unit may be too old; 4) yellowish loose dune sand with artifacts, grades into "3," deflated.

however, as robust, or as primitive in appearance, as the somewhat later skeletons from Nubia which will be discussed later (Butler, in press).

After the maximum of the Ballana-Masmas aggradation, the level of the Nile fell significantly. No sites are known from Upper Egypt or Nubia which can definitely be placed within this recession interval, although the Gemaian, Dabarosa, and Ballanan industries in Nubia are likely candidates, and there are two sites in Upper Egypt which date either to this interval or to the final part of the preceding Ballana-Masmas aggradation. (Fig. 17)

The Gemaian is known from eight sites, all of them small and all located in the vicinity of Wadi Halfa, Sudan (Shiner, 1968a, pp. 540-42). Although nearly half the tools are microlithic in size, it is more accurately described as a small *macrolithic* flake industry with lower to moderate frequencies of Levallois technology and a tool kit which emphasizes sidescrapers and endscrapers, burins, denticulates, and partially retouched Levallois points. Faunal remains suggest that large mammal hunting was the major economic activity, with secondary emphasis on fishing. Shiner sees the Gemaian as evolving into the Qadan industry, the most widespread lithic complex in Nubia of later Pleistocene age.

The Dabarosa complex is represented at three sites all clustered in a small area along the west bank of the Nile opposite Wadi Halfa (Irwin et al., 1968, pp. 25-40). The

lithic assemblages contain numerous bladelets and points produced by a modified Levallois technique from opposed platform cores with faceted platforms. These bladelets are often partially retouched and occasionally denticulated or notched. Few other tools occur except for an occasional sidescraper, burin, simple Levallois flake, or Halfa flake. There are four dates from sites of the Dabarosa complex, ranging from 4200 B.C. ± 300 years (I-864), and 7325 B.C. ± 600 years (GXO-122), both obviously too recent, to 13,150 B.C. ± 750 years (GXO-122) and 16,155 B.C. ± 1,200 years (I-863). The occurrence of Halfa flakes in these sites may indicate a contemporaneity with the Halfan industry, and if so, the earliest date may be correct.

The Ballanan is known from only four sites, all of them clustered in a small area on the west bank near Ballana, in southernmost Egypt (Wendorf, 1968, pp. 831-55). Most of the tools (68%) in this industry are made on blades, almost all of which (91%) are microlithic. Single and double platform cores were utilized, many of them with a bipolar technique. Distal truncated microblades are the predominant tools (42%), followed by backed microblades (17%) and burins (12%). Sidescrapers, denticulates, and notches occur, but all are rare. There are no dates which can be conclusively related to the Ballanan, although one surface hearth, in an area where many Ballanan artifacts were also present, dated 12,050 B.C. ± 280 years (WSU-329). If the association is correct, then at least that Ballanan site was probably occupied during the early phase of the subsequent Sahaba-Darau aggradation, rather than during the preceding recession.

A similar problem in dating confronts the chronological placement of two quite different assemblages from Esna, Egypt (Phillips, 1970, 1972, 1973). Since each is known from only one locality, they have not been given formal industry names; but both sites occur in the upper part of the dune facies of the Ballana-Masmas aggradation, and may either date to the end of that event or to the subsequent recessional episode. Both sites were clearly occupied before the interdune ponds developed in this area now regarded as an early feature of the Sahaba-Darau aggradation.

Nearly 80% of the tools at Site E71K13 are Ouchtata backed bladelets. Most of these are produced from wide, flat, opposed platform cores, or from similar but rare single platform cores. The debitage includes a high frequency (around 30%) of bladelets, well-made, with parallel sides and blunt distal ends. More than 90% of the debitage is made on local wadi chert. Other than the predominantly Ouchtata backed bladelets, the remainder of the tool kit is comprised of straight or arch-backed bladelets (around 8%) followed by backed and obliquely truncated bladelets, notches, denticulates, burins, retouched pieces, perforators, and endscrapers, all with frequencies ranging between 1% and 5%. (Fig. 19)

In marked contrast to the Ouchtata-oriented assemblage at Site E71K13 an adjacent site, known as E71K12, con-

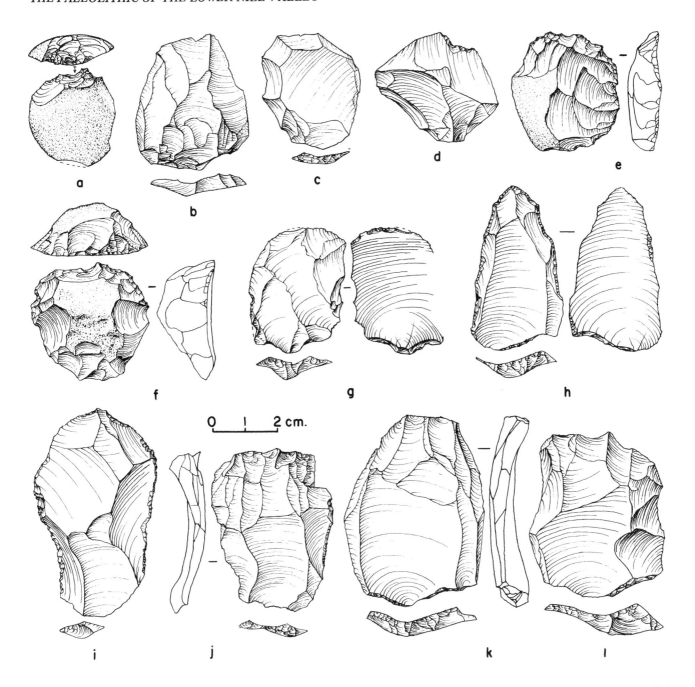

FIG. 11—Tools from Site E71P1C, Trench 5: *a*, groover; *b,k,l*, Halfa flakes; *c,d*, Levallois flakes; *e,f*, endscrapers; *g,i*, retouched Levallois flakes; *h,j*, retouched Halfa flakes.

tained an assemblage with quite different typology and technology, although it was in a closely similar stratigraphic and microenvironmental situation and was also based on bladelets. Most of the cores here are elongated and rounded (in contrast to the flat examples from E71K13), with either opposed or single platforms. A higher frequency of Nile pebbles (around 30%) also were utilized for raw material. Among the tools at Site E71K12 there are few Ouchtata pieces; instead the assemblage is dominated by straight backed and pointed bladelets (66%), many with retouched or truncated bases and/or retouched tips. Retouched tools (12%), notches and denticulates (10%), double-backed per-

forators (4%), Ouchtata retouched bladelets (4%), burins and endscrapers (each less than 2%) complete the tool kit. (Fig. 18)

The fauna from these two localities were all large mammals—hartebeest, *Bos*, and gazelle, in that order. While this suggests a heavy economic dependence on the hunting of savanna animals, it is also possible that poor preservation may be responsible for the absence of fish remains.

The levels of the Nile began to rise during the early phase of the Sahaba-Darau aggradation. The first preserved stratigraphic indication of this event is reflected by the development of numerous ponds which formed, apparently

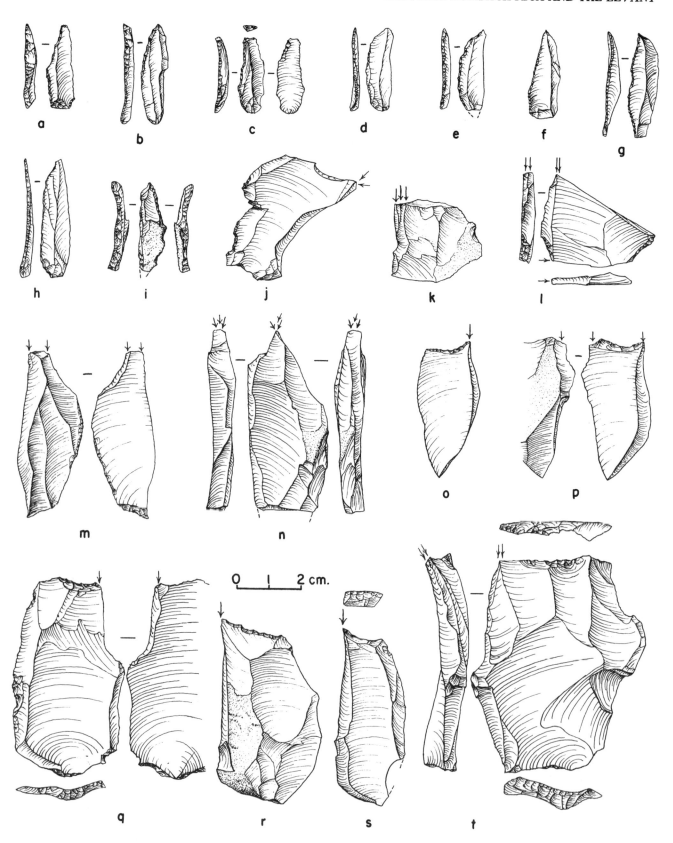

FIG. 12—Tools from Site E71P1C, Trench 5: *a,b,*, arch backed pointed microblades; *c*, backed, truncated and retouched microblade; *d-h*, Ouchtata retouched microblade; *i*, double backed perforator; *j-t*, burins.

FIG. 13—View of Site E71K5, looking southeast. Site occupies all of low sand mound where figures are standing.

by seepage, in the topographic lows behind the dune barriers that had been formed along much of the west bank of the Nile during the final phase of the preceding Ballana-Masmas aggradation. Later, as the level of the Nile continued to rise, most of these ponds and the surrounding dunes were covered by silts recording the maximum of the Sahaba-Darau event. It will be recalled that the beginning of this aggradation is not well dated, although several dates from Nubia and Kom Ombo suggest that it occurred between 13,000 B.C. and 12,000 B.C., and that it reached its maximum around or slightly after 10,000 B.C.

During this period a complex series of highly diverse lithic industries occurred along the Nile, only one of which, the Qadan, seems to have a clear-cut antecedent among the numerous earlier industries in the same area (Shiner, 1968a). The Gemaian, which appears to date during the preceding interval of low Nile levels, seemingly develops directly into the Qadan by a reduction in the frequency of Levallois, by a shift toward a preference for microlithic tools, and by the utilization of geometrics. The Qadan is a microlithic flake industry known at 19 localities, all sharing a similar technology and several tool types, but with considerable variation in the tool kits, probably reflecting a variety of seasonal and/or activity specializations. The characteristic tools are small scrapers, both end and side varieties, made on flakes and usually with some cortex remaining, lunates, arch-backed microflakes, scaled pieces,

and a variety of burins. Cores in these sites also vary in frequency, but in most sites they are about evenly divided between single platform, opposed platform, and bipolar varieties, with the single platform types being slightly more numerous.

The Qadan sites contain numerous remains of large savanna-type mammals, especially Bos and hartebeest, but fishing was also extensively practiced. The most important new development in the Qadan, however, was the appearance of a new economic activity based on the harvesting and grinding of grain of a type as yet unidentified but presumably not domesticated. Wheat rust spores, unfortunately of a form not limited to any particular variety of grain, together with plant cells from a large grain, were recovered from the interdune pond sediments in which occurred the Qadan artifacts, including numerous grinding stones and a few microliths with "sickle sheen." While the type of grass utilized in Nubia remains unknown, there are strong clues as to its probable identity from sites of about the same age, but located farther north in Upper Egypt and associated with a different lithic industry. These sites will be discussed later. The Qadan occurrences are of particular significance in that they record the earliest known extensive use of ground grain for food and probably illustrate an economic stage which just preceded food production.

There are several radiocarbon dates associated with the Qadan. These range from 13,250 B.C. ± 800 years

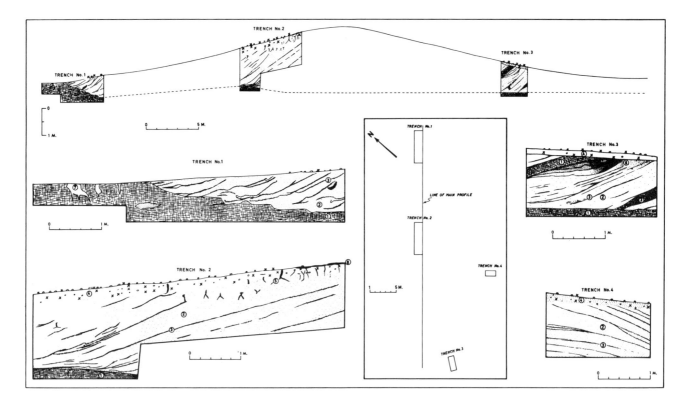

FIG. 14—Profiles for trenches at Site E71K1 showing interfingering of dune sand and Nile silt of the Ballana-Masmas aggradation: 1) brown, sandy silt, highly calcareous; 2) yellowish dune sand; 3) thin streaks and layers of silt within dune, truncated in back; 4) occupation horizon within dune, *Unio* shell yielded radiocarbon date of 16,070 B.C. ± 300 years (I-3416); 5) root drip casts; 6) brownish coarse sand and silt; 7) dehydration cracks filled with coarse sand; 8) thin patches of brownish grayish silt covering in places the surface of the dune and occupation horizons.

(GXO-413) to 4480 B.C. ± 200 years (WSU-190); however, both the oldest and the youngest dates are not regarded as indicative of the true range for the industry. The Qadan sites are consistently associated with the Sahaba-Darau aggradation. It seems likely also that the industry disappeared from the Wadi Halfa–Tushka area with the subsequent recessional event. This would suggest a time range between 12,000 B.C. and 9000 B.C.

The Qadan sites have also yielded our first adequate view of what the people looked like in the Nile Valley at this time. Three graveyards of this period have produced a combined total of over 100 skeletons (Wendorf, 1968, pp. 954-95). As a group the population is characterized by long, heavy craniums, with short, broad faces and well-developed supraorbital ridges. They closely resemble the "Mechta" variety of Cro-Magnon *Homo sapiens* which occur in several seemingly contemporary graveyards in the Maghreb (Anderson, 1968).

A second industry associated with the Sahaba-Darau aggradation is the Sebilian. Prior to the Nubian archaeological salvage program the Sebilian was one of the few well-developed lithic complexes known from the lower Nile Valley. It was represented at a series of sites near Kom Ombo, just north of Aswan (Vignard, 1923, 1928, 1934*b*, 1953, 1955*c*), and was divided into three stages. The earliest stage was characterized by tools made on large flakes,

generally removed from either Levallois or discoidal cores, and consisting predominantly of tools formed by basal and distal truncations, sometimes used in combination with backing, to achieve geometric outlines. Stage II of the Sebilian was closely similar, but the tools were smaller, while Stage III had many microlithic geometrics, some of which were made on microblades. The persistence of Middle Paleolithic–like technology in the Sebilian and the absence of typical Upper Paleolithic tools and technology probably were the major factors which led scholars to conclude that Egypt and the Nile Valley was a culturally conservative cul-de-sac during the Late Pleistocene.

Although originally proposed as a threefold developmental sequence covering a long span of time, it now seems likely that the Sebilian is a unique and apparently short-lived phenomenon in Nubia and Upper Egypt, and clearly not characteristic of either earlier or later Nilotic lithic industries. As used here, the Sebilian refers to Sebilian I and II of Vignard (1923). His Sebilian III apparently includes one or more of the several microlithic complexes mentioned by Smith (1966) and Reed (1966), some of which are stratigraphically earlier than Sebilian I and II.

In addition to the Sebilian sites at Kom Ombo, the number of which is not known, 14 were recorded in Nubia (Marks, 1968*d*), and three others are known from Upper Egypt—two just north of Qena and the other near Idfu

FIG. 15—View of Trench 1 at Site E71K1 showing interfingering of silt and sand of the Ballana-Masmas aggradation.

(Hassan, 1972). All are monotonously similar in technology and typology; although the artifacts at one of the Upper Egyptian sites are significantly smaller, they are closely alike in all other respects. (Fig. 27).

The faunal remains from the Sebilian sites indicate a heavy dependence on large mammal hunting, especially *Bos*, hartebeest, gazelle, and wild ass. Fish remains were not present in any of the Nubian sites, although they are reported from "Middle Sebilian" sites at Kom Ombo (Churcher, 1972). The occurrence of fish at Kom Ombo may indicate some utilization of this resource by the Sebilians; however, there may also be a problem in terminology, since the lithic materials from the Kom Ombo site where the fish occurred have not been described.

Sebilian sites, when they occur *in situ*, are inevitably associated with sediments of the Sahaba-Darau aggradation, and are thus in part contemporary with the Qadan. The dichotomy between the Qadan and Sebilian is so great, with almost no area of similarity between them in either typology or technology, that it is highly unlikely that the two industries are the products of two diverse activities by the same people. Instead, it seems probable that these two industries record a joint occupation of the same area by two quite distinct groups. The two groups may have had different economic specializations, with the Qadan people utilizing fish to a far greater extent than the Sebilians.

The origins of the Sebilian remain an enigma. Although technologically there are superficial resemblances with the Middle Paleolithic, it is separated from that stage by at least 20,000 years during which entirely different lithic traditions were present throughout Nubia and Upper Egypt. An origin outside of this area is clearly indicated. The general similarities with the Tshitolian of tropical Africa may indicate an origin from that general direction, although not necessarily from tropical Africa.

Downstream at Kom Ombo during the Sahaba-Darau aggradation there appear to have been several other and quite different lithic complexes in use, besides the Sebilian. As yet these complexes have not been described, but none of them appear to resemble closely the Qadan. Although the Kom Ombo sites are extremely important, in the absence of more complete descriptions it is difficult to relate them to the materials known elsewhere along the Nile. Based on the preliminary accounts, the Kom Ombo materials do seem to share a closer resemblance with the contemporary industries farther north in Egypt, particularly those found near Esna, than with those from Nubia to the south, and for this reason the

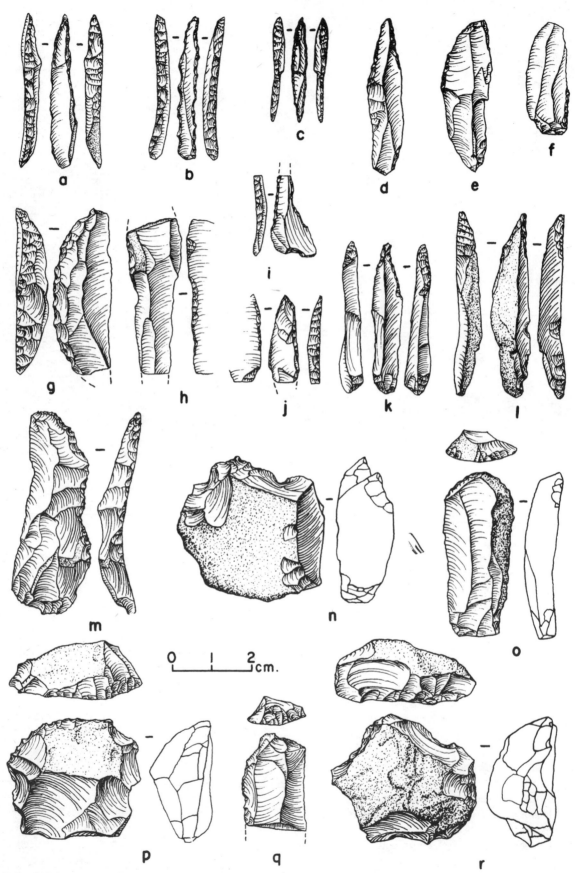

FIG. 16—Tools from Site E71K4: *a-c,i*, doubled backed perforators; *d*, backed and retouched bladelet; *e-f*, retouched bladelets; *g*, arch backed bladelet; *h* retouched bladelet; *j*, backed and retouched bladelet; *k-l*, simple perforators; *m*, denticulated bladelet; *n*, denticulated flake; *o-r*, endscrapers.

FIG. 17—View of Late Paleolithic Site E6102 in the sidewall of the Magahar-Dandara canal. Occupation floor is exposed at level where figures are standing.

Kom Ombo materials will be considered with the industries from Upper Egypt of this period.

Between Idfu and Dishna, a distance of approximately 140 km, there are at least four distinct lithic industries besides the Sebilian present during the Sahaba-Darau aggradation. Not all of these have identical chronological positions, but some of them seem to have identical stratigraphic positions.

Perhaps the earliest of these industries is represented by a single site found a few kilometers north of Esna, Egypt. The lithic assemblage from this site is closely similar to the illustrations of the Silsilian industry named by Smith (1966). There are two radiocarbon dates from a Kom Ombo Silsilian site of 13,360 B.C. ± 200 years (Y-1376), and 12,440 B.C. ± 200 years (I-5180).

At Esna most of the cores from the presumed Silsilian site have traces of typical side and back preparation and opposed platforms. Some were short and were used for flakes, while others were elongated and were used for blades and bladelets. The tool assemblage is dominated by truncated bladelets and backed bladelets, while blades and bladelets with altered bases are also common. The main indices are as follows:

Truncated bladelets, simple (including pieces with microburin scars)	28.1
Truncated bladelets with altered base (ogival, retouched, rounded, etc.)	3.2
Truncated bladelets, double	1.2
Truncated flakes	0.3
Backed bladelets	17.7
Ouchtata bladelets	1.8
Notches and denticulates	17.7
Retouched pieces	2.1
Blades and bladelets with altered base (ogival, retouched, rounded, etc.)	9.5

Of about the same age, or perhaps slightly later, is another industry known as the Affian, found in six separate small concentrations all situated along the margin of a fossil pond located just north of Esna, Egypt and partially imbedded in their basal sediments. Our interpretation of the stratigraphic evidence is that the pond formed by seepage during an early stage of the Sahaba-

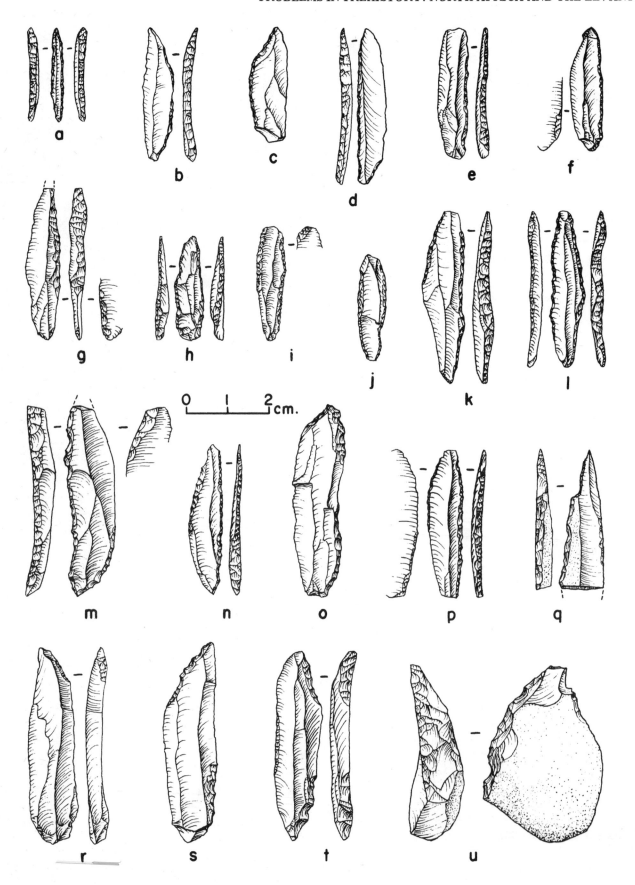

FIG. 18—Tools from Site E71K12: *a*, perforator; *b,c*, arch backed pointed bladelets; *d,f-i,k-q*, straight backed pointed bladelets, retouched; *e*, straight backed blunt bladelet; *j*, straight backed blunt bladelet, retouched, *r-t*, truncated bladelets; *u*, sidescraper.

Darau aggradation was subsequently covered by later silts of that event. An age of around 12,000 B.C. or slightly later is suggested. (Fig. 20)

Two facies seem to be represented, but both share a closely similar technology with common use of wide and flat opposed platform bladelet cores, many of which show traces of preflaking preparation reminiscent of Levallois. The platforms are usually faceted. Levallois cores are common in some assemblages (up to 20%), many of which are a distinct "bent-Levallois" variety (Schild, 1971), while other concentrations have little or no Levallois. The contrast between the two facies of the Affian is indicated by following main typological indices:

TYPOLOGICAL GROUP	E71K18A	E71K18D
Basal truncations, simple on bladelets and microflakes	17.9	5.3
Distal truncations, simple	4.2	–
Geometrics and semi-geometrics	13.5	5.1
Microburins, ordinary and central pressure	12.8	6.7
Backed elements, various	22.6	21.0
Endscrapers	9.0	16.5
Burins	0.7	0.7
Retouched pieces	5.6	16.6
Notches and denticulates	2.4	9.1

Many of the arch-backed and truncated pieces in both facies suggest an incipient stage in the development of compound tools, an extremely interesting suggestion in view of the indicated age of the industry. If indeed the Affian does date around 12,000 B.C. or before, then it and the Silsilian record the earliest massive manifestations of microburin technology known in Northern Africa. (Fig. 21)

The Affian sites at Esna lack all evidence of grinding stones, and there are no tools with traces of "sickle sheen." The industry appears, however, to be closely similar to an assemblage found in Kom Ombo and identified as "Sebilian," which has numerous grinding stones associated with it (Butzer and Hansen, 1968, p. 172; Reed, 1966; Phillips, personal communication). There are two radiocarbon dates of 11,610 B.C. ± 120 years (Y-1447) and 11,120 B.C. ± 120 years (Y-1375) on the Kom Ombo site, which might place it slightly later than is indicated for the Affian sites at Esna. For this reason it is difficult to evaluate whether absence of grinding stones at Esna only indicates different seasonal activities, or if it suggests that the sites were occupied before seed grinding was practiced by that group.

While seed grinding was apparently not done by the Affian groups at Esna, they did hunt large savanna animals, mostly *Bos* and hartebeest, and also fished extensively, primarily for large Nile catfish.

A third lithic manifestation found along this stretch of the Nile during the Sahaba-Darau aggradation is known thus far at only one site (E71K6, Area A). Almost all of the cores at this site are the opposed platform rounded variety for bladelets and flakes. There are a few cores with single platforms, but Levallois is not present, and the tool kit has no known analogies elsewhere along the Nile. Its main typological indices are as follows:

Endscrapers	40.0
Retouched pieces	14.0
Borers (on blades and bladelets)	10.0
Burins	7.0
Backed pieces (mostly arch-backed bladelets)	7.0
Notches and denticulates	7.0
Truncated blades and bladelets	6.0

This assemblage has a stratigraphic position closely similar to that of the Affian and was located on either the same or a closely adjacent interdune pond. Clearly, however, there are few elements in common between the two groups.

The fourth lithic complex which occurs along the Nile between Idfu and Dishna is known as the Esnan industry. The Esnan is the most numerous both in terms of numbers of sites and in the size of the occupation areas of all known lithic complexes for any period in Upper Egypt. In this respect the Esnan is similar to the contemporary Qadan in Nubia. It is perhaps significant that these two industries have radically different lithic technologies and typologies but share an important economic exploitative emphasis.

The Esnan sites are known from three widely separated areas—one group near Esna, another group near Nagada, and a third group at Dishna. Stratigraphically the occupations occur both before and after the extensive fire which swept this area during a late phase of the Sahaba-Darau aggradation, and one site was occupied during the subsequent recessional event. A time range from around 10,600 B.C. to 9500 B.C. is indicated. (Figs. 22 and 23)

Several variations of settlement situations are represented. At Esna the sites are very large, and yet they lack evidence of internal clustering suggestive of reoccupation. They suggest continuous and long-lasting settlements by a large population. At Dishna, while the sites are large, they represent, at least in some instances, several reoccupations of the same locality. At Nagada, on the other hand, the sites are not large, but they are numerous.

The lithic industry is produced exclusively by the use of hard hammer technique on large nodules and slabs of Eocene flint. The cores are large, almost all are for flakes, and more than half are of the unpatterned changed orientation variety. Preparation was usually limited to the striking platform. The tool kit from the sites at Esna is dominated by endscrapers (up to 64%), followed by notches and denticulates (from 11% to 19%), burins (between 3% and 13%, with burins being more frequent in the younger sites), and

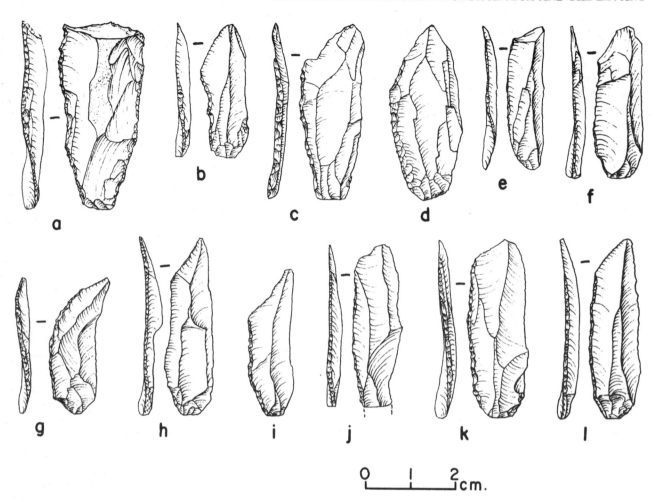

FIG. 19—Tools from Site E71K13: *a*, backed and truncated piece; *d*, retouched bladelet; *b-c,e-l*, Ouchtata retouched bladelets.

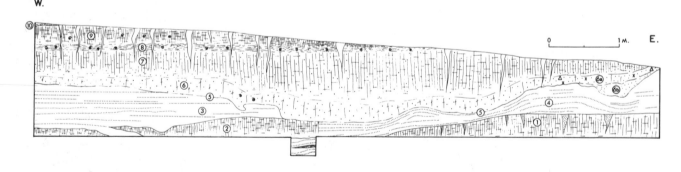

FIG. 20—Profile of Trench 3 at Affian site E71K18A: 1) light brownish silt with desiccation cracks filled with reddish dune sand; 2) same silt as "1"; 3 and 4) yellowish reworked dune sand; 5) surface of erosion; 6) gray sandy silt, "lower pond deposit"; 7) pinkish sandy silt, "middle pond deposit"; 8) light gray diatomite, with numerous snails; 9) gray sandy silt, "upper pond sediment"; 10) dark gray Nile silt, Sahaba-Darau aggradation.

retouched tools (around 5% to 7%). Backed elements, including arch-backed blades, and backed and truncated pieces are rare. Grinding stones also occur, and up to 15% of all *in situ* tools may display lustrous edges. (Fig. 24)

The Esnan sites contain numerous large mammal remains, especially *Bos* and hartebeest, but there are no fish except in the latest site. Perhaps in some way this puzzling absence of fish may be related to the evident heavy dependence on ground grain at most Esnan sites. While no examples of the grain utilized were recovered, a pollen profile from a pond where one of the Esnan communities was situated disclosed a sudden increase in a large cereal-type pollen (to around 15%) at the same level where the first appearance of the Esnan occupation occurs. This large

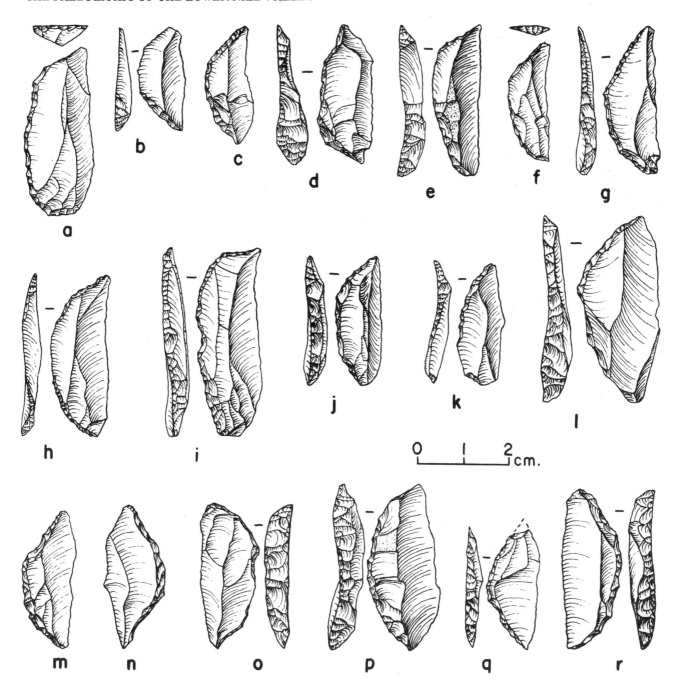

FIG. 21—Tools from Site E71K18A. *a,i*, arch backed and distal truncated bladelets; *b*, basal truncated bladelet; *c,g,l-r*, arch backed double pointed bladelets; *d*, arch backed and basal truncated bladelet; *e-f*, partially backed and distal truncated bladelet; *h*, partially backed double pointed bladelet; *j*, arch backed bladelet; *k*, arch tipped bladelet.

cereal-type pollen has been tentatively identified as *barley* by Dr. M. J. Dambrowski, of the Polish Academy of Sciences (Wendorf and Schild, in press).

If barley was present along the Nile south of Luxor, and was exploited as a wild plant, we must assume a significantly different climate than that of today for this region during the end phase of Late Pleistocene. Summer temperatures, particularly, would have to be much cooler. As previously noted there is other evidence, principally from the diatoms from these same pond sediments, which suggests both less tropical temperatures and reduced evaporation

during this period. This might explain why food production failed to develop at an early date along the Nile. Wild barley could not have survived in this area after the present hot and arid climatic regime became established. When this occurred is not known, but it may well have been already in process during the recession which follows the Sahaba-Darau aggradation.

The Esnan sites at Dishna occur in the same stratigraphic context as the sites at Esna, and the two groups are closely similar; but the Dishna sites differ by displaying higher frequencies of notches, denticulates, and retouched pieces,

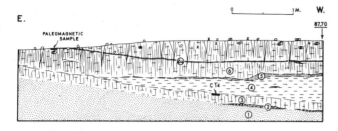

FIG. 22–Profile of Esnan Site E71K14A: 1) yellowish gray dune sand; 2) grayish diatomaceous sediment with admixture of sand, "lower diatomite;" 3) dark gray carbonaceous sand, yielded radiocarbon date of 10,740 B.C. ± 240 years (I-3421); 4) light gray diatomaceous sediment, at western edge interfingers with layer of loose beach sand; 5) grayish loose calcareous sand; 6) dark grayish brown sandy silt (Sahaba-Darau aggradation) with burned layer near middle of unit; 6a) cultural layer in upper 15 cm of silt, unit 6.

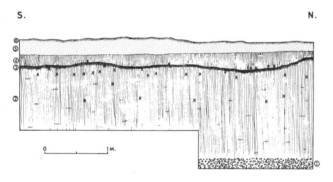

FIG. 23–Profile of Trench 1 at Site E61M9C, Esnan industry, near Dishna, Egypt: 1) local gravels, pebbles, and cobbles in pale olive sand; 2) olive gray silt (Sahaba-Darau aggradation) with burnt layer 2 at top, contains slightly polished artifacts; 3) baked clay lumps and silt with heated artifacts (burnt layer); 4) gray silt with artifacts in basal part; 5) light yellowish brown fine-grained sand, unstratified, cemented (playa sediment); 6) salt crust.

and by the absence of grinding stones and lustrous edge pieces. Many of them also contain higher proportions of debitage, possibly reflecting a greater emphasis on workshop activities. From the absence of grinding stones at Dishna one might infer either that the utilization of seeds was restricted to certain seasons not represented in the Dishna sites, or that grain grinding was an economic activity not practiced by all the Esnan peoples.

Because of the scarcity of exposures there is very little archaeological data which can be confidently attributed to the interval represented by the recession which follows the Sahaba-Darau aggradation. Only one site is known in Nubia for this period and it yielded too few artifacts to characterize as to the industry represented. A similar situation occurs in Upper Egypt where also only one site is known (E71P5), but this one did produce an adequate sample. The lithic assemblage from this site is closely related to the Esnan industry, with a tool kit dominated by retouched flakes and blades (39.3%), followed by endscrapers (16.5%), and notches and denticulates (12.1%). The categories of burins,

backed elements, truncated pieces (some identical to those in Sebilian sites), and geometrics (mostly trapezes) were all present, but minor, with each representing between 2% and 3% of the total tools. The site also contained two grinding stones and several pieces with lustrous edges. Blades are more frequently used for tools (27%) than in earlier Esnan assemblages, a feature also shared with the sites of this industry at Dishna. The site yielded a radiocarbon date of 9610 B.C. ± 180 years (I-3760). (Figs. 25 and 26)

THE FINAL PLEISTOCENE AND RECENT EVENTS

THE GEOLOGY

During the seven thousand year interval which follows the onset of the Birbet recession at the end of the Sahaba-Darau aggradation, there is another major episode of higher Nile sedimentation, which we propose to identify as the Arkin-Arminna aggradation, followed by a complex series of minor, or perhaps better characterized as short-lived, recessions each followed by a microaggradation. Traces of these events have been observed not only in Nubia, but also in Upper Egypt and still farther north in the Fayum. The sequence of levee remnants in the vicinity of Arkin in Nubia is particularly interesting.

The upper part of the Arkin aggradation there reached an elevation of 13 m above the modern floodplain and is dated at 7410 B.C. ± 180 years (WSU-175). This date, together with the sample noted earlier from near the base of these silts at a nearby locality which dated 9250 B.C., provides the best estimate of the time period represented in the Arkin-Arminna aggradation. This was followed by a recession and then another aggradation to 9 m above the floodplain, which is dated at 5750 B.C. ± 120 years (WSU-176). Below this a 6 m levee was formed and a sample from it is dated 5960 B.C. ± 120 years (SMU-4), regarded as slightly too old. The final event in this series is a 5 m levee which has three dates of 3650 B.C. ± 200 years (WSU-174), 3460 B.C. ± 150 years (SMU-1), and 3830 B.C. ± 150 years (SMU-2).

A complete sequence comparable to that at Arkin is not known elsewhere in Nubia and Upper Egypt, although portions have been noted at several localities. In Upper Egypt a thin lense of silt, presumably of the Arkin-Arminna aggradation, yielded two dates of 8450 B.C. ± 470 years (I-3428) and 7380 B.C. ± 160 years (I-3422). Not far away, at El Kab, a buried silt with an associated lithic industry similar to that in the 9 m levee at Arkin has three dates of 6400 B.C. ± 160 years (LV-393), 6040 B.C. ± 150 years (LV-464), and 5980 B.C. ± 160 years (LV-465). A later event is recorded at Catfish Cave in Egyptian Nubia, where silts at an elevation of 16 m above the floodplain, possibly recording a series of unusually high floods, are dated 5110 B.C. b 120 years (Y-1646).

Only in the Fayum depression, just south of Cairo, where an unusually sensitive record of Nile fluctuations is preserved, do we find a sequence similar to that at Arkin. Sediments in the depression record four succeeding Holocene lakes, the water for which was derived almost entirely,

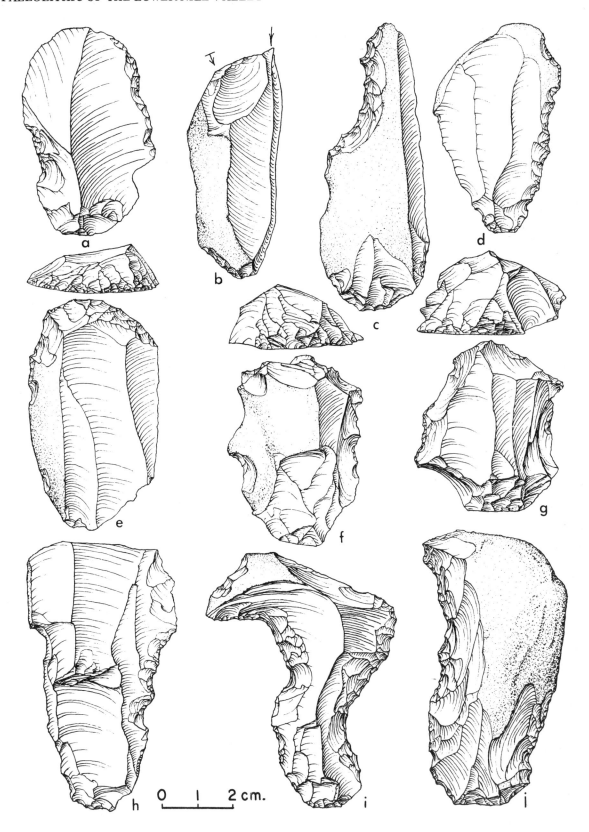

FIG. 24—Tools from Sites E61M6D, 10B, and 10C. *a,c*, notched pieces; *b*, burin or truncated blade; *d,h*, denticulated flakes; *e,g*, endscrapers; *f*, denticulated endscraper; *i*, strangled flake; *k*, sidescraper.

if not entirely, from the Nile. The fluctuations in these lakes, therefore, undoubtedly reflect changes in the level of the river. The earliest, known as the Paleomoeris Lake, is undated. It is known only by lacustrine sediments from the base of several pits and trenches, and has been tentatively correlated with the Arkin-Arminna aggradational event. It

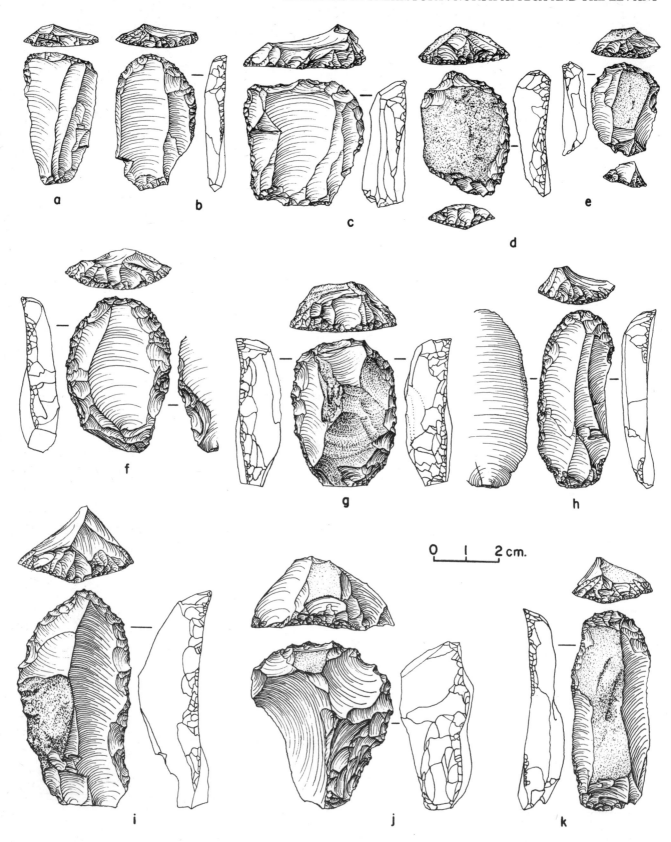

FIG. 25—Endscrapers from Site E71P5A.

was followed by a recession in which the deep water sediments were deeply cracked and dehydrated. (Fig. 28)

The succeeding Premoeris Lake reached a maximum ele-

vation of more than 17 m above sea level and has two dates
of 6120 B.C. ± 115 years (I-4126) and 6150 B.C. ± 130
years (I-4128). These dates seem to correlate closely in time

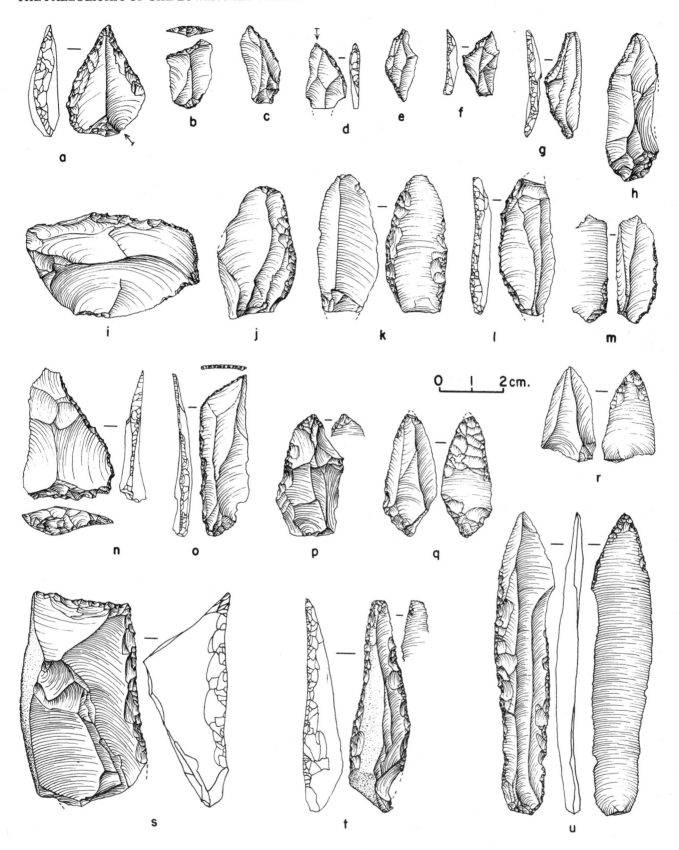

FIG. 26—Tools from Site E71P5A. *a*, perforator; *b*, oblique distal truncated flake; *c*, partially backed microblade; *d*, basal truncated microblade; *e*, trapeze, one edge poorly retouched; *f*, geometric; *g*, triangle; *h,j-k*, retouched blades; *i,s*, retouched flakes; *l*, arch backed double pointed bladelet; *m*, arch backed, truncated and retouched bladelet; *n*, backed, basal and distal truncated flake; *o*, backed and distal truncated bladelet; *p-r*, bifacially retouched point; *t*, bilateral retouched blade; *u*, pointed retouched blade with basal blunting.

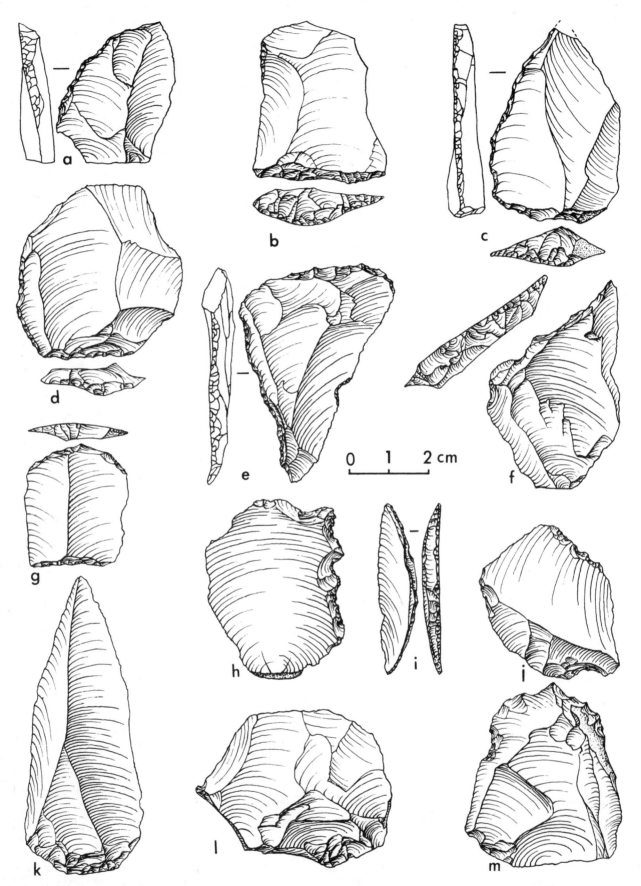

FIG. 27–Tools from Site E61M1A, B. *a*, distal truncated flake; *b*, basal truncated flake; *c*, backed, basal truncated flake; *d*, backed, basal truncated flake; *e*, backed, distal truncated flake; *f*, distal truncated flake; *g*, endscraper on truncated piece; *h*, denticulate; *i*, lunate; *j*, notched and retouched flake; *k*, Levallois blade; *l*, Levallois flake; *m*, notched flake.

FIG. 28–View of excavations at Qarunian Site E19G3, Area A, near Fayum, Egypt. Occupation floor is in dark humus layer (swamp soil) in foreground and extends under base of remnant.

with those from both the 9 m levee at Arkin and the El Kab silts in Upper Egypt, and presumably record an interval of comparatively high Nile around 6000 B.C. or slightly later.

During the following recession, which at one locality is dated 5550 B.C. ± 125 years (I-4130), the lake fell well below 12 m above sea level, and wadis, suggesting significant local rainfall, were cut through the sediments of the earlier lake. (Figs. 29 and 32)

The basin again refilled to form the Protomoeris Lake, perhaps to the highest level of all, around 24 m above sea level. This event has one date of 5190 B.C. ± 120 years (I-4129), which is closely similar to the indicated age of the high flood silts in Catfish Cave (5110 B.C.).

The Protomoeris Lake is followed by a long interval of comparatively low water levels, presumably slightly before 4000 B.C., at which time the basin again began to fill and formed the historic Lake Moeris. There are two dates on the early part of this event: 3910 B.C. ± 115 years (I-4131) and 3860 B.C. ± 115 years (I-4127), and a third from slightly higher of 3210 B.C. ± 110 years (I-3469). The upper part of the lake, at 23 m above sea level, is associated with elaborate harbor facilities of Old Kingdom age which, on the basis of the associated pottery, are estimated to date around 2800 B.C. After the Old Kingdom, the lake appears to have shrunk, presumably because of lower Nile levels,

until the time of Amenemhat I, who is reported to have initiated water engineering activities at a time when the lake stood around 18 m above sea level. It is interesting to note that the decline to the modern lake of Birket Qarun is due to the dam built across the Nile inlet to the Fayum. This dam seems to have been first constructed by Ptolemy I, who is reported to have lowered the level of the lake in order to reclaim the silt fan at the entrance to the Fayum depression (Ball, 1939).

THE ARCHAEOLOGY OF THE FINAL PLEISTOCENE AND RECENT EVENTS

The only known localities which definitely were occupied throughout the three thousand year period of the Arkin-Arminna aggradation and the subsequent recession are clustered in one small area along the west bank of the Nile opposite Wadi Halfa. These sites yielded a lithic complex known as the Arkinian industry. It is possible, but by no means well established, that some of the Qadan sites also refer to this period (Shiner, 1968a). The Arkinian technology made frequent use of bipolar techniques in producing flakes. Microblades and small flakes were often obtained from single platform cores (Schild et al., 1968). In the thirteen concentrations known, endscrapers and backed bladelets (and microblades) dominate the tool kit, with

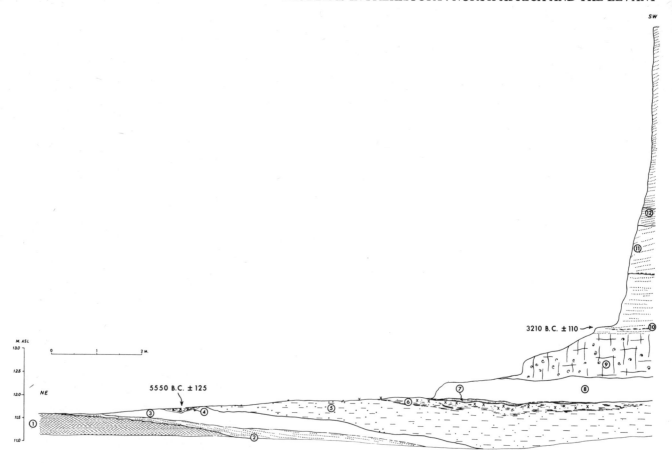

FIG. 29–Profile of Trench 1, Site E29G3, Area A, Qarunian industry: 1) pale yellow Eocene shale; 2) yellow silty sand with dip toward basin; 3) white diatomite, truncated by "5;" 4) dark gray laminated swampy sediment in small channel cut into "3," contains fresh Qarunian artifacts, adjacent extensive exposure of this unit contains charcoal which gave radiocarbon date of 5500 B.C. ± 125 years (I-4130); 5) light yellowish brown wadi fill with numerous pebbles and cobbles, grades into "6;" 6) gray wadi fill containing reworked "4" with numerous Qarunian artifacts slightly rolled and heavily patinated, surface clearly eroded; 7) pale brown coarse sand with gravels; 8) white diatomite, eroded at top; 9) light gray silty sand with numerous small lacustrine shells; 10) pale yellow foreset-bedded sand with layer of fish bones and charcoal, charcoal gave radiocarbon date of 3210 B.C. ± 110 years (I-3469); 11) pale yellow coarse-grained sand unconformably overlying "10," with charcoal and bones on an erosional surface, clear foreset-bedding; 12) yellow medium-grained sand unconformably over "11," foreset-bedded.

endscrapers representing from 23% to 52%, and backed elements from 34% to 66% of all tools. Other important tool classes include scaled pieces, perforators and lunates, together with a few triangles and trapezes. Grinding stones and lustrous edge pieces also occur. The Arkinian sites contain numerous bones from large savanna animals, especially *Bos*, hartebeest, and gazelle. Fish were also common.

Over a thousand years separates the Arkinian from the next known industrial complex along the Nile. After around 6000 B.C. the known sites are numerous, and they occur in four widely separated areas. The southernmost of these areas is in the vicinity of Wadi Halfa, where two lithic industries are found—the Shamarkian, known at six sites along the west bank (Schild et al., 1968), and an unnamed complex recorded at two sites in the Second Cataract area above Wadi Halfa (Marks, 1970, pp. 40-75).The unnamed industry is believed to be of about the same age as the earliest known Shamarkian site, and it shares with the Arkinian an emphasis on bipolar technique and backed bladelets and microblades, but has few other points of simi-

larity. Besides the backed bladelets (34% and 25%), the more important tools are burins (15% and 10%), scaled pieces (10.5% and 5.7%), truncated pieces (5.2% and 11.9%), notches and denticulates (11.8% and 20.2%). Lunates and trapezes are absent.

The Shamarkian, dated between 5700 B.C. and 3500 B.C., made no use of the bipolar technique, and there are also differences in material preferences in that both are primarily on chert, but the Shamarkian used more quartz and rarely employed Nile Agate. The Shamarkian tool kit also emphasize backed bladelets and microblades (62%); but it has few burins (less than 1%), low index of endscrapers, practically no scaled pieces, and much lower values for notches and denticulates (2.7%). The more recent Shamarkian sites continue the same general technological and typological characteristics found earlier, and in addition they contain side-blow flakes, numerous double backed perforators, triangle-rectangles, and pointed bladelets with retouched bases. The frequency of truncations also increases through time, and there is a general decline in workmanship. Grinding stones are present, but are not common. Significantly, neither mammal nor fish remains are numerous in the Shamarkian sites at Halfa, except for Site D1W51 which contained relatively large numbers of fish bones, in marked contrast with the situation at the earlier Arkinian sites. Pottery occurs with the most recent Shamarkian sites, around 3800 B.C.

An assemblage possibly related to the Shamarkian was recovered from Catfish Cave, located on the east bank of the Nile downstream from Wadi Halfa in Egyptian Nubia. The Catfish Cave lithic assemblage has not been described in detail, but the illustrated pieces indicate an emphasis on backed bladelets, microblades, and truncated bladelets. No scaled pieces or bipolar cores were noted. Catfish Cave also produced a large number of carved bone harpoons.

Still farther north, near the Old Kingdom fortress of El Kab in Upper Egypt, is another probable Shamarkian site with two occupation levels, both of which yielded lithic assemblages closely similar to that at the earliest Shamarkian site near Wadi Halfa (Vermeersch, 1970), although they differ by having a higher frequency of microburins and slightly lower values for arch-backed bladelets. The general similarities in technology and typology are so close, however, that a placement within the Shamarkian industry seems appropriate.

In northern Egypt in the Fayum, a generally similar industry, named the Qarunian, occurs during this period associated with sediments of both the Premoeris and Protomoeris Lakes. The industry is produced from small, single platform cores, with preparation limited to the platforms. It is primarily a backed bladelet industry, most of which are the pointed arch-backed variety, often with retouched or truncated bases (from 18% to 30%), followed by pointed straight backed bladelets with altered bases (from 14% to 18%). Shouldered and blunt tip backed bladelets also occur, as do a few true blades. Notches and denticulates are also common, ranging from 9% to 17% of all tools. The sites contain occasional geometrics, mostly triangles and trapezoids, perforators, and rare endscrapers. Grinding stones are also present, but not common. Worked bone, mostly small "harpoons" made from catfish jaws, and larger cylindrical double pointed pieces also occur. None of these sites contain any pottery. (Figs. 30 and 31)

The Qarunian sites were clearly oriented toward fishing, and most of them are situated where fish could be easily obtained. Fish remains are exceedingly common in the camp debris, and bones of large mammals also occur, of which the most common is hartebeest, followed by gazelle, hippopotamus, and a few Bos. There are four radiocarbon dates from these sites ranging from 6150 B.C. ± 130 years (I-4128) to 5190 B.C. ± 120 years (I-4129). (Fig. 32)

A gap of about 1,200 years separates the latest Qarunian assemblages from the next known complex in the Fayum, a fully developed Neolithic with pottery, domestic animals, and grains. These settlements have been named "Fayum A" (Caton-Thompson and Gardner, 1934), and they are associated with sediments of Lake Moeris. The associated lithic

assemblage in these Fayum A sites is radically different from that of the preceding Qarunian. The Qarunian blade technology is replaced by one based primarily on the exploitation of flakes produced by a hard hammer technique. Several new tool types appear, including stemmed and concave based arrowheads and bifacial tools, the latter made on tabular flint. The backed blades and bladelets of the earlier Terminal Paleolithic assemblages are either absent or very rare. The differences between the latest Paleolithic communities and the succeeding Neolithic settlements are so extensive that few points of continuity are evident. It seems likely, therefore, that a new population must have appeared in Egypt around 4000 B.C., and brought with them the Neolithic society which formed the basis for the earliest Egyptian civilization.

No data on the transition between the Terminal Paleolithic and the Neolithic are available for Upper Egypt, but in Nubia, in the vicinity of Wadi Halfa, there is a reasonably complete sequence for this period. The continuity in the Shamarkian from the Terminal Paleolithic into the Ceramic Period has already been discussed, but two other lithic complexes with early pottery also occur in this area. The Abkan is a microlithic flake industry emphasizing single platform cores (Shiner, 1968a). Besides simple pottery, these sites characteristically yield a high frequency of fractured quartz, even though this material was rarely used for retouched tools. Most of the tools are made on Nile chert. The Abkan has high frequencies of three tool groups: groovers (from 10% to 25%), lightly retouched scrapers (both end and side varieties at from 5% to 14% each), and denticulates (around 11%). Other less important tools are truncations, notches, and backed flakes (each around 6% to 8%). Lunates and burins are less common (2% to 3%), while geometrics are absent. There are a number of obvious resemblances between the Abkan and the Qadan in both technology and typology, and it has been suggested that the Qadan was the direct antecedent. There are also significant differences, some of which may be due to the considerable span of time which apparently separates the most recent Qadan site studied during the Nubian salvage program and the earliest Abkan site. This question conceivably could be resolved by reexamining the collections from the series of excavations conducted by Myers in 1948 and 1957 at several sites in the vicinity of Abka (Myers, 1958, 1960; di Cesnola, 1960). There are several radiocarbon dates from Myers's sites, ranging from 7350 B.C. to 2550 B.C. The upper levels are clearly assignable to the Abkan industry, with the first pottery occurring in a level dated 4000 B.C. The lithic materials from the earlier levels, however, are not described in sufficient detail to determine if they are Qadan or should be assigned to some other industry.

Still another quite different industry occurs with early ceramics in the Wadi Halfa area. This group, identified as the Khartoum Variant, was represented at eight sites. There are close parallels in the pottery and in some of the lithics with Shaheinab and similar sites farther south in central Sudan. The Khartoum Variant pottery is highly distinctive,

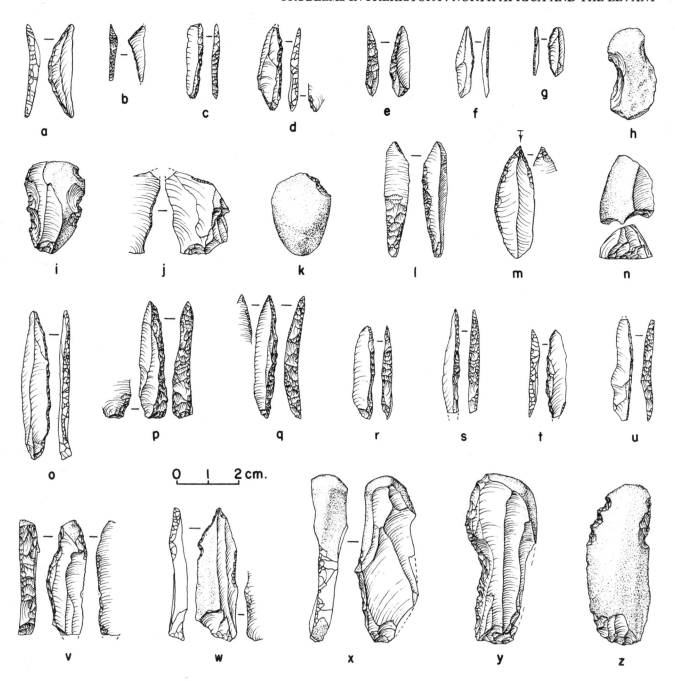

FIG 30—Tools from Site E29G3A, Trench 2. *a*, lunate; *b*, scalene triangle; *c,d*, straight backed microblade; *e*, arch backed pointed microblade; *f,g*, Ouchtata retouched microblade; *l,m*, pointed bladelet with normal and inverse retouch; *n*, basal truncated flake; *o-q*, arch backed pointed bladelet; *r-u*, straight backed pointed bladelet; *v*, arch backed bladelet with inverse notch; *w*, groover; *x*, partially backed bladelet; *y*, notched and retouched bladelet; *z*, denticulated and retouched bladelet.

with cord-impressed designs and micaceous paste. The associated lithics also differ from the Abkan in having much less frequent use of quartz, higher blade tool indices (around 12), and a tool kit which emphasizes backed flakes, truncated pieces, and a distinctive multi-edge scraper, the latter frequently made on Egyptian flint. None of the Khartoum Variant sites were dated, but the occupation is believed to have occurred between 3500 B.C. and 4000 B.C., or at about the same time as the Abkan. Faunal remains were absent from the Khartoum Variant sites.

CONCLUSION

Several rather obvious points seem to emerge from this brief survey of the Pleistocene sediments and associated Paleolithic materials in the lower Nile Valley.

1. The Early Paleolithic is virtually unknown in the Nile Valley except for a few workshops and quarries in the vicinity of Wadi Halfa. It seems highly likely, however, that this situation could be readily corrected if the remnants of the older Nile sediments preserved below Idfu, on both the

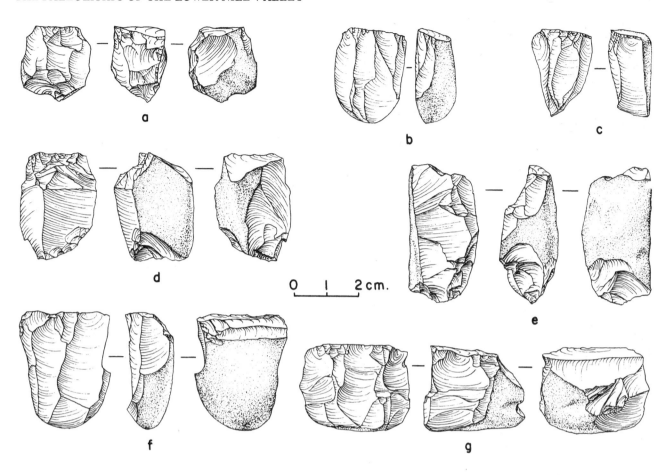

FIG 31—Cores from Site E29G3A, Trench 2.

east and west banks, could be examined closely for living sites. The Acheulean from the vicinity of Wadi Halfa, and the occasional finds from downstream in Upper Egypt, appear to be significantly different from the Acheulean in the adjacent Sahara, as illustrated by the finds at Kharga, Dakhla, and Bir Sahara.

2. Knowledge of the Middle Paleolithic is also limited to Nubia, where one lithic industry has some resemblances to Middle Stone Age materials from farther south; two other lithic industries are closely similar to the Typical and Denticulate Mousterian of Europe and the Near East; and a fourth complex seems to be similar to the Denticulate Mousterian at Bir Sahara. As in the Acheulean, Middle Paleolithic sites are known to occur in Upper Egypt, but as yet none have been systematically collected.

3. Exploitation of the specific Nilotic microenvironment, as indicated by an emphasis on fishing, occurs at least as early as the Middle Paleolithic in Nubia.

4. In spite of one radiocarbon date of greater than 36,000 years ago from a Late Paleolithic site, there appears to be a major gap in the Paleolithic sequence between the Middle Stone age and the earliest Late Paleolithic materials. In no instance does there appear to be a continuity between the two stages. In large part this probably reflects the emphasis which has been given in recent survey projects to the Later Paleolithic remains and the very limited examina-

tions given to earlier deposits, at least in Upper Egypt.

5. Insofar as the later Pleistocene sediments are concerned, episodes of maximum aggradation along the Nile do not correlate consistently with periods of either increased local rainfall or increased aridity, thus the relationship between increased rainfall in East Africa, water runoff down the Nile, and local climate in Egypt and the adjacent northeastern Sahara are not clear cut. Correlations of East African pluvials with either cool-moist periods or arid intervals in Egypt are premature.

6. A characteristic feature of Late Paleolithic lithic industries along the Nile is their diversity. Unlike Western Europe and the Near East, where a continuity of development over an extended period of time is usually evident, along the Nile we find that during any geologic episode the area was occupied by several diverse groups, each with radically different lithic traditions, and each seemingly exploiting closely similar if not identical microenvironments either at the same time, or possibly separated by only brief periods of time. This diversity continues throughout the Later Paleolithic and is even evident in the early Ceramic Period.

7. For most time periods the Late Paleolithic in Upper Egypt is generally different from that of Nubia. The more northern sites have a *tendency* toward greater emphasis on blades and bladelets, and in this respect are more similar to

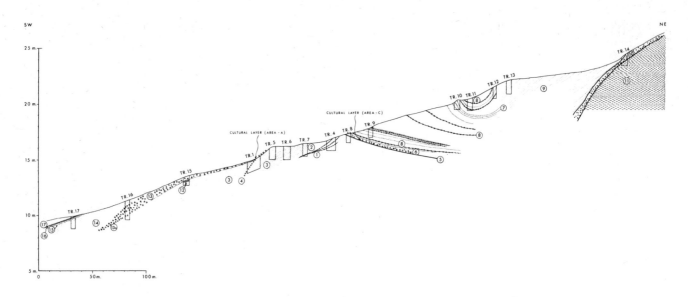

FIG. 32–General cross section of Site E19H1, Qarunian industry. A. *Premoeris Lake*: 1) deltaic beach sand; 2) dark swamp layers with *Pila ovata*; 3) deltaic beach; 4) cultural layer (Qarunian industry) with radiocarbon date of 6120 B.C. ± 115 years. B. *Protomoeris Lake*: 5) pronounced erosional surface; 6) coarse sand with crushed shells and younger occupation with Qarunian industry; 7 and 8) intercalated beds of sandy silts and swamp sediments, sometimes burnt; 9) beach sands; 10) older slopewash; 11) Eocene shale; 12) sandy silt with dehydration cracks; 13) fine sand with numerous shells; 14) deltaic sands; 15) soil; 16) pronounced erosional surface. C. *Moeris Lake*: 17) diatomite.

contemporary materials of Cyrenaica and the Levant than are the usually flake-oriented Late Paleolithic industries of Nubia.

8. Industries which emphasize macrolithic flake technology apparently briefly replace the blade industries in Upper Egypt and Nubia around 11,000 B.C. These flake industries have no known close analogies elsewhere in Africa, but in our present state of knowledge a southern source seems likely. Blade or bladelet technology again becomes dominant in several industries during the Terminal Paleolithic in both Nubia and Upper Egypt, and either persists or reappears in northern Egypt in the Fayum.

9. Two lithic traits of widespread significance have an early history in the Nile Valley. These are composite tools, possibly indicated by high frequencies of microlithic tools, which occur around 18,000 B.C. in the Halfan, and the microburin technique, which is present around 12,000 B.C.–11,000 B.C. in Upper Egypt.

10. Extensive utilization of wild grain, tentatively identified as barley, occurred in the Nile Valley before 11,000 B.C., and perhaps as early as 13,000 B.C. There is no evidence that this grain technology led to the development of food production in this area.

11. Nubia and Upper Egypt shared closely similar lithic industries during the Terminal Paleolithic, and these were generally similar to contemporary assemblages in the Fayum.

12. Neolithic food-producing communities initially appear at Fayum and probably elsewhere along the Nile in Lower Egypt around 4000 B.C. and contain lithic assemblages radically different from those of the preceding Terminal Paleolithic, dated around 5000 B.C., suggesting the appearance of a new population.

13. Neolithic or at least ceramic-using and probably food-producing communities occur farther upstream in Nubia only slightly later, ca. 3800 B.C., and at least some of these have an evident continuity in lithic traditions with those of the preceding Terminal Paleolithic in that area, which may indicate that in those instances a radical change in population may not have occurred. Other ceramic groups, particularly those with Khartoum-related pottery, have a different lithic technology with no known local antecedents. These probably have origins elsewhere.

BIBLIOGRAPHY

ALEEM, ANWAR ABDEL, 1958, "Taxonomic Paleoecological Investigation of the Diatom-Flora of the Extinct Fayorem Lake (Upper Egypt)." *University of Alexandria Bulletin* 2:217-44.

ANDERSON, J. E., 1968. "Late Paleolithic Skeletal Remains from Nubia." In *The Prehistory of Nubia*, edited by F. Wendorf, 2:996-1038. Dallas: Fort Burgwin Research Center and Southern Methodist University Press.

BALL, JOHN, 1939. *Contributions to the Geography of Egypt*. Cairo: Survey and Mines Department.

BUTLER, BARBARA, 1974. "Analysis of Skeleton from Site E71K1." In *The Fakhurian: A Late Paleolithic Industry from Upper Egypt and Its Place in Nilotic Prehistory*, by D. Lubell. Cairo: Papers of The Geological Survey of Egypt 58.

BUTZER, KARL W., and HANSEN, CARL L., 1968. *Desert and River in Nubia*. Madison: University of Wisconsin Press.

CATON-THOMPSON, G., 1946. "The Levalloisian Industries of Egypt." *Proceedings of the Prehistoric Society* 12(4):57-120.

————, 1952. *Kharga Oasis in Prehistory*. London: Athlone Press.

————, and GARDNER, E. W., 1934. *The Desert Fayum*. London: Royal Anthropological Institute.

CHAVAILLON, JEAN, and CHAVAILLON, JEAN MALEY, 1966. "Une Industrie sur Galet de la Vallée du Nil (Saudan)." *Bulletin de la Société Préhistorique Française* 63(2):65-70.

CHMIELEWSKI, W., 1965. "Archaeological Research on Pleistocene and Lower Holocene Sites in Northern Sudan: Preliminary Results." In *Contributions to the Prehistory of Nubia*, edited by Fred Wendorf, pp. 147-64. Dallas: Fort Burgwin Research Center and Southern Methodist University Press.

————, 1968. "Early and Middle Paleolithic Sites near Arkin, Sudan." In *The Prehistory of Nubia*, edited by Fred Wendorf, 1:110-47. Dallas: Fort Burgwin Research Center and Southern Methodist University Press.

CHURCHER, C. S., 1972. *Late Pleistocene Vertebrates from Archaeological Sites in the Plain of Kom Ombo, Upper Egypt*. Toronto: Royal Ontario Museum Life Science Contribution 82.

CURRELLY, C. T., 1913. "Catalogue général des Antiquities Egyptiennes du Musée du Caire, Nos. 63001-64906, Stone Implements." Le Caire.

di CESNOLA, ARTURO PALMA, 1960. "L'Industria Litica della Stazione di Abka." *Kush* 8:182-236.

GIEGENGACK, R. F., JR., 1968. "Late Pleistocene History of the Nile Valley in Egyptian Nubia." Ph.D. dissertation, Yale University.

GREEN, DAVID L.; EWING, GEORGE H.; and ARMELAGOS, GEORGE J., 1967. "Dentition of a Mesolithic Population from Wadi Halfa, Sudan." *American Journal of Physical Anthropology* 27(1):41-56.

GUICHARD, JEAN, and GUICHARD, GENEVIEVE, 1965. "The Early and Middle Paleolithic of Nubia: A Preliminary Report." In *Contributions to the Prehistory of Nubia*, edited by Fred Wendorf, pp. 57-116. Dallas: Fort Burgwin Research Center and Southern Methodist University Press.

————, and GUICHARD, G., 1968. "Contribution to the Study of the Early and Middle Paleolithic of Nubia." In *The Prehistory of Nubia*, edited by Fred Wendorf, 1:148-93. Dallas: Fort Burgwin Research Center and Southern Methodist University Press.

HASSAN, FEKRI A., 1972. "Note on Sebilian Sites from Dishna Plain." *Chronique d'Egypte* 47:11-16.

_____, 1974. *The Archaeology of the Dishna Plain*. Cairo: Papers of The Geological Survey of Egypt 59.

de HEINZELIN, JEAN, 1968. "Geological History of the Nile Valley in Nubia." In *The Prehistory of Nubia*, edited by Fred Wendorf, 1:19-55. Dallas: Fort Burgwin Research Center and Southern Methodist University Press.

_____, 1971. "Geology: Ed Debba to Korti." In *The Prehistory and Geology of Northern Sudan*, assembled by Joel L. Shiner. Mimeographed report to the National Science Foundation.

HESTER, JAMES, and HOEBLER, P., 1970. *Prehistoric Settlement Patterns in the Libyan Desert*. University of Utah Papers in Anthropology 92, Nubia Series 4. Salt Lake City: University of Utah Press.

IRWIN, HENRY T.; WHEAT, JOE BEN; and IRWIN, LEE F., 1968. *University of Colorado Investigations of Paleolithic and Epipaleolithic Sites in the Sudan, Africa*. University of Utah Papers in Anthropology 90. Salt Lake City: University of Utah Press.

LUBELL, DAVID, 1971. "The Fakhurian: A Late Paleolithic Industry from Upper Egypt and Its Place in Nilotic Prehistory." Ph.D. dissertation, Columbia University.

_____, 1974. *The Fakhurian: A Late Paleolithic Industry from Upper Egypt and Its Place in Nilotic Prehistory*. Cairo: Papers of The Geological Survey of Egypt 58.

MARKS, ANTHONY E., 1968a. "The Mousterian Industries of Nubia." In *The Prehistory of Nubia*, edited by F. Wendorf, 1:194-314. Dallas: Fort Burgwin Research Center and Southern Methodst University Press.

_____, 1968b. "The Khormusan: An Upper Pleistocene Industry in Sudanese Nubia." In *The Prehistory of Nubia*, edited by F. Wendorf, 1:315-91. Dallas: Fort Burgwin Research Center and Southern Methodist University Press.

_____, 1968c. "The Halfan Industry." In *The Prehistory of Nubia*, edited by F. Wendorf, 1:393-460. Dallas: Fort Burgwin Research Center and Southern Methodist University Press.

_____, 1968d. "The Sebilian Industry of the Second Cataract." In *The Prehistory of Nubia*, edited by F. Wendorf, 1:461-531. Dallas: Fort Burgwin Research Center and Southern Methodist University Press.

_____, 1970. *Preceramic Sites*. The Scandinavian Joint Expedition to Sudanese Nubia Publications, vol. 2, edited by Torgny Säve-Söderbergh. Helsinki: Scandinavian University Books.

_____; SHINER, JOEL L.; and HAYS, T. R., 1968. "Survey and Excavations in the Dongola Reach, Sudan." *Current Anthropology* 9(4):319-23.

_____; SHINER, JOEL L.; SERVELLO, FRANK; and MUNDAY, FREDERICK, 1971. "Flake Assemblages with Levallois Techniques from the Dongola Reach." In *The Prehistory and Geology of Northern Sudan*, assembled by Joel L. Shiner. Mimeographed report to the National Science Foundation.

MYERS, O. H., 1958. "Abka Re-Excavated." *Kush* 6:131-41.

_____, 1960. "Abka Again." *Kush* 8.

PHILLLIPS, JAMES L., 1970. "Oeuvre récente sur L'Epipaléolithique de la Vallée du Nil: Rapport préliminaire." *L'Anthropologie* 74(7-8):573-81.

_____, 1972. "North Africa, the Nile Valley, and the Problem of the Late Paleolithic." *Current Anthropology* 13(5):587-90.

_____, 1973. *Two Final Paleolithic Sites in the Nile Valley and Their External Relations*. Cairo: Papers of The Geological Survey of Egypt 57.

————, and BUTZER, KARL W., in press. "A 'Silsilian' Occupation Site (GS2B-II) of the Kom Ombo Plain, Upper Egypt: Geology, Archaeology, and Paleoecology." *Quaternaria* 16.

REED, CHARLES A., 1966. "The Yale University Prehistoric Expedition to Nubia, 1952-1965." *Discovery* 1(2):16-23.

SAID, RUSHDI; ALBRITTON, CLAUDE C.; WENDORF, FRED; SCHILD, ROMUALD; and KOBUSIEWICZ, MICHAL, 1972a. "Remarks on the Holocene Geology and Archaeology of Northern Fayum Desert." *Archaeologia Polona* 13:7-22.

————; ALBRITTON, C.; WENDORF, F.; SCHILD, R.; and KOBUSIEWICZ, M., 1972. "A Preliminary Report on the Holocene Geology and Archaeology of the Northern Fayum Desert." In *Playa Lake Symposium*, edited by C. C. Reeves, Jr., pp. 41-61. Lubbock: Icasals Publication No. 4.

————; WENDORF, FRED; and SCHILD, ROMUALD, 1970. "The Geology and Prehistory of the Nile Valley in Upper Egypt." *Archaeologia Polona* 12:43-60.

SANDFORD, K. S., 1934. *Paleolithic Man and the Nile Valley in Upper and Middle Egypt*. Chicago: University of Chicago Oriental Institute Publication 18.

————, and ARKELL, W. J., 1929. *Paleolithic Man and the Nile-Fayum Divide*. Chicago: University of Chicago Oriental Institute Publication 10.

————, and ARKELL, W. J., 1933. *Paleolithic Man and the Nile Valley in Nubia and Upper Egypt*. Chicago: University of Chicago Oriental Institute Publication 17.

————, and ARKELL, W. J., 1939. *Paleolithic Man and the Nile Valley in Lower Egypt*. Chicago: University of Chicago Oriental Institute Publication 46.

SCHILD, ROMUALD, 1971. "Nowa, Nieznana Odmiana Lewaluaskiej Metody Rdzeniowania z Poznego Paleolitu w Gornym Egipcie (A New Variety of the Levallois Method of Flaking from the Late Paleolithic of Upper Egypt)." *Archeologia Polski* 16:75-84.

————; CHMIELEWSKA, MARIA; and WIECKOWSKA, HANNA, 1968. "The Arkinian and Shamarkian Industries." In *The Prehistory of Nubia*, edited by F. Wendorf, 2:651-767. Dallas: Fort Burgwin Research Center and Southern Methodist University Press.

SCHWEINFURTH, G., 1903. "Steinzeitliche Forschungen in Ober-Aegypten." *Zeitschrift für Ethnologie* e. 798.

————, 1904. "Steinzeitliche Forschungen in Ober-Aegypten." *Zeitschrift für Ethnologie* 5:766.

————, 1905. "Recherches sur l'age de la pierre dans la Haute-Egypte." *Annales du Service des Antiquities de l'Egypte*. Le Caire.

————, 1909. "Uber Altpalaeolithische Manufakte aus dem Sandsteingebiet von Oberagypten." *Zeitschrift für Ethnologie* s. 735.

SHINER, JOEL L., 1968a. "The Cataract Tradition." In *The Prehistory of Nubia*, edited by F. Wendorf, 2:535-629. Dallas: Fort Burgwin Research Center and Southern Methodist University Press.

————, 1968b. "Miscellaneous Sites." In *The Prehistory of Nubia*, edited by F. Wendorf, 2:630-50. Dallas: Fort Burgwin Research Center and Southern Methodist University Press.

————, 1968c. "The Khartoum Variant Industry." In *The Prehistory of Nubia*, edited by F. Wendorf, 2:768-90. Dallas: Fort Burgwin Research Center and Southern Methodist University Press.

SIIRIANEN, ARI, 1965. "The Wadi Halfa Region (Northern Sudan) in the Stone Age." *Studia Orientalia* 30(4):3-34.

SMITH, PHILIP E. L., 1966. "The Late Paleolithic of Northeast Africa in the Light of Recent Research." *American Anthropologist* 68(2):326-55.

————, 1967. "New Investigations in the Late Pleistocene Archaeology of the Kom Ombo Plain (Upper Egypt)." *Quaternaria* 9:141-52.

STERNS, F. H., 1917. "The Paleolithic of the Eastern Desert." *Harvard African Studies* 1.

VERMEERSCH, P., 1970. "Une Nouvelle Industrie Epipaléolithique à elkab en Haute-Egypte." *Chronique d'Egypte* 45(89):45-67.

VIGNARD, EDMOND, 1921*a*. "Une Station Aurignacienne à Nag Hammadi (Haute-Egypte), Station du Champ de Bagasse." *Bulletin de l'Institut Français d'Archaeologie Orientale* 18:1-20.

————, 1921*b*. "Les Stations Paléolithique d'Abou del Nour à Nag Hammadi." *Bulletin de l'Institut Français d'Archaeologie Orientale* 20:89.

————, 1923. "Une Nouvelle Industrie Lithique, le Sebilien." *Bulletin de l'Institut Français d'Archaeologie Orientale* 22:1-76.

————, 1928. "Une Nouvelle Industrie Lithique, le Sebilien." *Bulletin de la Société Préhistorique Française* 25:200-220.

————, 1934*a*. "Les Microburins Tardenoiseiens du Sebilien: Fabrication, Enpolis, Origine de Microburin." *Congrès préhistorique de France 10e Session, 1934*, pp. 66-106.

————, 1934*b*. "Le Paléolithique en Egypt." *Mémoires de l'Institut Français d'Archaeologie Orientale* 66:165-75.

————, 1935. "Le Microburin est-il Sebilien?" *Bulletin de la Société Préhistorique Française* 32.

————, 1947. "Une Station du Sebilien III, à Reggan-Taourirt, dans le Tanezrouft, Sahara Central." *Bulletin de la Société Préhistorique Française* 44:293-313.

————, 1955*a*. "Menchia, Une Station Aurignacienne dans le Nord de la Plaine de Kom Ombo (Haute-Egypte). *Congrès Préhistorique de France 14e Session, Strasbourg, 1953*, pp. 634-53.

————, 1955*b*. "Un Kjoekkenmodding sur la rive droite du Wadi-Shait dans el Nord de la Plaine de Kom-Ombo (Haute-Egypte)." *Bulletin de la Société Préhistorique Française* 52:703-8.

————, 1955*c*. "Les Stations et Industries Sebiliennes du Burg el Makkazine, Region de Kom-Ombo (Haute-Egypte)." *Bulletin de la Société Préhistorique Française* 52:437-52.

————, 1957. "Point de vue nouveaux sur l'industrie du Champ de Bagasse près de Nag Hammadi (Haute-Egypte)." *Bulletin de la Société Préhistorique Française* 54:298-313.

VINOGRADOV, A. V., 1964. Sebilskaya Kultura Urajone Dakki." (In Russian).

WENDORF, FRED, (ed.), 1965. *Contributions to the Prehistory of Nubia*. Dallas: Fort Burgwin Research Center and Southern Methodist University Press.

————, (ed.), 1968. *The Prehistory of Nubia*, 2 vols. and atlas. Dallas: Fort Burgwin Research Center and Southern Methodist University Press.

————, and SAID, RUSHDI, 1967. "Paleolithic Remains in Upper Egypt." *Nature* 215:244-47.

————; SAID, RUSHDI; and SCHILD, ROMUALD, 1970*a*. "Egyptian Prehistory: Some New Concepts." *Science* 169:1161-71.

_____; SAID, RUSHDI; and SCHILD, ROMUALD, 1970*b*. "Late Paleolithic Sites in Upper Egypt." *Archaeologia Polona* 12:19-42.

_____; SCHILD, R.; and SAID, R., 1970*c*. "Problems of Dating the Late Paleolithic Age in Egypt." In *Radiocarbon Variations and Absolute Chronology*, edited by I. U. Olsson. Nobel Symposium 12, Upsala. Stockhom: Almqvist and Wiksell.

_____, and SCHILD, R., in press. "The Use of Ground Grain during the Late Paleolithic of the Lower Nile Valley, Egypt." In *Papers of the Burg-Wartenstein Symposium No. 56, held August 19-27, 1972, on the Origin of African Plant Domesticates*, edited by J. R. Harlan. The Hague: Mouton Publishers.

IBEROMAURUSIAN RELATED SITES IN THE NILE VALLEY

James L. Phillips
University of Illinois - Chicago Circle

The term given by North African prehistorians for the lithic assemblages which postdate the Late Pleistocene Aterian and predate the post-Pleistocene Typical and Upper Capsian is that of the "Iberomaurusian." Pallary introduced the term and based his definition on his own excavations at La Mouillah in the Maghreb, and also upon the work of Siret in Spain (Siret, 1893; [Pallary, 1909]).

Pallary defined the "Iberomaurusian" as an industry which contained hammerstones, cores, simple and notched blades, many small pointed backed blades, circular end-scrapers, discs, some pebbles with either ochre or hematite coloring, and some perforators of polished bone. True geometric microliths were exceedingly rare, but crescent-shaped bladelets did appear. No polished stone nor pottery occurred (Pallary, 1909, pp. 45-46).

Both the concept of the "Iberomaurusian" and the term itself have been brought up for review many times, notably by Gobert and Vaufrey (1932), Antoine (1952), Gobert (1952), Roche (1963), Tixier (1963), the Second Pan-african Congress in Algeria in 1952 (Balout, 1955), and Vaufrey (1955). During the early years after its introduction into the literature, the term was accepted. After further work had been concluded, however, prehistorians (Gobert and Vaufrey, 1932, for example) felt that the term was meaningless and did not account for the lithics found in the new sites. New terms were suggested, such as the "Oranian" and the "Mouillian," but it was felt that as the term "Iberomaurusian" was already in the literature from an early date it therefore had priority over the recently invented terms (Gobert, 1952, 1954a, 1962; Balout, 1955).

The "Iberomaurusian" has been divided by several authors, based on their own work at recently discovered sites (Antoine, 1934, 1952; Balout, 1955; Cadenat, 1948; Gobert, 1958, 1962; Roche, 1953, 1963). Antoine (1952, pp. 371-72) proposed a two-part division: *Ibéromaurusien ancien* (I), characterized as having no microburins (El-Khenzira) and only a few geometric microliths; and *Ibéromaurusien récent* (II), which is entirely microlithic and has microburins (Bouskoura). Cadenat (1948, pp. 3-66) proposed, on the basis of his excavations at Columnata, a "lower" and "upper" "*Oranien*." Engraving on bone appears only in the latter; the lithic assemblage was all microlithic and contained microburins, while the "lower" had no microburins and was not entirely microlithic.

J. Morel (1953, pp. 157-78) proposed a tripartite division of the "Iberomaurusian": "*Une Ibéromaurusien 'archaisant' à dominante levalloiso atérienne*" (an ancient or lower Iberomaurusian with predominantly Levalloiso-Aterian artifacts), which was well represented at Demnet el-Hassan; "*Une Ibéromaurusien moyen encore alourdi de formes anciennes qu'il étudie au Kef oum Touizar*" (a middle Iberomaurusian, still with ancient forms, such as those from Kef-oum Touizar); and "*Une Ibéromaurusien évolué, absolument microlithique, celui de La Mouillah*," etc. (an evolved Iberomaurusian, absolutely microlithic, such as that of La Mouillah, etc.). The "Iberomaurusian" at Demnet el-Hassan which contained the Aterian elements seems to have been a mixed site, or one where the latter occupants used the artifacts left by the people of the Aterian culture.

Lionel Balout (1955, pp. 382-83), cognizant of the above attempts at subdividing the "Iberomaurusian," proposed another tripartite division, but one based on much more evidence than any of the others. He proposed an "*Ibéromaurusien I, ou ancien, ou Proto-Ibéromaurusien*" which is typified by the assemblages from the *Horizon Collignon* at Sidi Mansour à Gafsa. This is an industry which is pre-Capsian, and is typologically characterized by the complete lack of all Capsian influence, particularly geometric microliths; no microburins occur. This unit is subdivided into a littoral facies (Ia), where there are also large tools of "Levalloiso-Mousterian" appearance. The industry is not entirely microlithic and is generally quite poor. Geometric microliths are quite rare, but a few microburins do occur. There is no bone tool assemblage present.

The unit which is next or younger is the "*Ibéromaurusien II, ou classique*." The industry is microlithic; a few geometric microliths occur, and in some sites there are numerous microburins, while in others they are missing. In several sites there is a bone tool assemblage, but it may well be absent from others. The bone assemblage is generally absent from surface sites, but bone needles and perforators do appear in cave sites. Balout thinks that Level C at Taforalt is the transitional site between Iberomaurusian I and II. He feels that Levels A and B at Taforalt contain assemblages which are equivalent to the assemblages in such sites as La Mouillah, El-Khenzira, Kifan bel Youdi, Kifan bel Ghomar, El-Hank upper level, El Kçar, Abri Alain, Columanta lower level, Ain Guedara (?), and El-Hamel lower level. All of the sites mentioned above are what Balout would also call "*Ibéromaurusien typique*" (Balout, op. cit., p. 382). Balout also sees an evolved phase of this stage and calls it "*Ibéromaurusien IIa*" (p. 382).

The Iberomaurusian IIa occurs in certain open air sites where the bone industry is not preserved (due to natural causes). The sites of Ouchtata, Oued Akarit A, El-Hamel middle level (?), Bouskoura, and perhaps Oueds Kerma are representative of this stage.

Balout's third unit, "*Ibéromaurusien III, ou évolué*," is found only at two sites in the Maghreb, Columnata, upper level, and Champlain. Balout feels that the stratigraphy at Columnata attests to this evolution within the industry. It is entirely microlithic, and is characterized by the delicacy and fineness of the lithic tools. There are great varieties of bone tools which "announce" the Neolithic (Balout, op. cit., p. 383).

In the same work where he proposed the tripartite division of the "Iberomaurusian," Balout also tried to remove the term from the literature. He proposed that the term "*epipaléolithique*" be substituted to include that period in Maghrebian prehistory which was post-Aterian, and pre-Neolithic (Balout, op. cit., p. 337). Both the Abbé Roche (1963) and J. Tixier (1963) use this term.

Thus, we have three terms which are synonymous with the "Iberomaurusian": *Mouillen, Oranien*, and a term with a somewhat larger meaning, *epipaléolithique*. It should be noted that, except for the sites of Taforalt, Columnata, El-Hamel, Djidjelli Ouest, Sidi Mansour à Gafsa (*Horizon Collignon*), Rassel, Tamar Hat, and Courbel-Marine, there are almost no stratified sites which have been excavated enough to show the place of the "Iberomaurusian" in any stratigraphic sequence. Therefore, the exact stratigraphic and chronological placement of this complex is at present very much in question. It has proved very difficult to correlate the geological occurrences of the stratified "Iberomaurusian" sites, perhaps because they occur over a 1,000-kilometer east-west range, and are found both along the littoral and inland. It is true, however, as both Gobert and Balout have claimed, that when we have a stratified site the "Iberomaurusian" overlies the Aterian and underlies the Capsian.

Furthermore, the concept of an evolution from an ancient to an evolved "Iberomaurusian" rests on rather fragile evidence; the interpretation can be questioned at many points. The relationship between such sites as Sidi Mansour (*Horizon Collignon*) and Lalla, with the rest of the "Iberomaurusian" (Phillips, 1972) is open for discussion; the queries rest on both the question of typology and the stratigraphic relationship between the sites near Gafsa which are under the "*manteau gypseux*" (gypsum crust) (Gobert, 1954*b*, 1962; Castany and Gobert, 1954), and those which occur stratigraphically above them.

The assemblages found at Lalla, near Gafsa, and within the *Horizon Collignon* at Sidi Mansour à Gafsa, both *in situ* sites, are characterized by a series of pointed backed bladelets (no further breakdown has been published), backed and obliquely truncated bladelets (*lamelles scalenes*), Ouchtata retouched bladelets; no perforators, geometric microliths, microburins, nor burins occur. Lalla contains 10% endscrapers, while Sidi Mansour à Gafsa has only 3.2%. Collections from both the *Horizon Collignon* and Lalla were analyzed with technological questions in mind (Phillips, 1970, 1972, 1973). Our observations, based on a rather inferior sample from both sites, show that the blades from Lalla are rather flat and parallel-sided, and 95% fall into the

bladelet category (defined as blades 3-5 cm in length). The few cores which have been preserved are opposed platform types, with the characteristic nibbling on the unfaceted platforms (the nibbling retouch was probably used for regularizing the edge of the platform). Many of the bladelets were obtuse and displayed Ouchtata retouch (see Gobert, 1962, p. 297, fig. 13; Castany and Gobert, 1954, p. 27, fig. 10, and p. 28, fig. 11, for illustrations).

The artifacts from the *Horizon Collignon* were generally microlithic except for some of the Ouchtata retouched pieces which were bladelets. Thus, even these two sites had quite different blade size qualifications, and different frequencies of pointed backed bladelets (Lalla contained 46.5% and the *Horizon Collignon* 62.5% of this group; see the type list in Gobert, 1962, p. 291 for the counts).

The Cave of Rassel is located on the Algerian coast on the east flank of the Chenoua Massif and the right bank of a small wadi (Brahimi, 1970, p. 37). The cave has two archaeological levels; the upper, ca. 1 meter thick (level II, *supérieur*), contains pottery, a flint assemblage dominated by backed bladelets and notched and denticulated tools, a bone-tool assemblage, and a human skeleton. Brahimi also mentions a "*à affinités néolithique*" level III, (*inférieur*), which contains a very rich lithic assemblage dominated by backed bladelets (66.7%) and microburin technique (9%). Endscrapers account for 5% of the assemblage, while notches and denticulates together equal 6%. Perforators, burins, backed blades, truncations, and geometric microliths together account for only 2.5% of the tools.

The excavator seems to feel that the lithic assemblage closest to Rassel is Taforalt VIII, stratigraphically earlier than the 10,120 B.C.–dated level VI.

The site of El-Hamel, located in central Algeria, southwest of the *Chotte el-Hadna*, is an open-air site in the presaharan Atlas mountains. The site is on a terrace of the Wadi Hamel and is stratified above Mousterian-Aterian horizons. The "Iberomaurusian" is found in Level E, in a matrix of brown-black clayey sand, from 1.10 to 1.40 m below the surface. According to Tixier (1954), over 30% of the 1,091 backed bladelets at the site have some sort of basal retouch. The backed bladelets make up 83.1% of all tools. Of the 208 entire and 883 broken backed bladelets, only three are over 50 mm; thus the assemblage is composed mainly of bladelets (we do not have the data for microlithic index). Only four of the unbroken bladelets have retouched tips. Tixier (personal communication) mentions that some of the backed bladelets had, in reality, Ouchtata retouch, but he had not separated these pieces out at the time he wrote the article on El-Hamel. Thus the backed bladelet frequency would drop some, and the Ouchtata frequency would rise.

Lionel Balout (1955, pp. 348-49), supporting his statements with the works of Gobert (1952) and Gottis (1953), states that the stratigraphy at Ouchtata is probably approximate to that of both the *Horizon Collignon* sites and Lalla. The dunes at Ouchtata, specifically the fossil dunes, were stabilized by vegetation during the Flandrian Transgression, and then covered by modern dunes. The sites were discovered when the wind action removed the recent cover and exposed the fossil dunes which were littered with lithic artifacts, shell and faunal remains. If Balout's interpretation is correct, then we see at this time a facies of the "Iberomaurusian" which is typologically entirely different from that of Lalla (see Balout's *Ibéromaurusien* II*a*, p. 192).

DATING

Table 1 indicates the dates for the Iberomaurusian.

TABLE 1

Radiocarbon Determinations for the Iberomaurusian
of the Maghreb

	B.P.	Lab	B.C.
Taforalt, Layer II	10,800 ± 400	(Sa.)	8,850
Taforalt, Layer VI	12,070 ± 400	(Sa.)	10,100
Taforalt, Layer VIII	10,500 ± 400	(Sa.)	8,550
Taforalt, Cemetery	11,900 ± 240	(L.)	9,950
Rassel, Layer III	14,270 ± 400	(Alg.)	12,320
Tamar Hat Layer I	12,450 ± 400	(Alg.)	10,500
Oued Guettara	10,190 ± 230	(GIF 882)	8,140

Haua Fteah Oranion Sequence

Haua Fteah Layer XV-XIV	12,750 ± 175	(NPL 43)	10,800
Haua Fteah Layer XIV	12,580 ± 175	(NPL 44)	10,630
Haua Fteah Layer XIV	12,300 ± 350	(W97)	10,350
Haua Fteah Layer XI-XII	10,600 ± 300	(W104)	8,650

The Haua Fteah material is very interesting, as it is a bladelet assemblage with a heavy emphasis on obliquely truncated and backed forms, in addition to a number of microburins. As McBurney himself indicates (1967, pp. 214, 327), a possible Levantine connection rather than any intense Maghrebian relation may obtain (see McBurney's discussion of possible connections, 1967, pp. 213, 327). Thus the Maghrebian sites seem to be younger than comparable sites in the Nile Valley.

THE NILE VALLEY

Since 1960, a number of terminal Paleolithic occurrences have been found in the Nile Valley, leading several investigators to speculate on both the nature and origin of the inhabitants (Marks, 1968; Phillips, 1970, 1972, 1973; Smith, 1966, 1968; Wendorf, 1968; Wendorf et al., 1970*a*, 1970*b*). A number of these scholars postulated probable direct relationships between the Nile Valley and the Maghreb, based on their analysis of lithic assemblages from both areas (Phillips, 1970, 1972, 1973; Schild et al., 1968; Smith, 1966; Wendorf, 1968; Wendorf et al., 1970*a*). The technocomplex to which all scholars refer is that of the Iberomaurusian. In fact, an investigator familiar with the North African material has labeled certain Nile Valley assemblages "Iberomaurusian, Nilotic Ouchtata facies" (Tixier, personal communication). A discussion of the Iberomaurusian was presented in the first part of the paper; this section will present the Nile Valley material.

Of the sites mentioned as candidates for the Iberomaurusian, one is in Nubia (Site Dibiera West I-Arkinian), while the remainder are found on the east bank of the River on the Kom Ombo Plain, and on the west bank near Esna, approximately 100 km north of Kom Ombo. Several different industrial terms have been applied to these sites, Arkinian, Sebekian, Complex D, Complex E, etc. They all share several features, mainly their lithic similarities, locale near permanent water, economic activities, and their relative contemporaneity (except for the Arkinian, all are dated between 17,000 B.P. and 14,000 B.P.).

The similarities in the lithic assemblages which appear to be significant to the various authors are the following: all assemblages are based on the production of blades/bladelets/microblades; the endscraper and burin indices are low; Ouchtata retouch is present and fairly substantial; microburin technique is rare, as are geometrics; and notches and denticulates are well represented. Depending on the raw material, cores are single, opposed, or with multiple platforms.

One of the type fossils of the Iberomaurusian, the Ouchtata retouched bladelet (Phillips, 1973, pp. 39, 68-74; Tixier, 1963, pp. 114-17), is found in most sites near Esna, although the frequency varies considerably. Since these pieces have been found in the Negev (Marks et al., 1971, 1972), and recently in North Sinai (Phillips et al., in press), this type of retouch can no longer be considered as an "indicator" of the Iberomaurusian. What is significant, however, is that at one site near Esna (E71K13), these pieces account for over 78% of the tool assemblage.

The period between 15,000 B.C. and 12,000 B.C. is placed by Wendorf et al. (1970*a*, 1970*b*) in the Deir el-Fakhuri recessional interval, and by Butzer and Hansen (1968) in the Darau Member of the Gebel Silsila Formation. This period was characterized by a series of episodes indicating that ponds were formed in topographic lows between dunes, perhaps by seepage from the Nile. Wendorf et al. (1970*b*, p. 63) point out that the accumulation of diatomite to a depth of 70 cm indicates more or less permanent ponds. The formation of the ponds may be interpreted, according to Wendorf, as a consequence of cooler summer temperature, but this may just as well indicate less evaporation due to other more local conditions. Sites are located on the shores of these ponds (Afian and Esnan industries) or on, or within, dunes stabilized by vegetation. All but one of the sites which might be correlated with the Iberomaurusian occur within this period, although it is at least conceivable that one or two of these occur at the end of the preceding Dibeira-Jer aggradation.

METHODOLOGY

One of the problems inherent in any comparative analysis, especially in one concerning areas nearly 2,000 km apart, is the lack of comparable units of analysis. Assigning a site in the Nile Valley to the "Iberomaurusian" complex requires not only a very high artifact correlation (using, of course, the same typology), but it also calls for a series of statistical tests which would indicate that these similarities cannot be due to chance.

It was decided to use as statistical tests correlation coefficients, multiple regression, factor analysis, and several other tests, in order to evaluate the hypothesis that the sites in the Nile Valley were *not* "Iberomaurusian." The multiple regression, factor analysis, and Kolmagorov-Smirnov tests are still being analyzed. This paper presents only the first part of the group of tests, namely coefficients of correlation. Two sets of tests were run. One with artifact frequencies expressed in terms of classes of tools, such as endscrapers, burins, backed bladelets, etc., while the other set used only the frequency of Tixier types 45-72, i.e., backed bladelets (Tables 2 and 3). These particular types were used for several reasons: (1) this is the most important class of tools in every Iberomaurusian site; (2) the variations between these types should reflect style differences rather than functional ones; (3) these style differences may be viewed as cultural proclivities and might help define several such units; and (4) the units could occur as clusters of attributes (or in this instance, types) reflecting quite obvious shape and retouch choices by the knapper.

Table 4 indicates that two major groups of sites occur, with several subsidiary or ancillary groups on the side. Thus, all North African sites except Ouchtata Rive Gauche and Ouchtata Rive Gauche 2 are highly correlated with one another. Nearly every correlation coefficient is greater than .9000. This is not the case, however, when the Nile Valley material is reviewed. Three units can be separated out from the Nile Valley material. Most interesting is the fact that three of these sites are very highly correlated with the two North African units.

Actually, Group III also could be grouped under Group I if a separate category for Ouchtata retouched bladelets were not used. Thus, if they were to be grouped under backed bladelets, ORG, ORG2 and K13 would belong to Group I. The test does indicate that the seriated postulated division of the Iberomaurusian into three stages does not obtain. A facies difference does, however, exist. Those sites which have an abundance of Ouchtata retouched bladelets, and consequently less backed bladelets, could be classified as an Ouchtata facies.

It might be postulated that given similar levels of technology, contemporaneity, ecological situation, and hunting proclivities, the gross tool kit also would be similar. If this is the case, the fact that two of the Nile Valley sites (K5 and K12) are grouped in the correlation test with most of the North African sites does not indicate a real connection at all. The importance of the Ouchtata facies is yet to be

determined. Since the technology from the site of Lalla (most likely the earliest of the Iberomaurusian occurrences) is quite different from that of Ouchtata itself, it is a bit difficult to reconcile the similarity in tool types. It is possible that the Ouchtata *facies* may be, in fact, a very specific activity variation within the Iberomaurusian.

Table 5 is most important, for it presents the correlation coefficients based on the 23 types of backed bladelets found in Tixier's typology (1963). A high correlation between sites would, in the writer's opinion, indicate a very real *cultural* relationship between them. One would not expect, however, to have as high coefficients as one would when dealing with tool classes. Thus, coefficients of correlation greater than .6500–.7000 would be equivalent to those of .8000–.9000 when discussing the larger groups.

It is immediately noticeable that most of the Maghrebian sites have coefficients greater than .8000 when set against each other. It is also interesting that the Nile Valley sites again fall into several groups.

Analyzing Tables 4 and 5, some very intriguing things are discovered. Site K5 (Fakhurian) has correlation coefficients greater than .6000 with all of the Maghrebian sites and with Sites K3 and K4 (Fakhurian) in the Nile Valley. It has a low correlation (.4266) with Sites K12 and K1 (Fakhurian). Most interesting about these figures is that Site K5 had a very *high* correlation with site K12 when tested with *classes* of tools (.9465). This tends to support the hypothesis that gross classes of tools from contemporaneous and similarly adapted sites, given close technological levels, will be very much alike.

Site K12 also has correlation coefficients greater than .6000 with all Maghrebian sites except Oued Kerma, although the coefficients are less than those of Site K5 with the same sites. The only site in the Nile Valley with a coefficient greater than .6000, set against K12, is El-Kab.

El-Kab has the highest coefficients with Maghrebian sites of all the Nile Valley sites tested, especially with Oued Kerma (.8091). This is really interesting, as El-Kab is the only site in the sample which is post-Pleistocene (dates: 6,400 B.C. ± 150 years (Lv-393) Level G; 6,040 B.C. ± 150 years (Lv-464) Level E; 5,980 B.C. ± 160 years (Lv-465) Level B; [Vermeersch, 1970, pp. 49, 51]). El-Kab has only one correlation coefficient greater than .6000 with any Nile Valley site, Site K12; all others fall below .5800.

The question which should be raised is whether the assumption that similarities between types of tools (even within one class) actually does indicate *cultural* connections, rather than similar responses to like environmental conditions. The point to be made here is that this is a relationship between 23 separate variables, not with a *fossil directeur*. Therefore, the particular complex of variables or attributes necessary to make up a series of backed bladelets in any group situation must necessarily reflect the peculiar proclivities of each group. Thus, the very nature of flint knapping has a built-in wild card, namely individuality. The entire concept of a lithic tool tradition is based on the

TABLE 2

COMPARATIVE INDICES OF NORTH AFRICAN, CYRENAICAN, AND NILE VALLEY FINAL PALEOLITHIC SITES

	Burins	Endscrapers	Notches and Denticulates	Truncations	Retouched Pieces	Ouchtata Retouched Pieces	Backed Bladelets	Microburins	Geometrics	Perforators	Scaled Pieces
El-H	0.84	2.97	7.08	0.23	?	?	83.09	3.81	0.76	0.00	0.00
Bous	0.23	2.19	5.16	2.50	10.11	6.47	70.10	2.88	0.08	0.00	0.00
LA M.	0.29	1.73	0.97	0.00	2.02	6.30	70.83	16.69	0.06	0.00	0.00
O.R.G.	0.12	1.64	3.32	2.58	0.00	68.69	14.30	9.58	5.05	0.00	0.00
O.R.G.2	0.14	0.42	1.70	1.84	0.00	82.40	4.10	7.65	0.28	0.00	0.00
K.B.G.	1.26	0.00	1.57	0.00	8.18	10.06	58.49	3.14	0.00	0.00	0.00
G.C.T.	0.55	11.52	5.85	1.10	23.77	5.48	42.96	2.56	0.00	0.00	0.00
E.R.E.S.	0.69	0.86	2.53	0.00	0.00	17.90	52.85	1.15	1.55	0.81	12.38
T.I	0.16	4.07	2.74	0.25	1.42	2.85	87.32	0.00	0.61	0.00	0.00
T.II	0.11	8.42	3.29	0.19	3.89	2.64	80.27	0.00	1.07	0.00	0.00
K12	1.10	1.10	9.40	4.10	11.90	3.80	65.70	0.21	0.01	4.10	0.00
K13	1.10	0.40	4.10	2.40	4.90	78.70	8.50	0.12	0.01	0.01	0.00
G.R.Int.	0.00	4.00	4.00	0.90	11.10	16.90	51.50	0.40	0.00	0.00	9.90
G.R.Plat.	0.00	3.70	4.20	1.30	12.50	16.60	53.70	1.00	0.70	0.20	4.80
Rassal	0.10	5.00	6.00	0.90	6.20	15.40	51.50	9.00	0.90	0.40	3.60
O.K.	0.50	4.00	4.30	3.60	1.10	13.90	60.60	2.00	2.20	0.00	6.90
C.M.	0.20	0.80	3.00	1.40	5.10	18.50	66.50	1.80	0.20	0.20	2.00
Djid.Ouest	1.10	5.70	15.20	0.70	14.90	9.40	42.20	3.30	0.70	1.10	2.20
T.H.	0.00	7.40	6.30	1.00	4.90	7.20	56.10	15.70	0.40	0.50	0.00
KI	3.10	10.50	9.60	6.00	32.10	0.40	20.00	0.00	0.00	9.20	2.90
KIII	2.50	3.30	15.20	6.50	27.20	1.80	22.40	0.30	0.10	15.50	0.10
KIV	2.80	8.00	13.90	6.00	29.70	4.10	21.10	0.00	0.00	9.80	1.10
KV	1.70	6.10	7.40	6.10	15.90	13.60	37.80	0.20	0.00	9.70	0.20
T.IV	0.00	8.15	2.84	0.31	2.46	3.97	80.67	0.69	0.12	0.06	0.00
T.V	0.04	9.19	4.75	0.00	3.25	1.62	79.22	0.98	0.04	0.00	0.00
T.VII	0.28	3.70	5.08	0.26	2.01	2.91	64.76	19.88	0.00	0.04	0.00
T.VIII	0.83	3.39	6.46	0.54	4.14	2.07	60.16	18.47	0.00	0.00	0.00
T.IX	0.42	10.65	8.58	0.83	7.75	4.29	37.41	25.62	0.00	0.00	0.00
D.OU.	0.95	5.90	15.62	0.76	14.89	9.52	43.24	3.43	0.76	1.14	0.00
H.F.XIV/ XV	1.05	0.42	0.00	0.00	1.03	?	94.10	0.13	0.11	0.11	0.03
H.F.XI, XII,XIII	0.58	0.86	0.00	0.86	0.86	?	96.60	0.65	0.00	0.13	0.00
EL-Kab	0.00	0.40	7.00	7.00	10.50	0.00	27.10	38.40	3.90	3.91	0.00
GS2B-2	3.00	3.00	9.00	27.00	8.00	4.00	18.00	30.00	0.50	0.00	0.00
Tera	1.30	5.40	4.40	3.70	3.20	0.00	76.60	0.00	1.00	0.00	0.00

TABLE 3
COMPARATIVE BACKED BLADELET FREQUENCIES
OF NORTH AFRICAN AND NILE VALLEY FINAL PALEOLITHIC SITES

TYPE	RASSEL	COUR. M.	T.H.	D.O.	O.K.	G.R. PLATFORM	G.R. INT.	K12	K5	K13
45	7.37	8.50	14.33	18.41	1.80	20.31	12.99	17.75	2.84	0.02
46	1.17	1.16	0.67	0.40	0.00	2.30	2.60	29.07	1.62	0.00
47	1.40	1.71	1.17	1.10	0.77	2.30	5.19	0.00	0.13	0.00
49	0.00	0.00	0.00	0.00	0.00	0.00	0.00	0.29	0.68	0.00
51	2.81	1.90	1.50	0.00	0.77	1.92	3.25	0.29	2.57	0.00
55	0.23	2.82	0.15	0.00	6.17	1.92	0.65	1.73	8.11	0.17
56	2.92	13.75	9.00	16.24	12.34	7.66	9.74	2.74	2.84	0.07
57	0.00	1.51	0.02	0.00	0.26	0.00	0.00	0.00	2.70	0.00
58	0.00	2.64	0.02	1.40	0.26	0.00	0.65	0.00	0.40	0.00
59	0.23	3.22	0.15	1.80	1.03	0.38	1.95	0.00	0.68	0.00
60	0.47	0.45	0.81	0.40	0.00	0.38	1.95	0.07	0.40	0.00
61	0.00	0.00	0.02	0.00	0.00	0.00	0.00	1.51	1.49	0.04
62	5.50	0.30	4.83	0.00	0.00	1.53	0.65	0.00	0.00	0.00
63	23.86	12.01	17.83	6.50	8.74	11.90	15.58	11.69	10.13	0.68
64	0.00	0.02	0.15	0.00	0.00	0.00	0.00	0.22	2.97	0.02
65	0.00	0.02	0.00	0.00	0.00	0.00	0.00	0.00	0.00	0.00
66	27.72	27.17	33.00	32.49	43.44	23.37	18.83	28.14	18.18	1.92
67	3.27	0.48	4.00	2.89	2.83	1.53	7.14	1.30	9.05	6.16
68	0.00	0.48	0.00	0.40	1.28	0.77	0.65	0.29	2.84	1.09
69	1.87	4.42	1.33	0.00	1.80	6.51	2.30	0.00	0.27	0.43
70	5.38	1.73	1.67	5.05	2.06	3.83	4.54	1.95	9.73	71.01
71	4.44	3.73	2.33	7.22	3.08	4.21	5.84	0.14	8.38	2.42
72	11.34	11.92	6.00	5.78	11.57	9.19	9.09	3.82	13.38	16.00

TYPE	K1	K3	K4	El-KAB	GS2B-II
45	0.09	0.59	1.27	2.62	0.29
46	0.00	0.44	0.14	0.44	0.00
47	0.00	0.00	0.00	0.00	0.00
49	0.00	0.00	0.00	0.00	0.00
51	0.00	0.59	0.84	0.00	0.00
55	1.53	2.06	2.10	0.87	7.30
56	2.07	0.88	1.13	0.44	0.29
57	0.09	0.00	0.00	0.00	0.00
58	0.00	0.00	0.14	0.00	0.00
59	0.36	0.15	0.42	0.00	0.00
60	0.00	0.00	0.14	0.87	0.29
61	0.00	0.15	0.00	0.00	0.00
62	0.00	0.00	0.00	0.00	1.46
63	3.50	3.28	4.22	1.75	4.37
64	0.18	0.44	0.56	5.24	0.87
65	0.00	0.00	0.00	0.00	0.00
66	2.16	5.14	4.07	11.35	1.17
67	0.81	0.59	0.70	0.00	0.00
68	3.31	4.73	2.24	0.00	1.74
69	0.00	0.00	0.14	0.00	0.00
70	0.45	0.29	1.82	0.00	3.50
71	0.00	0.59	0.70	0.00	0.00
72	0.00	0.89	1.40	0.00	0.58

SAMPLE SIZES FOR TABLES 2 and 3

ELH = El-Hamel (1,313)
BOUSK = Bouskoura (1,315)
LAM = La Mouillah (1,731)
ORG = Ouchtata Rive Gauche (2,434)
ORG2 = Ouchtata Rive Gauche 2 (705)
KBG = Kifan bel Ghomari (159)
GCT = Grotte des Contrebandiers à Temara (543)
ERES = Er Recheda es Souda (1,737)
T1 = Taforalt 1 (1,985)
T2 = Taforalt 2 (5,385)
T4 = Taforalt 4 (1,582)
T5 = Taforalt 5 (2,339)
T7 = Taforalt 7 (2,540)
T8 = Taforalt 8 (2,415)
T9 = Taforalt 9 (722)
HFXIVXV = Haua Fteah XIV/XV (3,795)
HFXIV = Haua Fteah XIV (1,919)
TERA = Hagfet et Tera (3,134)
RASSEL = Rassel Lower Level (1,279)
COURBETM = Courbet Marine, Gisement Ayme (9,686)
TAMARH = Tamar Hat, Petite Kabylie (948)
DO = Djidjelli Ouest (525)
GRINT = Grotte Roland Interieur (225)
GRPLAT = Grotte Roland Platform (374)
K12 = E71K12 (2,143)
K13 = E71K13 (6,040)
K1 = E71K1 (1,115)
K3 = E71K3 (673)
K4 = E71K4 (713)
K5 = E71K5 (1,800)

ELKAB = El Kab (229)
GS2B2 = Gebel Silsila 2B2 (343)
OK = Oueds Kerma (523)

TABLE 4

Units Defined by Correlation Coefficients of Tool Classes

Coefficient	*Value*	*Interpretation*
.7 – 1.0	< .01	Strong
.4 – .7	.01 – .10	Moderate
.3 – .4	.10 – .20	Weak

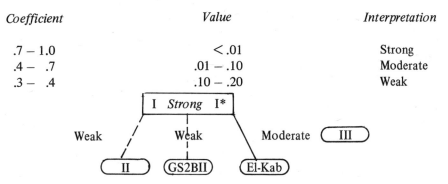

I = ELH, BOUSK, LAM, KBG, GCT, ERES, T1-T9, HF XIV-XV, HF XIV, TERA, RASSEL, COURBETM, TAMARH, DO, GRINT, GRPLAT

I* = K5, K12

II = K1, K3, K4

III = ORG, ORG2, K13

EL-KAB, GS2BII

TABLE 5

Units Defined by Correlation Coefficients of Types of Backed Bladelets

Coefficient	*Value*	*Interpretation*
.5 – 1.0	< .01	Strong
.3 – .5	.01 – .10	Moderate
.2 – .3	.10 – .20	Weak

I = RASSEL, COURBETM, TAMARH, DO, GRPLAT, GRINT, OK

I*= K5, K12

II = K1, K3, K4

III= K13

EL-KAB, GS2BII

premise that the technique of manufacture and the finished product reflects local training and learning experience, if not from father to son, then from generation to generation. If this is the case, it should be obvious that the total backed bladelet tool kit from any one group must reflect the group mentality. Variations within any given group's tool kit should be viewed as idiosyncratic insofar as no two individuals will manufacture the same tool type (as classified by the archaeologist) the same way. With all things being equal, high correlation coefficients between sites, using these 23 variables as the sample, should therefore indicate a degree of relationship which cannot be due to chance.

Does all this mean that there was direct contact between the various Iberomaurusian groups on the one hand, and between them and some Nile Valley groups on the other? Realistically viewed, the answer has to be no. That some of the Iberomaurusian groups on the North African littoral were in contact with one another, there should be no doubt. Correlation coefficients greater than .8000 occur between all of the North African sites mentioned in Tables 2 and 3. Between them and the Nile Valley? Highly unlikely. Then how are the relatively high correlation coefficients between El-Kab, K5, and K12 with several of the North African sites accounted for? This writer feels that the various groups must ultimately stem from a common source. There is no indication that the Iberomaurusian complex evolved in North Africa. On the contrary, most observers feel that this cultural complex migrated into the area, from the east along the coast, or from the Nile Valley (Phillips, 1973, pp. 93, 96 for discussion). Therefore, one must look to areas along the coast or in the Sahara for the "ancestral home" of both the Iberomaurusian and several of the Nile Valley groups.

The material from Haua Fteah and Hagfet et Tera, both in Cyrenaica, indicate that the backed bladelet component is very high, but the backed bladelets themselves are proportionally different from those from the Maghreb. Thus, while Layer B at Hagfet et Tera has 76.6% backed bladelets, 56.7% of them are backed and obliquely truncated. No site in the Maghreb comes close to this figure, while sites recently found in North Sinai (Phillips et al., in press) are quite similar. With greater effort and comparable units of analysis, it should be possible to pinpoint several home areas within the decade.

The writer would like to thank Dr. Harold Hietala of Southern Methodist University for his very useful comments and suggestions.

BIBLIOGRAPHY

ANTOINE, M., 1934. "Notes de préhistoire marocaine IX: La station ibéromaurusien de Bouskoura." *Bulletin de la Société Préhistoire Maroc* 8: 65-90.

————, 1952. "La grande ligne de la préhistoire marocaine." In *Actes du IIe Congrès panafricain de préhistoire, Alger, 1952*. Paris: Arts et Métiers Graphiques.

BALOUT, L., 1955. *Préhistoire de l'Afrique du Nord*. Paris: Arts et Métiers Graphiques.

BRAHIMI, 1970. *L'Ibéromaurusien Littoral de la Région d'Alger*. Alger: Mémoires du Centre de Recherches Anthropologiques, Préhistoriques, et Ethnographiques, tome 13.

BUTZER, K. W., and HANSEN, C. L., 1968. *Desert and River in Nubia*. Madison: University of Wisconsin Press.

CADENAT, P., 1948. "La station préhistorique de Columnata (Commune-Mixte de Tiaret, départment d'Oran)." *Bulletin trimestriel de la Société de Géographie et d'Archéologie de la Province d'Oran* 80-81:3-66.

CASTANY, G., and GOBERT, E. G., 1954. "Morphologie quaternaire, paléontologie, et leurs relations à Gafsa." *Libyca* 2:9-37.

GOBERT, E. G., 1952. "Notions générales acquises sur la préhistoire de la Tunisie." In *Actes du IIe Congrès panafricain de préhistoire, Alger, 1952*, pp. 221-39. Paris: Arts et Métiers Graphiques.

————, 1954*a*. "Capsien et Ibéromaurusien." *Libyca* 2:442-52.

————, 1954*b*. "Le site quaternaire de Sidi Mansour à Gafsa." *Quaternaria* 1:61-80.

————, 1958. "Er-Recheda es-Souda ou presqu'ile 26." *Karthago* 9:37-44.

————, 1962. "La préhistoire dans la zone littoral de la Tunisie." *Quaternaria* 6:271-308.

————, and VAUFREY, R., 1932. "Deux gisements extrèmes d'Ibéromaurusien." *L'Anthropologie* 42:449-90.

GOTTIS, C., 1953. "Sur l'âge des dunes de la region d'Ouchtata (Nefza, Tunisie septentrionale)." *Bulletin de la Société des Sciences Naturelles de Tunisie* 6:223-25.

McBURNEY, C. B. M., 1967. *The Haua Fteah (Cyrenaica) and the Stone Age of the Southeast Mediterranean*. Cambridge: At the University Press.

MARKS, A. E., 1968. "The Halfan Industry." In *The Prehistory of Nubia*, edited by F. Wendorf, 1:392-460. Dallas: Fort Burgwin Research Center and Southern Methodist University Press.

————; PHILLIPS, J.; CREW, H.; and FERRING, R., 1971. "Prehistoric Sites near 'En-'Avdat in the Negev." *Israel Exploration Journal* 21:13-24.

————; CREW, H.; FERRING, R.; and PHILLIPS, J., 1972. "Prehistoric Sites near Har Harif." *Israel Exploration Journal* 22(2-3):73-85.

MOREL, J., 1953. "L'outillage lithique de la station du Kef-oum Touiza, dans l'Est-Constantinous." *Libyca* 1:157-68.

PALLARY, P., 1909. "Note sur un gisement paléolithique de la province d'Oran." *Bulletin Archéologique du Comité des Travaux Historiques et Scientifiques du Ministère de l'Instruction Publique (puis de l'Education National)*:314-42.

PHILLIPS, J. L., 1970. "Oeuvre récente sur L'Epipaleolithique de la Vallée du Nil: Rapport préliminaire." *L'Anthropologie* 74(7-8):573-81.

————, 1972. "North Africa, the Nile Valley, and the Problem of the Late Paleolithic." *Current Anthropology* 13(5):587-90.

————, 1973. *Two Final Paleolithic Sites in the Nile Valley and Their External Relations*. Cairo: Papers of The Geological Survey of Egypt 57.

————; GOREN, N.; and BAR-YOSEF, O., in press. "Epipaleolithic Sites in Northern Sinai: A Preliminary Report." *Israel Exploration Journal*.

ROCHE, J., 1953. "La Grotte de Taforalt." *L'Anthropologie* 57:375-80.

————, 1963. *L'epipaléolithique Marocain*. Paris: Libraire Didier.

SCHILD, R.; CHMIELEWSKA, M.; and WIEÇKOWSKA, H., 1968. "The Arkinian and Shamarkian Industries." In *The Prehistory of Nubia*, edited by F. Wendorf, 2:651-767. Dallas: Fort Burgwin Research Center and Southern Methodist University Press.

SIRET, L., 1893. "L'Espagne préhistorique." *Revue des Questions Scientifiques*, series 2, t. 4.

SMITH, P. E. L., 1966. "The Late Paleolithic of Northeast Africa in the Light of Recent Research." *American Anthropologist* 68(2):326-55.

————, 1968. "A Revised View of the Later Paleolithic of Egypt." In *La Préhistoire: problèmes et tendances*, edited by F. Bordes, pp. 391-99. Paris: CNRS.

TIXIER, J., 1954. "Le gisement préhistorique d'El-Hamel." *Libyca* 3:81-128.

————, 1963. *Typologie de L'epipaléolithique du Maghreb*. Alger: Mémoires du Centre de Recherches Anthropologiques, Préhistoriques, et Ethnographiques, vol. 2.

VAUFREY, R., 1955. *Préhistoire de l'Afrique. Vol. I: Le Maghreb*. Paris: Masson.

VERMEERSCH, P., 1970. "L'Elkabien." *Chronique d'Egypte* 45:45-67.

WENDORF, F., 1968. "Summary of Nubian Prehistory." In *The Prehistory of Nubia*, edited by F. Wendorf, 2:1041-60. Dallas: Fort Burgwin Research Center and Southern Methodist University Press.

————; SAID, R.; and SCHILD, R., 1970*a*. "Egyptian Prehistory: Some New Concepts." *Science* 169:1161-71.

————; SCHILD, R.; and SAID, R., 1970*b*. "Problems of Dating the Late Paleolithic Age in Egypt." In *Radiocarbon Variations and Absolute Chronology*, edited by I. U. Olsson, pp. 57-79. Stockholm: Almqvist and Wiksell.

THE PREHISTORIC CULTURES OF NORTH AFRICA: RADIOCARBON CHRONOLOGY

G. Camps

Université de Provence

Translated by F. Vidal

Southern Methodist University

[Translator's Note: The author of this paper has availed himself freely of the French grammatical license to coin verbs and nouns out of other word forms, a common enough occurrence; cf. Teilhard de Chardin's expression: "la planétisation de l'humanité." Dr. Camps uses terms such as "néolithisé" or "néolithisation" ("neolithified" or "neolithification") when referring to sites or assemblages which in their stratigraphic sequence or their appearance show more and more elements of a Neolithic character. Rather than coin new words, I have in all instances paraphrased terms, such as "to become neolithified" or "neolithification," which appeared clumsy in the English context.]

INTRODUCTION

In 1968 we presented a preliminary chronological synthesis of the prehistoric cultures of North Africa and the Sahara (Camps et al., 1968). This initial review revealed the substantial progress achieved in our knowledge of the more recent prehistoric cultures of North Africa and the development of this knowledge from 1963 to 1968, due to the wider scope of fieldwork, particularly in the Algerian Sahara, and to the large increase in radiocarbon dates (table 1). We pointed out that the number of dates of only those samples found in association with prehistoric archaeological remains had increased from 16 in 1963 to 120 in 1968. Today the total has reached 286, to which must be added 32 dates pertaining to the Metal Age. These dates which refer to the North African protohistory will not be examined in this study, which, like the preceding one, will be limited to only prehistoric civilizations. At this time we are therefore able to substantiate the present new chronological synthesis on the basis of over 330 dates. Such a synthesis seems to be the more necessary inasmuch as, after a period of five years of work, the number of dates has more than doubled, and above all also because some areas previously neglected, or not dated at all, have since that time been the object of more or less intensive research work during which radiocarbon dates were obtained.

Such neglected areas are, from west to east, the province of Tarfaya (previously Cape Juby) in Southern Morocco, Northern Mauritania (where some specimens from the Copper Age were dated), Ouled Mya in the Algerian Sahara, the region Ouled Djellal and the Menencha in Eastern Algeria, the region of Arlit in the Aïr, and the Tibesti. Finally some other dates, isolated or in groups, in the Tunisian Sahil, Ténéré, the Tafassasset, Northern Senegal, the Hoggar, Tanezrouft, Tademaït, Saoura, the Algerian coast, etc., give us the opportunity to round out more fully the previously established chronological picture. The number of sites, samples of which were subjected to C14 analysis, has similarly increased from 6 in 1963 to 55 in 1968, and 121 in 1973.

The main points which drew our attention are the antiquity of the Aterian and of the Iberomaurusian, which are both confirmed as well as emphasized, and the new data on the various minor Epipaleolithic cultures of the Maghreb and the Sahara, which differ from the Capsian and the Iberomaurusian. The most important change refers to the age of the Typical Capsian and the significant importance of such age. Correspondingly, we find that the precedence or the contemporaneity of certain facies of the so-called Upper Capsian, with reference to the Typical Capsian, are definitely confirmed.

Finally, the development toward the Neolithic has been the object of intensive research work in the central Saharan massifs (Hoggar, Tassili n'Ajjer, Aïr, Tibesti) and their surroundings, as well as in the lower Sahara, the Atlas (Neolithic of Capsian tradition) and the coast (Mediterranean Neolithic).

THE ANTIQUITY OF THE ATERIAN

This writer has tried since 1955 to fight against the tendency to attribute too young an age to the Aterian industry (Camps, 1955) which, according to R. Vaufrey's con-

TABLE 1
BREAKDOWN BY CULTURE
OF THE NUMBER OF RADIOCARBON DATES

	1963	1968	1973
Paleolithic	0	9	11
Iberomaurusian	4	11	27
Epipaleolithic	0	8	17
Typical Capsian	2	2	14
Upper Capsian	3	23	68
Saharo-Sudanese Neolithic	6	43	92
Mediterranean Neolithic	0	4	6
Neolithic of Capsian Tradition	1	20	51
Total	16	120	286
Number of Sites	6	55	121

clusion, was "a prolonged Middle Paleolithic, contemporary with the European Upper Paleolithic" (Vaufrey, 1955). In 1968 we were able to show some chronological correlations between the observations made by McBurney at Haua Fteah, which would have no evidential value at all if they were isolated, and the studies conducted in the Saoura valley by H. Alimen and N. and J. Chavaillon. Moreover, the thesis of G. Conrad has furnished new data which further confirm recent observations made on the Algerian coast and the Moroccan site of Taforalt.

In the red cliffs near Bérard in the area of Algiers, Roubet distinguished a succession of red silt layers, intercalated within fossil dunes. From the top of the formation to the present sea level the following can be identified: brown soils mixed with recent sands which usually contain Iberomaurusian or Neolithic industries; then a silt layer with Aterian pieces associated with remains of heavily burnt patellae. These remains were subjected to radiocarbon dating and gave a date of 29,850 B.C. ± 190 years (I-3951). Beneath this level are two fossil dunes, separated by a layer of red silt. The older dune is in turn separated from the Neo-tyrrhénian beach by another red layer which contains an unusual industry. At the contact with the fossil beach, the upper part of which is here at 3.25 m, a wellflaked limestone blade was found. It is precisely the stratigraphic position of the Aterian I of Arzew and Karrouba which, in good logic, indicates that it must have appeared well before the thirtieth millennium.

This opinion is amply confirmed by new and valuable dates obtained by J. Roche (1970-1971) at Taforalt (Eastern Morocco). The last Aterian level of this important site, located below the "Epipaleolithic" levels, has been dated as from 30,400 B.C. Another date of the Upper Aterian gave an age of 32,600 B.C.

It is therefore easy to agree with the preliminary conclusions drawn from the dates of Dar es-Soltan (Aterian from the C-1 level, much older than 28,000 B.C.) and from the observations of H. Alimen and G. Conrad, who attributed to the Aterian in the Saoura an antiquity of forty millennia.

Today we must thus consider the Aterian as one of the recent facies of the Mousterian, which in its terminal phase may be contemporary with the beginning of the Aurignacian and the European Perigordian.

DURATION OF THE IBEROMAURUSIAN

If the Aterian can no longer be considered to be an "Upper Paleolithic of Mousterian tradition," another industry considered to be Epipaleolithic must from now on in part be accepted as being contemporary with the last Würmian stage. The Iberomaurusian, on which we now have 26 dates (as compared to 11 in 1968) actually appears in Taforalt since before the fourteenth millennium and has given the following six dates: 12,180; 12,170; 13,290 (level 11); 13,510; 13,550; and 13,750 (level 12), all B.C. This series, therefore, confirms the single date known up to this day, which belongs to the thirteenth millennium (Rassel). This date had made it possible for us, in 1968, to support McBurney's hypothesis placing the beginning of the Iberomaurusian between 12,500 and 13,000. Then again, at Taforalt, between level 12 and level 18, which contains final Aterian (30,400 B.C.), there are other important layers with bladelet industries from which the old Iberomaurusian must have emerged, which as we know today is contemporary with the Magdalenian.

The analyses performed on samples of the Algerian coast (Roland Cave, Cave of La Madeleine, Shelter of Tamar Hat) with reference to the Iberomaurusian confirm that the full development of this culture is to be placed around 10,000 B.C.

By contrast, three other dates appear to belong to the more recent phases of this industry. The most interesting one, since it rounds out a series as well as a stratigraphic sequence, is the one of the evolved Iberomaurusian of Columnata: 8850 B.C. ± 425 years. This recent dating is of importance because it confirms the date of the preNeolithic industry of Cave II of Ouled Guettara (Brédéah, Oran), i.e., 8240 B.C. ± 230 years, which is of Iberomaurusian tradition, but also, and more relevantly, because it sets apart, chronologically as well as stratigraphically, the Iberomaurusian from the Columnatian which follows it (6330–5350 B.C.).

The two most recent dates for the Iberomaurusian are isolated ones, even though they both belong to stratified sites (fig. 1). At El Hamel, the date obtained seems too recent (7950 B.C. ± 120 years) considering the very classical aspect of Level E. As to the industry from the El Haouita terrace, it has the aspect of a very evolved Iberomaurusian; the very late date (6270 B.C. ± 820 years) can therefore probably not be supported.

The new dates, particularly those of Taforalt and Columnata, allow us to delimit chronologically the Iberomaurusian on the coast and on the Tell, where the duration appears to have been very long, from the fourteenth to the end of the ninth millennium. We are not at all well acquainted with the industries which derived from the Iberomaurusian, and which during the seventh and sixth millennia acquired—within the same areas—a progressively more Neolithic aspect. The analyses of some industries belonging to this phase show a significant decrease in the proportions of backed bladelets, a considerable increase in the number of denticulated flakes and bladelets, and a slight increase in geometric microliths, although this facies cannot be mistaken for an industry of the Upper Capsian. This post-Iberomaurusian must be the Epipaleolithic substratum of the Mediterranean Neolithic in North Africa.

If we are able to understand how to fill the chronological gap between the Classic Iberomaurusian and the Mediterranean Neolithic, our knowledge is still very poor with respect to the many millennia which lie between the final Aterian (which would not be any later than 25,000 B.C.) and the beginning of the Iberomaurusian. To be sure,

Chronological Synthesis of the North African Epipaleolithic and Neolithic

	Morocco and Western Algeria	Central Algeria	Eastern Algeria and Tunisia	Lower Sahara and environs	Saharan Atlas	Saoura and Surroundings

Legend:

- ○ Neolithic of Capsian Tradition
- ⊘ Neolithic of the El Hadjar Type
- ⊙ Neolithic of the El Bayed Type
- ⊖ Mediterranean Neolithic
- ⬦ Melalian
- △ Upper Capsian
- ▲ Typical Capsian
- ▽ Columnatian
- ◇ Elassolithic
- ▽ Kristelian-Keremian
- ⊠ Iberomaurusian
- ▬▬ End of the Iberomaurusian
- ▬ ▬ Beginning of the Neolithic

we have found in Cyrenaica, between the Mousterian and a local facies of the Iberomaurusian, the so-called Dabba culture, which belongs to the Upper Paleolithic. But in the Maghreb we are only able at this time to mention the still unpublished industry found in the levels 17 to 12 of the Taforalt site (excavated by J. Roche), the industry of level 2 at El Guettar (excavated by Gruet) in the region of Gafsa—which is much earlier than that of the Collignon horizon—and, perhaps, a portion of the pre-Capsian industries of Southern Tunisia, among which that of the Collignon horizon is to be fitted. This heterogeneous collection, about which we have no reliable studies, could belong to the Maghrebian Upper Paleolithic of which the Iberomaurusian is the final phase.

We must confess that for between 30,000 and 14,000 B.C. there is a gap in our knowledge. Undoubtedly, it is during this long period that the Maghreb experienced the intrusion of an Epigravettian of oriental origin, around which hinges the development of the bladelet industries of Southern Tunisia and the Iberomaurusian of the Tell.

KEREMIAN, COLUMNATIAN, ELASSOLITHIC

We have already shown that between the disappearance of the Classic Iberomaurusian during the ninth millennium and the beginnings of the Capsian—the oldest dates for which, at the present stage of our knowledge, do not go beyond the beginning of the seventh millennium—there must be interposed a series of minor Epipaleolithic cultures of very short duration and limited regional area of extension. Aside from what we have called the post-Iberomaurusian, we are still able to identify a series of industries with very microlithic trends: the Columnatian, on which we have a series of dates derived from the Columnata site (6330; 6190; 5330 B.C. ± 200 years) and the Elassolithic level of Koudiat Kifen Lahda (6750 B.C. ± 200 years; and 6370 B.C. ± 150 years). The Keremian, limited to Western Algeria, has not yet been dated, but an Epipaleolithic level of Bou-Aichem at Kristel (Oran), equally rich in end-scrapers, but with very numerous backed microblades and microcrescents, has given two dates from samples of different types (marine molluscs: 8625 B.C. ± 400 years; ostrich egg: 7850 B.C. ± 400 years). The "Kristelian" may be described as a Keremian with an Elassolithic trend. The Keremian and the Kristelian may be compared, if not related to, a Nubian Epipaleolithic industry (Wendorf, 1968), the Arkinian, which shows considerable analogies. In these three assemblages the index of scrapers is very great, microburins and burins are rare, and the crescents predominate over triangles and trapeze forms. Nevertheless, the Arkinian has an index of backed blades (29 to 53) clearly larger than those of the Keremian and the Kristelian; it is actually this latter industry which seems to be closer to the Arkinian. The date of 7440 B.C. ± 180 years, obtained through radiocarbon dating from Site 1 of Dibeira West, does not contradict such closeness.

THE CAPSIAN: ITS FACIES AND ITS CHRONOLOGY

Our knowledge of the Capsian has advanced considerably during the past five years, not only on account of the increase of radiocarbon dates, which with regard to this culture have gone from 15 to 82, but also because of the excavation work of H. Camps-Fabrer (1974) and D. Grébénert (1972). The excavations at El Outed and the Relilaï (fig. 2) allow us to understand better what the Typical Capsian actually is, as well as its relationships with the Upper Capsian. The excavations of Rabah and Medjez II brought to light the evolution of the Upper Capsian in two different regions, those of Ouled Djellal and Setif.

Since 1968 the date samples of the typical Capsian have multiplied; today we have a total of 14, distributed as follows: from Bortal Fakher, 2; from El Outed, 4; from Relilaï, 7, and from Guentis, 1. Not one among these samples has given a date prior to 6500 B.C., which leads us, taking into account the dendrochronological corrections (Damon, Long, and Wallick, 1972), to just about the beginning of the eighth millennium. Even the oldest date of 6430 B.C. ± 150 years, belongs to the base of the Capsian levels of Relilaï, where the beginning of the Upper Capsian has been dated as from 5850 B.C. ± 140 years.

Among the industries of the Typical Capsian two very different assemblages can be distinguished: one group shows a high index of burins, either 30 or larger, the other group has an index of backed bladelets higher than that of burins, which is 20 or less. One could be tempted to attribute a different chronological position to these differences. The levels or horizons with a high index of burins (Typical Capsian at Bortal Fakher (Tixier, 1968), Relilaï II and IV; El Outed 2 and 3, Ain Sendes, Ain Zannouch, Bir Hammairia II, Bir Zarif El Ouar, Bou Hamran) actually appear to be more recent than those with a lower index (El Mekta, Relilaï I and III, El Outed 1, Shelter 402, and Redeyef, lower level of Table Sud). Unfortunately, the interfingering in certain stratigraphic sequences, such as at Relilaï, of levels belonging to both groups gives us cause for further reflection.

This is so, even though these two morphological subdivisions of the Typical Capsian, recognized by J. Tixier, seem to be quite clear and up to this date no level of the Typical Capsian with a high index of burins has been dated as belonging to a period preceding the sixth millennium, with the exception of phase II of Relilaï, which actually is anomalous in its stratigraphic position and should be of the same date as the phase III which succeeds it. We can summarize in Table 2 below the chronological and morphological data which perhaps may allow us at some time to give a greater precision to the evolution of the Typical Capsian.

The results obtained in recent years give us cause to attribute a younger age to the Typical Capsian and to consider it as a facies limited in its extension to a region south of Tebessa, in a semicircle of 100 kms radius, the center of which would be located at Tamerza. No shell heaps of the

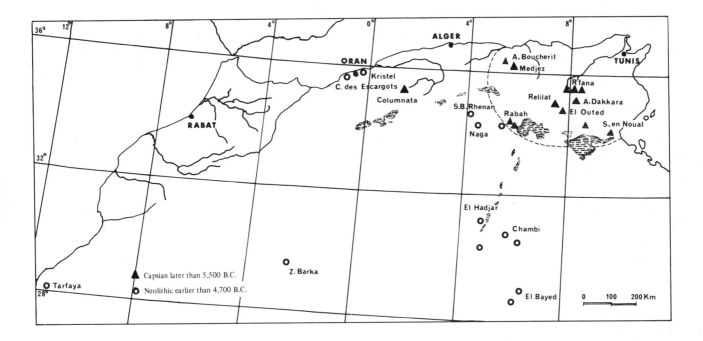

FIG. 2—Delay of the progress toward the Neolithic in the Capsian Area.

Typical Capsian are known to lie outside this semicircle. The easternmost shell heap is that of Aïn Zannouch, the northernmost is that of Cheria, the westernmost is that of Mahmel, while the southernmost ones are aligned from Bir Zarif to Bortal Fakher.

The other Capsian facies, grouped under the designation of Upper Capsian, have a quite different geographical extent inasmuch as certain industries of Capsian type are known to be in western Algeria (region of Tiaret) and probably even beyond. The most interesting discoveries of the last five years concern the age of the Upper Capsian. In 1968 the site of Medjez II (region of Setif), where a test pit had been dug, gave an initial series of dates, the oldest of which belonged to the deeper levels between 2.30 m and 3.20 m and went back to 6530 B.C. ± 300 years. This very high figure would be surprising if one were to accept that the Upper Capsian is derived from the Typical Capsian and that its origins are to be traced to the area where the latter culture is to be found.

The site of Medjez II, situated north of El Eulma (formerly Saint Arnaud), is actually very far from the area of the Typical Capsian and belongs to the northernmost facies of the Upper Capsian. It was later used to define the Setifian.

The excavation, directed by H. Camps-Fabrer, was also able to confirm the very great antiquity of the Upper Capsian in this area, since phase 1 which is the oldest one, lasted for a thousand years, from 6910 B.C. ± 150 years to 5900 B.C. ± 150 years. It is reminiscent of the Iberomaurusian. Phase 2 lasted only five centuries (5830 B.C. ±

140 years). It is during this phase that the Capsian characteristics become stronger. Phase 3, which is even shorter (end of the fourth millennium), proves to be only a transition to Phase 4, or evolved Setifian, which shows a considerable increase in the index of denticulates (50.2) and is characterized by a proliferation of triangles and of elongated trapezes, the smaller end of which is concave. This evolved Setifian phase is to be placed quite late; it spans the first half of the fifth millennium (4670 B.C. ± 300 years) and 4550 B.C. ± 150 years at Medjez, 5050 and 4850 B.C. ± 150 years at Aïn Boucherit).

The antiquity of the archaic phases of the Upper Capsian is not based only on the dates from the deep levels of Medjez II. Other sites, belonging to other facies, have actually given equally old dates. In the first place, we should mention the shell heap of Aïn Dokkara, excavated in 1948 by L. Balout. Shells of *helix* and charcoal samples gathered later at this site (Balout and Roubet, 1970) were sent to the Scientific Center at Monaco and to the laboratory at Gif-sur-Yvette. The deepest levels (1.10 to 1.30 meters) gave a date of 6580 B.C. ± 100 years; three other samples taken from a depth of one meter were dated as from 6395 B.C. ± 120 years; 6080 B.C. ± 120 years, and 6040 B.C. ± 90 years. The most recent levels belong to the middle of the sixth millennium (5620 B.C. ± 120 years, 5330 B.C. ± 120 years). The dates of the deep levels at Aïn Dokkara are not surprising if one considers the location of this site in the region of Tebessa and the previously obtained date for the Upper Capsian at El Mekta (6450 B.C. ± 400 years).

TABLE 2
TYPICAL CAPSIAN WITH LOW INDEX OF BURINS

	El Mekta	Relilai I	Relilai III	El Outed 1	Shelter 402	Redeyef Table Sud
Index of burins	14.5	20.0	16.0	19.4	18.2	11.2
Index of backed bladelets	33.9	20.4	25.2	25.0	15.8	28.6
B.C. Dates	Before 6500	6890	6430 6230	5900		

TYPICAL CAPSIAN WITH HIGH INDEX OF BURINS

	Bortal Fakher	Relilai II	Relilai IV	El Outed 2	El Outed 3	Bir Hammairia	Ain Sendes
Index of burins	48.7	34.7	40.6	41.9	31.7	28.7	34.2
Index of backed bladelets	22.9	30.5	20.3	15.8	23.9	18.1	22.8
B.C. Dates	5650 4980	(6230)	6000 5900	5450	before 4750		

Seemingly more disconcerting are the three dates obtained on the basis of *helix* shells found in the Capsian levels of Ain Naga, a site excavated by D. Grébénart in the vicinity of Messad, more than 400 km west of the area of the Typical Capsian (Grébénart, 1969). [If one accepts, as we still did in 1968, that the Upper Capsian developed on the basis of the Typical Capsian, the facies identified at Ain Naga in an area which is so far distant from that of the Typical Capsian should belong to a recent phase of the Capsian.] Now, this site has given the oldest Capsian dates known up to this day: 7220 B.C. ± 200 years (Gif 1220); 7350 B.C. ± 300 years; 6950 B.C. ± 280 years.

These different radiocarbon analyses, accompanied by the usual stratigraphic observations and by typological and morphological studies of the industries, have led us to modify considerably the ideas we had about the Capsian and its chronology.

The first fact which seems to have been established is the variability of the Upper Capsian, which is subdivided into numerous regional facies. Actually, although this classification should not be taken as being definitive, one can distinguish the Tebessian facies (upon which lies the old *Intergétulo-néolithique*, or Capsian of the Ain Aachena type), the so-called central facies which is found on the high plains between Constantine and the Aurès massif, the Setifian facies which is the northernmost one, the southern facies which spread from Biskra to Djelfa et Laghouat (region of Ouled Djellal and Ouled Naïl), the industries of which were made known by the work of D. Grébénart, and finally the Tiaretian or westernmost facies brought to light

by P. Cadenat. Moreover, outside Algeria and Tunisia, other industries showing Capsian affinities appear also in Cyrenaica (Haua Fteah—6450 B.C. ± 150 years to 5050 B.C. ± 100 years) and perhaps in Morocco (Ain Fritissa, Telouet) and in the Sahara (Reggan?, Ngouça?, Merdjouma?).

The second fact which also appears to be certain is that the "Capsianization" must not be considered as the simple geographic expansion of a cultural group which had its center of origin between Gafsa and Cheria, and whose first evidences of appearance always belonged to the Typical Capsian. Everything leads us to believe, in effect, that the Typical Capsian or at least the facies with a high index of burins (type Bortal Fakher) is in part contemporary with certain phases of the Upper Capsian. It must be kept in mind, above all, that the oldest dates which have been obtained on the Capsian assemblage belong to the levels called "Upper Capsian" in such sites as Ain Naga, Medjez II, Haua Fteah, and Ain Dokkara, which lie outside the area of the Typical Capsian, sometimes several hundred kilometers away.

The third proposition derived from recent observations is that the "Capsianization" took place on top of underlying levels with different industries: Typical Capsian in the southeast (El Mekta, Relilaï), but also farther west (Dakhlat El Saâdane); Epipaleolithic in the north, reminiscent of the Iberomaurusian (Bou Nouara, Medjez II, and probably Mechta el-Arbi), and more often unknown ones (southern facies). However, above these different substrata the "Capsianization" occurs in accordance with the same model. It is actually possible to follow in each facies a process of evolution which, even though not absolutely identical, ends with stages where the differences have been appreciably reduced, as if these cultures, after originating in different horizons, all had the same model and were tending toward certain uniformity.

THE INDUSTRIES OF PRE-NEOLITHIC BLADELETS

Some industries of an Epipaleolithic character, contemporary with the Upper Capsian and preceding the Neolithic, have been identified particularly in the Lower Sahara. These industries are generally rich in backed bladelets, but so poor in geometric microliths that these are on occasion totally lacking. On the other hand, these industries are familiar with the microburin technique.

The Mellalian (Camps et al., 1966) [sometimes also spelled Melalian by the author] is a bladelet industry first identified at Hassi Mouilah, at the edge of the Sebkha [salt-flat] of Mellala, near Ouargla. The investigations of G. Aumassip in this region, and farther to the south, in the valley of Oued Mya, led to the discovery of this industry in several other sites. In three sites these Epipaleolithic assemblages have been found in a stratigraphic context. They were separated from a Neolithic level by a layer of sterile sand—Hassi Mouilah, the El Hadjar hill, *Les Deux Oeufs* [probably El Baydhatain].

By coincidence, we have at hand some radiocarbon dates for two of these sites; the one at *Les Deux Oeufs* could only be dated on the basis of its Neolithic level, as shown below:

	Hassi Mouilah	*Les Deux Oeufs*	El Hadjar Hill
Neolithic Level of Capsian Tradition	3320 ± 150	3350 ± 125	Neolithic without pottery (Hadjarian) 4720 ± 120
	sterile	sterile	sterile
Level E (Mellalian)	5700 ± 150 6650 ± 150	Mellalian	5350 ± 170
Level F (Mellalian)	?		

Three other Epipaleolithic levels discovered by G. Aumassip could be dated in the same area of Ouargla: the "Burin Site" of 5000 B.C. ± 170 years; Site 7205 of 5140 B.C. ± 170 years; and Site 7206 of 4730 B.C. ± 170 years.

The Mellalian, quite distinct from the Capsian, appears therefore to have developed from the end of the seventh millennium to the end of the sixth millennium. It must be distinguished from another Epipaleolithic industry, which is also richer in backed bladelets than the Upper Capsian, and

to which has been given the name of "Facies d'el Oued" (Bobo, 1955). This industry of the Souf can be distinguished from the Mellalian by a higher index of backed bladelets (65 to 75), and in particular by the high index of geometric microliths (14 to 15), especially represented by triangles; trapezes are totally absent.

The Epipaleolithic of Oued Akarit, north of Gabès, has very close characteristics. Unfortunately, however, no samples from the sites at El Wad or from Oued Akarit have as yet been dated.

At the other end of the Maghreb, a new Epipaleolithic facies has just begun to be identified in the region of Tarfaya (Cape Juby, Southern Morocco) (Grébénart, 1973). The two dates taken from fragments of ostrich egg shells seem too low—4400 B.C. ± 120 years and 4200 B.C. ± 120 years, particularly because a close Neolithic site gave a date of 6150 B.C. ± 110 years on the basis of marine shells. It is therefore difficult at the present time to reach any conclusions regarding these isolated dates.

CHRONOLOGY OF THE NEOLITHIC IN NORTH AFRICA

The investigations carried out in the Sahara in recent years have confirmed the very great antiquity of the progress toward the Neolithic around the central massifs and in the southern part of the desert. This writer has proposed the name of "Saharo-Sudanese Neolithic" for the conglomerate of cultures previously grouped under the name of "Neolithic of Sudanese Tradition." This term was actually based on the assumption that the Nilotic Sudan had reached an earlier Neolithic development and that the elements common to the Neolithic cultures of the Sudan and of the Eastern and Central Sahara were due to a westward [the author says "eastward", but this seems to be an obvious lapse] extension of traits acquired from the lands of the Nile. Such a so-called "Sudanese tradition" seems to be even more questionable after it has been shown that the Neolithic sites of the Hoggar were of a very early date (Camps, 1968). It was in these sites where decorated potsherds with wavy line impressions were found, while all the dates obtained on the basis of Neolithic samples of the Nilotic regions are much later ones.

Today we have at least five sites of the Saharan Neolithic which date back to the seventh millennium, namely those of Amekni, the Launey site, Timidouin in the Hoggar Massif, Fozzigiaren in the Tassili n'Ajjer, and the Gebroug cave in the Tibesti. Another site, at Tamaya Mallet (Niger), has produced much too high a date (7400 B.C. ± 170 years) to be acceptable. The same tabulation reveals eight other sites which are earlier than the sixth millennium. These thirteen acceptable sites are not restricted within a narrow Saharan sector; they are widely dispersed from Ennedi to the Western Hoggar.

Thus, the antiquity of the Neolithic development in the Saharan Massif can no longer be questioned. The skepticism with which the announcement of the first dates was received has since been replaced among the majority of prehistorians by a more flexible response.

The duration of this Neolithic, the evolution of which is not considerable, seems to be very long; we actually have a number of stratigraphic sequences which span several millennia. Such is the case at Amekni, the sites of Launey Abouleg (Hoggar), Ouan Muhuggiag (Tassili n'Ajjer), and Arlit (Air).

The Neolithic sequences of the Tefedest are now becoming better known following the exploration work and the investigations carried out by J. P. Maître (1971), who was able to get radiocarbon dates on a number of samples. In this part of the Hoggar massif the regional extension of paintings of the "bovid" style has been largely confirmed.

We are inclined, farther eastward, to associate this artistic style more closely with the Ténéréan industrial facies. To the artistic analogies, which suggest transhumance, must now be added indisputable chronological correlations. Until 1968 we had only one absolute date for the Ténéréan, that of Adrar Bous III, of 3180 B.C. ± 300 years. In the same massif the British expedition was able to obtain for this culture two more dates: the skeleton of a domestic ox was dated as from 3810 B.C. ± 500 years, and the charcoal from a hearth gave a date of 2960 B.C. ± 140 years. The Ténéréan at Areschima is to be located at the middle of the third millennium: 2520 B.C. ± 115 years. However, at Ténéré itself this very beautiful industry was preceded by a coarser culture. At Bogouboulo, near Fachi, J. Maley and M. Servant have identified a stratified site beneath a level of diatomites; the basic assemblage of tools consisted of millstones, picks, and polished axes associated with pottery and with fish remains. This level gave a date of 4900 B.C. ± 250 years.

Several sites of the middle phase of the Saharo-Sudanese Neolithic, but not belonging to the Ténéréan, could be studied and dated. The site of Madaouéla, in the Air, belongs to a facies rich in arrowheads, which seems to have developed in the middle of the fourth millennium: 3570 B.C. ± 250 years. A test pit dug to a depth of 1.50 m in the important and neighboring site of Arlit (Air) does not show an appreciable evolution in its pottery, even though its dates are ranged from 3250 B.C. ± 140 years to 1080 B.C. ± 110 years.

To the west of Hoggar, near Tanezrouft, the small volcanic massif of Adrar Tiouiyne was occupied along the borders of Oued Amded by a population of Neolithic fishermen. The habitation site excavated in 1968 produced a beautiful and well-fired pottery, a very unusual lithic tool assemblage consisting almost exclusively of arrowheads, polished axes, and—at the surface—a considerable number of stone rings in various stages of manufacture. Two dates were obtained on the basis of charcoal samples: 3370 B.C. ± 130 years and 3200 B.C. ± 140 years.

As far as the most recent phase of the Saharo-Neolithic is concerned, we prefer to rely upon a new date from a charcoal sample from the burial at Tamanrasset II, which confirms its rather late date: 1960 B.C. ± 100 years. A previous analysis had given the date of 1380 B.C. ± 250 years.

The vast regions of the Western Sahara, despite their archaeological wealth, have not benefited from research work as intensive as that carried out in the Algerian Sahara. An exception is the group of Neolithic villages of Dhar Tichitt, which have been studied by P. Munson (1971). The older habitation sites were located at the edge of the lacustrian zone (1500 to 1100 B.C.).

Even more recent are the fortified villages situated atop the summit of the cliffs. After several radiocarbon analyses, P. J. Munson has proposed to give them a date of 100 to 850 B.C. The small fortified structures, located within the clefts of the cliff, are contemporary with the Copper Age in Mauritania (650 to 380 B.C.).

Near Saint-Louis, in the channel of the Khant, a very interesting bone industry, which included knives and "axes," was dated as from 2350 B.C. ± 180 years, according to the analyses of shells of *Arca senilis*.

With the exception of a site located near Nouvadhibou (Port-Étienne), dated as from 4280 B.C. ± 130 years, all other dates from the Neolithic in Mauritania belong to the second and first millennia. The necropolis of Tiŋtane, and that of Chami belong to a few centuries before the beginning of our era and are contemporary with the Mauritanian Copper Age, brought to light by N. Lambert in the region of Akjoujt. In the vicinity of this mining center, in the Bat-Cave, charcoal samples found during the excavation of the old mining tunnels were dated as of the fifth century B.C., and one of the dates was even of the ninth century (826 B.C. ± 130 years).

In the northern part of the Sahara and the highlands of the Maghreb, we find a Neolithic which differs from the Saharo-Sudanese Neolithic and which develops during the fifth millennium until it achieves its full bloom during the fourth millennium. It is possible to retain with respect to the whole group of the Neolithic facies of these regions the term of Neolithic of Capsian Tradition, proposed by R. Vaufrey. Results from radiocarbon datings have grown tremendously over the past few years; the number of dates attributed to this Neolithic period has actually gone up from 20 in 1968 to 51 in 1973. Thanks to these dates we have a better knowledge of the evolution of these industries and these facies, since the Neolithic of Capsian tradition covers an immense area within which the individual cultures do not show precisely the same aspect. If we want to simplify, we may be able at the present stage of our knowledge to identify the following areas: southern Tunisia and the part of eastern Algeria previously occupied by the Capsian; the lower Sahara and its surroundings; the western Saharan Atlas and the high plains; and the north of the Western Sahara. Outside these areas we have only a slight knowledge of the Neolithic in Tripolitania (Abiar Miggi) and Cyrenaica (Haua Fteah). The Neolithic of southern Morocco has only been subjected to some surface surveys, or in the case of the coast of the province of Tarfaya, to test pits dug by D.

Grébénart, which were able to round out the traits made known by the Spanish archaeologists (Almagro, 1968).

Within the Capsian zone of eastern Algeria, where one finds the variety of Neolithic which best deserves to be referred to as being of Capsian tradition, the research work of C. Roubet in the cave of Khanguet Si Mohamed Tahar (Aurès) has been able to determine a chronological sequence (Roubet, 1971). The deeper levels, dated as from 4850 B.C. ± 250 years, contain potsherds and some unusual points belonging to a beginning Neolithic. Another more evolved phase is represented in the middle levels of this site (3800, 3450 B.C. ± 140 years) and at Damous el Ahmar (3700 and 3470 B.C. ± 190 years). It is about 3500 B.C. where we find clustered in all areas the more numerous dates belonging to the Neolithic of so-called Capsian Tradition (Oued Zeggag, Columnata, Ain Guettara, Xo La Touffe, Hassi Mouilah, *Les Deux Ouefs*, Aschech III, Haua Fteah, etc.). It may thus be considered that this culture achieved its full development during the fourth millennium.

The third phase of the Neolithic within the Capsian region is clearly separated from the Capsian tradition; the industries of the two caves of Bou Zabaouine (2245 B.C. ± 130 years) and those of the upper levels of Khanguet Si Mohamed Tahar (2720 B.C. ± 130 years and 2390 B.C. ± 200 years) are the most representative of the evolved phase during which the number of ornamental pieces is increased.

Up to this time no Neolithic level earlier than the middle of the fifth millennium has been identified within the Capsian zones of Tunisia and eastern Algeria. This gives additional support to the conclusions reached with respect to the recent age of the evolved Upper Capsian in this region, some of which sites are contemporary with the initial Neolithic (Medjez II, phase 4, 4670 B.C. ± 300 years; 4550 B.C. ± 150 years, and Ain Boucherit, 4850 B.C. ± 150 years).

We do not have the same situation in the Sahara and the Saharan Atlas. In the lower Sahara and its surroundings important research work carried out mainly by G. Aumassip since 1966 has recently been able to identify a special Neolithic facies without pottery (Hadjarian), principally located along the chain of Sebkha which forms the drainage of Oued Mya (Aumassip, 1972). This Neolithic, lacking in pottery, is not really very old, and we do not think that it can be considered to be proto-Neolithic. It is to be differentiated from the Neolithic of Capsian tradition, *sensu stricto*, by a large percentage of backed bladelets and of geometric microliths. The small projectile heads, on the other hand, which are so prevalent in the Neolithic of Saharan Capsian tradition, particularly in the type of El Bayed, are extremely rare and are of little variation. They mostly belong to the so-called écusson type, which is probably a double perforator worked on a bladelet. The ostrich egg shells are, however, so abundant in this facies that they take the place of pottery. We have at hand for the Hadjarian Neolithic five dates, of which only one—that of site 6910 (Ashech III)—is later than the fifth millennium; all others are evenly distributed between 4700 and 4200 B.C.

This Neolithic of Oued Mya, lacking pottery, is nevertheless not the oldest facies of the Saharan Neolithic. Between the Eastern Grand Erg and the Tassili n'Ajjer, especially around Temassinine (Fort Flatters), we find during the course of the sixth millennium the development of a Neolithic industry which is noteworthy on account of the exceptional quality of its lithic tool assemblage. Its beautiful arrowpoints, its foliated pieces, its fragile perforators of astounding delicateness—all are show pieces in numerous museum display cases. The sites belonging to this facies are often widely dispersed, particularly at El Bayed, to which it owes its name and which covers several score hectares. Two dates have been obtained—the first one on charcoal gathered during the excavation and the second one on fragments of ostrich egg shell. They appear to be the same: 5350 B.C. ± 150 years and 5300 B.C. ± 100 years. The neighboring site of El Beida dates from the same period— 6160 B.C. ± 180 years. Thus, the facies of El Bayed is the oldest Saharan Neolithic known north of the tropical line. It is probable that it was through this facies that the move toward the Neolithic progressed in the Southern Sahara and the Capsian region.

There is in this area of the Sahara a last facies very close to the Neolithic of Capsian tradition in the Capsian region. The most characteristic site is that of Ain Guettara on the southern slope of the Tademait. The same industry is found again in the area of Ouargla (Hassi Mouilah, *Les Deux Ouefs*) and Hassi Messaoud. The seven dates which we now have on the Neolithic of the Ain Guettara type are spread between 4000 and 3350 B.C. This contemporaneity with the Neolithic of Capsian tradition in the north has also confirmed the very considerable cultural analogies which at times reach the point of being identical.

In the Saharan Atlas the Neolithic of Capsian tradition shows a different facies. It starts earlier than in the Capsian region of the East. We know the ages of several Neolithic levels in this region, and some are very old: Ain Naga 5500 B.C. ± 170 years; Safiet Bou Rhenan 5020 B.C. ± 170 years and 5270 B.C. ± 100 years; and in a more southerly area, Botma Si Mamar 4930 B.C. ± 100 years. This Atlas facies, which is occasionally mixed with considerable Mediterranean influences (Columnata 3900 B.C. ± 170 years and 3300 B.C. ± 100 years), is richer in pottery than that of the East, particularly in the caves of El Arouta at Brezina. The relations between this industrial facies and the examples of rock paintings from the Atlas are of primary interest with respect to the Atlas Neolithic.

In the Western Sahara, and particularly along the Saoura Valley, several Neolithic sites have been studied in recent years, and some of them have been dated. The oldest date is that of the site of Zmeilet el Barka, where an initial sampling had produced a very recent date (1000 B.C.); two more recent measurements taken at Gif have given dates of 5570 and 5250 B.C. ± 180 years. Both dates lead us to believe that the progression toward the Neolithic in the Western Sahara took place more or less at the same time as in the Eastern Sahara (Neolithic of the El Bayed type). They also confirm the quite early dates already known from Hassi Bou Bernous (4470 B.C. ± 190 years) and Hassi Manda (4380 B.C. ± 300 years). However, not all manifestations of the Neolithic are equally old. The site of Foum Seïada, near Béni-Abbès belong to the beginning of the third millennium (1980 B.C. ± 250 years), and farther toward the north that of Oued Zeggag (Hammaguir), which produced 56 pieces of pottery and about 9,000 beads, was dated on the basis of ostrich egg shell as from 3370 B.C. ± 150 years.

The Neolithic of southern Morocco has just begun to show its significance both with respect to its rock art as well as to its industry and its portable art. The survey work carried out in the Anti-Atlas and the Draâ Valley has not yet produced samples which could be radiocarbon dated. The coastal shell heaps of the province of Tarfaya (fig. 1) have been the subject of several test pit excavations; D. Grébénart has identified there, after an Epipaleolithic as yet not well determined, a Neolithic rich in arrowpoints and geometric microliths, possibly very old, if one is willing to accept the very high date calculated on the basis of marine shells of the site of Tarfaya II (6150 B.C. ± 110 years). This Neolithic lacks pottery. We should remember that two samples (marine shells and ostrich egg shells) of the site of Tarfaya I, considered to be Epipaleolithic, gave dates of 4400 and 4200 B.C., while fragments of an ostrich egg shell with an engraved ornament representing an antelope from a neighboring Neolithic site gave a date of only 840 B.C. ± 105 years. We must therefore wait for some newer measurements before reaching a conclusion with respect to the real age of this Neolithic, which could have lasted until a very belated age, after the fashion of that of Mauritania.

Our knowledge of the Mediterranean Neolithic has not progressed over the last few years. Its antiquity is confirmed by a date from Kristel, Travertine Station (Oran), as having given 5810 B.C. ± 190 years. The Neolithic site of *Deux Mamelles* [probably Nuhaydayn] near Mostaganem is more recent: 3600 B.C. ± 225 years.

In Tunisia, a site in the vicinity of Hergla at the border of Sebkhet Hank el Menzel was excavated by our Tunisian colleagues. Despite its marine location and the presence of obsidian (which probably originated on Pantelleria), this Neolithic almost totally lacking in pottery seems to belong to a facies of the Neolithic of Capsian tradition, which will probably be better defined as research work in Tunisia progresses. The site at Hergla was dated as from 3320 B.C. ± 140 years.

It should be easy to present at this point the conclusions of the first summary of the dates obtained by means of radiocarbon runs. The increase in the number of these dates has not only confirmed the conclusions regarding the absence of an alleged retardation of the prehistoric Maghreb and Sahara, as compared to their oriental and European neighbors, but—to the contrary—these dates have reinforced the antiquity of the Aterian and the Iberomaurusian. They have also supported the long duration of the so-called Upper Capsian and the earlier date of the progress toward the Neolithic in the Central and Southern Sahara by comparison to the more northerly regions, particularly that of eastern Algeria. The new facts are: (1) the discovery of the frequently late date of certain levels of the Typical Capsian, which seems to be only a regional facies of the general Capsian; (2) the independence of most of the facies of the so-called Upper Capsian with respect to the Typical Capsian; (3) the confirmation of the existence and the chronological determination of new Epipaleolithic industries which are distinct from the Iberomaurusian and the Capsian; and (4) the identification—within the Neolithic of Capsian tradition—of several facies, the southernmost of which appear to be the oldest, while the facies which became established in the Capsian region seems to be the most recent.

The often clumsy attacks directed against radiocarbon datings and the use which archaeologists can make of these datings can be countered by the significant results which the growth in the number of such dates has brought about in our much better knowledge of North African and Saharan prehistory.

BIBLIOGRAPHY

ALMAGRO, M., 1968. *Prehistoria del Norte de Africa y del Sahara espanol.* Madrid.

AUMASSIP, G., 1972. "Néolithique sans poterie de la région de l'oued Mya." *Mém. 20 du CRAPE, SNED.* Alger.

BALOUT, L., 1972. "Chronologie absolue et préhistoire saharienne." *Rev. de l'Occid. musulman et de la Médit.* 11:13-19.

_____, and ROUBET, C., 1970. "Datation radiométrique de l'Homme de l'Aïn Dokkara et de son gisement ("Escargo-tière du Chacal" région de Tébessa, Algérie). *Libyca* 18:23-34.

BOBO, J., 1955. "Un facies mésolithique saharien: le 'facies d'El Oued.' Sa place dans l'ensemble des industries du Souf." *Actes de la IIe session, Congrès Panafricain de Préhistoire, Alger, 1952,* pp. 493-502. Paris: Arts et Métiers Graphiques.

CAMPS, G., 1955. "Le gisement Atérien du Camp Franchet d'Esperey." *Libyca* 3:17-56.

_____, 1968, "Tableau chronologique de la préhistoire récente du Nord de l'Afrique. Première synthèse des datations absolues obtenues par le carbone 14." *Bulletin de la Société Préhistorique Française* 65:609-22.

_____, 1970. "Notes de Protohistoire nord-africaine et saharienne V. Dates absolues concernant la Protohistoire du Maghreb et du Sahara." *Libyca* 18:235-40.

_____, 1972. "Extension territoriale des civilisations épipaléolithiques et néolithiques dans le Nord de l'Afrique." *6eme Congrè panaf. de Préhist. et d'Études quatern., Dakar, 1967,* pp. 284-87.

_____; AUMASSIP, G.; and ROUBET, C., 1966. "Présentation de deux industries à lamelles des régions sahariennes." *Bulletin de la Société Préhistorique Française* 63:631-42.

_____; DELIBRIAS, G.; and THOMMERET, J., 1968. "Chronologie absolue et succession des civilisations préhis-toriques dans le Nord de l'Afrique." *Libyca* 16:9-28.

CAMPS-FABRER, H., 1974. *Un gisement capsien supérieur de facies sétifien, Medjez II.* Paris: CNRS.

DAMON, P. E.; LONG, A.; WALLICK, E. I., 1972. "Dendrochronologic calibration of the Carbon 14 Time Scale." *Radiocarbon Dating Conference, Wellington,* Contribution 57.

GRÉBÉNART, D., 1969. "Aïn Naga. Capsien et Néolithique des environs de Messad (Départ. de Médéa)." *Libyca* 17:135-98.

_____, 1972. "Le Capsien des régions de Tébessa et d'Ouled Djellal, Algérie orientale." *Trav. du LAPMO.* Aix-en-Provence.

_____, 1973. *Une armature nouvelle de l'Épipaléolithique saharien: la pointe de Tarfaya.* (In press).

MAÎTRE, J.-P., 1971. "Contribution à la Préhistoire de l'Ahhagar I, Téfedest centrale." *Mém. 17 du CRAPE, AMG.* Paris.

MARMIER, F., and TRECOLLE, G., 1968. "Stratigraphie du gisement d'Hassi Mouillah. Région de Ouargla (Algérie)." *Bulletin de la Société Préhistorique Française* 65:121-27.

MUNSON, P., 1971. "The Tichitt Traduction, a Late Prehistoric of the Southwestern Sahara." Thesis, University of Illinois.

ROCHE, J., 1970-1971. "La grotte de Taforalt (Maroc oriental)." *Bull. de la Soc. d'Hist. nat. du Maroc* 3:7-14.

ROUBET, C., 1971. "Sur la définition et la chronologie du Néolithique de tradition capsienne." *L'Anthropologie* 75:553-74.

TIXIER, J., 1968. "Notes sur Le Capsien typique." In *La Préhistoire: problèmes et tendances*, edited by F. Bordes, pp. 439-51. Paris: CNRS.

VAUFREY, R., 1955. *Préhistoire de l'Afrique. Vol. I: Le Maghreb*. Paris: Masson.

WENDORF, F. (ed.), 1968. *The Prehistory of Nubia*, 2 vols. and atlas. Dallas: Fort Burgwin Research Center and Southern Methodist University Press.

NEOLITHIC SETTLEMENT OF THE SAHARA AS IT RELATES TO THE NILE VALLEY

T. R. Hays

The University of Texas at Arlington

INTRODUCTION

During the past few years numerous studies in the central Sahara have indicated that the present desert conditions may have occurred rather recently. Results of paleoenvironmental research evoke a picture of the area as grasslands associated with lakes fed by rivers draining forested highlands during the seventh through third millenium B.C. Living in this area were numerous animals of a type now found primarily in East Africa and the humans who hunted them. Interpretation of rock paintings and archaeological excavations also suggests numerous groups of people who may have practiced a Neolithic way of life of farming and herding. If there is evidence of early Neolithic populations in the Sahara, it has potential importance for studies of the Nile Valley. It is the purpose of this paper to review the evidence in an effort to determine the extent of Neolithic settlement of the Sahara and its relationship to Nilotic cultures.

The topography of the Sahara does not consist of a monotonous plain, but is accented by plateaus and mountains. The central Sahara features a large semicircular plateau surrounded by mountain ranges rising over 2,000 meters. Aside from the Atlas range in the extreme northwest, the central Sahara contains the uplands of Tassili Ahaggar, Tibesti, and Aïr (fig. 1). This plateau extends from Darfur in the Sudan west through the Ennedi range. An extension runs north to Gebel Oweinat and the Gilf Kebir, while the main portion extends westward to the Tibesti and Hoggar ranges. The latter is then joined to the subtropical savanna zone to the south through the Aïr highlands (Hester, 1968, fig. 1). This crescentic area, adjoining the savanna belt on both ends, may have functioned as a zone of migration of plants, animals, and man during times of climatic fluctuation. During wetter intervals, there would have been a northward advance of the tropical savanna-type Ethiopian flora and fauna (Clark, 1967).

POST-PLEISTOCENE ENVIRONMENT

Numerous recent studies have provided data which indicate that the present Sahara Desert experienced a fluctuating climate even after the Pleistocene. Geological, paleontological, and palynological analyses combined with radiocarbon dating have provided evidence for a cooler and more humid climate. Faure (1966) has dated two subpluvials in the Sahara. Most dates for the earlier subpluvial cluster between 7000 B.C. and 5500 B.C., the second between 3500 B.C. and 1200 B.C.

Before 6100 B.C. in Tibesti, the Hoggar, and Tchad (Delibrias and Dutil, 1966; Servant et al., 1969*a*; Servant et al., 1969*b*) a cooler, moister phase occurred producing the upper (710 m) lake at Adrar Bous in Ténéré. These lake deposits reached a maximum depth at ca. 6600 B.C., but the lake began to dry up ca. 5000 B.C. (Faure, 1966). Drier conditions followed, the lake dwindled, and dunes moved across the old lake margins. Between 4000 B.C. and 2000 B.C. the dunes stabilized, small swamps formed, and the "Tenerian Neolithic" lived around the margins of the 700 m lake at Adrar Bous (Williams, 1971). This chronology for the two lake levels at Adrar Bous is thus consistent with dates for other lake deposits in the area.

At Ténéré there also is evidence of a transition from a Mediterranean steppe climate to a dryer climate characterized by subarid tropical plants. This spread of Ethiopian-Sudanic flora and fauna into the southern Sahara is based on fossil pollen from diatomites (Fuare et al., 1963). The Ténéré lacustrine deposits at Adrar Bous, dated ca. 3200 B.C. (Delibrias and Hugot, 1962), contained mostly pollen of tropical species (Acacia, Balanites) together with a large percentage of chenopods. Mediterranean species were represented, however, and consisted of myrtle, cypress, and juniper (Quezel and Martinez, 1962). At higher elevations in the Hoggar, Quezel and Martinez (1958) identified pollen from Méniet of cypress, pine, wild olive, and hackberry in association with bones of extinct wild buffalo and dated to ca. 3500 B.C. In the Acacus hills of Fezzan pollen of Typha, a swamp plant, accounted for over 50 percent of the samples, which also included Acacia and Balanites. Radiocarbon dates suggested a time range of 5600 B.C. to 3800 B.C. (Mori, 1965). A later horizon at Uan Muhuggiag (Fezzan) still indicated some swamp areas, but pollen representing semiarid vegetation was predominate.

In general, the evidence points to a cool period with an open woodland and savanna in the Sahara followed by a drying trend. The decrease in moisture caused a slow decline in Mediterranean flora toward the higher elevations and the formation of sand dunes in isolated basins at lower altitudes (below 1,000 m). Interdunal swamps containing tropical (Ethiopian) fauna occurred in these basins during the subsequent "Neolithic subpluvial" (Rognon, 1967). This last wet phase produced a connection of the basins with the highlands. The junction of these areas allowed an intermingling of Mediterranean flora and Ethiopian fauna which is still evident in some isolated areas.

In summary, during the "Neolithic wet phase" climatic conditions fluctuated between dry periods and those more moist than today. Prior to the sixth millenium conditions were much more moist than at present. The Sahara was

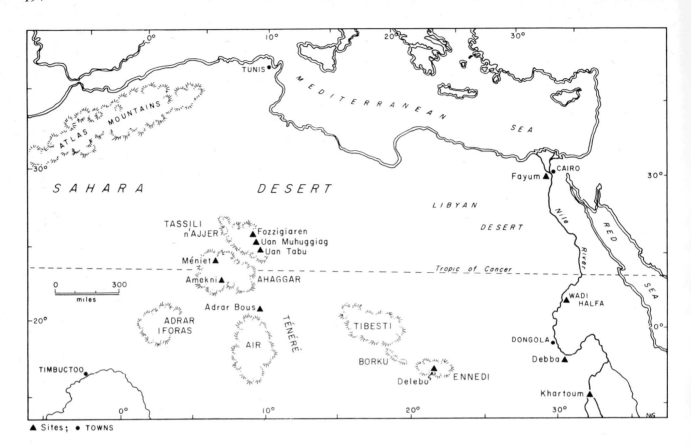

FIG. 1–Map of Saharan Africa.

relatively moist between 5500 B.C. and 2300 B.C. when the "Saharan Neolithic" occupation occurred. Butzer (1966) suggested the presence during this time of savanna woodlands in some of the highlands and grasslands providing good seasonal pastures on the uplands and wadi drainages. After ca. 2300 B.C. the climate became hyperarid in the Fezzan and probably in Tassili and Hoggar as well.

ARCHAEOLOGICAL EVIDENCE

Much of the above paleoenvironmental data has been provided as a consequence of excavation of archaeological sites. For the most part these sites date between 6000 B.C. and 2000 B.C. (Table 1) and are characterized by microliths, arrowpoints, pottery, and grinding stones. Bone industries with well-made harpoons have been found, as well as ground stone axes and gouges. Sites containing these characteristics have been attributed to the so-called "Saharan Neolithic." Several of these sites were situated in the central highlands and were associated with numerous localities containing rock paintings and engravings believed to derive from the "Neolithic" period. The distribution of these sites is illustrated in figure 1.

Many of the sites in the central and southern Sahara have been assigned to a "Neolithic of Sudanic Tradition" (Hugot, 1962) or more simply the "Sudanese Neolithic" (Camps, 1969). The basis for the terminology stems from the presence of unburnished comb-impressed pottery having decorative motifs similar to that described for sites near Khartoum (Arkell, 1949, 1953). Other sites in the northern Sahara containing "Neolithic" traits appear to derive from the Capsian and are called "Neolithic of Capsian Tradition." Camps makes a good case for the separation of the "Neolithic of Capsian Tradition" of the northern Sahara from the "Sudanese Neolithic" of the central and southern Sahara. Several distinct differences can be cited in lithic, bone, and ceramic industries. The "Sudanese Neolithic" utilized microlithic flakes rather than the microlithic geometrics formed on bladelets which characterized the "Neolithic of Capsian Tradition." The bone and ivory harpoons and fishhooks can be easily distinguished from the "Neolithic of Capsian Tradition," and incised stone and ostrich egg shell is absent or rare in the "Sudanese Neolithic." Finally, the ceramics of the south have spherical forms and are completely decorated with comb impression in "Sudanese" motifs, whereas those of the "Neolithic of Capsian Tradition" possess conical bases and collars with the decoration being sparse and often limited to the neck of the vessel (Camps, 1969).

Even though there are differences which can be used to distinguish the "Neolithic of Capsian Tradition" from the "Sudanese Neolithic," the latter covers a vast area of the Sahara and does not represent a uniform unit of material culture. Several facies of the "Sudanese Neolithic" have been postulated (Camps-Fabrer, 1966) although only a small number of sites have been examined in different regions of the Sahara. It should be pointed out, however,

TABLE 1

RADIOCARBON DATES FROM EGYPT, SUDAN, AND THE SAHARA

SITE	DATE	SAMPLE	MATERIAL
Egypt			
Fayum	4,441 B.C. ± 180 years	(C-550,C-551)	Grain
	4,145 B.C. ± 250 years	(C-457)	Grain
	3,910 B.C. ± 115 years	(I-4131)	Charcoal
	3,860 B.C. ± 115 years	(I-4127)	Charcoal
Sudan			
Wadi Halfa	3,650 B.C. ± 200 years	(WSU-174)	Charcoal
Shaheinab	3,445 B.C. ± 380 years	(C-754)	Shell
	3,110 B.C. ± 450 years	(C-753)	Charcoal
Sahara			
Méniet	3,450 B.C. ± 150 years	Hugot, 1962	Charcoal
Ténéré			
Adrar Bous III	3,190 B.C. ± 300 years	(SA-100)	Charcoal
Adrar Bous	3,810 B.C. ± 500 years	(UCLA-1958)	Bone
Amekni			
30-60	3,550 B.C. ± 250 years	(Gif-464)	Charcoal
60-90	4,850 B.C. ± 200 years	(Gif-1222)	Charcoal
H2	6,100 B.C. ± 80 years	(U.W.-87)	Charcoal
Chenachène	4,630 B.C. ± 50 years	(Grn-4386)	Charcoal
Adrar Tin			
Terin	2,770 B.C. ± 250 years	(Gif-304)	Charcoal
Delebo	5,230 B.C. ± 300 years	(Gif-351)	Charcoal
	4,950 B.C. ± 300 years	(Gif-352)	Charcoal
Jabbaren I	3,550 B.C. ± 200 years	Lhote, 1961	Charcoal
Sefar	3,070 B.C. ± 300 years	Lhote, 1961	Charcoal
Uan Muhuggiag	5,448 B.C. ± 120 years	Mori, 1965	Charcoal
VIII	4,002 B.C. ± 120 years	Mori, 1965	Charcoal
Uan Tabu	5,095 B.C. ± 175 years	Mori, 1965	Charcoal
Uan Telocat	4,804 B.C. ± 175 years	Mori, 1965	Charcoal

that these "Neolithic" occurrences have a wide range of dates (Camps et al., 1968), as well as distinct differences in ceramics and lithic industries which make such affinities very tenuous.

Even within rather close geographical boundaries, a comparative analysis of lithic artifacts reveals major differences. Both the sites of Méniet and Amekni are located in the Hoggar of the central Sahara. Even though these sites are scarcely 200 km apart, only the most general characteristics can be used as evidence of relationship. The major distinctions from Amekni lie in the higher frequency of bifacial points and scrapers at Méniet coupled with a lower frequency of notched pieces and scaled pieces. These differences were dismissed by Camps (1960, p. 201), who believed Méniet to be a "later facies" of Amekni. This position contradicts the radiocarbon dates, however, which indicate that the site of Méniet was contemporary with the middle level of Amekni (Camps, 1969, p. 206). In addition, a Chi square test of relationship conducted on these assemblages (Hays, 1971) indicated a lack of homogeneity. The computed Chi square value was 165.73 at 16 degrees of freedom as compared to an expected Chi square value of 39.25 at .001 level of significance. It must be concluded that the data are insufficient at present to support the proposed concept of "facies" for the central Sahara.

NEOLITHIC

The preceding summary of paleoenvironmental and archaeological evidence leaves little doubt that man and tropical plants and animals were able to live in the Sahara during several millennia after the Pleistocene. The question is, however, can these populations be attributed to a Saharan Neolithic? Consequently, an important and necessary aspect of an examination of the "Saharan Neolithic" is a consideration of the term *Neolithic*. This label has had different meanings to different prehistorians, and these differences are important since they concern the criteria used to define the term.

"Neolithic" was first used by Sir John Lubbock to mean the "New Stone Age," characterized by ground and polished stone tools and pottery (Daniel, 1963, p. 58). At the present time, however, prehistorians consider the presence of domesticated plants and/or animals to be most important. Thus, the Neolithic would include polished stone tools, bifacial flaking of arrowheads, pottery, farming, and stock breeding. Some Saharan prehistorians, however, insist that evidence for all of these "Neolithic" elements need not be found in the same site. For example, the presence of pottery and ground stone at the Nilotic site of Early Khartoum caused it to be considered Neolithic although there was no evidence for domestication (Balout, 1965, p. 156). Thus, the "Sudanese Neolithic" has included both the sites of Early Khartoum and Shaheinab. This combination has been confusing to later workers because these two sites are quite different in stone tools, ceramics, and economies. Only Shaheinab had any evidence for domestication—the presence of dwarf goats (Arkell, 1953, p. 15).

Further confusion has arisen regarding the decorative characteristics of the "Sudanese" pottery to which ceramics in the Sahara were compared. Some of the difficulties in using Arkell's classification have been presented elsewhere (Hays, 1971, 1974). Arkell has attempted to reduce the problem by reiterating the differences between the ceramics from the Sudanese sites. "Khartoum Mesolithic" pottery from the site of Early Khartoum is unburnished and characterized by "dotted wavy line" design motifs (fig. 1). On the other hand, although "dotted wavy line" motifs also occur in the "Khartoum Neolithic" pottery from Esh Shaheinab, the pottery is burnished (Arkell, 1972). Many workers now believe that confusion of the pottery from the different sites may have resulted from the same place-names being used for the two cultural manifestations (i.e., "Khartoum

Mesolithic" and *Khartoum* Neolithic"). Consequently, it is suggested that the place-name *Khartoum* apply only to the "Khartoum Mesolithic" whose type site is Early Khartoum, and that the term "Shaheinab Neolithic" be used to refer to the Neolithic industry whose type site is Esh Shaheinab.

The position taken by the present author concurs with the resolution presented at the 1965 Wenner-Gren African Symposium, which suggested that applying the term *Neolithic* to isolated pieces or to groups of artifacts possessing one or more characteristics of Neolithic industrial complexes (grinding and polishing of stone, pottery, grindstones), but without any indication of domestication or agricultural activity, is unjustified and should be discontinued. Consequently, in this analysis of the "Saharan Neolithic," the term *Neolithic* will be reserved for sites containing evidence of domestication.

This principle of domestication has been applied only rarely to ceramic-bearing sites in the Sahara. Analyses of pollen collected within stratified deposits at Méniet (Pons and Quezel, 1957) indicated the existence "...in a Sudanic-Neolithic context, of a cereal of the 'type of cultivated grass distinctive among grass-pollens' (Firbas, 1937, quoted in Erdtman, 1943)" (Hugot, 1968, p. 485). Combined with the pottery, the abundance of associated grinding stones thus received added significance, causing Hugot to declare, "I am in a position to speak of the Neolithic of Sudanic Tradition" (Hugot, 1968, p. 485). This conclusion was of fundamental importance. If, ca. 3450 B.C., the inhabitants of Méniet had cultivated grain, it is conceivable that other people of the "Neolithic of Sudanic Tradition" could have cultivated grain in the areas which they occupied. This could explain the abundance of grindstones found throughout the southern Sahara (Hugot, 1968) as well as differences from the northern Sahara. In sites of the "Neolithic of Capsian Tradition" in the north pottery was very rare, grinding stones were infrequent, and the diverse and numerous arrowheads seemed to reflect the maintenance of an Epipaleolithic (hunting and gathering) way of life (Camps, 1969).

Camps also agreed that prehistorians now define the term *Neolithic* so that a change in the way of life from one based on hunting and gathering to one based on the production of food, as in agriculture or animal husbandry, is the essential determining criterion. On the other hand, because of the difficulties of documenting domestication archaeologically, Camps predicted the term *Neolithic* would rarely be used in the Sahara. Camps also believed, however, that agriculture could be linked to the presence of ceramics since it seemed to be a technique associated with food modification. Consequently the abundance of pottery in the so-called "Neolithic of Sudanese Tradition" at Méniet, Amekni, Tanezrouft, and Tilemsi was considered by Camps as *indirect* proof of the development of agriculture in the southern Sahara. This conclusion seemed reasonable to Camps since grinding stones and pottery appeared in the same large proportions. Furthermore, Camps reasoned, if

FIG. 2–"Dotted Wavy Line" Pottery from the Dongola Reach, Sudan (motifs defined in Hays, 1971): 1-3) Straight line motif; 4-9) Wavy line motif; 10-13) Dotted wavy line motif.

these populations continued to live a way of life unchanged for millennia, what would stimulate them to invent ceramic vessels (Camps, 1969, p. 204).

Camps states,

> Potsherds, arrowheads, and polished axes by their presence make a neolithic level recognizable, but the absence of one of these documents or of the three together must not necessarily negate the assignment of the studied deposit to the Neolithic. . . . Despite the absence of domestic fauna and the weakness of documents attesting to the existence of true agriculture, we do not hesitate to consider the industrial assemblage of Amekni as apparently Neolithic of great age. (Camps, 1969, p. 205).

Despite such statement to the contrary, it should be stressed that pottery in no sense

> . . .implies a knowledge of agriculture. In large quantities it may indicate a tendency to settled life. Owing to its fragility, the nomad avoided it. It may be associated with agriculture only insofar as impressions of cereal grains are found in the paste, because fragments of straw were used in its manufacture (Hugot, 1968, p. 485).

Grains of domesticated plants have not been found in the Sahara. In fact, only the *single* pollen of a "cereal" identified at Méniet and *two* pollens interpreted as cultivated Pennisetum (Millet) recovered at Amekni can be presented as possible documentation of agriculture.

Since it must be concluded that the evidence for domestication of plants is very tenuous, it is necessary to examine the possibility of domesticated animals. As we have seen, the progressive desiccation of the Saharan savanna is a fairly recent phenomenon, and until the Roman period the conditions necessary for cattle raising obtained near the highlands. At present in the Aïr mountains are sheltered valleys with dense growth of Acacia, Balanites, and Panicum. Typical fauna includes moufflon, gazelle, and some of the last herds of Addax are found to the east of the Aïr mountains (Hall, 1971). In addition, small herds of Fulani cattle have been reported near the Azaouak wadi system northwest of Agades, Niger (Clark, 1970). Thus, very little change from the present climate would allow widespread animal husbandry.

One source of data for animal domestication which has been cited a great deal is the rock art of the Sahara. These engravings and paintings apparently depict scenes of tropical wild animals as well as herds of domesticated cattle at Tassili (Lhote, 1961) and Fezzan (Mori, 1965). It is assumed the paintings were representative of scenes known to the painters, hence cattle herders who lived between 4000 B.C. and 2000 B.C. Unfortunately most of the rock art is not accurately dated. A few radiocarbon dates, however, do tend to document domesticated cattle and styles of rock art to this time period. Lhote has distinguished four periods or styles for the rock paintings of Tassili: Hunter (6000 B.C.–4000 B.C.); Herder (4000 B.C.–1500 B.C.); Horse (1500 B.C.–600 B.C.); and Camel (600 B.C. on). These periods are based on two radiocarbon dates for sites which correspond to the "Herder" style: Jabbaren I, 3350 B.C. ± 200 years; and Sefar, 3070 B.C. ± 300 years (Lhote, 1961, p. 12; Delibrias et al., 1957, pp. 267-270). In the Fezzan, rock paintings of "Herder" style at Uan Muhuggiag were dated before 2750 B.C. ± 310 years, and Level VIII, dated at 4002 B.C. ± 120 years, contained a skull of the shorthorned *Bos brachyceros* (Mori, 1965). The only other remains of domestic cattle in the Sahara consist of an almost complete skeleton of *Bos brachyceros* from a "Tenerian" site at Adrar Bous which gave a bone date of 3810 B.C. ± 500 years (UCLA 1958) (Clark, 1971, p. 457). The question remains whether these cattle were the result of domestication in the Sahara or diffusion from other areas. Indigenous cattle, *Bos africanus* and *Bos ibericus*, could have been domesticated (Mori, 1964; Beck and Huard, 1969).

NILOTIC RELATIONSHIPS

Clark (1965, p. 158) believed that the spread of Neolithic cultural traits generally throughout northern Africa could best be explained as the outcome of economic and social adjustment following rapid diffusion of a pastoral and agricultural way of life from the east, along the Mediterranean littoral, and into the Sahara from the north and east. Following Clark's idea of diffusion of Neolithic traits into Africa from the north and east, it is necessary to check the dates for these traits in the Sahara and in the areas of proposed routes of diffusion. The earliest evidence for possibly domesticated animals in the Near East is domesticated sheep (8900 B.C.) at Zawi Chemi Shanidar in Iraq (Solecki, 1964). The earliest evidence to date for domesticated plants in the Near East is 7500 B.C. at Tepe Ali Kosh in Iran (Hole et al., 1969). In the Levant domesticated plants occur at Jericho ca. 7000 B.C. (Hopf, 1969), whereas domesticated animals are dated to no earlier than the seventh millennium (Ducos, 1969). In North Africa McBurney (1967, p. 271) placed the Neolithic (pottery and sheep or goat) of Haua Fteah in Cyrenaica beginning at 4850 B.C., but did not see it as a local development.

Domesticated grain may have been in the Sahara at Méniet in the fourth millennium and possibly at Amekni in the fifth millennium B.C. Domesticated cattle are dated to the fourth millennium at Adrar Bous and Fezzan. On the other hand, the earliest evidence for the Neolithic near the Nile is at Fayum in Egypt (emmer wheat), dated to 3910 B.C. ± 115 years (I-4131) (Wendorf et al., 1970, p. 1168). Bones of cattle and sheep were found, and according to Dr. Acheul Gautier, belong to domesticated species (Wendorf, personal communication). The "Shaheinab Neolithic" of

Sudan, with small domestic goat, dated ca. 3300 B.C. (Arkell, 1953, p. 107) has the only evidence for early domestication along the southern Nile.

Hugot and others accepted Clark's idea that the Nile Valley was an immense "nursery-garden," a line from which cultivated plants from the

...nuclear area of the Near East (Clark, 1962b) were transported after adaptation, west and south, especially westward along the great invasion route of the Neolithic people of Sudanic tradition (Hugot, 1968, p. 488).

The problem with this interpretation concerns the lack of evidence in the Sahara at this time for the use of barley and wheat, the plants cultivated near the Nile. The answer may be that another grain was utilized. There are numerous species of millet and sorghum which cover a vast zone including parts of northern and tropical Africa, the Near East, and India. Wild forms can still be found on wadi banks in the southern Sahara (Hugot, 1968, p. 487). It is possible that both plants could have been the first grain brought under cultivation in the Sahara.

The possibility of an independent development of agriculture within the central Sahara during a wet phase (6000 B.C.–3500 B.C.) rather than a diffusion from southwestern Asia via the Nile Valley has been proposed (Camps, 1968; Hoebler and Hester, 1969). Hester believed the independent domestication of local grasses such as sorghum and millet in the Sahara was possible. Once developed, however, such agriculture would have been short-lived, as increasing aridity would have favored reliance on a nomadic pastoral economy within two to three thousand years (Hester, 1968, p. 498). As we have seen, however, direct evidence for such plant domestication is extremely rare.

Clark, on the other hand, believed that the Neolithic of the Sahara and of the Nile Valley are so interrelated that they should be studied as a unit (Clark, 1965, p. 159). Later, Clark suggested

...these pastoral populations were largely indigenous stock that had taken unto itself certain cultural traits from the fully food producing economies of the Nile Valley.

Clark then listed

...cattle and sheep, probably the milking trait, ground and polished axes and adzes, stone platters and dishes, the hollow-based arrowhead, Wavy Line and Dotted Wavy Line pottery and a ware decorated with stab marks made with a cuneiform tool, perhaps also the bone harpoon head—all these can be cited at certain or probable introductions from the Nile (Clark, 1967, p. 603).

The proponents of the idea of a diffusion of pastoral ideas from the Nile Valley into the Sahara overlook several important points. First, there is no undisputed evidence of pottery, domesticated animals, or plants along the Nile before 3900 B.C. (Fayum, located some 50 km southwest of Cairo in Lower Egypt). Secondly, no reasons have been given for the contact of people between these areas, although several routes of movement have been proposed. Finally, Camps's question remains as to why would people utilize pottery who were not sedentary farmers.

First, it should be emphasized that the cattle identified as domestic at Fayum are the long-horned type, whereas those in the Sahara are short-horned (Gautier, n.d.). The cattle from the predynastic site of Badari in Upper Egypt also are not short-horned. The earliest evidence for short-horned cattle in Egypt would be in the V Dynasty, ca. 2600 B.C. (Epstein, 1971). Moreover, Smith (1973) and others suggest the progenitors of the Saharan short-horned cattle came from the Maghreb (i.e., Bos ibericus).

Secondly, the cultural sequence at Adrar Bous in Ténéré indicated a continuation in lithic technology from a fishing population to a later cattle-herding population ca. 3900 B.C. Smith (1973) interpreted this data as reflecting the acceptance of "neolithic" traits by an indigenous group. This data, coupled with the lack of evidence for short-horned cattle at this time along the Nile, suggest that it was the concept of domestication which spread into the Sahara rather than a migration of peoples.

Finally, the earliest utilization of pottery in the Near East seems to correlate with a settled way of life based primarily on the utilization of wild or domestic grains, as at Jarmo and Hacilar (Braidwood, 1958; Melaart, 1963). On the other hand, modern pastoralists in the Sahara store grain for later use in ceramic containers at various locations in the desert (Lhote, 1947; Nicolaisen, 1963). This same system was used prehistorically in the Hoggar (Hugot, 1962; Camps, 1969) and Ténéré (Clark, 1970) for the storage of wild products (Celtis berries). In addition, the earliest pottery in the Sahara is found in sites with numerous wild savanna and aquatic faunal remains, as at Amekni in Hoggar (Camps, 1960) and Adrar in Kiffi in Ténéré (Clark, 1971). Based on this data, it is postulated that perhaps wild grains *and* aquatic fauna from the lakes and rivers of the Sahara furnished regular and predictable food sources which permitted a semi-sedentism in which ceramics would be of value.

Dates for the early ceramics sites in the Near East go back to the seventh millennium B.C. with the earliest radiocarbon date being 6486 B.C. ± 102 years from Level IX at Catal Huyuk in Anatolia (Mellaart, 1967, p. 52). The earliest radiocarbon date for ceramics in the Sahara is now 6100 B.C. ± 80 years (U.W.-87) at Amekni (Camps, 1969, p. 207). The possibility of an independent invention of pottery in the Sahara has caused some workers to question the radiocarbon dates from Amekni. It has been suggested that the use of large dead trees as firewood could produce spurious dates (cf. Libby, 1963). Conversely, Suess (1970) indicated that due to the variations in accumulation of carbon 14 by large trees, the "true age" may be considerably older than the "radiocarbon age." Remnants of very large old trees do still exist in the central Sahara (Hugot, 1962; Clark, 1970), but at altitudes above 2,000 meters. It is interesting to note that a sample taken from a large limb of one of these olive trees produced a radiocarbon date of only 180 B.P. ± 60 years (UCLA-1655) (Clark, 1970, p. 21). The best evidence for the validity of the early dates, however, lies in the fact that several widely separated Saharan sites have produced similar sequences of early dates. It is highly unlikely that the early dates at Amekni, Adrar in Kiffi, Uan Muhuggiag, and Delebo (Bailloud, 1967) could be the result of chance or the utilization of "fossil" trees.

As pointed out elsewhere (Hays, 1973), there is now good evidence that the ceramic traditions of the Sahara and the Nile Valley were the results of separate developments. Current data strongly support the position that ceramic technology was independently developed in the central Sahara as well as in the Near East. Subsequently, the Near Eastern technology spread to the Lower Nile Valley while the Saharan tradition spread to the Upper Nile in Sudan. Only several millennia after the beginnings of pottery making did the two ceramic traditions meet and blend along the Upper Nile River Valley of northern Sudan.

A mineralogical examination of the so-called "Sudanese Neolithic" ceramics further documented the disparate nature of the Saharan and Nilotic sites (Hays and Hassan, 1974). Numerous potsherds from the Sahara and Nile Valley were subjected to petrographic and mineralogical analyses. The microscopic study of thin sections made from the sherds indicated that the mineralogic composition and texture of the temper varied from one area to another. Secondly, X-ray diffraction analysis indicated different clay sources for the ceramics. Finally, differences in the fabric of the ceramics indicated production by several groups rather than the dispersal of the products of one group. Techniques of pottery making tend to be stabilized and maintained by cultural traditions (Shepard, 1963, p. 338). Coupled with differences seen in lithic typology and technology, the ceramic analysis further strengthened the model of different cultural developments in the Sahara and along the Nile Valley.

Thus far relationships between the Neolithic occupations of the Sahara and the Nile Valley have centered on items of material culture. One additional source of comparative data, however, concerns human skeletal remains. The characteristics of human populations living in the central and southern Sahara during the "Neolithic period" can be important in postulating relationships. Lhote (1961) ascribed the "Têtes Rondes" style of the early "Herder" period to Negro populations. On the other hand, the paintings of people with domesticated animals, of the later pastoralist period, indicated populations with mixed racial characteristics. Lhote suggested "...some are European,

others are Negroid, but the majority have long straight hair and copper colored skin, and apparently represent an intermediate type...". The headgear, clothing, and most typical physical characteristics of the human figures of the pastoral period are said to resemble the present day Fulani (Lhote, 1961, pp. 139-40). These people pride themselves on their non-Negroid traits: light skin, straight hair, thin nose and lips. These characteristics are only the "ideal," however, as every group exhibits a wide range of physical characteristics (Stenning, 1965). Lhote's interpretation is that there was a mixture of racial characteristics as pastoralists from the Upper Nile area entered the Sahara (1961, p. 148).

Along the vast stretch of the Nile Valley three separate physical types are represented during the Predynastic. In Upper Egypt the Predynastic populations were rather small in stature, quite dolichocephalic and non-Negroid (Childe, 1953). Skeletons from Lower Egypt suggest that the inhabitants were somewhat taller, heavier, and more brachycephalic than the people of Upper Egypt (Hayes, 1965). These remains showed close resemblances with people from the Levant and suggested intermixture from that region rather than from the south (Trigger, 1968).

Of considerable importance is the lack of change in physical type in Upper Egypt during Predynastic times (Batrawi, 1945-1946). The continuity in material culture during this period has also been stressed (Frankfort, 1956; Kantor, 1965). On the contrary, the rare skeletal remains from Sudan have been interpreted as being "robust" and showing Negroid traits (Derry, 1949; Chamla, 1968). The meager skeletal remains from Sudan indicate the continuation there of Negroid populations during the fourth and third millennia B.C.

The question then arises as to the origin of the "non-Negroid" groups who entered the Sahara. After a comprehensive study of the human skeletal remains from Neolithic and Protohistoric Saharan sites, Chamla (1968) concluded that there was a change from Negroid populations during the Neolithic to mixed or non-Negroid populations in the Protohistoric period (ca. 3000 B.C.). Chamla suggests that these later changes resulted from contact with people from the northern Sahara where racial affinities were with the eastern Mediterranean populations (1968, p. 201). Significantly, a movement of people from Egypt was not postulated. Consequently, if a movement of Neolithic peoples had occurred from the Nile River into the Sahara, the Saharan skeletal evidence would dictate that the migration would have had to involve Negroid groups from the Sudan rather than non-Negroid ones from Upper Egypt. The lack of evidence for Sudanese cattle pastoralism at this time has been noted, however. These data suggest that populations of different racial stocks carried out similar types of economic pursuits during the so-called "Neolithic period" of Saharan and Nilotic cultural history.

Further evidence against population movements between Egypt and the Sahara resulted from recent archaeological exploration in the Egyptian Sahara. If there were, in fact, routes of communication between the Predynastic cultures of Egypt and the Neolithic cultures in the Sahara, it would be expected that some evidence of that communication would be found in the intervening areas. A test of this hypothesis occurred as part of the Combined Prehistoric Expedition 1973 season research under the direction of Professor Fred Wendorf. The author's participation was funded in part by the University of Texas at Arlington. Survey and excavation were undertaken near the westernmost oases in southern Egypt, some 350 km west of Abu Simbel. Numerous archaeological sites of various ages were discovered in the vicinity of Bir Terfawi, indicating that the prehistoric environmental conditions were far better than today. Results of the research indicated, however, that this area may not have experienced the climatic amelioration during the "Neolithic sub-pluvial" that was known in the central Sahara.

The earliest ceramic-bearing sites were dated only to 2500 B.C. (Haynes, personal communication). These sites contained rare grinding stones, no bifacial arrowpoints, high frequencies of denticulates and notches, and bipolar cores. Although large amounts of ostrich egg shell were present, no animal bone was recovered. The stone tools were made on local quartzite and also on Eocene flint. The nearest outcrop of this flint was approximately 150 km to the east near Bir Sheb. A brief reconnaissance to the Bir Sheb area revealed a number of sites in the vicinity of the oasis which contained ceramic and lithic assemblages similar to that of the Terfawi group. Further afield, the Abkan (Shiner, 1968) at the Second Cataract in Nubia has a similar high frequency of denticulates and notches. The expected evidence for connections between the central Sahara and the Nile Valley, however, was not forthcoming. Resemblances could not be found with either the "Saharan Neolithic" or the predynastic cultures of Egypt. The origins of these oasis people is unclear, but may be from the south.

CONCLUSIONS

It was the purpose of this paper to examine the validity of proposed Neolithic settlement in the Sahara and its relationships with the Nile Valley. This objective involved an evaluation of the evidence for establishing a Saharan Neolithic (e.g., "Neolithic of Sudanese Tradition"). Results of the study can be summarized as follows.

Paleoenvironmental data suggest the existence of two

cooling trends in the Sahara between approximately 7000 B.C. and 2000 B.C. This climatic amelioration allowed the Saharan plateau to support a Mediterranean flora in the higher elevations and a tropical (Ethiopian) flora and fauna at lower altitudes. Numerous archaeological habitation sites suggest the presence of a rather large human population during this time period. While these separated groups of people appear to have had communication with one another and with Nilotic cultures, their cultural and skeletal remains would indicate that they were autochthonous rather than immigrants from the Nile Valley.

All of the sites exhibit generalized "Neolithic" characteristics (e.g., ceramics, grinding stones, polished axes, bone harpoons), but direct evidence of domestication is rare. Significantly, there is no evidence for a pre-ceramic Neolithic in Saharan Africa; pottery occurs in many areas before domestication. For those people who maintained a "Mesolithic" economy but borrowed certain technological aspects of Neolithic artifacts, perhaps a term such as *Subneolithic* would be more appropriate (Bailloud, 1966, p. 159). That appellation would reserve the term *Neolithic* for those sites which contain evidence of domestication.

Only two sites (Méniet and Amekni) can be cited as possibly representing the use of domesticated grain. Evidence is better, however, for the domestication of animals. Rock art depicts scenes of pastoral groups with herds of cattle. Radiocarbon has been used to date these paintings between approximately 3800 B.C. and 2400 B.C. Actual remains of domesticated cattle have been dated around 3900 B.C. for the Sahara. Near the Nile River domestication of plants and animals also is dated to approximately 3900 B.C.

In conclusion, several points should be stressed for the Sahara. First, present evidence suggests the presence of "Neolithic" artifact assemblages before the domestication of plants or animals. Secondly, there is direct evidence for the use of domesticated cattle and possibly domesticated grain in the Sahara. Thirdly, the presence of the early "Subneolithic" and later Neolithic peoples was neither dependent upon nor the result of diffusion from the Nile Valley. Finally, the data suggest that the invention of ceramics, the domestication of cattle, and possibly the domestication of millet may have resulted from experimentation by indigenous groups living in the highlands of the central Sahara.

BIBLIOGRAPHY

ARKELL, A. J., 1949. *Early Khartoum*. London: Oxford University Press.

————, 1953. *Shaheinab*. London: Oxford University Press.

————, 1972. "Dotted Wavy-line Pottery in African Prehistory." *Antiquity* 46:221-22.

BAILLOUD, G., 1966. "Le Néolithique." In *La Nouvelle Clio La Préhistoire*, edited by Robert Boutruches and Paul Lemerée, pp. 157-203. Paris: Presses Universitaires de France.

————, 1969. "L'Évolution des Styles Céramiques en Ennedi (République du Tchad)." *Actes I^e Colloque International d'Archaeologie Africaine*:31-45.

BALOUT, L., 1965. "Comments on Nile Predynastic Development." *Current Anthropology* 6(2):156-57.

BATRAWI, AHMED, 1945-46. "The Racial History of Egypt and Nubia." *Journal of the Royal Anthropological Institute* 75:81-101, 76:131-56.

BECK, P., and HUARD, P., 1969. *Tibesti: Carrefour de la Préhistoire Saharienne*. Paris.

BRAIDWOOD, R. J., 1958. "Near Eastern Prehistory." *Science* 127:1419-30.

BUTZER, K. W., 1966. "Climatic Changes in the Arid Zones of Africa during Early to Mid-Holocene Times." In *World Climate from 8000 to 0 B.C.*, edited by J. S. Sawyer, pp. 73-83. London: Royal Meteor. Society.

CAMPS, GABRIEL, 1969. *Amekni, Néolithique Ancien du Hoggar*. Paris: Arts et Métiers Graphiques.

CAMPS-FABRER, H., 1966. *Métière et Art Mobilier dans la Préhistoire Nord-Africaine et Saharienne*. Mémoires du C.R.A.P.E. 5. Paris: Arts et Métiers Graphiques.

CHAMLA, M. C., 1969. *Les Populations Anciennes du Sahara et des Regions Limitrophes*. Mémoires du C.R.A.P.E. 9. Paris: Arts et Métiers Graphiques.

CHILDE, V. G., 1953. *New Light of the Most Ancient East*. London: Routledge and Kegan Paul.

CLARK, J. D., 1962. "The Spread of Food-Production in Sub-Saharan Africa." *Journal of African History* 3:211-28.

————, 1965. "Comments on Nile Predynastic Development." *Current Anthropology* 6(2):158-59.

————, 1967. "The Problem of Neolithic Culture in Sub-Saharan Africa." In *Background to Evolution in Africa*, edited by W. W. Bishop and J. D. Clark, pp. 601-28. Chicago: University of Chicago Press.

————, 1970. *Preliminary Report on an Archaeological Reconnaissance in the Northern Aïr and Ténéré*. (Mimeographed).

————, 1971. "An Archaeological Survey of Northern Aïr and Ténéré." *The Geographical Journal* 137(4):455-57.

DANIEL, GLYN, 1963. *The Idea of Prehistory*. New York: World Publishing.

DELIBRIAS, G., and DUTIL, O., 1966. "Formations Calcaires Lacustres du Quarternaire Supérieur dans le Massif Central Saharien (Hoggar) et Datations Absolues." *Centre Academie Science Paris* 262D:55-58.

————, and HUGOT, H. J., 1962. "Datation par la Méthode dite 'du C14' du Néolithique de l'Adrar Bous (Ténéréen)." *Missions Berliet Ténéré Tchad*.

DERRY, D. E., 1956. "The Dynastic Race in Egypt." *Journal of Egyptian Archaeology* 42:80-85.

DUCOS, P., 1969. "Methodology and Results of the Study of the Earliest Domesticated Animals in the Near East (Palestine)." In *The Domestication and Exploitation of Plants and Animals*, edited by Ucko and Dimbleby, pp. 265-75. Chicago: Aldine.

EPSTEIN, H., 1971. *The Origin of the Domestic Animals of Africa*. New York: Africana Publishing.

FAURE, H., 1966. "Évolution des Grands Lacs Sahariens à l'Holocène." *Quarternaria* 8:167-75.

————; MANGUIN, E.; and NYDAL, R., 1963. "Formations lacustres du Quaternaire supérieur du Niger Oriental: diatomites et âges absolues." *Bulletin du B. R. G. M.* 3:41-63.

FRANKFORT, H., 1956. *The Birth of Civilization in the Near East*. New York: Doubleday.

HALL, D. N., 1971. "The British Expedition to the Air Mountains." *The Geographical Journal* 137(4):445-50.

HAYES, W. C., 1965. *Most Ancient Egypt*. Chicago: University of Chicago Press.

HAYS, T. R., 1971. "The Sudanese Neolithic: A Critical Analysis." Ph.D. dissertation, Southern Methodist University. Ann Arbor: University Microfilms.

————, 1973. "Dispersal of Ceramics in Northeast Africa." Paper presented at the IXth International Congress of Anthropological and Ethnological Sciences, Chicago.

————, 1974. "Wavy Line Pottery: An Element of Nilotic Diffusion." *Bulletin of the South African Archaeological Society*.

————, and HASSAN, F. A., 1974. "Mineralogical Analysis of Sudanese Neolithic Ceramics." *Archaeometry*.

HESTER, JAMES J., 1968. "Comments on Origins of African Agriculture Symposium." *Current Anthropology* 9(5):497-98.

HOEBLER, P., and HESTER, J. J., 1969. "Prehistory and Environment in the Libyan Desert." *South African Archaeological Bulletin* 23:120-30.

HOLE, F.; FLANNERY, K.; and NEELY, J. A., 1969. *Prehistoric Human Ecology of the Deh Luran Plain*. Memoirs of the Museum of Anthropology, No. 1. Ann Arbor: University of Michigan.

HOPF, M., 1969. "Plant Remains and Early Farming in Jericho." In *The Domestication and Exploitation of Plants and Animals*, edited by Ucko and Dimbleby, pp. 255-59. Chicago: Aldine.

HUGOT, H. J., 1962. *Missions Berliet Ténéré-Tchad*. Paris: Arts et Métiers Graphiques.

————, 1968. "The Origins of Agriculture: Sahara." *Current Anthropology* 9:483-89.

KANTOR, H. J., 1965. "The Relative Chronology of Egypt and its Foreign Correlations before the Late Bronze Age." In *Chronologies in Old World Archaeology*, edited by R. W. Ehrich. Chicago: University of Chicago Press.

LHOTE, H., 1947. "La Poterie dans l'Ahaggar." *Travaux de L'Institut de Recherches Sahariennes* 4:145-54.

————, 1961. "The Rock Art of the Maghreb and Sahara." In *Art of the Stone Age*, edited by H. G. Bandi, pp. 99-152. New York: Crown Publishers.

McBURNEY, C. B. M., 1967. *The Haua Fteah (Cyrenaica) and the Stone Age of the Southeast Mediterranean*. Cambridge: At the University Press.

MELLAART, J., 1963. "Early Cultures of the South Anatolian Plateau." *Anatolian Studies* 13:199-236.

_____, 1967. *Catal Hüyuk*. London: Thames and Hudson.

MORI, F., 1964. "Some Aspects of the Rock Art of the Acacus (Fezzan Sahara) and Dating regarding It." In *Prehistoric Art of the Western Mediterranean and the Sahara*, edited by L. Pericot-Garcia and E. Ripoll-Perello, pp. 247-59. New York.

_____, and TORINO, G., 1965. *Tadrart Acacus*. Einaudi.

NICOLAISEN, J., 1963. *Ecology and Culture of the Pastoral Tuareg*. Copenhagen: National Museets Skrifter Etno.

PONS, A., and QUEZEL, P., 1957. "Prémière Étude Palynologique de Quelques Paléosols Sahariens." *Travaux de l'Institut de Recherches Saharaiennes* 16:15-40.

QUEZEL, P., and MARTINEZ, C., 1958. "Étude Palynolgique de Deux Diatomites du Borkou." *Bulletin de la Société l'Histoire Naturelle d'Afrique du Nord* 6:240-43.

_____, and MARTINEZ, C., 1962. "Premières resultats de l'analyse palynologique de sediments recuellis au Sahara méridional à l'occasion de la Mission Berliet." In *Missions Berliet Ténéré Tchad*, pp. 313-21. Paris: Arts et Métiers Graphiques.

ROGNON, P., 1967. "Climatic Influences on the African Hoggar during the Quaternary, Based on Geomorphological Observations." *Annals of the Association of American Geographers* 57(1):115-27.

SERVANT, M.; ERGENZINGER, P.; and COPPENS, Y., 1969. "Datations Absolues sur un Delta Lacustre Quaternaire au Sud du Tibesti." *Centre Recherche Sommaire Société Française* 313-14.

SHEPARD, A. O., 1963. *Ceramics for the Archaeologist*. Washington, D.C.: Carnegie Institution of Washington.

SHINER, J. L., 1968. "The Cataract Tradition." In *The Prehistory of Nubia*, edited by F. Wendorf, 2:535-629. Dallas: Fort Burgwin Research Center and Southern Methodist University Press.

SMITH, A. B., 1973. "Domesticated Cattle in the Sahara, and their Introduction into West Africa." Paper presented at the IXth International Congress of Anthropological and Ethnological Sciences, Chicago.

SOLECKI, R. L., 1964. "Zawi Chemi Shanidar, a post-Pleistocene Village Site in Northern Iraq," *VIth International Congress on the Quaternary, Warsaw, 1961*.

STENNING, D. J., 1965. "The Pastoral Fulani of Northern Nigeria." In *Peoples of Africa*, edited by J. L. Gibbs. New York: Holt, Rinehart and Winston.

SUESS, H. E., 1970. "Bristlecone pine calibrations of the Radiocarbon Time-scale 5200 B.C. to the Present." In *Radiocarbon Variations and Absolute Chronology*, edited by I. U. Olsson, pp. 303-12. New York: John Wiley and Sons.

TRIGGER, B. G., 1968. *Beyond History: The Methods of Prehistory*. New York: Holt, Rinehart and Winston.

WENDORF, FRED; SAID, RUSHDI; and SCHILD, ROMUALD, 1970. "Egyptian Prehistory: Some New Concepts." *Science* 169:1161-71.

WILLIAMS, M. A. J., 1971. "Geomorphology and Quaternary Geology of Adrar Bous." *The Geographical Journal* 137(4):450-55.

PART II

The Levant

THE PLEISTOCENE PALEOENVIRONMENTS OF ISRAEL

Aharon Horowitz
Institute of Archaeology
Tel Aviv University

INTRODUCTION

Israel is situated on the southeastern coast of the Mediterranean Sea, between 29°30′ and 33°30′N. and 34°10′ and 35°40′E. The country is comprised of three main morphographic units, running in a general north/south direction: the Coastal Plain, wide in the south but narrowing northward; the mountainous region, dividing the country as a longitudinal backbone, generally 600 m–900 m high; the Jordan–Arava Rift Valley, running along the whole country to the Bay of Elat in the south. In fact, these morphographic units also continue to the north, characterizing the whole Levantine coast.

The present climate of Israel and the Levantine coast is generally described as of the Csa type, regarded as "Mediterranean" (Trewartha, 1961). The north/south gradient of temperatures and rainfall is very steep in Israel and, in fact, the southern part of the country has a desert environment, the middle part semi-arid, and the northern part Mediterranean, with an annual rainfall of 600 mm–800 mm. Consequently, the vegetation varies considerably from north to south. A Mediterranean "maquis" is developed in the north, grading southward into a garigue steppe, while further south there is desert.

The present fauna and flora of Israel comprise elements of a fourfold origin (Tchernov, 1970; Zohary, 1959)—Tropical, relics of the Miocene; Euro-Siberian, that penetrated the country through an open waterway from the north during the Pliocene (Horowitz, 1973); Mediterranean, that developed in the region in Plio-Pleistocene times; and Endemic elements, developed in the Late Pleistocene in some ecologic niches in the country.

The great variability of the fauna and flora and the steep rainfall and temperature gradients along the country, together with the influence of the three different morphographic units—the coastal plain, mountains, and the Rift valley—create a great variability of environments in a relatively small area. Most of these are border environments, very sensitive to changes in physical conditions. Thus, changes in the environments are recorded in the erosional and depositional processes and in the composition of the vegetation and fauna, which are taken here as the basis for reconstructing past environments.

Previous studies of the Pleistocene of Israel dealt mainly with regional problems: the lithostratigraphy of the Coastal Plain (Issar, 1968; Issar and Kafri, 1972; Slatkine and Rohrlich, 1966; and others); the marine terraces on Mount Carmel (Michelson, 1970); the biostratigraphy of the marine sediments (Reiss and Issar, 1961); the Pleistocene shorelines (Avnimelech, 1962; Itzhaki, 1961); the stratigraphy of the Jordan Valley (Picard, 1943, 1963; Horowitz, 1973; and others); the palynostratigraphy of the Coastal Plain (Rossignol, 1962, 1964, 1969) and the Jordan Valley (Horowitz, 1966, 1968, 1971, 1973); and studies dealing with more specific subjects such as vertebrate remains, prehistoric sites, etc. An attempt to redefine and correlate all the Pleistocene formations of Israel and to delineate the paleogeographic development of the country throughout this period has been attempted (Horowitz, in press), and some of the results presented in the above-mentioned study are the basis for the present account.

The physical processes that influenced the Pleistocene environments in Israel can be grouped under climate, tectonics, and volcanism. The role of climate is the most complicated, since it must be deduced from second order climatically influenced processes which are not always believed, by all investigators, to be the result of the same climatic events. The Pleistocene climate of Israel can be generally divided into pluvials and interpluvials that may be correlated with the European glacials and interglacials (Horowitz, 1971, 1973). A pluvial climate results in a southward spreading of the maquis, and consequently all the vegetation formations; formation of red soils (locally called "Hamra") in the Coastal Plain; spreading of lakes in the Jordan Valley and marshes in the Coastal Plain; formation of gently dipping slopes in the mountains, due to soil formation processes and rich vegetation; and regression of the Mediterranean, due to the ice formation in the polar areas. The interpluvials result in a northward retreat of the vegetation belts, turning most of the country into desert; formation of sand dunes in the Coastal Plain, pushed forward by the marine ingressions, that later solidify into elongated calcareous sandstone ridges, locally called "kurkar"; great shrinkage of the Jordan Valley lakes and an almost total disappearance of the Coastal Plain marshes; and formation of steep canyons in the mountains due to floods and the lack of protection from vegetation cover.

The tectonic processes throughout the Pleistocene comprise a steady upwarping of the mountainous backbone of the country (Schulman, 1962; Horowitz, 1973, in press) accompanied with normal faulting, downfaulting of the Jordan–Arava Rift Valley (Picard, 1943; Schulman, 1962; Garfunkel and Horowitz, 1966; and others), and differential movements of blocks along the Coastal Plain (Kafri and Ecker, 1964; Karcz and Kafri, 1973; Horowitz, in press; D. Neev, personal communication, 1972).

A large scale volcanism is known in Israel in Preglacial Pleistocene times, and some minor phases of eruption occurred in Late Mindel, in Riss—Würm, and in Mid-Holocene times (Horowitz, 1973; Siedner and Horowitz, in preparation). The Pleistocene volcanic activity is limited to the northeastern areas of Israel.

THE PLEISTOCENE
BOUNDARIES AND SUBDIVISIONS

The term Pleistocene is used here in the broad sense, as suggested by a number of investigators and summed up in West (1968). The Villafranchian, Calabrian, and Sicilian stages, earlier regarded as the upper part of the Pliocene (Gignoux, 1955), comprise the Early, Preglacial Pleistocene. The beginning of the Pleistocene corresponds, therefore, in the sense used here, with the beginning of the Calabrian Transgression. This definition seems the only one that relates to natural processes that could be correlated on a worldwide basis. The use of fauna and flora to define the chronostratigraphic stage of the Pleistocene, or the beginning of the Pleistocene, is rejected here, as are the first appearance of man, or the first manifestations of hominids as tool makers. The biostratigraphic and cultural indicators cannot be used to define the beginning of the Pleistocene, since they differ in various areas and cannot define a chronostratigraphic plane. The radiometric age for the beginning of the Pleistocene is accepted here as 2.8—3.0 million years, defined both in East Africa (G. L. Isaac, personal communication) and in Israel (Siedner and Horowitz, in preparation).

The Cover Basalt of northeastern Israel, that correlates with the Calabrian sediments (Horowitz, in press) was K/Ar dated, and its upper flows yielded ages of 1.7—2.0 million years. These upper flows have reversed magnetic polarity which is typical for most of the sequence of the Cover Basalt (Freund et al., 1965), while the lower flows—usually only two or three—cooled under normal magnetic polarity, probably during the Gauss Normal Epoch. The Gauss—Matuyama reversal occurred some 2.5 million years ago (Tarling, 1971) and, therefore, the beginning of the Cover Basalt formation is older than 2.5 million years ago, suggested to be about 2.8 million years (Siedner and Horowitz, in preparation).

The term "Villafranchian" is used here to define the continental correlative of the Calabro-Sicilian Transgression. No further subdivisions of the Calabro-Sicilian or the Villafranchian (Zagwijn, 1960) are presented here, since these stages are represented in Israel only by a thin cover of sediments that do not permit further subdivision (Horowitz, in press).

The Calabrian and Sicilian marine transgressions are treated separately by some investigators (Gignoux, 1955) but it seems, according to recent studies (Selli, 1971), that they represent the same transgressive phase, with no possibility of distinction between the Calabrian and the Sicilian. Furthermore, malacalogical studies of the Calabrian and Sicilian in Israel (Moshkovitz, 1968) show that those two stages should be regarded as a single stage. Therefore this stage will be regarded as the Calabro-Sicilian Stage.

Sediments of Glacial Pleistocene age overlie unconformably the Preglacial Pleistocene Cover Basalt in Israel. A radiometric age of approximately 1.5 million years may be accepted for the beginning of the Glacial Pleistocene Stage (Siedner and Horowitz, in preparation). The subdivision of the Glacial Pleistocene in Israel is done according to the European glacial chronostratigraphy, and the Stage is divided into the Günz, Mindel, Riss, and Würm pluvials, with the corresponding interpluvials. A correlation of the interpluvials with the Mediterranean marine ingressions is suggested in Horowitz (in press) and presented in Figure 1. The correlation of glacial and pluvial climates is discussed in Horowitz (1971, 1973) and it appears that the Alpine Pleistocene chronostratigraphy is the most suitable for the Levantine area. It also correlates very well with the Mediterranean marine stages as summed up in Oakley (1964). The Holocene Stage, beginning about 12,000 years ago, is not separated here from the Pleistocene and is accepted as a natural continuation of this period.

THE PREGLACIAL PLEISTOCENE OF ISRAEL

The Marine Calabro-Sicilian

Marine sediments deposited during the Calabro-Sicilian Ingression on the Coastal Plain of Israel are designated as the Ga'ash Formation (Horowitz, in press). The type section for the Ga'ash Formation was proposed from the Ga'ash borehole, about 20 kms north of Tel Aviv, at depths from 159 m to 195 meters. At the type locality, the Formation comprises sandy marls and limestones, very rich in foraminifera and mollusca. The Ga'ash Formation crops out in the northwestern Negev, in the Besor area, and was referred to as the "C. P. Unit" by Shachnai (1967). It grades eastward into lateral conglomerates that are regarded by Horowitz (in press) as the "Lateral Conglomerate of the Ga'ash Formation," which comprise in part the Ahuzam Conglomerate, suggested in Issar (1968).

The malacofauna of the Ga'ash Formation was studied in detail by Moshkovitz (1968) from boreholes drilled along the coast in the vicinity of Tel Aviv. The malacofauna comprises about 50 species of molluscs, of which the most important are *Turitella pliorecens, Nucula placentina, Plicatula mytilina, Dentalium novemcostatum, Barbatia mytiloides*, and *Arcopagia corbis*, all pointing toward a Calabro-Sicilian age. Detailed analysis of the microfauna of the Ga'ash Formation is given in Reiss and Issar (1961) from the Reading 33/0 borehole to the north of Tel Aviv. They regarded the Calabro-Sicilian Ingression as the M1 Stage, accepted also by Horowitz (in press) to define the Ga'ash Formation microfaunal assemblage. A whole assemblage of foraminifera is described, of which the most important is the appearance of *Hyalinea balthica*, indicating a cool sea. Moshkovitz (1968) states also that the Calabro-Sicilian sea was cooler than the Pliocene sea. Reiss and Issar (1961) studied the planktonic microfauna, while Perath (1965) studied the benthonic microfauna in the Jaffa 1 borehole. Most of the benthonic foraminifera are relics from the Pliocene, but the Calabro-Sicilian assemblages are much poorer in the number of species than the Pliocene assemblages. This also may indicate a drop in the mean temperature of the sea water.

Pollen analyses of the Ga'ash Formation are given in Rossignol (1969) from the Reading 33/0 borehole. The assemblages comprise very high percentages of allochtonous pollen grains and spores, brought by the Nile and deposited in the eastern Mediterranean, which is typical for the whole sequence of marine Pleistocene deposits along the Israeli coast (Rossignol, 1962). The authochtonous spectrum is characterized by the high percentages of nonarboreal pollen, mainly derived from Gramineae and Cyperaceae with some Compositae, *Artemisia* and *Asphodelus*. About 10% of Chenopodiaceae and *Ephedra* appear as well. Arboreal pollen grains comprise mainly *Pinus halepensis*, which is probably a relic from the Pliocene, where it appears in high percentages (Horowitz and Zak, 1968; Horowitz, in press*b*). Minor percentages of *Quercus calliprinos* and *Olea europaea* appear too. This pollen assemblage indicates a dry climate, according to Rossignol (1969). Evidently, the pollen spectrum presented in Rossignol is indicative of the dry Mediterranean climate (Horowitz, 1971). In addition, a number of hystrichospheres and unicellular algae are described by Rossignol, which appear from the Pliocene until the present day with no major changes.

The Calabro-Sicilian Ingression left terraces on Mount Carmel at altitudes of 80 m to 105 m (Michelson, 1970; Slatkine and Rhorlich, 1966) that were correlated with the terraces appearing at the same elevations in Lebanon (Wetzel and Haller, 1944; Fleisch, 1957); in Egypt (Zeuner, 1958; Shukri et al., 1956); in Cyrenaica (McBurney and Hey, 1955); and on the French-Italian Riviera.

FLUVIATILE FORMATIONS OF VILLAFRANCHIAN AGE

The Lateral Conglomerates of the Ga'ash Formation

The Lateral Conglomerates of the Ga'ash Formation cover limited areas in the northwestern Negev, in the Besor area, and were referred to by Issar (1968) as part of the Ahuzam Formation, or Ahuzam Conglomerate. Gvirtzman and Buchbinder (1969) amended the term Ahuzam Conglomerate to include only the Pliocene conglomerates, interfingering and overlying the Pliocene Pleshet Formation in the Coastal Plain. In this respect the Lateral Conglomerates of the Ga'ash Formation are not included within the Ahuzam Conglomerate and are referred to presently as a separate stratigraphic unit. Bar-Yosef (1964) and Shachnai (1967), discussing detailed occurrences of these conglomerates, describe a number of outcrops in which almost no fauna was found except for some rolled Mediterranean molluscs. The limited distribution of this Formation and the lack of any determinable fossil remains do not favor any further discussion.

The Bethlehem Conglomerate

Several outcrops of conglomerates occur on the present watershed of Judea, in Bethlehem and around Jerusalem, filling shallow erosion channels and floodplains. Some of these conglomerates were referred by Horowitz (1970) to the Hazeva Formation, but further study by the author (Horowitz, in press) shows connections of these conglomerates with a similar conglomerate occurring in Bethlehem. This yielded a rich vertebrate fauna, discussed in Hooijer (1958), comprising *Archidiskdodon planifrons, Leptobos, Hipparion, Girafa* cf. *camelopardalis* and others, indicating a Villafranchian age and a steppe-like morphology of the area. Some crocodile bone fragments were found by Horowitz (1970) in these sediments. These conglomerates seem to comprise a part of a drainage system leading to the Mediterranean. They consist of pebbles mostly derived from the nearby rocks, especially the Campanian flints, but sometimes also contain quartzite pebbles the provenience of which is not known in the near vicinity. The conglomerates contain very high amounts of titanium (up to more than 1%), and the clays that are associated with the pebbles are mainly Kaoline, which points toward a long-distance transportation of the clastics (Horowitz, in press). This river system drained to the Mediterranean probably in the course of the present Nahal Soreq and caused the formation of wide meanders that are presently incised. Such meanders are very rare in other wadis in the Judea and Hebron areas. The rich titanium content of the clays may indicate a basaltic provenience of the material or at least part of the material. The high titanium content is typical of soil that is derived from basalts in Israel, rather than soils that are derived from limestones, which are poorer in titanium. It should be noted that no basalt outcrops are known from the Judea area, but these are widespread on the eastern Jordan plateau. Some flint pebbles of the Bethlehem Conglomerate were broken in a style that led people to believe that they might represent artifacts, resulting in excavations in Bethlehem. No definite proof, however, was forthcoming and presently the excavated material is not regarded as of hominid origin (Bar-Yosef, personal communication).

The Hameshar Conglomerate

The Hameshar Conglomerate (Garfunkel and Horowitz, 1966) comprises a series of conglomerates developed in the southern Negev. These conglomerates were deposited in a drainage system which led to the Mediterranean from the present area of the Arava and southern Transjordan, indicating that no topographic depression was present in the Dead Sea or Arava areas in those times. These conglomerates were regarded as of an Early Pleistocene age in Garfunkel and Horowitz (1966). They overlie the Pliocene Arava Conglomerate, over an erosional relief, and are overlain in places by some younger conglomerate horizons, or are eroded by channels connected with the drainage system that leads toward the Dead Sea Basin.

The Garof Conglomerate

The Garof Conglomerate (Garfunkel, 1970) is developed only in the Elat area where it overlies unconformably the Eilot Conglomerate of Pliocene age. This stratigraphic relationship is similar to that between the Hameshar Conglomerate and the underlying Arava Conglomerate. The Garof Conglomerate is overlain by some wadi terraces leading to the present area of Elat Bay. Garfunkel (1970) regards the Garof Conglomerate as correlative with the Arava Conglomerate, but this is rejected by Horowitz (in press), who correlates the Garof and Hameshar Conglomerates together with the Bethlehem Conglomerate, as representing synchronous drainage systems, leading to the Mediterranean and to the Red Sea. No fauna was found within either the Hameshar or the Garof Conglomerates. The Hameshar Conglomerate is developed and deposited in vast floodplains that probably were developed over very flat country.

The Cover Basalt

The Cover Basalt occurs in northeastern Israel and is an extension of the Golan Plateau and Jebel Druze basalts of southwestern Syria, which cover an area of about 80,000 sq kilometers. The Formation comprises up to 10 basaltic flows; the lower two or three are magnetically normal, while most of the sequence is magnetically reversed (Freund et al., 1965). Radiometric ages of the upper part of the Cover Basalt (Siedner and Horowitz, in preparation) are 1.7 million years and 2 million years. The thickness of the Cover Basalt varies from about 200 m at the area of Yavne'el down to only a few meters in the area of Hukok (Saltzman, 1964). The Cover Basalt always overlies an erosional relief, and the youngest formation overlain by the Basalt is the Late Pliocene Gesher Formation (Schulman, 1962). The Cover Basalt is overlain in the Jordan Valley area by the Erk el Ahmar and the Gadot formations—which are the oldest, of Günz age (Horowitz, 1973)—of the continental Glacial Pleistocene deposits of the Jordan Valley, and they were laid down over a taphrogenic relief. The Cover Basalt deposition was not confined to the area of the Jordan Rift Valley, however; the deposition extended southward in Transjordan down to the area east of the Dead Sea (Horowitz, 1973; in press). It consists mainly of olivine basalts, with only minor amounts of pyroclasts.

CHRONOSTRATIGRAPHY

The Calabro-Sicilian age of the Coastal Plain marine sediments—the Ga'ash Formation— is discussed in detail in Moshkovitz (1968). The Villafranchian age assigned by Hooijer (1958) to the bone-bearing Bethlehem Conglomerate is regarded as chronostratigraphically correlative with the Calabro-Sicilian sediments of the Coastal Plain. The Cover Basalt of northwestern Israel falls within the same stratigraphic limits as the Calabro-Sicilian and Villafranchian sediments since it overlies, over an erosional relief, the Late Pliocene deposits and is overlain by Günzian sediments. The radiometric ages given for the Cover Basalt strengthen its assignment to the Preglacial Pleistocene.

PALEOGEOGRAPHY

The paleogeography in Preglacial Pleistocene times is summarized by Horowitz (in press). The Late Pliocene regression caused channeling toward the retreating Mediterranean and proto-Elat Bay. The whole Negev was drained via wadi El Arish toward the Mediterranean, while another river developed over Judea, also carrying clastics from Trans-Jordan, as can be seen from the quartzite pebbles (Garfunkel and Horowitz, 1966) and the high titanium content of the Bethlehem Formation sediments. The kaolinitic nature of the clays filling this system is an indicator of long-distance transportation, that probably extended towards Transjordan. The meanders of Nahal Soreq are an indication of its great length, as discussed by Butrimowitz (1973). The northern and central Jordan Valley did not exist as topographic depressions, as in Pliocene times, because it was gradually filled with the Cover Basalt that flattened the relief. A number of erosional channels probably developed in this region, but relics of these were not detected.

The Calabro-Sicilian Ingression deposited marine-littoral sediments, the Ga'ash Formation, on the Coastal Plain and caused filling of the earlier channels by the Hameshar and Bethlehem Conglomerates. The same ingression in the Elat Bay caused filling of the channeling system by the Garof Conglomerate.

The relief of the country in Preglacial Pleistocene times was very low. This is indicated by the Hameshar, Garof, and Bethlehem Conglomerates that fill very low channels, mostly deposited over very wide floodplains as sheetwash conglomerates. In northeastern Israel, the Cover Basalt flooded the country and filled the preexisting relief. The maximum thickness of the Cover Basalt is only 200 m, and in no place is the Basalt known to fill canyons or deep gorges. It was flowing mostly over a relatively mild relief which is, in fact, an inheritance of the Pliocene plateau. The Bethlehem Conglomerate fauna included long-legged animals such as *Hipparion*, giraffes and elephants (Hooijer, 1958) that live in an open landscape, in contrast to the present-day hills.

Analysis of the occurrences of the Hameshar Formation in the southern Negev (Garfunkel and Horowitz, 1966) indicates that a slight westward tilting of the country must have occurred during the time of its deposition.

Generally, the landscape in Preglacial Pleistocene times is indicative of a vast steppe. The climate, as deduced from the pollen assemblages and the vertebrate remains, is of the Dry Mediterranean type, and the vegetation that developed because of the dry climate and the flat landscape was of savanna type. No equivalent to the Preglacial Pleistocene landscape and vegetation can be found presently in Israel or nearby countries, but it was perhaps similar to the East African plateaus. The sea was somewhat cooler than at present, but it does not seem that the difference was great, since most of the foraminiferal and molluscal assemblages are almost similar to the present-day ones. This description applies to most of the country, while in the northeast large-scale volcanism was probably the most prominent feature that influenced the environment.

Two processes acted in the Late Preglacial Pleistocene: the post-Calabro-Sicilian regression stopped the deposition of sediments connected with the Mediterranean transgression, the Hameshar and Bethlehem Conglomerates and the Ga'ash Formation, and erosion began toward the retreating sea.

In the Jordan Valley, the Arava, and the Bay of Elat a faulting phase developed that created the Jordan–Arava Rift Valley as it is presently known (Picard, 1943; Schulman, 1962; Garfunkel and Horowitz, 1966; Garfunkel, 1970; Horowitz, 1973; and many others). This faulting phase, which is the most prominent of the young faulting phases in Israel, occurred later than the Calabro-Sicilian Ingression and before the Günz, which places it at an absolute date of approximately one and one-half million years. Following the downfaulting of the Jordan–Arava Rift Valley, the mountainous region of Israel began to upwarp, at the end of the Preglacial Pleistocene. The upwarping of the country's backbone hills—the Galileean, Judean, Samarian, and Hebron—took place only after the cooling of the Cover Basalt, as noted already by Schulman (1962) and Horowitz (in press). Schulman based this assumption for the Galilee on the upwarping of the Cover Basalt together with the underlying rocks, while Horowitz based his assumption for Judea on occurrences of the Bethlehem Conglomerate at an elevation of about 800 m in Bethlehem and Jerusalem, and down at about 200 m in the Ma'ale Adumim area on the road to Jericho. In the western part of Judea, the Bethlehem Conglomerate occurs at elevations of around 400 to 500 meters. The correlative Lateral Conglomerates of the Ga'ash Formation occur, however, at elevations of around 100 m in the Shephela.

THE GLACIAL PLEISTOCENE OF ISRAEL

The flat landscape of Preglacial Pleistocene times no longer existed after the transition to the Glacial Pleistocene. The volcanism in the north terminated approximately 1.6 million years ago (Siedner and Horowitz, in preparation), while the Jordan–Arava Rift Valley was downfaulted, creating an internal depositional basin disconnnected from the Mediterranean, toward which a channeling system began to develop. The median part of the country began to be upwarped, creating the mountain barrier between the Coast and the Jordan–Arava Rift Valley. These processes created the three physiographic regions—the Coastal Plain, the mountains, and the Jordan Valley—that ever since have controlled environmental conditions in Israel.

Oscillations of the Mediterranean during eastward ingressions deposited the Hayarkon Formation, which is known mainly from the subsurface of the Coastal Plain of Israel. The foraminifera of this Formation were studied by Reiss

and Issar (1961) in the Reading 33/0 borehole, and a subdivision into stages was proposed. The microfauna bears characteristics similar to those of the present-day microfauna of the eastern Mediterranean. The stages proposed by Reiss and Issar are accepted as members of the Hayarkon Formation by Horowitz (in press). The malacofauna of the Hayarkon Formation is described in Moshkovitz (1968), who regards the assemblages as typical Mediterranean, assigned by him to the Tyrrhenian-type fauna. Pollen assemblages of this formation are presented in Rossignol (1962, 1969) and generally have present-day characteristics. The resemblance between the faunal and floral assemblages of the Hayarkon Formation and the recent flora and fauna of the eastern Mediterranean proves that the marine ingressions occurred during interpluvials, corresponding to the European interglacials, and not during the pluvials which have completely different pollen spectra (Horowitz, 1971, 1973, in press).

In the Carmel area, which was continuously tectonically uplifted throughout the whole Pleistocene, the marine ingressions left terraces, discussed in Michelson (1970). The marine ingressions pushed forward dune ridges that were later solidified into calcareous sandstones, locally called *kurkar* that are preserved today along the Israeli Coastal Plain.

During the marine regressions, in the pluvial periods, those *kurkar* ridges were eroded and soil was formed over them. Those paleosols are typically red, locally called "Hamra," and grade in some places to marsh deposits. It seems that their red color is the result of decomposition of iron-bearing minerals under conditions of high humidity. Some clays are included within these soils and are probably of eolian origin.

The sequence of calcareous sandstone and paleosols is defined as the Gaza Formation by Horowitz (in press), which was subdivided into a number of members, as presented in Figure 1.

The mountainous area was subjected to erosion during the Glacial Pleistocene, differing in style from pluvials to interpluvials. During the interpluvials floods and lack of vegetation cover created steeply dipping wadi shoulders, while under pluvial climatic conditions vegetation cover and soil formation helped in creating gently dipping slopes on which some conglomerates were deposited. The older conglomerates were totally washed out, while the younger conglomerates, of Rissian and Würmian age, are still preserved (Buchbinder, 1968; Horowitz, in press).

In the Jordan Valley, three sub-basins have been discerned: the southernmost (the Dead Sea Basin), which during the entire Glacial Pleistocene was the final erosional base level for the whole valley and in which Pleistocene sediments accumulated continuously (Horowitz, 1968); the central Jordan Valley, which was a rather shallow sub-basin in which lakes were formed only during pluvial times; and the Hula Valley, which was a very deep basin, in which sediments were deposited continuously. Taphrogenic subsidence of the Jordan–Arava Rift Valley continued

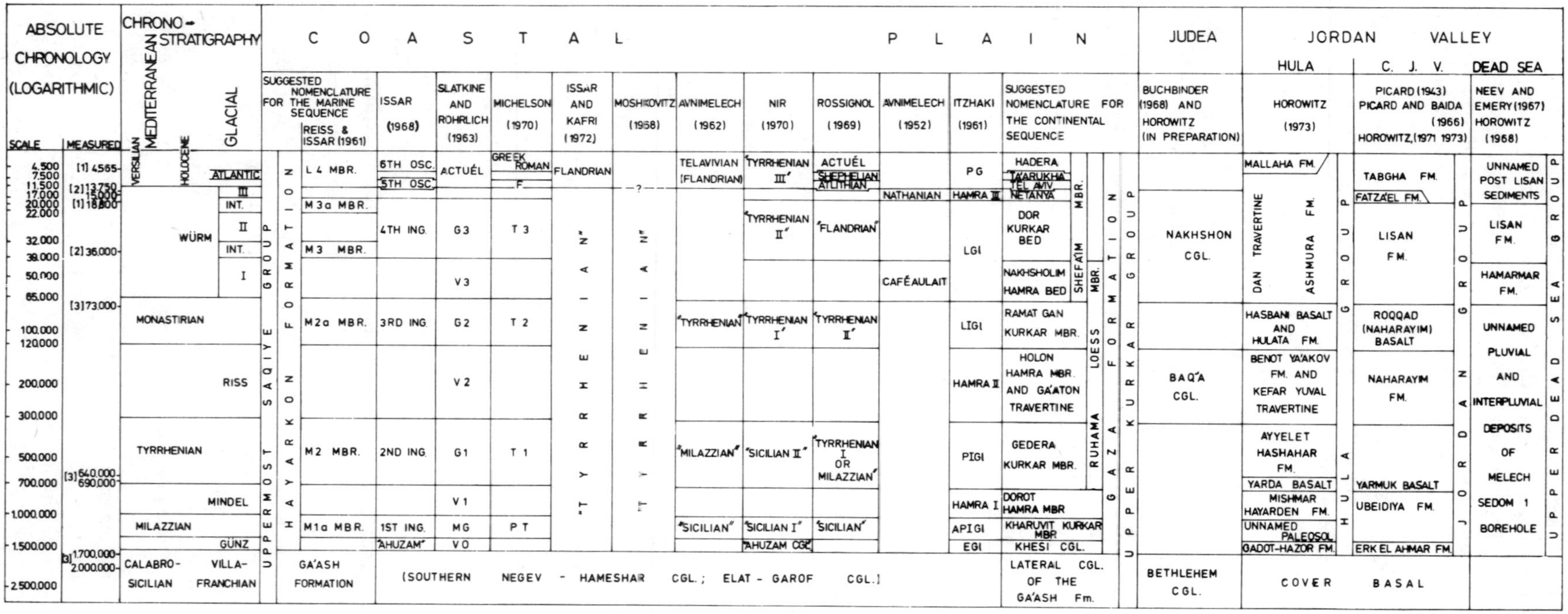

Fig. 1: Chronostratigraphic correlations and absolute chronology of the Pleistocene formations in Israel. Absolute chronology (logarithmic scale) after:

(1) Horowitz, 1971.
(2) Vogel and Waterbolk, in *Radiocarbon, 14* (1): 46–47.
(3) Siedner and Horowitz, in preparation.

throughout the Glacial Pleistocene and two stronger phases are discerned, in post-Mindel times, probably in the Early Mindel–Riss interpluvial and in Late Würmian times, approximately 18,000 years ago. Intermittent basaltic and pyroclastic volcanic activity is discerned in the northern Jordan Valley, during Late Mindel and Riss–Würm times.

THE GÜNZ PLUVIAL

Günzian sediments are rather rare in the Coastal Plain of Israel and except for the Hessi Conglomerate, that attains only a few meters in thickness, no Günzian sediments are known in this region. The Hessi Conglomerate is very limited in distribution and follows the Günzian Mediterranean regression. No fossils are known from this Formation. It seems that the shoreline in Günzian times was several kilometers west of that now present, and the southern and central Coastal Plain were occupied by a number of wide floodplains which were still a reminder of the Calabrian landscape. In the Jordan Valley, Günzian sediments were identified in the three sub-basins: The Gadot Formation and Hazor Conglomerate in the Hula Basin; the Erk el Ahmar Formation in the central Jordan Valley; and the lower part of the Upper Dead Sea Group, penetrated by Melech Sedom 1 borehole in the Dead Sea area.

The Gadot Formation and the Hazor Conglomerate interfinger with each other and crop out south of the Hula Valley, on the Gadot elevated block (Horowitz, 1973). The Gadot Formation comprises white to buff chalks with very scarce *Melanopsis* and *Melania tuberculata*. No other faunal or floral remains were found in this Formation, but it seems that it was deposited in the Hula Basin in times of greater extension of the Hula Lake. The Gadot Formation overlies unconformably the Cover Basalt and is overlain, separated by a paleosol horizon, by the Mishmar Hayarden Formation of Mindel age and the Yarda Basalt of Late Mindel or Mindel–Riss age. Pollen grains are rather scarce in the samples and are, for the most part, badly preserved due to oxidation of the sediments. Some poorly preserved assemblages are dominated by oak and Gramineae grains (Horowitz, 1973).

The Erk el Ahmar Formation comprises gray to brown clays and marls that were deposited in a lake occupying the central Jordan Valley. These sediments underlie the Mindel Ubeidiya Formation and overlie the Cover Basalt and are, therefore, correlated with the Gadot Formation and attributed a Günzian age (Horowitz, 1973, in press). Pollen analysis of the Erk el Ahmar Formation yielded the following spectrum: *Quercus*, mainly *calliprinos*, 30%; Umbelliferae, 38%; Gramineae and Cyperaceae, 21%; Others, including Liliaceae, Chenopodiaceae, Tubuliflorae, *Artemisia*, *Ephedra* and Papilionaceae, about 10%. This pollen spectrum is of a typical pluvial character, as discussed in Horowitz (1971), dominated by the oak pollen grains. The other elements were derived from a well-developed field vegetation that probably surrounded the Erk el Ahmar lake.

Pollen spectra for the Günzian sediments from the Dead Sea Basin are more or less similar to those from the Erk el Ahmar Formation, only the percentage of oak grains is a little lower, approximately 20%–25%, while the share of Chenopodiaceae is much higher, probably due to the development of salty playas south of and around the Dead Sea area, in the same manner that also can be seen presently (Horowitz, 1968).

The landscape in Günzian times was a typical pluvial landscape for Israel. The Jordan Valley was occupied by lakes, and the areas between the lakes were occupied by an open field vegetation. Toward the south, the vegetation cover was denser than today, and south of the Dead Sea lagoons or playas developed in which halophyte vegetation grew. The center of the country, the mountainous region, was covered by a dense maquis or an open forest comprising mainly oaks, the density of the forest diminishing southward. No indication as to the vegetation of the Coastal Plain in Günzian times is available. Presumably, the Coastal Plain was covered with steppe vegetation, with scattered trees. The shoreline was west of the present, and no indication is available as to the sea water mean temperature, since no marine sediments of Günzian age are known. No hominid occupation is known in Israel in Günzian times.

THE GÜNZ–MINDEL INTERPLUVIAL

Sediments that were deposited during the Günz–Mindel Interpluvial are very rare in the Jordan Valley and are, in fact, encountered only in the deeper parts of Melech Sedom I borehole, in the Dead Sea region. They occur most probably also in the subsurface of the Hula Basin (Horowitz, 1973). The scarcity of the Günz–Mindel Interpluvial sediments in the Jordan Valley indicates the limited extension of lakes during that time, which is a result of the dry interpluvial climate.

Pollen assemblages from the Melech Sedom I borehole, from a depth corresponding to the Günz–Mindel interpluvial (Horowitz, 1968), display scarcity of arboreal pollen, only about 10%, and a higher abundance of Chenopodiaceae as compared to their paucity in the pluvial sediments. This shows that most of the southern, and probably also the central, Jordan Valley was either subject to erosion or occupied by playas in which the Chenopodiaceae prevailed. Mountainous areas of Israel were subject to erosion which removed any sediments, like conglomerates or soils that formed and accumulated on the mountains and in the wadis during the Günz Pluvial.

In the Coastal Plain, the Mediterranean ingressed rather far eastward, depositing the M1A member of the Hayarkon Formation. This is also the First Ingression of Issar (1968), the MG Ingression of Slatkine and Rohrlich (1963), and this ingression also deposited the PT Unit (Michelson, 1970) in the subsurface of the Carmel Coastal Plain. The PT Unit consists of calcareous sandstones containing some corals–fossil algae, *Cladocora*, and *Lithotamnuium*–the latter two also being found presently in the Mediterranean.

The Günz–Mindel Ingression is probably responsible for the 55–60 m terrace on Mount Carmel which is correlative, according to Michelson (1970), with the Milazzian Stage of the Mediterranean. This terrace corresponds to the 60 m and 55–60 m terraces of Lebanon (Wetzel and Haller, 1944; Fleisch, 1957); and the 58 m and 60 m terraces from Egypt (Zeuner, 1959; Shukri et al., 1956); the 44–55 m terraces of Cyrenaica (McBurney and Hey, 1955); the 55–60 m terraces of the French-Italian Riviera; and to the 53 m terrace from Haifa described by Slatkine and Rohrlich (1966). All these terraces were attributed a Milazzian age.

The Milazzian Ingression pushed forward dunes that built the Kharuvit Kurkar Member of the Gaza Formation in the southwestern Coastal Plain, approximately 20 km east of the present shoreline (fig. 2). The Kharuvit Kurkar Member overlies the Hessi Conglomerate in the southern Coastal Plain and is known mainly from this area. In other areas, it is only poorly preserved due to subsequent erosion. The Kharuvit Kurkar Member is known from the western Galilee, at the quarry of Evron (Issar and Kafri, 1969, 1972), where it comprises about 5 m of calcareous sandstones, underlying the Mindelian hamra. The Kharuvit Kurkar Member is overlain by the Dorot Hamra Member of Mindel age, known from the northwestern Negev and the western Galilee.

The Coastal Plain landscape in Günz–Mindel or Milazzian times was a function of the ingressive sea and the dunes east of the shoreline. The Milazzian shoreline ran approximately parallel to the present one, but was about 20 km to the east in the southern part of the country, while in the northern part it was only about 2–3 km east of the western Galilee coast, about 15 km in the Kishon area, and only about 2 km in the Carmel area. The Milazzian shoreline is presented in Avnimelech (1962) and Itzhaki (1961).

The Günz–Mindel Interpluvial is represented in the northern Jordan Valley south of the Hula Basin by a thin (ca. 1½ m thick) paleosol horizon, separating the Gadot Formation from the Mishmar Hayarden Formation. This paleosol yielded neither faunal nor pollen remains.

The Jordan Valley was occupied by two small lakes in Günz–Mindel times, one in the Dead Sea area and the other in the Hula area. The vegetation of the country was most probably very poor. Pollen spectra of the Günz–Mindel sediments were obtained from the Dead Sea area where they point to a very dry climate (Horowitz, 1966, 1968). Pollen analyses of the M1A Member, representing the Milazzian Ingression, from a number of boreholes in the southern Coastal Plain (Rossignol, 1969), show a great poverty of arboreal pollen and a prevalence of pine pollen, while the most common are pollen of Chenopodiaceae and *Ephedra*, indicating a dry climate. Some pollen of Gramineae, Cyperaceae, Compositae, *Artemisia* and *Asphodelus* also occur, but in minor percentages. It seems that the vegetation in Günz–Mindel times was a typical interpluvial vegetation (Horowitz, 1971), and most of the country was covered by steppe in which some pines grew. The northern limit of the

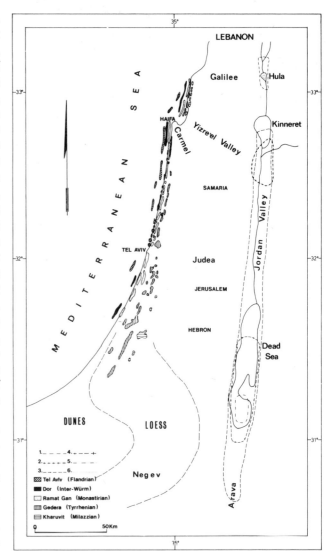

Fig. 2 Extension of Pleistocene deposits in Israel. Kurkar ridges in the Coastal Plain are denoted by their formational names. The northwestern Negev is an area of dunes or loess deposition. The extension of lakes in the Jordan Valley is displayed by broken lines: 1. Maximum of the Hula pluvial lakes. 2. The central Jordan Valley basin, active independently in Günz and Mindel times. 3. Maximum of the Würmian Lisan Lake. 4. Approximate limits of the Dead Sea Basin. 5. The Dead Sea interpluvial lakes. 6. The Hula interpluvial lakes.

desert in the maximum of the Günz–Mindel Interpluvial was farther north than at present. The marine microfauna described by Reiss and Issar from the Reading 33/0 borehole, and the malacofauna discussed in Moshkovitz (1968), indicate a sea which bears the same characteristics as the present-day Mediterranean.

THE MINDEL PLUVIAL

Sediments of Mindel Age are known from the northern Jordan Valley in the Gesher Benot Ya'akov area (the Mishmar Hayarden Formation); from the central Jordan Valley (the Ubeidiya Formation); from the Dead Sea area only from the subsurface; and from the Coastal Plain (the Dorot Hamra Member of the Gaza Formation)—(Horowitz, in press).

The Mishmar Hayarden Formation crops out in the vicinity of the Benot Ya'akov Bridge, comprising a sequence of lacustrine and paludine sediments which are some 10 m thick. Most of the section consists of a white, soft limnic chalk with several horizons very rich in molluscs. The strata overlie reddish brown clays that overlie the Gadot Formation. The uppermost layer consists of peat, covered by a basalt sheet of the Yarda Basalt. The sequence is strongly tilted, from 45° up to 90°, and only the base and the lower part of the Formation crop out, as its upper part is buried due to the faulting. It seems that the lower part of Hula I borehole, in the north, penetrated some lateral facies of this formation, consisting mainly of conglomerates. A basalt flow at a depth of about 300 m in this borehole may be correlative to the flow at the Benot Ya'acov Bridge. The fossil mollusc assemblage of this formation is dealt with by Tchernov (1972). The assemblage abundantly contains *Theodoxus jordani, Valvata saulcyi, Bulimus hawaderiana, Melanopsis praerosa, Limnaea lagotis, Gyraulus piscinarus, Anisus spirorbis, Pysidium casertanum* and a number of other species that are less common.

Although not definitely identical, this assemblage is thought by Tchernov to be correlative to the Ubeidiya Formation assemblage, in the central Jordan Valley. Bones of fossil vertebrates were also encountered in these strata, but none have been identified specifically. The most common are bones of *Hippopotamus*. Pollen analyses of samples collected from the outcrop of the Mishmar Hayarden Formation show a prevalence of *Quercus* grains, up to 70% of the total pollen counted. Pollen of other trees are extremely rare, not more than 1% of the spectrum. The non-arboreal pollen are generally those derived from the vegetation growing on the shores of the sedimentation basin. Typical are pollen of Gramineae, Cyperaceae, Umbelliferae, Tubuliflorae, *Typha* and minor quantities of Chenopodiaceae, *Artemisia*, Liliaceae, *Populus*, Cruciferae, and *Rubus*.

The Ubeidiya Formation is known from the central Jordan Valley and is dealt with by many authors. The paleoecological conditions under which the Ubeidiya Formation was deposited were summed up by Bar-Yosef and Tchernov (1972). The Ubeidiya Formation comprises about 200 m of lacustrine sediments, mainly chalk, clays, and conglomerates, most of which were deposited in a shallow lake, as well as some terrestrial paleosols. The malacological assemblage is very rich, mainly comprising species which are littoral, mud and rock dwellers such as *Theodoxus jordani, Melanopsis praerosa, Valvata saulcyi, Melania tuberculata, Melania dadiana, Lymnaea lagotis, Planorbis planorbis, Gyraulus piscynarum*, and minor amounts of deep water rock dwellers, such as *Ancylus fluviatilis, Unio terminalis, U. semirugatus, Legumaia chantrei, Corbicula fluminalis*, and *Bulimus hawaderiana* (Bar-Yosef and Tchernov, 1972). Most of the horizons of the Ubeidiya Formation did not

yield pollen grains, due to oxidation of the sediments. Pollen assemblages which were recovered from the Ubeidiya Formation comprise mainly grains of *Quercus*, more than 80%, Gramineae and Cyperaceae, about 10%, with the rest shared by Umbelliferae, *Olea europaea*, Cruciferae, *Juniperus, Rubus*, Papilionaceae, Chenopodiaceae, Compositae and Malvaceae. Vertebrate remains are abundant in the Ubeidiya Formation, of which the most important are *Stegodon, Archidiskodon, Dicerorhinus etruscus, Hipparion, Equus stenonis, Hippopotamus amphibius, Sus strozzi, Leptobos, Bison, Gazellospira*, an *Oryx*-like antelope, *Giraffa camelopardalis, Camelus, Cervus* cf. *ramosus, C. philissi, C. senezensis, Dama, Megaceros, Crocuta, Megantereon, Felis, Enhydrictis ardea, Canis* and others. The Ubeidiya Formation is also very rich in artifacts, discussed by Stekelis (1966), Bar-Yosef and Tchernov (1972), and others.

The Mindel sediments of the Dead Sea area, penetrated by the Melech Sedom 1 borehole at a depth of approximately 800 m—1,200 m, are rich in arboreal pollen, up to 40%, of which the main constituent is *Quercus*, with some minor amounts of pine pollen. The non-arboreal pollen spectrum is shared among Gramineae, Cyperaceae, and Chenopodiaceae, with some minor elements.

No sediments that could be attributed undoubtedly to the Mindel are known from the mountainous area, and it seems that this area was mainly subject to erosion. Conglomerates and soils which might have formed during Mindel times were probably eroded during the consequent Mindel—Riss Interpluvial.

The Dorot Hamra Member of the Gaza Formation is very widespread in the southern Coastal Plain. It was called "Hamra I" by Itzhaki (1961) and corresponds to the V1 regression of Slatkine and Rohrlich (1963). The Dorot Hamra Member yielded artifacts in the areas of Dorot and Ruhama, in the southern Coastal Plain, and at the quarry of Evron in western Galilee. In the quarry of Evron teeth and bones of mammals, such as *Elephas trogontherii, Hippopotamus* and a wart hog, *Metridiochoerus evronensis*, were found (Issar and Kafri, 1969, 1972; Haas, 1970). Bones of *Leptobos* were found in a well that was dug into the Dorot Hamra Member near Gedera (A. Issar, personal communication).

Marine sediments that were deposited in Mindel times were not encountered in the boreholes drilled in the Coastal Plain, and it seems that the shoreline was farther west than it is presently, corresponding to the Mediterranean regression in Mindel times.

The paleogeography of Israel in Mindel times resembled that of Günz times. The upwarping of the mountainous area continued, and the mountains were covered with very dense oak forest. Soil was formed on the mountains and the rich vegetation protected them from being abruptly eroded, so that gently dipping hills were formed, slightly moderating the relief of the Günz—Mindel Interpluvial erosion. The Coastal Plain was wide and red soils were formed that later became the Dorot Hamra Member paleosols. Some areas of the Coastal Plain were covered by extensive marshes in which animals such as *Hippopotamus* could live. It seems that the vegetation of the Coastal Plain was rather rich and comprised woods dominated by oaks and some pines. Other trees, like olive and pistachio, might have grown in these woods; but they are always underrepresented in the pollen spectra (Horowitz, 1971) and their existence is masked by the great amount of oak pollen.

The people of the Mindel times probably dwelt on the rims of the marshes on the Coastal Plain and on the shores of the lakes in the Jordan Valley. Two lakes existed in the Jordan Valley in Mindel times. The first is Hula Lake, which extended farther southward than at present, in which the Mishmar Hayarden Formation was deposited, and in a littoral facies of which some artifacts were found (Horowitz et al., 1973). The other, and best known, is the lake south of the present Lake Kinneret in which the sediments of the Ubeidiya Formation were deposited. The paleoecology of this lake is discussed in detail in Bar-Yosef and Tchernov (1972). The population that lived on the shores of this lake was probably large; this is evident from the enormous number of artifacts recovered from the Ubeidiya Formation. Many layers of the Ubeidiya Formation yielded artifacts which show that hominid occupation on the shore of the Ubeidiya Lake took place for a long time during the Mindel Pluvial.

The vertebrate fauna in Mindel times was very rich, especially in the Jordan Valley. The high humidity of the pluvial climate and the high temperature of the Jordan Valley, being an internal depression, provided an almost tropical environment in which the tropical vertebrates found an ecological niche. There they could survive longer than in other places where they already had become extinct. Relics from the Villafranchian times show that such animals as the *Hipparion, Archidiskodon* and *Rhinoceros etruscus* lived in the Jordan Valley in Mindel times, together with Middle Pleistocene horses. The favorable climate, the rich vegetation, and the availability of water supported this rich variety of animals.

In the Dead Sea area the Mindel sediments are known only from a number of boreholes, such as Melech Sedom I, Ein Gedi II, and the Mezada group of boreholes (Horowitz, 1966, 1968). Pollen analyses of samples from these boreholes indicate high percentages of oak pollen, while the nonarboreal spectrum is shared between Gramineae, Cyperaceae and Chenopodiaceae, the latter being rather low in quantity.

The climate of Israel in Mindel times was pluvial, with a relatively high humidity, estimated at 30%–40% more rainfall and availability of water, as compared with the present. The temperatures might have been a little lower than at present, but the probable difference was no more than 4°–5° C.

The Mindel temperatures, although somewhat lower than at present, and the high amount of rainfall really created a tropical climate over the country. This resulted in the rich vegetation and animal life, the possibilities for hominid occupation, and the formation of red, lateritic soils on the Coastal Plain, known presently as the Hamra paleosols.

Volcanic activity of Late Mindel age (Horowitz et al., 1973) is known from two localities in the northern Jordan Valley—south of the present Lake Hula and near the Yarmuk River. Near Lake Hula the Yarda Basalt covers an area of about 100 sq kilometers. This Basalt is magnetically normal, its radiometric age is 640,000 years, and it cooled at the beginning of the Brunhes Normal Epoch. The Yarda Basalt overlies conformably the Mishmar Hayarden Formation at the Benot Ya'akov Bridge area, and probably ceased its deposition in this locality. It overlies unconformably a steep erosional relief, the Gadot Formation of Günzian age, on the northern part of the Korazim–Gadot elevated block (Horowitz, 1973). Another system of small scale flows is known from the vicinity of the Yarmuk River, of the central Jordan Valley (Picard, 1943; Michelson, 1972) which is morphologically above the level of the Ubeidiya Formation, therefore correlated by Horowitz (1973) with the Yarda Basalt. Radiometric datings of this basalt (Horowitz et al., 1973) indicated an age of 680,000 years, confirming the correlation. The Yarmuk Basalt also cooled under normal magnetic polarity and was poured off from some fissures on the Golan Plateau, down into the gorge of the Yarmuk River that already existed in Mindel times. The Yarmuk Basalt did not cover the Ubeidiya Formation at the site, but the Yarda Basalt covered the Mishmar Hayarden Formation in the Benot Ya'akov Bridge area where artifacts were found.

THE MINDEL–RISS INTERPLUVIAL

Sediments of the Mindel–Riss Interpluvial age are known from the Jordan Valley only from the subsurface of the Dead Sea and Hula Basins, and it seems that the rest of the Valley was subjected to erosion. In the Dead Sea Basin (Horowitz, 1966, 1968) these sediments are known from a number of boreholes and yielded pollen assemblages that are very poor in arboreal pollen, in which pine prevails, while most of the nonarboreal pollen is represented by grains of Chenopodiaceae and *Artemisia*. These pollen assemblages are reminiscent of the same paleoecological conditions as those of the Günz–Mindel Interpluvial in the southern Jordan Valley.

In the Hula Valley the Mindel–Riss Interpluvial is represented by the Ayyelet Hashahar Formation, which was defined at the Emek Hula 1 borehole from its total depth of 455 m up to 340 meters. The base of the Formation was not penetrated by this borehole and is unknown. At the type locality, the lithology is mainly highly organic chalk, grading frequently into peat. The thickness is assumed in Horowitz (1973) to be approximately 200 m–250 m and probably maintains the same lithologic characteristics. Lateral time equivalents of the Formation are recorded in some of the conglomerates penetrated by the Hula 1 and Ne'ot Mordekhai boreholes in the north. No part of this formation crops out at the Benot Ya'akov area or elsewhere. The restricted distribution and the lithological characteristics of the Ayyelet Hashahar Formation indicate that it was deposited in times of great shrinkage of the Hula Lake, which remained only as marshes, depositing organic sediments.

Pollen analyses of sediments of Ayyelet Hashahar Formation (Horowitz, 1973) show rather low arboreal pollen percentages, less than 20%, shared by *Quercus* and *Olea*, with very little *Pistacia*. The prevailing elements are pollen of marsh vegetation, Gramineae, and Cyperaceae. This assemblage is typical of an interpluvial. Except for some unidentified mollusc debris, no faunal remains were recovered from this Formation. Since no outcrops are known, no larger remains could be sought.

During Mindel–Riss Interpluvial times the mountainous area was subjected to erosion which created steeply dipping wadis. Relics of the steep wadis of this period are still preserved in the Judean and Hebron mountains (Horowitz, in press).

In the Coastal Plain the Tyrrhenian Ingression of the Mediterranean controlled the paleogeography. The marine sediments that were deposited during the Tyrrhenian Ingression are defined as the M2 Member of the Hayarkon Formation (after Reiss and Issar, 1961, in Horowitz, in press). Issar (1968) called this ingression the "Second Ingression with *Marginopora*." It is also called the G1 ingression by Slatkine and Rohrlich (1963), and it formed the T1 Kurkar Ridge on the Carmel coast (Michelson, 1970), defined by Horowitz (in press) as the Gedera Kurkar Member of the Gaza Formation. The Kurkar ridge that was formed during the Tyrrhenian Ingression, in Mindel–Riss times, extends about 10-12 km eastward in the southern part of the country, while in the north it is much closer to the present shoreline. In western Galilee, the Tyrrhenian shoreline was approximately at the same locality as at present, and littoral Tyrrhenian sediments are found on the beach of Rosh Hanikra (Issar and Kafri, 1972). The Tyrrhenian Ingression left the 35 m–45 m terraces on Mount Carmel, called Tyrrhenian 1 by Michelson (1970) and correlated by him with the 35 m–45 m terraces of Lebanon (Wetzel and Haller, 1944; Fleisch, 1957), the Egyptian terraces at 35 m elevation (Zeuner, 1958; Shukri et al., 1956), the 35 m–40 m terraces of Cyrenaica (McBurney and Hey, 1955), and the 28 m–32 m terraces of the French–Italian Riviera. The marine sediments, and especially the littoral sediments that were deposited during the Tyrrhenian Ingression, are characterized by occurrences of the foraminifera *Marginopora*, indicating that the sea was somewhat warmer than the present-day Mediterranean. The occurrence of *Strombus bubonius* (Issar and Kafri, 1972) in the Tyrrhenian deposits of northern Israel strengthens this conclusion. *Strombus bubonius* is much more frequent in the marine Tyrrhenian of Lebanon and Cyprus (Moshkovitz, 1968). The occurrence of its ecological equivalent in Israel, the *Marginopora*, is taken as a paleotemperature indicator for the marine environment.

The Gedera Kurkar Ridge of the Gaza Formation created a barrier along the southern Coastal Plain behind which, to the east, loess accumulated from Mindel–Riss Interpluvial times until, at least, the Early Würm. This loess is defined as the Ruhama Loess Member of the Gaza Formation (Horowitz, in press).

Sometime during the Mindel–Riss Interpluvial a relatively strong faulting phase took place in the Jordan Valley. It resulted in the downfaulting and tilting of the Ubeidiya and the Mishmar Hayarden Formations, together with the underlying Erk el Ahmar and Gadot and the overlying Yarda Basalt. The Rissian sediments in the outcrops overlie the faulted sediments unconformably and, therefore, it occurred in post-Mindel, pre-Riss times. The Mindel–Riss formations are known only from the subsurface, and it is impossible to define more exactly the time of this faulting phase which caused further deepening of the Jordan–Arava Rift Valley but did not change essentially its general morphology.

The paleogeography in Mindel–Riss times was determined by the Tyrrhenian Ingression that narrowed the Coastal Plain and pushed dunes eastward. The loess that was accumulated in the northwestern Negev created, most probably, a landscape that is parallel to the areas presently around Be'er Sheva.

Pollen analyses of Tyrrhenian sediments by Rossignol (1962, 1969) indicate that the vegetation was rather poor and somewhat similar to the vegetation of Millazzian Ingression times. Low percentages of arboreal pollen, in which pine prevailed, and high percentages of Chenopodiaceae and *Artemisia* indicate a dry land and a steppe-like landscape for the central parts and maybe even the northern parts of the country, while the south was a complete desert. It seems that the mountains were almost barren of any vegetation except for some small stands of oaks and pines. The Hula Valley was occupied by some marshes but probably no distinct lake existed, while in the Dead Sea area a small lake still existed in parts of which rock salt was deposited (Neev and Emery, 1967).

No prehistoric sites are known from this time in Israel, and hominids were most probably pushed northward by the deteriorating climatic conditions. Sites of Mindel–Riss age are known north of Israel at Latamne in the Orontes Valley (de Heinzelin, 1968; Clark, 1969).

A paleoecological comparison between the Latamne site of Mindel–Riss age and the sites of Ubeidiya of Mindel age and Gesher Benot Ya'akov of Riss age is presented in Bar-Yosef and Tchernov (1972). It seems that the interpluvial site of Latamne corresponds very closely, paleoecologically, to the pluvial sites of Israel which are a number of hundreds of kilometers south of it. This strongly indicates that the climatic belts wandered in a north-south direction and that the pluvial climate of Israel corresponds to the interpluvial climate of the more northern countries. This is discussed also for the distribution of forests in Horowitz (1971). The oak forest, typical today for northern Lebanon and northward up to Turkey, was probably the climax vegetation of Israel during pluvial times. In interpluvial times, on the other hand, the country was an almost complete desert.

THE RISS PLUVIAL

Lacustrine sediments deposited during the Riss Pluvial in the Jordan Valley are known from the Hula area and from the Dead Sea Basin. Fluviatile conglomerates were accumulated in the central Jordan Valley Basin and are known also from the mountainous areas where they are rather rare, preserved only in high places sheltered from subsequent erosion.

In the Coastal Plain erosive and pedogenetic processes caused red soil formation, preserved as paleosols ("Hamra"). In some localities marshes developed, depositing black, highly organic clays. In the southern Coastal Plain and northwestern Negev loess deposition continued (Horowitz, in press).

Marine sediments that were deposited during the Riss Pluvial are not known from the Coastal Plain, and the shoreline was probably farther west as a consequence of the Rissian regression.

Spring activity was very strong, especially in the north of the country, and large-scale travertine deposition is known from western Galilee and from the northern Hula Valley.

Rissian sediments of the Hula area comprise the Benot Ya'akov Formation and the Kefar Yuval Travertine. The Benot Ya'akov Formation crops out along the Jordan River from the Hula Valley south to the Benot Ya'akov Bridge. It is generally known as the "*Viviparus* Beds" (Picard, 1963), named after its unique malacalogical fauna, comprised mainly of *Viviparus apameae*. Only the littoral facies is known from this area, and the type section was proposed in the Emek Hula 1 borehole (Horowitz, 1973) where the Formation is fully developed. In this borehole it extends from a depth of 340 m where it overlies conformably the Ayyelet Hashahar Formation, up to 155 m, where it is overlain conformably by the Hulata Formation of Riss—Würm Interpluvial age. The Benot Ya'akov Formation consists mainly of limnic chalk, very rich in mollusc remains of which the most prevalent is *Viviparus apameae*. At a depth of 215 m down to 235 m the sediments are particularly rich in organic material. The upper part of the Formation named "Lower Lacustrine Series," with the typical *Viviparus*, was penetrated by a number of boreholes drilled to the north of the present lake and in the area of the marshes (Picard, 1952).

About four to five m of the littoral facies of the Benot Ya'akov Formation, at the Benot Ya'akov Bridge area, were described by Picard (1963) and discussed in detail in Horowitz (1973). These comprise very coarse littoral conglomerates which merge northward into limnic chalk and bear enormous quantities of *Viviparus* shells. These strata also contain some other molluscs, the most abundant of which are *Valvata saulcyi, Bythinella, Bulimus hawarderiana, Melanopsis praerosa,* and *Pisidium casertanum* (Tchernov, 1972). The mammalian fauna recovered from the

Benot Ya'akov Formation outcrops revealed, according to Hooijer (1958, 1960), bones and teeth of *Elepahs trogontherii, Equus cabalus, Dicerorhinus merckii, Sus scrofa, Hippopotamus amphibius, Dama mesopotamica, Cervus elaphus, Bison priscus* and *Stegodon mediterraneus*. The outcrop also yielded a rich assemblage of implements, as discussed by Stekelis (1960) and Gilead (1970).

Pollen spectra of the Benot Ya'akov Formation from the Emek Hula I borehole and outcrop samples show 40%—50% to be of arboreal origin, almost all derived from oaks. Typical, although appearing only in small quantities in this Formation, is pollen of *Fagus*. It is found also in sediments of the same stratigraphic position in the Dead Sea boreholes (Horowitz, 1966, 1968). The nonarboreal pollen spectra are rather rich in a number of species, indicating a well-developed field vegetation in addition to marsh vegetation. The pollen spectra indicate a pluvial climate at the time of deposition of the Benot Ya'akov Formation, with an interstadial recorded in the Emek Hula I borehole (Horowitz, 1973). The interstadial is characterized by a drop in the arboreal pollen, an increase in Gramineae and Cyperaceae pollen, and a high percentage of organic materials in the sediments derived from marshes that moved closer to the center of the basin due to the shrinkage of the lake during the drier interstadial.

In the northern Hula Valley, near Ma'ayan Baruch and Kefar Yuval, there is an outcrop of travertines up to 20 m—30 m thick containing Early Paleolithic implements (Stekelis and Gilead, 1966). Picard (1963) named these Kefar Yuval Travertines and Horowitz (1973) correlated them with the Benot Ya'akov Formation. These travertines were deposited by strong spring activity, probably the result of the higher humidity and availability of water in Riss times. They are overlain by the Hasbani Basalt. It seems that during most of the Riss Pluvial, except for the interstadial separating Riss I from Riss II, the Hula Valley was covered by a lake that received much of its water from a series of springs in the north.

Sediments of Riss age were encountered in the central Jordan Valley as a series of river fills to the south and east of Lake Kinneret, that area comprising the Naharayim Formation (Picard, 1943).

Lacustrine sediments of Riss age were also recovered from boreholes in the Dead Sea area (Horowitz, 1966, 1968) and bear the same palynological characteristics as the Rissian sediments of the north.

The Rissian conglomerates of the Judean and Hebron mountains are defined as the Baq'a Conglomerate (Horowitz, in press). The Baq'a Conglomerate was deposited in shallow valleys, most probably covered by vegetation, in which pedogenetic processes produced red loams. They were preserved only in small areas that were sheltered from erosion and, in some places, yielded artifacts like those found in the Baq'a—Refa'im area in Jerusalem (Arensburg and Bar-Yosef, 1967). Sediments of Rissian age, bearing artifacts, are also preserved in the lower part of the sequence in the Umm Qatafa Cave in the Judean Desert (Neuville, 1951).

The most important processes that influenced the Coastal Plain during Riss times are pedogenetic processes which resulted in the formation of red soils, preserved as Hamra paleosol horizons and defined by Horowitz (in press) as the Holon Hamra Member of the Gaza Formation. This Hamra bed was defined by Itzhaki (1961) as the "Hamra II" and corresponds to the V2 regression of Slatkine and Rohrlich (1963) recorded in the subsurface sediments of Haifa Bay. Marshes in which black clay was deposited developed in the wide Coastal Plain during Riss Pluvial times. The marsh deposits yielded vertebrate bones of *Hippopotamus amphibius*, some unidentified elephants, antelopes, and horses. Hominid occupation was widespread in Rissian times along the Israeli Coastal Plain and sites are known from the areas of Nizanim, Ruhama, Holon, from western Galilee at the quarry at Evron, as well as at other localities. In the northern and northwestern Negev the deposition of the Ruhama Loess Member also continued during Rissian times. In the vicinity of Be'er Sheva, in the northern Negev, artifacts also were found in the Rissian loess.

Spring activity was very strong in western Galilee, depositing the Ga'aton Travertine (Horowitz, in press).

The paleogeography during Rissian times was determined by the Mediterranean regression and the soil formation processes on the Coastal Plain, which was a wide plain occupied by marshes, rich vegetation comprising woods in the north, and open savannas with some trees in the south. This is concluded from the vertebrates encountered in these sediments, as well as from palynological data. The mountains were covered totally with oak forests in which some northern elements penetrated, such as the beech (*Fagus*), while in the Jordan Valley two lakes existed. The lake in the Hula Valley occupied the whole of the Hula Basin, and the extent of the lake in the Dead Sea Basin is unknown due to the subsequent faulting and a lack of outcrops. The central Jordan Valley was not occupied by a lake but was, rather, a river valley. This is a probable result of the faulting phase that preceded Rissian times. As a result of this faulting the central Jordan Valley basin no longer acted as an independent depositional basin, but was strongly connected with the Dead Sea which was the final erosion base level.

The rich vegetation, the rich and variable fauna, the strong spring activity in western Galilee, in the northern Hula Valley and probably also in other localities, and the large quantities of river conglomerates in the central Jordan Valley all indicate a very high humidity and availability of water during Rissian times, resulting, most probably, in a permanent runoff of most of the rivers and wadis in Israel. The northern elements that penetrated Israel at this time, especially the *Fagus* and the *Viviparus* which are known today only from the northern areas of Syria and from the Pontic region of Turkey, indicate that the mean temperature was somewhat lower than at present; the difference is estimated at about 5°–6° C.

The Riss–Würm Interpluvial

Lacustrine sediments that were deposited during the Riss–Würm Interpluvial are very rare and restricted in distribution in the Jordan Valley. They are found only in a number of boreholes in the Dead Sea area. The mountainous area was subject to erosion that removed most of the Rissian sediments and conglomerates, while the Coastal Plain area was controlled by the Monastirian Ingression. Some volcanic activity is known from the northern Jordan Valley. The previous Rissian Hula Lake that extended over the whole Hula Valley shrank in the Riss–Würm Interpluvial and only a marshy area in which the Hulata Formation peat was deposited remained in the center of the Hula Basin.

The Hulata Formation (Horowitz, 1973) was previously termed the "Main Peat" (Picard, 1952) and is known from many boreholes within the Hula Valley. Its type section was taken at the borehole, named by Picard "Number Zero First Test," which was drilled at the northern border of the recent lake. The sequence at the type locality comprises 54 m, of which the lower 20 m and the upper 19 m consist of massive peat. The middle 15 m consist mainly of peat, with some limnic chalk intercalations. The formation thins to the north but thickens to the south and somewhat also to the east, toward the deeper parts of the basin where the share of limnic chalk in its sequence increases. It is thickest in Emek Hula I borehole where it attains 75 meters. The type section was proposed where the peat is best developed (Horowitz, 1973), where it was deposited in the marshes of the Riss–Würm Interpluvial. No outcrops of the Hulata Formation are known and its subsurface distribution within the valley is rather limited. A conglomerate horizon, about one meter thick, consisting mostly of flint pebbles, is exposed in the Benot Ya'akov area. It separates the upper conglomerate of the Benot Ya'akov Formation from the base conglomerate of the Würmian Ashmura Formation, perhaps representing a lateral equivalent of the Hulata Formation. No faunal remains are known from the Hulata Formation except for some mollusc debris. Pollen analyses of the Hulata Formation in the K-Jam and Emek Hula 1 boreholes are discussed in Horowitz (1971, 1973). Worth noting is the paucity of arboreal pollen and the almost total predominance of marsh vegetation pollen, Gramineae and Cyperaceae. These indicate a dry, interpluvial climate unable to maintain a forest vegetation. A poor maquis existed and the lake shrank to a small relic, with the marshes remaining the only body of water in the valley. Mountain vegetation was very poor, comprising scattered stands of some oak, pistachio, cypress, and olive trees.

The northern sector of the Hula Valley was covered by a basalt sheet extending into Lebanon, named the Hasbani Basalt by Picard (1963). The Hasbani Basalt overlies the Kefar Yuval Travertine at the Banias waterfall in the northern Hula Valley and underlies the Würmian Dan Travertine. This places it within the Riss–Würm Interpluvial. Radiometric dating indicates an average age of 70,000 years for the Hasbani Basalt (Siedner and Horowitz, in preparation).

Volcanic activity of the same age is known from the Golan (Mor, 1973) and also from the Yarmuk area where it is called the Roqqad Basalt (Michelson, 1972).

Sediments deposited during the Riss–Würm Interpluvial in the Judean Mountains are known only from the Umm Qatafa Cave (Neuville, 1951). Cave sediments of the same age are known also from the lower part of the sequence in Tabun Cave on Mount Carmel (Jelinek et al., in press). Pollen analyses from the Riss–Würm Interpluvial sediments of the Tabun Cave indicate a very poor maquis vegetation, expressed by very low percentages of arboreal pollen, while among the nonarboreal pollen Chenopodiaceae, *Artemisia*, and some other xerophile plants prevail (Horowitz, in Jelinek et al., 1973).

The Monastirian Ingression of the Mediterranean that took place during Riss–Würm Interpluvial times deposited the M2A Member of the Hayarkon Formation which is comprised mainly of shales and some calcareous sandstones. This is the "Third Ingression, containing *Marginopora*" of Issar (1968), and it corresponds to the Monastirian according to many authors. Issar and others referred to this ingression as the "Second Tyrrhenian Ingression" because of the appearance of *Marginopora*. This is the G2 ingression of Slatkine and Rohrlich (1963) and it corresponds to the T2 Ridge of Michelson (1970). The Monastirian Ingression left terraces on Mt. Carmel at an elevation of about 15 m. These correspond, according to Michelson (1970), to terraces at the same elevations in Lebanon that contain *Strombus bubonius* (Wetzel and Haller, 1944; Fleisch, 1957); in Egypt (Zeuner 1959; Shukri et al., 1956); in Cyrenaica (McBurney and Hey, 1955), and on the French-Italian Riviera. All these terraces are correlated according to altimetric data and the occurrence of a warm sea fauna, such as the *Strombus bubonius* and the *Marginopora*.

The Monastirian Ingression pushed forward sand dunes that later solidified to form the Ramat Gan Kurkar Member of the Gaza Formation. This kurkar ridge runs parallel to but not far from the present shoreline, and it seems that the Monastirian Ingression did not reach far eastwards—only 2–3 km in the southern and approximately 1–1.5 km in the northern Coastal Plain. In the northwestern Negev the Ruhama Loess Member was still being deposited.

The paleogeography during Riss–Würm Interpluvial times was determined in the Coastal Plain by the Monastirian Ingression that caused spreading of sand dunes over almost the whole area. The upwarping of the mountains continued and a strong erosion, resulting from the floods and the lack of vegetation cover on the mountains, caused opening to the air of some karstic caves that were formed in the subsurface during the humid Mindel and probably also the Günz pluvials. From this period onward the number of exposed caves is rather large in Israel, and most of them were later occupied by men. The water bodies of the Jordan Valley were very poor during the Riss–Würm Interpluvial, while the Hula Basin was occupied by marshes in which peat was formed. In the Dead Sea area a number of

playas existed in which rocksalt was deposited together with some hypersaline lacustrine clays. The vegetation of the country in Riss–Würm time was very poor, and it seems that the whole of the country was rather like a desert. Almost no trees grew even in the north of Israel, and the south was a total desert. Some volcanic activity around the Hula Valley contributed to the difficulty of living in these areas during this time. Actually the number of sites of the Riss–Würm Interpluvial age in the country is very limited. In fact, such sites are known only from the caves of Umm Qatafa and Tabun.

The Würm Pluvial

Würmian sediments are widespread in Israel. Lacustrine sediments, the Ashmura and the Lisan formations, cover most of the Jordan Valley area. Fluviatile conglomerates, the Nakhshon Conglomerate (Buchbinder, 1968), cover wide areas in the mountains and the Hashephela. The Coastal Plain is covered with paleosols developed during the humid phases of the Würm, and by fossil dunes that were formed during the interstadials when the sea ingressed eastwards.

Detailed palynostratigraphic studies of the Würmian sediments, especially those in the Jordan Valley, have resulted in a subdivision of the Würm Pluvial into three pluvial phases: an Early, Main, and a Late Würm, separated by two warm and humid interstadials. The Early Würm began 60,000 to 70,000 years ago and continued for approximately 10,000 years (Horowitz, 1971, 1973; Neev and Emery, 1967). A rather long interstadial that lasted approximately 20,000 years is recorded in the pollen diagrams. After this comes the main Würm phase that was rather short, lasting approximately 10,000 years. Then followed another interstadial that lasted until 16,000 years ago when the Late Würm occurred and lasted until 11,500 years ago. The Early, Main, and Late Würm phases are characterized by pollen spectra in which arboreal pollen comprises more than 50% and is dominated by oaks; the interstadials are characterized by pollen spectra in which the arboreal pollen drops to about 30% and comprises a mixture of oak, pine, pistachio, and olive. It seems that the climate during the pluvial phases was humid and somewhat cooler than at present, while the interstadials were slightly more humid than at present but not cooler.

The Ashmura Formation, deposited from the Würm until present, in the Hula Valley was studied in detail and described in Horowitz (1973). During the humid Würm the Ashmura Formation was deposited over wide areas in the Hula Valley, but in post-Würm times, as the lake shrank, it was deposited only in the middle of the basin where it continues to be deposited until the present day. The Ashmura Formation overlies the Hulata Formation in the subsurface. It crops out at the Benot Ya'akov Bridge area where it overlies unconformably the Benot Ya'akov Formation over a thin base conglomerate. The formation is comprised of white to gray chalk and is almost barren of mollusc remains, except for some in the upper few meters. Some peat intercalations are known in the Ashmura Formation, representing the interstadial phases. The Ashmura Formation was named by Picard (1952) the "Upper Lacustrine Series." Its lower part correlates with the Lisan Formation of the central and southern Jordan Valley, and its upper part with the Tabgha Formation of the Kinneret area (Horowitz, 1971).

A series of springs developed along the foothills of the Hermon Range in Würmian times, depositing travertines that were termed by Picard (1963) "Younger Travertines." These travertines, attaining about 25 m in thickness, are defined in Horowitz (1973) as the Dan Travertine. The travertines are loose, yellow to brown, contain some *Melania tuberculata* and *Melanopsis*, and in places are very rich in leaf impressions, mainly of *Populus* and *Salix*.

Artifacts that were found within the Ashmura Formation (Horowitz, 1973) include almost the whole sequence from Mousterian up to Chalcolithic and Early Bronze Age cultures.

The Lisan Formation covers most of the central and southern Jordan Valley, from the southern end of the Kinneret south to Hazeva in the northern Arava. It is comprised of two members in the Dead Sea area (Neev and Emery, 1967)—the lower, Hamarmar Member or Hamarmar Formation which is mainly clastic; and the upper, Lisan Formation, *sensu stricto*, which consists of varved limnic sediments. The deposition of the Lisan Formation in the central and southern Jordan Valley ceased rather abruptly approximately 18,000 years ago (Neev and Emery, 1967; Horowitz, 1973, in press) due to a faulting phase that caused the development of two subbasins within the Jordan Valley, the Kinneret and the Dead Sea. The Late Würm through Recent is represented in the Dead Sea area by the "Unnamed post-Lisan Sediments" (Neev and Emery, 1967) and in the Kinneret area by the Tabgha Formation (Horowitz, 1971, 1973). Rivers flowing to the retreating Lisan Lake in the cental Jordan Valley deposited the Fatza'el Formation during the Late Würm (Horowitz, in press). The Fatza'el Formation consists of conglomerates and red loams very rich in Epipaleolithic industries. The red coloration of the Fatza'el Formation is probably a result of disintegration of iron-bearing minerals in the tropical climate that existed in the Jordan Valley during the Late Würm.

In the mountainous areas the Nakhshon Conglomerate was formed and deposited in the wadis. The rich vegetation, the high humidity, and the permanent runoff of the rivers caused the development of gently dipping slopes on which the Nakhshon Conglomerate developed. Artifacts of Mousterian through Epipaleolithic were found within the Nakhshon Conglomerate. These conglomerates interfinger to the east with the Lisan sediments of the Jordan Valley and to the west with the hamra paleosols of the Coastal Plain.

The Würm is represented in the Coastal Plain by the lower part of the Shefaim Member of the Gaza Formation.

This lower part comprises three beds. The earliest, the Nakhsholim Hamra Bed, called "Café au lait" by Avnimelech (1952), is a paleosol which was formed in the Coastal Plain in Early Würm times under pluvial conditions. Within it are found Mousterian artifacts. It is overlain by the Dor Kurkar Bed that was deposited during the first and second interstadials of the Würm when the sea ingressed eastward. The regression of the second Würmian pluvial phase is recorded with the Dor Kurkar Bed by an unconformity between the lower and upper parts of the kurkar. This Kurkar Bed was termed T3 by Michelson (1970). Marine sediments deposited during the Würmian interstadials are known from the Coastal Plain boreholes as the M3 and M3A Members of the Hayarkon Formation. These ingressions also left terraces in the Carmel area (Michelson, 1970) at elevations of approximately 5 m–6 m above the present sea level. The Dor Kurkar Bed is overlain by the Netanya Hamra Bed that was formed during the Late Würm pluvial phase and contains many Epipaleolithic artifacts. This Hamra is widespread in the Coastal Plain and was defined by Itzhaki (1961) as the "Hamra III" horizon and by Avnimelech (1952) as the Netanyan Stage.

In the northwestern Negev, the Ruhama Loess Member of the Gaza Formation continued to be deposited until approximately the termination of the Early Würm. Since that time the Ruhama Loess has eroded, forming the typical badlands of the northwestern Negev. In the central Negev, loess deposition occurred during the pluvial phases of the Würm. The Early Würm loess contains Mousterian artifacts, the Main Würm loess contains Upper Paleolithic artifacts, and the loess deposited in the Late Würm times contains Epipaleolithic artifacts (Marks, 1971). Pollen analyses of the loesses of the central Negev highlands yielded pollen spectra for the Mousterian loess that are almost similar to those obtained today from the Carmel area. It seems therefore that the Negev highlands were covered with a rather dense vegetation, including developed stands of trees. The Upper Paleolithic and Epipaleolithic loesses of the central Negev yielded pollen spectra that resembled those obtained presently from the Hashephela. It seems that the vegetation of the central Negev highlands during the second and third pluvial phases of the Würm was still Mediterranean, with occasional trees growing here and there, but somewhat less humid than during the first pluvial.

Würmian sediments also are known from many caves in Israel and have yielded rich artifact assemblages. Early Würm sediments were palynologically analyzed from the Tabun Cave on Mount Carmel (Howowitz in Jelinek et al., 1973) and yielded pollen spectra rich in arboreal pollen that resemble Recent spectra from northern Lebanon. Pollen spectra of the Würm sediments from the Hula Valley are also very rich in arboreal pollen, especially in oak pollen, and it seems that during the pluvial phases of the Würmian a very well-developed oak forest grew in most of the mountainous areas of Israel and probably down to Be'er Sheva area, or even south of it.

The Würm interstadials are characterized by pollen assemblages in which the arboreal pollen share is slightly lower than that of the pluvial sediments, but still higher than today. Arboreal pollen that are mainly represented with the interstadial spectra are those derived from oaks and olives. The great distribution of olive pollen in the interstadials indicates the higher temperature that prevailed during these periods.

The Würmian paleogeography of the Coastal Plain was determined by the marine ingressions of the interstadials and the regressions during the pluvial phases. The regressions were followed by pedogenetic processes that produced red or sometimes grayish soils, preserved as hamra or Café au Lait paleosols (Avnimelech, 1952), while the ingressions caused an eastward spreading of dunes. These ingressions, however, never propagated far to the east.

In the mountainous area most of the wadis flowed constantly throughout the whole year and the area was densely covered with a forest composed mainly of oaks during the pluvial phases, and oaks and olives during the interstadial phases.

The Jordan Valley was occupied throughout most of the Würm by lakes: the Ashmura Lake in the northern Jordan Valley, the Hula area—and south of it—and the Lisan Lake that occupied most of the central and southern Jordan Valley down to central Arava (fig. 2). The existence of these lakes terminated about 18,000 years ago owing to the faulting phase that created the present Dead Sea and Kinneret basins and also limited the Ashmura lake area to the Hula Basin.

A series of springs poured their waters in the north of the Hula Valley, depositing the Dan Travertine. The climate was much more humid than at present, and it seems that during the pluvial phases—especially in the Early Würm—rainfall was 30% to 40% higher than it is today. The temperature dropped about 4°–5° C. During the interstadials the temperature was approximately as it is today, while the rainfall was still 30% higher.

These environmental conditions were excellent for the settlement of hominids in the area of Israel; indeed the Würmian sediments almost everywhere in Israel yield rich assemblages of artifacts, proving that the whole country was inhabited down at least to the central Negev.

The Holocene

The Holocene, that began approximately 11,500 years ago, is a period during which postglacial and postpluvial processes controlled environmental conditions. This is true except for a short time—1,500 or 2,000 years during the Atlantic Stage—approximately 4,500 to 7,000 years ago. Pollen spectra indicate that the climate and vegetation throughout the Holocene were similar to those of the present day, except during the Atlantic when the share of arboreal pollen in the pollen spectra was much higher. Such a high share indicates a higher humidity (Horowitz, 1971). During this period the Hula Lake area also expanded (Horo-

witz, 1971) and small lakes were formed in the central Jordan Valley (Neev, 1967). Higher humidity and richer vegetation in the Atlantic times also controlled human settlements; Chalcolithic and Early Bronze settlements are widespread in the Negev and even in Sinai at that time.

In the Jordan Valley the "Unnamed post-Lisan Sediments" continued to be accumulated in the Dead Sea basin and the Tabgha Formation continued to be deposited in the Kinneret Lake. Peat of the Mallaha Formation was deposited in the marshes that were formed in the Hula Valley, owing to the retreat of the Hula Lake which resulted from the deteriorating climate and lower humidity (Horowitz, 1973).

On the Coastal Plain, the postglacial rise of the sea level caused the deposition of what is generally known as "Flandrian," defined as the L4 Member of the Hayarkon Formation (after Reiss and Issar, 1961, in Horowitz, in press). In places where finer subdivision of the Holocene sediments of the Coastal Plain could be distinguished, the first postglacial rise of sea level deposited the Tel Aviv Kurkar Bed. A slight regression during Atlantic times caused the formation of the Ta'arukha Hamra Bed, while the Recent rise of sea level, since approximately 4,500 years ago, caused the deposition of the Hadera Dune Bed. These three beds comprise the upper part of the Shefaim Member which is the upper member of the Gaza Formation.

The Nakhshon Conglomerate in the mountainous areas has been subjected to erosion throughout the Holocene, while Würmian deposits of the central Negev have been subjected mainly to wind deflation. It seems that except for the Atlantic period with its higher humidity, the Holocene environments resemble those of the present.

CONCLUSION: THE HOMINID OCCUPATION OF ISRAEL IN PLEISTOCENE TIMES AS A FUNCTION OF THE ENVIRONMENT

Hominid occupation is known in Israel only from Mindel and Riss times. Hominids lived on the shores of lakes in the Jordan Valley and close to the marshes of the Coastal Plain. Sites of Mindel age are known from the central and northern Jordan Valley, from the northwestern Negev, and from western Galilee—all connected to open water bodies such as lakes and marshes. No sites are known in Israel from Mindel–Riss times, which may be a combined result of the scarcity of Mindel–Riss deposits, except for sand dunes that are not suitable for hominid occupation, and the dry and hot climate of the interpluvial that probably prevented occupation of Israel and pushed the people northward to northern Syria where sites of this time are known.

In Rissian times hominids came back to Israel and settled once more in the same environments as those of the Mindel times, around the lakes of the central and northern Jordan Valley, near the springs of the northern Hula Valley and western Galilee, and close to the marshes of Galilee and the Coastal Plain. The Rissian hominids also inhabited the mountainous areas; open sites are known from the vicinity of Jerusalem, while the first occupation of caves is known from the Judean Desert at the Umm Qatafa. It should be noted that the Umm Qatafa Cave is presently high above the wadi bed, but in Rissian times it was very close to the wadi bed in which water probably flowed throughout the whole year, as can be seen from the style of gentle erosion. Rissian open sites are known also from Upper Galilee, in the areas of Bar'am and Yir'on (A. Ronen, personal communication).

In Riss–Würm Interpluvial times occupation of the country by hominids was once more very poor, probably because of the dry and warm climate. Sites of this age are known only from the Tabun Cave in Mount Carmel and the Umm Qatafa Cave in the Judean Desert. The paucity of sediments of this period in Israel may also be one of the reasons for the scarcity of sites of this age.

In Würmian times almost the whole area of Israel was occupied—during Early Würm by the Mousterian people, in Mid-Würm by Upper Paleolithic people, and in the Late Würm by Epipaleolithic people. Both open-air sites and cave sites are known for this period, and it seems that the climate, vegetation, and animal life were favorable for hominid occupation.

In Holocene times, especially the central and northern parts of the country were occupied by people, but during the wetter Atlantic period even the southern Negev and part of Sinai were occupied. It seems that the reason for the occupation of the Negev and Sinai by the Chalcolithic and Early Bronze people is not only the favorable climate but also the quarrying of copper from the copper mines in these areas. However, many settlements are known from this period in the Negev and Sinai that are not connected with copper mining. Settlements could exist in these areas only because of the higher humidity which enabled pastoralism.

BIBLIOGRAPHY

ARENSBURG, B., and BAR-YOSEF, O., 1967. "Yacimiento Paleolitico en el Valle de Refaim, Jerusalem, Israel." *Ampurias* 29:117-33.

AVNIMELECH, M., 1952. "Late Quaternary Sediments of the Coastal Plain of Israel." *Bulletin of the Research Council of Israel* 2(11):51-57.

————,1962. "The Main Trends in the Pleistocene-Holocene History of the Israelian Coastal Plain." *Quaternaria* 6:479-95.

BAR-YOSEF, O., and TCHERNOV, E., 1972. "On the Paleoecological History of the Site of Ubeidiya." *Proceedings of the Israel Academy of Sciences and Humanities.*

BAR-YOSEF, Y., 1964. *The Geology of Ahuzam-Nir'am Area.* Tel Aviv: Tahal (Water Planning for Israel). (In Hebrew).

BUCHBINDER, B., 1968. *Young Conglomerates in the Hashelphela Area.* Jerusalem: Israel Geological Society.

BUTRIMOWITZ, Y., 1973. *On the Meanders of Nahal Soreq.* Tel Aviv: Tel Aviv University.

CLARK, J. D., 1969. "The Middle Acheulean Occupation Site at Latamne, Northern Syria." *Quaternaria* 10:1-76.

FLEISCH, H., 1957. "Dépots préhistoriques de la côte Libanaise et leur place dans la chronologie bassée sur le Quaternaire marin." *Quaternaria* 3:101-32.

FREUND, R.; OPPENHEIM, M. J.; and SCHULMAN, N., 1965. "Direction of Magnetization of Some Basalts in the Jordan Valley and Lower Galilee (Israel)." *Israel Journal of Earth Sciences* 14:37-44.

GARFUNKEL, Z., 1970. "The Tectonics of the Western Margins of the Southern Arava." Ph.D. dissertation, Hebrew University. (In Hebrew, English summary).

————, and HOROWITZ, A., 1966. "The Upper Tertiary and Quaternary Morphology of the Negev, Israel." *Israel Journal of Earth Sciences* 15:101-17.

GIGNOUX, M., 1955. *Stratigraphic Geology.* San Francisco: Freeman.

GILEAD, D., 1970. "Handaxe Industries in Israel and the Near East." *World Archaeology* 2:1-11.

GVIRTZMAN, G., and BUCHBINDER, B., 1969. "Outcrops of Neogene Formations in the Central and Southern Coastal Plain, Hashephela and Be'er Sheva Regions, Israel." *Bulletin of the Geological Survey of Israel* 50:1-52.

HAAS, G., 1970. "*Metridiochoerus evronensis*, A New Middle Pleistocene Phacochoerid from Israel." *Israel Journal of Zoology* 19:179-81.

de HEINZELIN, J., 1968. "Geological Observations near Latamne." In "The Middle Acheulean Occupation Site at Latamne, Northern Syria." by J. D. Clark. *Quaternaria* 10:1-76.

HOOIJER, D. A., 1958. "An Early Pleistocene Mammalian Fauna from Bethlehem." *Bulletin of the British Museum National History and Geology* 3:267-92.

HOROWITZ, A., 1966. "Preliminary Palynological Investigations of the Dead Sea Rift Valley Pleistocene Deposits." Report, Department of Geology, Hebrew University.

————, 1968. "Palynostratigraphy of 'Melech Sedom 1' Borehole." Report, Geological Survey of Israel, Jerusalem.

————, 1970. "Outcrops of Hazeva and Taqiye Formations in the Jerusalem Area and Their Possible Significance." *Israel Journal of Earth Sciences* 19:35-39.

————, 1971. "Climatic and Vegetational Developments in Northeastern Israel during Upper Pleistocene—Holocene Times." *Pollen et Spores* 13:255-78.

————, 1973. "Development of the Hula Basin, Israel." *Israel Journal of Earth Sciences* 21:150-86.

————, in press *a*. "Late Cenozoic Stratigraphy and Paleogeography of Israel." *Israel Journal of Earth Sciences*.

————, in press *b*. "Some Pollen Spectra from the Neogene of Israel." *Pollen et Spores*.

————; SIEDNER, G.; and BAR-YOSEF, O., 1973. "Radiometric Dating of the Ubeidiya Formation, Jordan Valley, Israel." *Nature* 242:186-87.

————; and ZAK, I., 1968. "Preliminary Palynological Analysis of an Evaporitic Sequence from Mount Sedom, Israel." *Review of Palaeobotany and Palynology* 7:25-30.

ISSAR, A., 1968. "Geology of the Central Coastal Plain of Israel." *Israel Journal of Earth Sciences* 17:16-29.

ITZHAKI, Y., 1961. "Pleistocene Shorelines in the Coastal Plain of Israel." *Bulletin of the Geological Survey of Israel* 32:1-9.

JELINEK, A. J.; FARRAND, W. R.; HAAS, G.; HOROWITZ, A.; and GOLDBERG, P., 1973. "New Excavations at Tabun Cave, Mount Carmel, Israel, 1967-1972: A Preliminary Report." *Paleorient* 1(2).

KAFRI, U., and ECKER, A., 1964. "Neogene and Quaternary Subsurface Geology and Hydrogeology of the Zevulun Plain." *Bulletin of the Geological Survey of Israel* 37:1-13.

KARCZ, I., and KAFRI, U., 1973. "Recent Vertical Crustal Movements between the Dead Sea Rift and the Mediterranean." *Nature* 242:42-44.

McBURNEY, C. B. M., and HEY, R., 1955. *Prehistory and Pleistocene Geology in Cyrenaican Libya*. Cambridge: At the University Press.

MARKS, A. E., 1971. "Prehistoric Settlement Patterns and Intrasite Variability in the Central Negev, Israel." *American Anthropologist* 73(5):1237-44.

MICHELSON, H., 1970. *Geology of the Carmel Coast*. Tel Aviv: Tahal (Water Planning for Israel). (In Hebrew).

————, 1972. *The Hydrogeology of the Southern Golan Plateau*. Tel Aviv: Tahal (Water Planning in Israel). (In Hebrew).

MOR, D., 1973. "The Volcanism in the Central Golan Plateau." Master's thesis, Department of Geology, Hebrew University.

MOSHKOVITZ, S., 1968. "The Mollusca in the Marine Pliocene and Pleistocene Sediments of the Southeastern Mediterranean Basin (Cyprus-Israel)." Ph.D. dissertation, Department of Geology, Hebrew University.

NEEV, D., 1967. "The Late Holocene Fluviatile History of the Kinneret and Bet Shean Basin." *Proceedings of the Israel Geological Society*.

————, and EMERY, K. O., 1967. "The Dead Sea." *Bulletin of the Geological Survey of Israel* 41:1-147.

NEUVILLE, R., 1951. *Le Paléolithique et le Mésolithique du Désert de Judée*. Archives de l'Institut de Paléontologie humaine, mémoire 24.

OAKLEY, K. P., 1964. *Frameworks for Dating Fossil Man*. Chicago: Aldine-Atherton.

PERATH, I., 1965. *Microfauna of the Jaffa 1 Well: Benthonic Foraminifera.* Jerusalem: Oil Companies Micropaleonotological Laboratory Report OS/4/65.

PICARD, L., 1943. *Structure and Evolution of Palestine.* Jerusalem.

_____,1952. "The Pleistocene Peat of Lake Hula." *Bulletin of the Israel Research Council of Israel* 2G:147-56.

_____, 1963. "The Quaternary in the Northern Jordan Valley." *Proceedings of the Israel Academy of Sciences and Humanities* 1(4):1-34.

REISS, Z., and ISSAR, A., 1961. "Subsurface Quaternary Correlations in the Tel Aviv Region." *Bulletin of the Geological Survey of Israel* 32:10-26.

ROSSIGNOL, M., 1962. "Analyse pollinique de sédiments marins Quaternaires en Israel, II, sédiments Pleistocènes." *Pollen et Spores* 4(1):121-48.

_____, 1964. "Analyse pollinique de sédiments marins Quaternaires en Israel, sédiments Pleistocènes." *Israel Journal of Earth Sciences* 12(4):207-14.

_____, 1969. "Sédimentation palynologique dans le domain marin Quaternaire de Palestine." *Notes et Mémoires du Moyen Orient* 10:1-261.

SALTZMAN, U., 1964. *The Geology of Tabgha–Hukok–Migdal Area.* Tel Aviv: Tahal (Water Planning for Israel). (In Hebrew, English summary).

SCHULMAN, N., 1962. "The Geology of the Central Jordan Valley." Ph.D. dissertation, Department of Geology, Hebrew University. (In Hebrew, English summary).

SELLI, R., 1971. "Calabrian." *Giornale di Geologia* 37(2):55-64.

SHACHNAI, E., 1967. "Geology and Hydrogeology of the Western Besor Area." Master's thesis, Department of Geology, Hebrew University. (In Hebrew).

SHUKRI, N. M.; PHILIP, G.; and SAID, R., 1956. "The Geology of the Mediterranean Coast between Rosetta and Baridia." *Bulletin Institut d'Egypte* 37:395-427.

SIEDNER, G., and HOROWITZ, A., in press. *Stratigraphic Significance of K/Ar Datings of Late Cenozoic Basalts from Israel.*

SLATKINE, A., 1966. "Données nouvelles sur les niveaux marins Quaternaires du Mont Carmel." *Israel Journal of Earth Sciences* 15:57-63.

_____, and ROHRLICH, V., 1963. "Sédiments du Quaternaire de la Plaine de Haifa." *Israel Journal of Earth Sciences* 12(4):159-206.

STEKELIS, M., 1960. "The Paleolithic Deposits of Jisr Banat Yaqub." *Bulletin of the Research Council of Israel* 9G:63-90.

_____,1966. *Archaeological Excavations at Ubeidiya, 1960-1963.* Jerusalem: Israel Academy of Sciences and Humanities.

_____, and GILEAD, D., 1966. "Ma'ayan Baruck, a Lower Paleolithic Site in Upper Galilee." *Mitqufat ha-Even* 8.

TARLING, D. H., 1971. *Principles and Applications of Palaeomagnetism.* London: Chapman and Hall.

TCHERNOV, E., 1970. "Pleistocene Biostratigraphy of Molluscs and Vertebrates." In *Pleistocene Stratigraphy in Israel,* edited by A. Horowitz. Jerusalem. (In Hebrew).

————, 1972. "On the Fossil Molluscs of the Jordan Valley." *Proceedings of the Israel Academy of Sciences and Humanities*.

TREWARTHA, G. T., 1961. *An Introduction to Climate*. New York: Mc-Graw Hill.

WEST, R. G., 1968. *Pleistocene Geology and Biology*. London: Longmans.

WETZEL, R., and HALLER, J., 1944. "Sur le Quaternaire côtier de la région de Tripoli (Liban)." *Publication École Française d'Ingénieures Beyrouth* 6:34-39.

ZAGWIJN, W. H., 1960. "Aspects of the Pliocene and Early Pleistocene Vegetation in the Netherlands." *Mededelingen de Geolosche Stichting* C-111-1:5.

ZEUNER, F. E., 1959. *The Pleistocene Period*. London: Hutchinson.

ZOHARY, M., 1959. *Geobotany*. Merhavia, Israel: Sifriat Poalim. (In Hebrew).

THE PALEOLITHIC ARCHAEOLOGY AND CHRONOLOGY OF ISRAEL

Avraham Ronen
Institute of Archaeology
Tel Aviv University

In this review we shall draw principally upon stratigraphic and archaeological data from the coastal plain of Israel, since the region is extremely rich in prehistoric finds and provides, by far, the best chronological sequence. While development projects are being carried out at present on the coastal plain at an unprecedented pace, menacing many sites, at the same time these provide valuable sections for the study of stratigraphic sections.

Previous studies of the Quaternary of the coast were based primarily upon boreholes drilled for water and considered only gross stratigraphic units.

This paper is based on recent work carried out by the present writer, as well as various students, as part of a long-term prehistoric and geological study of the coastal plain that has just begun. It is being made possible by the generous support of the Volkswagen Stiftung.

GENERAL CONSIDERATIONS ON THE QUATERNARY OF THE COASTAL PLAIN

The coastal plain, stretching from north to south, is the westernmost of three major morphological zones of Israel. On the east, the plain is bordered by a range of mountains—from Galilee through Carmel, Samaria, and Judea—which constitutes the second zone. The third zone is the Jordan Graben, east of the chain of mountains and separating it from the Golan and Transjordanian plateau (fig. 1).

The coastal plain is 35 km wide in south Israel and 4 km wide in the extreme north. Like the south Mediterranean flat coasts, that of Israel has a thick accumulation of alternating marine and continental deposits, with two major types of rock: on the one hand, quartz sand originating from the Mediterranean and, on the other, loams or clays of continental origin. Each of these rock types includes many facies which frequently change over short distances and are interbedded in a complex way. The sandy element is present as loose sand or as calcified sandstone, with all the degrees of cementation found. The soils, on the other hand, show all the stages—from light and poorly developed sandy regosols through fully developed mature red loams, to alluvial clayey soils. No wonder, then, that chronostratigraphic units are difficult to trace on the coastal plain, especially in west-east transects.

Indeed, only lithostratigraphical units have hitherto been defined within the Quaternary of the coastal plain (Issar, 1961, 1968): all sand deposits were grouped into the Pleshet Formation, and all continental deposits were grouped into the Rehovot Formation.

The morphology of the coastal plain is dominated by several ridges running largely parallel to the present shoreline. Built mainly of hard sandstone, these ridges affect the course of rivers, the development of soil catenas, and the vegetation. The ridges are widely accepted to denote the high sea levels and to have originated from near-shore dunes rich in shell fragments that subsequently dissolved and caused cementation of the ridges.

Since four such ridge formations were recognized (Izhaki, 1961; Issar, 1961), it was concluded that four ingressions and three regressions of intercalated paleosols constituted the Quaternary of the coastal plain, with the easternmost ingression being naturally the oldest.

This scheme is taken here to be essentially correct, but several observations call for a refinement. First, there exist, in reality, more than four ingressions, or periods of inland sand penetration. Second, on geomorphological grounds, the upper parts of some ridges ought to be eolian accumulation and, thus, the formation of a ridge cannot be safely attributed to direct proximity with the sea. Third, several paleosols may exist *within* one ridge, so that the attribution of a ridge to any single geological phase is untenable (Ronen, 1973; Farrand and Ronen, in press; Ronen, in press). Therefore, caution should be exercised in attempting to date the ridges whenever the sampling is based on the assumption that each ridge represents a homogeneous formation. These observations call for reconsideration of the possible origin and genesis of the various formations of the coastal plain.

All agree that quartz sand is carried by the long-shore Mediterranean current, dropped on land, and subsequently taken by the prevailing west wind as far inland as topography or vegetation allow. Under subaerial conditions the sand will subsequently calcify if it contains more than 10% $CaCO_3$ in the form of seashell fragments (Yaalon, 1967), but below that level of $CaCO_3$ it will remain loose.

Simultaneously, soil formation takes place. The original sand contains only 2% of alumo-silicates capable of yielding clay minerals, whereas lehms on top of the sand have 20%–50% clay minerals. Opinions vary as to the origin of the additional clay. Some see it in eolian transportation from the southwest deserts (Yaalon and Dan, 1967), others in alluvial clay from the nearby mountains east of the coastal plain (Ravikovitch, 1969). Still others maintain that the initial 2% clay minerals in the parent rock are enough, given sufficient time, to contribute the entire clay quantity in the lehms (Amiel, personal communication). All pedologists seem to agree, however, that the sandy parent material contains enough heavy minerals to stain the particles and give the mature loam its characteristic red or reddish-brown color (Pomeranchlum, 1966). On the whole, soil formation

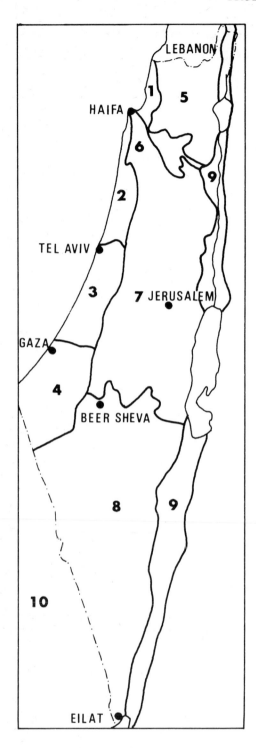

FIG. 1—Major Regions of Israel: *1*—Northern Coastal Plain; *2*—
Carmel and Sharon Plains; *3*—Pleshet Coastal Plain; *4*—
Southern Coastal Plain; *5*—Galilee; *6*—Mt. Carmel; *7*—Judea
and Samaria; *8*—Negev; *9*—Jordan Graben; *10*—Sinai.

takes place when sand supply is minimal or absent, because
with sand supply beyond a certain critical limit, lehmification is hampered. The sand is expected to change character depending on the distance from its source—coarser
and richer in shells near shore, finer and poorer in shells
inland. Subsequent lithification is apt to occur in the
former environment.

The above simplified mechanism of deposition would
have resulted in a flat coastal plain of alternating sands and
soils with rivers running directly east-west (fig. 2). In
reality, however, the penetrating sand accumulated in elongated ridges instead of flat sand-sheets. Observations of
bedding angles in various fossil dunes (Yaalon and Laronne,
1971) showed that all sands were deposited under the same
wind directions as prevail at present. Also, the cyclic formation of ridges repeatedly caused rivers to shift course from
east-west to roughly north-south in direction (Nir, 1970).
The existence of ridges supported further eolian accumulation on and around them, but the mechanism of the
initial formation of an elongated ridge is not yet clear.
Several possibilities exist.

1. A ridge is formed by the offshore dunes. This is the
most widely held hypothesis (Issar, 1961; Izhaki, 1961; Nir,
1970), but it is hardly supported by the nature of dunes
present today, which, far from creating a ridge, are extremely irregular in width.

2. A ridge is formed by offshore dunes whose penetration inland was stopped by the dense vegetation of the
pre-Neolithic era, before extensive grazing and agriculture
(Farrand and Ronen, in press).

3. The basal, or initial, part of a ridge is a long-shore bar
created *in the shallow sea* (Leontyev, 1969) and forming a
barrier for subsequent eolian cyclical transportations
(Ronen, in press).

4. The sand was, in effect, deposited in wide sheets, but
subsequent north-south erosion removed the nonconsoli-
dated sand and left only the consolidated parts which,
being dependent on the distance from the sea, resulted in a
fairly regular ridge-form (Ronen, in press).

It seems that a combination of the last two hypotheses
would best account for the features observed on the coastal
plain, both in the Quaternary and at present. Thus, the
irregular pattern of present-day sand penetration, covering
ridges and troughs alike, would in time remain confined
only to the ridges when erosion empties the troughs. Occasional filling of troughs also provides the best explanation
for the thick marshy alluvium or for the pseudo-gleys that
are found today on crests of ridges, high above the surrounding ground.

All cultural remains hitherto found on the coastal plain
were in or on soils and never in sand or in sandstone. It is of
prime importance then to define the chronology of the
various stages of the cyclical process described above,
within the framework of Quaternary sea level changes. We
propose the following chronology for a sedimentary cycle
(sand supply and subsequent soil formation):

Some sand will penetrate inland, and a barrier-bar (or
long-shore bar) will be formed during an ingressive halt. The
main sand penetration occurs, however, at the onset of the
regression when the off-shore sand belt, trapped between 0
and -40 m depth, is exposed to eolian transportation. Sand
will penetrate until the source is exhausted or until the sea
returns and covers what it had formerly exposed. When
sand supply is gone, or at least drops below a certain crucial

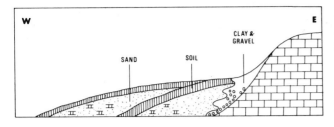

FIG. 2–Theoretical Evolution of the Coastal Plain of Israel.

level, soil formation will begin and will continue uninter-rupted throughout that regression and until the peak of the following transgression (fig. 3). At the onset of the next regression, sand penetration recommences, and the entire sedimentological cycle is repeated. It follows that the age of prehistoric industries found in paleosols may range almost over an entire geological cycle. Naturally, the number of sedimentological cycles is greatest in the western part of the coastal plain, easily reached by sand.

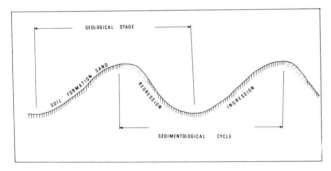

FIG. 3–Supposed Relation of Sedimentological and Geological Events.

In summary, the sequence of events would be as follows:

1. Maximum transgression. Sand is brought by sea on submerged land, concentrated between 0–40 m depth. Formation of a barrier-bar.

2. Beginning of the regression. Sand is exposed to the atmosphere and blown inland.

3. Beginning of soil formation. When the eolian sand supply drops or stops, soil formation begins simultaneously with cementation of the sand wherever $CaCO_3$ content is sufficient—intensive erosion along north-south troughs insure the ridgelike topography.

STRATIGRAPHY

THE NORTHERN COASTAL PLAIN

The most complete section known at present in the coastal plain is in the vicinity of Kibutz Evron, not far from the Lebanese frontier. Here four, possibly five, sandstone ridges are discernible from west to east (fig. 4). These are:

1. A series of off-shore sandstone islands, representing one (Issar and Dafri, 1972) or possibly two submerged ridges.

2. A ridge at the present shoreline, largely abraded at present. It is the only locality in Israel where abundant *Strombus bubonius* has been found (Issar and Picard, 1969).

3. The Evron ridge, up to 40 m a.s.l. Four superimposed sedimentary cycles, each with its red loam, were observed here (Ronen and Amiel, in press) with a total depth of 6 m, although additional paleosols may exist below. No industry was found in any of these soils.

4. The easternmost ridge, covered by an alluvium that had accumulated behind (eastward) the Evron ridge. A quarry has penetrated the entire depth of the easternmost ridge, revealing an important series of strata which have been studied by Issar and Kafri (1972). Their description (see fig. 5) is somewhat modified here (Ronen and Amiel, in press): (1) black alluvial soil, 1.0 m thick, with upper Acheulean industry; (2) thick gravel layer, 2.0 m thickness; (3) dark red soil, 1.0–2.0 m thick, with an Acheulean of an undetermined stage (in the western extension of the quarry); (3a) sandstone, 1.0 m thick (in the western extension of the quarry—not shown in fig. 5); (4) a very thick soil, 2.5 m, with well-developed pseudo-gley (in the Upper part of this soil—A horizon—is a middle Acheulean industry); (5) dark red soil, 1.5 m maximum thickness, gradually passing into its parent material, the underlying sandstone; (6) sandstone, 2.0–3.0 m thick; (7) reddish brown soil preserved only in small patches, 0.1–0.5 m thick; (8) sandstone, 3.0–4.0 m thick; and (9) Miocene marls with basalt fragments and volcanic ash at its top. Bottom of the quarry.

The Evron quarry shows four sedimentological cycles, each with an important soil formation. The uppermost alluvial fill is contemporaneous with the accumulation of the basal part of the Evron ridge, where four additional sedimentary cycles are visible. Thus, the vicinity of Evron reveals eight cycles altogether, as a minimal number. The ridges farther west are believed to be contemporaneous with the upper cycles of the Evron ridge, while elsewhere along the coast only partial sections are known which can be roughly fitted into the Evron sequence.

THE CENTRAL COASTAL PLAIN

The central coastal plain between Haifa and Ashdod has, locally, from two to five sandstone ridges. Only the stratigraphy of the westernmost one is exposed, showing seven sedimentary cycles (fig. 6). The lowest buried soil exposed anywhere contains Mousterian artifacts, so that, chronologically, the entire section matches the upper part of the Evron sequence. The uppermost cycle, with a poorly-developed regosol, postdates the Neolithic. The upper red loam has *on* it, rarely *in* it, Epipaleolithic industries. The sedimentary cycles between the Mousterian and the Epipaleolithic ought to be of Last Glacial age, but unfortunately the soils in question have not, as yet, yielded any cultural remains.

East of the ridge that marks the 35 m–45 m terrace on Mt. Carmel, and passes through Pardess-Hana, Tel-Mond,

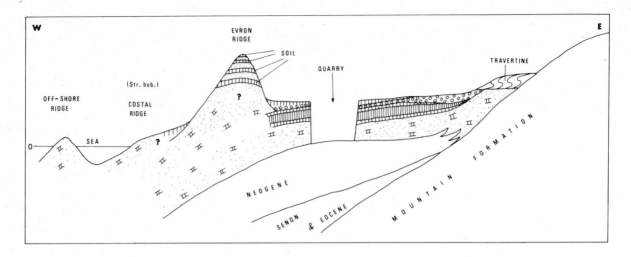

FIG. 4–Generalized Cross-Section, Northern Coastal Plain (after Issar & Kafri, modified).

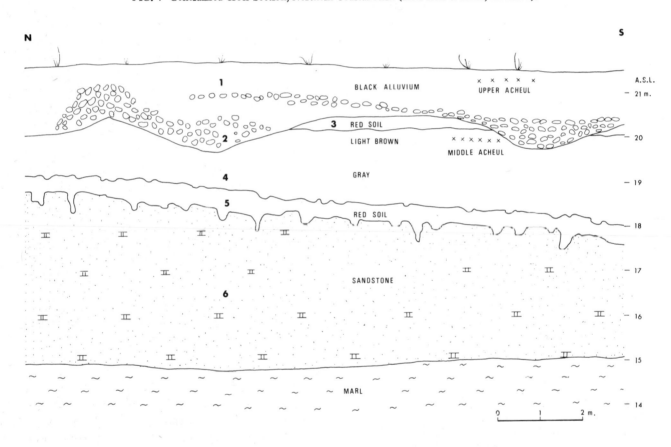

FIG. 5–Evron Quarry, Central Part of East Wall (Upper Acheulean is found west of here.)

and Azor (fourth ridge from west), Acheulean-bearing deposits were not covered by any later sandy deposits. This ridge, then, parallels that of Evron.

THE SOUTHERN COASTAL PLAIN

This is the widest part of the Israel coast, with six well-defined ridges as a minimal number (fig. 7). Only a limited area around Kissufim, near Gaza, has been studied in detail (Ronen et al, 1972). This lies between the Ali-Muntar ridge and the Ein-Hashelosha ridge (third and fourth from west).

Recently, new facts have been observed that complicate the section and render questionable the location of the industry as it was published. The description of strata visible at the Nahal Judeida section (fig. 8), reading from the top, is as follows: (1) loess cover, 0.5 m thick; (2) thin reddish brown lehm, 0.5 m thick; (3) sandstone, 1.0–2.0 m thick, extremely rich in shell fragments of a uniform size (around 3 mm), and near-shore deposition—ca. 55 m a.s.l.; (4) brown clay, 2.0 m thick; (5) gray clay rich in calcareous concretions, 1.5 m thick; (6) sandstone, with no shell

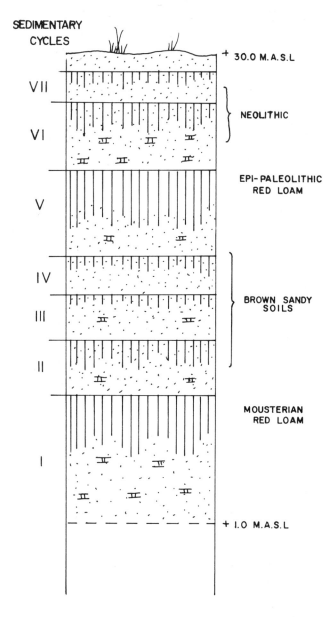

SEDIMENTARY CYCLES

+ 30.0 M.A.S.L

VII

VI } NEOLITHIC

EPI-PALEOLITHIC RED LOAM

V

IV } BROWN SANDY SOILS

III

II

MOUSTERIAN RED LOAM

I

+ 1.0 M.A.S.L

FIG. 6—Schematic Section in the Shoreline Ridge, Central Coastal Plain.

cretions, 1.0–2.0 m thick; (3) sand, unconsolidated with abundant small shell fragments, 2.0 m thick; (4) brown clay, 3.0 m thick; (5) reddish loam 1.5 m thick, passing gradually to the underlying sandstone; and (6) sandstone, thickness unknown.

In this section implements clearly derive from the top of the gray clay (Layer 2) and from the brown clay of Layer 4. It seems that the loose sand of Kissufim (Layer 3) is the lateral equivalent of the upper sandstone at Judeida, but the dissimilarities in both sections call for caution. One thing seems fairly certain—namely, that the entire Kissufim section fits into the middle part of the Evron sequence. It is worth noting that at Kissufim this sequence is found between ca. 50 m–80 m a.s.l., whereas at Evron, the equivalent cycles are found between 17 m–25 m a.s.l.

CHRONOLOGY OF THE COASTAL PLAIN SUCCESSION

Prehistoric industries constitute practically the only chronological clue in the coastal plain of Israel. Unfortunately, cultural remains have not been found in every soil.

In the Carmel and Central coastal plain (fig. 5), the two uppermost cycles are Holocene, both by virtue of the finds in them (Neolithic to recent) and by their position on top of the Epipaleolithic cycle (V) which, being pre-Natufian and post-Upper Paleolithic, should date from the late Würm.

The next soil to contain any industry is that of Cycle I in the coastal ridge, with fairly abundant Middle Paleolithic implements (Mousterian of Levallois technique). The intermediate phases II to IV should range within the Middle Würm period. It seems most probable that the sandstone underlying the Mousterian soil belongs to the *Strombus bubonius* ingression of the last Interglacial, which recently has been dated to 90,000 ± 20,000 B.P. (Sanlaville, 1971). The sandstone overlying the Mousterian soil (Cycle II) is here assigned (fig. 6) to the phase of Vermets in Lebanon, thought to be an early Würm ingression (Sanlaville, 1971).

In Lebanon, as in Israel, a Mousterian occupation is "sandwiched" between these two marine phases (the "Enfeau" and "Naamian" of Sanlaville). The red lehm seen on the west flanks of the Evron ridge (fig. 4) probably is of the same age and is the lowest soil that exists within the Evron ridge—whether it is the one observed or is another soil still further below. The red soil west of Evron ridge is probably not covered by the Strombus ridge on the present shore, as claimed by Issar and Kafri, 1972, but, on the contrary, had covered it before most of the shore ridge had been eroded and extensively quarried.

The soils which, in the westernmost ridge of Israel, are found between the Mousterian and the Epipaleolithic have a poorly developed character. They are brown instead of the normal reddish color, they have undergone a slight decalcification (numerous molluscs are preserved), and they have no more than 10% fines (Bakler, personal communication). They probably denote conditions that, while

fragments, 3.0 m thick; and (7) dark brown clay with black spots (organic material?), 1.0 m visible.

Layers 4 and 5 were originally considered to be the only artifact-bearing layers (Ronen et al., 1972). A few artifacts, though, were found recently on top of the upper sandstone (Layer 3), probably originating from the bottom of Layer 2. Since none of the upper Acheulean finds were *in situ*, it is not possible to tell whether only Layer 2 or all three layers (2, 4, and 5) contained artifacts. If the former is the case, the ridge "barring" on the Acheulean layers is that of Bani-Suheila-Ali Muntar (third from the west). If all three layers did contain artifacts, however, the shore of the 55 m transgression becomes post-Acheulean, a unique case in Israel.

The *Kissufim* section (fig. 8) is 3 km east of Nahal Judeida. The description of the strata, reading from the top is: (1) loess cover, 1.5 m thick; (2) gray clay rich in calcareous con-

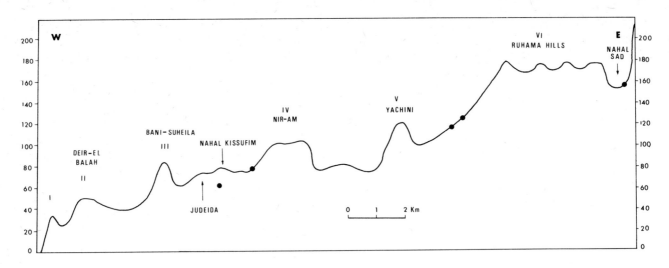

FIG. 7—Ridges in the Southern Coastal Plain. Dots indicate shore deposits.

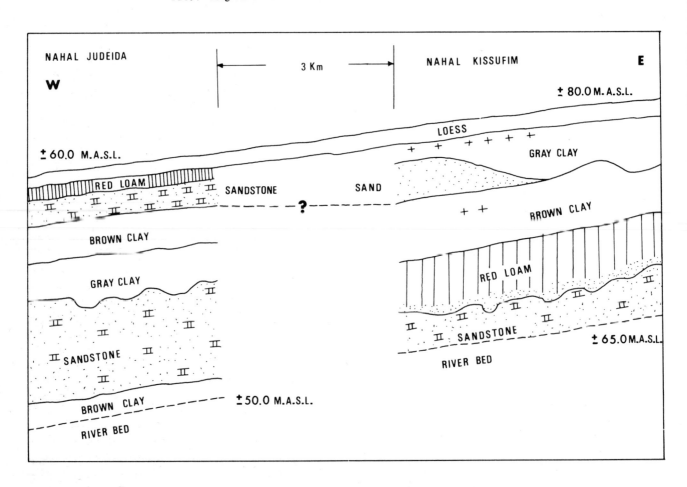

FIG. 8—Schematic Sections of the Soutern Coastal Plain, near Kissufim. + indicates implements found *in situ*.

having permitted lehmification, did not allow for a mature soil development. Farrand has suggested (personal communication) that this may disclose a continuous sand supply very close to the crucial limit that would have hampered lehmification, as was the case between the soils in question. Hence, it may be concluded that during these sedimentary cycles (II–IV), the seashore was not far away to the west

but sometimes far enough so that only very fine sand reached the ridge in question.

We suggest that the series of these soils (*café-au-lait*, of Avnimelech, 1952) reflect mid-Würm fluctuations of the sea which never receded far enough nor long enough for a mature lehm to develop. On the other hand, precisely these conditions were fulfilled during the late Würm, when the typical thick red lehm of the Epipaleolithic developed.

Below the Mousterian soil and *behind* the last Interglacial sand dunes is found the Upper Acheulean of Evron, embedded in the black alluvial-marshy soil. It may be assumed that it is contemporaneous with the basal sand accumulation of the Evron ridge. It is, thus, possible that the base of the Evron ridge belongs to the Strombus ingression or perhaps to a former high sea, but in any event *within the last Interglacial*. It should be noted that as yet no soil has been dated definitively to the last Interglacial, except perhaps the red loam that covers the Holon Acheulean site (Yizraeli, 1963). Unfortunately, the exact number of sedimentary cycles between the Upper Acheulean and the Mousterian is yet to be established.

The four sedimentary cycles which, in the Evron quarry, precede the Upper Acheulean occurrence, can surely be assigned to "pre-last-Glacial" times.

It seems fairly sure that Cycle IV (fig. 9) is Rissian, with its undetermined type of Acheulean. Cycle III, though, with its Middle Acheulean industry, could be assigned to Riss as well as to Mindel, and the dating of the lower cycles is even more obscure. We prefer, for the time being, to use the cycles as local stratigraphical units, as shown in fig. 9.

A clear feature along the entire coast of Israel is the lateral disappearance of Acheulean finds under later sedimentary cycles that originate at the sea (i.e. sandstone, etc.). East of that limit, Acheulean finds are found either in the surface layer (Evron, Sharon area) or are covered by alluvium (Tirat-Carmel) or eolian loess (Kissufim). West of that limit, no Acheulean finds have ever been recorded. The west limit of occurrence coincides with a sandstone ridge which seems to pass through Bani-Suheila-Ali-Muntar near Gaza, Azor near Tel-Aviv, the 35 m–45 m sandstone (terrace) in the Carmel coast, and the Evron ridge. This line, called "the third ridge" by Gilead (1970), roughly coincides with the Tyrrhenian I shore of Issar and Picard (1971) which, in the author's opinion, marks a last Interglacial shoreline (fig. 10).

The approximate elevations of the ridge bordering on the Acheulean finds are shown below as Table 1.

TABLE 1

Localities (South to North)	Junction of Acheulean Layer and Ridge	Crest of Ridge
Ali-Muntar	40-50 m	90 m
Azor	40 m	50 m
Mt. Carmel	35-45 m	eroded
Evron	25 m	40 m

A considerable difference exists only in the Evron area, lower than the rest. The high elevation in the Gaza area may result from the extremely thick accumulation of clays—regardless of whether this is alluvial or eolian—and/or from a greater sand accumulation in the southern part of the country (Nir, 1970). A comparison of elevations of sea terraces in the Mt. Carmel area (Slatkin and Rohrlich, 1966;

Michelson, 1970) and in the southern coastal plain is given below as Table 2, although the comparative ages are highly conjectural.

TABLE 2. Comparison of Sea Terrace Elevations

Mt. Carmel	Southern Coastal Plain
120 m	170 m
100 m	120-130 m
79 m	80 m
50-60 m	50-60 m
(Acheulean disappears)	(Acheulean disappears)
35-45 m	
12 m	
4 m	

There have been attempts to correlate the lowest three terraces in the Mt. Carmel area with the three ridges on the Carmel coast (Michelson, 1970), but this remains uncertain until the basal part of all the ridges is exposed. It should be noted that in the southern coastal plain, too, three ridges are recognizable west of the 50–60 m shoreline, clearly marked by beach rock exposed on several localities. Thus, the rejection or acceptance of altimetric data for sea level changes in Israel depends upon further research.

INLAND QUATERNARY STRATIGRAPHY AND CHRONOLOGY

The Quaternary stratigraphy of the Jordan Graben was studied mainly by Picard (1952, 1963, 1965, 1966), Neev and Emery (1967), and Horowitz (1973). It is from these sources particularly that material will be drawn.

It seems that no Villafranchian deposits exist in the Jordan Graben, which started to act as an independent base-level only after the eruption of the Cover Basalt, 1.7–2.0 million years ago. The oldest fill thereafter is a thick series of lake deposits, with one pollen sample showing 75% arboreal pollen (Horowitz, 1973).

The lower lake deposits (Erq el-Ahmar Formation or member) have many extinct malacological species and a rather Neogene spectra of Charophytes (Bar-Yosef, in press). Since the later Ubeidiya formation lacks these characteristics, a long time interval is assumed between these two lake formations, which perhaps may be seen in the lowest paleosol in the Hula Basin (Horowitz, 1973). A basalt flow (Yarda basalt) overlying the oldest lake formations, including Ubeidiya, has been dated to 640,000 ± 120,000 years ago (Horowitz, 1973), and was followed by an important tectonic activity that faulted the Ubeidiya and contemporaneous formations.

A series of marshy deposits (Ayelet-Hashahar Formation; Horowitz, 1973) separates the Ubeidiya lake formation from the following Benot-Yaakov lake formation which is distinguished by its *Viviparus* fauna. Within it were found Acheulean implements of the Gesher Benot Yaakov site (Stekelis, 1960a). Pollen shows 40%–50% arboreal

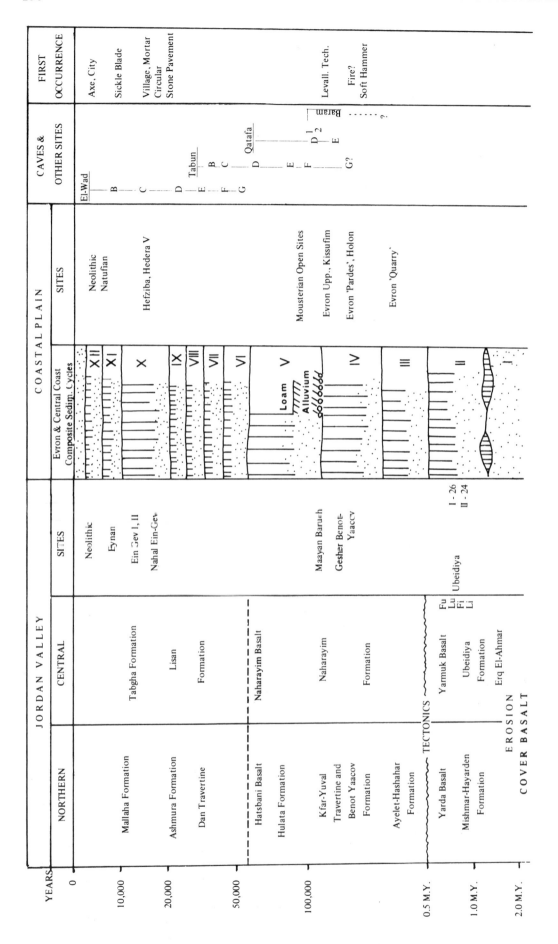

FIG. 9—Comparison of Inland and Coastal Plain Pleistocene Stratigraphy and Position of Main Sites.

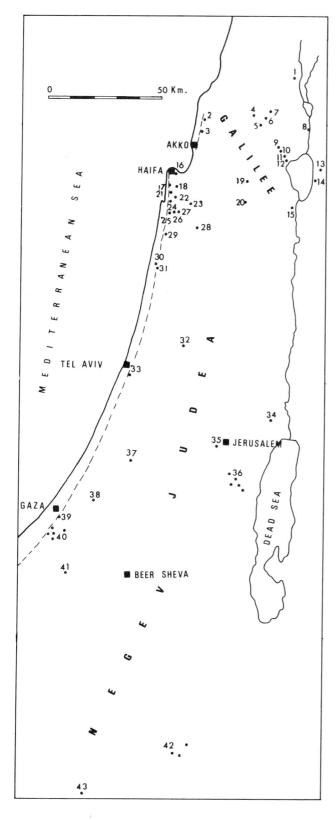

forms, mostly oak. Horowitz considers as contemporaneous with it both the Naharayim gravels and the Kfar Yuval travertine with its Acheulean industry at Maayan Baruch (Stekelis and Gilead, 1966), all indicating pluvial conditions.

There follows a phase of shrinkage in the water body when an important series of peat was deposited. A pollen spectra of poor maquis indicates an Interpluvial phase, the termination of which is dated by a basalt flow to 70,000 years ago (Horowitz, 1973).

A new series of lacustrine deposits (Hamarmar, Lisan, and contemporaneous formations) mark the last pluvial phase in the Jordan Valley, which can be accepted as the equivalent of Würm Glacial. Holocene deposits in the Graben include marsh deposits and soil formations, which on palynological grounds were divided into the five classical stages with a clear, humid Atlantic phase (Horowitz, 1968).

In summation, it may be stated that Horowitz distinguishes—mainly on grounds of palynological samples which are rather sparsely spaced—four major Pluvials in the Jordan Graben and four Interpluvials, including the Holocene (Horowitz, 1973). The use of the European Glacial nomenclature for these phases is rather misleading, since the attribution of the Ubeidiya Formation (older than 640,000 years) to Mindel does not fit the accepted date of 0.5 million years for the beginning of Mindel (cf. Butzer, 1971). As Bar-Yosef (in press) has noted, the similarity between the Olduvai Upper Bed II and Ubeidiya industries would also favor a pre-Mindel age for the latter.

ARCHAEOLOGY

LOWER PALEOLITHIC

There seems no question that Ubeidiya is the oldest site known in Israel. A series of occupations on lake shores, near swamps, or on alluvial fans has been continuously excavated there since 1960, the longest excavation hitherto held in Israel. Fourteen assemblages have been recorded, which may be divided into three main stages. The lowest consists of choppers–chopping tools, spheroids, and light-duty tools—but no handaxes (fig. 11). In the middle phase handaxes and trihedrals of a crude manufacture appear. Spheroids and light-duty tools become scarcer than in the lower phase, while chopping tools remain abundant. In the third and latest phase, handaxes disappear, although a few trihedrals survive; light-duty tools become more numerous

16–Geula Cave; 17–Tirat-Carmel; 18–Sheich Suleiman Cave; 19–Hayonim Cave; 20–Qafza Cave; 21–Oren & Abu-Usba Caves; 22–Sefunim Cave; 23–Rakefet Cave; 24–Mislia Cave; 25–Tabun Cave; 26–El Wad Cave; 27–Skhul Cave; 28–Ein Tut; 29–Kebara Cave; 30–Hedera V; 31–Hefziba; 32–Shukba Cave; 33–Holon; 34–Jericho; 35–Rephaim-Baqaa; 36–Umm-Qatafa & other Judean Desert Caves; 37–Kfar-Menahem; 38–Tel Hesi; 39–Beeri; 40–Kissufim Sites; 41– Ein Sharuhen; 42–Avdat Sites; 43–Har Harif Sites; - - - –Western Limit of Acheulean.

FIG. 10–Location Map: 1–Maayan Baruch; 2–Saar; 3–Evron; 4–Sasa; 5–Dalton; 6–Baram; 7–Yiron; 8–Benot Yaacov; 9–Shovach Cave; 10–Amud Cave; 11–Zuttiyeh Cave; 12– Emira Cave; 13–Nahal Ein Gev; 14–Ein Gev; 15–Ubeidiya;

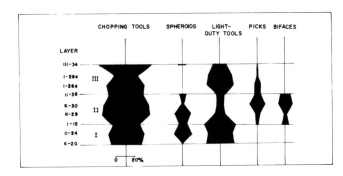

FIG. 11—Ubeidiya, Frequency of Main Tool Types (after Bar-Yosef).

than in the middle stage; and chopping tools remain abundant. Spheroids may or may not be present (Bar-Yosef, in press). According to the excavator, the industry closely resembles those from Middle and Upper Bed II at Olduvai.

The industry following Ubeidiya is the "Middle Acheulean" of the Evron quarry. Only a small number of bifaces have been collected in this locality (Prausnitz, 1969). These are extremely large (140–220 mm, Gilead and Ronen, in press), made exclusively by hard hammer and thus could be termed "Abbevillian" or "Early Acheulean" as well (Bordes, 1968). The handaxes include pointed ones, trihedral picks, or ones with a chisel-like tip. Their edges are uneven due to the big flake scars which form them. Ubeidiya seems well ancestral to the Evron quarry series, but the time that separates them is unknown. The Evron quarry industry is located in the upper part of an extremely thick soil (2.0–2.5 m, Ronen and Amiel, in press) with a pseudo-gley horizon about half that thickness. This should have had a long uninterrupted development which brings to mind the "long Interglacial."

Immediately above this occurrence there comes, in Cycle IV of Evron (fig. 9), another Acheulean which, like the former, is known only from several handaxes. While generally maintaining a large size, they are very well made and have straight and regular edges, and a soft hammer was clearly employed. Ovoids are numerous (30%), while cordiforms and amygdaloids combined account for 45% (Gilead and Ronen, in press). This assemblage possibly compares with that at Maayan Baruch (Stekelis and Gilead, 1966), which exhibits a similar technique, size range, and form distribution. The Maayan Baruch site is situated in a thin reddish-brown soil that had developed on thick travertine layers (Kfar Yuval travertine), assigned by Horowitz to the Riss Pluvial. It should be mentioned that a few handaxes and flakes were embedded in a travertine east of Evron, on the west slope of Galilee. This may parallel the Kfar Yuval travertine and thus be roughly contemporaneous with Cycle IV of Evron.

The site of Holon, embedded in a gray marshy deposit intercalated between two red loams, poses a stratigraphic problem. The lowest loam is on a sandstone abrasion platform at 37.0 m a.s.l. The upper loam overlying the site is unfortunately archaeologically sterile. It is proposed to be of Upper Acheulean phase, or Evron Cycle V, and the underlying Acheulean is proposed to be the equivalent of Evron Cycle IV. The lower loam may belong to either Cycle IV or III of Evron. The industry of Holon has been only briefly described (Yizraeli, 1967). The handaxes are well made; use of soft hammers is evident, and flake tools are numerous. Levallois technique is barely present.

The lower layer of Gesher Benot Yaakov, embedded in the *Viviparus* beds that are the lateral equivalent of Kfar Yuval travertine (Horowitz, 1973), is not typologically comparable to any other Acheulean occurrence in Israel. It has as many cleavers as handaxes, while cleavers are normally few in the Acheulean of Israel. Similarly, the utilization of basalt as practically the sole raw material is unique in Israel, since basalt is but rarely utilized even when easily available.

The affinities of the lower layer at Benot Yaakov with some African Acheulean have already been noted (Gilead, 1970; Bar-Yosef, in press). In fact, to consider it as an intrusion into the ordinary Israeli Acheulean may well be justified.

Above this occurrence, but still in the *Viviparus* beds, is a "normal" Upper Acheulean with flint utilized as the main raw material.

A common denominator of the Acheulean industries related to Evron Cycles III and IV (i.e., pre-Upper Acheulean) seems to be the lack of Levallois technique, or at least a limited use of it. An affirmation of this impression should, however, await the study of more flake samples.

Turning to the Upper Acheulean, its chronological situation should first be discussed. As seen from the Evron section, the alluvium accumulated behind the Evron ridge could date from the beginning of sand penetration onward. The upper limit of the Acheulean occupation is unclear at the open-air sites, and cave stratigraphy perhaps can be relied upon for that. In Tabun (Farrand, in Jelinek et al., 1973), Layer F with its Upper Acheulean occupation consists of sand dunes similar to those of the sandstone ridges. (Up to now, this is the only known occurrence of a deposit that originated in the sea inside a cave along the Israeli coast.) According to Farrand, the most probable sources for this sand were dunes which were deposited in the now-consolidated ridge on the nearby 35–45 m terrace by the high sea level. This ridge is, thus, correlated with the basal part of Evron ridge, as already mentioned. It is supposed that in Tabun as well as in the Evron ridge the *Strombus* phase ingression is present—the last one that reached as far east as Tabun, ca. 3 km from the sea. (The Mousterian layers in Tabun show that practically no Würmian sand was carried into the cave.) The fact that the overlying Yabrudian (Layer E) at Tabun is also very sandy indicates that here, at least, the Acheulean occupation had ceased *before* the end of the Interglacial. We may, thus, place the end of the Upper Acheulean in general during the end of the last Interglacial, at the latest.

The best known Upper Acheulean assemblages are Kissufim (Ronen et al., 1972) and Evron, Upper Layer (Cycle V) (Gilead and Ronen, in press). Both show a manufacture of fine handaxes, sometimes very thin, with pointed forms largely dominating over rounded ones. Flake tools are practically nondiscernible from Middle Paleolithic ones, and the Levallois technique is widely utilized. Flakes are thin, with butts frequently prepared. Blades are not common. A Yabrudian element is present in both assemblages.

The flake tool element of other Upper Acheulean assemblages has been more briefly reported. On the basis of the handaxe component, Umm-Qatafa (D2 and D1) belongs here (Neuville, 1951; Gilead, 1970), and perhaps Rephaim-Baqa in Jerusalem also belongs here because of the fine flakes, including Levallois examples (Arensburg and Bar-Yosef, 1967). Many Acheulean sites and find-spots that seem to belong here await study. These would include the Avdat sites in the Negev (Marks, this volume), sites in or on the surface layer in the eastern part of the coastal plain (e.g., Beeri, Ein Hashlosha, Naan, Maabarot, Kfar Glikson, to name only a few), and the Mt. Carmel sites of Ein-Tut and Tirat-Carmel (which apart from Tabun, contain the only occurrence of handaxes on the west slope of Mt. Carmel). At Tirat-Carmel, which is planned for excavation, the tools are embedded in an alluvial fill, the lowermost altitude of which is 55 meters. A Mousterian layer overlies the Acheulean alluvium (Ronen, in press).

The Upper Galilee group includes the Baram, Yiron, Sasa, Dalton, and Alma sites. Assigned by Gilead (1970) to the Upper Acheulean phase, recent studies of the Baram (Ronen et al., in press) and Yiron assemblages show some peculiar traits, and it is suggested that these two, at least, are earlier than the typical Upper Acheulean of Kissufim-Evron type. The Baram and Yiron assemblages are crude in appearance, with thick handaxes, although made by soft hammer. Backed handaxes are typical here. The flakes are particularly big, thick, and almost exclusively with prepared, Clactonian-type bases and with a negligible Levallois component. Peculiar to Baram is a high proportion of end-scrapers. All the known Galilee sites are located on the edge of basalt covers (Gilead, 1970), except for the Sasa assemblage. Until more studies are carried out here, the Baram-Yiron assemblages cannot be more precisely dated than pre—Upper Acheulean.

The Acheulean of Yabrudian facies—with some characteristic flat, small bifaces and a rich flake industry of Yabrudian-Charentian characteristics—is the latest industry with handaxes found in Israel. It has been found only in caves so far, except for one possible open-air occurrence near Eyal in the eastern Central coastal plain. It is best represented in Layer E of Tabun, where its evolution can be traced over 7 m of deposits. There seems no point in summarizing Garrod's observations here, since the report of the newly conducted excavations by Jelinek is now awaited. Chronologically, the Yabrudian occupies the end of the last Interglacial (Farrand, in Jelinek et al., 1973).

Several early Paleolithic occurrences of nonhandaxe assemblages are known to exist—in the lowest layers of Umm-Qatafa and of Tabun, as well as the Amudian or pre-Aurignacian within the Yabrudian complex in Tabun and Zuttiyeh. All the assemblages hitherto published are too poor to allow for a fruitful discussion. The Amudian of Tabun and its relations to the Yabrudian will be better known when Jelinek's excavation is reported.

SUMMARY OF EARLY PALEOLITHIC

Except for the cave deposits of Umm-Qatafa and Tabun, all Acheulean sites are open settlements, likely to have been used repeatedly and over long periods of time.

Some sites (Ubeidiya, Evron, Gesher Benot-Yaacov) are sealed in distinct layers, but the majority of assemblages could represent more than one phase of Acheulean (Maayan Baruch, Galilee group, Kissufim, Upper Evron, etc.). Patina might be of help here were this phenomenon better understood.

One is struck by two trends when examining the distribution of Acheulean find-spots in Israel and in Jordan. First is the growing number of find-spots as one proceeds in time, and second is the independence of this pattern from the present-day hydrographical system.

The first trend—the increase in the number of find-spots with time—may of course be explained by the vagaries of chance finds and by varying depth of burial, which are both legitimate considerations. In spite of this, it is believed that the pattern represents, at least to some extent, a real trend. Otherwise, later industries should be better represented than the Upper Acheulean (while the contrary is true, as we shall see). Thus, there is one site of the Ubeidiya type, with a few others suspected to have existed (Bar-Yosef and Tchernov, 1972). The next phase, the "Middle Acheulean," contemporary with Evron Cycles III and IV, comprises less than ten sites. The Upper Acheulean of Evron Cycle V type is represented by at least 50 and possibly more sites and find-spots (Gilead, 1961, 1970a), including the two cave occurrences. This slowly growing population made use of many water bodies that then existed—lakes, long-standing seasonal marshes, and rivers. The preferred biotopes were those of open woodland or savanna (Negev, coastal plain) or the forest margins (mountain sites). Remains of elephant characterize almost all Acheulean occupations, together with deer, horse, hippopotamus, and other grassland species. Ubeidiya is the only site where fish and water turtle remains were found. There seems little justification for rejecting these from the food supply, as is hinted by the excavator (Bar-Yosef, in press).

The other trend mentioned above, that concerning the distribution of Acheulean sites, is its lack of conformity to present-day conditions to an extent that is not repeated in the prehistoric record except, perhaps, during Epipaleolithic times. The Acheuleans occupied territories that are today devoid of any water sources, such as the Transjordanian Plateau (Garrod, 1956), Avdat in the Central Negev

(Marks, this volume), the Upper Galilee plateau (Ronen et al., in press), and the Kissufim area (Ronen et al., 1972). In Avdat and Baram occupation must have depended on the Zin and Dishon Rivers, respectively, before their deep incision started. Both rivers flow eastward to the Jordan Graben, and a clue is thus provided for chronological development of these major stream systems, today incised in steep gorges 100 m or more below the Acheulean occupations. The areas mentioned above remained practically unoccupied later on until historical times. To the extent that Mousterian or Upper Paleolithic sites do exist, their distribution closely follows that of present-day perennial water sources (for example, Ein-Avdat, Ein Sharuhen, etc.). The Upper Galilee plateau was not occupied again until the Neolithic, with a settlement in the river bed (Ronen et al., in press).

Post-Acheulean times in Israel seem to have been less favorable, as shall be seen further. The general trend toward a growing desiccation claimed by Tchernov (1968) on grounds of microfaunal studies seems to be confirmed by apparent population density (Table 3).

THE MIDDLE PALEOLITHIC

The beginning of the Middle Paleolithic in Israel can be dated to the onset of Last Glaciation on the following basis. In Tabun, the sand penetration that probably marks the last Interglacial ceases between the Yabrudian of Layer E and the lowest Mousterian of Layer D. Pollen analysis confirms this sedimentological observation, showing gradually increasing pluvial conditions from F to D (Horowitz, in Jelinek et al., 1973). Further, in the coastal plain, Mousterian is found in a thick red lehm intercalated between two sandstones. There is good reason to assign the lower at these to the *Strombus* stage of last Interglacial and the upper one to an early Würm high sea, which in Lebanon, too, overlies Mousterian deposits. This last phase has not been satisfactorily dated, but the date of 90,000 + 20,000 B.P. for the *Strombus* phase seems acceptable (Sanlaville, 1971).

Mousterian occupation is known at present from twenty-four caves and approximately twenty-five open sites or find-spots. The longest Middle Paleolithic sequences in Israel—Tabun, Kebara, and Qafza are not yet published, so that the basic data for the evolution within the Mousterian is practically negligible. The forthcoming analysis of Tabun industries doubtless will throw new light on this problem.

From the few sites that have been published or analyzed within the last few years, the Mousterian of Israel can be defined broadly as a typical Mousterian with Levallois technique, according to West European terminology. None of the other Mousterian groups of the classical area has been found so far in Israel. Within this broad definition, several subtypes are clearly distinguished. The major variables are the relative frequencies of (*a*) the Levallois technique; (*b*) sidescrapers; and (*c*) the Upper Paleolithic component.

The Levallois technique is present in all Middle Paleolithic assemblages. Normally, in fairly high percentage (about half of all flakes), it reaches up to 70%–80% in some of Garrod's series from El-Wad (personal observation based on the samples kept in Jerusalem). It is hard to evaluate whether these high percentages are real or perhaps are due to selective collection. On the other hand, a Levallois index of twenty is found at Tirat-Carmel (Ronen, in press).

The open site Rosh Ein-Mor, near Avdat in the Negev (Marks and Crew, 1972), has a Levallois index varying between eleven and sixteen. For the south of Israel, however, Levallois technique takes a special facies which may cause some problems of classification. By this is meant the "elongated Mousterian" of the Judean Desert type (e.g., Abu Sif [Neuville, 1951], Larikba [Vandermeersch, 1966]) to which Rosh Ein-Mor also belongs. This type of Mousterian exhibits a complete transition from typical Levallois points, through elongated points, to blades, all manufactured by essentially the same technique. The Levallois index will vary depending on how these blades and pointed blades are classified, a matter which still awaits agreement.

The Mousterian, rich in elongated points and blades, seems to be dominant in the south and not represented in the north, although it is present in Tabun D (Jelinek et al., in press).

In most of the known series sidescrapers are present in fairly high proportions (25%–40%). In several instances, though, the percentages drop to between 5% and 12%. Such is the case at Rosh Ein-Mor, Amud cave (11%), El-Wad, Layer G (11%), and Layer F (5%). For El-Wad and Amud, this is based on personal observations of samples kept in Jerusalem. It may be noted that the series mentioned have nothing else in common with the West European Mousterian, which is equally poor in sidescrapers.

Some Mousterian assemblages in Israel have a very high proportion of the Upper Paleolithic group. Rosh Ein-Mor has 21%–26%, and Tirat-Carmel has 20%. This character

TABLE 3. NUMBER OF SITES PRESENTLY KNOWN BY REGION AND PERIOD

	Coastal Plain	Galilee Cave	Galilee Open	Carmel Cave	Carmel Open	Judea Cave	Judea Open	Negev	Jordan Valley	Total
Lower Paleolithic	>50	1	>10	1	2	1	Several	Several	>4	>70
Middle Paleolithic	> 3	6		11	1	7		20		48
Upper Paleolithic		2		5		6		14	1	28
Epipaleolithic	>30	2		5		6		21	>5	>70

does not seem to have a temporal significance since Rosh Ein-Mor gave a Carbon 14 date of >50,000 B.P. (Marks, this volume). Curiously, it may be noted that several series claimed to be "transitional" to Upper Paleolithic are very poor in Upper Paleolithic elements—El-Wad G (1%) and El-Wad F (11%). On the other hand, Upper Paleolithic elements are well represented in some far older assemblages such as the Amudian or the Acheulean of Baram, 25%, (Ronen, in press).

In spite of the presence of Charentian-type Early Paleolithic in Israel (Yabrudian), no Charentian-type Mousterian is known at present.

The end of the Middle Paleolithic phase is unknown both typologically and chronologically. In many caves a marked water activity has reworked and redeposited the upper Mousterian layers (Vandermeersch, personal communication; cf. Bar-Yosef and Vandermeersch, 1972). It is expected that the latest Mousterian occupation in the caves was washed away or mingled with earlier phases. It is fully agreed with Bar-Yosef and Vandermeersch that the entire notion of "Transitional Culture" (Garrod, 1952, 1953, 1955) emerged from a mixture of Upper and Middle Paleolithic layers either by turbulent water or by excavators. As has been noted, the Upper Paleolithic element may be quite low in some "transitional" assemblages; the Emirah point, that "trace element" of the Transitional Culture, has actually been found from Upper Acheulean at Evron (Gilead and Ronen, in press) through Upper Paleolithic at Sefunim (author's excavation). The Emirah Point is perhaps of some regional significance, since its frequency seems to decrease from Lebanon southward (Copeland and Wescombe, 1965, 1966).

Chamfered pieces, typical elements of the earliest Upper Paleolithic in Lebanon, have been unconvincingly claimed to exist only in one Israeli site, Amud Cave (Watanabe, 1970), which is probably a typical Middle Paleolithic cave rich in Levallois products.

It seems to have been established that two distinct types of man are associated with the Mousterian of Israel—a Neanderthaloid found in Tabun C (Keith, 1939) and Amud (Suzuki and Takai, 1970), and a modern man such as found at Qafza and apparently at Skhul (Vandermeersch, 1972). The earliest burials found in Israel are Mousterian, and after the 1973 season Qafza has become the largest Mousterian cemetery known today, with at least 12 individuals (Vandermeersch, personal communication).

In the north of Israel, five open-air Mousterian sites—or rather find-spots—are known, all but one in a red lehm (Garrod and Gardner, 1935; Farrand and Ronen, in press). Since this layer is mostly buried, the low number of sites cannot be regarded as representative. Of these, only the one at Tirat-Carmel could be studied (Ronen, in press). Located in alluvial-colluvial deposits on the west slope of Mt. Carmel, a habitation site and a nearby workshop are known (Table 4).

Recently several open-air Mousterian sites were found in the south (19 near Avdat, Marks et al., 1971; one near Ein Sharuhen, Collins, personal communication). The only one published is Rosh Ein-Mor, already mentioned above.

The distribution of the Mousterian open sites is distinguished in that it closely follows the location of present-day perennial springs (Ein Avdat, Ein Sharnhen, Tirat-Carmel spring, etc.). This Mousterian habitation pattern differs from that of the Acheulean. Some wide areas that were occupied by the Acheulean (Baram Plateau, Kissufim area) were totally or largely deserted during the Middle Paleolithic. At the same time, there are indications for a lowering of the water table since Mousterian time (as evidenced by the fossil springs in the Avdat area). On the whole, though, one may assume that topography and hydrology have changed little since the Mousterian, whereas a radical change occurred between the Acheulean and the Mousterian.

THE UPPER PALEOLITHIC

With the "Transitional Phase" eliminated, the Upper Paleolithic in Israel consists solely of the Aurignacian phase. To date, no "chanfreins" phase has been discovered. It is not clear whether the erosion that had effected the Mousterian layers in caves occurred between the Middle and Upper Paleolithic or during Early Upper Paleolithic, thus possibly washing away some of the latter as well.

The beginning of the Aurignacian is as yet undated. It is fairly homogeneous in Israel, with endscrapers, carinated endscrapers, and burins as dominant elements. Endscrapers are normally more numerous than burins. The frequency of carinated, relative to flat endscrapers, is largely variable, with no clear temporal significance.

Among the burins, dihedral types almost always greatly outnumber those on truncation. Retouched blades are quite frequent, but Aurignacian retouch is rare. The El-Wad points (formerly Font-Yves or Krems) are, according to Garrod (1954), more frequent in the lower Aurignacian than in the upper. At present, this can be seen only at the El-Wad and Kebara caves. Other occurrences with numerous El-Wad points (e.g. Qafza, Layers 9 and 8, Ronen and Vandermeersch, in press) await dating. In most Aurignacian assemblages El-Wad points appear in small quantities (Table 5).

Bone tools—mainly points—are clearly shaped for the first time. Some bones were clearly used, or even flaked, in the Mousterian of Geula Cave (Wreschner et al., 1967) and even earlier (e.g. Ubeidiya, Holon).

The only Upper Paleolithic site with a different aspect is Qafza (Ronen and Vandermeersch, in press). Typologically it lacks carinated scrapers altogether and has abundant El-Wad points and microliths. Although the series recently excavated by Vandermeersch are poor, the more abundant series of Neuville show the same characteristics (Bar-Yosef, personal communication). Perhaps the Upper Paleolithic of Qafza should not be termed "Aurignacian."

The Upper Paleolithic of Israel is further typified by the lack of art or ornament and by the extreme paucity of

TABLE 4. PRINCIPAL ESSENTIAL[1]INDICES OF EARLY AND MIDDLE PALEOLITHIC ASSEMBLAGES

	Acheulean			Mousterian		
	Baram[2]	Kissufim[3]	Evron[4]	Tirat-Carmel[5]	Shovach[6]	Rosh Ein Mor[7]
Levallois Index	2	54	33	20	41	11–16
Facetting Index	15	73	47	34	65	46–56
Blade Index	3	16	23	15	12	11–22
Typological Levallois Index	14	49	27	16	45	49–60
Racloir Index	20	35	45	33	24	5–12
Mousterian Group	26	45	49	35	30	6–14
Upper Paleolithic Group	25	8	13	20	15	21–26
Denticulate Group	6	5	5	10	7	8–10

[1] Except for the Typological Levallois Index.
[2] Ronen et al., in press
[3] Ronen et al., 1972
[4] Gilead & Ronen, in press

[5] Ronen, in press
[6] Binford, 1966
[7] Marks & Crew, 1973

human remains. As for art, the Middle Paleolithic pattern is continued, whereby abundant fragments of ocher are the only hint of aesthetic values. In the lowest Upper Paleolithic of Qafza, a well-shaped pallet made of basalt served for grinding ocher.

When human remains are concerned, one cannot help but wonder at the seeming disappearance of the custom of burial. Compared with the abundant burials of the Middle Paleolithic, only one is known from the Upper Paleolithic, apparently of a late stage. It is a woman, found in a semi-flexed position near a living floor at the site of Nahal Ein Gev in the Jordan Valley (Bar-Yosef, personal communication). Extremely few other human remains are known. It is assumed, but with no direct evidence, that burials in the Upper Paleolithic were outside of caves, either on cave terraces or farther away. In fact, none of the caves in the northern part of Israel have Upper Paleolithic deposits on their terraces—Mousterian layers directly underlie Kebaran or Natufian layers. Furthermore, in the coastal plain of Mt. Carmel no deposit of Upper Paleolithic age is known, and naturally there are no open-air sites of this period. At Tirat-Carmel the Mousterian colluvial layers form the top of the section, with no later deposits. It is not known if they were eroded or simply absent. If burials were indeed on terraces, this may account for their disappearance, at least in the Mt. Carmel area.

The distribution and pattern of Upper Paleolithic habitation seem to indicate, in the northern part of the country, some deterioration of living conditions. Eighteen caves north of Jerusalem are known to have been inhabited during the Mousterian, and only seven were inhabited during the Upper Paleolithic, with a far smaller area occupied in each cave than during the Mousterian. There appears to be no case for claiming a wealth of Upper Paleolithic sites now submerged on the continental shelf. It has been noted that occupations exist in red lehms, both Mousterian

and Epipaleolithic, and that, in between these red lehms, soils that should date from the Upper Paleolithic did not develop into red lehm but indicate a near-shore environment. Hence there are no grounds to support the contention that the coastal plain of Israel was far wider than the present one during the Upper Paleolithic. It is possible that in the northern part of the country and along the entire coastal plain conditions during the Middle Würm differed markedly from those of Early and Late Würm. A similar reduction in the number of Upper Paleolithic settlements occurred in Lebanon (Suzuki and Kobori, 1970) and apparently in Jordan, too (Garrod, 1956).

In the southern half of the country Upper Paleolithic settlements are almost as numerous (Judea 6, Negev 14) as Middle Paleolithic ones (Judea 6, Negev 20), but not necessarily in the same localities (Table 3). It may be added that open-air Upper Paleolithic sites are near present-day perennial springs and that all areas where Mousterian habitation is unknown are also devoid of Upper Paleolithic habitation.

THE EPIPALEOLITHIC

The late Würm, from about 20,000 B.P., is characterized by the microlithic group of industries, best known from the work of Bar-Yosef (1970). Although no minute stratigraphical continuum can be observed in Israel, the Epipaleolithic industries seem to stem from the local Aurignacian. The ordinary tools—endscrapers, burins, and retouched blades— continue the former tradition in form and technique. Their relative frequencies, however, become more diversified than in the Aurignacian, with a general tendency toward an increase in burins and a decrease in endscrapers. Within the burins, those on truncation are generally more numerous than in the Aurignacian.

The best guide for subdividing the microlithic industries was found to be the microliths. The following criteria were chosen by Bar-Yosef: (a) Kebaran proper, with a high ratio

TABLE 5.
PRINCIPAL INDICES OF SOME UPPER PALEOLITHIC ASSEMBLAGES

	El Wad E(249)	El Wad D₂(230)	El Wad D₁(258)	El Wad C(338)	Kebara Upp. Pal.(290)	Hayohim D₃(125)	Sefunim 8(173)
Endscraper Index	23	26	35	22	26	22	25
Carinated Endscrapers	14	40	21	7	5	17	18
Burin Index	28	11	21	52	5	13	14
Dihedral Burins	20	8	15	40	2	8	12
Truncated Burins	6	3	5	11	1.5	4	1.5
Retouched Blades	8	12	7	3	6	10	18
El Wad Points	7	0.4	1.5		17		1.5
Microliths		0.4		3	3	11	6
Sidescrapers	4	4	1	2	10	6	0.5

[1] Author's count of samples in Jerusalem. [3] Bar-Yosef, personal communication.
[2] Bar-Yosef, personal communication (Stekelis's excavations). [4] Author's excavations.
[Total number of series indicated in parentheses]

of microliths (30%–70%) and few or no geometrics. The main type of microlith in Israel may be the micropoint or the obliquely truncated bladelet. Falita points are found only in the Jordan Valley (Ein Gev I and II) and are therefore considered to belong to the Transjordanian-Lebanese province rather than to the Israeli one; (b) Geometric Kebaran A. In this facies geometric microliths become numerous, mainly trapezes and rectangles, occasionally with some triangles and lunates; (c) Geometric Kebaran B. Here geometric forms are always more numerous than non-geometric, and lunates dominate together with triangles and trapeze-rectangles. Since lunates are the typical element of the Natufian, a contemporaneity of these assemblages was proposed (Bar-Yosef, 1970).

In addition to the mentioned territorial differences, further techno-typological features may denote even smaller territorial traditions or temporal variations (for example, the extent to which microburins are present).

The Epipaleolithic in Israel brings the first direct evidence for the onset of vegetal food processing. At three sites (Ein Gev I, near Tiberias and Hafziba and Hedera V, in the Central coastal plain) mortars and pestles made of basalt were found. These are deep mortars, unlike the shallow pallet-like form that is known earlier from Qafza and which carries clear traces of ocher (Ronen and Vandermeersch, in press). The deep mortars (about 25 cm high and 20 cm in upper diameter) were possibly intended for cereal processing. The Ein Gev assemblage, classified as Kebaran proper, was dated to 13,750 B.C. and had two sickle blades in a thousand tools (Bar-Yosef, 1970). The neighboring sites of Hefziba and Hedera V (Geometric Kebaran A and Kebaran, respectively) are not yet dated, but there are no sickle blades in either. Hence, the deep mortar preceded the invention of the sickle blade.

Ein Gev is the only Kebaran site so far known to have a circular stone structure. Hefziba, a 2,000 sq. m occupation of which 40 sq. m were excavated, did not reveal any signs of stone structures; hence, it is assumed that only light structures existed there. Also, Hedera V did not yield any signs of a structure during a short testing (Bar-Yosef and Phillips, personal communication). It is possible that the stone structure in Ein Gev is a "northern territory" feature, together with the Falita point and the microgravette. Seemingly, the circular stone structure appeared in Israel only in the Natufian.

The Epipaleolithic habitation pattern differs radically from the former Aurignacian one. Large open-air sites exist in the Jordan Valley, the coastal plain, and the Negev, together with small and poor cave dwellings that seem secondary. The number of sites during this period increases to the point of approximately matching the number of Acheulean sites. On the coastal plain Epipaleolithic sites are on or in a thick red lehm.

Along with cereals, *Bos, Gazella*, and *Sus* were the main food supply. No specific fishing tools had yet been devised, and no typical shell middens exist on the Israeli littoral. Concentrations of *Glycimeris* do exist, but their significance is conjectural. There are grounds to believe that a good deal of the Epipaleolithic is to be found on the submerged continental shelf.

The socioeconomic changes that must have taken place during the Epipaleolithic (Binford, 1968) are reflected by the growth of site size, by the diminution of implements, and by the growing tendency toward highly standard geometric forms. Apart from the evident growth of the community, a "geometric mental template" would disclose a society better and more tightly organized than ever before. Possibly, as Binford has suggested, such an organization became necessary due to a growing diversity of food resources and a growing complexity in manpower division—trends that culminated in the Natufian.

The Natufian, with a tool kit similar to Kebaran Geometric B, introduced several novelties. It was the first phase to evidence wide use of the sickle blade, manufacture of mortars and stone bowls not readily transported, massive construction, and the presence of cemeteries with between 50 and 100 individuals. These innovations probably disclose a sedentary way of life. The Natufians further introduced special fishing tools and art, in the form of decoration on stone vessels and sculptures in bone or stone (Stekelis, 1960b). Perhaps the increasing complication of daily life brought about social organization so complex as to give rise to a formal leadership, reflected in the non-egalitarian Natufian burial customs.

It seems likely then that domestication of cereals, if not that of animals, was already practiced by the Natufians (Ducos, 1968). The lack of "domestic" characters in Natufian remains can no longer be regarded as a convincing negative argument (Helbaek, 1966; Hole, Flannery and Neely, 1969).

The Natufian occupies the time between 10,000 B.C. and 8,000 B.C., the end of the Paleolithic. With the onset of the Holocene at 8,000 B.C., the Neolithic begins in Israel with the invention of the ax, which possibly denotes the necessity to fell trees in order to prepare new fields. Simultaneously, the first manifestation of urban life appears in Jericho, and soon after in Catal Huyuk. These developments lie outside this survey.

BIBLIOGRAPHY

ARENSBURG, B. and BAR-YOSEF, O., 1967. "Yacimiento Paleolitico en el Valle de Refaim, Jerusalem, Israel." *Ampurias* 29:117-33.

AVNIMELECH, M., 1952. "Quaternary Sediments of the Coastal Plain of Israel." *Bulletin of the Research Council of Israel* 2(11):51-57.

BAR-YOSEF, O., 1970. "The Epi-Palaeolithic Cultures in Palestine." Ph.D. dissertation, Hebrew University.

————, in press. *Archaeological Occurrences in the Middle Pleistocene of Israel.* Burg Wartenstein Symposium No. 58, July 2-11, 1973.

————, and TCHERNOV, E., 1967. "Archaeological Finds and the Fossil Faunas of the Natufian and Microlithic Industries at Hayonim Cave (Western Galilee, Israel)." *Israel Journal of Zoology* 15:104-40.

————, and TCHERNOV, E., 1970. "The Natufian Bone Industry of Ha-Yonim Cave." *Israel Exploration Journal* 20:141-50.

————, and TCHERNOV, E., 1972. "On the Palaeo-ecological History of the Site of Ubeidiya." *Proceedings of the Israel Academy of Sciences and Humanities.*

————, and VANDERMEERSCH, B., 1972. "The Stratigraphical and Cultural Problems of the Passage from Middle to Upper Paleolithic in Palestinian Caves." In *The Origin of Homo Sapiens*, edited by F. Bordes, pp. 221-26. Proceedings of the Paris Symposium, 2-5 September 1969. Paris: UNESCO.

BINFORD, L. R., 1968. "Post-Pleistocene Adaptations." In *New Perspectives in Archaeology*, edited by S. R. Binford and L. R. Binford, pp. 313-41. Chicago: Aldine-Atherton.

BINFORD, S. R., 1966. "Me'arat Shovakh (Mugharet-esh-Shubbabiq)." *Israel Exploration Journal* 16:18-32;96-103.

BORDES, F., 1967. "Considerations sur la Typologie et les Techniques dans le Paléolithique." *Quartär* 18:25-55.

BUTZER, K., 1971. *Environment and Archaeology.* Chicago: Aldine-Atherton.

COPELAND, L., and WESCOMBE, P. J., 1965. "Inventory of Stone Age Sites in Lebanon." *Mélanges de l'Université Saint-Joseph* 41:29-175.

————, and WESCOMBE, P. J., 1966. "Inventory of Stone Age Sites in Lebanon, Part II, North, South and East-Central Lebanon." *Mélanges de l'Université Saint-Joseph* 42:1-174.

DAN, J., and YAALON, D. H., 1971. "On the Origin and Nature of the Palaeopedological Formations in the Coastal Desert Fringe Areas of Israel." In *Palaeopedology—Origin, Nature and Dating of Paleosols*, edited by D. H. Yaalon. Jerusalem.

DUCOS, P., 1968. *L'Origine des Animaux Domestiques en Palestine.* Bordeaux: Publications de l'Institut de Préhistoire de l'Université de Bordeaux.

FARRAND, W. R., and RONEN, A., in press. "Observation on the Kurkar-Hamra Succession in the Carmel Coastal Plain, Israel."

GARROD, D. A. E., 1952. "A Transitional Industry from the Base of the Upper Palaeolithic in Palestine and Syria." *Journal of the Royal Anthropological Institute* 81:121-29.

————, 1953. "The Relations between Southwest Asia and Europe in the Later Palaeolithic Age, with Special Reference to the Origins of the Upper Palaeolithic Blade Cultures." *Journal of World History* 1:13-38.

————, 1954. " Excavations at the Mugharet el-Kebara, Mount Carmel, 1931: The Aurignacian Industries." *Proceedings of the Prehistoric Society* 20:155-92.

————, 1955. "The Mugharet el-Emireh in Lower Galilee; Type Station of the Emiran Industry." *Journal of the Royal Anthropological Institute* 85:141-62.

————, 1960. "The Flint Implements." In *North Arabian Desert Archaeological Survey, 1925-50*, edited by H. Field, pp. 111-24. Papers of the Peabody Museum of Archaeology and Ethnology, Harvard University 45, no. 2.

————, and BATE, D. M. A., 1937. *The Stone Age of Mount Carmel*, vol. 1. Oxford: Clarendon Press.

————, and GARDNER, E. W., 1935. "Pleistocene Coastal Deposits in Palestine." *Nature* 135:908.

GILEAD, D., 1970*a*. "Early Palaeolithic Cultures in Israel and the Near East." Ph.D. dissertation, Hebrew University.

————, 1970*b*. "Handaxe Industries in Israel and the Near East." *World Archaeology* 2:1-11.

————, and RONEN, A., in press. *Acheulean Industries from Evron, Western Galilee Coastal Plain.*

HELBAEK, H., 1966. "Pre-Pottery Neolithic Farming at Beidha." Appendix A to "Five Seasons at the Pre-Pottery Neolithic Village of Beidha in Jordan," by D. Kirkbride, pp. 61-66. *Palestine Exploration Quarterly*.

HOLE, F.; FLANNERY, K. V.; and NEELY, J. A., 1969. *Prehistory and Human Ecology of the Deh Luran Plain*. Memoirs of the Museum of Anthropology, No. 1. Ann Arbor: University of Michigan.

HOROWITZ, A., 1968. "Upper Pleistocene-Holocene Climate and Vegetation of the Northern Jordan Valley (Israel)." Ph.D. dissertation, Hebrew University.

————, 1973. "Development of the Hula Basin, Israel." *Israel Journal of Earth Sciences* 22:107-39.

HOWELL, C., 1959. "Upper Pleistocene Stratigraphy and Early Man in the Levant." *Proceedings of the American Philosophical Society* 103:1-65.

HUCKRIEDE, R., and WEISEMANN, G., 1968. "Der Jungpleistozäne Pluvial-See von El-Jafr und Weitere Daten zum Quartär Jordaniens." *Geologica et Palaeontologica* 2:73-95.

ISSAR, A., 1961. "Subsurface Geology and Hydrology of the Shefela and Sharon Plains." Ph.D. dissertation.

————, 1968. "Geology of the Central Coastal Plain of Israel." *Israel Journal of Earth Sciences* 17:16-29.

————, and KAFRI, U., 1972. "Neogene and Pleistocene Geology of the Western Galilee Coastal Plain." *Bulletin of the Geological Survey, Ministry of Development, Israel* 53:1-14.

————, and PICARD, L., 1969. "Sur le Tyrrhénien des Côtes d'Israel et du Liban." *Bulletin de l'Association Française pour l'Étude du Quaternaire* 6:35-41.

————, and PICARD, L., 1971. "On Pleistocene Shorelines in the Coastal Plain of Israel." *Quaternaria* 15:267-72.

ITZHAKI, Y., 1961. "Pleistocene Shorelines in the Coastal Plain of Israel." *Bulletin of the Geological Survey of Israel* 32:1-9.

JELINEK, A. J.; FARRAND, W. R.; HAAS, G.; HOROWITZ, A.; and GOLDBERG, P., 1973. "New Excavations at the Tabun Cave, Mount Carmel, Israel, 1967-1972: A Preliminary Report." *Paleorient* 1(2).

LEONTYEV, O. K., 1969. "Flandrian Transgression and the Genesis of Barrier-Bars." In *Quatenary Geology and Climate*, edited by H. E. Wright, pp. 146-49. Washington, D. C.

MARKS, A. E., and CREW, H., 1972. "Rosh Ein Mor, an Open-Air Mousterian Site in the Central Negev, Israel." *Current Anthropology* 13:591-93.

————; CREW, H.; FERRING, R.; and PHILLIPS, J., 1972. "Prehistoric Sites near Har Harif." *Israel Exploration Journal* 22:73-85.

————; PHILLIPS, J.; CREW, H.; and FERRING, R., 1971. "Prehistoric Sites near 'En-'Avdat in the Negev." *Israel Exploration Journal* 21:13-24.

MICHELSON, H., 1968. "The Geology of Mount Carmel Coastal Plain." M. Sc. thesis, Hebrew University.

NEEV, D., and EMERY, K. O., 1967. "The Dead Sea." *Bulletin of the Geological Survey of Israel* 41:1-47.

NEUVILLE, R., 1951. *Le Paléolithique et le Mésolithique du Désert de Judée*. Archives de l'Institut de Paléontologie humaine mémoire 24.

NIR, D., 1970. *Geomorphology of Israel*. Jerusalem (in Hebrew).

OLAMI, J., 1962. "Grotte du Sheikh Suleiman (Ornith), Mont Carmel, Israel." *Atti VI Congr. Int. Sc. Preist. e Protost., Roma*, pp. 173-76.

PERROT, J., 1955. "Le Paléolithique Supérieur d'El Quseir et de Masaraq en Na'au (Palestine)." *Bulletin de la Societé Préhistorique Française* 52:493-506.

————, 1968. "La préhistoire Palestinienne." *Supplément au Dictionnaire de la Bible* 8(43):286-446.

PICARD, L., 1952. "The Pleistocene Peat of Lake Hula." *Bulletin of the Research Council of Israel* 2G:147–56.

————, 1963. "The Quaternary in the Northern Jordan Valley." *Proceedings of the Israel Academy of Sciences and Humanities* 1(4):1-34.

————, 1965. "The Geological Evolution of the Quaternary in the Central-Northern Jordan Graben, Israel." In *International Studies of the Quaternary*, edited by H. E. Wright, Jr., and D. G. Frey, pp. 337-66.

————, and BAIDA, U., 1966. "Stratigraphic Position of the Ubeidiya Formation." *Proceedings of the Israel Academy of Sciences and Humanities*, Section of Sciences No. 4.

POMERANCHBLUM, M., 1966. "The Distribution of Heavy Minerals and their Hydraulic Equivalents in Sediments of the Mediterranean Continental Shelf of Israel." *Jour. of Sedi. and Petri.* 36:162-74.

PRAUSNITZ, M. W., 1969. "The Sequence of Early to Middle Paleolithic Flint Industries along the Galilean Littoral." *Israel Exploration Journal* 19:129-36.

RAVIKOVITCH, S., 1969. *Manual and Map of Soils of Israel*. Jerusalem.

RONEN, A., 1973. "Observations on the Pleistocene of the Coastal Plain of Israel." *Mitqufat ha-Even* 11:43-47 (in Hebrew).

————, in press. *Réflexions sur l'Origine, la Genèse et la Chronologie des Grès Dunaires Calcifiés Dites "Première" et "Deuxième" sur le Littoral Israelien*.

————, and AMIEL, A., in press. *Pleistocene Stratigraphy and Fossil Soils in the Vicinity of Evron, Western Galilee Coastal Plain*.

————, and DAIVIS, M., in press. *Tirat-Carmel, a Mousterian Open-Air Site in Israel*.

————; GILEAD, D.; BRUDER, G.; and MELLER, P., in press. *Notes on the Pleistocene Geology and Prehistory of the Central Dishon Valley, Upper Galilee, Israel*.

————; GILEAD, D.; SHACHNAI, E.; and SAUL, A., 1972. "Upper Acheulean in the Kissufim Region." *Proceedings of the American Philosophical Society* 116:68-96.

_____, and VANDERMEERSCH, B., in press. *The Upper Palaeolithic Industries of Qafza, Israel.*

SANLAVILLE, P., 1969. "Les bas niveaux marins pleistocènes du Liban." *Mediterranée* 3:25-792.

_____, 1971. "Sur le tyrrhénien libanais." *Quaternaria* 15:239-48.

SLATKINE, A., and ROHRLICH, V., 1966. "Données nouvelles sur les niveaux marins Quaternaires du Mont Carmel." *Israel Journal of Earth Sciences* 15:57-63.

STEKELIS, M., 1960a. "The Paleolithic Deposits of Jisr Banat Yaqub." *Bulletin of the Research Council of Israel* 9G:63-90.

_____, 1960b. "The Mesolithic Art of Eretz-Israel." *Eretz-Israel* 6:21-24.

_____, and GILEAD, D., 1966. "Ma'ayan Barukh, a Lower Palaeolithic Site in Upper Galilee." *Mitqufat ha-Even* 8.

SUZUKI, H., and KOBORI, I. (eds.), 1970. *Report of the Reconnaissance Survey on Palaeolithic Sites in Lebanon and Syria.* Bulletin No. 1, University Museum, University of Tokyo.

TCHERNOV, E., 1968. *Succession of Rodent Faunas during the Upper Pleistocene of Israel.* Hamburg: Mammalia Depicta.

VANDERMEERSCH, B., 1966. "L'Industrie Moustérienne de Larikba." *L'Anthropologie* 70:123-30.

_____, 1969. "Découverte d'un objet en ocre avec traces d'utilisation dans le Moustérien de Qafza (Israel)." *Bulletin de la Société Préhistorique Française* 66:157-58.

_____, 1972. "Récentes découvertes de squelettes humains à Qafzeh (Israel): Essai d'interprétation." In *The Origin of Homo Sapiens*, edited by F. Bordes, pp. 49-54. Proceedings of the Paris Symposium, 2-5 September 1969. Paris: UNESCO.

WATANABE, H., 1970. "A Palaeolithic Industry from the Amud Cave," In *The Amud Man and his Cave Sites*, edited by H. Suzuki and F. Takai. Tokyo.

WRESCHNER, E.; AVNIMELECH, M.; SCHMID, E.; HAAS, G., and DART, R. A., 1967. "The Geula Caves, Mount Carmel." *Quaternaria* 9:69-140.

YAALON, D. H., 1967. "Factors Affecting the Lithification of Eolianite and Interpretation of its Environmental Significance in the Coastal Plain of Israel." *Jour. of Sedi. and Petr.* 37:1189-99.

_____, and DAN, J., 1967. "Factors Controlling Soil Formation and Distribution in the Mediterranean Coastal Plain of Israel during the Quaternary." In *Quaternary Soils*, edited by R. B. Morrison and H. E. Wright, pp. 322-38. VIIth Congress INQUA 9.

_____, and LARONNE, J., 1971. "Internal Structure in Eolianites and Palaeowinds, Mediterranean Coast, Israel." *Jour. of Sedi. and Petr.* 41:1059-64.

YISRAELI, T., 1963. "Holon." *Israel Exploration Journal* 13:137.

_____, 1967. "Mesolithic Hunters' Industries at Ramat Matred (The Wilderness of Zin), First Report." *Palestine Exploration Quarterly* 99:78-85.

THE LOWER PALEOLITHIC OF LEBANON AND SYRIA

Francis Hours sj
Université Saint-Joseph
Beirut, Lebanon

INTRODUCTION

The early prehistoric periods are the ones during which man was most dependent upon climatic conditions in his environment. Knowledge of these paleoenvironments is, therefore, most important when dealing with these early periods.

As far as Lebanon and Syria are concerned, the essential fact is that the topographic relief forms a series of north-south barriers, parallel to the Levantine coast. Eastward, with each mountainous obstacle, Mediterranean influence diminishes and the climate becomes drier. Of the several zones which are distinguishable, we will divide the region into five, each one of which has its own climatic and vegetational characteristics (Pabot, 1957 and 1959; Niklewski and Van Zeist, 1970). These, described below from west to east, will form a framework for this study.

1. The first zone comprises the coast and the lower foothills of the mountains. However great was the amount of climatic variation during the course of the Quaternary, proximity to the sea and its latitude have always prevented the coast from suffering from intense cold. Moreover, even in dry periods, the reserves of water contained in the limestone mountains of Lebanon and in the Jebel Alaouiye have invariably given rise to perennial water sources. This zone was, therefore, always habitable.

It is also to be noted that the variations in sea level have left traces in the form of raised beaches or marine terraces, which can furnish dating information. Particularly visible in Lebanon, these strandlines have recently been studied in a comprehensive fashion by Sanlaville (1973). A chronology consisting of the Pleistocene part of his scheme is to be found in Table 1.

2. Higher up, conditions change; cold and precipitation make survival difficult here during the winter, and a large part of the mountainous area may be occupied only seasonally. It is not easy to establish the fluctuations in altitude which, during the course of the Quaternary, marked the upper limits of possible permanent habitation, no serious study having been carried out on the subject. In any case, in the mountains above ca. 1,000 m, Paleolithic sites are rare.

3. A third zone is formed by the inland depression, the northern extremity of the African Rift system. This extends from the South Béqaa, through the Orontes Valley into Syria, and ends in the valley of the Kara Su in Turkey.

It is traversed by permanent rivers, and inundated at various points by swamps—in the South Béqaa, the Bouqeia, the Ghab, and the Amuq Plain. This has always constituted an environment favorable to animal life, and there are signs that human occupation began early.

4. The eastern slopes of the mountain complex, bordering the Arabian desert, constitute a fourth zone. Today, just inside the limits of the nondesert zone, it is an arid steppe region where life can hardly be pursued except around springs or along the banks of rivers—the Damascus basin, the Yabroud-Nebek plain, the valley of the Euphrates and its tributaries. The relict forests which still exist on the Jebel Chaar and the Jebel Abd el Aziz show that conditions must have been different during the pluvial periods, particularly during those which correspond to Riss and Würm. So far as we know at the moment, it would seem that the steppe areas were occupied rather late, hardly before the Riss. These occupations were sometimes intensive, but also, apparently, sporadic.

5. Finally, a large part of Syria consists today of true desert, in which certain oases (such as Palmyra and Sukhne) could have been occupied. Up to the time of writing, not enough is known to say more than this.

The basis of our knowledge of the Lower Paleolithic in this large area rests on a relatively substantial amount of research carried out, the results of which are at our disposal. Père Zumoffen was the first to have searched for sites in Lebanon between 1890 and 1910 (Zumoffen, 1900, 1908). Père Bovier-Lapierre visited Upper Galilee in 1907 (Bovier-Lapierre, 1908). From 1925 until 1940 Père Bergy explored the environs of Beirut and the Béqaa (Bergy, 1932). Just before the last war, Rust studied the Yabroud-Nebek region (Rust, 1933), and Père Nasrallah the Qala-moun. Results of this work were assembled in the inventory of Burkhalter (1946-48, 1949-50), who had himself investigated the Alaouite region (Baudouin and Burkhalter, 1930; Burkhalter, 1933). After the war, Fleisch brought his efforts to bear on the Lebanese littoral, Ras Beirut in particular, and on the Béqaa (Fleisch, 1956, 1962). From 1950 until 1966, Van Liere took full advantage of his job as F.A.O. pedologist for the Syrian government to prospect the Damascus basin, the Ghab, the Nagr el-Kebir, and the Jezireh; to him is due the discovery of Latamné, later excavated at his request by Clark (1966a, 1966b). Since 1956 the present writer explored Mount Lebanon and the South Béqaa. Later, the available information concerning Leba-

249

TABLE 1
The Pleistocene Shorelines of Lebanon

Shorelines in m.	The type of formation	Local name	Correlations Mediterranean	Europe		Associated industries
TRANSGRESSION				POST GLACIAL		
R ⎡ −40 to −70 ⎢ −15 to −22 ⎢ ⎣ −5 to −8	SUBMARINE SURFACES and COASTAL DUNES		SOLTANIAN (continental Morocco)	NEO WURM / MESO WURM	WURM IV / LASCAUX / WURM III / LAUFEN PEYRARDS / WURM II	
T ⎡ 8.5 − 10.5 ⎣ ? − 8.5	vermetids vermetids	NAAMIAN	NEOTYRRHENIAN	EO WURM	BRØRUP	Naamé
R 13 − 2			PRESOLTANIAN (continental)		WURM I	
T ⎡ 10 − 13 ⎣ ? −8-10	terrace 10-12 strombus 90,000 B.P.	ENFEAN II b / a	EUTYRRHENIAN (OULJIAN) 85,000 B.P.			Adloun Ras Beirut V
R 20 − 0 T ⎡ 10 − 20 ⎣ ? − 8-10 R 20 − 2 T ? 20	terrace 20-22	ENFEAN I b / a PRE ENFEAN	EEMIAN			
R 45 − ?	conglomerate (Zghorta)		TENSIFTIEN (continental) 140,000	RISS	WARTHE / SAALE	Ras Beirut IV / III Bahsas
T ? − 40-45 R 85 − ? T 5 − 85	II 40-45 I 60-85 MIDDLE TERRACE	JBAILIAN II AB / D JBAILIAN I ABC	PALAEO TYRRHENIAN (ANFATIAN) II / I	HOLSTEIN		Sahel el-Jouané Ras Beirut II / Ras Beirut I a Ras Beirut I b Wadi Aabet Latamné
R			AMIRIAN (continental)	MINDEL (ELSTER)		Ubeidiya
T ⎡ 135 ⎢ 120 ⎣ 100 − 110	II I HIGH TERRACE	ZAQRUNIAN III II I	SICILIAN (MAARIFIAN)	CROMERIAN		Borj Qinnarit
			SALETIAN (continental)	GUNZ		Hama
150 − 170 190 − 220 240 − 260 290 − 320		CHAABIAN	CALABRIAN (MESSAOUDIAN)	PRE GUNZ VILLAFRANCHIAN		

non's prehistory was assembled into an inventory (Copeland and Wescombe, 1965, 1966). Perrot's synthesis appeared in 1968.

During the last few years a team from Saarbruck University has worked in the Béqaa, Wendt in the Nahr el-Kebir region in Syria (Wendt, 1971), while Copeland and Schroeder approached the extreme end of the Lower Paleolithic, one studying the material from the excavations of Garrod at Adloun, the other reinvestigating the site of Jerf Ajla, following its original excavation by Coon (Schroeder, 1969). Finally, in collaboration with J. Besançon, the present writer has tried to clarify the geomorphological stages and early phases of the occupation of the Béqaa (Besançon and Hours, 1970, 1971).

An attempt to place the prehistory of the Levant within the wider geographic framework of the Near East, based on the typology of its industries, was recently made (Hours et al., 1973).

Now, after seventy-five years of research, one can say that the coast (Zone 1) and the central depression (Zone 3) are fairly well known. The mountains and the desert fringes (Zones 2 and 4) have been subjected to only partial examination, while the desert (Zone 5) remains largely an unknown quantity. Figure 1 shows the extent to which Lebanon and Syria have been surveyed for Lower Paleolithic sites. Although the area covered is far from complete, it is enough to give us a general idea of the early periods.

Specifically, the work done so far has produced about 170 Lower Paleolithic sites, of which seven or eight have been the subject of useful preliminary reports, and of which

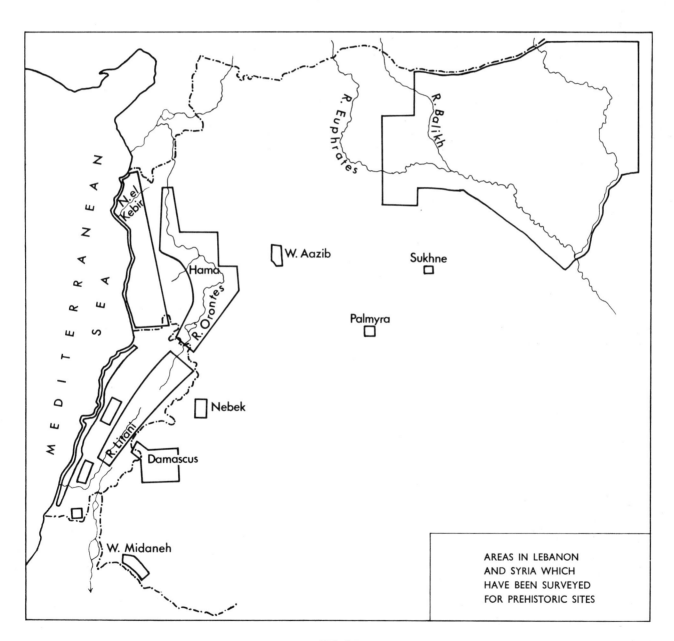

FIG. 1.

only Latamné has been adequately studied (Clark, 1966a, 1966b). This is at once a lot, and yet not so much. A lot in that it indicated the importance of the role played by Syro-Lebanese regions in Levantine prehistory since the Middle Pleistocene, and yet not so much in that all these sites have contributed very little precise information up to the time of writing. Most are really surface sites, identified in the course of surveys, sometimes rapid and unsystematic, in which only the most striking pieces were picked up. Thus, we know the Lower Paleolithic of our region only in its broadest outlines.

The material collected is accessible, some of it in the country of origin, in the Museums of Damascus, Aleppo, and Beirut, in the collections of the American University of Beirut, and above all in those of the Université Saint Joseph, Beirut. Outside of the Levant, collections exist at Cologne (Institut für Ur-und Frühgeschichte) and in Paris (Institut de Paléontologie Humaine and the Musée de l'Homme). Collections in London and Harvard do not include Lower Paleolithic material.

Our imprecise knowledge explains the rather vague divisions into which we have chosen to divide the phases of the Lower Paleolithic of Lebanon and Syria.

Firstly, an early phase is distinguished which we have called Para-Acheulean, attested to by three sites in sure stratigraphic position. Then, given that in the Acheulean itself there is neither any very early material (such as at Ubeidiya), nor anything very late (such as at Tabun F), and given the scarcity of sites in well-dated geological context, we have kept to a bipartite division of the Acheulean proper—an Early Middle Acheulean and a Middle-to-Late Acheulean. We have then dealt with some so-called Tayacian sites. The contact between the end of the Acheulean and the Middle Paleolithic (i.e., the Yabrudian, etc., as at Yabroud) will be discussed by Copeland (this volume).

THE PARA-ACHEULEAN

The three most ancient sites in our region, which are in sure stratigraphic position, seem to have material which is sufficiently different from that found a little later at Ubeidiya (the Ubeidiyan material will be treated separately). As their typology is still rather vague, they have been provisionally classed here as Para-Acheulean, which leaves the door open for more precise classification later.

The first of the early sites to be reported is Sharia, in the neighborhood south of Hama (Van Liere and Hooijer, 1961; Modderman, 1964; Van Liere, 1966, p. 16). On the banks of the Orontes is a high terrace consisting of pebbles and gravels with thin beds of sand and silt. Two old surfaces, indicated by fossil soils, mark the ancient riverbanks of the Paleo-Orontes. The industry recovered from what are now gravel quarries, by different people and at different times, has not been completely published and part of it is housed in the Damascus Museum. It consists of two spheroids, some irregular globular cores (polyhedrons?), and small flakes with plain, high angle butts. Some are cortex

flakes from river pebbles. There are no bifaces. Of great interest is the fact that the gravels of Sharia also contain remains of fauna, in particular an Archidiskodon meridionalis (Nesti), dated by Hooijer to late Günz (Van Liere and Hooijer, 1961).

Again on the Orontes banks, at Rastan, between Homs and Hama, some flakes were found in a thin bed of gravels (Van Liere, 1966, p. 16), which marked a fossil course of the Orontes about 70 m above the present level of the river. As in Hama, the flakes, the exact number of which is not known but which could not amount to more than twenty, include pebble cortex flakes. No cores and no bifaces accompanied them. Geologically speaking, the Rastan formation is referred, as is that at Sharia, to the start of the Middle Pleistocene, toward the end of Günz (Van Liere, 1966, p. 16).

Finally, on the Lebanese coast, 17 artifacts were found at Borj Qinnarit, southeast of Sidon, in a fossil beach at 95 m above present sea level (Hours and Sanlaville, 1972). The shorelines which are preserved all along the Lebanese coast at this altitude and up to 120 m have been grouped by Sanlaville as a succession of episodes referring to a transgression contemporary with the Günz/Mindel Interglacial: to this he gives the local name "Zagrounian" (Sanlaville, 1973). The raised beach at Borj Qinnarit represents an oscillation of the Zagrounian II, as is shown in Table 1. The flint consists of two pebble tools, two cores, one large anvil, two heavy flakes (one with a faceted butt), and ten small éclats de taille or preparation flakes (fig. 2). The appearance of one of the cores and the presence of a faceted butt indicate that the typology is more evolved than that at Sharia.

These three industries have enough traits in common to be grouped together (see fig. 5 for their distribution). They date to the start of the Middle Pleistocene, the end of Günz, or Günz/Mindel; there are no bifaces; they are certainly in the line of pebble industries, already differentiated from the African Oldowan which is, of course, much older. For the moment, one can see them as representing a non-biface industry, contemporary with the early Acheulean, somewhat similar to the Clactonian of Europe. To be more precise, however, we need much more evidence.

Following the latest conclusions concerning Ubeidiya (Bar-Yosef and Tchernov, 1972, pp. 30-31), which date that site to the equivalent of Mindel, the three flake assemblages of Lebanon and Syria represent the most ancient traces of Man yet known in the Levant.

ACHEULEAN

THE EARLY MIDDLE ACHEULEAN

There is now enough evidence which, when assembled from isolated occurrences reported from the Levant by various people at various times, indicates the presence of a distinct and typologically consistent tradition, a tradition which lasted through Mindel and up to the second half of Mindel-Riss, from the Nile to the Euphrates (Bovier-Lapierre, 1925; Hours et al., 1973).

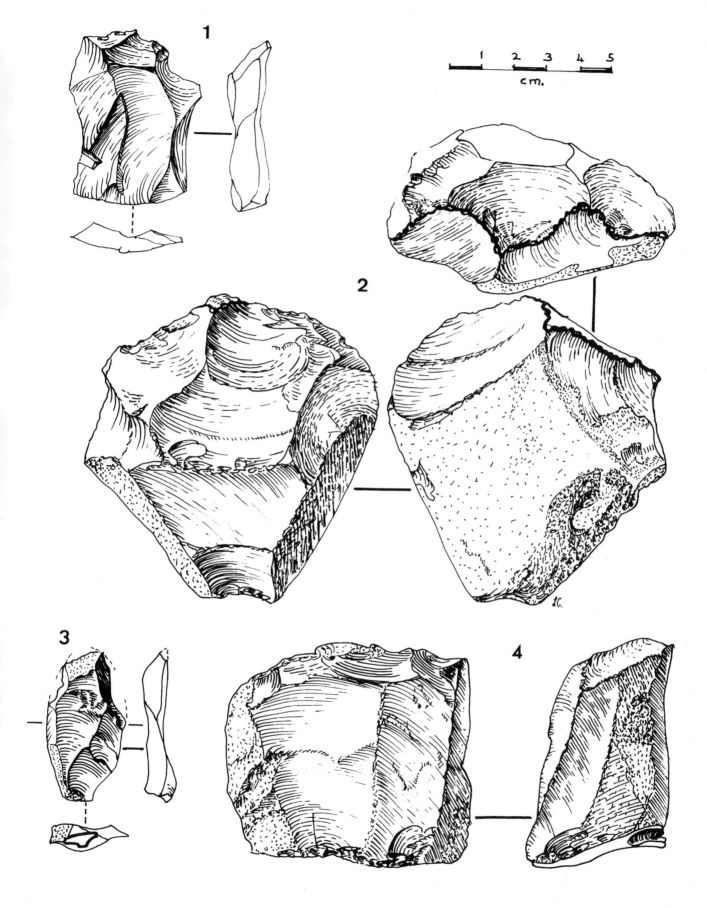

FIG. 2—Para-Acheulean: Borj el-Qinnarit. *1* and *3*: Flakes. *2*: Chopping tool. The chopping edge is well marked, but rolled. *4*: Core (rolled).

The point of departure can be seen in the well-known site of Ubeidiya in Israel. We are now able to add to this 35 sites from Lebanon and Syria, the most important of which is Latamné on the Orontes. Although the latter has been well published, only two others have been the subject of preliminary reports—Joub Jannine II (Besançon et al., 1970; Besançon and Hours, 1970) and Wadi Aabet (Fleisch et al., 1969, pp. 19-26).

In any case, from Ubeidiya and Latamné, a very good idea can be gained as to what the stable components in the typology of this tradition are.

The industry is characterized by heavy and large core tools. These are, nevertheless, precisely made to consistent patterns, and the economy of effort used to produce them from the often massive, rounded nodules which usually form the primary material, is notable.

The bifaces are generally elongated, with globular cortex bases. The lateral edges have, in most cases, been fashioned by the alternate removal of large, thick flakes, resulting in sinuous edges. The tips, often shaped by soft hammer, take on the form of a kind of spatula or duckbill—in Bordes's terms, these would be classed as *ficrons* and *lagéniformes* (Bordes, 1961, pp. 57-63). The bifaces are accompanied by trihedrals. These are carefully made tools with three flaked surfaces, sometimes just at the distal end, divided by three well-defined ridges; they usually have unretouched, globular bases. The pointed tips are often narrow and sharp. These pieces are too well made to go into the class of the blunt and thick tools which are usually designated as picks, and it is for this reason that they are simply called "trihedrals" and not "trihedral picks." The archaic character of the Early Middle Acheulean is confirmed by the presence of chopping tools and polyhedrons; these artifacts, as large as a fist, have been described only in summary fashion until now. Since they do not easily lend themselves to precise typological definitions, all the gradations in the transition from polyhedron, polyhedron with one pronounced ridge, chopping tool and core being encountered, it is understandable that some of the authors who have had to deal with them have classified them differently.

We define polyhedrons as pieces of globular form, fashioned by the removal of flakes around the whole surface, which results in the production of a sort of faceted ball or cube, and which can be distinguished from a "spheroid" by its well-marked ridges. In addition, spheroids are commonly made of limestone, while polyhedrons are made in flint. Polyhedrons are of variable size, and their diameters can vary from 5 cm to almost 20 centimeters. Besides all these characteristic forms, a whole range of lighter tools on flakes, sidescrapers in particular, are found in the Early Middle Acheulean.

The industry which we have just described does not conform to a rigidly fixed pattern. The proportions in which bifaces, chopping tools, trihedrals, polyhedrons, and flake tools appear, varies—both from site to site, and, it is thought, from period to period. There are also differences in the subtypes within the biface group. In short, it seems clear that we are dealing with an evolving tradition of long duration.

Not all the sites presently known are of the same value. Only one living floor has come down to us undisturbed—Latamné, which is also the only site excavated and published (Clark, 1966a, 1966b). Some others are, however, in sure stratigraphic geological context, the material being included in a river terrace, or in a fossil beach deposit. In other cases, the context is less clear—these are the surface sites, slope deposit sites, or sites where the material has been, whether to a large or small extent, redistributed. Mixtures are always possible and, in fact, occur. Nevertheless, this writer has come to realize that even problem sites such as these need not be neglected, since, studied with the help of other disciplines, such as geomorphology, enough can be recovered to give useful information as to the formation of the landscape and the evolution of the relief during the course of the Quaternary.

What we now recognize as an Early Middle Acheulean assemblage was first discovered by Passemard during the course of a survey at the mouth of the Nahr el-Kebir near the village of Khillaleh in Syria, not far from Lattakiyeh. At the time, he likened it to his Challossian (Passemard, 1926, 1926-27, 1927a, 1927b, 1927c), which precipitated quite a controversy. Neuville (1932), in particular, held it to be Neolithic. Other authors (Bovier-Lapierre, 1925, 1926) spoke of it as Chellean or pre-Chellean. The Khillaleh site has been visited often since (Baudouin and Burkhalter, 1930; Burkhalter, 1933; Wetzel and Haller, 1945-1948; Burkhalter, 1946-1948; Van Liere, 1961; Suzuki and Kobori, 1970). Unfortunately, the most thorough study is not generally available, as it is contained in the unpublished part of Wendt's thesis (Wendt, 1971).

Starting anew, Wendt restudied the whole lower part of the Nahr el-Kebir valley and identified four levels of fluviatile terrace deposits. He refers the highest to Mindel, the intermediate to Riss, and the two lowest to Würm. In the Mindel terrace, he found Acheulean at many points—around Khillaleh, at Khillaleh Sites 4, 5, 6, 7, and Ayak South; a little farther upstream, on the same bank of the Nahr el-Kebir, at Dahr Qadi Hassan; opposite, on the north bank of the river, another site (Roudo 5) near the village of Roudo.

Still in northern Syria, the same industry has been recovered from the Euphrates terraces by Pervès (1945, 1946-1948, 1964). It is found mixed with later Acheulean, and even with Middle Paleolithic, materials. An investigation of the Euphrates terraces was undertaken by Van Liere (1961, pp. 41-49). He, too, found some sites, but his study was not carried far enough to interpret the position of the industry, the typology of which related it to the Early Middle Acheulean. Van Liere (1961, p. 45) simply stated that only in the gravels of the High Terrace did he find it unmixed with later materials. In any case, trihedrals have now been reported from Abu Kemal, Ayèche, Deir ez-Zor,

Dibsi, Hammam, and opposite Raqqa. These localities form a chain of widely spaced sites to a point far down the course of the Euphrates.

It was Van Liere again who made known the most ancient Acheulean industries of the Orontes valley (Van Liere, 1961, p. 32, and more especially, 1966), even though the site of Kazo had already been found, without its significance being recognized, by Burkhalter (1933). Early Middle Acheulean sites in the Orontes valley now known include Sharia (above the level with the *Archidiskodon*), Kazo, Chaizar, Arba'in, Miramil, Latamné, and Qadib el Ban. In almost every case they consist of sites in association with the Orontes river terraces, and found thanks to the quarries which have been opened to exploit the gravels. Just as in the case of the Euphrates, no comprehensive, definitive, study of the Paleo-Orontes is available in which the age and relationship of the terraces has been established.

The only well-preserved living floor site, Latamné, is also the site which has been the most studied (Van Liere, 1961, 1966; Hooijer, 1961-62; Modderman, 1964; Van Dusen Eggers, 1966; de Heinzelin, 1966). Clark (1966a, 1966b) published the excavation and industry. The geology and the fauna combine in pointing to the end of Mindel, or more probably the start of the Great Interglacial (Mindel/Riss) as the date of occupation.

The southern part of the central depression, the South Béqaa in Lebanon, has produced the same industry. When the first site (Joub Jannine II) was found, it was reported, on account of its trihedrals, as Neolithic by Fleisch (1960), who followed in this the opinion of Neuville (1932). More recently a systematic survey has discovered the same assemblage of bifaces, trihedrals, chopping tools, and polyhedrons in about ten other localities (Besançon and Hours, 1970, 1971)—El Birke, Dahr el Hassane, El Hamrat I and II, Jabal Saad, El Khalliye, Sahm el Chaouk, and Ez Zanbout I and II. The site of Joub Jannine II has been studied in some depth, a sounding having been made (Besançon et al., 1970), and many concentrations of tools inventoried, measured, and classified (Besançon and Hours, 1970, pp. 84-86). To these, one may add the site of Ard es-Souda, where ancient forms of Acheulean have been noted by Fleisch (1966), and which is particularly interesting because of its geographic position on the sill dividing the watersheds of the Litani river and the Hasbani, Lebanese branch of the upper Jordan.

Even though they are all open sites, mostly on the surface, the South Béqaa sites are located in positions which are significant geomorphologically. The collaboration of a prehistorian (the present writer) with a geomorphologist (J. Besançon) has had the happy result that we have been able to distinguish a succession of three morphological cycles, each consisting of phases of erosion, valley fill, and planing-down. The first two cycles, dating to Mindel and Riss, resulted in the formation of deposits characterized by the presence of calcareous granules and pisoliths. It is sometimes possible to distinguish one from the other, for

example by their position relative to the Litani. In areas where the erosion, provoked by recent stream activity, has evacuated the later Würmian and Holocene deposits, the underlying calcareous granule beds are laid bare, and it is here, exposed on their surfaces, that one can find the Acheulean artifacts which they contain. Aerial photographs, topographic maps, and the very valuable new soil maps recently produced by the laboratory of Tell Amara (C.N.R.S. and the Lebanese Ministry of Agriculture) now allow us to predict almost infallibly on just which spot we will find bifaces and trihedrals.

Occasionally, the unpronounced relief in the lowest part of the Béqaa valley renders these surfaces barely visible, and it can happen that the Rissian cycle has overtaken and reworked the Mindel deposits. Here, one finds the industries mixed, early forms such as trihedrals occurring with oval or cordiform bifaces of the Late Acheulean. Never, however, have we found a calcareous granule outcrop associated with axes, arrowheads, or sickle-blades such as would give credence to the designation "Neolithic"—once, oddly enough, applied to the Béqaa trihedrals.

The Joub Jannine II site is the one which has furnished the most abundant industry (figs. 3 and 4). Leaving aside, for the moment, the slightly retouched or "utilized" flakes, we have listed 152 cores and 944 tools which consist of the following types: 255 polyhedrons, 148 chopping tools, 113 trihedrals, 16 quadrihedrals, 17 picks, 160 bifaces, 25 cleavers, and 18 *rabots*. The flake tools number: 85 sidescrapers, 37 endscrapers, 11 burins, 5 borers, 18 naturally backed knives, 5 backed knives, and 31 notches and denticulates. Among the bifaces we have distinguished (following the typology of Bordes, 1961) 10.3% Abbevillian, 45.7% Lanceolate, 3.9% Ficron and Lageniform, 17.0% Amygdaloid, 7.3% Partial, 4.4% Backed Bifaces, and 5.1% Bifacial Cleavers (*biface à biseau terminal*), as well as 0.7% Triangular and 0.7% Discoid bifaces.

Apart from certain types which seem to be more evolved (such as the rare triangular and discoid bifaces or the backed knives), which could indicate a sprinkling of Later Acheulean, the typology relates well with that of Latamné and Ubeidiya and can without hesitation be referred to the Early Middle Acheulean.

Along the Lebanese coast, another series of sites appears to belong to the same tradition. The first known was located in the suburbs of Beirut on the banks of the Beirut river, between Sinel-Fil and Furn esh-Shebbak (Desribes, 1921). There were probably several geological levels in the fluviatile deposits here which were not distinguished.

A recent discovery at Ras Beirut revealed another site of this period—Ras Beirut Ib. It is not yet published and is not to be confused with the site already discovered by Fleisch (Fleisch, 1956, 1962). On an abrasion platform, the position of which will be gone into below, rests a firmly consolidated fossil beach at 52 m above present sea level (Fleisch and Sanlaville, 1969, pp. 98-100). Last year a building foundation excavated another area of this beach

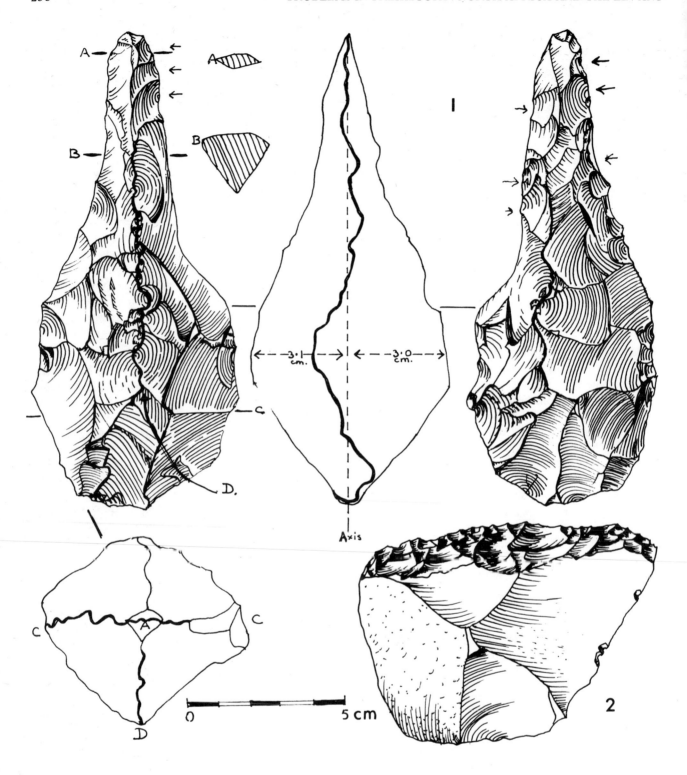

FIG. 3—Early Middle Acheulean: Joubb Jannine II. *1*: Trihedral. Although of small size, this trihedral is particularly regularly made and passes half way down its length into a quadrihedral. *2*: Sidescraper on a flake, with some cortex on the dorsal surface, and plain butt.

and revealed a site from which about 15 bifaces of the Latamné type have been recovered. The 52 m level has been attributed by Sanlaville (1973) to the Jbailian Ic transgression, equivalent to near the middle of Mindel/Riss (table 1).

North of Beirut, a site exists near Batroun which is identical in its stratigraphical position to the new Early Middle Acheulean site at Ras Beirut. A mountain stream, the Wadi Aabet, in course of eroding its valley, has eaten away marine deposits of the Jbailian transgression and exposed a

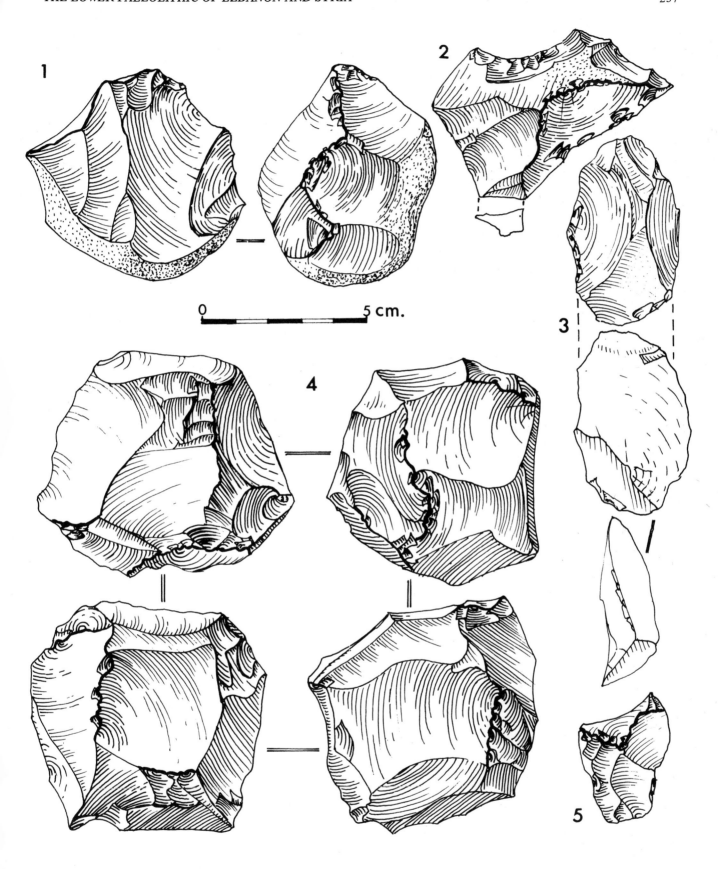

0 ___ 5 cm.

FIG. 4—Early Middle Acheulean: Joubb Jannine II. *1*: Chopping tool on a small flint pebble. *2* and *5*: Preparation flakes struck from a polyhedron. The ridges are clearly marked. *3*: Biface preparation flake. The ridges are less marked than in nos. *2* and *5*, and the plain butt forms an obtuse angle with the flake surface. *4*: Polyhedron, roughly cubic.

small Acheulean site at 52 m above sea level (Fleisch et al., 1970, pp. 19-26). The typology of the not very abundant assemblage, however, is different from the Early Middle Acheulean groups we have been describing, being more evolved. Apart from a lanceolate biface of basalt, the bifaces are of the short amygdaloid type, with thick globular bases and rounded, thin tips fashioned by soft hammer (at least, so far as can be told from the pieces in their present, rather rolled condition). Furthermore, the bifaces are of small size (7-10 cm long). From the strictly typological viewpoint, this group should be classed with the Middle-to-Late Acheulean, which we will be discussing below. The contradiction seen between the stratigraphy and the typology evidently poses a problem. It may also allow us, however, to pinpoint the end of the Early Middle Acheulean era, since, in association with the same marine episode (the Jbailian Ic transgression), one finds at Ras Beirut an industry in the Latamné tradition, while at Wadi Aabet is found an industry distinctly different, with a far less archaic appearance.

On the Syrian coast other sites can be placed as Early Middle Acheulean of the Latamné type—at Hennadi, and at the mouth of the Nahr al Moudiq (Van Liere, 1960-1961, p. 17), as well as Ouemie, south of Lattakia (Burkhalter, 1933).

Inland, three points were reported as "Chellean" in the Nebek region (Rust, 1933, Nasrallah, 1951). One has furnished trihedrals (unpublished part of Wendt's thesis, 1971).

From the chronological viewpoint, all of these industries occupy broadly the same period. The Latamné fauna, the Nahr el-Kebir terraces, the Jbailian Ic beach levels at Ras Beirut and Wadi Aabet, the calcareous granule formations of the South Béqaa, all relate to the end of Mindel (or more likely to the Mindel/Riss) in succession to the period of Ubeidiya.

From the typological viewpoint, one can certainly say that an internal evolution took place in the tradition. The differences separating Ubeidiya and Latamné have already been evaluated (Bar-Yosef and Tchernov, 1972, p. 31 and fig. 7), but it is also possible to detect significant changes, even within the Syro-Lebanese group. Even though the two sites are of different character, one a living floor *in situ*, and the other redistributed and coming down to us with a complicated geological history behind it, yet it seems of value to compare Latamné with Joub Jannine II (Clark, 1966b, pp. 88-93; Besançon and Hours, 1970, pp. 84-86). In order to facilitate the comparison, the industry has been regrouped according to Clark's terminology. Clark's "formless cores" seem to resemble closely our "polyhedrons"; as does Clark, this writer includes the trihedrals with the bifaces; *rabots* and core-scrapers seem to be the same tool. Apart from sidescrapers, all the other light flake tools have been regrouped in the same category, with the exception of notches and denticulates, which Clark puts with retouched flakes, and which are omitted from the total. This gives the following result:

Tool Types	Latamné	Joub Jannine II
Polyhedrons (formless cores)	10.3%	27.5%
Chopping Tools	4.3%	15.7%
Bifaces (including trihedrals)	27.4%	32.7%
Cleavers	0.5%	3.0%
Rabots (core scrapers)	12.3%	2.2%
Sidescrapers	37.1%	13.0%
Other small tools	8.0%	8.5%

The two sites have the same tool types, and this shows that they are part of the same tradition. At Joub Jannine, however, the heavy tools are more numerous (this may be due to the fact that at Latamné, the collection is complete, while for that at Joub Jannine, a surface site, this can hardly be the case); nevertheless, the considerable numbers of ancient forms, such as polyhedrons and chopping tools at Joub Jannine, as well as the abundance of trihedrals (which disappear in the Later Acheulean) could indicate that the industry of Joub Jannine is more archaic than that of Latamné. Again, the sidescrapers, more important as a group at Latamné, could indicate a more evolved stage. Strange to say, the small tools are represented in similar proportions at the two sites, in particular the burins and proto-burins, which amount to 1.6% at both sites.

Unfortunately, it is impossible to push such quantitative comparisons much farther, or to examine in more detail the correlations which might exist in this respect at the other sites. In any case, a qualitative analysis of the latter produces the same impression of variability within the framework of a single tradition.

From the ecological point of view, the only available data are that of Clark (1966b, pp. 87-88). The physical distribution (fig. 5) of the other sites suggests analogous conclusions. One can, in fact, detect concentrations—along the Euphrates, on the edge of the swampy areas of the South Béqaa and the Orontes, as well as on the seashore, and at the mouths of rivers. The importance attached to a fresh water supply is manifest, but, apart from that, we do not know to what extent the Mindel/Riss Acheuleans exploited marine resources. For the Inland, however, on the Euphrates or in the Béqaa, Clark's deductions seem well founded; we could see here the remains of temporary camps, located along the edges of swamps and river, in connection with forested and grassland zones, a landscape selected by the large animals which are represented in the faunal remains from Latamné—rhino, elephant, bison, horse, camel, and gazelle (Hooijer, 1961-62).

It remains to note that, except for the practically unknown sites of the Nebek region, the Early Middle Acheulean did not penetrate farther inland than the Anti-Lebanon and Qalamoun regions. This, added to the dependence on fresh water mentioned above, makes an occupation during an interpluvial period (such as Mindel/Riss) more likely.

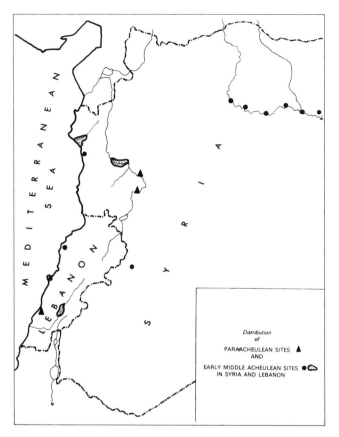

FIG. 5–The Early Middle Acheulean is concentrated in the South Béqaa, the Orontes valley around Latamné, and the mouth of the Nahr el-Kebir. The rest is sparsely dispersed; compare with Fig. 8.

THE MIDDLE/LATE ACHEULEAN

With the disappearance of the industry with trihedrals and polyhedrons, another style of Acheulean appears, much more abundantly represented in Lebanon and Syria. About 130 sites are known today which can be referred to this more evolved phase of the Acheulean. This does not mean that the Middle/Late Acheulean is well known, since of this 130, only one—Jerf Ajla (Schroeder, 1969, pp. 101-22)—has been studied in detail, and only four others—Ras Beirut Ia, III A, III B, and IV (Fleisch, 1950, 1956, 1962; numerotation according to Copeland and Wescombe, 1965)—have been described in brief preliminary reports. A good idea can also be obtained of the Lebanese part of Ma'ayan Barukh, thanks to a work published in Israel (Stekelis and Gilead, 1966). Finally, an unpublished study of the Nahr el-Kebir sites exists (Wendt, 1971). The other sites are noted in the inventories already mentioned above, but sometimes in only a few words, making these difficult to use.

Even the little we know is vague enough. Of this, the imprecise typology in this paper is the outcome. Seen as a whole, the impression gained from all these assemblages is that a Final or very Late Acheulean of the Tabun F type is rare, but it is impossible on present evidence to draw the line between the Middle and Late Acheulean, or to present in coherent form, the evolution from one to the other. The present writer has resigned himself, therefore, to putting into one group all the assemblages which come into the period from the end of Mindel/Riss to the Riss/Würm.

The 130 sites to be discussed are of various kinds. Unlike Israel, where cave sites are more numerous, only at Jerf Ajla is Acheulean-like material found in a cave. Some sites are in more or less clear geological context, included in exclusively continental deposits, slope deposits, or river terraces; not one is in *direct* connection with a fossil shoreline. Six of them, in the South Béqaa, are found in formations which, since they are the results of a later erosion having reworked Mindel deposits, contain Early Middle Acheulean material as well. Again, others are well dated and without mixture, but sparse, and although a fair idea of the typology can be gained in each individual case, this group is not large enough to be used for working out the stages of a typological evolution.

The surface sites are the most numerous, consisting of 93 localities, of which four contain Early Middle Acheulean traces. In their turn, the surface sites are not of uniform content or character. Certain of them, near primary flint sources, contain few finished tools and a lot of flake waste. They are evidently factories or knapping sites and some are vast, covering several acres. Others consist of small concentrations with more tools, and these could represent remains of habitation sites, at least in those cases where the geomorphological evidence gives a clear indication that the locus has not been disturbed much since the end of Riss/Würm. Finally, there are isolated occurrences which bear witness to the perambulations of the Acheuleans of that era.

The factories and the traces of Acheulean wanderings are new factors and could be seen as indicating an increase in population, the start of specialization, and new ways of territorial colonization. We will briefly review these 130 sites in the climatic-geographic context sketched at the beginning of the paper.

The Coast (Zone I): 33 Sites

Acheulean material has been reported from areas south of Beirut since before the 1914 war, at Akbyeh, south of Sidon (Zumoffen, 1897, p. 436), at Zahrani, and at Sidon itself (Neophytus and Pallary, 1914). Except for Zahrani, these surface sites are not of great interest. Northward, the Ras Beirut group, first noted by Lartet (1865, 1877), were studied in more detail by Bergy (1932) and by Fleisch (1950, 1956, 1962). Our concern here is with high levels where the Lower Paleolithic is found (fig. 6); the morphology of this important station can be summarized here according to the present state of our knowledge (Fleisch and Sanlaville, 1969).

An upper Terrace extends between 70 and 78 m above the present sea level. Below this, a rock-cut step or ledge is seen at 58 meters. Then an abrasion platform is seen to

Ras Beirut

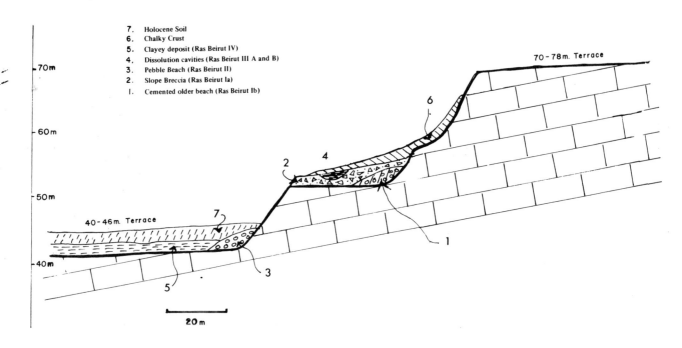

7. Holocene Soil
6. Chalky Crust
5. Clayey deposit (Ras Beirut IV)
4. Dissolution cavities (Ras Beirut III A and B)
3. Pebble Beach (Ras Beirut II)
2. Slope Breccia (Ras Beirut Ia)
1. Cemented older beach (Ras Beirut Ib)

FIG. 6—Schematic Section of the Higher Levels at Ras Beirut. *After Sanlaville*.

truncate the whole, forming a small dead-cliff, the foot of which is at an altitude of 52 meters. At the foot of this dead-cliff there is an ancient, very consolidated beach (the one noted above, which contained the Early Middle Acheulean bifaces, Ras Beirut Site Ib) All these features are covered by a consolidated breccia formation, containing Middle/Late Acheulean material. This is the site found by Fleisch (1950), his "Brèche de Pentè;" Ras Beirut I by the numerotation of Copeland and Wescombe (1965, pp. 116-23), which hereafter will be renamed Ia. The altitude of the surface of the breccia is between 52 m and 56 meters. The breccia has been eroded, and two dissolution cavities in its surface contain artifacts. These are Fleisch's *Dépôts A* and *B*, or Ras Beirut Sites III A and III B. The first contains "*Levalloisien à bifaces*" and the second "*Tayaco-Levalloisien*," according to Fleisch's terminology.

The slope breccia (Site Ia) appears to have been, in its turn, truncated by the sea, which left, at ca. 46 m above the present sea level, a strandline of uncemented pebbles (the "*Cordon Littoral*" of Fleisch, or Ras Beirut site II), in which was mingled an industry classed as "Tayacian."

Below this, a wide terrace slopes gently down toward the sea, from 46 m to about 40 meters. The bedrock is covered by a reddish yellow clayey continental deposit containing an industry classed as "*Vieux Levallois*," found in a locus referred to as Bergy's Trench, and in other places on the terrace (Bergy, 1932), numbered as Ras Beirut IV by Copeland and Wescombe (1965). This ancient deposit has been planed off and then unconformably recovered by more recent soil. The wide abrasion platform or Middle Terrace

of 46-40 m has in turn been truncated by more recent marine episodes, dated to the Middle Paleolithic and, hence, outside the scope of this paper.

Sanlaville (1973) attributes the above-mentioned features to the following marine phases: the beach of Ras Beirut Ib to a Jbailian I Transgressive phase, i.e., the first half of Mindel/Riss; the formation of the "slope breccia" of Site Ia to the regression which divides Jbailian I and Jbailian II; and the beach of Ras Beirut II at ca. 46 m to the Jbailian II Transgression, i.e. to the second half of Mindel/ Riss. We may add that the dissolution cavities (*Dépôts A* and *B*, Ras Beirut Sites III A and III B), as well as the clayey formation of Bergy's Trench (Ras Beirut IV), date to Riss.

If Sanlaville's geomorphological description and interpretation of the Ras Beirut promontory brings up not too many problems, the summary way in which the industries involved have been published (Bergy, 1932; Fleisch, 1956, 1962) calls for further precision, since we have neither a complete inventory nor a detailed analysis of any site.

As mentioned, the Acheulean of Site Ib is an Early Middle Acheulean Latamné type. That of Site Ia, on the other hand, has been classed as "*Acheuléen Moyen*" by its discoverer. The industry consists of about 200 artifacts so far recovered from the breccia; they are unrolled, not even smoothed. The industry includes seven bifaces, which are very different from the types we have described so far, except for some aspects of those of Wadi Aabet. They are short amygdaloids with thick, unretouched bases—the tip, in contrast, having been finely retouched by use of a soft hammer and made razor sharp. It is clearly an evolved typology, and it is surprising that it is encountered in a Mindel/Riss context. If it is Middle Acheulean, it is certainly a late Middle Acheulean.

We will discuss the Tayacian of the *Cordon Littoral*, Ras Beirut II, later on. As for the various names given to the industries of Ras Beirut III A, III B, and Beirut IV (*Vieux Levallois, Levallois à bifaces, Tayaco-Levalloisien*), these doubtless can be seen more realistically as covering the same thing, a Middle/Late Acheulean with Levallois debitage (fig. 7). Bifaces in fact exist in the *Vieux Levallois* of Ras Beirut IV as Bergy has already noted, as well as in Ras Beirut III A, and the Levallois influence has been recognized by Fleisch, according to the names he gave to the industries (Fleisch, 1962). It is, in any case, in keeping with what we know of the rest of the world, Europe in particular, to find Levallois debitage appearing in the Acheulean during the Riss.

In the suburbs north of Beirut, Middle/Late Acheulean material was found by Desribes (1921), not only at Sin el-Fil (where he had already found Early Middle Acheulean material) but also at Dekouané, Ain Sheikh, and Jdaidé; all were small assemblages without great significance. The same may be said for the Acheulean material reported by von Heidenstam, one of the pioneers of Lebanese prehistory, at Dbayé.

In 1963, Wendt found two Acheulean sites near Bibnine, on the Akkar Plain in North Lebanon. It would be of interest to hear more about these, since he reports the presence of Levallois debitage at both.

Along the Syrian coast around Tartous, Burkhalter (Baudouin and Burkhalter, 1930) and Van Liere (1961) reported surface sites of Late Acheulean typology from Tartous, the mouth of the Nahr Ismailie; at Saoudah, on the banks of the Nahr Markie and Nahr Senn; at Hraissoun; and at Jebleh. The last two sites could in fact be Yabroudian, but the data given by Van Liere (1961, pp. 21 and 23) are too vague to be sure.

It is not until one arrives at the Nahr el-Kebir terraces, west of Lattakia, that one finds the Middle/Late Acheulean in significant locations. Wendt found it in the Riss terraces at Dahr an-Nalasse, Killaleh I (Ain Turkman), Bdamioun 1 and 3, Sinjouan 3 and 4, Souayate 1, and Roudo 1. Unfortunately, all these are described in the unpublished part of his thesis. Van Liere had also (1961, p. 17) discovered a site on the butte of Esh-Shir. The most northerly coastal site is 20 km north of Lattakia on the banks of the Nahr el-Arab (Baudouin and Burkhalter, 1930).

The Western Slopes of the Mountains (Zone 2)—20 Sites

These represent a new factor in Levantine prehistory—the mountain areas are occupied for the first time.

The first group of sites was found in Upper Galilee in the course of an excursion in 1907 by Bovier-Lapierre (1908). The list was later added to by Fleisch (1954), and the

Tokyo University team recently found another (Suzuki and Kobori, 1970, pp. 34, 61, 72-73). These are Khallet el-Hamra, Wadi Koura, Khallet el-Michte I and II, Debel, Mseel, and Chalaboun, all located around the village of Ain Ebel. One may add the nearby site of Tibnine. These are mainly factory sites, and most were reactivated later, during the Neolithic. The occupation must have been relatively long and intensive, since bifaces are far from rare in the wadi beds. Their typology resembles that of the coastal sites—short amygdaloids, with thick bases and rounded tips, while, in addition, more rounded forms such as ovaloids are found.

Further north, in the inland valleys of South Lebanon, similar Middle/Late Acheulean material has been reported from Jezzine and Jbaa, the latter also being a factory which was reused during the Neolithic. The mountains of central and northern Lebanon have no important factory sites such as those mentioned above, but isolated finds along natural routes from the coast to the Béqaa show that Acheulean man had begun to use them. Bifaces have also been found in the Beirut river valley, near Mkalles and Beit Meri villages, in the valley of the Nahr el Kelb at Dik el-Mehdi, on the slopes of Jebel Sannin at Jebel Baniya, and on the plateaus bordering the Qadisha at Bsarma and Zghorta (see Copeland and Wescombe 1965, 1966 for specific locations).

As in South Lebanon, a relatively dense occupation of Middle/Late Acheulean occurred in the Alaouite mountains. The sites of Sasniye, Kalaat Yahmour, Tarye, and Slenfé were found by Burkhalter (Burkhalter and Baudouin, 1930; Burkhalter, 1933). Slenfé is on a route from the coast through to the Ghâb, analogous to routes in Mount Lebanon. The most important site is the vast station of Kalaat Yahmour, not far from the Nahr al Abrash, which is reminiscent, in its abundance and quality of material, of the large sites of Africa.

If all these mountain sites bear witness to the colonization of a new territory, it is remarkable that it is not total—valleys, passageways and the low hills of Upper Galilee and the Jebel Alaouiye only were preferred. The last two areas were frequented with a density that only Ras Beirut and the Nahr el-Kebir on the coast can equal.

The Central Depression, Litani and Orontes Valleys (Zone 3)—45 Sites

As in the Early Middle Acheulean, during the Middle/Late Acheulean this was the most fully occupied zone in the Syro-Lebanese region.

One group of sites forms a link between Western Palestine and the Upper Jordan Valley. It consists of Ard es Saouda (which also has Early Middle Acheulean material), the Lebanese part of Ma'ayan Barukh, and Nabatiye.

Another group is found in the South Béqaa (Besançon and Hours, 1970, 1971). The density of sites here was certainly greater than before, and occupation seems to have occurred up to the end of the Acheulean era. During the course of geomorphological evolution, the character of

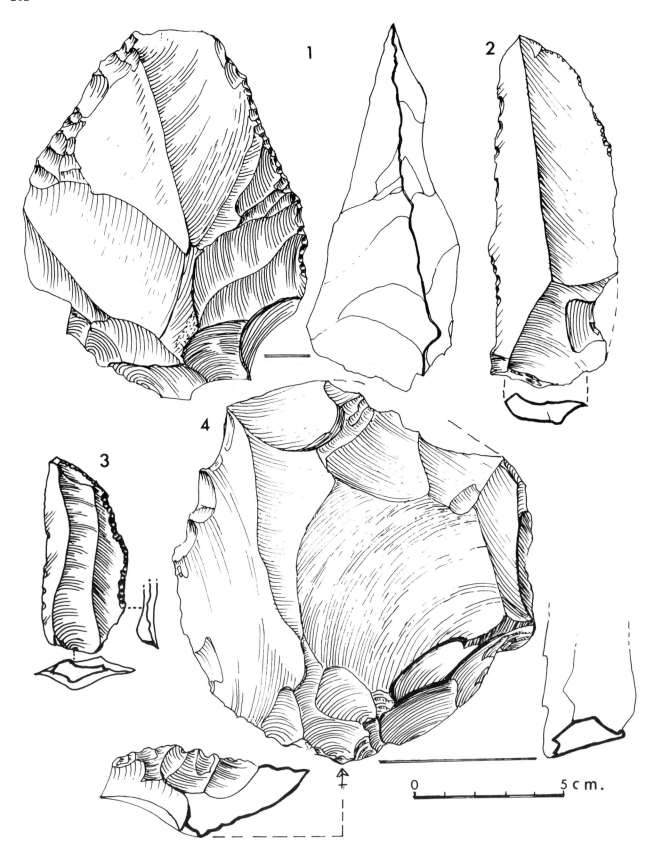

FIG. 7—Middle/Late Acheulean, Ras Beirut IV. *1*: Biface. The amygdaloid form and thick base are typical, as is the shaping of the edge by soft hammer. The rounded tip is also frequent, here, exceptionally, not retouched. *2*: Blade. *3*: Backed knife. *4*: Large, thick Levallois flake.

various sites has been altered. For the present they may, therefore, be classed only in broad categories. At Zraizer and Qaraoun III, on surfaces which are apparently Rissian and undisturbed, there are traces of what may have been living sites. In contact with the outcrops of Eocene conglomerates (which contain numerous nodules of good quality flint), a whole series of factories occur, many of which were also used during the Neolithic. From south to north, on both flanks of the Béqaa, the list includes Amlaq el-Qatih, Kefraya, Wadi Msil al-Hadd, Hajar Tawil, Kamed el-Loz I, Aachaich, Qata'a Eliassi, Tellet Haql el-Aaqel, Es-Saouane, Dakoue, Mejdel Anjal I, and Nebi Zair. Certain of these factories are very important and cover several acres; an example is Kefraya, known since 1900 (Zumoffen 1900), and another is es-Saouane, discovered in 1972.

Other sites occur in relation with the granule formations of the Rissian cycle. Even if the stratigraphical position is more sure, it is not possible to tell whether these were factories or living sites.

Along the Litani, sites are also found on the surface, brought to light by the erosional activities of small streams. These are Sahm el-Baidar, Sahm er-Raml, Joub Jannine I, Es-Slaiaa, and two on three points around el-Khalliyé. Finally, on old surfaces, which, from around the village of Joub Jannine form a passage from the Litani valley to that of the Wadi et-Taym (a prolongation of the Upper Jordan depression), one finds dispersed traces of Acheulean, possibly representing temporary stops en route through the passes: Haql al Agha, Birket al Jouani, and Birket Harizi.

Going north, it is not until one reaches the Orontes valley that one again finds Acheulean remains. Here the finds are due to Van Liere (1961, p. 40; 1966, pp. 20-24). At Kattineh, south of Homs, Middle/Late Acheulean material is found in Orontes terraces, and traces also occur at Jarnyeh, north of Homs between Rastan and Hama. Around Hama, a fairly dense occupation seems to have occurred, known long ago, judging by the six sites found in the immediate vicinity of the town (Pervès, 1945, p. 204; 1948, p. 120; Van Liere, 1961, p. 32; Modderman, 1964, pp. 51-55).

Between Hama and the Ghâb, many other Acheulean assemblages have been reported—Sheikh Abdallah, Arzé, Khattab, Wadi Sarouteh, Kafer Zita (Modderman, 1964, pp. 53-56; Van Liere, 1961, p. 50; Burkhalter, 1949-1950, p. 136). In contrast, the Ghâb depression itself has produced no Acheulean sites, except at the extreme north, where Fleisch collected thick, ovate bifaces from a terrace east of the Orontes, and where Van Liere found some pieces in the Paleo-Orontes gravels, thanks to the drainage works dug near Karkour (Van Liere, 1966, pp. 21-24, fig. 33). The occupation of the central depression in the later Acheulean continues into Turkey—for example, the neighborhood of Gaziantep. It will be noticed that the North Béqaa, like the Ghâb, appears to be devoid of human occupation in this epoch. For the former, the numerous surveys made by Copeland and Wescombe, Besançon and Hours, the Tokyo

University team, Schroeder, Kuschke and Azoury have not produced any Acheulean material. Perhaps, the climate, distinctly drier than the rest of the central depression (Plassard, 1972), and the absence of soil made this region unattractive. The case of the Ghâb is different. Even today it is a zone of subsidence, and the ancient bed of the Orontes is to be found only many meters below present ground level. This explains why it has been impossible to reach traces of Acheulean occupation here.

The situation in the South Béqaa is quite special. At the southern end of the Béqaa the Litani crosses a limestone sill which has not shifted since the beginning of the Middle Pleistocene and which has acted as a kind of dam, preventing any violent erosion. Hence the traces of Acheulean which are included in the formations of the Rissian cycle remained in the same place, even though redistributed during the Würm, and the stages of the reworkings can be distinguished by the geomorphology. It is, therefore, possible to deduce that different activities led to the installation of these sites in which can be seen the start of specialization differentiating living sites from factories. It is also possible to infer an evolution within the tradition, and it is perhaps in this region that traces of the most evolved Acheulean in Lebanon occur, with flat cordiform, triangular, or even Micoquian bifaces, as well as bifaces on flakes. Once more, the humid areas, attracting as they did the large game animals, played an important part in mankind's development.

The Western Fringe of the Desert (Zone 4)–25 Sites

No site preceding a Middle/Late Acheulean occupation has yet been recorded. The penetration of the desert fringe zone is (apart from Rust's two or three sites near Nebek mentioned above) a new departure, the meaning of which is yet unclear. Was it due to an amelioration of climatic conditions during the Riss Pluvial, or to more advanced techniques which made man less dependent on his environment?

The Acheulean has been reported at two points near the southern frontier of Syria—at Deraa on the banks of the W. Zaidé (Mallon, 1925) and at Tell Chehab in the Wadi Midaneh (Van Liere, 1960-61, pp. 49-50).

Farther north, the Damascus basin saw a fairly dense occupation, which can be explained as being due to the wadis flowing from Hermon and the Anti-Lebanon. These wadis even today irrigate the gardens of the Ghouta. An ancient lake existed in the basin, the deposits of which can be seen near Aateibeh and Hijane. Van Liere has there identified shorelines of two ancient levels of the lake, at 15 m and at 100 m above the present level of the plain. The swampy margins of this lake, of which fossil peat layers remain, doubtless provided the same attraction for man and animal as did those of the South Béqaa and the Orontes. The Middle/Late Acheulean is found at Ain ech Sharaa, at the springs of Awej (Van Liere, 1966, fig. 36), and in Wadi

Cherkess (Potut, 1937, p. 131), both sites being near Qatana. Bifaces have often been found in the Barada gravel terraces, e.g., at Barze (Van Liere, 1966, p. 25) or at el-Haméh (Pervès, 1945, p. 205). The northern fringe of the Damascus basin produced Acheulean at Wadi el-Hajjar and Achrafié (Potut, 1937, p. 131).

The wadis flowing from the Qalamoun between Damascus and Nebek also saw the passage of the Acheuleans, at Qteife (Van Liere, 1966, p. 25) and Maaloula (Nasrallah, 1951; Van Liere, 1966, p. 24). The last site is a special case, a factory for limestone artifacts. These are found dispersed on the plateau overlooking the gorge which shelters the village.

The well-watered Nebek-Yabroud plain formed a center of attraction, as the many sites found there show (Nasrallah, 1951, pp. 80-106)—Qreina, Wadi Skifta, Ain Falita, Wadi Falita, Seil el-Blat, and Deir el-Msidé. Nebek was prospected by Rust (1933), who discovered a dozen Middle/Late Acheulean stations, all within a range of 10 km from the village. An isolated biface (Field and Garrod, 1960, p. 145) found at Qaryatein, between Nebek and Palmyra, is a valuable sign that men of this epoch passed across what is now a desert.

The Euphrates terraces have furnished bifaces of Late type. Meskene (Passemard, 1926-27, p. 463), Giaour Köy, and Jerablus (Karge, 1917) have long been known. A very good site, Jebel Saouane, was found this year by Cauvin near Mureybat, and five other sites were reported in the Balikh valley near Chnine by Dr. Malenfant (Cauvin, 1970).

As was the case with the Lebanese mountains, these Middle/Late Acheulean occupations at the edge of the desert appear to have been sporadic, forming more an eastward extension of the more populated central depression than a real colonization. One can note, in fact, concentrations where the water supply is abundant with large empty spaces in between, especially north of Nebek.

The Desert (Zone 5)

We know very little about this area.

The cave of Jerf Ajla, 12 km north of Palmyra, produced 11 bifaces and bifacial tools at the base of the cave filling (Coon, 1957, pp. 290-316; Schroeder, 1969, pp. 101-22). They seem to be late, but one cannot tell from the published reports, given the conditions under which the material was excavated, whether one is dealing with a Late Acheulean or a Yabroudian facies. Van Liere (1961, p. 501) found what he considered to be a Late Acheulean in the Wadi al Aazib. In the Oasis of Soukhne, bifaces were reported from early on (de Morgan, 1927, p. 3) while the recent surveys have not reported anything new.

Summary of the Middle/Late Acheulean

It is difficult to say anything exact about the date of the many Middle/Late Acheulean sites, dispersed across the Syrian and Lebanese territories, mentioned in the foregoing list. Apart from the Ras Beirut station, which contains

marine fauna and unfortunately not characteristic as to date (Fleisch, 1962), none of the other sites which we have mentioned produced faunal remains. The beach deposits, so helpful for the earlier periods, are here of limited value, for no industry is directly associated with them. In some cases, the well-dated Rissian continental deposits allow a sure attribution—Ras Beirut, Orontes Valley, and Nahr el-Kebir terraces.

The occupation of the desert fringes, where residual forests still exist, suggest a wetter epoch, where more widely spread wooded areas must have contained more game (Van Liere, 1966, p. 25, fig. 36). On the contrary, the mountain sites seem more related to an interpluvial.

In sum, in most cases, we cannot be sure whether this or that site dates to Mindel/Riss, Riss, or Riss/Würm.

To resolve this dilemma, the typology is not an infallible guide. On one hand, it is a ticklish problem to divide the Acheulean by typology alone, and on the other hand, the latter is, in this case, somewhat monotonous. The great majority of the bifaces are short amygdaloids with thick, reserved bases. Some more evolved forms (such as flat cordiform, Micoquian, ovate, flat bifaces on flakes, or bifaces with completely retouched bases) certainly occur, but no site can be clearly referred to the Late, or Final, Acheulean of the Palestinian caves. There is not even a surface site which is the equivalent of the Upper Acheulean of Ma'ayan Barukh, and very evolved forms, when found, are exceptions.

The distribution of the sites (fig. 8) shows that throughout the period (impossible to subdivide) which goes from Mindel/Riss to Riss/Würm, the population increased significantly, and man was able to colonize new areas—mountain, oasis, and desert fringe. The traffic between the densely populated zones has left its traces. Human occupation, therefore, was both more widely and more firmly based.

There are some indications as to the way of life. Flint-knapping sites reveal specialized tasks and needs, and the placement of many sites shows less dependence on water supply than in the past, except on the edge of the desert. The occupation of the drier areas, probably zones of contact between the dry grasslands and the open woodlands, suggest that the game hunted was of a different character, consisting more of medium-sized animals—equids, bovines, and antilopoids. This is, however, no more than guesswork.

THE TAYACIAN

Finally, it is necessary to discuss several sites labeled "Tayacian" by their discoverers. There are seven of these, spread widely and of heterogeneous character. On the coast, there are Ras Beirut Sites II and III B (Fleisch, 1956, 1962); Harf al-Mosri, near Batroun (Fleisch et al., 1969, pp. 17-19); Bahsas, near Tripoli (Wetzel and Haller, 1945-48, p. 28); and Bdamioun, in the Nahr el-Kebir Valley (Van Liere, 1961, p. 16). On the Euphrates, Tayacian has been reported at Raqqa (Van Liere, 1961, p. 46) and also near Nebek at Yabroud Shelter IV (Solecki, 1966, pp. 131-38; 1968, pp. 401-10).

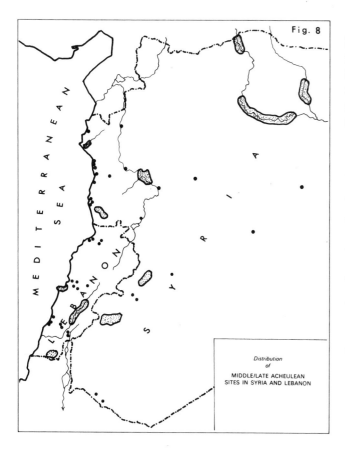

FIG. 8—Compare with Fig. 5 and note increase in density over the Early Middle Acheulean.

The vagueness which characterizes typological definitions of the Tayacian calls for the exercise of caution, since any assemblage of uncharacteristic flakes tends to be called Tayacian. The mediocrity of the Tayacian sites of the Levant suggests even more reservations.

We could, perhaps, at once omit from consideration Harf al-Mosri, Bdamioun, and Raqqa; the first is a block of breccia resting on bedrock, from which some 40 pieces including 20 flakes were extracted, and it would be somewhat venturesome to assign them to any industry. The other two are in fluviatile terraces where an undetermined number of non-Levallois flakes were found. There is no case, however, for claiming here the existence of a Tayacian independent of the Acheulean, which, as we have seen, exists in the same terraces.

Ras Beirut III B, with the strange label *"Tayaco-Levalloisien,"* produced a few flakes with visible Levallois influence which were quite similar to those of the neighboring and contemporary sites of Ras Beirut III A and IV, where they were accompanied by bifaces. In the opinion of this writer, this site seems to belong to the same Rissian Acheulean group in which the Levallois debitage appeared.

Yabroud, Shelter IV, contained one biface, illustrated by Solecki (1968, p. 408, fig. 7); why cannot this facies also be seen as an Acheulean, also Rissian, as the marshy context of the deposits containing it suggests.

Bahsas has known an extraordinary fame. In a red clay layer, overlain by a Riss conglomerate, Wetzel and Haller found more than 100 flakes, 40 of which were artifacts (Wetzel and Haller, 1945-1948, p. 28 and fig. 22). Of the four illustrated, one is very likely Levallois. Since this handful of flint was reported, it has been cited by de Vaumas (1947), Vaufrey (1948), Neuville (1951), Fleisch (1956), Howell (1959), Van Liere (1961), Fleisch (1962), Garrod (1962), Copeland and Wescombe (1965), Perrot (1968), and Wendt (1971). This is probably because of the impression made by the antiquity of the red clay layer, which had been attributed to Mindel/Riss. In fact, as it has since been shown (Sanlaville, 1973), the red layer formed a part of the same formation as the overlying conglomerates, and it, too, was Rissian. Further, Wendt (1971, p. 78; unpublished part of thesis) mentioned a biface which, according to him, had been found with these flakes. It may, therefore, be that here, too, we have a Rissian Acheulean with some Levallois debitage.

There remains Ras Beirut II, the *Cordon Littoral* (Fleisch, 1956, 1962). In a beach level consisting of uncemented pebbles at 46 m above present sea level, Fleisch recovered more than 2,000 artifacts. The majority are large flakes, much rolled, sometimes to the point where the edges and ridges are all but obliterated. Most have wide, high angle, plain butts, but a good proportion are faceted or dihedral (fig. 9).

Many of the flakes are manifestly elongated, and blades (flake-blades) are common, as are naturally backed knives. With these flakes a certain number of chopping tools and cores, but no bifaces, were found. A small proportion of Levallois debitage is present. The large sample collected authorizes us to confirm that this is not Acheulean. However, if it is Tayacian, it is a kind completely different from that from Tabun G, which is morphologically dissimilar and more evolved. This original industry is clearly dated to the end of Mindel/Riss or the very earliest part of the Riss retreat (table 1).

Were the form of the flakes not so different at Ras Beirut, it would be somewhat reminiscent of the Clactonian of Europe (with its larger and broader flakes), to which the *Cordon Littoral* is fairly close in age.

CONCLUSIONS

It is now time to come to some conclusions and to make clear what we know of the Levantine Lower Paleolithic.

1. The first new fact is the presence of an ancient industry, apparently non-Acheulean, dating to Günz and Günz/Mindel. Quantitatively, the amount of evidence is small, but given the scarcity of informaton relating to this early era, the very existence of three sites such as Sharia, Rastan, and Borj Qinnarit is interesting.

2. An Early Middle Acheulean can be distinguished, which dates to Mindel and Mindel/Riss, and which is in the line of succession from Ubeidiya both typologically (trihedrals, polyhedrons, and chopping tools accompanying bi-

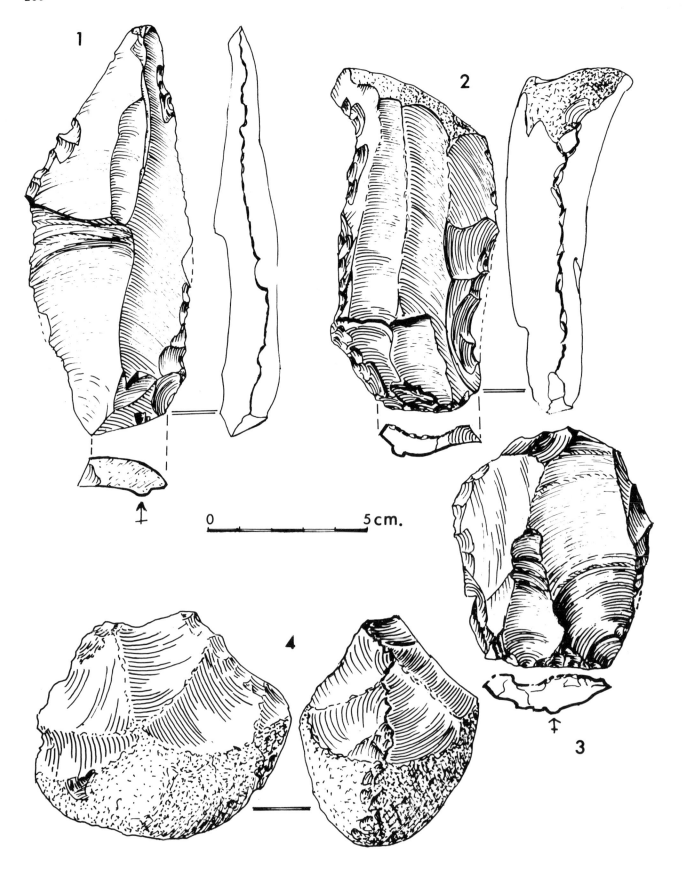

FIG. 9–"Tayacian," Ras Beirut II (*Cordon Littoral*). *1* and *2*: Large blades. *3*: Proto-Levallois flake. *4*: Chopping tool. No. 2 is slightly rolled, 3 is smoothed, 4 is rolled.

faces) and chronologically. One can perhaps conclude that in Syria and Lebanon this Early Middle Acheulean, the "Latamné phase of the Syrian Middle Acheulean" (Clark, 1966b, pp. 80-87), came from the south. It consists of a typologically characteristic assemblage, close to that of Abbasiyeh, near Cairo (Bovier-Lapierre, 1925, 1926) and even to that of Ternifine (Balout et al., 1967), or to that of Chalosse (Thibault, 1968, pp. 436-38), confirming the ideas of Passemard forty years before. The data furnished by Ras Beirut Ib and Wadi Aabet are particularly valuable, since, in the same geological situation toward the middle of Mindel/ Riss, Ras Beirut Ib follows the Latamné tradition, while Wadi Aabet is quite different. The end of the Early Middle Acheulean with trihedrals could thus be dated in the Levant to the end of the first Jbailian transgression.

3. It is impossible for the moment to trace, on Syrian and Lebanese evidence, the line between the Middle and Late (*Récent*) Acheulean. The sites are too unconnected to any stratigraphic context for such an attempt to be worthwhile. Perhaps sites in Israel such as Jisr Banat Yaqub, Evron, and Holon will furnish a model typological framework which we can use in classifying our northern industries.

We must await more, and more precise, analyses, as well as more complete surveys which, hopefully, will find new sites in sure contexts before we can have any clearer view of the evolution of the Middle/Late Acheulean which, at the moment, appears as an undifferentiated agglomeration.

4. Taking into account the distribution of the Acheulean sites in the Levant, it is not unlikely that the Euphrates represents the northeastern frontier of the biface industrial province, given that in spite of numerous prehistoric expeditions which have surveyed the Zagros over the past few years (e.g., those of Braidwood, Hole and Flannery, Solecki, and McBurney), practically no trace has been found of the Acheulean in Iraq and Iran, except at Barda Balka. It remains to be seen whether this is, in fact, the case—if so, it needs some explanation.

5. Taking into account the three earliest flake sites and Ras Beirut II, it could be that we have here the remains of a Levantine Lower Paleolithic tradition without bifaces. Such a tradition is known elsewhere, e.g., the Clactonian in Europe, some assemblages in South Arabia and in India (Caton-Thompson, 1953). Here again, much more evidence is needed before this can be confirmed or reasonably interpreted.

6. The lack of anthropological, ecological, let alone paleoethnological, data is only too cruelly apparent, and the point need not be pressed further. The excavation of Clark at Latamné is the only glimmer of light in the darkness. It is surely in the direction of filling the gaps in our knowledge of these subjects that new excavations and research must be oriented.

BIBLIOGRAPHY

BALOUT, L; BIBERSON, P.; and TIXIER, J., 1967. "L'Acheuléen de Ternifine (Algérie). Gisement de l'Atlanthrope." *L'Anthropologie* 71:217-37.

BAR-YOSEF, O., and TCHERNOV, E., 1972. "On the Palaeo-ecological History of the Site of Ubeidiya." *Proceedings of the Israel Academy of Sciences and Humanities.*

BAUDOUIN, A., and BURKHALTER, L., 1930. "Station chelléenne et acheuléenne de surface à Kalat Yahmour." *Bulletin de la Société Préhistorique Française* 27.

BEAUDET, G., 1971. "Le quaternaire marocain: état des études." *Revue de Géographie du Maroc* 20:3-55.

BERGY, A., 1932. "Le Paléolithique ancien stratifié à Ras Beyrouth." *Mélanges de l'Université Saint-Joseph* 16(5):169-216.

BESANCON, J; COPELAND, L.; and HOURS, F., 1970. "L'Acheuléen de Joub Jannine II. Compte-rendu d'un sondage effectué en 1968." *Bulletin du Musée de Beyrouth* 23:9-24.

_____, and HOURS, F., 1970. "Préhistoire et géomorphologie: les formes du relief et les dépôts quaternaires dans la région de Joub Jannine (Béqaa méridionale, Liban), 1." *Hannon* 5:63-95.

_____, and HOURS, F., 1971. "Préhistoire et géomorphologie: les formes du relief et les dépôts quaternaires dans la région de Joub Jannine (Béqaa méridionale, Liban), 2." *Hannon* 6:29-135.

BORDES, F., 1961. *Typologie du Paléolithique ancien et moyen.* Bordeaux: Mémoire 1, Publication de l'Institut de Préhistoire de l'Université de Bordeaux.

BOVIER-LAPIERRE, P., 1908. "Stations préhistoriques du Beled Becharra (Haute Galilée)." *La Géographie* 17:77-79.

_____, 1925. "Le Paléolithique stratifié des environs du Caire." *L'Anthropologie* 35:37-46.

_____, 1926. "Les gisements paléolithiques de la plaine de l'Abbassieh." *Bulletin de l'Institut d'Egypte* 8:257-75.

BURKHALTER, L., 1933. "Note sur les stations préhistoriques du Gouvernement de Lattaquié." *Bulletin de la Société Préhistorique Française* 30:582-87.

_____, 1946-1948. "Bibliographie préhistorique." *Bulletin du Musée de Beyrouth* 8:129-53.

_____, 1949-1950. "Bibliographie préhistorique (suite)." *Bulletin du Musée de Beyrouth* 9:1-52.

CATON-THOMPSON, G., 1953. "Some Paleoliths from South Arabia." *Proceedings of the Prehistoric Society* 19:189-218.

CAUVIN, J., 1970. "Mission 1969 en Djézireh (Syrie)." *Bulletin de la Société Préhistorique Française* 67:CRSM 286-87.

CLARK, J. D., 1966a. "The Middle Acheulean Occupation Site at Latamné, Northern Syria." *Annales Archéologiques Arabes Syriennes* 16(2):31-75. (Id. in *Quaternaria* 9 (1967):1-68).

_____, 1966b. "Further Excavations (1965) at the Middle Acheulean Occupation Site at Latamné." *Annales Archéologiques Arabes Syriennes* 16(2):76-121. (Id. in *Quaternaria* 10 (1968):1-76).

COON, C., 1957. *The Seven Caves. Archaeological Exploration in the Middle East.* New York: A. Knopf.

COPELAND, L., 1966. "Inventory of Stone Age Sites in Lebanon. Part Two: North, South, and East Central Lebanon." *Mélanges de l'Université Saint-Joseph* 42:1-174.

_____, and WESCOMBE, P., 1965. "Inventory of Stone Age Sites in Lebanon. Part One: West Central Lebanon." *Mélanges de l'Université Saint-Joseph* 41:29-175.

DESRIBES, R., 1921. "Quelques ateliers paléolithiques des environs de Beyrouth." *Mélanges de l'Université Saint-Joseph* 7:189-210.

FIELD, H., 1960. *North Arabian Desert Archaeological Survey, 1925-1950.* Cambridge, Massachusetts: Peabody Museum Papers 45 (2).

FLEISCH, H., 1950. "Préhistoire et brèche de pente du niveau de 45 m à Ras Beyrouth, Liban." *Atti del I Congresso Internazionale di Preistoria e Protoistoria Mediterranea (Firenze)*, pp. 79-80.

————, 1954. "Nouvelles stations préhistoriques au Liban." *Bulletin de la Société Préhistorique Française* 51:564-68.

————, 1956. "Dépôts préhistoriques de la côte Libanaise et leur place dans la chronologie basée sur le quaternaire marin." *Quaternaria* 3:101-32.

————, 1960. "Les industries lithiques récentes de la Béqaa, République Libanaise." *VIe Congrès International des Sciences Anthropologiques et Ethnologiques, Paris* 2(1):389 sq.

————, 1962. "La côte Libanaise au Pleistocène ancien et moyen." *Quaternaria* 6:497-524.

————, 1966. "Notes de préhistoire Libanaise." *Bulletin de la Société Préhistorique Française* 63, CRSM 239-42.

————; REMIRO, J.; and SANLAVILLE, P., 1969. "Gisements préhistoriques découverts dans la région de Batroun (Liban)." *Mélanges de l'Université Saint-Joseph* 45:1-27.

————, and SANLAVILLE, P., 1969. "Vues nouvelles sur Ras Beyrouth." *Hannon* 4:93-102.

GARROD, D., 1962. "The Middle Palaeolithic of the Near East, and the Problem of Mount Carmel Man." *Journal of the Royal Anthropological Institute* 92:232-51.

GILEAD, D., 1970. "Handaxe Industries in Israel and the Near East." *World Archaeology* 2:2-11.

GUERRE, A., and SANLAVILLE, P., 1970. "Sur les hauts niveaux marins quaternaires du Liban." *Hannon* 5:21-27.

de HEINZELIN, J., 1966. "Geological Observations near Latamné." *Annales Archéologiques Arabes Syriennes* 16(2):115-20.

HOOIJER, D., 1961-1962. "Middle Pleistocene Mammals from Latamné, Orontes Valley." *Annales Archéologiques Arabes Syriennes* 11-12:117-32.

HOURS, F.; COPELAND, L.; and AURENCHE, O., 1973. "Les industries paléolithiques du Proche-Orient; essai de correlation." *L'Anthropologie* 77(3-4):229-80.

————, and SANLAVILLE, P., 1972. "Découverte de silex taillés dans une plage située à + 95 m à Borj Qinnarit (Liban)." *Compte-rendus de l'Academie des Sciences* 275(D):2219-21.

HOWELL, F. C., 1959. "Upper Pleistocene Stratigraphy and Early Man in the Levant." *Proceedings of the American Philosophical Society* 103:1-65.

KARGE, P., 1917. *Rephaim. Die vorgeschichtliche Kultur Palästinas und Phöniziens.* Paderborn: Schöning.

LARTET, L., 1865. "Note sur la découverte de silex taillés en Syrie." *Bulletin de la Société Géologique Française* 2e série 22:537.

————, 1877. "Vestiges des temps préhistoriques en Syrie et en Palestine." In *Voyage d'exploration à la Mer Morte*, edited by A. de Luynes, t. 3, ch. 11:213-40.

MALLON, A., 1925. "Quelques stations préhistoriques de Palestine." *Mélanges de l'Université Saint-Joseph* 10:183-214.

MODDERMAN, P., 1964. "On a Survey of Palaeolithic Sites near Hama." *Annales Archéologiques Arabes Syriennes* 14:51-56.

MORGAN, J. de, 1927. *La Préhistoire Orientale. T. III l'Asie antérieure*. Paris: Geuthner.

NASRALLAH, J., 1951. "Recherches préhistoriques dans le Qalamun." *Annales Archéologiques Arabes Syriennes* 1:80-106.

NEOPHYTUS, F., and PALLARY, P., 1914. "La Phénicie préhistorique." *L'Anthropologie* 25:1-23.

NEUVILLE, R., 1932. "Affinités néolithique du 'Chalossien d'Egypte." *Bulletin de la Société Préhistorique Française* 29.

_____, 1951. *Le Paléolithique et le Mésolithique du Désert de Judée*. Archives de l'Institut de Paléontologie humaine, mémoire 24.

NIKLEWSKI, J., and VAN ZEIST, W., 1970. "A Late Quaternary Pollen Diagram from Northwestern Syria." *Acta Botanica Neerlandica* 19(5):737-54.

PABOT, H., 1957. "Rapport au gouvernement de Syrie sur l'écologie végétale et ses applications." *F.A.O. rapport, No. 663*, Rome.

_____, 1959. "Rapport au gouvernement du Liban sur la végétation sylvopastorale et son écologie." *F.A.O. rapport No. 1126*, Rome.

PASSEMARD, E., 1926. "Les terrasses alluviales de l'Euphrate et les industries qu'elles contiennent." *Compte-rendus de l'Académie des Sciences* 183:365-68.

_____, 1926-1927. "Recherches préhistoriques dans les territoires de Syrie, du Liban et des Alaouites." *Association Française pur l'Avancement des Sciences, Congrès de Lyon*, pp. 462-65.

_____, 1927a. "La station chelléenne de Khillalé près Lattakieh." *Syria* 8:169-73.

_____, 1927b. "Le Chalossien en France, en Egypte et en Syrie." *Syria* 8:342-51.

_____, 1927c. "Mission en Syrie et au Liban." *Bulletin de la Société Préhistorique Française* 24:70-74.

PERROT, J., 1968. "La préhistoire palestinienne." In *Supplément au Dictionnaire de la Bible* 8(43):286-446. Paris: Letouzey et Ane.

PERVES, M., 1945. "Notes sommaires de préhistoire syro-Libanaise." *Bulletin de la Société Préhistorique Française* 42:201-8.

_____, 1946-1948. "La préhistoire de la Syrie et du Liban." *Syria* 25:109-29.

_____, 1964. "La préhistoire de la région du moyen Euphrate." *Bulletin de la Société Préhistorique Française* 61:422-35.

PLASSARD, J., 1972. *Carte pluviométrique du Liban au 1.200,000*. Service météorologique du Liban, Beirut.

POTUT, L., 1937. "La préhistoire dans la région de Damas." *Bulletin de la Société Préhistorique Française* 34:130-32.

RUST, A., 1933. "Beitrag zur Erkenntniss der Abwicklung der vorgeschichtlichen Kulturperioden in Syrien." *Praehistorische Zeitschrift* 24:205-18.

SANLAVILLE, P., 1969. "Les bas niveaux marins pleistocènes du Liban." *Miditerranée* 3:257-92.

_____, 1973. "Étude Géomorphologique de la région littorale du Liban." French State Doctoral Dissertation.

SCHROEDER, B., 1969. "The Lithic Industries from Jerf Ajla and Their Bearing on the Problem of a Middle to Upper Palaeolithic Transition." Ph.D. dissertation, Columbia University.

SOLECKI, R. S., 1968. "The Shamsi Industry, a Tayacian Related Industry at Yabroud, Preliminary Report." In *La Préhistoire, problèmes et tendances*, edited by F. Bordes, pp. 401-10. Paris: CNRS.

————, and SOLECKI, R. L., 1966. "New Data from Yabroud, Syria: Preliminary Report of the Columbia University Archaeological Investigations." *Annales Archeologiques Arabes Syriennes* 16(2):121-54.

STEKELIS, M., and GILEAD, D., 1966. "Ma'ayan Barukh, a Lower Paleolithic Site in Upper Galilee." *Mitqufat ha-Even* 8.

SUZUKI, H., and KOBORI, I. (eds.), 1970. *Report of the Reconnaissance Survey on Paleolithic Sites in Lebanon and Syria*. Bulletin No. 1, University Museum, University of Tokyo.

THIBAULT, C., 1968. "Un gisement paléolithique inférieur et moyen de plein air en Chalosse; Nantet, commune d'Eyres-Moncube (Landes)." In *La Préhistoire, problèmes et tendances*, edited by F. Bordes, pp. 427-38. Paris: CNRS.

VAN DUSEN EGGERS, A., 1966. "Artifacts Collected from the Middle Orontes Area, near Latamné, Northern Syria." *Annales Archéologiques Arabes Syriennes* 16(2):104-9.

VAN LIERE, W. J., 1960. "Un gisement paléolithique dans un niveau Pleistocène de l'Oronte à Latamné, Syrie." *Annales Archéologiques Arabes Syriennes* 10:165-74.

————, 1961. "Observations on the Quaternary of Syria." *Berichte von de Rijkdienst voor het Oudheidkundig Bodemonderzoek* 10-11:1-69.

————, 1966. "The Pleistocene and Stone Age of the Orontes River (Syria)." *Annales Archéologiques Arabes Syriennes* 16(2):7-30.

————, and HOOIJER, D., 1961. "A Paleo-Orontes Level with *Archidiskodon meridionalis* (Nesti) at Hama." *Annales Archéologiques Arabes Syriennes* 11:168-73.

VAUFREY, R., 1948. Review of "Le quaternaire côtier de la région de Tripoli (Liban)," by R. Wetzel and J. Haller, *Notes et Mémoires (Beyrouth)* 4:1-49. *L'Anthropologie* 52:303-7.

VAUMAS, E. de, 1947. "Les terrasses d'abrasion marine de la côte Libanaise." *Bulletin de la Société Royale de Géographie d'Egypte* 22:21-85.

WENDT, W., 1971. *Das Paläolithikum im Tal des Nahr el Kebir (Nordsyrien) und seine Beziehungen zu den Quartären Fluss-und Strandterrassen*. Cologne: Institut für Ur-und Frühgeschichte.

WETZEL, R., and HALLER, J., 1945-1948. "Le quaternaire côtier de la région de Tripoli (Liban)." *Notes et Mémoires (Beyrouth)* 4:1-49.

ZUMOFFEN, G., 1897. "L'âge de la pierre en Phénicie." *L'Anthropologie* 8:272-83 and 426-38.

————, 1900. *La Phénicie avant les Phéniciens. L'âge de la pierre*. Beirut: Imprimerie Catholique.

————, 1908. "L'âge de la pierre en Phénicie." *Anthropos* 3:431-55.

LOWER AND MIDDLE PALEOLITHIC SETTLEMENT PATTERNS
IN THE LEVANT

David Gilead
Institute of Archaeology
Tel Aviv University

INTRODUCTION

The Levant, which is the subject of this survey, includes three main elongated belts running north/south; from west to east are the coastal plain, the hilly regions, and the Jordan Rift Valley. Southward they border on the Negev and Sinai deserts. Eastward, the Transjordanian plateau stretches into the Syrian desert. To the north and northeast, beyond the desert-steppe, rise the hills and mountains of Southeastern Anatolia and Kurdistan. The region is heterogeneous in topography, relief, climate, and biogeography. The environmental differences were well expressed by Garrod (1962), who wrote that the Levant covers "in a small space a contrast in altitude and climate . . . unequalled in the world."

Climatic fluctuations in the Eastern Mediterranean during the Pleistocene have been inferred from a variety of biological and geological data. The prevailing impression is that there have not been any remarkable changes in the overall environmental pattern, although the borders between the various climatic and vegetational zones have shifted in the past. Elaboration of more detailed environments, so important in the study of Paleolithic settlement patterns, requires ample evidence obtained by various disciplines (palynology, geology, geomorphology, pedology, etc.) and an overall interdisciplinary approach. It is still quite difficult to place the archaeological occurrences within good chronological frameworks; detailed paleogeographic or faunal analyses are rare; a considerable amount of various data have yet to be published. Consequently, there is a large degree of generalization in this work. Nevertheless, even with the incomplete records and the realization that many points are open to criticism and revision, the first step must be taken, if only to facilitate subsequent work.

A detailed survey and discussion of Acheulean occurrences in Israel, Jordan, Lebanon, and Syria has been done elsewhere (Gilead, 1970*a*, 1970*b*). Since the survey includes about 200 find-spots, it will not be repeated here, and the extensive bibliographical references will be omitted as well. Figure 1, however, shows a simplified distribution of Acheulean sites in the Near East. No comparable survey of the Mousterian exists, and therefore these occurrences will be described in somewhat more detail.

THE ACHEULEAN OCCURRENCES

Early Acheulean industries are known at Ubeidiya in the Jordan Valley (Bar-Yosef and Tchernov, 1972) and prob-

ably also at Joub Jannine in the Béqaa (Besançon et al., 1970) and Kefar Menahem in the coastal plain (Gilead, unpublished). Middle Acheulean evidences were discovered at Latamne in the Orontes Valley (Clark, 1967); Evron-Quarry (Gilead and Ronen, 1973); and Holon (Yizraeli, 1967) in the coastal plain; and in the Hula Valley at Gesher Benot Yaaqov (Stekelis, 1960; Gilead 1970*a*) and in eastern Judea at Umm Qatafa, Layer E (Neuville, 1951). Most of the other find-spots mentioned in this survey belong to the rather complex Late Acheulean (see Gilead 1970*a*, 1970*b*). In fact, the analyzed sample consists essentially of Late Acheulean occurrences. A detailed breakdown of the sample would probably provide more meaningful results, but because of numerous difficulties, this has not been attempted here. Some of the characteristics of Acheulean geographical distribution and settlement patterns are outlined below:

1. The majority of Acheulean habitations are in the open, as attested to by about 200 find-spots. The use of natural shelters is known in the final Middle and Late Acheulean: Umm Qatafa Cave, Tabun Cave, Zuttiyeh Cave, Jabrud Rockshelter I, Abri Zumoffen, and Bezez Cave.

2. In general, the geographical distribution includes the present-day favorable and marginal areas. It is quite possible that the marginal semidesert areas were frequented during humid phases, but it might be remarked that some of them could be favorable for occupation at present were it not for the destruction wrought by man in historical times. In the arid regions traces of occupation are rare, except near extant or extinct water sources (springs, mudflats, flooded depression).

3. Several find-spots in the hilly zone are located at rather high elevations: Jabrud at 1,400 m; several find-spots in Upper Galilee, Southern Lebanon, Golan, and Moav at about 1,000 m; and in the Judean Hills some are located at 600 m–800 m above sea level. The occupation of these highlands by Late Acheulean groups was probably confined to warmer or drier periods.

4. In the analysis of the distribution in the uplands of Judea, Samaria, Galilee, Lebanon, and Syria, two phenomena are most striking. First, when plotted on geomorphological maps, the find-spots are found bordering the small intermontane plains and basins or are located on plateaus. Secondly, when plotted on geological maps, they occur almost exclusively on two formations: basalt and Eocene limestone. The most reasonable explanation of the second phenomenon is that the vegetation on those formations was of the type favored by herbivores upon which

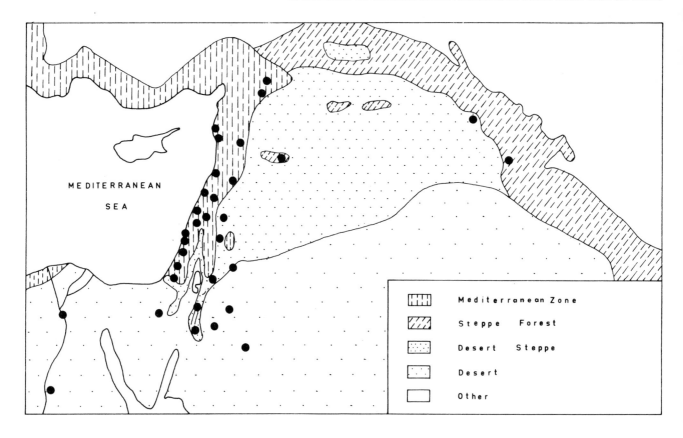

Fig. 1–The general distribution of Early Paleolithic find-spots in the major ecological zones of the Near East (based on M. Zohary, Vegetation maps, Atlas of Israel).

man largely depended for his food supply. This hypothesis is based on biogeographical studies (Brosh, 1960; Berliner, 1972) which stress the difference between vegetation on the basaltic or Eocene soils and that on *terra rosa* soils. It is assumed (Berliner, 1972; Zohary, 1964) that the climax vegetation of the former was of the open forest type (*Quercus ithaburensis* and *Pistacia atlantica* association). In fact, there is a large degree of correlation between the Acheulean find-spots in Israel and regions with an assumed climax vegetation of the Tabor oak park forest. Those are the Manashe Hills, Shafaram Hills, the vicinity of Mount Tabor, the basaltic plateaus of Galilee and Golan, and large parts of the coastal plain. We can, thus, tentatively reconstruct the ecological setting of these find-spots: in a more open type of vegetation, often in the vicinity of forests.

Other possible explanations for the frequent location of find-spots on or near basaltic and Eocene formations are less convincing. These are the proximity to flint sources, availability of water, and—for physiogeographical reasons—a more favorable preservation of Paleolithic remains. The last-mentioned factor has yet to be tested. Also, problems regarding preferred use of various kinds of flint have not yet been studied in detail. Though the use of Eocene flint for tool manufacture is well attested, other flint was used as well. As to the availability of water, the evidence at present is not conclusive. Early Paleolithic man frequented springs and other water sources, but whereas those occur in other

formations as well, Early Paleolithic find-spots there are rare.

Among the find-spots situated on basalt are Dalton, Alma, several find-spots in Golan, and Jezzinne. In some cases (Yiron, Baram, Kh. Maskana, Ardes Saudc) the sites are located on small basaltic plateaus, often surrounded by Eocene formations. Several sites are situated close to extensive basalt formations: Maayan Barukh, Gesher Benot Yaaqov, and Zuttiyeh. Find-spots on or near the margins of Eocene formations are quite numerous: several in Menashe Hills, Shafaram Hills, northern parts of Shomron Hills, Shephela; several in Lebanon and Syria (such as Hallet el Hamra, Akbiyeh, Nebatiyeh, Jabrud, Dara); several find-spots on the Upper Euphrates, a site near Maan in Jordan; and others.

5. There was a considerable occupation of the coastal plain (Gilead, 1973b), and several common features can be discerned there in the location of Early Paleolithic find-spots. In Israel, all are situated east of the third Kurkar ridge in the Sharon and its equivalents in the northern and southern coastal plain. This is certainly due to the fact that the upper deposits west of that ridge are post-Acheulean in age. The find-spots are very often associated with *hamra* soils; in many cases they occur on the *hamra* paleocomplex, partly covered by grumosols. The find-spots occur in the eroded parts of this complex. Since *hamra* soils develop throughout time, however, it is still unknown at which

exact stage in their development they were occupied by Acheulean peoples. More work is greatly needed to clear up this point.

The detailed paleoenvironment of each find-spot has yet to be reconstructed with the combined help of geology, geomorphology, pedology, palynology, and, where possible, paleontology. An interesting attempt to reconstruct former drainage systems in the coastal plain was made by Gvirtzman (1969). He demonstrated that the major drainage systems of the past have not changed their positions very much. Figure 2 shows an interesting degree of correlation between the Early Paleolithic find-spots and Gvirtzman's (1969, map 23) reconstructed drainage system 2, preserved at the base of the Pleshet Formation. It is assumed that this drainage system was still largely preserved during the coastal plain Acheulean and that it represents more accurately the course of the streams at that time than does the present-day drainage which was determined, to some degree, by later sands.

The available data suggest that the coastal plain had a park-forest character in its northern parts, with scattered streams, swamps, and some more or less perennial water bodies. There were probably gallery forests in the river valleys. The more southern parts of the region might have been in the nature of a park-savanna or of a drier savanna. These plains supported a varied plant complex and, thus, had a high potential of various species of food animals and edible plants. During the winter season good pasture for herds of wild ungulates was certainly available even in the more southern parts of the region. Estimates of available food in various ecological zones, as obtained by the index of carrying capacities based on biomass statistics of hoofed animals, and by some general data on the vegetable food sources, emphasize the potential of ecological regions such as that reconstructed for the coastal plain. With all the necessary reservations due to the still insufficient data we can, nevertheless, assume that the coastal plain was, for Acheulean man, one of the main resource areas in the country.

Caves (Tabun), rockshelters (Adlun), and open-air find-spots (Ras Beirut) located on the edge of the coastal plain were occupied as well, and their inhabitants certainly exploited the plain's potential.

From the Early Paleolithic deposits at Evron, remains of elephant, hippopotamus, warthog, and ruminants have been reported. Excavations at Holon unearthed rich faunal remains, and preliminary reports mentioned elephant, hippopotamus, deer, equid, and bovid. Preliminary identification of faunal remains at Nahal Hesi revealed small equids. At Abri Zumoffen cave, bear, rhinoceros, pig, equid, cattle, gazelle, goat, and deer were reported. This site is situated at the edge of the coastal plain, bordering on hills, so that the faunal assemblage expresses, to a certain extent, hilly habitats as well. A similar situation exists at Tabun Cave, where the faunal remains of layers F and E include gazelle, hippopotamus, elephant, pig, deer, goat, equid, and other species. It is evident that man exploited

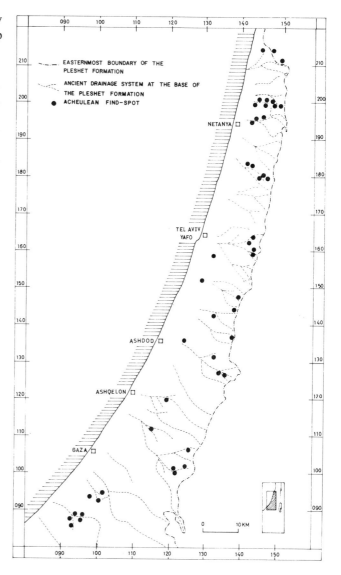

Fig. 2—Acheulean find-spots in the coastal plain of Israel in relation to an ancient drainage system (after Gvirtzman, 1969).

the permanent resources of the rivers and marshes and hunted the wild ungulates of the plain.

Some quantitative data were provided by Garrod and Bate (1937) on Tabun. Using the data of Perkins and Daly (1968), and assuming that the number of bones at Tabun actually reflects the number of individuals, the supply in terms of edible meat of the three main species would be as follows:

	Gazella	*Bos*	*Dama*
Tabun Ea	11%	67%	22%
Tabun Eb	6%	66%	28%

6. The major river valleys were frequented, as attested to by finds from the Upper Euphrates, Hama and Latamne on the Orontes, the Nahr el Kebir occurrences, Joub Jannine on the Litani, and Kissufim-Beeri on Nahal Besor. Lake shores occupied were Ubeidiya, Gesher Benot Yaaqov, and Azraq. Holon and Nahal Hesi were situated near small

lakes or marshes. The choice of sandbanks or sandy soils near the course of a stream was apparently quite common in the location of Acheulean sites.

7. The Acheulean of Jabrudian facies is confined to Tabun, Zuttiyeh, Jabrud, Adlun, and Maslukh. All these are natural shelters. They are located in what would be moderate climatic regions during pluvial times. It is of interest to note that the Amudian/Pre-Aurignacian occurrences are confined to those sites too (with the exception of Maslukh) and that there is a subsequent Mousterian occupation in them (also with the exception of Maslukh).

8. There are open-air occurrences where a vertical or, more often, a horizontal scatter of cultural material indicates that they were occupied on several occasions. Good examples are Ubeidiya, Gesher Benot Yaaqov, Evron, Maayan Barukh, and Joub Jannine. The same is true of most of the natural shelters.

9. Numerous find-spots which have yielded a small number of artifacts can probably be regarded as shifting, ephemeral, or seasonal occupations. Some sites might be regarded as situated along valleys leading from the coastal plain, and other plains, into the foothills and uplands, perhaps in connection with seasonal game movements.

10. The factor of proximity to sources of raw material has yet to be worked out. There are numerous sites (Rephaim-Baqa, Scopus, Adlun, sites in the Béqaa, in the Negev, and others) which are located close to large outcrops of flint. Other sites, however, are situated at some distance from suitable flint (Maayan Barukh, numerous sites in the coastal plain, several find-spots located on basaltic formations but with flint artifacts), and it appears that this factor was not always decisive in the location of sites.

11. Careful and detailed paleoecological reconstruction of the archaeological occurrences at the early site of Ubeidiya has been attempted by Bar-Yosef and Tchernov (1972) and will not be repeated here. They demonstrated that archaeological occurrences were found on a lake beach, at the edges of an alluvial fan, on mudflats or temporarily dried swamps, and on the hilly flanks.

12. The faunal evidence summarized, in brief, in Table 1 confirms the general impression that the location of sites often enabled the exploitation of several ecotypes.

THE MOUSTERIAN OCCURRENCES

The archaeological occurrences included in this survey belong to the industrial complex known as Levalloiso-Mousterian, now termed Levantine Mousterian. Chronologically, it postdates the last major marine transgression and, thus, might be assigned by the European glacial chronology to the Early Würm (though apparently not to its earliest phase). Its time span can be estimated as not less than 25,000 years. In the absence of a clear chronological and cultural subdivision of this complex, no grouping of the various occurrences is attempted. This certainly impairs the results of this study, especially since it is often assumed that intersite variability on the same cultural level reflects differences in settlement type. The Mousterian occupation

TABLE 1
Some Faunal Elements at Early Paleolithic Sites

	Elephants	Rhinoceros	Hippopotamus	Equid	Pig	Bovid	Bear	Deer	Goat	Gazelle - antelope
Ubeidiya	x	x	x	x	x	x	x	x	x	x
Latamne	x	x	x	x		x		x		x
Gesher Benot Yaaqov	x	x	x	x		x		x		
Holon	x		x	x		x		x		
Umm Qatafa E				x				x	x	x
Umm Qatafa D			x			x	x	x	x	x
Tabun E	x	x	x	x	x			x	x	x
Abri Zumoffen			x		x	x	x	x	x	x
Masloukh			x		x	x	x		x	x
Barda Balka	x	x		x		x			x	
Evron	x		x	x						
Zuttiyeh			x	x	x	x	x	x	x	

involves not only a relatively long period of time, but also apparently more than one climatic phase. In fact, climatic fluctuations during this cultural phase are claimed to have been demonstrated at several sites (e.g., Tabun and Geula).

Very little has been done so far in the study of the geographical distribution or the settlement patterns during the Levantine Mousterian. In the distribution map of Paleolithic sites published in the *Atlas of Israel*, compiled by Stekelis (1964), Mousterian occurrences are not distinguished from other Paleolithic find-spots. Mousterian find-spots in Lebanon were recorded by Copeland and Wescombe (1965, 1966) in their inventory of the Lebanese prehistoric sites. Howell, in his comprehensive survey of the Upper Pleistocene in the Levant, expressed the view of several of the earlier workers when he stated that the Mousterian "was common over much of southwest Asia" (Howell, 1959, p. 37). Binford (1968) touched on the distributional aspect, and Marks (1971) drew new attention to this interesting problem and to the Mousterian occurrences in the Negev.

It is not feasible, in the present stage of archaeological record and publication, to make any intelligent distinctions between home base, transit site, kill site, etc.; the recognition of workshop sites, however, seems to be less problematic. The distributional characteristics outlined here can be regarded as the cumulative effect of long-term trends, and some overall patterns can be discerned. Those will be described later; first, a brief description of Mousterian occurrences, grouped by the main geographical regions, will be provided (fig. 3).

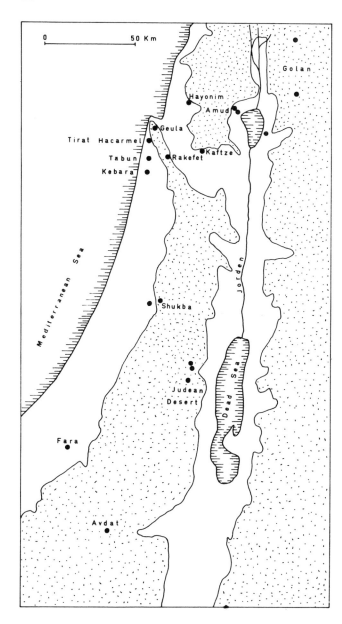

Fig. 3–Location map of some Mousterian occurrences in Israel. Dotted areas are over 200 m mean sea level.

GALILEE

Mousterian industries were reported from the lower reaches of Wadi Amud, at altitudes below sea level, at Zuttiyeh Cave (Turville-Petre, 1927), and at Shubbabiq (Binford, 1966). Kaftze Cave (Neuville, 1951) is located at the southern extent of Lower Galilee, south of Nazaret (fig. 4). Hayonim Cave (Bar-Yosef, 1971) is located in Western Galilee, on the banks of Nahal Izhar. Surface finds were reported from Gesher Benot Yaaqov (Stekelis, 1960; Gilead, 1970*a*) and workshops from the eastern shores of Kineret Lake, near the Neogene conglomerates (Bar-Yosef, 1972, p. 253); and some artifacts were collected by N. Zori (personal communication) in the Beth Shean area.

MOUNT CARMEL

Several sites are located on the western slopes of Mt. Carmel: Tabun, Skhul, and El Wad (Garrod and Bate, 1937; Jelinek et al., 1973); Kebara Cave (Stekelis, unpublished); Abu Usba Cave (Stekelis and Haas, 1952); Upper Fellah Cave (Olami, 1958); Sh. Suleiman (or Ornit) Cave (Olami, 1962); open-air occurrences at Tirat Hacarmel (Ronen, 1970); Missiliya and other largely ruined caves and rockshelters on the western cliff-line of Mt. Carmel; and Geula Cave at Haifa (Wreschner et al., 1967). Rakefet Cave is located on the eastern flanks of the Carmel, close to Nahal Yokneam (Higgs and Noy, 1973).

JUDEA

Shukba Cave is located on the western flanks of the Judean Hills (Garrod, 1942), and nearby is the Watwat Cave (Stekelis, 1942) in Nahal Beit Arif. On the eastern flanks of the Judean Hills are Erq el Ahmar rockshelter, Abu Sif Cave, Sahba Cave, Tabban Cave, Umm Naqous Cave (for all, see Neuville, 1952), and Larikba (Vandermeersch, 1966).

NEGEV

There are several excavated occurrences reported from the Avdat area (Marks, 1971), while surface collections were made in other parts of the region (Gilead, 1973*a*). Mousterian occurrences were reported on the banks of Nahal Besor, near Tell Fara (Price-Williams, 1973).

JORDAN

Surface finds were reported near Mafraq (Zeuner, 1957), in the Azraq depression (Clutton-Brock, 1970) and in the Jafr depression (Huckriede and Wiesemann, 1968).

GOLAN

Several surface finds were reported (Kochavi, 1973).

SYRIA

Jabrud, located on the eastern flanks of the Anti-Lebanon, is the most important locality (Rust, 1950). Finds were reported from the Palmyra region (Coon, 1957; Suzuki and Kobori, 1970). Of those farther east, Shanidar (Solecki, 1964) and Hazar Merd (Garrod, 1930) in Iraqi Kurdistan should be mentioned.

THE MEDITERRANEAN COASTLANDS

Mousterian occurrences are very rare in the coastal plain of Israel, and only a few find-spots were recorded (Ronen and Farrand, 1973). The Carmel sites facing the coastal plain were mentioned above. Farther north (fig. 4), Mousterian occurrences were recorded by Copeland and Wescombe (1965, 1966)—the more important sites being Ksar Akil, Bezez, Ras el Kelb, Nahr Ibrahim (Solecki, 1970), and Naamé (Fleisch, 1970). Surface finds were reported from *hamra* paleosols in the Beirut area (Fleisch, 1956). Still farther north, Mousterian industries were discovered in two

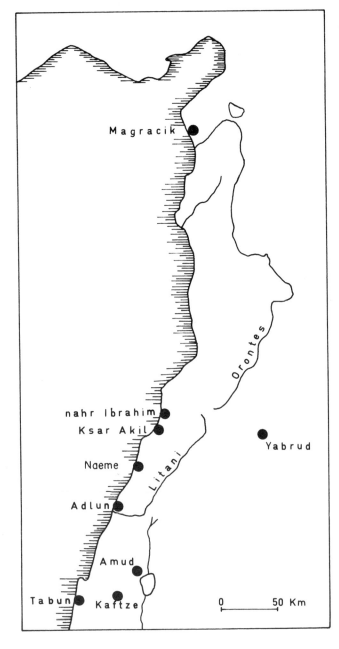

Fig. 4—Location map of some Mousterian occurrences in the Northern Levant.

caves near Magracik on the flanks of Samandag (Senyurek, 1959). Perrot (1968) mentioned surface finds in the Sakce—Gäzu plain and in the vicinity of Gaziantep.

Several characteristics that can be discerned in the site location of Mousterian occurrences are discussed below:

1. The majority of occurrences are situated in what is at present a Mediterranean climatic zone. This includes the numerous occupations from Shukba to Magracik. Sites in this zone are located at altitudes not exceeding 250 m, and most are located lower than that. The higher Mediterranean uplands (above 250 m) west of the Jordan Rift Valley were apparently not occupied, with rare exceptions of what looks like ephemeral, seasonal, or workshop remains.

2. The known distribution indicates a tendency toward the occupation of natural shelters (caves and rockshelters). In those parts of the Mediterranean zone where natural caves are absent, there seem to be only rare traces of occupation and often no occupation at all. In Ramot Menashe, for example, where lithology does not favor caves, hardly any traces of occupation were discovered. This sharply contrasts with the rich and numerous occurrences in the adjacent Mount Carmel area.

In the Carmel area, open-air occurrences were reported at Tirat Hacarmel. Farther north, in similar location, is the open-air site of Naamé. In the same region, however, numerous occurrences are known from natural shelters. There are no natural shelters in the coastal plain of Israel, and the rarity of Mousterian finds there is quite pronounced (though, perhaps, other factors are of importance here, and not just a preference for caves).

3. Numerous sites are in regions with present-day mean annual rainfall of 500 m—600 m, or less, and with mean annual temperatures not lower than 19° C. Only the sites along the coastal strip of Lebanon and Syria have, at present, a higher annual precipitation.

4. There is evidence of Mousterian occurrences in the present-day semiarid and arid regions. There is accumulating evidence, however, that at the time of this occupation these regions enjoyed a more humid climate, or perhaps it is that several of the sites were located at spots atypical of the area in which they lie—often next to rich water sources (Avdat, Azraq, Jafr, Kseimeh, Fara, Jabrud). In contrast to the generally low lying find-spots in the Mediterranean zone, sites in the marginal regions are often at higher elevations: Avdat, at about 500 m; Judean Desert sites, 500 m to 700 m; Shanidar, 800 m; Mafraq, 800 m; Golan, up to 1,000 m; and Jabrud, 1,400 meters.

5. A significant number of sites are located on the flanks of hills close to a plain and thus lie at the junction of at least two ecological zones. This is quite evident along the coastal plain where numerous sites are thus located. Examples of these would be Tabun, Kebara, Upper Fellah Cave, Abu Usba, Missiliyeh, Sefunim, Ornit, Tirat Hacarmel, Ras el Kelb, Amrit, Bezez, Magracik, and others. In other regions, one can mention Kaftze and Rakefet close to the Plain of Esdraelon, the Wadi Amud occurrences close to the Plain of Ginossar (apparently much wider at that time), sites on the Avdat Plateau, and Tell Fara in the Besor Plain. The majority are located very close to the plain. In a few instances the distance is somewhat greater but still within the limits of normal exploitation: Geula, about three kilometers; Rakefet and Hayonim, about four kilometers; and Shukba, about nine kilometers.

6. The proximity to flint sources was considered by Marks (1971) to be a major factor in the location of the Mousterian occurrences at Avdat. This factor was probably stronger in the location of open-air sites (such as Avdat or Tirat Hacarmel) than in the occupation of the relatively rare natural shelters. The general impression is that flint was often obtained from sources near the site or only a short

distance away. Mousterian workshop sites, for example, were reported (Archaeological Survey of Israel, unpublished) in the Carmel area, not far from sites such as Tabun, Kebara, Sefunim, or Geula. Workshops reported (Bar-Yosef, 1972) near Neogene conglomerates on the eastern shore of Lake Kineret might have supplied Mousterian groups on the basaltic plateau nearby.

7. It is difficult to reconstruct the water sources of the Mousterian sites. The proximity to springs, now active, is attested at several sites. On the other hand, there are regions rich in springs with no recorded Mousterian occurrences. Numerous sites are to be found in wadi valleys in the hilly regions, but this is a natural location of many caves and rockshelters. The available evidence does not indicate any intensive occupation along the major perennial rivers.

8. Faunal remains of food animals from an archaeological site can provide useful information on its paleoecological setting. Several authorities have expressed serious doubts as to the value of such an approach and stressed the effects of the cultural filter. It does not appear that the analysis of the faunal composition of food animals supports this opinion. Microfauna is a more sensitive indicator of paleoenvironments, but the area it reflects is generally rather limited in size (cf. Vita-Finzi and Higgs, 1970, p. 14), and what matters for the archaeologist are the wider biotopes exploited by the inhabitants of a site. In the analysis of faunal remains one encounters some difficulties, since only a portion of the results of such analyses have been published. Nonetheless, even the general data are of interest (see table 2).

For Tabun C, Haas (in Jelinek et al., 1973) assumed somewhat moister conditions than those of today, with woodlands and some grasslands; similar conditions were reconstructed by him for Geula (in Wreschner et al., 1967, p. 104). A humid, cool climate and the proximity of steppe was assumed for Kaftze (Bouchud, cited in Farrand, 1971). The faunal assemblage at Shubbabiq indicates a slightly cooler climate than exists today and a more wooded environment (Haas, in Binford, 1966, p. 97). The Shanidar and Hazar Merd fauna indicate a Mediterranean type vegetation, a country of woodlands, streamside thickets, and areas of open grasslands (Reed, in Braidwood and Howe, 1960). Thus, both the geographical setting and the faunal remains imply that at most sites more than one ecological zone was exploited.

9. Continuity or discontinuity in the occupation of a certain site during different periods might show environ-

TABLE 2
Some Faunal Elements at Mousterian Sites

	Gazelle	Equid	Bovid	Rhinoceros	Goat	Deer	Pig	Porcupine	Bear	Hippopotamus
Nahr Ibrahim		x	x	x						
Ras el Kelb			x		x	x			x	x
Ksar Akil		x	x	x	x	x	x	x	x	x
Naame			x	x	x		x		x	x
Tabun D-B		x	x	x	x	x	x	x	x	x
Geula			x	x	x	x	x	x	x	x
Rakefet		x						x		
Kaftze			x			x	x			
Shukba		x	x	x		x	x	x		
Shubbabiq		x		x		x	x	x		
Zuttiyeh		x	x	x		x	x	x	x	x
Abu Sif		x				x				
Sahba			x	x						
Erq el Ahmar	x	x	x		x	x				
Rosh Ein Mor		x								
Azraq			x	x	x	x				
Hazar Merd		x				x	x			

mental changes or cultural preferences. Several sites occupied by the Mousterians were previously occupied by Late Acheulean groups—for example, Tabun, Zuttiyeh, Jabrud Rockshelter I, Gesher Benot Yaaqov, and Bezez. It is, perhaps, of interest to note that none of these, with the possible exception of Bezez, show subsequent Upper Paleolithic occupation as well. At other sites, however—such as Kebara, Kaftze, Erq el Ahmar, Ksar Akil, and Shanidar—subsequent Upper Paleolithic occupation has been found. In several cases the Mousterian is the first occupation of sites at Sefunim, Rakefet, Abu Usba, Geula, Erq el Ahmar, Kaftze, Shanidar, and, perhaps, also at Kebara and Hayonim.

It is probably still too early to generalize on the available data. Morever, in several instances when there is no cultural continuity at a certain site, the other cultural phases can be found in the vicinity. On the whole, the distributional patterns of the Acheulean and Mousterian respectively seem to differ to a significant degree, probably more so than in the case of Mousterian and Upper Paleolithic occurrences.

BIBLIOGRAPHY

BAR-YOSEF, O., 1971. "Hayonim Cave." *Hadashot Archaeologiot* 40:2-3. (In Hebrew).

————— , 1972. "Prehistoric Man in the Kineret Region." *Salit* 1:52-56. (In Hebrew).

————— , and TCHERNOV, E., 1972. "On the Palaeo-ecological History of the Site of Ubeidiya." *Proceedings of the Israel Academy of Sciences and Humanities.*

BERLINER, R., 1972. "Vegetation of Basalt Areas in Galilee." *Teva Vaaretz* 15:19-21. (In Hebrew).

BESANCON, J., COPELAND, L., and HOURS, F., 1970. "L'Acheuléen de Joub Jannine II." *Bulletin du Musée de Beyrouth* 23:9-24.

BINFORD, S. R., 1966. "Me'arat Shovakh (Mugharet esh Shubbabiq)." *Israel Exploration Journal* 16:18-32, 96-103.

————— , 1968. "Early Upper Pleistocene Adaptations in the Levant." *American Anthropologist* 70:707-17.

BRAIDWOOD, R., and HOWE, B., 1960. *Prehistoric Investigations in Iraqi Kurdistan.* Chicago: University of Chicago Press.

BROSH, A., 1960. "The Soils of Eastern Upper Galilee." *Bulletin Israel Exploration Society* 24:229-39. (In Hebrew).

CLARK, J. D., 1967. "The Middle Acheulean Occupation Site at Latamne, Northern Syria." *Quaternaria* 9:1-68.

CLUTTON-BROCK, J., 1970. "The Fossil Fauna from an Upper Pleistocene Site in Jordan." *Journal of Zoology* 162:19-29.

COON, C. S., 1957. *The Seven Caves.* New York: Alfred A. Knopf.

COPELAND, L., and WESCOMBE, P. J., 1965. "Inventory of Stone Age Sites in Lebanon." *Mélanges de l'Université Saint-Joseph* 41(2):29-176.

————— , and WESCOMBE, P. J., 1966. "Inventory of Stone Age Sites in Lebanon, Part II, North, South, and East-Central Lebanon." *Mélanges de l'Université Saint-Joseph* 42(1):1-174.

FARRAND, W. R., 1971. "Late Quaternary Paleoclimates of the Eastern Mediterranean Area." In *The Late Cenozoic Glacial Ages*, edited by Karl K. Turekian. New Haven: Yale University Press.

FLEISCH, H., 1956. "Dépots préhistoriques de la côte Libanaise et leur place dans la chronologie basée sur le Quaternaire marin." *Quaternaria* 3:101-32.

————— , 1970. "Les Habitats du Paléolithique moyen à Naamé (Liban)." *Bulletin du Musée de Beyrouth* 23:25-98.

GARROD, D. A. E., 1930. "The Paleolithic of Southern Kurdistan: Excavations in the Caves of Zarzi and Hazar Merd." *Bulletin of the American School of Prehistoric Research* 6:8-43.

————— , 1942. "Excavations at the Cave of Shukbah, Palestine." *Proceedings of the Prehistoric Society* 8:1-20.

————— , 1962. "The Middle Paleolithic of the Near East and the Problem of Mount Carmel Man." *Journal of the Royal Anthropological Institute* 93:232-51.

————— , and BATE, D. M. A., 1937. *The Stone Age of Mount Carmel*, vol. 1. Oxford: Clarendon Press.

————— , and HENRI-MARTIN, G., 1961. "Rapport préliminaire sur la fouille d'une grotte au Ras el-Kelb, Liban." *Bulletin du Musée de Beyrouth* 16:61-67.

GAUTIER, A., 1970. "The Faunal Remains at Masloukh." *Bulletin du Musée de Beyrouth* 23:135.

GILEAD, D., 1970*a*. "Early Palaeolithic Cultures in Israel and the Near East." Ph.D. dissertation, Hebrew University.

————, 1970*b*. "Handaxe Industries in Israel and the Near East." *World Archaeology* 2:1-11.

————, 1973*a*. "Prehistoric Finds in the Negev and Sinai." *Mitqufat ha-Even* 11:36-42. (In Hebrew).

————, 1973*b*. "The Early Palaeolithic in the Coastal Plain of Israel." (In prepration).

————, and RONEN, A., 1973. "Acheulian Industries from Evron, Western Galilee Coastal Plain." (In preparation).

GVIRTZMAN, G., 1969. "The Saqiye Group (Late Eocene to Early Pleistocene) in the Coastal Plain and Hashephela Regions, Israel." *Bulletin of the Geological Survey of Israel* 51.

HIGGS, E., and NOY, T., 1973. "Rakefet Cave." *Hadashot Archaeologiot* 46:5. (In Hebrew).

HOWELL, F. C., 1959. "Upper Pleistocene Stratigraphy and Early Man in the Levant." *Proceedings of the American Philosophical Society* 103:1-65.

HUCKRIEDE, R., and WIESEMANN, G., 1968. "Der jungpleistozäne Pluvial-See von El-Jafr und weitere Daten zum Quartär Jordaniens." *Geologica et Palaeontologica* 2:73-95.

JELINEK, A. J.; FARRAND, W. R.; HAAS, G.; HOROWITZ, A.; and GOLDBERG, P., 1973. "New Excavations at the Tabun Cave, Mount Carmel, Israel, 1967-1972: A Preliminary Report." *Paleoorient* 1(2).

KOCHAVI, M., ed., 1973. *Judea, Samaria and the Golan Archaeological Survey 1967-1968*. Jerusalem.

MARKS, A. E., 1971. "Prehistoric Settlement Patterns and Intrasite Variability in the Central Negev, Israel." *American Anthropologist* 73(5):1237-44.

NEUVILLE, R., 1951. *Le Paléolithique et le Mésolithique du Désert de Judée*. Archives de l'Institut de Paléontologie humaine, mémoire 24.

OLAMI, J., 1958. "Prehistoric Survey of Mount Carmel." *Bulletin Israel Exploration Society* 22:174-80.

————, 1962. "Grotte du Sheikh Suleiman (Ornit), Mount Carmel, Israel." *Atti VI Congr. Int. Sc. Preist. e Protost., Roma*.

PERKINS, D., and DALY, P., 1968. "A Hunters Village in Neolithic Turkey." *Scientific American* 219:97-106.

PERROT, J., 1968. "La Préhistoire palestinienne." In *Supplément au Dictionnaire de la Bible* 8(43):286-446. Paris: Letouzey et Ane.

PRICE-WILLIAMS, D., 1973. "Environmental Archaeology in the Western Negev." *Nature* 242(5399):501-3.

RONEN, A., 1968. "Excavations at the Cave of Sefunim (Iraq-el-Barud), Mount Carmel, Preliminary Report. " *Quartar* 19:275-88.

————, 1970. "La Station moustérienne de Tirat Carmel." *Actes VII Cong. Int. Sc. Preh. et Protoh., Prague*, pp. 275-80.

————, and FARRAND, W. R., 1973. "Observations on the Kurkar-Hamra Succession in the Carmel Coastal Plain, Israel." (In press).

SENYUREK, M., 1959. "A Note on the Palaeolithic Industry of the Plugged Cave." *Belleten* 23:27-58.

SKINNER, J., 1970. "El-Masloukh: A Yabrudian Site in Lebanon." *Bulletin du Musée de Beyrouth* 23:143-72.

SOLECKI, R. S., 1964. "Zawi Chemi Shanidar, a post-Pleistocene Village Site in Northern Iraq." *VIth International Congress on the Quaternary, Warsaw, 1961*.

————, 1970. "Summary Report of the Columbia University Prehistoric Investigations in Lebanon, Season 1969." *Bulletin du Musée de Beyrouth* 23:95-128.

STEKELIS, M., 1942. "Preliminary Report on Soundings in Prehistoric Caves in Palestine." *Bulletin American School Oriental Research* 86:2-10.

————, 1960. "The Paleolithic Deposits of Jisr Banat Yaqub." *Bulletin of the Research Council of Israel* 9G:63-90.

————, 1964. "Prehistoric Sites." In *Atlas of Israel*, edited by N. Kadnom. Jerusalem.

————, and HAAS, G., 1952. "The Abu Usba Cave (Mount Carmel)." *Israel Exploration Journal* 2:15-47.

SUZUKI, H., and KOBORI, I., (eds.), 1970. *Report of the Reconnaissance Survey on Palaeolithic Sites in Lebanon and Syria*. Bulletin No. 1, University Museum, University of Tokyo.

TURVILLE-PETRE, F., 1927. *Researches in Prehistoric Galilee (1925-1926), and a Report on the Galilee Skull*. Bulletin of the British School of Archaeology in Jerusalem 14.

VANDERMEERSCH, B., 1966. "L'Industrie Moustérienne de Larikba." *L'Anthropologie* 70:123-30.

VITA-FINZI, C., and HIGGS, E. S., 1970. "Prehistoric Economy in the Mount Carmel Area of Palestine: Site Catchment Analysis." *Proceedings of the Prehistoric Society* 36:1-37.

WRESCHNER, E.; AVNIMELECH, M.; SCHMID, E.; HAAS, G.; and DART, R.A., 1967. "The Geula Caves, Mount Carmel." *Quaternaria* 9:69-140.

YIZRAELI, T., 1967. "A Lower Palaeolithic Site at Holon, Preliminary Report." *Israel Exploration Journal* 17:144-52.

ZEUNER, F. E., 1957. "Stone Age Exploration in Jordan." *Palestine Exploration Quarterly*, 89:17-54.

ZOHARY, M., 1964. "Vegetation of Israel and the Near East." In *Atlas of Israel*, edited by N. Kadnom. Jerusalem.

THE MIDDLE PALEOLITHIC SITE OF NAHR IBRAHIM (ASFOURIEH CAVE) IN LEBANON

Ralph S. Solecki
Columbia University of New York

This chapter concerns a Middle Paleolithic site (fig. 1), one of several cave sites on the Lebanese coast in which were found a large number of Levalloiso-Mousterian type artifacts. Virtually all productive cave sites along the eastern Mediterranean have been explored. A number of these were dug before the method of controlled excavations was known. The cave site described here is no exception, since it has been known to archaeologists for more than a hundred years. In the situation common to such sites, the "secondhand" nature of the conditions presented a number of problems which were not realized until the actual excavations were begun. Nonetheless, information of great value to prehistory has been salvaged, literally, from the dragline and blade of the bulldozer.

The Nahr Ibrahim—or Asfourieh cave (with variations in spellings)—has been the subject of three seasons of investigations by Columbia University during 1969, 1970, and 1973 (Solecki, 1971; Solecki and Solecki, 1971; Stearns, 1971). It lies about 25 km north of Beirut on the road to Tripoli (fig. 2), about 800 m north of the Nahr Ibrahim bridge in the karsted forest region of the so-called Adonis Ravine (Nahr Ibrahim valley). Actually, the cave lies just within the border of the township of Halat, adjacent to the town of Nahr Ibrahim. The site was first investigated by Zumoffen (1900), who called it the Nahr Ibrahim station. His *sondages* were discovered during these later investigations. It has been visited subsequently by Fleisch and Copeland (Copeland and Wescombe, 1965), who brought the present author there on one of their trips. The Japanese prehistorians of the University of Tokyo had originally planned to excavate a small cave adjacent to the main cave, but decided upon an alternate site instead (Suzuki and Kobori, 1970).

The cave of Asfourieh fell within the right-of-way of the new autostrade between Beirut and Tripoli, hence was in danger of being destroyed. It became apparent that unless something was done to salvage the prehistory of this important cave site, it and its information would be lost. A permit was secured from the Director General of Antiquities and Museums to excavate at Asfourieh cave, and work was begun there during the summer of 1969 with a group of interdisciplinary scientists and students. A longer field season during 1970 was followed by a relatively shorter summer season during 1973. Actual work on the roadway, which had been postponed up to this time, began in the neighborhood of the cave during the 1973 season.

Personnel included in the field investigations in one or more of the seasons were Rose L. Solecki of Columbia University, Michal Kobusiewicz of the Polish Academy of Sciences, Poznan, and James Skinner, formerly of Hunter College. Geologists were Charles Stearns of Tufts University and Eugene Bonifay of the University of Marseilles, with consulting geologists Wallace Broecker of Columbia University and William Farrand of the University of Michigan. The other disciplines represented were palynology—Arlette Leroi-Gourhan of the Museé de l'Homme, Paris; and paleozoology—Achilles Gautier of the University of Brussels. A number of students on a Ford Foundation grant plus several volunteer students comprised the rest of the expedition during the three seasons.

James Skinner was authorized to excavate the nearby Masloukh cave site north of the Asfourieh cave, recovering about 19,000 artifacts of flint as well as one tooth, which was later identified as Neanderthal. It was decided to excavate there because the site was going to be destroyed by the same autostrade that threatened the Nahr Ibrahim station. The material recovered is unique since it belongs to the Yabroudian (Jabrudian) culture horizon, which predates the Levalloiso-Mousterian in the Levant. Skinner's report (1971) is a preliminary one.

There are three major galleries, and one minor, in the Nahr Ibrahim station (fig. 3). From north to south these are referred to respectively as the *north, central, main,* and *south* galleries. The former three galleries are interconnected, and one can pass readily from one to another. The south gallery, a relatively small aperture, evidently had also been connected with the main gallery in prehistoric times, but breccia now clogs the way between them so that the south gallery stands as an individual cave. Including the distance from the south to the north gallery, the combined measurement is about 30 meters. Excluding the south gallery, which was not excavated, the combined measurement across the front of the cave is approximately 25 meters. The greatest depth within the habitable part of the cave (main gallery) is about 16 meters. The combined presently habitable or living floor area within the dripline zone of the Nahr Ibrahim station is about 200 square meters. Using the generally accepted areal measurement for population estimates in habitations, theoretically a population of 20 to 25 people could be easily accommodated in this cave complex. This does not take in a suspected collapsed cave area to the immediately adjoining side to the northeast, which was termed the "garden patch" from its present use. This would have added at least 40 more square meters to our calculations, and probably an additional 150 square meters if assessment of the findings made during the 1973 season is correct.

The main gallery measures about 5.5 m across the mouth, and its major living area extends to about 16 m deep from the portal. There is an interior grotto going back

FIG. 1—The Nahr Ibrahim (Asfourieh) Cave at Halat, Lebanon.

to a distance of about 30 m from the same point. Although quite a number of artifacts were found in this interior grotto, it is not believed that this was a habitation area since the aperture entryway is a very restricted one. Two of the 1973 expedition members, both graduate students, surveyed this area intensively and reached the conclusion that the floor area of this interior grotto was approximately equal to the floor area of the main gallery. The main part of the latter gallery and the portal area (ca. 14.20 m above sea level) had been modified greatly by man well back in antiquity. Purposeful architectural modifications were obvious. The floor had been cut and leveled and then plastered over with a thickness of white gypsum, traces of which were found near the cave front. During more recent and contemporary times, the gallery had served as an animal shelter, complete with iron tethering rings, a feed bin, and a water trough next to one wall.

The central gallery measures about 10 m across the mouth, and extends back into a crevice about 16.8 m from the portal. The floor is a step above the main gallery floor, with an elevation of about 16 m above sea level. There is a

decided upward slope to the cave floor from front to rear, or from west to east. The floor of this gallery, like the floor of the main gallery, had been artificially leveled, perhaps subsequent to the prehistoric human occupation, although no traces of a gypsum floor were noted. Huge fallen blocks of stone mark the boundary between the central gallery and the north gallery. These blocks are kept from collapsing into the central gallery by a marvelous accidental wedging of stones and rubble, which appear to need only a slight shock to bring the whole suspended works crashing down.

Zumoffen had reported that he had made a *sondage* (more about its measurements, location, etc. could not be learned) in this gallery, mute proof of which was found in the 1973 season. The specimens he collected are in the St. Joseph's University museum.

Patches of breccia containing flints and bones were found at about the 18 m above sea level elevation along the walls, practically butting up against the ceiling at several points. This gallery could not, of course, have functioned as a habitable cave when so clogged with deposits which had washed in from the higher elevation garden patch area to

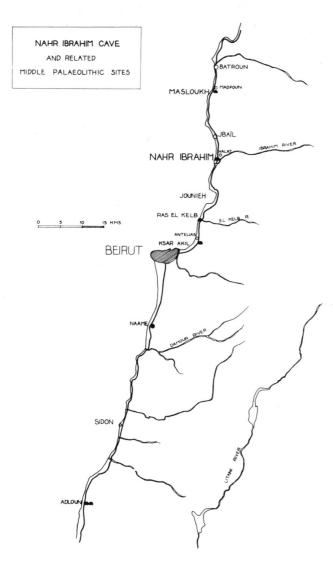

FIG. 2–Location of Nahr Ibrahim cave and related Middle Paleolithic sites in Lebanon.

the northeast. Before the stone blocks had fallen, thereby
closing in that side, the central gallery actually had been an
extension of the garden patch cave (now collapsed), providing one huge area joined to the northern gallery.

Deposits still evidenced in a cut at the north wall of the
central gallery under the huge block heretofore mentioned
show that only about half a meter of habitation cave earth,
or *in situ* material, had been removed. In other words, the
in situ cave earth had originally attained an elevation of
about 16.5 m above sea level. The rest of the overburden
appears to be derived material washed in from the garden
area where archaeological deposits were found much higher,
at about 21 m above sea level.

The front, or seaward opening of the central gallery, has
no scree slope, as is normally found in cave sites. The slope,
as in the main gallery, had been cut away in ancient times,
presumably at the same time that the similar work was
done in the main gallery. In its vertical face bones and flints

could be seen, but these were virtually impossible to
remove undamaged from the concrete-hard matrix.

The north gallery is a double-ended cave, with an
opening at both its eastern and western ends through which
funnels a fine draught of air. The western portal is about 7
m across and has an elevation of about 16 m above sea
level. The eastern portal, at an elevation of about 19 m, is
linked by a passageway 12 m long to the western opening.
Access to the central gallery from the north gallery is made
by a connecting passage 6 m long by 3 m wide.

As was found in the other galleries, the forward scree
slope had been cut away in mining for rich, man-fertilized
cave earth which was excellent for agriculture. It appeared
that a line of least resistance had been followed inward,
leaving a sort of open horseshoe or U-shaped area between
two arms of rock (original cave walls) projecting on the
forward part of the cave.

Aside from the cave itself, the second most prominent
feature is the curious block-shaped rampart cut out of the
limestone surmounting the main gallery. This feature, with
an adjoining quarry, was evidently part of the same activity
which was responsible for the modification of the interior
and front of the main gallery, and for the robbing of rich
cave earths from this station.

A survey in the cave area resulted in the discovery of
two other solution cavities in the Halat area, just north of
the Asfourieh cave. Both were considerably smaller but
could have taken the overflow of population from the large
complex. One of these was a shelter with Levalloiso-
Mousterian flints scattered about its front. It too had been
soil-robbed, probably also in antiquity. The cave, the other
feature, was used as a contemporary sheep shelter and
yielded no artifacts. The presence of many animal fleas
influenced our decision not to linger.

One thing which can be cleared of doubt and confusion
is the matter of presence of the fossil marine mollusc
Vermets sp., a kind of sea level marker, which was found
associated with the Nahr Ibrahim station. Before excavation
this evidence had been noted by the French geographer
Paul Sanlaville (1969) at the portal of the main gallery, and
was attributed by him to a high level of the sea in the cave.
The *Vermets sp.* fossils were found at ca. 14.20 m above sea
level and on the southern wall of the same gallery at about
15.5 m–16.0 m (see also Solecki, 1971, Pl. 2b; Stearns,
1971). The presence of these sea level gauges in the cave
would appear to indicate that they had formed subsequent
to the laying down of archaeological deposits which were
discovered below the lowest level (below 14.0 m). The
obvious flaw in this argument was that the soft cave earth
should have been washed away if the sea had truly invaded
the cave at that level in postoccupation times. This question
was resolved very simply in the 1970 season with the aid of
an air hammer, with which it was possible to pick around
and extract the 14.20 m *Vertes sp.* patch. Fortunately,
Sanlaville was present, and the specimen was identified as
an *intrusive* limestone block upon which the *Vermets sp.*

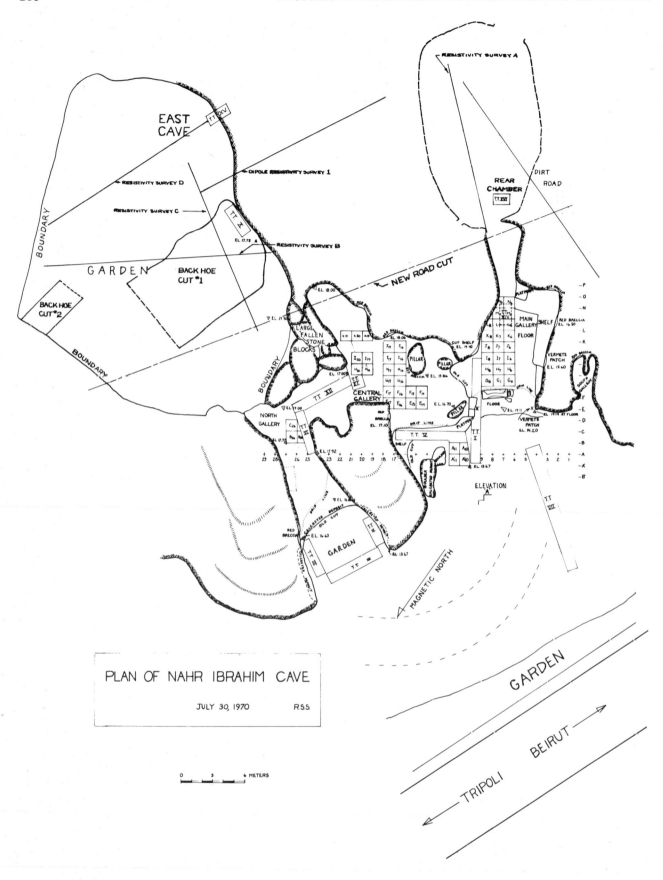

FIG. 3—Ground floor plan of the Nahr Ibrahim cave site.

had grown. The matrix, which was within the dripline of the cave, was heavily calcreted soil, which probably contributed to the original misinterpretation.

Two more deeper or low elevation *Vermets sp.* patches which, it was felt, were *in situ* were found adhering to the bedrock of the main gallery. One was at the base of the gallery a couple of meters in from the opening at an elevation of about 13 m, and the other was found at about 13.5 m at the side of a gulley-like runnel cut through the bedrock on a possible joint plane.

On the basis of this evidence, multiple sea stands between 13.0 m and 16.0 m can be postulated, all presumably related to a larger major episode. Because a transgressive sea in such a close confine most certainly would have wiped out the marine molluscs through scouring and erosion, it seems reasonable to believe that these evidences are of sea regressions below the 16 m above sea level high elevation stand. Sanlaville (1969) stated that the *Vermets sp.* dates here from the Last Interglacial, or more likely during one of the Würmian Interstadials. In any case, these fossils must predate the human occupation of the cave. Fleisch and Sanlaville (1967) and Sanlaville (1969) observed that the open Levalloiso-Mousterian site of Na'ame, about 14 kms south of Beirut, figured in at least two sea transgressions at about 8 m–10 m above sea level from evidence of *Vermets sp.* and *Strombus bubonius Lmk.* Comparing the occupation of the two sites with regard to that sea level, and discounting any tectonic activity which could influence the levels, brings to the fore an interesting question. Since the lowest archaeological deposit at Nahr Ibrahim was at about 11+ m above sea level, one would think that for the sake of its inhabitants' comfort, the occupation in the cave (at least in the main and central galleries) would have begun well after there was an appreciable sea regression, below the 8 m–10 m stand. In other words, with a stand at that elevation, the seaward exposure of the cave would have called for better protection as a buffer against high stormy seas to prevent the Neanderthals(?) from being preemptorily flushed out from their beds on occasion. As a counter argument, there is evidence that some flints were found mixed in the basal bedrock deposits, the yellow sands, indicating that occupations with wettings might have taken place. Or, did these flints wash down from the garden patch area, which has occupational deposits of Levalloiso-Mousterian origin several meters above the 8 m–10 m above sea level sea stand? Unfortunately, all of this is still undated except by tenuous extrapolation. However, with the great leaps in knowledge being made in geochemistry and prehistory, the answers to these questions may not be too far in the future.

It was not realized until later that younger paleolithic materials, such as could be identified, were not to be found in the Asfourieh cave. True, some typologically Upper Paleolithic flints were recovered deep in the inner grotto in the main gallery, but these were derived from elsewhere and were not *in situ* materials. In short, the very first cut in the cave floor unearthed Middle Paleolithic flints at the outset, which seemed then to be very convenient, if unnatural. Indeed, Middle Paleolithic flints were found right on the floor of the cave. There was neither sterile overburden nor thick deposits of younger archaeological layers with which to contend.

It is now evident that the archaeological deposits of the three galleries were truncated during the Roman age and brought down to the levels encountered today. It was evident that the new occupants were after more headroom in the main gallery than in the central gallery. There is an elevation difference of about two meters between the two floors, producing a kind of split-level effect. From the interior of the galleries alone, it is estimated the cave earth yield was about 400 cubic meters of organically rich earth. Zumoffen remarked about the spread of artifacts and bones scattered in front of the cave.

The century of the cave earth evacuation can be fixed with some certainty from evidence of architectural alteration, especially in the main gallery. The sides of this gallery opening were cut vertically, and a plaster floor with interior stone benches was made at about the 14.20 m level. The modifiers had to have some kind of sophisticated digging and cutting equipment, better than the stone age variety, as well as a mode of transporting the cave earth. The clue was provided by the sill stone uncovered at the opening to the main gallery (Solecki, 1971). This ca. two ton block had been very carefully shaped with metal cutting tools, brought to the portal, and set into a previously prepared rectangular hole in the truncated Middle Paleolithic deposits. That the soil was already hard is evidenced by the fact that the hole had vertical walls and was not dug out more than necessary for the reception of the sill stone. Tests with a carpenter's level showed that the sill stone was set in place by experienced engineers. According to the Director General of Antiquities, specialist in these matters who visited the site, the stone was cut and fashioned in the style of about 100 B.C., giving a fairly comfortable time fix for the probable evacuation and alteration of the cave interior.

While it cannot be known exactly how much *in situ* archaeological deposits may have been lost due to soil robbing, it is believed, by deduction, that no more than about one meter thickness was lost in the main gallery, and perhaps half of that amount in the central gallery. These amounts, if added on to the present elevations, would have given convenient squatting space and headroom for no more than a short man between the hypothesized floor and the cave ceiling (assuming that there were no great ceiling collapses). The upper part of the cave earth, whose evidence is found in the cave breccia on the side walls, appears to have been washed in from the upward slope and the garden patch area to the north and east, as mentioned earlier. Water flow was observed from the rear of the galleries toward the front during times of heavy rain and also during occasional periods when the irrigation ditches above the cave were opened and the water allowed to drain seaward.

The total original deposit of the main gallery was about four meters, two meters of which were excavated. The total original thickness of the central gallery deposits was about seven meters, a little over five meters of which were excavated. The northern gallery appeared to have a concentration of heavily deflated deposits, washed by sheet water which modified the archaeological deposits. Flints and bones were found in great abundance there.

The least disturbed and greatest depth of deposits was contained in the central gallery, with a thickness of nearly five meters. Seven layers, distinguished on the basis of soil color and character, were recognized in the L-shaped cut put in the middle of this gallery (figs. 4, 5, and 6). Good correspondences with marker layers were found in the main gallery layers, where fewer layers were present, since the top deposits were truncated away. Of these seven layers, layers 3 to 6 (called "units" in the fieldnotes) were most important in cultural remains. Layers 1 and 2 contained soilwashed materials, while layer 7 was sterile bedrock soil. It was primarily in the four major layers that some 58 lenses and soil horizons were counted. These included curious white bands of what appeared to be calcreted soil, which were identified in the field by Bonifay as hearths. These were sometimes very large in section, as much as a couple of meters in diameter and about 2 cm thick. Burned bones and flints were seen in these features, but singularly, it was not possible to detect any wood charcoal in association with these hearth features. Layer 6 had about eight features which could be identified as hearths.

In brief, the seven layers of the central gallery could be described as follows:

Layer One, undoubtedly truncated, measured about 50 cm thick, between 15.75 m and 16.25 meters. It consisted of a dark brown rubble containing small angular chunks of limestone and a number of roots and rootlets. The soil was loamy in texture and appeared to be the result of a series of soil washes rather than an occupational deposition.

Layer Two, found at about 16 m above sea level, was a truncated lens of soil about 25 cm thick next to the cave wall. It was a light brownish red loamy soil containing small angular fragments of limestone. It is thought that this soil, like Layer One, was the result of a soil wash, presumably from the northeastern side of the gallery.

Layer Three, with a thickness of about one meter (maximum), occurred between the 15 m and 16 m levels. It contained a number of calcreted soil horizons and many bones, flints and angular chunks of limestone. The soil was a light grayish brown in color, which was moist to the touch.

Layer Four, found between the 14 m and 15 m horizons, measured about one meter thick. Its dark gray color contrasted sharply with Layer Three, and it contained numerous thick, widespread lenses of calcreted soil. These were probably hearths, since they could not be characterized as stalagmitic soil or dripstone.

Layer Five, with a thickness of about 75 cm, was identified between the 14 m and 13.25 m level. Contrasting very sharply with the above layers, it was a dark reddish soil of uniform texture. It contained flints and limestone fragments but no calcreted soil. Hearths were identified in this layer.

Layer Six, measuring about 1.25 m thick, was uncovered between the 13.25 m and 12 m levels. It was a dark gray to almost black soil horizon, with widespread black lenses of soil. As noted above, there were a number of calcreted soil horizons rich in flints and bones, and at least eight hearths.

Layer Seven, found below 12 m, was bedrock which consisted of a light gray to yellowish sterile soil containing many small angular fragments of limestone and chert. Some flint artifacts and bone fragments were found mixed in this clean soil, apparently worked down into the soil from above. The contact between Layer Six and Layer Seven was at about 11.75 m above sea level and was traceable in the several points tested at the base of the central gallery excavation. Marine shells were found in this layer, like the type discovered at the base of the sondage in front of the central gallery (the seaward side).

In the main gallery (fig. 7), beneath a thin veneer of white plastered floor attributed to the Roman age, was found a horizon identified as Layer Five in the central gallery. The soil is a reddish gray color, with a 50 cm band of darker soil capping it to the surface. Angular fragments of limestone and numerous flints and bones were collected in this horizon. The second layer, which is identified as the extension of Layer Six in the central gallery, rests on solid limestone bedrock with a bedrock capping of yellowish sterile soil toward the rear. This layer includes a widespread 15 cm thickness of ceiling collapse composed of flat slabs, which was easily traced as a marker bed to the central gallery. This layer had a very dark gray color and contained numerous fire-burned flints and mammal bone fragments, including rhinoceros. The rockfall mentioned appears to mark a period of unsettled conditions in the cave. Because there were no strong occupational traces just prior to and subsequent to the ceiling collapse in the main gallery, it is presumed that the cave was shunned by man. Brecciated occupational evidences were plastered, as though with cement, on the surface of the bedrock. One marine cobble was noted in situ resting on the surface of the bedrock, as well as two occurrences of Vermets sp.. One of these was at 13.0 m, and the other was at about 13.5 m above sea level. A yellow greenish layer of loose granular soil material containing numerous limestone platelets was found in a deep runnel cutting through the gallery at about 13.2 meters. This was called "continental" in origin and "post-Vermet," according to Sanlaville on one of his several visits to the cave during the work. He observed that there were lithofarge against the south wall of the main gallery bedrock and under clefts near the runnel. He concluded that the sea had come in at about the 13.0 m level invading the cave, leaving the Vermets sp. as fossil evidence. Actually, it appeared

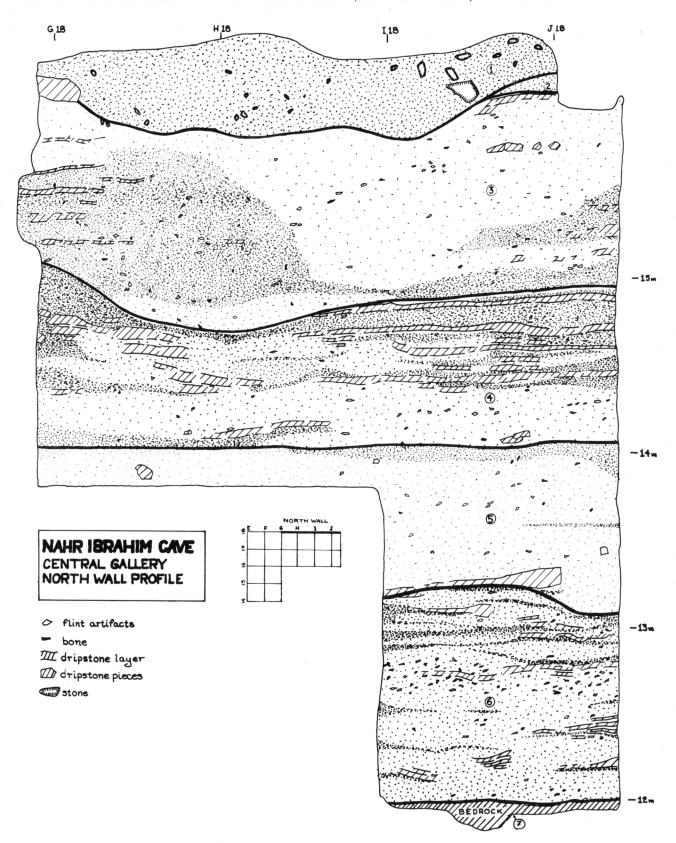

NAHR IBRAHIM CAVE
CENTRAL GALLERY
NORTH WALL PROFILE

⬠ flint artifacts
➖ bone
▥ dripstone layer
▱ dripstone pieces
⬭ stone

FIG. 4—East part of the Central Gallery "L" cut, north wall.

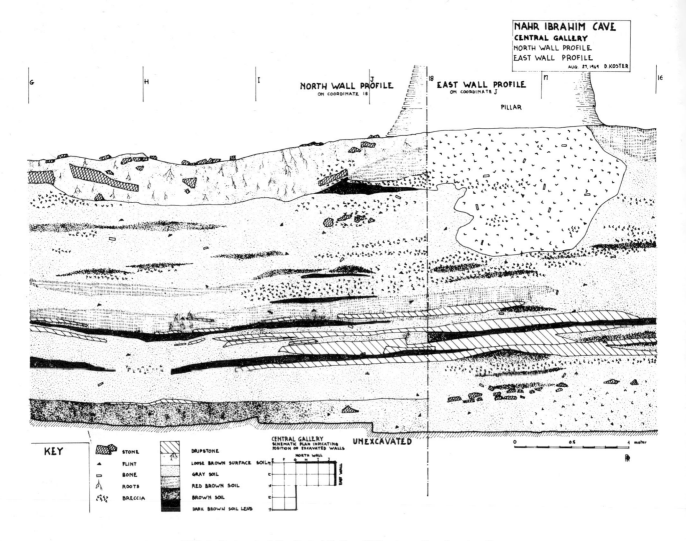

FIG. 5—East part of the Central Gallery "L" cut, north and east walls.

that all of the bedrock at this level in the main gallery seemed to show traces of *Vermets*. There is no evidence of sea action on the archaeological deposits, although some flints, presumably intrusive, were found mixed in the very top part of the clean basal yellowish soil in the runnel and in the back of the main gallery. Bedrock was reached at the base of the runnel at about 11.80 m above sea level, just about the same level as this soil was met in the central gallery.

It was a great pity that the deposits of the main gallery were both originally truncated and gouged into during, it is believed, Roman times. Moreover, the large pit in the center of the gallery (which had been filled in and floored over) was subsequently rechurned by others in recent times—a wine bottle cork was found near the base of the secondary pit. Whether this may be attributed to Zumoffen, another clandestine archaeological work, or treasure trove hunters is not known. In effect, what really remained in pristine condition were the sides and basal areas of the main gallery section.

The most interesting feature found in the cave of Nahr Ibrahim was a collection of bones which appears to be the remains of a ritual fallow deer burial (*Dama mesopotamica*). This feature was found in the inner part of the central gallery, at about 15.20 m elevation, or about a meter deep from the present surface. Included were several long bones, foot bones, a large section of backbone still in articulated order, and the whole surmounted by the skull cap of the same animal. Sprinkled in direct association with these remains were small bits of red ochre, a natural coloring matter, which was certainly out of place in this environment. Normally, animal bones occur in almost random distribution, in broken and fragmentary state, crushed open for their last food value. In the instance of the deer skeletal remains, the bones were found in relatively whole condition. There was a main cluster of bones in an area about 50 cm in diameter, lying in association with numerous flints and a heavy concentration of small limestone fragments. The idea has been entertained that this may have represented a hearth area for the cooking of deer. No carbon or ash evidences were found, however, and the bones (at least the joint ends) did not look burned. The implication is that this was part of a ritual activity in which the whole animal may have figured. Considering the large

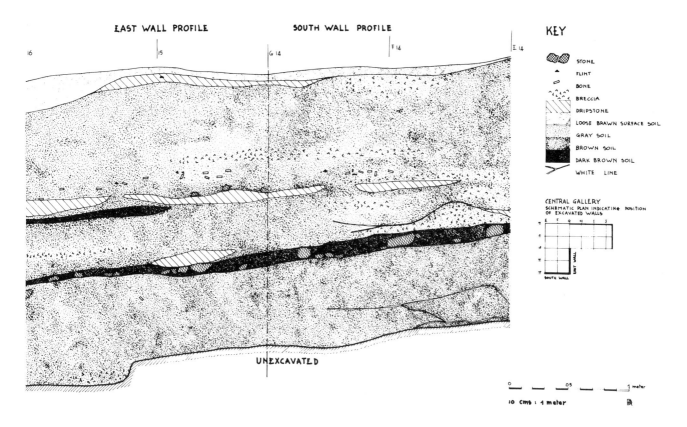

FIG. 6—West part of the Central Gallery "L" cut, east and south walls.

number of fallow deer bones found in the cave, it must have been the most important game animal at this station. It is possible that the early cave dwellers were ensuring a successful hunt by a propitiation rite to one of these animals. In the assumed ceremonial ritual, whole joints of meat were collected over a stony bed (the meaning of which is not known), capped with the top of the animal skull, and sprinkled with the red earthy mineral. The occurrence of whole bones of fallow deer scattered in the near vicinity of this collection implies that after the ceremony was finished, some disruption of the bones occurred, as would be the case when they have been left exposed. The red earthy matter, which was identified as red ochre, is known to have connotations of blood, or life in the ethnographic literature, and the material has been found in associations with Neanderthal cultures. The red ochre is a reminder of the legendary cult of Adonis—including the story that the Adonis River (presently called Nahr Ibrahim) was said to run red each spring from the blood of the slain hero. The cause for this seasonal coloration probably was due to an unknown store of red ochreous soil which was tapped by spring floods. A thick bed of red ochre was found associated with the Middle Paleolithic deposits in the

garden to the northeast of the cave complex. This may have been the local source for the red ochre fragments found among the deer remains.

One of the major questions in these investigations at the Asfourieh cave was the slopewash into the cave complex from the garden area. Steve Kopper, graduate student at Columbia University and professor at Long Island University, was present during the 1973 season. He applied the techniques of the electrical resistivity meter in the garden area and found that the meter readings indicated a breakdown in stratigraphy. A backhoe tractor, a very adaptable digging machine, the use of which was acquired through gracious arrangement with the Director General of Antiquities and Museums, cut two trenches in the garden area. The larger of the two was excavated to about two meters deep. This cut, next to the promontory at the northeast end of the cave complex, was forced to halt because it struck a number of large limestone blocks. It is believed that these blocks are part of an original cave collapse in that quarter. Exposed in the section was over a meter of stratified archaeological deposits, including a heavy band of the red ochre mentioned above. A hearth measuring about 1.25 m in diameter and about 5 cm thick was mapped in this

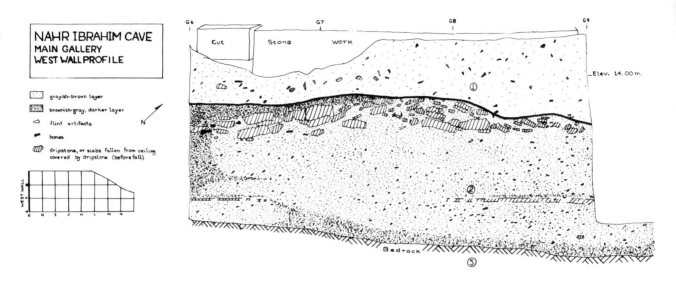

FIG. 7–West wall of the Main Gallery cut.

profile section. These garden deposits were higher than the three cave galleries with which there was a direct connection originally. This confirms the original hypothesis that the upper parts of the three galleries had received slopewash from the garden area.

The sequence of events for the habitation of the Nahr Ibrahim cave complex is tentatively reconstructed as follows: Following the last sea regression, in which the *Vermets sp.* were left on bedrock in the main gallery, occupation began some time during the early Würm by inhabitants bearing the Levallois-Mousterian culture. After both the middle and central—and perhaps also the north—galleries became uninhabitable because the debris began to choke up the living space, the occupation shifted around to the originally less desirable shelter in the garden patch area where a new start was made. There must have followed a tipping of the scales toward erosion of the latter deposits, possibly because of climatic change. The water, in seeking its own level, washed down toward the front of the cave complex, bringing with it the top deposits of the garden patch occupation in reverse stratigraphy. This accumulation gradually filled up both the central and middle galleries practically to the brim, sealing in the *in situ* deposits. Naturally, it cannot be known how much cut-and-fill action happened in the process. Eventually, though, all of the galleries became filled nearly to the ceiling with the derived soil. Evidence of streamwash was found in the central gallery in the form of a cut-and-fill set of remnants. A trench could not be cut between the two areas because of massive rocks which were poised on the brink between the central gallery and the garden patch area. Any slight movement would bring the boulders down, indicating that the area had not suffered any earth tremors of consequence for a fairly long time—at least since the Roman period.

The work on the autostrade was progressing during the 1973 field expedition, and a conference with the road engineers in July of that year indicated that the front of the

cave was going to be spared, including the area of the ongoing excavations. The road was going to cut away the rear of the main and central galleries, sections which were considered the least important from an archaeological point of view. The northern gallery was not to be touched at all. The engineers were very sympathetic to things of antiquity, and assured that they would not cut any more than was absolutely necessary to make the road cut.

The roadbuilders had made preliminary levelings to the north and south of the cave complex, which were examined in the course of the investigations. Flints were found scattered immediately south of the Nahr Ibrahim station and were probably derived from the suspected collapsed caves and shelters just to the east along the escarpment. Certainly they were mixed by the farming of centuries in this area. A deep trench cut farther to the south, made in conjunction with the roadbuilding, was examined. This was just to the east of the village of Nahr Ibrahim, between the river and the promontory. Well-marked deposits were measured, and in them a gravel beach was found at just about 16 m above sea level elevation. A number of Middle Paleolithic flints, some of which were identified as Levalloiso-Mousterian, were found in red sand just above the beach gravels. This beach appears to mark a sea level at the same approximate height as the sea level marked by the *Vermets* in the main gallery of the Asfourieh cave. No bone nor charcoal nor any other occupation evidences to indicate a habitation site were found; hence it may be inferred that the artifacts could have been derived from elsewhere up the slope to the east. The flints appeared to be quite fresh looking, so assuming that they were derived, they were not carried too far. No artifacts were found below the beach gravels, which is of some significance since there had been some original speculation that part of the early occupation of the Nahr Ibrahim cave predated the *Vermets sp.* deposition there. A total of 11 layers were found in this cut. The deposits appeared to have a southerly slope of about 50 minutes, which led to the supposition that there were tectonics represented here. On further observation, however, it was deduced that the cut was made at an angle to the natural slope of the deposits, cross-cutting the beds at an oblique angle, producing the apparent effect of tilted deposits. The flints were found in what was called Layer 8, which was a 50 cm thickness of red clay and sand. The flints actually occurred in a 5 cm–10 cm band at the junction of the red sand with the clay. Above this was a horizon of frost-fractured soil. Only about 20 cm thickness separated the artifact-bearing red sand and the pebble beach horizon, indicating that there was not too much time lapse before man arrived there. Analysis of the findings is continuing.

In the three seasons at Nahr Ibrahim, approximately 325,000 flints were recovered from the cave complex. These flints represent all of the specimens, including the tools and debitage. From this sum total, it must be remembered that a goodly number will have to be discounted because they were found in derived conditions. Thus, a good percentage was collected from the interior grotto of the main gallery, a proportion from the cut and fills made by Zumoffen and others, and a considerable number derived from elsewhere in the cave complex, principally those found in the deflated deposits of the northern gallery (top part) and adjacent areas. Work is presently going on in the study of this collection, and although it is still premature to make any conclusions about the percentage of tool types, etc., some preliminary observations may be drawn. There is good analogy to the specimens from Ras el Kelb, the site to the south of Nahr Ibrahim. The single C-14 date of older than 52,000 years (GrN 2556) places a considerable antiquity on the deposits, carrying the implication that the occupations at Nahr Ibrahim are of the same order at least.

In the manner of truncating, faceting, and thinning of the artifacts—traits peculiar to the Nahr Ibrahim specimens—examples were seen in the Ras el Kelb collections. There appeared to be an overwhelmingly large proportion of sidescrapers of several types among the tools from top to bottom of the central gallery excavation. Other tools in lesser numbers include denticulate and notched pieces, and naturally backed knives. Levallois points, which occur only in small numbers near the bottom, increased markedly in proportion toward the top. Mousterian points in a definite minority occurred, as did an occasional burin. Levallois cores and flakes were found throughout. There was a definite increase of specimens below the dripstone layers toward the bottom of the excavation. The predominant color of the flints in the lower horizons was a blue-black to black. Arlette Leroi-Gourhan, on the matter of the dripstones, remarked that she had found a surprisingly good source of pollens in these layers, better than in the cave earths proper.

What appears to be a large percentage of blade elements and burins made on broad blades was found in the north gallery. The tool inventory was reminiscent of, but definitely not, Upper Paleolithic in typology. The tools also included elongated Mousterian points, backed and naturally backed knives, and a number of sidescraper or *racloir* types. The collection from the north gallery is so pronouncedly different from the cast of the specimens from the other two galleries, it is safe to conclude that they represent a separate facies of the Levalloiso-Mousterian tradition. It was suggested that this industry might represent the end of the Levalloiso-Mousterian tradition at Nahr Ibrahim.

The faunal material is in the hands of Achilles Gautier for study. His first publication shows that the El Masloukh people knew and hunted mainly the now extinct rhinoceros, wild cattle, Iranian fallow deer, and horse or other equids. Rhinoceros seems to be present mainly in the lower part of the deposits of the main and central galleries at Nahr Ibrahim and seems to have dwindled away to extinction, or at least absence, in the upper levels at Nahr Ibrahim. Gautier (1970) mentions that at El Masloukh the faunal representations may reflect either a preferential hunting (for the larger species) or may be tied in with ecological factors such as the climate. The same probably holds true for Nahr Ibrahim. A comparison of the faunal evidence with the climatic information is yet to be done, but it is supposed that there will be some highly suggestive correspondences.

In connection with this, one of the Ford Foundation students, Mr. J. Steve Kopper, who had been a professional geologist, made some field studies at Nahr Ibrahim. He made a field analysis of the soil column from the central gallery between the 12 m and 16 m levels. He drew up an experimentally derived climatic curve based upon granulometric analysis of the thirteen different soil fractions examined. Of course, Eugene Bonifay had collected a larger series of soil samples from the same column during the 1970 season, and undoubtedly his report will be more detailed and comprehensive than Kopper's assessment. It must be realized that Kopper's work was not meant to supersede, diminish, or contradict Bonifay's investigations in any way. With this understood, Kopper's independent analysis indicates that there were three very marked cold and wet periods, dividing warmer periods in which there were oscillations of lesser coolness and humidity. He found a very cold and very wet "permanent" regime at about 12 m, or just about the base of the occupation. At about 13.0 m, there was what he calls a very cold and wet "seasonal" regime, lying above a warm and wet environment zone. The next very cold and wet "permanent" period occurred toward the 15.0 m level. Between Cold No. 2 and Cold No. 3 there appears a record of oscillations of warm and dry, cold and wet, warming dry, cold wet, seasonal to the suddenly very cold and wet of the Cold No. 3. The travertines (or dripstone layers) are equated with wet horizons. From the 15 m horizon to the 16 m mark (the present surface) a warming up period is indicated, with one oscillation toward a cool wet seasonal regime at about the 15.60 m level. Today the soils show that as a point of reference a warm and dry period is being undergone, a regime which has been exceeded in warmth and dryness approaching the 16 m level, and at various points in the past. It will be very instructive to correlate the cultural, floral, and faunal findings against such a climatic curve for Nahr Ibrahim. This is still in the future.

Mr. Kopper also made electrical resistivity measurements in the interior and exterior of the cave. He believes that the original roof over the garden patch area collapsed in a series of steps. As the roof retreated the occupational deposits underneath were exposed and thus were carried down toward the three connecting galleries. Under this hypothesis there should be reverse stratigraphy in the upper part of the main, central, and north galleries. It is not possible to check this in the first two galleries mentioned because their upper contents have been emptied long ago, as noted. His investigations inside the inner grotto of the main gallery showed that there were water entry points mainly in the northern and eastern sides of the grotto, namely from the garden patch area. Mr. Kopper also carried out some floatation tests on soils from the central gallery, but these tests revealed only indifferent results.

Thus, it has been seen that the cave complex at Nahr Ibrahim involves a broad range of scientific disciplines; and with them will be integrated the human side in prehistory at this site. The final results should be very interesting.

BIBLIOGRAPHY

COPELAND, LORRAINE, and WESCOMBE, PETER J., 1965. "Inventory of Stone Age Sites in Lebanon. Part One: West Central Lebanon." *Mélanges de l'Université Saint-Joseph* 41:29-175.

FLEISCH, H., and SANLAVILLE, P., 1967. "Nouveaux Gisements de *Strombus bubonius* Lmk au Liban." *Comptes rendus de la Société Géologique de France* 5:207-8.

GAUTIER, ACHILLES, 1970. "The Faunal Remains at Masloukh." *Bulletin du Musée de Beyrouth* 23:135-36.

SANLAVILLE, PAUL, 1969. "Les bas niveaux marins pleistocène du Liban." *Méditerranée* 3:257-92.

SKINNER, JAMES, 1970. "El-Masloukh: A Yabroudian Site in Lebanon." *Bulletin du Musée de Beyrouth* 23:143-72.

SOLECKI, RALPH S., 1970. "Summary Report of the Columbia University Prehistoric Investigations in Lebanon, Season 1969." *Bulletin du Musée de Beyrouth* 23:95-128.

SOLECKI, ROSE L., and SOLECKI, RALPH S., 1970. "A New Secondary Flaking Technique at the Nahr Ibrahim Cave, Lebanon." *Bulletin du Musée de Beyrouth* 23:137-72.

STEARNS, CHARLES E., 1970. "Observations on the Mughara el-Asfurieh and on the Littoral between Halat and Amchit (Region of Jbail)." *Bulletin du Musée de Beyrouth* 23:129-34.

SUZUKI, H., and KOBORI, I. (eds.), 1970. "Report of the Reconnaissance Survey on Paleolithic Sites in Lebanon and Syria." Bulletin No. 1, University Museum, University of Tokyo.

ZUMOFFEN, G., 1900. *Le Phénicie avant les Phéniciens. L'âge de la pierre.* Beirut: Imprimerie Catholique.

A PRELIMINARY REPORT ON SOME LOWER AND MIDDLE PALEOLITHIC INDUSTRIES FROM THE TABUN CAVE, MOUNT CARMEL (ISRAEL)

Arthur J. Jelinek
University of Arizona

The Paleolithic industries of the three caves at the mouth of the Wadi Mughara on the western edge of Mount Carmel in Palestine (El Wad, Es Skhul, and Et Tabun) have retained a basic importance in the definition of the cultures of Pleistocene man in the Near East since they were first described by Dorothy Garrod almost forty years ago (Garrod and Bate, 1937). Garrod's Mount Carmel sequence, along with the work of Rust at Yabrud in Syria (Rust, 1950), Neuville and Stekelis in the Galilee, and Neuville in the Judean Desert (Neuville et al., 1951), provided much of the basic data for an initial synthesis of the Near Eastern Paleolithic cultural sequence (Howell, 1959). Later work in various areas of the Near East has tended to supplement and expand the data accumulated in this early research, and to contribute to the definition of major problems (e.g., see Bordes, 1955a, 1961, and Garrod, 1956, 1961, 1962). The excavations at Tabun from 1967 to 1972 were undertaken in order to apply techniques of excavation and analysis not available in the earlier excavation to some of these problems at a site basic to the original definition of the Lower and Middle Paleolithic cultural sequence.

Garrod interpreted her excavation at Tabun to show a sequence of six major cultural layers beneath a superficial mixed deposit (Layer A). These were—in sequence from youngest to oldest—Layer B and the Chimney Deposits, Upper Levalloiso-Mousterian; Layer C, Lower Levalloiso-Mousterian, characterized by broad flakes; Layer D, Lower Levalloiso-Mousterian, characterized by triangular flakes; Layer E, Upper Acheulean (Micoquian); Layer F, Upper Acheulean; and Layer G, Tayacian. Layer E was initially subdivided into four sublayers on the basis of typological changes in the artifact materials—"broadly speaking, implements were larger and better made in E*a* than in E*b*, in E*c* (a very shallow zone) handaxes of La Micoque type were abundant, and in E*d* there was a return to the conditions of E*b*." (Garrod and Bate, 1937, p. 67). Later, Garrod recognized the essential homogeneity of her Layer E assemblage, which she grouped as Acheuleo-Yabrudian (1956, p. 40). The basic distribution of retouched tools, as classified by Garrod in these layers, is seen in Table 1. Garrod's excavation technique, based on arbitrary horizontal units of varying thickness and broad extent (1956, fig. 1), limited her recognition of the natural stratigraphic units containing these artifacts and led to her definition of "mixed zones" at the stratigraphic junction of the industries she described (Garrod and Bate, 1937, p. 65). The artifacts recovered in the initial excavation (in excess of 50,000) were distributed among forty institutions in Europe, North America, and Palestine, which has to some degree inhibited further exam-

ination of this material. This dispersal of material in itself reflects the intellectual climate in which these initial studies were carried out, where the presence or absence of specific artifact types was of greater interest than the quantitative variations of types within populations from each stratigraphic locus.

Two significant attempts to examine portions of this material in the light of more recent typological and quantitative concepts were made in the early 1960s. Skinner (1965) examined almost 4,400 artifacts in six collections from all layers at Tabun, other than F and G, as a part of his comprehensive study of early Late Pleistocene flake industries from Southwest Asia, and Wright (1966) reported a study of about 2,100 artifacts from Layers E and F in the collections of the University of Michigan Museum of Anthropology. Both studies utilized the typological and quantitative system developed by Bordes for the study of the Lower and Middle Paleolithic industries of Western Europe (Bordes, 1950, 1953, 1961; Bordes and Bourgon, 1951).

Wright's study tended to confirm the uniformity seen by Garrod in her reexamination of Layer E. However, his attempt to equate his sample from Layer E*a* with the Acheuleo-Yabrudian of Layers 11 and 24 at Yabrud, Shelter I, as classified by Bordes (1955a), revealed marked discrepancies, particularly in the proportion of denticulate tools, which was lower in the Tabun sample. Of the two samples from Yabrud I, he found Layer 11 to be most similar to Tabun E*a*. His several explanations for the differences between the samples did not include the likely possibility that the range of denticulates recognized by Bordes as tools was not recognized by Garrod in the early 1930s, and these tools were therefore not preserved (most flakes and cores were discarded in Garrod's Wadi Mughara excavations). Wright did advance other possible explanations of discrepancies in tool proportions between Tabun and Yabrud I based upon differences in the typological concepts of Bordes and Garrod, e.g., the distinction between handaxes and bifacial scrapers (op. cit., p. 421). In summary, Wright's study confirmed a relatively uniform industry throughout the limited samples available to him, which had been assigned by Garrod to Layer E, and indicated that, aside from discrepancies in the proportion of denticulate tools and bifacial scrapers, the sample from Layer E*a* seemed similar to the Acheuleo-Yabrudian from Layers 11 and 24 at Yabrud I. In this respect he supported Garrod's earlier equation of Layer E with the Acheuleo-Yabrudian.

Skinner's study was on a much larger scale than that of

297

TABLE 1
PERCENTAGES OF TOOLS FROM TABUN CLASSIFIED BY GARROD

Layer	Points	(Chatelperron and Audi)	Single	Double	Transverse	Steep	Other	Endscraper	Burin	Notch	Chisel	Squamous Flake	Disc	Chopper	Handaxe	N
CH	20.3	-	40.1	10.3	1.1	1.6	1.6	1.4	3.2	9.8	2.4	4.9	-	1.9	-	369
B	15.4	.2	55.9	11.2	1.1	-	4.4	.2	2.7	2.5	.8	4.4	.8	-	.2	475
C	10.6	1.6	38.8	19.9	1.8	2.4	1.5	.1	3.8	14.2	1.9	1.6	.3	.3	1.2	679
D	28.0	1.7	34.1	10.8	2.1	.5	6.8	.2	4.0	2.8	.4	.9	.5	4.0	4.3	1,115
Ea	1.2	1.0	33.9	3.4	6.8	7.2	24.0	.3	.9	-	-	-	-	5.1	16.0	6,251
Eb	.9	.7	36.2	4.2	5.8	6.0	23.0	.5	.7	-	-	-	-	7.8	13.9	13,470
Ec	.4	-	38.2	5.9	4.8	4.5	25.2	.2	.7	-	-	-	-	7.9	12.9	4,785
Ed	.3	-	30.7	3.2	3.2	4.4	27.2	.4	.6	-	-	-	1.1	9.0	19.8	18,259
F	.3	-	18.5	1.9	1.5	4.0	16.3	.3	.9	-	-	-	3.7	20.8	32.0	3,859
G	1.3	-	48.0	2.7	-	9.3	13.3	-	4.0	6.7	-	-	-	16.0	-	75

Wright and approached the general problem of the basic kinds of industries present in the late Lower and the Middle Paleolithic of Southwest Asia through a detailed examination of collections from a large number of strata from many many sites, including Tabun and Yabrud. His basic synthesis combined these assemblages into three major categories: *Group A*, represented solely at sites in the Zagros mountains north and east of the Mesopotamian Plain, is a Typical Mousterian in a Western European sense, without high incidence of Levallois technique; *Group B*, represented in his study only by Layer E at Tabun and in the lower Levels at Yabrud I, is a Yabrudian or Quina Mousterian in which Levallois technique is absent; *Group C*, widely distributed through the Levant, is less uniform but appears to be essentially a Typical Mousterian in Bordes's sense, with high incidence of Levallois technique. Within Group C, Skinner distinguished four major types: *Abou Sif*, confined to that site and characterized by many points and blades and moderate frequency of Levallois technique; *Tabun*, from several sites in northern Palestine, characterized by numerous sidescrapers, few blades, and a high frequency of Levallois technique; *Yabrud*, confined to Yabrud I, Layers 3-6, and Shukbah, characterized by moderate numbers of sidescrapers and a very high frequency of Levallois technique; and *Erq el-Ahmar*, represented at that site and by Yabrud I, Layer 10, characterized by a high frequency of Levallois technique and few retouched tools. He felt that, on the basis of their general similarity and various sampling problems, the last two types might be combined and both referred to as *Yabrud*. In addition to the samples which he considered reliable for quantitative studies, Skinner (op.

cit., pp. 105-9) tentatively included a number of other collections in his Group C classification. These include: *Abou Sif* type, Sahba, Tabban, and Ghar; *Erq el-Ahmar*, Oumm Naqous; Tabun, Mousterian assemblages from Ksar Akil, Ras el-Kelb, Jerf Ajla, Kebara F, Abu Usba, Geula, Qafzeh G, H, J, K, Emireh, Zuttiyeh, and possibly Magraçik (Plugged Cave) near the southeast coast of Turkey.

While Skinner's classification has provided us with a most useful corpus of comparative data, there are several aspects of his methods and synthesis open to criticism. Unfortunately, his terms for the *Tabun* and *Yabrud* types of *Group C* industries are likely to lead to a confusion of the former with the "Tabunian" proposed by Howell (1959, p. 15) for the industry of Layer G at Tabun (designated Tayacian by Garrod) and Layers E, F, and G at Oumm Qatafa, and of the latter with the "Yabrudian" from Yabrud and Tabun (represented by Group B). More important, in terms of substantive content of his work and its employment in a comparative sense, he does not appear to recognize that the flakes retained in many of the early excavations, particularly by Garrod (e.g., Tabun) and Neuville (e.g., Abou Sif), are only a small portion of the total original samples and are not necessarily representative of the total population of flakes or even of Levallois flakes and points from the excavation units. Thus his Levallois Index, Faceting Index, and Blade Index are not really comparable for all sites, but in many instances are heavily biased by the kinds of flakes that were selected for preservation by the excavator. This undoubtedly also biased the ratio of Levallois flakes, points, and naturally backed knives, to implements. His calculation of the Levallois and

Faceting indices deviates from the usage proposed by Bordes (1950, 1953; Bordes and Bourgon, 1951) in that cores are included in the comparison and the specimens compared are restricted to those on the list of tool types plus cores. This means that, while his indices are useful for comparison within his study (bearing in mind the flake biases mentioned above), they are not directly comparable to those calculated by the methods recommended by Bordes. The above qualifications should be considered in assessing Skinner's inventory and interpretation of Garrod's collections from Tabun, and in comparing his data with that of other workers. Even these differences in techniques of recording do not markedly affect the clear difference between Layers B through D, and Layer E recognized by Skinner.

A comparison of Skinner's and Wright's quantitative studies of two independent samples from Layer E may be of interest, first, as it may reflect on the uniformity of the samples; and second, as a possible indication of the variations in the way the same typology (Bordes's) is applied by different workers. Table 2 presents the results of Skinner's classification and Table 3 that of Wright. In both instances, for reasons cited above, the classification shown here is restricted to retouched tools, with the additional omission of denticulates (Type 43) and Bordes's Types 46-49, which are irregularly retouched and were also likely to have been saved only occasionally. In addition, Wright's new types of "naturally backed scrapers" and "oblique scrapers" were omitted from this classification. The former range from about 5% to 12% of the sample and are probably mostly classifiable as Types 9 and 10; the latter include only three artifacts. The specific discrepancies between the two classifications include a markedly higher total of Mousterian Points (6) in all levels in Skinner's sample, and a significantly higher total of convergent convex sidescrapers (19) in Wright's inventory, suggesting a vulnerability in the typology recognized elsewhere (Laurent, 1965, p. 39). Wright's consistently higher percentages of bifacial scrapers (28) may be accounted for in Skinner's consistently higher Biface Index, indicating that some of the artifacts that Skinner would classify as bifaces would be bifacial scrapers for Wright. It is less easy to explain the marked discrepancy in dejeté scrapers (21), with 10%-20% more of the total number of artifacts included in this category in Skinner's sample throughout the four levels of Layer E. While some dejeté scrapers might have been considered as normal side- or transverse scrapers with minor convergences by Wright (e.g., see Bordes, 1961, plates 14, no. 11 and 25, no. 2), his meticulous notes on variation within these categories (op. cit., pp. 413-14) suggest that little of the difference can be accounted for by different typological concepts and that this is one aspect in which the two samples are consistently different. This also appears true for the higher percentages of double sidescrapers (13, 15) in the Michigan collection. Wright's consistently higher percentages of *diverse* artifacts (62) may suggest somewhat greater conservatism on his part

in classifying artifacts with multiple utilization, or may reflect another real difference in the two collections. In any event, these independent studies of collections from Tabun agree upon the similarity of the several subdivisions of Layer E originally suggested by Garrod and upon its affinity with Yabrudian Layers from Yabrud. Their disagreement in detail points up some of the areas where further refinement may be needed in the typological systems currently employed in lithic classification, as well as the dangers of working with small samples from large collections.

As a result of his study of Middle Paleolithic collections from sites scattered over most of the Near East, Skinner drew several general conclusions which have a bearing on the cultural sequence at Tabun. They may be summarized as follows (op. cit., pp. 256-61):

1. The Yabrudian precedes the Levalloiso-Mousterian wherever they are found together. There is some chance that this relationship may not always hold, since the Yabrudian may have continued into the last Pluvial at Tabun and the Levalloiso-Mousterian seems to have started at the very beginning of the last Pluvial at Ksar Akil and Ras el-Kelb.

2. The Yabrudian is the end result of a developmental succession from the Final Acheulean or Micoquian. "The evolution is crystal-clear in basal Tabun and in Qatafa." (ibid., p. 258).

3. The origins of the Levalloiso-Mousterian are not yet clear; there may be some relationships between this tradition and an earlier Acheulean, with some emphasis on Levallois manufacture. There seems to be good reason to think that this tradition may be intrusive into the Levant, perhaps from Europe or Africa.

The most recent synthesis of Near Eastern Paleolithic industries pertinent to the problems of Tabun is that of Perrot (1968), which forms the best point of departure for a discussion of the industries recovered in our excavation, since it was written at about the time our work began.

Perrot sees the earliest industry at Tabun (Layer G) as similar to that from Layers E3, F, and G at Oumm Qatafa (op. cit., col. 329), as did Neuville (1951, p. 35) and Howell (1959, p. 15) in earlier syntheses. Perrot believes, however, that Howell's grouping of these materials as a "Tabunian" flake industry is probably premature, on the basis of the impoverished nature of the samples, and the uncertainty of their position in the Pleistocene chronology. Perrot combines the Late Acheulean of Tabun (Layer F), and that of Oumm Qatafa (E1, E2, and D2) to form one of four kinds of Late Acheulean industries in the Levant, all others deriving from the contexts of open sites. He agrees with Neuville in specifically equating Layer D2 at Qatafa with Layer F at Tabun. All of these industries are assigned to the last interglacial interval. Among them he sees examples of handaxe industries with Levallois technique, Levallois flaking industries without handaxes, and handaxe industries without Levallois technique. The Oumm Qatafa and Tabun samples fall into the last category.

TABLE 2

PERCENTAGES OF TOOLS FROM TABUN LAYER E
CLASSIFIED BY SKINNER
(Restricted typology less denticulates and naturally backed knives)

Type	Ea	Eb	Ec	Ed
4. Retouched Levallois Point	-	.1	-	-
6. Mousterian Point	4.2	4.2	8.2	4.1
7. Elongated Mousterian Point	-	1.1	.8	-
8. *Limace*	3.4	2.5	1.8	1.8
9. Simple Straight Sidescraper	8.0	11.8	10.3	9.8
10. Simple Convex Sidescraper	23.0	19.6	20.3	24.0
11. Simple Concave Sidescraper	-	.1	-	.4
12. Double Straight Sidescraper	-	.7	.5	.3
13. Double Straight-Convex Sidescraper	1.1	2.2	.8	-
15. Double Biconvex Sidescraper	1.5	.1	-	.8
16. Double Biconcave Sidescraper	-	-	-	.2
17. Double Convex-Concave Sidescraper	-	.1	-	-
18. Straight Convergent Sidescraper	.4	.4	1.0	.1
19. Convex Convergent Sidescraper	.4	.3	1.0	.7
21. *Dejeté* Convergent Scraper	23.6	26.4	30.0	25.6
22. Straight Transverse Sidescraper	1.7	3.0	1.5	4.5
23. Convex Transverse Sidescraper	11.6	13.1	9.2	7.9
24. Concave Transverse Sidescraper	-	.1	.3	-
25. Sidescraper on Interior Face	1.3	1.5	-	9.0
26. Steep Sidescraper	1.7	3.2	-	4.3
27. Thinned Backed Sidescraper	-	.2	.3	.8
28. Bifacially Retouched Sidescraper	8.0	1.3	5.1	2.1
29. Alternate Retouched Sidescraper	1.1	.1	1.0	.2
30. Endscraper	1.9	1.2	.8	1.5
31. Atypical Endscraper	1.9	2.4	2.1	4.1
32. Burin	.2	.4	2.6	.3
33. Atypical Burin	.4	.4	-	2.1
34. Reamer	.2	-	-	-
36. Backed Knife	.8	.8	-	.1
37. Atypical Backed Knife	3.0	.5	.3	-
39. *Raclette*	-	-	-	.1
40. Notch	.6	.7	.5	1.8
61. Chopping tool	-	1.3	1.8	1.9
TOTAL CLASSIFIED	474	1115	390	1055
Biface Index (IB)	9.7	12.3	12.1	19.1
Sidescraper Index (IR)	83.7	84.1	81.0	81.4
Group III	8.4	4.3	5.3	7.9

Under "Middle Paleolithic" Perrot classifies all of the industries above Layer F at Tabun. He equates, in general, Layer E with Layers 11-25 at Yabrud and recognizes that the impression of a "very large number of handaxes and Yabrudian sidescrapers" thought by Garrod (1956, p. 46) to have been associated with *"Pre-Aurignacian"* (or *"Amudian"*) blade tools, endscrapers, and burins at Tabun might well have resulted from a lack of control of the natural stratigraphy. The question is left open as to whether this was an independent culture representing a distinct human population (as it had been interpreted by Garrod [1962, p. 242] and others), or whether these tools represented merely an industrial facies of the Yabrudian, as suggested by Skinner (1965, p. 176). Perrot questions Garrod's concept of a "symbiosis" between Pre-Aurignacian (Amudian) and Yabrudian peoples (op. cit., Garrod, 1962),

TABLE 3
PERCENTAGES OF TOOLS FROM TABUN LAYER E
CLASSIFIED BY WRIGHT
(Restricted typology less denticulates and naturally backed knives)

Type	E*a*	E*b*	E*c*	E*d*
6. Mousterian Point	.5	.5	-	-
9. Simple Straight Sidescraper	5.7	8.1	15.3	12.4
10. Simple Convex Sidescraper	29.7	33.4	23.6	22.0
11. Simple Concave Sidescraper	.5	.7	.7	.9
12. Double Straight Sidescraper	-	.2	2.1	1.6
13. Double Straight Convex Sidescraper	1.9	2.0	4.2	1.6
14. Double Straight Concave Sidescraper	-	.5	-	-
15. Double Biconvex Sidescraper	3.8	3.2	6.3	3.0
17. Double Convex-Concave Sidescraper	-	.5	1.4	.7
18. Straight Convergent Sidescraper	-	-	.7	.7
19. Convex Convergent Sidescraper	8.6	7.6	12.5	7.9
20. Concave Convergent Sidescraper	-	-	.7	-
21. *Dejeté* Convergent Scraper	7.7	10.3	9.7	12.4
22. Straight Transverse Sidescraper	-	-	-	.9
23. Convex Transverse Sidescraper	8.6	8.1	7.6	12.4
24. Concave Transverse Sidescraper	-	-	-	.2
25. Sidescraper on Interior Face	1.9	-	.7	1.4
28. Bifacially Retouched Sidescraper	18.2	14.0	8.3	11.2
29. Alternate Retouched Sidescraper	2.4	1.5	-	.5
30. Endscraper	1.0	1.0	.7	1.6
32. Burin	-	.2	-	-
33. Atypical Burin	-	-	.7	.2
34. Reamer	.5	.2	-	.5
35. Atypical Reamer	-	-	1.4	-
36. Backed Knife	.5	1.2	-	.5
40. Truncated Flakes and Blades	-	-	-	.7
42. Notch	1.4	2.0	-	1.6
61. Chopping Tool	-	1.5	2.8	4.4
62. *Diverse*	7.2	3.2	.7	.5
TOTAL CLASSIFIED	209	407	144	428
Biface Index (IB)	7.5	8.6	5.2	15.5
Sidescraper Index (IR)	87.1	89.1	91.3	85.5
Group III	6.0	10.4	5.4	4.7

as evidenced by the industry of the beach deposits at Adlun in Lebanon, both on the basis of the small samples of distinctive tool types and the differing interpretations of the geology of the deposits (Perrot, 1968, col. 339). It is his opinion, based on geological evidence, that the Pre-Aurignacian industry in Lebanon was probably older than 45,000 years and therefore very much older than similar early Upper Paleolithic industries in Western Europe.

Perrot distinguishes five types of Mousterian following the Final Acheulean, Yabrudian, and Pre-Aurignacian industries. These are rather different from the Groups and Types outlined by Skinner and reflect a stronger link with Bordes's Mousterian classification for southwestern Europe. In particular, following Bordes's earlier analysis (1955*a*), he designed a *Mousterian of Acheulean Tradition*, without Levallois flaking, and characterized by moderate numbers of sidescrapers and the presence of handaxes, denticulates, and backed knives. He suggests Layers 12 and 18 of Yabrud I as examples. Industries with moderate levels of Levallois flaking and high faceting indices, which included moderate numbers of sidescrapers, he designates *Typical Mousterian*, and as examples cites Layer C at Tabban, Layer C at Oumm Naqous, Layer F at Qafzeh, Layer 7 at Yabrud I, and the industry from Shubbabiq. A *Denticulate Mousterian* is defined on the basis of numerous denticulate tools and few sidescrapers in a context of moderate Levallois flaking and faceting. While this industry is seen as rare in caves and shelters (e.g., Yabrud I, Layers 5, 9), it is more commonly reported for open sites, particularly in river valleys in Palestine and Syria and north of the Levant in Turkey. His *Mousterian of Levallois Facies* is a departure from Bordes's typology, as is his *Mousterian with Elongated Points*, which may be a subgroup of the Levallois Facies type. In the former category, characterized by over 30% Levallois tools, he places Layers B, C, and D at Tabun, G at el Wad, Skhul, the lower levels at Kebara, Layer D at Shuqbah, Layers L to G at Qafzeh, Layers 10, 8, 6, 4, 3, and 2 at Yabrud I, and on the basis of preliminary information, the industries of Amud, Ras el Kelb, Layer 14 and below at Ksar Akil, the "Yellow 1" layer at Jerf Ajla, and Layers 4 and 5 at Magraçik in southern Turkey. This classification corresponds fairly closely with Skinner's Group C, the only exceptions being Skinner's inclusion of Qafzeh Layer F, Shubbabiq, and Abou Sif Layers B and C with these industries. The former two are classified as Typical Mousterian by Perrot, and the latter as Mousterian with Elongated Points. Since the Elongated Point type is closely linked to his Levallois Facies type, Perrot's classification of these industries agrees fairly closely with that of Skinner.

While Perrot's Mousterian with Elongated Points can be seen as analogous in a sense to Skinner's Abou Sif type of Group C, the difference in taxonomic emphasis of Perrot's classification can be seen in the group of industries he associates within this classification. These include Abou Sif, Sahba, and Larikba in the Levant, but also, on the basis of the presence of long points, Hazar Merd, Shanidar D, and the Bisitun cave in the Zagros areas, while all of the latter are placed in Group A by Skinner. It is possible that Perrot's classification reflects the lack of publication and the limited portions of the collections which have been illustrated from these sites, and he might well have separated them, as does Skinner, if the full information used by Skinner had been available to him. On the basis of Skinner's inventories, the Zagros collections do not appear to belong even in a category "between Mousterian of Levallois Facies and Typical Mousterian," as Mousterian with Elongated Points is classified, when less than 20 of the more than 950 implements examined from those sites could be classified as Levallois. The Elongated Point sites in the Levant all share relatively high Levallois indices and, as Perrot points out, have weak indices of sidescrapers and numerous blades, some of which reach a length of 15 cm or more (op. cit., col. 345). This criterion seems open to question, however, as a defining aspect of the industry, since it may be dependent upon the size of the raw material available. Altogether, Perrot's formulation of a distinct Mousterian with Elongated Points is an interesting hypothesis which may find wide acceptance with further evidence. It should be noted that Skinner also isolated the industry of Abou Sif as a distinct type within his Group C. Perrot's separation of the Yabrudian and related Pre-Aurignacian industries from those of the Mousterian may represent a major difference between his views and those of Skinner.

Aside from this major point and the classification of the Zagros industries, it appears that the different groupings resulting from the classification of the same material are largely the result of differing minor emphases on the quantitative and morphological aspects of the collections. There is little that can be said in this context with reference to Perrot's Mousterian of Acheulean Tradition and Denticulate Mousterian, since they were based on collections from Yabrud I not reported, or discussed, by Skinner. Considering the material treated by both writers, Perrot's Mousterian of Levallois Facies category includes a majority of Skinner's Tabun and Yabrud type collections. Perrot's Typical Mousterian cateogry shows the least similarity to any of Skinner's units, since it includes collections assigned to the Tabun, Abou Sif, and Erq el-Ahmar (Yabrud) types. It would be difficult, on the basis of Perrot's criteria for Mousterian of Levallois Facies, to see why Shubbabiq and Qafzeh F were not included in that category if Skinner's typological analysis were accepted (p. 111). However, when the analysis of the excavator of Shubbabiq is considered (Binford, 1966), it is apparent that there are marked discrepancies with most of Skinner's crucial indices. Since Skinner examined less than 25% of the collection, it seems reasonable to treat his results with caution and to give preference to Perrot's designation of this industry. The other samples are more difficult to assess, either because of their small size or inadequate publication, leaving the issue of the extent of a Typical Mousterian, as seen by Perrot, still open to some question.

There is strong agreement with respect to the industries from Tabun in the context of these attempts at overall classification of the early Late Pleistocene cultures of the Near East. Both Perrot and Skinner see three major groups of industries, and Perrot touches upon the possibility of a fourth (the "Tayacian" of Layer G) not discussed by Skinner. Both agree that the Late Acheulean of Layer F is distinct from subsequent industries. Each sees the industries of Layer E as a cultural unit distinct from the succeeding industries of Layers D, C, B, and the Chimney deposits, which are in turn lumped as a single industry in both classifications. In this instance, whether Layer E is termed "Group B Mousterian" or "Middle Paleolithic: Final Acheulean and Yabrudian" is of little immediate import if the basic unity and affiliation implied by each of these terms is clear. Similarly, the particular designation applied to Layers D through the Chimney would seem to be equally valid as "Mousterian of Levallois Facies" or "Tabun type, Group C Mousterian," since both terms appear to have the same general taxonomic basis. The following sections of this paper will examine in some detail how well several samples of the recently recovered industries from Tabun conform to these basic earlier classifications.

In order to understand the significance of the cultural sequence recovered in our excavation, it is necessary to have some familiarity with the geological context of the materials as revealed by structural and sedimentological analysis (for greater detail in this regard, see Jelinek et al., 1973). It appears, on the basis of our section, that the sequence of sedimentation in the cave may have been interrupted by the collapse of underlying chambers not once (as distinguished by Garrod following Layer F [Garrod and Bate, 1937, p. 701]), but several times. One period of apparent erosion and contorted sediments is visible near the middle of Garrod's Layer E, and a massive collapse of the deposits in the interior of the cave took place following the deposition of her Layer D. A general summary of the depositional sequence and the nature of accompanying environmental conditions as seen by Jelinek, Farrand, Haas, Horowitz, and Goldberg would include:

1. Deposition of sandy eolian sediments of Layers G and F, probably derived from coastal dune deposits beginning with the peak of the Tyrrhenian II transgression, corresponding to the early Eemian interglacial of Europe.

2. A collapse of these sediments into the "swallow hole" in the outer chamber, as described by Garrod, which left some of the sequence in place on the east and west sides of the chamber.

3. A continuation of primarily eolian sedimentation, with particles of gradually decreasing size through Layer E, possibly interrupted by a collapse of sediments in the interior chamber at a point which may correspond to the position of Garrod's Layer E*c*. The sediments of Layer E differ from those of Layer F in their higher organic content, suggesting either a difference in depositional conditions or in the character of the occupation of the cave.

4. The transition from the cultural Layer E to Layer D is virtually indistinguishable in the stratigraphy of the cave deposits, suggesting that no significant amount of time is involved in this marked industrial change. By this period the sediments were extremely fine, suggesting a stabilization or removal of the dunes which contributed to the lower deposits. This may have been occasioned by the retreat of the sea with the onset of glacial conditions in the northern latitudes. By mid-Layer D pollen evidence indicates markedly cooler conditions in the vicinity of the cave, and, on the basis of limited samples of microvertebrates, these conditions persist through the upper levels of Layer D.

5. The presumably slow deposition of Layer D was followed by a collapse of most of the sediments in the inner chamber of the cave, presumably into an underlying chamber. The pit formed at the back of the cave was nearly filled at the time of the deposition of Layer C. During the filling of the pit the roof of the interior chamber began to collapse, and ultimately opened through to the top of the slope above the cave to form a chimney.

6. Once the pit in the inner chamber had filled and the roof had begun to collapse, deposition in that area was probably quite rapid, with increasing quantities of roof fall and *terra rosa* from above the cave contributing to the sediments of upper Layer C. These sediments probably filled the chimney relatively quickly during the Layer B and Chimney occupations. Pollen and faunal evidence suggests that Layer C was deposited under conditions similar to those at present, though somewhat more moist. This in turn suggests an interstadial equivalent, perhaps, on the basis of

radiocarbon determinations of 40,000-45,000 years for Layer C (Garrod, 1961, pp. 244-45), corresponding to the early Würm II-III interstadial of Europe (following the French literature).

Within this sequence we tested a section of the main profile left by Garrod between the inner and outer chambers of the cave. Our test was confined to a section six meters wide, which penetrated the profile to a depth of two meters. Excavation was conducted in one-meter squares, scheduled in alternation in each row in order to record stratigraphic profiles at one-meter intervals in both directions through the excavation. All artifacts (including flakes over 2 cm in maximum dimension and identifiable bone) were measured in place to the nearest cm of locus and recorded by geological bed and their attitude with respect to the landmarks of striking platform or maximum dimension. Altogether, we recovered over 40,000 artifacts from somewhat more than 90 m^3 of deposit in a section 10 m in depth. This section reached from the lower margins of Layer B through deposits of Layers C, D, and E and crossed a disconformity at the base of Layer E into deposits on the west side of the cave that are probably equivalent to Layer F or G. Within this section we were able to define approximately 60 stratigraphic units showing broad continuity, and, assuming on the basis of the section at the center of the cave that a minimum of 20 additional strata were represented by the disconformity under Layer E, we designated the deposits under the disconformity on the west side of the cave as "Bed 80."

The present study is concerned with six samples of material drawn from our section in an effort to begin to clarify some of the questions with regard to the nature of the industries at Tabun and their depositional context that are apparent in the literature cited in the background section of the paper. Specifically, the following units will be treated: all artifacts from Beds 1 through 18 (these are relatively few in number and represent the transition from Garrod's Layer C to Layer B); all artifacts from Bed 19 (this is the last major occupation of Layer C); artifacts from a four square m section in Bed 39 (mid-Layer D); artifacts from two square m which include two layers in Bed 48 (the top of E*b*, representing Yabrudian and "Pre-Aurignacian" levels); and artifacts from two partial square m in Bed 80 (representing the earliest materials recovered in our excavation).

In view of the above, and in order to maintain consistency in typological studies, it is suggested that in a statistical treatment it is logical to remove *all* unretouched flakes (as well as casually or possibly accidentally retouched specimens; i.e., Types 45 through 50) in order to separate the restricted (*essentiel*) from the complete (*réel*) list of tools.

The two types of tools that are, in effect, unretouched flakes which are retained in the restricted typology by current practice are Type 5, the pseudo-Levallois point, and Type 38, the naturally backed knife. In our collections from Tabun the latter type is present above 10% in all complete samples and above 25% in all but one of the restricted samples. It is suggested that this kind of flake is the result of the technology used to develop cores and of the nature of the raw material used for cores. Thus it is far more likely that flakes of this type will occur in assemblages flaked from nodular flints, rather than from tabular or massive material sources. In fact, with some of the latter material types it could be fairly difficult to manufacture such pieces deliberately. High percentages of these kinds of flakes have been reported for only a few sites in Western Europe: e.g., the Acheulean industry on the floor of the structure in the cave of Lazaret (de Lumley, 1969, p. 163), Layer 4 of the cave of the Madonna Dell'Arma (Isetti et al., 1962, p. 70); and Layers 6, 7, and C of Pech-de-L'Azé I (Bordes, 1955b, pp. 26-30). At both Lazaret and Madonna Dell'Arma, rounded beach pebbles contributed to the raw material on which the industry was made and may have been partially responsible for the high occurrence of this type of flake (although other layers at each of these sites exhibited lower percentages). The recent report of Marks and Crew (1972) on a preliminary quantitative analysis of a Mousterian industry from Rosh Ein Mor in the Negev indicates that high percentages of naturally backed knives may be more common in sites in the Levant than had been realized. Marks counted among his tools only those examples which exhibited clear "use retouch" (ibid., p. 591), stating that many others were present which showed little or no modification of the cutting edge. It is suggested that this kind of selection might merely distinguish those flakes that were used on resistant materials and, while this might be useful for some interpretations of the collections, it tends to obscure the typological-technological analysis of the population of artifacts. Therefore, as an alternative, in an attempt to show the effects of this tool type on the overall character of each collection samples have been presented graphically with three cumulative curves; one showing the complete assemblage, one showing the traditional restricted assemblage, and one showing the restricted assemblage without Type 38 (industries without significant Levallois components are portrayed only by the latter two curves). In addition an index numbered 38 has been added to place these flakes in perspective with other special types of unretouched flakes.

One additional observation with regard to the technological observations must also be mentioned here; this concerns the laminar or blade index. Bordes's definition of a blade, as a flake twice as long as it is wide, with length measured along the axis of flaking and width perpendicular to length (Bordes, 1961, p. 6), sometimes does not accurately coincide with the overall shape of the flake, particularly when the axis of symmetry of the flake diverges significantly from the axis of flaking. One can assume from this definition that it is the maximum dimension perpendicular to the axis of flaking that is meant here for width, and this can be particularly misleading in terms of the shape of the flake in an elongated asymmetrical example. In an effort to preserve some information on flake shape, complete flakes in our samples have been measured in the following

manner: length is the distance from the point of percussion to the point of last detachment from the core; width is measured perpendicular to length on the interior surface at the midpoint of the length; and thickness is measured perpendicular to width at the same point. In order to control for the divergence of the direction of the flake from the axis of flaking, we have also recorded the "angle of skew" (Leach, 1969, p. 55) within a system of eleven classes covering 180°. What this means, in terms of practical comparison with flakes measured by Bordes's system, is that our system tends to produce more of a tendency toward laminarity, since our measurement of length is almost always close to the maximum dimension of the artifact; while width, at the midpoint of this line, seldom represents the maximum dimension perpendicular to length. It can be argued, on the basis of the distribution of the ratio of length to width in most populations of flakes, regardless of the techniques of measurement employed, that the effect is one of a distribution around a central mode slightly skewed in the direction of higher values (e.g., see fig. 1, and Watanabe, 1968, pp. 504-5). The implications of this distribution with respect to the ratio $L = >2W$ have more to do with the tendency of varying portions of the population to fall on one side or the other of the arbitrary line representing this ratio, which passes through the distribution, than with a significant separation or bimodality within the distribution as would be the case if there were two distinct kinds of flakes. Thus it is perhaps more appropriate to speak of the laminar "tendency" of any particular population of flakes, which reflects the way the distribution lies with respect to this ratio, rather than a laminar "index," which implies the presence of a class of typologically or technologically distinct flakes. Samples of complete flakes as measured by our method will show a somewhat high laminar tendency than they would if they had been measured by Bordes's technique. However, experiment tends to indicate that this divergence is no more than a few percent in most instances.

There is a particular class of typologically distinct flakes mentioned by Bordes (1961, p. 6) frequently referred to as "true" blades, which show a deliberate preparation of the core in the form of parallel exterior flake scars. These flakes are typically long with parallel edges and, with few exceptions (6% in our samples to date), also show Bordes's ratio for blade classification. These blades have been separated and divided into Levallois (faceted platform) and normal (plain platform) blades in the hope that this may add additional depth to the technological view of each industry. All data on laminar tendency (Ilam) and blades reported here are confined to complete flakes. Within our collections two classes of incomplete flakes have been distinguished: one (Class B) which is measured along the axis of flaking in the manner suggested by Bordes, and the other (Class C) on which there is insufficient evidence of axis of flaking remaining for accurate measurement by that technique, and therefore length is measured as the maximum diameter of the artifact. In the case of both of these classes of incom-

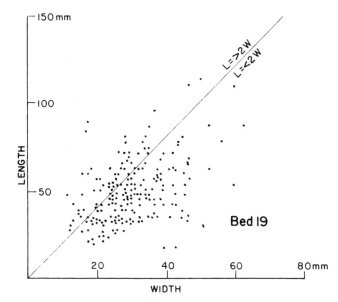

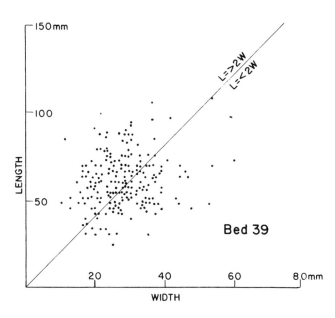

FIG. 1—Length/Width Ratios of Complete Flakes (Tabun).

plete flakes, width and thickness are measured at the midpoint of the length axis, with width the maximum diameter perpendicular to length on the interior surface and thickness perpendicular to width. In defense of the mid-point measurements of width and thickness it can be said that the product of the three dimensions taken in this manner reflects more accurately the volume of the flake than do maximum diameters on three axes.

THE TECHNOLOGY

The standard technological indices, plus indices for naturally backed knives (38), and Levallois and normal "true" blades, are presented in Table 4. Each index indicates the percentage of all classifiable specimens (flakes,

blades, points, and tools) in that category. N indicates the number of classifiable specimens in the preceding categories, e.g., in Beds 1-18. IF and IFs are based upon 257 classifiable platforms, while IL, 38, and True Blades are based on 353 classifiable flakes, and Ilam is based on 174 complete flakes.

It is apparent that a marked difference in IL, 38, IF, and IFs is present between Beds 1-18, 19, and 39 on the one hand, and 48A, 48B, and 80 on the other. The laminar tendency and blades do not show this kind of grouping, but show high occurrence in Beds 39 and 48B, and moderate Ilam and weak representation of blades in the other samples. Within the IL-38-IF-IFs groups, it appears that Beds 1-18 and 19 are quite similar and differ rather strongly in IL from Bed 39. It is also clear that Beds 48A and 48B are almost identical and differ to some degree from Bed 80 in all categories but IF.

An additional perspective on the technology can be gained by examining the ratios of major categories of lithic material; i.e., retouched tools (restricted), flakes, and cores. This information is presented in Table 5.

These ratios also suggest a stronger difference between the upper three and lower three units than within either group, based on the lower representation of tools in the later beds and lower representation of flakes in the earlier beds. There are, however, clear differences between each of the samples in these categories. It is assumed that to some degree these differences reflect different kinds of activities relating to the manufacture and use of chipped stone materials.

THE TYPOLOGY

The numbers of specimens in each represented category of the standard type list are shown in Table 6. Figures 2 through 5 show the complete, restricted, and restricted less Type 38 cumulative percentage curves for each sample, with the following exceptions: in the case of Beds 1-18, 151 artifacts classifiable in the standard typology were recovered, of which only 54 fall within the traditional restricted typology. Of these, 26 are naturally backed knives (Type 38). Therefore, on the basis of the general technological similarity between the two layers and the similar complete typological curves, the materials from Beds 1-18 and Bed 19 have been combined for the restricted curves. Complete curves for Beds 48A, 48B, or 80 have not been presented since they are essentially identical to the restricted curves. Table 7 presents the complete typological indices, and Table 8 lists the restricted indices.

It is readily apparent upon looking at the cumulative graphs that the similarities seen in many of the technological indices in the upper three units are strongly reinforced by the complete curves (fig. 2), which are quite similar except for higher percentages of Levallois points in Bed 39. This similarity is also reflected in the complete typological indices, where the only differences within this group lie in the higher occurrences of "Upper Paleolithic" indicators in Bed 39 and relatively lower sidescraper, Charentian, and

TABLE 4
TECHNOLOGICAL INDICES FOR SAMPLES FROM TABUN

Bed	IL	38	Lev.	Nor.	N	IF	IFs	N	Ilam	N
1-18	35.7	7.7	6.5	5.4	353	60.3	51.0	257	34.5	174
19	34.5	6.4	2.6	2.8	609	61.1	47.3	419	29.1	199
39	53.3	7.4	16.0	11.5	381	64.6	54.5	347	57.2	194
48A	3.2	22.7	.4	2.0	256	22.6	8.3	253	20.3	59
48B	5.0	23.3	3.2	20.4	279	25.2	10.4	270	49.6	127
80	1.0	15.4	.2	1.9	951	22.2	4.3	916	20.9	302

denticulate indices in that unit. The restricted curves (fig. 3) and indices show these differences more clearly. The lower three units appear to be alike only in the lack of Levallois typology, which hardly can be considered a unifying feature. Bed 48A is unlike any of the other samples in its high sidescraper and Charentian indices. Once the factors of Levallois and naturally backed knife technology are removed, the restricted indices of Bed 48A bear some resemblance to Beds 1-19; however, the latter do not have as many scrapers, and have more denticulates than 48A. The resemblance between the restricted curves and indices of 48B and those of Bed 39 is more striking, with somewhat fewer sidescrapers and markedly fewer (though still abundant) Upper Paleolithic types in Bed 39. Bed 80 is unique, with moderate percentages in all of the restricted indices other than dejeté scrapers. While there is a superficial resemblance between the restricted cumulative curves of Bed 80 and Bed 39, it should be noted that the marked rise in Bed 80 occurs after Type 40, while in Bed 39 it largely precedes Type 40.

Some bifaces were present in all of the units treated here, with the exception of Bed 19 (see table 8). The single biface from Beds 1-18 came from near the top of Square 2 (Bed 1) and is a short, thick nucleiform specimen that exhibits evidence of heavy chemical weathering (desilicification) and perhaps slight rolling. The appearance of this artifact suggests that it was derived from an earlier context and does not represent the industry of the beds in which it was found. The sample collection from Bed 39 produced two small, well-made bifaces, which were found about 50 cm apart in Square 16. The condition of these specimens is so fresh that it seems unlikely that they could have been collected from weathered areas of earlier deposits. It is here assumed that they form a part of the industry of Bed 39. The few bifaces recovered in the sample from Bed 48A are remarkable for their variation. One, an elongated cordiform, is reworked from an earlier artifact with marked patination, apparently also a biface. One is well flaked as a biface in the butt area and amygdaloidal in shape, but appears to be more of a bifacial scraper toward the tip. Another amygdaloidal specimen is quite carefully flaked with a very thick butt and thin tip. The final specimen in this group is a partial biface with the general contour of an

asymmetric *hachereau* or crude "*prodnik.*" The four bifaces from Bed 48B are similar in that they are all partial in type; each exhibits a considerable area of unmodified surface. The Bed 80 bifaces demonstrate an almost complete range of proficiency from crude nucleiform and Abbevillian types to thin symmetrical specimens with extremely fine flaking. There is a relatively high frequency of partial specimens. Virtually all of the *hachereaux* show tranchet sharpening. The *diverse* forms include a rectangular specimen, perhaps classifiable as a *biface carré*, two crescent-shaped specimens suggesting a particular pattern, and a large "*prodnik.*"

TABLE 5
PERCENTAGES OF MAJOR CATEGORIES OF LITHIC MATERIALS

Bed	Tools (Restricted)	Flakes	Cores	N
1-18	7.4	80.8	11.8	458
19	7.2	87.0	5.8	863
39	14.4	80.3	5.3	487
48A	47.1	48.0	4.9	452
48B	25.7	65.9	8.4	428
80	20.1	60.9	19.1	2080

Each of the industries in our samples is briefly characterized on the basis of the technological and typological information as follows:

BEDS 1-18

The rather poor sample of only 151 tools from the first 18 beds in our stratigraphic sequence includes a very large percentage of unretouched flakes (Types 1-3, 38). The few retouched tools remaining are largely simple sidescrapers and denticulates. The relatively large percentage of cores may indicate that some primary flaking was being carried out in the cave. Several cores from the upper beds are quite small Levallois flake cores. Their fine execution and that of several other cores suggests the possibility that these artifacts might also have served as tools. The sparse distribution of artifacts may indicate relatively infrequent use of this

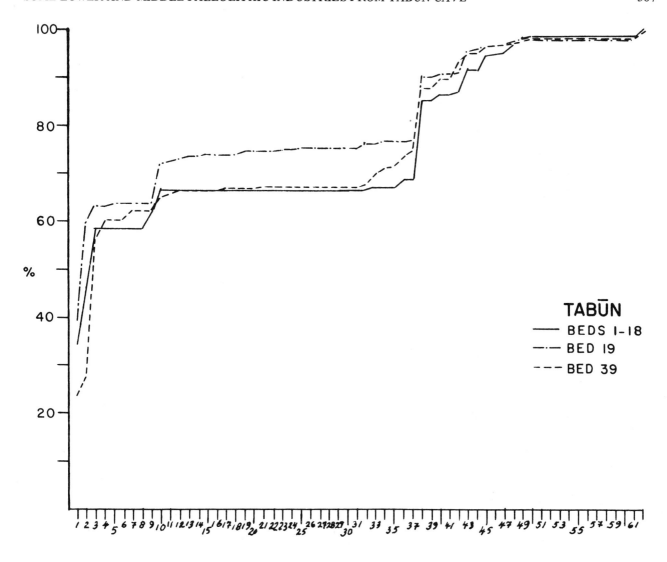

FIG. 2—Cumulative Graph of Beds 1-18, 19, and 39.

portion of the cave during the accumulation of these strata; this would be in keeping with the proximity of our section to the roof fall from the interior chamber, and the accompanying accumulation of *terra rosa* from the slopewash into the chimney. The heavily burned layers throughout these strata, which were interpreted by Garrod as "hearths" (Garrod and Bate, 1937, p. 63), can each be traced for considerable distances across the profile and appear to be the result of recurring overall conflagrations at the entrance to the inner chamber. These may have resulted from deliberate attempts to clear the inner chamber; however, no correlated prolonged or intensive period of habitation is observed.

BED 19

The industry from this level is similar in almost every way to that of Beds 1-18. The features in which Bed 19 differs signficantly from 1-18 are in the absence of straight sidescrapers, the relatively lower incidence of cores, the almost complete absence of very small Levallois flake cores,

and in the presence of a much greater variety of scrapers and significant numbers of fragments of very large Levallois flakes. The lower incidence of Levallois points and of true Levallois and normal blades, as well as the lower laminar tendency (Ilam), may also be significant. The greater intensity of occupation is evident in the fact that the total number of artifacts from Bed 19 is almost double that from Beds 1-18, although the Bed 19 sediments were very small in volume as compared to those that produced the 1-18 collection. To some degree this concentration may be due to a lower rate of sedimentation during this period, but it probably also reflects a significantly greater utilization of this portion of the cave.

BED 39

This industry is characterized by a high proportion of Levallois points (exceeding Levallois flakes) and a strong representation of Group III ("Upper Paleolithic") tool types. There are relatively few scrapers, and although a fair number of notches are present, denticulates are rare. The

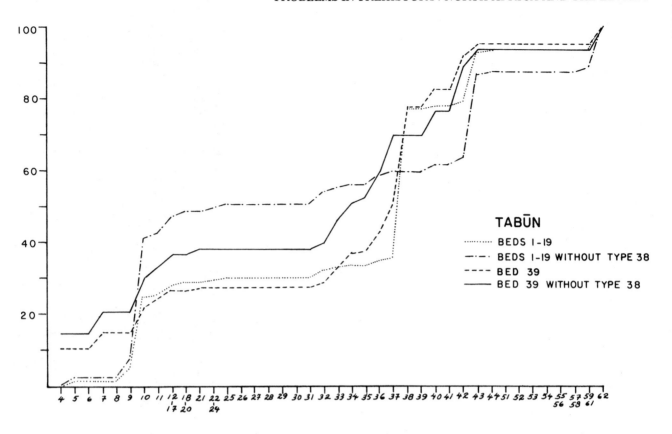

FIG. 3–Cumulative Graph of Restricted Type Lists for Beds 1-19 and 39.

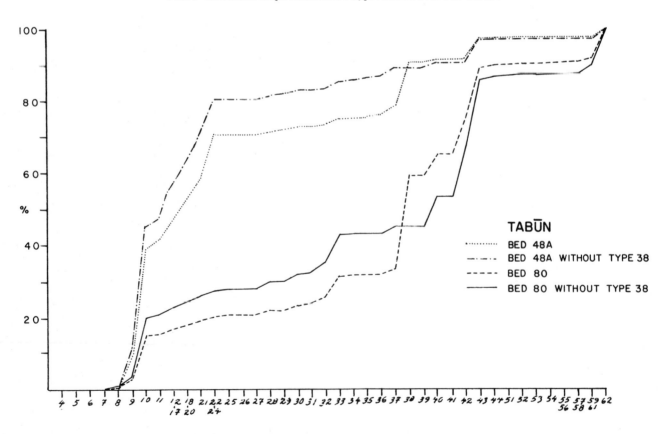

FIG. 4–Cumulative Graph of Restricted Type Lists for Beds 48A and 80.

TABLE 6
TOOL COUNTS IN SAMPLES FROM TABUN

Bed	1-18	19	39	48A	48B	80
TYPE						
1. Typical Levallois Flake	49	106	51	4	3	5
2. Atypical Levallois Flake	15	57	8	-	-	-
3. Levallois Point	22	9	61	1	-	1
4. Retouched Levallois Point	-	-	9	-	-	-
5. Pseudo-Levallois Point	-	2	-	-	-	-
7. Mousterian Point	-	-	4	-	-	-
8. *Limace*	-	-	-	-	-	1
9. Simple Straight Sidescraper	5	-	-	23	10	12
10. Simple Convex Sidescraper	7	23	6	70	8	58
11. Simple Concave Sidescraper	-	1	2	5	1	2
12. Double Straight Sidescraper	-	1	1	4	-	-
13. Double Straight-Convex Sidescraper	-	2	-	2	-	3
15. Double Biconvex Sidescraper	-	1	-	8	-	3
17. Double Convex-Concave Sidescraper	-	-	1	-	-	1
18. Straight Convergent Sidescraper	-	-	-	2	-	2
19. Convex Convergent Sidescraper	-	1	-	10	2	4
21. *Dejeté* Convergent Scraper	-	-	1	15	1	7
22. Straight Transverse Sidescraper	-	-	-	4	-	-
23. Convex Transverse Sidescraper	-	1	-	23	3	4
15. Sidescraper on Interior Face	-	1	-	-	-	2
28. Bifacially Retouched Sidescraper	-	-	-	3	1	7
29. Alternate Retouched Sidescraper	-	-	-	1	-	-
30. Endscraper	-	-	-	2	2	7
31. Atypical Endscraper	-	-	-	-	2	3
32. Burin	-	3	1	1	4	8
33. Atypical Burin	1	-	4	4	1	28
34. Reamer	-	1	3	1	-	2
35. Atypical Reamer	-	-	1	1	1	-
36. Backed Knife	2	-	4	1	18	-
37. Atypical Backed Knife	-	1	7	5	33	7
38. Naturally Backed Knife	26	36	24	29	47	125
40. Truncated Flake and Blade	1	1	4	2	9	30
42. Notch	1	1	8	-	1	49
43. Denticulate	7	13	3	14	3	68
44. Alternately Flaked Tip	-	1	-	-	-	3
45. Retouch on Interior Face	4	1	3	1	-	2
46-47. Flakes with Heavy Retouch	2	1	1	-	1	3
48-49. Flakes with Light Retouch	4	3	2	4	1	1
50. Flakes with Bifacial Retouch	1	-	1	-	-	-
51. Tayac Point	-	-	-	1	-	1
52. Notched Triangles	-	-	-	-	-	1
54. End-Notched Flake	-	-	-	-	1	1
58. Stemmed Piece	-	-	-	-	-	1
61. Chopper Tool	-	1	-	-	3	7
62. *Diverse*	4	6	4	5	1	37
TOTAL CLASSIFIED	151	274	214	246	157	496
Broken Implements	1	11	4	42	6	5
Utilized Flakes	23	32	63	32	38	260

TABLE 7
TYPOLOGICAL INDICES FOR SAMPLES FROM TABUN
(Complete Typology)

Bed	ILty	IR	IC	IAu	II	III	IV	N
1-18	57.0	7.9	4.6	1.3	7.9	2.0	4.6	151
19	62.8	10.9	8.8	.4	12.2	1.8	4.7	274
39	60.3	5.1	2.8	5.1	7.1	9.3	1.4	214
48A	2.0	68.7	39.4	2.4	68.8	6.1	5.7	246
48B	1.9	16.6	7.0	32.5	16.5	38.9	1.9	157
80	1.2	21.2	12.7	1.4	21.3	11.1	13.7	496

TABLE 8
TYPOLOGICAL INDICES FOR SAMPLES FROM TABUN
(Restricted Typology Less Type 38)

Bed	IR	IB	21	II	III	IV	N	IQ	N
1-18	42.9	3.4	-	42.9	10.7	25.0	28	-	12
19	50.8	-	-	54.1	8.2	21.3	61	5.7	33
1-19	48.2	1.1	-	50.4	8.9	22.5	89	4.4	45
39	19.0	3.1	1.6	23.8	31.7	4.8	63	21.4	14
48A	82.1	1.9	7.2	70.3	7.2	6.8	207	35.6	278
48B	24.8	2.8	1.0	24.0	58.1	2.9	105	45.8	24
80	29.2	13.5	1.9	29.5	15.3	18.9	359	10.1	119

high incidence of true blades and high laminar tendency are in marked contrast to Bed 19, but more closely resemble 1-18. It is interesting in this regard to note that a skilled lithic technologist has recently observed that the production of Levallois points results in the production of significant quantities of true blades (Bruce Bradley, personal communication). The similar ratios between true blades and Levallois points in Beds 1-18 and Bed 39, where significant quantities of both types are present, suggest this type of technological relationship between these two kinds of artifacts. The presence of several elongated Mousterian points tends to emphasize the "elongated" nature of this assemblage and its unique position among the samples described here. The material from Bed 39 occupies a significant depth of fine-grained sediments and can be assumed to have accumulated over a fairly prolonged interval. The lack of heavy concentration of artifacts in any single zone within this stratigraphic unit argues against intensive habitation in this period.

BED 48A

Perhaps the most remarkable feature of this collection is the very high ratio of tools to flakes and cores. The overwhelming preponderance of scrapers of diverse forms among these tools and the near absence of Levallois technique also isolate this industry from the later samples. In addition, the Quina index is quite high. The heavy concentration of artifacts as well as the abundance of tools implies a specialized intensive habitation, although the fine sedi-

mentation suggests that this may have occurred during a significant time interval. It is this writer's impression that a more detailed scraper typology applied to this and other similar collections in Layer E may produce some interesting contrasts in the assemblages. It is already possible to recognize some particular patterns among the artifacts that must, of necessity, now be classified as diverse. One of these is a crescent-shaped, thick lunate suggesting a "demi-limace."

BED 48B

This industry, non-Levallois in character, is dominated by high percentages of knives, with markedly lower ratios of scrapers and denticulates. Although almost half of the scrapers have Quina or demi-Quina retouch, nine of these eleven specimens are so near the contact with 48A that the significance of this ratio may be open to question. The contact between these two cultural layers is not reflected by any change in sedimentation in Squares 16 and 23, from which these samples were drawn. The contact was defined as closely as possible from the dominant nature of the industries above and below, and the attitude of the flat plane of the artifacts. Thus, artifacts in this contact zone (about 5 cm thick) cannot be unequivocably assigned. Virtually all of these nine scrapers fall within this zone. The similar technological indices (other than those affected by blade production) of 48A and 48B suggest that perhaps a single basic technology may characterize both, including the frequent use of Quina retouch. Many of the blades from 48B are heavily prismatic, in effect qualifying as large burin

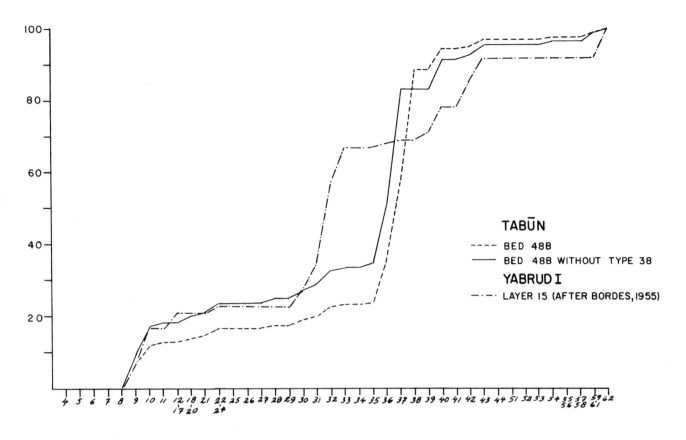

FIG. 5—Cumulative Graph of Restricted Type Lists for Tabun Bed 48A and Yabrud I, Layer 15.

spalls. In this sense they differ significantly from the flatter blades of Beds 1-18 and 39. An overall view of the industry from 48B leaves a strong impression of an emphasis on the manufacture of elongated thin-edged flakes. This is reflected in the high laminar tendency (Ilam), high frequency of normal blades, and high incidence of naturally backed knives. This last is an aspect of technology shared with 48A. The general effect, in a functional sense, is to emphasize an interest in slicing or cutting soft materials in 48B, in contrast to heavy planing or abrading in 48A.

BED 80

This sample of materials from Bed 80 is drawn from deposits over 1 m in thickness in order to acquire an idea of the general nature of these cultural layers. There is every reason to believe that, with more detailed structural and locational analysis, this collection, with those from adjoining loci, can be separated into several cultural layers of somewhat differing character. Bed 80 is quite similar to 48A in technology. In typology, however, it lacks the very high ratios of sidescrapers, though these are present in some abundance, and it has moderately strong ratios of bifaces, denticulates, and Upper Paleolithic (Group III) types (fig. 4). The Quina and Charentian indices are moderately low in contrast to 48A. A considerable portion of the Group III artifacts are burins of various types, and a significant number of the *diverse* (Type 62) tools also have burins as a part of their utilization. Among these is one clear example

of a *grattoir-burin*. A particular pattern of burin manufacture or burin-like utilization involves the removal of the striking platform with a single flake and the utilization of this flat surface to strike a burin blow. Truncated striking platforms without burins are also present. About 60% of the notches in the assemblage are Clactonian, and there is at least one good example of a "bill-hook." The striking feature of this industry is its diversity, exemplified by the presence of numbers of small, thick, well-flaked tools that do not characterize any of the other collections thus far examined.

DISCUSSION

These preliminary samples from Tabun need to be compared first with the previous classifications of the Tabun sequence based on the artifact collections recovered by Garrod. Secondly, there will be a broader comparison within the Lower and Middle Paleolithic of the Near East to determine whether this material conforms to the basic patterns of previously described industries.

Considering, first, Garrod's own reports on her material, which are basic to equating our specimens with her succession of Layers and cultures, the general similarities between her material and ours are clear. The patterns of high frequencies of Levallois technique in the samples from Beds 1-18, 19, and 39 (her Levalloiso-Mousterian of Layers B/C, C, and D); the higher frequency of Levallois flakes in 1-19 and of Levallois points in 39 (Layer D); the low frequency of Levallois technique in Beds 48 and 80; the high frequency of scrapers and the presence of backed knives in portions of Bed 48 (representing Layer E*b*); and a higher percentage of bifaces low in the sequence in Bed 80, are all factors that might be anticipated from her work.

In terms of her quantitative summaries (see table 1), the restricted IR for Beds 1-19 is similar to her figure of about 60% for Layer C, but her high percentage of notches is not reflected in our material. It is possible that some of the "notches" in her report are, in fact, denticulates, which do not figure in her typology but are present in our study in percentages slightly higher than her "notches." The percentages of minor artifact types in Beds 1-19 are generally quite close to those in Layer C in the initial report. A comparison of counts for Layer D and Bed 39 shows much higher frequencies of retouched points in her collection, as well as higher frequencies of scrapers (approximately double the Bed 39 IR of 19.0). Our collections, on the other hand, show higher percentages of burins and notches and denticulates. Our IB and her percentage of handaxes are quite similar at 3.1 and 4.3%, respectively. A surprising feature of our Bed 39 sample is the high percentage of true blades (Garrod seems to have observed only blades of this type), which are not remarked upon by Garrod in her discussion of Layer D, but which form one of the most striking features of this assemblage. In comparison with Bed 48, Garrod's 75.2% of sidescrapers for Layer E*b* is reasonably close to the IR of 82.1 for Bed 48A. Her percentage of bifaces in this unit is much higher than was found in either 48A or 48B and suggests that other beds within this layer will have higher frequencies of bifaces. The industry of Bed 48B is not represented in isolated form in Garrod's samples; the question of whether such an industry could be isolated was one of the primary problems facing our excavation at Tabun. It now appears that this is possible, though the clarification of the relationship of this industry to surrounding cultural materials will require further analysis.

Bed 80 is perhaps the greatest problem in equation with Garrod's material. It is clear from her stratigraphic diagrams that she was not aware of the industrial significance of this unit below the disconformity that marked the erosion following the collapse of Layers F and G; she did remark on this disconformity in an adjacent section, terming it a "fault" and mentioning that it was not noticed "until a few days before the completion of work." (Garrod and Bate, 1937, p. 70). The question involving this industry is whether it equates with the base of Layer E*d* or F, both of which might have been involved in the collapse, or is it possibly related to the enigmatic Layer G which formed a thin deposit above the irregular cave floor? The presence of rounded beach pebbles among the artifacts in this layer and tentative palynological analysis suggest that it belongs in the last interglacial period and, thus, is not drastically earlier than the F and E*d* deposits, which share similar attributes. The sediments of Bed 80 are quite sandy, fairly compact, and lightly cemented, differing in texture and hardness from the overlying Layer E Beds. The industrial

composition does not match any of Garrod's layers very closely; all of her lower layers have significantly higher frequencies of scrapers, and Layers E*d* and F have higher frequencies of bifaces. In the former category Bed 80 is close to Layer F, in the latter to Layer E. It is tempting to see some significance in the higher frequency of burins in Layer G, and especially in the presence of a significant number of notches in that layer, though they are absent throughout Layers E and F. Probably the best hypothesis that can be offered at present is that Bed 80 represents an industry that shows features of both Layer F (represented by scraper ratios and fine bifaces) and Layer G (represented by small, peculiar tools, burins, and notches). It is possible that a small sample of our Bed 80 material in which no handaxes were present might appear to be similar to Layer G, which included only 75 tools.

In comparing these industries with the cultural units defined by Skinner and by Perrot, it is difficult to find disagreement in the assignment of Beds 1-19 to the Mousterian of Levallois Facies defined by Perrot, or the similarly defined Tabun type of Group C Mousterian of Skinner. Bed 39, however, does not conform to either of these definitions, and is quite clearly related to Perrot's Mousterian with Elongated Points and Skinner's Abou Sif type of Group C Mousterian. Bed 48A belongs in Group B, as defined by Skinner and as all of Layer E was designated by him, and in the Yabrudian of Perrot. The low frequency of bifaces in Bed 48A in contrast to Garrod's counts for Layer E*b* suggests that Perrot is correct in his supposition that there are both Final Acheulean or Mousterian of Acheulean Tradition and Yabrudian cultural layers within Layer E.

At this point it is possible to treat the comparison of Wright's and Skinner's studies of collections from Layer E somewhat further. If the cultural layers in E are heterogeneous, as seems implied by the relationship of our sample from Bed 48A with Garrod's counts, most of the discrepancy between Wright's and Skinner's counts might well be based on a difference in the provenience from which each collection was derived. In this case Wright's collection appears to be from layers more similar to Bed 48A than was Skinner's material. With regard to Bed 48B, neither Perrot's nor Skinner's classifications are relevant, and it is necessary to compare our sample with the Pre-Aurignacian of Yabrud I, Layer 15, as described by Bordes (1955*a*). His Ilam of 37 is somewhat lower than ours of 49.6. The restricted IR of his sample closely matches ours (23.3 and 24.8, respectively); his Group III tools at 45 are less well represented than ours at 58.1; and denticulates are less well represented in our sample (2.9) than in his (8.3). A comparison of the two restricted curves, less Type 38 in our sample— apparently there were none in the Yabrud sample—is shown in Fig. 5. This clearly indicates a distinct difference between the two samples. The industry from Yabrud I, 15 is characterized by higher percentages of endscrapers and burins, particularly the latter, while Tabun Bed 48B is characterized by high percentages of backed knives and relatively few endscrapers and burins. Thus we can see two distinct kinds of industries, sharing a high laminar tendency and the use of tools which were later common in the Upper Paleolithic, but whose individual tool kits seem quite different. In this respect, Tabun 48B may more closely resemble the "Amudian" industry from the beach at Abri Zumoffen (Garrod and Kirkbride, 1961), though here too more significant quantities of endscrapers and burins occur. A further definition of this industry at Tabun will be possible as the complete collection is subjected to analysis. There is now good reason to believe that similar layers exist above and below Bed 48B, though whether there will ultimately be three such layers, as suggested by Garrod (1956), or more, remains to be seen.

The industry of Bed 80 also poses comparative problems. In general terms it conforms to Perrot's Late Acheulean of Oumm Qatafa and Tabun F, although the differences with the latter layer have already been discussed. It would appear, on the basis of Neuville's description (1931), that there may be more similarities with the Qatafa Acheulean, though here too bifaces appear to be proportionately more numerous and generally better executed than in Bed 80.

It has been the aim of this presentation to indicate some of the directions that our recent analysis of the collections has taken, and some of the results bearing upon basic problems in the interpretation of the early Late Pleistocene cultures of the Near East. It is hoped that as this research progresses and more additional information is made available from other areas of the Near East we will have a better understanding of the role of this site in the interpretation of man's biological and cultural development.

ACKNOWLEDGMENTS

The field work at Tabun from 1967 to 1972 was sponsored by the Foreign Currency Program of the Smithsonian Institution (Grants SFCP 19, SI-FCP 4791, SFC 5746, SFG 0-4977 and SFG 1-5267), the Ford Foundation (Grant 68-342), the National Science Foundation (Grant GS-2696), and a research grant from the University of Michigan. Throughout our work we benefited from a close association with the French Center for Prehistoric Research in Jerusalem, directed by Jean Perrot, and the assistance of Drs. Avraham Ronen and David Gilead of Tel-Aviv University. The Laboratory research has been sponsored by National Science Foundation Grant GS-2696. The author has profited greatly over several years from discussions with Professor François Bordes of the University of Bordeaux and has benefited from his knowledge of Paleolithic cultures with relation to the typological studies at Tabun (although the typological inventories presented herein are those of the author). Much of the routine work behind this presentation was patiently and carefully carried out by three research assistants at the University of Arizona—Donald Graybill, Gary Rollefson, and Bruce Jones.

BIBLIOGRAPHY

BINFORD, SALLY R., 1966. "Me'arat Shovakh (Mugharet esh-Shubbabiq)." *Israel Exploration Journal* 16:18-32; 96-103.

BORDES, FRANÇOIS, 1950. "Principes d'une méthode d'étude des techniques de débitage et de la typologie du Paléolithique ancien et moyen." *L'Anthropologie* 54:19-34.

————, 1953. "Essai de classification des industries Moustériennes." *Bulletin de la Société Préhistorique Française* 50:457-66.

————, 1955*a*. "Le Paléolithique inférieur et moyen de Jabroud (Syrie) et la question de pré-Aurignacien." *L'Anthropologie* 59:486-507.

————, 1955*b*. "Les gisements du Pech-de-l'Azé (Dordogne)." *L'Anthropologie* 59:1-38.

————, 1961, *Typologie du Paléolithique ancien et moyen.* Bordeaux: Mémoire 1, Publication de l'Institut de Préhistoire de l'Université de Bordeaux.

————, and BOURGON, MAURICE, 1951. "Le complexe Moustérien: Moustériens, Levalloisien, et Tayacien." *L'Anthropologie* 55:1-23.

GARROD, D. A. E., 1956. "Acheuléo-jabroudien et pré-Aurignacien de la Grotte de Taboun, Mont Carmel: Étude stratigraphique et chronologique." *Quaternaria* 3:39-59.

————, 1961. "Comment on M. Bordes' Article 'Sur la chronologie au Paléolithique en Moyen Orient'." *Quaternaria* 5:71-73.

————, 1962. "The Middle Palaeolithic of the Near East and the Problem of Mount Carmel Man." *Journal of the Royal Anthropological Institute* 92:232-51.

————, and BATE, D. M. A., 1937. *The Stone Age of Mount Carmel*, vol. 1. Oxford: Clarendon Press.

————, and KIRKBRIDE, D., 1961. "Excavation of the Abri Zumoffen, A Palaeolithic Rock-Shelter near Adlun, in South Lebanon, 1958." *Bulletin du Musée de Beyrouth* 16:7-45.

HOWELL, F. CLARK, 1959. "Upper Pleistocene Stratigraphy and Early Man in the Levant." *Proceedings of the American Philosophical Society* 103:1-65.

ISETTI, GIUSEPPE; de LUMLEY, H.; and MISKOVSKY, J. C., 1962. "Il giacimento musteriano della grotta dell'Arma presso Bussana (Sanremo)." *Rivista di Studi Liguri* 28:1-112.

JELINEK, A. J.; FARRAND, W. R.; HAAS, G.; HOROWITZ, A.; and GOLDBERG, P., 1973. "New Excavations at the Tabun Cave, Mount Carmel, Israel, 1967-1972: A Preliminary Report." *Paleorient* 1(2).

LAURENT, P., 1965. *Heureuse Préhistoire.* Périgueux: Pierre Fanlac.

LEACH, B. F., 1969. "The Concept of Similarity in Prehistoric Studies." In *Studies in Prehistoric Anthropology*, vol. 1. Anthropology Department, University of Otago.

de LUMLEY, HENRY, 1969. "L'industrie acheuléenne découverte sur le sol de la cabane du Lazaret." *Mémoires de la Société Préhistorique Française* 7:145-69.

MARKS, A. E., and CREW, H. L., 1972. "Rosh Ein Mor, an Open-Air Mousterian Site in the Central Negev, Israel." *Current Anthropology* 13:591-93.

NEUVILLE, RENÉ, 1931. "L'Acheuléen supérieur de la grotte d'Oumm-Qatafa." *L'Anthropologie* 41:13-51, 249-63.

————, 1951. *Le Paléolithique et le Méolithique du Désert de Judée.* Archives de l'Institut de Paléontologie humaine, mémoire 24.

PERROT, J., 1968. "Le préhistoire palestinienne." In *Supplément au Dictionnaire de la Bible* 8(43):286-446.

RUST, ALFRED, 1950. *Die Höhlenfunde von Jabrud (Syrien).* Neumünster: Karl Wachholtz.

SKINNER, JAMES H., 1965. "The Flake Industries of Southwest Asia: A Typological Study." Ph.D. dissertation, Columbia University. Ann Arbor: University Microfilms 65-9177.

WATANABE, HITOSHI, 1968. "Flake Production in a Transitional Industry from the Amud Cave, Israel. A Statistical Approach to Paleolithic Techno-Typology." In *La Préhistoire: Problèmes et tendances*, pp. 499-509. Paris: CNRS.

WRIGHT, GARY A., 1966. "The University of Michigan Archaeological Collections from et-Tabun, Palestine: Levels F and E." *Papers of the Michigan Academy of Science, Arts, and Letters* 51:407-23.

THE MIDDLE AND UPPER PALEOLITHIC OF LEBANON AND SYRIA IN THE LIGHT OF RECENT RESEARCH

Lorraine Copeland
London Institute of Archeology

INTRODUCTION

This paper will cover the Middle Paleolithic (beginning with the Yabrudian) and the Upper Paleolithic (ending with the Levantine Aurignacian) of the northern Levant, an area comprising Lebanon, Syria, and the Hatay region of southern Turkey. To discuss such a time span (some 80,000 years) in a conference paper necessitates some shortcuts.

Emphasis will be on recent work. Recent excavations include those of Columbia University at Nahr Ibrahim and Yabrud; Tokyo University at Keoue Cave; Tixier (auspices of CNRS) at Ksar Akil; and Fleisch (St. Joseph's University) at Naamé. Surveys were carried out by Tokyo University (Suzuki and Kobori, 1970; Suzuki and Takai, 1973), Toronto University (Schroeder, 1970), and Besançon and Hours in the South Béqaa (Lebanese University and St. Joseph's University). It is assumed that readers are familiar with the results of earlier research into the Levantine Paleolithic, such as was summarized, with emphasis on Palestine, recently (Perrot, 1968). This includes the work of Rust (1950), Garrod (Garrod and Bate, 1937), Père Zumoffen at Antelias and Adlun (Zumoffen, 1900), Wetzel and Haller (1945-48), and also a recent bibliography (Hours et al., 1973), to which a list of Near Eastern sites with their references is appended.

Discussion of archaeological data will be confined to material found in stratified cave or rockshelter deposits, or to material found in geological context, associated with fossil Quarternary sea levels; material from less secure locations will be mentioned but not dwelt upon.

The geographic and environmental context is summarized in terms of three north-south strips, Zones 1, 2, and 3; those correspond, in the main, to the five plant geographic zones of Mouterde (1954). Zone 1 consists of the coastal area, and includes the Mediterranean-facing foothills of the mountains. This region is favorable to permanent human occupation, having a mild climate even in winter and plentiful water sources. Moderate climatic shifts would hardly affect it, but the coastal plain would expand or contract with changing sea levels. Zone 2 is the mountainous ridge stretching from the Amanus southward through the Lebanon and Anti-Lebanon ranges into Upper Galilee. This region is forested, except on the mountain peaks, and could be regarded as seasonably habitable; in the winter, the higher parts are frequently under snow.

Since Middle and Upper Paleolithic material is rare to absent in the Litani and Orontes basins (situated between Zones 2 and 3), this strip has not been included in the tripartite scheme. Zone 3 is a high altitude region consisting

of the eastern flanks of the Anti-Lebanon mountains, including their extension, and the Palmyrids, at the fringes of the steppes of the Syrian desert; it has been classified as "Mediterranean Savannah" (Van Liere, 1966). Its open forest cover was more susceptible to climatic changes than were the other zones, and intensity of occupation apparently fluctuated. This was suggested not only by, for example, the sterile Levels 21-19 and other fluctuations at Yabrud I (Rust, 1950) but by pollen core interpretations from the Orontes valley; one is from Karkour (Van Liere, 1961, 1966), citing alternations of oak and pine forest, and the other is from 15 km south of Jisr esh-Shaghour (Niklewski and Van Zeist, 1970), also demonstrating climatic changes in the Riss/Würm and Early Holocene periods. The latter work provides a useful reconstruction of the probable fluctuations in the forest cover of Zones 1-3 in the Syrian Paleolithic.

The chronological framework consists of a combination of relative dating by typological comparison, and absolute dating by connection with the glacio-eustatic Mediterranean sequence. In practice, this means that:

1. Long sequences at multilevel sites will be used as models for the industrial succession—that of Tabun for the Middle Paleolithic (Garrod and Bate, 1937; Jelinek et al., 1973), and that of Ksar Akil for the Upper Paleolithic (Ewing, 1947; Azoury, 1971); the assumption underlying this is that like industries are probably (in a Paleolithic sense) contemporary.

2. As to the marine succession, the extensive fieldwork of P. Sanlaville has resulted in a massive, fully documented, comprehensive study of the Lebanese coast (French state doctoral thesis, more than 900 pages, several hundred illustrations, etc.: unpublished, dated June, 1973). This includes a chronology for the Lebanese Lower and Middle Paleolithic, based on his reconstruction of the Pleistocene transgressions. It generally fits so well with the archaeological indications that it has been eagerly adopted by workers in Lebanon; without repeating points already made in Hours (this volume) on the Lower Paleolithic, those parts which concern the Paleolithic archaeology are briefly described below.

It is assumed that readers are aware of the meaning and usage of terms such as "Levalloiso-Mousterian," "Emireh Point," etc. Artifacts are described using English equivalents of names used by French authors (Bordes, 1961; de Sonneville-Bordes and Perrot, 1956 et seq.). They are discussed in terms of the Bordean method (Bordes, 1950).

None of these frameworks or interpretations represent entrenched opinions on the part of this author, but are merely devices for ordering the material so that it can be described succinctly.

SUMMARY OF
SANLAVILLE'S MARINE CHRONOLOGY

Sanlaville's chronology is founded on the apparent stability of long stretches of the eastern Mediterranean coast, which appear to have risen equally, *en bloc*, and along which a series of dead cliffs and abrasion platforms of past sea levels form a staircase topography. Correlations were worked out after taking local deformations and other relative factors into account. These indicated that the sequence was more complex than previous workers had suspected, especially as concerns the concept of a series of sea levels which decrease in age altimetrically downward. Sites on the old "six m beach level" had been thought of as younger than those on the "15 m beach." This is no longer always the case, as the sea returned on its platform at least twice to much the same level.

The Late Pleistocene transgressions involving the Lower and Middle Paleolithic are:

1. *The Jebailean*, equated with Mindel/Riss. It is associated with Middle Acheulean, Late Acheulean, and Tayacian industries (Hours, this volume, table 1).

2. *The Enféan*, in two subphases, Enféan I and Enféan II, equated with Riss/Würm. The sea rose to fluctuate around 8-10.50 m, with rises to ca. 20 m in each subphase. *Strombus bubonius (Lmk)* and nine other thermophile molluscan species (P. Elouard, in Fleisch et al., 1971), as well as a heterometric pebble conglomerate, are characteristic of the Enféan II rise to 8-10.50 meters. The industries associated with the regression following this are Acheuleo-Yabrudian, Yabrudian, and Amudian at Adlun, and later (e.g., at Naamé), Levalloiso-Mousterian. Typesite: Enfé (Sanlaville, 1973, fig. 238, p. 776; and Hours, this volume, table 1).

The phase separating the Enféan and Naaméan Transgressions is called the Eowürm.

3. *The Naaméan*, which may represent either the first Würm (I/II) interstadial or a final Riss/Würm episode. (Würm is held to have started ca. 80,000 years B.P.) McBurney (1967) proposed the date of 50,000 for the start of Würm I, since, apparently, early fluctuations such as Brôrup are not reflected in the Libyan record (personal communication, 1970). This could be inappropriate in Lebanon, where, to begin Würm so late would relegate a block of time (80,000-50,000 years) to Riss/Würm when pollen analysis and other factors indicate that conditions had already changed. On the other hand, Sanlaville hesitates to place this era unequivocally in Würm I (his alternative dating being Riss/Würm), since, as mentioned, the change was not a severe one and may have consisted of wetter, rather than colder, conditions. The sea advanced up to its old level of 8-10.50 m, and its benches cut into the deposits of the previous phases; the bench is often marked by fossil *Vermetus* and *Petaloconchus*, which attach their shells to rocks at the exact sea level and, hence, permanently record its height during their lifetime.

DATING

So far, the dates obtained are considered, because similar, to be inconclusive; both the *Strombus* beach (Enféan) and *Vermet* bench (Naaméan) at Naamé gave similar Th^{230}/U^{234} dates (Sanlaville, 1971): 90,000 B.P. ± 20,000 years (Lamont) for a Strombus from the Enféan strand; 90,000 B.P. ± 10,000 years (Lamont) for *Vermets* from the Naaméan strand.

However, a Levalloiso-Mousterian occupation (still 2 m thick) occurred at Naamé *between these two stands of the sea* (fig. 4). It lies *on* the Enféan conglomerate with *Strombus*, etc., and a *Vermet* bench is found *on* the brecciated occupation deposit. In one locus, a cervid maxilla in the breccia supports the *Vermets* (Sanlaville, 1971; fig. 2, p. 243 and footnote 2, p. 244). Typesite: Naamé.

Sanlaville sees no pronounced climatic change during the Eowürm (at least to the degree which occurred during Würm II and Würm III [Main Würm]); the earlier placement of the phase (to the end of Riss/Würm) would be less acceptable archaeologically, since it would necessitate the back-dating of the start of the Middle Paleolithic.

As to the above-mentioned Th/U dates, Stearns (1970) has pointed out that ca. 90,000 years is ". . .the age of the youngest emergent strandline in the Western Mediterranean and on the Atlantic coast of Morocco (the dates cluster around 85,000 years)." When Stearns wrote his 1970 article, it had not yet been discovered that the Vermets in the sill of Nahr Ibrahim were not *in situ* but had fallen in on a lump of breccia (Solecki, personal communication, 1970). From this one could conclude that the Naaméan date is the more reliable.

Although Sanlaville's names for the transgressions are adopted here, for lack of alternatives the Alpine names "Riss" and "Würm" will be used for the intervening glacial (or pluvial) regression periods. Since today Alpine weather patterns arrive on the Lebanese coast usually after a lapse of only a day or two, these terms are not inappropriate.

THE MIDDLE PALEOLITHIC

In Southwest Asia, the Mousterian complex of industries occurs in three forms: the Zagros Mousterian, the Yabrudian, and the Levalloiso-Mousterian (Garrod, 1962; Skinner, 1965). The Zagros Mousterian differs geographically from the other two, being found in the mountainous regions of Iraq, Iran, and probably parts of Anatolia, flanking the Fertile Crescent. The Yabrudian sites known to date are restricted to a narrower region within the Levant, straddling Zones 1-3, in a square formed by Yabrud, Azraq, Tabun, and Masloukh (Rust, 1950; Zeuner et al., 1961; Garrod and Bate, 1937; Skinner, 1970, respectively). A possible northerly extension into the Ghab at Karkour (Van Liere, 1966, p. 21) remains to be confirmed.

Unlike the Zagros Mousterian, which apparently was the sole occupant of its zone during the Middle Paleolithic, the other two types seem to be successive; when found together in strata, the Yabrudian is always underneath: (1) At Tabun (Garrod and Bate, 1937; Jelinek et al., 1973) in E; (2) Yabrud, shelter I (Rust, 1950; Solecki, 1970) below level 10; (3) Bezez Cave, Adlun (Garrod, 1966) in C.

A fourth site may be Level E at Abou Sif (Neuville, 1951), and a fifth may be Layer Yellow 2 at Jerf Ajla (Coon, 1957; Schroeder, 1966 et seq.); alternatively, the material at the base of these sites may represent an Acheulean phase.

Unlike the Zagros region, where biface industries seem to have been almost nonexistent, the Levalloiso-Mousterian and Yabrudian occupied the same zone as did the earlier Acheulean complex in the Levant.

The Levalloiso-Mousterian differs from the other two by being "of Levallois facies" and can (depending largely on the zeal with which workers retain their waste flakes) be either "of non-Levallois debitage" or "of Levallois debitage." The two non-Levallois groups differ from each other in that the Yabrudian has immediate typological connections with an Acheulean tradition, while the Zagros Mousterian does not. An exception to the last two statements may have to be made in the case of Anatolia; while its Middle Paleolithic material appears to belong typologically to the Zagros group, the site of Kara'in is reported to have Lower Paleolithic (bifacial) material at its base (Kökten, 1963).

Of the two Levantine forms, the Levalloiso-Mousterian was the more widespread, the large cave sites (especially those in Zone 1) often containing deep deposits and abundant artifacts. Many shelters (and sites in Zones 2 and 3) were less heavily occupied, but there are numerous large and small open sites. Faced with such a plethora of material, several workers have attempted to subdivide the Levalloiso-Mousterian (for example, Garrod, 1962; Skinner, 1965; Perrot, 1968, p. 341). A new approach was that of S. Binford (1968) who indirectly classified the Levalloiso-Mousterian by ordering the sites according to their use or function. The new Tabun results confirm that any system (such as that of Skinner) which puts all three of the Tabun levels into one group is of questionable value. As stated, the writer will employ here the pragmatic approach, using the industrial succession manifested at Tabun in levels D, C, and B; however, use will also be made where appropriate of a suggestion in Hours et al. (1973) that the divisions be based on the morphology of the Levallois flake.

THE YABRUDIAN PHASE

This covers the span of time represented by Tabun E; layers Ed-Ea contain facies transitional (typologically at least) between the Lower Paleolithic bifacial industries (e.g., Tabun F) and the lighter flake industries such as those in Tabun D-B. There are three stratified sites to consider: Yabrud, Shelter I (Solecki and Solecki, 1966); Adlun

(Bezez Cave and Abri Zumoffen) (Garrod, 1966); and El-Masloukh (Skinner, 1970).

Adlun

Bezez Cave

This is a karstic formation in the Adlun promontory, an Eocene limestone cliff about 800 m from the present seashore between Tyre and Sidon. Its sill opens near the foot of the cliff about 15 m above present sea level. An excavation was carried out here by Garrod and Kirkbride (report in preparation) in an attempt to link the Levant, by way of raised beach correlations, to that of Europe (Garrod, 1962); there is a good chance that this relationship can be established (table 1), since, not only can Adlun's industrial sequence be equated typologically with those of Tabun and Yabrud I, but at Adlun the industries are in direct association with fossil-raised beaches which, when incorporated into Sanlaville's scheme, are attributed to two episodes in the last interglacial (Enféan I and Enféan IIa).

The sequence at Bezez (figs. 1 and 2, as adapted from the published plan and section of Garrod, 1966) is as follows: From base to top: (1) Beach material on bedrock, ca. 15 m above present sea level; (2) Level C, Acheuleo-Yabrudian, on top of beach, ca. 30 cm thick; (3) Level B, Levalloiso-Mousterian, phase 1 (or Tabun D) type, in dark lenses and occupation deposit, ca. 30 cm-50 cm thick. (Further Mousterian layers continued to ca. 17 meters; vestiges remain as hanging breccias.) B and C subside in some areas into a swallow-hole; (4) Upper Paleolithic; (5) Neolithic.

Some of the following interpretations are the writer's own. They derive from a three-year study of the material and the site at first hand, made during the preparation of the final report which is now nearing completion. The author also benefited greatly from being present during the excavation of Bezez in 1963.

Level C contains three variants of an Acheuleo-Yabrudian industry of non-Levallois debitage. These variants are distributed *laterally* in the deposits running from front to back of the cave. The industry consists predominantly of sidescrapers in great variety, including a special type (fig. 3-*11*) with knife-edge tip. The most impressive sidescrapers are the large transverse and offset pieces with Quina retouch, made on massive flakes. Sidescrapers grade into bifacial sidescrapers and into bifaces of late Acheulean typology. Most are amygdaloid, but other forms are pointed ovates, minute cordiforms, as well as large roughouts. The other tools include robust burins, Adlun burins (see below), denticulates, backed knives, and naturally backed knives.

In the view of the author this material is closely similar to that of Tabun Eb, seen in museum collections; it includes almost none of the rounded forms so characteristic of Tabun F and Ed.

The variation of facies is seen in the proportion of certain tool types vis-a-vis others (e.g., the biface/side-

TABLE 1. Tentative Chronology for the Adlun Sites

MARINE CHRONOLOGY (After Sanlaville, 1973, fig. 238)	NAAME	ADLUN — BEZEZ CAVE (main site)	ADLUN — ABRI ZUMOFFEN (annex)	LEVANT SITES WITH SIMILAR TYPOLOGY
Regression: Würm Naaméan Transgression to 8–10.5 m *Vermets* (FINAL RISS/WÜRM OR EARLY WÜRM)	*Vermets* dated to ca. 90,000 yrs. B.P.		?*Vermets* truncated breccia in Trench C, Layer 2, with reworked Amudian	Tabun C, Ras el Kelb, basal Nahr Ibrahim
Eowürm - wet or cold regressive phase	Lev.-Moust. occupation of Tabun C type	Bezez B — Lev.-Moust. of Tabun D type		Tabun D, Abou Sif C, Jerf 'Ajla base, Yabrud I, 10–8
			Acheuleo-Yabrudian (Layers 2–surface)	Yabrud I, 12–11
Regression from 13 m Enféan IIb transgression beach at 13 m (RISS/WÜRM, second half)		Bezez C — Acheuleo-Yabrudian variants	Yabrudian (Layers 9–2)	Tabun Ea
Enféan IIa transgression to ca. 10 m with *Strombus*	*Strombus*, dated to ca. 90,000 years B.P., in beach		Amudian (Layers 21–11)	Tabun Eb/Ea, Yabrud I, 15 and 13
Regression, 20–0 m (RISS/WÜRM, first half)		Beach deposited	Beach Industry, in and on beach	Tabun Eb, Masloukh, Yabrud I, 18–16
Enféan Ib transgression to 20 m				

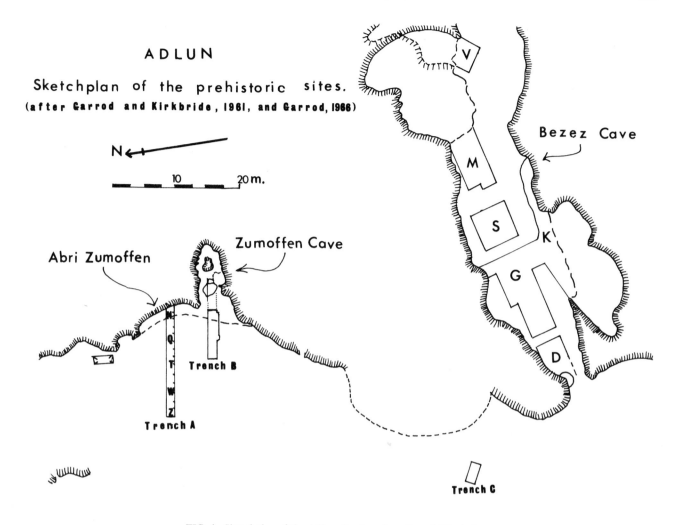

FIG. 1–Sketchplan of the Adlun sites based on the published plans.

scraper ratio), while the techniques of debitage, style of retouch, flake morphology, etc., are similar throughout. On statistical bases, these three variants resemble facies which occur *vertically* at Yabrud I, and which have been interpreted as different industries (Rust, 1950; Bordes, 1955). This author has suggested (Copeland, in press) that these variations in Bezez reflect activity zones (such as would be expected in a large Zone 1 base cave with extensive floor area), but this should be verified by further investigation. If the lateral disposition of these variants is confirmed, it will be difficult to reconcile this with the "alternating tribes" model, usually applied to the Yabrud sequence, except that the coexistence of the facies would be established. Meanwhile, the use of the term "Acheuleo-Yabrudian" is a compromise between various possibilities and reflects the presence of bifaces in all three variants as known at present.

The pebble beach in Bezez at ca. 15 m is considered by Sanlaville to have been laid down at the start of the Enféan transgression; the industry therefore could have begun some time after the sea's retreat from this level, i.e., the middle or latter half of the Enféan, when the sea was at a lower level (see chronology in table 1).

Abri Zumoffen

This is a rockshelter and includes a small fissure known as Zumoffen Cave, 60 paces north of Bezez Cave in the same cliff line, but at a slightly lower height (ca. 12 m) above sea level. It was excavated in 1958 (Garrod and Kirkbride, 1961). As shown in the left hand part of Fig. 2 (adapted from the published section of Garrod and Kirkbride, ibid.), the main features of the stratigraphy of Trench A from base to top are as follows: (1) Beach material, overlying a travertine, top at 11.65 meters. Bedrock not reached; (2) Beach Industry, an Amudian variant, in and on the beach; (3) Amudian in layers 21 to 11, each ca. 12 cm thick, separated by sterile, calcreted layers, each of similar thickness; (4) Yabrudian, from top of layer 9 to layer 3, in gray breccia; (5) Acheuleo-Yabrudian, layer 2 to the surface, in *terra fusca* soil.

Although sparse, the retouched tools of the Beach Industry are indistinguishable from those of the Amudian layers. However, they are accompanied by large numbers of flakes of fossiliferous Nummulitic Eocene flint, many of them biface preparation flakes, as well as cores on pebbles;

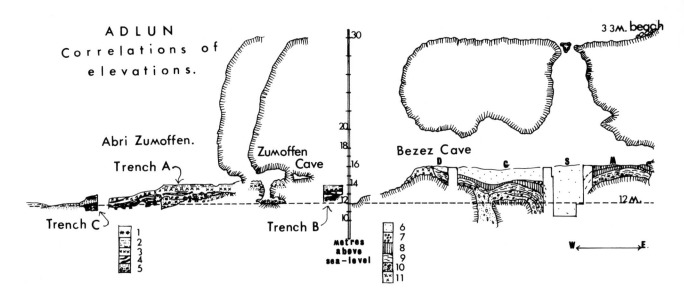

FIG. 2—The altimetric relationships of each trench at Adlun, placed in random order along a horizontal line at 12 m above sea level; based on the published sections in Garrod and Kirkbride (1961) and Garrod (1966). *1.* Reworked Amudian in gray breccia. *2.* Acheuleo-Yabrudian in *Terra Fusca. 3.* Yabrudian in gray breccia. *4.* Amudian between calcrete bands. *5.* Beach Industry in and on beach. *6.* Neolithic and mixed. *7.* Aurignacian (Level A). *8.* Levalloiso-Mousterian (Level B). *9.* Acheuleo-Yabrudian (Level C). *10.* Marine beach material.

the latter seem too sparse to account for the numerous preparation flakes. The objects from which the flakes were struck appear to have been removed from the deposits.

This writer has suggested (Copeland, in press) that, during the Beach phase, the shelter was an annex to the main occupation at Bezez, used as a factory for the knapping of large tools of Nummulitic flint, such as those which are present in Bezez C.

The Amudian occurs as a series of thin occupation lenses overlying the beach, separated by sterile calcrete bands which were (according to Zeuner et al., 1961) built up both from soils falling from the cliff top and sand blown from the shore, cemented together by the action of sea spray. The Amudian layers, which were laid down on top of these soils, contain hearths and animal bones *in situ.*

The tools consist mainly of backed knives; the retouch is often on the extreme margin of the blade (nibbled blades, fig. 3-*2* and *3*), but thick, Chatelperron-like specimens also occur (fig. 3-*1*). Most of the tools are made on blade blanks struck from small prismatic blade-cores (fig. 3-*6* and *9*) on pebbles, larger versions of which are often seen in the local coastal Acheulean; other blades (fig. 3-*10*) seem to have been struck off marginally Levallois cores of the one axis type. Some of the cores were listed as steep scrapers in the excavation report (Garrod and Kirkbride, 1961). Tool types include robust dihedral burins, Adlun burins (made on a distal notch; *ibid.*, and our fig. 3-*4*), endscrapers (rare and atypical) and sidescrapers, most with very fine retouch.

As this author sees it, this industry has little to do (except on the broadest lines) with the Pre-Aurignacian of Yabrud I, Layer 15, where burins dominate, backed knives are absent, 25% of the tools are sidescrapers, and end-scrapers are typical (compare the cumulative graphs for the

two, fig. 4). The Amudian of Abri Zumoffen bears a close resemblance, however, to the blade lenses of Tabun E*a*-E*b*, as can be seen in published illustrations and in museum collections. Although the miniaturization of some of the tools tends to obscure the fact, the Amudian has no radically new forms, or forms which do not also exist in Bezez C, if rarely. One explanation for the situation at Adlun could be that the varied assemblages in Bezez Cave contain examples of the whole Acheuleo-Yabrudian repertoire, while in the shelter tools are confined to concentrations of certain types (a tool kit for cutting and slicing?).

A Yabrudian industry overlies the Amudian (except in Trench C). The facies is unlike that in Bezez C. The tendencies toward blade production and miniaturization seen in the underlying Amudian persist, and large tools and bifaces (fig. 3-*8*) are rare (ca. 2%). Although every type can be matched in Bezez C, here the focus is on small side-scrapers (fig. 3-*5* and *7*). Another special tool kit could be indicated. Since it has rare bifaces, this facies is not "pure" Yabrudian in Rust's sense; the name is used to distinguish it from the facies in Bezez C.

An Acheuleo-Yabrudian is found eroding out of the *terra fusca* soil. It is like that in Bezez C except that bifaces are rare and large sidescrapers are more numerous. Père Zumoffen's first collection evidently came from this horizon (Zumoffen, 1900).

The interpretation of the marine geology is based on the presence of *Strombus* and other typical Tyrrhenian types embedded in exposures of the fossil Enféan beach near Adlun (Fleisch and Sanlaville, 1967), identical in composition and height to the beach in Abri Zumoffen's trenches. The beach at the base of Trenches A, B, and C is held to represent the Enféan II transgression, originating from a standstill at ca. 10.50 meters (Sanlaville, 1971; Sanlaville, 1973, fig. 233 and table 16).

According to this scheme, the Beach Industry would date to the start of the retreat from the Enféan II level, with the succeeding industries dating to the start of Würm. In the case of the Yabrudian, conditions were already cold (or wet), judging from the pollen analysis of a sample from the gray breccia, which contained abundant *Cedrus* and no subtropical flora (Leroi-Gourhan, 1971).

The fauna found at Adlun suggests that the Yabrudian phase inhabitants were unspecialized hunters; Garrod and Kirkbride (1961) quote Hooijer as having noted cave bear, *Bos*, rhino, pig, gazelle, and *Dama* at Abri Zumoffen. The faunal analysis was turned over to Higgs and his assistant, A. Garrard; the latter has noted an abundance of *Bos*, with a few signs also of *Dama*, gazelle, pig, and rhino at Bezez Cave in the sill breccia (personal communication, 1973). Garrard has also added some detail to Hooijer's first note: the cave bear specimens at Abri Zumoffen came from the Amudian levels; the Amudian and Yabrudian levels have broadly similar numbers of bones of *Dama*, *Bos*, rhino, roe deer, and pig, but in the Yabrudian levels, bones of *Equus hydruntinus* occur in a ratio of eighteen-to-one.

To sum up, the writer is suggesting that the disjointed sequence at the two Adlun sites represents a base camp and its annex; the industries which are present duplicate typologically the E*b*-E*a* part of the sequence at Tabun, where it is seen in the form of a vertical column.

El-Masloukh

This site is a small cave and terrace in limestone, ca. 500 m inland from the sea, 12 km north of Byblos, discovered by Remiro in 1969 and later investigated (Fleisch et al., 1969). It was subsequently excavated by Skinner (1970).

Like Tabun and Bezez, it consists of karstic formations in a cliff just at the junction of foothills and coastal plain. Whereas at Bezez the Yabrudian deposit is directly associated with a 15 m beach, the Yabrudian of Masloukh unconformably overlies a Jebailean marine platform out into the cliff at a height of 39 m, which it probably postdates by a whole glacial cycle. As reported by Fleisch, the stratigraphy (adapted from fig. 2, p. 7, Fleisch et al., 1969) is (from base to top) as follows: (1) Limestone bedrock, 39 m above sea level; (2) Beach of homometric flint and limestone pebbles, strongly brecciated, 50-70 cm thick; (3) Marine gravel, strongly cemented, containing shell fragments and worked flint (not yet excavated); (4) Gray bone breccia with Yabrudian, ca. 50 cm thick, running up walls of cave in some places; (5) Modern garden soil, product of the dissolution of the breccia; contains many flints.

Skinner's main exposure was made inside the small cave. He reports the following stratigraphy, given here from base to top: (1) Pebble conglomerate, a continuation of Fleisch's (2) above, 1.60 m thick in parts; sterile; (2) Interface. Not described; (3) Gray breccia, equated with (4) above. Rich in Yabrudian artifacts; (4) Layer C. Black

earth with Yabrudian, 80 cm thick; (5) Layer B. Reddish brown earth with Yabrudian, 40 cm thick; (6) Layer A. Loose dark brown earth with Yabrudian 40 cm thick.

In a test trench made on the terrace, Fleisch's third (gravel) layer did appear between Layers 1 and 3 of Skinner, but it was found to be sterile (Skinner, 1970, p. 149). The homogeneous state of the deposit, lack of hearths, soil lenses, etc. led Skinner to suppose that the material was not in place (1970, p. 148), and that it had eroded out of the extensive gray breccia covering the whole platform and cave floor.

The industry is considered to resemble that of Yabrud I, 22, except that ca. 4% of the tools consisted of typical bifaces and bifacial scrapers.

Faunal remains were fairly abundant, the most common species being *Dama*, equids, *D. hemitoechus* and a large bovid (Gautier, 1970, p. 96). Roe deer and wild goat appear to be far less common. A human tooth "presumably from a Neanderthal" (Solecki, 1970, p. 95) was also found at Masloukh. This is the first human fossil to be referred to a Yabrudian context since the finding of the Zuttiyeh skull.

In commenting, it would seem that there may be a relationship between the gray breccia of Masloukh and the same material containing Yabrudian at Abri Zumoffen; the two may have been subjected to the same climatic processes and could be contemporary. The fauna is also very similar. Meanwhile a full description of the Masloukh flint industry is eagerly awaited.

Yabrud, Shelter I

This rockshelter, 23 m long, in Zone 3 was first excavated by Rust and more recently by Solecki (Rust, 1950; R. S. and R. L. Solecki, 1966). Rust's material has for years formed part of the Levantine reference base. Since it was published, controversy has ensued over the industrial alternations proposed by Rust (in which he was later supported by Bordes, 1955) in the lower Levels 25-11; here, various Acheulean and Acheuleo-Yabrudian facies (i.e., layers with bifaces) interdigitated with Yabrudian layers (i.e., facies without bifaces and with numerous offset and other sidescrapers). Such alternations had not been reported at other sites of the Yabrudian phase, at which bifaces occurred throughout the levels concerned.

Workers in the Near East have long been admirers of Dr. Rust, whose work at Yabrud was carried out in the face of tremendous difficulties. However, a study of the preliminary reports and the geologists' reports on the results of the new excavations have shown that Rust's interpretation, at least that of Yabrud I, is open to reevaluation. Given its importance, the author will go into this aspect in some detail.

The Soleckis' operations resulted in an 8 m x 23 m transverse cut to the valley floor, which revealed that a large rockfall had formed an outer protective wall to the shelter; this placed some of the internal geology in a new light. Solecki (1970) has given the brief notes on the stra-

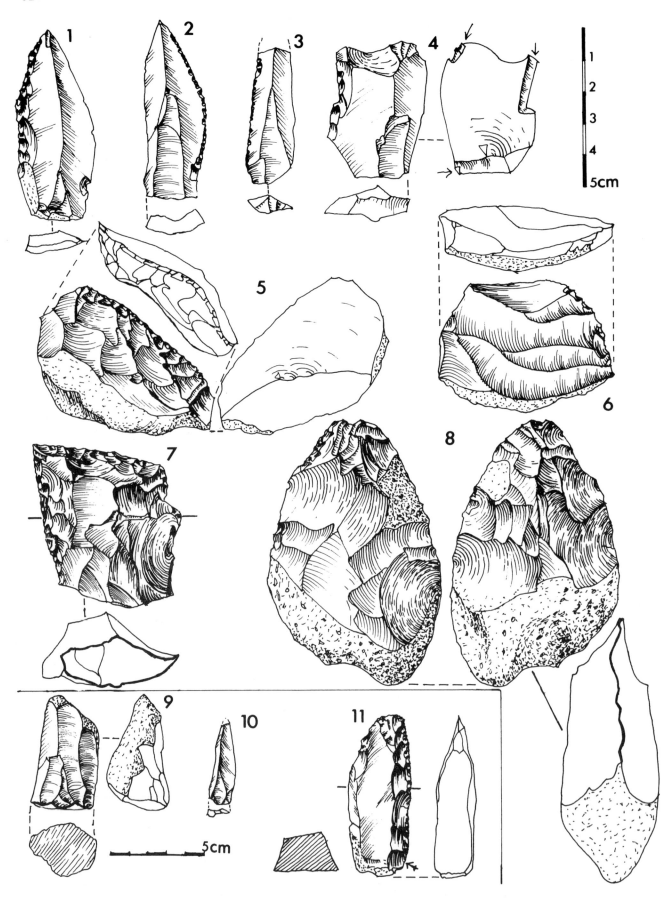

FIG. 3—Some typical Amudian and Yabrudian forms. Numbers *1-4*, *6* and *9-10* are from the Amudian of Abri Zumoffen; numbers *5*, *7*, and *8* are from the Yabrudian levels at Abri Zumoffen; number *11* is from the Acheuleo-Yabrudian of Bezez Cave, Adlun. *1*. Backed

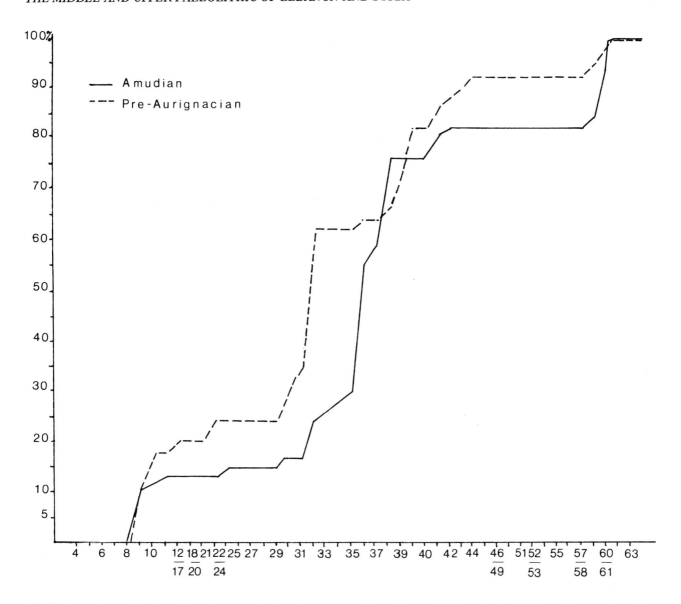

FIG. 4–Comparison of the Cumulative Graphs of the Pre-Aurignacian of Yabrud I, Level 15 (after Bordes, 1955) and the Amudian of Abri
   Zumoffen, Trench A (after a figure in Copeland, in press). Compare also with the Amudian of Tabun, Bed 48B, as illustrated by
   Jelinek (his fig. 5, this volume).

tigraphy he found, summarized here and given from surface to base: (1) 0-1.35 m—Levalloisian industrial material, thinning out downward; (2) 1.35 m—change to non-Levallois debitage, no change in soil; (3) 1.80-2 m—concentration of Yabrudian artifact types; (4) 2 m— widespread and horizontal hearth lenses appeared; (5) 2.40-2.80 m—denticulates abundant; (6) 2.80-3.30 m—demi-Quina retouch predominant; (7) 3.84-3.96 m—a rich layer, with demi-Quina tools, burins, prismatic cores—at this level in Rust's excavation, the pre-Aurignacian oc-

knife on a non-Levallois blade. *2.* Nibbled blade, a form of pointed backed knife with abrupt marginal retouch on one edge. *3.* Nibbled blade with very fine abrupt retouch, made on a semi-Levallois blank with faceted butt. *4.* Adlun burin, made on a flake which has been truncated by a notch; in this piece, burin spalls have been removed from the butt and the other distal corner, making it a multiple burin. Blanks for this type are often robust, non-Levallois flakes; the spall facet is usually inclined onto the flake surface. *5.* Transverse racloir with Quina retouch made on a thick flake; the high-angle butt is so close to the working edge as to render the edge convex (the "rocking-chair" edge of Garrod, 1962). *6.* Semi-Levallois blade-core made on a pebble; this piece may have begun as a bipolar core. *7.* Offset (*déjeté*) racloir on a non-Levallois blank. The *winkelkratzer* of Rust (1950, p. 15) and Tafel 10, 8. *8.* Biface with cortex butt, made on a Nummulitic flint pebble. The shape of the profile seems to indicate that the tip has been reworked. *The following three pieces are drawn to a smaller scale. 9.* Prismatic blade-core, "miniaturized," but similar in shape to the ones on cobbles often seen in the Levantine Acheulean. Its smaller size causes it to resemble some Upper Paleolithic blade cores. *10.* Unretouched blade, possibly a blank, which was apparently struck from a core similar to number 9. *11.* "Bezez-type racloir," a form of straight convex convergent racloir with a natural back (see profile). Note the very sharp and thin tip, and the position of the butt.

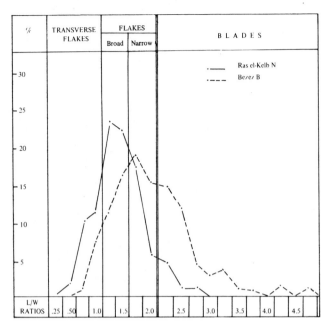

FIG. 5—Variation in Flake Morphology in the Levalloiso-Mousterian. The length/width ratios of a Levalloiso-Mousterian of
Phase 1 type (500 unretouched flakes from Bezez B), compared to those of a Phase 2 type (200 unretouched flakes
from Ras el-Kelb N).

curred; (8) 4 m—abundant traces of occupations; 5 m—long
ash layers, groups of stones (encircling hearths?)—soil damp
and dark brown, tools become less abundant below to 8 m,
fragments of limestone more abundant below; (9) 8.20-8.40
m—change to loose rubble, concentration of mammal
bones, some articulated, in this horizon, flints more abundant, especially at 9.20 m; (10) 9.60 m—wet brown loamy
soil and limestone chips, tools more abundant to 9.80 m;
(11) 10.00-10.20 m—soil change, rolled flints and bone
fragments, no tools in some areas; (12) 10.20-10.40 m—a
few tools in some squares.

To this may be added the more detailed findings of the
geologists. The first of those to be taken will be of de
Heinzelin (1966, p. 159)—his "Y" Member, which he inter-
prets as subaerian, with hearths and artifact concentrations
in discontinuous lenses (1966, p. 160) would correspond to
Solecki's above-mentioned comments 1-8. Of this group, in
Rust's Levels 4-10 he sees "various Mousterian facies;" in
Levels 11-12 are Mousterian facies with bifaces; Levels
13-16 have *le prétendu Pre-Aurignacien* (the name of which
he does not approve); Levels 14-16 (Quina facies) and
Levels 17-18 ("Mousterian with bifaces"), end this cycle.

His "X" Member at 6.50 m and "V" Member at 7.20 m
would fall into Solecki's comment 8; they consist of Rust's
Levels 19-20, with almost sterile deposits and poor, mixed
flint. De Heinzelin's lowest (U.N. and U.L.) Members begin
with Level 21 at 8.80 m, also with poor flint. However, in
Rust's Level 22, at 9.20 m, (corresponding to Solecki's
comments 9-10) to the base at ca. 10 m, "La partie infé-
rieure est essentiellement de nature torrentielle—contient

une concentration d'artifacts Yabroudiens plus ou moins
déplacés et incorporés" (1966, p. 159).

These interpretations differ from each other, and both
differ from that of Rust (can there be Yabrudian without
Quina retouch?), and also from that of Farrand. The latter's
section is given as Fig. 16 in the report of Solecki and
Solecki (1966), and is tabulated as Table I in his INQUA
paper (Farrand, 1969). From the base at 11 m he sees
coarse, angular cryoclastic *éboulis* to 2.3 meters. Between
8.15 and 5 m these deposits are nearly sterile. From 2.3 m
to the top the *éboulis* are relatively fine grained and cemented. Farrand adds that the sedimentological analyses
carried out (on Rust's samples by Brunnacker, 1970, and
on Solecki's samples by Goldberg, 1969) give results according closely to his findings; all three see cryoclastic,
instead of torrential, material even at the base. Although
different deposits were studied by these workers (Rust's old
profile as cleaned by Solecki's team in Farrand's case, and a
series of new sections in other areas of the shelter, produced by the excavations, in the case of de Heinzelin), this
hardly accounts for the differences in interpretation noted
above.

Turning to the archaeological implications, Solecki has
pointed out that to use Rust's industrial sequence as a
model is hazardous, for the following reasons:

1. The stratigraphy changes laterally along the length of
the shelter as well as along the transverse cut; some layers
lens out (e.g., the famous *flugsand*) and others appear. Furthermore, Rust could not see his section in its entirety, as it
would appear that he filled up one *Kammer* while excavating the next. Thus, the altimetric order of the layers—
particularly those farthest apart—is not necessarily chronological.

2. The published section is synthetic; some artifact-
bearing layers occurred in the northern part of the shelter,
some in the southern, and so forth, as Rust admitted
(Solecki and Solecki, 1966, p. 125). We have no guarantee,
therefore, as to the order in which the occupations occurred. It *may* not be exactly as it appeared to be to Rust
when he was excavating.

3. The material was incompletely recovered; Rust's difficulties obliged him to "be selectively economical in collecting flints," which must affect the original counts (ibid.).
Solecki himself used no sieves in the first season and nevertheless recovered 2,185 artifacts (mainly debitage) from the
backfill. Hence, any technical indices computed from
Rust's (and Solecki's) material are based on a selection.

In view of the above three points, it is regrettable that
two of the more illuminating pieces of work to appear recently were carried out on Yabrud I material—one being
Bordes's analysis (Bordes, 1955) and the other the Binfords' multivariate factor analysis, which is discussed
further below.

The faunal remains found by Rust have been published
(Lehmann, 1970). Equids predominated *in almost all levels*
of Shelter I, all other species, including *Gazella, Dama,* and
Capra were rare; this has a bearing on the argument as to

whether availability or cultural choice determine Paleolithic menus, and it may be added that in Shelter III (Epipaleolithic) the predominant type was *Capra*. Hooijer (1966) also studied the rhino remains from Shelters IV (Tayacian) and I, placing these as remains of the steppe and tundra type, *D. hemitoechus*.

In summing up, it seems clear that not all the answers from Yabrud I are yet on hand. The new operations have eroded to some extent the position (unique in the Near East up to the time of writing) of this site in appearing to have interdigitations of Lower and Middle Paleolithic industries as well as "pure," or biface-deficient, Yabrudian. Yet until the new work produces a study as careful and well documented on these industries as was the work of Rust, final judgment on Yabrud I will have to be suspended.

Concerning the geological data, this author's own comment would be that the findings of both Farrand and Goldberg relate more closely with Tabun and Adlun evidence than do those of de Heinzelin.

Two possibly Yabrudian open sites were found by Van Liere in Syria. One is Karkour, in the Orontes valley, where the tools (which include "terminal Acheul" bifaces, Quina sidescrapers, blades and waste flakes (Van Liere, 1966, fig. 32, nos. 2, 3, and 4) are found redistributed in Paleo-Orontes river gravels, attributed at first (Van Liere, 1961) to the second half and more recently (Van Liere, 1966) to the first half of his Young Pleistocene phase, QIIIa, i.e., Riss/Würm. Peat from Horizon 5, a layer below the artifact-bearing Horizon 4, was found to be too old to be dated by C14, hence is listed as "more than 56,000 years (Gro. 2640)" (Van Liere, 1966, p. 21 et seq.). The other is at Hraissoun, on the Syrian coast (1966, p. 25); this site is unusual in having bifaces at a height above the sea of only six meters, assuming that they are *in situ*.

Jerf Ajla

This cave is in Zone 3, in the Palmyrid foothills (Coon, 1957); Coon found six soil layers in ca. 6 m of deposit; it was subsequently reexamined (Schroeder, 1966a; 1966b), and 14 soil layers were distinguished in the same depth (Schroeder, 1969). In the basal layer (Coon's Yellow 2, Schroeder's G, H1, and H2, more than a meter thick) were found the following tool types: bifaces, bifacial scrapers, cleavers, transverse Quina sidescrapers, as well as Levallois flakes. The first four do not belong with the rest of the Levalloiso-Mousterian material, and one is reminded of the same kind of occurrence at Abou Sif in Level E (Neuville, 1951). In neither case is there enough material for a determination (as between Acheulean and Yabrudian) to be made.

An analysis of the soils (Goldberg, 1969) indicates that cold conditions applied throughout, with cryoclastic rubble (*éboulis*) predominating, except for two weathering horizons, one at three meters (i.e., top of Brown 2) and one less marked at five meters (top of Yellow 2). The deposits are attributed to Würm.

THE LEVALLOISO-MOUSTERIAN PHASE

The "dramatic" change in the industry at Tabun when the Levalloiso-Mousterian appears has been remarked on by both Garrod and Bate (1937) and by Jelinek (1969). As at Yabrud I, this change is not accompanied by a soil change.

In spite of an abundance of Mousterian material, we seem to lack answers to the most basic questions, concerning, for example, the fate of the Yabrudians, the origin of the Levalloiso-Mousterian, the way of life (sedentary or nomadic) led by them, the meaning of the variability of facies, etc. Moreover, as we now know, Mousterian industries in the Levant are not tribe-diagnostic, as they are thought by some to be in France; usually we do not know which human type made this or that Levalloiso-Mousterian variant (Neanderthal as in Tabun C, "Sapienized Neanderthal" as in Skhul, or *Homo sapiens sapiens* as in Qafzeh (Keith and McCown, 1939; Vandermeersch, 1966, respectively).

At this point the author trespasses briefly into Palestinian territory, where Tabun, the model for this phase, is found.

The Levalloiso-Mousterian levels in the Tabun vertical column consist of many meters of deposit in three blocks, D, C, and B. The first contains a laminar and elongated triangular Levallois point facies, the second a facies of broad, oval flakes (noted by Garrod and Bate, 1937, and confirmed by Jelinek et al., 1973), and the third and latest a lighter (and less retouched) triangular point facies on broad based Levallois flakes. Blocks D and C were considered by Garrod to represent the Lower Levalloiso-Mousterian (Garrod and Bate, 1937). Although there is no proof that this model is invariably repeated at other sites, the writer proposes, as a convenience to number the Levalloiso-Mousterian phases according to the order in which they occur in Tabun: Phase 1 (to which will be referred industries like that of Tabun D); Phase 2 (i.e., like Tabun C); Phase 3 (like Tabun B). Only time will tell if the chronological implications are valid regionally. For example, Phase 2 over Phase 1 occurs only at Tabun (this sequence may also have been present in Bezez, but the deposits overlying the Phase 1 are lost). Elsewhere in Lebanon, several sites *start* a long sequence with Phase 2 at the base; to date, a Phase 2 industry has never been found directly overlying a Yabrudian industry. It is possible, therefore, that Phases 1 and 2 coexisted, at least in Lebanon. Furthermore, at one site, Bergy's Plus-Eight (Bergy, 1932), there are hints that Phase 2 may be older than Phase 1 or at least contemporary with Enféan IIa; according to Sanlaville, the industry (which, to the author, seems to resemble Phase 2 typologically) is in a beach in which he has found *Strombus bubonius*. If the final report on Jelinek's Tabun material shows it to be warranted, these phases may usefully be renamed "D-type," "C-type," and "B-type" Levalloiso-Mousterian.

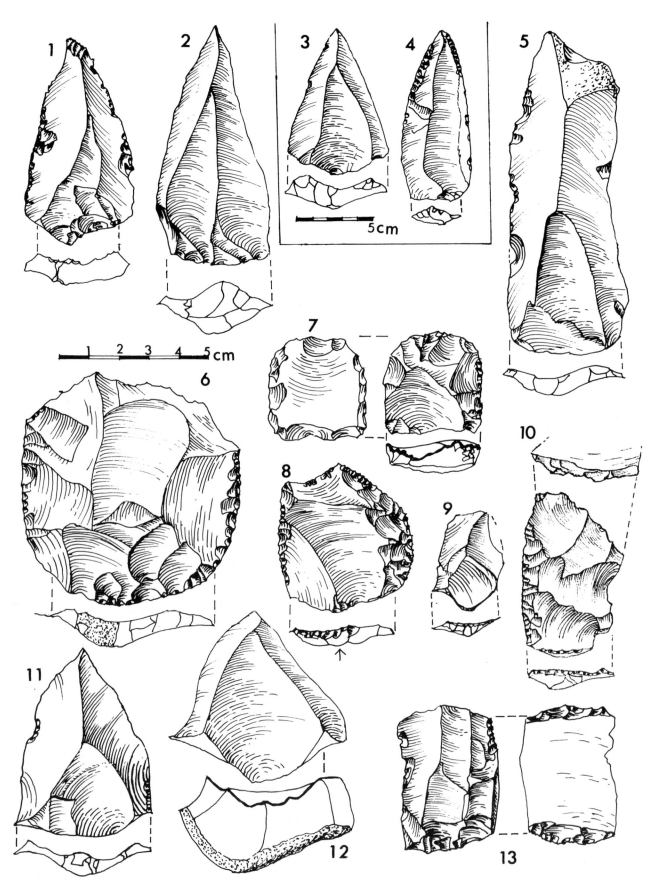

FIG. 6–Some Forms Characteristic of the Levalloiso-Mousterian Phases: numbers *1-5* (from Bezez Cave, Level B) are of Phase 1 type; number *6* (from Michmiche) and numbers *7-10* (from Ras el-Kelb) are of Phase 2 type. Of numbers *11-13* (from Michmiche),

Phase 1 (Model—Tabun D)

In five out of six stratified sites with this Phase known to the author (the sixth being an isolated case at Sahba), it occurs immediately above either a Yabrudian layer (Tabun D, Bezez B, Yabrud I, 10-8); over an Acheulean or Yabrudian layer (Abou Sif C, Jerf Ajla Yellow 2—Brown 2) or mixed with a Yabrudian assemblage (Zuttiyeh; Turville Petre, 1927). Surely this is not just a coincidence.

Characteristic of Phase 1 are: (1) predominantly one-axis methods of preparation of the Levallois cores; and (2) the laminar, triangular parallel sided blank which is struck off along the same axis as the core preparation, evidently by stone hammer (fig. 6-*1* through *5*). This produces fairly heavy flakes and points, some with pronounced bulbs (fig. 6-*2*); plain butts are quite common on flakes, blades, or points. (The presence of blades from far down in Level E at Tabun [Jelinek et al., 1973] means that the equation laminar = late must be dropped.)

In Lebanon, the only clear example is Bezez B (fig. 5), the layers of which overlie the Acheuleo-Yabrudian in Level C. The material seems to be virtually interchangeable with that of Tabun D. Bezez B has a high IL and ILty and low to moderate IR, and burins and denticulates are fairly frequent; there are some rather battered bifaces, which do not seem to be intrusive from Level C, since some occur in exposures which are separated from the Yabrudian by a sterile layer.

In Syria, Jerf Ajla Yellow 2 and Yabrud I, Levels 10, 9, and 8, refer to this phase (which therefore spans Zones 1-3). Bordes has given an excellent description of the elongated Levallois points of Yabrud I Level 10 (Bordes, 1955, p. 492). To quote Bordes's words describing Level 10: "le débitage est nettement Levallois. . . l'indice laminaire devient élevé. . . l'indice Levallois typologique très fort (66.7%) le classe parmi le faciès 'Levalloisien.' Cette industrie se caractérise par de grandes lames Levallois allongées, souvent retaillées, en pointes mousteriennes allongées, rappelant le niveau C d'Abou Sif" (ibid., p. 955). In Level 9, denticulates were numerous (another special tool kit?), but the debitage is the same as that of 10 and 8. At Jerf Ajla, the same kind of material appears in Yellow 2, and probably continues into White 1.

There are very little data on the environment except from Bezez and Tabun; the soil of Tabun, Level D, is said to be little different from that of E (Jelinek et al., 1973). There is also little sign either of fires or burning in Bezez B—and, it would appear in Tabun D, according to Garrod and Bate; this is in contrast to the striking evidence for fires in Tabun C and in other Phase 2 sites.

A large part of the fauna of Bezez B consists of *Dama*; there is also a good deal of gazelle and hyena, as well as less common remains of *Bos*, pig, panther, lynx, wolf, and other carnivores, rodents, cave bear, insectivores, and even a trace of *Procavia capensis* (A. Garrard, personal communication, 1973).

This phase is tentatively assigned to the pre-Brörup phase, ca. 75,000-65,000 years, especially if the Brörup equates with the Naaméan transgression.

Eastward from Zone 1 the data become scarce: the south Béqaa has virtually no Mousterian *in situ*; two typical pointed sidescrapers have been found in travertine spring deposits (Masqoua'a; Site 82, Besançon and Hours, 1971) and others have been dredged (together with Late Acheulean bifaces) from the River Litani (Besançon and Hours, 1970, pp. 83-84). This is attributed to erosion during Main Würm, when the river evacuated the soils on its middle and lower terraces (Besançon and Hours, 1970*a*, 1970*b*).

Farther north, at Qalaat al-Mudiq (ancient Apamea, overlooking the Ghab, a part of the Orontes river valley) abundant Mousterian material has been reported (J. and J. C. Balty and M. Dewez, 1970; Dewez, 1970). It is found in a red soil which can probably be tied into the Paleo-Orontes chronology proposed by workers at Latamné (see Hours, this volume). The material, so far only briefly described by the above authors, seems to represent an extensive Middle Paleolithic factory site (153 cores, several hundred flakes [64 Levallois] and four retouched pieces); it seems to be redistributed, although this point has not been made clear. Moreover, the authors, in classifying the material as Levalloiso-Mousterian, invoke the assemblage found by Van Liere at Karkour, which in 1960 he thought was mixed and

---

numbers *11* and *12* are typical forms of Phase 3, while number *13* is a rare type occurring in all three phases but more common in Phase 2. *1*. Elongated retouched Levallois point on a triangular flake with wide butt, made on a unidirectionally prepared Levallois point core, and struck off on the same axis. *2*. Unretouched elongated non-Levallois point with thick, faceted butt, probably made on a prismatic blade-core, also unidirectionally prepared. *3*. Triangular point of more classical Levallois debitage (except for the rather thick butt). Note that this and the following piece are drawn half-size. *4*. Biconvex racloir made on a Levallois blade. The retouch is semi-abrupt, parallel. *5*. Unretouched blade on a non-Levallois, or atypical Levallois, blank, struck from a unidirectionally prepared core, on the same axis as the preparation. *6*. Biconvex racloir made on a broad Levallois flake struck from a multidirectionally prepared core. *7*. Core on a flake; the core is prepared in classic Levallois fashion by multiconvergent faceting, and a broad flake was produced. *8*. Denticulated racloir, made on a broad Levallois flake struck from a multi-directionally-prepared core. *9*. Preparation-flake (*éclat-de-taille*); the size and form are typical and abundant in Phase 3 sites. *10*. Single straight racloir, made on a flake struck off a discoid core on an axis different from that of the core-preparation. It is difficult to say whether the distal end was truncated and faceted or whether it is the remains of the core edge. *11*. Triangular Levallois point; the debitage differs from that of *3*, above, in that this piece was struck from a multidirectionally prepared core. This form seems to be more characteristic of Phase 3 Levalloiso-Mousterian. *12*. Levallois point core, summarily prepared on a pebble, from which a pointed flake with *chapeau-de-gendarme* butt has been struck. *13*. Truncated-faceted flake (Schroeder, 1969), also called *éclat bitronqué* by Fleisch, 1971; in typical specimens, the butt and/or distal end is removed by direct retouch, and small flakes are struck off on the axis from the resulting platform or platforms.

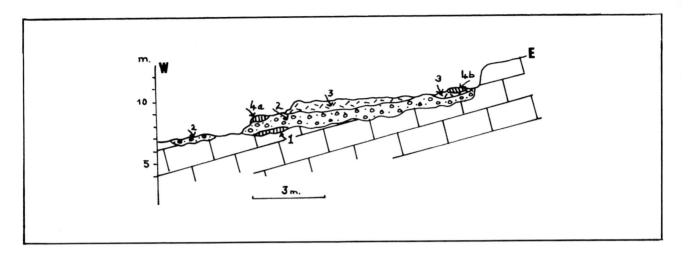

FIG. 7—Stratigraphy of the Mousterian site of Naamé, as synthesized by Sanlaville, 1971, his Fig. 4. Translation from the French of his caption reads: "Synthetic section of the beach at Naamé. *1*. Location of *Vermets* at +7.50 m-8 meters. Substratum of calcareous Cenomanian dolomite at an angle of tilt of 15° W; *2*. Enféan beach: conglomerate with warm weather fauna (*Strombus bubonius* Lmk); *3*. Reddish breccia with Middle Paleolithic artifacts; *4*. Naaméan formations (*4a*. Pavements of *Vermets* [8.50 m]; *4b*. Location of Vermetides [10.50 m])."

later (1966) described as "Terminal Acheul" (Van Liere, 1961, 1966); they also quote a nonexistent date of "56,000" for Karkour (Balty, Balty and Dewez, 1970, p. 19) and apparently are unaware that Van Liere had corrected the dating of Karkour from QIIIb to QIIIa in 1966. Finally, Van Liere's description of Horizon 4 material at Karkour (Van Liere, 1966, p. 21) precludes any connection with an unmixed Levalloiso-Mousterian.

It would therefore be of much interest to hear more of this apparently rich site in a region where other Mousterian material is (just as in the Litani valley) sparse, redistributed, or absent altogether.

In the Palmyra area of Zone 3, sites in addition to Jerf Ajla and Taniat el Baidah (Coon, 1957) have been found by the Buccellatis (1967) and by the TUSEWA (Tokyo University) survey team; one of the latter's finds was Douara, at present being excavated (Suzuki and Takai, 1973), and producing a sequence of Mousterian levels. Other Levalloiso-Mousterian material (not as yet attributable to any one phase) has been recovered by both groups from the debris thrown out of well borings in the inland basins near el-Koum; bifaces are also present. An example is TUSEWA Site 81 (fig. 42 and p. 85, Suzuki and Kobori, 1970).

In the same context, excellent Levallois flakes and large sidescrapers very similar to some Jerf Ajla material, have been retrieved from around the well-heads north of Aïn Sukhne in the el-Koum region by Cauvin (personal communication, 1973); a high gloss, apparently caused by long immersion in sulphurous water, has given them a striking, obsidian-like appearance.

All these indications make it clear that our knowledge of the Middle Paleolithic of inland Syria is, to say the least, far from complete.

Phase 2 (Model—Tabun C)

At Tabun there is said to be a distinct climatic shift

between C and D. On Lebanese evidence to date, we cannot clear up the connection of Phases 1 and 2, as mentioned previously. However, the two industries differ greatly in their approach to flint knapping. The Lebanese Phase 2 industry is a Levalloiso-Mousterian of Levallois facies, characterized by the virtual absence (0-2%) of triangular points, the majority of the flakes consisting of broad, transverse, oval, or offset types (fig. 6-*6* and *8*), either radially prepared (fig. 6-*6*) on the dorsal surface (i.e., they are first flakes from classic Levallois tortoise cores), or struck off obliquely to the axis of the preparation of the flake (i.e., they are pseudo-Levallois, from discoid cores; fig. 6-*10*). One axis cores, the main type of Phase 1, are virtually absent. Very small flakes (fig. 11-*9*) are abundant. Sidescrapers and denticulates are the only common tool types, Upper Paleolithic forms being virtually absent. Surprising is the apparent lack of differentiation between flakes and cores—flakes are used as cores (fig. 6-*7*) and cores reworked into tools. "Truncated-faceted flakes" (fig. 6-*10* and *13*) are quite common. First noted by Schroeder (1966, Plate 1, 1, p. 205) at Jerf Ajla, this type of flake is the *éclat bitronquée* of Fleisch (1970) and the subject of an article by R. S. and R. L. Solecki (1970). This artifact seems more common in Phase 2, although it occurs throughout the Middle Paleolithic. Retouched Levallois tools (so prominent in Phase 1) are almost absent, apparently replaced by sidescrapers. Hence, although the ILty is low, the index of Levallois blanks made into retouched tools is high. The retouch is commonly flat, or very flat, Quina retouch being nearly absent. (See fig. 5, where the morphology of Phase 1 and Phase 2 flakes are compared.)

The three main sites of this phase are: Ras el-Kelb, Naamé, and basal Nahr Ibrahim. Although known for some time, the first site is still under study (the classification of the flint material is now in course by the present writer). There are certainly proportional fluctuations, as at Naamé,

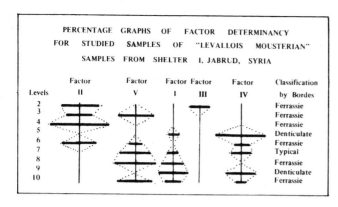

FIG. 8—Frequency Polygons, indicating a shift through time in the factors determining Levalloiso-Mousterian phases. Based on the sequence of Levels 10-2 at Yabrud Shelter I (after upper part of fig. 11 of L. and S. Binford, 1966, p. 284).

but a preliminary examination indicates that the 20 levels contain one facies; all of Ras el-Kelb will, for the moment, be referred to Phase 2. Being the only one of the three published to date, Naamé will represent the others here.

Naamé

Brecciated occupation deposits were found by Sanlaville, exposed in a bay in a low limestone cliff ca. 50 m from the seashore at Khalda, south of Beirut. *Three loci* were excavated by Fleisch (1970). The geology, as reported by Sanlaville (1970, fig. 4, p. 243, reproduced as our fig. 7), is as follows, from base to top: (1) Cemomanean limestone bedrock, dipping 15° W, patch of *Vermets* at +7.40-8 meters; (2) Enféan beach conglomerate with thermophile fauna (*Strombus bubonius* Lmk), 2 m thick in places; (3) Pink breccia with Middle Paleolithic flint. About 1 m thick in places; (4) Naaméan formations—Vermetid bench, 9.50 m, on conglomerate; patch of Vermets at 10.50 m, on breccia.

Point III, Locus 1

Taking Fleisch's Point III, Locus 1, as a representative section, the archaeological layers appear (so far as the writer has been able to understand the published report) to be as follows, from base to top: (1) Level O—Excavated to contact of bone-breccia with conglomerate at 11.10 m above sea level. Deposit cemented to surface of pebbles and in interstices; (2) Soil layer—0.35 m thick, local decalcification; (3) Level 1—Bone-breccia, intensely hard, with burned bone and flint. The *Niveau Inférieur*, which includes Level O and the soil layer, noted above; (4) Level 2—Bone-breccia, ca. 30 m thick, very rich in flint and bone—the *Zone Médiale*; and (5) Level 3—Bone-breccia, surface at 12 m 80 cm above present sea level—the *Niveau Supérieur* (Fleisch, 1970, fig. 1, p. 30).

In the *Niveau Inférieur* and *Niveau Supérieur* was a Levalloiso-Mousterian resembling that of Ras el-Kelb Tunnel Trench layers; in the *Zone Médiale* was a more Levalloisian version of the same facies with fewer retouched tools and

some points. The profile was truncated into a microcliff with the base (still in breccia) at 11.30 m above sea level, by a return of the Naaméan sea; during this (Naaméan) transgression, Vermets occupied the breccia in two places (see fig. 4).

Ras el-Kelb

The material of this truncated cave site was recovered from breccia in a rescue excavation, necessitated by road improvements (Garrod and Henri-Martin, 1961). Two loci were excavated, the Tunnel Trench (15 levels) in the interior of the cave, and the Rail Trench (5 levels) closer to the original cave mouth. If there is an industrial development upward in the 3.50 m deep deposit, as the excavators hoped (and as appears to occur at Nahr Ibrahim), it may be possible on typological grounds to relate these two exposures. As shown in the published section and plan (Garrod and Henri-Martin, 1961), from base to top the stratigraphy is as follows: (1) Rail Trench, Level E—beach material on cave floor, top at 5.80 m above sea level; (2) Rail Trench, 5 Levels, D-A—Top ca. 8 m above sea level—occupation deposits with bone and flint in D, alternating calcrete bands and hearths in C, B, and A; (3) Tunnel Trench, 15 Levels, O-A, Base at ca. 7 m, Top at ca. 10.75 meters—alternating hearth layers with flint and bone, and bands of calcareous soil or calcrete, becoming more brecciated and clayey above Level J; and (4) Disturbed deposits in a clay fill to roof, ca. 15 m above sea level.

The beach material, thought to have derived from the abrasion platform onto which the cave opened, has been thought of as pertaining to the "6 m-beach" (or Würm I/II interstadial beach). The occurrence of a similar industry at Naamé, however, on an Enféan beach puts the matter in a new light. If, as Sanlaville holds, the sea oscillated on its *polygénique* platform, returning twice to this level, the beach material in Ras el-Kelb could as well belong to the Enféan, just as at Naamé. The C14 "date" (more than 52,000 years; Gro. 2556), taken from burned bones 1-1½ m above bedrock, would relate well with this interpretation; it would not disagree with the earlier Th^{230}/U^{234} dates for eastern Mediterranean *Strombus* beaches (e.g., at Madonna del'Arma, overlain by Mousterian [de Lumley, 1969], at which the time range was between 60,000 and 90,000 years [L. 884 A and L. 934 R; Stearns and Thurber, 1965]).

However, if the beach is Enféan, we are obliged to put Ras el-Kelb and Naamé also into the early Würm I phase already occupied by the Amudian, Yabrudian, and Phase 1 Levalloiso-Mousterian (Bezez B) at Adlun.

Pollen analyses indicate that Phase 2 was cold (or wet) at Ras el-Kelb. Samples from 8 m and 7 m at Ras el-Kelb contained abundant arboreal pollen (Leroi-Gourhan, 1971). In the Ghab, a pollen core was obtained from the Karkour Main Drain; a layer of peat, also dated to "more than 56,000 years" (see above) indicated an increase of conifers vis-a-vis oak (Van Liere, 1961, 1966). We do not know if

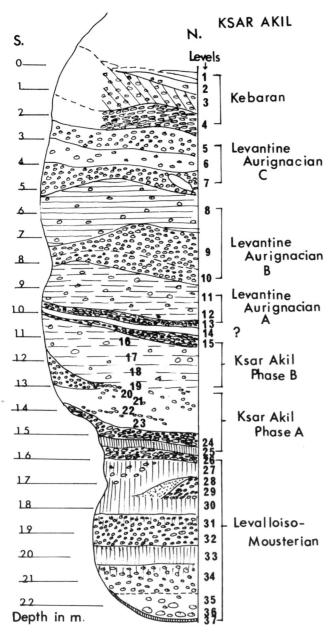

FIG. 9—Section of Ewing's 1947-1948 Excavations at Ksar Akil. After Newcomer (1972), with the present writer's interpretation of the industrial sequence of industries added to the right.

this is related to the signs of the extensive use of fires at all three Phase 2 sites (and at Tabun C); large numbers of the flints are burned, blackened, calcined, and deformed.

Judging by the human tooth found at Ras el-Kelb (a premolar of a sixteen-to-twenty-year-old individual [Vallois, 1962]), the makers of these fires were Neanderthals; this tooth had already begun to show signs of wear.

The Ras el-Kelb Neanderthals were primarily hunters of *Dama*, almost to the exclusion of other types (A. Garrard, personal communication). Since the region was apparently well forested (as it still is today), it contained a variety of species besides *Dama*, e.g. Merck's Rhino (Fleisch, 1955),

although it hints at specialization in favor of *Dama* by this Middle Paleolithic population.

Nahr Ibrahim (Asfourieh Cave)

Details of the long Mousterian sequence at this site, excavated in two seasons by Solecki, are not yet published; meanwhile it is expected that the occupation spanned the periods of Tabun C and Tabun B. Some of the flint material at the base of Nahr Ibrahim (which is illustrated in figs. 12 and 13, Solecki, 1970a) can be seen to resemble closely that of Ras el-Kelb and Tabun C.

Other Phase 2 Sites

Another group of sites on the seashore appears to belong to Phase 2; one of these is the site known as Bergy's Plus-Eight (Bergy, 1932). The others are sites found by Fleisch in beach deposits at the foot of the 15 m dead-cliff at Ras Beirut (Fleisch, 1956 et seq.).

In the opinion of two independent geologists—Gigout (Fleisch and Gigout, 1966, p. 14) and Sanlaville (Fleisch and Sanlaville, 1969)—the Ras Beirut promontory has risen *en bloc* in relation to the coastline north and south, since the era of the Middle Pleistocene, so that sites which appear to be at 13-15 m may correspond to those at 8-10 m elsewhere on the coast. If so, it would fit very well with the typological correlations: Père Fleisch (who has kindly allowed the author to examine the material) has given an excellent description—"un Levalloisien léger, aux éclats courts—assez minces, parfois très minces. Cette minceur apparît surtout dans les éclats discoides ou ovales; racloirs; grattoirs; utilisation de tout petits éclats. Les pointes triangulaires sont peu nombreuses et pas de belle facture, ce qui contraste avec les éclats discoides ou ovales très soignés. Ce Levalloisien . . . s'en distinque nettement, notamment par deux caractères: la grande pauvreté en pointes triangulaires, . . . l'absence d'influence moustérienne . . ." (Fleisch, 1946, p. 301). (The term "Moustérienne" here refers to retouch.)

It could be argued, therefore, that Phase 2 sites occur overlying Enféan beaches, or in them, except when the site is higher than 10.50 meters (e.g., basal Nahr Ibrahim). Except for the drop in sea level, which would separate the sites from the shore at the time of their occupation, some connection with the sea in Phase 2 is suggested.

In Syria, no typical Phase 2 sites can be cited, even on the coast. The Mousterian levels at Yabrud I (10 to 1), however, which are unsatisfactory as a model sequence for reasons given above, yet seem to contain material in Levels 7-5, which is reminiscent of the typology of the coastal Phase 2. Confirmation or denial of this may follow the publication of the new material from Yabrud I.

Phase 3 (Model–Tabun B)

It is during the last Levalloiso-Mousterian phase that aggradation of stream valleys permitted the first occupation of valley sites (Wright, 1962). This fill is attributed to upstream erosion in the mountains (Wright, 1962; Butzer,

1	2	3	4	5
Previous System	Ksar Akil Levels	KSAR AKIL proposed sequence	ANTELIAS	ABU HALKA
Athlitian (Phase V)	6 / 7	Levantine Aurignacian C	I / II	
Upper Antelian (Phase IV)	8	(gravettoid points)	III	
Lower Antelian (Phase III)	9	Levantine Aurignacian B		
	10	(el Wad points)	IV	IVc
—	11	(el Wad points)		
	12	Levantine		
	13	Aurignacian A	?Zumoffen's Red layer	
—	14	sparse	sparse	IVd
	15			sparse
Phase II	16	(Ksar Akil Points)		
	17	Ksar Akil Phase Bii	?	?
	18	Bi		
	19			
	20	(Backed knives)		
Emiran, Emiran or Phase I	21	Ksar Akil Phase A		
	22		V	IVe
	23	(chanfreins)		
	24		VII-VI	IVf
	25	sparse		
Levalloiso-Mousterian	26			
	27-36	Levantine Mousterian		

FIG. 10—Suggested Correlation of the Sequences at three Lebanese Early Upper Paleolithic Sites. In column 2 Ksar Akil levels are phased according to Azoury, 1971; in column 3 the phases are as suggested at the London Symposium of 1969 and include some suggestions made in Copeland (1970), and Copeland and Hours (1971). This figure is a corrected version of, and should supercede, Fig. 8 in Copeland (1970).

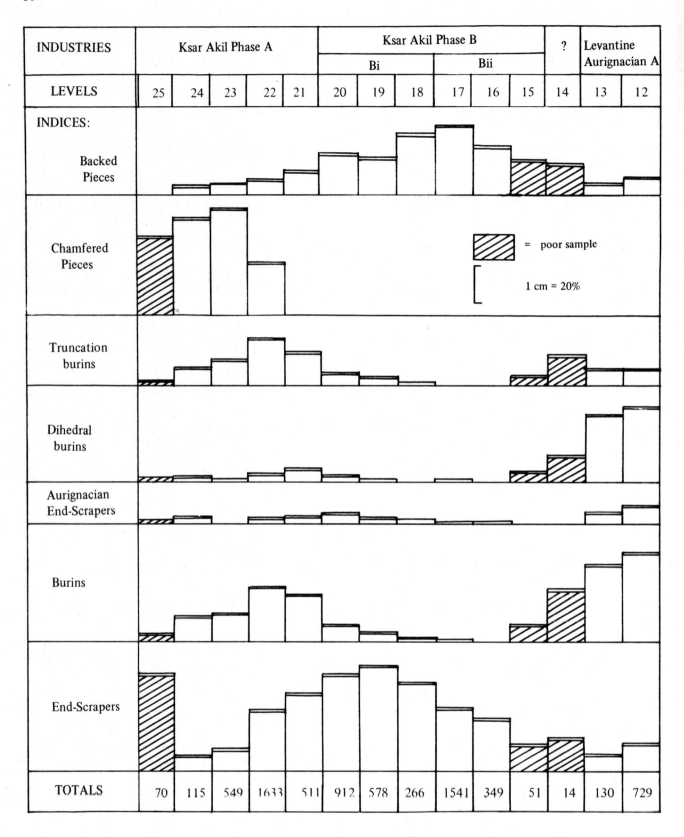

FIG. 11–The Indices of some Tool Groups in Ksar Akil Levels, according to I. Azoury's analysis of the Early Upper Paleolithic phases (after an unpublished figure based on data in fig. 180, Azoury, 1971).

1964; Sanlaville, 1973) caused by more severe climatic conditions (including torrential seasonal rain) at the start of Würm II (the Würm I of McBurney). The latter two date this to after the last transgression (i.e., the Naaméan). It is, hence, coincident with a drop of the sea level, and with the deposition of eolean sand on the littoral which interfingered with the torrential gravels (Wright, 1962).

The typology of Phase 3 sites produces two impressions—monotony, and the precision with which a standard product (the triangular Levallois point) could be produced. The technical characteristics seem to combine those of Phases 1 and 2; the points are struck from either one axis or radially prepared cores (fig. 6-*11* and *12*). The flakes are light and thin, resembling in this the broader forms of Phase 2, but now laminar and narrow forms prevail.

It may eventually be possible to confirm or disprove that there is a steady development from Phase 2 into Phase 3, from the long sequence at Nahr Ibrahim; e.g., see Fig. 9 of the preliminary report (showing part of the stratigraphy), Fig. 10 (showing an increase in triangular points upward), and a typical Phase 3 assemblage (fig. 13) near the top (Solecki, 1970*a*, p. 113 et seq.).

The alluvium building up on the Wadi Antelias terraces coincided with the first occupation of Ksar Akil shelter (Level 36, ca. 22 m below datum; Ewing, 1947), so that the sequence of Mousterian Levels 36-26 at Ksar Akil may be used as a model in addition to that of Tabun B.

Ksar Akil

The shelter consists of a series of vertical overhangs in a sheer limestone cliff (fig. 9). The Levalloiso-Mousterian deposits of eleven levels is 8 m deep in the lowest overhang; these occupations began while the site was still susceptible to flooding, but the top level (26) is without alluvia (Wright, 1951). These layers contained hearths in thin black lenses (Murphy, 1939) and ended with a three-level feature of angular limestone chips and red soil known as Stoney Complex 3 (see section adapted from Ewing's section, used by Azoury and Newcomer, fig. 9). The lower (*éboulis*) layer (26) of this feature is Levalloiso-Mousterian and is dated to ca. 44,400 B.P. ± 1,200 years (Gro 2574/75; Wright, 1962, p. 536).

The industry of Layers 26-36 is being studied by J. Waechter, who has kindly allowed the author to examine the drawn pieces, and who has stated (personal communication, 1969) that both flint and fauna are sparse in these levels. The industry is characterized by triangular unretouched Levallois points, many of them elongated, with few retouched tools. There may be a development from base to top, more retouched tools occurring from Level 31 upward. It would appear that Ksar Akil was not intensively occupied during the phase, contrary to what had been concluded by S. Binford (1968), who was working from an incomplete data base.

The faunal and molluscan remains (Hooijer, 1961; Alteena, 1962) indicate that the bulk of the Levalloiso-Mousterian menu was provided by moist woodland animals,

e.g., *Bos, Dama*, rhino, as well as upland types such as *Capra*. (The rhino is Merck's or *D. Hemitoechus*; see Hooijer 1961 and his errata in 1966.) The "outbreak" of *Bos* in the last Levalloiso-Mousterian levels is thought to be due to desiccation farther east, which has driven them westward (Higgs, in McBurney, 1967); a similar outbreak of rhino in these levels is attributed to the presence of swamps caused by eoleanite-blocked river mouths and erosion-blocked stream courses (Butzer, 1964). Bovines were reported to be numerous at Geula (Wreschner, 1967), which by date and typology should belong to Phase 3. Vulture bones occurred in all Ksar Akil levels: these possibly derive from times when the shelter was deserted.

Other Phase 3 Sites—Zones 1 and 2

A goodly number of sites probably relating to this phase are those associated with dunes-of-regression, or similar post-transgression locations (e.g., Amrit [Haller, 1941], and the Sands of Beirut [Fleisch, 1970]); when *in situ*, the material is embedded in *hamra* soils (decalcified eoleanites) or in cemented *ramleh* dunes, which are seen to continue under the sea to an unknown depth, graded to a sea level lower than that of today (Wright, 1962; Butzer, 1964).

Inland sites in the Lebanese foothills may refer to this phase, e.g., Nahr el-Joz and Deir Billah (Copeland and Wescombe, 1965, p. 82, p. 112), es-Souass and Keoue Cave, both discovered by the Japanese team (Suzuki and Kobori, 1970, p. 33). Of these, Deir Billah, at 800 m altitude, can be considered as a Zone 2 site; it is a cave, now unfortunately disturbed.

Keoue Cave

This is located in a now deforested limestone foothill area in north Lebanon, and has so far had one season's excavation (Watanabe, 1970). The upper terrace and front of the cave had the following stratigraphy, from surface to base (bedrock not yet reached): (1) Brown loam with heterometric rubble—Levalloiso-Mousterian; (2) Yellowish brown loam—Levalloiso-Mousterian; (3) Hard brown silty loam with hetermometric rubble, calcareous concretions and small particles of weathered limestone—Levalloiso-Mousterian notches more abudant; (4) Reddish brown clayey loam with cobbles and many animal bones—all the retouched pieces here were points; (5) Olive green silty clay with heavily weathered, white limestone cobbles and boulders—many animal bones—only one artifact, a narrow flake; (6) Grayish brown silty clay—material not mentioned.

Layers 1-4 contained similar material, an Upper Levalloiso-Mousterian industry consisting of pointed flakes and parallel sided flakes struck from "Abu-Halka" (i.e., one axis) cores, while blades and rounded flakes were scarce. Tools consist of retouched Levallois points, sidescrapers, Mousterian points (amounting to ca. 30-40%), and burins (amounting to 6-7%).

Watanabe comments that the majority of the retouched points are small, 3-4 cm long, and that the most numerous faunal type was a large bear, species not yet established. The next most numerous species is *Bos*. He adds: "The occupants of the site seem to have been big bear hunters with small points" (Watanabe, 1970, p. 214).

Farther north, in the Hatay west of Antioch, the First Cave and the Plugged Cave (Tikali Mghara) had Upper Levalloiso-Mousterian occupations (Senyürek, 1958; Senyürek and Bostançi, 1958) and interesting geological implications. The First Cave was 39 m above sea level (an altitude like that of Masloukh and similar to that of Tabun) and had the following stratigraphy (according to the excavators' report) from base to top: (1) Freshwater sandstone (*sic*) adhering to ceiling and walls, containing land snails and bones. Attributed to pre-Mindel/Riss times; (2) Several layers of marine (*sic*) sands, 6 m deep, containing foraminifera. Attributed to the Mindel/Riss transgression (i.e., Jbailean); (3) Rockfalls; (4) Yellow earth, 58 cm-1.91 m deep, with Upper Levalloiso-Mousterian—stalactite lenses; (5) Dark brown soil, ca. 47 cm thick, with Upper Levalloiso-Mousterian; (6) Rockfall, of sterile stones; (7) Black earth, with Aurignacian, 50-39 cm thick; (8) Light brown soil, 51-1.18 m, Aurignacian; (9) Black soil. Roman, etc.

The Plugged Cave was found at 83 m above sea level and also had a marine sand at its base. Over this was the same Upper Levalloiso-Mousterian facies as in First Cave, in a layer 1.35 m thick, without hearths, and with few bones.

The industry, as illustrated, consists of thin, broad-based triangular Levallois points, a few sidescrapers, and (in Level 4) "utilized bones," attributed to the overlying Aurignacian layers. The flakes were measured, found to be generally small (averaging ca. 5.2 cm), and likened to those of Tabun B. Layer 4 is attributed to a cold peak in Würm on the evidence of the stalactite layer between 4 and 5.

The sandstone was analyzed by Tavani (1958) and found to derive from the Miocene limestone of the region, but it contained the Quaternary-to-Recent species *Rotalia papilosa*. It was similar to the sand from the actual beach of today.

Phase 3 Sites in Zone 3

Jerf Ajla has a chronologically late Levalloiso-Mousterian in Level Brown 1, according to its C14 date of 43,000 B.P. ± 2,000 years (NZ. 76)—which relates well with Ksar Akil's date. Judging by the illustrations, however, the material does not particularly resemble the coastal Phase 3 facies. The same could be said for Yabrud Shelter II, where there are *éboulis* at the base and a poor Recent Mousterian industry, and for Shelter I, where the flakes of Levels 2 and 1 are heavier than is usual in the coastal Phase 3. On the other hand, there is a diminution of burins in the middle levels—just as in the Phase 2 of Lebanon. At Douara, the uppermost Mousterian level might be of Phase 3; unfortunately the C14 dates obtained so far are conflicting (Suzuki and Takai, 1973).

As to the environment of the last Mousterian phase, the evidence is conflicting, some workers seeing it as hot (Higgs, in McBurney, 1967), others as cold (Farrand, 1969, table 5, p. 12). There are hints as to differences in the way of life of the latest Mousterians. The sparsely occupied sites suggest short-lived occupations and frequent movement. The multivariate factor analysis conducted by the Binfords on the Levalloiso-Mousterian Levels 8-1 of Yabrud I gave results indicating that "... Factor II tends to replace Factor V through the Jabrud sequence ..." and that this could represent "... a shift in the way this specific location was utilised through time" and that "... the upper levels ... suggest more specific work groups occupying the shelter for shorter periods of time" (Binford and Binford, 1966, p. 283; see also their figure 11, p. 284, reproduced as fig. 8 here).

The clustering of dates around 42,000 for the late Mousterian sites in the Near East is surely significant, even though the reliability limits of the C14 dating method is approached here. In addition to those already mentioned from Jerf Ajla and Ksar Akil, are Geula (Wreschner, personal communication, 1969, with a date of 42,000 B.P. ± 1,700 years [Grn. 4142]); Kebara F (42,000 B.P. ± 1,000 years [Gro 2552]); and Haua Fteah (41,450 B.P. ± 1,300 years [Grn. 2564], McBurney, 1967, p. 71). If these dates are reliable, the Mousterian period was in its final phase in the Levant about this time (Farrand, 1969). The above list excludes unsatisfactory dates for Tabun and Douara.

Besides Level 26 at Ksár Akil, associated with a layer of *éboulis*, several other sites have similar evidences of pronounced climatic shifts at the end of the phase—see the striking stoney peak in Level 28 at Haua Fteah (McBurney, 1967, fig. 3, p. 53), Yabrud II, 10-8 (*Mousterien Récent*), Erq al-Ahmar H, probably Qafzeh I-H (Neuville, 1951), Magraçik, First Cave, Level 3 (Senyürek and Bostançi, 1958), and the eroded Level D in the Douara test trench (see Endo, p. 93, and Akawawa, p. 23, in Suzuki and Takai, 1973).

Other sites have suffered the loss of their Late or Final Levalloiso-Mousterian layers due either to collapse of the floor (Bezez), the deposits surviving as hanging breccias, or to erosion (Bar-Yosef and Vandermeersch, 1972). This article is quoted (in spite of the fact that it contains misleading comments on the Lebanese Upper Paleolithic) for the light it throws on the Palestinian cave situation in the transition era. The result of these agencies has been that there is no site known to date in the Levant with reliable stratigraphy from which the transition, without a break, from Middle to Upper Paleolithic can be illustrated; the end of the Levalloiso-Mousterian remains something of a mystery.

THE EARLY UPPER PALEOLITHIC

The transition between the Middle and Upper Paleolithic in the Levant has been the subject of much controversy in the past, based on incomplete data, found (as it now appears) in the wrong place. Since the way of life did not, apparently, change to any marked degree in the early Upper

Paleolithic (much the same game was hunted and many of the same sites were occupied as in the Mousterian era), it is not surprising that most of the discussion has centered on the flint typology of the layers concerned.

The evidence now available from Ksar Akil and Antelias suggests that there is a distinctive Stage I industry, characterized by *chanfreins* at three sites in Lebanon [chamfered pieces—first noted at Abu Halka as "*lames et éclats à chanfrein*" (Haller, 1941-43). They are blades or flakes which have had the distal end removed so as to leave a bevel (*chanfer*) at the tip. The removal blow is struck from a small retouched platform on the lateral edge near the tip (see fig. 12). In a full account, Newcomer (1970) calls them "chamfered pieces." This industry, which is transitional in several senses of the term (Copeland, 1970), has not been reported thus far in Palestine—where the earliest unequivocally Upper Paleolithic industry seems to relate to the second Upper Paleolithic stage of Lebanon (Bar-Yosef and Vandermeersch, 1972). After seeing the Ksar Akil material for the first time in 1968, Professor Garrod (personal communication) came to essentially the same conclusion, an outcome which she had envisaged earlier (Garrod, 1955, p. 21). After evaluating the evidence from Palestinian transitional sites and Abu Halka, she suggested that there were "...too many features in common to be regarded as other than closely related ... " and that "... it may ultimately prove possible to distinguish a 'northern' and a 'southern' facies in the Emiran ... " (ibid.). The nature of the 'southern' facies remains to be established, but Amud B may be a good model.

THE LEBANESE EVIDENCE

The three sites which conern us are: (1) Ksar Akil shelter: Levels 25-21 = Ksar Akil Phase A; Levels 20-15 - Ksar Akil Phase B (Ewing, 1947, 1963; Azoury, 1971; Azoury and Hodson, 1973; Newcomer, 1970, 1971, 1972; Newcomer and Hodson, 1973; and others); (2) Abu Halka Shelter, Levels IVe and IVf: Ksar Akil Phase A (Haller, 1941-43; Azoury, 1971); (3) Antelias Cave, Levels VII-V; Ksar Akil Phase A (Zumoffen, 1900; Ewing, 1947; Copeland, 1970).

The terms "Ksar Akil Phases A and B" are names provisionally agreed upon by participants of the Symposium on Levant Paleolithic Terminology held in 1969 (Hours and Solecki, forthcoming). Ksar Akil Phase A replaces Neuville's "Phase I," Garrod's "Emiran," and Ewing's "Transitional." Ksar Akil Phase B replaces Neuville's "Phase II" and Ewing's "Chatelperronian" (see fig. 10).

The model here is the sequence at Ksar Akil, one of the most complete in the Levant. The figures quoted are based on the work of Azoury and Newcomer as well as on the author's own observations.

Ksar Akil

Stratigraphy

1—Ksar Akil Phase A, Levels 25-21

The general stratigraphy is shown in Fig. 9, as adapted by Azoury (1971) and Newcomer (1972) from the old section of Ewing. The Upper Paleolithic levels begin in Level 25, where there is a distinct change in the typology (fig. 11).

Level 25 is a red clay layer between the two stoney layers below it (Level 26) and above it (Level 24), the whole being known as Stoney Complex 3 (Ewing, 1947, 1963). It passes into Level 24 at 15 m below datum. It contained sparse flint, fauna, and a Neanderthaloid maxilla ("Ethelruda"), according to Ewing (1963, 1966).

Wright (1951) has described the soils of the next four meters upward as being brown earth with ash layers and angular stones in scatters. They contained a high calcium carbonate percentage with caliche formations. The excavators divided this block into four archaeological levels, 23-20. As shall be seen, the occupation took place during the Würm II/III interstadial (Hengelo?).

2—Ksar Akil Phase B, Levels 20-15

After Level 20 there are signs of climatic activity in a layer of small angular limestone chips, 12.50 m below datum against the shelter wall. Levels 18-15 consist of soils which are brecciated against the shelter wall to 11 meters. ("Egberta," a *Homo sapiens sapiens* fossil, was found in breccia in Level 17 [Ewing, 1963].) At 11 m begins Stoney Complex 2, another three-layer feature, but thinner than Complex 3; Level 15 is the lower stoney layer, 14 a nearly sterile red clay layer, and 13 the upper stoney layer. This complex saw the end of the transition, the probable abandonment of the site in Level 14, and the appearance of the Levantine Aurignacian A in Level 13.

Typology

1—Ksar Akil Phase A

Although some atypical endscrapers and even a *chanfrein* were found in Level 26, it contained a typical Levalloiso-Mousterian assemblage (personal communication, J. Waechter) of Phase 3 type. In Level 25, however, 59% of the tools consist of burins, endscrapers, and *chanfreins* (fig. 12-2 through 6), while Mousterian tools are virtually absent (there is not even a category for these in Azoury's typelist, the rare specimens present being placed as "Divers"). Although the endscrapers and burins are typically Upper Paleolithic, they are made on Levallois blanks (fig. 12-1), struck from Levallois cores of the one-axis type (fig. 12-7), which differ little from those of the Levalloiso-Mousterian levels below. The unretouched debitage is strongly Levallois (the average ILty is 40%; Azoury, 1971), with numerous thin elongated points. It is these points which give the assemblage its evolved appearance and which distinguish its debitage from that of Level 26. Blades of Upper Paleolithic type (i.e., with punctiform butt) are virtually absent (2%-5% in these levels; Azoury, 1971).

We are not dealing here with a mixture of Middle Paleolithic tools made by Middle Paleolithic technology, and

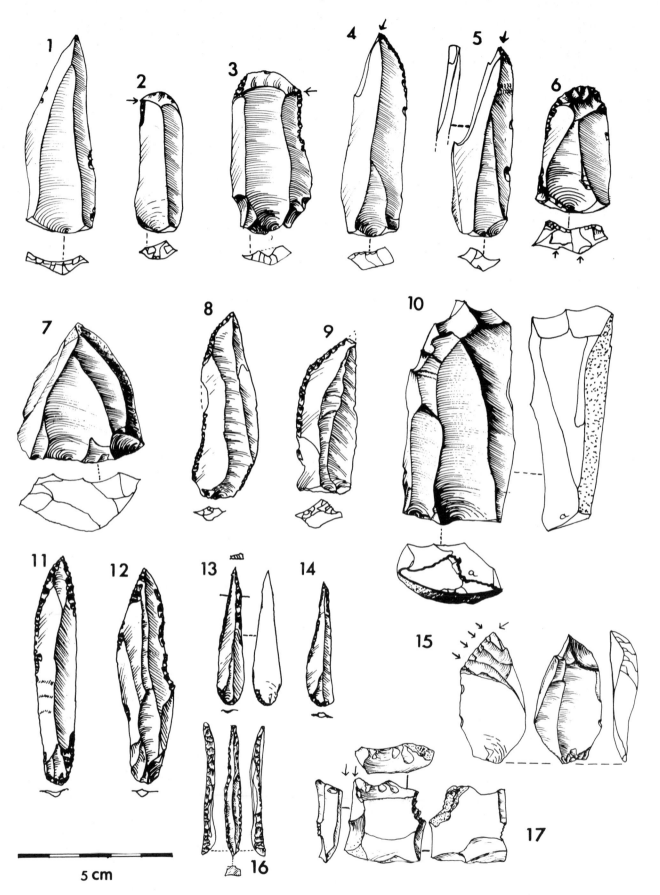

FIG. 12—Some Forms Typical of Various Upper Paleolithic Phases. Numbers *1-6* of Ksar Akil Phase A; numbers *8* and *9* of Ksar Akil Phase Bii; numbers *7* and *10* are core types seen in Ksar Akil Phases A and Bi; numbers *11* and *12* are typical forms of Ksar Akil Phase Bii.

Upper Paleolithic tools made by Upper Paleolithic technology, but the characteristically Upper Paleolithic tool types are found on blanks made by a Middle Paleolithic tradition of flint knapping (direct percussion, on prepared cores, to produce Levallois blades or points). Thus, the transitional aspect occurs *on the same piece of flint*. These attributes persist through three meters of deposit. Besides the *chanfreins* (fig. 12-*2* and *3*), a special burin "on lateral preparation" (Newcomer, 1972, and see fig. 12-*4* and *5*) occurs in these levels. An Emireh Point, so poor that in the opinion of some it does not qualify as an Emireh Point at all, occurs in Level 25. As to the other technical aspects, flakes outnumber blades two to one, and faceted butts amount to 50% (Azoury, 1971).

Contrary to what has been asserted by some authors, therefore, there is no "rapid switch to punched blade production" and no persistence of Mousterian tools in the earliest or Ksar Akil Phase A Upper Paleolithic of Lebanon.

Abu Halka, Antelias, and Other
Ksar Akil Phase Sites

Although the "*chanfrein*" industry of Abu Halka IVf and IVe was reported by Haller in 1942-43, it remained an isolated occurrence, mainly because of the delay in the publication of the material excavated by Ewing in Ksar Akil and Antelias, where, as it now transpires, the Abu Halka facies also existed. The existence of three sites having this facies, rather than just one, put the matter of the transition into a new light (Copeland, 1970). The stratigraphy and industrial sequence at Abu Halka and Antelias (both of which start their sequence with Ksar Akil Phase A, and continue with Aurignacian Phase B) is interpreted in Fig. 10, which is a corrected version of Fig. 8 in Copeland, 1970, p. 141.

At Abu Halka, the industry is found at ca. 6 m above sea level in a red clayey layer (IV) with hearths (f and e), each less than 40 cm thick. It contains a few (intrusive or reused) heavily patinated Mousterian pieces. It also differed from the Antelias Valley sites by having four typical Emireh Points. At Antelias one (unstratified) Emireh Point was found—it also appeared to belong to Ksar Akil Phase A Levels VII-V, judging by flint and patina. Recent evidence suggests that the time span for the Emireh Points, the erstwhile typofossil of "Stage I," may have to be lengthened at both ends (Bar-Yosef and Vandermeersch, 1972), but this depends on the resolution of the true chronology of the Palestinian transitional phase; *in Lebanon* numerous specimens occur in open sites, but in stratigraphic positions they occur only in Ksar Akil Phase A. This author takes the view that the Emireh Point still forms a link, perhaps the only *typological* link, between Lebanon and Palestine in the transitional period *sensu lato*. These remarks apply only to typical specimens, and not to *any* piece with bifacial retouch on the base (see Garrod, 1951, p. 142).

There may be a fourth Ksar Akil Phase A site at Kubbah II, a coastal cave near Batroun, reported by the Japanese survey team, their Site 6 (Suzuki and Kobori, 1970). The characteristic transitional burin is present (their fig. 43, nos. 2 and 4) as well as 'Abu Halka' (i.e., one-axis) point cores and narrow Levallois blades; this site is halfway between Abu Halka and Antelias near the mouth of the el-Joz river. Significantly, it had been reported (by Zumoffen) as containing Middle Paleolithic material (Copeland and Wescombe, 1965, p. 101).

Non-Ksar Akil Phase A
Transitional Sites

The Ksar Akil Phase A industry does not seem to have occurred elsewhere than along the Lebanese littoral. It has not been reported from Palestine, Syria, or from Zone 2 in Lebanon. Bar-Yosef and Vandermeersch (1972) have suggested various possible explanations for this situation, one of which was that evolved Mousterian industries continued to exist in Palestine during the era of the "*chanfrein*" industry.

Confirmatory evidence would seem to exist at:

1. *Amud B*, in Lower Galilee, where the industry is clearly not a normal Levalloiso-Mousterian facies. Even if the '*chanfreins*' at first reported (Watanabe, 1964) from Amud B have now been reclassified, this writer agrees with

---

Numbers *13-15* occur in the Levantine Aurignacian, particularly in the early phases. Number *16* is a Late type (Aurignacian B-C) and number *17* occurs only in Aurignacian C at Ksar Akil. All pieces are from Antelias Cave, except *11* and *12*, which are from Ksar Akil, Level 17, and numbers *13* and *14*, from Abu Halka IVc. *1.* Unretouched elongated Levallois point; the type of blank upon which the next five pieces were probably made. *2.* Chanfrein, or chamfered piece, made on a Levallois blade. The distal blow is struck from a platform of fine lateral distal retouch to form a bevel at the tip. *3.* Chanfrein made on a Levallois flake; the remains of an earlier chanfrein platform can be seen on the left distal edge (the existence of spalls at Ksar Akil Phase A sites shows that chanfreins were frequently refreshed). *4* and *5.* Burins on lateral preparation (*burin d'angle sur préparation lateral*) made on Levallois blanks; the blank is not truncated, which distinguishes this type from the burin on an oblique truncation. *6.* Endscraper made on a Levallois blank. *7.* Summary Levallois unipolar point-core. *8* and *9.* Backed knives, reminiscent of Chatelperron knives, made on blanks struck from evolved Levallois or prismatic cores. *10.* Elongated, semiprismatic point core, from which a Levallois blade might have been struck. *11* and *12.* Ksar Akil points, a type especially common in Level 17 at Ksar Akil. Note the change in the debitage; the retouch is fine and usually abrupt, and appears to have been done to form a point on the axis. *13* and *14.* El-Wad points (ex-Font Yves points). Typically, they are made on bladelets or small blades with wide butts. Number *13* has some fine inverse retouch at the base, a feature characteristic of Levantine Aurignacian Phase B at Ksar Akil. Number *14* has the (more commonly seen) unmodified base. The retouch is abrupt to semiabrupt, and often irregular. *15.* Flat-faced burin or *burin caréné plan*, a form not seen at Ksar Akil below Level 13. The burin spalls are struck off onto the flake surface. *16.* A form of microgravette—a development of the el-Wad point—with abrupt bilateral retouch, which has removed the original tip and butt of the piece. *17.* Burin on a (usually Clactonian) notch; especially common only in Level 6 at Ksar Akil (see fig. 9).

Watanabe (in Suzuki and Takai, 1970) that the industry relates—somehow—to the transitional phase.

2. *Mountain Sites.* In Zone 2 in Lebanon many large and small open sites are found on the pine forested, sandstone plateaus at high altitudes (ca. 1,000 m), such as Meyrouba, Mazraat Kfardebiane, and Michmiche. They contain artifacts made by very evolved Middle Paleolithic technology, rare Emireh Points, and an unusual number of endscrapers and burins. To complicate matters, however, there is certainly a sprinkling of Neolithic (and later Paleolithic?) material, and there is always the chance that some of these (40 odd) sites may represent the (now virtually lacking) Phase 3 Levalloiso-Mousterian sites of Zone 2. However, their location just below the treeline of today suggests that they could have been occupied only during an interstadial (Hours, 1973); this could well have been the same one which saw the Ksar Akil Phases A and B on the coast, the link being the Emireh Points. In any case, two have been published as Upper Paleolithic or Transitional: Jebel Mazloum (Fleisch, 1962) and Michmiche (Hours, 1962).

3. *Jerf Ajla Cave*, in Zone 3. Transitional material was reported to occur toward the top of the Mousterian levels; Schroeder (1966) states that there is a development from base to top of Level Brown 1 (1½ m thick) in the form of a steady increase of endscrapers and punched blades (the latter amounting to 30% of the butts at the top), with a corresponding decrease of the IL and ILty, as well as the IR. This is not the kind of transition which is seen at Ksar Akil, and Jerf Ajla may follow the non-Ksar Akil Phase A groups, in which Mousterian forms continued to exist into the Upper Paleolithic era. On the other hand, a break or some telescoping may have occurred; the flat-faced burin (not seen at Ksar Akil until the Aurignacian) is present (Schroeder's fig. 67-*2*, 1969) in the "transitional" layer.

Goldberg's study of the sediments (Goldberg, 1969) showed that the transition took place without change of sediments, and began 1 m above the position of the C14 sample. He sees all of Jerf Ajla as consisting of cryoclastic rubble, indicating cold conditions.

4. *Yabrud Shelter II.* One wonders if the "Recent Mousterian" noted above as having a Phase 3 Levalloiso-Mousterian appearance in Levels 10-8 at Shelter II (Rust, 1950, *Tafels* 76-78) may refer to this phase; contrasted to this idea is de Heinzelin's view that the base of Shelter II equated geologically with the top 13 levels at Shelter I.

Opinions regarding Level 7, where a striking change is discernible (*Tafel* 79), are conflicting; termed *Aurignacien ancien* by de Sonneville-Bordes (1956), it is described as a poor blade industry with some Mousterian tools, truncation burins, a *Chatelperron* point, etc.; the statistics are remarkably similar to those of Amud B: 25% endscrapers, 10% burins, no "Font Yves" points or nosed scrapers, IF 70%, and very high ILam. Significantly, there is a *rupture typologique* between Level 7 and Level 6 at Yabrud II (de Sonneville-Bordes, 1956). On the other hand, Level 7 includes pieces of Ksar Akil Phase B ambience (see below).

The Second Transitional Phase
Ksar Akil Phase B:
Ksar Akil Levels 20-15.

It is convenient to divide this into two subphases: Bi = Levels 20-18 and Bii = Levels 17-15.

In Bi, termed *Chatelperronian* by Ewing, there is an increase in backed blades and backed flakes (fig. 12, *8* and *9*), coincident with the decline of *chanfreins*, which disappear by Level 21/20, and with an increase of endscrapers. Level by level, the number of Upper Paleolithic types of blades increases, those with punctiform butts amounting to 37% by Level 18 (compared with 30% at Jerf Ajla), while those with faceted butts drop from ca. 49% in Level 20 to ca. 14% in Level 18. The ILty drops from 48% in Level 20 to ca. 22% in Level 18 (Azoury, 1971). The cores are either involved Levallois or prismatic, and the blanks are elongated, with small butts.

In Bii a remarkable number of robust points on blades appear (fig. 12-*11* and *12*). The distal end is made pointed on the axis of the blank by abrupt fine retouch, often on only one edge. Azoury terms these Ksar Akil Points, while at Antelias this writer termed them Ksar Akil 17 Points. A few heavier ones can be classed as *Pointes à face plan* (D. de Sonneville-Bordes and Perrot, 1956 et seq.). The backed blades continue; they are now made on finer blanks and they grade into the points. Burins virtually disappear in these levels, but endscrapers are numerous and well made. In Level 15 there is a reappearance of flakes made by the Levallois method, which brings the ILty up to 29% in this level (Azoury, 1971), and it is worth remembering that the same kind of debitage is found in Palestinian Phase II sites (e.g., Erq al-Ahmar E and F), not only judging from the museum collections, but also as expressly mentioned by Neuville (1951, p. 93).

Bone tools occur throughout the transitional levels (those at Ksar Akil are under study but are as yet unpublished); similar pieces from Antelias are described by Copeland and Hours (1971).

Other Ksar Akil Phase B Sites

Phase B cannot clearly be shown to have existed either at Abu Halka or at Antelias, though there are a few pieces of Phase B typology in each. At Abu Halka a near-sterile level, IVd, separated the "*chanfrein*" levels from the Aurignacian, and at Antelias the "sparse, red layer" noted by Zumoffen at the base of his sounding may correspond to this interruption.

Similar material seems to occur in Palestinian sites, however—at Erq al-Ahmar, already mentioned, and et-Tabban B of Neuville (1951). Here the robust points have often been lumped with the small pieces on bladelets, and both are called "Font Yves Points." It must be stressed that Font Yves (or el-Wad) points proper (that is, points with fine distal retouch on bladelets, often curved at the distal end [fig. 12-*13* and *14*], and not retouched at the butt as is fig. 12-*16*) do not occur in Lebanon until the Aurignacian, so that we are surely dealing with two kinds of artifacts, which should be kept separate. The name "El-Wad Point" has been adopted to replace Font Yves Point by all workers (including the present writer), except Azoury (who reasoned that the first appearance of this tool type was at Ksar Akil in Levantine Aurignacian A, which phase did not occur in el-Wad at all); she uses the term "Antelias Point" instead (Azoury, 1971). In any case, it is necessary to restrict the term to the special form in which these tools appear in the Levantine Aurignacian A and B at Ksar Akil, and to exclude both the earlier Ksar Akil Points of Level 17 and the gravettoid, late, forms of Aurignacian C; if this is not done, the tool loses its diagnostic value. It would be useful to know what secure stratigraphic connections exist in Palestine, and what is the relationship between the two types (e.g., does one develop out of the other?). This has a bearing on the origin of the Aurignacian.

There may be a Phase B in Level 7, at Yabrud II (Rust, 1950) as mentioned above, or this level may contain in telescoped form the spaced-out sequence of the coast; it contains a bone point (*Tafel* 79, 24).

At Magraçik in the Hatay, an earlier and a later Aurignacian was reported, and the first one may in fact represent a Ksar Akil Phase Bii industry; however, the drawings, without indication as to which is the distal end of the piece, and with insufficient delineation of the retouch, prevent useful classification (Senyürek and Bostanci, 1958).

Environment and Date of the
Ksar Akil Phases A and B

It is to be noted that workers in Palestine tend to minimize climatic effects brought about during Würm (particularly Würm III) in the Levant (Perrot, 1968, col. 349), while workers in the northern Levant (and even more in the Zagros) see evidence of substantial climatic and other changes in the Würm (Butzer, 1964 and his references; Niklewski and Van Zeist, 1970; Van Liere, 1966; and Besançon and Hours, 1970a, 1970b and 1971).

Date

At Ksar Akil, the transitional levels with *chanfreins* occupy the same relative position stratigraphically as does the Early Dabban in Libya (which also contains *chanfreins*: McBurney, 1967); the Early Dabban is considered to be the first Upper Paleolithic industry at Haua Fteah, and occupied the interstadial Würm II/III (our system), which followed the final Mousterian phase dated by C14 to ca. 44,000, as noted above. This date also relates with the similar one in Ksar Akil, from a level just below the changeover to Upper Paleolithic. Farrand confirms this when he places Qafzeh G, F, and E (containing Levallois, Mousterian, and Upper Paleolithic I facies) in the interstadial succeeding 43,000 B.P. (Farrand, 1969, table 5). Thus, the Upper Paleolithic appeared after this date. The date of ca. 33,000 for a Middle Paleolithic level at Kebara (Bar-Yosef, personal com-

munication, 1973) leaves some questions unanswered, however.

A transgression no doubt accompanied this interstadial, but its strand is invisible, and it probably did not reach the level of today's sea (Sanlaville, 1969b).

It is not clear when the interstadial ended; it may have occurred in the period of Ksar Akil, Level 19 (layer of stones), or alternatively, the beginning of a cold peak may be reflected in Stoney Complex 2.

Fauna

The break with the subtropical Mediterranean interglacial moist woodland fauna was probably complete in the northern Levant by the start of Würm III (Butzer, 1964). The Levalloiso-Mousterian hunters of Ksar Akil took four times as many *Bos* as *Capra*, and ten times as many *Dama* as *Capra*; their Upper Paleolithic successors turned more and more to temperate woodland types inhabiting the mountain regions (Hooijer, 1961, p. 58). Butzer sees this as evidence of the depression of the treeline and a reduction of the lush early Würm woodland. Nevertheless, in common with other Lebanese sites, *Dama* was the main item on the menu.

The Ksar Akil Phase A fauna (Levels 25-19) is predominantly of *Dama* and *Capra*, but red deer and *Capreolus* are more numerous, as is *Gazella*. The carnivores are more varied than in the lower levels (bear, fox, wolf, hyena, martin, and a variety of felids). The same features occur at Abu Halka (Haller, 1941-43).

Unfortunately, Hooijer describes the fauna of Levels 18-10 as one block, which cuts across the Stoney Complex, and the change to Aurignacian. During this period, *Dama* forms 50% of the cervid and bovid remains, and *Capreolus* just exceeds *Capra* as the second most numerous type. Rodents have disappeared, *Bos* forms only 2%-3%, and there is the usual selection of carnivores, to which *Meles* is added.

Hooijer (1961, p. 61) sums up by saying that "Apart from the difference in relative frequency of *Gazella, Capra, Dama*, and *Capreolus*, there is no significant difference between the assemblage of Ksar Akil and that of the Upper Levalloiso-Mousterian and Aurignacian of Mount Carmel," but he adds that the older faunal types, e.g., rhino, occur at Mount Carmel in earlier layers than they do at Ksar Akil while some arid zone types do not occur at Ksar Akil at all, and *Gazella* are never numerous. This suggests that Mount Carmel's ecology should not be considered as similar to that of Ksar Akil, and that the relative scarcity of *Gazella* there could just as easily reflect availability instead of choice on the part of the Paleolithic hunters. Hooijer's contrary opinion on this subject has been quoted as though it were fact by some authors; see fuller account in Higg's article (in McBurney, 1967).

Human Type

Besides the *Homo sapiens sapiens* fossils from the Levalloiso-Mousterian layers at the base of Qafzeh who were making a Mousterian industry (Vandermeersch, 1966), there were other fossils: a complete skeleton from Amud B, stated to be an advanced Neanderthal (Suzuki and Takai, 1970), who was making an evolved Mousterian industry with many Upper Paleolithic tools; at Ksar Akil, if the stratigraphy reported by Ewing (1963, 1966) and the locus reported by Hooijer are reliable, the first Upper Paleolithic industry was being made by Neanderthaloids ("Ethelruda"). Because it is not what would be expected, this evidence may necessitate reevaluation as to the role played by flint knapping traditions in evolution; in the Levant, different but coexisting human types used similar *technology* in this phase, even if their *tool-types* differed (e.g., *chanfreins* were used at some sites but not at others). (In this connection the author is informed that a constellation analysis [Azoury and Hodson; in preparation for 1974] shows a definite link between *time* and *technology* in the transitional [Ksar Akil A and B] phases.)

In any case, modern types, by now using Upper Paleolithic flint knapping techniques, were present by the second half of the transition at Ksar Akil ("Egberta"–Level 17, phase Bii).

THE LATER UPPER PALEOLITHIC–KSAR AKIL

The advent of the Levantine Aurignacian culture is placed in Ksar Akil, Level 13, on the basis of a distinct break, not only in the sediments, but also, according to Azoury (1971), in the typology and the technology. New techniques were also appearing, according to Newcomer's study (1971) of the flint technology, particularly of the burins. For example, in Levels 25-19 a core is rejuvenated by refaceting the striking platforms, whereas in Levels 13-1, the technique has changed—the whole platform is removed, producing a core tablet.

It is not the writer's intention to deal with the Aurignacian in detail for the following reasons: (1) There is a stratigraphic break at Ksar Akil, Abu Halka, and Antelias between the transitional phases and the Aurignacian, so that present Lebanese evidence cannot be used to determine whether the Aurignacian developed out of Ksar Akil Phase Bii, as this writer believes it did, or whether it had some other origin; (2) The Middle Aurignacian (or Antelian, or Stages III and IV) of Ksar Akil has not yet been studied in detail; and (3) The new excavations of Tixier at Ksar Akil have just reached the top of the Aurignacian levels, and shortly we may have important new information. What follows, therefore, is a summary of the results of recent work.

LEVANTINE AURIGNACIAN PHASE A

This exists only at Ksar Akil, in Levels 13-11, i.e., following directly on the break in Level 14, a red soil layer which was almost devoid of artifacts. This curious industry has been studied by Azoury (1971). It is typologically in strong contrast to the preceding levels (Ksar Akil Bii) which contained few burins and many large points; in the first

Aurignacian phase, the burin is the dominant form and includes the flatfaced or Ksar Akil burin (fig. 12-*15*), not seen in lower levels, which forms a horizon marker at Ksar Akil (Newcomer, 1971). Also present are el-Wad points. Even endscrapers are scarce. The A phase exists nowhere else in Lebanon, and apparently is not seen in Palestine.

Once again, Ksar Akil is making its own rules of succession, bringing up entirely new questions; for example, how are we to reconcile the facies which, at Ksar Akil, must be called the Aurignacian B, with probably the same facies in Palestine, where it is Early Aurignacian, according to Perrot (1968)?

LEVANTINE AURIGNACIAN PHASE B

Ksar Akil Levels 10 and 9

This can conveniently be subdivided—broadly speaking, Level 10 can be equated with Neuville's Stage III, Garrod's Lower Antelian, while Level 9 can be equated with Stage IV, the Upper Antelian. It also occurs in Abu Halka IVc (Haller, 1941-43) and at Antelias in levels IV and III (Copeland and Hours, 1971).

Antelias Levels IV and III

Endscrapers outnumber burins two to one. Typical Aurignacian forms (Aurignacian blades, carinated and nosed scrapers, etc.) increase, and the el-Wad points now form 12% of the tools; some have a form of inverse basal retouch, not seen in the A phase (fig. 12-*13*). Level IV has many flakes which were struck from prepared cores by stone hammer, and which have faceted butts.

The debitage of Phase Bii is dominated by tiny bladelets even though the tools are made on flakes, many of them (although very small) of "Clactonian" (*sensu lato*) type. This kind of debitage has produced large numbers of carinated scrapers made on short, thick flakes. The el-Wad points undergo a further development, becoming narrower and straighter, and the retouch more abrupt, especially at the proximal end.

Other Levantine Aurignacian Phase B Sites

Outside of Lebanon, this phase seems to have occurred at Yabrud II in Rust's Levels 6-4, where the percentages for the endscrapers, burins, and el-Wad Points (de Sonneville-Bordes, 1956) are remarkably similar to those computed for Ksar Akil 10 and 9 (Copeland and Hours, 1971). Level 4 also contained obsidian, bitumen, pierced shells, ochre, and bone points (Rust's *Tafel* 86 and de Sonneville-Bordes, 1956). A succession of hearths, one above the other (Rust's *Tafels* 74 and 75), distinguished Layers 7-1 at this rockshelter; the more recent investigations produced no new data (Solecki and Solecki, 1966).

In contrast, a different facies may be present at Magraçik in the First Cave and the Plugged Cave; both are said to have a second Aurignacian layer overlying an earlier one. This is likened to the facies in Kara'in (Kokten, 1963).

They are overlain by Roman or Recent deposits (Sen-yürek and Bostanci, 1958a, 1958b). The scarcity of end-scrapers, if real, suggests connections with the Baradostian, and hence with the Zagros zone and its different traditions; however, there is a real gap in our knowledge here which ought to be filled.

LEVANTINE AURIGNACIAN PHASE C

At Ksar Akil, this provisionally comprises Levels 8-6; these levels were the subject of a thesis by C. Dortch (1970), who sees them as stages in the development of the Late Aurignacian toward the Epipaleolithic (Kebaran). Level 8 is said to belong more with the B phase, 7 is transitional, and 6 a "Final Aurignacian" of a special kind, not similar, except on broad lines, to the Athlitian of Mount Carmel (Neuville's Phase V). Microliths increase markedly, and bladelet cores are very numerous. A reversal of the endscraper-burin ratio in favor of burins occurs in Level 6, where there are many carinated scrapers, very few other Aurignacian types, and a special burin "on a Clactonian notch" (Newcomer, 1971 and our fig. 12-*17*), as well as many other burins.

This phase seems to be more widespread than was Phase B. Besides Ksar Akil, it occurs at Antelias in Level 2 (Copeland and Hours, 1971), and perhaps at three other sites, all in south Lebanon: (1) Hammam Cave near Damour (Suzuki and Kobori, 1970; their Site 16, fig. 44); (2) Mugharet-el-Abed near Debel (Copeland and Wescombe, 1965, p. 47; see also Suzuki and Kobori, ibid., fig. 45); (3) Bezez Cave near Adlun; here, although little remains *in situ*, the material recovered is quite typical.

In Zone 3, Levels 3 and 2 at Yabrud II seem to have a C phase; burins just outnumber the endscrapers, and proximal, inverse retouch (a Late Aurignacian trait) appears on a developed form of el-Wad Point, now more of a Gravette Point (fig. 12-*16*).

An industry of Phase B or Phase C type has been collected at Saaidé (Level 5c) from below three meters of gravels in a pit dug for a well in the Béqaa, near Baalbek (Besançon and Hours, 1971a); it is heavily patinated and some pieces are rolled, so that its original locus is unknown.

Date

Level 8 at Ksar Akil is dated by C14 to 28,840 B.P. ± 380 years (Vogel and Waterbolk, 1963). This date relates very well with the new dates obtained by Tixier for his levels not far above Ewing's Level 8, but such early dates for a Late Aurignacian pose some problems (J. Tixier, personal communication, 1973).

ENVIRONMENT

Only one Aurignacian site (a small surface scatter) has been found in the mountains (Zone 2), and these were probably uninhabitable during Main Würm, when there was a depression of the snowline by about 600 meters (Butzer, 1964). Tchernov has reported a cold peak at about 22,000 years (Bar-Yosef, personal communication, 1969) on rodent evidence from Palestinian caves, which could not have been much later than the end of the C Phase at Ksar Akil, if the new dates are acceptable.

The scarcity of Aurignacian sites in Zone 1 (in comparison with the large numbers of both Middle Paleolithic and Epipaleolithic sites) may be in part due to the drowning of the coastline at the end of the Ice Age. Caves, which *could* have been occupied by the Aurignacians during the emergence of the coast in the Main Würm regression, have been observed in a line of cliffs below sea level at -25 meters. Freshwater submarine springs are also reported nearby.

Van Liere, in commenting on the sharp decline in the number of Aurignacian sites known in inland Syria, and the absence of open sites, suggests a virtual disappearance of the forest cover in Zone 3 during Main Würm (Van Liere, 1961); even in the Ghab, very low arboreal pollen values frequently obtained between ca. 47,000 and ca. 10,000 years (Niklewski and Van Zeist, 1970).

We await with interest new data from Ksar Akil (Tixier, 1970) which promises to throw light on this complex period of transition to the Epipaleolithic in Lebanon and Syria.

BIBLIOGRAPHY

AKAZAWA, T., 1973. "The Paleolithic Assemblages from the Douara Cave Site, Syria, and Their Relationship to the Prehistory of Western Asia." *Paleorient* 1(2).

ALTEENA, C. O. Van R., 1962. "Molluscs and Echinoderms from Paleolithic Deposits in the Rockshelter of Ksar Akil, Lebanon." *Zoölogische Medeilingen* 38(5).

AZOURY, I., 1971. "A Technological and Typological Analysis of the Transitional and Early Upper Paleolithic Levels of Ksar Akil and Abu Halka." Ph.D. dissertation, University of London.

————, and HODSON, R., 1973. "Comparing Paleolithic Assemblages: Ksar Akil, a Case-Study." *World Archaeology* 4(3):292-306.

BALTY, J.; BALTY, J. C.; and DEWEZ, M., 1970. "Un chantier de recherches archéologiques Belges en Syrie—Apamé sur l'Oronte." *Textes et Documents* 255.

BAR-YOSEF, O., and VANDERMEERSCH, B., 1972. "The Stratigraphical and Cultural Problems of the Passage from Middle to Upper Paleolithic in Palestinian Caves." In *The Origin of Homo Sapiens*, edited by F. Bordes, pp. 221-26. Proceedings of the Paris Symposium, 2-5 September 1969. Paris: UNESCO.

BERGY, A., 1932. "Le Paléolithique ancien stratifié à Ras Beyrouth." *Mélanges de l'Université Saint-Joseph* 16(5):169-216.

BESANCON, J., and HOURS, F., 1968. "Quelques sites préhistoriques nouveaux dans la Béqaa." *Mélanges de l'Université Saint-Joseph* 44(7):77-84.

————, and HOURS, F., 1970*a*. "Une coupe dans le Quaternaire récent, Saaidé I (Béqaa méridionale, Liban)." *Hannon* 5:29-61.

————, and HOURS, F., 1970*b*. "Préhistoire et géomorphologie: les formes du relief et les dépôts quaternaires dans la région de Joub Jannine (Béqaa méridionale, Liban)." *Hannon* 5:63-95.

————, and HOURS, F., 1971. "Préhistoire et géomorphologie: les formes du relief et les dépôts quaternaires dans la région de Joub Jannine (Béqaa méridionale, Liban), 2." *Hannon* 6:29-135.

BINFORD, L., and BINFORD, S., 1966. "A Preliminary Analysis of Functional Variability in the Mousterian of Levallois Facies." *American Anthropologist* special vol. 68(2,2):238-95.

BINFORD, S., 1968. "Early Upper Pleistocene Adaptations in the Levant." *American Anthropologist* 70:707-17.

BORDES, F., 1950. "Principes d'une méthode d'étude des techniques de débitage et de la typologie du Paléolithique ancien et moyen." *L'Anthropologie* 54:19-34.

————, 1955. "Le paléolithique inférieur et moyen de Jabrud (Syrie) et la question du Pré-Aurignacien." *L'Anthropologie* 59:486-507.

————, 1961. *Typologie du Paléolithique ancien et moyen.* Bordeaux: Mémoire 1, Publication de l'Institut de Préhistoire de l'Université de Bordeaux.

————, in press. "Que sont le Pré-Aurignacien et le Yabroudien?" *Stekelis Memorial Volume.*

BRUNNACKER, K., 1970. "Die Sedimente das Schutzdachs I von Jabrud (Syrien)." *Frühe Menschheit und Umwelt (Fundamenta A2)*, pp. 189-98.

BUCCELLATI, G., and BUCCELLATI, M. K., 1967. "Archaeological Survey of the Palmyrene and the Jebel Bishri." *Archaeology* 20:305-6.

BUTZER, K., 1964. *Environment and Archaeology*. London: Methuen.

COON, C., 1957. *Seven Caves*. London: Cape.

COPELAND, L., 1970. "The Early Upper Paleolithic Flint Material from Levels VII-V, Antelias Cave, Lebanon." *Berytus* 19:99-143.

————, in press. "The Middle Paleolithic of Adlun and Ras el-Kelb, Lebanon: First Results from a Study of the Flint Industries." *Bulletin du Musée de Beyrouth*.

————, and HOURS, F., 1971. "The Later Upper Paleolithic Material of Antelias Cave, Lebanon, Levels IV-I." *Berytus* 20:57-138.

————, and WESCOMBE, P., 1965. "Inventory of Stone Age Sites in Lebanon, Part I." *Mélanges de l'Université Saint-Joseph* 41:29-175.

DEWEZ, M., 1970. "Premières observations sur les industries lithiques de Qalaat al-Moudiq." *Annales Archeologiques Arabes Syriennes* 20:127-32.

DORTCH, C., 1970. "The Late Aurignacian Industries of Levels 8-5 at Ksar Akil, Lebanon." Master's thesis, University of London.

EWING, J. F., 1947. "Preliminary Note on the Excavations at the Paleolithic Site of Ksar Akil, Republic of Lebanon." *Antiquity* 21:186-96.

————, 1963. "A Probable Neanderthaloid from Ksar Akil, Lebanon." *American Journal of Physical Anthropology* 21(2):101-4.

————, 1966. "Erratum." *American Journal of Physical Anthropology* 24(2):275.

————, in press. "List of Fossil Men in Lebanon." In *Catalogue of Fossil Hominids*, edited by B. G. Campbell and K. P. Oakley. Volume for Asia, in preparation.

FARRAND, W., 1965. "Geology, Climate and Chronology of Yabroud Rockshelter I." *Annales Archeologiques Arabes Syriennes* 15(1):35-50.

————, 1969. "Geological Correlation of Prehistoric Sites in the Levant." "Symposium on Environmental Changes and the Origin of Modern Man." *UNESCO/INQUA, Paris, 1969*:227-33.

FEVRET, M., and SANLAVILLE, P., 1966. "L'utilisation des Vermets dans la détermination des anciens niveaux marins." *Méditerranée* 4:357-64.

FLEISCH, H., 1946. "Le Levalloisien du niveau +15 m. à Ras Beyrouth (Liban)." *Bulletin de la Société Préhistorique Française* 43:299-301.

————, 1955. "Le rhinocéros de Merck dans la grotte Levalloiso-moustérienne de Ras el-Kelb." *L'Anthropologie* 50:169.

————, 1956. "Dépôts préhistoriques de la côte Libanaise et leur place dans la chronologie basée sur le Quaternaire marin." *Quaternaria* 3:101-32.

————, 1962. "Les stations paléolithiques de montagne du Liban." *Atti del VI Congresso Internationale delle Scienze Preistoria e Protoistoria, Roma* 2:178-86.

————, 1970 (submitted 1964). "Les sables de Beyrouth (Liban) et leurs industries préhistoriques." *Frühe Menschheit und Umwelt (Fundamenta A2)*, pp. 171-80.

————, 1971. "Les habitats du Paléolithique moyen à Naamé (Liban), à paraître." *Bulletin du Musée de Beyrouth* 33:25-93.

————; COMATI, J.; REYNARD, P.; and ELOUARD, P., 1971. "Gisements à *Strombus bubonius* Lmk (Tyrrhénien) à Naamé, Liban." *Quaternaria* 15:217-37.

————and GIGOUT, M., 1966. "Revue de Quaternaire marin Libanais." *Bulletin de la Société Géologique de France* 8(7):10-16.

————; REMIRO, J.; and SANLAVILLE, P., 1969. "Gisements préhistoriques découverts dans la région de Batroun (Liban)." *Mélanges de l'Université Saint-Joseph* 45:1-27.

————, and SANLAVILLE, P., 1967. "Nouveaux gisements de *Strombus bubonius* Lmk au Liban." *Comptes rendus de la Société Géologique de France* 5:207-8.

————, and SANLAVILLE, P., 1969. "Vues nouvelles sur Ras Beyrouth, Liban." *Résumés de Communications, 8th INQUA Congress, Paris, 1969*, p. 196.

GARROD, D., 1930. "The Paleolithic of Southern Kurdistan." *Bulletin of the American School of Prehistoric Research* 6:9-43.

————, 1951. "A Transitional Industry from the Base of the Upper Paleolithic in Palestine and Syria." *Journal of the Royal Anthropological Institute* 81:121-29.

————, 1954. "Excavations at the Mugharet el-Kebara, Mount Carmel, 1931: The Aurignacian Industries." *Proceedings of the Prehistoric Society* 20(2):155-92.

————, 1955. "The Mugharet el-Emireh in Lower Galilee; Type Station of the Emiran Industry." *Journal of the Royal Anthropological Institute* 85:141-62.

————, 1962. "The Middle Paleolithic of the Near East and the Problem of Mount Carmel Man." *Journal of the Royal Anthropological Institute* 92:232-51.

————, 1966. "Mugharet el-Bezez, Adlun; Interim Report, July 1965." *Bulletin du Musée de Beyrouth* 19:5-9.

————, and BATE, D., 1937. *The Stone Age of Mount Carmel*, vol. 1. Oxford: Clarendon Press.

————, and HENRI-MARTIN, G., 1961. "Rapport préliminaire sur la fouille d'une grotte au Ras el-Kelb, Liban." *Bulletin du Musée de Beyrouth* 16:61-67.

————, and KIRKBRIDE, D., 1961. "Excavation of Abri Zumoffen, a Palaeolithic Rockshelter near Adlun, in South Lebanon, 1958." *Bulletin du Musée de Beyrouth* 16:7-46.

GAUTIER, A., 1970. "The Fauna of Masloukh." *Bulletin du Musée de Beyrouth* 23:135-36.

GOLDBERG, P., 1969. "Sediment Analysis of Jerf 'Ajla and Yabroud Rock Shelters, Syria." *Résumé de Communications, 8th INQUA Congress, Paris, 1969*, p. 279.

HALLER, J., 1941. "Notes de préhistoire phénicienne: le gisement levalloisien d'Amrit." *Bulletin du Musée de Beyrouth* 5:31-33.

————, 1941-43. "Notes de préhistoire phénicienne: L'Abri d'Abou Halka (Tripoli)." *Bulletin du Musée de Beyrouth* 6:1-20.

de HEINZELIN, J., 1966. "Révision du Site de Yabroud." *Annales Archeologiques Arabes Syriennes* 16(2):157-65.

HOOIJER, D., 1961. "The Fossil Vertebrates of Ksar Akil, a Paleolithic Rockshelter in Lebanon." *Zoologische Verhandelingen* 49:1-67.

————, 1966. "The *Dicerorhinus hemitoechus* (Falconer) at Yabroud." *Annales Archeologiques Arabes Syriennes* 16(2):155-56.

HOURS, F., 1962. "Le gisement de Michmiche: mélange ou industrie de transition?" *Atti del VI Congresso Internationale delle Scienze Preistoria e Protoistoria, Roma* 2:187-98.

————, 1973. "Le peuplement de la montagne Libanaise durant le Würm; essai de paléogéographie." *Mélanges André Leroi-Gourhan.*

————; COPELAND, L.; and AURENCHE, O., 1973. "Les industries paléolithiques du Proche-Orient, essai de corre-lation." *L'Anthropologie* 77(3-4):229-80.

————, and SOLECKI, R. (eds.), forthcoming. *Proceedings of a Symposium on the Terminology of the Paleolithic of the Levant.*

JELINEK, A., 1969a. "New Excavations at et-Tabun, Israel." Paper read at 8th INQUA Congress, Paris, 1969.

————, 1969b. In "Notes and News; Excavations at Tabun." *Israel Exploration Journal* 19(2):114.

————; FARRAND, W.; HAAS, G.; HOROWITZ, A.; and GOLDBERG, P., 1973. "New Excavations at the Tabun Cave, Mount Carmel, Israel, 1967-1972: A Preliminary Report." *Paleorient* 1(2).

KIETH, A., and McCOWN, T., 1939. *The Stone Age of Mount Carmel*, vol. 2. Oxford: University Press.

KOKTEN, K., 1963. "Die Stellung von Karaïn Innerhalb der Turkischen Vorgeschichte." *Anatolia* 7:59-86.

LEHMANN, U., 1970. "Die Tierreste aus den höhlen von Jabrud (Syrien)." *Frühe Menscheit und Umwelt (Fundamenta A2)*, p. 181.

LEROI-GOURHAN, A., 1971. "Pollens et terrasses marines au Liban." *Quaternaria* 15:249-60.

de LUMLEY, H., 1969. *Le paléolithique inférieur et moyen du Midi Méditerranéen dans son cadre géologique* 1. Paris: CNRS.

McBURNEY, C., 1967. *The Haua Fteah (Cyrenaica) and the Stone Age of the Southeast Mediterranean*. Cambridge: At the University Press.

MOUTERDE, P., 1954. "Les zones de végétation en Syrie et au Liban." *Rapports et Communication 7, 8th Congress Internationale Botanique*, pp. 103-5.

MURPHY, J., 1939. *The Method of Prehistoric Excavation at Ksar Akil*. Boston College Anthropology Series 3.

NEUVILLE, R., 1951. *Le Paléolithique et le Mésolithique du Désert de Judée*. Archives de l'Institut de Paléontologie humaine, mémoire 24.

NEWCOMER, M., 1970. "The Chamfered Pieces from Ksar Akil (Lebanon)." *Bulletin of the Institute of Archaeology, University of London* 8-9:177-91.

————, 1971. "Un nouveau type de burin à Ksar Akil (Liban)." *Bulletin de la Société Préhistorique Française* 68:267-72.

————, 1972. "Analysis of a Series of Burins from Ksar Akil (Lebanon)." Ph.D. dissertation, University of London.

————, and HODSON, R., 1973. "Constellation Analysis of Burins from Ksar Akil." In *Archaeological Theory and Practice, Grimes Memorial Volume*, edited by D. E. Strong, pp. 87-104. London: Seminar Press.

NIKLEWSKI, J., and VAN ZEIST, W., 1970. "A Late Quaternary Pollen Diagram from Northwestern Syria." *Acta Botanica Neerlandica* 19(5):737-54.

PERKINS, D., Jr., 1968. "The Pleistocene Fauna from the Yabrudian Rockshelters." *Annales Archeologiques Arabes Syriennes* 1-2:123-30.

PERROT, J., 1968. "La préhistoire palestinienne." In *Supplément au Dictionnaire de la Bible* 8(43):286-446. Paris: Letouzey et Ane.

RUST, A., 1950. *Die Höhlenfunde von Jabrud (Syrien)*. Neümunster: Karl Wachholtz.

SANLAVILLE, P., 1969a. "Sur le tyrrhenien libanais." *Résumés de Communications, 8th Congress INQUA, Paris, 1969*, p. 243.

————, 1969b. "Les bas niveaux marins pleistocènes du Liban." *Méditerranée* 3:257-92.

————, 1971. "Sur le tyrrhenien libanais." *Quaternaria* 15:239-48.

————, 1973. "Étude géomorphologique de la région littorale du Liban." French State Doctoral Dissertation.

SCHROEDER, B., 1966. "The Lithic Material from Jerf 'Ajla: A Preliminary Report." *Annales Archeologiques Arabes Syriennes* 16(2):201-10.

————, 1969a. "The Lithic Industries from Jerf 'Ajla and their Bearing on the Problem of a Middle to Upper Paleolithic Transition." Ph.D. dissertation, Columbia University. Ann Arbor: University Microfilms.

————, 1969b. "The Paleolithic Industries from the Syrian Desert Cave of Jerf 'Ajla." *Résumés de Communications, 8th INQUA Congress, Paris, 1969*, p. 377.

————, 1970. "A Prehistoric Survey of the Northern Béqaa Valley." *Bulletin du Musée de Beyrouth* 23:193-204.

SENYUREK, M., 1958. "Test Excavation Made in a Cave in the Vicinity of Samandag in 1958: Preliminary Report." *Anatolia* 3:64-70.

————, and BOSTANCI, E., 1958a. "Prehistoric Researches in the Hatay Province." *Belleten* 22:147-69.

————, and BOSTANCI, E., 1958b. "The Paleolithic Cultures of the Hatay Province." *Belleten* 22:191-210.

SKINNER, JAMES, 1965. "The Flake Industries of Southwest Asia: A Typological Study." Ph.D. dissertation, Columbia University. Ann Arbor: University Microfilms.

————, 1970. "El-Masloukh, A Yabroudian Site in Lebanon." *Bulletin du Musée de Beyrouth* 23:143-72.

SOLECKI, R. S., 1970a. "Summary Report of the Columbia University Prehistoric Investigations in Lebanon, Season 1969." *Bulletin du Musée de Beyrouth* 23:97-128.

————, 1970b. "A Sketch of the Columbia University Archaeological Investigations at Yabroud (Syria)." *Frühe Menschheit und Umwelt (Fundamenta A2)*, pp. 199-212.

————, and SOLECKI, R. L., 1966. "New Data from Yabroud, Syria: Preliminary Report of the Columbia University Archaeological Investigations." *Annales Archeologiques Arabes Syriennes* 16(2):121-54.

————, and SOLECKI, R. L., 1970. "A New Secondary Flaking Technique at the Nahr Ibrahim Cave Site, Lebanon." *Bulletin du Musée de Beyrouth* 23:137-42.

de SONNEVILLE-BORDES, D., 1956. "Paléolithique supérieur et Mésolithique à Jabrud (Syrie)." *L'Anthropologie* 60:71-83.

————, and PERROT, J., 1956 et seq. "Lexique typologique du paléolithique supérieur." *Bulletin de la Société Préhistorique Française* 51, 52, and 53.

STEARNS, C., 1970. "Observations on the Mughara el-Asfurieh and on the Littoral between Halat and Amchit (region of Jbail)." *Bulletin du Musée de Beyrouth* 23:129-34.

————, and THURBER, D., 1965. "Th^{230}-U^{234} Dates of Late Pleistocene Marine Fossils from the Mediterranean and Moroccan Littorals." *Quaternaria* 7:29.

SUZUKI, H., and KOBORI, I. (eds.), 1970. *Report of the Reconnaissance Survey on Paleolithic Sites in Lebanon and Syria*. Bulletin No. 1, University Museum, University of Tokyo.

————, and TAKAI, F., 1970. *The Amud Man and His Cave Site*. Tokyo: University of Tokyo.

————, and TAKAI, F. (eds.), 1973. *The Palaeolithic Site at Douara Cave, in Syria, Part I*. Bulletin No. 5, University Museum, University of Tokyo.

TAVANI, G., 1958. "Note sulle Sabbie Marine Antiche e Attuale di Samandag." *Belleten* 22.

TIXIER, J., 1970. "L'abri-sous-roche de Ksar Akil: Rapport préliminaire sur le campagne 1969." *Bulletin du Musée de Beyrouth* 23:173-91.

TURVILLE-PETRE, F., 1927. *Researches in Prehistoric Galilee (1925-1926), and a Report on the Galilee Skull*. Bulletin of the British School of Archaeology in Jerusalem No. 14.

VALLOIS, H., 1962. "La dent humaine levalloiso-moustérienne de Ras el-Kelb, Liban." In *Folia Primatologica, vol. Jub. Prof. A. Schultz*, p. 155. Basel and New York: Karger.

VANDERMEERSCH, B., 1966. "Nouvelles découvertes de restes humains dans les couches levalloiso-moustérienne du gisement de Qafzeh (Israel)." *Comptes rendus des Séances de l'Académie des Sciences* 262:1434-36.

VAN LIERE, W., 1961. "Observations on the Quaternary of Syria." *Berichten von de Rijkdienst voor het Oudheidkundig Bodemonderzoek* 10-11:1-69.

————, 1966. "The Pleistocene and Stone Age of the Orontes River (Syria)." *Annales Archeologiques Arabes Syriennes* 16(2):7-30.

VOGEL, J., and WATERBOLK, H., 1963. "Groningen Radiocarbon Dates." *Radiocarbon* 5:173-74.

WATANABE, H., 1964. "Les éclats et lames à chanfrein et la technique de fracturation transversale dans un horizon paléolithique en Palestine." *Bulletin de la Société Préhistorique Française, Compte rendus des Séances*, pp. 84-88.

————, 1970. "The Excavation of the Keoue Cave, Lebanon. Interim Report, June, 1971." *Bulletin du Musée de Beyrouth* 23:205-14.

WETZEL, R., and HALLER, J., 1945-48. "Le quaternaire côtier de la région de Tripoli (Liban)." *Notes et Mémoires (Beyrouth)* 4:1-49.

WRESCHNER, E., 1967. "The Geula Caves, Mount Carmel." *Quaternaria* 9:69-90.

WRIGHT, H. E., 1951. "Geological Setting of Ksar Akil, a Paleolithic Site in Lebanon: Preliminary Report." *Journal Near-Eastern Studies* 1:115-22.

————, 1962. "Late Pleistocene Geology of Coastal Lebanon." *Quaternaria* 6:525-39.

ZEUNER, F., 1957. "Stone Age Exploration in Jourdan I." *Palestine Exploration Quarterly*.

————; CORNWALL, I.; and KIRKBRIDE, D., 1961. "The Shoreline Chronology of the Palaeolithic of the Abri Zumoffen Rockshelter near Adlun, South Lebanon." *Bulletin du Musé de Beyrouth* 16:49-60.

ZUMOFFEN, G., 1900. *La Phénicie avant les Phéniciens. L'âge de la pierre*. Beirut: Imprimerie Catholique.

AN OUTLINE OF PREHISTORIC OCCURRENCES AND CHRONOLOGY IN THE CENTRAL NEGEV, ISRAEL

Anthony E. Marks

Southern Methodist University

INTRODUCTION

The Central Negev of Israel is situated between the Beersheva Plain and the Paran Desert (fig. 1). It consists of some 2,000 sq km of high ground (500 m to 1,021 m) which have been strongly eroded, while much of the surface soil cover has been removed by aeolean action. Today, it is semi-desert receiving between 50 mm and 200 mm a year precipitation during the winter months, although considerable fluctuation occurs in absolute precipitation from year to year. Since Byzantine times, the area has been very sparsely inhabited by Bedouins and, more recently, by Israelis. This paucity of occupation makes the Central Negev an ideal area for prehistoric studies, as the only significant disturbance of the countryside has taken place in the wadi bottoms which were terraced in Historic times.

Prehistoric investigations of the area are at best in an early formative period. Prior to 1969 only very limited exploration had been undertaken, mainly unsystematic survey supplemented by occasional surface collections (Glueck, 1953; Anati, 1963; Yizraeli, 1967; Stekelis, 1948). This work merely documented the presence of some Middle Paleolithic and Epipaleolithic occurrences without providing sufficient data to define clearly the nature of either. It must be pointed out, however, that both logistic and security considerations made even this much work difficult. Since 1967 these problems have become less intense, permitting long term, systematic prehistoric investigations, and in 1969 Southern Methodist University began such a project. Since then four long field seasons have been carried out, resulting in the systematic survey of 65 sq km, the recording of 58 prehistoric sites, the systematic collection of 44 surface sites, and the extensive excavation or testing of 9 sites with significant *in situ* deposits. This work was undertaken in two discontinuous geographic blocks, one of 15 sq km in the Har Harif and the other of 50 sq km in the Avdat/Aqev region (fig. 2). These regions cannot be considered typical for the Central Negev, as the Har Harif has the highest elevations in the Negev (900 m to 1,021 m), while there are five perennial springs in the Avdat/Aqev area, four of which fell within the survey zone. Both these situations are in contrast with the Central Negev generally, where elevations rarely exceed 900 m, and where perennial springs are few. Thus, the view presented here is derived from specific regions which were probably most favorable for prehistoric man, and the observations on settlement density, site size, and intrasite complexity should not be considered predictive for the whole of the Central Negev.

While much field work and laboratory analysis is already completed, some is yet to be undertaken, including the excavation of two important sites. Therefore, there will most probably be need for some minor revisions of this outline after all work is completed.

Sites were located which can be attributed to all major prehistoric periods: Lower Paleolithic, Upper Paleolithic, Epipaleolithic, and Neolithic. Within the two geographic areas, however, these are not equally represented, even considering their absolute size differences (Table 1). In spite of these marked variations in the occurrence of sites by periods, and differences in settlement patterns, an overall view of the prehistoric occupations may be presented.

LOWER PALEOLITHIC

Lower Paleolithic occurrences are restricted to the Avdat/Aqev zone, and even there they are quite poor. At two localities there are very sparse scatters of large unfinished bifaces, biface thinning flakes, biface fragments, and non-Levallois flakes, within larger concentrations of hamada. Density of artifact concentration is so low at each that reasonable samples could not be obtained. The third locality, on the Sde Boker plain, consists of an area of ca. one sq km over which a very thin scatter of generally small bifaces, Levallois flakes, points, and cores, as well as non-Levallois debitage appears to be deflating from fine aeolean sediments. No concentration was located, although collections by various amateur archaeologists had been going on for some time, which probably had a serious effect on horizontal distributions. On this weak evidence, it seems that at least two Lower Paleolithic aspects were present in the Central Negev; one with large bifaces without Levallois method present and another of generally small bifaces associated with a very fine Levallois method. This latter aspect appears broadly similar to that recovered from the coastal Negev (Ronen et al., 1972). In short, while it is possible to document some Lower Paleolithic occupation of the Avdat/Aqev area, both the condition of the localities and the extremely low artifactual density at each make more detailed definition of questionable utility.

MIDDLE PALEOLITHIC

Again, Middle Paleolithic sites are restricted to the Avdat/Aqev zone, although a very few Levallois flakes and cores were found widely scattered on the Har Harif plateau (Marks et al., 1972). In the Avdat/Aqev area, Middle Paleolithic sites can be divided into three groups: those which probably functioned as workshops, those which were primarily camp sites, and those where both workshop and

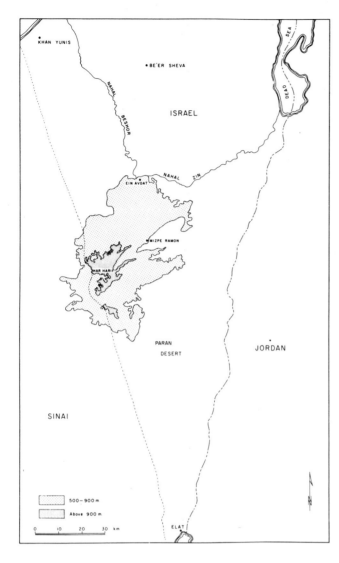

FIG. 1—The Negev, showing the Central Highlands.

camp site activities may have been rather evenly balanced. Workshops, which are always spatially associated with flint outcrops, have many large Levallois cores in various stages of production and much primary debitage, but extremely few retouched tools and complete Levallois flakes, blades, and points. Tools are usually either typologically atypical or broken during manufacture. Camp sites, while not nearly as common as workshops, are spatially associated with fossil springs and have many exhausted, unclassifiable cores, few typical Levallois cores, many unretouched or lightly retouched Levallois pieces, and numbers of other retouched tools. These sites, unlike the workshops, are characterized by generally thin debitage, indicative of extensive core reduction. The third group of sites tend to be spatially associated with both fossil springs and raw material sources. Their assemblages show characteristics which include a combination of good Levallois cores, Levallois pieces, and retouched tools, as well as a balance between thin and thick flake debitage.

There is a clear functional interrelationship between the workshops and the camp sites, as only combined do they

TABLE 1
PREHISTORIC SITES BY PERIOD AND ZONE

Period	Avdat/Aqev	Har Harif
Neolithic (Pre-Pottery)	1	1 (?)
Epipaleolithic	2	18
Upper Paleolithic	12	2
Middle Paleolithic	19	0
Lower Paleolithic	3 *	0
Totals	37	21

* Two of these sites were just outside the zone of systematic survey.

represent the full range flaking processes apparently used during core reduction.

The Middle Paleolithic of the Central Negev may be broadly classified typologically as a Mousterian of Levallois facies. Technologically, it is characterized by a strong tendency toward bidirectional and unidirectional core preparation, which resulted in the production of a high proportion of Levallois blades and points, a number of which are quite elongated, as well as some true blades and even bladelets (Marks and Crew, 1973). These traits, as well as typological considerations, link the Central Negev Mousterian with that known from Tabun, Level D (Jelinek et al., 1973). In addition, what has been referred to as the Nahr Ibrahim technique of flake modification is very prevalent (Solecki and Solecki, 1970).

Typologically, sidescrapers are rare, as are all other "typical" Middle Paleolithic tools. Burins, on the other hand, are fairly common and include a wide variety of types, although single examples on snap, single blow notch (Adlun type), or truncation are most common. Endscrapers, naturally backed knives, denticulates, and notched pieces occur in some number, but backed pieces are almost totally absent (fig. 3). It should be noted, however, that the prevalence of naturally backed knives may well reflect merely the bidirectional and unidirectional tendency in core preparation, rather than any intentional tool form.

Only a single Mousterian site, Rosh Ein Mor, contained faunal materials, and these were restricted to ostrich egg shell and what appears to be the remains of a single *Equus hemionus*. Two sites, Rosh Ein Mor and D35, produced pollen spectra which clearly indicate the presence, during this Middle Paleolithic occupation, of a rich Mediterranean environment (Horowitz, personal communication).

Mousterian sites show the widest locational distribution for any prehistoric period, although the majority cluster around raw material and/or water sources.

UPPER PALEOLITHIC

Upper Paleolithic sites occur in both the Avdat/Aqev and Har Harif zones. Only two were located in the Har Harif, both fairly scattered surface concentrations, while a much larger number were found in the Avdat/Aqev area, of which many were either still *in situ* or very recently deflated. Studies of these latter assemblages indicate extremely heterogeneous typological association (Marks et al., 1971; Marks and Ferring, in press). In spite of this, it

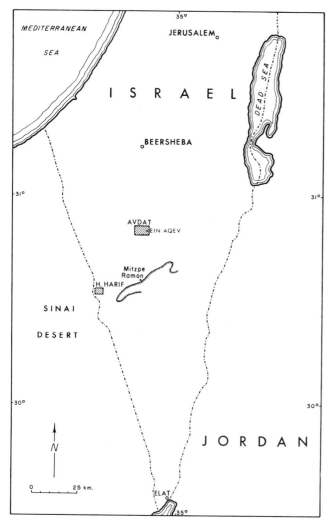

FIG. 2—The Negev, showing areas of systematic survey.

appears that these assemblages broadly correspond to the range of Upper Paleolithic assemblages traditionally called U. P. III through U. P. V for Palestine (Neuville, 1934; Garrod, 1962). Given the problems with this developmental sequence, it is prudent to recognize only two stages of Upper Paleolithic assemblages in the Central Negev: a Levantine Upper Paleolithic and a Late Levantine Upper Paleolithic. The Levantine Upper Paleolithic in the Avdat/Aqev area includes a series of assemblages which, while different, all share moderate amounts of polyhedric burins, thick scrapers, a tendency toward a proportionately low occurrence of blade tools, and a rarity of backed tools (fig. 4). Within this group, however, occurs one site, Sde Divshon, with a significant percentage of el Wad points.

Late Levantine Upper Paleolithic assemblages are characterized by variable occurrences of carinated tool forms (at times extremely high), a tendency for a rather high proportional utilization of blades and bladelets in tool production, and a common use of backing, Ouchtata retouch, or semi-steep inverse retouch on blades or bladelets (fig. 5).

While no faunal remains have been recovered from the Levantine Upper Paleolithic sites, pollen spectra from three

sites indicate a developed Mediterranean environment, only somewhat drier than that which pertained during the Mousterian (Horowitz, personal communication).

Some fauna has been found at a Late Levantine Upper Paleolithic site, including *Equus* sp., *Capra* sp., *Gazella* sp., and *Lepus europa*. While these forms are not particularly diagnostic of any particular environmental setting, pollen from two Late Levantine Upper Paleolithic sites indicates a climatic deterioration, resulting in a steppic environment with only a scattering of trees.

This climatic shift between the Levantine Upper Paleolithic and Late Upper Paleolithic is reflected in respective settlement locations. The earlier sites are situated on the edges of the Divshon plain, while the later sites are found within the Nahals Zin and Aqev, in close proximity to the extant fossil springs. One of these later sites, Ein Aqev, is of particular interest as it contained both two basalt grinding stones and numbers of shells from the Mediterranean, some of which were covered with ochre. As these materials are exotic to the Avdat/Aqev area, they indicate either a wide seasonal round or, perhaps, some form of exchange between areas.

EPIPALEOLITHIC

It is possible to place some Negev Epipaleolithic assemblages into industry groups which have been defined already for the northern Levant. On this basis the Central Negev contains four Epipaleolithic industries: a Negev Variant of the Kebaran, a Geometric Kebaran "A," a Natufian, and an apparently local southern industry, the Harifian (Marks, in press).

The Negev Variant of the Kebaran is known from a number of surface sites in the Har Harif. While it is typologically Kebaran in a general sense, a number of features separate it from the northern Kebaran: the absence of spikelike points; the tendency for concave backing associated with convex oblique truncations in short, wide scalene bladelets; the use of a purposeful microburin technique; and the presence of small numbers of lunates and other microliths with Helwan backing (fig. 6). Sites are small with relatively low artifactual densities, and all are situated on the highest available ground.

The Geometric Kebaran "A" is known only from one site in the Avdat/Aqev area. While it is a small site, the artifactual density is very high and it is situated within the Nahal Zin, in a position comparable to those of the late Upper Paleolithic. It is characterized by large numbers of trapezes and rectangles, backed and truncated bladelet fragments and scrapers. There is no microburin technique, Helwan retouch, or lunates, and even arch backed bladelets are extremely rare (fig. 7).

While faunal material was sparse, it included *Capra* sp. and a few dentalium shells from the Mediterranean. In addition, a small amount of red ochre was recovered.

Natufian occupation occurred in both the Har Harif and the Avdat/Aqev areas. In both, a single large Natufian site was located: Rosh Zin, of some 800 sq m in Avdat/Aqev (Henry, 1973a); and Rosh Horesha, with some 7,000 sq m

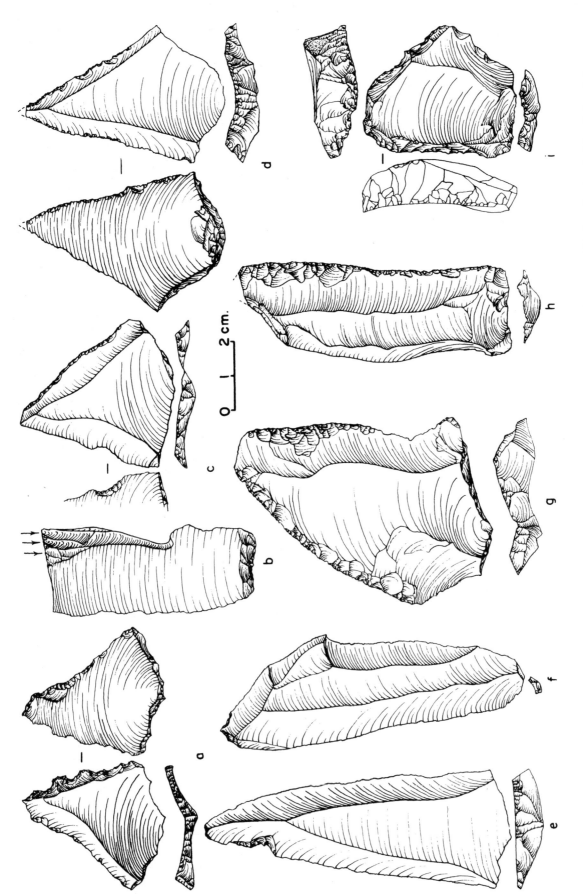

FIG. 3.—Middle Paleolithic Artifacts from Site Rosh Ein Mor: *a*, denticulated Levallois point; *b*, burin on basally truncated blade; *c,d*, retouched Levallois points; *e*, notched Levallois point; *f*, Levallois blade; *g*, converging convex sidescraper; *h*, straight sidescraper on Levallois blade; *i*, endscraper.

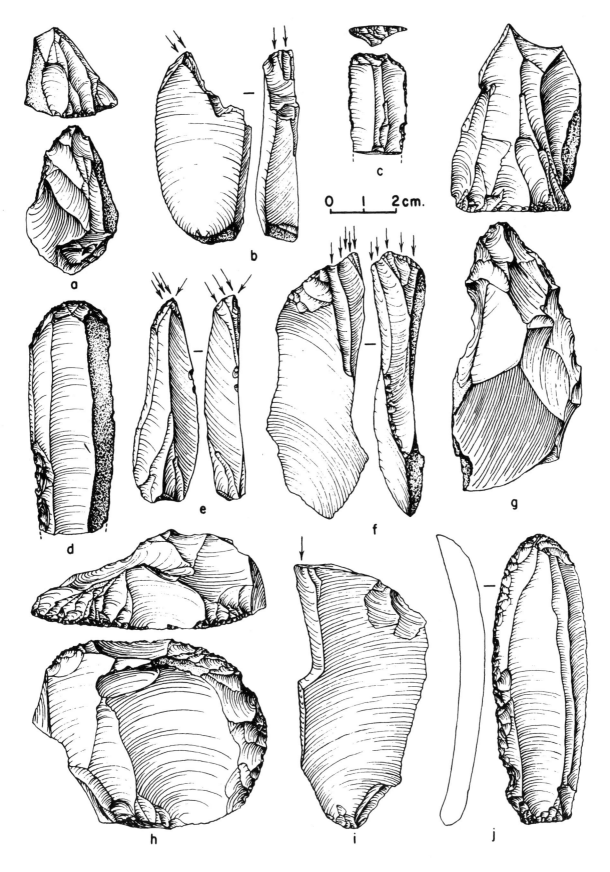

FIG. 4–Upper Paleolithic Artifacts from Site D-27A: *a-g*, carinated scrapers; *b,e,f,i*, burins; *c*, truncated blade; *d,h,j*, endscrapers.

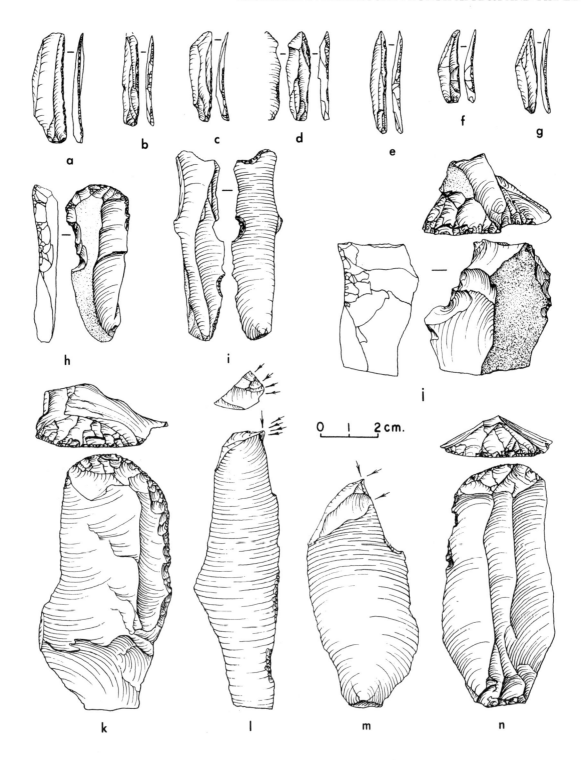

FIG. 5—Late Upper Paleolithic Artifacts from Site Ein Aqev East: *a-g*, bladelets with Ouchtata retouch; *h*, endscraper on notch; *i*, multiple notched piece; *j*, carinated scraper; *k,n*, endscrapers; *l-m*, burins.

of *in situ* deposits in the Har Harif (Marks, in press). Both contain clear architecture, consisting of circular to oval rooms with uncut boulder walls.

At Rosh Zin, four adjoining structures were excavated, as well as a stratigraphically earlier stone pavement. During the same period as the room construction, a 1.3 m stone column of bedrock was placed upright inside one of the rooms, the foundation for it cutting through the pavement, while the pillar was held in place by a packing of large cobbles. In this fill was found a "cache" or "offering" of a number of very large blade cores and a matched pair of grooved stones. As these occurred in the pillar packing and under a wall foundation, it is most likely that an offering of some sort was involved. Rosh Zin also contained a sizable number of bedrock mortars, ground stone, faunal remains, shells from both the Mediterranean and Red Seas, ochre,

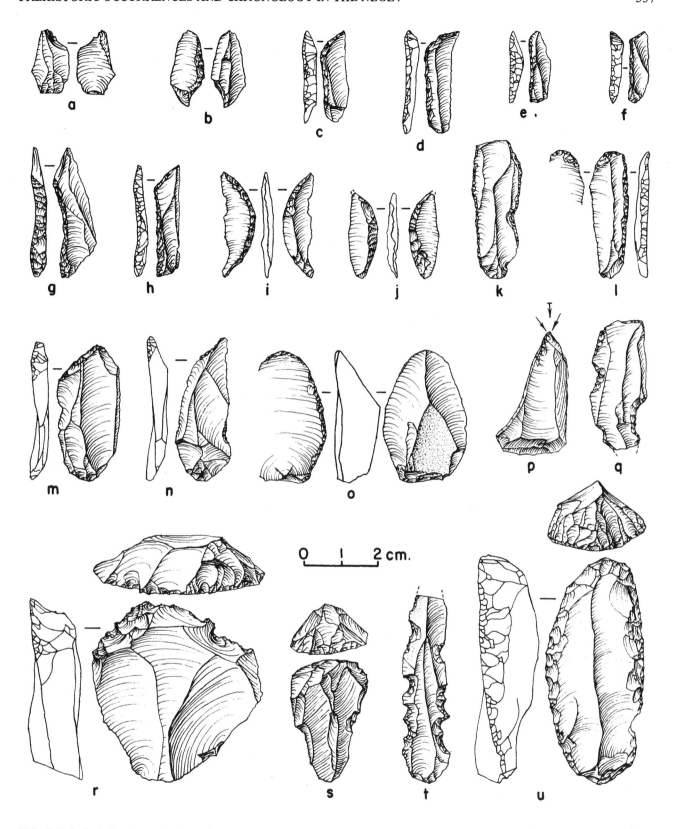

FIG. 6—Epipaleolithic (Negev Variant of the Kebaran) Artifacts from Site K7: *a,b*, microburins; *c-f,h*, scalene bladelets; *g*, La Mouillah point; *i-j*, Helwan lunates; *k,o*, retouched pieces; *l*, backed microlith; *m-n*, truncations; *p*, burin; *q,t*, multiple notched blades; *r-s,u*, various scrapers.

and a number of decorated ostrich egg shell fragments.

Rosh Horesha occurs in a wadi system, low in the Har Harif topography. Its size is amazing considering the ex-

treme artifactual density encountered all across it. To date, it has only been tested; but two structures have been located and a huge chipped stone artifact sample obtained,

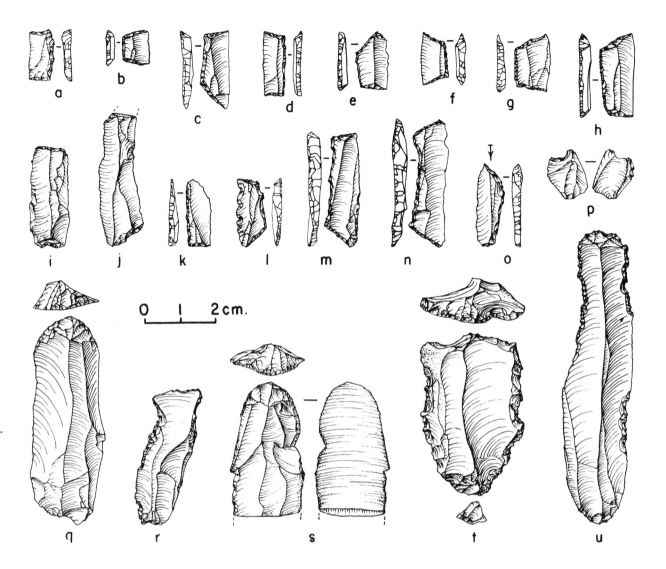

FIG. 7—Epipaleolithic (Geometric Kebaran A) Artifacts from Site D5: *a-h,l*, geometric microliths; *i-j*, truncations; *k*, backed and truncated bladelet; *m-o*, backed and double truncated bladelets; *p*, microburin; *q,s-u*, scrapers [*s* has bilateral sheen]; *r*, retouched bladelet.

as well as ground stone, rare bone tools, ochre, faunal materials, and shells from both the Mediterranean and Red Seas.

Typologically and technologically both sites are homogeneous. They are a Natufian without Helwan technique but with a very high microburin content. In all other ways, they are typically Natufian, although a number of sickle blades from both sites are without secondary retouch (fig. 8).

Faunal materials were recovered in abundance. The main megafauna hunted were gazelle and wild goat, although onager occurs at Rosh Horesha, and *Dama mesopotamica* is present at Rosh Zin. Other faunal material includes hare, rodents, a small carnivore, bird, and numerous mandibles of the large lizard, *Agama stellio*.

The last assemblage group, the Harifian, is known only from the Har Harif (Marks et al., 1972) and has recently been noted as well in northern Sinai (Bar-Yosef, personal communication). In the Har Harif it is known from four sites: three villages and a small campsite. These villages are

on the highest ground of the Har Harif plateau, while the camp is some 100 m lower within a wadi system. Only one of the villages has significant amounts of material still *in situ*. It covers an area of some 3,000 sq m and within the 214 sq m which are now in the process of excavation, eight circular to oval structures and two trash pits have been uncovered. The lithic assemblage (fig. 9) differs markedly from that of the Natufian in the rarity of burins, the large numbers of endscrapers, the presence of only minute lunates and triangles, and the large numbers of the special Harif point which is backed and has either a stemmed or triangular base (Marks, 1973). Other artifacts include ground stone, many shells from both the Mediterranean and Red Seas, ochre, a few pieces of malachite, a few bone tools, and a single piece of incised bone. Faunal remains are comparable to those from Natufian sites, although deer is missing and bird bones are somewhat more common.

Only a single Neolithic site was located in each area. That in the Har Harif is badly scattered and, because the sample was small, cannot be firmly placed into any particu-

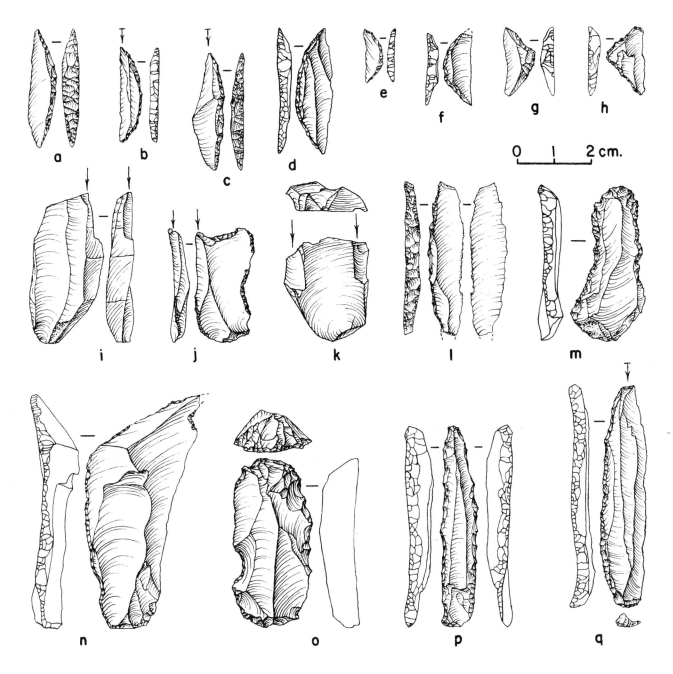

FIG. 8—Epipaleolithic (Natufian) Artifacts from Site G7: *a-h*, geometrics; *i-k*, burins; *l*, sickle blade; *m,o*, endscrapers; *n,q*, backed pieces; *p*, double backed perforator.

lar Neolithic group. That in the Avdat/Aqev area is clearly a Pre-Pottery Neolithic "B" hunting camp. It consists of a number of firepits without associated architecture. Artifacts are heavily weighted toward points, serrated blades, and burins. No sickleblades were found and the only ground stone are those with grooves. Faunal material is all of wild forms: gazelle, cattle, goat and *Dama mesopotamica*. No other nonlithic artifacts were recovered.

RELATIVE AND ABSOLUTE CHRONOLOGY

Because of the absence of caves or rockshelters within the two areas of investigation, no site was located which contained any long multi-industrial stratigraphic sequence, although a few open sites exhibited considerable depth of deposit of the same industry. Cross assemblage serration even by geological criteria was usually impossible, because of the generally limited horizontal extension of most archaeologically associated deposits. Thus, the relative chronological placement of the various assemblages has been carried out by reference to the relative sequence established for northern Israel. This, of course, permits only a very generalized sequence to be established, both because of the problems of specific assemblage comparison with those in northern Israel and because of the existing weaknesses in the relative sequence in the north. Thus, every effort was made to obtain radiocarbon dates. A certain

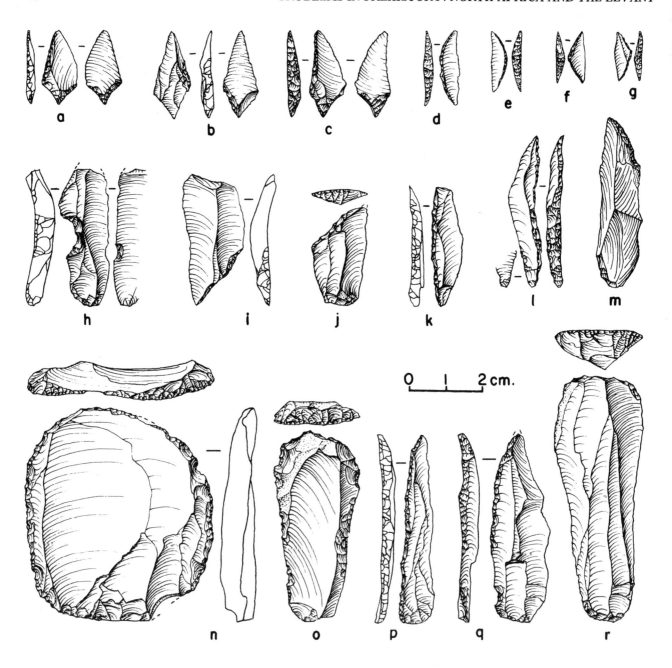

FIG. 9—Epipaleolithic (Harifian) Artifacts from Site G8: *a-c*, Harif points; *d-g*, geometrics; *k*, notched bladelet; *i-j*, truncations; *k-m* ,*p-q*, backed pieces; *n-o,r*, endscrapers.

degree of success was achieved, although additional dated assemblages are clearly needed before the details of the Central Negev chronology can be established. Those dates obtained, however, certainly confirm synchroneity with the assumed dating for major periods in northern Israel and, when dates in the north are available, clearly show that the Central Negev rarely exhibits any "time lag" in comparison with the northern sequence (Table 2).

While certain problems appear in the dating of a few sites, for the most part the dates are internally consistent. Some considerations are necessary, however.

The dates from the Mousterian site of Rosh Ein Mor were obtained from ostrich egg shell. While shell may acquire older carbonates from the surrounding limestone

bedrock, the dates of greater than 50,000 B.P. and greater than 44,000 B.P. are consistent with the assemblage's similarity to that in Tabun, Level D, while the rich Mediterranean environment in the Central Negev correlates with the peak cold period in the Carmel which, again, occurs during the deposition of Tabun D (Jelinek et al., in press). Thus, these dates seem fully acceptable and indicate that the Central Negev Mousterian is early in the Levalloiso-Mousterian complex.

There is clearly a major gap in the radiometric controls in that no dates are available from the main period of Upper Paleolithic occupation. The radiometric age of Ein Aqev, late in the Upper Paleolithic period, must be accepted, because of the number of overlapping radio-

TABLE 2
RADIOCARBON DATES FROM PREHISTORIC SITES IN THE CENTRAL NEGEV

Period	Industry	Site	Date and Lab No.
Neolithic	Pre-Pottery Neolithic "B"	Nahal Divshon (D1)	6,200 B.C. ± 180 years (Tx-1123)
			6,670 B.C. ± 140 years (I-5501)
			6,950 B.C. ± 180 years (SMU-3)
Epipaleolithic	Harifian	Adu Salem (G12)	8,020 B.C. ± 150 years (I-5498)
			8,280 B.C. ± 150 years (I-5499)
			8,280 B.C. ± 150 years (I-5500)
	Natufian	Rosh Horesha (G7)	8,540 B.C. ± 430 years (SMU-9)
			8,930 B.C. ± 280 years (SMU-10)
			11,140 B.C. ± 200 years (I-5496)
	Geometric Kebaran "A"	D5	11,220 B.C. ± 230 years (I-5497)
			13,870 B.C. ± 1,730 years (Tx-1121)
			16,890 B.C. ± 680 years (SMU-7)
Upper Paleolithic	Late Levantine Upper Paleolithic	Ein Aqev (D31)	14,950 B.C. ± 250 years (I-5494)
			15,440 B.C. ± 560 years (SMU-8)
			15,560 B.C. ± 290 years (I-5495)
			15,940 B.C. ± 600 years (SMU-6)
			18,030 B.C. ± 1,200 years (SMU-5)
Middle Paleolithic	Levantine Mousterian	Rosh Ein Mor (D15)	>37,000 B.P. (Tx-1119)
			>44,000 B.P. (Pta-543)
			>50,000 B.P. (Pta-546)

carbon dates. The single date of 18,030 B.C. ± 1,200 years appears aberrant, although it too overlaps with the others at two sigma.

The dating of Ein Aqev does pose a problem when compared to the Epipaleolithic dates from Nahal Oren (Bar-Yosef, this volume). If all dates are acceptable, then it would appear that the Upper Paleolithic in the Central Negev is contemporary with the Kebaran at Nahal Oren. While this is not out of the question, the only other Kebaran date, from Ein Gev I, suggests a much later time for the Kebaran than does the Nahal Oren date (Bar-Yosef, this volume). This problem is not clarified by the dates from the Geometric Kebaran A site of D5, as their wide range permits either interpretation. In fact, those dates are so spread that it is not possible to use any of them with assurance.

The dates for the Natufian place its occupation of the Central Negev at ca. 9000 B.C., a date which is consistent with all those from the north, although other evidence suggests that the Natufian in the Central Negev may not represent an early Natufian manifestation (Henry, 1973*b*).

The dates from the Harifian firmly place it as contemporaneous with the end of the northern Natufian and the beginning of PPNA. It would appear, therefore, that at least in the western portion of the Central Negev and in Sinai, as well, post-Natufian development had a character different from that in the north.

Another problem rests with both the relative and absolute dating of the various Epipaleolithic manifestations in the Central Negev. While the Harifian and the Natufian are reasonably dated, the placement of both the Negev Variant of the Kebaran and the Geometric Kebaran "A" is still impossible. This is of particular concern given the various conflicting and confusing models concerning Kebaran/Natufian relationships and relative chronology (Bar-Yosef, 1970*b*; Prausnitz, 1966, 1970).

In spite of these problems and uncertainties, the work carried out so far in the Central Negev has contributed considerable data to a wide range of prehistoric periods in the Levant. It is hoped that additional work will add even more.

BIBLIOGRAPHY

ANATI, E., 1963. *Palestine before the Hebrews*. New York: Alfred A. Knopf.

BAR-YOSEF, OFER, 1970. "Prehistoric Sites near Ashdod, Israel." *Palestine Exploration Quarterly* 102:53-69.

GARROD, D. A. E., 1962. "An Outline of Pleistocene Prehistory in Palestine-Lebanon-Syria." *Quaternaria* 6:541-46.

GLUECK, N., 1953. "Explorations in Western Palestine." *Bulletin of the American School of Oriental Research* 131:6-15.

HENRY, D., 1973*a*. "The Natufian Site of Rosh Zin: A Preliminary Report." *Palestine Exploration Quarterly* 105:129-40.

————, 1973*b*. "The Natufian of Palestine: Its Material Culture and Ecology." Ph.D. dissertation, Southern Methodist University.

JELINEK, A. J.; FERRAND, W. R.; HAAS, G.; HOROWITZ, A.; and GOLDBERG, P., 1973. "New Excavations at the Tabun Cave, Mount Carmel Israel, 1967-1972: A Preliminary Report." *Paleorient* 1(2).

MARKS, A. E., 1973. "The Harif Point: A New Tool Type from the Terminal Epipaleolithic of the Central Negev, Israel." *Paleorient* 1:99-102.

————, in press. "The Epipaleolithic of the Central Negev: Current Status." *Eretz Israel* 13.

————, and CREW, H., 1973. "Rosh Ein Mor, an Open-Air Mousterian Site in the Central Negev, Israel." *Current Anthropology* 13(5):591-93.

————; CREW, H.; FERRING, R.; and PHILLIPS, J., 1972. "Prehistoric Sites near Har Harif." *Israel Exploration Journal* 22(2-3):73-85.

————, and FERRING, R., in press. "Upper Paleolithic Occupation near Avdat, Central Negev, Israel: An Interim Report." *Eretz Israel* 13.

————; PHILLIPS, J.; CREW, H.; and FERRING, R., 1971. "Prehistoric Sites near 'En-'Avdat in the Negev." *Israel Exploration Journal* 21:13-24.

NEUVILLE, R., 1934. "Le Préhistorique de Palestine." *Revue Biblique* 43:237-59.

PRAUSNITZ, M. W., 1966. "The Kebaran, the Natufian and the Tahunian: A Study in Terminology." *Israel Exploration Journal* 16(4):220-30.

————, 1970. "Turning Points in the Mesolithic Cultures of the Israeli Littoral." *Actes du VIIe Congrès International des Sciences Préhistoriques et Protohistoriques, Prague, 1966, Institut d'Archéologie CSAV*, pp. 353-55.

RONEN, A.; GILEAD, D.; SCHACHNAI, E.; and SAUL, A., 1972. "Upper Acheulean in the Kissufum Region." *Proceedings of the American Philosophical Society* 116(1):68-96.

STEKELIS, M., 1948. "The Prehistoric Collection of Yzkhak Halevi." *Yedioth Havevra Lahaqirath Eretz-Israel We'athigoteh* 14:1-7. (In Hebrew).

YIZRAELI, T., 1967. "Mesolithic Hunters' Industries at Ramat Matred (The Wilderness of Zin), First Report." *Palestine Exploration Quarterly* 99:78-85.

THE EPIPALEOLITHIC IN PALESTINE AND SINAI

Ofer Bar-Yosef
Institute of Archaeology
The Hebrew University
Jerusalem, Israel

INTRODUCTION

The term "Epipaleolithic" is used presently in the Near East to include the microlithic industries which postdate the Levantine Aurignacian C and predate the Pre-Pottery Neolithic. It encompasses, therefore, those units referred to in the past as the Upper Paleolithic VI (Neuville, 1951) and the Mesolithic (Garrod, 1932). The first of these units, the Upper Paleolithic VI, included the following assemblages: Kebaran (Garrod and Bate, 1937), Micro-Kebaran (Kirkbride, 1958), Nebekian and Falitian (Rust, 1950), Gravettian (Ewing, 1947), and Bergian (Copeland and Waechter, 1968). It has been suggested that these be defined as the Kebaran and Geometric Kebaran A (Bar-Yosef, 1970a, 1970b). The second unit, the Mesolithic, included the Natufian (Garrod, 1932; Garrod and Bate, 1937; Neuville, 1934, 1951), and the Khiamian (Echegaray, 1966). These have been renamed as the Natufian and the Geometric Kebaran B (Bar-Yosef, 1970a, 1970b).

Those cultural designations suggested in 1970 were based upon quantitative studies of the material available in Israel, and upon additional collections and publications from adjacent countries.

Since then excavations and surveys have uncovered much more material. In the south, the major excavations and surveys have been undertaken in the Negev in the Avdat area and Har Harif (Marks et al., 1971, 1972) and in Gebel Meghara in Northern Sinai (Phillips et al., in press). In north Palestine, sites in the Lower and Central Jordan Valley should be noted, as well as the excavations at Hefsibah (Ronen, personal communication) and Nahal Hadera V. Simultaneously, excavations have been conducted in Lebanon and Syria, in either known or newly discovered sites.

It seems worthwhile to summarize the new data and to attempt, if possible, to fit them into the scheme the author has suggested, pointing out some avenues of research which seem profitable. This chapter is not, therefore, intended as an encyclopedic summary, but rather as a personal one. It is based upon the assumption that in order to study man's past behavior, as recorded in the archaeological evidence, three goals must be achieved: (1) a chronological framework; (2) an attempted reconstruction of the changing environment; and (3) cultural definition.

In this case the term "culture" as used by the author implies that the archaeological data are regarded in a system in which tools, debitage, burials, structures, art objects, site sizes and locations, and sources of subsistence are incorporated as different variables subject to change and interaction. Although the general order is adopted from Clarke (1968), because of the current status of research only cultures may be defined within the technocomplex (i.e.—Kebaran, Natufian etc. within the Epipaleolithic). The term "industry" is used only in reference to artifacts, including both technology and typology.

Research during the past decade has provided some basic data with respect to these aims. Several additional questions should now be posed. These may concern either general cultural history, a rechecking of the validity of previously suggested schemes, or the economic and social dynamics of different cultural entities.

First it will be necessary to refer to past work and to evaluate the cultural scheme used for the Epipaleolithic in the light of new discoveries (known through either published reports or personal communication). A suggested interpretation of the location of sites and sources of subsistence will follow.

STRATIGRAPHY AND CHRONOLOGY

There is perhaps only one site which presents a full succession of the Epipaleolithic industries—Nahal Oren Terrace—but a detailed report is still forthcoming. Rockshelter Yabrud III produced a somewhat similar sequence, but further excavations have not cleared up the problems raised in the initial work (Rust, 1950; Solecki, 1966). Therefore it seems necessary to record briefly the known stratigraphical evidence (the industry names in brackets are suggested by the author).

1. *Kebara Cave*: B—Natufian; C—Kebaran; D—Levantine Aurignacian (Turville-Petre, 1932; Garrod, 1954).

2. *Hayonim Cave*: B—Natufian; Ca-Cf—Kebaran; D—Levantine Aurignacian (Bar-Yosef, 1970a; Bar-Yosef and Tchernov, 1967, 1970; Bar-Yosef and Goren, 1973).

3. *Sefunim Cave* (Iraq el Baroud): (A1)—Neolithic; (A2)—Kebaran Natufian; (B-C)—Palestinian Aurignacian (Stekelis, 1961; Ronen, 1968).

4. *Nahal Oren Terrace*: Layers 1-3—Pre-Pottery Neolithic (Noy et al., 1973); Layers 4,5,6—Natufian; Layer 7—Geometric Kebaran A; Layers 8-9—Kebaran.

5. *El-Khiam Terrace*: 1—Tahunian; 2-3—Proto-Tahunian [Pre-Pottery Neolithic A]; 4—Khiamian II [Pre-Pottery Neolithic A]; 5—Khiamian I [Natufian]; 6—Kebaran III [Natufian]; 7—Kebaran II [Natufian]; 8—Kebaran I [Natufian]; 9—Upper Aurignacian/Atlitian [Geometric Kebaran A]; 10—Upper Aurignacian [Levantine

Aurignacian C]; (Perrot in Neuville, 1951; Echegaray, 1964, 1966; Bar-Yosef, 1970a).

6. *Rockshelter Yabrud III*: 1—Neolithic; 2—Natufian; 3—Falitian [Geometric Kebaran A]; 4—Nebekian [Kebaran]; 5—"Late Capsian (?)" [Kebaran]; 6—Nebekian [Kebaran]; 7—Nebekian [Kebaran]; 8—Skiftian [Levantine Aurignacian] (Rust, 1950).

7. *Hefsibah* (Nahal Hadera I): Geometric Kebaran A above Kebaran (Ronen, personal communication).

8. *Fazael III*: 1—Chalcolithic; 2—Alluvial soil accumulation; 3—Geometric Kebaran A in and above angular gravels; 4—Alluvial soil accumulation; 5—Kebaran; 6—Kebaran in and above angular gravels (personal observations).

Because of the fragmentary nature of the stratigraphical record, the reasons for which will be discussed below, C-14 dates have immense importance. This is especially true when the large number of single component open-air sites are taken into consideration. A list of the available C-14 dates is given below as Table 1.

These radiocarbon dates support our earlier guesswork suggestion of a date of 18,000 B.C.–15,000 B.C. for the beginning of the Kebaran. Furthermore, a date of 12,000 B.C.–11,000 B.C. would perhaps indicate the appearance of the Geometric Kebaran A, and 10,000 B.C.–9500 B.C. the beginning of the Natufian. The end of the 9th millenium probably saw the early manifestations of the Pre-Pottery Neolithic A and at least one new desertic variant of Epipaleolithic culture ("Harifian").

Acceptance of such a chronological framework would suggest several comments: (a) the Kebaran existed for at least three millenia; (b) the Natufian is basically a Pleistocene culture; (c) the term Mesolithic in its European sense (Kozlowski, 1973) is inadequate in the Levant (e.g., Prausnitz, 1970); and (d) with the aid of several additional C-14 dates from natural deposits, one might use the climatological evidence accumulated in the Levant to reconstruct the changing environment during the period under discussion.

LATE PLEISTOCENE ENVIRONMENTAL CHANGES

Environmental studies are not yet detailed enough to give an overall picture of what happened during this crucial period. The models which have been put forward to explain the changes in human behavior, from the Kebaran or Late Aurignacian to the Natufian and Pre-Pottery Neolithic, are lacking in basic evidence such as many and scattered pollen diagrams, detailed sedimentological studies, bone counts, and quantitatively sufficient paleobotanical material. Inferences made only from the appearance of the recent vegetational cover and the general landscape are rather dangerous (e.g., Vita-Finzi and Higgs, 1971). Conclusions drawn from such a basis ignore the changes which occurred during historical times (see, for example, Vita-Finzi, 1969; Reifenberg, 1953). However, it seems that a general outline can be drawn for both the coastal plain and the Jordan Valley. Other areas, such as part of the hilly zone, the Negev, and Northern Sinai, should await further studies.

The major change in the coastal plain was the rise of sea level. At about 15,000 B.C. sea level was 90 m–130 m below its present height. Judging from bathymetric maps, this means that the coastal plain was about 10 km–12 km wider than it is today. It may be assumed that near the shoreline there were marshes, but as the situation of the 19th century shows, there were probably also marshes elsewhere. These would have existed in low basins between the *kurkar* ridges. The actual picture can be drawn only at such a time as C-14 dates are provided from known swampy deposits. Along with the changing size of the coastal plain, several tectonic movements took place (Neev, personal communication). The variegated vegetational cover was possibly the open forest of Tabor oak along with Mediterranean savanna which probably dominated the southern reaches of the plain (Zohary, 1962). Evidence comes from geomorphic studies (Nir, 1967) as well as from faunal remains which include mainly gazelles, fallow deer, and bovids (E. Tchernov and E. Saxon, personal communications). It would seem that the main change from the Kebaran to the Natufian was the decrease of the fallow deer and the dominance of the gazelles, as also evidenced in Nahal Oren (Noy et al., 1973).

This description minimizes discussion of the faunal remains, being only an indication of the change of the vegetational cover. The less frequent remains of other animals (such as *Alcelaphus, Capra*, equids, turtles, and birds) show that certain special microenvironments were encountered within the coastal plain. Moreover, the exploitation of the hilly areas, even on their flanks, could have changed the faunal spectrum within a given site. It is worth mentioning that the rodents also provide supporting evidence for a gradual desiccation (Tchernov, 1968). The evidence for a wetter period during the Natufian will be considered later.

The Jordan Valley has been an arena for several impressive geomorphic changes. The Lisan Lake which covered the entire valley from Hatzeva in the south to the line between Migdal and Kursi in the north, gave way to a different lacustrine system. Climatic change (probably decreasing annual rainfall), along with tectonic movements, caused the Lisan Lake to shrink to half its size and created two additional lakes—the Sea of Galilee and the Beth-Shean Lake (Neev and Emery, 1967). A recently acquired date—15,300 B.C. (RT-386) from *Melanopsis* shells from the earliest shoreline of the Sea of Galilee (A. Kaufman, personal communication)—supports earlier estimates (Neev and Emery, 1967; Horowitz, 1971). It is still questionable what effects the appearance of two fresh water lakes had on the human economy. On the basis of fish vertebrae found in Ein Gev IV (Geometric Kebaran A), and recently in Nahal Ein Gev II (Natufian), it was suggested that fishing began only after the establishment of the Sea of Galilee as a fresh water lake. However, among the megafauna the same shift from a mixed diet of fallow deer and gazelle to dominance of gazelle seems to have occurred as elsewhere. Unlike the coastal plain, the faunal evidence from Ein Gev I is quantitatively substantial. The other nearby sites provided only

TABLE 1

Radiocarbon Dates from the Epipaleolithic of the Levant

Nahal Oren Terrace

(Kebaran)	Layer 9	16,300 B.C. ±	332 years	(UCLA-1776C)
(Kebaran)	Layer 8	14,930 B.C. ±	340 years	(UCLA-1776B)
(Geometric Kebaran A)	Layer 7	13,850 B.C. ±	300 years	(UCLA-1776A)

Ksar Akil I

(Kebaran)	4, IV - VII	12,150 B.C. ±	500 years	(MC-411)

Ein Aqev

(Late Upper Paleolithic)	D31/20/2-4	14,950 B.C. ±	250 years	(I-5494)
	D31/21A/4-5	15,560 B.C. ±	290 years	(I-5495)
	D31/x75-80	15,440 B.C. ±	560 years	(SMU-8)
	D31/x60-70	15,940 B.C. ±	600 years	(SMU-6)
	D31/x80-85	18,030 B.C. ± 1,200 years		(SMU-5)

Rosh Horesha

(Natufian)	G7/13/35-45	8,540 B.C. ±	430 years	(SMU-9)
	G7/15/35-45	8,930 B.C. ±	280 years	(SMU-10)
	G7/5-8	11,140 B.C. ±	200 years	(I-5496)

Abu Salem

(Harifian)	G12/3-4	8,020 B.C. ±	150 years	(I-5498)
	G12/5	8,280 B.C. ±	150 years	(I-5499)
	G12/6-7	8,280 B.C. ±	150 years	(I-5500)

Site D5

(Geometric Kebaran A)	D5/8A1	11,220 B.C. ±	230 years	(I-5497)
	D5/8A&8B	13,870 B.C. ±	730 years	(Tx-1121)
	D5/8A2	16,890 B.C. ±	680 years	(SMU-7)

Ein Gev I

(Kebaran)		13,750 B.C. ±	415 years	(GrN-5576)

Jericho

(Natufian)		7,800 B.C. ±	240 years	(F-69)
		7,850 B.C. ±	240 years	(F-72)
		9,216 B.C. ±	107 years	(P-376)
(Early PPNA)[1]		8,300 B.C. ±	200 years	(BM-105,106)
		8,230 B.C. ±	200 years	(BM-110)

[1] *These represent only the earliest PPNA dates.*

small collections, as the excavations were not carried beyond the stage of test pits.

Considering the geomorphic evidence and the fauna of the Late Aurignacian, such as layer D of Hayonim Cave (Davis, personal communication), a shift from drier to humid and a return to drier conditions can be plotted for the period of 20,000 B.C.–18,000 B.C. to 8000 B.C. These fluctuations emerge more clearly from the pollen spectra from Lebanon, Syria, and the Hula Valley (Horowitz, 1971; Leroi-Gourhan, 1973).

The hilly and mountainous region of Palestine is not represented in such a survey, not only because research has been less extensive but also because of the minimal number of known sites. This rarity is explicable, in the author's view, as a result of site distribution, reflecting a mode of economic life. This will be discussed below.

The semiarid and arid regions provide important supplementary data to the climatic interpretation, if site distribution is taken as an indicator. The dominance of Geometric Kebaran B, Natufian, and Harifian on the Har Harif plateau—remote from water sources—is apparent (Marks et al., 1972). The Geometric Kebaran A and B sites, as well as the Harifian at Gebel Meghara, reflect the same situation. So does the location of many similar sites in the dune areas of the Western Negev (Burian and Friedman, 1973). It seems to the author that population density during the Late Pleistocene was not especially different from earlier or later (Early Holocene) times. Other than the improved hunting options and the more readily available stands of wild cereals, nothing would have attracted the Geometric Kebarans to the semiarid areas.

CULTURAL CHARACTERISTICS

The division into cultural units has been made on the basis of technology, typology, and other archaeological elements such as size of site, location, ground stone tools, bone industry, and art objects. It is obvious when discussing both technology and typology that only quantitative studies should be utilized. Therefore isolated artifacts appearing in very low percentages (sometimes less than 1%) are not regarded as cultural designators unless they have special stylistic features, such as Falita points. Tool types such as triangles and lunates, if they appear in less than 1% of the total microlithic assemblages, are not considered characteristic.

Among the additional elements, heavy duty tools, bone industry, art objects, burial customs, and site size and location will be taken into account. Through such a process the different cultural groups based upon the various assemblages may be depicted. We may take the fundamental technology as the basis for the existence of the cultural groups and the culture itself. Several of these assemblages may represent base camps, while others represent transitory camps. The underlying assumption is that man does not change his way of stone knapping even if he is a wanderer. A higher analytical level deals with the types of tools and their method of modification. The stylistic differences discerned in the secondary trimming may be taken as indicative of different variants or of cultural phases within the framework of the same culture. It does not seem that the tools in our hands always enable us to draw a clear distinction between these, however.

From the technological viewpoint, there are differences which are the results of a development, and other differences which originate in the geographical distribution. We may say that in Western Palestine the basic technological change following the Levantine Aurignacian is the appearance of the bladelet core, generally with one or two striking platforms. In the Geometric Kebaran A this tendency continues, but within the Natufian the number of striking platforms increases. The long, narrow bladelets evolve into short, broad ones. This is pronounced as well in the retouched bladelets. We may look for the origins of this phenomenon in the industries of the Geometric Kebaran A, either in the coastal plain or in the Negev (see, for example, Kiryat Arieh I, Hofith, or D-5).

The bladelets in the Negev and Sinai are generally wider than those from the northern part of Palestine, within both nongeometric and geometric assemblages. This phenomenon is apparent even when taking into consideration the retouched or backed bladelets.

Another important event is the appearance of blades. As stressed previously (Bar-Yosef, 1970a), the early appearance of sickle blades in the Kebaran, and especially in the Natufian, brought the need for the production of blades. While Western Palestine is relatively poor in blades, the eastern part of the Sea of Galilee is rich in blades. This tendency becomes clearer through a comparison of the site of Ein Gev I-IV and Haon III. The technological difference between the east and west became more apparent when new sites were discovered in Wadi Fazael and Wadi Malieh which descend eastward into the Jordan Valley. Kebaran and Geometric Kebaran A sites with undoubtedly Palestinian type industries were uncovered.

However, sometimes the technological differences are accompanied by typological variations. For example, on the eastern side of the Sea of Galilee certain tool types such as the Falita Point appear (Ein Gev I and II) as well as several variants of microgravette points (Ein Gev III and IV). This suggests a tie between this area and the rockshelter of Yabrud III, Wadi Dhobai K, and Madmagh.

Microburin technique, as known from the archaeological evidence from the rockshelter Yabrud III, already has appeared in small quantities within the Kebaran. It may be that this is an early stage of the Kebaran; however, this does not contradict the suggestion (Henry, in press) that the origin of this technique is in North Africa. Although a high percentage of microburin technique was found in Sinai and the Negev, and was found to be decreasing northward within Natufian assemblages, one should remember the assemblage from Ein Gev IV where approximately 55% of the industry belongs to the microburin technique. It is undoubtedly important that microburin technique used in the Kebaran industries has a general appearance of uniformity. This may mean that the snap was always made in the same direction, while within Natufian assemblages the bladelets were snapped from both directions. If Ein Gev IV is considered a Geometric Kebaran A site or one belonging to a special culture which preceded the Natufian, then the standardized microburin technique for the production of oblique truncations had to be introduced before the Natufian and should not be considered a Natufian feature. This suggestion is supported by the high percentages of microburin technique in the sites related to the early phase of Geometric Kebaran B (see Table 4).

Within the typological studies the most important group is the microlithic tools which characterize the Epipaleolithic cultures. Actually, it was differences within this group which suggested the basic division into Kebaran and Geometric Kebaran. It is possible to observe a clear tendency toward the domination of the geometric component, although such a development is not linear but dendritic. This means that there is no way to place a certain industry within a chronostratigraphic sequence on the basis of quantitative relationships between nongeometric microliths and geometric microliths alone. For such an order C-14 dates are a necessity. In their absence, one may take into account some auxiliary considerations, such as the existence of a local or regional tradition in flint knapping or the function of the site as represented by the assemblage. This kind of information is provided in areas where clusters of sites exist, close in time and typology. Such clusters are available near wadi courses in the coastal plain, or near Ein Gev, as well as at the Natufian sites in the Judean Desert.

Breaking down the microlithic tool group by itself, it is possible to discern quantitative and stylistic changes within each subgroup. It seems that these changes indicate chronological gaps as well as differences in regional tradition of the cultural group. Beginning with the nongeometric microliths (Group J in the London Type List, 1969; Group H in Bar-Yosef, 1970a), we may designate several significant subgroups: retouched and backed bladelets, bladelets with inverse and alternate retouch, arched or curved bladelets (including micropoints), and retouched and obliquely truncated bladelets. The differences between the industries are presented in the quantitative relationship between those subgroups. It is worth mentioning that the subgroup of truncated backed bladelets gave the entire culture its definition, following the industry uncovered in the cave of Kebara (Turville-Petre, 1932; Garrod and Bate, 1937).

From the first publication it was clear that other elements are present besides the obliquely truncated backed bladelets. However, we may note that if the term Kebaran is assigned only to those assemblages where the obliquely truncated backed bladelet forms the major component within the microliths, a great many additional names will be required. It seems preferable to the author to use the term Kebaran for all the nongeometric microlithic assemblages. Presumably when the Kebaran has been studied more fully we shall be able to define it as a cultural group and to depict the various cultures within it.

The tracing of those subgroups of microliths reveals some interesting information. A stylistic change was noted earlier (Bar-Yosef, 1970a; Hours, 1966; Chavaillon and Hours, 1970) where most of the oblique truncations were made on the proximal end of the bladelets in the earlier levels (Hayonim C, Jaita II, Nahal Oren); while in later levels we find the majority of the truncations on the distal end (Ein Gev I, Ein Gev III, Fazael II-5). Also from abrupt retouch on the back and on the truncation, there is a transition to semiabrupt and fine retouch. Such stylistic changes will provide, on the basis of chronostratigraphy, for a division of the Kebaran into earlier and later phases.

As for the other subgroups of microliths, it is still difficult to suggest chronological meanings. C-14 dating hints that some of these quantitative situations are simply local. Several assemblages which differ in the dominant micro-

lithic subgroup are certainly contemporaneous. For example, the dominance of inverse retouch or alternately retouched bladelets at Ksar Akil (Tixier, 1970) is most probably contemporaneous with the dominance of obliquely truncated bladelets at Ein Gev I and Nahal Oren. We may suggest that even the dominance of curved or arched bladelets, such as in Kefar Darom 3, Kefar Darom 8, Kiryath Arieh II, and Fazael III-6, is contemporaneous with the former industries. Finally, the retouched bladelets are most probably a permanent component within each assemblage. Their quantity rarely varies. Perhaps they are actually unfinished microliths.

Within the group of geometric forms the following three subgroups have been distinguished: trapeze-rectangles, triangles, and lunates. The first and last appear more or less uniformly in many sites, while the triangles are known from fewer sites, with a great variation in their quantities. The trapeze-rectangles also appear in a wide range of quantities, but in several assemblages they form the dominant geometric component. They may be in the minority in some assemblages in relation to the nongeometric microliths (20% vs. 80%), but in the majority at other sites. In this subgroup trapezes and rectangles are either elongated and narrow, or short and wide. The dominance of these was suggested as the common denominator for assemblages assigned to the Geometric Kebaran A.

The lunates as a typologically dominant element characterize the Natufian. It is also suggested that they are the characteristic tool of the Geometric Kebaran B, which will be discussed later. They are made either by abrupt retouch, on an anvil, or by Helwan and inverse retouch. The Helwan retouch is broadly accepted as a chronological indicator.

The triangle is the most difficult to fit into our framework. We may note that its appearance in the stratigraphy of Rockshelter Yabrud III in Layer 5 is in an intercalation within Kebaran layers ("Nebekian," following Rust, 1950). A similar case was noted in Hayonim Cave in the assemblage of Layer Cb. A recent occurrence is their appearance at the site of Nahal Hadera V under nongeometric Kebaran layers which we may refer to as Late Kebaran (but pre-Geometric Kebaran). At Nahal Oren, in Layers 8 and 7 (Noy et al., 1973) the triangles are the dominant geometric form where they follow stratigraphically the obliquely truncated backed bladelets.

INDUSTRY CHARACTERISTICS

Following are the basic descriptions of the various cultures, which form approximately the same scheme suggested earlier (Bar-Yosef, 1970a). A few modifications are, of course, inevitable because of the accumulation of additional material. Although these definitions are not as yet fully supported quantitatively, since part of the new data are still unavailable, it seems useful to present them at this time to elicit further discussion.

KEBARAN

The suggested chronology and the typological variability

indicate that the Kebaran most probably endured at least three thousand years. It is premature to attempt a division into several phases, although there are several indications that this will be possible.

Typologically, the Kebaran is defined on the basis of its microlithic tool group, microliths (retouched and backed bladelets) forming from 50% to 90% of the total assemblage. The index of microliths depends on the method of collection. With the advancement of excavation methods we now may rely on the results from wet sieving, and only rarely on those from dry sieving. Although this group forms a large part of the tool kit, generally 30% to 50% of the microliths are broken, which results in their indices varying from one assemblage to another. In addition, often only those microliths capable of specific definition are taken into account in more restricted analyses.

On the basis of the major components of the microlithic group, the known Kebaran sites in northern Palestine can be divided as follows:

a. Small curved and pointed bladelets (narrow micropoints): Kiryath Arieh II and Kefar Darom 3.

b. Obliquely truncated backed bladelets, plus micropoints: Hayonim Cave, Layer C; Rockshelter Meged (near Hayonim Cave); Nahal Oren, Layer 9; Rakefet Cave; Sefunim Cave; Kebara Cave (?), Nahal Hadera V (lower levels); Giveath Ha'esev; Soreq 33M2; Poleg 18MII; Kefar Darom 8; Kefar Darom 13; and Fazael III, Layer 6.

c. Obliquely truncated bladelets: Ein Gev I and II; Unn Khlaid; Nahal Hadera V (upper levels); Fazael III-5; Haifa I (Olami, 1973); and Soreq 33M1.

Judging from some stratigraphic evidence, it may be that a chronological ordering exists between sites of subgroups a and b. This is suggested in the finds from Yabrud III, where obliquely truncated bladelets become dominant in the uppermost assemblage (Rust, 1950). In Fazael III there also appears to be the same kind of typological shift. Kefar Darom 8 is thus probably later than Kefar Darom 3 (Bar-Yosef, 1970b). If these observations are proven correct, then the Kebaran could be divided into early and late phases.

Geometric microliths occur in many of these assemblages, and some are basically modifications of an already existing type. Such is the case of the elongated narrow trapeze, which is similar to the obliquely truncated backed bladelet but which has an extra basal truncation. A similar example is the elongated scalene triangle.

Other tool groups such as scrapers, burins, truncated pieces, and notches and denticulates are well represented in Kebaran sites. Although the indices may vary from one assemblage to another, there is no assemblage without these tools. It is especially worth noting that while burins are sometimes less than 1% or absent in the Negev or Sinai sites, there is no similar case in northern Palestine. This holds true as well for Geometric Kebaran A sites.

Very few sites in the Negev and Sinai can be referred to as true Kebaran sites. Some sparse assemblages from the western Negev show Kebaran affinities on typological grounds. An assemblage studied from Gebel Meghara (Moshabi I in Phillips et al., in press) shows a dominance of nongeometric forms, mainly arched backed and obliquely truncated bladelets. In the writer's view, the extensive use of microburin technique would indicate a later date. This site, however, as well as Geometric Kebaran sites in the Negev and Sinai, demonstrates the major technological difference between the Kebaran north of Beer-Sheva and that of the south. After the secondary trimming the bladelets from the Negev and Sinai are generally wider than are those from northern Palestine. The backed bladelets from the north average 4 mm–8 mm in width, while the ones from the south average 7 mm–10 mm in width. This distinction is also seen in the sizes of unretouched bladelets, but much more precise work is needed to depict the entire phenomenon, as well as to draw exact limits between the two technological provinces.

Several typological features have enabled us to suggest another territorial division for the Kebaran. The Falita Point found at Ein Gev I and II, Wadi Madamagh, Yabrud III-3, —and its derivative the microgravette point (Ein Gev III and IV and Wadi Dhobai K)—indicate an eastern province of the Kebaran. It is possible that this province has direct affinities with the Lebanon (Ksar Akil) and the Galilee (Hayonim C). However, a comparative study undertaken recently shows that both the Falita Point and the microgravette are absent from sites in the western part of the Jordan Valley. This dissimilarity is constant when comparing Geometric A sites from both sides of the Sea of Galilee (Haon III and Emirah Cave).

Other classes of artifacts in the Kebaran tool kit are bone tools and grinding and pounding stones. Bone tools are rare but when present are most often points and burnishers. Pounding and grinding tools have been uncovered in several sites to date. Ein Gev I was the first instance where mortars and pestles were found in a Kebaran site (Stekelis and Bar-Yosef, 1965). Since then ground stone tools have been uncovered in Umm Khalid, Caesarea-south (Prausnitz, personal communication), Hefsibah, Nahal Hadera V, and Haon III. These finds are always fewer in number when compared to the numerous mortars and pestles in Natufian sites. It would be premature to infer the presence of early domestication of plants from this phenomenon when such an interpretation is still dubious in regard to the Natufian economy. Paleobotanical finds are extremely rare. We may suggest, however, that two kinds of vegetable food were possibly ground in the mortars—acorns and wild cereals.

The size of Kebaran sites is generally 150 m² –400 m². Ein Gev I provided relatively clear evidence of a hut dug into a sandy hill, delineated by a shallow basin 5 m–7 m in diameter. This depression contained the remains of several living floors which were littered with tools, debitage, bones, and stone. A few pestles and one mortar were uncovered, as well as a burial of a woman (Arensburg and Bar-Yosef, in press). Subsequent erosion has caused a large surface scatter of artifacts. Wide artifactual surface scatter also characterizes the coastal plain sites. This, in our view, is a result of erosion and is not a reflection of the actual size of the occupations. When found intact, Kebaran deposits are over one meter in thickness and are limited to a restricted area. While post-Kebaran erosion is rather obvious, natural destruction also affected sites during periods of abandonment. It is, therefore, possible that some of the scattering was concurrent with Kebaran occupancy.

GEOMETRIC KEBARAN A

The stratigraphic position of this culture is recorded from Abri Bergy (Copeland and Waechter, 1968); Yabrud III, Layer 3; Fazael III, Layer 5; and Hefsibah. In several assemblages there seems to be a direct typological connection with the Kebaran, particularly where there is a low percentage of trapeze-rectangles. This occurs at the sites of Umm Khalid, Kebara C, Haifa I, and Ein Gev III. It is preferable to denote an assemblage as Geometric Kebaran A when the trapeze-rectangles (rarely with a few triangles and lunates) constitute at least half of the microlithic category. In several sites these tools (either complete or broken) are absolutely dominant (Haon III, Malih V, Nahal Lavan II, 105, and D5). Whether this designates a cultural phase or more probably a special activity is yet to be studied. The same typological and technological provinces found within the Kebaran are evident in the Geometric Kebaran A. In Ein Gev III there is a continuation of the Falita Point in the form of microgravettes. The Negev and Sinai present wider trapeze-rectangles than those of the north. In a few cases, however, such as Lagama Ic, one may also find narrow trapeze-rectangles.

As in the previous cultures, other tools are also common. Among the scrapers those made on blades are most numerous. The appearance of microburin technique cannot yet be considered traditional.

Data from the Geometric Kebaran A sites are yet very limited, but it is evident that they reflect the Kebaran tradition. Pounding and grinding tools are again a part of the material culture (Hefsibah, Haon III). The average size of sites is approximately 500 m^2.

GEOMETRIC KEBARAN B

When the term Geometric Kebaran B was suggested only a few assemblages with typological traits different from, yet reminiscent of the Natufian, were known. These were Ein Gev IV; Kefar Darom 28 (Bar-Yosef 1970a,b); Layers 8–6 at El-Khiam terrace (Echegaray, 1966); Matred 141 and 190 (Yizraeli, 1967); and Poleg 18M (Prausnitz, 1970; Bar-Yosef, 1970a). Since then more sites have been discovered or reexcavated and studied (Marks et al., in press). It has become evident that the relationships within this group of assemblages and between this group and the Natufian were rather poorly defined.

Within the microlithic tool element from these non-Natufian assemblages, a distinction may be made between assemblages with a dominance of triangles and those with a dominance of lunates. The chronostratigraphic relationship

of these two groups has been and still is problematical because of deficiencies in both absolute and relative dating evidence. Therefore a brief review of the available evidence is needed here to clarify the author's view.

Nahal Oren Layers 8 and 7, dominated by triangles, overlay a Kebaran assemblage and were, in turn, covered by Natufian layers. The C-14 dates (see Table 1), in spite of appearing to be somewhat too early, suggest a possible time-correlation with the trapeze-rectangle assemblages. Ein Gev IV, as yet undated, demonstrates an extensive use of the microburin technique and a dominance of blades among the scrapers.

Typologically and technologically, the Ein Gev IV assemblage seems to be later than that of Ein Gev III which lacks evidence of the microburin technique and includes rectangles as a distinct component of the microlithic group. Also within other sites of Geometric Kebaran A there are no signs of the systematic use of a microburin technique. It seems that only triangles and lunates in the Levantine Epipaleolithic are associated with this technique. This association provides an approach which can be used in tracing the possible origins of some Natufian assemblages.

The sites with lunates—either with abrupt retouch like Poleg 18M or with Helwan retouch like those from Matred, Har Harif, Gebel Meghara, and Zeelim sands—were suggested as being related to the Natufian. Most probably the ambiguous definition of the nature of these relationships made by the author caused some confusion (Bar-Yosef, 1970a). It is commonly believed that the appearance of Helwan lunates is a time "guide fossil." If this is true, then the sites from the Negev and Sinai are contemporaneous with the Early Natufian of northern Palestine, characterized by the presence of Helwan lunates (Garrod and Bate, 1937; Neuville, 1951; Henry, 1973).

Summarizing the above information, it seems that there are two possible chronological frameworks: in one, the assemblages typified by triangles are contemporaneous with those with trapeze-rectangles, while in the other the triangles designate a later chronological stage. In both schemes the association between triangles and the microburin technique precedes the Natufian (Table 2).

The Geometric Kebaran B is best understood on the basis of comparison with the Natufian. The studies in the Negev (Marks et al., 1972; Marks, in press) confirmed the technological differences between these two entities. Similar results are expected from comparison between western Lebanon, where there are no Natufian sites, and the Beqaa Valley, where Natufian sites are known (Schroeder, 1970). Moreover, the size and the distribution of the Geometric Kebaran B sites are different from those of the Natufian. Since more stratigraphic evidence and radiometric datings are needed, a typological seriation must be used to order the known assemblages. Those, apart from Poleg 18M and the terrace of El-Khiam, are limited to the Negev and northern Sinai.

The possibly earlier phase of this culture contains mainly

TABLE 2
SUGGESTED ALTERNATIVES OF
CHRONOLOGICAL AND CULTURAL ORDERING OF THE LEVANTINE EPIPALEOLITHIC

Pre-Pottery Neolithic A	Harifian (Negev & Sinai)
Late Natufian	
Early Natufian	Geometric Kebaran B (Negev & Sinai)
Geometric Kebaran A_2 (triangles)	Geometric Kebaran A_1 (trapeze-rectangles)
K e b a r a n Subgroups A, B, & C	

Pre-Pottery Neolithic A	Harifian (Negev & Sinai)
Late Natufian	
Early Natufian	Geometric Kebaran B (Negev & Sinai)
Geometric Kebaran A_2 (triangles)	
Geometric Kebaran A_1 (trapeze-rectangles)	
K e b a r a n Subgroups A, B, & C	

scrapers on blades, a few burins, numerous obliquely trun-cated backed bladelets (sometimes scalene triangles and a few crude lunates), La Mouillah points (more often in Sinai), and an extensive use of the microburin technique. The best example is the assemblage of Moshabi I (Phillips et al., in press).

The apparent later phase of the Geometric Kebaran B is characterized by scrapers on blades, denticulates and mul-tiple notches, obliquely truncated backed bladelets, some triangles, La Mouillah points, Helwan lunates (either few or numerous), the use of microburin technique, but few or no burins. Worth mentioning is a rare use of quartz as an ad-ditional raw material seen, to date, only in Gebel Meghara. The size of the sites varies from 100 m² –300 m², and the number of tools varies from ca. 4 m² –8 m². In one site (Moshabi IV) the spatial distribution of ashes in the sand indicates the possibility of brush shelter about 7 m x 3 m in size. This area contained most of the artifacts.

Dentalia shells from both the Mediterranean and Red Seas are common in the Geometric Kebaran B sites in Sinai, but are lacking at similar sites in the Negev. Mediterranean *Dentalia* shells are already present in small numbers in the Kebaran and Geometric Kebaran A. The extensive utili-zation of these shells is recorded only from the Natufian and Geometric Kebaran B. It seems that the appearance of Helwan lunates, along with the augmentation of microburin technique in Sinai and the Negev, the numerous La Mouil-lah points in Sinai, the casual use of quartz, and the Red Sea *Dentalia* shells in Sinai reinforces the suggestion of con-nections between Egypt and Palestine during the period of the Early Natufian (Garrod, 1957; Henry, 1973).

NATUFIAN

It is almost redundant after the recent important sum-mary of the Natufian culture (Henry, 1973) to try to give a short summary here. We may linger only on the points pertinent to the subject of this chapter, those concerning the cultural sequence.

It seems that new stratigraphic data, as well as some unpublished dates, support the division of the Natufian into early and late phases (Henry, 1973; Henry, in press). Ac-ceptance of the presence of Helwan retouch as a chrono-logical indicator will show that Early Natufian sites are found only within the Mediterranean vegetational zone (Eynan, Hayonim, el-Wad, Kebara, Erq-el Ahmar and Beidha). Late Natufian sites are located both in Mediter-ranean and Irano-Turanian zones including the high Negev (Nahal Oren, el-Wad, Shukbah, Rosh Zin, Rosh Horesha). Taking into account the technological similarities among all these sites, one may conclude that the Natufian way of life was established first in the most favorable Mediterranean zones, and only later did they penetrate into the Negev. This suggests that research concerning the origins of the Natufian should be made through technological studies of the Geometric Kebaran A assemblages in northern Pales-tine, as one possible source. Only studies of this kind will indicate whether the Natufian culture is of Palestinian origin.

The Natufian tool kit is similar in many aspects to the Geometric Kebaran A (i.e., Kiryath Arieh I). The dominant tool group is the microlith, which contains some non-geometric forms (such as obliquely truncated backed bladelets) along with dominating geometric forms (lunates with triangles, trapezes, and rectangles). At several Natufian sites lunates are almost the only geometric form present in the known assemblages (Eynan, Hayonim B, Erq-el Ahmar A_2). However, reservation should be made in relation to two sites: at Eynan a recent analysis showed that the micro-lithic group is larger than was formerly recorded, about 40% of the assemblage, even without wet sieving (Valla, in press); while Hayonim Cave, Layer B, may represent an area of specialized activity (Bar-Yosef and Goren, 1973).

A diagnostic characteristic of Natufian base camps is a wide range of typological forms. Among the tools first common in the Natufian, borers and awls should be men-tioned along with elongated picks (proto-axes?), while at some sites burins play an important role (Hayonim Cave, Eynan, Rosh Zin, and Rosh Horesha). Mortars—either mobile or bedrock—pestles, mullers, and bowls are the pounding and grinding tools found in each base camp. These ground stone pieces are sometimes decorated. "Stone pipes" are located *in situ* only in graves (see, for example, Stekelis and Yizraeli, 1961, Pl. 3, B-C) and should be considered as tombstones.

An important difference between the Natufian and the Kebaran is demonstrated by the intrasite activity patterning. Much energy was spent by the Natufians in digging, constructing, and manufacturing stone tools (such as "stone pipes" and mortars). This offers possibilities for future study of different areas of activities, possible specialization in stone crafts, possible mobility of part of each Natufian community, as well as anthropological studies of burial practices with the possible existence of residentially distinct family groups, such as are hinted at in the dental evidence from Hayonim (Smith, 1973).

HARIFIAN

It may be premature to suggest this term for a certain group of assemblages recently discovered (Marks et al., 1972; Marks, 1973), but such a suggestion is within the scope of this chapter as defined above. The data provided by Marks from two village sites in the Har Harif and the two ephemeral sites found recently in Gebel Meghara indicate the presence of a cultural group in the Negev and in Sinai, which corresponds in time with the beginning of the PPNA. Both the technology and typology of these sites relate them to the Epipaleolithic techno-complex. At least for one site, Abu Salem, the presence of considerably complex architectural features has been confirmed, although to date burials are unknown. The Harif point is the quantitative guide fossil, and its presence in the western Negev and absence from northern Palestine delineates the northern expansion of this culture. It is worth mentioning in this context that another type of arrowhead is found in what was named "late Natufian" (Natufian IV of Neuville) and perhaps the appearance of these two arrowheads occurred during the same period (i.e., within a few hundred years).

DISCUSSION

The following discussion presents a series of interpretations of the aforementioned reviews. It takes into account a mixture of facts such as site locations and content, as well as several interpretations already made. These interpretations, made only for the purposes of evaluating the Levantine Epipaleolithic, are as follows:

1. The number of tools in a given site represents the intensity of occupation. This takes into account both site size and length of occupation. It means that a small site (50 m² –200 m²) with thousands of tools indicates a considerable length of occupation (even when seasonal abandonment is considered).

2. Most of the edible meat came from hunting gazelles, although in northern Palestine the percentage of fallow deer in Kebaran sites is considerable. This probably decreased southward because of the scarcity of forested areas, although little data are available. Gazelles have distinct territories, such as southeastern Galilee (about 200 km²) or the northeastern side of the Sea of Galilee (300 km²). This situation also enabled the Kebarans to use a limited territory. In southern Palestine, where there was less annual precipitation and grassy areas were more scattered and limited, a Kebaran territory should have been larger than in northern Palestine.

3. A localization may be discerned in the technological and typological continuation of certain clusters of Kebaran and Geometric Kebaran sites. Such examples are available near Ein Gev (I–IV), Nahal Poleg (18MI, 18MII, 18MIV, and Wingate), and Nahal Lachish (sites numbered as Kefar Darom 3, 8, 13, 26, 27, and 28). It is therefore possible to demonstrate stylistic differences, some of which originate in the variability of raw material, between Kebaran territories.

4. A distinction can be made between Kebaran core areas where sites have a high density of artifacts (calculated in relation to the volume of the deposit), pounding and grinding tools, and have special locations near water resources, beside a major wadi course, in a lookout position, etc. Transitory or ephemeral camps are smaller, with low artifactual densities, and are normally farther up-wadi than is the case for the larger sites. Natufian base camps have a different location which will be discussed later, but they contain the same high tool densities, pounding and grinding tools, structures, and burials. Trying to define the geographical distribution of the Kebaran and Geometric Kebaran A, the following longitudinal strips within Palestine can be depicted:

a. Western Galilee, Mount Carmel, the western Samarian Hills, the western Judean Hills, and the coastal plain along these hilly areas. South of the Beer-Sheva Valley, the mountainous Negev forms the highland and the Zeelim and Haluza sands the lowland. The landscape there dictates a more radial distribution, following wadi courses rather than the parallel structure of northern Palestine.

b. Eastern Galilee, the eastern Samarian Hills, and the Judean Desert are the highlands, while the Hula Valley and the western Jordan Valley are the lowlands.

c. The Golan and Gilead Heights with the eastern Jordan Valley.

d. The Trans-Jordanian plateau with the fringes of the Syro-Arabian desert.

Within each region we may pick up the core area sites and the transitory camps. (The term "core area" is used here to designate a limited area—1 km² - 3 km²—where the major Kebaran sites are located. These sites are interpreted as base camps, but as they shifted their place within a given territory it seems appropriate to reserve the term "base camps" for only the Natufian and Harifian sites.) There is a certain impression of zonation within each strip, but only detailed stylistic study will enable us to discern these smaller geographical boundaries. Such case studies are suggested for southern Lebanon and the Galilee, where microgravettes seem to be a diagnostic tool, or for the central coastal plain (between Nahal Alexander and Nahal Lachish), where narrow and broad micropoints (curved, pointed, retouched, or backed bladelets) are the most common microlith in several sites. The overlapping of cultural units, exchange or trade, and possible long-range movements are indicated, for example, by the existence of Mediterranean shells at the Ein Gev sites. A clear cultural border is formed by the Sea of Galilee, as is evident from a comparison between the Geometric Kebaran A from Ein Gev II and IV and the recent finds from Emirah. Ein Gev III and IV have a dominant blade element among the scrapers, while in Emirah they are made on flakes. The whole industry at Emirah is microlithic and has an appearance similar to other sites in western Palestine (I. Gisis, personal communication). The difference may arise from the different raw material, which is larger and better near Ein Gev. The mere fact that at the sites around Ein Gev a clear change is visible (from the narrow, carinated core to single platform prismatic blade core), however, indicates that the size of raw material cannot, alone, account for such a difference.

Following is a more detailed survey of these particular areas, given in order to make the generalizations more restricted. In the western Galilee two ephemeral Kebaran camps are known to date: Hayonim Cave, Layer Ca–Cf, and Rockshelter Meged (about 300 m eastward from Hayonim). There are only a very few such camps in the lowlands and the coastal plain. This may be due either to insufficient research or to the fact that one *kurkar* ridge has been destroyed by the sea and another is now densely settled.

In the coastal plain, most of the large Kebaran camps are located along the first *kurkar* ridge, close to the outlets of the actual wadi courses. Taking into account that the coastal plain was wide at that period, these sites were actually in the central part of the plain. It is worth noting that, when located on a map, these sites form a north-south line with comparable camps in Mount Carmel (Nahal Oren and Kebara). It should be kept in mind, however, that any distribution map is biased, as the central part of the actual coastal plain has been built up since the 1890s and probably a considerable number of sites have been destroyed. It seems that the Kebaran sites had their subsistence sources within the coastal plain and the flanks of the hilly region. More work is needed in the western Samarian and Judean Hills to verify this conclusion. However, it is clear that the Kebarans were basically hunters (as shown by the amount of bones recovered recently from Hefsibah and Nahal Hadera V), but were also using grinding and pounding tools—for acorns or wild cereals, or both. No fish bones have been recovered, and even in places like Ein Gev IV or in Natufian sites like Hayonim Cave, fish remains are scarce.

In the Jordan Valley a similar pattern of site location is noticed. Kebaran and Geometric Kebaran sites are found at the outlet of Wadi et-Malih. More sites are expected at the outlets of several other major wadis. This is the period when Lisan Lake shrunk and flat steppic areas developed in the central Jordan Valley. The economic influence of the fresh water lakes of Beth-Shean and the Sea of Galilee is yet unknown.

Near Ein Gev it seems that the fresh water lake played a minute role. No plant remains have been recovered as yet, but the pounding tools indicate some exploitation of vegetal food. The Ungulates hunted at Ein Gev I were 43.0% gazelle, 36.0% cervids, 15.5% *Capra* and *Ovis*, 4.5% cattle, and 1.0% wild boar (Davis, 1972). The sites studied to date are considered by the author to be campsites within a core area; transitory camps have not yet been found in the area, but the survey of the upstreams of the wadis just recently began. The semiarid region of the mountainous Negev and the lowlands of the western Negev have not provided any confirmed Kebaran site. Only Geometric Kebaran A sites were found, mainly in the sandy region known as Zeelim and Halutza sands. Five sites were recorded (Table 4) near the wadi courses of Nahal Lavan and Nahal Besor. Two sites are found in the higher Negev, only one of which, D5, is well recorded (Marks et al., 1971; personal communication). It seems that the populations would have been less dense than in northern Palestine, and sites therefore would be smaller and more scattered as the exploited territory is larger. In consequence it will be difficult to distinguish between a distinct limited core area with densely occupied sites and an ephemeral camp on the basis of tool density, unless other elements are uncovered (i.e., pounding tools, structures, and burials).

Table 3 summarizes published and unpublished data on the above geographical zonation. Table 4 lists sites in each zone.

Major changes took place with the establishment of the Natufian culture. Distinct base camps were formed and located in northern Palestine within the wadi valleys, sometimes near existing springs. In the Negev they followed the present Irano-Turanian vegetational zone. Natufian sites are larger than Kebaran sites and occupy areas of 500 m^2–7000 m^2 and normally have deposits of at least one meter thickness. Structures, either for dwelling or for burials, are frequent, as are paved areas. In northern Palestine burials and pounding stones are common. It is possible to locate seasonal camps, although it seems that in several instances they overlay Kebaran sites and were mixed later due to deflation or insufficient accumulation (as in Sefunim). However, the following sites are considered by the author to be transitory Natufian camps: Yabrud III, 2; Sefunim, Layer 8A; Abu Usba; Rakefet; Poleg 18M(?); Azor; Tor Abu Sif; Umm ez-Zuwetina; Ain Sakhri; Fazael IV; and Point 508. The territories seem to be larger than during the Kebaran, as they had to provide a variety of food in large quantities for larger communities. The Galilee

TABLE 3

	Coastal Plain and Western Hills		Jordan Valley and Western Hills		Jordan Valley and Golan Heights		Lower & Higher Negev and Northern Sinai
	Sites in Core Area	Sites not in Core Area	Sites in Core Area	Sites not in Core Area	Sites in Core Area	Sites not in Core Area	Sites in Undifferentiated Areas
Geometric Kebaran B							20
Geometric Kebaran A	7		4	2	2		9
Kebaran	12	4	2		2		

seems to be split into two territories: Western Galilee—Hayonim terrace plus a possible other site; and Eastern Galilee—Eynan (and there should be one or two more sites). Mount Carmel, the Samarian and Judean Hills are divided in latitudinal strips: Mount Carmel—two sites (Early Natufian: Kebarah and el-Wad; and Late Natufian: Nahal Oren and el-Wad). Samaria and Judea provided only two sites, but unpublished surveys indicate the existence of two or three more sites. The same situation probably occurred in Hebron hills, but the area has not been surveyed. As for the Golan and the Trans-Jordanian Plateau, the sites of Nahal Ein Gev II and Beidha hint that a similar distribution should be revealed. The long-range connections between the different areas of Palestine and Sinai can be judged from the transportation of materials. Basalt mortars, bowls, pestles, and whet stones are common in Natufian base camps which are far from the sources of this raw material (eastern Galilee). The Natufian could have gotten these, either by exchange or by local fabrication in the source areas. *Dentalia* shells were also transported from the Mediterranean Sea inland and from the Red Sea northward. No ostrich eggshells similar to those found in the Natufian sites in the Negev have been recorded from northern Palestine. Taking into account these three observations (basalt tools, *Dentalia* shells, and ostrich eggshells) it seems that the major exchange direction was east/west and only rarely south/north.

It may be concluded that the Natufian in Palestine consisted of two entities, sharing the same technology (i.e., a culture group in which two separate cultures are defined). The socioeconomic structure of the northern Natufian was different from the southern one, mainly in regard to burial practices and utilization of mobile mortars and sickles. If the Geometric Kebaran B is undoubtedly technologically different from the Natufian, then the Late Natufian sites in the Negev (Rosh Zin and Rosh Horesha) are the result of population expansion. It is possible that demographic

pressures in the Mediterranean zone of Palestine, caused by the large Natufian communities, forced some groups to move into the southern Irano-Turanian zone.

A similar situation is expected in Lebanon where the cedar forest did not encourage the establishment of Natufian economy as did the *pistachio-quercetum* zone (Van Lierre and Contenson, 1964).

It seems to be relevant to the discussion of the Epipaleolithic to add a brief review of site distribution during the Pre-Pottery Neolithic A period. The archaeological remains of the PPNA as represented in Jericho, or Nahal Oren, are thought to demonstrate a direct continuation of the Natufian (e.g., Kenyon, 1960; Mellart, 1965; Perrot, 1968; Flannery, 1972). This continuity is reflected through the architectural remains (rounded houses) and the geographical distribution of sites (mainly in the Mediterranean zone). There is a distinct difference in the Neolithic tool kit, however, following the appearance of the axe tool group, the arrowheads, and a new type of grinding tool (the step-like querns).

If the PPNA as a term is reserved only for a certain group of assemblages defined by the existence of axes, sickle blades, a few arrowheads, rounded structures, and subfloor burials, then its distribution will be clearly limited to the Mediterranean zone. Within it the sites are located on the edges of alluvial terraces and in proximity to springs where a primitive form of irrigation may have been practiced. In this case the Neolithic settlements will differ from Natufian ones mainly by the dominance of axes, the change in grinding tools (which may imply different vegetal food), and the decrease in the use of microliths.

During the same period, the marginal zones (marginal to the Mediterranean region) were still occupied by groups of hunters and food-gatherers. The new forms of arrowheads and the continuation of use of microliths are the most indicative typological features which demarcate these groups. There are two common types of arrowheads. First

TABLE 4

GEOGRAPHICAL DISTRIBUTION OF EPIPALEOLITHIC AND EARLY NEOLITHIC SITES IN PALESTINE AND NORTHERN SINAI

CHRONOLOGY Years/B.C. (based on C-14)	COASTAL PLAIN	GALILEE CARMEL JUDEA	JORDAN VALLEY	JUDEAN DESERT	LOWER NEGEV	HIGHER NEGEV	NORTHERN SINAI
8,300		*PPNA* Nahal Oren, 1-3	*PPNA* Jericho	El Khiam, 1-3 El Khiam, 4		*Harifian* Abu Salem (G12) G8	*Harifian* Lagama IV Moshabi III
	Late Natufian *Azor *Poleg 18M	*Late Natufian* Nahal Oren, 4-6 El-Wad B$_1$ Shukbah *Point 508	*Late Natufian* Nahal Ein Gev II *Fazael IV	*Late Natufian* *Tor Abu Sif *El-Khiam, 8-5		*Late Natufian* Rosh Zin (D16) Rosh Horesha (G7)	
		Early Natufian Hayonim El-Wad B$_2$ Kebara *Rakefet *Abu Usba Erq el Ahmar	*Early Natufian* Jericho Eynan	*Early Natufian* *Ain Sakhri *Umm ez-Zuwetina	*Geom. Keb. B* Nahal Lavan IV Zeelim No. 4,7,12 Ain Sekher Kurnub	*Geom. Keb. B* K5 K6 K7 G1,3 G14 K9 G9	*Geom. Keb. B* Lagama IX Moshabi IV Arif en Naga Lagama Ie Moshabi I
10,000	*Geom. Keb. A* †Kefar Darom 28 Cesarea-South Hefsibah Hofith Kefar Vitkin III (mixed) Kiryath Arieh I Gath Rimon Soreq 33MI Soreq 33M	*Geom. Keb. A* †Nahal Oren, 8-?	*Geom. Keb. A* †Ein Gev IV Haon III Emireh Cave Fazael III, 3 Malih I-II Malih V Malih IV	*Geom. Keb. A* El-Khiam, 9	*Geom. Keb. A* Nahal Lavan VII Nahal Lavan 105 Point 104 Nahal Lavan II Zeelim No. 5 (mixed)	*Geom. Keb. A* D5 Ras Abu Zerabit	*Geom. Keb. A* Lagama I,c&f
12,000	*Kebaran* Haifa I Omm Khalid Maagan Michael Nahal Hadera V Poleg 18MII Wingate Kiryath Arieh II Soreq 33M$_1$, 33M$_2$ Giveath Haesev Kefar Darom 3	*Kebaran* Kebara C Nahal Oren, 9 Sefunim Iraq el Baroud, A$_2$ Rockshelter Meged Hayonim, C a-f	*Kebaran* Ein Gev III, 1-5 Ein Gev II Ein Gev I Fazael III,5 Fazael III,6				
15,000	Kefarom 8 Kefarom 13						

* Natufian transitory camps

† Assemblages with dominance of triangles

is the retouched point with bilateral notches and concave base, or retouched point with concave base (Perrot, 1952; Echegaray, 1966); these are assumed to be of Late Natufian age and to represent a distinct entity (Khamian), and are suggested as contemporary with an early phase of the PPNA period. The second type is the Harif point as described by Marks (1973).

The first type was found with microlithic assemblages (lunates and trapeze-rectangles) either in an arid area (El-Khiam) or within high mountainous, plateau-like areas in the Anti-Lebanon (Schroeder, personal communication). In both cases, as in the many more expected ones, these points are associated with what seems to be a continuation of the Geometric Kebaran industrial tradition (i.e., production of bladelets and microliths). At least from the stratigraphic evidence of El-Khiam this kind of assemblage is probably later than the Natufian. This observation is supported by the C-14 dates from Abu-Salem in Har Harif (Table 1).

The diversity of economic activities as it can be estimated now from the distribution of different types of assemblages between ca. 8300 B.C.–7500 B.C. is between simple farming communities that exploited the vegetal resources of the Mediterranean regions, with a minor additional source of game, and hunters carrying on the same mode of life as their forerunners in the arid zones. The variegated area of the Anti-Lebanon and the Syrian plateau probably enabled these hunters to coexist with the Neolithic villagers.

To sum up both the facts and the interpretations presented in the above pages, it seems that there were tremendous changes in both adaptation and exploitation from the Kebaran to the Pre-Pottery Neolithic B period. There was a shift from what seems to have been small bands of hunters and food-gatherers, spread all over the countryside, with special preference for lowlands, to larger communities in the Mediterranean and Irano-Turanian zone which demonstrate extended dynamics in hunting, food collecting, trade, and architectural construction. The other vegetational zones, either heavily forested highlands or desertic areas, remained hunting fields for both the Natufians and their contemporaries. Intensive adaptation is accentuated in the PPNA period with the invention of new grinding and hunting tools. The onset of Holocene conditions, as well as possible overexploitation, emphasizes the differences between the villagers and the hunters.

BIBLIOGRAPHY

ARENSBURG, B., and BAR-YOSEF, O., in press. "Human Remains from Ein Gev I, Jordan Valley, Israel." *Paleorient* 2.

BAR-YOSEF, O., 1970*a*. "The Epi-Paleolithic Cultures of Palestine." Ph.D. dissertation, Hebrew University.

————, 1970*b*. "Prehistoric Sites near Ashdod, Israel." *Palestine Exploration Quarterly* 102:53-69.

————, and GOREN, N., 1973. "Natufian Remains in Hayonim Cave." *Paleorient* 1:49-68.

————, and TCHERNOV, E., 1967. "Archaeological Finds and the Fossil Faunas of the Natufian and Microlithic Industries at Hayonim Cave (Western Galilee, Israel)." *Israel Journal of Zoology* 15:104-40.

————, and TCHERNOV, E., 1970. "The Natufian Bone Industry of Ha-Yonim Cave." *Israel Exploration Journal* 20:141-50.

BURIAN, F., and FRIEDMAN, E., 1973. "Prehistoric Hunters in the Dunes of Halutza." *Mitqufat ha-Even* 11:27-34 (in Hebrew).

CHAVAILLON, J., and HOURS, F., 1970. "Jiita II (Dahr el Meghara). Campagne 1971, rapport préliminaire." *Bulletin du Musée de Beyrouth* 23:215-31.

CLARKE, D., 1968. *Analytical Archaeology*. London: Methuen.

COPELAND, L., and WAECHTER, J., 1968. "The Stone Industries of Abri Bergy, Lebanon." *Bulletin of the Institute of Archaeology, London* 7:15-36.

DAVIS, S., 1972. "Faunal Remains of Upper Palaeolithic Sites at 'En Gev (Israel)." Master's thesis, Hebrew University.

ECHEGARAY, J. G., 1964, 1966. *Excavaciones en la Terraza de 'El-Khiam' (Jordania)*. Madrid.

EWING, J. F., 1947. "Preliminary Note on the Excavations at the Palaeolithic Site of Ksar Akil, Republic of Lebanon." *Antiquity* 21:186-96.

FLANNERY, K. V., 1972. "The Origins of the Villages as a Settlement Type in Mesoamerica and the Near East: A Comparative Study." In *Man, Settlement, and Urbanism*, edited by J. P. Ucko, R. Tringham, and G. W. Dimbleby, pp. 23-53. London: Gerald Duckworth.

GARROD, D. A. E., 1932. "A New Mesolithic Industry: the Natufian of Palestine." *Journal of the Royal Anthropological Institute* 62:257-69.

————, 1954. "Excavations at the Mugharet el-Kebara, Mount Carmel, 1931: The Aurignacian Industries." *Proceedings of the Prehistoric Society* 20:155-92.

————, 1957. "The Natufian Culture: The Life and Economy of a Mesolithic People in the Near East." *Proceedings of the British Academy* 43:211-27.

————, and BATE, D. M. A., 1937. *The Stone Age of Mount Carmel*, vol. 1. Oxford: Clarendon Press.

HENRY, D., 1973. "The Natufian of Palestine: Its Material Culture and Ecology." Ph.D. dissertation, Southern Methodist University.

————, in press. "An Examination of the Artifactual Variability in the Natufian of Palestine." *Eretz-Israel* 13.

HOROWITZ, A., 1971. "Climatic and Vegetational Developments in Northeastern Israel during the Upper Pleistocene-Holocene Times." *Pollen et Spores* 13:255-78.

HOURS, F., 1966. "Rapport préliminaire sur les fouilles de Jiita." *Bulletin du Musée de Beyrouth* 19:11-28.

KENYON, K., 1960. *Archaeology in the Holy Land*. London.

KIRKBRIDE, D., 1958. "A Kebaran Rock Shelter in Wadi Madamagh near Petra, Jordan." *Man* 58:55-58.

KOZLOWSKI, S. K., 1973. *The Mesolithic in Europe*. Warsaw: Warsaw University Press.

LEROI-GOURHAN, A., 1973. "Les possibilités de l'analyse pollinique en Syrie et en Liban." *Paleorient* 1:39-48.

MARKS, A. E., 1973. "The Harif Point: A New Tool Type from the Terminal Epipaleolithic of the Central Negev, Israel." *Paleorient* 1:99-102.

————, in press. "The Epipaleolithic of the Central Negev: Current Status." *Eretz-Israel* 13.

————; CREW, H.; FERRING, R.; and PHILLIPS, J., 1972. "Prehistoric Sites near Har Harif." *Israel Exploration Journal* 22:73-85.

————; PHILLIPS, J.; CREW, H.; and FERRING, R., 1971. "Prehistoric Sites near 'En-'Avdat in the Negev." *Israel Exploration Journal* 22(2-3):73-85.

MELLAART, J., 1965. *Earliest Civilizations of the Near East*. New York: McGraw-Hill.

NEEV, D., and EMERY, K. O., 1967. "The Dead Sea." *Bulletin of the Geological Survey of Israel* 41:1-147.

NEUVILLE, R., 1934. "Le Préhistorique de Palestine." *Revue Biblique* 43:237-59.

————, 1951. *Le Paléolithique et le Mésolithique du désert de Judée*. Archives de l'Institut de Paléontologie humaine, mémoire 24.

NIR, D., 1967. "Remarques sur le quaternaire de la plaine côtier du Néguev septentrional (Israel)." *Bulletin de l'Association de Géographes Française* 352:2-10.

NOY, T.; HIGGS, E.; LEGGE, A.; and GISIS, I., 1973. "Recent Excavations at Nahal Oren, Israel." *Proceedings of the Prehistoric Society* 39:75-99.

OLAMI, Y., 1973. "The Epi-Palaeolithic Site Haifa 1." *Metqufat ha-Even* 11:8-15 (in Hebrew).

PERROT, J., 1952. "Tètes de flèches Natoufien et du Tahunien (Palestine)." *Bulletin de la Société Préhistorique Française* 49:439-49.

————, 1966. "Le gisement Natoufien de Mallaha (Eynan), Israel." *L'Anthropologie* 70:437-84.

————, 1968. "La préhistoire palestinienne." In *Supplément au Dictionnaire de la Bible* 8(43):286-446. Paris: Letouzey et Ane.

PHILLIPS, J.; GOREN, N.; and BAR-YOSEF, O., in press. "Epipaleolithic Sites in Northern Sinai: A Preliminary Report." *Israel Exploration Journal*.

PRAUSNITZ, M. W., 1970. "Turning Points in the Mesolithic Cultures of the Israeli Littoral." *Actes du VIIe Congrès International des Sciences Préhistoriques, Prague 1966, Institut d'Archeologie CSAV*, pp. 353-55.

REIFENBERG, A., 1953. "The Struggle between the Desert and the Sown." *Desert Research*.

RONEN, A., 1968. "Excavations at the Cave of Sefunim (Iraq-el-Baroud), Mount Carmel, Preliminary Report." *Quartar* 19:275-88.

RUST, A., 1950. *Die Höhlenfunde von Jabrud (Syrien)*. Neümunster: Karl Wachholtz.

SCHROEDER, B., 1970. "A Prehistoric Survey of the Northern Béqaa Valley." *Bulletin du Musée de Beyrouth* 23:193-204.

SMITH, P., 1973. "Family Burials at Hayonim." *Paleorient* 1:69-72.

SOLECKI, R., and SOLECKI, R. L., 1966. "New Data from Yabroud, Syria: Preliminary Report of the Columbia Archaeological Investigations." *Annales Archéologiques Arabes Syriennes* 16(2):121-54.

STEKELIS, M., 1961. "Iraq-el-Baroud, nouvelle grotte préhistorique au Mont Carmel." *Bulletin of the Research Council of Israel* G10:1-12.

_____, and BAR-YOSEF, O., 1965. "Un habitat du Paléolithique supérieur à Ein Gev (Israel), note préliminaire." *L'Anthropologie* 69:176-83.

_____, and YIZRAELI, T., 1963. "Excavations at Nahal Oren, Preliminary Report." *Israel Exploration Journal* 13:1-12.

TCHERNOV, E., 1968. *Succession of Rodent Faunas during the Upper Pleistocene of Israel*. Hamburg: Mammalia Depicta.

TIXIER, J., 1970. "L'abri-sous-roche de Ksar Akil: Rapport préliminaire sur le campagne 1969." *Bulletin du Musée de Beyrouth* 23:173-91.

TURVILLE-PETRE, F., 1932. "Excavations in the Mugharet el Kebarah." *Journal of the Royal Anthropological Institute* 62:270-76.

VALLA, F., in press. "L'industrie Natoufienne d'Eynan (Mallaha), Fouilles 1972." *Israel Exploration Journal*.

VAN LIERRE, W. J., and CONTENSON, H., 1964. "Holocene Environment and Early Settlement in the Levant." *Annales Archéologiques Arabes Syriennes* 14:125-28.

VITA-FINZI, C., 1969. *The Mediterranean Valleys, Geological Changes in Historical Times*. Cambridge: At the University Press.

_____, and HIGGS, E., 1971. "Prehistoric Economy in the Mount Carmel Area of Palestine: Site Catchment Analysis." *Proceedings of the Prehistoric Society* 36:1-37.

YIZRAELI, T., 1967. "Mesolithic Hunters' Industries at Ramat Matred (The Wilderness of Zin), First Report." *Palestine Exploration Quarterly* 99:78-85.

ZOHARY, M., 1962. *Plant Life of Palestine, Israel, and Jordan*. New York: Ronald Press.

FAUNA IN NEAR EASTERN ARCHAEOLOGICAL DEPOSITS

Don Henry
Institute of Archaeology
The Hebrew University
Jerusalem, Israel

INTRODUCTION

For a number of years prehistorians have been concerned with the implications of the variability in animal remains derived from archaeological deposits. Faunal material has primarily been viewed as evidence for the reconstruction of paleoenvironments which existed during the prehistoric occupations of archaeological sites. The reconstruction of past environments by faunal analysis is based on the assumption that animals presently indigenous to specific environmental zones would have been associated with similar zones in the past. The recovered faunal sample, however, must be representative of an animal population surrounding an archaeological site at the time of occupation, if the paleoenvironmental reconstruction is to be reliable. It has been suggested that prehistoric man could have biased faunal samples in an archaeological context by preferential selection or hunting. This biasing mechanism, termed a "cultural filter," implies that prehistoric behavioral patterns must be considered prior to environmental reconstruction (Reed, 1963). Examination of cultural filters can also yield considerable insight into prehistoric behavioral patterns (Uerpmann, 1973).

A classic example of paleoenvironmental reconstruction without consideration of a cultural filter is the hypothetical climatic curve based on faunal material recovered from the Mount Carmel caves in Palestine. This proposed climatic sequence was based on the proportional occurrences of *Dama* (Persian fallow deer) and *Gazella* (gazelle) remains appearing in the archaeological deposits of the caves (Garrod and Bate, 1937). *Dama* is associated with forested areas and a more moist biotype than the steppe adapted *Gazella* (Harrison, 1968). It was assumed, then, that high frequencies of *Dama* were indicative of forest conditions and a moist climate, while a prevalence of *Gazella* remains implied a steppic environment induced by a period of aridity. Subsequent excavation of the site of Ksar Akil in Lebanon yielded an archaeological sequence which, in part, could be temporally correlated with the Mount Carmel sequence. Upon analysis, the associated faunal material failed to correspond to the Mount Carmel evidence. As a result of the differences in faunal assemblages from the two areas, the validity of the *Dama-Gazella* climatic sequence was questioned (Hooijer, 1961). Proponents of the climatic sequence, however, have suggested that the inherent environmental differences of the Mount Carmel and Ksar Akil regions could account for the disparity in faunal assemblages at any point in time (Higgs, 1967). The question of a cultural filter has also been considered in relation to the climatic sequence.

DETECTION OF A CULTURAL FILTER

Recently, it was suggested that a cultural filter could be detected if culturally related archaeological sites exhibited similar faunal assemblages even though the sites were situated in significantly different environments (Higgs, 1967). This testing procedure has been applied to gross archaeological entities (Upper Paleolithic, Levalloiso-Mousterian), recognized in North Africa and the Levant, in an attempt to demonstrate that a cultural filter was not operative and that the Mount Carmel climatic sequence was indeed valid. These archaeological entities, however, cannot be viewed as cultures because of their considerable spatial distribution and temporal span.

The upper part of the Mount Carmel climatic sequence is based on faunal material recovered from the Natufian deposit, layer B, of el-Wad Cave. The Natufian represents a prehistoric culture with limited and defined spatial distribution and temporal span (Henry, in press). The Natufian site settlement pattern is distributed in two macroenvironments, or phytogeographic zones, of Palestine (Zohary, 1962) (fig. 1). Examination of the faunal assemblages from Natufian sites makes it apparent that a cultural filter is present, for *Gazella* remains are consistently predominant over *Dama* remains regardless of environmental setting (Table 1). The *Gazella* peak, during the Natufian, appears not to reflect a steppic environment or greater aridity in the Mount Carmel area from 10,000 to 12,000 years ago. Recent studies of microfauna (Bar-Yosef and Tchernov, 1966), evaporites (Neev and Emery, 1967), and pollen (Horowitz, 1971) in various areas of Palestine for this time period indicate that the climate was actually more humid than at present.

VARIETY OF CULTURAL FILTER

It is apparent that the presence of a cultural filter induced the prevalence of gazelle remains in Natufian deposits, but the specific factor responsible for the prominence of gazelles is more difficult to define. Several possible causes exist, including butchering bias, domestication/herding, and prehistoric hunting patterns.

Butchering bias could have existed if the Natufian hunters had processed deer to a greater extent than gazelle while in the field before returning to camp. The Persian fallow deer is somewhat greater in size than the Near

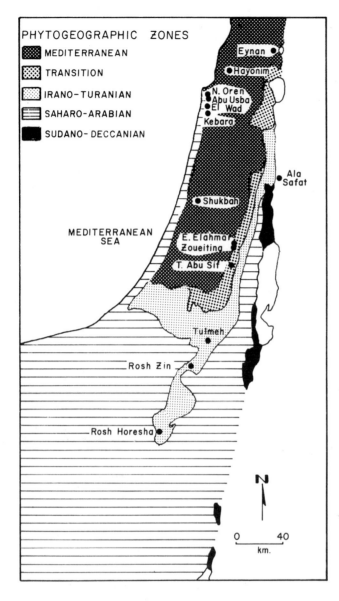

FIG. 1—Natufian site distribution in relation to phytogeographic zones of Palestine.

Eastern gazelle forms. It is, therefore, feasible that the Natufian hunters selectively butchered a deer carcass to remove excess weight, but, on the other hand, returned to camp with nearly all of the gazelle carcass. If this were the case, one would expect *Dama* and *Gazella* remains to exhibit different types of bones in the Natufian camps. If *Dama* were being butchered in the field to reduce its weight, it is probable that the least productive parts of the carcass (lower limb bones and crania) would have been removed (Uerpmann, 1973; Chaplin, 1971; Perkins and Daly, 1968). While this model is theoretically appealing, the available data do not support it. Examination of *Dama* and *Gazella* remains from Natufian deposits (Hayonim Cave and Eynan) reveals that there are no significant differences in the types of bones recovered. At Hayonim Cave the *Dama* and *Gazella* remains are represented mostly by mandibles (Bar-Yosef and Tchernov, 1966), and at Eynan lower limb

bones constitute the most common skeletal parts of both animal varieties as reported by Ducos (1968). While there are differences between Hayonim and Eynan in regard to the specific skeletal parts present, the differences are not between animals at either of the sites. The similar varieties of *Dama* and *Gazella* bones would imply that differential butchering did not account for the prominence of *Gazella* remains in Natufian occupation deposits. It is interesting that those bones most subject to elimination away from the camp appear as the most prominent in Natufian occupations. This could possibly be accounted for by the differential durability of bones due to their shape and structure. Brain (1967, 1969) notes that cranial parts (particularly mandibles) and certain lower limb bones are the most durable to the various destructive agencies in modern Hottentot villages.

Recently it has been suggested that domesticaton or herding of gazelles could have accounted for their abundance in Natufian deposits (Legge, 1972), although the distinction between domestication and herding of gazelle is considered to be an arbitrary division by some authorities (Coles and Higgs, 1969). This proposal is based primarily on the high frequencies of young gazelles recovered. The appearance of high frequencies of immature sheep and goats in archaeological deposits has been used as evidence for domestication when diagnostic morphological data were lacking (Reed, 1959; Bokonyi, 1969). It is assumed that greater cropping of immature animals would occur in a domestication situation than in hunting. Frequencies of immature gazelle (under 2 years) range from 30% to 55% in Natufian deposits (Ducos, 1968; Legge, 1972). While these frequencies seem to be high, they are lower than the frequency of immature gazelles (70%) represented in existing East African herds (Robinette and Archer, 1971). Although the age distribution data on modern herds were derived from a study of Thomson's gazelles (*Gazella thomsonii*) in East Africa and not Near Eastern forms (*Gazella subgutturosa, Gazella gazella, Gazella dorcas*), the data offer pertinent insights into the problem of age distribution. Considering the large numbers of predators that feed on gazelles, it is not surprising that the natural age curve would reflect high frequencies of immature forms (Brooks, 1961; Wright, 1960). Until recent times, a wide variety of predators, including many of those cited by Brooks and Wright, were found in Palestine.

Another potential problem with using age distribution data as evidence for domestication or herding of gazelles is that this approach disregards their social system or intraherd behavior. As is typical of gregarious, territorial antelopes, three groupings can be recognized among gazelles: nursery herds of females and young, bachelor herds of mainly immature males, and a small class of mature territorial males (Estes, 1967). The proximity of these groups varies, depending on the kind of gazelle and the size of its territory. These divisions along age and sex lines could easily distort the archaeological interpretation of a prehistoric faunal assemblage, especially if the assemblage was made up

TABLE 1

DISTRIBUTION OF *DAMA* AND *GAZELLA* REMAINS
RECOVERED FROM NATUFIAN DEPOSITS
IN RELATION TO PRESENT MEAN ANNUAL RAINFALL
AND MAJOR FLORAL COMMUNITIES OF PALESTINE

SITE AREA	Hayonim Cave Western Galilee	Eynan Eastern Galilee	el-Wad Mount Carmel	Shukbah Western Judea	Erq El-Ahmar Eastern Judea	Rosh Zin Negev Hills
Modern Ishohyte	600-800 mm	600-700 mm	500-700 mm	500-600 mm	300-500 mm	100-200 mm
Modern Flora	Mediterranean	Mediterranean	Mediterranean	Mediterranean	Mediterranean and Irano-Turanian	Irano-Turanian
Identifiable Bones						
Dama	2	96	60	12	Absent	Rare
Gazella	35	382	2,050	303	Abundant	Abundant
Reference	(Bar-Yosef and Tchernov, 1966)	(Ducos, 1968)	(Garrod and Bate, 1937)	(Bate, 1942)	(Neuville, 1951)	(Marks, personal communication)

of a small bone sample. A single prehistoric hunt that, by chance or intention, focused on any one of these segregated groups would produce a faunal assemblage that could be highly misleading to an osteo-archaeologist emphasizing age/sex distribution data alone.

If the age distribution of modern East African herds is indicative of herds existing in Palestine from 10,000 B.C. to 8,000 B.C., it would seem that Natufian exploitation of gazelles was not focused on immature animals. As shown in fig. 2, the age distribution of gazelles recovered from the Natufian site of Eynan underrepresents immature animals and overrepresents mature forms. Although the reasons for this biasing are unknown, it could be related to the greater meat production of the mature forms, to conservation prac-

tices of prehistoric hunters, or to the reluctance of mature male gazelles to leave their territory in face of danger (Estes, 1967). Regardless of the factors influencing selection of mature animals, this information does necessitate a reevaluation of the significance of high frequencies of immature gazelles in denoting domestication or herding. Until more adequate evidence becomes available, the proposal that Natufian populations were involved in herding or domestication of gazelle should be viewed as purely hypothetical.

If, as it appears, gazelles were not herded or domesticated by Natufians, then an explanation for the prevalence of gazelle in Natufian deposits must be associated with hunting strategy. The intensive exploitation of the gazelle in the Natufian can be accounted for in two ways. First, the Natufian site catchment (area of exploitation surrounding the site) was larger than site catchments of preceding groups, enabling Natufians to develop hunting strategies more efficient in exploitation of gazelles.

In reviewing the Hole and Flannery (1967) settlement pattern model, Mortensen (1972) distinguished between "circulating" and "radiating" settlement patterns. He notes that in the circulating pattern seasonal movement accounts for numerous ephemeral camp sites, while in the radiating pattern a single, permanent base camp is maintained by various transitory camps situated about it radially. The site catchments of the two patterns would be expected to differ significantly, as well (fig. 3). In the circulating pattern, the site catchment would include an area in close proximity to the site (perhaps on the order of five km, as suggested by Vita-Finzi and Higgs [1970]). The site catchment of the radiating pattern, on the other hand, would include a considerable territory through the channelling of resources (animal, plant, and raw material) from the various radial exploitation camps back to the base camp.

A radiating pattern is in fact suggested by the two major kinds of sites reported for the Natufian (Bar-Yosef, 1970, p. 175; Henry, 1973, pp. 192-93). Base camps and exploitation camps can be distinguished by their respective site

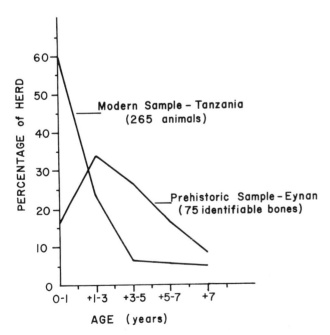

FIG. 2–Comparison of the age distributions of modern and archaeologically derived *Gazella* remains.

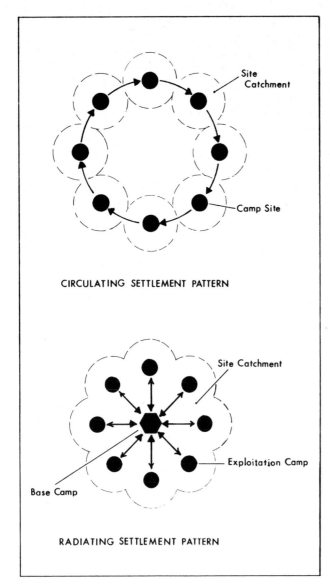

CIRCULATING SETTLEMENT PATTERN

RADIATING SETTLEMENT PATTERN

FIG. 3—Idealized schematic comparing circulating and radiating settlement patterns (modified after Mortensen, 1972).

areas, associated features, and artifactual assemblages. Examination of Table 2 indicates that Natufian base camps normally exhibit occupation areas in excess of 200 m² and contain burials, ground stone, and ornamental objects. Exploitation camps, on the other hand, generally display occupation areas under 200 m² and lack the burials, architecture, and ground stone.

Thanks to an intensive utilization of plant resources (as evidenced by grinding stones, sickle blades, and pollen information) Natufian groups were able to develop a storable surplus which allowed for permanent residence and large group size. In comparison to the Natufian exploitive strategy, preceding groups of the Palestinian Upper Paleolithic tradition did not emphasize the collection and processing of plant resources; this is reflected in the near absence of grinding stones and sickle blades (Bar-Yosef, 1970). Site

size and density also indicate that groups of the Upper Paleolithic tradition were highly transitory, with little permanency of residence.

The Natufians, being sedentary or semisedentary, were induced to exploit a larger site catchment than groups of the Upper Paleolithic tradition. Therefore, Natufian base camps contain remnants of resources derived from a much more extensive area surrounding the site than the smaller and more transitory Upper Paleolithic campsites.

The differences in site catchment size might explain, in part, the differences in faunal assemblages recovered in the Upper Paleolithic and Natufian deposits of the Mount Carmel caves. The site catchments of the Upper Paleolithic levels would have been more restricted to the Mediterranean maquis biotype (*Dama* habitat) of the Mount Carmel area, while the Natufian site catchments would have been more extensive, including much more of the coastal plain (*Gazella* habitat). Today, the coastal plain fronting the Mount Carmel area, is narrow and displays considerable marsh land. However, with the lower sea level of terminal Pleistocene times the coastal plain would have been much more extensive and probably better drained than today. Thus, it is not surprising that the Natufian occupations in the Mount Carmel display higher frequencies of gazelle than the Upper Paleolithic levels.

The factor of prehistoric group size is also considered to have generated different hunting strategies in the Natufian and the Upper Paleolithic. The areas of Natufian base camps are considerably larger than sites of the Upper Paleolithic tradition. The areas of Natufian base camps average ca. 700 m² (one in excess of 7,000 m², while Kebaran and Geometric Kebaran average 200 m²). The greater areas of Natufian camps would imply larger group population which would have been supported by the stable subsistence base of the Natufian economy. With the greater numbers, the Natufian hunters could consistently have exploited gazelle herds by drives and surrounds. The Upper Paleolithic groups, no doubt, hunted gazelle, but with less efficiency. Stalking of gazelle herds on the open, flat plains would have been difficult and possibly less rewarding for small groups of hunters than searching the forest and shrub areas for deer. Pfeifer (1969) describes the stalking procedure employed by the late Louis Leakey in approaching a gazelle over a two-hour period. Spinage (1963) upon observing Thomson's gazelles in East Africa notes that the Tommy is almost strictly an animal of the open plains, avoiding the bush even under chase and relying on speed and stamina for escape. Spinage goes on to point out that when surrounded by several hunters, the animals will become confused and run in small circles. This circling tendency has also been observed in the Near East. Hole, Flannery, and Neely (1969) observed that while the gazelles (*G. subgutturosa*) had tremendous speed, they had a habit of running in wide circles. Recognizing their circling tendency, Neely was able to predict the path of a herd and intercept it.

It appears that the behavior of gazelle, and possibly

TABLE 2

NATUFIAN SITE AREAS AND RELATED ATTRIBUTES

SITE	AREA (m²)	BURIALS	ARCHITECTURE	GROUND STONE
Hayonim Cave	150	+	+	+
Eynan	2,000	+	+	+
el-Wad	350	+	+	+
Shukbah	1,000	+	+	+
Erq el-Ahmar	50	+	−	+
Rosh Zin	800	−	+	+
Rosh Horesha	7,000+	−[1]	+	+
Oumm ez-Zoueitina	50	−	−	−
Tor Abou-Sif	50	−	−	?
Ain Sakhri	50	−	−	−
Ala Safat	50	−	−	−
Jabrud III/2	?	−	−	−
Nahal Oren	1,000	+	+	+
Kebara	200	+	−	+
Abu Usba	140	−	−	−

[1] Insufficiently tested to permit any definite conclusion.

other antelopes, makes them subject to exploitation by drives and surrounds. Ethnographic information suggests that large numbers of people are required for effective drives, as indicated by aborigines in North America where rabbit and antelope drives were undertaken with the cooperation of a number of autonomous groups (Steward, 1933).

SUMMARY

Before archaeologically derived fauna can be used for paleoenvironmental interpretations, the various biasing aspects of a cultural filter must be considered. While a cultural filter tends to distort paleoenvironmental reconstructions, biased faunal remains can reveal a great deal about prehistoric behavioral patterns.

With respect to Natufian deposits in Palestine, it would appear that a cultural filter was operative from 10,000 B.C.–8,000 B.C. as indicated by the homogeneity of faunal assemblages retrieved from Natufian deposits situated in diverse environments. The recognition of a cultural filter in the Natufian, in conjunction with modern paleoenvironmental data, necessitates a rejection of the climatic implications of the hypothetical *Dama-Gazella* curve, at least in respect to the Natufian deposits.

In drawing on human biasing factors, prehistorians have proposed that differential butchering or domestication/ herding could have accounted for the prevalence of *Gazella* in Natufian deposits. Because neither of these models is supported by the available data, an alternative model, which emphasizes prehistoric demographic and sociocultural evidence in relation to *Gazella* behavior, is advanced. It is proposed that the prevalence of *Gazella* in Natufian occupations resulted from: (1) the Natufian site catchments' incorporation of large areas of *Gazella* habitat; and (2) the effective utilization of drives and surrounds in *Gazella* procurement by Natufian communities.

BIBLIOGRAPHY

BAR-YOSEF, O., 1970. "The Epi-Paleolithic Cultures of Palestine." Ph.D. dissertation, Hebrew University.

————, and TCHERNOV, E., 1966. "Archaeological Finds and the Fossil Faunas of the Natufian and Microlithic Industries at Hayonim Cave (Western Galilee, Israel)." *Israel Journal of Zoology* 15:104-40.

BATE, D. M. A., 1942. "Excavations at the Cave of Shukbah, Palestine, 1928. (Appendix on the Fossil Mammals of Shukbah)." *Proceedings of the Prehistoric Society* 1:1-20.

BOKONYI, S., 1969. "Archaeological Problems and Methods of Recognizing Animal Domestication." In *The Domestication and Exploitation of Plants and Animals*, edited by P. J. Ucko and G. W. Dimbleby. Chicago: Aldine.

BRAIN, C. K., 1967. "Hottentot Food Remains and their Bearing on the Interpretation of Fossil Bone Assemblages." *Scientific Papers of the Namid Research Station* 32:1-11.

————, 1969. "The Contribution of Namid Desert Hottentots to an Understanding of Australopithecine Bone Accumulations." *Scientific Papers of the Namid Research Station* 39:13-22.

BROOKS, A. C., 1961. *A Study of Thomson's Gazelle in Tanganyika*. London: Her Majesty's Stationery Office.

CHAPLIN, R. E., 1971. *The Study of Animal Bones from Archaeological Sites*. London: Seminar Press.

COLES, J. M., and HIGGS, E. S., 1969. *The Archaeology of Early Man*. New York: Praeger.

DUCOS, P., 1968. *L'Origine des Animaux Domestiques en Palestine*. Bordeaux: Publications de l'Institut de Préhistoire de l'Université de Bordeaux.

ESTES, R. D., 1967. "The Comparative Behavior of Grant's and Thomson's Gazelles." *Journal of Mammalogy* 48:189-209.

GARROD, D. A. E., and BATE, D. M. A., 1937. *The Stone Age of Mount Carmel*, vol. 1. Oxford: Clarendon Press.

HARRISON, D. L., 1968. *Mammals of Arabia*, vol. 2. London: Ernest Benn Ltd.

HENRY, D., 1973. "The Natufian of Palestine: Its Material Culture and Ecology." Ph.D. dissertation, Southern Methodist University.

————, in press. "Examination of Artifactual Variability in the Natufian." *Eretz Israel*, vol. 13, edited by O. Bar-Yosef and B. Arensburg.

HIGGS, E. S., 1967. "Faunal Fluctuations and Climate in Libya." In *Background to Evolution in Africa*, edited by W. W. Bishop and J. D. Clark, pp. 149-64. Chicago: University of Chicago Press.

HOLE, F., and FLANNERY, K., 1967. "The Prehistory of Southwestern Iran: A Preliminary Report." *Proceedings of the Prehistoric Society* 33:147-206.

————; FLANNERY, K.; and NEELY, J., 1969. *Prehistoric Human Ecology of the Deh Luran Plain*. Memoirs of the Museum of Anthropology, No. 1. Ann Arbor: University of Michigan.

HOOIJER, D. A., 1961. "The Fossil Vertebrates of Ksar Akil, a Paleolithic Rock Shelter in Lebanon." *Zoologische Verhandelingen* 49:1-67.

HOROWITZ, A., 1971. "Climatic and Vegetational Developments in Northeastern Israel during Upper Pleistocene-Holocene Times." *Pollen et Spores* 13:255-78.

LEGGE, T., 1972. "Prehistoric Exploitation of the Gazelle in Palestine." In *Papers in Economic Prehistory*, edited by E. S. Higgs. Cambridge: At the University Press.

MORTENSON, P., 1972. "Seasonal Camps and Early Villages in the Zagros." In *Man, Settlement, and Urbanism*, edited by P. Ucko et al. London: Duckworth and Co.

NEEV, D., and EMERY, K., 1967. "The Dead Sea." *Bulletin Geological Survey of Israel* 41:1-147.

NEUVILLE, R., 1951. *Le Paléolithique et le Mésolithique du Désert de Judée*. Archives de l'Institut de Paléontologie humaine, mémoire 24.

PERKINS, D., 1964. "Prehistoric Fauna from Shanidar, Iraq." *Science* 144:1629-39.

————, and DALY, P., 1968. "A Hunters' Village in Neolithic Turkey." *Scientific American* 219:97-106.

PFEIFER, J., 1969. *The Emergence of Man*. New York: Harper and Row.

REED, C. A., 1959. "Animal Domestication in the Prehistoric Near East." *Science* 130:1629-39.

————, 1963. "Osteo-archaeology." In *Science in Archaeology*, edited by D. Brothwell and E. S. Higgs. New York: Basic Books.

ROBINETTE, W. L., and ARCHER, A. L., 1971. "Notes in Ageing Criteria and Reproduction of Thomson's Gazelle." *East African Wildlife Journal* 9:83-98.

SPINAGE, C. A., 1963. *Animals of East Africa*. Cambridge: Riverside Press.

STEWARD, J. H., 1933. "Ethnography of the Owens Valley Pauite." *University of California Publications in American Archaeology and Ethnology* 33:233-350.

UERPMANN, H. P., 1973. "Animal Bone Finds and Economic Archaeology: A Critical Study of 'Osteo-Archaeological' Methods." *World Archaeology* 4:307-22.

VITA-FINZI, C., and HIGGS, E. S., 1970. "Prehistoric Economy in the Mount Carmel Area of Palestine: Site Catchment Analysis." *Proceedings of the Prehistoric Society* 36:1-37.

WRIGHT, B., 1960. "Predation on Big Game in East Africa." *Journal of Wildlife Management* 24:1-15.

ZOHARY, M., 1962. *Plant Life of Palestine, Israel, and Jordan*. New York: Ronald Press.

PART III

Syntheses

PATTERNS OF ENVIRONMENTAL CHANGE IN THE NEAR EAST DURING LATE PLEISTOCENE AND EARLY HOLOCENE TIMES

Karl W. Butzer

University of Chicago

About 20,000 years ago continental glaciers covered much of Europe and North America. In all, approximately 30% of the earth's land surface was covered by ice. As paleoclimatic evidence continues to accumulate from a variety of disciplines, the magnitude of environmental change becomes increasingly apparent. Well beyond the ice sheets periglacial conditions with permafrost applied, and the Würm–Wisconsin faunas of Eurasia and North America attest to ecological conditions radically different from those of today. In the highlands of lower mid-latitudes the last Pleistocene glaciation was recorded by cirque, valley, and piedmont glaciers; or by screes, talus, and solifluction mantles. Elsewhere, in the lowlands of the subtropics, there are a variety of alluvial terraces, colluvial beds, and dunes. And in the innertropical zone, the available evidence now suggests that the tropical rain forest and forest-savanna were drastically modified and, at times, almost eliminated.

Although the broad lines of glacial phenomena have been known since the early 1900s, understanding of environmental changes in nonglaciated areas of the planet has proceeded at a rapid pace only since about 1950. Radiocarbon, potassium-argon, uranium series, and paleomagnetic dating now provide estimates of real time and, as a result, many fundamental stratigraphic concepts of Pleistocene glacial and interglacial sequences are either obsolete or in serious need of revision (see Butzer and Isaac, 1974).

Paleotemperature data, derived from deep-sea cores, indicate that ocean surface-water temperatures were appreciably different in the middle and tropical North Atlantic, the Mediterranean and Red Seas, as well as the tropical Pacific. Palynological evidence is rapidly becoming available from several sectors of the Mediterranean Basin. The accumulating pollen results from Africa are fascinating if enigmatic, while even in midlatitude Europe the interpretation of full-glacial vegetation continues to advance rapidly (see Butzer, 1971, pp. 287 ff.). Aided by these auxiliary sciences and refined by new techniques or revised theoretical concepts, geomorphological studies have found new and challenging problems in periglacial, desert, and tropical environments. Finally, both the number and sophistication of faunal and prehistoric studies have made a quantum jump in several areas.

Pleistocene studies are, consequently, in a state of flux and any synthesis is soon rendered obsolete by more recent findings. Under these circumstances any regional review can be little more than an assessment of currently available information. It renders the work of synthesis ephemeral and often thankless, but nonetheless vital if future work is to be directly along meaningful lines.

A review of late Pleistocene and early post-Pleistocene environmental changes in southwestern Asia and Egypt, written in 1973, faces these very same difficulties. For a critical discussion of the key late Pleistocene and Holocene sequences of the central and western Sahara, see Butzer (1971, pp. 312-34), and for the Sudan, see Butzer and Hansen (1968, pp. 254-58, 323-27) and Whiteman (1971, pp. 109-54). Furthermore, field work in most of this area has lagged, compared with research in many other regions of the Old World. Remarkably few stratigraphic events have been radiometrically fixed outside of Israel and the Nile Valley. In addition, the various episodes of the Late Pleistocene as well as the minor climatic variations of the Holocene are no easier to discern or interpret than are the gross changes of glacial and interglacial stages. It is generally difficult to pinpoint minor climatic variations, and in an intermediate environment such as the subtropical woodlands they are doubly difficult to recognize.

By the standards of northern Europe and the northeastern or northwestern United States, the Pleistocene and the Holocene of the Near East are poorly understood. Evidence is fragmentary and frequently of variable quality, and chronological data are inadequate for the purposes of a regional stratigraphy. At best we can outline the present status of information from different categories of evidence—glaciological, geomorphological, and biological. The broad, generalized impressions that obtain for the major physical provinces will then be presented by way of a tentative synthesis. The results, with the exception of a few areas, are unsatisfactory and, although we have attempted to take a positive approach wherever possible, it must be emphasized that the patterns suggested by the present evidence are best considered as working hypotheses.

Some fifteen years ago the writer assembled the available evidence on Pleistocene and Holocene climatic variation in the Near East (Butzer, 1958), attempting to organize the scattered data into a stratigraphic framework analogous to that of northern Europe. Despite a modest proliferation of field studies since that date, the evidence remains fragmentary for the late Pleistocene, and either nonexistent or next to incoherent for earlier time ranges. However, the results now available suggest that climatic changes within the Near East do not necessarily follow the same pattern from region to region; hence, broad interregional correlations are precluded. It is also apparent that, whatever environmental trends may be recorded in the Holocene, these cannot be simply fitted into the postglacial chronology of northern Europe. Similarly, no clearcut sequence of pluvials and interpluvials has emerged in any region, and glacial-pluvial correlations are as untenable in the Near East as elsewhere in the Mediterranean Basin and Africa (Butzer, 1971, chaps. 19-20). This same picture of complexity, wherever adequate detail and absolute dating become available, also reduces the stratigraphic value of sea-level fluctuations (Butzer, 1974). In effect, although climato-stratigraphic concepts such as "early," "full," or "late" glacial, or last glacial (Würm) and last interglacial, retain a qualified value in the Near Eastern Highlands, chronometric frameworks offer the only means of realistic, interregional correlation.

GLACIAL-GEOMORPHOLOGICAL EVIDENCE

Glaciation in the Near East is today confined to a few of the highest peaks in the mountain ranges of Turkey, the Caucasus, and northern Iran.

Small glaciers have been reported from Turkey in the Kackar Dagh (3,937 m) and Karagol (3,095 m), both in the Pontic Ranges; in the Ak Dagh (3,024 m), the Bolkardagh (3,585 m), Ala Dagh (3,900 m), Erçiyas Dagh (3,916 m), Artos Dagh (3,475 m), and Çilo Dagh (4,168 m) of the Taurus Ranges, and on the Suphan Dagh (4,434 m) and Mt. Ararat (5,165 m), among the summits of the Armenian Plateau (Messerli, 1967, pp. 166 ff.). From this evidence Messerli (1967, p. 167) estimates that the contemporary snowline rises inland from 3,200-4,000 m in the Pontic Ranges while also increasing from 3,500-4,000 m toward the interior within the Central and Eastern Taurus.

In Transcaucasia there currently are important glaciers along the crestline of the High Caucasus (Gora Elbrus, 5,633 m; Gora Shkhara, 5,201 m; Gora Kazbek, 5,047 m; Gord Bazar-Dyuzi, 4,480 m) (Klebelsberg, 1949, pp. 787 ff.), with a snowline provisionally estimated at 4,000—4,300 m (Frenzel, 1959, Map 2).

Finally, although there is a perennial snow patch or firn ice on Mt. Lebanon (3,088 m), it responds very rapidly to minor changes in precipitation and appears to be unsuitable for a snowline determination (Messerli, 1966). Highlands located at more southerly latitudes in southwestern Asia and northeastern Africa lie well below the snowline.

At the height of the Würm glaciation, existing glaciers expanded considerably and a great number of new glaciers came into existence, both in the peripheral zones of western Turkey, Lebanon, and the Zagros Ranges of Iraq and Iran, as well as among the lower ranges of eastern Turkey, northern Iran, and Transcaucasia. In Turkey the snowline depression of the Würm full glacial varied between 800 m and 1,200 m (Messerli, 1967, pp. 167 ff.), while in the Iraqi Zagros (Algurd Dagh, 3,730 m) this value was at least 1,200 m (Wright, 1962a). The snowline depression in northern Iran may have been little more than 800—900 m (Schweizer, 1970), with slightly or moderately greater values reported from older work in the Caucasus (Klebelsberg, 1949, pp. 747 ff.). Both the High Lebanon (2,088 m) and Mt. Hermon (2,814 m) were glaciated, with a snowline estimated at 2,700 m—at least 1,000 m below that of today (Messerli, 1966, also 1967, p. 166, with critique of Kaiser, 1963).

Information for the late Würm Glacial and for the post-Würm is rather more scanty. Reinhard (1925) identified three retreat stages of the Caucasus glaciers, marked by successive snowline depressions of 800—900 m, 550—600 m, and 300—400 meters. The last of these was tentatively correlated with the terminal phase of the Würm.

In the eastern Pontic Ranges, Leutelt (1935) and Gall (1966) refer to three widespread retreat stages but give few details, while de Planhol and Bilgin (1964) describe similar "recessional" moraines form the Karagol. Work by Birman (1968) indicates the presence of moraines of probably late Würm and early post-Würm age, together with definite evidence of post-Würm ice activity, both in the Pontic Ranges (south of Rize) and in the Bolkardagh of the Central Taurus. In the Ulu Dagh (2,543 m) of the western Pontic Ranges there are two successive moraines of probable late Würm or early post-Würm age together with evidence of a later, minor advance (Birman, 1968). Moraines postdating the Würm Pleniglacial are found on Ak Dagh (3,024 m), Western Taurus (Messerli, 1967, pp. 148 ff.). In the Erçiyas Dagh, Central Taurus, Birman (1968) suggests the presence of early post-Würm moraines although Messerli (1967, pp. 120 ff.) believes that an even younger rock glacier may still be of late Würm age. In the Ala Dagh, Spreitzer (1958) identified several minor morainic stages, which he believed to pertain to readvances of the seventeenth to nineteenth centuries A.D. A rock glacier, similar to that described by Messerli from the Erçiyas Dagh, was ascribed to the nineteenth century.

In the Eastern Taurus, Bobek (1940) noted a complex of "recessional" moraines in the Çilo and Sat Dagh, suggesting a snowline depression of 350 meters. In the northern Zagros there are also small upper-story cirques at 3,000 m in the Algurd Dagh, which suggest a snowline depression of at least 300 m in fairly recent times (Wright, 1962a); Desio (1934) reported recessional moraines of possible late Würm age in the Zardeh Kuh (4,286 m), southern Zagros. On the slopes of Mt. Ararat, Birman (1968) suggests the presence of late Würm or post-Würm moraines, while minor moraines postdating the Würm full glacial are fairly common in the Elburz Range of northern Iran (Bobek, 1937). The presence of these moraines seems to imply successive snowline depressions of 700 m, 450—500 m, 300 m, 250 m, 170 m, 100 m, and 50 m in the Tacht-i-Suleiman and of 700 m and 450—500 m in the Tochal group (3,970 m).

Seen in overview there is considerable, although highly fragmentary, evidence for late and post-glacial fluctuations of glaciers in the Near Eastern Highlands. Unfortunately, dating techniques are based on indirect geomorphic criteria or weathering phenomena that lack geochronological precision, and Birman (1968) was hampered in establishing a relative stratigraphy of moraines by a lack of suitable rocks for weathering criteria. Under these circumstances no definite chronology is possible. However, it seems reasonable to assume one or more readvances of the highland glaciers during the late Würm glacial, and at least one if not several stages of minor reglaciation or glacial advance in Holocene times. Messerli (1967, p. 207) estimates a summer temperature depression of 6°–7° C. for Asia Minor during the Würm Pleniglacial; and, presumably, conditions were still noticeably cool during late glacial times.

High mountain geomorphological processes of "periglacial" type are still so poorly understood in the Near East (see reviews and discussion by Tuzer, 1958, pp. 48 ff.; Bobek, 1963; and Messerli, 1966, 1967, pp. 122, 138 f., 148, 152, 199 ff.; also de Planhol and Bilgin, 1964, and Besançon and Hours, 1970–71) that they are of limited value for the present discussion.

Kaiser (1963) states that late Pleistocene cryoturbation phenomena, "ice wedges," and ice-wedge-like networks occur at elevations of 750–1,000 m in Lebanon and Syria. The writer saw these features illustrated by color slides at a colloquium (Geological Institute, University of Cologne, November 30, 1960). They are remarkably similar to colluvial or "solifluctoidal" phenomena studied in detail by the writer in Spain (Butzer, 1964a), where they are not even remotely connected with cryoturbation or ice wedges, and where it is only rarely necessary that soil frost be invoked for their genesis. The ice-wedge-like networks may be simple frost cracks, but they may possibly be dehydration fissures instead. Similar confusion exists concerning the interpretation of possible periglacial features in Sinai (see Butzer and Hansen, 1968, p. 427), the Sahara (see Butzer, 1973b), Ethiopia (see Butzer and Hansen, 1968, p. 450, and Butzer, unpublished), and southern Africa (see Butzer, 1973a).

LACUSTRINE EVIDENCE
FROM THE INTERIOR BASINS

Fossil lake beds and high shorelines are common in semiarid, lower middle latitudes. The interiors of Turkey, Iran, and the Levant are no exception.

Broad, shallow lakes, possibly of seasonal type, existed in some of the extensive alluvial basins of central Anatolia. From such evidence Wenzel (1935, pp. 40 ff.) concluded that the regional drainage had once been integrated, although it lacked an outlet to the sea. Alluvial fans appear to have been deposited during or after the recession of these lakes, and the hydrography has subsequently deteriorated into a number of minor, isolated basins.

A second type of nonoutlet lake can be found in many small tectonic basins of considerable relief, and the literature contains frequent references to high shorelines, at elevations of as much as 100 m above present lake level, in such basins (Louis, 1938; Ardel, 1938, 1954; Lahn, 1951). In no case did external drainage develop, although, on occasion, some of these lakes overflowed into an adjacent, nonoutlet basin. Such older studies offer no stratigraphic frameworks and lack sedimentological analyses.

The lacustrine beds of Anatolia may some day provide substantial evidence for late Pleistocene and Holocene climatic changes. This can be inferred from the results obtained by de Planhol (1956, pp. 39 ff.), from the Burdur Basin. Early observations had indicated the presence of shorelines at 45 m, 80 m and 90-95 m above the modern lake. These surficial beds are characterized by abundant shells of *Dreissensia burdurensis*, and an overflow threshold was recognized at the highest level, at ca. 947 meters. Louis (1938) found "microliths" on dune sands blown up from this lake, presumably during its ultimate recession, and considered them as Mesolithic. (Needless to say, small stone artifacts—when not precisely identified—have a potential time range of at least 15,000 years in the Near East.) In view of the freshness of the shorelines, he consequently concluded that the high lake levels were of late Pleistocene age and that the level dropped rapidly in early post-Pleistocene times. However, de Planhol (1956) discovered massive lake travertines to an elevation of 980 m (+125 m), which are disconformable under the younger shorelines. Paleobotanical examination of the uppermost travertine beds by G. Depape and J. Arènes (de Planhol, 1956, p. 41) showed the presence of warm-temperate species such as the trees *Quercus* cf. *pedunculata* and *Salix babylonica*, and the mesic grass *Glyceria* cf. *fluitans*. Considering that the absolute elevation of the travertines is 980 m and that a lowering of temperature would exclude such species from interior Turkey, they can hardly be of glacial age. They should tentatively be assigned to the early post-Pleistocene warmup. Implicitly, the younger shorelines could be of Holocene age. Without radiometric dating a definite chronological position can hardly be suggested. But de Planhol's work serves to show how inadequate earlier studies have been, and how promising future investigation will be. The detailed geomorphological, sedimentological, and isotopic studies of similar lacustrine phenomena in southern California and in the Great Basin (see Morrison, 1965, with references) provide good examples.

In the interior of Iran, Bobek (1937) described shorelines at 45 m, 55 m, and 60–70 m above Lake Rezaieh (Urmia), which today has a maximum depth of only 16 meters. This enlarged lake covered an area twice the size of the modern one. Bobek computed a simplified hydrological budget for this former lake and concluded that a 5°C. lowering of mean annual temperatures could adequately explain a water volume almost 10 times as great as that of the present. The age of the high shorelines is uncertain.

Evidence of lacustrine deposits has long been discussed for the great salt pans or kavirs of Iran (Sedlacek, 1955; Gabriel, 1957; Stratil-Sauer, 1957; Bobek, 1959, 1963, 1968; Huckriede, 1962), but the age and paleoclimatic significance of these sediments has remained controversial until the more comprehensive study of Krinsley (1970). Although there is generally no absolute dating, the sedimentary sequences of the intermontane basin floors (Qum Playa, Great Kavir, Lut and Seistan Basins, Lakes Shiraz and Neirz) indicate overall semiarid conditions that were periodically ameliorated by lower temperatures, reduced evaporation ratios, and increased spring runoff from expanded mountain snowpacks. Existing shallow lakes were deeper and greatly expanded; present salt flats harbored shallow sheets of water during winter and spring, while higher water tables inhibited wind erosion. The last lacus-trine phase thus appears to date from the full Würm glacial, although "dating" of the 60 playas Krinsley studied is limited to early Upper Paleolithic artifacts associated with the high shorelines of Lake Neriz. Maximum aridity is indicated in early Holocene times.

More informative are the lacustrine marls and peaty beds described by Huckriede (1962) from a subdesert environment at Kerman (1,760 m). Over 3 m thick, these deposits include a rich mushroom flora, abundant ferns of the species *Pteridium aquilinum* (now confined to the rain forest of the southern Caspian littoral), a host of mollusca requiring permanently moist conditions, as well as the "northern" snail *Valvata piscinalis pulchella*—today found at over 4,000 m elevation in the Zagros Mountains. Saline soils with a completely different, xerophile molluscan fauna are present today. The radiocarbon age of these incontestably pluvial beds is "greater than 25,000 years" (Huckriede, 1962), suggesting an early Würm glacial date.

This evidence from Kerman is compatible with the results of Wright (1966) and his associates, obtained at Lake Zeribar (1,300 m) in the Zagros. From about 22,500 (the base of the longest core) to 12,000 years ago the climate was drier than today at this mountain locale, as shown by the aquatic flora and microfauna, as well as by the nature of the chloride and carbonate precipitates. Higher lake levels, with development of a floating sedge mat, were established during the terminal stages of the late Würm glacial or at the very beginning of the Holocene. These inferences are corroborated by the pollen profiles discussed further below.

From the Kerman and Zeribar data in particular it becomes apparent that generalizations concerning pluvial and nonpluvial periods in the high country of southwestern Asia require far more extensive radiocarbon dating before the apparent parallelisms with high glacial age lakes in the American Southwest (Morrison, 1965) can be confirmed.

The pattern of a moist early glacial followed by a dry full and late glacial appears to be corroborated along the southern shores of the Caspian Sea. A recent study by Ehlers (1971a) identifies three high levels of the Caspian Sea at 45–50 m, 25 m, and 0 m above sea level—or +73–78 m, +53 m, and +28 m above the modern Caspian level—and known as the Early, Middle, and Late Chvalyn Transgressions respectively. The highest level corresponded to an overflow of the Early Chvalyn Sea into the Black Sea during early Würm times (Frenzel, 1959, p. 103; 1960, pp. 45 ff.), apparently in response to a cool, moist climate in mid-latitude Russia. Considerable fluvial activity in northern Iran is indicated by delta fans contemporary with this shoreline (Bobek, 1937; Ehlers, 1971a), and this shoreline is also directly linked to a glacio-fluvial terrace. Ehlers (1971a) was also able to correlate stream alluvia with the late Chvalyn shorelines, although as the Caspian receded in late glacial times, primarily eolian loess was deposited in what is now the Hyrcanian rain forest. Bobek (1937) rightly emphasizes that the lack of any soil development in

the lower 6–7 m of the loess near Asterabad indicates an arid climate. But the youngest loess is much older than Bobek supposed—in the neighboring Belt Cave the uppermost loess has a radiocarbon date of 10,320 B.C. ± 825 years (Ralph, 1955), while a loess-like sediment was being deposited in the Kara Kamar Cave near Haibak, Afghanistan, from before 30,000 B.C. to about 9000 B.C. (Coon and Ralph, 1955). The exact age of a Caspian Sea level 22 m below the present is uncertain.

Although there are lake beds of early Pleistocene age in the interior basins of Syria and Iraq, lacustrine deposits of late Pleistocene or Holocene age are poorly developed (Van Liere, 1961; Voute and Wedman, 1963), except for the Damascus Basin, where there are extensive lake marls, chalks, and gyttjas (at 610–620 m elevation), dating from a little before 22,000 B.C. to a little after 16,000 B.C. (Kaiser et al., 1973). These lacustrine beds of the lower Barada drainage are correlated with piedmont terraces. The mollusca and ostracods suggest shallow, standing waters of eutrophic character, with abundant vegetation; a temporary recession of palearctic forms midway in the sequence coincides with evidence of increased salinity. The pollen (see below) does not support a major shift of vegetation. Of further interest are massive spring tufas on the mountain flanks (1,100 m), with one terminal C14 date of 1530 B.C.; the pollen includes substantial quantities of oak, pine, and walnut or cedar. If these 80 m-thick tufas are indeed all of Holocene age, as unconvincingly claimed by Kaiser et al. (1973), they would imply a somewhat wetter climate.

The Jordan–Dead Sea Valley shows a massive suite of finely laminated silts, marls, and gypsum, deposited by a great lake 300 km in length and with a volume of 325 km³ water, compared with 136 km³ for the modern Dead Sea (Neev and Emery, 1967). Known as the Lisan Marls, these beds are primarily of late Pleistocene age, and Ben-Arieh (1964a) computed that a 200 mm increase in annual precipitation would be necessary to explain the hydrological budget of this lake, not taking into account any temperature changes.

A series of C14 dates extending back to "greater than" 40,000 years, with extrapolation from the varve-like laminae of the Lisan Marls, indicate that the typical, deep-lake beds were laid down ca. 50,000–17,000 years ago (Neev and Emery, 1967; Huckriede and Wiesemann, 1968; Horowitz, this volume). Shallow-water salt units were deposited from before 100,000 to ca. 70,000 years ago, and intermediate conditions with increasing water depth are indicated ca. 70,000–50,000 years ago by alternating clays and salts. Lake level was temporarily low ca. 13,000 B.C., due at least in part to major tectonic changes, then moderately high ca. 10,000–5000 B.C. and again for a short while ca. 3000 B.C. Related lake shorelines have been studied by Bowman (1970) but are not dated. Conditions similar to those of today prevailed ca. 4500–3500 B.C. and again after 2500 B.C. These results show that the last interglacial was by and large as dry as or drier than the present, while the full glacial was relatively wet, with an optimal runoff-evaporation ratio ca. 20,000 B.C. coincident with the maximal, Würm glacial advance. Part of the late glacial may have been dry, while undisputable early to mid-Holocene "subpluvial" conditions are shown for a time range with temperatures at least as warm as today.

The Dead Sea evidence finds corroboration in the Hula-Tiberias region where lake chalks and peats were laid down, providing key pollen evidence (see below), in conjunction with spring travertines along the Hermon foothills. Horowitz (this volume) evaluates the total evidence to suggest a rainfall increase of 30–40%, and a temperature decrease of 4–5°C. for the early last glacial, with rainfall still 30% higher during the interstadial. If, however, the temperature depression was twice as great, as is suggested for other parts of the Mediterranean Basin (Butzer, 1971, chaps. 18-19), then there would be no need to postulate a full glacial increase of rainfall (see Haude, 1969; also Galloway, 1970, for similar views on interpretation of "pluvial" lakes in the American Southwest).

The Lisan Lake of the Jordan–Dead Sea Basin finds a parallel in the Jafr depression of southeastern Jordan. Here a lake as much as 1,800 km² in area led to the accumulation of over 25 m of marls, silts, and limestones, with a rich freshwater snail fauna, that includes Palearctic species (Huckriede and Wiesemann, 1968). This lake turned shallow and brackish a little after 24,450 B.C. ± 870 years, with a *Melanoides*, *Hydrobia* and *Corbula* fauna, and increasing proportions of sand and gravel. Ultimately the lake disappeared, and the deposits were covered with fanglomerates, later deflated. A last moist interval, attributed to the terminal Würm glacial, led to deep solution of the older lacustrine limestones; the associated mud flats deposits contain Upper Paleolithic implements. There is no evidence for substantial Holocene climatic changes.

Finally, in Egypt and elsewhere in the eastern Sahara, extensive lacustrine deposits are relatively rare. A notable exception is the case of the Fayum Depression, where deep lakes, considerably larger than the modern Birket Qarun, can be verified for late Pleistocene to mid-Holocene times (Said et al., 1972; Butzer, 1974b). However, these lake fluctuations reflect changes of Nile floodplain elevation and Nile influx. At no time were they controlled by local rainfall variation (Butzer, 1958, pp. 68 ff., 109 ff.). Other contemporary lacustrine beds in Egypt are essentially wadi ponds, such as those of Kurkur (Butzer and Hansen, 1968, chap. 7), or oasis floor deposits, such as those currently being studied from southwestern Egypt by Fred Wendorf and others.

The presence of mid-Holocene lake beds and fossil spring deposits in South Arabia (McClure, 1968; el-Masry, 1973) suggests the possibility that the Arabian record may be analogous to that of Egypt.

The evidence of Near Eastern high shorelines and lacustrine sediments reviewed here is unsatisfactory. Nonetheless there are strong indications for significant changes of climate during the broad time span of the Würm glacial and the Holocene. The patterns and nature of these climatic

changes remain to be elucidated by detailed, radiometrically-controlled studies such as have been published from the American Southwest. At the moment, however, the evidence appears to show that the highlands of Anatolia and northern Iran were cold and dry during the last glacial, with reduced evaporation permitting some enlargement of lakes, whereas the southern Levant and possibly the southern sectors of Iran were apparently wetter and certainly cooler. This dichotomy finds support in other lines of evidence.

ALLUVIAL AND COLLUVIAL PHENOMENA: SOUTHWESTERN ASIA

The evidence of river terraces and other alluvial or colluvial deposits in the Near East is of variable quality from region to region. In some areas, such as Turkey, Iraq, and Iran, data are limited to scattered reports of an exploratory nature. In the Levant somewhat more systematic observations are available, but there are few or no isotopic dates. In Egypt and Nubia the chronology of alluvial deposits is fairly reliable. In Transcaucasia and Arabia, there is almost no published information. A discussion of late Würm and early Holocene alluvial deposits must therefore be selective and uneven.

TURKEY

In Turkey general terrace studies have been made by Pfannenstiel (1940) in the Ankara Valley and by Izbirak (1962) and by Erdbrink and van Heekeren (1965) in the Kizil Irmak Valley.

In the Ankara Valley there appear to be four alluvial terraces at relative elevations of 20–23 m, 65 m, 80 m, and 100–110 m, each composed of coarse, angular, and relatively little-rolled gravel. The lowest terrace gravels include artifacts of late Levalloiso-Mousterian type, and have therefore been ascribed to accelerated frost-weathering and detrital transport during the Würm glacial.

The Kizil Irmak terraces are little more informative for the time range in question. The present floodplain is recognized at 5 m above mean low-water, and consists of clayey material, intercalated with coarse to cobble gravels near the fans developed at the mouths of tributary streams. Dissected gravels and sands, at relative elevations of 7–10 m and at about 20 m, occur at intervals along the river, particularly in basin areas. These and other alluvial deposits from Turkey discussed by Vita-Finzi (1969a) record Holocene and late Pleistocene aggradations of tectonic or climatic origin, but both age and interpretation are uncertain.

IRAN

A detailed study of alluvial deposits in Iran has been made in the Meshed Basin of Khorassan by Scharlau (1958). The terrace suite present there suggests several periods of accelerated erosion and deposition, with development of coarse, well-rounded valley fills and lateral solifluction mantles. The youngest terrace complex is thought to be of late Pleistocene age. Scharlau (1958) suggests that older observations by Bobek (1940) of alluvial terraces and associated solifluction deposits, found along the southern slopes of the Elburz Range, should be interpreted in a similar manner, a view substantiated by Ehlers (1971*a*) and Vita-Finzi (1969*b*).

IRAQ

In the Zagros Ranges of Iraq a variety of alluvial deposits, primarily of glacio-fluvial origin, have been referred to by Bobek (1940) and Wright (1962*a*), and 60 m of initial gravels and younger silts, intercalated with lacustrine beds, occur in the Iraqi foothills of the Zagros. Wright (1952) considers these as late Pleistocene, reflecting a more humid climate. Similar observations of alluvial terraces, scree and solifluction mantles, or massive landslide phenomena, have been made in the Zagros foothills by Wirth (1958) and Voute and Wedman (1963). The same authors postulate a period of accelerated geomorphologic activity and greater moisture, presumably in late Pleistocene times.

The Tigris Valley, upstream of Baghdad, shows a well-developed terrace suite that extends into the lower courses of the major tributaries (Buringh, 1960, pp. 123 ff.). The "low" or Mahdy terrace, with a general elevation of 10–15 m above floodplain, may possibly correlate with terraces in Syria that Van Liere (1961) considers as late Pleistocene. The basic components of this Tigris terrace are fine sands or silts, capped by 2–4 m of clayey beds and a reddish-brown soil (Buringh, 1960, pp. 123 ff.). On the Jezira Plain, between the middle Tigris and Euphrates, as well as along the larger wadis of the Syrian Desert, Wirth (1958) noted two alluvial terraces. The younger of these consists of gravels, sands, and silts, forming a 3–5 m terrace above the modern gravel channel. Above this lower fill, thought to be of Holocene age, older gravels form a slightly higher surface that grades smoothly onto the surrounding plains. The rather extensive, older fill is attributed to greater discharge and detrital transport in late Pleistocene times. Significantly, these wadis lack hills or mountain terrain in their catchment areas, so that greater runoff rather than a greater supply of weathering detritus seems to be the best explanation. Only locally have minor tributaries dissected the younger fill.

THE LEVANT

The alluvial terraces of Syria and Lebanon are better understood. The middle Euphrates has a broad, well-developed gravel terrace, with abundant derived artifacts of both Acheulean and Levalloiso-Mousterian typology. Some 5–8 m of stratified silt generally terminate this aggradation unit, which typically lies up to 20 m above modern floodplain. A late Pleistocene age is assumed (Van Liere, 1961, pp. 44, 46 f., 59). This silt is indirectly attributed to a greater supply of valley fill.

The results of Van Liere are a little difficult to reconcile with de Heinzelin's (1965) observations on the middle Euphrates. The latter author defines two formations representing a single alluvial complex of pre-Neolithic and possible late Pleistocene age. The Shajara Formation has a relative elevation of 20–30 m above modern floodplain and incorporates rolled Paleolithic artifacts. Well-patinated, unrolled Middle Paleolithic artifacts occur on the surface. The Mureibat Formation varies from 1–10 m above modern floodplain and is older than a series of Neolithic tells found on its surface. In a broad way the Mureibat fill corresponds to Van Liere's 5 m Holocene silt terrace, while the Shajara deposits probably can be correlated in part with the Main Gravel Terrace as well as with some of Van Liere's older alluvia. More detailed publications on the middle Euphrates will be necessary before satisfactory conclusions can be drawn.

In the Orontes system a "Main Gravel Terrace" is ascribed to the late Pleistocene (Van Liere, 1961, pp. 32, 42 f.). Gravels are again overlain by several meters of stratified silt or fine sandy loam, and a broad floodplain, four times the size of the modern alluvial valley, suggests greater runoff. More detailed facies changes have been recorded from the Ghab depression, where the Orontes once deteriorated into a swampy or lacustrine environment. Here, pollen data (see below) imply appreciable environmental changes during late Pleistocene times, and further radiocarbon dating should provide valuable insights into late Pleistocene and, perhaps, early Holocene environments and tectonic history of central Syria. Holocene fill terraces are not now recognized in the Orontes system.

In the areas of interior drainage near and south of Damascus there are a variety of late Pleistocene alluvial and colluvial deposits. The Wadi Midaneh, a major tributary of the Yarmuk, has a gravel terrace, with rolled Acheulean and fairly fresh Levalloiso-Mousterian artifacts, capped by 5–6 m of stratified clay (Van Liere, 1961, pp. 49 ff.). The silty cap is pre-Neolithic. Similar gravels take the form of alluvial fans adjacent to the Damascus Basin (Van Liere, 1961, pp. 52 ff.; Kaiser et al., 1973). They are overlain by colluvial brown clays, which may be broadly synchronous with black fluvial clays that line the floor of the Damascus Basin. The exact age of these late Pleistocene to early Holocene beds is uncertain. Analogous basin sediments have been described from different parts of the Jordanian desert (Van Liere, 1961, p. 55; Zeuner, 1957; Vita-Finzi, 1964; Huckriede and Wiesemann, 1968). On the other hand, contemporary alluvial deposits appear to be absent from the great wadis that drain the Syrian Desert toward the Euphrates Valley (Wirth, 1958).

A succession of late Pleistocene to Holocene alluvial sediments has been described from the Jordan graben and the adjacent tributaries, particularly those of the eastern bank (Picard, 1963; Vita-Finzi, 1964; Nir and Ben-Arieh, 1965; Horowitz, this volume). During late Pleistocene times a complex of massive gravels was transported through the tributary systems both east and west of the Jordan. As much as 30 m thick, and including the Nakhsholim Conglomerate of Judea, these alluvia are at least locally interdigitated with the Lisan Marls, and have been observed to overlie scarp-edge tufas. They typically form broad, shallow fans, often incorporating derived *terra rossa* soils, on the margins of the Jordan Valley. Upstream, in the tributaries proper, the lateral equivalents average 10–20 m thick and consist of poorly sorted, subangular to subrounded gravel with limited stratification. Fluvial beds are frequently intercalated with lateral screes, suggesting torrential stream flow and sheetwash. The last general fill east of the Jordan, known as the Younger Terrace, has an average thickness of 3–4 m and consists of better-rounded materials, and contains abundant Roman potsherds. The presence of two fresh-water snails (*Melanoides tuberculata* and *Melanopsis praemorsa*) suggests some permanent or semipermanent waters (Sparks, in Vita-Finzi, 1964, pp. 32 f.). A post-Roman age is inferred. In Wadi Hasa there are two further fills, intermediate in age between the older and younger terrace alluvia. The first of these is 2 m thick and consists of angular to subangular gravel with Upper Paleolithic blades. The younger attains a maximum thickness of 5 m and consists of well-stratified sandy silts or subrounded to rounded gravel, with Upper Paleolithic ("Kebaran") artifacts. Radiocarbon dates are, unfortunately, not available to clarify the details of alluvial stratigraphy either east or west of the Jordan Graben.

Along the coast of Syria (Van Liere, 1961, pp. 15 ff.) the Würm regression was heralded by alluviation of coarse gravel fans across the coastal plains in areas of resistant bedrock. By contrast there was rapid downcutting (at least 35 to 40 m below the present bed) in areas of unconsolidated substrata. These features suggest a much heavier runoff than at present. Later on during the Würm regression eolianites were deposited on the coastal plains, while only fine gravelly clays were carried and deposited by the local streams. This would suggest a noticeable decrease in discharge. Analogous features are described from the Lebanese coast by Wright (1962b), where one or more red soil profiles (or colluvial soil horizons) may interrupt the eolianites.

Along the littoral of Israel there is further evidence of accelerated discharge as well as dune stabilization by deep soils, at the beginning of the Würm glacial, with relatively drier conditions, including a record of several generations of coastal dunes and loess, dominant thereafter (Horowitz, this volume; also M. Pfannenstiel, discussed in Butzer, 1958, pp. 33 ff.). In Holocene times the undercut valleys were filled in with fine sediments, often marked by colluvial wash, coastal dunes, or stormbeach gravels (Van Liere, 1961, pp. 24 ff.; Horowitz, this volume).

In review, the Levantine evidence suggests one or more periods of greater stream discharge in late Pleistocene times, indicating a moister or a cooler climate, or both. Interpretation and regional correlation of paleoclimatic events must await further radiocarbon dates, although on present evidence, there may have been a moister phase in early Würm times, and one or more minor moist intervals at the very end of the Pleistocene. Evidence for comparatively moist phases during the Holocene appears to be confined to Israel and Jordan.

THE ALLUVIAL RECORD: EGYPT

The late Pleistocene and Holocene of the Nile Valley in southern Upper Egypt and Lower Nubia are characterized by a complex sequence of nilotic sediments—primarily derived from Ethiopia and the southern Sudan in the wake of the summer flood regime—and lateral wadi deposits—derived from sporadic, local rains (Butzer, 1967; Butzer and Hansen, 1967, 1968) (fig. 1). This suite of intercalated nilotic and wadi fill is younger than intensively rubefied and locally ferricreted gravels. Weathering was followed by a period of Nile and wadi fill dissection (at least 10–12 m), reflecting lower Nile floods and limited wadi activity. The subsequent sequence of events is more detailed than that of any other Near Eastern area and can be outlined as follows:

WADI FLOOR CONGLOMERATE

At the base of the late Pleistocene sequence up to 5 m of ferricreted, well-rolled cobble conglomerates overlie the bedrock floors of several Nubian wadis. These gravels were graded to a floodplain level at least as low as that of today. They suggest major wadi activity and a pluvial climate, probably corroborated by gravels and calcareous tufas (Wadi Tufa III) at the Kurkur Oasis of the Libyan Desert, dating "greater than 40,000 years" (Butzer, 1964c, 1965b; Butzer and Hansen, 1968, chap. 7). Deposition of the Wadi Floor Conglomerate was followed by a period of erosion and consolidation.

KOROSKO FORMATION

Extensive spreads of subaqueous to fluvial marls, gravelly marls, and sandy gravels were deposited by a rapidly aggrading, braided Nile to +34 m near the Sudanese border and to +20 m on the Kom Ombo Plain. Local wadis injected great quantities of sand and gravel into temporary lacustrine environments along the valley margins. Coarse, well-rolled wadi conglomerates are prominent at the base of the Korosko Formation, and similar gravels are interdigitated in the middle of the sequence. These gravels record the terminal phase of late Pleistocene "pluvial" conditions in Egypt, with contemporary "pluvial" conditions in the Kurkur Oasis recorded by Wadi Tufa IV. Swift and turbulent summer floods of Ethiopian origin introduced silt, clay, and solubles, while local materials (made available by wadi discharge during the winter months) were reworked and redeposited in the Nile Valley. The heavy mineral and clay mineral spectra suggest a greater influx of Bahr el-Ghazal waters and sediments, relative to those of the modern Nile. A very approximate age of 50,000 to 25,000 years ago can be extrapolated from a "greater than or equal to" date of 25,250 B.C. Comparable deposits have not been recognized in Sudanese Nubia or north of Edfu, although the Makhadma Formation of Said (1974) is a possibility.

The subsequent period of Nile and wadi incision (at least 19 m and 5 m respectively) lowered the local base level to below modern floodplain, reflecting on lower Nile floods and limited wadi activity.

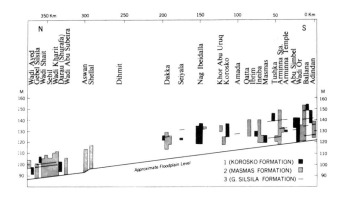

FIG. 1—Late Pleistocene Nilotic Deposits in southern Egypt. Whereas *1* and *2* indicate the vertical range of sediments recorded, *3* shows only the maximum elevation of the different substages. (From *Desert and River in Nubia*, by K. W. Butzer and C. L. Hansen [Madison: University of Wisconsin Press, 1968], p. 267).

MASMAS FORMATION

Extensive horizontal flood silts, rich in Ethiopian heavy minerals, filled the Nile Valley to +33 m in Nubia to +22 m on the Kom Ombo Plain. The sedimentary environment indicated pertains to a floodplain (alluvial flats or backswamps), and only rarely to channel or levee beds. A broader floodplain was regularly inundated and levee-breaching was common, indicating somewhat greater summer flood discharge. The clay mineral composition again suggests more Bahr el-Ghazal waters. However, in Egypt, wadi activity was minimal throughout this period with next to no interdigitation of wadi deposits where the Masmas flood silts extend well into tributary valleys. The Masmas beds attain a thickness of over 40 m at Kom Ombo and can be traced from Upper Nubia into Lower Egypt. They suggest an intensified summer flood regime, and a time range from perhaps 22,000 to 16,000 B.C. can be inferred from radiocarbon dates. The Masmas Formation is equivalent to the Dibeira-Jer Formation, as identified in Sudanese Nubia and the Esna-Edfu area by Fred Wendorf and his associates (see comparison and discussion in Butzer and Hansen, 1972).

During a subsequent period of Nile downcutting (to below present floodplain level, vertical differential at least 20 m) the local wadis dissected these older floodplain silts. At about this time or shortly thereafter slickensides and epigenetic dehydration cracks developed within these deposits. The latter take the form of large polygons and minor crack networks, penetrating to depths of 1.5 meters. These phenomena suggest development of a floodplain vertisol of Mazaquert type under arid climatic conditions.

GEBEL SILSILA FORMATION

The third and final episode of nilotic alluviation includes a sequence of fine gravels, silts, and sands related to channel and levee environments of a rather more vigorous and competent Nile. Horizontal flood silts are rare; instead, former shoals of bed gravels or sands interfinger with laterally embanked topset and backset strata. Relative proportions of clay minerals and heavy minerals are, for the first time, almost identical to those of today. However, the gravels are marked by an influx of exotic flint, chert, chalcedony, agate, jasper, and carnelian—most of which are totally absent from all earlier deposits.

The Gebel Silsila Formation includes three major periods of nilotic aggradation, separated by periods in downcutting and interdigitated with a complex of wadi deposits.

Darau Member

15,000–10,000 B.C.
(+22.5 m in Egyptian Nubia,
+13 m on the Kom Ombo Plain)

The deposits exceed 18 m in thickness and include geologically stratified Sebilian and other Late Paleolithic sites, formerly located along the banks of the Nile. On the Kom Ombo Plain three distinct channel stages are recognized, with median floodplain elevations of +11–13 m (ca. 15,000–12,500 B.C., four C14 dates), +9–10 m (ca. 12,500–11,000 B.C., ten C14 dates, see also Smith, 1968), and +8 m (ca. 10,500 B.C., one C14 date). A final, high flood phase occurred ca. 10,000 B.C. (three C14 dates at Kom Ombo alone). Younger members of the Gebel Silsila Formation, recognized in Nubia, are not represented on the Kom Ombo Plain, being suballuvial north of Aswan and the Kalabsha gorge (see Vermeersch, 1970). The temporal equivalence of the Deir el-Fakhuri, Sahaba, and Dishna Formations of the Edfu-Esna area is apparent. Contemporary deposits of the Eastern Desert wadis record more frequent heavy rains in the Red Sea Hills—the 9 m *Malki Member* of the *Ineiba Formation*, (Butzer and Hansen, 1968, pp. 116 ff.), with a basal date of 15,450 B.C. ± 300 years and a terminal date of 10,070 B.C. ± 205 years. However, paleoclimatic evidence from the Esna area is inconclusive: (*i*) the noncalcic, humic, "mediterranean" type soil (Said et al., 1970, p. 54; Wendorf et al., 1971, p. 63) remains to be described in even basic terms; (*ii*) the diatom-rich ponds do not prove "cooler summer temperatures" (Said et al., 1970, p. 56), but can be adequately explained by lateral seepage from the Nile-controlled water table, even during the low-water season (cf. modern lagoons and swales west of Dairut, e.g., Butzer, 1959*a*). Comparable pond deposits near Ballana Police Post in Egyptian Nubia are included as facies within the Darau Member by Butzer and Hansen (1968, pp. 29 f. and fig. 6-10). Subsequent wadi dissection, reflecting lower Nile base level and limited wadi activity, locally exceeded 12 meters.

Arminna Member

9200–6000 B.C.
(+15 m in Egyptian Nubia, absent at Kom Ombo)

Accelerated fluvial activity, with accumulation of at least 12 m of fill (*Sinqari Member* of *Ineiba Formation*). Wadi aggradation reflecting rainfalls in the Red Sea Hills as well as local rains can be approximately dated ca. 9500–6500 B.C. This was later followed by development of a minor red paleosol with a 30 to 50 cm-deep (B)-horizon. Oxidation and decalcification were accompanied by formation of kaolinitic clays, indicating biochemical weathering, some form of vegetative mat, and more frequent gentle rains. The age of this almost ubiquitous paleosol in southern Egypt may be about 5000 B.C. Subsequent wadi downcutting under drier conditions exceeded 6 meters.

Kibdi Member

Ca. 4000–3000 B. C. (Nile +6–7 m in Egyptian Nubia)

Accelerated fluvial activity in the wadis (over 6 m of fill), accompanied by extensive sheetwashing of surface, as a result of sporadic, but protracted, torrential rains (Member I, *Shaturma Formation*). Alluviation of the modern Nile floodplain began after dissection in late Old Kingdom times (Bell, 1970, 1971). The last episode of accelerated wadi discharge is recorded by up to 2.5 m of deposits that date ca. 1000–1200 A.D. (see Butzer, 1974a).

The nilotic deposits of southern Egypt were derived from the sub-Saharan drainage basin of the Nile and indicate that flood amplitudes and velocities were significantly greater than today for most of the period between ca. 50,000 and 5,000 years ago. This can be explained only by greater runoff from Ethiopia and the southern Sudan. From this we can infer three complex wetter or cooler periods for the summer monsoonal belt of the Nile Basin, interrupted by periods of reduced discharge ca. 23,000, ca. 15,000, ca. 9500, ca. 5500, ca. 4500, and ca. 2500 B.C. If we compare these fluctuations of Nile discharge with the activity of local streams in southern Egypt, several facts may be noted:

(*1*) Maximum "pluvial" conditions in southern Egypt, as recorded by the Wadi Floor Conglomerate (ca. 60,000 B.C.?), probably corresponded to the early Würm in Europe. There is no evidence for higher Nile floods at the time. Egyptian climate was also "pluvial," although subarid in nature during the first half of the Korosko sedimentary hemi-cycle, in this case correlated with much more vigorous Nile floods. But later, during the Korosko stage, local wadi activity was limited. Consequently, there was only a broad, incomplete correspondence between Egyptian and sub-Saharan pluvial oscillations during most of the time span of the Würm full glacial (ca. 60,000 [?]–25,000 B.C.).

(*2*) It is notable that the maximum glacial advance of the Würm (ca. 22,000–16,000 B.C.) was dry in Egypt and throughout the Sahara (Butzer, Isaac, et al., 1972), although relatively moist in the Ethiopian drainage basin of the Nile, possibly as a result of reduced evaporation.

(*3*) Between 15,000 and 3000 B.C. greater Nile discharge of Ethiopian origin coincided very closely with accelerated wadi activity in Egypt. It could be shown in the field that, despite the synchroneity of events, local winter spates and summer Nile floods were, in fact, seasonally out of phase. In other words, the evidence of late Pleistocene

and Holocene wadi activity in Egypt can be largely, if not entirely, attributed to winter rains, and not to a simple, northward extension of the sporadic summer shower activity evident in Sudanese Nubia today.

(*4*) The accelerated activity of the Egyptian wadis ca. 9500–6500 B.C. and ca. 4000–3000 B.C. suggests very minor "subpluvial" episodes that were contemporary with higher Nile floods. The intervening red paleosol (ca. 5000 B.C.) has no obvious nilotic counterparts. These three episodes account for most of the time represented by the Younger Dryas, Boreal, and Atlantic phases in Europe. Then, during the third millenium B.C., Nile flood levels dropped, wadi activity was reduced to a minimum, while sand dunes were periodically activated around the margins of the Nile Valley (Butzer, 1959a, 1966; de Heinzelin, 1964; Bell, 1970, 1971). The climate of Egypt and Nubia has remained hyperarid ever since.

In conclusion, the Nile Valley record provides strong evidence for a modest increase of precipitation in Egypt during the late glacial and the early to middle Holocene. The primary evidence is provided by fairly homogeneous wadi sands, sometimes with abundant root impressions of xerophytic shrubs or with profusions of terrestrial shells (*Zootecus insularis, Pupoides sennaariensis, P. coenopictus*), now extinct in Egypt. All this would suggest a vegetative mat along the wadi floors and periods of fairly frequent winter rains of moderate intensity. The coarse wash deposits and colluvium incorporated into the Kibdi Formation, by exception, indicate violent sheetfloods, suggesting a time of frequent torrential rains. Finally, the reddish paleosol of mid-Holocene age can best be explained by biochemical weathering, some form of vegetative mat, and more frequent gentle rains. Nonetheless, all of these pluvial phenomena, except the Wadi Floor Conglomerate, are indicative of arid or subarid conditions. Consequently, the amplitude of these moister intervals should not be overestimated—despite their obvious ecological significance. Furthermore, there were frequent interruptions of subpluvial conditions by interludes of hyperarid climate.

THE RED SEA COAST

An independent geomorphologic record of late Pleistocene stream activity is provided by the Red Sea littoral, near Mersa Alam. Here dated, tectonically undisturbed, high beaches allow stratigraphic correlation with alluvial deposits or episodes of fill-cutting (Butzer and Hansen, 1968, chap. 8). The sequence is as follows:

1. +10 m coral reef (coralline limestone). Minimal wadi activity.

2. +6 m coral reef (calcarenite and coral), with Th^{230}/U^{234} dates of 80,000 B.P. ± 8,000 years (on reef shell) and 118,000 B.P. ± 10,000 years (on shell from older beach gravels back of the reef). Last interglacial transgression. Minimal wadi activity.

3. +8.5 m gravel bars and estuarine gravels, indicating accelerated wadi activity.

4. Regressive oscillation.

5. +3.5 m coral reef (calcarenite, some coral). Minimal wadi activity. Terminal last interglacial transgression?.

6. Regressive oscillation with wadi dissection.

7. Alluviation of coarse gravels of Middle Terrace, indicating "pluvial" conditions with increased stream competence. Basal beds appear to be contemporary with estuarine conglomerate at modern high-water, while later fluvial sediments extend to below modern sea level. Early Würm regression?.

8. Dissection of alluvium and calcification (weak paleosol).

9. Alluviation of Low Terrace, again indicating a "pluvial" climate. Gravels indicate oversteepened gradient at coast, and deposits extend to below modern sea level. Contemporary with early or Middle Würm regression.

10. Long-term dissection of coastal deposits to well below modern sea level during middle to late Würm regression. During Holocene times sea level returned to its present mark, drowning the lowermost wadis, since post-Pleistocene wadi activity has been minimal.

This stratigraphic sequence clearly shows that in southeastern Egypt the last "pluvial" episodes of the later Pleistocene are broadly contemporary with the first half of the Würm glacial regression, while the greater part of last interglacial experienced a climate about as arid as that of today. At the same time the Mersa Alam evidence shows that there was a brief moister interval during the late, last interglacial while the last half of the Würm regression was comparatively dry. This again emphasizes that pluvial-glacial or pluvial-interglacial correlations are gross oversimplifications of a rather more complex pattern of events.

Although Holocene moisture fluctuations were not significant enough to leave an imprint on the hyperarid Red Sea littoral, a generalized record of climatic trends in the Red Sea region is given by a deep-sea core in the gulf of Aden. Here Olausson and Olsson (1969) were able to show that moister phases produced a greater phosphate component while drier intervals increased eolian materials. On this basis it can be inferred that the early Holocene was dry and the mid-Holocene relatively moist, with maximum moisture in the fourth millenium B.C. Of similar interest is another core, from the Persian Gulf, where there was little terrestrial influx in the seventh millenium B.C., when the post-Würmian transgression first invaded the area (Diester, 1972); however, a little later terrestrial components became dominant in each of the cores analyzed.

EVIDENCE OF CAVE SEDIMENTS AND ASSOCIATED FAUNAS

Microstratigraphic and paleoclimatic evidence of exceptional value has, in Europe, been obtained from a number of cave sites. However, in the Near East sufficiently detailed studies are lacking from all but the Levant, while the available sediment studies suggest only limited environmental changes. Reviews of the older literature have been published by Howell (1959) and Butzer (1958, pp. 80 ff.),

and a number of reports by Van Liere (1961, pp. 63 ff.), Hooijer (1961), Solecki and Leroi-Gourhan (1961), Wright (1962b), Farrand (1970, 1972), Gonzalez (1966), Brunnacker (1970), and Leroi-Gourhan (1971) have subsequently added to the available information. Unfortunately, few of sedimentary sequences or faunal successions extend into the late glacial, let alone the Holocene. Consequently, the available information for the time range under study is highly fragmentary and, in general, disappointing.

At the abri of Ksar Akil, in coastal Lebanon, there is a key sediment and archaeological sequence that still remains to be fully studied and published. Based on Wright (1962b), Copeland (this volume), and Hooijer (1961), the following sequence can be tentatively outlined:

1. 6 m of stream-laid deposits with some Levalloiso-Mousterian occupation. Key faunal elements *Dama mesopotamica*, *Bos* sp. and *Capra aegagrus*, in order of prominence. Capped by (frost-weathered?) rubble horizon, dated ca. 44,000 years.

2. 4 m of cave deposits, beginning sequence of Upper Paleolithic occupation. Fauna: *Dama*, *Capra*, *Capreolus capreolus* ssp., *Gazella*. Basal (frost-weathered?) rubble horizon, with similar *éboulis* level interdigitated at back of cave.

3. 9 m as before, with *Dama*, *Capreolus* and *Capra* in order of prominence. Interdigitated in lower third with a complex of (frost-weathered?) rubble horizons enveloping a lens of red clayey soil, due to weathering in place (moister?) or colluvial introduction (accelerated runoff outside). C14 date of 28,500 B.C. in upper third.

4. 3 m as before. One (frost-weathered?) rubble horizon. Kebaran, with unpublished C14 dates.

Other interesting sequences, equally difficult to interpret, are found in the coastal cave at Adlun (Copeland, this volume), where travertines or calcrete horizons underlie and rest on a last interglacial beach. These are followed by a gray (frost-weathered?) breccia and ultimately a *terra fusca* soil (sediment?), with Acheuleo-Yabrudian industry. There caves and other Lebanese sites have fortunately yielded good pollen spectra (see below).

The last littoral site, Tabun Cave in Mt. Carmel, is about to be published in interim form, so that few details can be given. Preliminary work (Farrand, 1971; A. J. Jelinek, personal communication) indicated that the Acheulean deposits were strictly eolian and comparable to modern coastal sands. The early Levalloiso-Mousterian strata are increasingly poorly sorted, at first finer-grained, then predominantly cultural (hearths, ash) and coarser. The later Levalloiso-Mousterian strata consist of chaotic, corroded limestone blocks with a matrix of clayey *terra rossa* soil-wash, reflecting the collapse of a karstic sink-hole into the cave. The well-publicized *Dama-Gazella* curve is directly related to his physical history of the cave, and has no bearing on climatic fluctuations. A reevaluation of the faunas, based on the materials excavated since 1967, is still outstanding, and the information pollen data is in press (Horowitz, this volume). There may also be paleoclimatic evidence in later time ranges, and Bate (1940) concluded that there was a significant faunal change during early Holocene (Natufian, ca. 9550–7500 B.C.) times. A half-dozen species of gazelles, a hedgehog, and a species of hyena became extinct, possibly suggesting the oncoming of a more humid phase. Less securely dated than the Natufian is the "early Neolithic" of the Abu Usba Cave, also of Mt. Carmel, where Stekelis and Haas (1952) suggest an appreciably moister environment on faunal grounds. Typical steppe species were absent, but numerous thrushes, reptilian types such as *Chameleo chamaeleon*, *Agama stellio*, *Ophisaurus apus*, as well as the snail *Cyclostoma olivieri* would presume a dense vegetation with more bountiful moisture.

In the interior highlands of Israel, long sedimentary sequences are evident in the caves of Umm-Qatafa (551 m elevation, Judea) and Qafzeh (220 m, near Nazareth). The alternating strata of angular rubble, clays, and calcareous enrichment suggest repeated environmental changes, but modern analytical studies still remain to be reported (Farrand, 1971). The fauna of the last glacial levels at Qafzeh is uniformly dominated by *Cervus*, *Dama* and *Bos* (Bouchud, 1971). Elsewhere in Judea, the cave of el-Khiam (Gonzalez and others, 1966) shows that the late glacial and Holocene (Kebaran, Khiamian, and Tahunian levels, ca. 12,000–5500 B.C.) environment of that area was not unlike that of today. The sediments are rich in carbonates, with uniformly high pH values (over 8.0), and no evidence of weathering. The terrestrial and fluvial mollusca include *Helix*, *Helicogena*, *Eupharypha*, *Pyramidula*, and *Theba*, indicating a dry, warm environment. The megafauna, with *Gazella* sp., boar (*Sus scrofa libycus*), fox (*Vulpes vulpes*), donkey (*Equus asinus* cf. *somaliensis*), and domesticated goat (*Capra hircus*), is compatible with this interpretation, as is the palynological evidence, which suggests a treeless setting of steppe or desert vegetation, dominated by *Chenopodiaceae*.

In the interior of Syria, the cave of Jabrud I (1,427 m elevation) has been studied in unique detail by Farrand (1970, 1971) and Brunnacker (1970). The bottom stratum D, at -8.8 to 11 m (Acheulean and Jabrudian), consists of frost-weathered *éboulis* and travertines, suggestive of a cold and moist climate. The next unit C, at -5 to 8.8 m (Jabrudian), contains only a few horizons of finer and less angular *éboulis*, with eolian lenticles, inferring a drier and less cold climate. Unit B, at -2.3 to 5 m (Jabrudian, Acheulean, Pre-Aurignacian) is more comparable to D, while the uppermost stratum A, at 0 to -2.3 m (Levalloiso-Mousterian), is another fine frost-weathered *éboulis* horizon; both B and A also suggest a cold, moist climate. The relative age of C and D is uncertain, whereas B and A suggest the first half or mid-part of the last glacial. The fauna is dominated by equids throughout, with minor components of gazelle, fallow deer, and goat (Lehmann, 1970).

Equally interesting is the Jerf Ajla cave in the Palmyra foothills at 550 m elevation. The sequence is as follows (Farrand, 1971):

1. 1 m of frost-weathered rubble, with Levalloiso-Mousterian, capped by weathering horizon (corrosion of rubble, partial decalcification of matrix).

2. 2 m as before.

3. 1.75 m of frost-weathered rubble, with Levalloiso-Mousterian, and date of 43,000 years. Secondary calcification.

4. 1.25 m of frost-weathered rubble, with Upper Paleolithic. Secondary calcification. The entire sequence may span some 50,000 years prior to 30,000 B.C., and again records a colder climate during much or most of the early and full Würm glacial; the early Würm horizons of increased chemical weathering are of considerable interest.

In effect, Jabrud and Jerf Ajla summarize the total import of the Near Eastern cave sequences, both in terms of their implications for glacial cold and their equivocal record of moisture fluctuations.

Although various caves in the Zagros Mountains have been excavated over the years, sites such as Shanidar, Palegawra, Warwasi, Hazar Merd, etc., have not yet produced even rudimentary geological descriptions. For a discussion of the Caspian littoral caves, see Butzer (1958, pp. 107 f.).

POLLEN DATA

LAKE ZERIBAR

At the moment one of the most detailed and continuous records of late glacial and Holocene environmental changes in western Asia is provided by the studies of Lake Zeribar, located at 1,300 m elevation in the Zagros Ranges, 160 km northwest of Kermanshah. Three overlapping piston cores with a total depth of 26 m were subject to meticulous pollen analysis (van Zeist and Wright, 1963; van Zeist, 1967; Wright et al., 1967), while microfaunal and chemical changes within the same sediments were also studied in detail (Hutchinson and Cowgill, 1963; Megard, 1967; Wasylikowa, 1967; Wright, 1966). The deposits in question range from silt and clay to gyttja and peat, laid down in a small lake basin within mountainous terrain (to 2,100 m). Modern rainfall is estimated to vary locally from 600 to 800 mm, with mean January and July temperatures of about 2° and 28° C., respectively.

Three major pollen zones are recognized. Zone A shows next to no arboreal pollen, but is dominated by *Chenopodiaceae* (about 70%) and *Artemisia* (about 30%). The closest analogy is provided by the intermontane steppes of Tabriz, in northwestern Iran, with similar elevations but only 300 mm precipitation. The modern vegetation here is dominated by *Artemisia herba-alba*, with *Chenopodiaceae* in poorly drained areas with saline soils, and local prominence of *Ephedra*. The modern pollen rain near Tabriz includes some oak, 25% *Artemisia*, and 45% *Chenopodiaceae*. The pollen rain of the somewhat restricted modern alpine zone in Iran or Turkey was not sampled, a fact that leaves an element of uncertainty in the application of modern analogues to an interpretation of the cores. Since Lake Zeribar is now located in the Zagros oak-woodland belt, Wright et al. (1967) suggest that Zone A reflects a depression of the altitudinal treeline by at least 1,000

meters. Increased aridity is corroborated by abundant carbonates with chlorides in the mineral sediments of this
time, while greater cold is indicated by the presence of two
"northern" cladoceran species. Three C14 dates of 20,650
B.C., 12,850 B.C., and 11,700 B.C., are available, and by
interpolation and extrapolation Zone A can be dated from
before 20,500 to about 10,000 B.C. It therefore appears to
record the later full glacial and part of the late glacial.

Zone B marks a transition period with *Quercus* present
and increasing irregularly from an initial value of about
15%. While *Artemisia* fluctuates around 10%, the *Chenopodiaceae* decrease from about 70% to 50%, *Plantago*
averages near 10%, with *Salix*, Gramineae, and Compositae
present in addition. Wright et al. (1967) indicate that there
is no good regional analogue for this type of pollen spectrum. The modern pollen rain in the Zagros oak woodland
(800–2,000 m elevation) includes 35% *Quercus*, 15% *Artemisia*, with abundant Gramineae, *Plantago*, and some
Pistacia. In the almond-pistachio (*Amygdalus-Pistacia*)
savanna of the Zagros foothills (700–800 m), *Quercus* is
limited to 1 or 2% and *Artemisia* to 5%, with *Plantago*
dominant. This suggests closer analogies with the oak woodland than with the piedmont savanna or the plateau steppe,
and conditions were obviously warmer than during Zone A.
Northern species of *Cladocera* phase out in Zone B, and
southern species make their first appearance in significant
numbers. Carbonates and chlorides decrease steadily in the
sediments. A C14 date of 6,150 B.C. allows interpolation
for a time span of about 10,000 to 4000 B.C. (?Alleröd,
Younger Dryas, Boreal, early Atlantic). The second half of
Zone B, broadly corresonding to the middle Holocene, has
appreciably higher *Quercus* values, while evaporites average
no higher than they do in more recent sediments.

Zone C, with a basal date of 3510 B.C., suggests that
conditions have remained similar to those of today during
the last 6,000 years. *Quercus* averages near 60%, *Artemisia*
and *Plantago* about 10% each, and some *Pistacia* is generally
recorded from the organogenic sediments.

The Zone A spectrum suggests arid conditions in the
Zagros during the second half of the Würm glacial. This
finds strong confirmation in the contemporaneous pollen
record of southern Europe (see discussion in Butzer,
1974c), as well as in more recent pollen spectra from Syria
and Lebanon. The Zeribar diagrams are, furthermore, regionally representative, since unpublished results from two
other Iranian cores are comparable (van Zeist, 1967).
Therefore it appears that most of Turkey, northeastern
Iraq, and Iran were treeless during the Würm full glacial and
during most of late glacial time. However, the lacustrine
and glaciological evidence precludes truly arid climate even
if absolute precipitation was significantly reduced (compare
Messerli, 1967, pp. 204, 209 ff.; Wright, 1962a; Butzer,
1971, chap. 19). In other words, we are confronted with
evidence of physiological rather than climatic aridity, such
as in many parts of mid-latitude Europe (see Butzer, 1971,
pp. 285 ff.). Mountain tundra, steppe, and scrub-steppe
were almost certainly the dominant vegetation of the Near

Eastern highlands during the full and late glacial. This is
compatible with the evidence of accelerated frost-
weathering, solifluction, and alluviation from these areas.
Similarly it would explain the full and late glacial loess
deposits of northern Iran and Afghanistan.

The interpretation of Zone B is more difficult. Wright et
al. (1967) implicitly suggest that the local environment was
drier than at present, tentatively drawing analogies from the
almond-pistachio savanna of the Zagros piedmont. However, on the basis of the evidence presented, the similarities
of upper Zone B with the pollen rain of the modern oak-
woodland belt are conspicuously stronger. In conversation
and correspondence both Jack R. Harlan and Marvin W.
Mikesell have expressed the opinion that degraded oak
scrub produces more pollen than an undisturbed oak forest,
since there are many more flowering shoots. Daniel Zohary,
on the other hand, believes that fully-developed, undisturbed oaks of the *Quercus persica–Quercus ithaburensis*
group will produce more flowers and pollen than heavily-
cropped oaks or a fully degraded oak scrub. With such differences of opinion, this question requires further study in
the field. As an alternative hypothesis, it is therefore possible that the marked increase in oak pollen between Zones
B and C reflected intensive cultural disturbance (browsing,
cropping, charcoaling), initiated in late prehistoric times.
The sediment chemistry does not substantiate a drier environment for the upper half of Zone B. Similarly, pollen
profiles from northwestern Turkey suggest that the first
half of the Holocene was slightly moister and possibly
cooler than the second part (Beug, 1967). On the available
evidence it would therefore seem that essentially modern
conditions had been established by the beginning of the
Holocene, and that there may have been few significant
changes since.

THE ORONTES VALLEY, COASTAL LEBANON, AND LAKE HULA

The overall implications of the Zeribar profile find
corroboration in a 12 m core from the Ghab depression of
the central Orontes Valley, at 190 m elevation (Niklewski
and van Zeist, 1970). A rudimentary chronology is provided by interpolation and extrapolation from two finite
C14 dates, and several reconstructions in time are given by
the vegetation cross section of Figure 2. Superimposed fluctuations complicate but do not obscure a progressive
opening of the vegetation during the course of the late
Pleistocene. During the early Würm the 500–800 m Jebel
Zawiye to the east was an open woodland of deciduous and
live oak; the 500–1700 m Jebel Alaouite a deciduous oak
forest with some pine, cedar, and juniper; and the Mediterranean coastal plain a live oak–pistachio woodland. By the
late Würm the mountains and coastal plain were cheno-
pod-*Artemisia* steppes with a mixed, temperate woodland
confined to the intermediate level, windward slopes of
Jebel Alaouite. In detail, the Würm interstadial time spans
were notable by increased woodland vegetation, while the
glacial maxima saw an increasingly open vegetation (fig. 2).

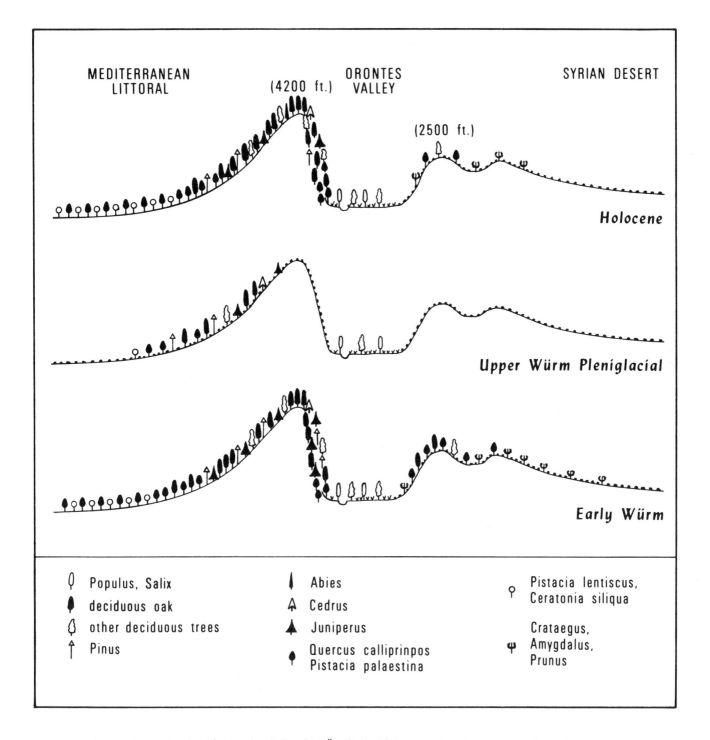

FIG. 2—Reconstruction of vegetation during the Würm in the Khab Depression, Orontes Valley, from a 12 m core.

The Ghab profile and its interpretation are verified by 14 well-chosen pollen spectra from several late Pleistocene substages recorded by sediments along the Lebanese coast (Leroi-Gourhan, 1971). The last interglacial, +1.8 m *Strombus* beach was next to a mediterranean woodland of live oak, pistachio, wild olive, and carob, with a minor representation of hornbeam, *Celtis*, walnut, and wild grape. By contrast, late interglacial or early glacial deposits suggest a forest steppe, with wild olive and pine the dominant trees. Nonarboreal pollen vary from 42 to 94% in the full glacial

spectra, reflecting a predominantly open vegetation. This picture of coastal vegetation promises to be complemented by pollen from Mt. Carmel, where the Tabun sequence includes a high proportion of temperate trees in the early Würmian levels (Horowitz, this volume). It is also compatible with Leroi-Gourhan's pollen spectra from the Damascus Basin (Kaiser et al., 1973), where arboreal pollen in the full glacial deposits accounts for only 3 to 36%. However, the presence of *Pterocarya* and *Tilia tomentosa*, now found in the Caucasus, as well as cedar and walnut, now found at more mesic elevations and exposures, suggest a cooler and slightly less xeric regional environment.

The 123 m Hula profile, from below sea level at the northern end of the Jordan graben, is essentially dated by extrapolation from a single C14 date (Horowitz, 1971, 1973; see also Cowgill, 1969, for other dates and a discussion of the variable sedimentation rates). For the Holocene, several other dated profiles are available from Hula and Lake Tiberias. The early Würm was marked by a maximum of live oak and wild olive, probably representing an open mediterranean woodland, not substantially different from that prevalent in the relatively moist mid-Holocene. Another period of open oak forest is indicated ca. 25,000 B.C., with a return to almost equally mesic conditions during part of the late glacial. Nonarboreal pollen dominated during the last interglacial, the mid-Würm interstadial, for a short while ca. 18,000 B.C., and during early Holocene times.

These Levantine pollen profiles, seen as an ensemble, show that some woodland persisted in the coastal hill country throughout the late Pleistocene, unlike the open vegetation of Anatolia and Iran. Nonetheless, with possible exception of the early Würm, the last glacial can hardly have enjoyed greater rainfall than the Holocene. Most of the apparent pluvial phenomena must therefore be attributed to lower temperatures and reduced evaporation, possibly combined with greater seasonal periodicity of precipitation and runoff. However, there is an apparent zonal change from north to south within the Levant, whereby late Pleistocene vegetation was generally denser in Israel—where open woodland extended into the northern Negev for a while (Horowitz, this volume)—than in Syria and Lebanon; similarly, the Würm interstadial time-range saw an increase of woodland in the north, a decrease in the south. These regional contrasts presumably document a real zonal trend from glacial aridity in the latitude of Anatolia to increasingly moist glacial conditions in Israel. By extension, substantial increases of absolute precipitation during much of the late Pleistocene should be expected in the latitude of Sinai and Egypt, which is consonant with the geomorphologic record of the Nile Valley.

SYNTHESIS: TURKEY AND IRAN

In concluding and attempting to synthesize the Near Eastern evidence for environmental conditions from the late Pleistocene to mid-Holocene time range, it is necessary to review our information within broad regional contexts: (1) the highlands of Anatolia, Armenia, Kurdistan, and Iran; (2) the hill country and plains of the Levant and Mesopotamia; and (3) the lower Nile Valley and the adjacent deserts.

The evidence from the highland belt can be summarized as follows:

1. Widespread glacial features in Turkey, Transcaucasia, Iran, the adjacent parts of Iraq, as well as in the high Lebanon, all indicate a colder climate during the Würm full glacial. Mean summer temperatures may have been in the

order of 6–7° C. lower than at present. The existence of multiple minor ("recessional") moraines in association with most of these late Pleistocene glaciers suggests one or more readvances during the late glacial as well as one or more stage of temporary readvance or reglaciation during the Holocene.

2. The Lake Zeribar pollen diagram and associated evidence suggests that an open vegetation of steppe and mountain tundra, perhaps with scrub-steppe in more favored localities, characterized Turkey, northeastern Iraq, and most of Iran during the full glacial. The warmup during the Alleröd and particularly during the early Holocene appears to have been accompanied by an increase in precipitation, leading to gradual reforestation of the highlands.

3. The remaining categories of geomorphologic evidence from the highlands do not appear to contradict the Lake Zeribar interpretation. Few lacustrine deposits have been dated, and many but not all seem to be of early Würm or of Holocene date. In no case do the higher lake levels indicate a very appreciable increase in rainfall, and those of glacial age are readily explained by reduced evaporation alone. The alluvial deposits of the high highlands are all dated, on rather indirect criteria, as late Pleistocene. Some or even the majority may turn out to be of early Würm age. Others may pertain to the full glacial, reflecting seasonally concentrated stream discharge and accelerated morphogenesis under a more severe climate. Although dissected Holocene alluvia appear to be infrequent or lacking, there is at least a strong possibility of higher lake levels during some parts of the Holocene (e.g., Lake Burdur).

4. The data now available show clearly that the Near Eastern Highlands, north of about latitude 35°, did not experience "pluvial" conditions during the last 50,000 years or so. The full and late glacial were conspicuously cold and comparatively dry. The Holocene environment appears to have remained fairly constant, with conditions similar to those to be expected today without human disturbance. Perhaps the only significant post-Pleistocene changes in this regional setting have been those accompanying and following intensive or rapacious land-use. Under any circumstances, considerable environmental change must have accompanied the Pleistocene-Holocene transition. Unfortunately, the exact nature of these changes can only be conjectured at the moment.

SYNTHESIS: THE LEVANT AND MESOPOTAMIA

In the hill country and plainlands of Syria, Lebanon, Israel, Jordan, and Iraq, the climatic vicissitudes of the late Pleistocene and early Holocene are documented by several categories of evidence:

1. There are no imposing lake deposits outside of the Jordan Valley, and geomorphologic changes appear to be most manifest in fairly widespread alluvial fills that accompany many larger and smaller streams. The implications of these now-dissected alluvia are not unequivocal, and they may be a result of one or more of the following factors: (a) more torrential rains, (b) more concentrated discharge

and/or precipitation, (c) greater precipitation, (d) more detritus as a result of accelerated weathering, and, in areas with an effective vegetation mat today, (e) changes of the vegetative cover reflecting on differing temperatures and evaporation rates. Until more detailed work has been done and isotopic dating has become available, the geomorphic environment of the Levant and Mesopotamia in recent geological times must remain somewhat enigmatic. An important exception is provided by the Damascus Basin and particularly by the Jordan Valley, where several moist interludes can be clearly recognized in the late Pleistocene to Holocene time range. Interpretation of at least the lacustrine beds and massive spring deposits seem to be clear in this area, although further sedimentological study of the alluvial terraces will be necessary.

2. The available cave sequences show that most of the early Würm, and parts of both the full and late Würm, were sufficiently cold (and moist) to generate significant frost-weathering. The resulting angular rubbles are interrupted by horizons reflecting on chemical weathering or fine-grained sedimentation under more temperate conditions. The state of cave sedimentological studies leaves a great deal to be desired, however.

3. The biological evidence from the Levant and Mesopotamia now includes both faunas and some pollen. Although the full glacial cave deposits of the Levant show a number of intrusive Palearctic forms (see Howell, 1959, and Hooijer, 1961), the glacial age faunas everywhere suggest ecological conditions remarkably similar to those of today. Far more impressive are the pollen data, which show that forest vegetation was generally diminished during the glacial periods, except for the Negev. This trend to relatively diminished vegetation is far more evident in northern Syria and Lebanon, where absolute rainfall must have decreased markedly during the full glacial, than in Israel where rainfall amounts did not decline appreciably but where reduced evaporation favored expansion of existing woodlands. There may also be some biological evidence for moister conditions during part of the early and middle Holocene in Israel and the Damascus Basin, but elsewhere the paucity of evidence for change should be evaluated in a positive light, namely that there has been little ecologically significant change in post-Pleistocene times north of perhaps 32° latitude.

4. In view of the evidence there is absolutely no support for once current theories that agricultural origins must be explained by post-Pleistocene desiccation. There is no evidence for a deterioration of suitable agricultural lands in the Levant or Mesopotamia during the Pleistocene/Holocene transition. Instead, the close of the Pleistocene opened up extensive arable lands and lush pastures in the high country. Similarly, there is no reason whatsoever to believe that agricultural dispersals were motivated or aided by progressive desiccation of the nuclear agricultural area in southwestern Asia. These problems have already been outlined and discussed elsewhere (Butzer, 1971, chaps. 32-33).

SYNTHESIS: EGYPT

In a hyperarid environment such as Egypt even very modest increases of precipitation have had disproportionately great effects on geogmorphologic equilibrium as well as on ecological conditions. Yet even here true "pluvial" conditions were last experienced during the first half or so of the Würm. The later full glacial was as dry as today in Egypt. The more recent evidence can be summed up as follows:

1. Wadi discharge in Egypt and Nubia was more significant during much of the period between 15,000 and 3000 B.C., except for three major dry interludes centered at approximately 9500 B.C., 5500 B.C., and 4500 B.C. The geomorphologic evidence is substantiated by fragmentary biological data and, altogether, suggests that rains were more frequent and perhaps of greater duration during much of this time. A reddish paleosol, with distinctive evidence of biochemical weathering, can be dated 5000 B.C. The existence of one or more mid-Holocene moist spells appears to be borne out by the lake beds and spring deposits of Arabia as well.

2. The impact of subpluvial intervals on the fauna of Egypt during late prehistoric times has been studied in some detail (Butzer, 1959a) and the significance of these moister spells elsewhere in the Sahara has been frequently discussed in the literature. There is no evidence, however, that episodes of late Pleistocene desiccation in Egypt led to enforced concentration of prehistoric settlement in the Nile Valley, as was once claimed. Lower and Middle Paleolithic habitation seems to have already been confined to the vicinity of reliable water sources, and the late Paleolithic settlers of the Nile Valley did not expand into the nearby deserts during moister intervals (see Butzer and Hansen, 1968, chap. 4). However, the biomass and diversity of game resources outside of the riverine zone would have varied significantly, with potential implications for at least some activities of certain prehistoric groups.

3. Contemporary ecological conditions were finally established in Old Kingdom times and a long arid phase with accelerated dune activity, accompanied by comparatively low Nile floods had begun by the end of the Fifth Dynasty (ca. 2350 B.C.).

GENERAL CONCLUSIONS

In final overview, it is apparent that the available evidence allows several general conclusions.

1. The last interglacial period, although poorly recorded in most areas, more often than not experienced environmental conditions similar to those of today. Nonetheless, wherever there is detailed information it becomes equally evident that climates changed through time.

2. The last glacial allows chracterization of three distinct paleoclimatic provinces in the Near East: (a) the highlands of Anatolia and Iran, intensely cold most of the time, were also very dry during the full glacial, with next to no tree growth possible; (b) the Levant, moderately cold

and relatively dry in the north, cool and comparatively moist in the south—this dichotomy possibly extending east-wards across Mesopotamia and southern Iran; (c) Egypt, experiencing long periods of increased rainfall, except for the Würm glacial maximum—a pattern possibly repeated in Sinai and Arabia. Different trends again are apparent in the southern Sahara and East Africa (Butzer, Isaac, et al., 1972).

3. The mid-Holocene saw repeated moister trends in Egypt and Arabia, comparable to those in sub-Saharan Africa, that affected Israel but are not evident farther north.

4. The early to middle Pleistocene, although not the subject of this review, is next to intangible in view of the fragmentary evidence, and above all in view of the almost total lack of radiometric and palynological criteria that proved to be essential to any realistic unravelling of the late Pleistocene and Holocene of the Near East.

5. All of the climatic changes recorded were of rela-tively short wave length, and none exceeded the duration of the standard late Pleistocene substages utilized in the European chronology. This makes direct correlations with the European chronology difficult if not undesirable, par-ticularly in default of radiometric dating.

6. Except for Egypt, there is no sound evidence for pluvials as such in the Near East, even though the term "pluvial" is useful as an adjectival form to describe partic-ular phenomena (see also Butzer, 1971, pp. 350 ff.).

BIBLIOGRAPHY

ARDEL, A., 1938. "Au sujet des variations de niveau du lac de Van durant la période quaternaire. *Comptes Rendus, Congrès International de géographie, Amsterdam 1938* (Leiden) 1(2a):261-69.

————, 1954. "Partie occidentale de la région des lacs, Turquie." *Review of the Geographical Institute, Istanbul,* International Edition 1:66-84.

BATE, D. M. A., 1940. "The Fossil Antelopes of Palestine in Natufian (Mesolithic) Times." *Geological Magazine* 77:418-33.

BELL, B., 1970. "The Oldest Records of the Nile Floods." *Geographical Journal* 136:569-73.

————, 1971. "The Dark Ages in Ancient History." *American Journal of Archaeology* 75:1-26.

BEN-ARIEH, Y., 1964*a*. "A Tentative Water Balance Estimate of the Lisan Lake." *Israel Journal of Earth Sciences* 13:42-47.

————, 1964*b*. "Some Remarks on the Last Stages of Formation of Lake Tiberias." *Israel Journal of Earth Sciences* 13:53-62.

BESANCON, J., and HOURS, F., 1970. "Préhistoire et géomorphologie: les formes du relief et les dépôts quaternaires dans la région de Joub Jannine (Béqaa méridionale, Liban), 1." *Hannon* 5:63-95.

————, and HOURS, F., 1971. "Préhistoire et géomorphologie: les formes du relief et les dépôts quaternaires dans la région de Joub Jannine (Béqaa méridionale, Liban), 2. *Hannon* 6:29-135.

BEUG, H. J., 1967. "Contributions to the Postglacial Vegetational History of Northern Turkey." In *Quaternary Paleoecology*, edited by E. J. Cushing and H. E. Wright, pp. 349-56. New Haven: Yale University Press.

BIRMAN, J. H., 1968. "Glacial Reconnaissance in Turkey." *Bulletin of the Geological Society of America* 79:1009-26.

BOBEK, H., 1937. "Die Rolle der Eiszeit in Nordwestiran." *Zeitschrift für Gletscherkunde* 25:130-83.

————, 1940. "Die Gegenwärtige und eiszeitliche Vergletscherung im Zentralkurdischen Hochgebirge." *Zeitschrift für Gletscherkunde* 27:50-88.

————, 1959. *The Great Kawir of Central Iran: A Contribution to the Knowledge of Its Features and Formation.* Arid Zone Research Centre, University of Teheran, 2.

————, 1963. "Nature and Implications of Quaternary Climatic Changes in Iran." *Arid Zone Research (UNESCO)* 20:403-13.

————, 1968. "Vegetation." In *The Cambridge History of Iran*, edited by W. B. Fisher, 1:280-93. Cambridge: At the University Press.

BOUCHUD, J., 1971. "Étude préliminaire de la faune du Djebel Qafzeh, près de Nazareth." *Supplément Bulletin de l'Association Française pour l'Étude du Quaternaire* 1:455-58.

BOWMAN, D., 1971. "Geomorphology of the Shore Terraces of the Late Pleistocene Lisan Lake (Israel)." *Palaeogeography, Palaeoclimatology, and Palaeoecology* 9:183-209.

BRUNNACKER, K., 1970. "Die Sedimente das Schutzdachs I von Jabrud (Syrien)." *Frühe Menschheit und Umwelt (Fundamenta A-2)*, pp. 189-98.

BURINGH, P., 1960. *Soils and Soil Conditions in Iraq.* Baghdad: Ministry of Agriculture, Republic of Iraq. Wageningen: Veenman and Zonen.

BUTZER, K. W., 1958. *Quaternary Stratigraphy and Climate in the Near East*. Bonner Geographische Abhandlungen 24.

—————, 1959*a*. *Die Naturlandschaft Aegyptens während der Vorgeschichte und dem dynastischen Zeitalter*. Abhandlungen Akademie der Wissenschaften und die Literatur (Mainz), Mathematische-Naturwissenschaftliche Klasse 1959, 2.

—————, 1959*b*. "Contributions to the Pleistocene Geology of the Nile Valley." *Erdkunde* 11:46-67.

—————, 1964*a*. "Pleistocene Cold Climate Phenomena of the Island of Mallorca." *Zeitschrift für Geomorphologie* 9:7-31.

—————, 1964*b*. "Pleistocene Palaeoclimates of the Kurkur Oasis." *The Canadian Geographer* 8:125-41.

—————, 1965*a*. "Physical Conditions in Eastern Europe, Western Asia, and Egypt before the Period of Agricultural and Urban Settlement." *Cambridge Ancient History*, rev. ed., fasc. 33, vol. 1, chap. 2.

—————, 1965*b*. "Desert Landforms at the Kurkur Oasis, Egypt." *Annals of the Association of American Geographers* 55:578-91.

—————, 1966. "Geologie und Palaeogeographie archäologischer Fundstellen bei Seiyala (Unternubien)." *Denkschriften, Oesterreichische Akademie der Wissenschaften (Wien), Philosophische-Historische Klasse* 92:89-98.

—————, 1967. "Late Pleistocene Deposits of the Kom Ombo Plain, Upper Egypt." *Alfred Rust Festschrift, Fundamenta B-2*, pp. 213-27.

—————, 1971. *Environment and Archeology*. Chicago: Aldine-Atherton.

—————, 1973*a*. "Periglacial Phenomena in Southern Africa." *Boreas* 2:1-12.

—————, 1973*b*. "Past Climates of the Tibesti Mountains, Central Sahara." *Geographical Review* 63:395-97.

—————, 1974*a*. "Modern Egyptian Clay Sources and Predynastic Buff Ware." *Journal of Near Eastern Studies*. In press.

—————, 1974*b*. "Birket el-Karun." *Lexikon der Ägyptologie*. In press.

—————, 1974*c*. "Pleistocene Littoral-Sedimentary Cycles of the Mediterranean Basin: A Mallorquin View." In *After the Australopithecines: Stratigraphy, Ecology, and Culture Change in the Middle Pleistocene*, by K. W. Butzer and G. L. Isaac. The Hague: Mouton. In press.

—————, 1974*d*. "Delta." *Lexikon der Ägyptologie*. In press.

—————, and HANSEN, C. L., 1967. "Upper Pleistocene Stratigraphy in Southern Egypt." In *Background to Evolution in Africa*, edited by W. W. Bishop and J. D. Clark, pp. 329-56. Chicago: University of Chicago Press.

—————, and HANSEN, C. L., 1968. *Desert and River in Nubia*. Madison: University of Wisconsin Press.

—————, and HANSEN, C. L., 1972. "Late Pleistocene Stratigraphy of the Kom Ombo Plain, Upper Egypt: Comparison with Other Recent Studies near Esna-Edfu." *Bulletin de Liaison, ASEQUA* 35-36:5-14.

—————, and ISAAC, G. L., 1974. *After the Australopithecines: Stratigraphy, Ecology, and Culture Change in the Middle Pleistocene*. The Hague: Mouton. In press.

—————; ISAAC, G. L.; RICHARDSON, J. L.; and WASHBOURN-KAMAU, C. K., 1972. "Radiocarbon Dating of East African Lake Levels." *Science* 175:1069-76.

COON, C. S., and RALPH, E. K., 1955. "Radiocarbon Dates from Kara Kamar, Afghanistan." *Science* 121:921-22.

COWGILL, U. M., 1969. "The Waters of Merom: A Study of Lake Huleh." *Archiv für Hydrobiologie* 66:249-72.

de PLANHOL, X., 1956. "Contribution à l'étude géomorphologique du Taurus occidental et de ses plaines bordières." *Revue de Géographie Alpine* 44, no. 4.

_____, and BILGIN, T., 1964. "Glaciaire et périglaciaire quaternaires et actuels dans le massif du Karagol (Chaînes pontiques-Turquie)." *Revue de Géographie Alpine* 52:497-512.

DESIO, A., 1934. "Appunti geografici e geologici sulla catena dello Zardeh Kuh in Persia." *Memorie Geologiche e Geographiche di G. Dainelli* 4(13):141-67.

DIESTER, L., 1972. "Zur spätpleistozänen und holozänen Sedimentation im zentralen und öostlichen Persischen golf." *Meteor Forschungs-Ergebmsse* C-8:37-83.

EHLERS, E., 1971*a*. "Südkaspisches Tiefland und Kaspisches Meer." *Tübinger Geographische Studien* 44:1-184.

_____, 1971*b*. "Die Historischen Spiegelschwankungen des Kaspischen Meeres und Probleme ihrer Deutung." *Erdkunde* 25:241-49.

ERDBRINK, D. P. and van HEEKEREN, H. R., 1965. "The Presence of Supposedly Primitive Human Tools along the Upper Reaches of the Kizil Irmak in Anatolia." *Eiszeitalter und Gegenwart* 16:78-87.

FARRAND, W. R., 1970. "Geology, Climate and Chronology of Jabrud Rockshelter I." *Frühe Menscheit und Umwelt (Fundamenta A-2)*, pp. 212-23.

_____, 1972. "Geological Correlation of Prehistoric Sites in the Levant." In *The Origin of Homo Sapiens*, edited by F. Bordes, pp. 227-35. Proceedings of the Paris Symposium, 2-5 September 1969. Paris: UNESCO.

FRENZEL, B., 1959-60. *Die Vegetations und Landschaftszonen Nord-Eurasiens während der letzten Eiszeit und während der post-glazialen Wärmezeit*. Abhandlungen der Akademie der Wissenschaften und der Literatur (Mainz), Mathematische Naturwissenschaftliche Klasse. 1959, no. 13, 1960, no. 6.

GABRIEL, A., 1957. "Zur Oberflächengestaltung der Pfannen in den Trockenräumen Zentralpersiens." *Mitteilungen Geographische Gesellschaft Wien* 99:146-60.

GALL, H., 1966. "Gletscherkundliche Beobachtungen im Hochgebrige von Lasistan." *Mitteillungen Österreichische Geographische Gesellschaft* 108:261-86.

GALLOWAY, R. W., 1970. "The Full Glacial Climate in the Southwestern United States." *Annals of the Association of American Geographers* 60:246-56.

GONZALEZ-ECHEGARAY, J., 1966. *Excavaciones en la terraza de "el-Khiam" (Jordania)*. Madrid: Bibliotheca Praehistorica Hispana 5, vol. 2.

HANSEN, C. L., and BUTZER, K. W., 1966. "Early Pleistocene Deposits of the Nile Valley in Egyptian Nubia." *Quaternaria* 8:177-85.

de HEINZELIN, J., 1964. "Le Sous-sol du Temple d'Aksha." *Kush* 12:102-10.

_____, 1965. "Observations sur les terrasses du Moyen Euphrate." *Bulletin de la Société Géologique de France* 7(7):37-44.

_____, 1967. "Pleistocene Sediments and Events in Sudanese Nubia." In *Background to Evolution in Africa*, edited by W. W. Bishop and J. D. Clark, pp. 313-28. Chicago: University of Chicago Press.

_____, 1968. "Geological History of the Nile Valley in Nubia." In *The Prehistory of Nubia*, edited by F. Wendorf, 1:19-55. Dallas: Fort Burgwin Research Center and Southern Methodist University Press.

HOOIJER, D., 1966. "The Fossil Vertebrates of Ksar Akil, a Paleolithic Rockshelter in Lebanon." *Zool. Verhandelingen* 49:1.

HOROWITZ, A., 1971. "Climatic and Vegetational Developments in Northeastern Israel during Upper Pleistocene-Holocene Times." *Pollen et Spores* 13:255-78.

_____, 1973. "Development of the Hula Basin, Israel." *Israel Journal of Earth Sciences* 22:107-39.

HOWELL, F. C., 1959. "Upper Pleistocene Stratigraphy and Early Man in the Levant." *Proceedings of the American Philosophical Society* 103:1-65.

HUCKRIEDE, R., 1962. "Jung-Quartär und End-Mesolithikum in der Provinz Kerman (Iran)." *Eiszeitalter und Gegenwart* 12:25-42.

_____, and WIESEMANN, G., 1968. "Der Jungpleistozäne Pluvial-See von El-Jafr und Weitere Daten zum Quartär Jordaniens." *Geologica et Paleontologica* 2:73-95.

HUTCHINSON, C. E., and COWGILL, U. M., 1963. "Chemical Examination of a Core from Lake Zeribar." *Science* 140:67-69.

IZBIRAK, R., 1962. *Geomorphologische Beobachtungen im oberen Kizilirmak und Zamanti-Gebiet*. Münchener Geographische Hefte 22.

KAISER, K., 1963. "Die Ausdehnung der Vergletscherungen und 'periglazial' Erscheinungen während der Kaltzeiten des quartären Eiszeitalters innerhalb der syrisch-libanesischen Gebirge." *Report of the VIth International Congress on the Quaternary, Warsaw 1961*, 3:127-48.

_____; KEMPF, E. K.; LEROI-GOURHAN, A.; and SCHUTT, H., 1973. "Quartärstratigraphische Untersuchungen aus dem Damaskusbecken und seiner Umgebung." *Zeitschrift für Geomorphologie* 17:263-353.

KLEBELSBERG, R. V., 1949. *Handbuch der Gletscherkunde und Glazialgeologie*, vol. 1, pp. 407-1028. Vienna: Springer.

KRINSLEY, D. B., 1970. *A Geomorphological and Paleoclimatological Study of the Playas of Iran*. Washington: U. S. Department of the Interior Geological Survey.

LAHN, E., 1951. "Sur la géologie et géomorphologie de quelques lacs de la Turquie." *Mining Research and Exploration Institute of Turkey* 41:127-28.

LEROI-GOURHAN, A., 1971. "Pollens et terrasses marines du Liban." *Quaternaria* 15:249-60.

LEHMANN, U., 1970. "Die Tierreste aus den höhlen von Jabrud (Syrien)." *Frühe Menscheit und Umwelt (Fundamenta A-2)*, pp. 181-88.

LEUTELT, R., 1935. "Glazialgeologische Beobachtungen im Lasistanischen Hochgebirge." *Zeitschrift für Gletscherkunde* 23:67-80.

LOUIS, H., 1938. "Eiszeitliche Seen in Anatolien." *Zeitschrift der Gesellschaft für Erdkunde zu Berlin, 1938*, pp. 267-85.

LUTTIG, G., 1965. "Der Stand der Holozän-Forschung in Westdeutschland 1961." *Report of the VIth International Congress on Quaternary, Warsaw, 1961*, 1:447-61.

el MASRY, A. H., 1973. "Prehistory in Northeastern Arabia: The Problem of Interregional Interaction." Unpublished dissertation, University of Chicago Oriental Institute.

McCLURE, H. A., 1971. "The Arabian Peninsula and Prehistoric Populations." In *Field Research Projects*, edited by H. Field. Miami: Coconut Grove.

MEGARD, R. O., 1967. "Late Quaternary *Cladocera* of Lake Zeribar, Western Iran." *Ecology* 48:179-89.

MESSERLI, B., 1966. "Das Problem der eiszeitlichen Vergletscherung am Libanon und Hermon." *Zeitschrift für Geomorphologie* 10:37-68.

—————, 1967. "Die eiszeitliche und die gegenwärtige Vergletscherung im Mittelmeerraum." *Geographica Helvetica*, pp. 105-228.

MORRISON, R. B., 1965. "Quaternary Geology of the Great Basin." In *The Quaternary of the United States*, edited by H. E. Wright and D. G. Frey, pp. 265-85. Princeton: Princeton University Press.

NEEV, D. and EMERY, K. O., 1967. "The Dead Sea." *Bulletin of the Geological Survey of Israel* 41:1-147.

NIKLEWSKI, J., and van ZEIST, W., 1970. "A Late Quaternary Pollen Diagram from Northwestern Syria." *Acta Botanica Neerlandica* 19(5):737-54.

NIR, D., and BEN-ARIEH, D., 1965. "Relicts of an Intermediate Terrace between the Ghor and the Zor in the Central Jordan Valley." *Israel Journal of Earth Sciences* 14:1-8.

OLAUSSON, E., and OLSSON, I. U., 1968. "Varve Stratigraphy in a Core from the Gulf of Aden." *Palaeogeography, Palaeoclimatology, and Palaeoecology* 6:87-103.

PFANNENSTIEL, M., 1940. "Die diluvialen Schotterterrassen von Ankara." *Geologische Rundschau* 31:407-32.

RALPH, E. K., 1955. "University of Pennsylvania Radiocarbon Dates I." *Science* 121:150-52.

REINHARD, A. V., 1925. "Glazialmorphologische Studien im westlichen und zentralen Kaukasus." *Zeitschrift für Gletscherkunde* 14:81-148, 211-28.

SAID, R.; ALBRITTON, C.; WENDORF, F.; SCHILD, R.; and KOBUSIEWICZ, M., 1972. "A Preliminary Report on the Holocene Geology and Archaeology of the Northern Fayum Desert." In *Playa Lake Symposium*, edited by C. C. Reeves, Jr., pp. 41-61. Lubbock: Icasals Publication No. 4.

—————; WENDORF, F.; and SCHILD, R., 1970. "The Geology and Prehistory of the Nile Valley in Upper Egypt." *Archaeologia Polona* 12:43-60.

SCHARLAU, K., 1958. "Zum Problem der Pluvial-zeiten in Nordost-Iran." *Zeitschrift für Geomorphologie* 2:258-77.

SCHWEIZER, G., 1970. "Beiträge zur Gletscherkunde und Glazialgeomorphologie vorderasiatischer Hochgebirge." *Tübinger Geographische Studien* 34:163-78.

SEDLACEK, A. M., 1955. "Sande und Gesteine aus der südlichen Lut und Persisch-Belutschistan." *Sitzungsberichte der Osterreichischen Akademie der Wissenschaften, Mathematisch-Naturwissenschaftliche Klasse*, Abteilung 1(164):607-58.

SMITH, P. E. L., 1958. "New Investigations in the Late Pleistocene Archeology of the Kom Ombo Plain (Upper Egypt)." *Quaternaria* 9:141-52.

SOLECKI, R. S., and LEROI-GOURHAN, A., 1961. "Paleoclimatology and Archeology in the Near East." *Annals of the New York Academy of Sciences* 95:729-39.

SPREITZER, H., 1958. "Frührezente und rezente Hockstände der Gletscher des Kilikischen Ala Dag im Taurus." *Schlern Schrfiten* (Innsbruck) 190:265-81.

STEKELIS, M., and HAAS, G., 1952. "The Abu Usba Cave (Mt. Carmel)." *Israel Exploration Journal* 1(1):15-47.

STRATIL-SAUER, G., 1957. "Die pleistozänen Ablagerungen im Inneren der Wüste Lut." *Festschrift, 100-Jahr-Feier*, pp. 460-84. Geographische Gesellscheft zu Wien.

VAN LIERE, W. J., 1961. "Observations on the Quaternary of Syria." *Berichten, Rijksdienst Oudheidkundig Bodemonderzoek* 10-11:1-69.

VAN ZIEST, W., 1967. "Late Quaternary Vegetation History of Western Iran." *Review of Palaeobotany and Palynology* 2:301-11.

————, and WRIGHT, H. E., 1963. "Preliminary Pollen Studies at Lake Zeribar, Zagros Mountains, Southwestern Iran." *Science* 140:65-69.

VERMEERSCH, P., 1970. "L'Elkabien." *Chronique d'Égypte* 45:45-67.

VITA-FINZI, C., 1964. "Observations on the Late Quaternary of Jordan." *Palestine Exploration Quarterly* 96:19-33.

————, 1969*a*. "Late Quaternary Continental Deposits of Central and Western Turkey." *Man* 4:605-19.

————, 1969*b*. "Late Quaternary Alluvial Chronology of Iran." *Geologische Rundschau* 58:951-73.

VOUTE, C., and WEDMAN, E. J., 1963. "The Quaternary Climate as a Morphological Agent in Iraq." *Arid Zone Research (UNESCO)* 20:395-402.

WASYLIKOWA, K., 1967. "Late Quaternary Plant Macrofossils from Lake Zeribar, Western Iran." *Review of Palaeobotany and Palynology* 2:313-18.

WENDORF, F.; SCHILD, R.; and SAID, R., 1970. "Problems of Dating the Late Paleolithic Age in Egypt." In *Radiocarbon Variations and Absolute Chronology*, edited by I. U. Olsson, pp. 57-79. New York: Wiley Interscience.

WENZEL, H., 1935. *Forschungen in Inneranatolien: Aufbau und Formen der Lykaonischen Steppe*. Schriften, Geographisches Institut der Universität Kiel 5, H. 1.

WHITEMAN, A. J., 1971. *The Geology of the Sudan Republic*. Oxford: Clarendon Press.

WIRTH, E., 1958. "Morphologische und bodenkundliche Beobachtungen in der syrisch-irakischen Wüste." *Erdkunde* 12:26-42.

WRIGHT, H. E., 1952. "The Geological Setting of Four Prehistoric Sites in Northeastern Iraq." *Bulletin American School of Oriental Research* 128:11-24.

————, 1962*a*. "Pleistocene Glaciation in Kurdistan." *Eiszeitalter und Gegenwart* 12:131-64.

————, 1962*b*. "Late Pleistocene Geology of Coastal Lebanon." *Quaternaria* 6:525-39.

————, 1966. "Stratigraphy of Lake Sediments and the Precision of the Palaeoclimatic Record." In *World Climate from 8000 to 0 B.C.*, edited by J. S. Sawyer, pp. 157-73. London: Royal Meteor. Society.

————; ANDREWS, J. H.; and VAN ZEIST, W., 1967. "Modern Pollen Rain in Western Iran and Its Application to Plant Geography and Quaternary Vegetational History." *Journal of Ecology* 55:415-43.

ZEUNER, F. E. 1957. "Stone Age Exploration in Jordan." *Palestine Exploration Quarterly* 89:17-54.

CURRENT STATUS OF THE LOWER AND MIDDLE PALEOLITHIC
OF THE ENTIRE REGION FROM THE LEVANT THROUGH NORTH AFRICA

C. B. M. McBurney

University of Cambridge

If I understand my brief correctly, I suppose the rather alarmingly wide frame of reference I have been asked to deal with means that I may confine myself to the broader issues and try to avoid some of the pitfalls of more precise fields of inquiry with which I am sure other contributors are better acquainted than I. Apart from short periods of work some years ago in Lebanon and in Egypt, my personal fieldwork in the Mediterranean has been concentrated along the Libyan coast from Cyrenaica to western Tripolitania, and in Asia to the Zagros Mountains and the Caspian Basin. From these points of vantage I have tried to form what opinion I could of problems and ongoing investigations elsewhere in order to integrate my own results with a wider and more significant panorama. I suppose that it is inevitable that from whatever angle one views so wide a scene, one's impression is bound to be colored and biased to some extent by the results available from the area one knows best, and this must be my excuse for putting forward some generalizations which may appear too sweeping to those engaged in other fields.

Nevertheless, it is supposed that one of the objects of a symposium is to enable the participants to express their ideas freely in the hopes of achieving through discussion a wider and more accurate overall synthesis.

In discussing the "status" of these two immense subdivisions of the archaeological record in the particular context of the southern and eastern Mediterranean, immense, that is, both in duration of time and in implication for world prehistory, it will be necessary to focus on certain fundamental issues. The nature of even these fundamental issues is such that their finality is far from being determined. This is not to belittle the great discoveries of the last ten years, or those that continue to emerge; on the contrary, it is immediately obvious that quite apart from forcing researchers to abandon many long-accepted notions, the new results are continuously opening new and more significant areas of inquiry. Ideally, one should not merely engage in a discussion of the status quo but should also suggest at least some of the apparently more promising avenues ahead.

Arguably, the most far-reaching discovery of recent years has been the gradual establishment of a time scale *in solar time units* (as opposed to mere *succession* in time) extending, at least in broad outline, throughout the Lower and Middle Paleolithic. One has only to glance at the discussions of ten to fifteen years ago to see how vastly different is the perspective now revealed from anything dreamed of then. The cultural implications are clearly fundamental, and this writer believes that their full import is a long way from

being appreciated. The first question to be considered is exactly how these time estimates affect matters in this area.

First, let us take the figure of two and a half to two and three-quarters of a million years as the date put forward for the earliest toolmakers in East Africa, indicated by the latest discoveries in the Lake Rudolf area. If this is coupled with the wealth of fossil evidence in favor of East and South Africa as a primary focus of hominid evolution, then the case for initial expansion of toolmaking man from that time forward appears very strong. Such expansion toward the Asiatic Far East and Europe can hardly have failed to pass along the southern and eastern shores of the Mediterranean. However, at first sight, direct evidence of this appears singularly lacking. In the following text it will be seen just how far indirect evidence from marginal and adjacent areas can be made to fill this void.

It is true that for rigorous demonstration one must ask quite a lot of the evidence—namely, adequate samples of typologically diagnosable material in direct or indirect association with chronometric data. One of the most striking cultural consequences of the new East African evidence has been the marked shift in emphasis with regard to the so-called "Pebble Tool assemblages." Twenty years ago, as a glance at Leakey's first volume on Olduvai will show, these seemed like a sort of vestibule or introduction to the main episode of the Lower Paleolithic distinguished by the first appearance of handaxes. It was not guessed that this formative phase was, in fact, comparable in duration to the rest of all human activity. What then can be known or reasonably guessed concerning the role of the Middle East in this connection?

At the time of writing this synthesis, this writer believes that there is no doubt that in importance the field is still held by the discoveries of Northwest Africa. What has happened is that the new developments in East Africa have established the significance of these discoveries on an altogether new and firmer basis. Although there is little direct isotopic evidence of date, the relative indications provided by geology and paleontology are outstanding in their implications.

From the geological point of view, the key area is the Casablanca region which is exceptional in offering a succession of no less than five superimposed fossil shorelines ranging in height from approximately 100 m downward to a well-reserved feature some six to eight m above modern mean sea level. Although subjected at the time of their discovery, and subsequently, to a conventional interpretation which has since been widely criticized (see R. W. Hey's recent summary of the findings of the International Commission on Fossil Shorelines, established by INQUA), a number of well-established features of the Casablanca succession retain fundamental importance for our purposes. First, as P. Biberson (1961) and others have demonstrated, each of the high level marine still-stands, whether they ultimately prove to be of eustatic or local tectonic origin, is separated from the next by prolonged periods of emergence, giving rise to massive terrestrial deposits. They cannot conceivably be interpreted as deriving from minor periods of equilibrium during, for example, a gradual period of continual emergence. This conclusion is further supported by the invertebrate paleontology.

Secondly, the actual heights of the high levels themselves are in accord to a considerable extent with the original features made famous by de Lamothe in Algeria, those of McBurney and Hey (1955) in Cyrenaica, and are not far removed from those recorded by Rushdi Said and others near Alexandria (Said, 1957) at the northeastern extremity of the continent. Despite the existence of divergent successions elsewhere in the world, and indeed in the Mediterranean basin itself, this coincidence is still sufficiently marked to call for comment. It may at the least be taken to favor interpretation in terms of widespread geological events of major dimensions and chronological implication. It should be added that despite some traces of localized tectonic movement, the suggestion of important eustatic factors in the succession as a whole remains very much a possibility.

Turning to the paleontological aspects of the Moroccan evidence, insofar as is known by this writer, the situation remains very much as described by Biberson in 1961. Between the Pliocene mammalian assemblages and those similar in evolutionary status to the European Middle Pleistocene, there occur in both Algeria and East Africa mixed or intermediate mammalian communities comparable to the European Villafranchian.

In Algeria at least two subphases of this African Villafranchian have been distinguished, but in Morocco only the first of these has so far been positively recognized. Unfortunately this cannot be directly correlated to the marine succession, and although it underlies the earliest element of that succession, the main terrestrial complex known locally as the Moulouyian precedes the highest of the shorelines at around 100 meters.

It is suggested that the Moulouyian belongs to the same age as the later phase of the Villafranchian. The conclusion, if validated, is of importance in the present discussion since it is these deposits that contain the earliest traces of undoubted human industry in the form of well-defined Pebble Tools, at the site of Douar Doum, for example, and elsewhere. Judging from Biberson's published figures, the artifactual nature of these Pebble Tools cannot reasonably be called in question (Biberson, 1961, p. 46, plate IV, nos. 4 and 5), nor can there be much doubt about the minimum duration, in geological terms at least, of this type of industrial activity in the Maghreb. Every shoreline and inter-

vening terrestrial deposit from the Moulouyian through the 100 m down to the retreat stage below the 50-60 m Maarifian sea level is characterized by abundant Pebble Tools, and by them alone. It is not until the terminal phases of that retreat, in the famous "MNO" complex, that the first traces of handaxes and cleavers are encountered. From then on they dominate the local industrial pattern until the final retreat from a well-marked 8 m feature widely correlated here, as elsewhere in the Mediterranean, with the much later Eemian interglacial. Thus the parallel with the European succession is striking.

Remarkable as the Moroccan coastal succession is, it would be misleading to consider it in isolation. Although the Algerian succession is far less complete, it serves to complement the Moroccan in a number of cardinal ways, both with regard to the Pebble Tool complexes under discussion and also the later handaxe assemblages to be assessed below. The first point to be emphasized surely must be the conclusive demonstration revealed at Ain Hanech that the former had indeed reached the Maghreb *before* the replacement of the Villafranchian by the Middle Pleistocene mammalian congeries. This conclusion is complemented, moreover, by the character of the faunal associations of the *earliest* Algerian handaxes when, as in Morocco, they finally become established as part of the pattern of human activity. One of the most significant features of the finds in the earlier of the two Ternifine horizons, although overshadowed in interest by the spectacular human fossils, was the presence in the associated fauna of three crucial survivors of the ancestral Villafranchian; namely, an archaic Phacochoeroides, a giant Cynocephalus ape, and, above all, a species of *Machairodus*, here as elsewhere in the Old World, one of the key phyla of the earlier assemblage (Arambourg, 1949, 1963).

It would seem then that we have here pinpointed with unusual precision a common reference zone between the industrial and paleontological record, and that handaxe making in Algeria goes back to the final episode of the Villafranchian–Middle Pleistocene transition. In general order of magnitude this accords well enough with the Moroccan sequence, but what it implies in terms of more precise quaternary chronology is another matter. In this connection, however, attention may be called to two general points of comparison. The corresponding biological transition in Europe clearly antedates these, the Elster-Saale Interglacial complex (or complexes), and in all probability at least part of the Elster or Mindel episodes as well. However these climatic events are defined, such isotopic indications of age point to a *minimum* age in the order of 400,000 years. Moreover, if the probability is accepted that some degree of correlation between world sea level movement and the glaciations was present, even at this remote period, it is interesting to observe that both in Morocco and in Europe the industrial change from pure Pebble Tool activity to one including handaxes seems to occur during the early stages of a glaciation *preceding* the Saale or Riss. Thus, within the somewhat wide frame of reference available at present, it is still true to say that the beginning and end of this initial period of human culture appears to be synchronous, in the very broadest terms, north and south of the Sahara, at least in the sense that the earliest traces belong unquestionably to the Lower Pleistocene. The first major innovation of any substance, the emergence of true handaxes, does not take place until toward the end of this vast epoch. At the same time, if we consider the situation in closer detail, it is pertinent to draw attention to a few signs which already tend to suggest a certain degree, and perhaps even a substantial degree, of time lag, especially regarding the end of the cultural episode in question.

At Olduvai (Leakey, 1971) a case of considerable substance can now be formulated for a date in the order of a million and a quarter years ago for the emergence of handaxes. If such a figure were assigned to the early Amirian in Morocco, then the latter could hardly be equated with Elster or Mindel in Europe, given the K/Ar dates offered thus far as 300,000-400,000. It may quite reasonably be urged that the K/Ar dates in question are numerically too few to be reliable, and indeed the date attached to the Torre in Petra handaxes in Italy (though not directly related to a climatic episode) is even earlier, at 450,000. On the other hand again, one may well reject the whole "classic" scheme of four or five major glaciations and turn in preference to the far more complex picture offered by deep sea cores—for example, Pacific core V28-238—with their suggestions of a much greater number of climatic oscillations than is traditionally allowed by terrestrial geologists. Quite recently this point of view has been dramatically reinforced by the publication of Van der Hammen et al. of the 120 m pollen core from Phillipi, Greece (Turekian, 1971). However, it should be noted that if this latter stance is adopted, researchers are almost inevitably committed to the assumption of extreme discontinuity of which, indeed, there is little sign in the later phases.

As the evidence stands at the present time, there is an apparent dilemma. Although a substantial overlap in time between the Pebble Tool traditions of East and Northwest Africa is almost certain, the possibility is also raised that both the beginning and the end of the episode may eventually prove to have been significantly earlier to the south than to the north of the Sahara. It is difficult to see how the problem can be resolved until the chronometric data have been greatly expanded, especially in the Maghreb. It is probable that no one would seriously wish to propose a reverse pattern; hence the probability of a south-to-north expansion of the earliest toolmakers already suggested by distributions and paleontology is, to that extent, enhanced.

It is against this backdrop that one may now proceed to a discussion of the remaining indications thus far obtained from the rest of this area. The direct evidence, as has already been pointed out, does not as yet amount to much. To the east of the Atlas Massif in the minor prolongation of that feature which is the Gebel Nefusa range of Northwest Libya, this writer was able to recover some thirty years ago

(McBurney, 1947) indications which appear to agree with those discussed above. *In the middle reaches of the Wadi Merdum, facing toward the Sirtican plain*, traces were found of a terraced topography yielding very abundant Pebble Tools together with rarer traces of handaxes and finally more numerous remains of Middle Paleolithic type. These three categories were predominantly in very different states of mechanical and chemical weathering and afford some slight grounds for deducing a spread of the early complex this far to the east.

Again, a thousand miles to the east, in Egypt, there are of course the frequently quoted finds made long ago by Père Bovier-Lapierre (1925) at Abbasiaya. There is little to add to what has been said by others, except that after a fairly detailed examination of the exposure as it survived thirty years ago, a massive series of characteristic Pebble Tools from the basal horizon was obtained, unaccompanied as far as could be established by any traces of bifaces. The possibility presented itself that the remarkably crude examples of the latter kind reported on by Bovier-Lapierre might perhaps have formed a separate and later series.

When this writer visited Bovier-Lapierre and discussed the matter during World War II, however, no decision was reached on the basis of his notes and recollections; nor is anything of the kind mentioned by Sandford and Arkell and their well-known pioneering monograph on the area.

Again moving east, into the Levant proper, the important series from Ubeidiya (Stekelis, 1966a, 1966b, 1969), which were originally cited as possible traces of a Pebble Tool assemblage in Palestine, have now been effectively shown to compare closely in composition with the earliest handaxe assemblages of East Africa—Olduvai Bed II for instance, rather than their predecessors, for which a recent K/Ar reading (not yet published) fits them perfectly. Nor has anything of the kind yet emerged from the important marine succession of the Beirut area, where, on the contrary, Fleisch (1956) has claimed the presence of undoubted handaxes as early as his 100 m level. It is perhaps somewhat difficult to know how to evaluate this remarkable claim due to signs of local tectonic disturbance, or even to be quite certain of the association (see Hours, this volume).

With these few hints at one's disposal, it seems clear that if any assessment is offered of the possible situation in the Levant during the Lower Pleistocene, it can only be done indirectly and by implication from the wider scene in the rest of the Old World. As far as Europe is concerned, at long last some few indications have begun to appear from which researchers can try to deduce a first estimate of the initial phase of human culture.

To begin with, it would seem that the original find at Mauer is really neutral to the issues concerned. Although the general character of the associated fauna is undeniably comparable to the earlier zone at Ternifine, conceivably it could also be somewhat earlier in date. This writer personally does not find the proposed artifacts, published by Rust from the same deposit, conclusively artifacts, by any means. But at least they are the product of a very carefully conducted search which produced no signs of the handaxes expected by the adherents of d'Ault du Mesnil and the Abbé Breuil.

The Vertészöllös finds (Kretzoi and Vertes, 1965) are another matter. If both the artifactual nature of the industry and the association with the Biharian microfauna are beyond question, the exact chronological status of the latter would seem to be in need of some further discussion. Where exactly does it fit in with the better known mammalian assemblages of Western Europe, and what precisely are the limits in terms of glacial age which we can assign to it? At least the implication seems to be of the order of an early Middle Pleistocene.

Although too small for cultural diagnosis, de Lumley's Vallonet find does afford fairly solid indication of human presence, and the geological date is certainly interesting. Even making substantial allowance for local tectonic movement, a shoreline at 100 m in Provence seems unlikely to be far removed in age from the first or second shorelines in Morocco, and correlation with the Messaudian seems perfectly reasonable. At the least, a late Lower Pleistocene date seems, on balance, difficult to avoid. For what they are worth, Breuil's old researches in the upper Garonne basin and Zbyzewski's on the Portuguese coast would be in in accord (Breuil and Zbyszewski, 1945). A comparable date for the earliest inhabitants of Europe and the Moroccan coast seems broadly indicated.

Thirdly, we may pass in review the loosely knit, if individually conclusive, discoveries of the Asiatic Far East, and here again there would seem to be several points not irrelevant to the problem of the opening stages of occupation in the Middle East. If, as I have proposed, we provisionally accept a model involving a general expansion from sub-Saharan Africa of Pebble Tool makers during a major part of the Lower Pleistocene, then we might reasonably expect signs of their arrival in the Far East after some degree of time lag.

Such indeed seemed to be the case suggested by the apparently Middle Pleistocene evolutionary status of the fauna at Chou Kou Tien. It is true that many specialists were inclined to place the Java material somewhat earlier, but it was not until Donald Walker and Ann Sieveking published (Sieveking, 1960) Kota Tampan in Malaya that substantial independent testimony was available in support. Once again it is sea level evidence that renders it unlikely that the human presence revealed is later than some period in the Lower Pleistocene, nor is the character of the industrial activity in this case in any serious doubt. Both the quantity and characterization of the products are in every way comparable to those we have been discussing as well as, of course, those at Chou Kou Tien itself.

What then can one usefully propose in connection with the search for corroborative material in this connection in the Middle East? Perhaps one should take a leaf from some recent studies of much later periods of prehistory and make a more specific attempt to identify the locations and eco-

logical setting of settlements of the initial humankind. Human artifacts should not be expected to be scattered at random, as are the remains of some widely prevalent animal species, but are almost certainly related to the environment in a much more specific fashion. Perhaps a scrutiny of deposits of the appropriate geological age from this point of view rather than from the point of view of convenient fossiliferous beds might yield more positive results. This suggestion is made without sufficient knowledge of the area, but it is made with the feeling that too much weight should not be attached to purely negative evidence until it has been shown to be exhaustive.

In conclusion, two minor points in this connection may be worth mentioning. During an examination of wide gravel spreads on the eastern slopes of the Kopet Dagh or Hazar-i-Masjid range of Northeast Iran, near Sarakhs on the Soviet border, gravel fans deeply dissected by subsequent erosion were identified which yielded at least one example of what is a probable Chopper in Movius's sense. Further to the east, however, in the course of a short survey of the Amu Darya basin in northern Afghanistan, nothing earlier than Middle Paleolithic was found in a setting which suggested a Last Interglacial date. To the north, in Soviet Turkmenistan, Uzbekhistan, and far to the northeast in Central Asia, and in the Yenisei basin in particular, assiduous search has been undertaken for traces of this very period by, among others, I. A. Astakhov, V. P. Liubin, and L. V. Ranov. During a visit to the Soviet Union recently, this writer discussed the problem and saw some of the recovered material. From these firsthand studies no very positive conclusion was reached, however. In any case, the bulk if not the totality of the material thus far is from the surface and is nearly impossible to date. The possibility of penetration of these areas, though, is something that should be borne in mind when one is seeking to reconstruct a total picture.

At this point, it would seem appropriate to offer some reflections on the Lower Paleolithic (of the older concept), that is, primarily in the handaxe-bearing assemblages of the Middle and earlier Pleistocene, as well as some elements in the broad picture which they provide for this region. Once again, there can be no doubt that the principal source of information lies in Biberson's work in Morocco, although supplemented largely in the Levant by finds belonging to the end of the phase.

It is the relative continuity and wide time span, above all, which lend special importance to the Moroccan succession. Mention has already been made of the well-known finds from the "MNO" horizon in the southeastern corner of the great Sidi Abd er Rahman cutting near Casablanca. Earlier accounts concentrated mainly on the geological implications, and it is to Biberson that we owe the first comprehensive account with really instructive figures of this and later finds in this succession.

His account, written some twelve to thirteen years ago, is still unduly influenced by ideas emanating from much earlier workers, such as Breuil and the pioneer investigators of South and East Africa, but it is still very necessary to take into account a whole host of solidly established factual data of permanent value. This is all the more so since Biberson had at his disposal an almost unique geological succession, much of which has since been destroyed by commercial exploitation. It is, therefore, a great advantage that he so meticulously recorded via photograph and scaled section.

In the previous extended discussion of the initial Pebble Tool assemblages attention was drawn to the precision, stratigraphically speaking, with which one could pinpoint their final replacement by assemblages of the succeeding type, namely to a retreat stage of the Maarifian high sea level at +60 meters. Further study has now confirmed an internal or fine structure of this event which is of considerably more than local interest. Moreover, there is no longer dependency upon a single geological exposure; and a number of others analyzed in detail by Biberson facilitate the study of both the technological and chronological aspects more closely.

The broad outlines of the geological context now seem well established. Resting on the outer or seaward margin of the sloping 60 m terrace cut in the pre-Pleistocene formations are (1) a complex of marine and littoral facies beginning at the base with a true beach conglomerate passing upward with minor unconformities into a lagoonal or lacustrine formation. This in turn is overlaid by (2) an immense and unbroken deposit of cemented dune up to 50 ft thick in places (the *Amirian* of Biberson and the *H* formation of earlier writers) whose geological age is clearly indicated by later episodes of these; (3) a further raised shoreline, the first reaching a height of 25 m, with a particularly well-developed coastal topography, the *Anfatian*, including a cliff and a system of seacaves. It is of course the latter which yielded a fine vertebrate fauna (including the well known *Atlanthropus* human fossils), and important molluscan fauna, and a fine stratified succession of industries. The infilling of the caves, like that of the previous episode, begins with a marine conglomerate followed by terrestrial formations (4) in a more or less unbroken sequence, the *Tensiftian*. It is these latter which are incised by a further high sea leavel, reaching only 18 m this time (5), which again is overlaid by terrestrial formations (6) known locally as *Pre-Soltanian*. For the purposes of the present summary we may class as an episode (7) the well-marked feature of a shoreline at approximately 8 m (the *Ouljian*) followed by a further terrestrial series (8) in process of erosion by the rising contemporary sea.

Some suggestions have already been made regarding the upper date of the *Maarifian* retreat and the onset of the *Amirian*, and now consideration will be given to the premise against the detailed pattern just outlined. Taking into consideration the relative magnitude of the *Amirian* sandstone feature, it can hardly be denied that it presents an episode of marine retreat of approximately the right order for a glaciation. To this can now be added a number of further arguments based on the *Anfatian* feature. Even though one is aware that the existence of a true eustatic episode of approximately these dimensions (30 m) has been

questioned recently on the basis of apparently discordant features in other areas, it is felt that one should not lose sight of the weighty positive considerations which support it. The later we come in the marine succession of many areas besides Morocco, the stronger such considerations appear. Not only is it true to state that analogous features have been reported from virtually every apparently tectonically stable area that has been examined thus far, but also when the West European and Egyptian evidence is reexamined, the remarkable parallel offered by the archaeological data cannot, in all fairness, be ignored either.

One example from current research will be quoted in detail, namely that at Slindon in Sussex, southern Britain. A well-preserved storm beach can be followed for many miles, and the original observations of Green and Calkin, claiming association with an industry comparable to the 30 m terraces of the Thames and Somme, were reconfirmed in the summer of 1973. There is certainly no evidence of tectonic disturbance at Slindon, and the pollen indications here and elsewhere are unqestionably in favor of a pre—Rissian interglacial date for such an event, both at Hoxne (with the same typology) and in Jersey (with appropriate flora).

It comes, therefore, as no surprise that the corresponding Moroccan feature at 30 m is associated with a typologically developed and well-characterized handaxe assemblage. To this can now be added a most interesting, if still controversial, element in the shape of the Uranium time estimates of Stearns and Thurber (1965). These gave mean figures of 80,000 ± for the 8 m feature, 120,000 ± for that at 18 m, and consistently over 200,000 for the feature under discussion. The parallel between these figures and those obtained for the last three major warm periods of the deep sea cores on the basis of Pa/Th readings adds up to a chronologic/climatic/geologic scheme of considerable potency. If this is accepted, for the sake of argument, then the archaeological consequences would seem to be as follows.

The broad limits of possible dating of the earliest handaxe-bearing industries have been outlined above. Looking now in closer detail at the scheme proposed initially ten years ago by Biberson, it can be noted that he believes that he is able to isolate the assemblages belonging to three separate geologic phases *all* contained within a short subsection of the retreat from 60 m through 18 m down to an unknown depth, but probably in the order of −100 m, as during the maximum of Würm. Although one can only guess at what period in that retreat the formation of the *H* sandstone was initiated, it would seem unlikely that the process occupied less than a substantial part, if not the greater part of the glacial phase indicated. The measured rates of comparable phenomena later in the glacial sequence make it difficult to believe that Biberson's three initial handaxe stages are spread out over an interval of much more than 200,000 years; the interval may equally well have been much shorter.

Even if this figure is accepted as a first estimate, it is

nonetheless worth comparing it with that offered recently by Glynn Isaac for Olorgesailie, where for this interval he was unable to discern any substantial or unreversed change in typology or technique. Biberson, writing, granted, at a time when no chronometric estimates of even an order of magnitude were available, believed that he could isolate three distinct stylistic phases of wide geographical validity. If he is right, then by the standards of the Lower Paleolithic, Moroccan cultural change was remarkably swift.

Apart from these detailed distinctions, the more generalized features of his older handaxe stages seem well established and compare rather strikingly with those of western Europe. The handaxes themselves can be arranged in the usual typological subgroups with perhaps traces of some local distinctions peculiar to the Atlas massif. Despite earlier assertions Biberson now shows that typical cleavers were present from the start, together with "classic" bifaces of much the same form as one finds in upper Bed II and Bed III at Olduvai, and these are virtually identical to those at Ternifine. Sharp-pointed lanceolate forms are noted passing gradually into rougher narrow shapes and ultimate coarse flake trihedrals. Many of the forms, it is true, are really very rough indeed, and there are still plenty of pebble tools indistinguishable from those of the preceding epoch, but these are unquestionably associated with a proportion of new forms which are sometimes remarkably well finished. These latter new elements, he asserts (and his illustrations afford support), appear to increase to a noticeable degree even during the short geological period in question.

A most interesting and forward-looking feature of his discussion is the attention he gives to the auxiliary material and the basic techniques of manufacture. Thus, he emphasizes the total absence of anything resembling prepared core technique in the manufacture of flakes, large or small. This indication of a prolonged intial phase during which great development in the form and finish of handaxes took place *without* significant accompanying evolution in the *primary* methods of flake-tool manufacture applies equally to Europe. This writer has been able to verify this recently, both at Swanscombe and Hoxne as well as other East Anglian sites. In Europe the chronological indications are that this technological status lasted until the threshold of Riss or Saale. Even then the new traits appear at first in only a very sporadic way. It is not until well into the penultimate glaciation that they suddenly come to dominate the patterns of industrial output, sometimes to the apparent exclusion of handaxes altogether.

It is interesting that in Biberson's picture is found a somewhat divergent developmental pattern from this point onward. The first timid traces of prepared core technique (in the sense of this discussion) become apparent in Morocco during, or soon after, the 30 m Anfatian level. It would be interesting if the geological horizon could be specified a little more closely so that a more precise comparison with Europe could be attempted. However, the present evidence does not make this practicable. Looking carefully at the data Biberson offers, one feels that he tends to overemphasize this element, which is made difficult to discern, in any case, by the relatively coarse materials from which the tools are made. Primarily, one must rely on the evidence of illustrated specimens for the statistical data, which in turn is too generalized to be of much use.

Here must be faced two sources of confusion sometimes introduced into discussion. The first is the notion that all well-defined production of flake blanks to be worked into a variety of precision flake tools is somehow linked to the new technique. That this is not the case was long ago established at a number of classic European stations, among which one can recall Commont's Workshop site (admirably republished, for instance, by François Bordes), Hoxne, Swanscombe, and the earlier handaxe assemblages collected from the Thames terraces and geologically dated by A. D. Lacaille.

In all of these, this writer can vouch from personal examination that there is positively no trace of the prepared core techniques until the very end of the Interglacial, or even the onset of Riss or Saale.

Before comparing the situation in the Middle East and Africa generally, however, it would no doubt clarify this discussion if an attempt were made to define a little more precisely the criteria which this writer has in mind. Everyone is familiar with the so-called "Clacton technique" involving wide plain platforms markedly oblique to the bulbar surface, or at most including two or three platform-facets of a similar nature. There is also a correspondingly low number (in general, two or three) of primary scars on the dorsal surface of the flake. It is also quite unnecessary to engage in, in this connection, such debatable and subjective notions as "block-on-block" or "anvil" detachment methods.

The fracture characteristics observed at this stage can, quite as easily, be produced by a wide variety of methods including the basic one of a hefty blow with any kind of heavy hammerstone. This is likely the easiest technique to teach a beginner in flaking. It usually does not take more than five or ten minutes to show a bonafide beginner how to produce flakes indistinguishable in description from those at the sites mentioned.

The production of a convincing "tortoise core," or even the simpler "disc core" with their characteristic narrow platforms angled at 90°-100° to the bulbar surface and correctly adjusted by numerous small facets, is quite another matter. The manual skill involved is substantial but once acquired results in a number of appreciable advantages to the worker. In the first place, as this author showed statistically in a paper to the Zurich congress in 1950, these improved methods result in a considerable saving of raw material and hence of the effort needed to collect it. In general, samples from flaking floors showing evident signs of the new technique yield a ratio of cutting edge to volume in the order of 50% greater than any assemblage relying solely on plain platform unprepared cores. Moreover, the effect of this economy of effort can be independently checked in a number of ways. Thus, sites in the immediate vicinity of abundant supplies of raw material tend to show a substantially lower degree of core preparation than those situated at some distance from the source of supply.

A good example of this can be found in the original work of McBurney and Hey (1955) in Libya in the region of Derna, Cyrenaica. Here it was possible to correlate geologically two sites widely different in the matter of raw material accessibility. It appeared that the source of raw material lay in horizontal beds exposed by marine erosion along the coast. Quarry sites at the foot of such exposures yielded fantastic numbers of flakes and abandoned cores which included, in addition to a small proportion of carefully worked classic tortoise cores, discs, and other carefully prepared variants, a large additional element of heavy flakes struck with little regard to regularity or economy. There were also abandoned nodules often of great size, with the work scarcely begun. Site 32, published in the same monograph, was one such site which was investigated in detail.

Inland at the geologically contemporary waterhole hunting site of Hajj Creiem, the situation and the reaction of the hunters was entirely different. Here the local source of lithic raw material was notably poor, and a glance at the bulk of the output showed that virtually the whole of it was on fine, nonlocal flint apparently the same as that of the coastal exposure many hours walk away. That such material had indeed been brought from the coast was neatly proven by the presence of unworn barnacle and marine worm tests on the outside of some of the nodules! The difference in treatment of the material thus laboriously imported was striking. The proportion of carefully faceted flakes and the proportion of such flakes carefully sharpened and resharpened was of a different order and very much greater. So, also, was the overall average size of the artifacts—something like half the size of those on the coast.

Quite recently this writer has been able to study an analogous situation in Europe, interestingly enough at a very early stage of development. This is at the Cotte de St. Brelade, Jersey (McBurney and Callow, 1971), where a multiple-layered occupation covering an estimated 10,000 to 15,000 years could be assigned on geological grounds to the final stage of the Riss immediately preceding Eem. Occupation was therefore during a period of marked eustatic sea level rise. Since there are no *in situ* sources of flint available on the island during periods of high mean sea level and there is reason to believe that such supplies would have been accessible during low mean levels, the occupants during the period in question were being gradually deprived of their preferred raw material. They were thus obliged to use a steadily increasing quantity of inferior local material and find measures to economize. The fine material brought from greater distances on the mainland, etc. proved to be essentially the same as the Libyan Middle Paleolithic makers just mentioned, namely, a fine-grained flint. Over the period in question each oscillation in the composition of the raw material is accompanied by the same basic reac-

tions, namely, a reduction in mean size, an increase in the proportion of secondarily retouched implements, and a more careful preparation of cores. These tendencies all show a negative correlation to the percentages of imported selected flint, itself a measure of availability.

That this reaction was not in the nature of long-term cultural buildup but rather an immediate or short-term functional response was made evident by the calculation of Partial Correlation coefficients holding Time. Of course, other examples could be adduced which also tend to show the functional advantages of prepared core techniques; it is the type of situation calculated to trigger off such long-term trends.

Thus, it would seem clear that the technological innovation first noted in Morocco in Biberson's Stage V during the Anfatian episode is not simply a trivial variant but points to a genuine watershed in technique, above all in the sense that it accomplishes certain necessary industrial functions at a substantially lower input of energy. It is further interesting, as the experimental evidence quoted above indicates, that this progress is achieved not merely as the result of some haphazard discovery but does need to be based on what is, in all probability, socially maintained skill.

In the Middle East, as in the Maghreb and in Europe, it is the subsequent development and contingent industrial changes—and their geographical and chronological position—that raise a number of basic problems. In Morocco, according to Biberson, the practices once introduced never disappear until the appearance of a quite different set of innovations associated with the much later introduction of blade-based industries. It is further important to see that throughout the two succeeding phases correlated by Biberson with the emergent interval between the 18 and 8 m high still-stands, handaxes continue to provide a main element in the tool kit. At the same time there is evidence that they undergo what appear to be genuine sustained trends of evolution.

These trends include two of special interest—a marked reduction in size, and a growing tendency to wide heart-shaped forms strongly reminiscent of the famous cordiforms of the European MTA. In this last connection, it is also interesting to recall that the apparently contemporary Temara skull has been diagnosed as of "classic Neanderthal," rather than of *Atlanthropus* type.

Another detail which should be given consideration is the association with this final stage of at least one apparently unmistakable Aterian tanged implement. The term Aterian has sometimes been used rather loosely, but in this case it can be applied in its strictest sense. This observation, moreover, can be coupled with the known presence as reported by Caton-Thompson, elsewhere in the Maghreb, and in Egypt, of a residual handaxe element in otherwise typical Aterian assemblages. It would appear that insofar as the local succession is concerned, the handaxe element did not wholly disappear until the final stage of the Aterian at post-Ouljian sites, such as Dar-es-Soltan for instance, with far more specialized bifaces of a quite different kind.

It would be misleading to project the Moroccan sequence into a wider area without positive evidence. At the present time, there is not comparable continuity in the archaeological record, even for so close a region as the eastern outliers of the Maghreb highlands. In the three basal zones at Sidi Zin, south of Tunis, with their highly accomplished handaxe assemblages, and in the similar series at Ma el Abiod in the same general area, there is no hint of prepared cores, despite the presence of small flake tools, great technical mastery, and fine raw material. It is not until the overlying fourth layer that this element becomes apparent at Sidi Zin, accompanied by a fauna which it would be difficult to place earlier than the beginning of the Upper Pleistocene.

If Morel and Hill's succession near Tunis is reliable, it appears likely that by the time of a local 8 m beach, remarkably similar to the Moroccan Ouljian, the local prepared core assemblages had lost all traces of a handaxe element. Further east an apparent unreversed cultural transition, leading from an assemblage characterized by abundant refined handaxes but no prepared cores to a prolonged succession of prepared core assemblages with no handaxes, has been observed or claimed in a number of regions. An example is that claimed from Kharga Oasis and the lower Nile by Caton-Thompson (1952). Here the lower end of the spectrum with the supposed lack of prepared cores is, perhaps, not as clear as it might be, but the subsequent development with the fairly rapid disappearance of the handaxes is most convincingly displayed and accompanied by a wide variety of other apparently unreversed evolutionary changes. Her sequence is calibrated to an independent geological succession, though not one that can be correlated, unfortunately, with any certainty even to the adjacent Nile, let alone further afield.

It is, however, worth noting certain broad elements of comparison with the succession proposed by Guichard and Guichard (1968) for Nubia. While the geological context of their finds is much vaguer than that described by Caton-Thompson, it would appear that they also have evidence for an initial stage lacking the prepared core element and associated, in their case, with relatively roughly formed handaxes, succeeded by assemblages with a more finished handaxe morphology and associated with some degree of prepared core manufacture. Admittedly, one must be cautious here not to get involved in a circular argument. Because a series of finds on the time scales with which we are dealing here can be easily arranged on a scale of typological resemblance is no argument whatever for deducing a corresponding time succession. Again the point made by Glynn Isaac of the wide range of contemporary variation at this stage of cultural status in East Africa has to be borne in mind.

At the same time Marks's data alone are sufficient to show that, unlike Europe, once the Mousteroid (if this term can be introduced now) had been established, there was no return to the much older industrial pattern. It is notorious that the same general picture holds true of North Libya, the

Levant, and inland regions of Southwest and Central Asia.

Thus far, discussion has been deliberately restricted to the most general level, and therefore the writer risks being accused of laboring the obvious. The object, though, has been to start the final discussion on the basis of solidly ascertained facts of primordial significance. It is with these in mind that now the far more difficult (because more detailed) field of the taxonomy of the Middle Paleolithic proper and its geographical setting will be examined. In this there is the advantage of being able to follow the interesting review of this very subject offered by Marks in 1968 in connection with his study of the Nubian Mousterian.

Three observed successions above all dominate the scene at this period in the Southeast Mediterranean—that of Rust (1950) at Jabrud I, that of Garrod (1934) at Tabun, and that of McBurney (1967) at Haua Fteah. It is this last which provides the most complete chronological data, and since a chronological framework is obviously essential to any model of cultural relations, this writer would like to start with a review of six years of discussion and further discovery following original publication. Moreover, some quite simple factual points seem to have been overlooked in some of the published comments, while in others significant points have, quite frankly, been misquoted. The opportunity is welcomed, therefore, for discussing the situation again and its possible bearing on the interrelations of finds elsewhere.

The industries that can be broadly grouped under the heading "Middle Paleolithic" extend from the lower part of Layer XXV at 18 ft below surface datum, down to excavated unit (Spit) 179 at the base of the deep sounding 42½ ft below datum. Direct Time calibration for the site was obtained by C^{14} readings, eighteen in all, spread out down to Layer XXXIII with a reading of 45,050 B.P. ± 3,200 years. Time estimates below this were obtained indirectly by isotopic calibration between food shells stratified in the deposits, and the independently time-calibrated deep sea sediments of the Central and Eastern Mediterranean published by F. L. Parker, C. Emiliani, and others. At a further remove, still on the basis of the oxygen isotopes, comparison was made with Pa/Th calibrated cores in the Atlantic. In addition, two further cross checks were attempted on the basis of climatic fluctuations. These were recorded by three kinds of indicators—the oxygen isotopic data already referred to, mammalian fauna, and sedimentology of the cave deposits themselves.

The climatic record obtained on this basis and time calibrated in the manner just described was then compared in detail to the nearest sequence available at the time, that of Dr. Ralph Solecki at Shanidar. Only a general comparison was originally attempted with the European succession, but since publication a number of sources have become available, two of the most important being those of Van der Hammen et al. (1967) and Bottema (1967).

Since the upper portion of the succession is likely to be the most reliable from a chronological point of view, the interpretation may begin in Layer XXV. This is where the long succession of Levalloiso-Mousterian samples of Palestinian type finally and suddenly give way to a true Upper Paleolithic assemblage, the Dabban. The climatic evidence shows that this cultural event occurred during a considerable temperate phase within a much more prolonged interval of relatively unrelieved cold. That the cold phase as a whole corresponds to Würm is made abundantly clear by the subsequent temperate phase starting about 10,000 B.C. and lasting, with some oscillations, up to the present. The same sector also serves to check the significance of the mammalian and sedimentary data.

At the time of publication attention was drawn to the earlier temperate phase within Würm which appeared to correspond closely to Emiliani's Isotopic Stage 3 and was equally discernible in the foraminiferal diagrams of Parker (1957) in the East Mediterranean at the same period. It is now widely recognized that both are the same as Van der Hammen's Moorshoofd/Hengelo/Denekamp Temperate Complex in the North, and this has now further been identified by Bottema in Greece as his "Zone II" at Joannina and by Van der Hammen and others in his magnificent succession at Phillipi (Turekian, 1971). The time limits of all these occurrences are well within experimental error of one another and correspond approximately to an interval from 32,000 B.C. to 42,000 B.C., taking all sources of error into account, both statistical and stratigraphical (the depth through which the charcoal was collected). Finally an independent check on this date was afforded by a direct reading for an early phase of the Dabban from Dabba itself—namely, 38,550 B.C.

If these are now compared with the latest readings from Palestine and the dates of the Baradostian at Khoramabad, a very considerable degree of correspondence emerges for the Mousterian/Upper Paleolithic substitution in all three nearly contiguous regions. Furthermore, the important point of the anteriority of this event in the Levant by some 5,000 years over the corresponding occurrence in Southwest Europe seems virtually demonstrated. This in turn has a further bearing on the separate question of the correlation between Haua Fteah and Jabrud I, since it may reasonably be taken to render Bordes's dating at the latter finally and completely untenable. This point shall be returned to again later, but it seems that what really makes the situation so clear is the concatenation of so great a variety of entirely independent lines of reasoning. Thus the date of 40,000 for the Levalloiso-Mousterian suggested by Marks (he does not say what limits he is prepared to offer for its duration) can, at best, apply only to the time of its disappearance. The question of the time of its emergence remains entirely open.

Addressing this latter problem, the situation at the Haua appears to be the following—the earliest horizon of Levalloiso-Mousterian occurs in Layer XXXIV associated with a suite of temperate climatic indicators. This contrasts with the nearly overlying layers XXXII to XXVIII inclusive, where the corresponding indications are of a climate as cold as at any subsequent time in the main Würm maximum.

From XXXIII downward, on the other hand, the indications are of temperate conditions indistinguishable from the present—alike in isotopic temperatures, mammalian fauna, and sedimentology, as far down as the 42.5 ft level. Thus, this record begins with a prolonged warm period extending back beyond the present record, followed by a relatively short but marked cold phase. This is followed in turn by a temperate complex, followed again by the obvious equivalent of Main Würm. Thus the prima facie model is unquestionably that of Eem, followed by Early Würm, followed by Bottema and Van der Hammen's Temperate Complex, followed by Main Würm.

The parallel to Parker's twelve cores in the eastern Mediterranean, as can readily be seen from her fifteen diagrams, is close and consistent, and the entire body of chronometric data available at present is equally consistent. All lines of observation point to a late or terminal Eem date for the first appearance of Levalloiso-Mousterian in North Libya. In attempting to translate this climatic correlation into a date in years, it will be well not to restrict considerations to the local evidence but to take as wide an account of the world scene as is possible. It will be recalled that both Pa/Th and the earliest C^{14} dates consistently estimate the end of Eem as in the order of 60,000 to 70,000 years ago. Admittedly, in applying these results one must bear in mind differences in latitude.

In southerly districts, such as Libya, it is only to be expected that the onset of cold conditions will register later than in the north, and minor cold events will cease to be discernible. In higher latitudes, on the other hand, the reverse is to be expected, and it is the warm subphases that may be expected to disappear so that the minor cold phases coalesce and become indistinguishable from each other and from the major cold phases. Thus, it is not surprising that quite apart from the degree of resolution of the data, no traces are found of such epi-Eem substages as Brörup, Ammersfoort, and Odderade, since the intervening cold episodes which register in North Holland are hardly likely to be discernible in Libya. It follows that the Libyan picture of Eem may well include these last. Even so, it is highly unlikely that the initial Levalloiso-Mousterian made its first appearance in Libya at a date appreciably later than 60,000 B.P.

The author has spoken specifically of its *earliest* emergence in the Libyan sequence and has to justify the statement that the occurrence in question is, in fact, the earliest and not just the earliest so far observed. In the first place, it is necessary to show that the contents of the immediately underlying formation—Layer XXXV—is significantly (and not just accidentally) different from all subsequent layers all the way up to Layer XXV. In the second place, it has to be shown that the industrial difference, even if statistically demonstrable, represents something more than a brief episode connected, perhaps, with some exceptional functional necessity.

In this particular case this writer is prepared to argue quite definitely that both these provisos can, in fact, be met. From Layer XXXV at the top of the Deep Sounding down to Spit 175 at the bottom there is an unbroken scatter of finds.

Although the occurrence is virtually continuous, it is uneven, varying from a dense concentration in the lowest eight spits to a thin trickle in the upper part of the Deep Sounding, and recovering to some extent at the top. Even so, if the assemblage is taken as a whole, it presents a re-markable set of differences, negative and positive, which constantly differentiate them from those in and above Layer XXXIV. Chronologically, on the basis of known sedi-mentation rates, they can hardly occupy an interval of less than approximately 10,000 years.

The most striking differences in question are probably those that affect the primary flaking. From Layer XXXIV upward there is an abundance of typical discoid cores of the normal evolved Mousterian kind. There is a high occur-rence of faceting, however it is calculated, and a high pro-portion of flakes classifiable as Levallois in the somewhat broad use of that term made by Bordes. There are also quite characteristic miniature tortoise cores and the flakes struck from them. Blade production is, however, low (as can be seen in detail from the rigorous method of con-tinuous variable analysis which has been applied in prefer-ence to the rougher and more subjective two-class method of Bordes). In all these characters there is a striking analogy with the Levalloiso-Mousterian of Palestine as exemplified from Layer D upward at Tabun and innumerable other sites. A similar link is offered by the high proportion of convex sidescrapers and points, as Marks (1968) has quite justly emphasized. This writer agrees with him that both characteristics are grounds for classing the Palestinian and Libyan finds within a single and specific taxon. Indeed, only two details of restricted occurrence differentiate the two. In Layers XXXI-XXX there are fairly evident traces of the Aterian found in unmistakable form at two sites else-where in Cyrenaica, while in Layer XXXIV itself there is a quite exceptional level for Group III provided mainly by the presence of surprising numbers of both endscrapers and burins at the expense of points and sidescrapers. There does not appear to be any numerical parallel in the published evidence from Palestine, but it would not be surprising if one were eventually to come to light.

The interpretation of the underlying complex is not so simple. That it falls just outside any reasonable limits of the Levalloiso-Mousterian is beyond question. Take, for instance, the Levallois index itself; however that rather nebulous concept is calculated, whether by using Bordes's categories or by straightforward measurement, it is very nearly negligible.

The same is true of faceting—14% in Spit 174 as com-pared with 67% in Layer XXXIV. On the other hand, the lamellar production is astonishing, and but for the detach-ment technique with massive plain platforms it would be indistinguishable from true Upper Paleolithic. The tool composition where it can be studied is equally idiosyncratic with dominant, if massive, angle burins and innumerable utilized blades. Among the rarer features, however, are fairly definite signs of handaxe manufacture.

Original search for a formal analogy to this strange industrial manifestation was somewhat hampered by the lack of information from the Maghreb, where the position is still as outlined above. In other words, there is really no picture at all for the transition, whatever it may have been, from handaxe to Middle Paleolithic patterns of equipment for this area. Nevertheless, there is certainly no hint of anything of the kind described, either dated or undated.

The picture in the Levant seemed at the time, and still does seem, far more suggestive. It will be recalled that a very reasonable comparison was found in at least two Layers (15 and 13) at Jabrud I. It was difficult to know exactly how to interpret the similarity in the absence of all dating evidence, although as has been pointed out, at least Bordes's improbable comparison with European Aurigna-cian can now be disregarded.

The analogy with the Abri Zummoffen, though less complete, was nevertheless marked by the presence of all the same technological features, and was furthermore of considerable interest because of the apparently similar geo-logical date. Whatever the precise dating of Zummoffen may eventually turn out to be, at least it can hardly be *later* than Last Interglacial. In view of the universality of typical Levalloiso-Mousterian throughout this region, the fact that the "Amudian" (as Garrod called it) is overlain not by Levalloiso-Mousterian but by a substantial zone of Ja-brudian, is surely sufficient guarantee. For whatever par-ticular interpretation that may be favored for the poly-morphic series of Layer E at Tabun and Layers 25-10 at Jabrud I, their taxonomic and chronologic separation from the overlying Levalloiso-Mousterian can hardly be doubted.

Having thus embarked on the chronological setting of homoeomorphs of the early complex at the Haua, it seems opportune to pursue one additional aspect of the chrono-logical setting, namely the widely recurring beach lines at or about 8 m above modern sea level. Regarding the Libyan occurrences, it seems that they preserve their horizontality along the Cyrenaican coast for some 100 km east of Derna in the eastern sector, and what is apparently the same feature can be picked up again at various points between Tocra and Benghazi far to the west. Such horizontal exten-sions seem to make a tectonic explanation, although perhaps not theoretically excluded, distinctly unlikely.

The position of the feature with regard to the archaeo-logical and climatic sequences is interesting. Immediately overlying the beach in the eastern sector are a series of wadi tufas containing abundant and well-characterized settle-ments of Levalloiso-Mousterian—at Hajj Creiem, Ain Mara, etc. (McBurney and Hey, 1955). Above these are alluvial deposits with further *in situ* Levalloisian but no Upper Pale-olithic. The latter occurs first, and in some quantities, in the form of cf. Dabban in a characteristic overlying forma-tion of screes, as Hey has been able to show. Thus the beach precedes the advent of the Upper Paleolithic (at 40,000 B.P.) by a very substantial time. Correlation with the Würmian interstadial complex as suggested some years ago at Burg Wartenstein is thereby rigorously excluded as far as the Libyan feature is concerned. Conversely, correlation with Parker's marine substage in her Zone IIa and Elimiani's Stage 5 must be regarded as virtually demonstrated. This important fact does seem to merit particular emphasis. It may now be coupled with a tentative, but still highly probable, correlation to the Northwest African Ouljian stage with the time estimate of 80,000± on the basis of Stearn's Uranium-Thorium readings (Kretzoi and Vertes, 1965).

There is thus a prima facie case for assigning the same correlation to the Levantine feature in the absence of any positive argument to the contrary. If this is correct, much earlier argument on this issue—such as, for instance, Garrod's in 1962—would thereby be rendered obsolete. Finally, if the marine correlations are what they appear to be, then a further correlation with the European Eemian is almost inevitable. Direct evidence to this effect is by no means rare either on the Northwest Mediterranean shore or along the French and English Channel coasts. The well-known succession at Fosselone in west Italy will serve as a good example. There the actual substitution of Upper Paleolithic for an underlying Mousterian can, in turn, be seen to overlie the raised beach in question. Since the date of the substitution can hardly be much later than 35,000 B.C. and the interval separating it from the underlying beach is clearly a very long one on both geological and cultural grounds, the chance of the beach belonging to Van der Hammen's Würmian complex interstadial is remote. Further examples from the same area have been published by the late A. C. Blanc.

Richard West has now provided pollen diagrams for the Channel area which associate the equivalent feature with the Eemian botanical phase. Most recently Callow and this writer have studied the relation of this beach to both the botanical and cultural record in the Island of Jersey, an area, it should be noted, of probable tectonic stability on other grounds. It was possible to show that the beach *underlay* formations with typical late Eemian flora and *overlay* others with Rissian flora. The former contained a typical early Würmian Mousterian and the latter an interesting industry of prepared cores and handaxe elements, antedating the MTA of Aquitaine by a whole climatic cycle. Sieveking and Kerney have recently shown that the same is true of the well-known series of Levalloisian and handaxe assemblages at Baker's Hole in the Thames.

This rapid *tour d'horizon* may at least serve to show that there is nothing prima facie anomalous about the East Mediterranean succession on this basis; on the contrary, this reading now appears in excellent general accord with the broad features in Europe and Northwest Africa.

Some further consequences of this model may now be explored with regard to particular variants of the broad Middle Paleolithic cultural taxon in the Southeast Mediterranean.

In the first place, as far as Zumoffen is concerned, the conclusion would be that both the Jabrudian and Pre-Aurignacian ("Amudian") patterns were in current use by a date no later than an early phase of Eem—say 80,000 to 100,000 on the original Pa/Th estimates, or 100,000 to 125,000 on Shackleton's recent revised estimates. On the face of it, the dimensions of the "E" feature at Tabun and the typologically corresponding strata at Jabrud cannot be said to contradict such an estimate. In this writer's recent studies of sedimentation rates in cave deposits, and bearing in mind that these are almost entirely due to natural causes, about 30 cm per 1,000 years is the most usual. For Tabun this would suggest about 30,000 to 40,000 years duration at a first estimate. This, in turn, would give a rough figure in the order of 60,000 to 70,000 years for the emergence of typical Levalloiso-Mousterian in our record.

Apart from the premises from which this argument is presented, the meaning of this suggestion is considerably affected by the nature of the cultural distinction between Jabrudian and its successor. The technological differentiation is much greater than Bordes's analysis (on which Marks relied, for instance) would suggest. Even admitting that the examined Jabrudian samples have been statistically small, it is still rather striking that there appears to be a rarity of faceted platforms or, for that matter, clear traces of prepared cores (either on the dorsal surface of flakes or the cores themselves). It contrasts sharply with all variants of Levalloiso-Mousterian and also (it may be added) with the La Quina variant in the west as well, where disc cores showing full mastery of this technique are by no means as rare as is sometimes suggested. This aspect is emphasized since it has an obvious bearing on the taxonomic situation in the Levant at this stage. The same technical status is equally, if not more, markedly displayed by the Acheulean layers at Jabrud and also, it would appear, by the underlying handaxe Layer F at Tabun.

At the time of writing, the relation between the three constituent patterns of equipment as seen at Jabrud is still far from clear, although it should perhaps be added that a simple Chi Square test demonstrates that the difference between the published samples cannot reasonably be accounted for simply in terms of random variation, as has sometimes been suggested. Two alternative explanations may be suggested to account for the divergences. A completely *functionalist* point of view, on the one hand, might be adopted, supposing that there is evidence of only one continuum varying by highly specific response to different circumstances or needs. On the other hand, a purely *cultural* model may be offered requiring the presence of two, or perhaps three, specialized groups of hunters, each adapted to the highly differentiated environments which can indeed be encountered in the neighborhood (or would, were it not for the intervention of man)—e.g., forest, desert, and steppe. This would presuppose the sort of situation in which groups specifically adapted to these or comparable *climax* conditions occasionally entered the interzonal fringe in which the site seems to be situated.

Ethnographic parallels are not difficult to find for both alternatives. Other alternatives, again taking particular note of different sets of variables, could be proposed as well, of course. Formal statistical or other tests of these have yet to be proposed or applied—specifically something similar to the Binfords' analysis of the Mousterian, or the rather more specialized methods that have recently been applied by this writer to the Epipaleolithic of the surrounding regions. These will, though, require more comprehensive quantification of food and other environmental factors than are yet available. However, attention might be drawn even at this stage to one set of general circumstances that may not be irrelevant.

What is perhaps the most specific of the entities in question, the Pre-Aurignacian/Amudian type, occurs positively in several widely different environmental contexts— Jabrud on the edge of a desert and steppe, Zumoffen and Tabun close to the shore in a relatively well-watered maritime setting, and Haua Fteah, far removed across desert barriers but surrounded by dense Mediterranean scrub.

The Levalloiso-Mousterian, on the other hand, occurs in the same geographical setting but has the further peculiarity of straddling two widely different climatic periods, offering contrasted food resources and conditions of hunting. Thus it can hardly be supposed that the differences between the two generic taxa owe their existence to any very direct or simple environmental interaction, and a basically cultural model certainly seems more feasible, if not actually required. It is at least possible that the same is true of the subvarieties of the earlier Complex; that is, unless these relatively striking and synchronous resemblances are accepted as purely coincidental, an attitude which, to this writer at any rate, would seem far-fetched.

Some of the same considerations may be applied with equal reason to other more or less contrasted geographical variants of the evolved Middle Paleolithic (Mousteroid) industries. They have already been dealt with in broad outline by Marks (1968), and since this writer is in general agreement with him, there is little point in rehearsing the matter here apart from certain minor points which may help to fill out the general picture.

Regarding Iraq and Iran, the basic distinction between the Mousterian of the Zagros and the Caspian was first pointed out by Stringer—namely, the consistently much lower Levalloisoid tendency. Callow and this writer have recently reexamined the same material (with Stringer's help by correspondence), adding to it this writer's more recent discoveries at the specialized high montane site of Sangé Safid in the Ku-i-Dasht area, Ke Aram east of the Caspian, and a small open station near Miane, north of Lake Rezaiyeh. The upshot is to reinforce the consistency of the patterning throughout this region and its constant divergence from the Levalloiso-Mousterian. An interesting detail is that Sangé Safid occurs in a region and at an altitude which makes year-round occupation impossible. In winter the site is filled with snow up to the ceiling. In summer, however, the area is the resort of ibex migrating from the heat of the surrounding plains, as indeed the bones which are in the process of being analyzed suggest. There can be little doubt that here is a reliable example of seasonality, and it is interesting to see that although there are features in the cumulative curve which are not reproduced at, say, Hazar Merd and other sites of lower altitude, yet the distinction with the Levant is equally apparent. Briefly then, the same arguments can be applied here in favor of a cultural explanation, that is, one involving preferred trends of regional development engendered and maintained by proximity between hunting groups circulating within distinct geographical territories. Returning to North Africa, there seems to be a very reasonable case of the same kind on the basis of the geographic distribution of the Aterian, or, for that matter, of Marks's variant of the Mousterian in Nubia. The fact is that there are many answers to most practical problems at this level of technology, although this writer is prepared to admit the possibility, and indeed necessity, of many features (as yet not isolated successfully) which owe their existence or distribution to purely practical stimuli. Social factors may be expected to operate in the choice of these, and accordingly must be allowed a part in explanations.

This does not mean, of course, that one should neglect to examine possible correlation between environmental and typological limits; on the contrary, it is by their progressive isolation that the strictly cultural tendencies in their true proportions may be recognized.

The present assessment then, which is offered for discussion, is that there are already indications in the evolved Middle Paleolithic of the whole area in question of relatively specific local variants which do not obviously coincide with environmental territories. The proposed explanation is that whether or not cultural trends owe their *inception* to some localized or regional stimulus, their subsequent divergent development is attributable here to a substantial factor of social intercourse and exchange. If, for the sake of argument, this proposition is allowed with regard to the Southern and Eastern Mediterranean, what view should be taken of more generalized resemblance and divergence in the much wider context of Europe or Central Asia? This, it seems, is a problem on an altogether different scale. The probability of long-term and generalized convergence between widely separated areas may be taken to be roughly proportional to distance and other physical barriers. Moreover, there is the further possibility that a preexisting and shared cultural know-how over a wide area may, of itself, predispose to certain particular subsequent developments.

However, there is, on the face of it, no reason why such "automatic" developments should be synchronous in separate regions, let alone why they should form chronological clines between a chain of such regions. Here, then, is one possible approach to the selection of an appropriate model, and the value of a chronometric rather than a relative chronology needs no stressing. Accurate quantification of cultural pattern is another desideratum. One needs to know a lot more about actual patterns of change through time, on the one hand, and the nature of synchronous variation, on the other. A number of cases where class frequencies of the Bordes type do not appear to give reliable results have been mentioned in passing. In some of these the addition of further analysis by continuous variables certainly provides a clearer and more meaningful result, and yet other technical features involving a less rigidly morphological approach could be suggested.

All in all, however, and despite these and other uncertainties, this writer would be prepared to argue that a state of knowledge has now been reached in the area where cultural entities are beginning to appear at least by the final phase of the Middle Paleolithic epoch. That is to say, if this chronology is correct, these appear by the middle of the Eemian Interglacial. One would, however, be far more cautious regarding the Lower Paleolithic, where the basic requirements such as the most elementary mapping of find categories (let alone estimates of their age) have still to be met, except in a few isolated instances.

BIBLIOGRAPHY

ARAMBOURG, C., 1949. *Compte Rendu Sommaire des Séances de la Société Géologique de France.*

_____, 1963. "Le gisement de Ternifine." *Archives de l'Institut Paléontologie Humaine* Mémoire 32. Paris.

BIBERSON, P., 1961. "Le Paléolithique inférieur du Maroc atlantique." *Publications du Service des Antiquitiés du Maroc* 17.

BINFORD, L. R., and BINFORD, S. R., 1966. "A Preliminary Analysis of Functional Variability in the Mousterian of Levallois Facies." *American Anthropologist* 68(2-2):238-95.

BOTTEMA, S., 1967. "The Climate, Environment and Industries of Stone Age Greece." *Proceedings of the Prehistoric Society* 33.

BOVIER-LAPIERRE, M. P., 1925. "Le Paléolithique stratifié des environs du Caire." *L'Anthropologie* 35:37-46.

BREUIL, H., and ZYSZEWSKI, G., 1945. "Contributions à l'étude des industries portugaises." *Com. Serv. Geol. Portugal,* vol. 23, 1942 and vol. 26, 1945.

CATON-THOMPSON, G., 1952. *Kharga Oasis in Prehistory.* London: Athlone Press.

FLEISCH, H., 1956, "Dépôts préhistoriques de la côte Libinaise et leur place dans la chronologie basée sur le Quaternaire marin." *Quaternaria* 3:101-32.

GARROD, D. A. E., 1934. "Excavations in the Mugharet-et-Tabun." *Bulletin of the American School of Prehistoric Research* 11.

GUICHARD, J., and GUICHARD, G., 1968. "Contributions to the Study of the Early and Middle Paleolithic of Nubia." In *The Prehistory of Nubia*, edited by F. Wendorf. Dallas: Fort Burgwin Research Center and Southern Methodist University Press.

KRETZOI, M., and VERTES, L., 1965. "Upper Biharian (Intermindel) Pebble Industry Occupation Site in West Hungary." *Current Anthropology* 6(1).

LEAKEY, MARY, 1971. *Olduvai Gorge*, vol. 3. Cambridge: At the University Press.

McBURNEY, C. B. M., 1947. "The Stone Age of the Libyan Littoral." *Proceedings of the Prehistoric Society.*

_____, 1967. *The Haua Fteah (Cyrenaica) and the Stone Age of the Southeast Mediterranean.* Cambridge: At the University Press.

_____, and CALLOW, P., 1971. "The Cambridge Excavations at La Cotte de St. Brelade." *Proceedings of the Prehistoric Society.*

_____, and HEY, R. W., 1955. *Prehistory and Pleistocene Geology in Cyrenaican Libya.* Cambridge: At the University Press.

MARKS, A. E., 1968. "The Mousterian Industries of Nubia." In *The Prehistory of Nubia*, edited by F. Wendorf, 1:194-314. Dallas: Fort Burgwin Research Center and Southern Methodist University Press.

PARKER, F. L., 1957. "East Mediterranean Foraminifera." In *Reports of the Swedish Deep Sea Expedition* 8(4).

RUST, H., 1950. *Die Höhlenfunde von Jabrud (Syrien)*' Neumünster: Karl Wachholtz.

SAID, R., 1957. "Post-Tyrrhenian Climatic Fluctuations in Northern Egypt." *Quaternaria* 3.

SIEVEKING, A., 1960. "The Paleolithic Industry of Kota Tampan, Perak, Northwest Malaya." In *Asian Perspectives, 1958*. Hong Kong.

STEARNS, C. E., and THURBER, D. L., 1965. "$Th^{230}-U^{234}$ Dates of Late Pleistocene Marine Fossils from the Mediterranean and Moroccan Littorals." *Quaternaria* 7:29.

STEKELIS, M., 1966*a*. "Ma'Ayan Barukh, a Lower Paleolithic Site in Upper Galilee." *Metqufat ha-Even* 8.

————, 1966*b*. "Archaeological Excavations at Ubeidiya 1960-1963." *Proceedings of the Israel Academy of Sciences and Humanities*.

————, 1969. "Archaeological Excavations at Ubeidiya 1964-1966." *Proceedings of the Israel Academy of Sciences and Humanities*.

TUREKIAN, K. K. (ed.), 1971. *Late Cenozoic Glacial Ages*. New Haven and London: Yale University Press.

VAN DER HAMMEN, T., et al., 1967. "Stratigraphy, Climatic Succession and Radiocarbon Dating of the Last Glaciation in the Netherlands." *Geologie en Mijnbouw* 46(3).

AN EVALUATION OF THE RELATIONSHIP BETWEEN THE MOUSTERIAN COMPLEXES OF THE EASTERN MEDITERRANEAN: A TECHNOLOGICAL PERSPECTIVE

Harvey L. Crew
University of British Columbia, Alberta

INTRODUCTION

A half century of research into the prehistory of northern African and Asian portions of the circum-Mediterranean has delimited a number of Middle Paleolithic Complexes; the three most widely accepted being the North African, the Nubian, and the Levantine Mousterian Complexes. The age of these three Complexes seems comparable, and all are probably late Eem Interglacial or Early Würm in age. The Nubian Mousterian is not as well dated as the other two Complexes, but it may be roughly contemporaneous in time, since a subsequent industry in the same area, the Khormusan, has been dated provisionally to at least 34,000 B.C. (Irwin et al., 1968, p. 110). As the above Complexes share the use of Levallois methods, there has been speculation about their degree of relatedness (McBurney, 1960, p. 171; 1967, p. 131; Marks, 1968, pp. 301-8; Gruet, 1959, pp. 63-66; Garrod and Bate, 1937, p. 118).

The objective of this paper is to address the problem of what relationship these Complexes bear to each other. Two possible propositions are indicated: (1) are the shared similarities due to actual population movements or to simple diffusion of a new culture into the areas, or (2) are the similarities a result of the diffusion of new techniques and/ or new economic strategies which were incorporated into the existing sociocultural contexts and technology of indigenous populations? The above propositions or hypotheses have been stated in overly simple terms, but the simplicity will result in clarity when the archaeological requisites for each are examined. This paper does not purport to be a definitive work on the topic by any means. Given the lack of archaeological data for this area, a definitive work would be impossible at the present, even if the research methods described in this paper were proven capable of the task. It will be enough if the exercise can underline some factors which must be accounted for when relationships are considered between these Middle Paleolithic Complexes of the circum-Mediterranean.

Any postulated contact between the African Complexes and those of the Near East must acknowledge the geographic position of the Levantine Mousterian, which lies astride the entrance to the African continent from Asia. Levantine Mousterian assemblages have been found from the Syrian Desert in the north to the Negev Desert in the south, and thus the Complex spans the length and breadth of the area through which any movement toward either the west or east would have to pass. There is no evidence to suggest the existence of another Complex residing contemporaneously with the Levantine Mousterian in the area. Therefore, when there is a suggestion of contact between the Levantine Mousterian and one or both of the other Complexes during the Mousterian period, whether by a population movement or by diffusion, it must be recognized that the Levantine Mousterian has to be the eastern donor and/or recipient.

The focal point of the study is upon the Levallois methods (primarily the Levallois flake method) practiced within the Complexes: first, because it is one of their major points of similarity; second, because the behavior associated with some of the stages of the methods can be measured as to their degree of similarity and difference in execution (Crew, 1972, pp. 27-36); and, third, because methods are assumed to be conservative to change, at least more so than morphology and the frequency of occurrence of the artifacts created by the methods. In other words, the way an implement type is fabricated is not as likely to reflect the changing vagaries of style as the morphology of the implement, or greater or lesser need to perform the task for which the implement was created. This is not to say that methods of manufacture are simplistically invariant in execution. For example, several workers have established that there are variations in the Levallois methods (a matter of degree of core reduction) from quarry to base camp locations (McBurney and Hey, 1955, pp. 168-69; Munday, personal communication).

Another important factor not commonly considered is the possible effect of the relationship between the extent of the variation of the physical attributes which the function of the tool permits, in combination with culturally based concepts of acceptable levels of energy needed to perform the tasks for which the tool was made. In other words, a task might be more easily performed with a large tool, but in situations where the availability of suitable raw material is at a premium, the tool likely will be made smaller and the energy level increased to offset the less efficient size (see Isaac, 1972, p. 176 for an independent but basically similar statement). If we are to define methods so as to be diagnostically useful, the extent of their variation in an industrial entity has to be described as fully as possible, and this can be achieved only by having a sample of assemblages of an industry from several areas to insure that most manifestations of the method are present.

The above criteria would require many sites from different physiographic zones to be studied, and except perhaps for the Levant, this goal has not been fully realized by the present study. Only the Levallois flakes have been utilized for this—a point necessitated because the other Levallois forms, blades and points, are more difficult to define or are effectively absent from the other Complexes to which the Levantine Mousterian will be compared. The Levallois points will be discussed later since their presence, absence, or rarity can be critical in any discussion of relationships between the pertinent Complexes.

The analysis of the Levallois flakes was approached in a number of ways. First, the preparatory flaking suite of the methods was analyzed by direction and presented statistically to express its variability within the unit examined; and second, the dimensional measures of absolute length and indices of relative size (W/L and Th/W) of the Levallois flakes were analyzed. The method of analysis utilized to study the preparatory flaking has been presented earlier (Crew, 1973, p. 30), and thus it will be discussed only briefly here. It consists of dividing a circle into four 90° sectors, placing the Levallois flake in the center, butt downward, and counting the flake scars which were struck from each sector (fig. 1). When all of the Levallois flakes of the sample have been analyzed in this manner, the number for each sector is then totaled and a frequency graph is constructed to illustrate the relative frequency of each sector.

THE ASSEMBLAGES

Three assemblages from the Nubian Mousterian have been studied (1010-8, 1033, and 1038). The assemblages have been lumped together, for the purpose of this paper, to insure an adequate sample size. They are all located back from the Nile on the jebels and, thus, are in the same environmental situation. Typologically, all three of the assemblages appear to be the same (Marks, 1968, p. 284).

Regrettably, no Mousterian assemblages from the Maghreb proper (Tunisia, Algeria, Morocco) were examined for this study, but fortunately two assemblages—the Haua Fteah and the Hajj Creiem—from the Cyrenaican peninsula, Libya, were available for analysis. Since the Cyrenaican peninsula is located on the only feasible migration route between the Levant and the Maghreb, the Haua Fteah and Hajj Creiem material should provide evidence of any cultural phenomena emanating from the lower Nile Valley or the Levant toward the Maghreb (McBurney, 1955, 1967). The Mousterian layers from the Haua Fteah span a considerable period of time and in combination with the assemblage from the Hajj Creiem should insure that some of the possible temporal and spatial variation of the Levallois methods of this Mousterian Complex will be included. The samples studied from the Haua Fteah were derived from layers 35 to 32. They were combined with the assemblage from the Hajj Creiem to create an adequate sample size and to reflect better the variation of which the methods were capable in the Libyan Mousterian. The fact that the samples from the Nile Valley and Libya are small is definitely a weak point, since the possible variation in the Levallois methods of each Complex may not be represented in the assemblages studied.

The Southern Levant was divided into coastal and inland provinces to test for variations in methods due to different environmental situations. The division is similar to that presented by Binford (1968, pp. 707-17), but it is not meant to be a defense of her proposed seasonal round. The division as presented here is merely a device to insure that assemblages from at least two different physiographic zones are represented in the sample. While the size of the Levantine sample is far larger than those from the other two areas, this study does not maintain that it represents all of the variation of Levallois flake methods in the Levantine Mousterian. In fact, the examination of a larger series of assemblages from the Levant has revealed some variation not present in the assemblages selected for use in this study, but the variation is not of sufficient difference to affect the evidence presented.

The sample of coastal assemblages consists of Kebara (excavated by Stekelis), Skhul B, El Wad G, Tabun B, C, and D, and Shukba (all excavated by Garrod and her associates). Shukba is not presently located on the coast, but it is located on the western slopes of the coastal range, as are the others, and it has therefore been included. The inland assemblages, except for one, are all located in presently desertic areas. The assemblages from the sites of Erq-el-Ahmar H, Abou Sif B and C, Sahba B, and Ghar were all collected or excavated by Neuville, and they are situated in the Judean Desert. Rosh Ein Mor (Marks and Crew, 1972) and D35 (unpublished as yet but typologically and technologically similar to Rosh Ein Mor) are located in the Negev Desert and were excavated by the archaeological teams from SMU during the 1969 to 1972 seasons. The last site, Esh-Shubbabig, was excavated by Binford (1966, pp. 18-33; 96-103), and the cave is located in the lower reaches of the Wadi Amud, above the Sea of Galilee. The assemblages from each province have been combined for the purpose of this analysis.

Chronistics, whether absolute or relative, are only partially understood for the Mousterian era in the Levant, and even this sketchy knowledge usually is concerned only with the age of the Mousterian as a whole and not with any possible stages within its development (but see Copeland, this volume). Not withstanding this caveat, however, an attempt has been made to select suitable sites to insure that the list includes those which seem to span the duration of the Mousterian period. El Wad G, for example, was regarded by Garrod as late (52, pp. 121-30), and no one seems to doubt that Tabun D is early. Rosh Ein Mor, which has two dates of > 44,000 B. P. and > 50,000 B. P., is apparently similar to Tabun D (Jelinek, personal communication) and definitely appears to be early in the development of the Levantine Mousterian. The Judean sites have no C14 dates, and their geological context is equivocal for the Mousterian layers at least. If the rubble or éboulis layers which underlie the Mousterian layers of Abou Sif and Sahba indicate the same éboulis-causing phenomena as Layer B of Tabun, then they may be late. Esh Shubbabig,

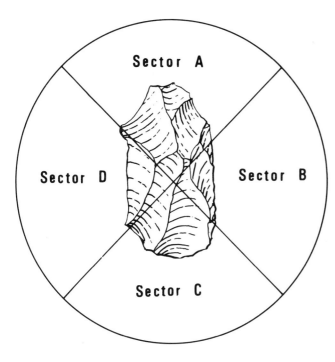

FIG. 1–Method for Flaking Analysis.

while the original monograph of the Haua Fteah (McBurney, 1967) treated the clusters of layers 35/34 and 33/32 as different entities, the analysis by dorsal preparation does not reveal any differences in the methods particular to each layer. The preparation pattern of the Nubian Mousterian is more centripedal than any other Complex studied, since the laterally directed flaking is almost equal to the distal/proximal. The Nubian Mousterian assemblages, when examined singly, still reveal the same pattern, and it can probably be considered the norm for the Complex. The Hajj Creiem sample, albeit small, displayed the same pattern when graphed separately, and the pattern cannot be considered confined to the Nubian Mousterian. When viewed together, the high frequency of lateral preparation in the Levallois methods of the African Complexes, above 40% (almost 50% for the Nubian), stands in contrast with the Levantine Mousterian where lateral preparation is less than 25%.

To summarize, in the Levantine Mousterian distally and proximally directed flaking accounts for over 70% of the total preparation, while lateral preparation is minimal (22% and 17%), and the Levallois flake method can be characterized as heavily bidirectional. In contradistinction, lateral preparation in the Nubian and Libyan Mousterian Levallois flake methods accounts for 49% and 39%, respectively, of the total preparation. If the Levantine method is called unidirectional or bidirectional, the methods of the African complexes can be characterized as centripedal.

Shukba, and Kebara also fall into the equivocal category, since no C14 dates are available and their geological context precludes any definitive temporal placement.

LEVALLOIS PREPARATION

As is clear from figure 2–the graphs for both Levantine provinces–proximal preparation accounts for over half of the total preparation in the Levallois flake method of the Levantine Mousterian. The dominance of proximal preparation (sector C) presents graphically, especially in the inland province, the recently noted unidirectional preparation (Watanabe, 1968, p. 499; Copeland, 1970, p. 105) characteristic of the Levallois flake method in the Levantine Mousterian. Distal preparation, albeit much lower in frequency than proximal, is the second most frequent. Together distal and proximal account for over 75% of the dorsal preparation, and the method is certainly not classic Levallois, if by that term centripedal preparation is meant. The pattern of preparation from the coastal province has been affected, to a degree, by the proximally dominated flaking of the assemblage from Kebara. If the Kebara assemblage were removed, proximal preparation would account for a little under 50%, which would emphasize the already clear difference in preparation between the coastal and inland Levantine Mousterian clusters.

The preparation of the Levallois flake method in the Nubian and Libyan Mousterian is also dominated by proximal preparation, but to a much lesser extent, since it accounts for less than 40%. The configuration of the preparation of the Libyan Mousterian is generally similar to the Levantine, because distal and proximal preparation account for more than lateral preparation. Incidentally,

RELATIVE WIDTH

The graphs of figure 3 have been divided into three intervals of proportions: >.50 to .70 is lamellar; >.70 to 1.00 is flakish; and >1.00 is transverse. The Levallois flakes from the Levantine Mousterian tend toward lamellar proportions with mean values of .64 and .58, respectively, for the coastal and inland Levantine provinces. The inland Mousterian, however, did manufacture flakes with more lamellar tendencies than the coastal variety. A difference of mean test indicates that the differences between the proportions of the flakes from the two provinces is significant at >.01 level. Nonetheless, the flakes from the coastal assemblage are still decidedly lamellar in proportions, since over half of the flakes fall into the lamellar interval of >.50 to .70. The analysis revealed that the frequency of transversely proportioned flakes (>1.00) in the Levantine samples, from both the coast and inland, is probably less than five percent. The examination of the larger number of assemblages from the Levant rather than those used for this report evidences the same low frequency of transverse flakes, and the production of wide flakes probably is not common in the technology of the Levantine Mousterian. In summary, the Levantine Mousterian has a strong tendency toward the production of lamellar proportioned flakes, but within the Complex there are significant levels of differences both in proportions and dorsal preparation.

The W/L proportion of the Levallois flakes of the Nubian and Libyan Mousterian Complexes, .85 and .84

LEVALLOIS FLAKES: PREPARATORY FLAKING

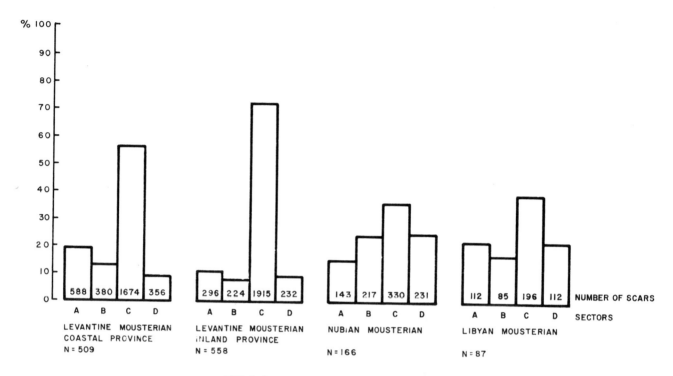

FIG. 2–Preparatory Flaking of Levallois Flakes.

respectively, are clearly dissimilar from the W/L proportions of the flakes of the Levantine Mousterian assemblages included in the study. Only 30.5% of the Levallois flakes from the Nubian samples and 19% from the Libyan fall into the lamellar interval. The flakes from both of the African Complexes are much broader than is characteristic of the Levantine Mousterian. In fact, over 15% of the flakes from both Complexes are in excess of 1.00, or broader than they are long, if length means the axis of percussion. A difference of mean test indicates that the means of the W/L indexes for the African complexes are nearly identical.

RELATIVE THICKNESS

For convenience, the scores have been divided into very thin (0.0 to 1.5), moderately thin (1.5 to 2.6), moderately thick (2.5 to 3.5), and very thick (3.5+). First, in the Levantine Mousterian, while the majority of the pieces fall into the "very thin" and "moderately thin" intervals for samples from both provinces (fig. 4), the coastal province definitely has thinner pieces, regardless of length. In fact, in the coastal Mousterian all but 1.8% of the pieces fall into these intervals. In contradistinction, the Th/W values for the Nubian Mousterian are almost totally restricted to "moderately thin" and "moderately thick" intervals. Forty-five percent of the flakes of the Libyan Mousterian fall into the "very thin" interval, and the Levallois flake element rightfully could be called delicate. The Levallois

flakes of the Levantine Mousterian essentially reveal a much wider latitude of thickness than do the flakes of the African Complex. The thickness index seems to vary somewhat independently of other attributes, and it may be partly correlated with the quality of the raw material; i.e., a coarse granular material like ferrocrete sandstone utilized in the Nubian Mousterian is not as amenable to the production of light thin flakes as is a fine-grained flint.

OTHER METRIC AND DIMENSIONAL MEASURES

The Levallois flakes of the inland province of the Levant have considerably less dorsal preparation and a lesser degree of butt faceting than those of the coastal province and are clearly not as carefully prepared (table 1). The lengths of the flakes from the inland province are, on the whole, a little longer, which correlates with their more unidirectional preparation. While the means of the lengths, 63.8 and 66.1, do not appear to be very different, a difference of means tests indicates that it is significant. The convergence of these characteristics would indicate that a more careful workmanship was generally practiced on the coast than inland.

The Nubian Mousterian, both in terms of dorsal scars and length, is similar to the coastal variety of the Levantine Mousterian (table 1). In fact, in regard to the difference between the means of length, the differences are not significant. In terms of relative thickness, the Levallois flakes of

LEVALLOIS FLAKES: W/L INDEX

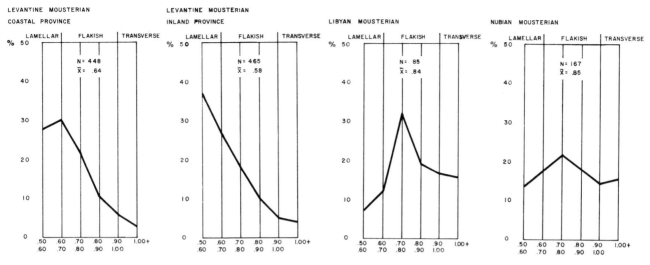

FIG. 3–Length/Width Ratios of Levallois Flakes.

LEVALLOIS FLAKES: Th/W INDEX

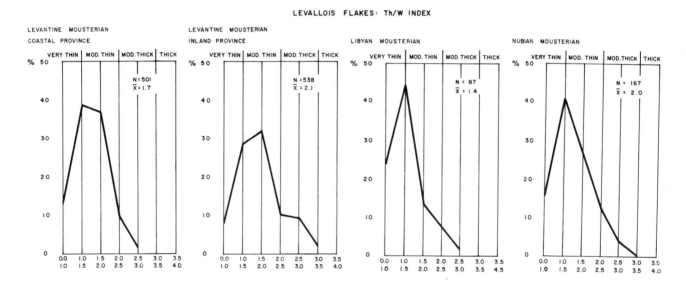

FIG. 4–Thickness/Width Ratios of Levallois Flakes.

the Nubian Mousterian are not significantly different from the Levallois flakes from the Levantine inland province. The degree of butt faceting in the Nubian Mousterian, however, is considerably less (very minimal indeed), and as earlier established the flakes tend to be very much broader than in any variety of Levantine Mousterian presented. The Levallois flakes of the Libyan Mousterian, while as broad as and prepared similarly to the Nubian flakes, are not similar in the rest of the attributes listed (see table 1). For example, the Levallois flakes have the most dorsal scars per piece, the shortest length, and the smallest Thickness Index. When these attributes are viewed in their entirety, they support the aforementioned "delicateness" of the Levallois flakes of the Libyan Mousterian.

While the combination of samples utilized for this study does not reveal any clear correlation between the amount of preparation and lamellar or transverse tendencies, there is some evidence to suggest that when the assemblages are viewed individually more preparation is required to prepare a transverse than to prepare a long narrow Levallois flake. The correlation between the size of the Levallois flake and the number of dorsal scars necessary to prepare the piece is positive, however. The smaller the piece is in length, the more dorsal preparation is necessary to prepare it. The correlation between size and dorsal scar number is also manifested in the Khormusan industry (Crew, 1972, p. 32) in which a similar tendency toward smaller size ($\bar{X} = 47$ mm) is correlated with a high dorsal scar number ($\bar{X} = 7.2$). In terms of proportions, the Levallois flakes of the Khormusan tend to be very broad. While such a correlation between size and amount of dorsal preparation may seem patently obvious, it must be made explicit since such correlations

TABLE 1
LEVALLOIS FLAKES
SELECTED ATTRIBUTES BY REGION

	Length	No. of facets	Dorsal Scars	Width/Length	Thickness/Width
Coastal	M=63.8 S.D.=17.3 N=673	M=6.0 S.D.=2.8 N=630	M=5.9 S.D.=3.0 N=636	M=.64 S.D.=.19 N=673	M=.17 S.D.=.06 N=673
Inland	M=66.1 S.D.=17.2 N=886	M=4.9 S.D.=3.0 N=816	M=5.0 S.D.=1.6 N=880	M=.58 S.D.=.21 N=886	M=.20 S.D.=.07 N=886
Libyan Moust.	M=49.1 S.D.=13.5 N=94	M=6.2 S.D.=2.6 N=89	M=7.0 S.D.=4.1 N=94	M=.83 S.D.=.19 N=94	M=.14 S.D.=.05 N=94
Nubian Moust.	M=63.1 S.D.=16.6 N=118	M=3.7 S.D.=3.0 N=105	M=5.9 S.D.=1.2 N=117	M=.85 S.D.=.21 N=118	M=.20 S.D.=.05 N=118

M—*Mean*
S.D.—*Standard Deviation*
N—*Number*

have bearing on what level of significance should be attached to technically dissimilar assemblages of the same general form in the same area. The same industrial tradition, by reason of such mechanical requirements of manufacture in conjunction with other impinging factors such as, but not limited to, the differential availability of suitable raw material, could produce technically different implements.

The author has attempted to reveal the extent of the variation of which the execution of the Levallois flake method was capable in the Levantine Mousterian. Whether the significant differences between the Levallois flake methods of the assemblages from the coast and inland areas represent two different traditions or, alternatively, seasonal variation cannot be answered at the present. The data given do express the probable range of variation of the Levallois flake method of the Levantine Mousterian as a whole.

In review, the dorsal preparation of the Levallois flakes in the Levantine Mousterian is dominated by proximal preparation (over 50% in the coastal province and even higher inland). This high degree of proximally directed preparation is directly correlated with a strong tendency to produce flakes of lamellar proportions and fairly long length. The amount of dorsal preparation is probably tied to the technical requirements which the above attributes induce. The

relative thickness is partially correlated with the above variables but also seems to be affected by the quality of the raw material.

The Levallois flake methods of the Libyan and Nubian Mousterian Complexes when viewed together are significantly different from the variation perceivable in the Levantine Mousterian. The centripedally directed preparation and the tendency for broad flakes approaching transverse proportions in both of the African Complexes represent a combination of technical traits not often encountered in the Levantine Mousterian. While some positive correlations between attributes were noted, for example, between the attributes of length and dorsal preparation, these similarities do not vary consistently together with the other important attributes and are thus spurious.

FURTHER EVIDENCE

The examination of the Levallois points and the other method of flake and blade manufacture, evidenced from the study of the non-Levallois cores, further supports the differences between the Complexes manifested by the analysis of the Levallois flake method. Triangular Levallois points are common components in most Levantine Mousterian assemblages, although they are apparently scarce in a few (Fleisch, 1972, pp. 25-96). These points are generally well made, usually prepared by two to four proximally removed flakes or, more rarely, distally delivered flakes; the butt is usually well faceted with a convex or *chapeau de gendarme* shape, while the size of the pieces spans a considerable range.

The Levantine assemblages which have only a few points should be discussed since in this respect they resemble the African Complexes which have a few or none. There have been only a few assemblages published which are characterized (or believed to be characterized) by a few points; these are Tabun C (Garrod and Bate, 1938) and Naame (Fleisch, 1972, pp. 25-96). Garrod (1938, p. 76) records that 138 out of a total of 405 Levallois flakes kept from Tabun C were triangular in shape. While her category of triangular Levallois flake probably does not equate entirely with the presently accepted category of triangular Levallois points, it does indicate that a fair number of points were part of the assemblage. The recent reanalysis of the extant Tabun C material supports this assertion (Skinner, 1965, p. 73). Moreover, the analysis by the author of the flaking patterns of 32 Levallois points from Tabun C reveals that they are prepared in a characteristic Levantine fashion, largely by proximally directed flakes. Naame, which assuredly has comparatively few points, does have frequencies ranging from approximately 5% to almost 8% (Fleisch, 1972, p. 74). In his recent study of a number of Levantine Mousterian assemblages, Skinner (1965, p. 95) lists only one site, Erq-el-Ahmar H, with less than 10% Levallois points. The common presence of triangular Levallois points in most, if not all, Levantine Mousterian assemblages is an important factor to consider in any discussion of the relationship of the complex to the other neighboring Mousterian Complexes.

The Nubian Mousterian Complex has comparatively few Levallois points, and they are of a style of manufacture different from those commonly found in the Levant. The triangular-shaped specimens appear to have been formed by two blows delivered on the distal end (see Marks, 1968, fig. 28*e*) and were obviously struck from Nubian Mousterain cores (Guichard and Guichard, 1965, pp. 68-9). The styles of point manufacture between the Nubian and the Levantine Mousterian appear to be clearly different in execution. The examination of the Haua Fteah and Hajj Creiem assemblages did not reveal any Levallois points of the triangular variety whatsoever. While classic Mousterian points are common, especially in the Hajj Creiem assemblage, the dorsal scar pattern on the points indicates that the original blank was often a centripedally prepared Levallois flake. The lack of triangular points in the Libyan Mousterian assemblages, since they are such common elements in the Levantine Mousterian assemblages examined, is a major difference between these respective Complexes of the Middle Paleolithic period.

Moreover, the discoid method of the Libyan Mousterian contrasts with the variety of core types found in the Levantine Mousterian. The Levantine Mousterian is characterized by a variety of flake cores which are difficult to classify satisfactorily by a morphologically based typology. For example, the typological lists from Naame, one of the Levantine Mousterian assemblages with only a few points and therefore like the African Complexes, reveal that around half of its cores are non-Levallois and nondiscoid. Tabun C, characterized by supposedly few points, also evinces a large number of non-Levallois and nondiscoid cores. An examination of the typological lists records that Garrod (1938, p. 76) kept 302 cores, of which 196 were classified as rough and atypical. Schroeder's (1969) reanalysis of the Jerf Ajla material (Coon, 1957, pp. 290-316), with deposits seemingly spanning a large extent of developmental history of the Levantine Mousterian, has revealed a fair number of atypical cores in all layers. In short, a fair percentage of non-Levallois and nondiscoid cores is common in Levantine Mousterian assemblages.

In contrast, the examination of the cores from the Libyan assemblages of the Haua Fteah and Hajj Creiem has revealed a much stricter variability, i.e., the greater majority would easily fit into a Levallois flake or discoid category—predominantly the latter. Since McBurney (1967), in his spit-by-spit analysis of the material from the Haua Fteah, notes only a few cores which are not discoid or Levallois, the two examinations agree on this point. Certainly McBurney's illustration of them demonstrates their small range of morphological variation quite adequately (McBurney, 1967, p. 118). The cores of the Nubian Mousterian are of a number of different types, and in this respect they have the diversity common to the Levantine Mousterian. However, the presence of Nubian cores, types I and II (Guichard and Guichard, 1966; Marks, 1968), and well-made para-

Levallois cores in the majority of the Nubian assemblages reveals that the diversity of core types is of a nature different from that in the Levantine Mousterian.

MODELS AND HYPOTHESES
AN EVALUATION

The population movement model, as defined here, presupposes that a migratory people will maintain, within an archaeologically recognizable form, the basic pattern of behavior associated with their manufacturing technology. Thus, a validation of a hypothesis based upon the model requires archaeologically similar industries on both ends of the migration route, and if not that, then a series of sites spanning portions of the route that demonstrate the transformation from the beginning format of the migrating industry to its final format at the end of the migration route. If the technology of the recipient industry is changed to such a degree that it is unrecognizable as the transformation of the technology of another industry, then it cannot, and probably does not, concern prehistoric studies. The last requirement of the model is that the presence of the industry in its original area must be chronologically earlier than its presence in the end of the route area. This requirement admittedly is difficult to establish for the period under examination, since the refinement of the chronistics has not proceeded that far.

The second model presented to account for the affinities between the Complexes could, with some qualification, be called a diffusion model. It cannot be confused with a simplistic diffusion model, which sees entities diffusing as intact wholes and is thus liable to the same kind of evidence demanded of a migratory hypothesis. The model as conceived here views the similarities between the adjacent Complexes as due to the constant interchange of ideas (interlinking), exploitative strategies, and techniques from one Complex to another. The implementation of the newly diffused traits would be based, in part, upon the previous counterparts in the indigenous industry. Since the artifactual configuration of the new industry is a result of a crucible reaction between two industries, the evidence for the earlier industry should at least be maintained in the more conservative aspects of the new industry's technology.

As the brief discussion hopefully has made clear, the population movement model requires certain kinds of evidence to lend support to its applicability. It requires similar industries on either end of a given route or a series of assemblages along the route which demonstrate the transformation of one industry to another. With these caveats in mind, the hypothesis of a proposed relationship between the Levantine and Libyan and Nubian Mousterian will be examined. The evidence for the transformation of technology characteristic of the Levantine Mousterian to the technology characteristic of the African Complexes along the Eastern Mediterranean littoral cannot be demonstrated, even if it occurred, since the requisite archaeological research has not found such assemblages, nor undertaken systematic survey in some of the intervening areas. The evidence for the support of the hypothesis therefore must be based upon a survey of the similarities and differences between the industries at both ends of the route.

The summation of the evidence presented in table 2 argues against any direct relationship between the methods utilized by the Levantine and Libyan Mousterian, respectively, since in every compared attribute the two Complexes display differences in these aspects of their respective technologies. The extent of the differences in something as conservative as the industries' technologies does not make direct relationship between these two Complexes feasible. This lack of requisite proof for a direct relationship signifies that the hypothesis should be rejected or placed in abeyance until new evidence can be offered to support it.

There appear to be some positive correlations between the technologies of Levantine and Nubian Mousterian Complexes that were lacking between the Libyan and the former (table 2). These similarities do not hold up under a more careful scrutiny, however. Admittedly, the means of the lengths are similar, but coupled with the drastic differences in proportions and direction of preparation, the similarities seem to be spurious. Further, while both Complexes have Levallois points in their repertoire, the distally prepared Nubian point is very rare in the Levantine Mousterian, and the strongly proximally prepared point of the Levantine Mousterian is lacking in the Nubian assemblages examined. Further, while the core component of both Complexes is not dominated by discoid cores as in the Libyan, this similarity is also deceptive. The Nubian cores, types I and II, and para-Levallois cores, as defined by the Guichards (1965, pp. 97-8), are found in variable quantities in every Nubian Mousterian assemblage, while they are usually lacking in the Levantine Mousterian. On the other hand, assemblages in the Levantine Mousterian will commonly have some cores made on flakes (Solecki and Solecki, 1970, pp. 137-42; Schroeder, 1969; Fleisch, 1972). These kinds of cores are totally lacking in the Nubian Mousterian. All in all, the similarities between the Complexes, the length and the amount of dorsal scars, are not significant when judged in relation to the extent of the differences between the methods practiced by the two Complexes.

The African Complexes (table 2), when viewed in terms of the technological attributes utilized for this analysis, seem to be generally similar, i.e., they have the same pattern of preparation and tendency toward broad flakes. The number of dorsal scars and the mean of the lengths differ, but these differences are probably correlated together, since the amount of dorsal preparation increases with smaller size. The lack of a Levallois point method in the Libyan Mousterian does contrast with the Nubian Mousterian. The complete lack of the Nubian core types in the Libyan Mousterian is another difference between the Complexes. The real level of affinity between the African Complexes is their heavily centripedal preparation and the tendency to create broad flakes; both Complexes may share in a broad tradition of lithic manufacturing methods of at least northern African origin.

The level of affinity between the industrial Complexes discussed here is probably at the level of an entity of the magnitude of Clarke's technocomplex (1968, pp. 321-57). Technocomplex already may be an overused term, but it is the best defined entity to encompass the characteristics that enable prehistorians to agree on what is a Mousterian industry. Clarke (1968, p. 357) has defined a technocomplex as "a group of cultures characterized by assemblages sharing a polythetic range but differing specific types of the same general families of artifact types, shared as a widely diffused and interlinked response to common factors in environments, economy, and technology." The differing specific types are, of course, the Mousterian tools. Since the tool components of lithic assemblages from North Africa to the Levant have been classified into Bordes's tool categories, the similarities between types from these spatially disparate industries are already established.

The evidence for an early tradition from which each of the Complexes developed is lacking at present. This situation exists, in part, because of a lack of intense research in some areas and also because our archaeological focus is so diffuse for this period that it makes the detection of a relatively rapid transformation from one industrial format to another difficult. The common sharing by the Complexes of the Levallois method, however, is insufficient proof of migration or simple diffusion—at least in the Middle Paleolithic period—since the Levallois method was

TABLE 2

COMPARISON OF THE LEVANTINE, LIBYAN, AND NUBIAN MOUSTERIAN

	Preparation	W/L Index	Dorsal Scars	Butt Facets	Length	Tri. Lev. Pts.	% Lev./Disc. Cores
Levantine Mousterian	Bidirectional	Lamellar	5.9/5.0	6.0/4.9	63.88/66.1	Few to many	@ 50%
Libyan Mousterian	Centripedal	Flakish	7.0	6.2	49.1	None	@ 90%
Nubian Mousterian	Centripedal	Flakish	5.9	3.7	63.1	Few	@ 50%

already present in the Acheulean from all of the areas. This is not to say the impetus toward the intensification of the method may not have been diffused from one Complex to another. Since other papers will undoubtedly touch on these problems, they will not be covered here. The hypothesis of a widely diffused way of life, represented by industries in the same general level of technological complexity, seems to account for local variation perceivable in the technology better than the migration or simple diffusion hypotheses.

ACKNOWLEDGMENTS

This writer would like to thank the following for their helpful assistance which enabled the research on which this paper is based to be completed—Professors O. Bar-Yosef, L. Copeland, C. B. M. McBurney, L. Rahmani, A. Ronen, R. and R. Solecki, J. Tixier, B. Vandermeersch, and F. Wendorf. To Anthony Marks, the greatest debt is owed. His encouragement, material aid, and friendship made the research possible.

BIBLIOGRAPHY

BINFORD, S., 1966. "Me'arat Shovakh (Mugharet esh-Shubbabiq)." *Israel Exploration Journal* 16:18-32;96-103.

————— , 1968. "Early Upper Paleolithic Adaptations in the Levant." *American Anthropologist* 70:707-17.

CLARKE, D., 1968. *Analytical Archaeology*. London: Methuen.

COON, C. S., 1957. *The Seven Caves Archaeological Exploration in the Middle East*. New York: A. Knopf.

COPELAND, L., 1970. "Early Upper Paleolithic Flint Material from Levels VII-V, Antelias Cave, Lebanon." *Bertyus* 19:99-143.

CREW, H., 1972. "A Statistical Analysis of Levallois Preparatory Flaking." In *Bulletin of the Commission on Nomenclature of the Pan-African Congress on Prehistory and the Study of the Quaternary*, edited by J. D. Clark and G. Isaac, 5:27-37.

FLEISCH, S. J., 1970. "Les habitats du Paléolithique moyen à Naamé, (Liban)." *Bulletin du Musée de Beyrouth* 23:25-98.

GARROD, D. A. E., 1952. "A Transitional Industry from the Base of the Upper Paleolithic in Palestine and Syria." *Journal of the Royal Anthropological Institute* 81:121-29.

————— , and BATE, D. M. A., 1937. *The Stone Age of Mount Carmel*, vol. 1. Oxford: Clarendon Press.

GRUET, M., 1959. "Le gisement moustérien d'el Guettar." *Karthago*.

GUICHARD, J., and GUICHARD, G., 1965. "The Early and Middle Paleolithic of Nubia: A Preliminary Report." In *Contributions to the Prehistory of Nubia*, edited by Fred Wendorf, 1:57-116. Dallas: Fort Burgwin Research Center and Southern Methodist University Press.

IRWIN, H.; WHEAT, J.B.; and IRWIN, L.F., 1968. *University of Colorado Investigations of Paleolithic and Epipaleolithic Sites in the Sudan, Africa*. University of Utah Papers in Anthropology 90. Salt Lake City: University of Utah Press.

ISAAC, G., 1972. "Early Phases of Human Behavior: Models in Lower Paleolithic Archaeology." In *Models in Archaeology*, edited by D. Clarke, pp. 167-200. London: Methuen.

McBURNEY, C. B. M., 1960. *The Stone Age of Northern Africa*. Harmondsworth, Middlesex: Penguin Books.

————— ,1969. *The Haua Fteah (Cyrenaica) and the Stone Age of the Southeast Mediterranean*. Cambridge: At the University Press.

————— ,and HEY, R. W., 1955. *Prehistory and Pleistocene Geology in Cyrenaican Libya*. Cambridge: At the University Press.

MARKS, A., 1968. "The Mousterian Industries of Nubia." In *The Prehistory of Nubia*, edited by Fred Wendorf, 1:194-314. Dallas: Fort Burgwin Research Center and Southern Methodist University Press.

————— , and CREW, H., 1972. "Rosh Ein Mor, an Open-Air Mousterian Site in the Central Negev." *Current Anthropology* 13:591-93.

SCHROEDER, B., 1969. "The Lithic Industries from Jerf 'Ajla and their Bearing on the Problem of a Middle to Upper Paleolithic Transition." Ph.D. dissertation, Columbia University.

SKINNER, JAMES, 1965. "The Flake Industries of Southwest Asia: A Typological Study." Ph.D. dissertation, Columbia University. Ann Arbor: University Microfilms 65-9177.

SOLECKI, R. and SOLECKI, R. L., 1970. "A New Secondary Flaking Technique at the Nahr Ibrahim Cave Site, Lebanon." *Bulletin du Musée de Beyrouth* 23:137-42.

WATANABE, H., 1968. "Flake Production in a Transitional Industry from Amud Cave, Israel: A Statistical Approach to Paleolithic Techno-typology." In *La Préhistoire: problèmes et tendances*, edited by F. Bordes, pp. 499-509. Paris: CNRS.

THE CURRENT STATUS OF UPPER PALEOLITHIC STUDIES FROM THE MAGHREB TO THE NORTHERN LEVANT

Anthony E. Marks
Southern Methodist University

INTRODUCTION

It is somewhat illusionary to discuss the current status of prehistoric studies in any area, much less one as large as the title suggests. Prehistoric investigations are currently in progress throughout northern Africa and the Levant, while much fieldwork of the past few years has yet to see the light of publication. Thus, this chapter will review the basic data and the ideas for the area as available in press, adding what little information the author has on unpublished materials. In addition, an attempt will be made to correlate the data from the various regions in order to see what parallels, connections, and differences exist in the Upper Paleolithic record of northern Africa and the Levant and how these fit the various published ideas of interregional interaction. While the major focus of this chapter will be on northeast Africa and the Levant, the former cannot be understood without also considering the Sahara and the Maghreb. Thus, these areas will be briefly examined as well.

For the sake of expediency, the term Upper Paleolithic will refer to the lithic industries or complexes which fall temporally between the end of the true Mousterian and the beginning of the Epipaleolithic. In this case, the Epipaleolithic is defined as including all those industries which are based on a true bladelet technology. Not included, however, is the Halfan of the Nile Valley which, while having a microblade aspect, also retains highly specialized Levallois technology. Owing to the apparent differences in tempo of prehistoric development and change within specific regions of this very large area, the temporal boundaries of the Upper Paleolithic will vary from region to region. In the most general terms, however, the absolute time range involved will be from about 35,000 B.C. to sometime between 15,000 B.C. and 12,000 B.C., while the actual duration of the Upper Paleolithic in any one region will be judged on radiometric dates which are often in short supply.

In broad perspective, four regions will be considered which are as much defined by their prehistoric materials as by geographic or environmental boundaries: 1) Northern Africa, from the Western Desert of Egypt to the western border of Morocco and from the Littoral, excluding Cyrenaica, south into the Sahara as far as 15° N. latitude; 2) The Nile Valley, as far south as the Second Cataract, in the northern Sudan; 3) Cyrenaica; and 4) the Levant, extending from northern Sinai to southern Syria. Even using such broad regions, there will be considerable variation in the amount of data available, as each region has not undergone equally intense prehistoric studies.

NORTH AFRICA AND THE SAHARA (EXCLUDING CYRENAICA)

Within this huge area there is a single archaeological manifestation which fits the definition being used for the Upper Paleolithic—the Aterian. The date of its inception is not well controlled, either by terminal dates for the earlier Mousterian or by dates on the Aterian itself. While there is a clear, if sparse, Mousterian occupation of the Maghreb (Balout, 1965), as well as of the extreme eastern edge of the Western Desert of Egypt (Wendorf, personal communication), only a single radiocarbon date is available: > 32,000 B.P. (Ny-73), from Jebel Irhoud, Morocco (Camps et al., 1968). There are, however, a series of dates from the Aterian bearing sediments of Unit II of the Saourian cycle at El Ouata, in the northwest Sahara. These dates show two clusters: > 38,000 B.P. and > 39,000 B.P. (Alimen et al., 1966) and 33,900 B.P. ± 1,900 years and 32,700 B.P. ± 1,700 years (Alimen, 1965), but as the samples were not taken from actual Aterian occurrences, they merely provide a probable approximation of dating for the nearby occurrences. As Aterian artifacts seem to occur in the lower half of Unit II, it is possible that the earlier dates are most applicable. Recent work in the Egyptian desert has produced two dates from a deposit which is felt to parallel some containing Aterian artifacts: 30,870 B.P. ± 1,000 years (SMU-75) and > 44,700 B.P. (Wendorf, personal communication). While these cannot be taken as conclusive evidence for the date of Aterian occupation of Egypt, they do parallel, somewhat, the Unit II Saourian dates.

Somewhat better evidence comes from the Aterian site of Dar-es-Soltan, located on the Littoral in Morocco, which provided a minimal date of > 30,000 B.P. (UCLA-678A) for the earliest Aterian level and another minimal date of > 27,000 B.P. (UCLA-678B) for the succeeding Aterian level (Camp et al., 1968). The new dates from the Aterian at Taforalt—30,400 B.C. and 32,600 B.C.—and a date of 29,850 B.C. ± 190 years from an Aterian bearing level near Bérard, Algeria supply firm evidence for Aterian at ca. 30,000 B.C. (Camps, this volume). These later dates, as well as that from Ain Maarout [32,000 B.P. ± 600 years (GrN-3165)], associated with typical Aterian materials, clearly call for its inception well prior to 30,000 B.C. The earlier dates from the Egyptian desert and the Saourian deposits, while suggestive of an origin by 40,000 B.C., certainly need confirmation.

The full duration of the Aterian is, again, poorly controlled. There are two dates of between 19,000 B.C. and 17,000 B.C. on diatomites at Fachi, in the eastern Sahara, which have been correlated with Aterian occurrences some distance away (van Zinderen Bakker, 1966). These are, at best, suggestive of Aterian occupation post−20,000 B.C., but this is hardly conclusive evidence, while other dates all suggest a terminal period at least prior to 25,000 B.C.

Within the Sahara, and particularly its western portion, it has been argued that the Aterian survives until the beginning of the Neolithic in post−Pleistocene times (Hugot, 1967). While this is not entirely out of the question, in this area the evidence is still based on undated stratigraphic sequences and surface occurrences which certainly need additional confirmation.

The distribution of Aterian sites in North Africa and the Sahara shows a heavy concentration along the Littoral of Algeria and Morocco, with a decreasing density toward the south (Tixier, 1967), and with the southern limit of Aterian occupation at about 15° N. latitude (Hugot, 1967). To the east of Algeria, Aterian sites are present in small numbers in Tunisia (Tixier, 1967) and western Libya (McBurney and Hey, 1955), as well as to the south along the eastern margin of the Libyan Desert in Egypt and the Sudan (Caton-Thompson, 1952; Arkel, 1962; Hester and Hoebler, 1971).

The Aterian, as an industry, may be characterized as having a Mousteroid technology; that is, its primary technological base consists of both Mousterian discoid and Levallois methods of debitage, with the use of the Levallois method dominant (Tixier, 1967). In this regard, the Aterian cannot be separated realistically from the true Mousterian and is, without doubt, a direct continuation of the Mousterian technological tradition. In fact, at least one authority considers the Aterian no more than a "facies" of the Mousterian (Tixier, 1967), although a late "phase" might be a more appropriate term.

The Aterian might be considered a distinct industry, however, as there are, among other attributes, two secondary technological traits present which are only rarely found in the Mousterian. The more important of these two is the tendency to produce stems (pedunculates) on artifacts, resulting in the characteristic Aterian tool form. The second technique is the use of bifacial flaking to produce foliates, small bifaces, and lanceolates, as well as completely bifacial retouched stemmed points. This latter technique is not usually so developed as the former, at least in terms of its proportional occurrence at Aterian sites (see Ferring, this volume).

Another distinction between some Aterian assemblages and the Mousterian is the somewhat greater occurrence of Levallois blades in the Aterian. Along with these, some Aterian sites evidence the occasional use of a hard hammer blade technology (McBurney and Hey, 1955), but this trait is not common, nor does there appear to be any consistent developmental tendency toward a leptolithic technology.

Typologically, the Aterian also is related closely to the Mousterian. The most typical tools include Mousterian points, sidescrapers, and unretouched or lightly retouched Levallois pieces. There is, however, often a tendency toward a greater proportional occurrence of endscrapers at

Aterian sites than is common at those for the Middle Paleolithic (Tixier, 1967). As a typological trait, the stemming of tools is important in that it is not restricted to those which might be considered "points," but is practiced on a wide variety of tool types.

Considering the huge area in which and possible duration during which the Aterian occurred, it is not surprising that some evidence is present for artifactual and secondary technological variations between assemblages. To date, a number of different formal systems of classification have been presented to deal with these variations (e.g., Caton-Thompson, 1946a; Ruhlmann, 1947; Antoine, 1950; Balout, 1955), all of which have taken mainly a diachronic view, relating differences to evolutionary development, although some recognition has been given to apparent, but still only broadly defined, regional variations. In spite of these variations, almost all who have studied the problem agree that certain basic widespread changes can be seen through time. It appears that the major diachronic changes can be expressed broadly as beginning with a Middle Paleolithic assemblage pattern of Levallois facies with few pedunculated tools, bifacial foliates, and endscrapers, which then shifts to one where unifacial pedunculates and endscrapers are common, while bifacial pieces are still rare, and finally to one where bifacial retouch is more refined and also is used on pedunculated pieces. It must be noted, however, that even this generalized tripartite division does not always permit easy assemblage classification (Tixier, 1959). This is perhaps the case partially because the changes are not of a large order, effecting neither primary technology nor typology to any great extent. The shifts are more in the popularity of secondary technological methods, while there is little vectored change in the type or proportional occurrences of tool types. In this sense, the Aterian may be regarded as being highly conservative.

It has been noted that the Aterian industry represents "tribes...well versed in the exacting routine of a desert existence" (McBurney, 1960, p. 160). Certainly, the extremely widespread distribution of Aterian sites throughout the Sahara is suggestive of this. On the other hand, it is clear that the Aterian was not specifically desert-adapted, but exploited numerous environmental zones, while apparently utilizing the same basic tool kit.

The Aterian of the littoral and mountain regions of northern Africa reflects an adaptation to a basic Mediterranean environment, with specialized hunting of both riverine and gallery forest megafauna: rhinoceros, "horse," hippopotamus, hartebeest, gazelle, wild cattle, wild pig and southern warte hog, among other forms (Vaufrey, 1955).

To the south, within the Sahara and particularly along its eastern margin, Aterian sites are often situated on the edge of now dry Pleistocene swamps and lakes (e.g., Arkell, 1962; Hall et al., 1971; Wendorf, personal communication). While these localities are within the larger desertic zone, it appears that at least in some cases the Aterian population not only hunted dry-steppe megafauna, but also exploited aquatic resources (Wendorf, personal communication).

There are, however, numerous Aterian sites in the Sahara which are located on terraces along what must have been very ephemeral streams. Thus, Aterian adaptation appears to have been quite flexible and opportunistic, maximizing potential for expansion over wide areas with variable environmental conditions.

THE NILE VALLEY

The Nile River, north of the Second Cataract, flows through desert as dry as any within the Sahara. The river, however, provides a constant source of water which supports considerable plant growth along its banks and which has always attracted both animals and man. The unstable nature of the surrounding desert environments, even during pluvial periods, is in sharp contrast with the unchanging environment within the valley itself. It is not surprising, therefore, that prehistoric occupation of the valley is both long and complicated.

Perhaps the most extensive and intensive prehistoric studies in Africa have been carried out along the Nile, in Sudanese Nubia, during the Nubian Monuments Campaign of the 1960s (e.g. Wendorf, 1965, 1968; Irwin et al., 1968). Along the Egyptian Nile, prehistoric investigations have also been extensive if not as intensive, considering the larger area involved. In spite of years of study, there are still many areas of Nilotic prehistory which are only partially understood. This is particularly true for the early post-Mousterian, the sites of which are associated mainly with the silt and dune episodes of the Dibiera-Jer Formation, for these deposits have been extensively covered by the silts of the later Sahaba aggradation (Said et al., 1970).

While post-Mousterian industries can be placed in the Nile alluvial sequence during the Dibiera-Jer Formation and even in somewhat earlier contexts, their termination is a problem. There is no clear temporal interface between the Upper Paleolithic and the Epipaleolithic. Some Upper Paleolithic industries with considerable antiquity in the Nile Valley are found as late as 15,000 B.C., others of non-Epipaleolithic technology actually appear at about that time, while true Epipaleolithic assemblages are well documented by 16,000 B.C. For the sake of brevity, only those archaeological manifestations which are initially associated with the Dibiera-Jer Formation will be considered here, although a single group of assemblages dating to ca. 15,000 B.C. will also be noted as affinities have been claimed between it and Levantine materials.

There are three main archaeological manifestations which can be considered Upper Paleolithic: the Khormusan industry (Irwin et al., 1968; Marks, 1968b); the Halfan industry (Irwin et al., 1968; Marks, 1968c); and the Idfuan in Upper Egypt (Wendorf et al., 1970). Of the three, the Khormusan appears first, although overlapping in time with the other two near the end of its existence. The earliest Khormusan date, > 36,000 B.P. (GXO-409), from site 6G30 near Wadi Halfa, Sudan, while needing confirmation suggests that the shift from a true Mousterian to an Upper Paleolithic may have taken place at least prior to 34,000

B.C. While this is the only dated site of its early phase, at least one other Khormusan site, 34A (Marks, 1968b), may be stratigraphically somewhat older.

The duration of the Khormusan can be documented by two additional radiocarbon dates: 18,950 B.C. ± 280 years (WSU-203) for a middle phase at site 1017, and 16,850 B.C. ± 500 years (WSU-15) for a late phase from site ANW-3, both near Wadi Halfa, Sudan. While other undated Khormusan sites are known, none is in appreciably younger stratigraphic context. Thus, the duration of the Khormusan may be placed tentatively between ca. 34,000 B.C. and ca. 16,000 B.C.

The Khormusan appears to be geographically restricted to a small area extending north from the Second Cataract for a distance of some 50 kilometers. Sites all consist of small overlapping artifact concentrations, situated lineally along old Nile channels. While exhibiting some vectored change through time (Marks, 1968b), its basic technology and typology are stable throughout its existence. Khormusan technology is based on the production of flakes by the classic Levallois method. Levallois blades and points are rare and, while there is an initial, minimal use of a single platform core technique which increases through time, it never dominates the use of the Levallois method. A wide range of lithic materials were utilized, but there is a parallel shift toward Nile pebble chert accompanying the increase in single platform cores.

Typologically, the Khormusan is dominated by unretouched or lightly retouched Levallois flakes, variable but very significant numbers of burins and denticulates, and a general paucity of scrapers and other specific tool forms. Perhaps one of the most noticeable changes in tools through time is a decrease in tools over 50 mm in length and their replacement by tools under 30 millimeters. Most, however, fall between 30 mm and 50 mm throughout the sequence. This size shift does not effect the types of tools being produced, although there are minor increases in simple retouched pieces and scrapers in the late phase.

Khormusan adaptation was based on a combined exploitation of the Nilotic microenvironment (fish, hare, hippopotamus) and the surrounding steppe (hartebeest, gazelle, wild ass, and wild cattle). The settlement pattern and site configurations strongly indicate that site location was always in close proximity to the Nile and that each occupation was transitory, involving only small groups of individuals.

The Halfan Complex definitely overlaps temporally with the Khormusan; the earliest sites are clearly associated with the Dibiera-Jer Formation. A single radiocarbon date gives a tentative indication of its appearance in Nubia: 23,750 + 2500 - 3700 B.C. (GXO-410), from site 6B32, near Wadi Halfa, Sudan. Better dates are available for later phases: 17,200 B.C. ± 375 years (WSU-32) from site 2014 near Wadi Halfa; 16,650 B.C. ± 500 years (WSU-318) from site 8859 near Ballana, in Egyptian Nubia; 15,050 B.C. ± 600 years (I-1297) from Khor-el Sil III at Kom Ombo in Upper Egypt; and a series of five dates which cluster between

15,850 B.C. and 15,000 B.C. from site E71P1 (67/2A) near Idfu in Upper Egypt (Said et al., 1970). On the basis of these dates and the somewhat later stratigraphic position of the undated Halfan sites near Wadi Halfa, it appears that its duration in Nubia was from perhaps 20,000 B.C. to about 15,000 B.C., while in Upper Egypt it can be placed only between 16,000 B.C. and 15,000 B.C. The Halfan shows a wide distribution along the Nile Valley—from the Second Cataract in the Sudan to near Idfu in Upper Egypt, a distance of some 415 km (Smith, 1967; Marks, 1968c; Wendorf et al., 1970b).

The Nubian Halfan, in its earliest phase, is technologically dominated by a modified Levallois method of flake production which utilizes a special distal preparation and the removal of a channel flake prior to the detachment of the main Halfan flake (Marks, 1968c). A less common method of blank production utilizes simple single platform cores for the removal of microblades. Both these methods were carried out on Nile pebbles, and the resulting pieces rarely exceeded 30 mm in length.

The major technological change within the Nubian Halfan is a steady but marked shift from the Halfan method of flake production to the simple single platform method of microblade production, so that by 17,000 B.C. bladelet production is fully dominant. This makes the Halfan the earliest "bladelet" manifestation in northern Africa.

Typologically, the two basic Halfan tools are the Halfan flake, which is normally unretouched but occasionally has basal blunting, and the backed or Ouchtata retouched microblade. Other tools include low frequencies of burins, scrapers, denticulates, notches, and sporadically occurring scaled flakes (Marks, 1968c; Irwin et al., 1968). Fully reflecting the technological shift, the typology shows a vectored change from the dominance of Halfa flakes to a dominance of backed bladelets, with little change occurring in the other tool classes.

The Nubian Halfan adaptation is similar to that of the Khormusan—a combined exploitation of the Nilotic and steppic environments. There is, however, a major difference in site configuration. All Halfan sites are small, oval, with considerable artifactual densities and, when still in situ, have thick midden deposits. This suggests that while the residential units may have been small, each site was occupied on a more permanent basis than was the case for the Khormusan.

The Halfan of Upper Egypt appears to represent a facies of the Nubian Halfan, differing from it in a number of minor respects. The raw material normally utilized in Upper Egypt is Eocene flint, which is locally available in large blocks, and which appears to have resulted in overall larger tool and debitage sizes. Technologically, the Upper Egyptian Halfan has a fairly strong Halfan element, simple single platform microblade cores and, in addition, there is a macroblade technology which produced good blades by a soft hammer or punch technique.

Typologically, the Halfan flakes are often retouched into other tools, particularly burins. In fact, the sizable number of burins is in contrast with their normal paucity in the Nubian Halfan, although most are of simple type—on snaps or on truncations. Other tools include a fair number of scaled pieces, large numbers of backed or Ouchtata microblades, few scrapers of any sort, and a number of simple retouched blades.

While studies are not yet complete, it is already clear that the Upper Egyptian Halfan retained the Halfan method of flake production well after it had disappeared in Nubia, while the addition of a true blade technology and the proportional importance of burins place it somewhat apart from the Nubian aspect.

The third Upper Paleolithic manifestation, the Idfuan, previously referred to as Complex A (Wendorf et al., 1970), occurs only in Upper Egypt. It is known from both the Idfu area and at Isna, separated by some 50 km, possibly suggestive of two regional facies. While still only partially known, owing to incomplete studies, it is possible that it overlaps temporally with both the Khormusan and the Halfan. Its earliest dated occurrence is placed by thermoluminescence at 19,640 B.C. ± 1,510 years (Wendorf, personal communication), from site E71K9 near Idfu. This date, however, does not correlate well with the site's stratigraphic position, which is placed in the terminal Ballana aggradation. Such a placement is suggestive of a date closer to 15,000 B.C. than to 19,000 B.C. and a number of other Idfuan occurrences in similar stratigraphic position are considered to date between 16,000 B.C. and 15,000 B.C. If the date is not valid, then the Idfuan is clearly later than the Khormusan but would still overlap with the Halfan.

In its more northern and possibly earliest form, the technological base appears to combine macroblade and Levallois methods. That is, blade cores were apparently formed initially in classic fashion, which resulted in elongated lames à crête. Then, two opposed platforms were made, each finely faceted, and blades were struck off alternately from these platforms with a hard hammer. The resulting blades are often long, 70 mm to 90 mm, and about 40% exhibit convexly faceted or chapeau de gendarme platforms. Simple, single platform bladelet cores occur rarely, the Halfan method is not present, and there is a faint hint of occasional soft hammer or punch technique for blade removal.

Typologically, this more northern phase is dominated by burins and denticulates. The burins occur in numerous varieties, but a large number are polyhedric and about one-quarter of all are either busqued or busquoid. The denticulates include a sizable percentage on long blades, and a common type is a heavily retouched, converging denticulate on a blade which has a thin perforator made at the distal extremity. Other tools include unilaterally or bilaterally basally blunted pointed blades, which occasionally have additional retouch at the tip, a few blades with heavy inverse thinning, and a few scrapers.

The assemblages which are from sites farther south maintain the basic technology, but there are also many long blades, often blunt, which are produced with a soft hammer or punch. The tool kit remains essentially the same, but busquoid burins are rare and there are numerous continuously retouched blades, only a very few of which are basally blunted. This southern aspect seems to show some affinities both with the Sebekian of the same general areas, which is dated to ca. 13,000 B.C. (Smith, 1968), and also with the Menchian of Kom Ombo (Smith, 1966). Thus, the total duration of the industry might run from ca. 20,000 B.C. to, perhaps, as late as 13,000 B.C.–well into the Epipaleolithic.

While the nature of adaptation has not been fully explored, it seems that both the Nilotic and steppic environments were exploited. Owing to considerable deflation at most sites, site size cannot be accurately judged, although these sites do seem to be somewhat larger than comparably deflated Halfan sites.

While presently having no documented base within the Nile Valley, another assemblage group which might date to as early as 15,000 B.C. should be mentioned. Originally referred to as Aurignacian (Vignard, 1955), it has subsequently been renamed Menchian (Smith, 1966). It is known only at Kom Ombo, Upper Egypt, from a number of surface and *in situ* localities and, while undated radiometrically, its geological position places it within the Gebel Sisila Formation which has been reported to date between 15,000 B.C. and 10,000 B.C. (Butzer and Hansen, 1968). As Smith's excavations of the early 1960s have yet to be published in any but the most cursory form, description must rely on Vignard's collections. The assemblage described is characterized by large numbers of endscrapers, few burins, numerous retouched blades, and limited numbers of other blade tools. Of particular interest are the scrapers, which account for over half of all tools. Specific types include a very few on blades, as well as limited numbers of ogival, carinated, and nosed examples. The most common forms are simple endscrapers on short, thick flakes with lateral retouch. The retouched blades tend to be quite large with heavy overlapping retouch, and a number exhibit a heavy, inverse basal thinning. Many of those illustrated appear to be denticulated, including some bilateral examples not unlike those from the Idfuan.

This assemblage, with its high percentage of scrapers, does seem quite distinct from earlier industries in the Nile Valley. Vignard (1955) views it as being European Middle Aurignacian, while Smith (1966) prefers to correlate it typologically with the Antelian of the Levant. While this will be discussed later, the faunal remains (Churcher and Smith, 1972) from the excavated sites clearly indicate a mixed riverine and steppic exploitation (fish, hippopotamus, wild cattle, hartebeest, and gazelle), fully comparable with the adaptation of long standing Nilotic industries.

Mention should be made of the reported Aterian occurrences in the Nile Valley (Seligman, 1921; Siirianen, 1965; Carlson, 1967). The most compelling of these accounts is Seligman's, as he illustrates a number of pedunculate pieces. Carlson, while claiming Aterian from south of the Second Cataract, is quite vague as to its attributes, and the descrip-

tion given of both its stratigraphic position and its artifacts could easily apply to the Nubian Mousterian. Siirianen, while noting that no stemmed artifacts were found near Wadi Halfa, Sudan, suggests that some isolated bifacial foliates may be the result of "Aterian influence." While this is possible, in this area bifacial foliates do occur in a number of contexts which are not in any way Aterian (Chmeilewski, 1968; Guichard and Guichard, 1968).

Considering the large amount of work recently carried out in the Nile Valley, it is somewhat surprising that only one Aterian site has been located, and that some fifty years ago. At this time, at least, it would seem prudent to view any Aterian artifact in the Nile Valley as highly unusual, thus placing the general eastern extent of Aterian occupation at the playas and oasis of the Western Desert.

CYRENAICA

In Cyrenaica, it is really only the high ground of the Jebel Akhdar, between Bengazi and the Gulf of Bomba, which has received any serious prehistoric explorations. Limited though these may be, their results are of considerable interest as they indicate the presence of two Upper Paleolithic manifestations, one of which is quite distinct from all others in northern Africa. Of these two, the Aterian and the Dabban, the Aterian is poorly represented, undated, and seems to be restricted to the steppic areas of the coastal strip in front of the Jebel Akhdar (McBurney and Hey, 1955). It is the second industry, the Dabban, which is of particular interest. While it is known from only two sites, the caves of Ed Dabba (McBurney and Hey, 1955) and Haua Fteah (McBurney, 1967), both have supplied some sizable artifact samples, faunal materials, and radiocarbon dates; while at the Haua Fteah there is a long stratigraphic sequence.

The inception of the Dabban is not firmly controlled, but a date of 41,450 B.C. ± 1,300 years (GrN-2564) for a stratigraphically late Mousterian at the Haua Fteah probably provides the lower limit, while another date on the early phase of the Dabban from Ed Dabba (38,550 B.C. ± 1,600 years [GrN-3260]) indicates its presence by at least 36,000 B.C. On stratigraphic grounds, it has been suggested that its appearance can be dated to 38,000 B.C. ± 2,000 years (McBurney, 1967). Dates for the later phase from the Haua Fteah include 31,150 B.C. ± 400 years (GrN-2550); 16,070 B.C. ± 250 years (GrN-2585); and 14,120 B.C. ± 100 years (GrN-2586), with the latter two dates coming from late Dabban levels. While these do not give a terminal point, a date of 12,300 B.C. ± 350 years (USGS-I) from the stratigraphically younger Early Eastern Oranian might serve this function. Thus, the duration of the Dabban may be placed realistically between ca. 38,000 B.C. to 36,000 B.C. and ca. 12,000 B.C.

Unlike all other early post-Mousterian industries of northern Africa, the Dabban shows no signs of Levallois tradition. Quite to the contrary, it exhibits a fully developed blade technology from its earliest significant occurrences, including classic blade core preparation and the use of a soft hammer or punch for blade removals (McBurney, 1967).

Basic technological practices appear to remain constant throughout the full duration of the Dabban. Cores are mainly of opposed platform blade type, although single platform examples are also present. Perhaps the one really significant change is a shift toward broader pieces from the Early to Later Dabban, while a general lowering of the technological standard has also been noted (McBurney, 1967).

Typological differences are also apparent between the Early and Later Dabban. In the early phase, backed blades dominate, some of which attain considerable length: 70 mm to 90 millimeters. In addition, there are small numbers of burins, mostly on truncation, simple endscrapers, and a highly characteristic tool, the chamfered piece. This tool, formed by a transverse, semi-*plan* blow, exhibits considerable proportional variability between excavation samples, but is always present. In the Later Dabban, the chamfered piece virtually disappears and is replaced by an increase in scrapers and burins, while backed blades continue in a rather constant manner (McBurney, 1967). Although these differences seem well founded, any more detailed expression of tool type fluctuations throughout the Dabban deposits at the Haua Fteah must be viewed with extreme caution, owing to very poor sample sizes from most stratigraphic units.

Dabban adaptation was clearly oriented toward the hunting of megafauna, of which caprines were most common, while other less common forms include large bovines, gazelle, hartebeest, and wild horse. There is only minor evidence for the exploitation of small animals (tortoise and birds), so little that it is unlikely that they played an important role in the food supply (McBurney and Hey, 1955; McBurney, 1967). There is no evidence for exploitation of aquatic resources, in spite of the fact that the Haua Fteah is close to the Mediterranean shore.

In terms of adaptation, technology, and typology, the Dabban shows considerable conservatism, with the exception of the initial presence and later disappearance of the chamfered piece.

THE LEVANT

With the exception of the Maghreb, prehistoric investigations have been going on longer in the Levant than in any other region under consideration. While this has resulted in the excavation of numerous sites and the publication of considerable data, the long period over which this work has taken place is reflected in the often differing interests and descriptive standards found in publication. Owing to this alone, there are a number of conflicts and uncertainties concerning the data which cannot be resolved.

The inception of the Levantine Upper Paleolithic is a very complex problem. While it is generally agreed that it developed out of a local Mousterian (Neuville, 1934; Garrod, 1952; Perrot, 1968; Copeland, 1970), the nature of this transition is still under debate. The end of the Levan-

tine Mousterian would appear to be after ca. 40,000 B.C., as a series of rather consistent radiocarbon dates place the late Levantine Mousterian around that time—41,800 B.C. ± 1,500 years (GrN-2579); 39,050 B.C. ± 1,000 years (GrN-2561); 41,050 B.C. ± 2,000 years (NZ-76); 40,050 B.C. ± 1,700 years (Wreschner, 1967).

It is unfortunate, however, that very few radiocarbon dates are available for the Levantine Upper Paleolithic, the earliest being only 26,890 B.C. ± 380 years (GrN-2195) from a "middle" Levantine Aurignacian level from Ksar Akil. Thus, there is a gap between ca. 40,000 B.C. and 27,000 B.C. where there is no temporal control of what must include the terminal Mousterian, the actual transitional period, as well as much of the true Levantine Aurignacian. There also is a date of 18,000 B.C. ± 300 years (RT-227) from layer 26 at Kebara Cave, but as the artifacts from that layer have never been described beyond being termed Levantine Aurignacian the date is of little significance. The only other Levantine Upper Paleolithic assemblage thus far dated is from site Ein Aqev in the Central Negev, where four dates firmly place a late manifestation with many carinated scrapers and burins, as well as numerous *lamelles dufour* between 16,000 B.C. and 15,000 B.C.; 15,940 B.C. ± 600 years (SMU-6); 15,400 B.C. ± 560 years (SMU-8); 15,560 B.C. ± 290 years (I-5495) and 14,950 B.C. ± 250 years (I-5494).

In order to judge a probable terminal date for the Levantine Upper Paleolithic, it is necessary to look at those dates available for the succeeding early Epipaleolithic Kebaran. Dates here, too, are rare, coming from only three sites: Ein Gev I (Bar-Yosef, this volume); Rakefet and Nahal Oren (Noy et al., 1973). The Ein Gev date, 13,750 B.C. ± 415 years (GrN-5576), is consistent when the Ein Aqev dates are considered, as are two dates from Nahal Oren—13,850 B.C. ± 300 years (UCLA-1776A) and 14,930 B.C. ± 340 years (UCLA-1776B)—indicating that the transition from Upper Paleolithic to Epipaleolithic took place between 15,000 B.C. and, perhaps, 14,000 B.C. Unfortunately, the lowest Kebaran layer at Nahal Oren and a Kebaran layer at Rakefet both produced dates considerably older: 16,300 B.C. ± 320 years (UCLA-1776C) and 16,960 B.C. ± 300 years (I-6865), respectively. These are fully within the range of the late Upper Paleolithic dates from Ein Aqev. This conflict may be more apparent than real, as there is no valid reason to assume a synchronous shift throughout the Levant from the Upper Paleolithic to Epipaleolithic. The present evidence, while still weak, suggests that the Kebaran developed first in the north and spread to the south only in its evolved geometric aspect. This certainly seems to be true, since no non-Geometric Kebaran sites are known from the Negev (Bar-Yosef, this volume). Thus, the total duration of the Levantine Upper Paleolithic is in the order of 20,000 years, from ca. 35,000 B.C. to ca. 16,000 to 15,000 B.C., although the possibility of a somewhat earlier origin should not be excluded.

At this time, there is disagreement as to what types of assemblages constitute a valid Middle Paleolithic/Upper

Paleolithic transition. The traditional view (Neuville, 1934; Garrod, 1952; Garrod and Clark, 1965) sees the transitional phase, called Upper Paleolithic I (Emiran) and II, consisting of a combination of typical Mousterian and Upper Paleolithic artifact types and technologies along with a specialized basally thinned Levallois point (Emirah point). In this view, such assemblages contain Mousterian tool types (sidescrapers, Mousterian points, etc.) made on blanks from Levallois or discoidal cores as well as Upper Paleolithic tool types (endscrapers, burins, and backed knives) made on blades from typical Upper Paleolithic blade cores. This view derived from the results of early excavations at the Palestinian caves of Emirah and el Wad in northern Israel and the caves of Erq el Ahmar and Tabban in the Judean Desert, and has been questioned recently in a number of publications. Detailed review of the occurrence of Emirah points has shown they are not a valid type fossil (Binford, 1966), while the contextual association of the artifacts in these so-called transitional assemblages has been brought into question by Perrot (1968) and more recently, in considerable detail, by Bar-Yosef and Vandermeersch (1972).

A more recent view (Copeland, 1970) sees two transitional phases, the earlier containing blanks mostly produced by an "evolved" Levallois method, which tends toward unidirectional preparation, on which typical Upper Paleolithic type tools have been formed. In addition, there are small numbers of blades struck with a soft hammer or punch, suggestive of an initial development of the Upper Paleolithic method of blade removal. Typologically, the main tool classes are burins, flat end-scrapers, unretouched or lightly retouched Levallois pieces (mostly blades and elongated points), and the chamfered piece, which is considered more or less a type fossil of this phase. Assemblages of this type seem to be mainly restricted to Lebanon: Ksar Akil, levels 25-20 (Ewing, 1947); Antelias, levels V-VII (Copeland, 1970); and Abu Halka, levels IVe-f (Haller, 1941-43), although a somewhat similar manifestation may be present also in northern Israel at Amud Cave (Watanabe, 1968).

If this view of two transitional phases is valid for the Lebanese coast, as it now appears to be, there is still no clear documentation that it leads directly to the true Levantine Aurignacian. At Ksar Akil, the stratigraphically later phase (levels 20-16) has backed blades and points of Levantine Aurignacian type, but there is a more or less sterile stoney layer between this transitional phase and the true Levantine Aurignacian, as is the case at the other two sites as well. Additional recent studies of the Ksar Akil material have shown that when both typological and technological attributes are combined, the transitional assemblages below the stoney layer (levels 25-16) are significantly different from the early Levantine Aurginacian levels of 12 and 13 (Azoury and Hodson, 1973). Thus, while perhaps the nature of the initial transitional phases has been isolated and defined, the transition into the true Levantine Aurignacian is still to be found.

Given the data as now published, it is questionable whether the full nature and sequence of Upper Paleolithic development in the Levant can be determined with any accuracy. The traditional view (Neuville, 1934; Garrod, 1962) implicitly saw a unilinear evolution of the Levantine Upper Paleolithic out of the Upper Paleolithic I, progressing through five stages—II to VI. Stages I and II have already been discussed as the transitional period, with the Levantine Aurignacian actually beginning in Stage III. This stage, at times referred to as the Lower Antelian (Copeland, 1970), was broadly characterized by el Wad points (Font Yves), carinated and thick scrapers, polyhedric burins, and many scrapers on retouched pieces. Stage IV, or Upper Antelian, was similar but the El Wad point was no longer characteristic, although present, and thick scrapers became more important. Stage V, or the Atlitian, was a specialized development out of Stage IV, containing large numbers of steep scrapers and prismatic burins as well as some *lamelles dufour*. Stage VI, or Kebaran, marked a major change in the appearance of bladelet technology and is now considered to be Epipaleolithic (Bar-Yosef, 1970).

The sequence proposed by Neuville in 1934, on the basis of only a few excavated sites, had a marked effect on subsequent thought. Until recently, the pattern had been to place newly excavated assemblages into the sequence by ignoring "non-diagnostic" elements and using a few criteria as determining factors.

Recently, this rather simplistic developmental sequence has been seriously questioned. Perrot (1968) suggests that the considerable variability seen in assemblages of Stages III and IV, the Antelian, probably reflects regional facies, while de Sonneville-Bordes (1956) postulates a much more complicated development, as seen at Jabrud II, in Syria, by placing stratigraphically non-contiguous levels into generic groupings. In addition, recent work in the Negev (Marks and Ferring, in press) has uncovered some Upper Paleolithic assemblages which cannot be placed into the sequence, as defined, without doing grave injustice to the total assemblage configurations.

Within Lebanon, a new series of phases for the Levantine Aurignacian has been proposed (Copeland and Hours, 1971). This sees a three-part division (A–C) based on the material from Ksar Akil, with phase A being unique to Ksar Akil, phase B incorporating Neuville's Stages III and IV, and phase C equaling Neuville's Stage V. The phases are characterized both by shifts in the proportional occurrence of major tool classes (e.g., scrapers as opposed to burins) and by the presence of certain morphological shifts within other tool classes, particularly points. While this sequence may have validity for Lebanon, it is questionable whether it can be successfully applied on a pan-Levantine basis. In fact, it may represent no more than a very localized sequence, reflecting as much specific activity variables as any actual developmental progression. Clearly, only data from additional sites will resolve the question.

At this time, it is perhaps most realistic to view the Levantine Upper Paleolithic as consisting of only two major chronological groups. The first and earlier would be a transitional period, of two phases, as described by Copeland

(1970). The second would include all the remaining Levantine Aurignacian assemblages, including those assemblages with el Wad points, carinated and thick scrapers, polyhedric burins, and even those with *lamelles dufour*. This is not to say that this latter group is typologically or technologically homogeneous, but merely that the present level of knowledge, in the absence of controlled chronology and the uneven quality of assemblage recovery and published descriptions, does not permit realistic definitions of facies or phase differentiations over the whole of the Levant.

In spite of the present confusion over the local Upper Paleolithic complex, Upper Paleolithic adaptation can be described to some extent. On the general level, it seems clear that Upper Paleolithic adaptation was strongly oriented toward megafaunal hunting. It appears, however, that those large animals hunted at each site were at least partly determined by the immediate environmental setting. Thus, at Jabrud, Syria, along the cliffs at the edge of a major plain, wild ass and wild goat are present (Lehmann, 1970); at Ksar Akil, in the wooded mountains along the Lebanese coast, the faunal remains are heavily dominated by deer (Hooijer, 1961); while in the Carmel cave of el Wad, close to both Mediterranean woodlands and coastal steppe, there is a fluctuation between the dominance of deer and gazelle (Garrod and Bate, 1937). It is doubtful, however, that a strict one-to-one correlation can be made between dominant environmental zones and faunal remains from Upper Paleolithic sites. For example, the faunal material from the Levantine Aurignacian levels from Hayonim Cave, within the wooded hills of northern Israel (Bar-Yosef and Tchernov, 1966), is dominated by gazelle, rather than deer as the environment might suggest (Simon David, personal communication). A similar situation is present in the Judean Desert site of Erq el Ahmar, where a decided mixture of forms occurs: wild ass, gazelle, deer, goat, and even pig (Neuville, 1951). The problem in interpreting this collection lies in the absence of quantitative data, as well as in its marginal environmental location where minor climatic fluctuations may have caused significant changes in the megafaunal populations.

DISCUSSION

The foregoing simplified presentation of the available data suggests some possible correlations across this huge area, although the complexity within seeming trends and parallels should not be underestimated. In organizing this data, a number of major categories will be considered which, of course, do overlap: basic technological methods, typological complexes, tempo and vector of change, and adaptive patterns.

TECHNOLOGY

In the most general sense, the post-Mousterian industries may be grouped into two basic technological traditions: those where the Levallois method or some modification of it persists, and those where a leptolithic technology either develops rapidly or seems to appear full-blown at the end of the Mousterian. The former situation is clearly present in the Maghreb and the Sahara, while the latter describes what apparently took place in the Levant and Cyrenaica. This clear dichotomy, however, breaks down to some extent when the Nile Valley is considered, although a complex pattern is apparent when the Nile Valley is viewed through time. If the Upper Paleolithic is divided into three general periods (ca. 30,000 B.C., 20,000 B.C., and 15,000 B.C.), it is possible to see an increase in complexity taking place within the Nile Valley as compared with other regions (fig. 1a-c).

At ca. 30,000 B.C. (fig. 1a), the general statement as to a technological dichotomy appears valid, with the Nile Valley falling into the area of Levallois method, although nothing is known from Upper Egypt for that time. By ca. 20,000 B.C. (fig. 1b), however, Nile Valley materials evidence considerable technological complexity compared with other regions, which merely show continuation of the basic technological methods employed earlier. In this time frame, three different aspects appear in the Nile Valley, two in Nubia and the other in Upper Egypt. The Nubian aspect includes the Levallois-based Khormusan and the Halfan, which has two clearly distinct technological elements: a modified Levallois method of flake production and a microblade technology. Given the extreme distance which separates Nubia from all contemporaneous leptolithic technologies (Cyrenaica and the Levant), it is unlikely that the origin of this microblade aspect lies in external influence, although no evidence is present yet for a local progenitor. It should be noted, as well, that this is strictly a simple microblade technology without any indications of the complex core preparation which characterizes the leptolithic technologies far to the north. Until otherwise demonstrated, it is necessary to view this microblade technology as being probably of local origin, representing a discrete technological strain.

The Idfuan in Upper Egypt presents a curious amalgamation of basic technological traditions, with both Levallois and classic leptolithic technology utilized in the same production sequence. Perhaps here is the only potential evidence for an interaction and blending of otherwise disparate technological traditions. Unfortunately, the absence of known materials in Upper Egypt prior to ca. 20,000 B.C. makes an interpretation of this phenomenon difficult. It does seem to indicate, however, that at least part of the Nile Valley was open to influences from areas of leptolithic tradition at a possibly early date.

By ca. 15,000 B.C. the Nile Valley shows extreme technological variability, but the general trend is toward a shift to various forms of leptolithic technology (fig. 2c). In Nubia, the Halfan has become almost exclusively based on microblade technology, with evidence for Levallois method in Nubia now restricted to apparently non-Nilotic cultural manifestions which have no great time depth in the area (e.g., Early Sebilian and Gemaian). In Upper Egypt, however, the Halfan still evidences strong modified Levallois

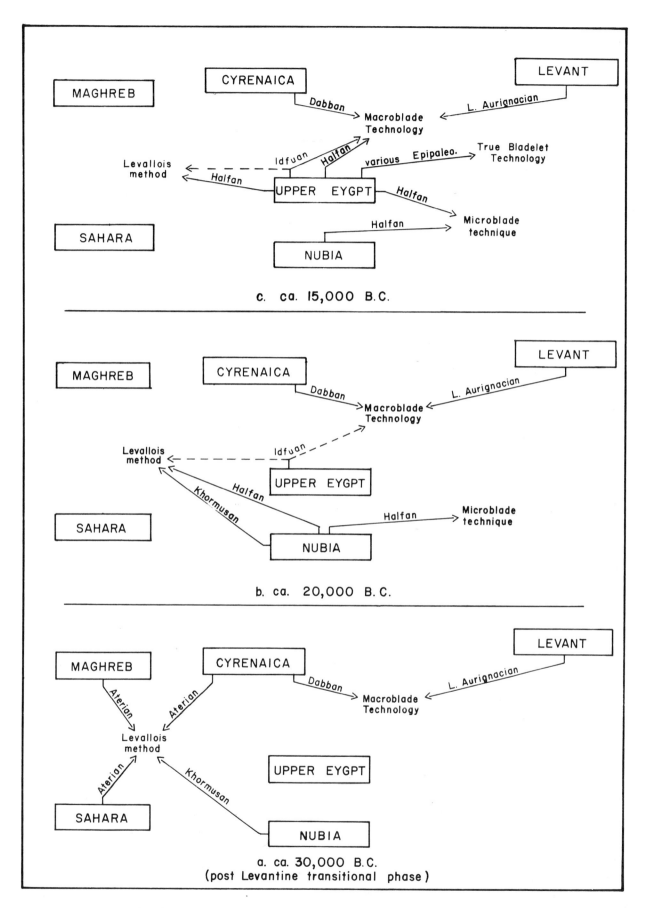

FIG. 1–Relationships between time, regions, and Upper Paleolithic technologies.

method along with the expected microblade technology. In addition, this facies of the Halfan indicates a new technological aspect in the production of macroblades with the use of a soft hammer or punch. The Idfuan, on the other hand, has lost most of its Levallois aspect, and a true macroblade technology dominates. At this period and as early as 16,000 B.C., Upper Egypt was occupied at least sporadically by groups whose technologies were already fully Epipaleolithic (Wendorf et al., 1970*b*; Phillips, 1973; Lubell, 1974). These groups appear to have no progenitors in the Nile Valley, yet have not been traced elsewhere, as they are by far the earliest Epipaleolithic so far known.

Perhaps more than at any other period, the cultural manifestations in Upper Egypt at ca. 15,000 B.C. suggest a meeting ground of technological traditions, with the leptolithic technologies dominating. In this regard, the Upper Egyptian Halfan seems to represent the last gasp of Levallois method for those industries with a long Nilotic background. It is curious, however, that the Sebilian, with its Levallois technological base, appears to survive well into the Epipaleolithic in both Nubia and Upper Egypt.

A slightly different problem exists concerning the technological relationships between those industries in Cyrenaica and the Levant. While both areas exhibit very early post-Mousterian blade-based assemblages, it is not at all clear that they are part of the same specific leptolithic tradition. It appears that the Dabban utilized an opposed, alternately struck blade core as a dominant form, with a subsidiary use of a single platform type core. This range of description, however, is generally lacking in published Levantine reports, making comparison difficult. Certainly, opposed platform blade cores are present in the Levant; but aside from a single reference stating that they were the most common form in layer F1 at el Wad (Garrod and Bate, 1937), there is no other indication that they were ever dominant. In the Central Negev, a wide range of Levantine Aurignacian assemblages have never more than ca. 20% opposed platform cores, while in the transitional phase of Antelias they clearly are in the minority (Copeland, 1970). As inconclusive as these observations may be, they tend to suggest that there were specific differences in blade core form between Cyrenaica and the Levant, with the opposed platform type from Cyrenaica most similar to those used in Central Egypt at ca. 20,000 B.C.

TYPOLOGY

Comparison of typological complexes is more difficult and, certainly, involves a number of variables unrelated to basic technological habits, particularly those associated with function. On the other hand, some patterns are present which transcend technological differences, although they are somewhat amorphous.

Throughout the geographic range of the Aterian, the basic tool kit is strikingly homogeneous, with only very minor regional and temporal variations. As a typological entity, it contrasts sharply even with those Nubian industries with which it shares a Levallois method. It is basically

a Mousterian tool kit of sidescrapers, points, denticulates, and only a small number of Upper Paleolithic type tools (endscrapers, burins, backed knives, etc.).

Within the Nile Valley, two typological complexes may be seen. One includes the Khormusan and the Idfuan, although their technological bases are quite distinct. Aside from those "tools" which are a direct result of the Levallois method (Levallois flakes, etc.), these two industries share a tool kit dominated by denticulates and burins. In both industries these exhibit considerable typological variation, but their importance as tool classes is clear. In addition, both share a marked paucity of backed forms, perforators, and scrapers of all kinds. The second complex is known only from the Halfan. In its early phase, ca. 20,000 B.C.–17,000 B.C., retouched tools are heavily dominated by blunted elements (microblades or Halfan flakes), with burins somewhat common, while denticulates and all scrapers are quite rare. In its more developed aspect, blunting takes on even greater importance in Nubia, while burins become a significant secondary element in Upper Egypt.

It should be noted that the tendency to blunt tools is not exclusively a Halfan trait, as the Idfuan has a few basally blunted pointed blades, although true backing is virtually absent. By 15,000 B.C., however, there are a number of assemblages, noted above, which are Epipaleolithic and where backed bladelets of various types are dominant; so the significance of the blunting in the Halfan lies more with its long time depth than with its presence at this period of time.

Perhaps the most striking aspect of these typological complexes is the paucity of endscrapers in both. It is curious that post 15,000 B.C., a number of assemblages occur where endscrapers are the dominant typological element. For the Menchian, some affinities with the Idfuan can be seen in other tool classes, but in at least one other case, Complex G (Wendorf et al., 1970b), there is no obvious affinity with any earlier Nilotic group.

The Nilotic dichotomy between industries where backed tools dominate and those where they are rare or absent has a parallel within the industries of clear leptolithic tradition in Cyrenaica and the Levant. In Cyrenaica, the Dabban, throughout its duration, has a large backed tool element. This is hardly the case in the Levant, where backed tools are always rare until the onset of the Epipaleolithic, although they are often cited as being "diagnostic."

A further comparison between the later Dabban and the Levantine Aurignacian indicates that while scrapers are among the major tool classes in both, the style of these tools appears to differ significantly. Throughout the Dabban sequence scrapers are poorly formed, preponderantly of flat cross-section, and rarely display specific nosed, shouldered, or ogival forms. In the Levantine Aurignacian, on the other hand, scrapers are always among the finest tools produced, with a wide range of specific types, including sizable proportions of carinated and thick-nosed or shouldered forms, and a significant but lower occurrence of ogival examples. On the basis of the available descriptions there is little question that the Dabban scraper group could be mistaken for any Levantine Aurignacian end-scraper sample.

Data pertaining to burins are not so clear. From the initial occurrence of the later Dabban, levels XXe/XXIA later stage, burins are proportionally important (ca. 20+%) and are described as including a number of polyhedric examples, as are the burins from younger levels. Unfortunately, no detailed burin typology is given, so that the proportional occurrence of polyhedric burins cannot be determined. A generally similar situation exists for the Levantine Aurignacian, in that polyhedric burins are a common form but, as there is a wide range of burin typologies utilized in published reports, there is no sure way of extracting comparable detailed information on intraclass structure. Given this state, all that can be said is that the burins of the Dabban and the Levantine Aurignacian may be similar in the importance of polyhedric forms. Aside from the burins, however, it is clear that the later Dabban and the Levantine Aurignacian are significantly different, in spite of variations in proportional occurrences within each region.

Two Nilotic groups, the Idfuan and the Menchian, have both been tentatively linked to the Antelian of the Levant. In both cases, this appears to have been done on the basis of certain typological affinities; for burins and backed blades in the Idfuan (Wendorf et al., 1970b), and apparently for scrapers and heavily retouched blades in the Menchian (Smith, 1966). Both the Idfuan and the Menchian are, at best, coeval with the end of the Levantine Aurignacian.

For the Idfuan, as viewed here, typologically only the burins appear to justify such a link. These are heavily dominated by polyhedric forms, with a sizable subset of carinated and busquoid examples. Without doubt, these are not typically Nilotic, even though, as a class, burins are always important. The backed microblades are, in fact, associated with the Upper Egyptian Halfan, which had not been separated from the Idfuan when it was first published (Wendorf et al., 1970b). An additional element which might suggest Levantine affinities is the important role blades play in both the overall assemblages and as blanks for retouched tools. This latter is illusionary, however, as Levantine Aurignacian assemblages normally are not dominated by blades, either as debitage or as blanks for tools. It is only at the very end of Levantine Aurignacian when backing and inverse retouch become common that assemblages contain a preponderance of blade debitage and tools. Given that only a single typological element is now suggestive of Levantine affinities, it is perhaps best to reserve judgment until complete reports are published.

The same may well be said about the Menchian/Antelian affinities, although these appear somewhat more convincing. This is particularly true for the scraper element, as even small numbers of carinated, nosed, and ogival forms are rare in Nilotic assemblages. In addition, the apparent considerable incidence of lateral retouch on scrapers is a Levantine trait. These observations must be balanced against the paucity of burins, which is certainly non-Levantine, as well as the presence of long, denticulated blades and inversely thinned blades, both of which are found in the Idfuan but not in the Levantine Aurignacian. It is possible that the Idfuan, the Menchian, and even the Sisilian are in some way related as phases and facies of the same Complex. Until complete publication is forthcoming, however, this cannot be judged with any degree of realism.

ORIGINS

A more pressing problem relates to the possible connections between the Early Dabban and the transitional Mousterian/Upper Paleolithic assemblages of the Levant, as it has been claimed that both derive from a yet unknown "common centre of mature Upper Paleolithic tradition" (McBurney, 1967, p. 178). This position is based on the premises that neither the Dabban nor the "Emiran"–the term used by McBurney after Garrod (1952) for the Levantine material–evolved in place and that the typological and technological similarities between the Dabban and the "Emiran" are such as to suggest a common ancestor. Evidence for the lack of a transition between the Cyrenaican Mousterian and the Dabban may be briefly summarized as follows: at the Haua Fteah there is a clear, major typological and technological break in the upper portion of level XXV between the long, homogeneous Mousterian sequence and the long, equally homogeneous Dabban sequence (McBurney, 1967, p. 135). The argument against a transitional phase in the Levant is somewhat more complex. Essentially, it rests with a rejection of the claims for a Mousterian technology in the transitional phase, owing to the absence of the "use of a truly Levallois-Mousterian pattern or cores, either *discoid* or *tortoise*" (McBurney, 1967, p. 178). While it is noted that blank production is mainly restricted to a hard hammer technique, unlike that of the Dabban, this is explained "as the result of a moderate degree of acculturation between an exotic and an indigenous population" (McBurney, 1967, p. 178). Additional arguments include the general similarity between Dabban and "Emiran" typology and, specifically, the common presence of the chamfered piece, as well as the overall similarity of blank length/width ratios.

While on the surface these points have considerable merit, there are problems which throw the resulting conclusions into doubt. Certainly, the strongest case has been made for the lack of transition between the Dabban and the Cyrenaican Mousterian. Yet even here, it is perhaps premature to consider the case closed. This does not rest on the available data but on the paucity of data for Cyrenaica as a whole. The Jebel Akhdar alone covers somewhat over 12,600 sq. miles (McBurney and Hey, 1955, p. 5), as compared to just over 12,000 sq. miles for all of Israel and Lebanon combined. If the vast amount of prehistoric work undertaken in the Levant and the paucity of known sites which pertain to the transitional Mousterian/Upper Paleolithic question are considered, is it, in fact, reasonable to view the single stratigraphic sequence at the Haua Fteah as fully elucidating the total prehistoric record of an area somewhat larger than the Levant? Clearly, additional work is needed to verify the apparent lack of Mousterian/Dabban transition in Cyrenaica.

The view of the Levantine transitional phase has been somewhat enlarged (Copeland, 1970; Azoury and Hodson, 1973) since the opinions expressed by McBurney (1967). Perhaps the most significant aspect of these recent works is the reaffirmation that the early transitional phase is, in fact, technologically characterized by a Levallois method, although it is of "evolved" form. It is quite true that the typical discoidal and tortoise cores typical of the north African Mousterian are missing, but these forms are not a major part of most Levantine Mousterian assemblages, even those of considerable age. Throughout, there is usually a strong tendency toward bidirectional and unidirectional preparation of cores, which gives the whole Levantine Mousterian of Levallois facies a special character. Thus, this form of core preparation within the early transitional assemblages of Antelias, Ksar Akil, and Abu Halka is consistent with a long-lived technological pattern.

In spite of the acceptance of a probable local Mousterian/Upper Paleolithic transition in at least part of the Levant, there are a number of traits which to some extent do suggest affinities between the Early Dabban and these transitional assemblages. It has been noted that the burins of both are similar at least in size and that, while the quality of the scrapers differs considerably, in both areas they exhibit an inverse co-variation with chamfered pieces (McBurney, 1967). Of course, this may be due to no more than a shift in manufactural style for two functionally identical types.

The most important and striking affinity between the Early Dabban and the early Levantine transitional phase is the common presence of chamfered pieces, a highly specialized tool form which, it is thought, is unlikely to have had two separate origins. They are found in coastal Lebanon and again only in Cyrenaica, and then only in the earliest Upper Paleolithic occurrences. Their absence from Israel is indeed strange, as they are missing even from those mixed sites which were originally considered transitional (el Wad, Emirah, and Erq el-Ahmar), as well as from those Mousterian sites which technologically closely approach the transitional pattern (Abu Sif, Sahba, and Larikba).

Given the gap in the distribution of the chamfered piece and the clearly different technological bases of the Dabban and the transitional assemblages of Lebanon, the present data suggest some possible models. One is that the Dabban is generically unrelated to the transitional phase of the Levantine Upper Paleolithic and that the presence of chamfered pieces in both is due to convergence through independent invention. Another possiblity is merely a modification of that above, with the chamfered piece representing a rapid and widely diffused horizon marker in otherwise unrelated industries, as the level of other affinities is quite low. The problem with this, again, rests in the discontinuity of its distribution, at least at the time level under considera-

tion. Chamfered pieces have been found at Nag Hammadi, Upper Egypt (Vignard, 1921, 1957) in association with transverse axes at a surface site, but these appear to be of predynastic age and so do not have significance here.

A third possibility, a mere modification of McBurney's position, might be to see the Dabban as intrusive into Cyrenaica, originating somewhere in the inland Near East, with the chamfered pieces and Upper Paleolithic typological emphasis of the Levantine transitional period resulting from influences from this unknown early Upper Paleolithic center. Owing to the absence of any hint as to where this Upper Paleolithic might lie, how it spread to Cyrenaica without leaving a trace in between, or, in fact, from what it might have developed, this possibility cannot be considered seriously yet. It should be noted, as well, that much of the inland Near East, particularly the Negev, northern Sinai, Jordan, western Iraq, and eastern Syria, has seen some sporadic survey (e.g. Field, 1960; Stockton, 1969; Van Liere, 1961; Marks et al., 1971, 1972), and to date there has been no indication of any such possible early Upper Paleolithic manifestation. In short, while one of these (or yet another model) might be valid, there is simply not enough data to choose one over another.

Aside from the Aterian, the origin of which clearly lies in the Maghrebian Mousterian, the other Upper Paleolithic, Levallois-based industries of northern Africa have no firmly identified progenitors. The Khormusan exhibits a highly developed Levallois method based on tortoise cores with consistent centripetal preparation of their upper surfaces. This classic form is found in the Mousterian of northern Africa (McBurney, 1967), in the "Levalloisian" of Egypt (Caton-Thompson, 1946*b*), and in the local Nubian Mousterian (Marks, 1968*a*). In this sense, Khormusan technology is merely a continuation of the Middle Paleolithic pattern, with only shifts in raw material utilization and increased faceting placing the Khormusan artifacts somewhat apart. The real difference between the Khormusan and the Mousterian lies in the tool kit, particularly in the consistent proportional importance of burins and denticulates. It may well be that the Khormusan is a direct evolution out of the local Nubian Mousterian, or perhaps the "Levalloisian" if it is earlier. As yet, however, there is no way to document fully the typological transition between the two, although site 34A is suggestive of such a transition. Two possible clues lie in the apparent importance of burins in what might be termed the "Nilotic adjustment" (Wendorf, 1968), and the marked shift in settlement pattern from a wide Mousterian site distribution to one in the Khormusan which is exclusively riverine. The paucity of riverine sites dated to before 30,000 B.C., however, makes this relationship still speculative.

The Nubian Halfan and the Idfuan of Upper Egypt appear so late in the record (ca. 20,000 B.C.) that it is unreasonable to expect any evidence which would trace their origins to a pre-Upper Paleolithic context. The absence of any sites predating 20,000 B.C. in Upper Egypt and *terra incognita* of Central and Lower Egypt present a gap which makes all but the most speculative assessments unrealistic. Clearly, additional excavation is sorely needed in Upper Egypt, while any prehistoric work at all in the remainder of the northern Nile Valley should prove invaluable. This may be particularly true in tracing the origins and development of the true Epipaleolithic industries which appear in Upper Egypt at ca. 16,000 B.C., as it is certain that their origins do not lie to the south.

TEMPO AND VECTOR OF CHANGE

This subject may be divided into two areas: that which concerns the evolution of a long-term, specific, regional industry such as the Aterian or the Dabban, and that where change may be seen only in a succession of possibly generically unrelated industries within a region such as the Nile Valley and even, possibly, the Levant.

The Aterian, as noted before, seems to show little change through its duration of perhaps 15,000 years, except in minor secondary technological traits and a very few shifts in typological emphasis. Thus, it is conservative in its technological and typological proclivities and seemingly shows no development toward any north African Epipaleolithic manifestation.

The Dabban, of demonstrably longer duration than the Aterian, still appears to be rather conservative. There are no radical technological shifts, and the only typological change of significance is the virtual disappearance of the chamfered piece at the end of the Early Dabban, at ca. 32,000 B.C. For the remaining 20,000 years, there are only fluctuations in the proportional occurrence of a few consistent tool types. This picture, however, must be modified by the recognition that it is based on a single excavation where only minimal tool samples were obtained from most levels. The emphasis on backed blades and bladelets, however, is consistent with later north African Epipaleolithic manifestations, although no trends are present which suggest an actual transition to any specific industry.

The relatively small area and numerous archaeological manifestations in the Nile Valley present two possible levels of analysis: one of intra-industry change and the other of regional change. The former aspect has already been described in the first section; this discussion will deal only with the overall pattern of change within the Nilotic Upper Paleolithic. Perhaps the most important consideration in viewing change in the Nile Valley is that it does not represent a generically related evolutionary development. It is quite clear that some industries appear fully developed, undergo internal change, and then disappear without directly leading to any temporally succeeding industry. In this sense, the Nile Valley is not a homogeneous culture area, although the early Upper Paleolithic manifestations all seem to exhibit a broadly similar technological base. This base, however, at ca. 20,000 B.C. is clearly in a state of flux with both Levallois and leptolithic strains already present. The question of how this came about cannot be answered at this point. Certainly, the Levallois element derives from

some local Middle Paleolithic base, although the Halfan modification cannot be directly traced back to it. The microblade aspect of the Nubian Halfan, again, seems to be of local origin, perhaps first developing in the Halfan itself. The macroblade tendency of the Idfuan in Upper Egypt, however, may well derive from influences from Cyrenaica or the Levant; but if so, it was amalgamated with a typical Nilotic typological and technological base. A similar pattern is seen for the Upper Egyptian facies of the Halfan at 15,000 B.C., where macroblades occur in association with typical Halfan and microblade technologies. It seems clear that this macroblade aspect is already present in Upper Egypt by 20,000 B.C., and may even have greater antiquity in the area, but is well established in numerous forms by 15,000 B.C. It is in the period around 15,000 B.C. that extreme complexity becomes apparent in industry manifestations in both Nubia and Upper Egypt.

In Nubia the newly appearing industries (Sebilian, Gemaian) still exhibit modified Levallois methods or simple flake technologies utilizing faceted platform cores, while the Halfan has already evolved a fully microblade technology. In Upper Egypt, on the other hand, the newly appearing industries are based on either macroblade or bladelet technologies (with the exception of the Sebilian), while some indicate strong typological affinities with later Maghrebian or earlier Levantine materials.

In short, the Upper Paleolithic of the Nile Valley provides evidence for both innovative change on an intra-industry level and influences from, or actual influxes of, industries of non-Nilotic tradition. This appears to be particularly true for Upper Egypt and it can only be speculated that Central and Lower Egypt may well contain even greater evidence for these non-Nilotic, leptolithic occurrences. It is possible, of course, that this northern area in fact falls into the leptolithic technological zone, with the Nubian province exhibiting a distinct history of technological development which is not characteristic for the whole Nile Valley and with Upper Egypt representing a frontier zone between the two. Again, however, only speculation is possible at this time.

As noted before, it is unrealistic to place the present data for the Levantine Upper Paleolithic into any detailed chronological scheme which reflects technological or typological change. From the onset of the Levantine Aurignacian until the appearance of the Epipaleolithic, a period of perhaps some 20,000 years, all assemblages tend to contain a similar range of tool types. It has been suggested in the past that certain of these may act as type fossils: el Wad (Font Yves) points for an early phase, thick nosed scrapers for a somewhat later phase, *lamelles dufour* for a terminal phase, etc. While in the most general terms these specific types may seem to be more common in one section of the sequence than another, the condition of most excavated assemblages permits neither sure, detailed comparisons nor accurate temporal correlations.

Recent finds in the Central Negev have uncovered a

series of assemblages where these potential type fossils either are not found at all or are found in associations which make the type fossil concept untenable. For example, el Wad points are found in what might be considered classic early Levantine Aurignacian (Marks et al., 1971) as well as associated with elongated *lamelles dufour* in a geological context which certainly also dates early in the local Upper Paleolithic. *Lamelles dufour*, of minute size, are also found in association with large numbers of carinated scrapers and burins at a third site, while thick nosed scrapers are found at yet another site associated with poor Emirah points. Clearly, the general value of type fossils is questionable in the Negev. There are, perhaps, other attributes which may be useful in tracing the overall pattern of Levantine Aurignacian development and change. Technological change may be one of these, but data are still generally lacking.

Some approach which integrates technological, typological, and stylistic attributes is, perhaps, more likely to provide a valid measure of change through time than is the proportional occurrence of tool sub-classes between assemblages of generally similar type.

ADAPTIVE PATTERNS

The more or less synchronous appearance of post-Mousterian industries across northern Africa and along the eastern Mediterranean coastal zone calls for some explanation. Certainly, the present data do not suggest it was the result of appearance of a new hominid type, as recent work in Israel has shown modern man associated with the Levantine Mousterian of Levallois facies (Vandermeersch, 1972). It is also not the result of rapid, wide-ranging population movements, which replaced Middle Paleolithic industries with those of Upper Paleolithic type over a huge area. More likely, the technological and typological changes which define the Mousterian/Upper Paleolithic boundary resulted from shifts in adaptive patterns combined, in some areas, with gradual increases in technological efficiency. It must be noted, however, that the functional relationships between adaptive changes in food procurement, typology, and technology have not been firmly established.

The adaptive changes are difficult to define, although some hint of them may be seen through settlement pattern studies. In the Maghreb, to date, documented Mousterian occurrences have mostly an inland distribution with sites in close proximity to springs (Balout, 1965), while the Aterian shows a much wider distribution and the association between Aterian sites and springs is not marked. In Nubia a shift is also seen between the Nubian Mousterian and the Khormusan, where Nubian Mousterian sites have a wide distribution well away from the Nile, while Khormusan sites are all in close proximity to the river. As there are only four sites in Cyrenaica which have been reported to contain either Mousterian or Dabban, no judgment can be made on settlement pattern. In the Levant, however, this shift is not apparently present, or at least it is not clear. Perhaps the

only hint comes from the Negev, where the Mousterian settlement pattern differs radically from that of the Upper Paleolithic. Mousterian habitation sites are always in close proximity either to springs or to major drainages, while workshop localities were determined solely by raw material sources. For most of the Upper Paleolithic, however, site location was apparently determined by balancing resource needs, with no convincing evidence for more than one type of settlement. This type, a small traditionally revisited camp, shows evidence of both workshop and habitation site activities. These may be fairly near water sources (Marks et al., 1971) or may be far removed from permanent water (Marks et al., 1972). These differences suggest considerably more mobility on the part of the Upper Paleolithic inhabitants than for those of the Mousterian.

What relationship these settlement pattern changes had with shifts in subsistence activities is not at all clear for most regions. In the Maghreb, faunal remains from both Mousterian and Aterian sites are very similar, although perhaps there is a slightly more riverine character to the Aterian fauna. The first real evidence for a major shift in Aterian adaptation comes in the eastern Sahara, where fishing is added to a megafaunal hunting base. Unfortunately, faunal reports for the Aterian are usually no more than lists of species present, so that the relative importance of specific forms cannot be judged. In Nubia, the Mousterian failed to yield faunal remains; but Khormusan sites certainly demonstrate that both the steppe and Nilotic environments were exploited, including aquatic resources. While settlement patterns cannot be judged for Cyrenaica, the faunal remains from the Haua Fteah do not indicate any significant change between Mousterian and Early Dabban hunting preferences, although there is a slight indication of an increased range of forms recovered, particularly of birds and small animals.

In the Levant, the pattern of megafaunal hunting appears to be linked more with environment than with culture type. On the other hand, in Syria, there is some evidence for a shift from a very dominant "horse" hunting in the Mousterian of Jabrud I to an additional exploitation of wild goat in the Upper Paleolithic of Jabrud II and III (Lehmann, 1970). This is, however, only impressionistic because reporting has been incomplete. In the Mt. Carmel caves, there is no major difference between the late Mousterian faunal assemblage of et Tabun and the Upper Paleolithic assemblage from el Wad, although the appearance of badger, marten, and hare in the Upper Paleolithic is suggestive of a minor expansion of the exploitative range to include more small animals (Garrod and Bate, 1937).

Without question, considerably more detailed data are needed before the relative importance of different fauna between Mousterian and Upper Paleolithic sites can be judged. This, of course, will have to be filtered through the probable effects of local climatic fluctuations (Higgs, 1967), but if any shift in hunting preferences took place, it should be traceable.

CONCLUSIONS

Even this brief examination of the Upper Paleolithic of the Maghreb through the Levant suggests a number of observations. Clearly, it is not possible to document a unified origin either for the Levallois-based industries of the Maghreb, Sahara, and Nile Valley or for the leptolithic industries of Cyrenaica and the Levant. At this time, most evidence indicates that early post-Mousterian manifestations may be derived from local Mousterian industries in each region, with the exception of Cyrenaica, where the evidence is not sufficient to permit any sure judgment.

In all regions, however, it seems that the Upper Paleolithic appears sometime between 40,000 B.C. and 35,000 B.C., although the nature of the initial technological and typological modification differs considerably from region to region. In the Maghreb and the Sahara the change is slight and mostly in secondary technological methods; in Nubia the technology remains fully Middle Paleolithic, but there are typological changes and shifts in raw material preferences; in the Levant there is a visible transition in technology, together with a marked shift in typology, while in Cyrenaica there presently appears to be a sharp break in both technology and typology.

While some parallels and affinities exist between certain industries in different regions, there is no compelling evidence for actual migrations from one region to another, although a widespread expansion of the Aterian clearly took place from out of the Maghreb. In fact, contemporaneous industries from different regions normally show very low levels of affinity, and these may relate as much to functional convergence as to any interregional interaction. The problem of the significance of the chamfered pieces still remains, however, but probably it should not be considered as a deciding factor in establishing generic relations between the Levant and Cyrenaica during the early post-Mousterian period.

Of all the regions under consideration, the Nile Valley shows the greatest evidence for a possible meeting ground of discrete technological traditions. This occurs both as different technological methods present in the same cultural group (e.g., Halfan) and as contemporaneous groups with different technological traditions sharing the same general area (Upper Egyptian Halfan and the more southern Idfuan). In fact, there is some evidence for a brief merging of the leptolithic and Levallois-based technologies in Upper Egypt at ca. 20,000 B.C., but whether this was due to long distance transmission of ideas cannot be judged, because of the lack of prehistoric work in Central and Lower Egypt.

This complex situation in the Nile Valley apparently accounts for rapid intra-industry changes, the general lack of a widespread, conservative industrial tradition, and the number of temporally ephemeral industries which are present by 15,000 B.C. Without doubt, this situation was made possible both by the geographic position of the Nile Valley intermediate between the Sahara and the Levant, and by the rich Nilotic environment which acted as a magnet to groups in peripheral areas. It appears that in the Nile Valley, more than in any other region, population pressures even at an early date restricted the spread of industries over wide areas.

While it has been possible to bring into partial focus the Upper Paleolithic of the various regions and to define broadly the nature of their development, there are still many problems to be resolved. Such resolution depends not only upon the quality of the available data, but also upon the kinds of questions asked, as these will partially determine what data are collected and reported. Historically, most questions have related to chronology, typology and, to a somewhat lesser extent, technology. In recent years, this interest in typology has led to a vast improvement in published description (Copeland, 1970; Copeland and Hours, 1971) and the utilization of well-defined type lists (e.g., Tixier, 1967), to an awareness that debitage and the total tool component need to be reported numerically, and to a consideration of metric attributes. On the other hand, no matter how fine and standardized typological description becomes, it is still only a base from which to work—albeit a very necessary one. The specific form of various tools and their apparent proportional occurrences within any assemblage may be dependent upon many factors (function, style, localized activity, area of site sampled, etc.); so many, in fact, that there is as yet no way of being sure which factors determine similarity or difference. This is somewhat less true for technological and stylistic attributes, as the production of blanks for tool manufacture seems to be less effected by momentary needs, as are stylistic proclivities.

In order to make reasonable comparisons, particularly those relating to assemblage affinities, temporal control is vital. While much improvement has been seen in chronological controls since the advent of radiocarbon dating, it is still curious how few dates are available from some regions for Upper Paleolithic materials.

Even the best typological descriptions and comparisons are only one facet of prehistoric investigation. They will be truly useful only when they are integrated with well-controlled chronology, technological and stylistic observations, settlement and intrasite patterning, and adaptive strategies seen through faunal remains as cultural artifacts rather than solely as paleoclimatic indicators. While some attempts have been made to integrate these avenues of investigation into a holistic approach, much more needs to be done before it will be possible to resolve the meaning of typological and technological similarities and differences which now seem apparent and so important in the prehistoric record of northern Africa and the Levant.

BIBLIOGRAPHY

ALIMEN, H., 1965. "The Quaternary Era in the Northwest Sahara." VII Congress of the International Association for Quaternary Research, Boulder. The Geological Society of America, Inc. Special Paper 84:273-91.

ANTOINE, M., 1950. "L'Atérien du Maroc atlantique, sa place dans la chronologie nord-africaine." *Société de Préhistoire du Maroc* n.s.:5-47.

ARKEL, A. J., 1962. "The Aterian of Great Wanyanga (Ounianga Kebir)." In *Actes du IVe Congrès panafricain de préhistoire et de l'étude du Quaternaire, Léopoldville, Congo, 1959, section 3, Pré- et Protohistoire*, edited by G. Mortelmans and J. Nenquin, pp. 233-42. Tervuren, Belgium: Musée royal de l'afrique centrale.

AZOURY, I., and HODSON, F. R., 1973. "Comparing Paleolithic Assemblages: Ksar Akil, a Case Study." *World Archeology* 4(3):292-306.

BALOUT, L., 1955. *Préhistoire de l'Afrique du Nord*. Paris: Art et Métiers Graphiques.

————, 1965. "Le Moustérien du Maghreb," *Quaternaria* 7:43-58.

BAR-YOSEF, O., 1970. "The Epi-paleolithic Cultures of Palestine." Ph.D. dissertation, Hebrew University.

————, and TCHERNOV, E., 1966. "Archaeological Finds and the Fossil Fauna of the Natufian and Microlithic Industries at Hayonim Cave (Western Galilee, Israel)." *Israel Journal of Zoology* 15:104-40.

————, and VANDERMEERSCH, B., 1972. "The Stratigraphical and Cultural Problems of the Passage from Middle to Upper Paleolithic in Palestinian Caves." In *The Origin of Homo Sapiens* edited by F. Bordes, pp. 221-26. Proceedings of the Paris Symposium, 2-5 September 1969. Paris: UNESCO.

BINFORD, S., 1966. "Me'arat Shovakh (Mugharet esh-Shubbabiq)." *Israel Exploration Journal* 16:18-32; 96-103.

BUTZER, K., and HANSEN, C. L., 1968. *Desert and River in Nubia*. Madison: University of Wisconsin Press.

CAMPS, G.; DELIBRIAS, G.; and THOMMERET, J., 1968. "Chronologie absolue et succession des civilisations préhistoriques dans le Nord de l'Afrique." *Libyca* 16:9-28.

CARLSON, R., 1967. "Excavations of Khor Abu Anga and at Sites in Nubia." *Current Anthropology* 8:352.

CATON-THOMPSON, G., 1946a. "The Aterian Industry: Its Place and Significance in the Paleolithic World." *Journal of the Royal Anthropological Institute* 76(2):87-130.

————, 1946b. "The Levalloisian Industries of Egypt." *Proceedings of the Prehistoric Society* 12(4):57-120.

————, 1952. *Kharga Oasis in Prehistory*. London: Athlone Press.

CHMIELEWSKI, W., 1968. "Early and Middle Paleolithic Sites near Arkin, Sudan." In *The Prehistory of Nubia* edited by F. Wendorf, 1:110-47. Dallas: Fort Burgwin Research Center and Southern Methodist University Press.

CHURCHER, C. S. and SMITH, P., 1972. "Kom Ombo: Preliminary Report on the Fauna of Late Paleolithic Sites in Upper Egypt." *Science* 77:259-61.

CLARK, J. D., 1964. "The Prehistoric Origins of African Culture." *Journal of African History* 5(2):161-83.

COPELAND, L., 1970. "The Early Upper Paleolithic Flint Material from Levels VII-V, Antelias Cave, Lebanon." *Berytus* 19:99-143.

————, and HOURS, F., 1971. "The Later Upper Paleolithic Material of Antelias Cave: Levels IV-I." *Berytus* 20:57-138.

EWING, J. F., 1947. "Preliminary Note on the Excavations at the Paleolithic Site of Ksar Akil, Republic of Lebanon." *Antiquity* 21:186-96.

FIELD, H., 1960. *North Arabian Desert Archaeological Survey, 1925-1950*. Cambridge, Massachusetts: Peabody Museum Papers 45 (2).

GARROD, D. A. E., 1952. "A Transitional Industry from the Base of the Upper Paleolithic in Palestine and Syria." *Journal of the Royal Anthropological Institute* 81:121-29.

————, and BATE, D. M. A., 1937. *The Stone Age of Mount Carmel* vol. 1. Oxford: Clarendon Press.

————, and CLARK, J. D. G., 1965. *Primitive Man in Egypt, Western Asia, and Europe*, rev. vols. 1 and 2, The Cambridge Ancient History, fasc. 30. Cambridge: At the University Press.

GUICHARD, J., and GUICHARD, G., 1968. "Contributions to the Study of the Early and Middle Paleolithic of Nubia." In *The Prehistory of Nubia*, edited by F. Wendorf, 1:148-93. Dallas: Fort Burgwin Research Center and Southern Methodist University Press.

HALL, D. N.; WILLIAMS, M. A. J.; CLARK, J. D.; WARREN, A.; BRADLEY, P. and BEIGHTON, P., 1971. "The British Expedition to the Air Mountains." *Geographical Journal* 137(4):445-57.

HALLER, J., 1941-43. "Notes de préhistoire phénicienne: l'Abri d'Abou Halka (Tripoli)." *Bulletin du Musée de Beyrouth* 6:1-20.

HESTER, J. and HOEBLER, P., 1970. *Prehistoric Settlement Patterns in the Libyan Desert*. University of Utah Papers in Anthropology Number 92, Nubia Series 4. Salt Lake City: University of Utah Press.

HIGGS, E. S., 1967. "Faunal Fluctuations and Climate in Libya." In *Background to Evolution in Africa*, edited by W. W. Bishop and J. D. Clark, pp. 149-64. Chicago: University of Chicago Press.

HOOIJER, D., 1961. "The Fossil Vertebrates of Ksar Akil, a Paleolithic Rockshelter in Lebanon." *Zoologische Verhandelingen* 49:1-68.

HUGOT, H. J., 1967. "Le Paléolithique terminal dans l'Afrique de l'Ouest." In *Background to Evolution in Africa*, edited by W. W. Bishop and J. D. Clark, pp. 529-56. Chicago: University of Chicago Press.

IRWIN, H.; WHEAT, J. B.; and IRWIN, L. F.; 1968. *University of Colorado Investigations of Paleolithic and Epipaleolithic Sites in the Sudan, Africa*. University of Utah Papers in Anthropology 90. Salt Lake City: University of Utah Press.

LEHMANN, U., 1970. "Die Tierreste aus den hölen von Jabrud (Syrien)." *Frühe Menscheit und Umwelt*, p. 181.

LUBELL, D., 1974. *The Fakhurian: A Late Paleolithic Industry from Upper Egypt and Its Place in Nilotic Prehistory*. Cairo: Papers of The Geological Survey of Egypt 58.

McBURNEY, C. B. M., 1960. *The Stone Age of Northern Africa*. Harmondsworth, Middlesex: Penguin Books.

————, 1967. *The Haua Fteah (Cyrenaica) and the Stone Age of the Southeast Mediterranean*. Cambridge: At the University Press.

————, and HEY, R. W., 1955. *Prehistory and Pleistocene Geology in Cyrenaican Libya*. Cambridge: At the University Press.

MARKS, A. E., 1968*a*. "The Mousterian Industries of Nubia." In *The Prehistory of Nubia*, edited by F. Wendorf, 1:194-314. Dallas: Fort Burgwin Research Center and Southern Methodist University Press.

————, 1968*b*. "The Khormusan: An Upper Paleolithic Industry in Sudanese Nubia." In *The Prehistory of Nubia*, edited by F. Wendorf, 1:315-91. Dallas: Fort Burgwin Research Center and Southern Methodist University Press.

————, 1968c. "The Halfan Industry." In *The Prehistory of Nubia*, edited by F. Wendorf, 1:392-460. Dallas: Fort Burgwin Research Center and Southern Methodist University Press.

————; CREW, H.; FERRING, R.; and PHILLIPS, J., 1972. "Prehistoric Sites near Har Harif." *Israel Exploration Journal* 22(2-3):73-85.

————; PHILLIPS, J.; CREW, H.; and FERRING, R., 1971. "Prehistoric Sites near 'En-'Avdat in the Negev." *Israel Exploration Journal* 21:13-24.

MAUNY, R., 1955. "Contribution a l'Étude du Paléolithique de Mauritane." In *Actes du Congrès Panafricain de Préhistoire, IIe session, Alger, 1952*, edited by L. Balout, pp. 461-80. Paris: Arts et Métiers Graphiques.

NEUVILLE, R., 1934. "Le Préhistorique de Palestine." *Revue Biblique* 43:237-59.

————, 1951. *Le Paléolithique et le Mésolithique du Désert de Judée*. L'Institut de Paléontologie humaine, mémoire 24.

NOY, T; HIGGS, E. S.; LEGGE, A.; and GISIS, I., 1973. "Recent Excavations at Nahal Oren, Israel." *Proceedings of the Prehistoric Society* 39:75-99.

PERROT, J., 1968. "La préhistoire palestinienne." In *Supplément au Dictionnaire de la Bible*, edited by Letouzey and Ane, 8(43):286-446.

PHILLIPS, J., 1973. *Two Final Paleolithic Sites in the Nile Valley and Their External Relations*. Cairo: Papers of The Geological Survey of Egypt 57.

SAID, R.; WENDORF, F.; and SCHILD, R., 1970. "The Geology and Prehistory of the Nile Valley in Upper Egypt." *Archaeologia Polona* 12:43-60.

SELIGMAN, C. G., 1921. "The Older Paleolithic Age in Egypt." *Journal of the Royal Anthropological Institute of Great Britain and Ireland* 51:115-53.

SIIRIANEN, A., 1965. "The Wadi Halfa Region (Northern Sudan) in the Stone Age." *Studia Orientalia* 30(4):3-34.

SMITH, P., 1966. "The Late Paleolithic of Northeast Africa in the Light of Recent Research." *American Anthropologist* 68(2):326-55.

————, 1967a. "A Preliminary Report on the Recent Prehistoric Investigations near Kom Ombo, Upper Egypt." Fouilles en Nubia (1961-63), extract from Antiquities Department of Egypt, pp. 8-14.

————, 1967b. "New Investigation in the Late Pleistocene Archaeology of the Kom Ombo Plain (Upper Egypt)." *Quaternaria* 9:141-52.

————, 1968. "A Revised View of the Later Paleolithic of Egypt." In *La Préhistoire: problèmes et tendances*, edited by F. Bordes, pp. 391-99. Paris: CNRS.

de SONNEVILLE-BORDES,, D., 1956. "Paléolithique supérieur et Mésolithique à Jaburd (Syrie)." *L'Anthropologie* 60:71-83.

STEKELIS, M., and BAR-YOSEF, O., 1965. "Un habitat du Paléolithique supérieur à Ein Gev (Israel), note préliminaire." *L'Anthropologie* 69:176-83.

STOCKTON, R., 1969. "A Bibliography of the Flint Industries of Transjordan." *Levant* 1:1001-1103.

TIXIER, J., 1959. "Les Industries lithiques d'Aïn Fritissa (Maroc oriental)." *Bulletin d'Archéologie marocaine* 3:107-248.

_____, 1967. "Procédés d'analysc et questions de terminologie concernant l'étude des ensembles industriels du Paléolithique Récent et de l'Epipaléolithique dans l'Afrique du Nord-Ouest." In *Background to Evolution in Africa*, edited by W. W. Bishop and J. D. Clark, pp. 771-820. Chicago: University of Chicago Press.

VANDERMEERSCH, B., 1972. "Récentes découvertes de squelettes humains à Qafzeh (Israel): essai d'interprétation." In *The Origin of Homo Sapiens*, edited by F. Bordes, pp. 49-54. Proceedings of the Paris Symposium, 2-5 September, 1969. Paris: UNESCO.

VAN LIERE, W. J., 1961. "Observations on the Quaternary of Syria." *Berichte von de Rijkdienst voor het Ouedheidkundig Bodemonderzoek* 10-11:1-69.

VAUFREY, R., 1955. *Préhistoire de l'Afrique, Vol. I, Le Maghreb*. Paris: Masson.

VIGNARD, E., 1921. "Une Station Aurignacienne à Nag Hammadi (Haute-Egypte), Station du Champ de Bagasse." *Bulletin de l'Institut Française d'Archéologie Orientale* 18:1-20.

_____, 1955. "Menchia, une Station Aurignacienne dans le Nord de la Plaine de Kom Ombo (Haute-Egypte)." *Congrès Préhistorique de France, 14ᵉ session, Strasbourg-Metz 1953*, pp. 634-53.

_____, 1957. "Points de vue nouveaux sur l'industrie du Champ de Bagasse près de Nag Hammadi (Haute-Egypte)." *Bulletin de la Société Préhistorique Française* 54:298-313.

WATANABE, H., 1968. "Flake Production in a Transitional Industry from Amud Cave, Israel: A Statistical Approach to Paleolithic Techno-typology." In *La Préhistoire: problèmes et tendances*, edited by F. Bordes. Paris: CNRS.

WENDORF, F. (ed.), 1965. *Contributions to the Prehistory of Nubia*. Dallas: Fort Burgwin Research Center and Southern Methodist University Press.

_____ (ed.), 1968. *The Prehistory of Nubia*, 2 vols. and atlas. Dallas: Fort Burgwin Research Center and Southern Methodist University Press.

_____; SCHILD, R.; and SAID, R., 1969. "Problems of Dating the Late Paleolithic in Egypt." In *Radiocarbon Variations and Absolute Chronology*, Nobel Symposium 12, edited by I. Olsson, pp. 57-79. Stockholm: Almqvist Wilksell.

_____; SAID, R.; and SCHILD, R., 1970*a*. "Egyptian Prehistory: Some New Concepts." *Science* 169:1161-71.

_____; SAID, R.; and SCHILD, R., 1970*b*. "Late Paleolithic Sites in Upper Egypt." *Archaeologia Polona* 12:19-42.

WRESCHNER, E.; AVNIMELECH, M.; SCHMID, E.; HAAS, G.; and DART, R. A., 1967. "The Geula Cave, Mount Carmel." *Quaternaria* 9:69-140.

van ZINDEREN BAKKER, E. M., 1972. "Late Quaternary Lacustrine Phases in the Southern Sahara and East Africa." *Paleoecology of Africa* 6:15-27.

CONFERENCE OVERVIEW

J. Desmond Clark

University of California, Berkeley

To begin with, I think it needs to be acknowledged that this conference is in the nature of a milestone in the practical realization that there is a great deal that North Africa and the Middle East have in common in prehistoric as well as in historic times. The organizers and sponsors of these meetings are to be sincerely congratulated, therefore, on gathering us here to discuss mutual problems and the ways of tackling them, to compare the evidence, and to establish collaboration for future research.

It is very evident, from the large amount of new knowledge and the new approaches that have come about in the course of the last ten years or so, that, prehistorically as historically, northern Africa has probably more in common with the Middle East—indeed, one might say, with the Mediterranean basin as a whole—than it does with sub-Saharan Africa, after the close of the Middle Pleistocene. Similar environments, plant and animal resources, and similar ways of exploiting them, if we can judge by the contents of the prehistoric tool kits, show that we are justified in identifying and defining a Mediterranean Culture Area (in the sense the term was used by Herskovits) in which at least two major sub-regions can be recognized—the North African littoral and the Levant—both having not a little in common though each with its own distinctive but related traditions. During the Middle Pleistocene, the evidence is more incomplete and there is less distinction between North and sub-Saharan Africa; but already, I believe, the beginnings of differentiation can be seen in the Acheulean tool kits. If the Sahara acted as a filter for the passage of techniques and peoples, so also did the Sinai, but the more closely related ecosystems and climates of North Africa and the Middle East were probably the main factors that were responsible for these two being more nearly identified with each other than either can be with tropical Africa.

Listening to the discussions, it is apparent that there is much concern with correlating local stratigraphic and cultural successions with the European sequences. There is, however, little to be gained from continuing to try to correlate local sequences with the classic Alpine sequence of glacials/interglacials, in view of the fact that deep sea cores and the loess sequence in central Europe show that since ca. 700,000 years B.P. there have been eight major interglacial episodes. Until it is possible, therefore, to date sequences more precisely than at present, correlation with episodes earlier than the last interglacial can be little more than informed guesswork. More advantageous will be the establishment of well-defined local sequences using local names/terminologies. The only reliable way of correlating these is by radiometric/isometric methods and by paleomagnetic reversal. In the Middle East, in particular, it is to be hoped

that in the next few years a number of new K/Ar dates will be forthcoming checked by uranium fission track and paleomagnetism.

Pollen data are especially valuable for archaeological interpretation since they can provide, more satisfactorily than fauna, the basic understanding of the paleoenvironment that is essential for understanding the cultural evidence. Our discussion has shown, however, that pollen diagrams in the tropics and subtropics are still liable to some misinterpretations, especially in regard to the overrepresentation of wind-blown, allochthonous pollen and the underrepresentation of certain dominant autochthonous species. Nevertheless, the importance of pollen evidence cannot be overemphasized, for not only can it provide one of the best ways of reconstruction of the habitat, but if the major plant communities are known it can also show which plant foods are more likely to have provided the staples.

In the past (less so today) it has been the practice of both prehistorians and geologists to use archaeological assemblages to correlate sedimentary sequences. In late prehistoric times technological equivalence and the presence of one or more very specialized types of artifacts may still be reliable means of correlating strata over short distances. It is becoming increasingly obvious, however, that this is not so for earlier Quaternary times. The Oldowan/Acheulean cultural sequence at Olduvai Gorge is showing that technological development does not consist in increasing refinement of large cutting and other tools from beginning to end of the succession: well-made tools may occur at a low level and poorly-made ones at a high level. Increasing refinement and skill appear, therefore, to depend on factors other than time—individual ability and experience, traditional patterning, the dictates of function, etc.—and this is now being shown so far as the Middle Pleistocene is concerned for other localities in East Africa that can be correlated with Olduvai on K/Ar and paleomagnetic data. Apart from the final, evolved Acheulean, which shows technological and typological developments not found with the earlier stages, and somewhat less certain criteria for dividing a "Lower" from an "Upper" Acheulean, any inferred progressive development toward increased refinement in the Acheulean still remains to be proven. Even more is this the case with the Oldowan/Developed Oldowan—the latter persisting contemporaneously with little apparent change from the beginning to the end of the Acheulean tradition.

Recently, also, the radiocarbon dates for the later Pleistocene cultural traditions in southern Africa are showing that technological equivalence is no longer a reliable indicator of contemporaneity. The so-called "Middle Stone Age" traditions can be seen to be time transgressive and are more probably, therefore, related to several different kinds of site exploitation patterns that are determined by the resources available. When more dates become available generally from the Levant and North Africa, it may be that anomalies will become apparent that can best be explained by similar models.

Correlation of stratigraphical sequences and correlation of artifactual assemblages has been, understandably, a frequent matter for discussion. It is, however, apparent that long-range correlation of assemblages, on the whole, is much less reliable and productive than is correlation over short distances. Identification of similarities and differences between assemblages from ecologically similar and distinct localities that are separated by no great distance is likely to be much more meaningful from the point of view of understanding the extent to which local behavior dictated the use of particular kinds of tools which, in turn, depended on the season at which the site was occupied and the kind of exploitation that it permitted. In this way, it should be possible to identify and define the tradition of local groupings. This is where, after more intensive local survey, detailed technological and typological studies, on both a qualitative and a quantitative basis, should be able to show the boundaries of the exploitation territory of a single group. Since each group can be expected to have established its own idosyncratic tradition and the products of different groups are likely to show various small differences in typology and technology, it should be possible to show, with radiometric control, continuity between generations and perhaps even to identify the work of individuals. More probably it is to be expected that there will be greater continuity through time at a site or adjacent sites within a limited geographical area, than there will be between contemporary archaeological occurrences in different geographical regions. Indeed, this has been shown recently for various stratified "Later Stone Age" regional assemblages both in East Africa and in South Africa. Since stone artifacts do not breed and cannot be classified as if they were butterflies or coins, but are the work of individuals and so open to all the idiosyncratic differences that distinguish them one from another, not only should we not expect the tools used by one group to be identical with those of another occupying a different territory, perhaps using a different grade or type of stone, but, if two such assemblages are closely identical, it might be expected that they were made by the same group, not by a different group.

A major problem touched on in discussion is the meaning of technological change and transitional industries. Can one identify a transitional industry—transitional, that is, between one major tradition and another? I certainly believed so at one time, but it seems now unlikely that such industries, if they ever existed, would have done so for anything more than a brief period of time. What would such an industry look like? One in which it is possible to see the gradual increase in importance of new types and the disappearance of old ones, presumably? However, radical technological changes, such as the manufacture of bifaces,

the Levallois technique, Aterian tangs, and Amudian blades, must, in the nature of things, manifest themselves suddenly in the record—they are either there or not there. Their presence most probably reflects specific behavior related to improved ways of doing things or new resources brought into use—more efficient extraction processes reflected by new, improved technology.

It is reasonable to suppose, and is historically documented, that if technological innovation were sufficiently advantageous and radical, it would spread with considerable rapidity—faster than the kind of time we can measure at present by radiometric methods. We are still dealing in thousands of years whereas significant, innovative changes come about in much shorter periods of time. Phillips has suggested that the similarities between the Epipaleolithic industries of northwest Africa and the Nile Valley are the outcome of convergent development that results from using similar resources by means of similar exploitation patterns and technology. Such a model for preagricultural populations carries much more weight than the implication, almost traditionally entrenched in European prehistory, that technological changes presuppose ethnic changes and, in particular, migration of whole populations. For example, it can be seen in north, west, and east Africa, how the changes in technology brought about by the introduction of agriculture were essentially of an economic nature and did not involve any major ethnic changes. Again, there is increasing evidence that the disappearance of the "Later Stone Age" hunting/gathering populations in the subcontinent and their replacement by Iron Age agriculturalists was due only in part to small-scale movements of negroid farming peoples. The archaeological and skeletal evidence indicates that in many parts the disappearance of lithic technology and its replacement by metallurgy was the result of the adoption of the new socio-economic pattern by the hunter/gatherers because of its obvious advantages. For related or contiguous communities practicing a generally similar way of life and using generally similar resources, the advantages that accrue from adopting similar economic and social improvements can hardly be denied and if these necessitated, as they often do, the introduction of new technological traits, then these traits will be transferred also. It is these traits and a common life style that distinguish Culture Areas and, I believe, permit us to define a Mediterranean Culture Area in prehistory.

How then can one best explain rapid technological change in Paleolithic times? The mechanism lies more probably in the open nature of the structure of hunting groups and the rapidly changing composition of the group which, with the sharing of food and water, is one of the main mechanisms for survival. For example, Yellen found that the composition of the !Kung Bushman group at Dobe changed as much as 80% in the course of one year, individuals coming from as far as 80-100 miles distant from the waterhole. The bands join into larger groupings and come together during the rains when the game disperse and more food and water sources become available; they practice communal hunting, barter, and general exchange of information at this time; and in the dry season they split into smaller groups and hunting is important as they fall back on the various permanent water sources. If one can generalize from such a pattern it is not difficult to see how new advantageous techniques and kinds of artifacts could be quickly diffused.

Ethnic migration as an explanation of technological change should not be assumed, therefore, unless it is confirmed by other and independent evidence. Populations do not generally move great distances unless the pressures are sufficiently great; and it is hard to see that they would have been sufficiently compelling, bearing in mind Paleolithic population densities, before Natufian times. Local readjustments are indeed to be expected (the preference in Palestine of the makers of the Acheulean for the coastal plain and of the Mousterian population for cave sites in the hills, for example), but large-scale migration is unlikely, unless previously favorable regions for settlement became unfavorable or unavailable or previously unfavorable habitats became favorable owing to climatic change or technological improvements that opened up hitherto empty or unused areas to occupation. As examples we could cite the occupation of the Zaire/Congo basin in the Upper Pleistocene after the retreat of the lowland forest, the occupation of the Sahara during later Acheulean and again in Aterian times and its unfavorable nature during the "Mousterian" and Epipaleolithic and also, of course, the occupation of the New World at the close of the Pleistocene. Also, Ferring's suggestion that the cold, dry climate of the Maghreb during the main Würm may have caused migrations of Aterian populations into the Sahara needs to be considered here.

More rewarding, perhaps, than long-range correlation or typological studies at present, is the shift seen in some of the presentations toward attempts to recover evidence that will permit interpretation of the economic, perhaps the socio-economic pattern and so provide an understanding of the behavior of the prehistoric community. This is to me much the most exciting part of prehistory; but we stand little chance of being able to interpret the meager surviving evidence—artifacts, fauna, features, etc.—unless a large part or all of the occupied area of the site is excavated. Different activities can be expected, on ethnographic evidence, to have been carried on in different parts of the camp site, and any excavation that does not take account of this will inevitably fail to record some, perhaps a significant part, of these data. Of course, only primary sites can provide the kind of information that can lead to interpretation of settlement patterning and identification of activity areas. And up to now, it is the open sites that have proved the most productive. In cave sites, where most of the work has been concentrated, the deposits are usually compressed and single occupation horizons are much less easy to isolate than on open sites that were occupied for a single occasion only. In this connection, it should be mentioned that it has been found, so far as Middle Pleistocene sites south of the Sahara are concerned, that some of the best evidence as to

activity patterning, in particular in regard to butchery techniques and tool kits, comes from low density sites occupied for a brief occasion only when a single animal was butchered; a direct relationship can be established between the tool kit and the remains of the dismembered beast. At those sites occupied over a period of time at which several different activities were carried out, judging from the distinctive artifact types, it is much less easy to distinguish separate activity areas. The same was found to be the case by Yellen studying Bushman camp sites in the Kalahari. Those occupied only briefly gave the best evidence of different activity residues; at camps occupied for longer periods the residues became mixed and dispersed.

Recovery of this kind of evidence requires excavation on a recurrent or long-term basis, involving several or many seasons' excavation before the work is completed. It also requires a team of investigators in different disciplines to establish the problems and the best techniques of recovery of data and, no doubt, a change of investigators before the program is completed. It also provides invaluable opportunities for the training of students. An excellent example of this kind of project is, of course, the work at 'Ubeideya which has produced the first real knowledge of earlier Pleistocene occupation sites in the Middle East. It is very much to be hoped that others will follow. For example, it would be of very great interest to know what a Mousterian occupation area on the Kurkur ridges in Israel looks like, and removal of the overlying sterile deposits by mechanical equipment to permit excavation of the site as a unit would surely be a practical proposition. Especially important also, I would suggest, are the sites in the desert where deflation has partly exposed the site and where there is thus a minimum of overburden to remove to recover the occupation pattern. The sites we have studied in the Sahara often show very little lateral displacement of artifacts, and those reported on by Marks and others at this conference show especially well how little disturbance has taken place and how well the patternings are preserved.

Artifact grouping and patterning on an occupation horizon shows relationships between some different kinds of tools—choppers and small flake tools, for example, on Acheulean sites—and it is possible to distinguish a small number of distinctive types of artifacts that, by the nature of their attributes and/or associations, can be seen as relating to different kinds of activities—e.g., large cutting tools, heavy duty picks and core-scrapers, small flake tools, etc., with the Acheulean—and these are repeated in innumerable variations wherever the Acheulean is found. When one looks at individual classes of tools, considerable variation in shape, size, refinement, etc., is apparent. Much significance has been attributed to this in the past, as is only too clearly borne out in the established classification systems and terminology, but we now need seriously to consider whether the typologies we have set up do not in part help to obscure the main issue—to determine functionally distinct kits of artifacts—by setting up "types" that would never have been considered different types by their original makers and users. Analogy with present-day ethnographic evidence shows that the populations of Australia, New Guinea, South West Africa, or Ethiopia still using stone artifacts recognize a minimum number of functionally distinct kinds of tools—two, three, or four, seldom more—though the morphology of the artifacts themselves is often sufficiently different for archaeologists to classify them into a number of distinctive "types" of tools. Another example is this collection of tribulum flints (circulated) from Syria. They were all made for a single purpose, ready for mounting, but not yet used. As you can see, it is easily possible to classify even this small collection into some half-dozen different "types." Clearly, if we are looking to interpret behavior/tool function, the standard classificatory systems have limited application, though they remain useful, however, in showing *differences between assemblages*. Since, therefore, so many of these differences are more probably idiosyncratic than functional, we need to be very careful, I feel, in our attempts to interpret them, especially when we consider that we are dealing with only the imperishable stone tool equipment, which is only a part, often a very small part, of the whole material culture of a group.

We have probably overemphasized and overextended the artifactual evidence at the expense of that provided by fauna and plant remains. Henry has summarized something of what can be learned from faunal analysis and some of the problems involved. I am sure it is every bit as important as the study of the artifacts and, as such, should form a regular part of all student training in archaeology.

Plant remains and plant foods are more of a problem since they are generally not preserved, except under fully arid or water-saturated conditions. Much can, I believe, be learned, however, from pollen studies, and if the "main" plant communities are known it should be possible, by correlating with the present-day pattern and making use of local ethno-botanical knowledge, to construct a model to show what were the plants most likely to have been used by prehistoric hunter-gatherers. There are a great many valuable ethno-botanical data for some parts of Africa e.g., the Sahara, West, and Central Africa, but much remains to be collated or collected so far as the Levant and North Africa are concerned. Studies of this kind should receive a high priority as also should "site catchment" studies of the kind initiated by Vita-Finzi and Higgs. At the same time, studies

of nomad movements need to be investigated by archaeologists, as they give an indication of the seasonality of prehistoric patternings as well as of game movements. At present we do not know whether much or nothing can be learned from such movements, but until they are studied through the eye of an archaeologist this potential source of information remains untapped. In North Africa and the Middle East, as in the rest of the African continent, there is, I feel, a great deal of very pertinent information to be obtained from ethnographical/archaeological studies and, indeed, such as have already been carried out in sub-Saharan Africa fully confirm the significance of this new and largely uninvestigated source of evidence.

In summary, therefore, the conference has shown the impressive amount and depth of the new material that has become available over the past few years. It has shown the need for the establishment of well-defined local sequences; the evident advantages of studying tool kits in the context of the occupation area and its contents, as a whole and from the point of view of what they can tell us about behavior, rather than as so many different typological assemblages; and in particular, the advantages of total excavation of one-time occupation sites in the open as distinct from cave sites, and the value of long-term programs of excavation of whole sites by interdisciplinary teams that use not only the directly archaeological but also all other sources of evidence that can provide relevant information on the past habitat and way of life.

This has been an immensely interesting and stimulating conference, and this exchange of ideas and data cannot fail to be productive of further advances in concepts and knowledge. It is to be hoped that some means will be found of insuring its continuity, similar to that enjoyed by the Pan-African Congress on Prehistory and Quaternary Studies. As a start it might be proposed to establish a Newsletter that could be circulated to all those actively working in North Africa and the Middle East. This could be mimeographed or otherwise inexpensively produced and could include brief information on current programs, requests for information and exchange, and brief discussions on current concepts, teaching, etc. It might be put out once or twice a year and would be of great benefit in keeping the respective research workers informed of what each is doing and thinking.